FROMMER'S
DOLLARWISE GUIDE™ TO
FRANCE

by Darwin Porter

Assisted by Danforth Prince

1987-88 Edition

Sponsored by

Published by Prentice Hall Press
A Division of Simon & Schuster, Inc.
Gulf + Western Building
One Gulf + Western Plaza
New York, NY 10023

ISBN 0–671–62059–2

Manufactured in the United States of America

*Although every effort was made to ensure the accuracy
of price information appearing in this book,
it should be kept in mind that prices
can and do fluctuate in the course of time.*

CONTENTS

Introduction   **DOLLARWISE GUIDE TO FRANCE**   **1**
The $25-a-Day Travel
Club—How to Save
Money on All Your Travels   **4**

Chapter I   **GETTING TO AND AROUND FRANCE**   **8**
1. Traveling to France   **8**
2. Traveling Within France   **9**
3. The Grand Tour of France   **13**

Chapter II   **SETTLING INTO FRANCE**   **17**
1. The French   **17**
2. Food and Drink   **28**
3. The ABCs of France   **32**

Chapter III   **PARIS AND ITS HOTELS**   **37**
1. Orientation   **38**
2. The Super-Deluxe Hotels   **47**
3. 8th Arrondissement   **55**
4. 16th and 17th
   Arrondissements   **59**
5. 1st Arrondissement   **63**
6. 2nd and 9th Arrondissements   **66**
7. 5th Arrondissement   **67**
8. 6th Arrondissement   **70**
9. 7th and 15th Arrondissements   **76**
10. 14th Arrondissement   **78**
11. 3rd and 4th Arrondissements   **79**
12. 18th Arrondissement   **81**
13. Orly Airport   **82**
14. Airport Charles de Gaulle   **83**

Chapter IV   **THE RESTAURANTS OF PARIS**   **84**
1. The Haute Cuisine   85
2. 1st and 2nd Arrondissements   89
3. 8th Arrondissement   93
4. 5th and 6th Arrondissements   97
5. 3rd and 4th Arrondissements   102
6. 7th Arrondissement   104
7. 9th and 10th Arrondissements   106
8. 12th Arrondissement   108
9. 15th Arrondissement   108
10. 16th Arrondissement   109
11. 17th Arrondissement   111
12. 18th and 19th
      Arrondissements   113
13. Vegetarian Dining   113
14. Tea Rooms and Pâtisseries   114

Chapter V   **DISCOVERING PARIS**   **116**
1. The Top Sights   117
2. Other Major Sights   139
3. More Museums   148
4. More Churches   157
5. The Gardens of Paris   158
6. The Markets of Paris   160
7. A Sightseeing Miscellany   161
8. Paris for Children   163
9. In the Environs   165
10. Shopping in Paris   167

Chapter VI   **PARIS AFTER DARK**   **177**
1. Cafés, Bars, and Pubs   177
2. Wine Bars   184
3. Spectacles   185
4. Folk Songs and Chansonniers   187
5. Supper Clubs   188
6. Jazz and Discos   189
7. Opera, Theater, and Music
      Halls   191

Chapter VII **THE ÎLE DE FRANCE** **193**
    1. Versailles **194**
    2. Fontainebleau **198**
    3. Vaux-le-Vicomte **202**
    4. Barbizon **203**
    5. Milly-la-Forêt **205**
    6. Rambouillet **206**
    7. Chartres **206**
    8. Illiers **209**
    9. Provins **209**
    10. Malmaison **210**
    11. Senlis **211**
    12. Compiègne **212**
    13. Chantilly **214**
    14. Beauvais **217**
    15. Château de Thoiry **218**
    16. Giverny **219**
Chapter VIII **THE CHÂTEAU COUNTRY** **221**
    1. Châteaudun **222**
    2. Tours **223**
    3. Montbazon **228**
    4. Azay-le-Rideau **229**
    5. Luynes **230**
    6. Villandry **231**
    7. Loches **232**
    8. Amboise **234**
    9. Blois **236**
    10. Chaumont **238**
    11. Chambord **239**
    12. Beaugency **240**
    13. Cheverny **242**
    14. Valençay **243**
    15. Chenonceaux **244**
    16. Orléans **246**
    17. Sully-sur-Loire **249**
    18. Les Bézards **250**

	19. Gien	250
	20. Langeais	251
	21. Ussé	253
	22. Chinon	253
	23. Fontevraud-l'Abbaye	255
	24. Saumur	256
	25. Angers	258
	26. Le Mans	261
	27. Loué	262
Chapter IX	**NORMANDY**	264
	1. Rouen	265
	2. Jumièges	272
	3. Saint-Wandrille	272
	4. Caudebec-en-Caux	272
	5. Pont-Audemer	273
	6. L'Aigle	274
	7. Orbec	274
	8. Caen	275
	9. Bayeux	278
	10. Port-en-Bessin	280
	11. D-Day Beaches	280
	12. Cherbourg	282
	13. Le Mont St-Michel	283
	14. Pont l'Évêque	285
	15. Cabourg	285
	16. Deauville	286
	17. Trouville	290
	18. Honfleur	291
	19. Le Havre	292
	20. Fécamp	294
	21. Dieppe	295
Chapter X	**BRITTANY**	297
	1. Nantes	298
	2. La Baule	301
	3. Carnac	303
	4. Quiberon	305

	5.	Belle-Île-en-Mer	306
	6.	Hennebont	307
	7.	Quimperlé	308
	8.	Pont-Aven	309
	9.	Riec-sur-Belon	309
	10.	Concarneau	310
	11.	La Forêt-Fouesnant	312
	12.	Quimper	312
	13.	Locronan	314
	14.	Dinan	315
	15.	Dinard	317
	16.	St-Malo	319

Chapter XI — **REIMS AND THE CHAMPAGNE COUNTRY** — 321
	1.	Épernay	321
	2.	Condé-en-Brie	323
	3.	Reims	324
	4.	Fère-en-Tardenois	328
	5.	Château-Thierry	328
	6.	La Ferté-sous-Jouarre	329

Chapter XII — **THE ARDENNES AND THE NORTH** — 330
	1.	The Ardennes	330
	2.	Amiens	332
	3.	St-Quentin	333
	4.	Laon	334
	5.	Arras	335
	6.	Lille	337
	7.	Dunkerque	339
	8.	Calais	340
	9.	Boulogne-sur-Mer	341
	10.	Le Touquet-Paris-Plage	342

Chapter XIII — **ALSACE-LORRAINE AND THE VOSGES** — 344
	1.	Verdun	344
	2.	Metz	346
	3.	Nancy	347
	4.	Lunéville and Baccarat	351

	5. Domrémy-la-Pucelle	352
	6. Strasbourg	353
	7. La Wantzenau	360
	8. Illhaeusern	361
	9. Colmar	362
	10. The Wine Road of Alsace	365
	11. The Crest Road	371
	12. Mulhouse	372
Chapter XIV	**THE FRENCH ALPS**	375
	1. Évian-les-Bains	375
	2. Morzine-Avoriaz	378
	3. Flaine	380
	4. Chamonix–Mont Blanc	382
	5. Megève	385
	6. Albertville	388
	7. Annecy	389
	8. Talloires	391
	9. Aix-les-Bains	393
	10. Chambéry	395
	11. Grenoble	396
	12. Courchevel	402
Chapter XV	**BURGUNDY AND MORVAN**	404
	1. Chablis	405
	2. Auxerre	406
	3. Joigny	407
	4. Vézelay	408
	5. Avallon	409
	6. Planchez	411
	7. Château-Chinon	411
	8. Autun	412
	9. Beaune	413
	10. Chagny	415
	11. Bouilland	416
	12. Gevrey-Chambertin	417
	13. Dijon	418
	14. Montbard	421
	15. Saulieu	422

	16. Aubigney	423
Chapter XVI	THE VALLEY OF THE RHÔNE	424
	1. Bourg-en-Bresse	424
	2. The Beaujolais Country	426
	3. Lyon	428
	4. Pérouges	438
	5. Roanne	439
	6. Vienne	440
	7. Condrieu	441
	8. Valence	441
	9. Montélimar	443
Chapter XVII	THE MASSIF CENTRAL	444
	1. Bourges	444
	2. Nohant (St-Chartier)	446
	3. Vichy	447
	4. Clermont-Ferrand	448
	5. Le Puy	450
	6. Aubusson	452
	7. Limoges	452
	8. Aurillac	455
Chapter XVIII	THE PÉRIGORD-DORDOGNE REGION	457
	1. Périgueux	458
	2. Lascaux (Montignac)	459
	3. Les Eyzies-de-Tayac	461
	4. Beynac-et-Cazenac	462
	5. Brive-la-Gaillarde (Varetz)	463
	6. Sarlat-la-Canéda	465
	7. Rocamadour	467
	8. Cahors	468
	9. Montauban	469
Chapter XIX	BORDEAUX AND THE ATLANTIC COAST	471
	1. Bordeaux	471
	2. The Wine Country	475
	3. Angoulême	479
	4. Cognac	481

		5. Saintes	482
		6. La Rochelle	484
		7. Poitiers	487
Chapter XX	THE BASQUE COUNTRY AND THE PYRÉNÉES		490
		1. Bayonne	490
		2. Biarritz	492
		3. St-Jean-de-Luz	496
		4. Pau	499
		5. Eugénie-les-Bains	501
		6. Lourdes	501
		7. Cauterets	504
		8. Ax-les-Thermes	505
		9. Perpignan	506
Chapter XXI	LANGUEDOC AND THE CAMARGUE		508
		1. Auch	508
		2. Toulouse	509
		3. Albi	513
		4. Cordes	515
		5. Castres	516
		6. Narbonne	517
		7. Montpellier	518
		8. Carcassone	521
		9. Nîmes	523
		10. Aigues-Mortes	526
Chapter XXII	PROVENCE		528
		1. Îles d'Hyères	528
		2. Toulon	530
		3. Marseille	533
		4. Aix-en-Provence	540
		5. Vauvenargues	545
		6. Arles	546
		7. Fontvieille	549
		8. Les Baux	549
		9. St-Rémy-de-Provence	551
		10. Avignon	554

	11. Gordes	559
	12. Orange	561
	13. Châteauneuf-du-Pape	563
Chapter XXIII	**THE FRENCH RIVIERA**	564
	1. Menton	565
	2. Roquebrune and Cap Martin	569
	3. Monaco	570
	4. Eze and La Turbie	579
	5. Beaulieu	581
	6. St-Jean and Cap Ferrat	583
	7. Villefranche	585
	8. Nice	587
	9. St-Paul-de-Vence	603
	10. Vence	605
	11. Cagnes-sur-Mer	607
	12. Biot	610
	13. Antibes and Cap d'Antibes	611
	14. Juan-les-Pins	615
	15. Golfe-Juan and Vallauris	617
	16. Mougins	618
	17. Grasse	620
	18. Cannes	621
	19. La Napoule-Plage	631
	20. St-Tropez	633
Chapter XXIV	**CORSICA**	639
	1. Bastia	643
	2. L'Île-Rousse	644
	3. Calvi	645
	4. Porto	645
	5. Corte	646
	6. Ajaccio	647
	7. Porticcio	648
	8. Propriano	649
	9. Sartène	650
	10. Porto-Vecchio	650
	11. Bonifacio	651

MAPS

France	2–3
Paris Métro	40–41
Paris	48–49
Paris: Right Bank	52
Paris: Left Bank	56
Environs of Paris	200
Châteaux of the Loire Valley	225
Brittany and Normandy	266
Chamonix	381
Courchevel	401
Provence and the Camargue	531
The Riviera	567
Corsica	641

The author of this guide gratefully acknowledges the research and editorial contributions of Margaret Foresman of New York City.

INFLATION ALERT!!!

In the wave of inflation that has battered Europe, France has been hard hit. The author of this guide has spent laborious hours of research trying to ensure the accuracy of prices appearing in this book. As we go to press, I believe we have obtained the most reliable data available. However, in a system that in 1986 saw one restaurateur in the Loire Valley raise the price of his salmon three times in one summer, I can't offer guarantees for the tariffs quoted. In the lifetime of this edition—particularly in its second year (1988)—the wise traveler will add *at least* 15% to 20% to the prices quoted.

THE FRANC AND THE DOLLAR: The franc, like all world currencies, is currently fluctuating on the world market. That means that the franc-to-dollar conversions appearing in parentheses throughout these chapters may or may not be exact. There is no way to predict what the rate of exchange will be when you visit France. Check with your bank to determine the up-to-date figure.

A DISCLAIMER: Although every effort was made to ensure the accuracy of the prices and travel information appearing in this book, it should be kept in mind that prices do fluctuate in the course of time, and that information does change under the impact of the varied and volatile factors that affect the travel industry.

Readers should also note that the establishments described under Readers Selections or Suggestions have not in many cases been inspected by the author and that the opinions expressed there are those of the individual reader(s) only. They do not in any way represent the opinions of the publisher or author of this guide.

DOLLARWISE GUIDE TO FRANCE

The Reason Why

FRANCE IS A NATION of contrasts, united by love of country . . . and a loaf of bread. Wherever you go, from the streets of Marseille to the fishing hamlets of Brittany, from the provincial capitals to the "capital of capitals," you'll see the French, the matronly and the chic, carry home their daily bread.

Of course, even this time-honored ritual is changing. Many modern homemakers in France buy their bread wrapped in waxpaper at supermarkets. Gaul is not entirely trapped by its traditions. You may find some elderly wives of fishermen in Brittany wearing the starched lace headdresses their grandmothers' mothers did before them. But at the next table you might meet their daughters, exquisitely attired in the latest Parisian fashions, discussing the state of the theater in New York.

Some things in France never change, however. Priests still walk the streets of provincial towns greeting aging women in black; lovers with their arms wrapped around each other still stroll along the banks of the Seine; and Left Bank students still spend an evening arguing philosophy over a bottle of wine. The *agent pivot* still directs traffic with a white baton, waving speeding motorists around the Arc de Triomphe; French people still spend hours in their favorite cafés; and little old winemakers practice the same basic techniques they have for generations. The nation, then, is a land rich in tradition, and it is that quality I'll search for in exploring—

THE BEST OF FRANCE: I have set myself the formidable task of seeking out France at its finest and condensing that between the covers of this book. The best towns, villages, cities, and sightseeing attractions; the best hotels, restaurants, bars, cafés, and nightspots.

But the best need not be the most expensive. My ultimate aim—beyond that of familiarizing you with the offerings of France—is to stretch your dollar power . . . to reveal to you that you need not always pay scalpers' prices for charm, top-grade comfort, and gourmet-level food.

In this guide I'll devote a great deal of attention to those old tourist meccas —Paris, Cannes, Monaco, Biarritz—focusing on both their obvious and hidden treasures. But they are not the full "reason why" of this book. Important as they are, they simply do not reflect fully the widely diverse and complicated country that France is. To discover that, you must venture deep into the provinces.

DOLLARWISE—WHAT IT MEANS: In brief, this is a guidebook giving specific details, including prices, about French hotels, restaurants, bars,

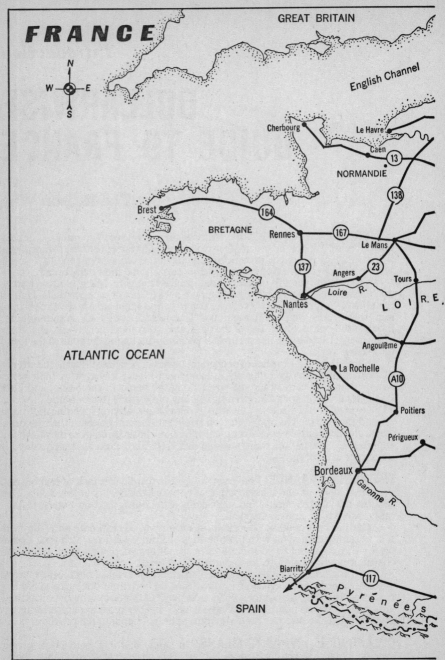

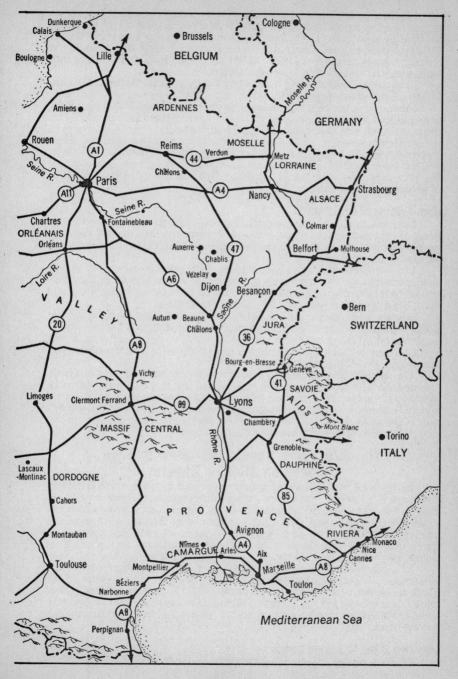

cafés, sightseeing attractions, nightlife, and tours. Establishments in many price ranges have been documented and described, although mainly I am searching for bargains such as the Hostellerie Gargantua, a family-style inn named after Rabelais' amiable giant, Gargantua, in the charming village of Chinon in the château country. It charges 210F ($28.96) per person for a double room with bath, with a continental breakfast with homemade croissants.

In all cases, establishments have been judged by a strict yardstick of value. If they measured up, they were included.

Now, more than ever, one needs an accurate guidebook including tips for saving money. By careful planning and selecting from these listings, you'll find the true French experience while remaining within your budget. This applies to independent travelers as well as those who visit France on a package tour. Even though you've obtained your flight ticket, and are offered a hotel for a few days, you'll still need helpful tips on restaurants, nightlife, and sightseeing attractions. If you're given a car, then you'll be in the market for suggestions in the country, or at least outside of Paris.

Some Words of Explanation

No restaurant, inn, hotel, nightclub, or café paid to be mentioned in this book. What you read are entirely personal recommendations; in many cases the proprietors never knew their establishments were being visited or investigated for inclusion in a travel guide.

Unfortunately, although I have made every effort to be as accurate as possible, prices change, and they rarely go downward, at least in France. The country has only limited government regulation of its hotel tariffs, unlike Spain and Italy, but more supervision than England or Scandinavia.

Always, when checking in, inquire about the rate—and agree on it. That policy can save much embarrassment and disappointment when it comes time to settle the tab. If the prices quoted are not the same as those mentioned in this book, remember that my prices reflect those in effect at the time this edition was researched. As I said, prices change.

This guide is revised cover to cover every other year. But even in a book that appears with such frequency, it may happen that that cozy little bistro of a year ago has changed its stripes, blossoming out with cut-velvet walls, crystal chandeliers, and dining tabs that include the decorator's fee and the owner's villa at Deauville. It may further develop that some of the people or settings I've described are no longer there or have been changed.

The $25-a-Day Travel Club—How to Save Money on All Your Travels

In this book we'll be looking at how to get your money's worth in France, but there is a "device" for saving money and determining value on *all* your trips. It's the popular, international $25-a-Day Travel Club, now in its 24th successful year of operation. The Club was formed at the urging of numerous readers of the $$$-a-Day and Dollarwise Guides, who felt that such an organization could provide continuing travel information and a sense of community to value-minded travelers in all parts of the world. And so it does!

In keeping with the budget concept, the annual membership fee is low and is immediately exceeded by the value of your benefits. Upon receipt of $18 (U.S. residents), or $20 U.S. by check drawn on a U.S. bank or via international postal money order in U.S. funds (Canadian, Mexican, and other foreign residents) to cover one year's membership, we will send all new members the following items.

Any two of the following books

Please designate in your letter which two you wish to receive.

Europe on $25 a Day
Australia on $25 a Day
England on $35 a Day

Eastern Europe on $25 a Day
Greece including Istanbul and Turkey's Aegean Coast on $25 a Day
Hawaii on $45 a Day
India on $15 & $25 a Day
Ireland on $35 a Day
Israel on $30 & $35 a Day
Mexico on $20 a Day (plus Belize and Guatemala)
New York on $45 a Day
New Zealand on $35 a Day
Scandinavia on $40 a Day
Scotland and Wales on $35 a Day
South America on $25 a Day
Spain and Morocco (plus the Canary Is.) on $35 a Day
Turkey on $25 a Day (avail. May '87)
Washington, D.C., on $40 a Day

Dollarwise Guide to Alaska (avail. April '87)
Dollarwise Guide to Austria and Hungary
Dollarwise Guide to Benelux (avail. June '87)
Dollarwise Guide to Bermuda and The Bahamas
Dollarwise Guide to Canada
Dollarwise Guide to the Caribbean
Dollarwise Guide to Egypt
Dollarwise Guide to England and Scotland
Dollarwise Guide to France
Dollarwise Guide to Germany
Dollarwise Guide to Italy
Dollarwise Guide to Japan and Hong Kong
Dollarwise Guide to Portugal, Madeira, and the Azores
Dollarwise Guide to Switzerland and Liechtenstein
Dollarwise Guide to California and Las Vegas
Dollarwise Guide to Florida
Dollarwise Guide to New England
Dollarwise Guide to New York State (avail. May '87)
Dollarwise Guide to the Northwest
Dollarwise Guide to Skiing USA-East
Dollarwise Guide to Skiing USA-West
Dollarwise Guide to the Southeast and New Orleans
Dollarwise Guide to the South Pacific (avail. June '87)
Dollarwise Guide to the Southwest
Dollarwise Guide to Texas
(Dollarwise Guides discuss accommodations and facilities in all price ranges, with emphasis on the medium-priced.)

A Guide for the Disabled Traveler
(A guide to the best destinations for wheelchair travelers and other disabled vacationers in Europe, the United States, and Canada by an experienced wheelchair traveler. Includes detailed information about accommodations, restaurants, sights, transportation, and their accessibility.)

A Shopper's Guide to Best Buys in England, Scotland, and Wales
(Describes in detail hundreds of places to shop—department stores, fac-

tory outlets, street markets, and craft centers—for great quality British bargains.)

A Shopper's Guide to the Caribbean
(A guide to the best shopping in the islands. Includes full descriptions of what to look for and where to find it.)

Bed & Breakfast—North America
(This guide contains a directory of over 150 organizations that offer bed & breakfast referrals and reservations throughout North America. The scenic attractions, businesses, and major schools and universities near the homes of each are also listed.)

Dollarwise Guide to Cruises
(This complete guide covers all the basics of cruising—ports of call, costs, fly-cruise package bargains, cabin selection booking, embarkation and debarkation and describes in detail over 60 or so ships cruising the waters of Alaska, the Caribbean, Mexico, Hawaii, Panama, Canada, and the United States.)

Dollarwise Guide to Skiing Europe
(Describes top ski resorts in Austria, France, Italy, and Switzerland. Illustrated with maps of each resort area plus full-color trail maps.)

Travel Diary and Record Book
(A 96-page diary for personal travel notes plus a section for such vital data as passport and traveler's check numbers, itinerary, postcard list, special people and places to visit, and a reference section with temperature and conversion charts, and world maps with distance zones.)

How to Beat the High Cost of Travel
(This practical guide details how to save money on absolutely all travel items—accommodations, transportation, dining, sightseeing, shopping, taxes, and more. Includes special budget information for seniors, students, singles, and families.)

Marilyn Wood's Wonderful Weekends
(This very selective guide covers the best mini-vacation destinations within a 175-mile radius of New York City. It describes special country inns and other accommodations, restaurants, picnic spots, sights, and activities—all the information needed for a two- or three-day stay.)

Museums in New York
(A complete guide to all the museums, historic houses, gardens, zoos, and more in the five boroughs. Illustrated with over 200 photographs.)

Swap and Go—Home Exchanging Made Easy
(Two veteran home exchangers explain in detail all the money-saving benefits of a home exchange, and then describe precisely how to do it. Also includes information on home rentals and many tips on low-cost travel.)

The Fast 'n' Easy Phrase Book
(French, German, Spanish, and Italian—all in one convenient, easy-to-use phrase guide.)

Motorist's Phrase Book
(A practical phrase book in French, German, and Spanish designed specificallly for the English-speaking motorist touring abroad.)

The New York Urban Athlete
(The ultimate guide to all the sports facilities in New York City for jocks and novices.)

Where to Stay USA
(By the Council on International Educational Exchange, this extraordinary guide is the first to list accommodations in all 50 states that cost anywhere from $3 to $30 per night.)

(2) A one-year subscription to *The Wonderful World of Budget Travel*

This quarterly eight-page tabloid newspaper keeps you up to date on fast-breaking developments in low-cost travel in all parts of the world bringing you the latest money-saving information—the kind of information you'd have to pay $25 a year to obtain elsewhere. This consumer-conscious publication also features columns of special interest to readers: **Hospitality Exchange** (members all over the world who are willing to provide hospitality to other members as they pass through their home cities); **Share-a-Trip** (offers and requests from members for travel companions who can share costs and help avoid the burdensome single supplement); and **Readers Ask . . . Readers Reply** (travel questions from members to which other members reply with authentic firsthand information).

(3) A copy of *Arthur Frommer's Guide to New York*

This is a pocket-size guide to hotels, restaurants, nightspots, and sightseeing attractions in all price ranges throughout the New York area.

(4) Your personal membership card

Membership entitles you to purchase through the Club all Arthur Frommer publications for a third to a half off their regular retail prices during the term of your membership.

So why not join this hardy band of international budgeteers and participate in its exchange of travel information and hospitality? Simply send your name and address, together with your annual membership fee of $18 (U.S. residents) or $20 U.S. (Canadian, Mexican, and other foreign residents), by check drawn on a U.S. bank or via international postal money order in U.S. funds to: $25-A-Day Travel Club, Inc., Frommer Books, Gulf & Western Building, One Gulf & Western Plaza, New York, NY 10023. And please remember to specify which *two* of the books in section (1) above you wish to receive in your initial package of members' benefits. Or, if you prefer, use the last page of this book, simply checking off the two books you select and enclosing $18 or $20 in U.S. currency.

Once you are a member, there is no obligation to buy additional books. No books will be mailed to you without your specific order.

Chapter 1

GETTING TO AND AROUND FRANCE

1. Traveling to France
2. Traveling Within France
3. The Grand Tour of France

A HOLIDAY IN FRANCE, for most of the readers of this book, must first begin with a transatlantic trip *to* France. That requires a brief examination of the available transportation—especially the question of air transportation.

Of equal importance, of course, is the matter of getting around in the country after you arrive. There is so much to see that it pays to have in mind before you go just how you will seek out that little village in Provence and what means of transportation is best to take you to the attractions of the French Riviera, to the imposing châteaux of the Loire Valley, and through the miles of vineyards in the wine country.

As I have traveled extensively and frequently in France, I will seek in this chapter to give you the benefit of my experiences and to share with you my suggestions as to the routes to follow on a "grand tour" of the country.

1. Traveling to France

In choosing an airline for your trip to France, your thoughts will immediately turn to **Air France.** The French national carrier operates more daily transatlantic flights to Paris—as many as eight a day—from more cities in North America than any other carrier, including New York, Washington, D.C., Anchorage, Montréal, Toronto, and Mexico City, as well as the only non-stop 747s from Chicago, Los Angeles, and Houston. The Air France network covers 435,968 miles and serves 155 cities in 75 countries.

Both for the regular transatlantic business commuter and the first-time aviation enthusiast, the **Air France Concorde,** the world's first and only supersonic air transport, has established a new lifestyle in air travel. Concorde, which cuts U.S.-to-Europe flying times in half and virtually eliminates jet fatigue, flies daily between New York and Paris.

Air France Première service pampers first-class passengers with the finest

French cuisine complemented by vintage champagnes and wines. The Première cabin on the 747 features the airline industry's first dual-control, electrically powered seat, assuring the height of comfort for Première passengers while dining, working, or relaxing.

Business travelers should be aware that the carrier offers **Air France Le Club,** with larger seats and a special section of the 747 cabin, as well as expanded meal and bar service. The airline is also now part of the United Airlines Mileage Plus and Continental's Travel Bank programs for frequent flyers, meaning that travel on Air France can earn awards on these carriers and vice versa. Even in economy class, however, Air France offers special extras such as complimentary headsets, champagne, cocktails, wine, and liqueur.

Upon arrival in Paris, you'll find Air France and Air Inter have scheduled many convenient ongoing flights to principal cities like Nice, Lyon, Marseille, Bordeaux as well as nearly 58 cities throughout Europe. The French airline is also well equipped to provide advance trip information.

Air France has ten district offices across the U.S., staffed by personnel who are constantly being briefed on travel facilities, accommodations, and what's new abroad. As you would expect, Air France is the airline that knows France best.

And remember, only Air France puts you in France from the moment you check in. Your Gallic adventure begins with a welcoming *"Bonjour!"* from a charming bilingual hostess and continues right through a gourmet lunch or dinner, featuring fine food and wines.

PLANE ECONOMICS: Air France offers travelers to France a number of economical alternatives. **Jet Vacations,** a major U.S. tour operator, runs charter flights to France during the summer using Air France 747 aircraft. These flights are available twice weekly between New York and Paris and between Boston and Paris and New York and Nice.

Round-trip fares are usually less than on regular flights. Check with a travel specialist or the airline.

2. Traveling Within France

PLANES: The cost of domestic air travel for U.S. travelers in France has been cut dramatically, thanks to **Visit France** air fares. Sold only in conjunction with Air France Visite or Youth Fares (or several other special reduced fares), Visit France rates can save 40% to 50% off regular economy fares.

Jet Vacations Flexi-Plan

A shopper's delight of budget tour options in Paris and throughout France is included in this plan. Options range from discount car rentals to a prepaid selection of a hotel, restaurant, or sightseeing tour. For more details, get in touch with Jet Vacations or your travel agent, or call 212/247-0999.

TRAINS: In a few hours, trains link Paris with all parts of France—the fastest way to go, except for travel by air on some long distances. On the network of the **S.N.C.F.** (French National Railroads), there are 24,000 miles of track, about 5,000 stations. Completely safe, the express trains go as fast as 168 miles per hour. Their on-time arrival record is fabled throughout the world. You can travel either first or second class by day or in couchette or sleeper by night. Many long-distance trains in France carry dining cars that serve food ranging from airline-type meals up to five-course dinners.

French National Railroads features an economical rail pass called **France Vacances,** which reduces the total cost of train travel considerably. Available for 7 or 15 days or one month in both first and second class, it entitles the holder to unlimited rail transportation throughout France as well as to free bus and subway travel in Paris, free transfer to and from the Paris airports via Orly-Rail or Roissy-Rail, free admission to the Pompidou Center, plus reductions on French Railroads-operated bus excursions and, for those carrying a first-class ticket, special discounted unlimited mileage fares on car rentals for budget Train + Auto service is available at more than 200 train stations throughout France. Special bonuses are included with this kind of ticket, whether for first- or second-class passengers, which include one day's free transport on the Chemins de Fer de Provence, between Digne and Nice. Also included are free transport on the Paris subway and bus systems. A seven-day France Vacances ticket offers two free days of interurban Paris transport, a 15-day ticket provides four such free days, and on a one-month pass you can ride free for seven days.

A **France Vacances Special** is now available, consisting of nine or 16 daily coupons for unlimited rail travel in either first or second class, depending on the program selected. Coupons must be used within a one-month period.

This French equivalent to Eurailpass is available to nonresidents of France. It may be purchased at French National Railroads, 610 Fifth Ave., New York, NY 10020 (tel. 212/582-2110), or through your local travel agency. Submit your passport number and country of residence. France Vacances travel is within France only.

If you plan to travel heavily on the French National Railroad and other European railroad lines, you will do well to secure the latest copy of the Thomas Cook Continental Timetable of European Railroads. This comprehensive 500+ page timetable details all of Europe's mainline rail services with great accuracy. It is available exclusively in North America from Forsyth Travel Library, P.O. Box 2975, Shawnee Mission, KS 66201, at a cost of $15.95, plus $2.50 postage.

For information in Paris about train departures, go to the Gare de l'Est, the Gare du Nord, the Gare Saint-Lazare, the Gare Montparnasse, the Gare d'-Austerlitz, and the Gare de Lyon. In Paris, you can telephone 43-80-50-50 for railway information in English. From outside Paris, you'll need to dial 16-1-43-80-50-50.

Some of the most popular sleepers in France are the *Train Bleu,* which leaves Paris-Lyon every night at 9:46 serving Cannes, where it arrives at 7:15 the next morning, and Nice, arrival time 7:55 a.m.; *L'Occitan,* which leaves Paris-Austerlitz at 10:53 p.m. and gets into Toulouse at 7:03 a.m.; and *La Palombe Bleu,* which leaves Paris-Austerlitz at 10:57 p.m. and arrives in Tarbes at 8:10 a.m. Of course, one of the standard bearers is *L'Aquitaine,* which leaves Paris-Austerlitz at 5:47 p.m. to reach Bordeaux at 9:56 p.m.

If you have questions about this method of transportation, you can have them answered before leaving North America by getting in touch with the **French National Railroads** at 610 Fifth Ave., New York, NY 10020; 360 Post St., San Francisco, CA 94102; 11 East Adams St., Chicago, IL 60603; 9465 Wilshire Blvd., Los Angeles, CA 90212; 2121 Ponce de Leon Blvd., Coral Gables, FL 33134; 1500 Stanley St., Montréal, Québec; or at 409 Granville St., Vancouver, B.C.

Eurailpass

For years, many in-the-know travelers have been taking advantage of one of the greatest travel bargains in Europe—the Eurailpass, which permits unlimited first-class rail travel in any country in Western Europe except the British Isles (good in Ireland). Passes are purchased for periods as short as 15 days or as long as three months and are strictly nontransferable.

Here's how it works: The pass is sold only outside of Europe and North Africa and only to residents of countries outside those areas. Vacationers may purchase a 15-day Eurailpass for $260; otherwise, a 21-day pass costs $330; a one-month pass, $410; two months, $560; or three months, $680. Children under 4 may travel free, and children under 12 pay only half fare.

The advantages are tempting. No tickets, no supplements (simply show the pass to the ticket collector, then settle back to enjoy the European scenery). Seat reservations are required in some trains. Some trains have couchettes (sleeping cars), for which an additional fee is charged.

Obviously, the two-or three-month visitor gets the greatest economical advantages; he or she can visit all of France's major sights, from the Alps to Brittany, then end the vacation in Norway—all on the same ticket. Eurailpass holders are entitled to considerable reductions on ferry steamers and some buses.

If you're under 26, you can purchase a **Eurail Youthpass,** entitling you to unlimited second-class travel for one month for $290, for two months at a cost of $370.

Eurail Saverpass is a money-saving ticket offered for three or more people traveling together. It is good for 15 consecutive days of unlimited first-class rail travel in the same countries and with the same privileges as Eurailpass. All it requires is that your group remain together throughout the trip. The price of the 15-day saver is $199 per person. From October 1 to March 31, Eurail Saverpass can also be purchased when only two persons travel together.

The Eurailpass is available from all travel agents and at the offices of CIT. Tours Corp., 666 Fifth Ave., New York, NY 10103 (tel. 212/397-9300), and from the French National Railroads, the German Federal Railroads, and the Swiss Federal Railways.

CAR RENTALS: Francophiles maintain that the best way to see France is by car, and I heartily concur. The most charming châteaux and the best country hotels always seem to lie away from the main cities and far away from train stations, and for that and other reasons you'll find that renting a car is usually the best way to travel once you get to France, especially if you plan to explore in depth and not just stick to the standard routes, such as the Paris-Nice run.

The major car-rental companies all have the same price arrangement. Of the major world-wide competitors, the cheapest weekly arrangements, as of this writing and subject to change, are offered by Budget Rent-a-Car, followed by National/Europcar. Hertz is more expensive, and Avis is the most expensive. In most cases, the best deal is a weekly rental with unlimited mileage.

Renting a car is easy. You'll need to present a valid driver's license and be at least 21 years old for the cheaper models and at least 23 for the more expensive vehicles. Renters must also present a valid passport and a valid credit card unless payment is arranged in North America before leaving home. It usually isn't obligatory, but certain companies, perhaps the smaller ones, have at times asked for the presentation of an international driver's license.

Budget Rent-a-Car has 11 locations inside Paris as well as at the two major airports, both Orly and Charles de Gaulle. Cars can usually be picked up in one city and dropped off in another city with no additional charge if you warn Budget in advance when you make the reservation.

One of the cheapest cars available is a two-door Opel Corsa with manual transmission. It costs about 1,100F ($151.69) per week with unlimited mileage.

It can conceivably hold four passengers plus their luggage, although if you travel in slightly bigger (and better) circumstances you can reserve a Peugeot 205 for 1,248F ($172.10) per week, plus another 178F ($24.54) for each extra day. Automatic transmissions are regarded as a luxury item in Europe. The least expensive car Budget offers with an automatic transmission is a four-door, five-passenger Renault 11, renting for about 1,950F ($268.91) per week. The above prices are meant as a guideline only and are subject to an additional 33⅓% tax in France.

Clients wanting to protect themselves against international currency-exchange fluctuations can ask Budget to "lock" the exchange rate in effect at the time of booking. In such cases, a reservation must be made and paid for in North America at least 21 days before the anticipated pickup of a car. For information about this and other car-rental matters, call Budget toll free at 800/527-0700 in the United States. In Canada call toll free 800/268-8900 (in Toronto, 482-0222; in British Columbia, 112/800/268-8900; and in Quebec, 800/268-8970).

National Car Rental is represented in Paris through its European affiliate, Europcar. Headquarters in Paris are at 145 Avenue Malakoff, 16e (tel. 45-00-08-06). It also maintains branches at both Paris airports, as well as at about another half-dozen locations in the city. Its headquarters can rent you a car on the spot, but to qualify for the cheaper weekly rental you must reserve at least two days in advance on National's toll-free number: 800/328-4567.

Hertz is well represented in Paris, with 12 locations as well as offices at both major airports. The main office is at 27 rue St. Ferdinand, 17e (tel. 45-74-97-39). Most visitors opt for the cheaper weekly rental which in peak season must be reserved at least seven days in advance (however, this is reduced to only two days in winter). For toll-free reservations in the U.S., dial 800/654-3001 (in Oklahoma, dial 800/522-3711).

Avis has offices in Paris at both Orly and Charles de Gaulle airports, as well as a Left Bank inner-city location at 5 rue Bixio, 7e (tel. 45-50-32-31), near the Eiffel Tower. Prices vary with the season, but the most favorable rates are given drivers who reserve a car at least two business days in advance. In the U.S., cars can be reserved by calling toll free 800/331-2112.

Rules for Driving

Everyone in the car, in both the front and the back seats, must wear seat belts. Children under ten years old are required to ride in the back seat.

Drivers are supposed to yield to the car on their right, except where signs indicate otherwise, as at traffic circles.

TOURS FOR SPECIAL INTERESTS: Whether shopping for mustard in Dijon or tasting wine in Burgundy, viewing Roman ruins or dining in starred restaurants, the **Continental Waterways** luxury barge tours offer stunning scenery and something special for every taste. Continental's fleet of six elegant canal barges covers France from the Chablis to the Bordeaux regions. For first-time visitors and old hands alike, the barges offer an exciting way to see France's castles, vineyards, and rural villages. Carrying from eight to 24 passengers, the barges all have English-speaking crews, expert chefs, and the finest regional cuisine and wines. Itineraries feature three- and six-night programs, with a choice of sailings midweek or weekends. The cruises are designed to cover a wide variety of interests. Passengers can participate in on-board aerobics, and there are activities for children on certain trips. In several places, hot-air ballooning is offered as an extra-cost option.

For reservations and information, get in touch with Continental Waterways (tel. toll free 800/227-1281).

3. The Grand Tour of France

To be blunt and in contradiction of our headline, a "grand tour" of France is almost impossible for the average visitor. It takes at least two weeks to tour each major province, and France has a lot of provinces—all of tourist interest either major or limited—and few persons have months in which to see the country, as delectable an idea as that might be. Some strong choices about where to go have to be made. The answer of where to go depends entirely on your time, whim, inclination, and, often, your pocketbook. I'll give you what I hope are helpful suggestions to get you across at least some of the highlights of a constantly changing but ever-fascinating countryside.

Covering 212,741 square miles, France is slightly smaller than Texas. But no other patch on the globe concentrates such a fabulous diversity of sights and scenery in so compact an area. Within her borders, France houses each of the natural characteristics that make up Europe: the flat, fertile north, the rolling green hills of the central Loire valley, the snow-capped alpine ranges of the east, the towering Pyrénées in the south, and the lushly semitropical Mediterranean coast of the southeast.

Name your taste and France has a spot for you. The châteaux country around Orléans for castles and vineyards. Normandy and Brittany for rugged seashores and apple orchards. The Mont Blanc area for mountain-climbing and skiing. The Champagne for sun-warmed valleys and the greatest of all wines. Languedoc for Spanish flavor, olive groves, and Mediterranean cookery. The Riviera for golden sands, palm-fringed beaches, and bodies beautiful.

Because the country is—by American standards—not very large, all these contrasts beckon within easy traveling range. By train from Paris, it's just four hours to Alsace, five hours to the Alps, seven hours to the Pyrénées, and eight hours to the Côte d'Azur. France's National Railroads (SNCF) actually *want* passengers and operate one of the finest services in the world. They're also impressively fast to and from Paris, but more inclined to crawl on transversal routes, that is, those unconnected with the capital.

There are some 44,000 miles of roadway at your disposal, most in good condition for fast, long-distance driving. But take a tip and don't stick to the Route Nationale network all the time. Nearly all the scenic splendors lie alongside the secondary roads, and what you lose in mileage you more than make up for in enjoyment.

PARIS, NORMANDY, BRITTANY (10 Days): The first tour is recommended for even the most superficial of visits.

Days 1 to 6: Paris is the major goal of most pilgrims, and, chances are, it will be for you too. Allow your arrival day for settling into the "City of Lights" and resting up after your air trip. Spend days 2, 3, and 4 exploring the top sights of Paris (see our check-list in Chapter V). Day 5 should be set aside for a day trip to **Versailles,** and day 6 for a day trip to **Fontainebleau** (see Chapter VII for information about these attractions). All of this program can be accomplished while still based in Paris at the same hotel.

Day 7: Strike out for Normandy and Brittany, two old provinces of France North Americans generally find the most intriguing (see Chapters IX and X). Head first for **Rouen,** a distance of 84 miles northwest of Paris. You can arrive in time to see where Joan of Arc died in 1431 and the famous Rouen Cathedral.

Day 8: Head east toward **Caen,** the seat of the government of William the Conqueror, a distance of 150 miles from Paris. You can overnight there or else travel west 17 miles to **Bayeux,** where you'll want to see the Cathedral and the Bayeux Tapestry.

Day 9: Either based in Bayeux or Caen, spend the day exploring the **D-Day**

Beaches, of great interest to Americans and Canadians. The highlights are described in Chapter IX.

Day 10: Continue west, heading toward **Le Mont-St-Michel,** one of the great sightseeing attractions of Europe, lying at the border of Normandy and Brittany, 209 miles from Paris. For an overnight stopover in the area, consider those enchanting resort towns in Brittany, **St.-Malo** or **Dinard,** on the northwest coast, facing each other across an estuary. St.-Malo, an ancient pirates' stronghold and walled fishing village, lies 53 miles from Le Mont-St-Michel. Dinard has a gambling casino and sheltered beach, along with golf and tennis courses.

Those with the time will find that the entire peninsula of Brittany has 600 miles of coast and chains of beaches, rustic fishing ports, and some of the greatest seafood you'll ever taste. But time may have run out for you. If so, those who spent the night in Dinard will find that Paris lies 259 miles southeast, easily reached in a day.

THE CHÂTEAU COUNTRY (One Week): About 120 miles southwest of Paris

stretches "the green heart" of France, the breathtakingly beautiful region of the Loire Valley. The towns of the area have magic names, but they also read like Joan of Arc's battle register—Orléans, Blois, Tours, Chinon. Every hilltop has a castle or palace, and there are vineyards as far as the eye can see. The Loire winds through the countryside like a silver ribbon, and the walled cities cluster around medieval churches.

It is estimated that the average North American spends only three nights in the Loire Valley. A week would be better. Even then, you will have only skimmed the surface. If you're severely hampered by lack of time, then try at least to see the following châteaux: Chenonceaux, Amboise, Azay-le-Rideau, Chambord, Chaumont, and Blois (see Chapter VIII for more details).

Day 1: If you're driving from Paris to the Loire Valley, I suggest you take the autoroute to **Chartres** and spend the first night there, taking time to see its fabulous cathedral. The distance is 60 miles south from Paris.

Day 2: Drive to **Tours,** the capital of the Loire Valley, a distance of 144 miles southwest from Paris. It is your best all-around base in the château country, because it has a more diversified selection of hotels. However, Tours is a big city, and many visitors prefer to anchor at **Amboise,** 15 miles east of Tours which is also a good center for exploring.

Day 3: Based in either Tours or Amboise, head for the major attractions in the southwest: **Azay-le-Rideau,** 17 miles from Tours (a private residence during the Renaissance), and **Chinon,** 30 miles from Tours, one of the oldest fortress-châteaux in France.

Day 4: Again based in Tours, head for the already cited **Amboise,** with its memories of Leonardo da Vinci, and **Chenonceaux,** 21 miles southeast of Tours. Chenonceaux is the chef-d'oeuvre of the Renaissance, forever linked to the legend of the *dames de Chenonceaux.*

Day 5: Leave Tours or Amboise, heading east along the autoroute to **Blois,** seat of the counts of Blois. But spend the morning sightseeing at **Chaumont,** with its memories of Diane de Poitiers. Overnight in Blois.

Day 6: Leave the next morning, heading east to **Orléans,** but stop first at **Chambord,** former seat of François I, the Chevalier King. Overnight in Orléans, forever associated with the legend of the Maid of Orléans.

Day 7: Return to **Paris** (the shortest route is the autoroute, a distance of 81 miles).

THE FRENCH RIVIERA (One Week): Now we come to France's sunny south,

her holiday region par excellence. Known to the world as the Côte d'Azur, this is a short stretch of curving coastline near the Italian border. Much to the delight of holiday makers from all parts of the globe, it's a land drenched in sunshine, sprinkled with vineyards and olive groves, and dotted with some of the world's most fascinating tourist meccas. Selecting your resort might be your most difficult decision, as there are at least 26 major ones, spread out along a distance of 70 miles from Menton near the Italian border to Saint-Raphael.

Days 1 to 3: Head for **Nice** and base there for three nights. It lies 578 miles south of Paris, so, if you're rushed, you'd better fly to save time and, incidentally, money. Day 1 will be spent getting there and settling into your hotel. I suggest you spend day 2 exploring **St-Paul-de-Vence,** with its Maeght Foundation, and **Vence,** with its Matisse Chapel. Nice has many attractions of its own (and you'll also want some sun), so spend day 3 on home ground.

Day 4: Drive to **Monte Carlo,** at least for a night, going along to **St-Jean** and **Cap Ferrat** on the same day if you have time. This is one of the poshest parts of southern France. Monaco is 12 miles from Nice along the Moyenne Corniche.

Days 5 to 6: Head for **Cannes,** 20 miles east of Nice. Spend the first day enjoying Cannes itself, and day 6 exploring at least some of the attractions in its environs, including the Lérins Islands off its shoreline (linked to the legend of *The Man in the Iron Mask).*

Day 7: Before saying good-bye to the Riviera, pay a visit to glamorous, chic **St-Tropez,** 46 miles east of Cannes, our last stopover. St-Tropez is strictly for fun and won't dazzle you with a lot of attractions.

LANGUEDOC AND PROVENCE (One Week):
The Rhône River forms the dividing line between Languedoc in the west and Provence in the east. Both portions are equally drenched in sunshine, sprinkled with vineyards and olive groves, and dotted with fascinating towns. The main difference is that Languedoc has an intriguing Spanish air and is somewhat less fashionable and expensive than Provence. Provence, on the east side of the Rhône, can be divided into two units from a vacation viewpoint. The portion closer to the Rhône is studded with both large and tiny towns, each of which provides a holiday setting.

Days 1 to 2: From Paris, fly to **Marseille,** a distance of 482 miles. If you're in Nice, the mileage is 117 miles (Marseille lies west of Nice). Spend the first day settling in, and Day 2 exploring the attractions of the second largest city of France, one of the world's major seaports, and the most colorful, turbulent, and exotic place in the country. Part of the day should be spent visiting Château d'If, an island used as a setting for *The Count of Monte Cristo.*

Day 3: It's an easy 19-mile drive to **Aix-en-Provence,** northeast of Marseille. Aix-en-Provence, the old capital city of Provence, linked with Paul Cézanne, makes a good overnight stopover and you can spend the day sightseeing there.

Day 4: Leaving Aix-en-Provence in the morning, go to **Les Baux,** 54 miles from Marseille. Spend part of the day exploring this "nesting place for eagles," then go to **Arles,** 47 miles west of Aix-en-Provence to discover why it cast a spell over Van Gogh. Spend the night in romantic old Arles.

Day 5: It's on to **Avignon,** surrounded by ancient ramparts and the seat of the popes during the 14th century. The distance is 24 miles from Arles. Arrive early because you'll have a busy day of sightseeing.

Day 6: Two of the most charming cities in the region are **Nîmes** and **Montpellier.** Nîmes contains the most impressive Roman remains in France, including an arena and the Temple of Diana. Montpellier is the center of southern wine production and lies in a scenic setting of unsurpassed beauty. They are only 31 miles apart and can be visited in one busy, busy day. Nîmes should be viewed first, as it lies 27 miles west of Avignon. You should overnight in Montpellier.

Day 7: For a wrap-up, head for one of the major attractions of France, **Carcassonne,** the greatest fortress city of Europe. The location is 57 miles southeast of Toulouse, and it is linked with Montpellier by autoroute. Overnight in Carcassonne after enjoying a platter of cassoulet.

MILEAGE BETWEEN FRANCE'S MAJOR CITIES
Distance in Miles

	Bayonne	Bordeaux	Calais	Grenoble	Limoges	Lyon	Marseille	Nancy	Nice	Orléans	PARIS	Rouen	Strasbourg	Toulon	Toulouse	Tours
Amiens	569	450	96	441	337	376	601	224	668	171	92	70	319	609	528	236
Bayonne		114	658	505	256	503	423	649	520	402	478	505	776	461	185	333
Bordeaux	114		539	374	137	338	402	530	498	283	359	386	657	440	151	214
Caen	447	358	212	492	271	428	623	316	719	224	159	77	450	661	476	145
Calais	658	539		530	426	466	661	151	757	260	181	135	387	699	617	325
Dijon	512	393	530	183	258	118	314	132	410	184	193	273	208	352	450	254
Grenoble	505	374	530		288	65	174	316	207	340	350	430	313	207	332	331
Lille	613	530	69	485	381	420	616	174	712	207	136	135	352	654	572	280
Limoges	256	137	426	288		220	283	391	490	165	246	300	436	432	191	127
Lyon	503	338	466	65	220		195	251	244	276	285	365	298	251	331	266
Marseille	423	402	661	174	283	195		446	116	413	481	561	494	40	251	456
Metz	678	559	290	347	422	283	478	35	574	281	205	260	101	516	614	316
Montpellier	321	300	650	186	268	185	104	436	200	325	334	414	483	142	149	394
Mulhouse	425	506	394	252	371	233	428	115	433	325	273	273	70	466	564	394
Nancy	649	530	151	316	391	251	446		531	235	189	273	91	484	582	316
Nantes	321	202	414	453	187	388	603	413	699	186	234	219	533	614	353	122
Nice	520	498	757	207	490	244	116	531		567	577	657	614	95	347	552
Orléans	402	283	260	340	165	276	413	235	567		81	135	303	509	356	69
PARIS	478	359	181	350	246	285	481	189	577	81		86	251	519	437	145
Reims	562	443	172	430	300	365	531	119	588	162	88	135	215	530	521	229
Rouen	505	386	135	430	300	365	561	273	657	135	86		357	598	491	172
Strasbourg	776	657	387	313	436	298	494	91	614	303	251	357		531	629	443
Toulon	461	440	699	207	432	251	40	484	95	509	519	598	531		288	495
Toulouse	185	151	617	332	191	331	251	582	347	356	437	491	629	288		332
Tours	333	214	325	331	127	266	456	316	552	69	145	172	443	495	332	

Chapter II

SETTLING INTO FRANCE

1. The French
2. Food and Drink
3. The ABCs of France

MANY OF THE DIFFERENCES between the provinces of France are based on geographical variations. The highly publicized area where blue sea waters lap the Côte d'Azur of the Mediterranean, known as the French Riviera, is totally unlike the northwestern corner of the country, Brittany, although both are coastal areas. Blessed with long, dry summers and inviting beaches, the international playground of the south was a drawing card in the slower-paced days of aristocratic and royal visitors, and it is still so for jet-setters of today.

The sea and tides have long governed the lives of the people in coastal provinces. In Brittany, and elsewhere to a lesser degree, the products of the sea are still a means of livelihood. In the southwest and south, this has given way to other sea-going enterprises, such as operation of yachts and other pleasure vessels, as well as cruise ships, all of which ply the waters and keep healthy the economy there.

France faces the Mediterranean on the south, the Bay of Biscay and the Atlantic Ocean on the west, and the English Channel and the Strait of Dover on the northwest. It is bordered on the north by Belgium and Luxembourg, on the northeast by West Germany, on tne east by Switzerland, on the southeast by Italy, and it is divided from Spain on tne south by the rugged Pyrenees Mountains. Besides the Pyrénées, other mountain ranges of the country are the Alps and the Jura. Scattered plains make up more than half of the country. All of these geographical definitions have brought about the development of France into a rich and fertile land.

Farming, wine and brandy production, and cheese making are only some of the pursuits of the country people in the interior, with modern factories, scientists, and laboratories bringing their own coloration to the cities, towns, and villages.

With its many-faceted civilization, its long history of war and conquest, and its prominence in the history books of the world, France is a lure and a challenge to travelers of all nations.

1. The French

HISTORY: The political unit that the world knows today as France resulted from an often bloody series of conflicts among fiercely competitive personalities and factions. When the ancient Romans considered it a part of their empire, their boundaries extended deep into the forests of the Paris basin and up to the edges of the Rhine. As it declined, Rome retreated to the flourishing colonies it had established along a strip of the Mediterranean coastline. Rome colonized them with what were reputed to be the best traders of the era, Greeks and Syrians, who intermarried with local residents and blond-haired, blue-eyed northerners. Centuries later, their ancestors contributed their offspring to the racial melting pot which became modern France.

Grateful for Rome's protection from the barbaric northerners, the residents of this coastal strip became the most cultivated and cultured inhabitants of Gaul. In the north, however, a cluster of tribal kingdoms were already established. Each of these was strengthened and became bolder after the retreat of Rome. The Visigoths, Burgundians, Franks, Ripuarians, Salians, and, in Brittany, the Celts, controlled regions whose boundaries sometimes overlapped those of modern Germany and Spain. Borders and alliances shifted according to an unrecorded array of skirmishes.

The Roman armies left as their legacy the Catholic Church, which, for all its abuses, was probably the only real guardian of civilization. A form of low Latin was the common language, and it slowly evolved into the archaic French which both delights and confuses today's medieval scholars.

In this semi-barbaric political vacuum, the form of Christianity adopted by many of the chieftains was considered heretical by Rome. Consequently, when Clovis, king of northeastern Gaul's Salian Franks, astutely converted to Catholicism, he won the approval of the Pope, the political support of the powerful archbishop of Reims, and the loyalty of the many Gallic tribes which had grown disenchanted with anarchy. At the battle of Soissons in 486, the armies of Clovis defeated the last vestiges of Roman power in Gaul. Other conquests which followed included expansions first westward to the Seine, then to the Loire. After a battle in Dijon, in 500, he became the nominal overlord of the king of Burgundy. Seven years later, after the battle of Vouillé, his armies drove the Visigoths into Spain, giving most of Aquitaine, in western France, to his newly founded Merovingian dynasty. Trying to make the best of an earlier humiliation, Anastasius, the Byzantium-based emperor of the Eastern Roman Empire, finally gave the kingdom of the Franks his legal sanction.

After the death of Clovis in 511, his kingdom was split among his squabbling heirs. The Merovingian dynasty, however, managed to survive in fragmented form for another 250 years. During this period, the power of the bishops and the great lords grew, firmly entrenching the complex rules and preoccupations of what we today know as feudalism.

From the wreckage of a Merovingian court swathed in intrigue, the Carolingian dynasty produced the first strong leader in centuries, Charlemagne. Crowned emperor in Rome on Christmas of the year 800, he returned to his capital at Aix-la-Chapelle (Aachen) to found the Holy Roman Empire. Distinct cultural differences were already visible within this sprawling Empire, most of which was eventually divided between two of Charlemagne's three squabbling heirs. Charles of Aquitaine agreed to accept the western region, while Louis of Bavaria took the east. Historians credit this official division with the development of modern France and Germany as separate nations.

Shortly afterward, the Vikings began plundering from the north, while the Muslim Saracens launched raids in the south. When the Merovingian dynasty died out in 987, Hugh Capet, Count of Paris and Duke of France, officially began the Middle Ages. In 1154, Eleanor of Aquitaine's marriage to Henry II of England placed the entire western half of France under English control, where vestiges of their power would remain for centuries. Meanwhile, vast forests and swamps were cleared for harvesting, the population grew, and monastic life contributed heavily to every level of a rapidly developing social order. Louis IX (Saint Louis) emerged as the 13th century's most memorable king, even though he ceded most of the hard-earned military conquests of his predecessors back to the English. He died of disease along with most of his army in 1270 during the Eighth Crusade in Tunis. Notre-Dame Cathedral and Sainte-Chapelle in Paris had been completed, and the arts of tapestry-making and stonecutting flourished.

During the 1300s, the struggle of French sovereignty against the claims of a rapacious Roman Pope tempted Philip the Fair to encourage support for a pope based in Avignon. (The Roman pope, Boniface VIII, is said to have died of the shock.) Two popes ruled simultaneously, competing fiercely for the financial and spiritual loyalty of Christendom, until the French pope stepped down in 1378. The centuries saw an increase in the wealth and power of the French kings, an increase in the general prosperity, and a decrease in the power of the feudal lords. The death of Louis X without an heir in 1316 prompted more than a decade of intrigue before the eventual accession of the Valois dynasty. The Black Death began in the summer of 1348, killing an estimated 33% of the population. A financial crisis coupled with a ruinous series of harvests almost bankrupted the nation.

During the Hundred Years' War, the English made sweeping inroads into France in an attempt to grab the throne. At their most powerful, they controlled almost all of the north (Picardy and Normandy), Champagne, and most of the Loire Valley. They also ruled the huge western region of France called Guyenne. The peasant-born Joan of Arc, with her visions and enthusiasm, rallied the French troops as well as the timid Dauphin, Charles VII, until she was burned at the stake in Rouen by the English in 1431. A barely cohesive France, led by the newly crowned king, initiated internal reforms which strengthened its finances and its vigor. After compromises among the quarreling factions, the French army drove the increasingly discontented English out of France, leaving them only the port of Calais.

In the late 1400s, Charles VIII married Brittany's last duchess, Anne, for a unification of France with its Celtic-speaking western outpost. In the early 1500s, the endlessly fascinating François I, through war and diplomacy, strengthened the monarchy, rid it of its dependence on Italian bankers, coped with the intricate policies of the Renaissance, and husbanded the arts into a form of patronage which French monarchs would continue for centuries.

Meanwhile, the allure of Protestantism and the unwillingness of the Catholic church to tolerate it led to some of the most intense civil strife in French history. In 1572, Catherine de Médicis reversed her policy of religious tolerance and ordered the St. Bartholomew's Day Massacre of hundreds of Protestants throughout France. The very urbane Henri IV, fearing that a fanatically Catholic Spain would meddle in France's religious conflicts, and tired of the bloodshed, converted to Catholicism as a compromise gesture in 1593. Just before being fatally stabbed by a half-crazed monk, he issued the Edict of Nantes in 1598. This granted freedom of religion to Protestants in France, as well as safeguarding their "places of security," notably La Rochelle.

By now, France was a modern state, finally rid of all but a few of the vestiges of feudalism. In 1624, Louis XIII appointed a Catholic cardinal, the Duke of Richelieu, as his chief minister. Richelieu virtually ruled the country until his death in 1642. Under Richelieu, the Protestants lost their stronghold at La Rochelle but were then assimilated into French society, and the power of France, with a minimum of bloodshed, was greatly increased within Europe. Richelieu's one focused objective, the total power of the monarchy, paved the way for the eventual absolutism of Louis XIV.

Although he ascended the French throne when he was only nine years old, with the help of his Sicilian-born chief minister Mazarin, Louis XIV was probably the most powerful monarch Europe had seen since the fall of the Roman emperors. Through first a brilliant military campaign against Spain, and then a judicious marriage to one of its royal daughters, he expanded France to include the southern provinces of Artois and Roussillon. Later, a series of diplomatic and military victories along the Flemish border expanded France toward the north and east as well. The estimated population of France at this time was 20 million, as opposed to eight million in England and six million in Spain. French colonies in Canada, the West Indies, and Louisiana flourished. The mercantilism which Louis' brilliant finance minister, Colbert, was able to implement is regarded as one of the most important fiscal policies of the era, one which hugely increased the power and wealth of France. The arts flourished. The palace of Versailles is probably the most visible monument to the most flamboyantly consumptive era of French history.

Louis' territorial ambitions so deeply threatened the other nations of Europe that, led by William of Orange (the Dutch-born English king), they united to hold him in check. France entered a series of expensive and demoralizing wars which, coupled with high taxes and years of bad harvests, engendered much civil discontent. England was now viewed as a threat both within Europe and in the global rush for lucrative colonies. The great Atlantic ports of the west, especially Bordeaux, grew and prospered because of France's success in the West Indian slave and sugar trade. Despite its power, France's total number of colonies diminished thanks to the naval power of the English. The rise of Prussia as a militaristic neighbor posed an additional problem.

Meanwhile, the Enlightenment was training a new generation of thinkers for the struggle against absolutism, religious fanaticism, and superstition. Europe was never again the same after the Revolution of 1789, although the ideas which engendered it had been brewing for more than 50 years. On August 10, 1792, troops from Marseille, aided by a Parisian mob, threw Louis XVI and his Austrian-born queen, Marie Antoinette, into prison. After bloodshed and bickering among violently competing factions, the two were executed. France's problems got worse before they got better. In the bloodbaths that followed, both moderates and radicals were guillotined within full view of the bloodthirsty crowd. It usually included voyeurs such as Dickens's Madame Defarge, who brought her knitting every day to the Place de la Révolution (later renamed the Place de la Concorde) to watch the beheadings.

It required the militaristic fervor of Napoleon to unite France once again. Possessed of genius and unlimited ambition, he restored to France a national pride which had been diminished during the horror of the Revolution. In 1799, at the age of 30, he entered Paris and was crowned First Consul and Master of France. Soon after, a decisive victory in his northern Italian campaign solidified his power at home. A brilliant politician, he made peace through a compromise with the Vatican, moderating the atheistic rigidity of the earliest days of the Revolution.

Napoleon's victories made him the envy of Europe. Beethoven dedicated one of his symphonies to him (*Eroica*), but later retracted the dedication when Napoleon committed what Beethoven considered atrocities. Napoleon's famous retreat from Moscow during the winter of 1812 reduced his formerly invincible army to tatters, as 400,000 Frenchmen died in the Russian snows. After a complicated series of ebbings and wanings of his almost mystical good luck, Napoleon was defeated at Waterloo by the combined armies of the English, the Dutch, and the Prussians. Exiled to the British-held island of St. Helena in the south Atlantic, he died in 1821, probably the victim of an unknown poisoner.

In 1814, the Bourbon monarchy was re-established, with reduced powers and a changing array of leaders, including the Prince of Polignac and, later, Charles X. In 1830, the regime was thrown out after it imposed censorship on newspapers and dissolved Parliament. Louis-Philippe, Duke of Orléans, the son of a duke who had voted in 1793 for the death of Louis XIV, was elected king of the French under a liberalized constitution. His reign lasted for 18 years of calm prosperity during which England and France more or less collaborated on matters of foreign policy. The establishment of an independent Belgium and the French conquest of Algeria (1840–1847) were to have resounding effects on French politics a century later.

It was a time of wealth, grace, and the expansion of the arts for most French people, although the industrialization of the north and the east produced some of the most horrible poverty of the 19th century. A revolution in 1848, encouraged by a financial crash and fueled by disgruntled workers in Paris, forced Louis-Philippe out of office. That year, on the dawn of the Second Republic, Emperor Napoléon's nephew, Napoléon III, was elected president by moderate and conservative elements. Appealing to the property-protecting instinct of a nation which hadn't forgotten the violent upheaval of less than a century before, he initiated a right-wing government where he was eventually able to gain complete power—as emperor—in 1851. Unlike those of the First Empire, the clergy of the Second Empire enjoyed great power, especially in the countryside. Steel production, a railway system, and Indochinese colonies were established and expanded.

By 1866, an industrialized France began to see the Second Empire as more of a hindrance to its continued development than as an encouragement. The dismal failure at colonizing Mexico and the increasing power of Austria and Prussia were setbacks to the Empire's prestige. In 1870, the Prussians defeated Napoléon III at Sedan and held him prisoner with 100,000 of his soldiers. Paris was besieged by an enemy who only just failed to march their vastly superior armies through the streets of the capital. After the Prussians withdrew, a violent revolt ushered in the Third Republic and its elected president, Marshal Mac-Mahon, in 1873. Peace and prosperity slowly returned, France regained its glamor, the Eiffel Tower was built, and the impressionists made their visual statements. French influence in North Africa, Southeast Asia, and Madagascar was greatly increased. However, France in humiliation lost Suez to the British.

International rivalries and conflicting alliances led to World War I, which, after decisive German victories for two years, degenerated into the mud-slogged horror of trench warfare. In 1917, the United States broke the European deadlock by entering the war. Immediately after the Allied victory, grave economic problems, coupled with a populace demoralized from years of fighting, offered fertile ground for the rise of socialism and an active communist party. The French government, led by a vindictive Clemenceau, demanded every centime of reparations it could wring from a humiliated Germany. That is said to have increased the Germans' passionate determination to rise from the ashes of 1918 to a place in the sun.

That sun cast its shadow over France again on June 14, 1940 when German armies, under the control of Hitler, marched arrogantly down the Champs-Élysées in Paris, and newsreel cameras recorded Frenchmen openly weeping at their humiliating defeat. Marshal Henri Pétain agreed to form a ministry. Under terms of the armistice, the north of France was occupied by the Nazis and the puppet French government was established at Vichy. Free-French forces, however, continued to fight with the Allies on such battlegrounds as North Africa.

A Committee of National Liberation was set up in Algeria in 1943, declaring itself the legitimate government of the Republic. Under Gen. Dwight Eisenhower, the D-Day landings in Normandy in June of 1944 launched the reconquest of France. The invasion troops were aided by French resistance forces. Paris rose in rebellion even before the Allied armies arrived, and on August 26 Charles de Gaulle entered the capital as head of the government. The Fourth Republic was begun as Nazi occupation forces retreated.

The post-war years were rough for France, and many French soldiers died on the battlefield as former colonies rebelled. It took 80,000 lives, for example, to put down a revolt in Madagascar. French industry was greatly aided by the Marshall Plan in 1948. France associated itself more and more with the United States in foreign affairs, and in 1949 it joined NATO. After suffering a bitter defeat in 1954, France ended the war in Indochina and freed its former colony. It also granted internal self-rule to Tunisia, and Morocco also became independent.

Algeria was to remain a greater problem. War in Algeria dragged on. The situation worsened in 1958, and De Gaulle was called back to form a new government. The Fifth Republic was launched. The Algerian war came to an end in 1962, and the sun had set on most of France's far-flung colonial empire.

GOVERNMENT: There may still be pretenders to the "throne" of France, but that kingdom is long gone. As everybody knows, France is a republic. Its Parliament, chosen through free elections, consists of a National Assembly and the Senate. The National Assembly makes the laws. The president of the Republic is elected by a clear majority and serves a term of seven years. After that, he can be elected only one more time. The president represents France in international negotiations, as he is considered the representative of the most "permanent and immutable interests of the state." Political parties are not always well organized in France on a national level. Their political opinions range from the far right to socialist to the extreme left, as exemplified by the most militant of the communists. Sometimes loose and temporary coalitions among some of the political parties are formed, but these alliances tend to be weak and can easily divide over one issue.

LANGUAGE: The nation has always been so varied that at times it seems that the main link which unites France is its mellifluous language. For centuries it was associated with diplomacy, fine literature, and romance. Even today, a proficiency in reading it is viewed both as a glittering social ornament and a psychological tool for plumbing the depths of the human spirit.

Like any language, its evolution into what you'll hear today on the streets of Paris was a function both of popular usage and concerted efforts by scholastic bodies to standardize its syntax and spelling. Its origins came from the mingling of Latin, the language of the ancient Roman conquerors, with the now forgotten languages of the native Celts. During the early Middle Ages, two main divisions developed, the sides being the "langue d'Oïl" in the north (particularly Paris), and the "langue d'Oc" of the south. (The ancient district of Languedoc derived its name from the language that was originally spoken there.) Eventually, the dictates of the academic and political stronghold of Paris acquired a supremacy in both the spoken vernacular and the written languages.

The potential of civil discord, provoked and encouraged by the era's linguistic differences, had always terrified French monarchs. It was Richelieu in 1635 who finally established a governing body to sometimes legally enforce the linguistic purity of the French language. Called the Académie Française and composed of the most notable men (and recently women) of French letters, it was recognized as the world's official arbiter and judge of which phrases and forms of French grammar would or would not be accepted into the official linguistic canon. In spite of that, a wealth of dialectical differences is still heard, but to a decreasing degree, despite the sometimes heroic efforts of a body of 17th-century grammarians who made the standardization of French their life's work. It required the homogenizing influence of media—especially television—to blur the ancient linguistic divisions of France. Even until the end of World War II, Provençale (a variation of the ancient langue d'oc) was widely spoken in the south. A Celtic language, called Breton, was spoken in Brittany, the linguistically baffling Basque tongue in the southwest, and even Catalán, the language of Barcelona, was heard along sections of the Spanish border. German dialects were used in Alsace and Lorraine, and the adaptation of Flemish was spoken near the Belgium border.

Although each of these languages was spoken within homes and cottages of the rural areas, the mainstream of French society has always prided itself on the exactitude of the phrases and nuances of grammar which are at first such a torment and later such a delight to foreigners who study them. Perhaps the greatest celebration of the language occurred in the literary forms of the 19th and early 20th century, when novelists and poets (especially Flaubert, Proust, and Baudelaire) toyed, tinkered, and reveled in paragraphs which are sometimes overwhelmingly evocative. Flaubert, while writing in his Norman garden, would compose the same paragraph as many as 20 times before achieving an elegance of phrasing and a precision of emotional states which an increasingly telegraphic world may never see again.

Some French-speaking people staunchly defend the purity of their tongue, while others have become increasingly vocal about the inability of their rigidly structured language to remain scientifically competitive with the vastly more flexible English language. The computer boom and developments in almost every form of scientific research have tended to be expressed in what has become the second language of educated people throughout the world—English. This is of enormous concern to French leaders who, despite their qualms, have sometimes levied fines on manufacturers whose advertisements include phrases from English or other languages. (The French translation for "computer software" is hopelessly convoluted, even for a person who speaks French fluently.)

In spite of its drawbacks as a scientific language, French is arguably the best vehicle for expressing subtle variations of feeling which never sound quite as meaningful when translated into another language. Cynics have claimed that no other language in Europe is as well suited to irony, skepticism, or sarcasm. But, as anyone who's ever fallen in love with a French-speaking person knows, affairs of the heart are always best expressed *en français*.

FRENCH LITERATURE: The development of a body of French literature is intricately tied with the emergence of French as a workaday vernacular language. Some historians consider the body of French literature to have existed only since the Renaissance, although a strong body of work, very definitely produced by the ancestors of the culture which is today called France, was popular as early as the 11th century. The langue d'oc, spoken as a well-defined language of the south, especially in Provence in the 11th century, produced an evocative and unique kind of poetry which the world had never seen before. Usually sung by wandering adventurers called troubadours, it praised the virtues of courtly love, perhaps laying the foundation of the legends which have always enveloped the supposedly exalted romantic powers of the French.

The crusade by the northern French against the Albigensian Heresy in the 1400s virtually destroyed both the political independence and the literary forms of Provence, although those that had already been recorded are still regarded as examples of the boldest and most charming literary form to emerge from the Middle Ages.

In the north, around 1007, an unknown writer composed the heroic poem, *Chanson de Roland* (Song of Roland), which consists of 4,002 unrhymed ten-syllable lines describing the heroic death of a warrior at Roncesvalles in the Pyrénées. Other contemporary works involved the *Breton Cycle,* a French adaptation of the legend of England's King Arthur and his Knights of the Round Table, and an Anglo-Norman version of the story of Tristan and his love for Isolde.

For the next 200 years, literature struggled to be recorded and encompassed everything from didactic essays meant to instruct to political satires, morality plays, and buffoonish dialogues between righteous men and wily foxes (who usually won). François Villon, born in 1431 of poor parents, educated by a helpful priest, and later attracted to a life of vice and crime, left a handful of genuinely evocative poems.

During the Renaissance, French poetry flowered in the hands of Clément Marot. Du Bellay, in his 1549 *Defense and Illustration of the French Language* elaborated upon new poetic theories without apology to his wish to express them in the vernacular. Later Rabelais (1494–1553), a man well-versed in classical literature, wrote graphically amusing tales loaded with the kind of political implications which both vastly amused his readers and later forced him into exile in Rome. Pierre de Ronsard (1524–1585) was a nobleman destined for an important military career. Faced with deafness and drawn to his writing, he produced some of the most elegant poetry of his era. Later, Montaigne, for a time the mayor of Bordeaux, delighted in exploring his own psyche, recording in his *Essays* his belief in the absolute negation of all knowledge not gained from personal experience. He is credited today with leaving to France what might be the most remarkable distillation of Renaissance values ever recorded.

By the 17th century, a new appreciation of the rational powers of man, partially sparked by the Age of Enlightment's scientific discoveries, produced a literature filled with lofty language and heroic struggles of conscience versus the dictates of society. Pierre Corneille and his contemporary, Racine, produced both tragedies and comedies which sometimes touched on the delicate balance of the era's religious passions. Later, Blaise Pascal wrote a piquant and brilliant text defending the Jansenists against an attack led by the Jesuits. Despite its popularity at the time, Pascal is much better remembered today for his *Pensées* and its exploration of the relationship of a suffering man and an all-powerful God.

The late 17th century was one of violent conflicts of religion and philosophy, and much of the urbane polish of its writers probably came from their success at negotiating the era's politics. Madame de Sévigné perfected the art of letter writing. La Fontaine wrote his charmingly insightful *Fables,* and François de la Rochefoucauld created his *Maxims*. The battle-scarred poet, the Duke of Saint-Simon (1675–1755), recorded his urbane memoirs, one of the best insights into the era of Louis XIV. One of France's most performed playwrights, Molière, left a still vivid portrayal of the foibles of human nature in his dryly entertaining comedies whose incidents almost always show a love of ostentatious show and ceremony. Despite his humor and the favor he enjoyed from Louis XIV, his satirical jabs at the established tenets of his day embroiled him in the undying enmity of several religious factions.

By the early 1700s, the novel took its first form in Prévost's great (and only) novel of love, *Manon Lescaut,* thus launching a literary tradition which in France would reach dizzying heights of expression a century and a half later. Prévost, as did earlier writers, accepted the social order with resignation and stoic calm, although with the advent of Voltaire, a new sarcasm and irreverence permeated the literary air, particularly as it applied to both religious pomposity and fanaticism. Rousseau preached the nobility of both animals and savages untouched by social teachings, and Montesquieu established a new field of study, the philosophy of history. Diderot compiled an encyclopedia in 17 volumes filled with essays whose conclusions were based on the scientific discoveries of the era. A few years later, the Marquis de Sade (1740–1814) both practiced and wrote about cruelties which made him a social untouchable at the time, but which influenced the Romanticism of later generations of writers.

Romanticism allied itself with the political and social preoccupations of the early 1800s. Probably weary of the heroic militarism of the Napoleonic wars, it celebrated a sentimental lyricism and a sometimes personal outpouring of emotion. Victor Hugo, who envisioned himself as "the embodiment of the French soul," became the movement's leader. His *Hunchback of Notre Dame* is the most famous to North American audiences, although *Les Misérables,* a novel of social injustice, has been called one of the greatest works of popular literature ever written. On his 80th birthday in 1882, more than 600,000 French people came to pay their respects.

By the mid-1800s, both the literary salon and a handful of literary journals disseminated new ideas to a wider group of readers than ever before in French history. Benjamin Constant's dry and cerebral recitation of the blistering emotions of his semiautobiographical hero in *Adolphe* ushered in a new generation of novelists. Stendhal led a life of revolt and adventure, and later wrote both *The Red and the Black* and *The Charterhouse of Parma*, where his appreciation of Italy was expressed through the aristocratic bravado of its hero.

A man who had failed in virtually every business he ever tried except writing, Balzac produced a voluminous collection of novels which were entitled *The Human Comedy*. Balzac was very much a product of the bourgeois age of industrialization which swept across France. His sometimes verbose novels were created almost as serials, where characters and plots were interwoven from novel to novel. Never before had French society been so insightfully analyzed on such a large scale. Sometimes riveting, Balzac's novels give deep insights into the commercial envy and social competition of the age of Napoléon III.

By now, a yearning for realism and naturalism was enveloping literary tastes. A new generation of writers shunned both sentimentality and frivolous romanticism, returning to a sometimes rigourous precision and almost scientific objectivity. Flaubert, who produced some of the most emotionally satisfying novels ever written, believed in concealing his own thoughts and feelings as completely as possible, bringing a vigor and depth to his characters—especially in *Madame Bovary,* which is almost pure joy to read. Flaubert was as concerned about the way he expressed an idea as he was with the idea itself. His prose in the original French is as highly polished, elegant, and emotionally precise as anything else from its era. Émile Zola, who probably understood the commercial value of media attention better than any other writer who preceded him, believed that a human personality is the product of the environment in which it developed. Almost constantly the target of obscenity suits, he described graphically the brutality of life in the lowest class of French urban society.

Meanwhile, clusters of impressionistic poets (Verlaine, Mallarmé, and Valéry) experimented with new forms of poetry. Baudelaire conveyed with symbols and images his own passions and despair. Apollinaire and Rimbaud produced surrealistic writing largely divorced from the moral outrage which had become popular with other writers. Their symbolic and elegant verse was considered decadent because of its divorce from the trials of everyday people.

Marcel Proust, considered by many critics to be the finest 20th-century writer in any language, tried to illuminate the recesses of his mind where memories lay hidden, sometimes devoting page after page to the childhood feelings which lay behind the odor of a freshly baked madeleine. *His Remembrance of Things Past* is sometimes viewed as an artful, very fertile effort to bring to light the emotions which only years of the very best and most dedicated psychoanalysis might bring out. Later, André Gide, in his sustained and painful self-investigation, explored his relationship to his innermost thoughts and to society.

The disturbing events leading up to World War II provoked the existentialist movement. It stressed the absurdity of life and the meaninglessness of any attempt to establish a real communication among people. Sartre and Camus are the movement's best remembered advocates. The movement quickly split into Christian and atheistic branches, each loaded with implications which have influenced theologians and philosophers ever since.

ART AND ARCHITECTURE: During the heyday of Rome, only the southernmost region of France was considered of any commercial or artistic merit. This region, through trade with the architecturally sophisticated Mediterranean, was quick to adopt the building techniques which were common in the Roman world. As it applies to architecture, it's been said that the Romans' triumphal arches, their rhythmically massive aqueducts, and their mausoleums fixed themselves in the French aesthetic for all time. As Christianity made inroads toward the Celtic tribes of the northern edges of Gaul, an abbreviated and naïve kind of naturalism permeated the old Roman ideals, resulting in a crude aesthetic of geometric carvings and primitive architectural masses of which only a few remain today. Those that do are occasionally influenced slightly with eastern motifs from Byzantium which flourished at the time.

The architectural form called Romanesque developed from these trials. Its rise is sometimes attributed to the growing spiritual power of the 11th- and 12th-century church which in many areas was the only constant factor in a region of shifting political alliances. The earliest manifestations appear more like thick-walled fortresses, and often served as refuges during times of invasion. At first they were unembellished with sculpture of any kind, relying on rounded arches and occasional windows for ornamentation. Many critics consider the echoing simplicity of the Cistercians—a reform-minded offshoot of the Benedictines—to be among the more spiritually alluring styles of the era. (Clairvaux and Fontenay are the best remaining examples.) By the 1100s, notably in Poitou, the façades and sections of the interiors of some Romanesque churches were almost completely covered with sculptures whose forms were designed to emphasize the architecture, rather than serve as separate works of art. Although some of the more visible Romanesque sculptures are solid, rigid, unyielding, and lifeless, the capitals above the massive columns are often charming, the most natural representations that can be found. These are studied today with great interest by art historians who are sometimes able to assign almost forgotten biblical allegories to some of them. The first French Romanesque church was built around 1002 in Dijon (the Monastery of St. Bénigne). The flowering of the style appeared in the vast ecclesiastical complex of Cluny in Burgundy which was begun in 1089 and destroyed by zealous townspeople just after the French Revolution.

Contemporaneously with the 10th- and 11th-century construction of churches, the era also produced secular fortresses whose crenellations and thick walls often concealed dank, drafty, cramped quarters where cooped-up occupants barely managed to stay sane during times of war. Often, when a fortress was destroyed during a pillage, the survivors rebuilt it into a more fashionable form. In this way, some of the greatest châteaux of France were built, altered, upgraded, and transformed into the sometimes elegant domiciles which are preserved today as symbols of the Renaissance.

About 400 years before the great châteaux of the Loire reached their present form, the hard-working architects of the royal abbey of Saint-Denis, outside Paris, completed the first section of a radically new architectural style—Gothic. The cathedrals of Noyon, begun a year later in 1145, and Laon, launched in 1155, almost immediately exemplified the new principles, as did Notre-Dame of Paris when construction on it was undertaken in 1163. Gothic churches usually, but not always, included a choir, a ring-around ambulatory, radiating chapels, pointed arches, clustered (rather than monolithic) columns, and ribbed ceilings. Probably most important is the presence of wide, soaring windows occupying the space which, in a Romanesque church, would have been devoted to thick stone walls. This new design usually required the addition of exterior flying buttresses to support the weight of the very heavy roof and ceiling.

It was at Chartres, 60 miles southwest of Paris, that an adaptation of earlier Gothic principles was developed for the first time into a flamboyant High Gothic style when a section of the existing cathedral was destroyed in a fire. The tendency toward increased altitude was more and more fully developed until the cathedrals of Reims and Amiens reached heights so dizzying that medieval man couldn't help but be awed by the might and majesty of God.

Meanwhile, the ecclesiastical sculpture which ornamented the portals and façades of Gothic churches progressed from an early, very static kind of stern rigidity to a more fluid, more relaxed, sometimes coquettish kind of naturalism. By the 14th century, ecclesiastical and especially secular carvings attained a kind of international refinement and courtliness that was appreciated and copied in aristocratic circles throughout Europe.

It wasn't long, however, before the Renaissance helped Frenchmen realize that the glass and stone marvels erected to the glory of God were also examples of the sophisticated building techniques of the time. When the 14th-century papal schism encouraged a portion of Europe's bishops to recognize that Avignon, not Rome, was the legitimate seat of the papacy, a fortress was required which would also be a palace. New political and social conditions encouraged aristocratic residences filled with sunlight, tapestries, paintings, and music. Adaptations of Gothic architecture, mingled with strong doses of the Italian Renaissance, were applied to secular residences more suited to peace than the times of war. (Chambord, the hunting château of François I, is a good example.) Architectural motifs as well as paintings abandoned religious themes. French painting modeled itself first after Flemish, then after the Northern Italian examples. It began to distance itself increasingly from the dictates of the church.

The early 17th century witnessed the architectural burgeoning of Paris, whose skyline bristled with domes in the restrained baroque of the Italianate style. Louis XIV employed Le Vau, Perrault, both Mansarts, and Bruand for his buildings, and Le Nôtre for the rigidly intelligent layouts of his gardens at Versailles. Meanwhile, court painters such as Boucher depicted allegorical shepherdesses and cherubs at play, while Georges de la Tour used techniques of light and shadow garnered from Caravaggio during a sojourn in Italy. The châteaux designed in this era included the lavishly expensive Vaux-le-Vicomte, and the even more lavishly expensive royal residence of Versailles.

By the 18th century, French architects returned to a restrained and dignified form of classicism. Public parks in Metz, Bordeaux, Nancy, and Paris were laid out, sometimes requiring the demolition of acres of twisted medieval sections of cities. Roman styles in painting, sculpture, and dress became the rage, although a brief fling with Egyptology followed the discovery of the Rosetta Stone during Napoleon's campaign in Egypt. The revolutionary school of David came and went and, within the new order, Ingres strove for a kind of classical calm.

Around 1850, a new school of eclecticism combined elements from scattered eras of the past into new, sometimes inharmonious wholes. Between 1855 and 1869, Napoléon III and his chief architect, Baron Haussmann, demolished much of the crumbling medieval Paris to lay out the wide avenues which today connect the various monuments in broad, well-proportioned vistas. New building techniques were developed, including the use of iron as the structural support of bridges, viaducts, and buildings such as the National Library, completed in 1860. Naturally, this opened the way for Alexandre Gustave Eiffel to design and erect the most frequently slurred building of its day, the Eiffel Tower, for the Paris exposition of 1889.

Among sculptors, the only authentic giant to emerge from the 19th century was Auguste Rodin, born in 1840. He brought new energy and vision to sculpture. His human figures were vital and lifelike, and he became known for such works as *The Thinker* and *The Kiss*.

Eugène Delacroix, born in 1798, became the greatest name in French Romantic painting, showing great skill as a colorist. In the second quarter of the 19th century, landscape painting rose in prominence, and none was better at this form than Jean-Baptiste Corot, the French painter of the Barbizon school. To many critics, the first modern painter in France was Edouard Manet, born in 1832. He painted portraits and scenes of everyday life but could also create a scandal *(Picnic on the Grass)* by depicting nudes among dressed figures. Manet is not to be confused with Monet, born in 1840. Claude Monet was a great innovator, known for his series of paintings of water lilies and of Rouen Cathedral. Pierre Augustine Renoir, born 1841, became celebrated for his sensuously rounded nudes in pearl white, and Edgar Degas, born 1834, turned to ballet dancers and scenes of racing and the theater for his inspiration.

Outside all movements, but equally important, was Henri de Toulouse-Lautrec, born in 1864. Satiric but amused, his style was exemplified by the posters and sketches of music hall life he depicted. His interest was in the demi-monde of his day. In the early part of the 20th century, the Fauves or "wild beasts" attracted the most attention, and the greatest of their lot was Henri Matisse, born 1869. He became known for his bright colors and flattened perspective.

Throughout the 20th century, exquisite beaux-arts buildings continued to be erected throughout Paris, most of them at roughly the same height, giving the city an evenly spaced skyline and rhythmically ornate façades which have caused it to be deemed again and again the most beautiful city in the world. The art nouveau movement added garlands of laurel and olive branches to the gray-white stone of elegant apartment buildings and hotels throughout France. In the 1920s and 30s, art deco's simplified elegance captivated sophisticated sensibilities throughout the world. Braque defined cubism, and Picasso worked at his mission of turning the art world upside down. Le Corbusier developed his jutting, gently curved planes of concrete, opening the door for a new, but often less talented school of modern French architects. As for recent years, critics have not been kind to the exposed, rapidly rusting structural elements of Paris's notorious Centre Beaubourg.

2. Food and Drink

Volumes have been written about French gastronomy, and I will not attempt to do so here, but a few general comments may be in order. First, as any French person will tell you, French food is the best in the world. That is as true today as it was in the days of the great Escoffier. More than ever, chefs de cuisine, especially the younger ones, are making creative statements in the kitchen, and never in the history of the country has there been such an emphasis on super-fresh ingredients. One chef I know in Bordeaux has been known to shut down his restaurant for the day if he didn't find exactly what he wanted in the marketplace that morning. There are certain rules to observe when dining in France, and I'll review a few of them.

Of course, the first question you may ask is, what will it cost? France, especially Paris, has gained a reputation as being a damnably expensive place in the food department. True, her star-studded, internationally famous establishments are very expensive indeed. Places like Tour d'Argent and Maxim's are not so much restaurants as temples of gastronomy, living memorials to the glory of French cuisine. Tour d'Argent, for example, boasts what is widely regarded as the finest wine cellar in the world. In these culinary cathedrals, you pay not only for superb decor and regal service, but also for the art of celebrated chefs on ministerial salaries.

There is also a vast array of expensive dineries—not only in Paris but increasingly throughout the country—that exist almost exclusively for the tourist trade. Their food may be indifferent or downright bad, but they'll have ice water and ketchup to anesthetize your tastebuds, trilingual waiters, and quadrilingual menus. Luckily, there are others. Hundreds of others. Even Paris, which is said to have more restaurants than any other city on earth, has many good, reasonably priced ones. And they don't take much finding. I've counted 18 of them in a single, narrow Left Bank street.

DINING TIPS: Most Paris restaurants automatically add a service charge of around 12% to 15% to your bill *(service compris)* which means you don't have to leave a tip, but it's customary always to leave something extra. If service is not included, it is customary to tip about 15%.

In many of the less expensive places I'll be taking you to in this guide, the menu will be handwritten in French only. Don't let that intimidate you. You needn't be timid either about ordering dishes without knowing precisely what they are. You'll get some delightful surprises. I know a woman who wouldn't have dreamed of asking for escargots if she'd realized they were snails cooked in garlic sauce. As it was, she ate this appetizer in a spirit of thrift rather than adventure—and has been addicted to it ever since. As for vegetables, the French regard them as a separate course and eat them apart from the meat or poultry dishes. But I wouldn't advise you to order them specially, unless you're an exceptionally hearty eater. Most main courses come with a small helping or *garni* of vegetables anyway.

You'll find a large number of specific dishes explained in the restaurant descriptions. No one, however, can explain the subtle nuances of flavor that distinguish them. Those you have to taste for yourself.

As a rule, it's better to order an apéritif—often the house will have a specialty—rather than a heavy drink such as a martini before a classic French dinner. Vodka or Scotch can assault your palate, destroying your tastebuds for the festive repast to come. Allow plenty of time for a gourmet dinner. Orders are often prepared individually, and it takes time to absorb the wine and the flavors. Sometimes sorbet (a sherbet) is served midway in your meal to cleanse your palate.

Making reservations is important, and please try to show up on time. Too many Americans make reservations and then become a "no-show," and this creates ill will, especially since many nine-table restaurants must be filled completely every night in order to make a profit. If you're window-shopping for a restaurant, you'll find the menu most often displayed outside. French people read it like a book. It's there for you to study and ponder over—so read it in anticipation. Most French people have their main meal during the day, and when in France you, too, may want to follow that custom, dining lighter in the evening.

Most French meals consist of several small courses. You can begin, for example, with hors d'oeuvres or else a light potage, or soup, although chefs don't serve soups as frequently as they used to. The classic restaurant used to serve fish, a small order, after the appetizer, then the meat or poultry course. But nowadays it is likely to be either fish or meat. A salad follows the main course, then a selection of cheese (there are 365 registered ones alone), and dessert, often a fruit concoction or a sorbet.

If you find the food "too rich, too many sauces," that may be because you've been ordering wrong. Elaborately prepared gourmet banquets should not be consumed for both lunch or dinner or even every day. The French don't. Sometimes an omelet or a roast chicken can make a delightful light meal, and you can "save up" for your big dining experience.

LA NOUVELLE CUISINE: The revolution against Escoffier has been raging for so long that many of the early rebels are now returning to the old style of cookery, as exemplified by the boeuf bourguignon, the blanquette de veau, and the pot-au-feu. Nevertheless, La Nouvelle Cuisine, even if it isn't that "new," remains a viable part of the French dining scene. Unlike another revolution, the battle between haute cuisine and La Nouvelle Cuisine didn't begin in Paris. Romantically, one would like to think it started when Michel Guérard's beautiful Christine murmured in his ear, "Vous savez, Michel, if you would lose some weight, you'd look Great."

For a man who loved food as much as Guérard, that was a formidable challenge. But he set to work and, ultimately, invented the "cuisine minceur," which is a way to cook good French food without the calories. The world now makes its way to Guérard's restaurant, at Eugénie-les-Bains in the Landes, just east of the Basque country. His *Cuisine Minceur* became a best seller in North America, and Gael Greene, the food critic, hailed Guérard as "the brilliant man who is France's most creative chef." The cuisine minceur is more of a diet cuisine than La Nouvelle Cuisine. However, the "new cuisine," like cuisine minceur, represents a major break with haute cuisine, yet it is still based on the classic principles of French cookery. Rich sauces, for example, are eliminated. Cooking times that can destroy the best of fresh ingredients are considerably shortened. The aim is to release the natural flavor of food without covering it with heavy layers of butter and cream. New flavor combinations in this widely expanding repertoire are often inspired.

Many chefs, and these include some of the finest in France, dislike the word "nouvelle" when applied to cuisine. They call theirs "moderne," which blends the finest dishes of the classic repertory with that of the nouvelle kitchen. Although widely defined, moderne basically means paying homage to the integrity of ingredients, certainly fresh ones, and working in the kitchen to bring out natural flavors and aromas.

PROVINCE BY PROVINCE: What exactly is "French food"? That's a hard question to answer. Even cities have their own specialties: Toulouse, for example, is known for its cassoulet, a shell bean stew made with pork, mutton, and goose or duck.

Gastronomy would be good enough reason for going to the Loire even if it didn't have châteaux. From Nantes to Orléans, the specialties are many, including, for example, shad cooked with sorrel, Loire salmon, chitterling sausage, lark pâté, goats'-milk cheese, partridge, rillettes (shredded and potted pork), herb-flavored black pudding, plus good Loire wines, including rosés.

The Normans are known not only as good soldiers but as hearty eaters. Their gastronomic table enjoys world renown. Many Parisians drive up for *le weekend* just to sample the rich Norman cuisine, which uses a lot of fresh butter and thick cream. Harvested along the seacoast are sole, brill, mackerel, and turbot. Shellfish are also common, especially those fat black mussels, the prawns of Cherbourg, the demoiselles of Dieppe. Try also Madame Poulard's featherweight omelet, sole normande (stewed in rich cream), tripe à la mode de Caen, chicken from the Auge Valley, and duckling from Rouen. Normandy apples, especially those from the Auge Valley, produce a most potent cider. Matured in oaken casks, the apples also are turned into Calvados, a sort of applejack, a distillation of cider flavored with hazelnuts. A true Norman drinks this cider spirit at breakfast. Bénédictine, the liqueur made at Féchamp, also enjoys acclaim. The rich Norman camembert is imitated but never equaled. Pont l'-Évêque cheese has been known here since the 13th century. The Livarot is just fine for those who can get past the smell.

The province of Brittany is rich in seafood, the mainstay of its diet, including Aulne salmon, pike (best with white butter), scallops, trout, winkles, cockles, spiny lobsters, and Lorient sardines. Of course, the pré-salé (salt-meadow lamb) is the best meat course, traditionally served with white beans. The finest artichokes come from Roscoff, the most succulent strawberries from Plougastel. Nearly every village has its own crêperie, specializing in those paper-thin pancakes with an infinite variety of fillings. Buckwheat griddlecakes are another popular item. The food is washed down with Breton cider (admittedly inferior to the Norman variety, but quite good nevertheless). Unlike much of France, the province lacks wine, except for muscadet, a light white wine produced from the vineyards around the old Breton capital of Nantes in the lower Loire Valley.

Alsace-Lorraine has a strong Germanic flavor in its cuisine, as reflected by its sauerkraut garni, its most popular dish. It is also the home of foie gras, an expensively delicious treat. The Savoy, taking in the French Alps, also has many specialties, especially in its use of rich cream and milk. Game such as woodcock is plentiful. The cookery is heavy but tasty.

The best food and best wines are found in Burgundy. You'll also see à la Bourgogne (bourguignon) after a dish (that means cooked in a red wine sauce and often garnished with buttonhole mushrooms and pearl onions). Lyon is regarded as the gastronomic capital of France. For example, tripe lyonnaise is known around the world. Lyonnais sausage is also well known, and the city's many famous dishes include quenelles (fish balls, often made with pike).

The Périgord and Dordogne regions are known for their foie gras and truffles. Many farmers' wives sell foie gras directly from their kitchen door. Foie gras, naturally, comes from either a goose or duck. The rose-hued goose liver is considered the greater delicacy. But the poor goose has a rough time of it in life, and it's a distasteful business to many sensitive souls. The goose is force-fed about one kilogram of corn every day: the French call this *gavage*. In about 22 days the liver is swollen to about 25 ounces (in many cases, far more than that). The foie gras is most often served with truffles. Otherwise, it's called au naturel. Even if you don't like foie gras, you'll surely want to try the fish from the rivers of the Dordogne, along with morels, strawberries, and flap mushrooms—called cèpes—from the field.

Gourmets, not just beach lovers, go to the Riviera too. The food, especially fish, tends to be exceptionally good. It also tends to be expensive. Bouillabaisse, said to have been invented by Venus, is the area's best-known dish. Each chef has his or her own ideas on the subject. Rascasse (hogfish), a fish found only in the Mediterranean, is invariably put in. One of the best seafood selections, rouget (red mullet) sometimes appears on fancy menus as bécasse de mer (sea woodcock). Yet another is loup (bass) de mer, cooked with fennel. Aïoli, mayonnaise with a garlic and olive-oil base, is usually served with hors d'oeuvres or boiled fish. Other specialties include soupe au pistou (vegetable soup with basil), salade niçoise (likely to include everything, but traditionally made with tomatoes, green beans, olives, tuna, anchovies, and radishes), pan bagnat (bread doused in olive oil and served with olives, anchovies, and tomatoes), and ravioli which needs no explanation.

THE DRINKING OF WINE: French cookery only achieves palate perfection when lubricated by wine, which is not considered a luxury or even an addition, but an integral part of every meal. Certain rules about wine drinking have been long established in France, but no one except traditionalists seems to follow them any more. For example, if you're having a roast, steak, or game, a good burgundy might be your choice. If it's chicken, lamb, or veal, perhaps you might choose a red from the Bordeaux country, certainly a full-bodied red with cheese such as camembert, and a blanc de blanc with oysters. A light rosé can go with almost anything, especially if enjoyed on a summer terrace overlooking a willow-fringed river bank.

Let your own good taste—and sometimes almost equally as important, your pocketbook—determine your choice of wine. Most wine stewards, called sommeliers, are there to help you in your choice, and only in the most dishonest of restaurants will they push you toward the most expensive selections. Of course, if you prefer only bottled water or perhaps a beer, then be firm and order either without embarrassment. In fact, bottled water might be a good idea at lunch if you're planning to drive on the roads of France later. Some restaurants include a beverage in their menu rates *(boisson compris)*, but that is only in the cheaper places. Nevertheless, some of the most satisfying wines I've drunk in France came from unlabeled house bottles or carafes, called a *vin de la maison*. Unless you're a real connoisseur, you can, for the most part, not worry about labels and vintages.

When in doubt, you can rarely go wrong with a good burgundy or bordeaux, but you may want to be more experimental than that. That's when the sommelier (who today is likely to be a woman) can help you, particularly if you tell him or her your taste in wine (semidry or very dry, for example). State frankly how much you're willing to pay and what you plan to order for your meal. If you're dining with others, you may want to order two or three bottles with an entire dinner, selecting a wine to suit each course. However, even the

French at most informal meals, and especially if there are only two persons dining, select only one wine to go with all their platters from hors d'oeuvres to cheese. As a rule of thumb, it is estimated that a French person dining out expects to spend about one-third of the restaurant tab for wine.

LABELS OF WINE: Since the latter part of the 19th century, French wine has been labeled (that is, French wine served in France; outside of France, who knows?). The general label is known as *Appellations Contrôlées*. These controls, for the most part, are by regions such as Bordeaux or the Loire. These are the simple, honest wines of the district. They can be blended from grapes grown at any place in the region. Some are composed of the vintages of different years.

The more specific the label, the greater the wine (in most cases). For example, instead of a bordeaux, the wine might be labeled a Médoc (pronounced may-dawk), which is a triangle of land extending some 50 miles north from Bordeaux. Wine labels can be narrowed down to a particular vine-growing property, such as a Château Haut-Brion, one of the most famous and greatest of red wines of Bordeaux (this château produces only about 10,000 cases a year).

On some burgundies, you are likely to see the word clos (pronounced clo). Originally, that meant a walled or otherwise enclosed vineyard, as in Clos de Beze, which is a celebrated Burgundian vineyard producing a superb red wine. Cru (pronounced crew and meaning "growth") suggests a wine of superior quality when it appears on a label as a *vin de cru*. Wines and vineyards are often divided into crus. A Grand Cru or Premier Cru should, by implication, be an even superior wine.

Labels are only part of the story. It's the vintage that counts. Essentially vintage is the annual grape harvest and the wine made from those grapes. Therefore, any wine can be a vintage wine unless it was blended. Like people, there are good vintages and bad. The variation between wine produced in a "good year" and wine produced in a "bad year" can be major, even to the neophyte palate.

Finally, champagne is the only wine that can be correctly served through all courses of a meal, but only to those who can afford its astronomical prices.

3. The ABCs of France

In this section, I have tried to give information which may be helpful to you in planning your trip to France and during your stay there. The following data pertains to the country as a whole. Information about Paris in particular will be found under "Practical Facts," Chapter III, and of course in many ways, as the capital goes, so goes the nation.

CIGARETTES: Bring in as many as Customs will allow if you're addicted to a particular brand, as American cigarettes are very expensive in France. A possible solution is to learn to smoke French cigarettes. Don't expect anything like the taste of your familiar brand, but you may acquire a taste for it. One of the most popular French cigarettes is called Gauloise Bleu.

CLIMATE: The climate of Paris is described in Chapter III, under "Practical Facts." The climate of France is greatly affected by all three of the climatic influences of northwest Europe: the continental land mass, the Atlantic Ocean, and the Mediterranean Sea. Thus, the variation throughout the country ranges from the cold winters and hot summers of the Aquitaine to the mild winters and fairly minor temperature changes of Brittany to mild winters and hot, dry summers of the Mediterranean area.

CONSULATES AND EMBASSIES: For information on where to get in touch with these offices, see "Practical Facts" in Chapter III, Paris.

CRIME: For crime in Paris, see the warning issued in "Practical Facts," Chapter III. Generally, it's never wise for a woman to leave her purse lying loose beside her or carelessly hung over a chair. Also, be sure your luggage is near you and safe from greedy hands in airports and train stations. Much of France, particularly central France, the northeast, Normandy, and Brittany, remains relatively safe, although no place in the world is *that* safe. Visitors contemplating a visit to the south of France, especially the French Riviera, should exercise extreme caution. Robbery and mugging are commonplace. It's best to check your baggage into a hotel and then go sightseeing instead of leaving it unguarded in the trunk of a car which can easily be broken into. Marseille is among the most dangerous cities of Europe, and visitors should keep this in mind.

CURRENCY: The basic unit of French currency is the **franc**, worth about $.1379 in U.S. currency. One franc breaks down into 100 centimes. Coins are issued in units of 1, 5, 10, 20, and 50 centimes, plus 1, 5, and 10 francs.

The franc, like all world currencies, is fluctuating on the market. That means that the franc-to-dollar conversions appearing in parentheses throughout these chapters may or may not be exact. There is no way to predict what the rate of exchange will be when you visit France. Check with your bank to determine the up-to-date figure.

Francs	Dollars	Francs	Dollars
0.10	$ .01	50	$ 6.90
0.25	.04	75	10.32
0.50	.07	100	13.79
0.75	.10	150	20.69
1	.14	200	27.58
2	.28	250	34.48
3	.41	300	41.37
4	.55	350	48.27
5	.69	400	55.16
10	1.38	500	68.95
15	2.07	750	103.43
20	2.76	1,000	137.90
25	3.45	2,000	275.80

CUSTOMS: As a general rule persons arriving in France via airports stand less chance of being inspected than those arriving by train or automobile. In any case, a visitor more than 15 years of age coming from a non-European country may import duty free 200 cigarettes or 50 cigars. You are allowed two liter bottles of wine and one of alcoholic spirits. In addition, you may bring in two still cameras of different makes, with ten rolls of film for each, plus a motion picture camera with ten reels of film. Aside from hunting guns, the government strictly forbids the importation of guns and ammunition.

Upon leaving France, citizens of the United States who have been outside the country for 48 hours or more are allowed to bring back to their home country $400 worth of merchandise duty free—that is, if they have claimed no similar exemption within the past 30 days. If you make purchases in France, it is important to keep your receipts.

DOCUMENTS FOR ENTRY: A valid passport is all an American, Canadian, or British citizen needs to enter France for stays up to three months.

DRUGSTORES: If you need one during off-hours, have your concierge get in touch with the nearest Commissariat de Police. An agent there will have the address of a nearby pharmacy open 24 hours a day. French law requires that the pharmacies in any given neighborhood designate which one will remain open all night. The address of the one that will stay open for that particular week will be prominently displayed in the windows of all other drugstores.

ELECTRICAL APPLIANCES: In the main expect 200 volts, 50 cycles, although you'll encounter 110 and 115 volts in some older establishments. Adapters are needed to fit sockets. Many hotels have two-pin (in some cases, three-pin) sockets for electric razors. It's best to ask at your hotel before plugging in any electrical appliance.

FILM: All types of film are available in France at prices that will cause only minor anguish. There are no special restrictions on visitors who want to take pictures of the country. However, processing of film can involve considerable delays, so unless you're going to be in France for an extended period, I suggest that you wait to develop your pictures upon your return home.

HOLIDAYS: The main holidays are January 1 (New Year's Day); Shrove Tuesday (the Tuesday before Ash Wednesday); Good Friday; Easter; May 1 (Labor Day); Ascension Day (40 days after Easter); Whit Monday; July 14 (Bastille Day); August 15 (Assumption Day); November 1 (All Saints Day); November 11 (Armistice Day); and December 25 (Christmas). Everything is likely to be closed on these days except your hotel and emergency services.

INFORMATION: Before leaving for France, you can gather information at the French Tourist Office, 610 Fifth Ave., New York, NY 10020 (tel. 212/757-1125); 645 N. Michigan Ave., Chicago, IL 60601 (tel. 312/337-6301); 9401 Wilshire Blvd., Beverly Hills, CA 90212 (tel. 213/272-2661); and Suite 500, 1 Hallidie Plaza, San Francisco, CA 94102 (tel. 415/986-4161).

LANGUAGE: In the wake of two World Wars and many shared experiences, not to mention the influence of English movies, TV, and records, the English language has made major inroads. It is almost a second language in some parts of Paris, but in the more remote parts of France you'll encounter only the tongue of Charles de Gaulle (except in hotels and major restaurants). Frommer's *Fast 'n' Easy Phrase Book* will help you with the meaning and pronunciation of commonly used French terms and menu translations. An American trying to speak French might even be understood.

LAUNDRY: Many hotels provide this service, and if they do, it's likely to be expensive. To cut costs, I'd recommend that you search the phone directory for a *laverie automatique* and find one near your hotel. Watch out for Sunday and Monday closings.

LIQUOR: One of the joys of visiting France is to savor its champagnes, brandies, and wines. They have no equal in the world. The national beverage is wine, and it's consumed at every meal except breakfast (and even that sometimes). Scotch is so very expensive that I recommend that while in France you avoid imports and stick to the local products. For a change-of-pace drink, try a French cognac with soda (or water).

METRIC MEASURES: Here's your chance to learn metric measures.

Weights	Measures
1 ounce = 28.3 grams	1 inch = 2.54 centimeters
1 pound = 454 grams	1 foot = 0.3 meters
2.2 pounds = 1 kilo (1000 grams)	1 yard = 0.91 meters
	1.09 yards = 1 meter
1 pint = 0.47 liter	
1 quart = 0.94 liter	1 mile = 1.61 kilometers
1 gallon = 3.78 liters	0.62 mile = 1 kilometer
	1 acre = 0.40 hectare
	2.47 acres = 1 hectare

OFFICE HOURS: In general, these are from 9 a.m. to 6 p.m., with a long time-out for lunch.

PETS: If you have certificates from a vet and proof of antirabies vaccination, you can bring most house pets into France.

REST ROOMS: Those French in dire need duck into a café or brasserie, using the lavatories there. It's customary to make some small purchase. Paris Métro stations and underground garages usually contain public lavatories, but cleanliness varies. France still has many "hole-in-the-ground" toilets, so be forewarned.

SENIOR CITIZENS: For those who reach what the French call "the third age," there are a number of discounts. At any railway station in France, a senior citizen (that means 60 for women and 65 for men) can obtain a **Carte Vermeil** (Vermilion Card), for a cost of 68F ($9.38). With this card, a person gets a reduction of 50% on train fares in both first- and second-class compartments. Further discounts include a 10% reduction on all rail excursions and 10% reduction on the Europabus running from Paris to Nice. The catch is that these discounts do not apply at certain peak periods of travel, including runs on express trains and on Paris commuter lines.

The French domestic airline, Air Inter, honors "third agers" by giving them 25% to 50% reductions on its regular, nonexcursion tariffs. Again, certain flights are not included. Carte Vermeil allows reduced prices on certain regional bus lines as well as on theater tickets in Paris. Reductions are available on about 20 Air France flights a week to Nice.

Finally, half-price admission to state-owned museums is yet another concession the French make to those aging. Detailed information is available at the French Government Tourist Office, 610 Fifth Ave., New York, NY 10020 (tel. 212/757-1125).

TAXES: Watch it: you could get burned. As a member of the European Common Market, France routinely imposes a "Value Added Tax" (VAT) on many goods and services—currently, 18.6%. However, for so-called luxury items—and these range from caviar to motorcycles—the tax is 33⅓%.

TELEGRAMS: These may be sent from post offices during the day. Look in the telephone directory in the town from which you wish to send a telegram. In large cities, the main post office may be open 24 hours, in which case night messages can be sent.

TELEPHONES: No longer an international joke, the French telephone system has been vastly upgraded in recent years. Public phone booths are found in cafés, restaurants, Métro stations, post offices, airports, train stations, and occasionally on the streets. Some of these booths work with tokens called *jetons*, which can be purchased at the post office or at any café from the cashier. (It's usually customary to give a small tip if you buy them at a café.) Phone booths accept coins of 50 centimes, 1F, and 5F. Generally, you pick up the receiver, insert the *jeton*, then dial when you hear the tone, pushing the button when there is an answer. Many of the public phones are modernized, taking coins instead of slugs, and on these it's possible to make long-distance calls, including transatlantic ones.

If possible, avoid making calls from your hotel, as some French establishments double or triple the charges on you.

When you're calling **long distance within France,** dial 16, wait for the dial tone, and then dial the eight-digit number of the person or place you are calling. To **call the U.S.,** first dial 19, then after the tone dial 1 (the same for Canada), then slowly dial the area code and the seven-digit number. Calls to the U.S. and Canada can be made fairly rapidly, depending on the time of day and period of year. There are apt to be more calls during the heavy tourist season, for instance.

For **information,** dial 12.

TELEX: Chances are, your hotel will send one for you.

TIME: The French equivalent of Daylight Saving Time lasts from around April to September, which puts it one hour ahead of French winter time. Depending on the time of year, France is six or seven hours ahead of Eastern Standard Time in the U.S.

TIPPING: This is practiced with flourish and style in France, and as a visitor you're expected to play the game. If your bill shows *service compris,* the tip has been included.

Waiters: In restaurants, cafés, and nightclubs, service is usually included. However, it is the custom to leave something extra, especially in first-class and deluxe establishments. Service usually is 15%; in deluxe places it is more likely 20%.

Porters: Usually a fixed fee is assessed, about 10F ($1.38) per piece of luggage. You're not obligated to give more; however, many French people do, ranging from 50 centimes (7¢) to 2F (28¢).

Theater ushers: Give at least 2F (28¢) if he or she seats up to two persons.

Hairdressers: The service charge is most often included; otherwise, tip at least 15%, more in swankier places.

Guides: In museums, guides expect 5F (69¢).

Cloakroom attendants: Often the price is posted. If not, give at least 1F (14¢) or 2F (28¢).

Bartenders: Give 12% to 15%.

Hotels: The service charge is added, but tip the bellboy extra, from 6F (83¢) to 20F ($2.76) for three bags (more in deluxe and first-class hotels). A lot depends on how much luggage he has carried and the class of hotel. Tip the concierge based entirely on how many requests you've made of him. Give the maid about 20F ($2.76) if you've stayed for three or more days. The doorman who summons a cab expects 5F (69¢); likewise your room-service waiter, even though you've already been hit for 15% service. Incidentally, most small services around the hotel should be rewarded with a 5F (69¢) tip.

Chapter III

PARIS AND ITS HOTELS

1. Orientation
2. The Super-Deluxe Hotels
3. 8th Arrondissement
4. 16th and 17th Arrondissements
5. 1st Arrondissement
6. 2nd and 9th Arrondissements
7. 5th Arrondissement
8. 6th Arrondissement
9. 7th and 15th Arrondissements
10. 14th Arrondissement
11. 3rd and 4th Arrondissements
12. 18th Arrondissement
13. Orly Airport
14. Airport Charles de Gaulle

PARIS IS THE MOST fabled city of Europe, romanticized beyond reality but somehow always managing to live up to its image. It is discovered anew by each young man or woman who walks along the quays of the Seine, slowly and uniquely making the city his or her own. It is a capital to be savored, like the *ne plus ultra* of claret, a bottle of Château Lafitte-Rothschild.

In the 1920s it was Ernest Hemingway who was to find Paris a "moveable feast." "There is never any ending to Paris," he wrote, "and the memory of each person who has lived in it differs from that of any other."

One reason that memories differ so is that there are so many faces of Paris —districts that live in ignorance or else indifference to other sectors. Paris, after all, is a city of *quartiers* or *arrondissements,* 20 in all. Deciding which quarter most appeals to you—the sector you want to make your living headquarters— will be your first task. Do you like the Left Bank or the Champs-Elysées? The city is split by the winding Seine, the river that knows what has been called the mystery of continuity. The north of the river is the Right Bank or Rive Droite, the lower part the Left Bank or Rive Gauche. You may be fickle, as I am, not wanting to adopt any arrondissement but to walk from quarter to quarter, learning the secrets of all of them.

Novelist Romain Gary put it this way: "The kid will come from Nebraska or Heidelberg, from Poland or Senegal, and Paris will be born again—new, brand-new and unexpected, and the Arch of Triumph will rise again, and the Seine will flow for the first time, and there will be new areas, unknown and unexplored, called Montmartre and Montparnasse . . . and it will all be for the first time, a completely new city, built suddenly for you and you alone."

1. Orientation

Paris isn't a big city—as world capitals go. It occupies only 38 square miles of land, eight less than the "Paris of the West," San Francisco. It's far more populous, containing some three million people. But it's compact, and the majority of tourist attractions are so concentrated that it's a sheer joy to navigate.

The city is bisected by the wide arc of the Seine. The northern part is called the **Right Bank** (Rive Droite), and the southern part is the **Left Bank** (Rive Gauche). The unusual designations make sense when you stand on a bridge facing downstream and watch the waters flow out toward the sea—to your right is the north bank; the south is on your left. Thirty-two bridges link the Right and Left Banks, as well as the two small islands at the center of the Seine, the **Île de la Cité**, out of which contemporary Paris grew, site of the imposing Cathedral of Notre-Dame, and the **Île St-Louis**, a moat-guarded oasis of sober 17th-century mansions and country-quiet streets. These islands can cause some confusion to walkers who think they've just crossed a bridge from one bank to the other, only to find themselves caught up in an almost medieval maze of old buildings and courtyard greenery.

The best way to orient yourself to Paris is to climb to a high point on a clear day and simply look around. The best places for this are the Eiffel Tower and the Arc de Triomphe. From the top of the Eiffel Tower, you can see all of Paris in one giant sweep. The view from the Arc de Triomphe is more detailed. From the Place de l'Étoile (renamed Place Charles de Gaulle) beneath you, 12 avenues radiate, sweeping majestically across the minor city streets, linking the arc, like giant wheel spokes, with the Place de la Concorde down the Champs-Élysées, the green lawns of the Bois de Boulogne, the stately white buildings of the Palais de Chaillot, and the honky-tonk joints of "Pig Alley." The city crowds around, condensed and intimate like a scale model, and you feel you could reach out and pick up a bridge to examine it or pluck some sugar off the birthday-cake peaks of Sacré-Coeur.

After taking in the overall view, take a boat ride up the Seine. Choose a sunny day when the breeze is warm and you can sit outside on deck. Tune out the gabble around you and the recorded guide in four languages. Specific buildings aren't the point—and anyway you can hardly mistake the luminous towers of Notre-Dame. Sit and absorb Paris, letting her sights and sounds seep into you. You'll see the shadowy quay where Voltaire worked and died. Gargoyles will gape down at you with the irritability of old age. Golden horses will take flight overhead from the stanchions of Pont Alexandre III. Students, curled up in puppy clusters on the banks, will tease your boatload as it glides past, with hoots and guitar fanfares. Not all these, of course, are remarkable sights, but each is an essential piece of the Parisian landscape.

PARIS BY ARRONDISSEMENT: The city is divided into 20 municipal wards called "arrondissements," each with its own mayor, city hall, police station, and central post office. Some even have the remnants of market squares left over from those independent days before the city burst its boundaries and engulfed the surrounding towns. Most city maps are outlined by arrondissement, and all addresses include the arrondissement number (written in Roman or Arabic numerals and followed by "e" or "er"). Paris also has its own version of a ZIP Code. Thus, the proper mailing address for a hotel or restaurant is written, say, "75014 Paris." The last two numbers, the 14, indicate that the address is in the 14th Arrondissement, in this case, Montparnasse.

Not all arrondissements concern the visitor. "Tourist" Paris is only a minute proportion of the city as a whole, but a passing acquaintance with the more relevant districts can help you get your bearings.

When people speak of the Right Bank, they are usually referring to that traditionally monied area on the north side of the Seine comprising the **First, Second,** and **Eighth Arrondissements.** Here are houses of fashion, the Stock Exchange, luxury trades such as the perfume industry, the most elegant hotels, expensive restaurants, smartest shops, and the most fashionably attired women and men. Along the river, in the First, are the classically precise Tuileries Gardens and the Louvre. The Second is a business district, with many offices and shops, but it also contains the Opéra. The Eighth includes the vast showplace of the Champs-Élysées, linking the mighty Arc de Triomphe with the delicate obélisque on the Place de la Concorde.

The **Third** Arrondissement embraces one of the most historic and increasingly fashionable districts of Paris, the Marais, with architectural interest centering around its old mansions and the Place des Vosges, called the Palais Royal in the days of Henri IV. Its main attraction today is the Picasso Museum.

The **Fourth** Arrondissement encompasses both small islands in the Seine. Cross the river to the south and you reach the **Fifth** Arrondissement which, along with the **Sixth,** is what people mean when they speak of the Left Bank— that part of the city dedicated to art and scholarship. The Fifth is the Latin Quarter, center of Paris University and site of the Sorbonne. Students, cafés, and cheap restaurants abound. The adjoining Sixth, heartland of the publishing industry, is the most colorful quarter of the city, an exciting, Greenwich Village-y area, where the School of Fine Arts sends out waves of earnest would-be artists. This is also the finest area for finding a good budget-priced hotel or meal, and later on I recommend many of both. Neighboring the Seine is the **Seventh** Arrondissement, which is primarily smart and residential, with embassies and government ministries operating out of what were once the fabulous mansions of French aristocracy. At the western river edge stands the Eiffel Tower. In the center is Napoleon's Tomb and the Invalides Army Museum (beside this is the city air terminal). Look at a city map, and you will see that these arrondissements, One to Eight, form a circular core in the center of the city.

Other districts have their attractions, of course. The famed **Sixteenth,** which shades out from the Seine to the vast park of the Bois de Boulogne, has the classiest living quarters, as well as the museums in the Palais de Chaillot. The part of the **Seventeenth** closest to l'Étoile is equally smart and riddled with executive-priced apartments. The delightful hill of Montmartre, crowned by Sacré-Coeur, is in the **Eighteenth.** But you could easily confine yourself to that magic inner circle and take in almost everything you came to Paris to see.

If you are staying more than two or three days, consider investing in one of the inexpensive pocket-size books that include the "plan de Paris" by arrondissements, available at all major newsstands and bookshops. Most of these guides provide you with a Métro map, a fold-out map of the city, and indexed maps of each arrondissement, with all streets listed and keyed.

TRANSPORTATION: Before you check into your hotel, you've got to reach it,

and therefore coping with the Parisian transport system becomes all important. Driving a car in Paris is definitely not recommended for tourists. There isn't room to drive in the city for the Parisians, much less for foreigners, and parking is equally difficult. Public transportation here is excellent. Of course, people walk and search in Paris, often for love, but chances are you'll need a more practical method of transport than your feet.

Airlines/Airports: Chances are, you'll land at either of the two major international airports: **Orly,** 8½ miles from Paris, or at **Charles de Gaulle,** 14¼ miles from the city. The least expensive way to get into the center of the city is to take

PARIS MÉTRO

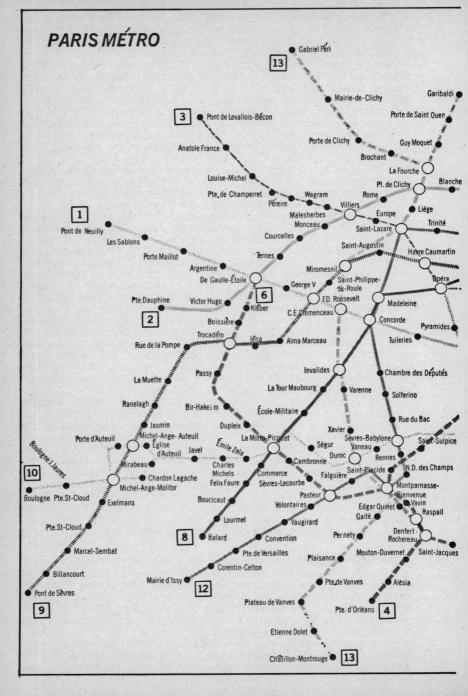

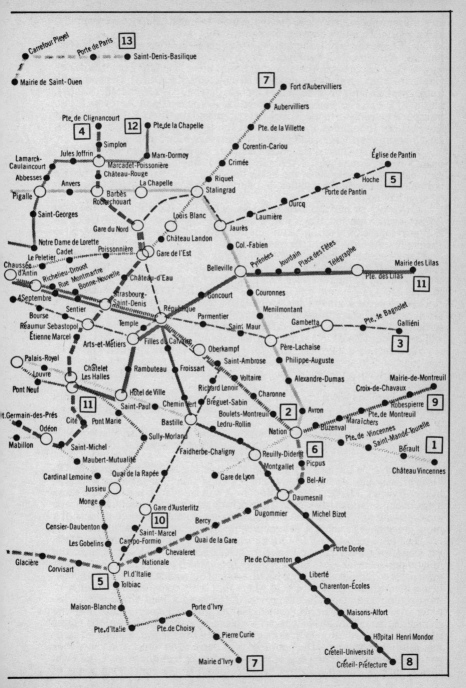

an Air France-operated bus to one of the main terminals. Service is (generally) about every 12 minutes between 5:45 a.m. and 11 p.m.

At Charles de Gaulle there are two terminals—Aérogare 1 for foreign carriers and Aérogare 2 for Air France. From Aérogare 1 you take a moving walkway to the passport checkpoint and Customs area. The fare from Charles de Gaulle for a trip normally taking about 30 minutes is 31F ($4.28). Depending on traffic, the half-hour taxi ride to the Opéra in daytime costs from 150F ($20.69), plus a 10% tip. The shuttle bus connecting Aérogare 1 and Aérogare 2 also transports passengers to the Roissy rail station and the direct R.E.R. train that leaves every 15 minutes on a high-speed run to the Gare du Nord, Châtelet, Luxembourg, Port Royal, and Denfert-Rochereau Métro stations.

Returning to Charles de Gaulle Airport, Air France buses leave for Aérogare 1 every 20 minutes, for Aérogare 2 every 15 minutes. You board at the bus terminal in the basement of the Palais de Congrès at Porte Maillot. The trip normally takes about 30 minutes, but during rush hours it's advisable to allow another half hour.

Orly Airport has two terminals also—Orly Sud (South) and Orly Ouest (West)—which are linked by a shuttle bus. Air France buses leave the De Gaulle airport for the Orly terminals and return every half hour. The ride takes 50 to 75 minutes. At Orly, board the bus at Exit B.

Orly's west terminal is for domestic flights. All others use Orly Sud, where passport and Customs checkpoints are on the first floor. Air France buses leave Orly Sud every 12 minutes from Exit I, heading for Gare de les Invalides, a trip costing 27F ($3.72). At Exit D you can board bus 215 for Place Denfert-Rochereau in the south of Paris. Don't take a freelance taxi from Orly Sud. It's much safer and surer to get a metered cab from the line, which is under the scrutiny of a policeman. The 40-minute cab ride from here to l'Opéra in daytime will cost about 120F ($16.55), plus extra for your bags, plus a 10% tip.

You can take a shuttle bus from Orly Sud to the Orly rail station, where you can board a high-speed R.E.R. train, leaving every 15 minutes, taking you to central stops along the Seine. Your ticket allows transfers to any other underground line.

To return to Orly Airport, you can get an Air France bus at the Invalides terminal to either Orly Sud or Orly Ouest every 15 minutes, for about a 30-minute run.

For more information about transport to Charles De Gaulle, telephone 47-58-20-18; and for Orly 45-50-32-30. For airport flight information, telephone De Gaulle at 48-62-12-12 and Orly at 48-67-12-34.

Subways: At the turn of the century, pedestrians went "underground." To lure Parisians into its subway, the city posted at street level flowery wrought-iron entryways. The Museum of Modern Art in New York has elevated these art nouveau creations to the pinnacle of artistic statements; museums in Europe are following suit. At the most prestigious stops, some of these reminders of a more gracious era remain to delight underground travelers of the future.

Le Métro (call 43-46-14-14 for information) is your most efficient and fastest means of transportation in the traffic-clogged Paris of today. Unlike the lunatic-designed subway system of New York, which often baffles the natives, even more so foreign visitors, Le Métro was laid out so that people might actually use it with some assurance as to where they were going. At the entrance to most stations is a map giving the routes of the various lines, which often criss-cross. You can trace your own route (chances are you'll have to make only one change, if that, although some tricky routes require three). Many of the bigger stations have pushbutton indicators that do the work for you, lighting up automatically when you press the button of your destination. Once you know your goal, follow the line to the end of its run, then take that *direction.* Where you change lines is known as *correspondances,* that is, the converging points of trains. Some of these Métro terminals tend to require long walks (the stop at Châtelet is the most notorious).

To ride to any point on one of the urban lines requires the same fare, the only difference being whether you prefer first or second class. You pay 7F (97¢) for a first-class ride, 4.90F (68¢) for a second-class fare. Actually, there isn't much difference in the level of comfort between the cars, except at rush hour. In first class, you may be only mildly pushed, shoved, and stepped on. In second class, death by smothering is likely!

Instead of buying individual tickets, it's a better bargain to purchase a *carnet* (pronounced "car-nay")—that is, a booklet of ten tickets at a reduced cost. In second class, a booklet costs 30F ($4.14), 45F ($6.21) in first class. A *carnet* may be purchased at any Métro ticket counter. A rider in the first-class compartments is often subjected to a ticket inspection (in second class, almost never)—so hold onto your stub. Trains begin their runs at 5:30 a.m., leaving their frontier stations at 12:30 a.m. for the ride back to the "corral."

Buses: Often buses are preferred by some visitors for the sights along the route. Of course, buses are necessarily slow, owing to the traffic congestion. At designated stops are signs listing the number of those buses servicing that point as well as the destinations of each (usually north to south, east to west). Most stops along the way are also posted on the sides of the buses.

The vehicles run from 6:30 a.m. until 9:15 p.m. (a few operate until 12:30 a.m., and a handful traverse the city during the early-morning hours). The service is greatly curtailed on Sunday and holidays. At rush hours you may have to draw a ticket from a dispensing machine, indicating your position in the line.

Most bus rides require one ticket, but there are other destinations calling for two. For bus riders, it's more economical to purchase a booklet of tickets, a *carnet*—the same one used on the Métro.

If you stay a week or a month, you can also buy a special "Go As You Please" tourist ticket valid for two, four, or seven days on all the RATP networks or a *carte orange* valid for two, three, four, or five zones in the Paris area.

If you intend to do any serious bus riding, pick up an RATP bus map at the office on the Place de la Madeleine or at the tourist offices at **RATP** headquarters, 53 bis quai Grands Augustins, Paris (6e). You can also write to the RATP to obtain maps of the transportation systems operated by this authority and other information and pamphlets on the networks. When in Paris, you can also telephone the inquiry center (tel. 43-46-14-14) to get precise details on the fares, routes, and schedules concerning buses as well as the Métro.

You may also want to use the bus system for excursions outside Paris. Many different trips are offered from the beginning of April to the end of October during weekends at reasonable prices to off-the-beaten-path places. You can, of course, go to such standard attractions as Chartres, even le Mont St-Michel. Also, you can visit various châteaux in the Loire Valley. To get more details on the prices and on the sightseeing tours, you can write to the RATP at its headquarters (address above). When in Paris, you can also have the details and book space by going to the office at the Place de la Madeleine. It is open from 4:30 a.m. to 6:45 p.m. weekdays and from 6:30 a.m. to 6 p.m. on Saturday and Sunday.

Taxis: A mixed blessing. It's impossible to secure one at rush hour—so don't even try. Taxi drivers are strongly organized into an effective lobby to keep their number limited to 14,300. Many riders—and not just the foreign ones—complain that the meters are concealed from view. When boarding a taxi, check out the meter to make sure you don't pay the previous passenger's fare.

In Zone A, inside Paris, from 6:30 a.m. to 10 p.m. the flag goes down at 8.50F ($1.17), and the meter ticks away at 2.44F (34¢) per kilometer. Another rate applies when you stray outside the 20 arrondissements. However, you do not have to pay the driver's return fare if he takes you either to Orly Airport or

Charles de Gaulle Airport. At night you can expect an increase of about 30% of the fare.

You pay an extra 3.80F (52¢) when leaving or arriving at railway stations. You are allowed several small pieces of luggage inside free, providing that none of them weighs more than five kilos (about 11 lbs.). Any suitcase weighing more is usually put in the trunk at the rate of 2.70F (37¢) per piece.

"Vulture" cabbies often are parked outside the doors to nightclubs catering to big spenders. They wait for their prey, such as a thoroughly inebriated Yankee. Most of these hacks are unmetered, and they charge what the market will bear—and then whatever else they can get. Agree on the price in advance, then have your attorney draw up an ironclad contract. Otherwise, get the doorman to hail you a legitimate taxi.

The method for getting a taxi in Paris is to wait at a cab stand. One can be called in advance (usually your hotel will arrange this the night before—say, if you have an early plane or train to catch), although taxi stands are prevalent near Métro stations. Tips average around 15% of the fare. One longtime resident of Paris, Herbert R. Lottman, who views taxi drivers with a jaundiced eye, said, "Your Paris chauffeur hardly needs the tip after everything else that he's got from you."

Railroad Information: Paris is served by seven principal rail stations. The average tourist will pass through **Gare des Invalides,** where trains depart for Orly Airport, as mentioned, or **Gare du Nord,** where trains leave not only for Charles de Gaulle Airport, but points in the north of the country, as well as Holland and Belgium. Trains for the northwest leave from **Gare St-Lazare;** for the west, from **Gare Montparnasse;** for the southeast (including the French Riviera), from **Gare de Lyon;** for eastern France and Germany, from **Gare de l'Est;** and for the southwest (the Pyrénées) from **Gare d'Austerlitz.** For general information about departures, telephone 42-61-50-50 in Paris.

THE HOTELS OF PARIS: Paris supports more than 1,400 hotels, among which
a handful are world famous. If you're willing to pay the tab, you can rent some of the finest rooms in Europe. But many modestly run hotels also provide top value. Their only drawback is that they are known among shrewd travelers and are likely to be full, especially in summer. I've surveyed some of the best of them. In these, I suggest reserving rooms at least a month in advance at *any* time of the year and as far as six weeks ahead during the tourist-jammed months from early May through mid-October. You might send a one-night deposit just to be sure. The majority of these hotels, in fact the majority of all Parisian hotels, also share another common problem. Noise. It's strange how Paris traffic sounds seem to magnify in the narrow streets, echoing and re-echoing through the chimney-topped canyons. Add in late-night revelers and early-morning markets, and I heartily recommend that light sleepers request rooms at the back.

Hotel breakfasts are fairly uniform and include your choice of coffee, tea, or chocolate, a freshly baked croissant and roll, and limited quantities of butter and jam or jelly—in short, a continental breakfast. It's nowhere near as massive as the English or American breakfast, but it has the advantage of being quick to prepare, is at your door moments after you call down for it, and can be served at almost any hour requested.

There could be a riddle, if the French were so crude, going something like "When is a hotel not a hotel?" The answer is when it's another kind of building entirely. The word *hôtel* in French has several meanings. It means a lodging house for transients, of course. But it also means a large mansion or town house, such as the Hôtel des Invalides, once a home for disabled soldiers, now the most important military museum in the world. Hôtel de Ville means town hall. Hôtel des Postes refers to the general post office, and Hôtel-Dieu is a hospital. So watch that word.

In my hotel listing in this chapter, those following the deluxe accommodations are grouped by arrondissements and in descending order of price.

Student Discounts

Armed with a student identification card in Paris, you can enjoy many bonuses, including savings of up to 40% on transportation and 50% off admission to many museums. You'll need proof of full-time student status (university or high school), best obtained by requesting an **International Student Identity Card** (which costs $10) from the **Council on International Educational Exchange,** 205 East 42nd St., New York, NY 10017; or 16 rue de Vaugirard, Paris 75006. Write first for the application form, which, properly filled out and submitted with payment and required documentation, will expedite your receiving the ISIC. Allow three to four weeks for delivery during peak season.

Year-round temporary housing (60 beds) for students, male and female, is available at the **Association des Étudiants Protestants de Paris,** 46 rue de Vaugirard, 6e (tel. 4354-31-49), on the Left Bank. They have a library and various cultural activities. Rates, including a continental breakfast and showers, are 44F ($6.07) for dormitories (four to six beds). During the summer period, singles at 58F ($8) and doubles at 52F ($7.17) per person are available. Students must be between 18 and 25 years old to be accommodated during the school year and between 18 and 30 during the summer. Métro: Luxembourg, St-Sulpice, St-Germain, or Odéon.

The **Bureau des Voyages de la Jeunesse,** a nonprofit organization created in 1948, runs four student accommodation centers in Paris, catering to young people 17 to 30 years of age. The first three listed below have rooms which contain one to eight beds, with toilets and showers on each floor. Prices charged are 65F ($8.97) for bed and breakfast, 100F ($13.79) for half board, and 140F ($19.31) for full board. These centers are:

The **BVJ Louvre,** 20 rue J.-J. Rousseau, 1er (tel. 42-26-88-18), has a capacity of 200 beds. Métro: Louvre-Châtelet or Les Halles. The **BVJ Opéra,** 11 rue Thérése, 1er (tel. 42-60-77-23), offers 68 beds. Métro: Palais Royal or Pyramides. The **BVJ Les Halles,** 5 rue du Pélican, 1er (tel. 42-60-92-45), has 55 beds. Métro: Louvre-Châtelet or Les Halles.

The fourth one, which receives students all year long in the heart of the Latin Quarter, is **BVJ Quartier Latin,** 44 rue des Bernardins, 5e (tel. 43-29-34-80), which also has rooms accommodating one to eight persons. Prices are 80F ($11.03) in a single, 70F ($9.65) per person in a double, and 65F ($8.97) per person in a dormitory room, with a continental breakfast included in the rates. Métro: Maubert Mutualité.

PRACTICAL FACTS: There are any number of situations—not only transportation—that might arise to mar your trip. Included in this category is a medical emergency, of course. Although I don't promise to answer all the needs you might meet in Paris, there is a variety of services that could ease your adjustment. The concierge of your hotel, incidentally, is a usually reliable dispenser of information, offering advice about everything—for example, whether you can "bring somebody back to the room." If he or she fails you, the following summary of pertinent survival facts may prove helpful. The ABCs of France, in Chapter II, can also be useful in Paris.

Crime in Paris: *Beware of child pickpockets.* They roam the French capital, preying on tourists around sites like the Louvre, Eiffel Tower, and Notre Dame, and they especially like to pick your pockets in the Métro, sometimes blocking you off on the escalator. A band of these young thieves can clean your pockets even while you try to fend them off. Their method is to get very close to a target, ask for a handout (sometimes), and deftly help themselves to your money, passport, whatever. Women should hang onto their purses with both hands. Gendarmes advise tourists to carry umbrellas and to keep anyone who looks like a pickpocket at umbrella's length away.

Emergency: If you need an ambulance on an SOS call, there are several things you can do. Many hotels rely on the Paris fire department which rushes cases to the nearest emergency room. Their number is 45-78-74-52. An independently operated, privately owned ambulance company is S.A.M.U. (tel. 45-67-50-50). Otherwise, a roving band of vehicle-borne doctors, each with a car radio connection, can be contacted at S.O.S. Medecin (tel. 47-07-77-77).

For information on how to make a **telephone** call, see the ABCs of France, Chapter II.

Telegrams: Telegrams may be sent from any Paris post office during the day (see the listing under post office), and anytime during the day or night at the 24-hour central post office. In telegrams to the United States, the address is counted. There is no special rate for a certain number of words. There are, however, night telegrams sent during the slack hours that cost less. If you're in Paris and wish to send a telegram in English, dial 43-33-21-11.

Dentists: If a toothache strikes you at night or in the early hours of the morning (and doesn't it always?), telephone 43-37-51-00 in Paris anytime between 8 p.m. and 8 a.m., Monday to Friday. Both holidays and weekdays you can telephone this number day or night. You can also call on the **American Hospital,** 63 Boulevard Victor-Hugo, Neuilly (tel. 47-47-53-00; Métro: Pont de Levallois). A dental clinic is on the premises, open 24 hours a day.

Doctors: Some large hotels have a doctor attached to their staff. If yours doesn't, I'd recommend the **American Hospital,** 63 Boulevard Victor-Hugo in Neuilly (tel. 47-47-53-00; Métro: Pont de Levallois), in Paris. At this facility outpatients are cared for between 9 a.m. and noon and 2 to 6 p.m. An emergency service is open 24 hours daily.

Tourist Office: The official tourist office in Paris is at 127 Avenue des Champs-Élysées, 8e (tel. 47-23-61-72; Métro: Charles-de-Gaulle). Hours are Monday to Saturday from 9 a.m. to 10 p.m., on Sunday and public holidays to 8 p.m. In winter, offices close an hour earlier. At this "Welcome Office," you'll receive much assistance from the helpful, English-speaking staff.

Newspapers: English-language newspapers are available at nearly every kiosk (newsstand) in Paris. Published Monday through Saturday, the *International Herald-Tribune* is the most popular paper read by visiting Americans and Canadians. Kiosks are generally open from 8 a.m. to 9 p.m.

Post Offices: These abound in Paris, as many as three or four per arrondissement. Some offices remain open late, including those in railway stations. Otherwise, regular hours are Monday to Friday, 8 a.m. to 7 p.m. (from 8 a.m. to noon on Saturday). The central post office, **Hôtel de la Poste,** 52 rue du Louvre, 1er (tel. 42-33-71-60; Métro: Louvre), is open 24 hours a day (and that means Sunday and holidays) every day of the year. Stamps can be purchased not only at post offices, but also at your hotel reception desk (usually) and at *café-tabacs* (tobacconists). At present, it costs 3.85F (53¢) to send an airmail letter to the U.S., providing it doesn't weigh more than five grams; 3.15F (43¢) to send a postcard.

American Express: For many a pipeline or lifeline to the United States, these offices are at 11 rue Scribe, 9e (tel. 42-66-09-99), which is close to the Opéra (also the Métro stop). Hours are from 9 a.m. to 5 p.m., Monday through Friday.

Banks: The already-mentioned **American Express** may be able to service most of your banking needs. If not, most banks in Paris are open from 9 a.m. to 4:30 p.m., Monday through Friday; a few are open on Saturday. Ask at your hotel the location of the one nearest to you. Shops and most hotels will cash your travelers checks, but not at the advantageous rate a bank or foreign exchange office will give you. So make sure you've allowed enough funds for *le weekend*.

Babysitters: For babysitters in Paris, there are several agencies you can call. It might be a good idea to verify if the sitter and your child speak the same language before you commit yourself. **Institut Catholique,** 21 rue d'Assas, 6e (tel. 45-48-31-70), runs a service from among its students. The price is around 25F ($3.45) an hour. The main office is open from 9 a.m. till noon and 2 to 6 p.m. weekdays only. **Ababa** (an other mother), 34 rue Delambre, 14e (tel. 43-22-22-11), is open from 8 a.m. to 9 p.m. daily and will watch over your child for 18F ($2.48) to 25F ($3.45) per hour, with discounts for extended time periods of 10 hours at a stretch, offering many auxiliary services by bilingual, carefully chosen babysitters.

Consulates and Embassies: I hope you'll not need such services. But in case of a lost passport or some other emergency, the **U.S. Embassy** is at 2 Avenue Gabriel, 8e (tel. 42-96-12-02; Métro: Concorde), and the **Canadian Embassy** stands at 35 Avenue Montaigne, 8e (tel. 47-23-21-21; Métro: F.-D.-Roosevelt). For the **United Kingdom,** the address is 35 Faubourg St-Honoré, 18e (tel. 47-23-01-01; Métro: Concorde).

Weather: For a forecast in Paris, telephone 45-55-95-90. Paris has an uncommonly long springtime, lasting through April, May, and June, and an equally extended fall, from September through November. The climate is temperate throughout the year, without those extremes so common to New York or Chicago. The coldest months are December and January, when the average high reaches 42° Fahrenheit. There's occasional snow during these months. The warmest months are July and August, when the daily averages range between 55 and 76°. Sunshine is plentiful in summer; rainfall is moderate but heavier in winter. The city looks best in autumn leaves, but its sweetest fragrance is the soft scent of spring air.

Religious Services: France is a **Roman Catholic** country, and churches of this denomination are found in every city and hamlet of the land. In addition, many churches in Paris conduct services in English. For example, the **American Church** in Paris, 65 Quai d'Orsay, 7e (tel. 47-05-07-99; Métro: Invalides), is nondenominational. The **First Church of Christ Scientist** is at 36 Boulevard St. Jacques, 14e (tel. 47-07-26-60; Métro: Glacière); **Second Church of Christ Scientist,** 58 Boulevard Flandrin, 16e (tel. 45-04-37-74; Métro: Dauphine); and the **Third Church of Christ Scientist,** 45 rue La Boétie, 8e (tel. 45-62-19-85; Métro: St-Augustin). The **Great Synagogue** is at 44 rue de la Victoire, 9e (tel. 42-85-71-09; Métro: La Peletier). An English-speaking Roman Catholic church is **St. Joseph's,** 50 Avenue Hoche, 8e (tel. 45-63-20-61; Métro: Charles-de-Gaulle). Another Catholic church with worship services in English is **Mission Anglophone,** 22 rue Claude Lorrain, 16e (tel. 45-27-05-09; Métro: Exelmans).

2. Super-Deluxe Hotels

These hotels are among the world's most celebrated and charge corresponding tariffs. Some, such as the Ritz, are legends. Their suites are far removed from the patronage of the average French person or the middle-class foreign visitor. Still, some of them ask prices in their more standard rooms that are comparable to some of Paris's leading first-class hotels. If you'd like to know how Edward VII and Lillie Langtry lived when they came to Paris, then check into one of the following selections.

Le Ritz, 15 Place Vendôme, 1er (tel. 42-60-38-30), is more than ever the greatest hotel in any European city. Opened in 1898, it is a continuing legend. The "little shepherd boy from Niederwald," César Ritz, converted the Lauzun Mansion—on one of the most beautiful and historic squares in Paris—into a hotel whose name was to become synonymous with elegance and chic. Teamed with that culinary master Escoffier, he created a miracle of luxury living. In the years to come, they would play hosts to some of the great names of the world, including Edward VII of England.

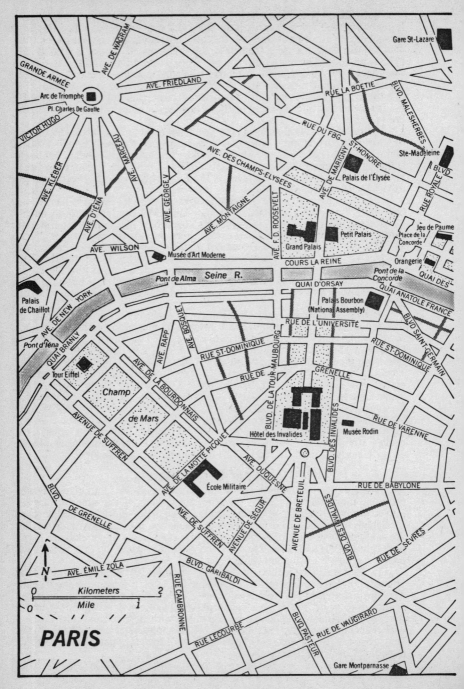

PARIS

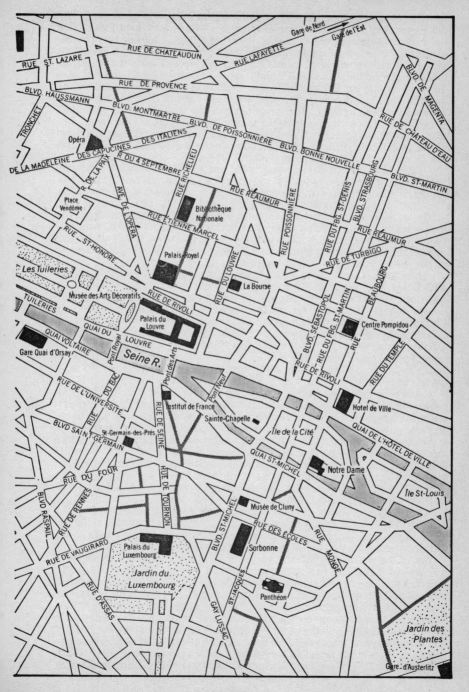

The Ritz broke precedent by providing a bath with every guest room. The drawing rooms, salons, three gardens, and courtyards were kept intact. Two town houses were eventually annexed, joined by a long arcade lined with miniature display cases representing 125 of the leading boutiques of Paris. The salons were furnished with museum-caliber antiques: gilt pieces, ornate mirrors, furniture from the periods of Louis XV and Louis XVI, hand-woven tapestries, ten-foot-high bronze torchéres. The regular bedrooms of the Ritz are among the finest in Paris. Elaborate bathrooms with every kind of little and big convenience have been installed. Artisans were brought in to give every room that French look, employing color coordination, tasteful fabrics, rich woods, lustrous marbles, antique chests, desks with bronze hardware, and crystal lighting. Singles cost from 2,300F ($317.17) and doubles from 2,800F ($386.12). Guests can dine in the Espadon grill room. Métro: Opéra.

Le Bristol, 112 rue du Faubourg St-Honoré, 8e (tel. 42-66-91-45), is a palace in every sense of the word. Not too large or too small, it is just the right size for the personalized old-world service that it rigidly and meticulously maintains. The location is on the shopping street that runs parallel to the Champs-Élysées and near the Palais de l'Élysée, the state residence of the French president. The tone is set by the classic 18th-century Parisian façade, with a glass and wrought-iron entryway, under which attendants liveried in green and red await arriving guests. Hippolyte Jammet founded the Bristol back in 1924, installing a wealth of near-priceless antiques and furnishings.

Everywhere you turn are valuable pieces, many signed, from the Louis XV and Louis XVI periods. All the bedrooms are luxuriously and opulently furnished—either with showcase antiques or well-made reproductions, inlaid woods, bronze and crystal, Oriental rugs, and original oil paintings. Even the bathrooms are sumptuously marbled, with separate stall showers, plenty of large towels, and such amenities as a lighted magnifying mirror for makeup or shaving. Singles start at 1,250F ($172.38), going up to 1,730F ($238.57). The least expensive double is 2,270F ($313.03), and some twin-bedded rooms cost as much as 2,800F ($386.12), with suites beginning at 5,400F ($744.66). To these prices, 18.6% VAT is added. Métro: St-Phillipe-du-Roule.

Marriott Prince de Galles, 33 Avenue George V, 8e (tel. 47-23-55-11). When it was constructed in the 1920s, the cognoscenti of the era's stratospheric social life adopted its art deco / neo-Byzantine courtyard as their preferred rendezvous point. Later in the 1950s diarist and composer Ned Rorem recorded the trysts and trials of the "unapproachable innermost snob-life of Paris" which transpired within the hotel walls. Eras change but the allure of the "Prince of Wales" remains. Marriott's recent adoption (and meticulous restoration) of this palace maintained the impeccable standards for which it was known, perhaps subtly imbuing it with doses of American efficiency and friendliness, but basically leaving it as a very Parisian monument to the good life.

The hotel occupies a platinum location only a short promenade from the Champs-Élysées, the Arc de Triomphe, and the glamorous boutiques of the Avenue Montaigne. Guests are greeted at the door with a smile by a team of uniformed attendants, who quickly arrange for cars to be parked and baggage sent to one of the plushly upholstered, very spacious accommodations. A cluster of French sofas and armchairs is grouped around bouquets of flowers, complementing the Regency detailing of the six-sided lobby. The paneled bar, with its leather-upholstered copies of 18th-century armchairs, is one of the great hotel bars of Paris. Many guests enhance their sybaritic fling with a meal in the paneled dining room which even Madame de Sévigné might have been tempted to write about. Both the dining room and the quietest bedrooms look out over the famous courtyard, whose sides are covered with elaborate mosaics whose glistening surfaces might resemble the background of a painting by Gustav Klimt.

Each of the high-ceilinged accommodations contains an ultra-comfortable bathroom whose surfaces repeat the Edwardian / art deco tilework which works so successfully on the hotel's façade. The elegantly furnished, air-conditioned bedrooms contain color TV with in-house movies, direct-dial phone, radio, and lots of sunflooded space. Singles cost from 1,800F ($248.22), doubles 2,300F ($317.17), with taxes and service included. A well-trained and sophisticated staff seems eager to respond to queries and requests, including the need for complete privacy that many of this hotel's well-heeled clientele demands. For reservations and information within North America, call toll free 800/228-9290. Métro: George V.

The **Crillon,** 10 Place de la Concorde, 8e (tel. 42-65-24-10), is unquestionably one of the great hotels of Paris, now owned by Jean Taittinger of the Taittinger Champagne family. First of all, the setting is unparalleled: right on the Place de la Concorde, across from the American Embassy. The building—designed by Gabriel—is more than 200 years old. Once the palace of the Duke of Crillon, it housed and entertained some of the major names in French history for two centuries. Since the first decade of this century, it's been a hotel, its most famous guest none other than Woodrow Wilson during his stay in Paris.

Behind its colonnaded exterior, with its classic fluted columns, the palace-like hotel envelops a large formal courtyard, favored for drinks or tea. Silently attended by two statues, tables and parasols are set around a reflecting pool and a border of flowers. The interior is 18th century, with well-preserved architectural details and authentic and reproduction antique decorations. Throughout the parquet-floored salons are paneled walls with large scenic murals, gilt- and brocade-covered furniture, glittering chandeliers, niches with fine sculpture, inlaid desks, Louis XVI chests and chairs. The bedrooms are classically furnished as well, the accommodations generously proportioned and equipped with handsome bathrooms lined with travertine marble. Singles rent for 1,800F ($248.22), while doubles range from 2,400F ($330.96) to 2,800F ($386.12).

The Crillon's two restaurants, the elegant Les Ambassadeurs and the more informal L'Obélisque, both serve high quality meals under the culinary inspiration of Jean-Pierre Bonin. Expect to spend from 400F ($55.16), including wine and service, for dinner in Les Ambassadeurs. In L'Obélisque, you can dine for 225F ($31.03) and up. Métro: Concorde.

George V, 31 Avenue George V, 8e (tel. 47-23-54-00). J. Paul Getty used to feel at home here. So did Darryl Zanuck. So do many visiting New York and Beverly Hills "simple folk." On a tree-lined avenue between the Champs-Élysées and the Seine, the hotel offers grandiose luxury in a semimodern building, almost like a smaller French version of the Waldorf Astoria. The George V tends to rise and fall in popularity with the fickle chic. At present, it seems to be enjoying a renaissance with many former clients who had deserted it for quieter hotels offering less "show biz." One of the legends of the George V is that it keeps a mysterious file of the preferences of its most favored habitués. How detailed it is or how far the hotel goes to meet those preferences, I simply don't know—except to say that the George V is matched by few hotels in Europe in service. The staff is not only large but attentive. Every guest has virtually his or her own personal servant. The pampering begins the moment you sit at the Empire reception desk to be registered and welcomed.

The public rooms are imbued with a museum air, with rich old tapestries, impressive paintings from the 18th and 19th centuries, even Pompeian inlaid marble walls. In good weather, luncheons are served in the roomy inner courtyard—haute cuisine meals spread under red parasols. Try to get a room or suite overlooking this courtyard, for many of these select accommodations have terrace balconies with summer furniture plus urns and boxes overflowing with red geraniums and other bright summer flowers. A single rents for 1,800F ($248.22) to 2,100F ($289.59), a double for 2,400F ($330.96), taxes and service included.

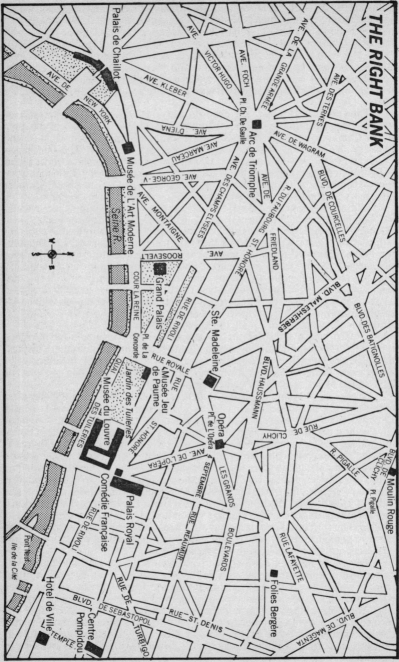

THE RIGHT BANK

The hotel is better than ever, a far cry from the way it was when in 1944 General Eisenhower made it his headquarters during the Liberation. A complete refurbishing program is under way, and the hotel rooms are fully air-conditioned. Trusthouse Forte has done much to retain its Versailles-like flavor. The aim is to maintain an atmosphere of pleasant luxury throughout the entire hotel—and not just in the stunning suites. Métro: George-V.

Plaza Athénée, 25 Avenue Montaigne, 8e (tel. 42-25-43-30). In the old days, Mata Hari used to drop in. It's also been known to about half of all the pampered visiting celebrities of Paris. It is pure gilded luxury set in the midst of the foreign embassies (the rich ones) and the temples of haute couture, from which it draws many of its guests. It is said that there are two employees for each guest in the 250-room citadel dedicated to the good life. The hotel doesn't exactly hide its luxuries. First, its location is auspicious, in an embassy area, halfway between the Champs-Elysées and the Seine, on an avenue graced with towering shade trees. The tone is set when a taxi (or limousine) delivers you to the formal entrance, with its striking awnings. A livéried attendant stands below a glass shelter to welcome you. The architectural details are in the pre-World War I style: arched windows and ornate balconies.

When you check in, you're seated in front of a Louis XVI marquetry desk, facing a rare Flemish tapestry. The hotel is built palace style, the pinnacle achieved by the Regency Salon, paneled in rich grained wood and dominated by a marble fireplace. The better bedrooms overlook a courtyard, with awnings and parasol-shaded tables. Vines climb over inner balconies, and there are formal flowerbeds—in all, a choice spot for breakfast or lunch. The well-maintained, air-conditioned bedrooms all have a private tile bath that is especially large and fine, with double basins and shower included. Such other amenities as small refrigerators, ample closet space, and taffeta draperies make the rooms elegant, comfortable places to stay. Singles rent for 1,650F ($227.54) to 1,950F ($268.91), and doubles go for 2,100F ($289.59) to 3,200F ($441.28), plus 15% service charge. Meals are an occasion, as the food is superb. The preferred choice for dining is Le Régence, a room of handsome period furniture and delicate pink, peach, and gold colors. It is known for its lobster soufflé. With its bright colors and decoration, the Grill Relais Plaza is the meeting place of "tout Paris," especially at lunch, drawing dress designers and personalities from the worlds of publishing, cinema, and art. The Bar Anglais is a favorite spot of mine for a late-night drink (it's open until 1:30 a.m.), with its plaid carpet and dark-green and red leather decor. Métro: Alma-Marceau.

Royal Monceau, 35–39 Avenue Hoche, 8e (tel. 45-61-98-00). The CIGA chain, renowned for its ultra-glamorous properties in Italy, has transformed this elegant property into its flagship hotel in France. The hotel was already famous in its own right. Completed in 1925, it has been host to a wide social and political spectrum of guests, ranging from occupying Nazi officers to Golda Meir, from King Farouk of Egypt to Ho Chi Minh. Today, the graceful hotel combines the best of French restraint with doses of Italian flair.

The hotel sits in an upperclass neighborhood within the sightlines of a kitty-corner view of the nearby Arch of Triumph. From the moment guests pass beneath the translucent art nouveau canopy of the intricately carved façade, an attentive staff is there to serve them. The airy lobby radiates the kind of lavish spaciousness you'd expect to find in the wings of a 19th-century museum. In its center, an oval-shaped dome is covered with murals of cerulean skies and fluffy clouds creating a canopy over huge bouquets of flowers.

The establishment's sophisticated designers transformed a courtyard into an attractive restaurant, Le Jardin, by building a glassed-in gazebo whose rounded walls combine space-age construction with a French neoclassissism. Views of the double tiers of plants are visible through the lattice windows, including a 20-foot magnolia and dozens of flowering shrubs. Two other restaurants and a piano bar provide ample dining choice. In the hotel's basement, a sybaritic health club combines the equipment of a state-of-the-arts gym with elements from the baths of a Roman emperor.

The wide array of accommodations are usually filled with Directoire furnishings and all the plush upholstery and electronics you'd expect. Each is air-conditioned with a marble-covered bathroom. Singles cost between 1,450F ($199.96) and 1,800F ($248.22), doubles between 1,800F ($248.22) and 2,100F ($289.59), breakfast not included. Tax is extra. For reservations and information in North America, call CIGA's reservation service, toll free 800/221-2340 (residents of New York City should dial 212/935-9540).

Hôtel Meurice, 228 rue de Rivoli, 1er (tel. 42-60-38-60). The expression "fit for a king" could have been coined to describe this hotel. Directors in the past were judged on the basis of how discreetly they could slip royal "favorites" in and out of the boudoir. Kings not being as plentiful as they were, you're more likely nowadays to run into diplomats, industrialists, and successful authors. The self-proclaimed "mad genius" Salvador Dali makes the Meurice his headquarters, occupying Suite 108, which was once used by the deposed and exiled king of Spain, Alfonso XIII. During the Nazi occupation, the office of German General von Choltitz, who was in charge of Paris, was Suite 108.

The Meurice is an unmarred, romanticized 18th-century way of life, with a totally French aura. You can see the Louvre from the upper floors of this hotel, which dates from 1907. Its gilded salons were copied from the château at Versailles. It's a world of gilt-edged paneled walls, monumental crystal chandeliers, ornate tapestries, and furnishings from the periods of Louis XIV, XV, and XVI. The location is impressive, just off the rue de Rivoli and the Tuileries Gardens, within walking distance of the Louvre. The formal drive-in entrance begs for a Mercedes, a plea that's usually granted. Once inside, a look at the garden evokes life in a country château. In the lounge you stand under a circular "star"-studded ceiling. The bedrooms, redecorated, air-conditioned, and soundproof, are richly furnished with some period and modern pieces—each containing a bed-sitting salon and a private bath. One person pays 2,300F ($317.17); two persons, from 2,800F ($386.12).

The Meurice Restaurant is just what you'd expect in the world's dining capital, the home of the true French haute cuisine. The Pompadour cocktail lounge is a gracious rendezvous for cocktails and tea, and the elegant Meurice Bar offers drinks in the warm atmosphere of its renovated decor. Métro: Tuileries or Concorde.

Paris Inter-Continental, 3 rue de Castiglione, 1er (tel. 42-60-37-80), is a miraculous mixture of French tradition, Gallic know-how, and 20th-century modernity and ingenuity. The result: The largest and splashiest deluxe hotel in Paris. The position is stunning, along the rue de Rivoli and across from the Tuileries Gardens. When it originally opened in 1878, it was known as "The Continental." In 1883 Victor Hugo was fêted at a luncheon. The belle époque hotel has always enjoyed an elite position in Paris, sheltering such guests as the Empress Eugénie of France and Jean Giraudoux. The alterations were drastic, the improvements dramatic. It just isn't the old Continental anymore, although the unusual and distinguished among the architectural features have been preserved. The great inner courtyard, known as "La Cour d'Honneur," is paved with white marble on several levels, with a circular splashing fountain and an 1864 statue by Cunny. In fair weather, luncheon, tea, or drinks are served al fresco here, under a gold and white canopy.

The public rooms have flair and style. The main lounge, for example, has Persian carpets, period furnishings, bronze sconces, and marble cocktail tables. The colonnaded front entrance, carpeted in blue, has a pair of bronze candelabra secured from a palace in Leningrad. The bedrooms and suites are among the finest in Paris. Although there are many antiques, the 500 bedrooms are tastefully and knowingly decorated in the classic French style, with reproductions of Louis XVI pieces. Each chamber has its own paneled walls, matching draperies and bedcovers, and a one-color theme to each room that creates that salon effect—enhanced by a discreet use of crystal, fine fruitwoods, bronze hardware, and inlaid consoles, desks, and tables. Every room is air-conditioned, with direct-dial phone, plus 24-hour room service and same-day valet. Single rooms range in price from 1,700F ($234.43) to 1,900F ($262.01); twins, from 1,900F ($262.01) to 2,500F ($344.75).

There is no main dining room as a survey indicated that guests prefer more intimate character rooms. That theory works successfully here. The most elegant dining spot is the Rôtisserie Rivoli, brightened by tones of light pink and green, with windows looking out on the Tuileries Gardens. Terrasse Fleurie is the interior courtyard landscaped to depict the four seasons. Estrela, the newest and most up-to-date disco in Paris, with mirror walls and green and gold colors, is open from 10 p.m. to 4 a.m. Café Tuileries is a typical French restaurant and bar, in the belle époque style, serving breakfasts, snacks, light meals, informal suppers, cocktails, and French pastries; open until midnight. Métro: Concorde.

l'Hôtel, 13 rue des Beaux-Arts, 6e (tel. 43-25-27-22). If you were either unkind or blunt, you would have called the 19th-century Hôtel d'Alsace a "fleabag." It was, but it had some style, attracting down-and-out artists—many drawn there because of its reputation as the building in which Oscar Wilde died. A broken man, the Victorian author scrawled his last letter at the Alsace, beseeching Frank Harris to send him "the money you owe me." Nowadays, the clientele—Leopold Rothschild, Mia Farrow, Julie Christie, Jack Lemmon, and Ava Gardner—is hardly in such straits.

Called simply l'Hôtel, and on the Left Bank (out-of-bounds for most deluxe Parisian hotels), it was the love child of one of France's favorite actors—Guy-Louis Duboucheron, who wanted to establish an intimate, supersophisticated place of jewel-box proportions and character, where guests would be pampered and pay the price. ("I wanted it to be like raiding the icebox at home in the middle of the night.") l'Hôtel drew upon the creative energies of a Texas architect, Robin Westbrook, who also aided with the interior furnishings. He gutted the core of the old hotel to make a miniature circular courtyard similar to the interior of the Tower of Pisa.

The smallest rooms rent for 1,000F ($137.90) to 1,500F ($158.59). Larger doubles, two with fireplaces, opening onto the garden rent from 1,800F ($248.22). Two rooms are conversation pieces. One, facing the garden rear, is where Wilde died. The other holds the original furnishings and memorabilia of Mistinguett, France's legendary stage star. Her pedestal bed is set in the middle of the room; and all her furnishings, including the bed, are covered with mirrors! But regardless of the room you get or the price you pay, you receive the same ingratiating service.

Drinks are served in a vaulted stone cellar, where fine antiques are set in nooks and crannies. The enclosed courtyard is a true delight: travertine bistro tables with bentwood chairs, glistening silver serving dishes on a mahogany pedestal, even caged monkeys and pigeons, brass street lanterns, lush plants, and flowers. In the petite reception salon, furnished with 18th- and 19th-century charm, and in a lusher, richer drinking lounge, you'll find paintings. Be warned that informality reigns: at any moment, a pet duck may waddle in from the courtyard, seeking your attention and upstaging many a super-star in the midst of an elaborate story. Métro: St-Germain-des-Prés.

3. 8th Arrondissement

CHAMPS-ÉLYSÉES / MADELEINE: The Champs-Élysées dominates the 8th Arrondissement. Restaurants such as Maxim's have made it famous. It is the

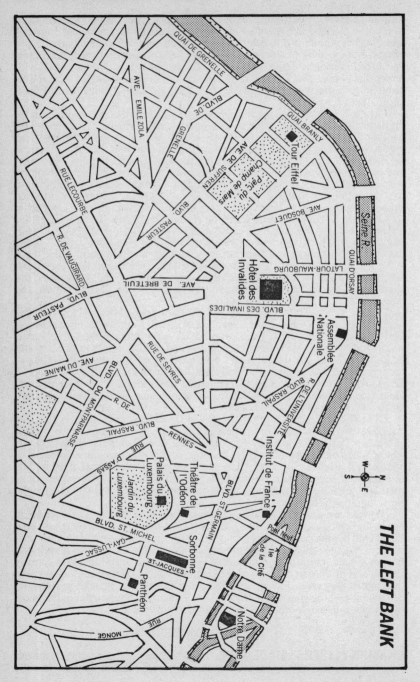

domain of such well-known hotels as the Crillon, the George V, and the Plaza-Athénée. But a notch down from these palaces are lesser-known establishments, such as the Lancaster (which many film stars consider the finest hotel in Paris). Converted town houses have been turned into fine hotels. All of the above are far beyond the average budget. However, you do have your choice of medium-priced selections—but don't come here for low-budget hotels.

Deluxe Hotels

Hôtel Lancaster, 7 rue de Berri, 8e (tel. 43-59-90-43), was once an exquisite private house off the Champs-Élysées, with an open forecourt and stables. Some years ago it was acquired by Swiss-born Monsieur and Madame Wolf, who transformed the stables into an almost regal dining room. They took in "paying guests," and their salon became known among artists and writers. As patrons of the arts, the Wolfs amassed a handsome collection of antiques and pictures, which are used throughout the hotel. There is also an assortment of fine clocks—although they don't always tell the exact time. Since its inception, the Lancaster has maintained much of the feeling of a private club and is perhaps the most British-influenced hotel in Paris. In 1970, the Wolfs, feeling they had made their statement, sold the hotel, now a member of the British Prestige group, which has made excellent improvements in the establishment's physical plant. Nowadays, it is likely to attract movie stars, everybody from Gregory Peck to Peter Ustinov.

A single ranges in price from 1,200F ($165.48) to 1,400F ($193.06); a double, from 1,730F ($238.57) to 1,900F ($262.01). A 15% service charge is added to all bills. The more expensive rooms are larger and better positioned, usually opening onto a quiet and restful courtyard. The average chamber is richly furnished in a traditional manner—containing paneled walls, brocaded Louis XVI-style furniture, gilt mirrors, and tasteful accessories. The baths are commodious, having their own special style. You can have predinner drinks in the Grand Salon and then enjoy fine food in the restaurant. In good weather, drinks and meals are served in the garden. Métro: George-V.

Hôtel Le Warwick, 5 rue de Berri, 8e (tel. 45-63-14-11), one of the newest major hotels in Paris (it opened in 1981), occupies a desirable location near a corner at the upper end of the Champs-Élysées. Perhaps because the hotel is owned by a group of investors from Hong Kong, many of the lacquered accents in the public rooms are of a deep Chinese red, alternating with mirrors and lots of plants. Even the young and attractive staff is attired, as is the establishment's façade, in shades of maroon. About 30% of the bedrooms have evergreen-covered terraces looking out at views of the Eiffel Tower and the 18th-century buildings across the street. Business people from across North and South America appreciate the soundproof windows, the opulent marble-covered baths, the bronze and peach-colored accents, the 24-hour video on the color TVs, and the attractively concealed mini-bars. All units are air-conditioned. Accommodations cost around 1,450F ($199.96) in a single and 1,880F ($259.25) in a double. Children under 12 stay free in their parents' rooms.

The ground floor contains the Swann Bar, with live piano music and views into the elegant in-house restaurant, where a five-course, fixed-price meal, costing around 230F ($31.72), includes such items as a paillard of salmon with caviar, cassoulet of duckling, and marinated mussels. The hotel has a parking garage. Métro: George-V.

Upper Bracket Hotels

Hotel Balzac, 6 rue Balzac, 8e (tel. 45-61-97-22). What might be the most successful renovation in this part of Paris opened late in 1985 in a neighborhood well acquainted with 19th-century grandeur. The gilding on the wrought-iron balustrades was barely dry before the hotel was adopted by cognoscenti as one of the most refreshing hotels which Paris has seen in this price category in a long time. Its desirable location a few steps from the Champs-Élysées, near the Arc de Triomphe, makes it even more worthwhile.

When they created it, a team of French and Lebanese designers added well-studied touches of the best decors of England, Italy, and France to a sophisticated series of public rooms which include elements of art deco, Palladian revival, and neo-Byzantine. A recessed alcove in the lobby is covered with hand-painted tendrils and vines, which seem to grow into the glistening white marble of a sun-flooded atrium. Kilim carpets, plum-colored upholstery, burnished paneling, and antique oil portraits add to the allure. The hotel restaurant, Le Sallambier, is named after Balzac's mother. A quartet of lions peers out from the restaurant's illuminated ceiling dome whose sides are covered with frescoes that might have been painted by Rousseau or Gauguin. A well-prepared (and well-received) cuisine features specialties from southwestern France as well as a smattering of nouvelle cuisine tempters. Even the breakfast room is replete with amber-colored translucent pilasters and curved 1920s-style furniture.

Accommodations are accessible via a glass-walled elevator which glides silently upstairs past acres of Turkish-patterned carpeting. Each of the rooms is outfitted with a glistening marble bathroom, thick upholstery, and tastefully monochromatic decors of blue gray or spice. Each contains a mini-bar, radio, phone, and color TV with half a dozen channels. A handful of suites lie on the uppermost floor. Singles cost from 1,100F ($151.69); doubles, 1,550F ($213.75). Suites begin at 2,400F ($330.96). Métro: George V.

Hôtel Château Frontenac, 54 rue Pierre-Charron, 8e (tel. 47-23-55-85), is a desirable, well-appointed, and sophisticated hotel set in the midst of the kind of neighborhood that every fashion star in Paris wants eventually to live in. The building is a grandly ornate corner structure graced with the stone carvings and elaborate wrought-iron detailing so common in this part of town. The public rooms open into a glamorous combination of richly super-modern paneling, concealed lighting, and warmly inviting colors. A bar and the Pavillon Russe restaurant off the main lobby are startlingly outfitted in shades of vermilion and black. Single rooms range from 510F ($70.33) to 680F ($93.77), while doubles cost 700F ($96.53) to 900F ($124.11). Métro: F.-D.-Roosevelt.

The **San Régis,** 12 rue Jean-Goujon, 8e (tel. 43-59-41-90), once a fashionable town house, stands in the midst of embassies and exclusive boutiques (Christian Dior is across the street), enjoying, in a quiet and modest way, its position as one of the best hotels in Paris. It is right off the Champs-Élysées, only a short walk from the Seine. Many guests find it much like a private club. There is a small but attentive staff who quickly learn your whims and fancies and make you feel at home.

Each room is unique (my personal favorite is Room 6), decorated with discretion and taste, lavishly sprinkled with antiques, and all have private bath, color TV, music, and air conditioning. A few have a separate sitting room, and many overlook a quiet side garden. The price for a single ranges from 800F ($110.32) to 950F ($131.01), doubles or twins costing from 1,000F ($137.90) to 1,500F ($206.85). The hotel has a lounge and a bar-restaurant. Métro: Alma-Marceau or F.-D.-Roosevelt.

Hôtel Royal Alma, 35 rue Jean-Goujon, 8e (tel. 42-25-83-30), is a well-positioned hotel that was completely renovated in 1984. It's just a whisper from the Seine, an eight-minute walk from the Champs-Élysées, smack in the heart of some of the most expensive real estate in Paris. There's a bar leading off the main lobby, an unpretentious modern decor, and sinuous wine-colored carpeting that winds up the stairwell and throughout the eight floors of comfortably appointed but simple and compact bedrooms. All of these have private bath,

TV, phone, and access to nearby parking. From the windows of a few of them you can see into the labyrinthine recesses of a neighboring office building, where the employees work busily while you enjoy the sights of Paris. Singles rent for 853F ($117.63), doubles for 981F ($135.28), and triples for 1,019F ($140.52), with a continental breakfast included. Métro: Alma-Marceau.

The Middle Bracket

Hôtel l'Horset Astor, 11 rue d'Astorg, 8e (tel. 42-66-56-56), a member of the Parisian hotel chain, is in an area of old inner-city villas not far from the Élysées Palace. The paneled reception area is spacious and well appointed. As in many hotels in Paris, the better rooms are beautiful and the less desirable ones are exactly that, so you may or may not like your accommodations. On the premises is a long wooden bar with leather-topped stools and a blowup of what looks like an 18th-century engraving. There's an in-house restaurant. All rooms have phone, color TV, and mini-bar. Singles rent for 750F ($103.43), doubles for 850F ($117.22), and triples for 950F ($131.01). Métro: St-Augustin.

Schweizerhof, 11 rue Balzac, 8e (tel. 45-63-54-22), is in the vicinity of the Champs-Élysées and the Arc de Triomphe, yet for many it evokes a small hotel in a quiet Swiss town. This former private residence with a garden in front has been converted into a well-run and friendly hotel. The owners have added antiques wherever possible. Each room is different, particularly in size. There is TV, radio, and a private bar in all the rooms. Prices are 575F ($79.29) for a single and 750F ($103.43) for a double. Métro: George-V.

Lord Byron, 5 rue de Chateaubriand, 8e (tel. 43-59-89-98), is a select little hotel you can be proud to stay in and recommend to your friends. On a quiet, gently curving street of distinguished buildings, it is just off the Champs-Élysées. The owner, Madame François Coisne, who migrated to Paris from the Île de France, has put her imprint everywhere. Each room has a personalized, tasteful concept, revealing an authoritative woman's touch. The furnishings are usually good reproductions of antiques or else restrained, likable modern. Placed throughout are framed prints of butterflies and historic French scenes.

Prices include taxes, service, and an especially good breakfast (no other meals are provided.) Breakfast is served either in your room, in a petit salon, or in a shaded inner garden. A large-bedded room for two with a private bath rents for 500F ($68.95). A few suites with two beds are also available for 800F ($110.32). The bathrooms are as functional as they are attractively decorated. Métro: George-V.

The Budget Range

Madeleine-Plaza, 33 Place de la Madelein, 8e (tel. 42-65-20-63), couldn't be more Right Bank central, unless you slept in Madeleine church itself. Just on the plaza, it offers many consolidated and streamlined bedrooms, with a view of the church. A renovation program also provided all units with private bath or shower. Compact doubles with shower begin at 325F ($44.82), going up to 480F ($66.19) with private bath. The bedrooms are not overly spacious. For those who do not want their breakfast in bed, a breakfast room overlooks the church. Métro: Madeleine, of course.

4. 16th and 17th Arrondissements

ÉTOILE/CHAILLOT/BOIS DE BOULOGNE: This is one of my favorite districts of Paris. Hemmed in by the Seine and the elegant park, the Bois de Boulogne, the 16th Arrondissement is largely a residential area of old town houses. In addition to the super-deluxe Raphael, the district also contains some of the finest hotels in Paris, known to well-heeled, discriminating travelers. Other selections, much preferred, are in the 17th Arrondissement, embracing the Parc Monceau.

The Upper Bracket

Raphael, 17 Avenue Kléber, 16e (tel. 45-02-16-00). When you face the cashier, you'll notice a large gold-and-orange painting on your right. It's an original Turner, and a fine one. As you gaze around at the main reception hall and the salons that open off it, you'll be stepping back into the luxury of romantic France. For example, the main hallway has lustrous dark-paneled walnut walls, with ornate bronze torchères and gilt-framed oil paintings. The music salon is also richly wood paneled, with fine carving, a marble fireplace, and turkey-red carpeting. A favorite with celebrities is the drinking lounge, also ornately paneled and furnished with claret velour sofas, carved oak chairs, and fluted columns.

A mahogany-and-brass elevator takes you to the many floors of impressive bedrooms. Each chamber is large enough to seem like a wing of a suite or a palace room, replete with silk draperies, gilt-and-brass-trimmed chests, tables, inlaid woods, and armoires. All important furniture periods are represented: Directoire, Louis XVI, Regency. A single room with private bath rents from 790F ($108.94), a moderate double room with private bath costs from 860F ($118.59), and a medium-grade double room is priced from 1,400F ($193.06). Rates include taxes, service, and continental breakfast. Métro: Charles-de-Gaulle.

Hôtel La Perouse, 40 rue La Perouse, 16e (tel. 45-00-83-47). My favorite hotel in the 16th Arrondissement occupies an ornate turn-of-the-century building graced with an elaborate iron-and-glass canopy stretching over the entrance. Charles de Gaulle lived here for a long time (between 1946 and 1958), occupying Suite 24 on the third floor. No wonder: it is grandly, warmly, and totally French. The high-ceilinged lobby is filled with plasterwork detailing, warm colors, deeply comfortable 19th-century reproduction leather chairs and sofas, and verdant potted palms.

The hotel occupies a strategic position, just off the Place Charles-de-Gaulle with its Arc de Triomphe. Many a statesperson and foreign ambassador has chosen the quiet salon or dining room for some diplomatic maneuvering, and the in-house restaurant, l'Astrolabe, offers the kind of elegantly sophisticated ambience for you to do some maneuvering of your own. Jean Giraudoux, author of *The Madwoman of Chaillot,* also lived here for a time. Doubles with bath, TV, radio, mini-bar, air conditioning, and phone, cost 1,300F ($179.27) to 2,300F ($317.17). Métro: Kléber.

Méridien, 81 Boulevard Gouvion-Saint-Cyr, 17e (tel. 47-58-12-30), is the largest hotel in France. Under Air France's aegis, the 1027-room, air-conditioned hotel is a first of its kind in Paris. It caters to groups as well as to individuals, and it is big enough to accommodate a separate check-in counter for the former. The location is opposite the Air Terminal and two steps from the Champs-Élysées. It's at Porte Maillot, on the Neuilly-Vincennes Métro line. A lot of Air France know-how has gone into the design and furnishings—so you're offered rather pampered living. The setting is contemporary French, and the dramatic, overscale lobby chandelier is an immediate eye-catcher. The bedrooms are designed to provide attractiveness, convenience, and comfort, plus good views of a great city. Featured are lots of slick built-in pieces, textured and handsomely colored fabrics, TV, direct-dial telephones, and partitioned bathrooms. Depending on their size and how they were renovated, singles cost from 1,170F ($161.34) to 1,675F ($230.98), with doubles ranging in price from 1,350F ($186.17) to 1,675F ($230.98). Suites begin at 2,600F ($358.54). All tariffs include taxes and service.

There are four restaurants, featuring everything from traditional French cuisine (Le Clos Longchamp) to Japanese specialties. The hotel has a coiffeur and a duty-free shop. A bar called Le Patio offers a musical ambience, and from 6 to 10 p.m. you hear piano music. An international jazz band plays from 10 p.m. to 2 a.m. Métro: Porte Maillot.

La Résidence du Bois, 16 rue Chalgrin, 16e (tel. 45-00-50-59), is an exquisite little villa, all shiny white with a mansard roof, tucked away in a shady lane off the park-like Avenue Foch, only two minutes from the Arc de Triomphe. Go here only if you like quiet luxury. Monsieur and Madame Desponts bought this 300-year-old mansion from the comte de Bomeau in 1964 and turned it into a retreat for discriminating guests. When they finished their careful restoration, they brought in their vast collection of antiques (mostly Louis XVI), gilt-edged paintings, crystal chandeliers, bronzes, sculpture, brocaded and silk draperies —making each room a charming world. Although the rooms evoke the 17th and 18th centuries, with classic patterns of silk fabric on the walls, the bathrooms are super-modern. Depending on the room assignment, doubles range in price from 850F ($117.22) to 1,200F ($165.48).

A favorite spot in cooler months is an intimate drinking lounge, with huge armchairs positioned around a fireplace. In the cellar is a historic room where the mansion's first owner, an eminent physician, performed operations. A small front garden is screened from the lane by a stone wall and a wrought-iron fence, a few aged trees lending it a country feeling. In the rear garden are tables for breakfast. Métro: Charles-de-Gaulle.

The Middle Bracket

Résidence Foch, 10 rue Marbeau, 16e (tel. 45-00-46-50), is a gracious and artistic 25-room hotel run by Mr. and Mrs. Schneider. Off the Avenue Foch, it's only a few minutes from the Arc de Triomphe and a short walk from the Bois de Boulogne. Popular with the diplomatic corps, the hotel is well decorated. All rooms contain private bath, direct-dial phone, radio, television, and clock. The regular doubles rent for 640F ($88.26) to 820F ($113.08), the singles for 540F ($74.47). Prices quoted include tax, service, and a continental breakfast. Guests drop in for afternoon drinks in the front bar-lounge, enjoying its warm, quiet atmosphere. Métro: Porte Dauphine or Porte Maillot.

Les Trois Couronnes, 30 rue de l'Arc de Triomphe, 17e (tel. 43-80-46-81). Jean-Louis and Paule Lafont renovated an older hotel near the Étoile in 1983. Today their creation combines a decor that embraces both art deco and art nouveau. They used personal objects they had collected for many years, including a 19th-century carved oak mantelpiece flanked with bearded statues (it's been turned into a reception desk) and a narrow marble fireplace that came at one time from a private house in Versailles.

The colors used throughout the 20 bedrooms are cheerfully appropriate and blend well with the elmwood trim. On the premises are a vaulted breakfast room, which you can reach via an elevator, a winding staircase with a light forged-iron balustrade, and an up-to-date security system. Each of the rooms comfortably houses one or two persons, and is equipped with private bath, TV, and mini-bar. They each rent for 400F ($55.16). Métro: Charles-de-Gaulle (Étoile).

Regent's Garden Hotel, 6 rue Pierre-Demours, 17e (tel. 45-74-07-30), has not one but two gardens, one with ivy-covered walls and umbrella tables—an inviting place to meet fellow guests for a cooling apéritif. Near the Convention Center, it is three minutes from the Arc de Triomphe. The owners, Mr. Garnarat and Mr. Erot, who treat guests with friendly simplicity, are proud of the heritage of the hotel: Napoléon III built the stately château for his physician. Today the interior is like a country house, with a classic touch. The entry has fluted columns, the living room a casual mixture of family-style furniture— neither too studied nor too impressive, always comfortable.

The bedrooms, all with soundproof windows, are cheerfully done, featuring French flower prints on the walls and beds and tall French windows graced by soft filmy curtains. Some modern pieces have been added here and there, but most rooms are traditionally furnished; some even have draped canopy beds. The prices, including taxes, service, and continental breakfast, are from 650F ($89.64) for a single with bath, from 800F ($110.32) for a double with bath. Métro: Wagram or Ternès.

Hôtel Alexander, 102 Avenue Victor Hugo, 16e (tel. 45-53-64-65), is a very correct, very conservative hotel in the heart of the comfortably well-off 16th Arrondissement. In the best sense of the word, this is really the perfect bourgeois hotel, the kind you'd send an elderly aunt to for her first trip to Paris. About 50% of the frilly and feminine rooms look out over a well-planted and quiet courtyard. Each room has its own small crystal chandelier, private bath, phone, color TV, and mini-bar. An elegant elevator carries you inside the curve of a wrought-iron winding stairwell to your carpeted bedroom. Singles rent for 635F ($87.57), while doubles cost 800F ($110.32), with a continental breakfast included. Métro: Pompe.

La Régence Étoile, 24 Avenue Carnot, 17e (tel. 43-80-75-60), is only two minutes from the Arc de Triomphe, on a shady tree-lined street. The hotel occupies an attractive building of white stone with white shutters and trim. Inside, a tiny reception area and three small salons are furnished with several antiques, augmented by murals of Paris. A miniature elevator takes you to the especially nice bedrooms, furnished with reproductions of good French furniture. All the rooms have a tile bath, including a bidet and often a shower as well as a tub, plus direct-dial phone and color television. Two sets of prices are charged for the double rooms, the higher rate for the larger ones: 420F ($57.92) to 530F ($73.09), including taxes, service, and a continental breakfast. Singles go from 340F ($46.89) to 420F ($57.92). There's a garage nearby. Métro: Charles-de-Gaulle (Étoile).

Hôtel Frémiet, 6 Avenue Frémiet, 16e (tel. 45-24-52-06). Lean out a front bedroom window and you'll see the Seine, its silent parade of barges and boats, perhaps even the spot where the late Anaïs Nin moored her houseboat. Across the river from the Eiffel Tower, the second house down from the Avenue du Président Kennedy, which borders the Seine, Frémiet stands in an exclusive residential district, one of only a few hotels here.

It's been owned by the same English-speaking Fourmond family for some 20 years. Each year the owners have done renovations, installing an automatic elevator and a new bar in the lobby. That French look is achieved with a generous use of Louis XVI-style furniture. All the freshly decorated bedrooms contain a private bath. TV is available in the rooms, and each unit has a direct-dial phone. Doubles range in price from 600F ($87.74) to 690F ($95.15); singles, from 540F ($74.47) to 580F ($79.98). The reception lobby is just that, nothing more, although there is a small antique-filled salon for guests. Métro: Passy.

Hotel Pierre, 25 rue Theodore-de-Banville, 17e (tel. 47-63-76-69), was given its name as a facetious counterpoint to the owners' favorite North American hotel, the Pierre in New York. To create it, the owners combined a trio of 19th-century buildings into a clean and modern hotel with art deco styling. Opened in 1986, it sits at the end of a residential street a short walk from the Arch of Triumph. Each of the 50 stylish accommodations contains a TV set with video movies, mini-bar, a safe with a combination lock, and a phone. Each is outfitted with monochromatically restful shades of blue and gray. A member of the Best Western reservations system, the hotel charges from 560F ($77.22) in a single, from 680F ($93.77) in a double, including breakfast. Richard Duvauchelle is the conscientious manager whose Boston-born wife is occasionally on the premises. Métro: Courcelles.

Tivoli-Étoile, 7 rue Brey, 17e (tel. 43-80-31-22). Many visitors to Paris like to stay right off the Champs-Élysées, in the vicinity of the Arc de Triomphe, yet find the hotels in this district beyond their limited means. The rue Brey is a side street branching off the Avenue de Wagram, one of the spoke-like avenues from the Étoile. Although this street has a number of moderately priced hotels (all of which seem to be full all year), the Tivoli-Étoile is the best one. It's been entirely redecorated, and all of its 30 small rooms contain a private bath, radio, TV, direct-dial phone, and up-to-date furnishings, along with such conveniences as radios. For this midcity location, you pay 425F ($58.61) for two persons, this tariff including a continental breakfast. The hotel has a pleasant contemporary lobby with a mural, and a restful inner patio. Métro: Place Charles-de-Gaulle.

In the same neighborhood, the management also runs the new **Hôtel Plaza Étoile,** 21 Avenue Wagram, 17e (tel. 43-80-42-24). Its up-to-date rooms are well cared for, and are furnished in modern pieces, containing color TV, radio, and either a complete bath or shower with toilet. Best of all, breakfast is served on a lovely terrace overlooking Avenue Wagram. The cost is 550F ($75.63) in a double, including a continental breakfast. The hotel has a pleasant bar, Le Tiffany. Métro: Charles-de-Gaulle.

The Budget Range

Des Deux Acacias (The Hotel of the Two Locust Trees), 28 rue de l'Arc-de-Triomphe, 17e (tel. 43-80-01-85), is a good bargain if your tastes are simple. A neat, semimodern little hotel, with a white marble façade, it is only a block from the Arc de Triomphe. Actually, it's in a district of budget hotels popular with foreign and provincial visitors who prefer more sedate living than that offered by the Left Bank hotels, which attract a younger crowd.

The emphasis is strictly on the rooms, as the hotel has only a small public lounge. All rooms have a private shower or bath and a toilet. Singles range from 255F ($35.17), doubles are 295F ($40.68); these tariffs include a continental breakfast. Des Deux Acacias is recommended for its cleanliness and certainly its stellar position. Métro: Place Charles-de-Gaulle.

5. 1st Arrondissement

PALAIS ROYAL/PLACE VENDÔME: This is the heart of Paris, rich in hotels appealing to traditional tastes (the deluxe Ritz, Meurice, and Inter-Continental). But you need not pay celestial tariffs for accommodations often furnished sumptuously with antiques. Housed in a room in the 1st Arrondissement, you'll be in the midst of the haut-monde sector of Paris, close to the Louvre, the Tuileries, and luxury boutiques.

The Upper Bracket

Hôtel Lotti, 7 and 9 rue Castiglione, 1er (tel. 42-60-37-34), has been called a "junior Ritz." Just off the historic Place Vendôme, it costs less than some of its swankier neighbors. Of course, it's not as voluptuous, although nevertheless very French in the best meaning of that expression when applied to decor. True to the tradition of most quietly elegant French hotels, its drawing room is generously endowed with a number of fine old tapestries, marble and gilt tables, plus the inevitable sparkling crystal.

Wide ranging, the bedrooms have that personalized styling of the 19th century. In furnishings, the era of the three Louises is often evoked. Mahogany desks, rosewood chests, gilt chairs, silk damask draperies, tufted slipper chairs, and tambour desks make for a rich and inviting ambience. There are 130 apartments in all, each with a private bath.

The different price levels depend on the location, size, and decor of the room. Singles range in price from 1,100F ($151.69) to 1,400F ($193.06) and doubles from 1,460F ($201.33) to 1,825F ($251.67). Private apartments cost 3,650F ($503.34) to 4,500F ($620.55). All bedrooms are air-conditioned. Métro: Opéra.

Hôtel Regina, 2 Place des Pyramides (also 192 rue du Rivoli), 1er (tel. 42-60-31-10). Sitting in the flagstoned courtyard of this old-fashioned, truly French hotel, you'd never think you were so close to the Tuileries, the Place Vendôme, the Opéra, or the Louvre. Water spurts from the dolphin fountain, and there are large pots of summer flowers, planters with geraniums, and white wrought-iron furniture to complete the rural scene.

Breakfast is pleasant in the morning room, overlooking the garden. The public rooms are gracious too, utilizing furnishings from many eras, including the Louis XV and Louis XVI periods. Spacious drawing rooms and salons open off the long corridor lounge, with its islands of furniture arranged on rich Oriental rugs. Throughout are good touches: bronze statues, 18th-century paintings, bowls of fresh seasonal flowers, inlaid marquetry desks and tables.

All rooms contain a private bath, and cost 650F ($89.64) to 775F ($106.87) in a single, 775F ($106.87) to 950F ($131.01) in a double. Apartments cost from 1,340F ($184.79) to 1,470F ($202.71). All tariffs include a continental breakfast. Métro: Pyramides, Tuileries, or Palais-Royal.

Hôtel de France et Choiseul, 239-241 rue St-Honoré, 1er (tel. 42-61-54-60), is a remake of a gracious 1720 town house, just off the Place Vendôme. It's been a hotel since the 1870s and became a fashionable oasis in fin-de-siècle Paris. Now, more than a century later, it has been completely remodeled. The 120 bedrooms—most of which open onto the inner courtyard—were gutted, then turned into tiny bandbox-size accommodations that are, nevertheless, attractively decorated. All sorts of conveniences are offered as compensation for the lost belle époque glamor: a refrigerator, television, radio, a dressing table, plus a decorative tiled bath with all the latest gadgets. All is color coordinated and every room has its token Louis XVI-style chair "to set the right tone." A few mini-suites have been installed on the top floor under the mansard roof, with a rustic staircase leading up to twin beds on a balcony. Singles go for 900F ($124.11), and doubles and twins for 1,050F ($144.80), peaking at 1,500F ($206.85) in a deluxe unit, including taxes and service. There is a small Pullman-style dining room for guests and a charming restaurant, Le Lafayette, opening onto the inner courtyard and consisting of the historic salon where Lafayette received the subsidies to participate in the American War for Independence. Métro: Concorde, Tuileries, Opéra, or Madeleine.

The Middle Bracket

Hôtel de Castille, 37 rue Cambon, 1er (tel. 42-61-55-20), is a pleasant, dramatically renovated hotel between the Paris headquarters of Chanel and the Chase Manhattan Bank, across the street from the "back door" of the Ritz. The interior was overhauled in the autumn of 1983, and what you'll see today is a series of beige marble panels and big mirrors in the low-ceilinged lobby, wall sconces, and a black-trimmed elevator bank. The sunny bedrooms are painted in a variety of pastel colors and outfitted in a streamlined art deco style that includes clean white baths with gray marble sinks, mini-bars, and TVs with in-house movies.

Quiet for a hotel so close to major shops, museums, and busy boulevards, it is only a few minutes' walk from the Place Vendôme, la Concorde, or la Madeleine. You'll recognize the façade by the double-arched entrance, the contemporary black and white accents on the two lower floors, and the 19th-century wrought-iron detailing on the ornate stonework of the upper floors. Singles cost 1,100F ($151.69), doubles 1,300F ($179.27), and a duplex suite 1,700F ($234.43) to 2,300F ($317.17). All prices include bathroom, a continental breakfast, service, and taxes. On the premises is a restaurant, Le Relais Castille, done in colors of flame and rust. Lunch and dinner are served in the inside garden court. Métro: Madeleine.

Hôtel Mont-Thabor, 4 rue du Mont-Thabor, 1er (tel. 42-60-32-77). No matter which way you walk from this Right Bank hotel, you're within minutes of some of the major attractions of Paris: the Louvre, the Tuileries, the Place de la Concorde, the Place Vendôme, the Opéra. The facilities are excellent, and every room—more than 100 in all—has a private bath.

The character of most of the bedrooms suggests the 19th century, each one in a "salon" mood, with color-coordinated fabrics on the bed and at the windows. All is comfortable and traditional. The tiled bathrooms feature separate circular or square stall showers. In a single room the tariff is 480F ($66.19), and 510F ($70.33) in a double, including a continental breakfast. There's a domed circular reception lounge with intricately patterned marble on the floor and walls. This classic effect is softened by the use of fruitwood provincial furnishings arranged on a blue-and-gray Chinese rug. There is a Japanese restaurant on the premises. Métro: Tuileries.

The Budget Range

Family Hotel, 35 rue Cambon, 1er (tel. 42-61-54-84). How such a pleasant, family-operated hotel can exist in such a swank neighborhood is still a mystery to first-time visitors to Paris. It's sandwiched between the House of Chanel and the Chase Manhattan Bank, diagonally across the street from the Ritz. The location of the hotel in part accounts for its "in-ness."

Since 1899 the Family has been a hotel, witnessing decade after decade of improvements and popularity. Madame Battesti doesn't mind a little bit of clutter—she prefers home-like informality. The bedroom furnishings vary in origin from the 19th century to the late 1960s, making for a comfortable atmosphere. Singles, with bath and breakfast included, cost from 200F ($27.58), with doubles on the same arrangement going for 340F ($46.89). Métro: Concorde.

Britannique, 20 Avenue Victoria, 1er (tel. 42-33-74-59), is an attractive little hotel, entirely renovated, lying right in the heart of Paris, within easy reach of Les Halles, the cultural center Georges Pompidou, and Notre-Dame. Rated three stars by the government, it offers small but clean, comfortable, and adequately equipped bedrooms. In a single with shower and toilet, the charge ranges from 380F ($52.40). In a double- or twin-bedded room, with bath or shower as well as toilet, the charge goes from 420F ($57.92) to 450F ($62.06). Families may prefer a triple room, also with plumbing, for 500F ($68.95). Service and taxes are included. All units contain TV. Métro: Châtelet.

Hôtel des Ducs d'Anjou, 1 rue Ste-Opportune, 1er (tel. 42-36-92-24), is an unpretentious 39-room hotel off a colorful workaday square near Les Halles. Many of the clients are actors and dancers from the nearby Théâtre de la Ville, and the receptionist remembers when the entire Roland Petit dance company once registered en masse. You'll take a tiny elevator from the simple lobby up to cramped hallways leading to the basic but well-lit bedrooms, each of which has a private bath and smallish double beds. The breakfast area is tiny, lying behind a linoleum divider in the lobby. This hotel, as you've guessed, is not luxurious, but it's clean and reasonably well maintained, and the location is suitable for exploring the back alleys of this part of town. Singles and doubles cost the same, with the price of an accommodation being determined by its exposure. Rooms facing the courtyard cost 245F ($33.79), and those facing the street cost 290F ($39.99). Métro: Châtelet.

Hotel Henri IV, 25 Place Dauphine, 1er (tel. 43-54-44-53). Four hundred years ago, the printing presses for the edicts of Henri IV filled this narrow building. Today, the orderly rows of trees in the outside contribute to one of the loveliest locations in Paris. A sojourn here lures a loyal clientele of budget-conscious academicians, journalists, and francophiles. The low-ceilinged lobby, one flight above street level, is cramped and a bit bleak. But that is dispelled by the friendliness of Mr. and Mrs. Maurice Balitrand. The 20 bedrooms, reached via a winding stairwell, saw better days under Clemenceau, but many devotees consider them romantically threadbare. None contains its own bath, shower, or toilet, but each has a sink. To reach the WCs, you have to negotiate a series of narrow stairs filling the confines of a sunless airshaft. The real allure of this place, aside from its dramatic location, is the price: singles go for 85F ($11.72), doubles 135F ($18.62), and triples for between 175F ($24.13) and 220F ($30.34), with breakfast included. Métro: Pont-Neuf.

6. 2nd and 9th Arrondissements

OPÉRA/GRANDS BOULEVARDS: These are two of the most international districts of Paris, especially the 2nd Arrondissement. The 9th stretches all the way to Pigalle, where Maurice Chevalier, as he confessed to an American TV audience, had his first affair. The Grands Boulevards are legendary, although the pinnacle of fashion they once enjoyed has now largely passed. The streets are crowded, the cafés bustling . . . no one ever said this was the quietest district of Paris. You can walk along rue de la Paix, go to the Opéra or the Opéra-Comique, and end up eventually at the infamous "Pig Alley" of World War II without ever leaving these arrondissements. Go to these quarters for lower-cost Right Bank living.

The Upper Bracket
Le Grand Hôtel, 2 rue Scribe, 9e (tel. 42-68-12-13), is a good example of a successful regeneration of an old hotel, under the aegis of Intercontinental Hotels. Time had passed Le Grand by, although it once had tremendous glamor. It was created by Charles Garnier, the architect of the Opéra, and was inaugurated by the Empress Eugénie. Now, with its new lease on life, it is again one of the leading first-class Parisian hotels. The lounge, with its central glass-covered courtyard, is quite beautiful. Fine contemporary furniture is arranged for conversational groupings, and the central reflection pool is traditionally correct. The decor is in flame colors, harmoniously blended with wood tones and contrasted with crisp white.

The bedrooms are neat in appearance, graciously designed and decorated with tasteful color schemes. All the chambers have radio and television, as well as a bar and refrigerator. The most desirable accommodations are the quieter rooms opening onto the courtyard. Singles with bath rent for 1,300F ($179.27) to 1,620F ($223.40), and double or twin-bedded rooms, also with bath, go for 1,450F ($199.96) to 1,780F ($245.46). Rates include taxes and service. On the premises is the world-famous Café de la Paix, where every visitor sooner or later is fated to meet someone for drinks. Métro: Opéra.

The Middle Bracket
Hôtel Richmond, 11 rue du Helder, 9e (tel. 47-70-53-20), is a substantial, three-star hotel, just a short walk from the Opéra—a superb location, as it lies near the American Express, the Café de la Paix, and many fine shops. The hotel has been much improved in recent years. Lying behind an attractive façade, it invites you to its pleasantly decorated lounge. Groups of sofas are conveniently placed for conversation. There are also marble columns, even a water fountain, Roman style—all tasteful, everything evoking an old-world mood. The rooms have comfort and convenience. The cost is 485F ($66.88) in a double, and a high 460F ($63.43) in a single, including a continental breakfast. Métro: Opéra.

London Palace, 32 Boulevard des Italiens, 9e (tel. 48-24-54-64), is a bit of contemporary France in a superb central location, just 50 yards from the Opéra departure point of tours. Within walking distance of many of Paris's fine restaurants and department stores, it has been renovated and overhauled and given a new lease on life. Occupying the upper floors of a classic building, with a row of dormers across the top, it fronts one of the Grand Boulevards, the haunt of 19th-century society.

Behind its classic façade modernity blazes with joyful colors and furnishings. White and vivid oranges are the color theme. The main lounge has a country-home look with picture windows opening onto a busy scene. The 50 bedrooms are equally well styled, again using for the most part contrasting white and orange. All of the rooms contain private bath. A single ranges from 310F ($42.75) to 380F ($52.40). Double rooms cost 490F ($67.57), and a room for three (two or three beds) is 600F ($82.74). Taxes, service, and a continental breakfast are included in these tariffs. Most important, in July and August discount rates are granted visitors. Métro: Opéra.

Hôtel L'Horset Opéra d'Antin, 18 rue d'Antin, 2e (tel. 47-42-13-01), near the American Express and the Opéra, is run, as its name implies, by the L'-Horset chain. Polished marble and well-crafted period reproductions give it a traditional charm, the kind where the paneling gleams, and you'll be impressed by the many well-detailed touches. The service is polite and friendly, and the hotel is efficiently managed. The well-appointed rooms have a turn-of-the-century ambience enhanced by the flowered Victorian-style wallpaper and the occasional brass bed. Rooms with bath cost 430F ($59.30) in a single and 560F ($77.22) in a double. Singles without bath cost 235F ($32.41), and doubles without bath go for 250F ($34.48). All tariffs include breakfast. Métro: Opéra.

Hôtel de Sèze, 16 rue de Sèze, 9e (tel. 47-42-69-12), is a rather good buy, considering its central location—right off the Avenue de l'Opéra, within sight of the Madeleine. There's an elegant but tiny lobby, with wood paneling, chunky brass hardware, and some Louis XVI-style furniture. The 25 bedrooms, with all kinds of plumbing, have a curious hit-or-miss quality, but whether they're furnished with well-chosen antiques or plain old modern, they're serviceable and practical.

Depending on the plumbing, singles rent for 275F ($37.92) to 300F ($41.37), doubles for 310F ($42.75) to 340F ($46.89), and triples for 365F ($50.33) to 410F ($56.54). Taxes, service, and breakfast are included. English is spoken quite well. Métro: Madeleine.

The Budget Range

Hôtel du Nil, 10 rue du Helder, 9e (tel. 47-70-80-24), has to be valued for its location and price, not its lounge and entryway. Although it resembles many small hotels of Paris, its situation is prime, right near the Opéra and just a short walk from the Boulevards Haussmann and des Italiens. There are no salons, but you can always meet a friend at the Café de la Paix for a coffee. All rooms contain a phone, small color TV set, and private bathroom, some with tub and some with shower. Depending on the plumbing, singles range from 180F ($24.82) to 210F ($28.96), and doubles cost 200F ($27.58) to 225F ($31.03), with breakfast included. There is no formal breakfast room, and it's usually served in the rooms. Métro: Opéra.

7. 5th Arrondissement

LATIN QUARTER: Now we cross over to the Left Bank, into the Quartier Latin, that traditional intellectual and artistic center of Paris. Through its narrow streets and on its wide, café-studded boulevards throng students and visitors from every corner of the world. The hotels are plentiful, and, if not always inexpensive, at least moderately priced.

The colleges of the Sorbonne dominate the area. This section of Paris appeals more to the young and adventurous than to older readers. If you take the Métro to the Place St-Michel, you will then emerge onto the Boulevard St-Michel (called "Boul Mich"), the heart of the university sector of Paris. In this district, the rue des Écoles is the most concentrated section for budget hotels, but I have many selections on little side streets branching off from it.

The Middle Bracket

Hôtel Le Colbert, 7 rue de l'Hôtel-Colbert, 5e (tel. 43-25-85-65). How can you miss by staying at this little, centuries-old, 38-room inn? It's not only on the Left Bank, a minute from the Seine, but it provides a fine view of Notre-Dame from many of its rooms. There's even a small courtyard, setting the hotel apart from the bustle of Left Bank life.

You'll enter a tastefully decorated lobby area, with marble floors, red cut-velvet wallpaper, and a view of the wrought-iron spear-topped fence separating the evergreen trees of the courtyard from the narrow street outside. A sunny bar area is filled with gilt-accented furniture. The rooms are well designed and tailored, furnished for the most part with good pieces. Most of them provide comfortable chairs and space for a breakfast area. The baths (one for every room) have recently been renovated; the beds are inviting, and units include such amenities as a phone, plenty of towels, and efficient maid service. Singles cost 415F ($57.23), with doubles going for 520F ($71.71) to 650F ($89.64). Métro: Maubert-Mutualité.

Select, 1 Place de la Sorbonne, 5e (tel. 46-34-14-80), is the only hotel in the Latin Quarter that stands directly on this square dominated by the Church of the Sorbonne, built between 1635 and 1642 by Le Mercier. Try to get a room overlooking this plaza, which has been replanted with trees and had a fountain and benches added. Although the square is quiet and dignified, it opens onto the busy "Boul Mich," where you can enjoy café sitting. The interior has been modernized, and all the comfortably furnished bedrooms contain private bath, a double renting for 360F ($49.64) to 520F ($71.71). Métro: St-Michel.

The Budget Range

Grand Hôtel du Mont-Blanc, 28 rue de la Huchette, 5e (tel. 43-54-22-29). Who has ever written a guide to Paris without including this little inn on the famous street of the Latin Quarter? The "grand" in its name is a pretension, of course. It's really modest. Behind its ivory-white façade and beckoning coach lamps, are simple but clean and comfortable bedrooms suitable for one or two persons, depending on the plumbing and the size. They cost from 255F ($35.17) to 310F ($42.75). Those filled with a nostalgia for the Paris of yesteryear recall the hotel's association with Hemingway. And, of course, Elliot Paul, the novelist and friend of Gertrude Stein (she called Paul "the New England Saracen") and author of *The Last Time I Saw Paris,* stayed at the Mont-Blanc. Métro: St-Michel.

Hôtel de Sully, 31 rue des Écoles, 5e (tel. 43-26-56-02), has been skillfully redecorated and modernized, with a sparkling, up-to-date lounge. It's mostly modern except for some traditional touches. The lobby has exposed stone, marble floors, and walls upholstered with attractively tasteful flowered fabrics. A streamlined glass entrance door slides sideways to open with an electric eye. The bedrooms are done in a country style, with provincial furniture. The television sets are placed near the ceiling so as not to intrude on the decor of the rooms. Most beds contain chintz-padded headboards. Single or double rooms rent for 345F ($47.58) to 550F ($75.63). Métro: Maubert-Mutualité.

Hôtel Elysa, 6 rue Gay-Lussac, 5e (tel. 43-25-31-74), is a traditional hotel, featuring the atmosphere of Brittany, and standing in one of the oldest parts of Paris. The furnishings are in the provincial style, making use of strong colors and wallpaper. There are only 36 bedrooms offered, and these are occasionally booked by teachers or the families of students going to the Sorbonne, in Paris to visit with their offspring. Most of the bedrooms are attractively furnished, with a full bath, shower, or phone. A double with bath costs 300F ($41.37), and a few doubles with shower cost 205F ($28.27). A continental breakfast and taxes are included. Métro: Luxembourg.

Hôtel du Levant, 18 rue de la Harpe, 5e (tel. 46-34-11-00), caters to art, theater, and concert buffs, among others. The walls of its lounges are covered with posters advertising concerts, openings, and art shows. On a street of budget restaurants, right in the heart of the St-Michel district, the hotel stands apart from the teeming life. Its wide front windows are filled with ferns. Those who want to be in the Latin Quarter will find moderately comfortable singles renting for 250F ($34.48) to 335F ($46.20), depending on the plumbing. A continental breakfast is included. Happily, there's an elevator. Métro: St-Michel or Odéon.

Hôtel Esmeralda, 4 rue Saint-Julien-le-Pauvre, 5e (tel. 43-54-19-20). Esmeralda, of course, was the beloved of Quasimodo, who used to hunch his way through the towers of Notre-Dame, directly across the river from this hotel. In a small 16th-century storefront, on a quiet square facing a church even older than Notre-Dame, this hotel is one of the most unusual in Paris. It has only 19 tastefully wallpapered rooms, many with antiques, as well as views of the cathedral. Exposed timbers still support the narrow walls of this very old house.

You'll reach your room by passing through a small stone-walled lobby and climbing a winding flight of stairs whose massive balustrades are as old as the house itself. This is a popular hotel, and it's usually difficult to get a room in high season. If you do, your favorite chamber might quickly become no. 14. The accommodations facing the front are usually bigger and well furnished. Most doubles cost from 300F ($41.37), although one is just a little more expensive, and a few contain a shower instead of a bathtub for a budget-conscious 200F ($27.58). Métro: St-Michel.

Hôtel d'Albe, 1 rue de la Harpe, off the Place St-Michel, 5e (tel. 46-34-09-70), is right in the center of one of the most teeming streets of the Latin Quarter, and as such, is preferred by those who like to be in the whirlwind of Left Bank life. The d'Albe is a six-story corner building that has recently been modernized. The lounge is inviting, with a breakfast salon where you can order your morning coffee and croissants. An elevator takes you to the rooms on the upper floors. All the bedrooms are comfortably furnished and well kept. Double with water basins rent for 175F ($24.13), rising to 275F ($37.92) with shower or complete bath. The most expensive unit, a twin-bedded accommodation with shower and private bath, peaks at 325F ($44.82). English is spoken. Métro: St-Michel.

Hôtel du Brésil, 10 rue Le Goff, 5e (tel. 46-33-45-78). Hemingway used to stroll by here after having killed a fat pigeon in the Luxembourg Gardens for his dinner (he wheeled the dead bird in a baby carriage). Between the years 1885 and 1886, Sigmund Freud lived here. In spite of some famous associations, the hotel is relatively unknown. However, it may become better known, as it is being completely modernized, and, hopefully, these recent renovations will make it a more attractive Latin Quarter choice for visitors. The more than 30 bedrooms rent for 290F ($39.99) in a single and 320F ($44.13) in a double. Each room has a phone and TV. Breakfast is included in the price of the rooms. Métro: Luxembourg.

Grand Hôtel St-Michel, 19 rue Cujas, 5e (tel. 43-54-47-98), with its old-fashioned furnishings, reflects the graciousness of its owner, Madame Salvage, and its reception manager, Madame Perette. The little salon has elegance and is almost reminiscent of the *ancien régime.* A huge crystal and bronze chandelier, travertine floors, 19th-century marble-topped Empire tables, and fresh flowers fill the public room. The bedrooms are simply furnished, all of them recently upgraded, with a direct-dial phone, a sink, a shower, and a toilet in each one. A double room costs 150F ($20.69) to 170F ($23.44), while singles go for 140F ($19.31). The hotel also rents quads from 220F ($30.34). No breakfast is included, but there are many nearby cafés serving coffee and croissants. Métro: St-Michel or Odéon.

Hôtel St-Jacques, 35 rue des Écoles, 5e (tel. 43-26-82-53), is a pleasingly decorated hotel in the heart of the Quartier Latin. It's definitely one of the best and least expensive in the area. Its lounge and reception area are painted white, and are prettily furnished with provincial reproductions. A few antiques are added to give it more charm. There's even a *Mona Lisa* reproduction in the hallway staring at every guest. Danielle Thouati is the charming and attractive English-speaking owner, who creates such an inviting ambience that some guests want to move in permanently. An elevator as well as an elegant stairwell with an iron railing lead to the slightly old-fashioned rooms, where the most expensive double, with full bath, costs 300F ($41.37), but only 195F ($26.89) in a double with shower. Singles range from 190F ($26.20) to 250F ($34.48), depending on the plumbing. A continental breakfast is included in the rates. Métro: Maubert-Mutualité.

8. 6th Arrondissement

ST-GERMAIN-DES-PRÉS/ODÉON: The 6th Arrondissement embraces the most interesting quartier of the Left Bank—St-Germain-des-Prés and the Luxembourg Gardens with its magnificent grounds. Although the student population of the Sorbonne has invaded, there is, as well, an elegant residential quarter.

For the budget hotel shopper, there are more quality choices here than in the 5th Arrondissement, just previewed. Somehow the hotels of St-Germain-des-Prés seem to have more style and character than those around the Sorbonne, although you may disagree.

In the 6th Arrondissement, art galleries, studios, restaurants, and celebrated cafés (such as Flore and Deux Magots) abound.

Many of my recommendations in this sector center around the Place de l'Odéon, a square dominated by the Théâtre de France, one of the three state-run theaters of Paris.

If you're searching for a room with some of the color and charm that you traditionally associate with Left Bank Paris, then you've come to the right quarter. Happy hunting!

The Upper Bracket

Victoria Palace Hôtel, 6 rue Blaise-Desgoffe, 6e (tel. 45-44-38-16). It can safely be said that this old Montparnasse establishment is the best hotel in the 5th and 6th Arrondissements of Paris. It has survived the past century through an outpouring of a mountain of francs and a desire to create an aesthetically pleasing setting for visitors who covet comfort and peaceful living. It lies behind an elegantly ornate façade on a quiet street between the busy arteries of the rue de Rennes and the rue de Vaugirard. As an aid to tranquility, an inner courtyard with greenery beckons.

Many of the original trappings remain, including an elegant selection of Louis XV and XVI commodes, although the hotel has been redecorated with attractively conservative taste and flair. The traditional-style bedrooms have white-paneled walls, antique-style beds and chairs, well-chosen wallpaper, and finely grained chests with marble tops and brass hardware. Most of the baths are covered from floor to ceiling with polished marble, and retain many of the most charming details of their construction. The rooms cost 575F ($79.29) in a single and from 650F ($89.64) to 765F ($105.49) in a double, with a continental breakfast included.

A spacious dining room opening onto the courtyard offers a fixed-price dinner, plus à la carte selections. There is also a reception lounge, along with an American-style bar, as well as a garage on the premises. In a hotel-poor district, the Victoria Palace is outstanding. Métro: St-Placide.

Hôtel de l'Abbaye, 10 rue Cassette, 6e (tel. 45-44-38-11), is a stylish remake of a 17th-century abbey, restored by Monsieur and Madame Lafortune. Fifteen-foot street doors lead to an open paved courtyard and an entry lounge with marble floors and 18th-century antiques. The lower-level lounges have informal dignity, opening onto a rear courtyard with summer furniture. Behind the central living room is a winter salon, with green-and-white floral paper, white wicker furniture, and plants. In the patio beyond, garden furniture is set against a backdrop of shrubbery.

The smallish bedrooms, each with a private bath, are reached by elevator. Madame Lafortune's choice of decorative accessories blends with uninhibited color schemes and fabrics. Doubles range from 520F ($71.71) to 650F ($89.64), taxes, service, and a continental breakfast included. Métro: St-Sulpice.

Relais Christine, 3 rue Christine, 6e (tel. 43-26-71-80), welcomes a sophisticated international clientele into what used to be a 16th-century Augustinian cloister. This is really one of the most unusual hotels in this part of town. You'll enter from a narrow cobblestone street into first a symmetrical courtyard and then an elegant reception area dotted with baroque sculpture, plush upholsteries, and a scattering of Renaissance antiques. The Auvergne-based Bertrand family converted the building from a warehouse for a nearby publishing company into this elegant hotel in 1979, and promptly appointed the friendly and experienced Pierre Blondeau as the manager. Just off the reception area is a paneled sitting room and bar area, which is ringed with 19th-century portraits and comfortable leather chairs. You won't have experienced the hotel, however, until you go down into the vaulted breakfast room on the lower level, whose ancient well is spotlit from within and whose massive central stone column witnessed all the activity in what used to be the cloister's kitchen.

Each of the 51 bedrooms is individually decorated with antiques or antique reproductions and lots of flair. Accessories might include massively beamed ceilings and plush wall-to-wall carpeting. Double rooms range from 950F ($131.01) to 2,000F ($275.80), depending on the accommodation. Métro: St-Michel.

The Middle Bracket

Scandinavia Hôtel, 27 rue de Tournon, 6e (tel. 43-29-67-20). From a wide street near the Luxembourg Gardens, you'll see a plate-glass façade covering thick weathered beams and chiseled stone. The building was constructed in the 16th century, when it was offered by François I to his favorite poet, Clement Marot. Later, Marie de Medici had all the façades on this street realigned so they wouldn't interfere with the visual perspective of her nearby palace. Both Paul Verlaine and Casanova once lived here. Today the lobby is furnished with a mind-boggling collection of medieval armor, velvet-covered chaise longues, old religious sculpture, and carved Gothic panels. Even the floor is set with fragments of old bas-reliefs. My favorite room is the adjoining salon whose baronial fireplace and Renaissance furniture practically transport you to another era.

You'll reach your room via a winding staircase whose cast-iron balustrade is set with images of female sphinxes. Each of the rooms has antiques, oil paintings, massive ceiling beams, and dozens of extraordinary touches. Doubles cost 375F ($51.71). Métro: Odéon.

Grand Hôtel de l'Univers, 6 rue Grégoire-de-Tours, 6e (tel. 43-29-37-00), wins on many counts. Its owner, Monsieur Beck, gutted the ugly latter-day overlay of this 15th-century inn, exposing the old beams and the rugged stone walls. Skillfully he slipped in private baths and central heating. Each bedroom is furnished distinctively. Most of the rooms have exposed beams and tasteful decor. However, all rooms have a tiled bath, TV, background music, and a small bar stocked with drinks. The color schemes are dramatically attractive. Singles cost 620F ($85.50), while doubles go for 650F ($89.64). All tariffs include breakfast. The location is bull's-eye center of the Left Bank, just a minute off the Boulevard St-Germain, Métro: Odéon or Mabillon.

Hôtel de Fleurie, 32 rue Grégoire-de-Tours, 6e (tel. 43-29-59-81), just about 70 feet off the Boulevard Saint-Germain on this colorful little Left Bank street, is one of the best of the "new" old hotels. Restored to its former glory, the façade is studded with statuary that is spotlit at night, recapturing its 17th-century elegance. The stone walls have been exposed in the reception salon, with its refectory desk where guests check in. They've added a stone-trimmed bar with rust-colored carpeting just off the reception area. It has latticework, climbing ivy, and an exposed beamed ceiling. A spiral staircase leads to a small TV and breakfast room. The lobby contains a collection of 19th-century antiques and "brown-gravy" paintings. An elevator takes you to the well-furnished, modernized bedrooms, where a double with a complete bath rents for 320F ($44.13), that tariff rising to 380F ($52.40) in a twin-bedded room with bath. A continental breakfast is extra, but the service charge is included in the rates quoted. Métro: Odéon.

Odèon-Hôtel, 3 rue de l'Odéon, 6e (tel. 43-25-90-67), will convince you you're spending the night in a colorful country inn in Normandy. The renovation uncovered old beams, rough stone walls, and high crooked ceilings. After modern plumbing was installed, rooms were designed and furnished, each with a character of its own. Furnishings have successfully blended the old with modern, ranging from oak and bookbinder wallpaper to bright, contemporary fabrics. Singles rent for 550F ($75.63) and doubles for 600F ($82.74), tax and service included. Rooms are equipped with either private bath or shower. The guest lounge is dominated by an old Parisian tapestry, an amusingly beamed and mirrored ceiling, and black leather furnishings. The hotel is one minute from the Théâtre de l'Odéon and Boulevard St-Germain. Métro: Odéon.

Aviatic, 105 rue de Vaugirard, 6e (tel. 45-44-38-21), maintains tradition down in Montparnasse, wherein are those legendary cafés. Guests are likely to include everybody from unpublished novelists to jazz musicians. It is a small, family-run hotel of character and elegance, one of my personal favorites in its category. It's totally Gallic, with a simple inner courtyard and an ivy-covered lattice on its walls. The entrance is impressive too, with its marble columns, ornate brass chandeliers, and old-style furniture. In a little salon you can meet your friends. Each bedroom has its own distinct style, as well as numerous conveniences, likely to include a wide range of plumbing. Singles cost from 550F ($75.63); doubles, 640F ($88.26), prices including tax, service, and a continental breakfast. Units are equipped with direct-dial phone, mini-bar, color TV, and the staff speaks English. Métro: Montparnasse-Bienvenue.

Hôtel du Pas de Calais, 59 rue des Saints-Pères, 6e (tel. 45-48-78-74). Many famous people have stayed here. Maurice Béjart, the dancer-choreographer-stage designer; even Sartre, along with a host of lesser-known singers, actors, and writers. The building dates from the 17th century. Chateaubriand (who lived here between 1811 and 1814) began the long parade of artistic and literary visitors to its doorstep. In 1815 the town house was converted into a hotel.

The Pas de Calais was redecorated and modernized with varying results. The rooms, although clean and well kept, rely heavily on bentwood pieces, blond woods, and plastic coverings. In the more expensive rooms with private bath, the rate is 500F ($68.95) for two. Singles are charged 475F ($65.50). Included in the tariffs are taxes, service, and breakfast. Guests are invited for afternoon drinks or breakfast on the small patio. Métro: St-Germain-des-Prés.

Hôtel d'Angleterre, 44 rue Jacob, 6e (tel. 42-60-34-72). No matter how hard some other hotels try to create an old-world atmosphere of gentility and simplicity, they are amateurs compared to this mellowed charmer, built in 1650. In a district of antique shops and private art galleries, d'Angleterre once sheltered the British Embassy. Since 1910 it has been managed by the Berthier family. Shut off from street traffic, most of its rooms open onto an exposed courtyard, planted with grass, climbing ivy, and spring or summer flowers. Many of the clients prefer to take their breakfast at one of the little tables set up on the edge of the courtyard in a Rive Gauche atmosphere.

Picture a small old-fashioned salon that hasn't succumbed to a decorator's touch, with a grand piano and comfortable chairs—and you can understand why d'Angleterre has long been favored by such illustrious guests as Anne Morrow Lindbergh, who didn't seem to mind the antiquated plumbing. Hemingway once stayed here and was ill, but Madame Berthier took care of him, as related in his son's book. Double rooms with bath and toilet range in price from 500F ($68.95) to 600F ($82.74), with suites costing much more. Métro: St-Germain-des-Prés.

Hôtel d'Isly, 29 rue Jacob, 6e (tel. 43-29-59-96), is a renovated corner hotel, on the street where Richard Wagner lived from 1841 to 1842 (look over the Bar Vert at no. 14). A good base from which to explore Left Bank art galleries, bookstores, and antique shops, d'Isly appears as white as vanilla ice cream. The hotel is entered from a busy street but many of its rooms overlook a quiet, inner courtyard which, although minuscule, evidences the owner's green thumb.

There is a small contemporary lounge, and the living room, where you can take your morning meal on a bentwood chair, evokes a bistro ambience. But the Hôtel d'Isly puts most of its care and concern into its bedrooms, which have that French feminine look—many with lacy flowered paper on the ceilings and walls. The overall effect is restful and comfortable. Most of the rooms have a private bath, in which the color-coordinated wallpaper scheme carries over. The all-inclusive cost, including continental breakfast, service, and taxes, for a single room with a large bed and a private bath is 410F ($56.54), but only 280F ($38.61) for a single with water basin. A double room or twin with bath or shower goes for 460F ($63.43). Métro: St-Germain-des-Prés.

Hôtel des Saints-Pères, 65 rue des Saints-Pères, 6e (tel. 45-44-50-00). The best recommendation for this time-tested favorite is the long list of habitués who swear by it. Just a minute off Boulevard St-Germain, it offers 40 bedrooms facing an inner courtyard. It has a welcoming entrance with all-glass doors, potted trees, and coach lights. All the rooms have been modernized and come complete with private bath. Cozy rooms suitable for either one or two persons rent for 430F ($59.30) to 530F ($73.09), depending on the plumbing. Larger double rooms with twin beds cost 650F ($89.64) to 865F ($119.28). While the rather modern furnishings may not be imaginatively selected, they are comfortable. It's recommended that you order breakfast in the courtyard, weather permitting, as the pots of flowers can cheer your expeditions for the day. Métro: St-Germain-des-Prés or Sèvres-Babylone.

The Budget Range

Regent's Hôtel, 44 rue Madame, 6e (tel. 45-48-02-81), is deep in the Left Bank district, one short block from the Luxembourg Gardens. On a relatively quiet street, it offers 36 rooms. Perhaps its best feature is a little paved patio with beds of flowers, shrubbery, and white wrought-iron furniture. Breakfast is leisurely in this secluded spot. The bedroom furnishings are a mixture of modified modern, antiques, and reproductions. In all cases, the rooms are comfortable, the beds large and soft. The Jacques and Cretey families offer some doubles and twins with private bath for 325F ($44.82). These rates include a continental breakfast and taxes. You can meet with friends (or make new ones) in the petit salon, highlighted by Louis XV-style furniture. Métro: St-Sulpice.

Hôtel Louis II, 2 rue Saint-Sulpice, 6e (tel. 46-33-13-80). One of the most skillful, and perhaps the most charming, renovations on the Left Bank transformed the interiors of a rundown pair of 18th-century buildings into a chintz-covered rustic fantasy. Its decorators exposed as many of the hand-hewn beams as was feasible, so that in each of the 20 cozy bedrooms wide expanses of mellowed patina contrast pleasantly with flowered wall coverings and plush carpeting. Many repeat visitors request one of the romantic rooms beneath the slope of the building's eaves for an upgraded version of the kind of attic room where scenes from *La Bohème* might have been staged. Each accommodation contains its own private bathroom, phone, mini-bar, and (if requested) TV. Single or double rooms range from 400F ($55.16) to 520F ($71.71), with triples going for 710F ($97.91). Afternoon drinks and morning coffee are served in an elegant reception salon, where gilt-framed mirrors, bouquets of fresh flowers, and well-oiled antiques add to what seems like a refreshingly provincial allure. A visitor's stay is made even more pleasant thanks to the dedicated efforts of the manager, Brigitte Siozade. Métro: Odéon.

Deux-Continents, 25 rue Jacob, 6e (tel. 43-26-72-46), is the domain of Madame Chresteil, who inherited these "two continents." She is a host with that rare combination of sense and candor, good humor, and kindliness. She's furnished the bedrooms in modern and not so modern, installed telephones, and ensured that there are reading lights over the beds. Cleanliness prevails. The prices include taxes, service, and a breakfast tray brought to the room. All the accommodations have shower or bath and cost 340F ($46.89) to 450F ($62.06) in twins or doubles, 280F ($38.61) to 390F ($53.78) in a single. The two buildings are so connected that there are myriad corridors, little staircases, and courtyards. Métro: St-Germain-des-Prés.

Grand Hôtel Taranne, 153 Boulevard St-Germain, 6e (tel. 42-22-21-65). Its enviable location next to the Brasserie Lipp, within the shadow of the tower of St-Germain-des-Prés, makes it a favorite for visitors wanting to be in the heart of a district known for its artistic chic. You'll approach the reception desk via a narrow hallway, at the end of which is a bar and breakfast room. Upstairs, 35 well-upholstered bedrooms make a stopover here a good choice. Each unit is slightly different from its neighbor, sometimes with a scattering of period-style reproductions, a tile- or marble-covered bathroom, a mini-bar, TV, and phone. The quieter rooms look out over a shadowy courtyard whose walls block out noise from the street. Either single or double accommodations range from 275F ($37.92) to 500F ($68.95). Métro: St-Germain-des-Prés.

Michelet-Odéon, 6 Place de l'Odéon, 6e (tel. 46-34-27-80), is a mansard-roofed corner building right on the 18th-century Place de l'Odéon, itself dominated by the Greek- and Roman-style Théâtre de France. The classic columns of the hotel's reception hall seem appropriate to the setting, and because of its proximity to the state-run theater, it is often home base for many performing artists.

Although there's a homey little lounge for meeting one's friends, the hotel is recommended mainly for its comfortable and fairly priced bedrooms. The rate for a double with shower and toilet is 285F ($39.30); with a complete bath, it increases to 360F ($49.64). Some doubles with shower (no toilet) cost from 220F ($30.34). The furnishings are adequate and pleasant but not distinguished. Métro: Odéon.

Hôtel de l'Academie, 32 rue des Saints-Pères, 6e (tel. 45-48-36-22). The exterior walls and the old ceiling beams are all that remain of this 17th-century former residence for the private guards of the Duc de Rohan. In 1983 it was completely renovated to include an elegant marble and light-grained oak reception area, Second Empire-style chairs, and a friendly, English-speaking staff. The comfortably up-to-date rooms have Directoire beds, an Île de France decor upholstered in soft colors, and views over the 18th- and 19th-century buildings in the immediate neighborhood. Each of the 33 rather small rooms has a private bath, mini-bar, phone, TV, radio, and alarm clock. Doubles range from 390F ($53.78) to 490F ($67.57), depending on the plumbing. Mr. Gérard is the young and attractive director. Métro: St-Germain-des-Prés.

St-André-des-Arts, 66 rue Saint-André-des-Arts, 6e (tel. 43-26-96-16), is old, rambling, and little, the atmosphere casual, friendly, and appealing to youthful travelers, actors, models, singers, and dancers in the French capital. The 33 bedrooms are scattered along a labyrinthine series of upstairs hallways and winding stairs. Most of the 17th-century walls are crafted of exposed stone with massive wooden beams between dividers of rough plaster. Most of the simple, clean units have a tile bath. Singles rent for 220F ($30.34), doubles for 280F ($38.61), triples for 355F ($48.96), and quads for 380F ($52.40). A handful of small bathless singles are a bargain at around 140F ($19.31). Breakfast is included in all the tariffs. Just off St-Germain-des-Prés, this modest Left Bank establishment is easy to spot: the façade is deep red and its name is in gold letters. It's right in the center of a district of dozens of small galleries and antique specialists. Métro: Odéon.

Hôtel du Vieux Paris, 9 rue Git-le-Coeur, 6e (tel. 43-54-41-66), is one of those hard-to-find little hotels just off the Seine. But this one is a winner, tucked away in a building with a chocolate-brown façade. Many artists and writers have stayed here, arising the next morning to contemplate the view of Notre-Dame after a short walk along the river. The rooms have been given decorator touches, such as large patterned wallpaper on the ceilings. The owner, Madame Odillard, runs a fine little hotel. Two persons can stay here at prices ranging from 180F ($24.82) to 300F ($41.37), the tariffs depending on the plumbing. A simple single costs from 125F ($17.24). Rates include a continental breakfast. Métro: St-Michel.

Hôtel Racine, 23 rue Racine, 6e (tel. 43-26-00-60), is a little hotel made by joining two buildings, lying just a few feet from the Place de l'Odéon with its marble Théâtre de France. Its entry suggests that it's a well-cared-for hotel. A splashy use is made of the red colors, and there's even a classic bust of Racine on a pedestal. In a small covered patio, a continental breakfast is served to guests, and the reception is from helpful students. Many of the rooms have much character, although the less expensive ones are simpler. A double with full bath goes for 320F ($44.13), but only 270F ($37.23) with a shower. A single with bath is priced at 270F ($37.23). Included in these tariffs are a continental breakfast and tax. Métro: Odéon.

Grand Hôtel des Balcons, 3 rue Casimir-Delavigne, 6e (tel. 46-34-78-50), is perhaps the best buy on this little street off the Odéon. The lobby is rust colored and decorated with art nouveau panels. The place is friendly and unpretentious. A two-star hotel, it once sheltered Endre Ady (1877–1919), Hungary's greatest lyric poet, who died a victim of alcoholism. His Paris years were characterized as his "angry young man" period, when he became the target of violent attacks. The rooms have been renovated by the owners, Mr. and Mrs. Corroyer. They offer 55 compact rooms, each with a private bath, direct-dial phone, color TV, and background music. Depending on the plumbing, singles begin at 220F ($30.34), rising to 250F ($34.48). Two persons pay from 300F ($41.37) to 320F ($44.13), with some triples peaking at 385F ($53.09). Métro: Odéon.

Welcome Hôtel, 66 rue de Seine, 6e (tel. 46-34-24-80), is a successful restoration of a 17th-century house. A second-floor reception lounge is furnished with tapestries between old beams, chandeliers, and comfortable armchairs. A continental breakfast is served on a long oak refectory table. The bedrooms, for the most part, are oddly shaped and furnished with French provincial pieces. Twin-bedded rooms with a complete bath go for 365F ($50.33); with a shower, 300F ($41.37). A single with private shower and toilet rents for 195F ($26.89). The location is memorable, just off the Boulevard Saint-Germain, next to a colorful open-air market filled with booths and vendors selling fruit and vegetables from all over France. Hopefully, you'll be there the morning the fresh strawberries come in. You can buy some to go with your breakfast. Métro: Odéon or Mabillon.

La Rèsidence du Globe, 15 rue des Quatre-Vents, 6e (tel. 46-33-62-69), after extensive remodeling and restoration, recaptures some of the character of a 17th-century town house. The renovation revealed rugged stone walls and twisted old oak beams, and modern decorators added a touch of sophistication by bringing in an eclectic collection, including ornate wrought-iron gates, an old chest, a bishop's chair, ornate gilt mirrors, and a bronze chandelier. Close to interesting shops, the hotel lies right off the Carrefour de l'Odéon. Its rooms are simply furnished and well kept, costing 230F ($31.72) in a double with complete bath, but only 185F ($25.51) in a double with shower. There are no twins, only doubles. Métro: Odéon.

9. 7th and 15th Arrondissements

EIFFEL TOWER/INVALIDES: This is largely a middle-class residential sector on the Left Bank, embracing the Eiffel Tower and the Champ de Mars, plus a military school that Madame de Pompadour founded and Napoleon attended. The 15th Arrondissement was hardly considered a hotel district—until the Hilton opened its doors. The 7th Arrondissement, however, has long been noted for its few select hotels. These Left Bank districts are characterized by tree-lined boulevards and large open squares, ranging around Les Invalides (founded by Louis XIV).

In the 15th Arrondissement, not far from the Eiffel Tower, a *front de Seine* development of high-rise modern buildings has gone up. One critic said that it looks like "a little bit of New York's East Side or Chicago's Lake Shore Drive."

First-Class Hotel

Paris Hilton, 18 Avenue Suffren, 15e (tel. 42-73-92-00). The Eiffel Tower is the very symbol of Paris itself, and it was on a tract of land only a short distance away that the Hilton built one of the city's most impressive modern hotels. Today the Hilton is one of the best established of Paris's gleaming contemporary palaces, the first to shatter the Right Bank's deluxe monopoly on grand hotels. It has also become a focal point of social life in this part of the city. You needn't worry that you will be one member of an isolated group of your compatriots inside this hotel, because 45% of the establishment's income comes from the thriving business its bars and restaurants do with the local community. This is only one example of the acceptance and approval the Hilton has gained since it opened in 1966.

Built in the Hilton format of maximum comfort, with strong doses of Parisian flavor and virtually every convenience and efficiency a hotel could hope for, this 11-story, completely air-conditioned hotel is designed around window walls of glass, streamlined throughout with contemporary gadgets, and backed up by a competent and professional staff along with a computer-age security system. This includes a keyless lock system that allows a hotel room to be opened only upon the insertion of a magnetic card whose individual entry code is automatically cancelled as soon as a client checks out. Hilton spent a million dollars and ten years developing the system before installing it here.

Each of the well-furnished bedrooms has a generous bathroom covered with an appealingly tinted series of marble slabs, an oversize sink, and dozens of square yards of towels, terrycloth bathrobes, and lots of sweetly scented toilet articles. The emphasis throughout the hotel is on personal service and amenities such as readily available ice cubes, a mini-bar, babysitting service, a nearby underground garage (most valuable in Paris), and same-day laundry and cleaning services, a representative of a major airline and car-rental company, a beauty parlor, and several chic boutiques.

Each accommodation has a color TV with two full-length feature films shown every day and a tasteful collection of contemporary and French-inspired furniture. The 479 rooms are also soundproofed. They cost from 1,700F ($234.43) in a single and from 2,000F ($275.80) in a double. The breakfast buffet served in La Terrasse is one of the best available in Paris. You get copious amounts of hot coffee, friendly service, and an array of international breakfast food, both hot and cold. Also on the premises of this top-notch hotel are three bars and two additional restaurants (see my restaurant selections in Chapter IV and my nightlife recommendations in Chapter VI). Métro: Bir Hakeim.

The Middle Bracket

Hôtel de l'Université, 22 rue de l'Université, 7e (tel. 42-61-09-39), is one of the most engaging little hotels of Paris. It's on the Left Bank, near the Seine, within walking distance of the Boulevard Saint-Germain. A remake of a 300-year-old town house, it has only 27 rooms, some looking over the miniature courtyard where you can have your own morning coffee and croissants. The hotel is the creation of Monsieur and Madame Bergmann, who reconstructed the interior to preserve the best of the original architectural features while installing modern conveniences. The bedrooms, many with antiques, are one of a kind, furnished in a personalized and tasteful manner. Both the decor and the colors used are sophisticated. A favorite is Room 54, in which rattan is mixed with period pieces, the bath is marble, and the color Gainsborough blue. The price you pay depends on the plumbing you require: singles go for 375F ($51.71), and doubles cost 600F ($82.74), all prices including tax and service. Drinks and light food are served in the lounge in the evening. Métro: rue de Bac and Saint-Germain.

Hôtel de Bourgogne et Montana, 3 rue de Bourgogne, 7e (tel. 45-51-20-22), is in a quiet, dignified sector of Paris, in the Place du Palais-Bourbon, opposite the mansion housing the president of the National Assembly. The hotel is two blocks from the Seine and directly across the river from the Place de la Concorde. The interior of this six-story, 35-room building is suitable for homey comfort. The main-floor reception, with its intimate circular writing room and classic columns, adjoins a cozy salon. A small elevator takes you to your bedroom, which is likely to be decorated with floral chintz and comfortable beds and armchairs. Doubles begin at 600F ($82.74) and go up to 750F ($103.43). Singles are 400F ($55.16) to 650F ($89.64), a continental breakfast, service, and taxes included. Métro: Invalides or Chambre des Députés.

St-Thomas-d'Aquin, 3 rue du Pré-aux-Clercs, 7e (tel. 42-61-01-22), has been entirely renovated and redecorated, offering one a chance to live in a refined, traditional ambience. Behind a cream-colored façade with shutters and balconies, it stands on a relatively traffic-free street between the busy Boulevard St-Germain and the rue de l'Université. The reception hall and small lounge are modestly and traditionally furnished, with flocked paper and paneled woodwork. The ceiling is also paneled, and there are bronze chandeliers casting soft light. The bedrooms are good for the price. Many contain provincial reproductions, and some have tester beds set in oaken alcoves. Most of the rooms are adorned with flowery French wallpaper, and all have a phone. Singles cost 300F ($41.37), and doubles go for 390F ($53.78). A continental breakfast is included. Métro: Bac or St-Germain-des-Prés.

The **Hôtel du Quai Voltaire,** 19 Quai Voltaire, 7e (tel. 42-61-50-91), doesn't depend on its namesake for its reputation but rather on Oscar Wilde, Baudelaire, and Richard Wagner, who occupied Rooms 47, 56, and 55, respectively. Most of the rooms—many of them renovated—of this charming if modest inn directly overlook the bookstalls and boats of the Seine.

The manager, Madame Trollat, likes to retain the atmosphere of the place. Staircase and corridors are decorated with blue paper walls and white doors. The bar and the little salon with its fine tapestry allow the guests to meet over drinks. Of the 33 bedrooms, most are equipped with a good-size modern bath.

Singles cost from 250F ($34.48) to 300F ($41.37), and doubles go for 375F ($51.71) to 425F ($58.61). A handful of bathless singles cost 140F ($19.31) to 165F ($22.75). All tariffs include a continental breakfast. Métro: Rue du Bac.

Hotel St. Simon, 14 rue de St-Simon, 7e (tel. 45-48-35-66). Set on a quiet residential street of the Left Bank, the hotel is famous as a mainstay of solid charm and reasonable rates. It's a small villa, really, boasting a tiny garden with vines and lattices in front, as well as an 1830s-style decor of glowing birchwood doors and trompe-l'oeil panels of *faux marbre*. Even the miniscule elevator which will transport you to one of the 34 gem-like accommodations is frescoed with views of a landscape. The vaulted cellar, formerly a storage for coal, contains an intimate bar with an adjacent Louis XIII–style breakfast room.

Before he spent a fortune renovating the property, Swedish-born Goran Lindqvist worked at several of the most glamorous hotels in France and Germany. Much of what he learned is apparent in the restrained but helpful service which the staff seems so good at offering. Each accommodation is different from its neighbors in size and styling, yet each is sure to contain at least one antique. Units also have a private bath and phone. With breakfast, singles rent for 550F ($75.63), doubles for 620F ($85.50). Suites go from 800F ($110.32) to 1,050F ($144.80). Métro: Bac.

The Budget Range

Lindbergh, 5 rue Chomel, 7e (tel. 45-48-35-53), honors the late American aviator whose nonstop solo flight across the Atlantic electrified Paris in 1927. Not so long ago this formerly insignificant establishment looked as if nothing had changed since that day. However, it's happily entered the 1980s, becoming modern. On a somewhat hidden-away Left Bank street, it is off the Boulevard Raspail. The reception lounge is inviting. The bedrooms have plumbing added, along with direct-dial phones. In 1986, the hotel added new draperies and carpets, along with new furniture in the bedrooms. The larger units have a minibar. A single with shower goes for 290F ($39.99). The price is 420F ($57.92) for an equivalent double. The doubles with complete bath cost from 400F ($55.16). The Lindbergh has a modern, elegant exterior and a TV salon, as well as a restaurant where you can have breakfast. Métro: Sevres-Babylone.

Hotel Verneuil Saint-Germain, 8 rue de Verneuil, 7e (tel. 42-60-82-14), is a sort of "annex" to the Hotel de l'Académie. This three-star entry, run by Mme. Gérard, lies a few blocks from the Seine on a narrow street lined with antique dealers. Behind its cream-colored façade are 26 cozy bedrooms, most of which have upholstered walls, exposed beams, tile bathroom, phone, and color TV. Single or double units range in price from 375F ($51.71) to 450F ($62.06). A bar, decorated with provincial French furniture, serves drinks to residents and their guests. Métro: Bac.

10. 14th Arrondissement

Rapidly undergoing massive renovation, the 14th Arrondissement of Paris has been given a tremendous push in its bid for the tourist dollar with the opening of the following hotels.

THE UPPER BRACKET: The **PLM St-Jacques,** 17 Boulevard St-Jacques, 14e (tel. 45-89-89-80), affiliated with Wagon-Lits, is an 800-room, 14-story glass-and-steel hotel, refreshingly stylish and very French—red, white, and blue everywhere. Not only are the public rooms attention-getting, but the bedrooms as well have strong textures and primitive colors, contrasting with bone-white in effective combinations. The rooms come complete with refrigerator, direct-dial telephone, television, radio, and individually controlled air conditioning. Tiled bathrooms have both shower and tub, plus a separate toilet area. All year, singles rent for 900F ($124.11) and doubles for 1,050F ($144.80), including service, tax, and a continental breakfast.

The most winning of the public rooms is a bistro called Le Café Français, a re-creation of a turn-of-the-century brasserie, with bentwood chairs, 1890s posters, potted palms, and belle époque lighting fixtures. A meal here would run about 225F ($31.03). Drinks are served in three bars. And on the lower level is a maze of little boutiques. Métro: Saint-Jacques.

Hôtel Montparnasse Park, 19 rue Commandant-Mouchotte, 14e (tel. 43-20-15-51), is the largest hotel on the Left Bank, its skyscraper tower dominating Montparnasse. Encased in the 25-story tower are 1,000 rooms, including 33 suites and apartments. Singles range in price from 1,200F ($165.48) to 1,300F ($179.27), and doubles go for 1,200F ($165.48) to 1,450F ($199.96), tax included. Rooms are soundproof and color coordinated, all with an exceptional view over Paris, and equipped with color TV with closed-circuit movies, radio, background music, direct international dialing telephone, mini-bar, individual alarm clock, automatic message service, and air conditioning.

The hotel has three restaurants. The Montparnasse '25 serves a high-level French cuisine. It takes its theme from the Montparnasse period of 1925, with black lacquered furniture, gold-leafed sculptures, and art reproductions of Modigliani and Van Dongen. La Ruche, a coffeeshop with a beehive theme, has a buffet and à la carte specialties, plus a view onto the gardens. Le Park, an outdoor garden restaurant, is open June to September. An adjoining place for pre-dinner drinks is Le Corail Bar with an oceanic theme. There is also a piano bar in the evening and a lobby bar, Le Retro. In the hotel is a shopping gallery and nearby an ice skating and curling rink, plus a bowling alley. The subway stop, Montparnasse-Bienvenue, is across the street, and Gaité, exactly underground, connects directly to the Champs-Elysées (six stops).

11. 3rd and 4th Arrondissements

ST-LOUIS/LE MARAIS: If you're fortunate, there is perhaps no more romantic place to live in all of Paris than on the historic Île Saint-Louis, a center of aristocratic town houses and courtyards, once a home to such famous people as Madame Curie. On this island in the Seine, you can experience the joy of Paris of yesterday.

Likewise, Le Marais also has aristocratic credentials. Once it was the heart of elegant Paris before falling into decay for centuries. Now many of its mansions are being restored, and some private apartments here rent at prices higher than nearly everywhere else in Paris. However, until further notice le Marais remains a bastion of inexpensive hotels and restaurants. If you go now, you can take full advantage of the low tariffs charged at some of the following hotels.

The Middle Bracket

Le Pavillon de la Reine, 28 Place des Vosges, 3e (tel. 42-77-96-40). Lovers of Le Marais have long lamented the lack of a hotel on this square where Victor Hugo lived. However, the inauguration of this hotel in 1986 changed that oversight. The entrance is through a tunnel leading under the northern border of the square. At the end of the tunnel, flanked with vine-covered lattices and a small formal garden, is a cream-colored villa whose simplified neoclassical façade blends perfectly into the neighborhood. The hotel of the Bertrand-Chevalier family is new, but it fits into the landscape so perfectly you can't tell. Inside, the Louis XIII decor evokes the era when the Place des Vosges was in its heyday. Wing chairs with flame-stitched upholstery couple with iron-banded Spanish antiques to create a feeling of hospitable rusticity. Each of the 49 bedrooms is uniquely different; some are duplexes with sleeping lofts set above a cozy salon. Each contains a warm decor of weathered beams from older buildings, reproductions of famous oil paintings, marble-sheathed bathroom, color TV, mini-bar, and phone. Accommodations for one or two guests, depending on the size and format, range from 800F ($110.32) to 1,400F ($193.06). Motorists appreciate the 25 underground parking spaces. Métro: Chemin-Vert.

Hôtel des Deux-Îles, 59 rue St-Louis-en l'Île, 4e (tel. 43-26-13-35), is a hotel adventure of the interior decorator Roland Buffat. On the same street, he has restored both the Hôtel St-Louis and Hôtel de Lutèce. This 17th-century building is larger, providing more space for his glamorous setting, a reflection of his impeccable taste. The lounge, with its refectory-table reception area at the door, has a central garden of plants and flowers. Monsieur Buffat has utilized an eclectic collection of furnishings, mostly bamboo and reed blended with period pieces. He shows his charm and sense of whimsy by an occasional touch such as a cage of white doves or an antique painting. On a lower level is a rustic building-length tavern with an open fireplace, a cozy retreat at which to meet new or old friends. The bedrooms reflect somewhat the same decorative theme as the public lounges, with much use made of bamboo and reed. Unusual paintings abound, and the colors are harmoniously blended. A double with bath costs 520F ($71.71), dropping to 420F ($57.92) in a single with shower. Tax and service are included. Métro: Pont-Marie.

Hôtel de Lutèce, 65 rue St-Louis-en-l'Île, 4e (tel. 43-26-23-52). When you open the front door, you'll think you're in a country house in Brittany. Reflected everywhere is the good, restrained taste of Roland Buffat. At the Lutèce, the single, all-purpose lounge is graciously furnished with sofas and armchairs facing an old fireplace with spicy contemporary paintings. The country antiques and the original tiled floors make the hotel mellow and ingratiating. Many famous people, such as the Duke and Duchess of Bedford, use it as their Parisian home base. Conversation in the lounge tends to be a fascinating grab bag. Monsieur Buffat has given each of the bedrooms its own individual stamp. He hasn't been sparing with antiques, either. Each room comes equipped with private bath. Either singles or doubles rent for 525F ($72.40), taxes and service included. Métro: Pont-Marie.

The Budget Range

Hôtel Saint-Louis, 75 rue St-Louis-en-l'Île, 4e (tel. 46-34-04-80), is a small hotel fashionably and romantically positioned on the historic Île St-Louis. Roland Buffat, a Parisian interior decorator, discovered this hotel and did a good job of converting its 25 rooms. However, the hotel today is run by Guy and Andrée Record, whose "devotion to guests," according to the *Los Angeles Times,* "goes unmatched anywhere in Paris." They maintain a charming, family-type atmosphere that is becoming harder and harder to find in Paris. Many of the accommodations upstairs offer views over the rooftops of Paris. I prefer the rooms on the fifth floor, which have the most atmosphere and are decorated with old wood and selections of attractive furniture. Pleasant accessories decorate the rooms, and there are antiques in the small reception lounge. All of the 21 bedrooms are equipped with bath or shower and toilet. There are no singles. A double ranges in price from 313F ($43.16) to 410F ($60.68), depending on the type of plumbing and the location. Twin-bedded rooms with bath cost 410F ($60.68). Métro: Pont-Marie.

Hôtel du Grand Turenne, 6 rue de Turenne, 4e (tel. 42-78-43-25). The façade is in an impressive French town-house style from the Louis XIV era. Inside this little two-star hotel you'll find unqualified respectability. It's one of the more expensive hotels in the Marais, as it has been considerably upgraded in recent years, with many comforts and modern conveniences added. The breakfast room and reception area are quite attractive. All rooms have private bath or shower. Singles cost 220F ($30.34), and doubles go for 270F ($37.23), all with breakfast included. Métro: St-Paul-le-Marais.

Hôtel du Vieux Marais, 8 rue du Plâtre, 4e (tel. 42-78-47-22), is a simple hotel behind an ornate Beaux Arts exterior, in a small street just off the rue des Archives. The warmly tinted lobby area has marble floors, wood accents, a friendly arts-oriented receptionist, and an enlarged engraving of the Place des Vosges centuries ago. The simple rooms all have their own bath, flowered wallpaper, and an easy access, if that's what you're looking for, to the underground culture of the Marais. Totally renovated, the hotel contains 30 bedrooms, priced 225F ($31.03) to 345F ($47.58) for a single and 345F ($47.58) to 380F ($52.40) for a double, with breakfast. Métro: Hôtel-de-Ville.

Hôtel des Célestins, 1 rue Charles V, 4e (tel. 48-87-87-04), within walking distance of the Bastille, stands on a seldom-used, narrow street. One reader called it "a jewel among Parisian hotels." After an extensive modernization program the hotel has emerged as most appealing. Guests are welcomed into a reception lounge area, decorated, like the private rooms, in the style of the Marais. The bedchambers are handsomely furnished and immaculately kept. Two persons occupying a room with bath pay 220F ($30.34) to 300F ($41.37). A single with shower costs from 210F ($28.96). Métro: Bastille or Sully-Morland.

12. 18th Arrondissement

MONTMARTRE: The 18th Arrondissement, which takes in Montmartre, is not the most recommendable place for hotels. Of course, finding a hotel around Pigalle and Place Clichy that isn't a "hot bed" candidate takes some talent, although such hotels do exist. However, the steep hill of Montmartre has a particular appeal all its own for certain readers, so I've included the following recommendations, which are safe havens in an otherwise rough district.

The Upper Bracket

Résidence Charles-Dullin, 10 Place Charles-Dullin, 18e (tel. 42-57-14-55). Named after a revered 19th-century actor who established a theater in the neighborhood, this apartment-style hotel is on a cul-de-sac at the corner of a quiet but colorful square in an unlikely part of Paris. Each of the rooms contains a fully equipped kitchen and a private bath, creating what might be the ideal arrangement for anyone planning to remain in Paris for an extended sojourn. Some of the larger rooms have folding Murphy-style beds and stationary day couches and are illuminated with big sunny windows. The staff is untrained and young, but if you prefer to come and go as you please, the accommodations may be just fine for you. A maid comes to clean six days a week, changing the sheets twice weekly. Each unit has its own color TV and phone.

Although any of the 76 rooms can be rented by the day, most visitors check in here on a weekly basis, utilizing the cheaper long-term rates. Studio and one-bedroom apartments cost 3,100F ($427.49) to 5,400F ($744.66) per week, while two-bedroom accommodations cost around 6,000F ($827.40) per week. The hotel will rent on slightly cheaper terms after a substantial payment in advance. Métro: Anvers.

The Budget Range

Hôtel de Flore, 108 rue Lamarck, 18e (tel. 46-06-31-15), is a good little two-star choice for those visitors who want to be in proximity to Sacré-Coeur, Pigalle, and la Place Clichy. It's not everybody's glass of vin rouge, but then the tastes of Paris visitors are wide ranging. Even though the hotel has been modernized, it still appeals to the ones nostalgic for La Butte. A short walk will take you to Lapin Agile, which was once patronized by Picasso and Utrillo. And it was on rue St-Vincent that little Rose de Bruant was murdered. Of course, some of the displaced families who occupy de Flore couldn't care less that the heroine of *La Dame aux Camélias* or Madame Récamier, the legendary beauty, were buried in the Cemetery of Montmartre. The rooms at de Flore are quiet and moderately comfortable in this turn-of-the-century town house with its little balconies from which you can peer down at the street below. Try to get one of the upper rooms, as they are sunnier. The hotel contains 42 double rooms (no singles), priced from 170F ($23.44) to 270F ($37.23). Métro: Lamarck-Caulaincourt.

Timhôtel Montmartre, 11 Place Émile-Goudeau, 18e (tel. 42-55-74-79), stands next to the Bâteau-Lavoir, which burned down but was reconstructed by the City of Paris. This "Boat Washhouse," where Picasso and many of his colleagues lived, has been called the cradle of cubism. The Timhôtel, formerly the Paradise, lies behind the chestnut trees of one of the loveliest country-village squares of Paris. The carefully detailed, white neoclassical façade shelters a well-designed hotel where the interior was almost completely gutted in 1983 in an attempt to form a collection of individually shaped and decorated rooms with taste and charm. This is one of the highest altitude hotels in Montmartre, and from the windows of many of the rooms on the fourth floor and above, you'll have faraway views of the Eiffel Tower or the rest of the old *quartier*.

All rooms have phone, automatic alarm, radio, and color TV, with in-house movies. All but 11 of the 61 rooms contain a private bath. The most charming units are on the top floor, sheltered between sloping walls corresponding to the mansard roof, plus panoramic views. A member of a Paris-wide hotel chain, the establishment charges around 170F ($23.44) in a single without bath, 295F ($40.68) for a double with bath if it's used by one person or 320F ($44.13) for the same double with bath for two persons. For some of the rooms the toilet may or may not be in the hallway outside. A third person in a double room costs an additional 85F ($11.72). Francis Falourd is the young and efficient manager. Métro: Abbesses

13. Orly Airport

A FIRST-CLASS HOTEL: The **Hilton International Orly,** 267 Orly Sud (tel. 46-87-33-88), midway between the two terminals at Orly Airport, is one of the most contemporary airport hotels on the continent, with a low "sawtooth" design outside and a sophisticated style and flourish inside. It offers high-level comfort and all the modern conveniences to clients who prefer to spend either their first or last nights near their departure or arrival point. A full range of conference facilities is available, and many of the guests tend to be international business people who prefer the traditional style and efficiency of a Hilton. The hotel has two restaurants, one of them in the Louisiana Plantation style, an accommodating bar area, and a wide range of extra facilities. The hotel is connected by free shuttle bus to the passenger terminals of the nearby airport.

Each of the 388 most comfortable bedrooms has been well insulated against noise, and they contain phone, air conditioning, multilanguage radio, TV with in-house movies, and access to 24-hour room service. The heart of Paris is about 30 minutes away by taxi anytime except during rush hours. Most clients will find enough to do on the premises, including swimming, ice skating, and tennis courts a few minutes away. Singles range from 640F ($88.26) to 800F ($110.32), while doubles cost 800F ($110.32) to 1,100F ($151.69). An extra bed can be set up in any room for another 130F ($17.93), and children can stay free in their parents' room.

The main restaurant, La Louisiane, features Créole and international specialties in a charming New Orleans setting. The restaurant is closed on Saturday and in August, and meals run around 225F ($31.03). Many Parisians come here from the center of Paris just to dine, enjoying such dishes as oysters Rockefeller, seafood or chicken gumbo, jambalaya, and grilled chicken Créole, finished off with exotic fruit sorbets and café Brûlot prepared right at your table. Adjoining

the restaurant, l'Atelier is an attractive rendezvous, offering drinks and entertainment in an artist's-studio, Montmartre picture-gallery ambience.

14. Airport Charles de Gaulle

A FIRST-CLASS HOTEL: The **Sofitel Roissy,** Aéroport Charles de Gaulle–
Zone Centrale, Roissy-en-France (tel. 48-62-23-23), is a 352-room hotel a few
minutes from the airport, from which there is free bus service. All its rooms are
air-conditioned and soundproof, and there are enough bars and restaurants to
save you from making a difficult trip into Paris. Double-bedded rooms and twins
are offered, and all of them contain TV set, phone, radio, and harmoniously
attractive furnishings. One person pays from 535F ($73.78) to 650F ($89.64),
and doubles rent for 630F ($86.88) to 725F ($99.98). Guests who use the room
only for the day pay 295F ($40.68) in a single and 330F ($45.51) in a double.

Chapter IV

THE RESTAURANTS OF PARIS

1. The Haute Cuisine
2. 1st and 2nd Arrondissements
3. 8th Arrondissements
4. 5th and 6th Arrondissements
5. 3rd and 4th Arrondissements
6. 7th Arrondissement
7. 9th and 10th Arrondissements
8. 12th Arrondissement
9. 15th Arrondissement
10. 16th Arrondissement
11. 17th Arrondissement
12. 18th and 19th Arrondissements
13. Vegetarian Dining
14. Tea Rooms and Pâtisseries

IN A CITY OFTEN CONSIDERED the gastronomic capital of the world, and one with more than 12,000 restaurants, it is a difficult task to pick out the very best. As you may imagine, a rather ghastly degree of elimination proved necessary.

I don't pretend to have surveyed all the good restaurants of Paris. What I have done is list my personal favorites in all price ranges. Some of my choices are fabled throughout the world; others are relatively unknown bistros. The selection is varied enough to keep you well fed for a weekend . . . or a decade.

Is Paris the gastronomic capital of the world? Many restaurants, such as Lasserre and Taillevent, are truly among the finest. Others, however, take advantage of the city's culinary reputation and trap visitors with shoddy cooking. I will not answer the question I posed. Instead, I offer two thoughts: do not overrate the restaurants of Paris, and do not hesitate to sing the praise of well-prepared French food.

I don't share the snobbish attitude that "no one" goes to the great restaurants of Paris, such as La Tour d'Argent or Maxim's. Both of these establishments offer such uniquely Parisian experiences that they number, along with the Eiffel Tower, among the top "sights." Still, for the best food and to keep your budget intact, I'll recommend far less expensive establishments.

1. The Haute Cuisine

Taillevent, 15 rue Lamennais, 8e (tel. 45-63-39-94), dates only from 1946, when the restaurant was founded by the father of present owner Jean-Claude Vrinat, but it has climbed steadily in the ranks of excellence until today it is recognized as arguably the most outstanding eating place in Paris in terms of the cuisine, the wines, the service, and the all-around pleasure provided its customers. The setting of this citadel of haute cuisine is a grand 18th-century town house off the Champs-Élysées, with paneled rooms and crystal chandeliers. Monsieur Vrinat welcomes guests to his dignified establishment as if they were arriving for a private dinner party. The place is not large, but that is as the owner wishes it, since it permits him to give personal attention to every facet of the operation, seeing to the continuation of the discreet, London-club atmosphere he so carefully maintains. He helps his staff pamper the guests while they are eating of the fine foods turned out under the direction of Claude Deligne, the chef.

Menus are deftly balanced between traditional and modern cuisine. A good opener to your gourmet repast might be cannellonis de céleri aux truffes (rolled celery with truffles). For a main course, I suggest a house specialty, bar aux langoustines (sea-bass with prawns) or poularde de Bresse au foie gras (Bresse chicken with foie gras). Another highly recommendable dish is the foie de canard chaud au gingembre (hot duck liver with ginger). To conclude your meal, you'll find the cheese course, fromages de nos provinces, always reliable, and there is also a blanc-manger aux fruits (light almond mousse with fruit) which I find just right after a filling repast.

Taillevent's wine list is one of the best in the city. Monsieur Vrinat and his wife make the selections carefully and knowledgeably, providing bottles pleasing to the palate and complementary to the fine cuisine. Count on spending from 700F ($96.53) for a gourmet dinner, plus 15% service. That service, incidentally, is impeccable. Reservations are necessary, and although M. Vrinat likes Americans, it isn't always easy for visitors from the States and other countries to book a table, since the owner prefers to see his clientele comprise about 60% French people. The restaurant is closed on Saturday and Sunday.

The name of the restaurant, in case you wondered, honors a famous chef of the 14th century, who was the author of one of the oldest known books on French cookery. Métro: George-V.

Lasserre, 17 Avenue Franklin-D.-Roosevelt, 8e (tel. 43-59-53-43), is perhaps the greatest citadel of the haute cuisine in Paris. Much to the chagrin of its more tradition-laden competitors, it continues its lead position year after year. Its success revolves around Monsieur Lasserre, who combines his flairs for drama and for food in both the cooking and the presentation.

Before World War II, what is now the restaurant was just a bistro and a rendezvous for chauffeurs. When Monsieur Lasserre purchased the dilapidated, two-story building, he began on the long road toward creating a miniature culinary paradise. Behind a pair of gleaming white front doors are two private ground-floor dining rooms with a "disappearing wall," plus a reception lounge, keynoted by Louis XVI furnishings and brocaded walls. You ascend to the second landing via a petite elevator lined with brocaded silk. The main dining room is elegantly appointed and designed—two stories high, with a mezzanine on two sides. Tall, arched windows are draped softly with silk. On a Louis XV salon chair, you sit down to an exquisite table set with the finest of porcelain, gold-edged crystal glasses, a silver bird, a ceramic dove, and a silver candelabrum.

Monsieur Lasserre selected a painter to decorate the ceiling with a blue sky and fleecy-white clouds; but in fair weather he slides back the roof to let in the real sky or the moonlight in the evening. He's been known to bring in a flock of white doves from his country place to release in the main dining room, with raffle numbers attached to their feet.

No matter what you select, it'll have its own decorative drama. Garnish vegetables become flowers in the hands of the artists back in the kitchen. To begin your repast, I'd suggest a specialty, the filets de turbot à la fouesnantaise. Of the fish dishes, many are on their way toward becoming house specialties, they are so well conceived. Try the poëlée de langoustines au coulis de homard. Incidentally, the proprietor is often called "the king of casseroles," his position reconfirmed by the fact that the "Club de la Casserole" dines here.

Especially recommendable is the noisettes d'agneau lamrani, the finest I've ever had anywhere. Another excellent choice is the steak de charolais au bourgueil. In addition, Lasserre presents two dozen gloriously fattening desserts. Try the timbale Élysée. Count on spending from 650F ($89.64) for an elegant repast here. The cellar of some 180,000 bottles is among the most remarkable in Paris, the red wine decanted into silver pitchers or ornate crystal.

Reservations are imperative. Wanting to be certain to have a table, one wealthy Californian wrote six months in advance. Closed in August and on Sunday and Monday. Métro: Franklin-D.-Roosevelt.

Maxim's, 3 rue Royale, 8e (tel. 42-65-27-94). Edward VII, then the Prince of Wales, used to revel in its atmosphere, enjoying his freedom away from his stern mother, Queen Victoria. Perhaps the single most legendary restaurant in the world, Maxim's is a belle époque bonanza. Gowned women who dine here are made to feel like precious jewels in a velvet-lined Cartier box. The whole aura suggests the Opéra Comique of the Gay '90s, where elegant cocottes, beplumed with ostrich feathers, sat in their boxes flashing smiles and diamonds.

Today, Maxim's remains the choice of the affluent, fashionable, and globetrotting set. The "greats" of another era are still here too, but in caricature form on the walls. Maxim's was the setting for *The Merry Widow* in which silent-screen stars Mae Murray and John Gilbert "dipped and swayed," and the orchestra is still fond of playing the waltz, reminiscent of the days when dark, almond-eyed men waited in vain to meet a wealthy widow. Louis Jourdan took Leslie Caron to Maxim's "the night they invented champagne" in *Gigi*. Pierre Cardin took over the restaurant in the spring of 1981.

There are several dining rooms, and the intricacy of which table is best escapes most first-time diners, who wouldn't get it anyway. The background is art nouveau, with paneled walls, gilt and colored vines, leafy cut-out overlays, and a stained-glass ceiling.

Then there's the question of what to order. At Maxim's you can almost forget about the cuisine, so dazzling is the atmosphere. But the chef, Michel Menant, is backed up by some of the finest young cooks in France, who train at Maxim's before heading back to the provinces to open their own bistros. For appetizers, the "Billi-By" soup is the time-tested favorite. Topped with whipped cream and grated parmesan cheese, it is made with mussels, coarsely ground pepper, white wine, cream, chopped onions, celery, and parsley. Anyone who knows anything about Maxim's has tried sole Albert (named after the famous, now-deceased maître d'). It is flavored not only with bread crumbs and chopped fine herbs but a large glass of vermouth. Bon vivants favor two other dishes as well—coquilles Saint-Jacques (scallops flavored with saffron) and poularde de vendée aux concombres (pullet with cucumbers). For dessert, I'd recommend either the crêpes veuve joyeuse or the tarte tantin, made with thick slices of Reinette apples and a pâté brisée dough. What to drink? Everybody—just everybody—orders champagne at Maxim's, although the cellar is stocked with other fine wines.

Maxim's is open all year, daily except Sunday. After-theater suppers are served to musical accompaniment (with dancing), and orders are taken until midnight. Reservations are imperative. A full meal will cost 750F ($103.43) to 850F ($117.22) per person. Métro: Concorde.

La Tour d'Argent, 15 Quai de la Tournelle, 5e (tel. 43-54-23-31), is the great-granddaddy of Parisian restaurants. Actually a restaurant in some form or another has stood on this spot since 1582, although an amusing "family tree" mural in the before-dinner drinking lounge traces the beginning back to Adam and Eve. Illustrations highlight culinary coups, such as the 1870 dinner—the Christmas during the war with Prussia—when the chef served elephant soup, antelope chops, camel hump, bear steaks, even wolves, cats, and side dishes of rats. Now this fabled restaurant is under the eagle eye of Claude Terrail, a debonair gentleman who was once called "the playboy of the Western world." Celebrities he's used to—Truman, Eisenhower, and Churchill all dined here. The restaurant grew in fame when it was owned by Frédéric Delair, who purchased the wine cellar of the legendary Café Anglais on its demise and started the custom of issuing certificates to diners who order the house specialty, pressed duck (caneton)—the birds are numbered.

A modern structure surrounds and absorbs the original building, which has been turned into a gastronomic museum. On the Left Bank, directly on the Seine, the restaurant seats its guests on the top floor, where all-glass walls provide a panoramic view of the 17th-century houses along the quays of the Île-St-Louis. As darkness approaches, the flying buttresses of Notre-Dame are illuminated, partially at the expense of La Tour d'Argent. So many well-heeled Americans flock here for "that French culinary experience" that, quite honestly, there are times when no French accents are heard except those of the staff.

The cookery is brilliant, the food immaculately served on Dresden china. Most first-timers seem to order the duck, and it's sensational. Incidentally, a quarter of the menu is taken up with various ways you can order the bird. If you don't like duck, you'll find a host of other selections, including filets de sole cardinal or filet Tour d'Argent. For a beginning, the potage Cladius Burdel is made with sorrel, egg yolks, fresh cream, chicken broth, and butter whipped together. For dessert, the pêches flambées is everything you'd expect it to be. The restaurant is closed on Monday, but otherwise receives orders until 10 p.m. Reserve, reserve, and expect to pay from 500F ($68.95) to 750F ($103.43) for a complete meal. Métro: Maubert-Mutualité or Sully Morland.

Alain Senderens' Lucas-Carton, 9 Place de la Madeleine, 8e (tel. 42-65-22-90), a Paris landmark from the belle époque era, is today a blend of the old and the new, since it was taken over by one of Paris's top restauranteurs. Senderens has added his own touches to the historic restaurant, which was created during the time of British King Edward VII by an Englishman named Lucas and a talented French chef, Francis Carton. The new owner has had the two dining rooms as well as the private rooms upstairs decorated with expanses of mirrors, sprays of spring flowers offsetting the carved wooden panels, pristine white ceilings and napery, and art nouveau lighting. If General Pershing, Marshal Foch, General de Gaulle, Winston Churchill, and other leaders in both World Wars were looking around today for a proper site to discuss world affairs over lunch, they would probably opt again for Lucas-Carton, as they once did.

The food they would be served, however, would be different from half a century and more ago. Senderens, who bakes his own bread, creates such tasty dishes as fresh cod with eggplant, caviar, and fried zucchini, ravioli filled with scallops and served with thyme-flavored zucchini, and mild smoked salmon with a sprinkling of salmon eggs, plus other delicacies from his own smoker and from the rôtisserie. However, Senderens is constantly searching for new culinary creations, so you will get to choose from what he has developed by the time you visit. For dessert, if it is on the menu then, I suggest hot pineapple fritters, beignets d'ananas Eventhia (named for his wife). The menu dégustation costs 500F ($68.95), and à la carte dinners go for 630F ($89.64) to 900F ($124.11). The restaurant is closed Saturday, Sunday, and holidays. Reservations must be made several days ahead for lunch and several weeks ahead for dinner. Métro: Madeleine.

Jamin, 32 rue du Longchamp, 16e (tel. 47-27-12-27), is where Joël Robuchon, the chef and proprietor, basks in his reputation as the country's most innovative cook. If you are a gourmet, your idea of heaven could well be to hire Monsieur Robuchon to be in charge of your kitchen. This creative master of the culinary arts has turned from La Nouvelle Cuisine to the latest trend, a blend of classic and nouvelle cooking known as Cuisine Moderne and even sometimes as Cuisine Actuelle, or what is actually being cooked now. Produced here are foods which are light and delicate, with outstanding flavors. In his pink dining room, where his wife Janine presides over the cash register, Robuchon's capable and courteous staff serves dishes which the chef takes pains to make colorful and pleasing to the eye as well as tempting to the palate. He even bakes his own bread fresh every day, and he is known to spend long hours in the kitchen testing out (or inventing) new recipes. He even has his own fish and shellfish shipped fresh from Brittany so it doesn't have to "linger" at the Rungis wholesale market.

Among the delectable offerings are such dishes as kidneys and sweetbreads diced and sautéed with mushrooms, canette rosée (duckling which has been roasted and braised, flavored with such spices as ginger, nutmeg, cinnamon, and other Chinese-influenced touches), shellfish-filled ravioli steamed in cabbage leaves, and chicken for two, poached in a pig's bladder. Set menus are offered for 200F ($27.58), 420F ($57.92), and 470F ($64.81). If you prefer to order à la carte, expect to pay from 500F ($68.75) to 650F ($89.64) for your meal. Reservations are imperative, and it's wisest to make them six to eight weeks in advance. Some guests make them from the United States before starting their trip to Paris. Monsieur Robuchon likes to have foreign diners, but he prefers to have about half the guest list made up of French customers. The restaurant is closed on Saturday, Sunday, and in July. Métro: Trocadéro.

Le Grand Véfour, 17 rue de Beaujolais, 1er (tel. 42-96-56-27), has been an eating place since the reign of Louis XV, and it has had its ups and downs. Although the exact date of its opening as the Café de Chartres is not definitely known, it is more than 200 years old and is a classified historical treasure. It got its present name in 1812, when Jean Véfour, former chef to a member of the royal family, owned it. Since that time, it has attracted such notables as Napoleon and Danton and a host of writers and artists, such as Victor Hugo, Colette, and Jean Cocteau (who designed the menu cover in 1953). Amid the arcades of the Palais-Royal, the restaurant had lost its earlier glamour by the start of the 20th century and was simply a little corner café. It had another "up" period after World War II, under Raymond Oliver, one of the most famous of modern French chefs, but as he aged, it again fell into a decline. Fortunately, Jean Taittinger of the Taittinger Champagne family (they also own the Crillon) purchased the restaurant, and it has now reached—perhaps surpassed—its former glories. The restoration, done under the close eye of the Department of Historical Monuments, involved cleaning, repairing and matching of furniture, reweaving of Aubusson carpets, and refurbishing of the painted-silk decor.

Under the careful direction of the manager, Yvan Courault, dining here is an experience. From Limoges china, white with a green-leaf border, you can feast at a table bearing a brass plaque with the name of a famous former occupant. The chef, André Signoret, produces dishes, some traditional and some new creations, which are limited but choice. You can select from such appetizers as baked eggs with truffles and artichokes, terrine de foie gras of duck, and cold oysters with caviar and salmon eggs. Fish and meat dishes include herb-stuffed bass, lobster, tournedos, lamb, and veal. You'll want to accompany your meal with one or more of the fine wines from the cellar. Expect to pay 600F ($82.74) to 700F ($96.53) for an à la carte meal. The restaurant is closed on Saturday and Sunday. Reservations are required. Métro: Palais-Royal.

2. 1st and 2nd Arrondissements

Les Halles, the Bourse, the Opéra, the Palais Royal, the rue Montmartre, the Place Vendôme, the Île de la Cité, and the rue St-Honoré are found within these two arrondissements, as are many fine restaurants.

THE UPPER BRACKET: Carré des Feuillants, 14 rue de Castiglione, 1er (tel. 42-86-82-82). Alain Dutournier, one of the leading chef de cuisines of Paris, established his reputation at Au Trou Gascon, which is now run by his wife, Nicole. He moved his showcase to this restaurant which immediately became an overnight success. The location near Place Vendôme and the Tuileries is platinum. Monsieur Dutournier launched his cooking career in the Gascony region of southwest France, working in the kitchen with his mother and grandmother. His parents owned an inn.

He likes to call his food a "cuisine du moment." That suggests a wild, experimental imagination which makes it next to impossible to suggest any specific dishes that might be served on the day of your visit. For example, you might get langoustines with unripened mangoes. Basically, he's not interested in rich sauces, preferring a more lighthearted cuisine (and I might add healthier as well). He has a whole network of little farms that supply him with the fresh produce from which he weaves his magic spell. A menu is priced at 400F ($55.16), and à la carte orders, with wine and service, usually average 550F ($75.63). The sommelier, Jean-Guy Loustau, has distinguished himself for his exciting *cave* containing several little-known wines along with a fabulous collection of armagnacs. A dozen places in the bar await those who casually walk in without a reservation. Otherwise, seating is in a selection of modern dining rooms with a trendy decor, including graphics of vegetables and fruits, the type the Jolly Green Giant might harvest. Métro: Tuileries.

Escargot-Montorgueil, 38 rue Montorgueil, 1er (tel. 42-36-83-51). No wonder the divine Sarah took many of her meals here, virtually adopting the kitchen as her own. That mural of those chubby cherub chefs on the ceiling is said to have come from her summer home on an island off the southern coast of Brittany. Mlle Bernhardt is gone, of course, and fashion is fickle; but the Escargot (Snail) of Les Halles still reigns supreme. Mme Saladin-Terrail, known as Kouikette, sister of Monsieur Terrail of La Tour d'Argent, has taken over the place, improving the style without disturbing the atmosphere.

The building is said to date from the time of Henri II and Catherine de Medici, and the restaurant itself opened back in the 1830s. The original Louis-Philippe decor is carefully preserved; two dining rooms on the ground floor have starched Breton lace curtains and (electrified) gaslight fixtures on sepia walls. An open spiral staircase leads to a formal paneled dining room upstairs. First-timers always seem to order the snails—they are good. I'd recommend the pieds de porcs and the feathery turbot soufflé. For dessert the specialty is strawberry beignets. Your complete meal is likely to run from 200F ($27.58) to 350F ($48.27) per person with wine. The restaurant is closed Monday and Tuesday and part of August. Reservations are imperative. Métro: Les Halles.

THE MEDIUM-PRICED RANGE: Pierre Traiteur, 10 rue de Richelieu, 1er (tel. 42-96-09-17). Its location behind the Comédie Française is the perfect setting for the kind of richly flavorful bourgeois cuisine for which France is famous. The Auvergne-born owner, Monsieur Nouyrigat, and his chef, Marc Faucheux, prepare updated versions of traditional recipes which residents of the surrounding neighborhood appreciate highly. A repeat visitor can take a gastronomic tour of France without ever leaving the restaurant, because so many different regions of the country are represented on the menu. You might begin with a filet of mackerel cooked in cider and served with apples, sausages (andouillettes) braised with mustard and chopped cabbage, roast leg of lamb with gratin potatoes, and marvelously flavorful preparations of beef. À la carte meals cost from 250F ($34.48), and are served daily except on weekends and in August. Reservations are necessary. Métro: Palais-Royal.

Pharamond, 24 rue de la Grande-Truanderie, 1er (tel. 42-33-06-72), a timbered neo-Norman structure founded in 1832, sits on a street in the Les Halles sector once frequented by the vagabonds of Paris. The dish to order here is tripes à la mode de Caen served over a charcoal burner. Tripe admittedly isn't popular with North Americans, but if you're at all experimental you'll find no better introduction to this good dish than at Pharamond. A more common and frankly more appealing offering is the coquilles St-Jacques au cidre (scallops in cider). For a good beginning, try half a dozen of the Breton oysters, served between October and April. Other main-dish specialties include grillade du feu de bois for two persons, as well as filets de sole normande. Your bill will range from 150F ($20.69) to 200F ($27.58). Closed Sunday and in July. Métro: Les Halles.

Le Soufflé, 36 rue du Mont-Thabor, 1er (tel. 42-60-27-19). What Paris needs, decided André Faure when he arrived from Cahors, is a good soufflé. So he set up shop near the Tuileries and the Place Vendôme, and he's been dispensing "cloud puffs" ever since, along with the deeply colored red wine from his region. Soufflés come in all shapes and sizes here, and you can go through the entire menu, from appetizers to desserts, ordering nothing but. For variety, however, you might elect to begin your meal with fond d'artichaut gourmande, an artichoke served with fresh mushrooms and freshly made mayonnaise. The cheese soufflé and the escalope de saumon (salmon) soufflé are justly praised. An especially good main dish is the poule sautée à l'estragon (sautéed chicken in a cream-laced white wine sauce that's been flavored with tarragon). The raspberry soufflé is spectacular, although you may prefer chocolate or hazelnut. Meals cost from 190F ($26.20). Closed Sunday. Métro: Tuileries.

Restaurant Lescure, 7 rue de Mondovi, 1er (tel. 42-60-18-91). Finding a reasonably priced restaurant near the Place de la Concorde is no easy task. Hence, this miniature bistro, operating since 1919, is a discovery. Off the rue de Rivoli, it's right around the corner from the 18th-century mansion where Talleyrand died. The tables on the sidewalk are tiny, and there isn't much elbow room inside either. What it does have is rustic charm. The kitchen is exposed to view, and round about are hung drying bay leaves, salami, and garlic pigtails. Don't expect anybody to speak English either. The patron is a very down-to-earth man who calls his food *"cuisine bourgeoise."* For example, you might begin with a pâté en croûte. Main-course house specialties include le confit de canard and salmon in a green sauce. My favorite dessert is one of the chef's fruit tarts. Count on spending 150F ($20.69) if you order à la carte. A set menu of four courses costs 76F ($10.48). The restaurant is closed on Sunday and in August. Métro: Concorde.

Au Pied de Cochon, 6 rue Coquillière, 1er (tel. 42-36-11-75), near the contemporary buildings that have replaced Les Halles market in the center of Paris and also close to the famous 16th-century church of St-Eustache, has succeeded in keeping the tradition of good food. On the ground floor, which is in the cheerful Parisian brasserie style, as well as on the first or second floors with their quiet, elegant dining rooms, you can enjoy such offerings as pigs feet grilled with béarnaise sauce or stuffed with goose liver and mustard sauce. Another specialty is the suckling pig St-Eustache (sliced pork filet and chops, roasted and cooked with mustard sauce). There is another well-known specialty served here too. It is andouillette, or chitterling sausage with a béarnaise sauce. The famous onion soup is a standard of the house to start your meal, or try one of the trays of shellfish. Oysters, clams, mussels, and sea urchins are brought every day from the sea directly to the Pied de Cochon. For a dessert, I'd suggest La Vie en Rose. Your bill is likely to average about 200F ($27.58). The restaurant is one of the last in Paris to be open day and night all year. Métro: Les Halles.

La Rose de France, 24 Place Dauphine, 1er (tel. 43-54-10-12), enjoys a setting worthy of an operetta, complete with candlelit tables, in the old section of the Île de la Cité near Notre-Dame. You can dine with a sophisticated crowd of young Parisians who know they can get good and reasonably priced meals here. In fair weather, the sidewalk tables overlooking the Palace of Justice are favored. The restaurant's just around the corner from the old Pont Neuf. Main dishes include deviled steak, spring lamb chops, a Norman-style veal chop with cooked apples, and a soufflé of scallops with muscadet. For dessert, try the fruit tart of the day, a sorbet, or iced melon (in summer only). A set menu costs 150F ($20.69). It's closed Saturday and Sunday. Métro: Cité or Pont-Neuf.

Joe Allen, 30 rue Pierre Lescot, 1er (tel. 42-36-70-13), long ago invaded Les Halles with his American hamburger. Even though the New York restauranteur admits "it's a silly idea," it works. First there was the money needed, but backers appeared in the form of such as Lauren Bacall and Roy Scheider. Then he had to get the tablecloths, those little red-checked ones you associate with Paris bistros. Not finding them in the French capital, he had to import them from New York. Likewise, the green awning outside. The brick walls, the oak floors, the movie stills, even the blackboard menu—all evoke a saloon atmosphere. Most of the work, however, went into creating the American burger, which is easily the best in Paris. Joe concedes, however, that it's not as good as the ones dispensed at P.J. Clarke's in New York. While listening to Garland or Streisand on the jukebox, you can order such delights as black bean soup, chili, a sirloin steak, barbecued spare ribs, and apple pie. By all means try the spinach salad with a creamy roquefort dressing and little crunchy bits of bacon and fresh mushrooms.

Joe claims his saloon is the only place in Paris that serves an authentic New York cheesecake or a real pecan pie. The pecans are flown in from the United States. They have a Telex link-up with New York, and the two kitchens often swap daily specials and other dishes that have proved successful. Joe claims that (thanks to French chocolate) "we make better brownies than those made in the States." Giving the brownies tough competition is the California chocolate mousse pie, along with the strawberry Romanoff and the coconut cream pie. The bill will range from 150F ($20.69) to 200F ($27.58) per person. Thanksgiving dinner at Joe Allen's in Paris is becoming a tradition (but you'll need a reservation way in advance). Hours are daily from noon to 2 a.m. Unless you're prepared to wait 30 minutes at the New York bar (not a bad idea), you should call ahead and reserve a table for dinner. Métro: Châtelet or Les Halles.

THE BUDGET RANGE: La Moisanderie, 52 rue de Richelieu, 1er (tel. 42-96-92-93), is a relatively unknown bistro of high quality and low prices. It's conveniently located—just off the Palais Royal arcades, opening onto a passageway leading to the 18th-century Théâtre du Palais Royal. (Diderot, the editor of the great 28-volume *Encyclopédie,* died at no. 39 on this street on July 31, 1781, and Molière lived and died, in 1673, at no. 40.) The tiny restaurant is the domain of Monsieur Baesch, a kindly, gray-haired gentleman who seats everyone himself, keeping a sharp eye out to see that every guest is served properly. His place is simple and small, the tables big enough for sparrows—but somehow everything goes smoothly. The bistro has a pleasant, homey, rustic French decor: wood paneling covered with 16th-century tapestries, a brick fireplace, red cloths, a basket of crusty bread, a counter of mouthwatering homemade pastries.

Set meals are offered for 75F ($10.32) and 90F ($12.41), plus service. For some fancier dishes, such as steak with cognac or orange duck, a supplement is asked. For openers you are offered eight different hors d'oeuvres, a soup (the vegetable soup with cream is excellent), or marinated herring. Next comes a meat or fowl course: stuffed chicken, pork with mushrooms, grilled liver, perhaps a veal cutlet in a cream sauce with mushrooms. For dessert you help yourself from a large glass bowl of fresh fruit salad, unless you prefer a wedge of green apple tart. Lunch orders are taken between noon and 2 p.m., dinner orders between 7 and 9 p.m. Closed Sunday and in August. It's crowded, so go early. Métro: Palais-Royal.

Le Drouot, 103 rue Richelieu, 2e (tel. 42-96-68-23), is one of the best budget restaurants in this arrondissement. A curving stairway leads to this second-floor dining hall. Under high ceilings, rows of tables await hungry diners who gravitate to this friendly, informal atmosphere. At mealtimes, between 11 a.m. and 3 p.m. and 6 and 9:30 p.m., it is usually packed with economy-minded Parisians who know they can get well-prepared food at low cost.

Almost in the tradition of the famous *bouillons* at the turn of the century in Paris, a breadman comes around to see that your plate is kept full. For an appetizer, you might select ham from the Ardennes or perhaps artichoke bottom vinaigrette. Among the main courses offered, I'd recommend the veal kidneys in a bordelaise sauce, although you might like the couscous or even the sauerkraut, which comes with a number of pork products. Chocolate mousse is the favored dessert. Expect to pay around 65F ($8.97) per person for a meal. Métro: 4-Septembre.

André Faure, 40 rue du Mont-Thabor, 1er (tel. 42-60-74-28), has a great virtue: modesty. Totally unheralded, Monsieur Faure's Right Bank establishment, decorated with paintings, serves simple French cooking—but of a fine standard. A special five-course dinner is featured nightly except Sunday at 95F ($13.10). Likely offerings are le poulet en cocotte grand'mére, lapin (rabbit) sauté, and coq au vin. The tables are crowded, especially at lunch with local business people attracted by the 70F ($9.65) set luncheon, which is not only a fine bargain but well prepared. Service is slapdash in the grand tradition of the French bistro. Closed Sunday. The restaurant is good for sightseers in the area, as it lies only a short block from the Place Vendôme and within an easy walk of the Place de la Concorde. Métro: Tuileries.

Restaurant Paul, 15 Place Dauphine, 1er (tel. 43-54-21-48). When the century was young, this address was to be dispensed with strictest confidence to first-time visitors to Paris. Over the decades it has become a virtual cliché for the hidden little bistro. The only secret today is that it's still here, still serving the same good food, and that madame is still behind the cash register. On the historic Place Dauphine, that triangular square on the Île de la Cité, Chez Paul has another entrance bordering the Seine on the Quai des Orfevres. Find a seat in its narrow confines, then relax and enjoy the escalope papillote, veal cooked in parchment. For a beginning, why not the quenelles de brochet à la Nantua? The dessert specialty is baba à la confiture flambé au rhum. Your tab is likely to run from 120F ($16.55) to 170F ($23.44) for a meal here. It's closed Monday, Tuesday, and in August. Métro: Pont-Neuf.

Au Grand Comptoir, 4 rue Pierre-Lescot, 1er (tel. 42-33-56-30). The opening of Les Halles Forum has given a new lease on life to this restaurant, a reminder of the "ventre de Paris." At this *grand comptoir* (grand, long bar) the last century has hardly mattered. In the dining room beyond, the decor hasn't been changed in more than 50 years. The restaurant has been functioning since 1868. It's still in a prime position, offering you a chance to sample food long savored by the merchants from the central markets, even the porters who used to line the long bar. A lot of Limousin specialties are offered, in addition to other dishes. Try the haddock with fondue butter, or perhaps the coq au vin. Most meals begin with an order of rillettes. This is diced meat, generally pork brisket, pounded and preserved in pots. The most typical salad is made with lentils. Of course, the century-old specialty, and it never changes, is grilled pigs' feet. If you arrive in the right season, you can order oysters on a bed of seaweed and crushed ice. The restaurant serves a lightly chilled Sancerre and a good beaujolais, among other wines. For dessert, I'd recommend the chocolate caramel parfait. A good, healthy meal of typically popular French food will cost

185F ($25.51) to 235F ($32.41) here. Closed Saturday night and Sunday. Métro: Les Halles.

3. 8th Arrondissement

Highlights of the 8th Arrondissement are the Champs-Élysées, the George V, the Place de la Concorde, the Madeleine, the Saint Lazare, the Faubourg Saint-Honoré, and the Place de l'Alma. Got your bearings? Then let's go dining.

THE UPPER BRACKET: Au Petit Montmorency, 5 rue Rabelais, 8e (tel. 42-25-11-19), was created as the dream of Daniel Bouché and his wife, Nicole. Before opening his own place just north of the Champs-Élysées, Bouché trained at a number of restaurants, including Maxim's in Chicago. But he seems to have discarded most of what he learned, preferring to chart his own course in the turbulent waters of La Nouvelle Cuisine. Paintings, engravings, and hanging lanterns give a decidedly old-fashioned touch to his restaurant, the ambience heightened by candlelight and the profusion of fresh flowers.

All on his own, Bouché turns out a delicate and subtle cuisine—daube with calves' feet (a dish served in winter only), sweetbreads with kidneys and morels, a chausson au roquefort (a sort of cheese turnover), stuffed turbot with vegetables, and a gourmandise aux légumes, a charlotte made with seven vegetables. If you can afford it, I'd suggest a carmelized foie gras of duck to begin your meal. For dessert, I'd recommend a heavenly smooth chocolate soufflé with vanilla ice cream. Of course, these dishes are cited only to give you an idea as to the type of cuisine served. The menu, in fact, changes quite often according to what they find desirable in the market on any given day. Expect to pay from 325F ($44.82) to 425F ($58.61) per person for a complete meal. The French wines are well selected, including some choice but little-publicized ones. The restaurant is closed on Sunday and in August. Métro: Franklin-D.-Roosevelt.

Chiberta, 3 rue Arsène-Houssaye, 8e (tel. 45-63-77-90), right near the Étoile, has a chef who has stunned some of the gastronomic circles of Paris. He is Jean-Michel Bédier, who once worked with the equally well-known Monsieur Delaveyne at Bougival's Le Camélia. In an elegantly modern setting, Bédier turns out inventive dishes, and is himself adding a chapter to La Nouvelle Cuisine.

The director of the restaurant is Louis-Noël Richard, who has taken this house and turned it into one of the most attractive restaurants in Paris. He has decorated each table with amaryllis. Each dish is admirably presented and described by Jean-Paul Fries, the charming maître d'. The menu changes twice a year, but typical opening courses might include smoked salmon rolled around fresh asparagus and served in a sauce of red pepper and paprika, ravioli with truffles, or salmon tartare. For a main course, you might order a fricassée of scallops with truffles. To finish off, try wild strawberries with honey ice cream covered with raspberry sauce. The wine list is well chosen.

Bédier certainly knows how to turn out a culinary masterpiece, and the service and attention you get here are also winning. One critic once claimed that "every woman looks beautiful" in the setting at Chiberta. However, for all this perfection, you will have to pay a hefty tab, ranging from 300F ($41.37) to 500F ($68.95), depending on what you order. The restaurant is closed in August and on Saturday and Sunday. Métro: Charles-de-Gaulle (Étoile).

Restaurant Copenhague and Flora Danica, 142 Avenue des Champs-Élysées, 8e (tel. 43-59-20-41), is the "Maison du Danemark," one of the finest eating establishments along the Champs-Élysées. The good-tasting food of Denmark is served with considerable style and flair. In summer you can dine outside on the rear terrace, an idyllic spot. If you want to go Danish all the way, you'll order an apértif of aquavit and ignore the wine list in favor of Carlsberg or

Tuborg, the two most famous beers of Denmark. For an appetizer, you might prefer terrine de canard (duckling) Copenhague. If you want to order the house specialty, it's called délices scandinaves—"a platter of joy" of foods the Danes do exceptionally well. The feuilleté Cercle Polaire is a fine finish. Expect to spend around 300F ($41.37) for a meal.

At the Boutique Flora Danica facing the Champs-Élysées you can have a small snack from noon until midnight. Open-faced sandwiches, Danish smørrebrød, with beer go for around 100F ($13.79). Sandwiches, pastries, beer, and aquavit are available in the small delicatessen. Flora Danica is open all year. Copenhagen is closed on Sunday, holidays, and in August. Métro: George-V.

Caviar Kaspia, 17 Place de la Madeleine, 8e (tel. 42-65-33-52). How chic can you get, sitting on the second floor of this caviar center, enjoying a view of the columns of the stately Madeleine while casually tasting Russian caviar and sipping Russian vodka? You're welcomed by the genial, English-speaking manager, Stellio Conforti, who will explain the selections to you and seat you at a tiny table to begin your life of decadence. Should you not prefer a taste of caviar, you'll also find smoked salmon, foie gras, even a more modest hot borscht and blinis. The more elaborate dishes, such as the salmon and caviar, are priced by the gram, and the tabs on these delicacies fluctuate from week to week, so I won't cite them here, except to say they are always super-expensive. However, for a "taste," expect to pay 350F ($48.27). A carry-out shop is on the ground floor. The place is closed Sunday, but otherwise it's open from 9 A.M. to 2 A.M., perfect for a late-night snack if you're flush. Métro: Madeleine.

THE MEDIUM-PRICED RANGE: La Fermette Marbeuf 1900, 5 rue Marbeuf,
8e (tel. 47-20-63-53), has a turn-of-the-century decor, reasonable prices, a fine cuisine, and a setting a short distance from the Champs-Élysées. The hand-painted tiles and stained-glass windows of the twin dining rooms contributed to the establishment's listing as a national historic monument. Guests come here for the fun of it all, as well as for the well-prepared and flavorful cuisine. Specialties include sweetbreads in puff pastry, a basil-flavored filet of sole with fresh noodles, a bavarois of salmon, a ragoût of wild mushrooms, and several beef dishes. A fixed-price menu costs a reasonable 140F ($19.31), while à la carte meals average 270F ($37.23). Reservations are a good idea, and the establishment is open every day of the year. Métro: F.-D.-Roosevelt.

L'Espace, 1 Avenue Gabriel, 8e (tel. 42-66-11-70). What's probably the most lavish buffet in Paris is served daily in a picnic-style decor of plastic chairs, oilcloth coverings, and decorative parasols—a setting you might find at a California beachside restaurant. In reality, however, nothing could be more French and more central to the hordes of lunchtime diners flocking here from offices in this prestigious neighborhood. It lies midway between the American Embassy and the Champs-Élysées, whose adjacent gardens are exposed to the views of clients who sometimes prefer to dine on an outdoor terrace. The luminary who established this consciously informal trend-setter is Pierre Cardin, whose other more formal culinary endeavors have been well documented thanks to his acquisition of Maxim's. For 165F ($22.76), you'll have access to a buffet of more than 70 hors d'oeuvres, a groaning table rich with salads, vegetables, cold roast meats, and the kind of antipasti you'd expect to find in Italy. The main course is served by a waiter who brings you a choice of a plat du jour. This is followed by a selection from the dessert buffet. Service and drinks are extra (champagne is sold by the glass). The establishment is open till 1 a.m., serving meals daily except Saturday at lunch. Métro: Champs-Élysées.

Moulin du Village, 25 rue Royale in the Cité Berryer, 8e (tel. 42-65-08-47), might be an ideal choice if you're strolling along the rue Royale toward the Madeleine district at lunch or dinnertime, and you can't afford Maxim's. Although not on the rue Royale with Maxim's, the "Moulin" is just around the corner, in a little alleyway that is the scene of a typical street market on Tuesday and Friday.

Owner Steven Spurrier has created a charming little place, with a few outside tables, serving original, creative, and well-prepared food at reasonable prices. Next door is the Blue Fox Wine Bar, named after a 19th-century furrier who used to occupy the premises. The well-selected wine list at the Moulin is entirely supplied by Steven Spurrier's renowned Caves de la Madeleine, also in the Cité Berryer.

Within the Moulin, in an elegant setting of immaculate napery and attentive waiters, you can enjoy à la carte meals for 230F ($31.72) each. Among the specialties are a salad of duck's breast, scrambled eggs with truffles, filet of salmon with chives, and duckling with cherries, peaches, or pears. You must always reserve a table in the Moulin section, but the Blue Fox is less formal. Both restaurants are closed on Saturday night, all day Sunday, and holidays. Métro: Concorde or Madeleine.

Au Vieux Berlin, 32 Avenue George-V, 8e (tel. 42-08-88-96). Good German cooking—with a French accent—is what you get in "Old Berlin." The setting is stylish, and so is the address, across from the George V hotel. The front windows with their changing display suggest the high fashion level of the interior. You dine in armchairs set against a modish background. The visiting celebrities prefer the dining room in the rear on a lower level.

Paris has precious few German restaurants, a fact which makes the outstanding specialties here that much more appealing. You are served such classic à la carte dishes as wienerschnitzel, followed by a typical apfelstrudel. Another interesting specialty the chef does well is filet de porc cooked in beer. Expect to spend from 250F ($34.48) for a meal. Closed Saturday and Sunday. Métro: George-V.

Chez Edgard, 4 rue Marbeuf, 8e (tel. 47-20-51-15). A chic coterie of neighborhood residents regard this belle époque eating place as their favorite *restaurant du quartier,* and owner Paul Benmussa makes it a point to welcome them during their frequent visits as if they were members of his extended family. This is one of the consistently best restaurants in the fashionable 8th Arrondissement. The customers are often French politicians and journalists. The decor is red and black, the kind you'd have expected in the private apartments of one of Paris's turn-of-the-century courtesans. All of it seems to stimulate both conversation (it can be noisier here than in less expensive environments) and appetites.

Specialties include breast of duckling, rouget with basil in puff pastry, and several terrines, including one made from scallops. There is also a range of well-prepared meat and fish dishes. The service is attentive and sensitive, and the ice cream sundaes (they're listed with other desserts on a special menu) are particularly delectable. There's a small outdoor terrace, although most of the guests prefer to eat inside on one of the semiprivate banquettes. The restaurant charges around 225F ($31.03) per person, wine not included. It is closed on Sunday. Métro: F.-D.-Roosevelt.

Mignonnette du Caviar, 13 rue du Colisée, 8e (tel. 42-25-30-35), serves more than just caviar, although it offers two different kinds of that. But since most people can't afford it, you can order instead a very good-tasting borscht or a plate of herring. A popular main-dish specialty is the chef's beef Stroganoff, and there are blinis with cream. Ever had a fruit salad with vodka? A simple meal is offered for only 55F ($7.56) at lunchtime, but count on spending from 175F ($24.13) if you order dinner à la carte. The restaurant occupies a small storefront behind a fire-engine-red façade. Métro: F.-D.-Roosevelt.

Chez Tante Louise, 41 rue Boissy-d'Anglais, 8e (tel. 42-65-06-85), is an intimate little place with a tiny mezzanine, just off the Madeleine and the Place de la Concorde. An oil painting on the wall and a bronze plaque on the brown marble façade pay homage to the restaurant's originator, "Aunt Louise," who reigned from the mid-1920s to the mid-1950s. Today, Monsieur and Madame Christian Fiorito carry on in Tante Louise's worthy tradition. They've inherited her secrets, and the menu reflects numerous specialties from Landes, such as the confit d'oie (slices of goose meat kept in a goose fat), served with sautéed potatoes. Other featured dishes include turbotin au champagne, magret de canard (duck), and filet of sole with fresh noodles, as well as escargots with foie gras. A good dessert is the chocolate profiteroles with "3 perfumes" or the Black Forest chocolate cake. Expect to pay around 200F ($27.58) to 325F ($44.82) per person, including wine. Closed on Sunday and in August. Métro: Madeleine.

Androuët, 41 rue d'Amsterdam, 8e (tel. 48-74-26-93), is one of the most unusual restaurants in the world, if only because cheese is the basic ingredient in most of the dishes. It all began in World War I when the founder, Monsieur Androuët, started inviting favored guests down to his cellar to sample cheese and good wine. The idea caught on, and at one time it was considered one of the most fashionable things to do in Paris. Nowadays, Androuet isn't merely chic: it's an institution.

Cheese experts, of course, flock here; I heard one claim that he could tell what the goat ate by the cheese made from its milk. If you're not an expert but would like to be, order *la dégustation unique de tous les fromages.* One man at one sitting allegedly sampled 120 varieties before being carried out. Some items you're familiar with: certainly the Welsh rarebit and the quiche Lorraine. Main-dish specialties include the côte de veau (veal) savoyarde and the rognons de veau Beauge. A set meal costs from 165F ($22.75), but you are likely to spend from 275F ($37.92) if you order à la carte. It's closed Sunday, and it is best to reserve for lunch and dinner. Métro: St-Lazare.

Chez André, 12 rue Marbeuf, 8e (tel. 47-20-59-57). What you see from the street is an intriguingly discreet red awning stretching over an array of shellfish on ice. On the corner of the rue Clement-Marot, this is one of the most charming bistros in the neighborhood, with an art nouveau decor that includes etched glass and masses of flowers. The clients are likely to include a visiting South American businessman, a Japanese fashion designer, or the innermost upper crust of this very expensive neighborhood.

The interior is a medium-size labyrinth of nooks and cubbyholes, where you'll probably be seated elbow to elbow with someone whose picture you've seen in a magazine. The old-fashioned menu is hand-scrawled in purple ink and includes a very French collection of items such as pâté of thrush, roquefort in puff pastry, several kinds of omelets, calf's head vinaigrette, a potage du jour, and an array of fresh shellfish, along with several reasonably priced wines. Desserts might be rum babas, chocolate cake, or a daily pastry. Full meals range from 170F ($23.44) to 200F ($27.58). It is open every day except Tuesday from noon to 3 p.m. and 7 to 11:30 p.m. Métro: F.-D.-Roosevelt.

THE BUDGET RANGE: Fauchon, 26 Place de la Madeleine, 8e (tel. 47-42-60-11). For epicures, this store has always been the "haut grocery of Paris." In fact, it's such a symbol of the Establishment that French Maoists once launched what the press called "a daring caviar and foie gras heist in broad daylight" at this exclusive store, the Fortnum & Mason of Paris.

What many people don't know about Fauchon is that it offers a reasonably priced cafeteria-style lunch. First, tell the waitress at the counter what you are going to order (apply to one of the two interpreters if you don't speak French), pay at the cashier's desk, and receive a ticket that you give to the clerk behind the counter. You may order a Fauchon's club sandwich and a coupe of ice cream. A simple meal can be composed for 150F ($20.69). Only hitch is that you stand at a counter while you eat. In the afternoon, Fauchon's cakes and pastries make tea a delight. Métro: Madeleine.

La Boutique à Sandwiches, 12 rue du Colisée, 8e (tel. 43-59-56-69), is a well-adjusted marriage of American and French tastes. Run by two Alsatian brothers, Hubert and Claude Schick, it's an inexpensive place at which to order absolutely delectable sandwiches in many unusual and imaginative varieties. A quarter of a block from the Champs-Élysées, it is upstairs, with bare wooden tables and colored mats—quite informal. There are at least two dozen different sandwich concoctions on the menu, as well as light snacks or "plate meals," some with distinctly Swiss and Alsatian overtones. Special hot plates include pickelfleisch (Alsatian corned beef). An unusual dish is la raclette valaisanne à gogo. A wheel of cheese—part of it melted—is taken to your table and scraped right onto your plate; accompanying it are pickles and boiled potatoes, the latter resting in a pot with a crocheted hat. A sweet conclusion to your meal might be the apple strudel. Sandwiches begin at 10F ($1.38) and go up, and there's also a set meal offered for 55F ($7.56). However, if you prefer to order the specialties of the house on the à la carte menu, expect to pay 85F ($11.72) to 125F ($17.24). It's closed Sunday and in August. Métro: Franklin-D.-Roosevelt.

Minim's, 76 Faubourg St-Honoré, 8e (tel. 42-66-10-09). Pierre Cardin created what he calls an "alimentary boutique" on this fashionable street near the Élysée Palace. It's really an ideal luncheon restaurant for rich suburbanites spending their day shopping, but it's also a good choice for midafternoon tea or a quick, well-prepared snack. The name, of course, is a tongue-in-cheek adaptation of "Lord Cardin's" acquisition, Maxim's, and like the decor of its big sister, the tea-house is filled with art nouveau lighting fixtures and stained glass.

You can eat alone at a beautifully wood-grained bar, or on small tables near a collection of turn-of-the-century silver maidens that I was told came from the collection of Cardin himself. It's totally appropriate here to order a plat du jour. These change daily but might include osso buco milanese or rabbit with a sauce made with two different mustards. You can also order sandwiches, as well as six kinds of coffee, wine by the glass, or tea with pastries. Set meals cost from 100F ($13.79). Minim's is open daily except Sunday from 10 a.m. to 6:30 p.m. A deluxe delicatessen fills an adjoining room, while an arts boutique is one floor above ground level. Métro: Concorde.

L'Assiette au Boeuf, 123 Champs-Élysées, 8e (tel. 47-20-01-13), offers one of the best food bargains in Paris. You can dine well on an inexpensive cuisine in a glamorous setting. You get real French food in reproduction belle époque settings. The menus are fixed, and no reservations are accepted. The Champs-Élysées entry has a sidewalk "box," offering dramatic views of the Arc de Triomphe, which is especially stunning at night. Much of the food is called "cuisine du marché" which means it is based on the freshest of produce available at the market on any given day. You might be offered a brochette of fish or else a tender slice of beef (served rare if you wish), with a sauce on the side, along with a mound of slender pommes frites. Menus cost 45F ($6.21) and 55F ($7.56). Desserts are extra, and you get a wide choice, including sorbets. There are four sizes of wine presented, beginning with a small carafe. If you become an Assiette au Boeuf aficionado, you'll find sister restaurants of this chain scattered at strategic locations throughout Paris. For the Champs-Élysées version, take the Métro to George-V.

4. 5th and 6th Arrondissements

These two quarters are the most popular from the tourist point of view and the most densely populated districts on the Left Bank. The largest quantity of restaurants (but not necessarily those of the highest quality) are centered in the teeming Latin Quarter. This area embraces parts of Montparnasse, the Quai des Grands Augustins, the Quai de la Tournelle, the Panthéon, St-Michel, the Sorbonne, St-Germain-des-Prés, and Odéon.

THE UPPER BRACKET: Jacques Cagna, 14 rue des Grands-Augustins, 6e (tel. 43-26-49-39). Both the clientele and the victuals are considered among the most sophisticated and/or grandest in Paris. The establishment is contained within a 17th-century town house whose interior is filled with massive timbers and a delectable color scheme of pinkish beige. A specialty is the Aberdeen-Angus beef, aged for a full three weeks, which chef Cagna imbues with a shallot-flavored sauce rich with herbs and seasonings. You might begin with a double-edged salad of Brittany lobster mixed with duck liver and artichoke bottoms, or else a feuilleté of crayfish with mussels in a sherry-flavored morel sauce. Other specialties include tender sweetbreads braised in essence of giant shrimp, a pungent leg of baby lamb with tarragon, or perhaps Brittany pigeon with honey and Sauterne. Desserts are overwhelmingly tempting. Two attractive fixed-price menus with a surprisingly varied choice of dishes are offered at lunch for 225F ($31.03) and 410F ($56.54). A la carte meals, costing between 400F ($55.16) and 460F ($63.43), are served daily except Sunday and in August. Métro: St. Michel.

Dodin Bouffant, 25 rue Frédéric-Sauton, 5e (tel. 43-25-25-14), was once a former rehabilitation center on the Place Maubert, which was acquired by the well-known French chef, Jacques Manière, who named it flippantly after the fictional character in 19th-century French gastronomic lore. There, in a transformed modern setting, a temple was dedicated to nouvelle cuisine. Manière is long gone, but Madame Dany Cartier, who trained under Manière, is the empress of this exceptional restaurant today. It has one of the finest cuisines in Paris, and is attractively priced for what it offers.

Try one of the shellfish dishes, which come from saltwater fish tanks. They are superb, especially the savory mussel soup. Main dishes reflect an imaginative, personalized touch—canard (duck) poêle au bitter, ris de veau (sweetbreads) à ma façon, calf head with rosemary, and filets de sole courtine. The desserts are elaborate preparations, as exemplified by the soufflé glacé à l'orange or the simpler but still superb tart made with the fresh fruits of the season. Expect to pay 275F ($37.92) to 350F ($48.27) for a complete meal, and always call in advance for a reservation. The restaurant is closed on weekends and in August. Métro: Maubert-Mutualité.

Closerie des Lilas ("Pleasure Garden of the Lilacs"), 171 Boulevard Montparnasse, 6e (tel. 43-26-70-50). Hemingway first knew when he wrote of meeting with Ford Maddox Ford at this early-19th-century café: "I have always avoided looking at Ford when I could and I always held my breath when I was near him in a closed room. . . ." The number of legendary people who have sat in the Closerie, watching the falling leaves blow along the streets of Montparnasse, is almost endless: Gertrude Stein, Ingres, Henry James, Chateaubriand, Apollinaire, Lenin and Trotsky at the chess board, Proust, André Gide, Sartre, Simone de Beauvoir, Verlaine, Braque, Valéry, and James Abbot McNeill Whistler, who would sit here expounding the "gentle art" of making enemies. We come here for the memories and the food.

To get a seat in what they call the "bateau" section of the restaurant, following in the footsteps of the prewar celebrities, is hard. However, you may enjoy waiting for a seat at the bar and ordering the best champagne julep in the world, prepared by Claude the barman. In the "bateau," you can order such rustic dishes as poached haddock or beef with a salad, even steak tartare. In the chic restaurant inside the Closerie, the cooking remains more classic. Try the escargots façon Closerie for openers. Of the main-course selections, highly recommended are the rognons de veau à la moutarde (veal kidneys with mustard) and ribs of veal in a cider sauce. Expect to pay around 200F ($27.58) per person in the "bateau," about 350F ($48.27) in the restaurant. The Closerie is open daily all year. Métro: Port-Royal or Vavin.

THE MEDIUM-PRICED RANGE: André Allard, 41 rue St-André-des-Arts, 6e (tel. 43-26-48-23). The street outside was the setting for George du Maurier's *Trilby,* but inside it is simply an unpretentious Left Bank bistro. In a down-to-earth atmosphere of sawdust-littered floors and old-fashioned marble-topped tables, the Bouchard family welcomes you—and BB, and Delon, and Gabin, etc. The bistro was opened in 1930. The building (or more especially the cellar) is from the days of Louis XIII and his domineering mother, Marie de Medici. The family makes yearly trips to Burgundy to select their own wine, and they bottle it themselves. Two rooms are found here, the front one with a zinc bar and low ceilings. In either you may order the house specialty, duckling with olives for two. Also good is the filet of turbot, prepared in smooth white butter (beurre blanc). To commence your meal try the terrine de canard (duckling), and to end it, perhaps a tart made with fresh strawberries. In the off-season, you get an apple. For a complete meal, your tab is likely to run from 275F ($37.92) to 325F ($44.82) per person. Closed Saturday and Sunday and in August. Reservations are always necessary. Métro: St-Michel.

L'Ambroisie, 65 Quai de la Tournelle, 5e (tel. 46-33-18-65), is a Left Bank choice with only nine tables (reservations are imperative) on the ground floor of a 17th-century mansion. Somberly decorated in shades of burgundy and gray, the restaurant offers a severely limited menu because of the smallness of the kitchen. But as Spencer Tracy once remarked about Katharine Hepburn, what there is is choice.

One of the most talented young chefs in Paris today, Bernard Pacaud, has attracted world attention. He's come a long way since he was an orphan who, at 14, had to wash dishes. He trained at the prestigious Vivarois before deciding to strike out on his own. It was a wise choice. His few tables are nearly always filled with satisfied diners who visit to see where his imagination will take him next. His fresh pasta is inspired, as is his veal sweetbreads with parsley and shallots. You might begin with his heavenly red pepper mousse served with a fresh tomato coulis. He also does a panache of fish flavored with saffron. For dessert, his chocolate cake is no ordinary chocolate cake. Try it. A menu served only at lunch is available for 220F ($30.34). If you order à la carte, expect to spend from 350F ($48.27). The restaurant is closed the last three weeks of August and for two weeks in February. Métro: Maubert-Mutualité.

Dominique, 19 rue Bréa, 6e (tel. 43-27-08-80). Shades of imperial Russia in Montparnasse. But don't be carried away by the turn-of-the-century St. Petersburg aura in the upstairs room; you might order a "tin" of Sevruga Iranian caviar before you know it. You'll still see some of the lost colony of Russian aristocracy here—or, more accurately, their offspring—as they know they'll get some of the best Russian food in the city.

All the familiar dishes are offered: borscht, blinis with cream, and a Russian salad. For a main course I recommend côtelette de volaille (poultry) Dominique, and for dessert, the house specialty, kasha gourieff flambé. Meals begin at 275F ($37.92), going up. Of course, no Russian repast is complete without vodka (try a glass of Zubrovka, imported from Poland and made with a special herb). If you have too much vodka, Gary, the manager, will send you back in an ambulance! But do stay awake to hear the gypsy music. Downstairs, where there is a counter and prices are slightly cheaper, delicacies are sold to take out. The place is open daily; try to get there before 10 p.m. Closed in July. Métro: Vavin.

THE BUDGET RANGE: Le Procope, 13 rue l'Ancienne-Comédie, 6e (tel. 43-26-99-20), is the oldest café in Paris. Originally created back in 1686 by a Sicilian, Francesco Procopio dei Coltelli, who is said to have popularized the art of drinking coffee among Parisians, the café is now a restaurant, lush with gilt-framed old mirrors, time-aged portraits of former guests, crystal chandeliers, red-leather banquettes, and strawberry-pink tablecloths.

Few restaurants can name-drop with such aplomb as Le Procope: La Fontaine, Voltaire, Benjamin Franklin, Rousseau, Anatole France, Robespierre,

Danton, Marat, Desmoulins, even the young Bonaparte. Balzac drank one cup of coffee after another here, Victor Hugo taking it a little easier, Verlaine preferring absinthe. Many of today's guests prefer the spacious second-floor restaurant, with its provincial furnishings and drinking lounge, although the ground floor (in the words of one habitué) has more immediacy. A 110F ($15.17) fixed-price dinner includes a main course and dessert, although an à la carte repast costs 160F ($22.06) to 180F ($24.82). It's open daily but closed in July. Métro: Odéon.

La Cabane d'Auvergne, 44 rue Grégoire-de-Tours, 6e (tel. 43-25-14-75). This self-proclaimed "rabbit hutch" is like a rustic tavern from the Auvergne, an ancient province of France (now divided into départements), which was known as a fertile land of copious and rich cookery. This tiny restaurant on an obscure Left Bank street keeps alive the tradition. Under beamed ceilings, you are served typical regional meals on bare plank tables with provincial stools. The stone and wood-paneled walls are decorated with rustic artifacts. It often gets very crowded, so show up early if you want a seat. The owner, Gilbert Guibert, is the hearty patron of the place, and he keeps the breezy chitchat going. The kitchen specializes in terrines. One is made from marcassin (young boar), another from fricandeau (larded veal loin), yet another from caneton (duckling). Main courses are generous and well cooked. You'll find it an effort to order dessert. You can enjoy a complete meal for as little as 130F ($17.93), but you can also easily find yourself spending 180F ($24.82). Closed Sunday and at lunchtime Monday. Métro: Odéon.

Bistro de la Gare, 59 Boulevard du Montparnasse, 6e (tel. 45-48-38-01). In addition to offering low-cost, well-prepared meals, this unusual establishment has an art nouveau decor that is classified as a national treasure by the government. It's often photographed by visiting busloads of Asian tourists. Its hand-painted tiles were installed in 1903 across a busy boulevard from the Montparnasse railway station. Today, the crowds who elbow into this place wait for an empty table at the standup bar where a friendly employee offers a free glass of kir to anyone obliged to wait for more than a few minutes. The most popular item is a two-course fixed-price menu, going for 45F ($6.21) to 60F ($8.27), depending on which of the several choices you select. Menu items are straightforward but flavorful, including several kinds of grilled steak, duck, and terrines. A wide assortment of desserts is offered, as well as house wine sold in carafes. The establishment doesn't accept reservations, and meals are served at both lunch and dinner seven days a week. Métro: Montparnasse-Bienvenue. You'll see other members of this popular chain at strategic locations throughout Paris.

La Cafetière, 21 rue Mazarine, 6e (tel. 46-33-76-90), in the heart of the Odéon district, is a tiny neighborhood bistro that serves good cookery at reasonable prices. Because of the limited space, it is imperative that you reserve a table. Dining is on two levels, and the restaurant serves both lunches and dinners daily, including Sunday when many other bistros nearby are closed. A coffee-pot theme forms the decor, and service is polite and friendly. The wine selection is limited but good and the dish of the day is always praise-worthy. Among the à la carte selections, you might begin with an endive salad or a salad of lentils with freshly chopped shallots. A terrine de canard (duck) is also good. Among the recommendable main courses are a côte de veau au citron and a peppersteak flambé, even a steak tartare. To finish, you might prefer a plate of French cheese or a fresh fruit tart. The chocolate mousse is generously served from a large bowl. Ordering à la carte is likely to run your bill up to 180F ($24.82). Métro: Odéon.

Au Cochon de Lait, 7 rue Corneille, 6e (tel. 43-26-03-65), feeds you heartily, elegantly, and well, giving you a selection of classic French dishes. The house specialty is cochon de lait (roast suckling pig with sauce). I enthusiastically endorse the crotin de chavignol chaud sur un lit de frisée (hot goat cheese with salad) and escargots de Bourgogne. The least expensive way to dine here is to order the set dinner at 95F ($13.10), including an appetizer, main course, dessert, or cheese. Your drink is extra. Red curtains and stained glass make the "Suckling Pig" all the more appetizing. It's open from noon to 3 p.m. and from 7 to 11 p.m. Métro: Odéon.

Aux Charpentiers, 10 rue Mabillon, 6e (tel. 43-26-30-05). Once it was the rendezvous of the master carpenters, whose guild was next door. Nowadays it's where the young men of St-Germain-des-Prés take their dates for inexpensive meals in a pleasant atmosphere. Presided over by motherly Frenchwomen, Aux Charpentiers keeps alive the fast-disappearing tradition of the neighborhood family dining room—it's like Paris of 30 years ago.

The restaurant takes up two floors; the street level is more animated, the lower level quieter, better for conversation. Although not especially imaginative, the food is well cooked in the best tradition of the Left Bank bistro. Appetizing appetizers include regal d'Auvergne. Especially recommendable as a main course is the roast duck with olives. Each day of the week a different plat du jour is offered, with traditional French home-cooking: petit salé aux lentilles, pot au feu, boeuf à la mode are among the main dishes on the menu. Desserts always include a homemade fruit tart. A service charge is added to all tabs. There is a large choice of Bordeaux wines direct from the château. For example, you may have Château Gaussens. If you order à la carte, count on spending 120F ($16.55) to 180F ($24.82). Closed Sunday. Métro: Mabillon.

Crémerie-Restaurant Polidor, 41 rue Monsieur-le-Prince, 6e (tel. 43-26-95-34), is the most characteristic bistro in the Odéon area, serving the cuisine familiale. You might call it a *vieille maison très sympathique.* It still uses the word *crémerie* in its title, an appellation dating back to the early part of this century when it specialized in frosted cream desserts. In time it became one of the Left Bank's oldest and most established literary bistros. In fact, it was André Gide's favorite. But many famous people have dined here, including Hemingway, Paul Valéry, Artaud, Charles Boyer, even Jack Kerouac.

The atmosphere is one of lace curtains, polished brass hat racks, and drawers in the back where repeat customers lock up their cloth napkins. Frequented in large part by students and artists, who always seem to head for the rear, the present restaurant was founded in 1930 and it's been little changed since then. The art deco ceiling fixtures are still there, and pottery pitchers of water are placed on the tables, which are most often shared.

Overworked but smiling waitresses serve such dishes as pumpkin soup, snails from Burgundy, rib of beef with onions, rabbit with mustard sauce, and veal in white sauce, followed by such desserts as a raspberry or lemon tart. The menu changes every day, a typical meal costing from 100F ($13.79). No reservations are accepted, and the restaurant is closed on Sunday and Monday and in August. Métro: Odéon.

Astoin Rive Gauche, 19 rue du Regard, 6e (tel. 45-48-87-67). A coterie of visiting American professors swear that this offers one of the best low-priced meals in the district. The establishment's owner gravitated toward high-quality cuisine after purging his wanderlust in every place from Vancouver to Texas. Today, Pierre Astoin, along with his partner-chef, Jean-Marc Giorgi, offers a 100F ($13.79) fixed-price menu worth a special detour. À la carte meals cost slightly more: from 125F ($17.24). Within the mirrored and vaguely art deco locale, meals are served on tables topped with polished slabs of pink granite whose surfaces shimmer from lights clustered along the high ceilings. The frequently changing menu includes such well-prepared dishes as smoked and marinated haddock, a feuilleté of snails with wild mushrooms, a Landais salad studded with foie gras, a fresh fish of the day, filet of sole with cheese and leeks, and a succulently grilled version of contre-filet of beef with rosemary butter.

The dessert specialty is a temptingly caloric marquis of chocolate with a champagne sauce. Reservations are suggested, and meals are served daily except Sunday. Métro: St. Placide.

5. 3rd and 4th Arrondissements

Now we head toward the Bastille, the Île de Cité, the Place des Vosges, the Île Saint-Louis—good sightseeing, good dining. (I don't mean to confuse you, but two of my recommendations, on the triangular Place Dauphine on the Île de la Cité, are technically within the 1st Arrondissement.)

THE UPPER BRACKET: Marc Annibal de Coconnas, 2 bis Place des Vosges, 4e (entrance on the rue de Birague; tel. 42-78-58-16). The restaurant, in the Louis XIII style, could have been called the Bistrot de Henri II (who lost his life on the Place des Vosges). It could have been called the Victor Hugo restaurant (the novelist lived in an apartment, now a museum, on this square of the grand siècle). Instead it's called Marc Annibal de Coconnas, honoring some esoteric figure of the 17th century. But what's in a name? Concentrate instead on the superb cuisine, courtesy of Claude Terrail, who also owns La Tour d'Argent.

A complete fixed-price meal, including drink and service, is 200F ($27.58) and might include a tartare of salmon with lemon juice, then duck, followed by a sorbet to finish—a good bargain. It costs from 300F ($41.37) to dine à la carte. I recommend that you phone for a table, as the place gets quite crowded. Closed Monday and Tuesday. Métro: Bastille or St-Paul.

THE MEDIUM-PRICED RANGE: La Colombe, 4 rue de la Colombe, 4e (tel. 46-33-37-08), is on the Île de la Cité. The rue de la Colombe, one of the smallest in old Paris, runs into the Quai aux Fleurs behind Notre-Dame. The house of La Colombe (the dove), dating from 1275, is an idyllic setting for a meal. Ludwig Bemelmans painted the walls of one of the dining rooms. At this old inn in the heart of one of the most beautiful districts of Paris, Renata, mistress of the house, will welcome you and look after your comfort. Robert, the maître d' for ten years, will be happy to help you choose a good wine. The chef, who has presided over the Colombe kitchen for 17 years, creates such delicacies as Norway lobster au gratin on a froth of sorrel, snails in a flaky pastry, tournedos served on fried bread with a Périgueux sauce, and young duck with peaches. Among the desserts, try the Bavarian tart made with red fruits and served with cream. A copious gastronomical menu is served for 200F ($27.58), the price including taxes. The restaurant is closed all day Sunday and Monday for lunch. Hours are noon to 2:30 p.m. and 7 p.m. to midnight. Métro: Cité or Hôtel-de-Ville.

L'Ambassade d'Auvergne, 22 rue de Grenier St-Lazare, 3e (tel. 42-72-31-22). In an obscure district of Paris, this rustic tavern not only oozes with charm but dispenses the hearty cuisine bourgeoise of Auvergne, the heartland of France. You enter through a busy bar, with heavy oak beams, hanging hams, and ceramic plates. At the entrance is a display of the chef's specialties: jellied meats and fowls, pâté cakes, plus an assortment of regional cheese and fresh fruit of the season. Rough wheat bread is stacked in baskets, rush-seated ladderback chairs are placed at tables covered with bright cloths. Stem glassware, mills to grind your own salt and pepper, a jug of mustard bedeck each table.

The chef has introduced among the more classical dishes some nouvelle cuisine plates, including a cassoulet with lentils, a pot-au-feu, confit de canard, and codfish casserole and stuffed cabbage. Some of these specials are featured only on one day of the week. As a side dish, I recommend aligot, a medley of fresh potatoes, garlic, and Cantal cheese. A complete meal with regional wine will cost from 200F ($27.58) per person. The tavern, open for both lunch and dinner, is closed Sunday. Métro: Rambuteau.

Bofinger, 5 rue de la Bastille, 4e (tel. 42-72-87-82), is the oldest Alsatian brasserie in Paris, tracing its origins back to 1864. It successfully retains the palace style of that era: lots of leaded glass, creamy macramé curtains, lampshades shaped like tulips, antique mirrors, mahogany pieces, dark-gray benches, a revolving main door, and a central dome of stained glass. Much restored, it now looks better than ever. At night many members of the Parisian slumming chic venture into the Bastille district for beer and sauerkraut at Bofinger.

The brasserie is run by Monsieur and Madame Urtizvéréa, who offer not only excellent Alsatian fare but hearty portions and friendly service by waiters in floor-length white aprons. The chef prepares a different main dish every day of the week; on a recent Wednesday a savory stew in casserole (le cassoulet Toulousain) was offered. But, slumming or not, most guests order the choucroute formidable (sauerkraut) complete with sausages, smoked bacon, and pork chops. Dessert? Frankly, I've never had room for it at Bofinger, although the apple tart always looks good, as do the fresh berries of spring. For a supper here, expect to pay from 180F ($24.82) per person. It's open all year. Métro: Bastille.

THE BUDGET RANGE: Au Gourmet de l'Isle, 42 rue St-Louis-en-l'Île, 4e (tel. 43-26-79-27). A good restaurant is hard to find on the Île St-Louis; many just look good. So does this one—the flickering candlelight at its tables, heavy dark beams overhead—but it also serves a fine meal.

A sign "A.A.A.A.A." is posted outside. That signifies that the restaurant is a meeting ground for a society of gastronomes, the friendly association of amateur devotees of the authentic andouillette. Andouillettes, chitterling sausages grilled on a low fire, are to the French what a clam chowder is to a Cape Cod resident, chili con carne to a Texan, and a Nathan's hot dog to a New Yorker. Accompanied by mashed potatoes, they're hearty fare. Another well-recommended dish is la charbonnée de l'Île, a savory pork dish. Personally, I visit the "isle" just to taste Mme Bourdeau's stuffed mussels in shallot butter. Your palate will fare as well as your wallet if you order the 100F ($13.79) fixed-price menu. Count on spending from 140F ($19.31) for dinner if you order à la carte. Closed Monday, Thursday, and in August. Métro: Pont-Marie.

La Taverne du Sergent Recruteur, 41 rue St-Louis-en-l'Île, 4e (tel. 43-54-75-42). Take a hitherto insatiable appetite to this 17th-century setting on the principal street of the Île St-Louis. For 160F ($22.06) plus service, you'll get enough to eat to last you through the next day. Note the Romanesque arches above on your way to the tables in the rear. The dining room is beamed and narrow, with leaded-glass windows, placemats that are reproductions of old French engravings, and ladderback country chairs. Pronged iron racks suspended from the ceiling hold everything from round loaves of crusty bread to pigtails of garlic, a horse collar, and oil lamps.

But back to the meal. First, the makings of a salad are placed before you: carrots, radishes (red and black), fennel, celery, cucumbers, green peppers, and hard-boiled eggs. Next comes a huge basket of sausages—you slice off as much as you wish. A bottomless carafe of wine (rosé, red, or white) is set on your table, along with a crock of homemade pâté. Then the waiter asks you for your selection of a main dish—steak, chicken, veal, whatever. A big cheese board follows, but that's not the end of it; you can select chocolate mousse or ice cream for dessert. The restaurant is open from 7:30 p.m. to 2 a.m. Métro: Pont-Marie.

A GASTRONOMIC TOUR: One street in the 4th Arrondissement is a virtual neighborhood gastronomic tour, the **rue des Rosiers** (Métro: St-Paul). Before the war the Marais sector was filled with many fine Jewish restaurants. In the Middle Ages this was the ghetto. The street still retains the air of a little village town. However, the neighborhood has changed considerably with the arrival of many North African Jews, specifically from Tunisia, Morocco, and Algeria.

John Russell once wrote, "The rue des Rosiers is the last sanctuary of certain ways of life; what you see there, in miniature, is Warsaw before the ghetto was razed . . . Samarkand before the Soviet authorities brought it into line."

If you're in the market for pastrami, corned beef, dill pickles, schmaltz, herring, chopped chicken livers, and matzoh balls, then go here. It's best viewed on Sunday morning when much of Paris is asleep. Actually, you don't have to enter a restaurant. You can wander up and down, eating as you go. Perhaps an apple strudel will tempt you, certainly a pastrami on Jewish rye bread, or smoked salmon, pickled lemons, perhaps the smoked sausages of Algeria known as *merguez*. Of course, a thick chunk of Jewish cheesecake is always a temptation.

On this "Street of the Rose Bushes" the best-known restaurant is **Jo Goldenberg,** 4 rue des Rosiers, 4e (tel. 48-87-20-16). The doyen of Jewish restaurateurs in Paris, Albert Goldenberg, has moved to another restaurant, in chicer surroundings, at 69 Avenue de Wagram, 17e (see below). But his brother Joseph has remained at the original establishment. The original Goldenberg delicatessen was opened in Montmartre in 1936. (The brothers Goldenberg were born in Constantinople. Their father was Russian.) On the rue des Rosiers, the carpe farcie (stuffed carp) is a preferred selection, although you may choose the beef goulash. I also like the eggplant moussaka. The pastrami is one of the most popular items. The menu also offers Israeli wines at 50F ($6.90), but Mr. Goldenberg admits they are not as good as French wines. A complete meal here begins at 150F ($20.69). Dining here is on two levels. Look for the collection of samovars and the white fantail pigeon in a wicker cage. Interesting paintings and strolling musicians add to the ambience.

6. 7th Arrondissement

The 7th Arrondissement includes such attractions as the Eiffel Tower, the Military School, the Invalides, and the Boulevard St-Germain—plus some especially good restaurants.

THE UPPER BRACKET: Le Divellec Cuisine de la Mer, 107 rue de l'Université, 7e (tel. 45-51-91-96), is one of the great seafood restaurants in all of France. In a long and narrow modern room whose walls are painted in shades of dark blue, gray, and white, you can select some of the most unusual combinations of seafood which nouvelle cuisine has ever produced. Brittany-born Jacques Divellec is the guiding force behind the place, and the ambience evokes the aura of a captain's table on a private yacht. Many of the most sophisticated diners of Paris consider the best dishes here the simplest ones. Of course, the ingredients are amazingly fresh. The more experimental try, as for example, the filet of stingray with truffles, a terrine of foie gras studded with crayfish, a gratin of codfish, a mousseline of shellfish with filet of John-Dory, and turbot with noodles tinted with squid ink. Most diners prefer to begin with a half-dozen oysters. Two fixed-price meals cost from 200F ($27.58) to 300F ($41.37), with à la carte dinners ranging from 400F ($55.16) to 500F ($68.95). The restaurant is open daily except Sunday, Monday, and during most of August. Métro: Invalides.

Le Jules Verne, Tour Eiffel, Champs-de-Mars, 7e (tel. 45-55-61-44). Today the institution of drinking and dining within the framework of the symbol of Paris is still alive and well. Many visitors view the elevator ride up to the second platform of the Eiffel Tower as one of the highlights of their experience. Once you have made the ride up, you are ushered into a decor as black as the Parisian night outside, with only strategically placed spotlights set on each of the minimalist tables. The end result seems to bring the twinkling Paris panorama into the restaurant itself.

All of this would be merely a fantasy for ex-aviators and the child in each of us if not for the exquisite food prepared by a culinary team headed by Louis

Grondard. The menu changes with the season, but might include a ravioli of sweetbreads with lobster sauce, scallops with sweet and sour sauce, duck liver with aged vinegar sauce, filet of turbot with seaweed and butter flavored with sea urchins, or else a cassolette of fresh hot oysters with cucumbers. Full meals are served only with an advance reservation, costing from 450F ($62.06). A fixed-price menu is served only at lunchtime for 210F ($28.96). The restaurant is open every day of the year, and features a high-tech metallic piano bar. Métro: Trocadéro, École-Militaire, or Bir-Hakeim.

Chez les Anges, 54 Boulevard de Latour-Maubourg, 7e (tel. 47-05-89-86). The encyclopedia *Larousse Gastronomique* reported that "Burgundy is undoubtedly the region of France where the best foods and the best wines are to be had." Well, whether or not that's true, the "House of Angels" does serve some of the finest Burgundian meals in Paris. On the Left Bank, almost opposite the Invalides, Les Anges is worth the trek. It is directed by François Benoist. The ambience is that of a bistro, and although there's a praiseworthy collection of contemporary paintings, the emphasis is placed where it should be: on the food. Before dinner, try a refreshing apéritif, le badule, made with champagne spiked with fresh raspberry juice

As an appetizer, les oeufs en meurette (poached eggs in a red wine sauce) are recommended. Among the main dishes, the most reliable are the sauté de boeuf bourguignon and the entrecôte au vin de Rully. The most expensive specialty is la tranche épaisse de foie de veau (thickly sliced calf liver) cooked very rare, for two. Be sure to order a fluffy light gratin dauphinois, an excellent accompaniment to most dishes. For dessert, you may choose from what is certainly the widest assortment of goat cheese in a Parisian restaurant. Not in the mood? Perhaps a fresh strawberry sorbet with the esteemed Cassis liqueur (made with black currants) from Dijon will tempt you. The Burgundy wines in the cellar are above reproach. The average bill is likely to be between 200F ($27.58) and 325F ($44.82) per person. Reservations are necessary, especially at lunch when French business people will do you out of a seat. Closed Sunday night and Monday, and from August 15 to September 15. Near the Invalides, the nearest Métro stop is Latour-Maubourg.

THE MIDDLE BRACKET: Le Bistrot de Paris, 33 rue de Lille, 7e (tel. 42-61-16-83). What is that magic element that makes discriminating diners zero in on a little place? Whatever it is, Michel Oliver knows the secret. He is the son of Raymond Oliver, one of the great restaurateurs of France, who ruled supreme for such a long time at the prestigious Grand Véfour at the Palais Royal.

It seems a long-ago summer afternoon when I first strolled into this chic, sophisticated, and elegant bistro, and Monsieur Oliver (the Younger) served me a memorable sweetbreads flavored with orange that I've always remembered. He also presented me with a cookbook for children, *La Cuisine Est un Jeu d'Enfants,* which he'd written with an introduction by the late Jean Cocteau. His magnificent kiddie book even included a recipe for quiche Lorraine. The various specialties have changed over the years, but the cookery has consistently remained of high quality, backed up by an impressive wine list. Count on spending from 300F ($41.37). The restaurant is closed Sunday and from the end of July until the last week of August. Métro: Solferino.

Au Quai d'Orsay, 49 Quai d'Orsay, 7e (tel. 45-51-58-58). Go here for stuffed duck neck. Yes, stuffed duck neck. It's a superb specialty, rarely found. Served at the beginning of your meal, it is a concoction whereby the skin has been stuffed with a blend of pork and chopped duck, flavored with several seasonings including pistachios. The effect is somewhat like a crude pâté. Another heartily recommendable beginning is pleurotes de peupliers, wild mushrooms, meaty and firm, served in a cream sauce. Among the bourgeois dishes is calf's head ravigote. Known in the heyday of Les Halles, this dish is tender and tasty. Expect to pay around 280F ($38.61) to 320F ($44.13) per person with wine included. On the banks of Seine, the restaurant is crowded and popular, so reservations are important. You should call the day before. The dining rooms are old-fashioned. Friday is the busiest night, and the restaurant closes on Sunday and in August. Métro: Invalides.

THE BUDGET RANGE: L'Auberge Basque, 51 rue de Verneuil, 7e (tel. 45-48-51-98), offers excellently prepared food. The à la carte menu depends on what the day's shopping expedition turned up. Monsieur Rourre, the owner, comes from the Basque country near the Spanish border—hence his meals reflect the wonderful cooking of that district. Before he came to Paris, he opened a restaurant for artists in Cannes, where he began to collect paintings. Backed by the tremendous moral support he gathered on the Riviera, Rourre finally ventured to Paris.

In a tavern setting with a beamed ceiling, you're likely to receive, say, a pâté, veal in a cream sauce with noodles, a lettuce and endive salad, pipérade basque, rognon de veau à la crème, thon (tuna) basque style, homemade foie gras, and a magret de canard (duck) as well as a confit de canard, a selection of cheese, and such desserts as tarts and sorbets. The wines are simple, a full bottle of Cahors noteworthy. Expect to pay from 140F ($19.31) up for a complete meal. Guitarists play for you in the evenings. The restaurant is open all year, but never on Sunday. Métro: Bac.

La Petite Chaise, 36-38 rue de Grenelle, 7e (tel. 42-22-13-35), is one of the oldest restaurants in Paris, dating from 1680. Very Parisian, it invites you into its ambience of terracotta walls, cramped but attractive tables, wood paneling, and gilt ornate wall sconces. Its special feature is its set meal for 100F ($13.79), which is likely to include such specialties as chicken Pojarski (minced, breaded, and sautéed), noisettes of lamb with green beans, quenelles de brochet (made with pike), trout meunière, escalope de veau normand, and pavé steak with roquefort sauce. The cheese tray, especially the cantal and brie, is always respectable, and the desserts are good and rich. Because of the long-enduring fame of this restaurant, it is always necessary to call and book a table. It is open every day, including Sunday. Métro: Sèvres-Babylone.

7. 9th and 10th Arrondissements

These two arrondissements go from the elegance of the Opéra district to the honky-tonk of Pigalle and Clichy. Within these confines are some of the worst restaurants in Paris . . . plus some good ones outlined below.

THE UPPER BRACKET: Nicolas, 12 rue de la Fidélite, 10e (tel. 47-70-10-72), lies in an unfashionable part of Paris, a few steps from Gare de l'Est, yet its good cuisine and charm draw conservative diners from throughout Paris. It was founded in 1919 and decorated in a turn-of-the-century bistro style which it has never lost even through various changes of ownership. Today, chef Bernard Jouannin prepares a classic and exemplary cuisine which includes such bourgeois staples as grilled turbot with sauce choron, crayfish salad, filet of sole Nicolas, mussel soup with saffron, seafood salad with lemon, homemade foie gras, and creamy filet of herring. Full meals, costing from 300F ($41.37), are served daily except Saturday at lunch. Métro: Gare de l'Est.

THE MIDDLE BRACKET: Julien, 16 rue du Faubourg St-Denis, 10e (tel. 47-70-12-06), offers you an opportunity to dine in one of the most sumptuous belle époque interiors in Paris. It stands in an area not too far from Les Halles. It began life at the turn of the century as an elegant place but declined after World War II, becoming a cheap restaurant, but the decor remained, albeit grimy and unappreciated. From a dingy working-class eating place, it has now been restored to its former elegance, the dirt cleaned off and the magnificence of the fin-de-siècle dining area brought back to life. Marble and brass gleam in the mirrored, high-ceilinged room, with 15-foot-high murals, peacock-shape coat hooks, twisted rococo pillars, and paintings of odalisques.

The food served here is traditional bourgeois but without the heavy sauces once used. Excellently prepared dishes include soups such as "Billi-By" (a creamy mussel soup as good as that served at Maxim's), soupe au pistou, and vichyssoise. Among main courses are cassoulet, calves' liver, seafood such as dorade (sea bream), and andouillette (sausage made of pigs' entrails). The wine list contains good and reasonable bottles. The price of your main dish includes an appetizer. Meals, with wine, cost from 150F ($20.69). Julien is open for lunch and dinner daily, serving food until the 1:30 a.m. closing. The restaurant shuts down in July. Métro: Strasbourg-St-Denis.

Brasserie Flo, 7 Cour des Petites-Écuries, 10e (tel. 47-70-13-59). Fin-de-siècle Paris lives on. The area is remote, hard to find. You walk through passageway after passageway, perhaps being solicited along the way. Then Flo emerges. In what might be a slum in any other city, chauffeurs open the doors for their clients, who often look like Lord Alfred Douglas with a spotted Dalmatian on the rein. You expect high prices, but you're wrong. Inside, the leather banquettes, the brass-studded chairs, the old mahogany bar—everything is right, including the beer mugs. The house specialty, la formidable choucroute, is served for two persons—a heaping mound of sauerkraut surrounded by boiled ham, bacon, and sausage. Another good main dish is pintadeau (guinea hen) with lentils. The onion soup is the traditional opener. The average dinner will cost between 170F ($23.44) and 220F ($30.34) per person, plus 15% for service. Closed Sunday and in August. Métro: Château d'Eau.

Haynes, 3 rue Clauzel, 9e (tel. 48-78-40-63). When a late-night jazz musician drops into Haynes and orders oysters, he doesn't mean those fancy *belons* that come from Brittany. Rather, he's referring to Kentucky oysters—and to soul-food devotees that means chitterlings, served with rice and gravy. Big, burly Haynes—straight from the Deep South, U.S.A.—is the proprietor, general watchdog, emissary of goodwill, confidant of the down-and-out, and a most remarkable man. His little bit of Louisiana bayou country holds forth deep in Paris (within walking distance of the Place Pigalle). It's a homing point for many a homesick Yank, jazz artist, or visiting movie company. Even French people, with their versatile and adventurous palates, are hooked on "le soul food." The setting is incongruous: mud-daub plaster walls, Moorish columns, alcoves on low mezzanines, a bar with stools, and signed photographs of visitors such as Elizabeth Taylor, Warren Beatty, and Rod Steiger.

Haynes often does the cooking himself: southern fried chicken, his own original cole slaw, barbecued spare ribs, a hell-hot Mexican chili, corn on the cob, and an old-fashioned homemade apple pie. You can dine here for 175F ($24.13). It's open from 8 p.m. till 1 a.m. Closed Sunday and Monday. Métro: Notre-Dame-de-Lorette or St-Georges.

THE BUDGET RANGE: Le Grand Zinc, 3 Faubourg Montmartre, 9e (tel. 47-70-88-64). True, the quarter is unfashionable. But the Paris of the 1880s survives here, as exemplified by the spirit lamps hanging inside. You make your way into the restaurant, passing baskets of seafood. You can inspect the belons or brown-fleshed oysters from Brittany. A traditional favorite and available year round, these oysters may be purchased inside. The atmosphere is bustling in the tradition of a brasserie. A full meal goes for only 120F ($16.55). My latest repast began with a selection of crudités (raw vegetables), and was followed by rognons sautés (fried kidneys), then a coupe de glace, an ice cream dessert. Included also was a quarter of a carafe of vin rouge. Métro: Montmartre.

8. 12th Arrondissement

The 12th Arrondissement wouldn't be considered chic by anyone's standards, containing a handful of rail stations for merchandise and for passengers, a proximity to the industrialized and traffic-choked Place de la Nation, and a gray dinginess that by now seems to be part of the building façades. It does, however, possess its discreet charms, as exemplified by the following recommendation.

THE UPPER BRACKET: Au Trou Gascon, 40 rue Taine, 12e (tel. 43-44-34-26). One of the most acclaimed chefs in Paris today, Alain Dutournier launched his cooking career in the Gascony region of southwest France, working in the kitchen with his mother and grandmother. His parents owned an inn, and they mortgaged it to allow Dutournier to open a turn-of-the-century bistro in an unchic part of the 12th Arrondissement that had been a rendezvous for chauffeurs.

At first he got little business, but the word soon spread that this man was a true artisan in the kitchen who practiced the real nouvelle cuisine and not some of its unfortunate derivatives. Today, he has opened another restaurant in Paris, but he left his secrets behind. The owner's smiling wife, Nicole, is still there to greet you, and the wine steward has distinguished himself for his exciting *cave* containing several little-known wines along with a fabulous collection of armagnacs. It is estimated that the cellar has some 350 varieties of wine.

The chef does not use cream, preferring to cook with herbs, spices, fresh vegetables, and rich stocks. It's almost impossible to cite specialties, as the menu changes about every two months. Food critics have suggested that a diner should leave the menu selection to Dutournier's *idées du moment*. Although the kitchen is devoted to La Nouvelle Cuisine, you will never get undercooked carrots or turnips in cream, and worse, "pink" duck. They like duck crispy here, and, chances are, you will too. Two specialties (which may or may not be on the menu at the time of your visit) are ravioli with truffles and foie gras (offered only from November to June) and wild salmon with smoked bacon. One of my favorite dishes is the cassoulet. Count on spending from 275F ($37.92) up for a meal here. Closed on Saturday and Sunday and from around mid-July to mid-August. Métro: Daumesnil.

9. 15th Arrondissement

Here, in the vicinity of the Eiffel Tower, I'll lead off—ironically—with a re-creation of the American West.

THE UPPER BRACKET: Le Western, Hilton Hotel, 18 Avenue de Suffren, 15e (tel. 42-73-92-00). American meat and French wine are what it's all about at Hilton's recreation of the Old West in Paris. The steaks served at this mixture of cattle ranch and French elegance are imported from Kansas, and are as good as anything you'd find in Abilene. The service, however, is impeccably French and most friendly. The welcome, performed by the maître d', Francis Faure, is as intelligent a synthesis of the best parts of France and the American Midwest as you'd find anywhere. Each of the waiters is dressed cowboy style, and Francis himself is in a sheriff's garb. Contrary to expectations, this has become one of those chic Parisian places where many of the French go to rubberneck the unusual (for Europe) costumes and decor.

You might begin your meal with a crab cocktail, jumbo shrimp, or a Caesar salad, to be followed by an array of grilled steaks. If not that, a roquefort-stuffed chopped sirloin or a saddle chop of salt marsh lamb with mint jelly. The portions are large, but if you are still hungry, your meal might be followed by a selection of French cheeses or pastries. At trail's end (according to the menu), you might want a steaming cup of outlaw's coffee (made with Kentucky bourbon instead of Irish whisky). À la carte meals average 175F ($24.13) and 350F ($48.27). Service is until 11 p.m. Métro: Bir Hakeim.

10. 16th Arrondissement

Whether you're attending the Longchamp racecourse or wanting to sample the food of one of the most creative chefs in Paris, you'll find superb dining in the 16th Arrondissement.

THE UPPER BRACKET: Vivarois, 192 Avenue Victor-Hugo, 16e (tel. 45-04-04-31), has been called a revelation by food critics. This restaurant opened in 1966 with a modern decor (including chairs by Knoll), and it was initially popular with the American colony. Now, however, it's been fully discovered by the French. The American magazine, *Gourmet*, once hailed it as "a restaurant of our time . . . the most exciting, audacious, and important restaurant in Paris today." It still maintains its original standards. The restaurant is the personal statement of its supremely talented owner-chef, Claude Peyrot. His menu is constantly changing. Someone once said, and quite accurately, "The menu changes with the marketing and his genius." He does a most recommendable coquilles St-Jacques (scallops) en crème and a pourpre de turbot Vivarais. His most winning dish to many is rognons de veau (veal kidneys). Expect to pay from 400F ($55.16) for a memorable meal.

Madame Peyrot is one of the finest maîtres d'hôtel in Paris. She'll guide you beautifully through wine selections so you'll end up with the perfect complement to her husband's superlative cuisine. It is necessary to reserve in advance. Closed Saturday, Sunday, and in August. Métro: Pompe.

Faugeron, 52 rue de Longchamp, 16e (tel. 47-04-24-53), is in the Trocadero district. Henri Faugeron is an inspired chef. I've followed his career since I first heard of him at Les Belles Gourmandes on the Left Bank and was delighted there with his mastery of French cooking in the classic style. Today, the handsome chef, along with his beautiful Austrian wife, Gerlindé, entertains a faithful list of gourmets: artists, diplomats, and business executives. Faugeron many years ago established this restaurant that is elegant yet not an obtrusive backdrop for his superb cuisine. This creative chef calls his cuisine "revolutionary." He is viewed as a culinary researcher, and his menu always has one or two platters from the classic French table, perhaps a leg of lamb baked seven hours or rack of hare in traditional French style. Much of his cookery depends on the season and his shopping for only the freshest ingredients in the market. Game dishes, frogs' legs, oysters, scallops—whatever—Monsieur Faugeron prepares platters with style. In this he is aided by Jean-Claude Jambon, one of the premier sommeliers of France—indeed, of the world. Menus begin at 350F ($48.27), with à la carte orders costing from 450F ($62.06) up. Closed weekends and in August. Métro: Iéna.

Prunier Traktir, 16 Avenue Victor-Hugo, 16e (tel. 45-00-89-12), opened in 1925, the traditional, classic fish restaurant of Paris. The decoration and style of this restaurant evokes an art deco of the 1920s and 1930s. There are those who have suggested that the fish recipes are just as old. However, why not? When something tastes good, why change it? The restaurant has always been known for using only the freshest fish and seafood, and that includes the delectable oysters from Brittany that are flown in. Marmite dieppoise is one specialty I've enjoyed over the years, and it's still served on Wednesday and Friday. It is similar to a bouillabaisse and is cooked in white wine. Also exceptional, if featured, is the filet de turbot Vérilhac, served with lobster tails and boned at the table.

The guiding light of the establishment is Claude Barnagaud-Prunier, who is a grand professional, attracting an elegant clientele. He sees that filet de sole Walewska is on the menu, but there are more imaginative and innovative dishes these days as well. Among the latter is lotte à l'orange with saffron. Count on spending 350F ($48.27) or more à la carte. It is closed Monday and Tuesday, or Sunday and Monday in July and August. Métro: Charles-de-Gaulle (Étoile).

Le Petit Bedon, 38 rue Pergolèse, 16e (tel. 45-00-23-66), is traditional but also innovative. Christian Ignace is one of the many aspiring chefs of Paris who is trying to make it on his own, and so far he's doing a good job. If you visit in early spring, you can order milk-fed lamb from the Dordogne region of France that is delicate and tender and prepared to perfection. Ignace has only 14 tables, and he's getting better known all the time, so it's important to call for a reservation. The menu changes every two weeks. The room is warm and inviting, but also fairly simply decorated. There is an explosion of fresh flowers delivered fresh from Rungis. Ignace is written almost as a signature on each dish. He got a lot of his training at La Grand Véfour, and he is well versed in tradition, but also is allowed to give full reign to his imagination now that he has his own place.

For an appetizer, you might prefer salmon, thinly sliced, which has been cured and smoked by the chef himself. A black pepper from South America brings out the right seasoning in the dish. He is also known to do marvelous twists with Challans duckling. His masterpiece of desserts is his plate of mixed sorbets. Not only is it a work of art in its presentation, but you are allowed to guess the flavors, and if you give up, the maître d' will reveal the secrets. Expect to spend from 325F ($44.82) up for a meal here. The restaurant is closed on Saturday, Sunday, and in August. Métro: Argentine.

Guy Savoy, 28 rue Duret, 16e (tel. 45-00-17-67), serves the kind of food that he himself likes to eat, and does so with consummate skill. When the five or six "hottest" chefs in Paris are named today, he most often is mentioned, and deservedly so. You never know what you are going to be served when you go there, as Monsieur Savoy seems to take his inspiration from the market and only then when he's right on the spot, selecting his poultry, meat, and fresh vegetables, which he will later blend with his special magic touches.

Don't eat all day—then come here and order his menu *dégustation,* which many clients prefer. Although it runs to nine courses, the portions are small and you don't get satiated with food before the meal has run its course. What do you get? Perhaps red mullet with wild asparagus. Maybe a cassolette of snails flavored with tarragon (no garlic, for a change), or chicken quenelles with chicken livers and cream, the rich-tasting dish sprinkled with strips of delectable black truffles. If you visit in the right season, you may have a chance to order masterfully prepared game such as mallard or venison, even game birds. He is fascinated with the champignon in all its many varieties, and has been known to serve as many as a dozen different types of mushrooms, especially in the autumn.

Mr. Savoy is from Grenoble, the son of a French mother and a Swiss father. Before acquiring his own restaurant, he cooked at some of the great restaurants of France, including Troisgros at Roanne. To dine at his restaurant will cost 320F ($44.13) to 390F ($53.78) if you order from one of the menus. On the à la carte, expect to spend 300F ($41.37) to 500F ($68.95) if you sample the specialties. He is closed Saturday and Sunday, and for the last week in December and the first week in January and the last two weeks of July. Métro: Argentine.

La Grande Cascade, Bois de Boulogne, 16e (tel. 45-06-33-51), stands opposite the Longchamp racecourse and serves, incidentally, the best food in this fashionable park. Named after the waterfall of the Bois de Boulogne, the restaurant is a belle époque shrine, the perfect spot for a long, lingering afternoon lunch or a fashionable tea. This indoor-outdoor restaurant was a hunting lodge for Napoléon III, but its fame as a restaurant dates from the early part of this century. Once it was attended by the theatrical chic, Mistinguette always making her entrance in a wide hat as she emerged from a grand carriage. If the sun is shining, most guests ask for a table on the front terrace with its view. Otherwise, on a foggy day the interior looks more inviting—made all the more so with its gilt and crystal and glass roof. Selecting La Grande Cascade is also a good idea at dinner, as it's more romantic then. Guests dine to the soft sounds of the nearby cascade, and the tall frosted lamps cast a soft, forgiving light.

The restaurant presents such à la carte selections as foie gras de canard (duckling) au torchon dans sa robe de poivre, panache de poisson à la vapeur d'algues au basilic, coeur de filet à la moelle au vin de moussy rouge, and puits d'amour au coulis de fruits rouges. A spectacular finish is provided by crêpes soufflées à l'orange. A complete meal will cost about 350F ($48.27). The restaurant serves lunch and dinner every day from April 15 to October 31. The rest of the year when it's open, it serves lunch only. The place is closed from mid-December to mid-January. You must take a taxi or drive to the restaurant.

Le Pré Catelan, Route de Suresnes, Bois de Boulogne, 16e (tel. 45-24-55-58). In a lovely park setting, you can dine in a classic château, built in the grand manner at the turn of the century by Nestor Roqueplan. Make it a special occasion—and try to avoid weekends when receptions, weddings, conventions, whatever, seemingly reign supreme. Reached by taxi, the restaurant has a definite belle époque style. Under Colette Lenôtre, the establishment has been totally refurbished. On a spring or summer day, the flowers in the surrounding garden invite guests to linger long. When you make your entrance, you're seated in a luxuriously appointed dining room, its tall, wide windows opening onto a vista of greenery.

In addition to the fine à la carte menu, a set meal is offered at 500F ($68.95). Ordering independently, you might dine on a terrine of Mediterranean sea bass with cucumbers, "flower eggs" with caviar, smoked fresh salmon, and a tomato fondue. However, your tab is likely to run in the neighborhood of 525F ($72.40) to 650F ($89.64) if you should get carried away and order the lobster roasted with herb butter, climaxed by a pâtisserie Lenôtre. Always reserve a table. The restaurant is closed on Sunday night and on Monday and in February.

11. 17th Arrondissement

The southern section of the 17th Arrondissement is one of the quintessentially residential sections of Paris, earmarked by many 19th-century bourgeois homes along with blocks of heavily ornamented apartment buildings, plus a scattering of glass-and-concrete postwar constructions. Its staunchly conservative and family-oriented population values its upper-crust location close to the Place Charles-de-Gaulle (Place de l'Étoile). The 17th is also one of the biggest arrondissements, containing at its northern end the increasingly seedy Place Clichy.

THE UPPER BRACKET: Le Bernardin, 18 rue Troyon, 17e (tel. 43-80-40-61), is elegant and may soon emerge as one of the great restaurants of Paris. In the Étoile sector, Monsieur and Madame Le Coze serve only fish and shellfish, and they may be the only restaurant in Paris to have attained such a high rating without serving meat dishes as well. A brother-and-sister act, the Le Coze team are from Brittany, and their fish dishes are recognized as the finest in Paris, outranking the fame of Prunier. Their grandfather was a fisherman along the coast of Brittany, and their own father ran a fish restaurant there.

In their blue salon, with its seascape engravings, they present a delectable menu in a comfortable dining room often frequented by celebrities. Try their fresh salmon smothered in thin slices of black truffles. Heavenly. Or order their stuffed scallops or the skate in hazelnut butter. They also serve as an appetizer sea urchins (called oursins) in a sea urchin butter. Their lobsters are celestial, but also celestial in price. Tout Paris calls this team "Gilbert et Maggy," and for the privilege of dining at their establishment you are presented with a bill likely to run a lot more than 400F ($55.16) unless you practice discretion. They are closed on Sunday, Monday, and in August. Métro: Charles-de-Gaulle (Étoile).

Michel Rostang, 10 rue Gustave-Flaubert, 17e (tel. 47-63-40-77), is one of the most creative chefs of Paris. He's the fifth generation of one of the most distinguished "cooking families" of France. His family has been connected with the famed Bonne Auberge at Antibes on the French Riviera. From Grenoble, Rostang eventually found himself in Paris in the 17th Arrondissement where the world soon came to the door of what he modestly calls his "boutique restaurant" (nevertheless, it can seat as many as 100 diners).

Small and intimate, the restaurant has a menu that changes constantly, depending on Rostang's inspiration. However, some of his specialties include ravioli filled with goat cheese and coated with a sprinkling of chervil bought fresh that morning in the market. If the mood strikes him, he might prepare a young Bresse chicken, considered the finest in France, served with a delicate chervil sauce (as you may have guessed, Rostang is much enamored with fresh chervil). From October to March, he is likely to offer quail eggs with a coque of sea urchins. He also prepares on occasion a delicate fricassée of sole. I recently enjoyed his guinea hen "raised on the farm" and served with a gratin dauphinois. Many interesting wines from the Rhône are available, including Châteauneuf du Pape and Hermitage. Another specialty worth citing is duckling cooked in its own blood. A set menu is offered at lunch (only) for 185F ($25.51). Dinner is à la carte and likely to cost from 450F ($62.06). The restaurant is closed Saturday for lunch, on Sunday, and from the last week in July to the last week in August. Métro: Ternès.

THE MEDIUM-PRICED RANGE: Goldenberg's, 69 Avenue de Wagram, 17e (tel. 42-27-34-79), is the best place to go in the Champs-Élysées area for Jewish-deli food. The "doyen of Jewish restaurateurs in Paris," Albert Goldenberg opened his first delicatessen in Montmartre in 1936. He's been going strong ever since, tempting Parisians with such dishes as cabbage borscht, blinis, stuffed carp, and pastrami. Naturally, Jewish rye bread comes with almost everything. The front half of the deli is reserved for a specialty take-out section, the rear half for proper in-house dining. There's also a large room downstairs for guests. The menu even offers Israeli wines. You'll spend from 200F ($27.58) up for a meal. Métro: Place Charles-de-Gaulle or Ternès.

Lajarrige, 16 Avenue de Villiers, 17e (tel. 47-63-25-61), is a bright, new little restaurant (12 tables) not far from Parc Monceau and the Rue de Lévis market. Jean-Claude de Lajarrige, long-time restaurateur, and his young chef, Philippe Feret, have combined their talents to present food which is well prepared using the best of ingredients. They are not followers of La Nouvelle Cuisine, yet their classic dishes are light and tasty. One of the waiters in this little place is also a sommelier, and already there is a respectable cellar whose offerings will be pointed out to you by someone who knows.

The menu contains a wealth of good dishes, including several foie gras French productions. One of the most outstanding courses, aside from the many game dishes offered in season, is a big cassoulet (you don't really have to clean up your plate), delicately contrived to let you enjoy the crunchy white beans, the duck confit, and the fatless, well-seasoned sausages. Another favorite is a duck preparation, magret de canard. A good lunch dish, or also good as an appetizer, is the salade de coquilles St-Jacques sur légumes tièdes, tender scallops on garden vegetables, all in a light sauce. A five-course menu is offered for lunch, costing 195F ($26.89). An à la carte dinner will cost 275F ($37.92) to 375F ($51.71). Closed for Saturday lunch and all day Sunday. Métro: Villiers.

THE BUDGET RANGE: L'Étoile Verte, 13 rue Brey, 17e (tel. 43-80-69-34). This "Green Star" stands for economy diners, and it serves food all day so you can arrive long after the lunch crowds have departed and still be served. The decor is so simple as to be forgettable, but a large array of well-prepared foods emerges from the kitchen in back, and the staff is friendly and helpful. The type of cookery is that on a typical French bistro menu of long ago: that is, rabbit pâté, veal marengo, fresh oysters, coq au vin in Cahors, sweetbreads with sautéed endive, mussels ravigote, chateaubriand béarnaise, and ris de veau (sweetbreads). The cheapest fixed-price meal is 45F ($6.21). A simple à la carte repast costs only 60F ($8.27), with more elaborate selections costing 80F ($11.03) to 100F ($13.79). The owners, the Figoni family, keep their restaurant open seven days a week all year long. Métro: Charles-de-Gaulle (Étoile).

12. 18th and 19th Arrondissements

Old Montmartre has its share of tourist-trap restaurants, but there are some exceptions described below.

THE UPPER BRACKET: Beauvilliers, 52 rue Lamarck, 18e (tel. 42-54-19-50). It's reputed to be the favorite Parisian restaurant of Paul Bocuse, the master chef, who drops in whenever he's visiting from Lyon. The decor is unabashedly romantic, dripping with art nouveau touches which the owners have accumulated since the space was first transformed from a bakery many years ago. Edouard Carlier is the secret behind the success of this Montmartre hideaway, whose tables are very much in demand. Amid 19th-century statues, old engravings, and massive bouquets of flowers, you can enjoy subtle transformations of traditional French dishes. Specialties include a flan of mussels with zucchini, duckling en cocotte with a confit of lemons, and a succulent leg of lamb with tarragon. À la carte meals cost between 350F ($48.27) and 450F ($62.06). In summer the restaurant moves outside to an airy location near a wide stairway leading up to the famous butte so fabled in Parisian lore. Métro: Anvers.

    Cochon d'Or (Golden Pig), 192 Avenue Jean-Jaurès, 19e (tel. 46-07-23-13). The slumming chic come here for some of the best beef in the city, even if they do have to journey out to the remote Porte de Pantin in the 19th Arrondissement. The restaurant's history goes back to the turn of the century when it was created as a bistro for butchers in skullcaps. Nowadays it's run by Monsieur Ayral, who extends personal greetings. You get hefty portions at sky-high prices, but good value nonetheless, considering the quality of the produce and the concern that goes into the preparation. The one dish that I'd assume you'd make the trip for is the charcoal-grilled côte de boeuf with a moelle (marrow) sauce for two. It is usually accompanied by a potato soufflé. Known mainly by gastronomes, an especially satisfying choice is the onglet grillé, one of the best beef cuts I've ever sampled in Paris. An expenditure of 275F ($37.92) to 375F ($51.71) per person is to be expected. The Golden Pig is open all year, every day. You must arrive before 10:30 p.m. Métro: Porte de Pantin.

THE BUDGET RANGE: Le Maquis (Underbrush), 69 rue Caulaincourt, 18e (tel. 42-59-76-07). Montmartre for all its local color and atmosphere has never been a great place for dining, with three or four exceptions. However, if you don't mind leaving the Place du Tertre and heading on a 12-minute walk down the Butte, you'll be richly rewarded at this attractive restaurant, which has a tiny terrace in the fair weather months. The menu is limited but select, and the chef is the owner, Claude Lesage.

    I like Le Maquis a lot because it is a bargain. You can dine here for 65F ($8.97) on a set menu, 180F ($24.82) to 210F ($28.96) à la carte. Among the delectable courses are puff pastry with roquefort, rabbit fricassée, homemade pasta, an émincé of monkfish with little vegetables, a filet of sole served with a tomato and onion purée, and pheasant with cabbage. The desserts are often elaborate concoctions. The restaurant is closed on Sunday. Métro: Lamarck-Caulaincourt.

13. Vegetarian Dining

    Le Jardin, 100 rue du Bac, 7e (tel. 42-22-81-56), offers health-conscious food which is so well prepared that some dedicated meat-eaters sometimes arrive for a taste. You'll dine beneath a greenhouse-style ceiling in a pleasant room filled with sunlight and plants. A 60F ($8.27) fixed-price meal includes generous portions of salads, grain dishes, vegetables au gratin, and a dessert cheese or pastry. A substantial à la carte meal, with a chocolate cake for dessert, plus wine, costs from 115F ($15.86) per person. The place is open for lunch and dinner every day but Sunday. Métro: Bac.

Le Grain de Folie, 24 rue de la Vieuville, 18e (tel. 42-58-15-57). Run by American and English owners, this restaurant has a pleasant ambience. It lies halfway up the slope of Montmartre's hill, within a relaxed decor where a fixed-price menu dégustation goes for a reasonable 55F ($7.56). The menu includes a full array of salads, cereal products, vegetable tarts, and vegetable terrines. Desserts include an old-fashioned apple crumble or a fruit salad. Either the house beaujolais or a frothy glass of vegetable juice might accompany your meal. The restaurant is open only at night between 7 and 10 seven days a week. Métro: Abbesses.

La Macrobiothèque, 17 rue de Savoie, 6e (tel. 43-25-04-96). Within a simple decor appropriately filled with plants, you can enjoy vegetarian specialties in a relaxed and pleasant environment. Most diners pay 40F ($5.52) for a three-course hot meal loaded with rice and vegetables, drinks included. An array of salads and vegetable tarts, as well as macrobiotic dishes, is carefully concocted with regional in-season produce. No one will mind if you enter just to order a platter of food instead of an entire meal. It is closed Sunday. Métro: St. Michel.

Aquarius, 54 rue Ste-Croix de la Bretonnerie, 4e (tel. 48-87-48-71), is one of the best known vegetarian restaurants in Le Marais which has a lot of health-conscious residents who insist on no smoking. Neither wine nor spirits is sold, but you can enjoy a fruit-flavored beverage. Meals, regardless of what you order, seem to overflow with raw or steamed vegetables. A fixed-price menu costs 40F ($5.52), and if you order à la carte you'll pay 50F ($6.90) and up. The establishment is open for lunch, afternoon tea, snacks, and dinner daily except Sunday. Métro: Hôtel de Ville.

14. Tea Rooms and Pâtisseries

The *salon de thé* has had a surprising revival in Paris. London no longer enjoys a monopoly.

Ladurée, 16 rue Royale, 8e (tel. 42-60-21-79). Here, more than at any other salon de thé in Paris, the men look more important, the ladies more affluent, and the desmoiselles more self-consciously casual. The croissants have been described as superb by batallions of French gastronomes who have watched this establishment flourish during world wars and multiple changes of government. In turn-of-the-century grandeur, you can sip tea or coffee at tables barely big enough to hold a napkin. Matronly waitresses in filly aprons take orders for light lunches and an array of just-baked pastries, as clients talk quietly beneath the ceiling frescoes of the main salon. There, pink clouds support chubby cherubs as they bake pastries in the heat in the powerful sun. Café au lait with a croissant costs 45F ($6.21). Hours are daily except Sunday between 8 a.m. and 7 p.m. Métro: Concorde.

Fanny Tea, 20 Place Dauphine, 1er (tel. 43-25-83-67). The tea it serves is so flavorful that it's featured as the leading tea room of Paris in Japanese-language guidebooks. The view from its windows encompasses the orderly rows of trees on one of the most idyllic and historic squares of Paris. Inside, the verdigris wall coverings, the incense, and the well-oiled wooden surfaces give a touch of Victoriana to the minuscule room which is the perfect place to wind down after a tour of the Île de la Cité. The charming French owner, half descended from Scots, derived the name of her establishment from "theophany" (manifestation of God), corrupting the word into "Fanny Tea." The handwritten menu lists 13 kinds of tea and five different coffees priced at from 25F ($3.45) each. Home-made pastries, lemon mousse, and toast with smoked salmon cost from 35F

($4.83) each. The tearoom is open from 1:30 to 7:30 p.m. daily except Monday, and is closed from July 20 until the end of August. Métro: Pont Neuf or Cité.

The Village Voice, 6 rue Princesse, 6e (tel. 46-33-36-47), opened in 1982 when Odile Hellier decided to emigrate from Washington, D.C., to set up this oasis of American art and literature on the Left Bank. It has a low-budget, hi-tech decor that seems to welcome virtually every American artist and writer of stature who comes to Paris. Many of them give readings and lectures from their works, or simply relax with a cup of herbal tea on one of the simple white banquettes. The upstairs room shelters a frequently changing art exhibition, while a space in front offers well-chosen American books and recent periodicals. Menu items at the café in back are usually posted on a blackboard, and are likely to include leek pie, eggs and cheese with salad, coffee, and cakes. Main courses cost around 45F ($6.21), with beverages starting at 12F ($1.66). It is open from 11 a.m. to 8 p.m. Tuesday to Saturday. Métro: Mabillon.

On the Right Bank, **W.H. Smith,** 248 rue de Rivoli, 1er (tel. 42-60-37-97), an English bookstore, also has a tea room which has grown from a couple of tables at the back of the shop when the British company bought the bookstore in 1903 to an upstairs tea shop serving scores of people daily (although there was a hiatus from World War II to 1950 because of shortages of tea and coffee). Breakfast is served from 10 a.m. to noon, lunch from noon to 5 p.m., and tea from 3 to 6 p.m. daily except Sunday. A full breakfast with orange juice, fried eggs, and bacon costs about 30F ($4.14). A pot of tea goes for 15F ($2.07), and you can enjoy it at teatime with English fruit cake or other baked goodies. Métro: Concorde.

The Tea Caddy, 14 rue St-Julien-le-Pauvre, 5e (tel. 43-54-15-56), might be one of the city's perfect spots for a spot of tea. You'll recognize it by the stained-glass windows set into the oak door of what probably used to be a stable for one of the nearby houses of what looks like a rural village square in the heart of the Latin Quarter. The view of Notre-Dame from a point a few steps away is supposed to be one of the most painted panoramas in Paris. Tea or coffee costs from 12F ($1.66), omelets from 18F ($2.48), and salads from 12F ($1.66). Closed every Monday and Tuesday, the establishment is open Wednesday through Saturday from noon till 7 p.m. and Sunday from 2 till 7 p.m. It is closed in August. Métro: St-Michel.

Pâtisserie Pottier, 4 rue de Rivoli, 4e (tel. 48-87-87-16). Anyone who has ever read *Remembrance of Things Past* by Marcel Proust is familiar with the madeleine. This little golden tea cake, often called "the national cookie" of France, enjoys an honored position in the tradition of the country. It is said that the madeleine is the first item that little French girls learn to bake. In his book, Proust was sent out by his mother to buy some madeleines. With his madeleine, he drank some tea made with the dried blossoms of a linden tree. That touched off the memories that led to his creation of the famed classic. The madeleine is a simple little cookie, made with butter, sugar, eggs, and lemon zest, along with flour, of course. It is never taken with coffee, only tea, and it's proper form to dip the cookie in the tea. If you'd like to try one of these madeleines, you can purchase them at the above address, a package costing 11F ($1.52). However, you might like chocolate cakes even better, a small one costing 9.30F ($1.28). Open daily from 8 a.m. to 1:30 p.m. and 3 to 7:30 p.m. (closes at 7 p.m. on Sunday). Métro: St-Paul.

Chapter V

DISCOVERING PARIS

**1. The Top Sights
2. Other Major Sights
3. More Museums
4. More Churches
5. The Gardens of Paris
6. The Markets of Paris
7. A Sightseeing Miscellany
8. Paris for Children
9. In the Environs
10. Shopping in Paris**

IF IT'S YOUR FIRST visit to Paris, you are lucky. If it's your second, third, fourth, or your fiftieth you're even more fortunate. Like any good lover, Paris doesn't reveal all her charms and subtleties at once. The full impact of her beauty takes years to understand.

Paris is an old city, yet very much in the present, trying at times—almost hysterically—to be the style-setter of the world. Fads come and go with such rapidity that only New York and London could harbor so much fickleness. Somehow the old has learned to adapt to the new, and vice versa.

I'll spend a lot of time discussing monuments and art in this chapter, fashionable promenades and beautiful gardens. But even though I glorify monumental Paris, remember that its main attraction is and has always been the Parisians themselves. They're a unique breed, as even the most cursory visitor to the French capital finds out. The French from the provinces regard Parisians with interest, detachment, sometimes outright jealousy.

ORGANIZED TOURS: Before plunging into more detailed sightseeing on your own, you might like to take the most popular get-acquainted tour in Paris. It's called **Cityrama**, 4 Place des Pyramides, 1er (tel. 42-60-30-14) (Métro: Tuileries). On a double-decker bus with enough windows for the Palace of Versailles, you're taken on a nice and lazy three-hour ride through the city's streets. You don't actually go inside specific attractions—rather, settle for a look at the outside of such places as Notre-Dame, the Eiffel Tower, and the studios of Montmartre.

The language barrier is overcome as individual earphones are distributed, with a canned commentary in ten different languages. In comfortable armchair seats you sit back as Paris unfolds before you. Tours depart on the hour (except noon) from 9:30 a.m. to 2:30 p.m. The cost is 150F ($20.69). Another Cityrama offering, a tour of the nighttime illuminations, leaves at 10 p.m. every night in summer, at 8:30 p.m. in winter. The cost is 118F ($16.27).

WALKING TOURS: Organized tours have their place, if only for orientation. But the only way to discover Paris is on foot, using your own shoe leather. The first part of this chapter is organized into a series of walking tours of the major attractions of the City of Lights. Of course, the first sight, the Louvre, is not a district of Paris but after going through its monumental block you'll feel you've been on one of the major strolls of your life. After that, the Île de la Cité is so structured in this chapter that you will be able to spend the good part of one day viewing its many attractions, including Notre Dame and Sainte Chapelle.

The following day you might be ready for "The Grande Promenade", which will take you from the Arc de Triomphe to the Tuileries. A third day can be spent exploring Montmartre (see the section coming up), and a fourth day visiting the many history-rich attractions of Le Marais. A fifth day might bring you into the Latin Quarter, visiting the Cluny Museum and the Sorbonne. Those with even more time for Paris can turn to the section called "Other Major Sights," beginning with Île Saint-Louis. Space prevents us from going into street-by-street details of all the walking tours of Paris, but Air France publishes a little guide to seven walking tours. It's called *Paris à Pied* and can be picked up at Air France ticket offices.

1. The Top Sights

Unless you're in Paris for several weeks, it's virtually impossible to visit all its many attractions. Most people will wing in on a busy schedule, and in a short time will be lucky to see merely the highlights. In order of importance, that busy itinerary should include the following "must see" attractions: (1) the Louvre; (2) Notre-Dame de Paris; (3) Sainte Chapelle; (4) the Conciergerie; (5) Arc de Triomphe; (6) the Champs-Élysées; (7) the Eiffel Tower; (8) Montmartre and Sacré-Coeur; (9) the Marais district; (10) the Latin Quarter; (11) the quays of the Seine and such famous bridges as the Pont Neuf; and, finally (12) Île Saint-Louis.

Now, I'll proceed to detail the itinerary listed above.

THE LOUVRE: From far and wide they come—from North Dakota to Pakistan, from Nova Scotia to Japan—all bent on seeing the wonders of the legendary Louvre (tel. 42-60-39-26, extension 3588). People on one of those "Paris-in-a-day" tours try to break track records to get a glimpse of the two most famous ladies of the Louvre: the *Mona Lisa* and the armless *Venus de Milo*. (The scene in front of the *Mona Lisa* is best described as a circus. Viewers push and shove, and there seems minimal supervision from the staff. Flashbulbs, which are forbidden, pop all over the place. In all this fracas, you'll have anything else but a contemplative moment to view this world-famed attraction.) Those with an extra five minutes to spare go in pursuit of *Winged Victory,* that headless statue discovered at Samothrace and dating from about 200 B.C. You might as well appraise the considerable charms of these ageless favorites before making a big decision: which of the other 200,000 works would you like to see?

The Louvre suffers from an embarrassment of riches. Hence, masterpieces are often ignored by the casual visitor—there is just too much of a good thing. It is the world's largest palace and the world's largest museum (some say greatest). As a palace, it leaves me cold, except for its old section, the Cour Carrée. As a museum, it's one of the great artistic heritages of the human race.

Marie Antoinette's head had rolled less than a month before the Revolutionary Committee decided that the king's collection of paintings and sculpture would be opened to the public. Between the Seine and the rue de Rivoli (Métro to Palais-Royal or Louvre, the latter the most elegant subway stop in the world), the Palace of the Louvre stretches for almost half a mile. In the days of Charles V it was a fortress, but François I, a patron of Leonardo da Vinci, had it torn down and rebuilt as a royal residence. At the lowest point in its history, in the 18th century, it was home for anybody who wanted to set up housekeeping. Laundry hung out the windows, corners were literally pig pens, and each family built a fire somewhere to cook a meal during the long Paris winter. Napoleon changed all that, chasing out the inhabitants and launching the restoration of the palace. In fact, the Louvre became the site of his wedding to Marie-Louise.

The collections are divided into six departments: Egyptian, Oriental, and Greek and Roman antiquities; sculpture; painting; and furniture and art objects. For an admission of 16F ($2.21) (free on Sunday), you can view the collections in most of the departments any day except Tuesday from 9:45 a.m. to 5 p.m. The Greek section, containing the *Venus de Milo* and the *Winged Victory,* and that of French and Italian paintings, where the *Mona Lisa* is found, are open till 6:30 p.m. Some rooms are closed between 11:30 a.m. and 2 p.m. daily. If you don't have to "do" Paris in a day, perhaps you can return to the Louvre for several visits, concentrating on different collections or schools of painting. Those with little time should go on one of the guided tours (in English) that leave daily except Sunday and Tuesday at 11:30 a.m. and 3:30 p.m.; for a well-spent additional 17F ($2.34), you can cover the highlights with a well-informed guide. The guided tour tickets and entrance tickets are on sale at the main entrance (Denon) at a special desk marked "Visites Guidées." Tours last about 1¼ hours. The vast museum has several entrances; most notable are the Porte Denon and Porte Jaujard (Tuileries Gardens). The Louvre's most important collections are in the wings devoted to painting and Greek and Roman sculpture. What to see after you've seen the "big three" *(Winged Victory, Venus de Milo, Mona Lisa)?* I'll give you a rough idea of some of the Louvre's masterpieces in the painting collection. After that you're on your own—it would take a book to describe the Louvre in any detail (many have been written).

Da Vinci's much traveled *La Gioconda* was acquired by François I. Note the guard and the bullet-proof glass: it was stolen in the summer of 1911, found in Florence in the winter of 1913. Less well known (but to many even more enchanting) are Da Vinci's *Virgin and Child with St. Anne* and the *Virgin of the Rocks.* For Americans, at least, there's a picture which must rank No. 4 (in interest) among the ladies of the Louvre: *Whistler's Mother.* (Regrettably, because of lack of staff, this painting is nowadays shown only for a brief period on Monday and Wednesday—that is, when the staff isn't taking a break or having lunch.) The palace must certainly be big to house this stern woman under the same roof as those voluptuous naked women painted by such artists as Rubens.

Incidentally, one gallery displays 21 paintings by Rubens, done for Marie de Medici for her Luxembourg Palace in only two years. The Louvre stacks masterpiece upon masterpiece: Ingres's *The Turkish Bath;* David's portrait of Madame Récamier lounging on her familiar sofa; the Botticelli frescoes from the Villa Lemmi; Raphael's *La Belle Jardinière;* Titian's *Open Air Concert;* a 1460 *Pietà* from Avignon; Dürer's self-portrait; Anthony Van Dyck's portrait of Charles I of England; Lucas Cranach's curious *Venus;* Fra Angelico's *Coronation of the Virgin;* Hans Memling's *Portrait of an Old Woman;* Jan Van Eyck's *Madonna with Chancellor Rolin;* Correggio's *The Mystic Marriage of St. Catherine;* Hans Holbein's (the Younger) *Portrait of Erasmus of Rotterdam;* Mantegna's *Calvary;* Ribera's *Clubfoot;* Rubens's portrait of Helena Fourment (his second wife) with her children; Vermeer's *Lacemaker;* Delacroix's barebreasted *Liberty Leading the People;* the Titian portraits of Protestant-burning François I and his exquisite *Man with a Glove.* Usually no visit is complete without a look at some "fluff": Boucher's *Diana Resting after Her Bath* and Fragonard's *Bathers*.

You ask, where did all these paintings come from? The kings of France, notably art patrons François I and Louis XIV, acquired many of them. Others have been willed to or purchased by the state. Many that Napoleon contributed were taken from reluctant donors (the church a heavy and unwilling giver). Much of Napoleon's plunder had to be returned, although France hasn't seen its way clear to giving back all the booty.

Of the Greek and Roman antiquities, the most notable collections, aside from the *Venus de Milo* and *Winged Victory,* are fragments of the frieze from the Parthenon. In Renaissance sculpture, two slaves by Michelangelo were originally intended for the tomb of Julius II but were sold into other bondage. Combine all that wealth of art with Sumerian and Babylonian treasures, Assyrian winged bulls and Persian friezes, bronze Egyptian queens and a world-renowned *Squatting Scribe,* Cellini's *Nymph of Fontainebleau,* and Marie Antoinette furniture—and you've got a busy three days . . . at least. Métro: Louvre or Palais-Royal.

The Jeu de Paume Museum of Impressionism

The Louvre didn't want them, and only "the crazy Americans" were buying these "weird" works for a while. Although often hungry and always ridiculed, the impressionists of the late 19th century continued to paint. Today, they warrant a separate gallery—the Galerie du Jeu de Paume—of the Louvre, and remain one of the most enduring and popular attractions in all of Paris. At the Place de la Concorde, 8e (tel. 42-60-12-07), the museum is open daily except Tuesday from 9:45 a.m. to 5:15 p.m., for an admission of 16F ($2.21), 8F ($1.10) on Sunday.

The Jeu de Paume does not house a school of painting. If nothing else, the Impressionists were independent, but unified in opposition to the dictatorial Académie des Beaux-Arts. For their subject matter they chose the world about them, and insisted on bathing their canvases in light, ignoring ecclesiastical or mythological scenes. They painted the Seine, Parisians strolling in the Tuileries, even railway stations such as the Gare St-Lazare (some critics considered Monet's choice of the latter unforgivable vulgarity). The Impressionists were the first to paint the most characteristic feature of Parisian life: the sidewalk café, especially those in what was then the artists' quarter of Montmartre.

Perhaps the most famous painting displayed is Manet's *The Picnic on the Grass,* which when it was first exhibited was decried as *"au grande scandale des gens de bien."* Painted in 1863, it depicts a forest setting with a nude woman and two fully clothed men. Two years later, his *Olympia* created another scandal, showing a woman lounging on her bed and wearing nothing but a flower in her hair and high-heeled shoes. Attending her is a black maid. Zola called Manet "a man among eunuchs."

One of Renoir's brightest, most joyous paintings is here—the *Moulin de la Galette,* painted in 1876. That mill is still standing in the Paris of today. Of course, there is always Degas with his racecourses and dancer series. His 1876 *Absinthe*—again, rejected when it was first shown—remains one of his most reproduced works, and *The Laundresses,* painted much later, is celebrated as well. Paris-born Claude Monet was fascinated by the changing light effects on Rouen Cathedral, and in a series of five paintings he makes the old landmark live as never before.

Other works (not all impressionistic) are by the American Mary Cassatt, with her familiar *Mother and Child* theme; Paul Cézanne (a forerunner of cubism); Fantin-Latour (note his *Studio at Batignolles*); Gauguin's *Tahitian Women*; Pissarro's sleepy village scenes; Henri Rousseau's *The Snake Charmer*; the modest Sisley, who was actually English although he lived and painted his dreamy scenes in France all his life; and Van Gogh, who wins new friends with each generation by such works as *The Restaurant de la Sirène, Room at Arles,* and the *Church of Auvers.* Métro: Concorde.

The Water Lilies of the Orangerie

When you leave the Jeu de Paume, turn left and walk to the river edge of the Place, where you'll find the **Orangerie des Tuileries,** Place de la Concorde, 1er (tel. 42-97-48-16). Often set aside for special exhibits, this museum has one celebrated display: Claude Monet's exquisite *Nymphéas,* executed between 1890 and 1921, a light-filtered tangle of lily pads and water, paneling the two oval, ground-floor rooms.

Creating his effects with hundreds and hundreds of minute strokes of his brush (one irate 19th-century critic called them "tongue lickings"), Monet achieved unity and harmony, as he did in his Rouen Cathedral series and his haystacks. Artists with lesser talent might have stirred up "soup." But Monet, of course, was a genius. See his lilies and evoke for yourself the mood and melancholy as he experienced it so many years ago. Monet continued to paint his water landscapes right up until his death in 1926, although he was greatly hampered by failing eyesight.

The renovated building also shelters the Walter-Guillaume collection, which includes more than 20 Renoirs and many works by Cézanne, Picasso, Matisse, Rousseau, and Soutine. Other artists, lesser known, include Derain and Marie Laurencin. The water lilies may be viewed daily except Tuesday from 9:45 a.m. to 5:15 p.m. (sometimes closed at lunch). Admission is 12F ($1.66), half price on Sunday. Métro: Tuileries.

ÎLE DE LA CITÉ: Medieval Paris, that architectural blending of grotesquerie and Gothic beauty, began on this island in the Seine. The venerated island ever since has been known as "the candle" of the city. Actually, the river formed a protective moat around it. Sauval once observed: "The island of the City is shaped like a great ship, sunk in the mud, lengthwise in the stream, in about the middle of the Seine."

Few have written more movingly about 15th-century Paris than Victor Hugo, who invited the reader "to observe the fantastic display of lights against the darkness of that gloomy labyrinth of buildings; cast upon it a ray of moonlight, showing the city in glimmering vagueness, with its towers lifting their great heads from that foggy sea."

Medieval Paris was a city of legends and lovers, none more notable than Abélard, who was emasculated because of his love for Héloïse (afterward, he became a monk, she a nun), of blood-curdling tortures and brutalities. Explore as much of it as you can, but even if you're in a hurry, try to visit Notre-Dame, the Sainte Chapelle, and the Conciergerie.

Notre-Dame de Paris

Notre-Dame is regarded as the venerable heart of Paris, even of France itself. For example, distances from Paris to all parts of France are calculated from its precincts.

Although many may disagree, Notre-Dame is, in my opinion, more interesting from the outside than in. Hence, you'll want to walk around the entire structure to appreciate this "vast symphony of stone" more fully. Better yet, cross over the bridge to the Left Bank and view it from the quay.

The history of Paris and that of Notre-Dame are inseparable. Many came here to pray before going off to lose their lives in the Crusades. Napoleon was crowned emperor here, taking the crown from Pius VII and placing it on his own head. Before that event, "Our Lady of Paris" had been sacked by revolutionaries, who destroyed the Galerie des Rois. But wars of religion, carelessness, vandalism, and "embellishments" had destroyed much that previously existed.

The cathedral was once scheduled for demolition, but, partly because of the Victor Hugo classic and the revival of interest in the Gothic, a movement mushroomed to restore the cathedral to its original glory. The task was completed under Viollet-le-Duc, an architectural genius.

The setting has always been memorable: on the banks of the Seine on the Île de la Cité. Founded in the 12th century by Maurice de Sully, bishop of Paris, Notre-Dame grew and grew. Over the years the cathedral has changed as Paris has—often falling victim to fads in decorative taste. Its flying buttresses were rebuilt in 1330.

Once the houses of old Paris crowded in on the structure, but Haussmann ordered them torn down to show off the edifice to its best advantage from the square known as Parvis. From that vantage point, you can view the trio of 13th-century sculptured portals. On the left, the portal of the Virgin depicts the signs of the Zodiac and the coronation of the Virgin. The association of the Virgin and the Cosmos is to be found in dozens of earlier and later medieval churches.

The restored central portal of the Last Judgment is divided into three levels: the first shows Vices and Virtues; the second, Christ and his Apostles; and above that, Christ in triumph after the Resurrection. The portal is a close illustration of the Gospel according to Matthew.

Finally, the portal of St. Anne is on the right, depicting such scenes as the Virgin enthroned with Child. It is the best preserved and probably the most perfect piece of sculpture in Notre-Dame. Over the central portal is a remarkable rose window, 31 feet in diameter, forming a showcase for a statue of the Virgin and Child.

Equally interesting (although often missed by the scurrying visitor) is the portal of the cloisters (around on the left), with its dour-faced 13th-century Virgin, a unique survivor of the many that originally adorned the façade. Unfortunately, the Child figure she is holding is decapitated. Finally, the portal of St. Stephen on the Seine side traces the martyrdom of that saint.

If possible, see the interior of Notre-Dame at sunset. Of the three giant medallions that warm the austere cathedral, the north rose window in the transept, dating from the mid-13th century, is best. The interior is in the typically Gothic style, with slender, graceful columns. The stone-carved choir screen from the early 14th century depicts such biblical scenes as the Last Supper. Near the altar stands the 14th-century Virgin and Child, highly venerated among the more faithful of Paris.

It costs 15F ($2.07) for adults and 3F (41¢) for children to visit the Treasury, with its display of vestments and gold objects, including crowns, behind glass. Exhibited are a cross presented to Haile Selassie, the former Emperor of Ethiopia, and a reliquary given by Napoleon. Notre-Dame is especially proud of its relic of the True Cross and the Crown of Thorns. The Treasury is open daily from 10 a.m. to 6 p.m., from 2 to 6 p.m. on Sunday.

Finally, to visit those grimy gargoyles immortalized by Hugo you have to scale steps leading to the twin square towers, flat on top, rising to a height of 225 feet. If you're sturdy-limbed and will spend 20F ($2.76), you can do so any day from 10 a.m. to 4:30 p.m. (closes an hour earlier off-season). In winter, the charge is only 9F ($1.24). Once there, you can closely inspect those devils (some sticking out their tongues), hobgoblins, and birds of prey. You expect to see the imaginary character of Quasimodo in one of his celluloid hunchback interpretations (Charles Laughton, Anthony Quinn, or Lon Chaney, depending on which version you saw).

The open hours of the cathedral, in general, are from 8 a.m. to 7 p.m. However, it is advised to refrain from visiting during Sunday mass from 10 a.m. to noon. From October to May, a lecture on theological or historical subjects is given at 4:45 p.m., followed by a free organ recital at 5:45 p.m. and by a solemn mass at 6:30 p.m. During these, visitors are not encouraged to circulate in the cathedral. For information, telephone 43-26-07-39. The complete address is 6 Place du Parvis Notre-Dame, 4e, but it's such a landmark no one needs a street number to find it.

Approached through a garden behind Notre-Dame is the **Memorial to the Deportation**, jutting out on the very tip of the Île de la Cité. Birds chirp nowadays, the Seine flows gently by—but the memories are far from pleasant. It is a memorial to French martyrs of World War II, who were deported to camps like Auschwitz and Buchenwald. In blood-red are the words: "Forgive, but don't forget." It may be visited from 10 a.m. to noon and 2 to 7 p.m.; no admission charge.

Métro: Cité, Hôtel-de-Ville, or Maubert.

Sainte Chapelle

It is customary to call this tiny chapel a jewel box. That hardly suffices—nor does such a contemporary expression as a "light show." Go when the sun is shining, and you'll need no one else's words to describe the remarkable effects of natural light in Sainte Chapelle.

Approach Sainte Chapelle from the Boulevard du Palais, 1er, and enter through the Cour du Mai (Courtyard of May) of the Palace of Justice. If it weren't for the chapel's 247-foot spire, the law courts here would almost swallow it up.

Built in only two or three years, beginning in 1246, the chapel has two levels. It was constructed to house relics of the True Cross, including the Crown of Thorns acquired by St. Louis (the Crusader king, Louis IX) from the Emperor of Constantinople. In those days, cathedrals throughout Europe were busy acquiring relics for their treasuries, regardless of authenticity. It was a seller's—perhaps a sucker's—market. Louis IX is said to have paid heavily for his precious relics, raising the money through unscrupulous means. He died of the plague on a Crusade and was canonized in 1297.

You enter through the lower chapel, supported by flying buttresses and ornamented with fleur-de-lis designs. The lower chapel was used by the servants of the palace, the upper chamber by the king and his courtiers. The latter is reached by ascending narrow spiral stairs.

Viewed on a bright day, the 15 stained-glass windows seem to glow with ruby red and Chartres blue. They vividly depict scenes from the Bible. The walls consist almost entirely of the glass, which had to be removed for safekeeping during the Revolution and again during both World Wars. In them are embodied the hopes, dreams, even the pretensions of the kings who ordered their construction. The chapel is open from 10 a.m. to 6 p.m. (until 5 p.m. in winter). The price of admission is 20F ($2.76). Métro: Cité.

The Conciergerie

London has its Tower of London, Paris its Conciergerie. Although it had a long and regal history before the Revolution, it is visited today chiefly by those wishing to bask in the horrors of the Reign of Terror. The Conciergerie lives on as a symbol of infamy, recalling the days when carts pulled up daily to haul off the fresh supply of victims to the guillotine.

On the Seine, at 1 Quai de l'Horloge, 1er, it is approached through its landmark twin towers, the Tour d'Argent and the Tour de César. The 14th-century vaulted Guard Room, which remains from the days when the Capets made the Palace of the Cité a royal residence, is the actual entrance to the chilling building. Also dating from the 14th century, and even more interesting, is the vast, dark, and foreboding Gothic Salle des Gens d'Armes (People at Arms), totally changed from the days when the king used it as a banqueting hall.

Architecture, however, plays a secondary role to the list of famous prisoners who spent their last miserable days on earth at the Conciergerie. Few in its history endured the tortures of Ravaillac, who assassinated Henry IV in 1610. He got the full treatment—pincers in the flesh, hot lead and boiling oil poured on him like bath water.

During the Revolution the Conciergerie became more than a symbol of terror to the nobility or the "enemies of the State." Meeting just a short walk from the prison, the Revolutionary Tribunal dispensed "justice" in a hurry. And the guillotine fell faster. If it's any consolation, these "freedom-loving" jurors did not believe in torturing their victims—only decapitating them.

In failing health and shocked beyond grief, Marie Antoinette was brought here to await her trial. Only a small screen (and sometimes not even that) protected her modesty from the glare of the guards stationed in her cell. The Affair of the Carnation failed in its attempt to abduct her and secure her freedom. In retrospect, one can perhaps feel sympathy for the broken and widowed queen. By accounts of that day, she was shy and stupid, although the evidence is that upon her death she attained the nobility of a true queen. Further, historians deny that she uttered the famous quotation attributed to her, "Let them eat cake," when told the peasants had no bread. It was shortly before noon of the morning of October 16, 1793, when her executioners came for her, grabbing her and cutting her hair, as was the custom for victims marked for the guillotine.

Today you can see lithographs and paintings depicting scenes from the Revolution, including a model of the dreaded guillotine. Also displayed is a facsimile of the final touching letter, or "testament," written by Marie Antoinette to Madame Elizabeth, sister of Louis XVI.

Later the Conciergerie housed yet more noted prisoners, including Madame Elizabeth; Madame du Barry, mistress of Louis XV; Mlle Roland ("O Liberty! Liberty! What crimes are committed in thy name!"); and Charlotte Corday, who killed Marat with a kitchen knife while he was taking a sulfur bath. In time the Revolution turned on its own leaders, such as Danton and Robespierre. Finally, even one of the most hated men in Paris, the public prosecutor Fouquier-Tinville, faced the same guillotine to which he'd sent so many others.

The Conciergerie is open daily from 10 a.m. to 5:30 p.m. Guided tours are given from 10 to 11:30 a.m. and from 1:30 to 5:30 p.m. (until 4:30 p.m. in winter). Admission is 20F ($2.76), 10F ($1.38) on Sunday. Métro: Cité.

Pont Neuf

After leaving the Conciergerie, turn left and stroll along the Seine past medievalesque towers till you reach the Pont Neuf or "New Bridge." The span isn't new, of course; actually, it's the oldest bridge in Paris, erected in 1604. In its day the bridge had two unique features: it was not flanked with houses and shops, and it was paved.

At the Hôtel Carnavalet, a museum in the Marais section (see below), is a painting, *Spectacle of Buffons,* showing what the bridge was like between 1665 and 1669. Duels were fought on the structure; great coaches belonging to the nobility crossed it; peddlers sold their wares; and as there were no public facilities, men defecated right on the bridge, as depicted in the painting. With all those crowds, it attracted entertainers, such as Tabarin, who sought a few coins from the gawkers. The Pont Neuf is decorated with corbels, a mélange of grotesquerie.

Square du Vert Galant

Finally, continue on to the "prow" of the island, the Square du Vert Galant, pausing first to look at the equestrian statue of the beloved Henri IV, killed by an assassin. A true king of the people, Henry was (to judge from accounts) also regal in the boudoir. Hence the nickname "Vert Galant," or gay old spark. Gabrielle d'Estrées and Henriette d'Entragues were his best-known mistresses, but they had to share him with countless others—some of whom would casually catch his eye as he was riding along the streets of Paris.

In fond memory of the king, the little triangular park continues to attract lovers. If at first it appears to be a sunken garden, that's because it remains at its natural level; the rest of the Cité has been built up during the centuries.

THE GRANDE PROMENADE: In 1891 that "Innocent Abroad" Mark Twain called the Champs-Élysées "the liveliest street in the world," designed for the favorite pastime of Parisians, promenading. It is rather too innocent to rank walking as a Parisian's number-one pastime, but surely it comes in second. Nowadays, tourists invariably take up that highly respectable custom of the 19th century. Visitors from Minnesota who normally would get into their automobiles to drive half a block to the drugstore are seen doing the sprint from Place Charles-de-Gaulle (Étoile) to Place de la Concorde. That walk is surely a grand promenade, and you won't know Paris till you've traversed it.

Arc de Triomphe

At the western end, the Arc de Triomphe suggests one of those ancient Roman arches—only it's larger. Actually, it's the biggest triumphal arch in the world, about 163 feet high and 147 feet wide. To reach it, don't try to cross the square, the busiest traffic hub in Paris (death is certain!). Take the underground passage and live longer. With one dozen streets radiating from the "Star," the roundabout was called by one writer "vehicular roulette with more balls than numbers."

After the death of Charles de Gaulle, the French government—despite protests from anti-Gaullists—voted to change the name of the heretofore Place de l'Étoile to the Place Charles-de-Gaulle.

The arch has witnessed some of France's proudest moments—and some of its more shameful and humiliating defeats, notably those of 1871 and 1940. The memory of German troops marching under the arch that had come to symbolize France's glory and prestige is still painful to the French. And who could ever forget the 1940 newsreel of the Frenchman standing on the Champs-Élysées openly weeping as the haughty Nazi stormtroopers goose-stepped through Paris?

Commissioned by Napoleon in 1806 to commemorate his victories, the arch wasn't ready for the entrance of his new empress, Marie-Louise, in 1810. It served anyway; in fact, it wasn't completed until 1836, under the reign of Louis-Philippe. Four years later the remains of Napoleon—brought from his grave at St. Helena—passed under the arch on the journey to his tomb at the Invalides. Since that time it has become the focal point for state funerals. It is also the site of the permanent tomb of the unknown soldier.

The greatest state funeral was that of Victor Hugo in 1885; his coffin was placed under the center of the arch, and much of Paris turned out to pay tribute to the author. Another notable funeral was the one in 1929 of Ferdinand Foch, the supreme commander of the Allied forces in World War I. Perhaps the happiest moment occurred in 1944, when the Liberation of Paris parade passed through. That same year Eisenhower paid a visit to the tomb of France's unknown soldier, a new tradition among leaders of state and important figures. An eternal flame is kept burning.

Of the sculpture on the monument, the best known is Rude's *Marseillaise*, also called *The Departure of the Volunteers. The Triumph of Napoleon in 1810*, by J. P. Cortot, and the *Resistance of 1814* and the *Peace of 1815*, both by Etex, also adorn the façade. The monument is engraved with the names of hundreds of generals (those underlined died in battle) who commanded French troops in Napoleonic victories.

You can take an elevator or climb the stairway to the top. From April to September, hours are 10 a.m. to 5:45 p.m. Otherwise, it closes at 4:15 p.m. Up there is an exhibition hall, with lithographs and photos depicting the arch throughout its history. From the observation deck, you have the finest view of the Champs-Élysées as well as such landmarks as the Louvre, the Eiffel Tower, and Sacré-Coeur. Admission is 20F ($2.76). For information, phone 43-80-31-31. Métro: Charles-de-Gaulle (Étoile).

Champs-Élysées

The greatest boulevard in Paris, perhaps in the world, has a two-faced character. Part is a drive through a chestnut-lined park, the other a commercial avenue of sidewalk cafés, automobile showrooms, airline offices, cinemas, lingerie stores, even a Wimpy. The dividing point between the park and the commercial sections is Rond-Point des Champs-Élysées. Close to that is a philatelist's delight, the best-known open-air stamp market in Europe, held Sunday and Thursday. To chronicle the people who have walked this broad avenue would be to tell the history of Paris through the last few centuries. Ever since the days of Thomas Jefferson and Benjamin Franklin, Americans have gravitated here (some of the business establishments report 75% patronage by Yankees). The Champs-Élysées has, of course, lost the fin-de-siècle elegance described by Proust in *The Remembrance of Things Past*. For one thing, not all the kids playing in the park today are rich. Puppet shows, carousels, and other amusements entertain the present brood.

A slight detour from the Champs-Élysées takes you to—

Palais de l'Élysée

The French "White House" is called Palais de l'Élysée, and it occupies a block along fashionable Faubourg St-Honoré. It is now occupied by the president of France and cannot be visited by the public without an invitation.

Built in 1718 for the Count d'Evreux, the palace had many owners before it was purchased by the Republic in 1873. Once it was owned by Madame de Pompadour. When she "had the supreme delicacy to die discreetly at the age of 43," she bequeathed it to the king. The world première of the Voltaire play *The Chinese Orphan* was presented there. After her divorce from Napoleon, Josephine also lived there. Napoléon III also lived at l'Élysée when he was president, beginning in 1848. When he became emperor in 1852, he moved to the Tuileries. Such celebrated English visitors as Queen Victoria and Wellington have spent their nights there as well.

Included among the palace's works of art are tapestries made at Beauvais in the 18th century, Raphael and Leonardo da Vinci paintings, and Louis XVI furnishings. A grand dining hall was built for Napoléon III, as well as an orangerie for the Duchess du Berry (now converted into a winter garden).

Place de la Concorde

In the east, the Champs-Élysées begins at Place de la Concorde, an octagonal traffic hub ordered built in 1757 to honor Louis XV. The statue of the king was torn down in 1792 and the name of the square changed to Place de la Révolution. Floodlit at night, it is dominated nowadays by an Egyptian obelisk from Luxor, considered the oldest man-made object in Paris. It was carved circa 1200 B.C. and presented to France in 1829 by the Viceroy of Egypt.

In the Reign of Terror, the dreaded guillotine was erected on this spot, and claimed the lives of thousands—everybody from Louis XVI, who died bravely, to Madame du Barry, who went screaming and kicking all the way. Before the leering crowds, Marie Antoinette, Robespierre, Danton, Mlle Roland, and Charlotte Corday rolled away. (You can still lose your life on the Place de la Concorde; all you have to do is chance the traffic and cross over.)

For a spectacular sight, look down the Champs-Élysées—the view is framed by the Marly horses. On the opposite side, the gateway to the Tuileries is flanked by the winged horses of Coysevox.

On each side of the obelisk are two fountains with bronze-tailed mermaids and bare-breasted sea nymphs. Gray-beige statues ring the square, honoring the cities of France. To symbolize the city's fall to Germany in 1871, the statue of Strasbourg was covered with a black drape that wasn't lifted until the end of World War I. Two of the palaces on Place de la Concorde are today the Ministry of the Marine and the deluxe Crillon Hotel. They were designed in the 1760s by Ange-Jacques Gabriel.

Tuileries

Bordering the Place de la Concorde, the Tuileries are as much a part of the Paris scene as the Seine. These statue-studded gardens were designed by Le Nô-tre, the gardener to Louis XIV, who planned the grounds of Versailles.

About 100 years before that, a palace was ordered built by Catherine de Medici. Connected to the Louvre, it was occupied by Louis XVI after he left Versailles. Napoléon I called it home. Twice attacked by the people of Paris, it was finally burnt to the ground in 1871 and never rebuilt. The gardens, however, remain.

Like the orderly French mind, the trees are arranged according to designs. Even the paths are straight, as opposed to winding English gardens. To break the sense of order and formality are bubbling fountains. (Two museums in the Tuileries—the Jeu de Paume and the Orangerie—were discussed above.)

The neoclassic statuary is often insipid and is occasionally desecrated by rebellious "art critics." Seemingly half of Paris is found in the Tuileries on a warm spring day, listening to the chirping birds and watching the daffodils and red tulips bloom. Fountains bubble, and mothers roll their carriages over the grounds where 18th-century revolutionaries killed the king's Swiss guards.

At the end of your walking tour of the Tuileries—two miles from Place Charles-de-Gaulle (Étoile)—you'll be at the **Arc de Triomphe du Carrousel,** at the Cour du Carrousel. Pierced with three walkways and supported by marble columns, the monument honors the Grande Armée, celebrating Napoleon's victory at Austerlitz on December 5, 1805. The arch is surmounted by statuary, a chariot, and four bronze horses. "Paris needs more monuments," Napoleon once shouted. He got his wish.

THE EIFFEL TOWER: Everyone visits the landmark that has become the symbol of Paris. For maximum enjoyment, however, don't just rush to it right at once. Approach it gradually. Take the Métro to Place du Trocadéro, dominated by a statue of Marshal Foch. Once you've surfaced from the underground, you'll be at the gateway to the—

Palais de Chaillot

Replacing the 1878 Palais du Trocadéro, the new palace was built in 1937 for the International Exhibition. If you have time, try to visit at least two of the three important museums lodged in the building: one a maritime showcase, another a gallery of reproductions of many of the monuments of France, a third devoted to people (see the museum section below for more detailed descriptions).

From the palace terrace (one writer called it "Mussolinian"), you have a panoramic view across the Seine to the Eiffel Tower. The **Jardins du Palais de Chaillot** in back sweep down to the Seine. They are noted for their fountain displays. From April to October, the gardens are a babel of international tongues.

The Tower

Cross the Pont d'Iéna and you'll reach your goal, the incomparable Eiffel Tower at Champ-de-Mars, 7e (tel. 45-50-34-56). Except for perhaps the Leaning Tower of Pisa, it is the single most recognizable structure in the world. Weighing 7,000 tons but exerting about the same pressure on the ground as an average-size person sitting in a chair, the tower was never meant to be permanent. It was built for the Exhibition of 1889 by Gustave Alexandre Eiffel, the French engineer whose fame rested mainly on his iron bridges, such as the one built in Porto, Portugal. (Incidentally, one of the lesser-known aspects of his career is his designing of the framework for the Statue of Liberty.)

The tower, including its 55-foot television antenna, is 1,056 feet high. On a clear day, you can see it from some 40 miles away. An open-framework construction, the tower ushered in the almost unlimited possibilities of steel construction, paving the way for the skyscrapers of the 20th century.

Skeptics said it couldn't be built, and Eiffel actually wanted to make it soar higher than it did. For years it remained the tallest man-made structure on earth, until such skyscrapers as the Empire State Building usurped that record.

Artists and writers vehemently denounced it, although later generations sang its praise. People were fond of calling it names: "a giraffe," "the world's greatest lamppost," "the iron monster." Others suggested, "Let's keep art nouveau grounded." Nature lovers feared it would interfere with the flights of birds over Paris.

The advent of wireless communication in the early 1890s preserved the tower from destruction.

You can visit the tower in three stages. Taking the elevator to the first landing, at a charge of 10F ($1.38), you have a view over the rooftops of Paris. A cinema museum can be visited for 12F ($1.66), and restaurants and a bar are open all year. The second landing, costing 22F ($3.03), provides a panoramic look at the city. The third and final stage, 37F ($5.10), gives the most spectacular view, with displays allowing you to identify monuments and buildings that are visible. Eiffel's office contains wax figures of Gustave Eiffel and Thomas Edison. On the ground level in the western pillar, a visit to the 1899 lift machinery is offered at a cost of 5F (69¢). You can visit the tower from 10 a.m. to 11 p.m. Métro: Trocadéro, École Militaire, or Bir Hakeim.

Champ-de-Mars and École Militaire

With time remaining, explore the Champ-de-Mars, the gardens between the Eiffel Tower and the Military School. Traditionally, these gardens, laid out around 1770, were the World's Fair grounds of Paris, the scene of many a military parade.

Thanks in part to one of France's best-known mistresses, Madame de Pompadour, the École Militaire (Military School) was established; the plans were drawn up by A.-J. Gabriel. This classical school was founded in 1751 for about 500 young men who wanted a military career.

Napoleon entered in 1784, the year his father died of cancer. He was graduated a year later as a lieutenant, aged 16. According to accounts, he wasn't popular with his classmates, many of whom openly made fun of him. One wrote, "All boots, no man." Pity those creatures when their names came up for promotions years later. Another French general, Charles de Gaulle, also studied at the school. Special permission is needed to go inside.

Behind the military school is the **UNESCO Building,** 7 Place de Fontenoy, 7e (tel. 45-68-10-00), a Y-shaped structure fronting the Place de Fontenoy. On the piazza may be seen Alexander Calder's mobile, standing out like a sentinel against a travertine wall; the big *Reclining Figure* by Henry Moore; and two perpendicular walls covered with ceramics designed by Miró and executed by Artigas. On the eastern façade is a garden arranged by Noguchi according to the rules of ancient Japan, in which may be seen a statuette of an angel, a survivor of the holocaust of Nagasaki in 1945. Métro: Ségure.

HÔTEL DES INVALIDES: The glory of the French military lives on here. It was the Sun King who decided to build the "hotel" to house soldiers who'd been disabled. It wasn't entirely a benevolent gesture, since these veterans had been injured, crippled, or blinded while fighting his battles. Louvois was ordered in 1670 to launch this massive building program. When it was completed—and Louis was long dead—the corridors stretched for miles. Eventually the building was crowned by a gilded dome designed by Jules Hardouin-Mansart.

The Invalides is best approached by walking from the Right Bank across the turn-of-the-century Alexander III Bridge. Of this span, critic Ian Nairn wrote, "The whole thing is carried to the limit of mock pomposity, like Offenbach satirizing a romantic situation yet at the same time providing a beautifully tender melody for lovers." In the building's cobblestone forecourt is a display of massive cannons—a formidable welcome.

Before rushing on to Napoleon's tomb, you may want to take the time to visit the greatest **Army Museum** in the world. In 1794 a French inspector started collecting all these weapons, uniforms, and equipment.

With the continued accumulation of war material over the centuries, the museum has become a horrifying documentary of man's self-destruction. Viking swords, Burgundian bacinets, blunderbusses from the 14th century, Balkan khandjars, American Browning machine guns, war pitchforks, salamander-engraved Renaissance serpentines, "Haute Époque" armor, a 1528 Griffon, musketoons, grenadiers . . . if it could kill, it's enshrined in a place of honor here. As a sardonic touch, there's even the wooden leg of General Daumesnil. The museum was looted by the Germans in 1940.

Among the outstanding acquisitions are the suits of armor worn by the kings of France, including Louis XIV. The best-known one—the "armor suit of the lion"—was made for François I. Henri II ordered his suit engraved with the monogram of his mistress, Diane de Poitiers, and (perhaps reluctantly) that of his wife, Catherine de Medici. The showcases of swords are reputedly among the finest in the world.

The mementos of World War I, including those of American and Canadian soldiers, are especially interesting. Included is the Armistice Bugle, which sounded the cease-fire on November 11, 1918.

Much attention is focused on that Corsican general who became France's greatest soldier. A plaster death mask by Antommarchi is one of the most notable pieces on display. So, too, an oil by Delaroche, painted at the time of Napoleon's first banishment (April 1814), which depicted him as he probably looked, paunch and all.

In the rooms relating to the First Empire are displayed the field bed of Napoleon with his tent. In the room devoted to the Restoration, the 100 Days, and Waterloo, you can see the reconstituted bedroom of Napoleon at the time of his death at St. Helena. On the more personal side, you can view Vizir, a horse he owned (stuffed), as well as a saddle used mainly for state ceremonies. The Turenne Salon contains other souvenirs of Napoleon, including the hat he wore at Eylau, his sword from his victory at Austerlitz, and his "Flag of Farewell" which he kissed before departing for Elba.

The Salle Orientale in the west wing shows arms for the Eastern world, including Asia and the Muslim countries of the Mideast, from the 16th to the

19th centuries. Turkish armor and weapons and Chinese and Japanese armor and swords are on display.

A walk across the Court of Honor delivers you to the **Church of the Dome,** designed by Hardouin-Mansart for Louis XIV. The great architect began work on the church in 1677, although he died before its completion. The dome is the second-tallest monument in Paris. In the Napoleon Chapel is the hearse used at the emperor's funeral on May 9, 1821.

To accommodate the **Tomb of Napoleon,** the architect Visconti had to redesign the high altar in 1842. First buried at St. Helena, Napoleon's remains were returned to Paris in 1840. Louis-Phillippe had demanded that of England. The triumphal funeral procession passed under the Arc de Triomphe, down the Champs-Élysées, en route to the Invalides. Snow swirled through the air. The tomb is made of red Finnish porphyry, the base from green granite. Napoleon's remains were locked away inside six coffins. Surrounding the tomb are a dozen amazon-like figures representing his victories. Almost lampooning the smallness of the man, everything is made large, big, awesome. You'd think a real giant was buried here, not a symbolic one. In his coronation robes, the statue of Napoleon stands 8½ feet high. The grave of Napoleon's son, "the King of Rome," lies at his feet.

Napoleon's tomb is surrounded by those of his brother, Joseph Bonaparte; the great Vauban; Foch, the Allied commander in World War I; Turenne; and La Tour d'Auvergne, the first grenadier of the Republic (actually, only his heart is entombed here).

The Army Museum is open every day from 10 a.m. to 6 p.m. April 1 to September 30; to 5 p.m. October 1 to March 31. It is closed January 1, May 1, November 1, and December 25. The entrance price of 15F ($2.07) includes the Army Museum, the Tomb, and the **Museum of Plans and Reliefs** in a top-floor gallery. Métro: Latour-Maubourg, Varenne, or St-François-Xavier.

A **son et lumière** program—titled "Shades of Glory"—is presented at the Invalides. From March 31 to May 5 and August 14 to October 5, two shows are performed nightly in English at 9:30 and 11 p.m., with a French presentation at 10:30 p.m. Between May 5 and August 13, there is only one evening performance in English, at 11 p.m., because there is too much light in the sky to permit an early show. Each program lasts about 40 minutes and is viewed from seats placed in front of Les Invalides. The price of entrance is 38F ($5.24) for adults, 28F ($3.86) for children. For the latest information, phone 39-79-00-15. The entrance for the shows is at the Esplanades des Invalides. There are no performances between October 6 and March 31.

MONTMARTRE: Soft-white three-story houses, slender, barren trees sticking up from the ground like giant toothpicks—that's how Utrillo, befogged by absinthe, saw Montmartre. On the other side of the canvas, Toulouse-Lautrec brush-stroked it as a district of cabarets, circus performers, and prostitutes. Today Montmartre remains truer to the dwarfish artist's conception than it does to that of Utrillo.

From the 1880s to the years preceding World War I Montmartre enjoyed its golden age as the world's best-known art colony. *La vie de bohème* reigned supreme. At one time the artistic battle in La Butte was the talk of the art world. There was, for one, the bold Matisse, and his band of followers known as "The Savage Beasts." Following World War I the pseudo-artists flocked to Montmartre in droves, with camera-snapping tourists hot on their heels. The real artists had long gone, perhaps to Montparnasse.

Before its discovery and subsequent chic, Montmartre was a sleepy farming community, with windmills dotting the landscape. The name h~~ ~~ been the subject of disagreement, some maintaining that it originated~~ ~~ "mount of Mars," a Roman temple that crowned the hill, others as~~ ~~ means "mount of martyrs." The latter is a reference to the martyrd~~o~~

Denis, patron saint of Paris, who was beheaded on the mountain along with his fellow-saints Rusticus and Eleutherius.

Up to Sacré-Coeur

The simplest way to reach Montmartre is to take the Métro line to the Anvers station, then walk up the rue Steinkerque in the direction of the funicular. Funiculars run every day from 6 a.m. till 11 p.m. You will be delivered to the precincts of Sacré-Coeur. Another, and preferable, way is to take the Métro to Place Pigalle, from which you proceed down the Boulevard de Clichy, turning right at the Cirque Médrano and beginning your climb up the rue des Martyrs. (On your left, at no. 75, is Madame Arthur, a club known throughout Europe for its female impersonators.) Turn left on the rue Abbesses, then go right along the steep rue Ravignan.

Eventually, you arrive at the **Place Émile-Goudeau,** a tree-studded square in the middle of the rue Ravignan. At no. 13, across from the Timhôtel, stood **Bateau-Lavoir** ("Boat Washhouse"), called the cradle of cubism. Fire gutted it in 1970, but it has been reconstructed by the City of Paris. Picasso once lived here, painting, in the winter of 1905–1906, one of the world's most famous portraits, *The Third Rose* (Gertrude Stein). Other residents have included Kees Van Dongen and Juan Gris. Modigliani had his studio nearby, as did Henri Rousseau and Braque.

A sign at the Place Jean-Baptiste-Clément points the way to the **Musée de Cire de la Butte Montmartre,** the waxworks of Montmartre, at 11 rue Poulbot, 18e (tel. 46-06-78-92). Charging 15F ($2.07) for adults, 10F ($1.38) for children, the museum documents historical Montmartre. In wax tableaux, the exhibit depicts the days that used to be: one, for example, is devoted to a café as it might have been in the 19th century. Captured in wax are such figures as George Sand, Delacroix, Toulouse-Lautrec (his studio has been re-created), Liszt, Chopin, Berlioz, Renoir, and Utrillo. St. Denis is relegated to stained glass, where he's been frozen walking head in hand. The museum is open daily from 10:30 a.m. to noon and from 2:30 to 5:15 p.m.

Poulbot crosses the tiny **Place du Calvaire,** which offers a panoramic view of Paris. On this square (a plaque marks the house) lived Maurice Neumont (1868–1930), the artist, painter, and lithographer. From here, follow the sounds of an oompah band to the **Place du Tertre,** the old town square of Montmartre. Its cafés are overflowing, its art galleries (in and out of doors) always crowded. Some of the artists still wear berets, and the cafés bear such names as La Bohème—you get the point. Everything is so loaded with local color—applied as heavily as on a Seurat canvas—it gets a little redundant.

Right off the square fronting the rue du Mont Cenis is the **Church of St. Pierre.** It has played many roles: a Temple of Reason during the Revolution, a food depot, a clothing store, even a munitions factory. Nowadays it's back to being a church, although originally, during the reign of Louis VI, it was a Benedictine abbey. In 1147 the present church was consecrated, which makes it one of the oldest in Paris. Two of the columns in the choir stall are the remains of a Roman temple. Among the sculptured works is one depicting a nun with the head of a pig, the symbol of sensual vice. At the entrance of the church are three bronze doors sculptured by Gismondi in 1980. The middle door depicts the life of St. Peter. The left door is dedicated to St. Denis, patron saint of Paris, and the right door to the Holy Virgin.

Finally, we reach the crowning achievement of the butte, the **Basilica of Sacré-Coeur** (tel. 42-51-17-20). After the Eiffel Tower, it is the most characteristic landmark of the Parisian scene. Like the tower, it has always been—and still is—the subject of much controversy. One Parisian called it "a lunatic's confectionery dream." An offended Zola declared it to be "the basilica of the ridiculous." Sacré-Coeur has had warm supporters as well, including Max Jacob, the

Jewish poet, and the artist Maurice Utrillo. Utrillo never tired of drawing and painting it, and he and Jacob came here regularly to pray.

In gleaming white, it towers over Paris,—its five bulbous domes suggesting some Byzantine church of the 12th century, and its campanile inspired by Roman-Byzantine art. But it's not that old. After France's defeat by the Prussians in 1870, the basilica was planned as a votive offering to cure France's misfortunes. Rich and poor alike contributed money to build it. The National Assembly approved its construction in 1873. The church was not consecrated until 1919, but perpetual prayer of adoration has been made day and night since 1885.

It costs 20F ($2.76) to visit both the dome and the crypt, which are open from 9:30 a.m. to 6 p.m. On a clear day the vista from the dome can extend for 35 miles. You can also walk around the inner dome of the church, peering down like a pigeon (one is likely to be keeping you company).

Even if you have only 24 hours in Paris and can't explore most of the sights recommended in this chapter, try to make it to Sacré-Coeur at dusk. There, as you sit on the top steps, the church at your back, the Square Willette in front of you, nighttime Paris begins to come alive. First, a twinkle like a firefly; then all of the lights go on. One young American got carried away with it all: "Here, away from the whirling taxis, concierges, crazy elevators, and tipping problems, the sound of Paris permeates by osmosis." Try to see it.

The Cemetery of Montmartre

Second only in fame to Père-Lachaise, the Montmartre Cemetery is the resting place of many famous personages. The burial ground lies west of the "Butte," north of the Boulevard de Clichy. Opened in 1795, the cemetery was the final call for such composers as Berlioz (died 1869) and Offenbach (died 1880). The poet Heinrich Heine was forced to leave Germany in 1848 because of his political convictions. The author of the *Lorelei,* who was born Jewish but converted to Christianity, was buried in Montmartre in 1856. The great Stendhal was buried here, as were the Goncourt brothers, and poets such as Alfred de Vigny and Théophile Gautier. But when I'm in the area, I like to pay my respects at the tomb of Alphonsine Plessis, the heroine of *La Dame aux Camélias,* and Madame Récamier, who taught the world how to lounge. Métro: Clichy.

On to the Moulin Rouge

The **Musée de Montmartre,** 12 rue Cortot, 18e (tel. 46-06-61-11 for information), is in the charming 17th-century house of Roze de Rosimond, a member of the acting troupe of Molière's "Illustre Théâtre." Utrillo once lived in the building. With its wide collection of Vieux Montmartre, it makes for an interesting visit that needn't take too long. Charging 15F ($2.07) for admission, it is open daily from 2:30 to 5:30 p.m. (from 11 a.m. to 5:30 p.m. on Sunday). Métro: Abbesses or Lamarck-Caulaincourt.

Nearby, at 4 rue des Saules, is the vine-covered **Lapin Agile** ("Agile Rabbit"), an old inn that once attracted Utrillo, Picasso, and a host of other artists (see my nightlife recommendations in Chapter VI). If you take the winding rue Lepic (ordered built by Napoléon III) in the direction of Place Blanche, you will pass along the way the **Moulin de la Galette** (1 Avenue Junot), immortalized in the Renoir painting at the Jeu de Paume Museum. In 1886 Van Gogh lived at 54 rue Lèpic with Guillaumin. The interesting old house is still standing today, although in dire need of repair. Métro: Lamarck.

At the Place Blanche stands an even better-known windmill, the **Moulin Rouge,** one of the most famous nightclubs in the world, immortalized Toulouse-Lautrec. Métro: Blanche.

Down to Pigalle

From Place Blanche, you can begin a descent down **Boulevard de Clichy,** fighting off the pornographers and hustlers trying to lure you into tawdry sex joints. With some rare exceptions—notably the citadels of the chansonniers— Boulevard de Clichy is one gigantic tourist trap. Still, as Times Square is to New York, Boulevard de Clichy is to Paris: anyone who comes to Paris invariably winds up there.

The boulevard strips and peels its way down to **Place Pigalle,** the nudity center of Paris. Ironically, the square is named after a French sculptor, Pigalle, whose closest association with nudity was a depiction of Voltaire in the buff. Place Pigalle, of course, was the notorious "Pig Alley" of World War II. Toulouse-Lautrec had his studio right off Pigalle at 5 Avenue Frochot. In the days when she was lonely and hungry, Edith Piaf (the "little sparrow") sang in the alleyways of Pigalle, hoping to earn a few francs for the night.

At Cirque Médrano, the boulevard changes its name and becomes **Boulevard de Rochechouart.** Seurat maintained his studio at no. 128 on this wide thoroughfare, much frequented today by prostitutes of both sexes.

LE MARAIS: When Paris began to overflow the confines of Île de la Cité in the 13th century, the citizenry settled in le Marais, the marsh that used to be flooded regularly by the high-rising Seine. By the 17th century le Marais had reached the pinnacle of fashion, becoming the center of aristocratic Paris. At that time, many of its great mansions—now in decay—were built by the finest craftsmen in France.

In the 18th and 19th centuries, fashion deserted le Marais for the expanding Faubourg St-Germain and Faubourg St-Honoré. Industry eventually took over the quarter, and the once-elegant hotels were turned into tenements. There was talk of demolishing this seriously blighted sector, but in 1962 the alarmed Comité de Sauvegarde du Marais banded together and saved the historic district.

Today the 17th-century mansions are being restored, and many artisans are moving in. The *Herald-Tribune* called it the latest refuge of the Paris artisan fleeing from the tourist-trampled St-Germain-des-Prés. The "marsh" sprawls across the 3rd and 4th Arrondissements, bounded by the Grands Boulevards, the rue du Temple, the Place des Vosges, and the Seine.

A good place to start your exploration of le Marais is at—

Place de la Bastille

Here, on July 14, 1789, a mob of people attacked the Bastille and so began the French Revolution. Here? In all this traffic? Precisely, for nothing remains of the historic Bastille, built in 1369. It was completely torn down. A symbol of despotism, it once contained eight towers, rising 100 feet high. Many prisoners —some sentenced by Louis XIV for "witchcraft"—were kept within its walls, the best-known being "The Man in the Iron Mask." And yet, when the fortress was stormed by the revolutionary mob, only seven prisoners were discovered. The Marquis de Sade had been transferred to the madhouse ten days earlier. The authorities had discussed razing it anyway. So in itself the attack meant nothing. What it symbolized, however, and what it started will never be forgotten. Bastille Day is celebrated with great festivity each July 14.

It was much easier to storm the Bastille, I think, than it is to skip by the speeding cars to the center, where the **Colonne de Juillet** (July Column) doesn't commemorate the Revolution at all. It honors instead the victims of the July Revolution of 1830, which put Louis-Philippe on the throne. The tower is crowned by a winged nude, the God of Liberty, a star emerging from his head.

Incidentally, on this square you can dine at La Tour d'Argent, but not *the* Tour d'Argent, as you'll quickly discover by looking at the prices.

From Place de la Bastille, walk up the rue St-Antoine, turn right on rue des

Tournelles, and note the statue (1895) honoring the 18th-century dramatist Beaumarchais *(The Barber of Seville* and *The Marriage of Figaro).* Cut left again, on the colorful and typical rue Pas-de-la-Mule ("Footsteps of the Mule"), and you'll soon note by the posters and graffiti that you're in a hotbed of left-wing French politics. Then, suddenly, you've entered the enchanted—

Place des Vosges

It is the oldest square in Paris and was once the most fashionable. Right in the heart of Marais, it was called the Palais Royal in the days of Henri IV. The king planned to live here, but his assassin, Ravaillac, had other intentions for him. Henry II was killed while jousting on the square in 1559, in the shadow of the Hôtel des Tournelles. His widow, Catherine de Medici, had the place torn down.

Place des Vosges, once the major dueling ground of Europe, is considered one of the first planned squares in Europe. Its grand-siècle rosy-red brick houses are ornamented with white stone. The covered arcades allowed people to shop at all times, even in the rain—quite an innovation at the time. In the 18th century chestnut trees were added, sparking a controversy that continues to this day: critics say that the addition spoils the perspective.

Over the years such personages as Descartes, Pascal, Cardinal Richelieu, the courtesan Marion Delorme, Gautier, Daudet, and the most famous letterwriter of all time, Madame de Sévigné, lived there. Its best-known occupant was Victor Hugo (his home, now a museum, is the only house that can be visited without a private invitation). The great writer could be seen rushing under the arcades of the square to a rendezvous with his mistress. In the center of the square is a statue of Louis XIII on horseback. An excellent but expensive restaurant facing the square is the Coconnas (see Chapter IV).

Victor Hugo Museum

Appraisals of Hugo have been varied. Some have called him a genius. Cocteau said he was a madman, and an American composer discovered that in the folly of his dotage he carved furniture—with his teeth! From 1832 to 1848 the novelist and poet lived on the second floor at 6 Place des Vosges, in the old Hôtel Rohan Guéménée, built in 1610 on what was then the Place Royale. His maison is owned by the City of Paris, which has taken over two additional floors.

A leading figure in the French Romantic movement, Hugo is known for such novels as *The Hunchback of Notre Dame* and *Les Misérables.* The museum owns some of Hugo's furniture as well as pieces that once belonged to Juliette Drouet, the mistress with whom he lived in exile on Guernsey, one of the Channel Islands.

Worth the visit are Hugo's drawings, more than 450, illustrating scenes from his own works. See, in particular, his *Le Serpent.* Mementos of the great writer abound: samples of his handwriting, his inkwell, first editions of his works, and the death mask in his bedroom. A painting of his funeral procession at the Arc de Triomphe in 1885 is on display. Portraits and souvenirs of Hugo's family are also plentiful. Of the furnishings, especially interesting is a chinoiserie salon. The collection even contains Daumier caricatures and a bust of Hugo by David d'Angers, which—when compared to Rodin's—looks saccharine.

The maison (tel. 42-72-16-65) is open daily, except Monday and legal holidays, from 10 a.m. to 5:40 p.m.; 8F ($1.10) admission, free on Sunday. Métro: St-Paul.

From the Place des Vosges, the rue des Francs-Bourgeois leads to the—

Hôtel Carnavalet and Musée de la Chasse

At the **Hôtel Carnavalet,** 23 rue de Sévigné 4e (tel. 42-72-21-13), the history of Paris comes alive in intimately personal terms—right down to the chessmen Louis XVI used to distract his mind in the days before he went to the guillotine. A renowned Renaissance palace, it was built in 1544 by Pierre Lescot and Jean Goujon; later it was acquired by Madame de Carnavalet. The great François Mansart transformed it between the years 1655 and 1661.

But its best-known memories concern one of history's most famous letterwriters, Madame de Sévigné, who moved into the house in 1677, losing her dear friend La Rochefoucauld two years later. Fanatically devoted to her daughter (until she had to live with her), she poured out nearly every detail of her life in letters, virtually ignoring her son. A native of the Marais district, she died at her daughter's château in 1696. It wasn't until 1866 that the City of Paris acquired the mansion, eventually turning it into a museum.

You enter any time between 10 a.m. and 5:40 p.m., and pay 15F ($2.07) admission (free on Sunday). Closed Monday. Métro: St-Paul.

Many salons depict events related to the Revolution: a bust of Marat, a portrait of Danton, and a replica of the Bastille (one painting shows its demolition). Another salon is devoted exclusively to the story of the captivity of the royal family at the Temple, including the bed in which Madame Elizabeth slept. The exercise book of the Dauphin is there—the pathetic legacy he left the world before his mysterious disappearance.

There is much to see: the Bouvier collection on the first floor, façades of old apothecary shops, extensive wrought-iron works, a bust of Napoleon by Charles-Louis Corbet, a Cazals portrait of Paul Verlaine that makes him look like Lenin, Jean Beraud's parade of 19th-century opulence, and Baron François Gerard's painting of Madame Récamier—lounging, of course.

You end your tour in the immaculate courtyard in front of a statue of Louis XIV (which Coysevox originally did for l'Hôtel de Ville).

Nearby, François Mansart also built the Hôtel Guénégaud, which the Sommer Foundation has restored and turned into the **Musée de la Chasse et de la Nature** at 60 rue des Archives, 3e (tel. 42-72-86-43). It is open daily except Tuesday and national holidays from 10 a.m. to 5:30 p.m.; 15F ($2.07) admission fee. Photographs at the entrance depict the shocking state of the building's decay before its subsequent restoration.

Mounted heads are plentiful, ranging from the antelope to the elephant, from the bushbuck to the waterbuck, from the moose to the hideous "bush pig." Rembrandt's sketch of a lion is here, along with a collection of wild-animal portraits by Desportes (1661–1743). The hunt tapestries are outstanding and often amusing—one a cannibalistic romp, another showing a helmeted man standing eye to eye with a bear he is stabbing to death. The rifles, some inlaid with pearls, others engraved with ivory, are exceptional, many dating from the 17th century. The museum also displays other historical weapons, along with a remarkable collection of paintings, including works by Rubens, Breughel, Oudry, Chardin, and Corot. Métro: Rambuteau.

A short walk from the hunting museum deposits you at a Paris landmark steeped in French history:

The National Archives

On Napoleon's orders, the Palais Soubise was made the official records depository of France. But the building, designed by the much-underrated Delamair, is as fascinating as, or even more so than, the exhibits contained within. Apartments once belonging to the Prince and Princess de Soubise have been turned into the **Musée de l'Histoire de France,** open 2 to 5 p.m. daily except Tuesday; 4F (55¢) admission, 2F (28¢) on Sunday. The entrance is at 60 rue des Francs-Bourgeois, 4e (tel. 42-77-11-30). You enter into the colonnaded Court of Honor. Before going inside, walk around the corner to 58 rue des Archives to see the medieval turreted gateway to the original Clisson mansion.

The Clisson mansion gave way to the residence of the dukes of Guise, who owned the property until it was purchased by the Soubise family. The Princess Soubise was once the mistress of Louis XIV, and apparently the Sun King was very generous, giving her the funds to remodel and redesign the palace.

The museum contains documents that go back to Charlemagne and even earlier. The letter collection is highly valued, exhibiting the penmanship of Joan of Arc, Marie Antoinette (a farewell letter), Louis XVI (his will), Danton, Robespierre, and Napoléon I. The museum possesses the only known sketch made of the maid from Orléans while she was still alive. Even the jailer's keys to the old Bastille are found here. For a much later Princess de Soubise, Germain Boffrand in 1735 designed a Salon Ovale, with *parfaites* (faultless) *expressions*. Adding to the lush decor, the gilt, and the crystal are paintings by Van Loo, Boucher, and Natoire.

From the Hôtel de Rohan to the Hôtel de Sully

Within the same precincts (entrance is at 87 rue Vieille-du-Temple) is Delamair's **Hôtel de Rohan,** once occupied by the cardinal of the "diamond necklace scandal," which implicated Marie Antoinette. That was the fourth Cardinal de Rohan. The first, the original occupant of the hôtel, was reputed to be the son of Louis XIV.

The interior is open to the public only for guided visits on Monday, Wednesday, Thursday, and Friday at 3 p.m. The main attraction is the amusing Salon des Singes (Monkey Room) of the 18th century. In the courtyard (open working days from 9 a.m. to 6 p.m.) you can see a stunning bas-relief depicting a nude Apollo and four horses against a background exploding with sunbursts. Métro: Hôtel-de-Ville or St-Sebastian.

Also on rue Vieille-du-Temple, at no. 47, is the **Hôtel des Ambassadeurs de Hollande,** where Beaumarchais wrote *The Marriage of Figaro.* It is one of the most splendid mansions in le Marais—and it was never occupied by the Dutch Embassy. You cannot go inside.

From rue Vieille-du-Temple, turn onto **rue des Rosiers** (Street of Rosebushes). Again the name misleads. Actually, it's one of the most colorful and typical streets remaining from the old Jewish quarter. The Star of David shines here; Hebrew letters flash (in neon, no less); couscous is sold from the shops run by Moroccan or Algerian Jews; bearded old men sit in the doorway watching time pass them by; restaurants serve strictly kosher meats; and signs appeal for the liberation of the Jews of Russia.

Whatever you're in the market for—goose sausage stuffed in a goose neck, roots of black horseradish, pickled lemons—you'll find it here.

Although the façade at the 17th-century **Hôtel de Beauvais,** 68 rue François-Miron, is badly damaged, it remains one of the most charming in Paris. A plaque commemorates the fact that Mozart inhabited the maison in 1763. Although he was only seven years old, he played at the court of Versailles. Louis XIV presented the mansion to Catherine Belin, wife of Pierre de Beauvais, who reportedly had the honor of introducing young Louis, then 16, to the facts of life.

Nearby, the **Hôtel de Sens,** a Paris landmark at 1 rue du Figuier, 4e (tel. 42-78-14-60), was built between the 1470s and 1519 for the archbishops of Sens. Along with the Cluny on the Left Bank, it is the only domestic architecture remaining from the 15th century. Long after the archbishops had departed, 1605 to be exact, it was inhabited by the scandalous Queen Margot, wife of Henri IV. Her new lover—"younger and more virile"—slew the discarded one while she looked on in great amusement. The restoration of the Hôtel de Sens was, as usual, the subject of great controversy; nonetheless, today it houses the Bibliothèque Forney. Leaded-glass windows and turrets characterize the façade; you can go into the courtyard to see more of the ornate stone decoration—the gate is open from 1:30 to 8 p.m., except on Sunday and Monday.

Finally, the **Hôtel de Sully,** 62 rue St-Antoine, 4e (tel. 48-87-24-14). Work began on this mansion in 1625, on the orders of Jean Androuet de Cerceau. In 1634 it was acquired by the duc de Sully, who had been Henri IV's minister of finance before the king was assassinated in 1610. After a strait-laced life as "the accountant of France," Sully broke loose in his declining years, adorning himself with diamonds and garish rings . . . and a young bride. Noted for her indiscretion, the young bride told not only her confidants but her husband as well of her preference for "very young" men, whom she openly invited to their home. Sully, incidentally, was 74 years old when he moved to the Marais address with her. He died seven years later.

The Hôtel de Sully was acquired by the French government just after World War II. Recently restored, the relief-studded façade is especially appealing. You can visit the interior of the hotel with a guide on Wednesday, Saturday, and Sunday at 3 p.m. There is entrance to the courtyard and the garden every day. In the building is an information center where you can learn about the Marais, Paris, and the monuments of France.

THE LATIN QUARTER: This is the precinct of the University of Paris (often called the Sorbonne), lying on the Left Bank in the 5th Arrondissement—where students meet and fall in love over coffee and croissants. Rabelais called it the "Quartier Latin," because of the students and professors who spoke Latin in the classroom and on the streets. The sector teems with belly dancers, exotic restaurants (from Vietnamese to Balkan), sidewalk cafés, bookstalls, *caveaux,* and the *clochards* and *chiffonniers* (the bums and ragpickers).

A good starting point for your tour might be **Place St-Michel,** where Balzac used to get water from the fountain when he was a youth. This center was the scene of much Resistance fighting in the summer of 1944. The quarter centers around **Boulevard St-Michel,** to the south (the students call it "Boul Mich").

From the "place," your back to the Seine, you can cut left down **rue de la Huchette,** the setting of Elliot Paul's *The Last Time I Saw Paris.* Paul first wandered into this typical street "on a soft summer evening, and entirely by chance," in 1923. Although much has changed since his time, some of the buildings are so old they often have to be propped up by timbers. Paul captured the spirit of the street more evocatively than anyone, writing of "the delivery wagons, makeshift vehicles propelled by pedaling boys, pushcarts of itinerant vendors, knife-grinders, umbrella menders, a herd of milch goats, and the neighborhood pedestrians." The local bordello has closed, however.

Branching off from Huchette is **rue du Chat Qui Pêche** (the "Street of the Cat Who Fishes"), said to be the shortest, narrowest street in the world, containing not one door and only one window. It is usually filled with garbage or lovers . . . or both.

Now, down rue de la Harpe to rue St-Séverin and—

The Church of St-Séverin

This flamboyant Gothic building, just a short walk from the Seine, hardly recaptures the lifestyle of its namesake, the ascetic recluse of the sixth century. An act of Henri I in the 11th century gave the church to Paris, and by the end of the 15th century it was imitating some of the architectural features of Notre-Dame across the river. In the 17th century Mlle de Montpensier (La Grande Mademoiselle) was one of its parishioners and certainly its heaviest financial contributor.

Before entering, walk around the church to see its gargoyles, birds of prey, and reptilian monsters projecting from the top. To the right, facing the church, is the "garden of ossuaries" of the 15th century. The entrance on the rue des Prêtres (Métro: St-Michel or Maubert-Mutualité) leads to the wide interior. Inside, the stained glass is its most obvious adornment—in cobalt, burgundy, amber, magenta, white-gold, royal-blue, indigo, oyster-pink, ruby-red. It is interesting to contrast the modern stained glass by Jean Bazaine in 1970 with the panels from the 14th and 15th centuries.

The present church was built from 1210 to 1230, then reconstructed in 1458. The tower was completed in 1487, the chapels between 1498 and 1520. Hardouin-Mansart designed the Chapel of the Communion in 1673 when he was 27 years old. For information, telephone 43-25-96-63.

Across rue St-Jacques lies the—

Church of St-Julien-le-Pauvre

This church, at 1 rue St-Julien-le-Pauvre, occupies a virtual oasis in Paris. Stand first at the gateway and look at the beginning of rue Galande, especially the old houses with the steeples of St-Séverin rising across the way—one of the most characteristic and most painted scenes on the Left Bank. You enter through a courtyard, listening to chirping birds, walking into a slice of medieval Paris, isolated and aloof. The garden to the left of the entrance offers the best view of Notre-Dame.

The church is like a country chapel, and everybody from Rabelais to Thomas Aquinas has passed through its doors. Before the sixth century a chapel stood on this spot. The present structure goes back to the Longpont monks, who began work on it in 1170, which makes it the oldest existing church in Paris. In 1655 it was given to the Hôtel Dieu, and in time became a small warehouse for salt. In 1889, however, it was turned over to the followers of the Melchite Greek rite, an eastern branch of the Byzantine church.

Do stop by—then head for the major attractions on the Left Bank:

The Cluny Museum

You stand in the cobblestone Court of Honor, admiring the flamboyant Gothic building with its clinging vines, turreted walls, gargoyles, and dormers with seashell motifs. Along with the Hôtel de Sens in le Marais, the Hôtel de Cluny is all that remains of domestic medieval architecture in Paris. Originally, the Cluny was the mansion—built over and beside the ruins of a Roman bath—of a rich 15th-century abbot.

By 1515 it was the residence of Mary Tudor, teenage widow of Louis XII and daughter of Henry VII of England and Elizabeth of York.

Seized during the Revolution, the Cluny was rented in 1833 to Alexandre du Sommerard, who adorned it with his collection of medieval works of art. Upon his death in 1842, both the building and the collection were bought back by the government.

The present-day collection of arts and crafts of the Middle Ages is considered the finest in the world. Most people come primarily to see the **Unicorn Tapestries,** viewed by critics (and I heartily concur) as the most outstanding tapestries in the world. A beautiful princess and her handmaiden, beasts of prey, and just plain pets—all the romance of the age of chivalry lives on in these remarkable yet mysterious tapestries. They were discovered only a century ago in the Château de Boussac in Auvergne. Five seem to deal with the five senses (one, for example, depicts a unicorn looking into a mirror held up by a dour-faced maiden). The sixth shows a woman under an elaborate tent with jewels, her pet dog resting on an embroidered cushion beside her. The lovable unicorn and his friendly companion, a lion, hold back the flaps. The background in red and green forms a rich carpet of spring flowers, fruit-laden trees, birds, rabbits, donkeys, dogs, goats, lambs, and monkeys.

The other exhibitions are wide ranging, including a 16th-century retable—
The Passion—from Anvers; a 15th-century Florentine (life-size) John the Bap-

tist; 14th-century French consoles; four statues from the Sainte Chapelle, dating from 1243–1248; 13th-century crosses, studded with gems; golden chalices, manuscripts, ivory carvings, vestments, leatherwork, jewelry, coins, a 13th-century Adam, and heads and fragments of statues from Notre-Dame de Paris recently discovered. In the fan-vaulted medieval chapel hang tapestries depicting scenes from the life of St. Stephen.

Downstairs are the ruins of the Roman baths, dating supposedly from around A.D. 200. You wander through a display of Gallic and Roman sculptures and an interesting marble bathtub engraved with lions. A votive pillar dates from the days of Tiberius. Both the museum and baths are open daily except Tuesday from 9:45 a.m. to 12:30 p.m. and 2 to 5:15 p.m.; 12F ($1.66) for admission, only 6F (83¢) on Sunday. The museum is at 6 Place Paul-Painlevé, 5e. Métro: Odéon or St-Michel. For information, phone 43-25-62-00.

Head down the Boul Mich, and shortly you'll arrive at—

The Sorbonne

The University of Paris—everybody calls it the Sorbonne—is one of the most famous institutions in the world. Founded in the 13th century, it had become the most prestigious university in the West by the 14th century, drawing such professors as Thomas Aquinas. Reorganized by Napoleon in 1806, the Sorbonne is today the premier university of France.

At first glance from Place de la Sorbonne, it seems architecturally undistinguished. In truth, it was rather indiscriminately reconstructed at the turn of the century. Not so the **Church of the Sorbonne**, built in 1635 by Le Mercier, which contains the marble tomb of Cardinal Richelieu, a work by Girardon based on a design by Le Brun. At his feet, the statue *Science in Tears* is remarkable. Métro: St-Michel.

At the end of rue Soufflot stands—

The Panthéon

Some of the most famous men in the history of France (Victor Hugo, for one) are buried here, in austere grandeur, on the crest of the mount of St. Geneviève. In 1744 Louis XV made a vow that if he recovered from a mysterious illness, he would build a church to replace the decayed Abbey of St. Geneviève. He recovered. Madame de Pompadour's brother hired Soufflot for the job. He designed the church in 1764, in the form of a Greek cross, with a dome reminiscent of that of St. Paul's Cathedral in London. Soufflot died, and the work was carried out by his pupil Rondelet, who completed the structure nine years after his master's death.

Came the Revolution, and the church was converted into a "Temple of Fame"—ultimately a pantheon for the great men of France. The body of Mirabeau was buried here, although his remains were later removed. Likewise, Marat was only a temporary tenant. However, Voltaire's body was exhumed and placed here—and allowed to remain.

In the 19th century the building changed roles so many times—first a church, then a pantheon, then a church—that it was hard to keep its function straight. After Victor Hugo was buried here, it became a pantheon once more. Other notable men entombed within include Jean-Jacques Rousseau, Soufflot, Emile Zola, and Louis Braille.

The finest frescoes—the Puvis de Chavannes—are found at the end of the left wall before you enter the crypt. One illustrates St. Geneviève bringing supplies to relieve the victims of the famine. The very best fresco depicts her white-draped head looking out over moonlit medieval Paris, the city whose patroness she became.

It is open daily from 10 a.m. to noon and 2 to 5:30 p.m. April to September, till 4:30 p.m. October to March. Admission is 10F ($1.38). For more information, telephone 43-54-34-51. Métro: St-Michel or Monge.

ALONG THE SEINE: A stroll along the banks and quays of the noble Seine is for many visitors the most memorable walk in Paris. Some of the city's most important monuments, such as Notre-Dame on the Île de la Cité, are best viewed from the riverbank. Many of them, such as the mighty façade of the Louvre, take on even more interest at night when they are floodlit.

Famous bridges, such as the **Pont Neuf,** the oldest in Paris, recall the Middle Ages. (In those days, you came to the bridge to have your tooth pulled.) Seven crossings lie between the Invalides and the Île de la Cité open to vehicular traffic.

The Seine is called the loveliest avenue in Paris. You walk past flower vendors, seed merchants, pet shops, sellers of caged birds (parakeets, finches, fantail pigeons, pheasants, and parrots), perhaps stopping at one of the *bouquinistes* or booksellers that line the parapets. Postcards, stamps, souvenirs, reproductions of paintings . . . the bouquinistes sell more than books. Suitable for framing are the prints and drawings of Vieux Paris. Incidentally, along the way you'll pass fishermen called by one writer "the most patient in the world."

If you should fall in love with the Seine, you can always moor your houseboat here, as did the writer Anaïs Nin, recording her experience in a memorable short story, "Houseboat."

You may also want to ride on the Seine. The glass-topped **Bateaux Mouches** (tel. 42-25-96-10) offer luxury cruises. The launches vary, some boasting delightful open sundecks and others having well-stocked bars and restaurants. All provide commentaries in five languages, including English. Departures are from the Pont d l'Alma, at the Place de l'Alma, 7e, on the Right Bank (Métro: Alma-Marceau). Boats leave at least every 30 minutes from 9:30 a.m. to 11:30 p.m. (every 15 minutes in good weather, depending on the demand). Rates are 25F ($3.45) to 30F ($4.14) for a ride lasting about an hour and 15 minutes. The higher price is for the evening illuminations cruise. Children go for half price. Luncheon cruises are popular, departing at 1 p.m. and costing 220F ($30.34). There is also a deluxe dinner cruise leaving at 8:30 p.m. at a cost of 450F ($62.06). Formal dress is preferred for this cruise.

2. Other Major Sights

Those with more time can plunge deeper into the soul of Paris, beginning at the—

ÎLE SAINT-LOUIS: As you walk across the little iron footbridge from the rear of Notre-Dame, you descend into a world of tree-shaded quays, aristocratic town houses and courtyards, restaurants, and antique shops.

The sister island of the Île de la Cité is primarily residential; its denizens fiercely guard their heritage, privileges, and special position. If you meet residents on the Riviera and ask them where they live, they don't answer just "Paris," they say perhaps "Île Saint-Louis," or more defiantly, "Île."

Saint-Louis was originally two "islets," one named "Island of the Heifers." It was popular as a dueling ground, prompting one foreigner to write home, "There isn't a Frenchman worth his salt who has not slain a man in a duel." The two islands were ordered joined by Louis XIII.

The number of famous people who have occupied these patrician mansions is now a legend. Plaques on the façades make it easier to identify them. Madame Curie, for example, lived at 36 Quai de Bethune, near Ponte de la Tournelle, from 1912 until her death in 1934.

The most exciting mansion (and there is almost universal agreement on that) is the **Hôtel de Lauzun,** built in 1657. It is surely one of the most elegant town houses of Paris. It is owned by the city, and permission to visit it requires bureaucratic red tape. At 17 Quai d'Anjou, it is named after the 17th-century rogue the Duc de Lauzun, famous lover and on-again/off-again favorite of Louis XIV (he once hid under the Sun King's bed while the monarch made love to his mistress of the moment). At the hôtel, the French courtier was secretly married to "La Grande Mademoiselle" (the Duchess of Montpensier), much to the dislike of Louis XIV, who dealt with the matter by hustling him off to the Bastille.

That "Flower of Evil" Charles Baudelaire, French poet of the 19th century, lived at Lauzun with his "Black Venus," Jeanne Duval. At the same time that he was squandering the family fortune, Baudelaire was working on poems that celebrated the erotic. Although he had high hopes for them, they were dismissed by many as "obscene, vulgar, perverse, and decadent." (It was only in 1949 that the French court lifted the ban on all the works.) Baudelaire attracted such artists as Delacroix and Courbet to his apartment, which was often filled with the aroma of hashish. Occupying another apartment was 19th-century novelist Théophile Gautier ("art for art's sake"), who is remembered today chiefly for his *Mademoiselle de Maupin*.

Voltaire lived at 2 Quai d'Anjou, in the **Hôtel Lambert,** with his mistress Emilie de Breteuil, the Marquise du Châteley, who had an "understanding" husband. The couple's quarrels at the Hôtel Lambert were known all over Europe (Emilie did not believe in confining her charms, once described as "nutmeg-grater skin" and "bad teeth," to her husband or her lover). But not even Frederick, king of Prussia, could permanently break up her liaison with Voltaire.

The mansion was built by Louis Le Vau in 1645 for Nicolas Lambert de Thorigny, the president of the Chambre des Comptes. For a century the hôtel was the home of the royal family of Poland, the Czartoryskis, who entertained Chopin, among others.

Farther along, at no. 9, stands the house where Honoré Daumier, the painter, sculptor, and lithographer, lived between 1846 and 1863. From that house he satirized the petite bourgeoisie of his day. In hundreds upon hundreds of lithographs he attacked corruption in the French government. His caricature of Louis-Philippe netted him a six-month jail sentence. Métro: Sully-Morland or Pont-Marie.

THE PALAIS ROYAL: At the demolished Café Foy in the Palais Royal, Camille Desmoulins jumped up on a table and shouted for the mob "to fight to the death." The date was July 13, 1789. The French Revolution had begun. But the renown of the Palais Royal goes back much further. Facing the Louvre, the gardens were planted in 1634 for Cardinal Richelieu, who presented them to Louis XIII. As a child, the future Louis XIV played around the fountain, once nearly drowning. Children frolic here to this day.

In time the property became the residence of the dukes of Orléans. Philippe-Égalité, a cousin of Louis XVI, built his apartments on the grounds, and subsequently rented them to prostitutes. By the 20th century those same apartments were rented by such artists as Colette and Cocteau. Of the gardens Colette wrote, "It is as though I were living in the provinces under the shadow of the parish church! I go into the temple en passant." (A plaque at 9 rue Beaujolais marks the entrance to her apartment, which she inhabited until her death in 1954.)

New York–born American actor and playwright John Howard Payne wrote *Home, Sweet Home* while living in one of the apartments.

Let us turn the clock back again: Napoléon Bonaparte, then an 18-year-old lieutenant, met his first prostitute in the Palais Royal. Robespierre and Danton dined here. An actress, Mlle Montansier, "knew" many of them, including the Corsican. Charlotte Corday came this way, looking for a dagger with which to kill Marat. During the Directoire, when gambling dens flourished at the Palais

Royal, foreigners reported seeing Frenchmen leaving the salons without their silk breeches—they had literally lost their trousers at the tables!

Today a sleepy provincial air remains. It's hard to imagine its former life. From the Place Colette, you enter the Court of Honor, colonnaded on three sides. The palace is the headquarters of the Councils of State these days, and the Court of Honor is a parking lot during the day. In the center of the Palais Royal is the Galerie d'Orléans, with two fountains and many a colonnade. You can stroll through the gardens or down the Galerie Montpensier, filled with little shops no one but stamp collectors ever seem to patronize.

Everything seems sadly neglected, although it has a physical location that could make it the most elegant boutique district of Paris.

Métro: Palais-Royal.

PLACE VENDÔME: Always aristocratic, sometimes royal, Place Vendôme enjoyed its golden age in the heyday of the Second Empire. Dress designers—the great ones, such as Worth—introduced the crinoline there. Louis Napoléon lived here, wooing his future empress, Eugénie de Montijo, at his address at Hôtel du Rhin. In its halcyon days the waltzes of Strauss echoed across the plaza. But in time they were replaced by cannon fire.

Today the most prestigious tenant on the plaza is the Ritz. Banks and offices abound. Still, the Place Vendôme is considered one of the most harmonious squares in France, evoking the Paris of le grand siècle—that is, the age of Louis XIV.

The square is dominated today by a column crowned by Napoleon. The plaza was originally planned by Mansart to honor Louis XIV—so it's a good thing he died earlier. There was a statue of the Sun King here until the Revolution, when it was replaced briefly by "Liberty."

Then came Napoleon, who ordered that a sort of Trajan's Column be erected in honor of the victor at Austerlitz. That Napoleon himself won the battle was "incidental." The column was made of bronze melted from captured Russian and Austrian cannons.

After Napoleon's downfall the statue was replaced with one of Henri IV, everybody's favorite king and every woman's favorite man. Later Napoleon surmounted it once again, this time in uniform and without the pose of a Caesar.

The Communards of 1871, who detested royalty and the false promises of emperors, pulled down the statue. The artist Courbet is said to have led the raid. For his part in the drama, he was jailed and fined the cost of restoring the statue. He couldn't pay it, of course, and was forced into exile in Switzerland. Eventually, the statue of Napoleon, wrapped in a Roman toga, finally won out.

The plaza is one of the best known in Paris. It has attracted tenants such as Chopin, who lived at no. 12 until his death in 1849. Who was Vendôme, you ask? He was the son (delicate writers refer to him as "the natural son") of the roving Henri IV and his best-known mistress, Gabrielle d'Estrées. Métro: Opéra.

AROUND THE HÔTEL DE VILLE: Back in the good old days, you could stroll down to the Hôtel de Ville for an evening's amusement. If it was a good day, you could see Robespierre being hauled off to the guillotine, Foulon getting lynched on a lamppost, or revelers tossing cats into a bonfire.

You can still visit the district, but the entertainment isn't what it used to be. Take the Métro (one of four lines) to **Place du Châtelet**—a theatrical square, dominated by Napoleon's palm fountain, at the foot of which rest four sphinx-like figures.

On one side of the square is the **Théâtre de la Ville,** honoring Sarah Bernhardt; on the other, the **Théâtre Municipal du Châtelet,** the largest in Paris. A fortress once stood on this spot, overlooking the Seine, and in it was imprisoned the highwayman Cartouche. Before he was removed to the Conciergerie, the fashionable ladies of Paris considered it "sport" to peer in at his cell, giggling their little hearts out.

In a satellite square stands the **Tower of St. Jacques,** isolated and alone today. In the flamboyant Gothic style, it was erected between 1508 and 1522, but the church to which it was attached was destroyed by revolutionaries. For some reason, somebody decided to spare the tower, and it remains as an anachronistic landmark at the point where rue de Rivoli meets the Boulevard de Sébastopol. You can't scale it as Pascal did to make experiments, but you can sit in the surrounding park and either watch the cars whiz around you or contemplate the marble statue of Pascal, his robes clustered around him, a curious position for the founder of the modern theory of probability.

From Place du Châtelet, take the Avenue Victoria, named after the English queen, to the **Hôtel de Ville,** at Place de l'Hôtel-de-Ville. In the 1920s two elegantly dressed American visitors arrived demanding rooms. They had seen photographs of the pseudo-Renaissance-style building and had mistakenly assumed that it provided deluxe accommodations. Hôtel de Ville, of course, means town hall in French.

One of the most flamboyant buildings in Paris, the municipal building boasts a façade studded with 136 statue-filled niches honoring such Frenchmen as Pigalle. It is not the original building that stood on this spot. After France's defeat by the Prussians in 1871, the Communards burned down the building. It was rebuilt in the following decade.

Town Hall Square was once the infamous **Place de Grève,** center of public executions. Before cheering crowds, Leonora Galigai, confidante of Marie de Medici, was beheaded following her conviction on a charge of witchcraft. When "the Jack the Ripper of France," Cartouche, was brought to the execution stand, he "squealed" for almost a full day, naming his accomplices. They killed him nonetheless.

The most publicized execution was that of Ravaillac, the mystic who killed Henri IV. As French historian Roger-Armand Weigert put it: "He was tortured with red-hot pincers, burned with 'fire and brimstone,' sprinkled with hot lead, boiling oil, pitch, burning resin, wax and brimstone melted together, and then pulled apart and dismembered by four horses." The year was 1610. Some 60 years later, the Marquise de Brinvilliers was beheaded for being a bad cook. She was. Her arsenic-flavored cuisine killed her father and two of her brothers.

Behind the Town Hall on the Place St-Gervais is the **Church of St. Gervais and St. Protais,** named after two Roman martyrs. The façade—the first of the classical style in Paris—incorporates Doric, Ionic, and Corinthian features that have nothing to do with the Gothic interior. The church was begun in 1494, completed in 1657, when much of Paris turned out to see the new and "daring" style.

Inside, the chapels are richly decorated, the artwork including a 19th-century sculptured *Christ on the Cross* by Antoine-Auguste. The mausoleum of Louis XIV's chancellor, Michel Le Tellier, the work of Pierre Mazeline and Simon Hurtrelle, is memorable. The oldest chapel, dating from the late 15th century, was dedicated to St. Madeleine. Adjoining it is the Chapel of St. Pierre, finished in 1510.

Many great names in French history have attended the church; Madame de Sévigné was married there. During the Middle Ages, it is said, French justice was dispensed under an elm tree outside.

Head back to the Tower of St. Jacques, walk down rue de Rivoli, then turn left on rue St-Bon, which turns into steps. A narrow alley leads to rue de la Verrerie and (at no. 76) the **Church of St. Merry,** crowded in by houses but easily seen from Centre Pompidou on the north. Once this was the liveliest district of Paris, and St. Merry's was known as "the worshipping hole of sluts."

Inside the 16th-century Gothic church are some notable artworks, including a painting, *The Blue Virgin,* by Van Loo (to the right of the choir). The large

Chapel of the Communion was constructed between 1741 and 1754. It contains a painting, *The Pilgrims d'Emmaüs,* by Charles-Antoine Coypel (1694–1752). Within the church are two haut-reliefs—one a monument to Joan of Arc by Paul-Amboise Slodtz, dated 1743. The church is open every day from 8 a.m. to 7 p.m. Free concerts are presented every Saturday at 9 p.m. and on Sunday afternoon at 4 p.m.

LES HALLES: In the 19th century Zola called it "the underbelly of Paris." For eight centuries Les Halles was the major wholesale fruit, meat, and vegetable market of Paris. The smock-clad vendors, the carcasses of beef, the baskets of what many regarded as the most appetizing fresh vegetables in the world—all that belongs to the past. Today the action has moved to the steel-and-glass contemporary structure at Rungis, a suburb near Orly Airport. The original edifice, Baltard's old zinc-roofed Second Empire "umbrellas of iron," has been torn down.

Replacing these so-called umbrellas is **Le Forum des Halles,** which opened in 1979. This large complex, much of it underground, contains dozens of shops, plus several restaurants and movie theaters, along with a wax museum (previewed separately). Many of the shops aren't as good as one would wish, but others contain a wide display of merchandise that has made the complex popular with both residents and visitors alike.

For many tourists a night on the town is still capped by the traditional bowl of onion soup at Les Halles, usually at Au Pied de Cochon ("Pig's Foot") or at Au Chien Qui Fume ("Smoking Dog"), in the wee hours. One of the most classic scenes of Paris was night-owling tourists or elegantly dressed Parisians (many just released from Maxim's) standing at a bar drinking cognac with bloody butchers. Some writers have suggested that one Gérard de Nerval introduced the custom of frequenting Les Halles at such an unearthly hour. (De Nerval was a 19th-century poet whose life was considered "irregular." He hanged himself in 1855.)

A newspaper correspondent described the market scene today this way: "Les Halles is trying to stay alive as one of the few places in Paris where one can eat at any hour of the night."

There is still much to see in Les Halles district, beginning with the **Church of St-Eustache,** which, in the opinion of many, is rivaled only by Notre-Dame. In the old days cabbage vendors came there to pray for their produce. Even before that it knew the famous and the infamous of its day—everybody from Madame de Pompadour (she was baptized here; so was Richelieu) to Molière, whose funeral was held here in 1673.

In the Gothic-Renaissance style, the church dates from the mid-16th century, although it wasn't completed until 1637. It has been known for its organ recitals ever since Liszt played here in 1866. Inside is the black-marble tomb of Jean Baptiste Colbert, the minister of state under Louis XIV. A marble statue of the statesman rests on top of his tomb, which is flanked by a Coysevox statue of *Abundance* (a horn of flowers) and a J. B. Tuby depiction of *Fidelity.* The main entrance to the church is at 2 rue du Jour (another entrance on rue Rambuteau).

The district around the protective mother church of Les Halles has always had an unsavory reputation. Centuries ago a Parisian was saying how "ideal it was for assassinations." The best-known murder was that of Henri IV ("Vert Galant") in front of 11 rue de la Ferronnerie (the street of ironmongers). The assassin was Ravaillac, whose punishment I described above.

Close at hand, rue des Lombards is worth seeking out. Once it was the banking center of Paris.

ST-GERMAIN-DES-PRÉS: In the époque of l'après-guerre, a long-haired girl in black slacks, black sweater, and black sandals drifted into St-Germain-des-Prés. Her name was Juliette Greco. She arrived in the heyday of the existentialists, when all the world seemed to revolve around Jean-Paul Sartre, Simone de Beauvoir, and Albert Camus. The Café de Flore, the Brasserie Lipp, and Deux-Magots were the stage settings for the newly arriving postwar bohemians who came there to "existentialize."

In time Sartre was eulogizing Miss Greco ("She has millions of poems in her throat"); her black outfit was adopted by girls from Paris to California; and eventually she earned the title of "la muse de St-Germain-des-Prés."

In the 1950s new names appeared: Françoise Sagan, Gore Vidal, James Baldwin. By the time the 1960s had arrived the tourists were as firmly entrenched at the Café de Flore and Deux-Magots. The old days are gone, but St-Germain-des-Prés remains an interesting quarter of nightclubs in "caves," publishing houses, bookshops, art galleries, Left Bank bistros, and coffeehouses—as well as two historic churches.

St-Germain-des-Prés Church

Outside it's an early-17th-century town house, a handsome one at that. But beneath that covering it's one of the oldest churches in Paris, going back to the sixth century when a Benedictine abbey was founded on the site by Childebert, son of Clovis, the "creator of France." Unfortunately, the marble columns in the triforium are all that remains from that period. At one time the abbey was a pantheon for Merovingian kings. Restoration of St. Symphorien Chapel, which is the site of the Merovingian tombs, at the entrance of the church, began in 1981. During that work, unknown Romanesque paintings were discovered on the triumphal arch of the chapel, making it one of the most interesting places of old Christian Paris.

Its Romanesque tower, topped by a 19th-century spire, is the most enduring landmark in the village of St-Germain-des-Prés. Its church bells, however, are hardly noticed by the patrons of Deux-Magots across the way.

The Normans were fond of destroying the abbey, and did so at least four times. The present building, the work of four centuries, has a Romanesque-style nave and a Gothic-style choir with fine capitals. Among the people interred at the church are Descartes and Jean-Casimir, the king of Poland who abdicated his throne.

The address of the church is 3 Place St-Germain-des-Prés, 6e; for information, telephone 43-25-41-71.

When you leave St-Germain-des-Prés Church, just turn right in the rue de l'Abbaye and have a look at the 17th-century Palais Abbatial, a pink palace.

Church of St. Sulpice

Pause first on the 18th-century **Place St-Sulpice** (Métro: St-Sulpice). On the 1844 fountain by Visconti are sculpted likenesses of four 18th-century bishops: Fenelon, Massillon, Bossuet, and Flechier. Napoleon, then a general, was given a stag dinner there in 1799. He liked the banquet but not the square. When he was promoted he changed it. One of the two towers of the church was never completed.

Work originally began on the church in 1646; the façade, "bastardized classic," was completed in 1745. Many architects, including Le Vau, worked on the building. Some were summarily fired; others, such as the Florentine Servandoni, were discredited.

One of the most notable treasures inside the 360-foot-long church is Servandoni's rococo Chapel of the Madonna, with a marble statue of the Virgin by Pigalle. One critic wrote that you'd have to go to Versailles to find a peer of that chapel. The church contains one of the world's largest organs, with more than 6,500 pipes. The Sunday mass concerts—made known by Charles Widor—draw many visitors. Chalgrin designed the organ case in the 18th century.

One of the largest and most prestigious churches in Paris, St. Sulpice was sacked during the Revolution and converted into the Temple of Victory. Camille Desmoulins, the revolutionary who sparked the raiding of the Bastille, was married here.

But the real reason you come to St. Sulpice is to see the Delacroix frescoes in the Chapel of the Angels (first on your right as you enter). Seek out his muscular Jacob wrestling (or is he dancing?) with an effete angel. On the ceiling St. Michael is having his own troubles with the Devil, and yet another mural depicts Heliodorus being driven from the temple. Painted in the final years of his life, the frescoes were a high point in the career of the baffling, romantic Delacroix.

If you are impressed by Delacroix, you can pay him a belated tribute by visiting the—

National Museum of Eugène Delacroix

To art historians, Delacroix is something of an enigma. Even his parentage is a mystery. Many believed that Talleyrand had the privilege of fathering him. The Frank Anderson Trapp biography saw him "as an isolated and atypical individualist—one who respected traditional values, yet emerged as the embodiment of Romantic revolt." By visiting his atelier, you will see one of the most charming squares on the Left Bank and also the romantic garden of the museum.

The apartment is at 6 Place de Fürstenberg (Métro: St-Germain-des-Prés; tel. 43-54-04-87). You reach the studio through a large arch on a stone courtyard. The house may be visited daily except Tuesday from 9:45 a.m. to 5:15 p.m. for an admission of 6F (83¢). In spring and summer a special exhibition takes place in the museum, each year on a different theme about Delacroix.

Delacroix died in this apartment on August 13, 1863. Lithographs, watercolors, oils, and reproductions fill the house where the artist sat up into the late hours writing his memorable and penetrating journals. In the Louvre is a portrait of Delacroix as a handsome, strong, mustachioed man. You'll also have to go to the Louvre to see some of the artist's best-known paintings, such as *Liberty Leading the People*.

A short walk away is the **rue Visconti**, a street obviously designed for pushcarts. At no. 17 is the maison where Balzac established his printing press in 1825. The venture ended in bankruptcy—which forced the author back to his writing desk. In the 17th century the French dramatist Jean-Baptiste Racine lived across the street. Such celebrated actresses as Champmeslé and Clairon were also in residence.

MONTPARNASSE: For the "lost generation," life centered around the literary cafés of Montparnasse. Hangouts such as Dôme, Coupole, Rotonde, and the Select became legendary. Artists, especially American expatriates, turned their backs on Montmartre, dismissing it as "too touristy." Picasso, Modigliani, and Man Ray came this way, and Hemingway was a popular figure. So was Fitzgerald when he was poor (when he was in the chips, you'd find him at the Ritz). William Faulkner, Archibald MacLeish, Isadora Duncan, Miró, James Joyce, Ford Madox Ford, even Trotsky—all were here. Except Gertrude Stein, who would not frequent the cafés. To see her, you would have to wait for an invitation to her salon at 27 rue de Fleurus. She bestowed her favor on Sherwood Anderson, Elliot Paul, and, for a time, Hemingway. However, Papa found that there wasn't "much future in men being friends with great women." John Malcolm Brinnin wrote in *The Third Rose*: "To have paid respects to Gertrude and to have sat with Alice [Alice B. Toklas] was to have been admitted into the charmed circle of those whose pretenses, at least, were interesting and fashionable."

When not receiving, Miss Stein was busy buying paintings—works by Cézanne, Renoir, Matisse, and Picasso. One writer said that her salon was engaged in an international conspiracy to promote modern art. At her Saturday evening gatherings you might meet Braque.

The life of Montparnasse still centers around its cafés and exotic nightclubs, many of them only a shadow of what they used to be. Its heart is at the crossroads of the Boulevard Raspail and the Boulevard du Montparnasse, one of the settings of *The Sun Also Rises*. Hemingway wrote that "the Boulevard Raspail always made dull riding." Rodin's controversial statue of Balzac swathed in a large cape stands guard over the prostitutes who cluster around the pedestal. Balzac seems to be the only one in Montparnasse who doesn't feel the impact of time and change.

The **Maine-Montparnasse Tower,** 33 Avenue du Maine, overshadows the Left Bank Quarter of Montparnasse where Gertrude Stein once reigned at her Saturday evening gatherings. The tower, completed in 1973, covers an entire block and houses some 80 shops, including Galeries Lafayette, and more than 200 offices. Its 56 floors are serviced by ultra-rapid elevators that speed visitors from the lobby to the top floor in less than 40 seconds. Sightseers go to **Montparnasse 56**, the covered, glassed-in observation deck on the 56th floor, where a panoramic view of Paris opens from every side. A ticket includes an audio-visual presentation of the girls and glamour of Paris, expositions of how the tower was built, and highlights of the Paris skyline far below. The Belvedere bar-café, good for lunch, a quick snack, or a drink, is also in the Montparnasse 56 complex. The charge for the elevator to the 56th floor is 22.50F ($3.10) for adults and 12F ($1.66) for children under 15. Montparnasse 56 is open daily from 9:30 a.m. to 11 p.m. in summer, from 10 a.m. to 10 p.m. in winter. For an additional 5F (69¢), you can climb a set of stairs leading to the heliport a couple of flights up, where you can have an open-air view of Paris.

Also on the 56th floor is **Le Ciel de Paris**, the highest (altitudinally) restaurant in the city, where for 225F ($21.03) to 275F ($37.92) you can enjoy a full meal of such specialties as rognons de veau with morels or paupiettes of salmon and scallops. When you have finished your meal, if you wish, the waiter will give you a ticket for entrance into Montparnasse 56. Le Ciel de Paris is open from noon to 3 p.m. and 7 p.m. to midnight seven days a week. Reservations (tel. 45-38-52-35) are suggested but not absolutely essential ordinarily. There is no charge to take the elevator going directly to the restaurant from the lobby. The Métro stop for the tower is Montparnasse-Bienvenue.

THE GRANDS BOULEVARDS: Once there was nothing more fashionable than dining at a restaurant along these boulevards. Their chic began in the mid-18th century, reaching a pinnacle with the carriage trade, which later abandoned them for the Champs-Élysées. Stretching from the Madeleine to Baron Haussmann's Place de la République, the boulevards are lined with many fine department stores and shops.

The Madeleine Church

The promenade begins at the Madeleine, one of the most imposing Grecian-inspired temples in the world. The Madeleine church stands right in the heart of the Right Bank on the landmark Place de la Madeleine, 8e. Actually, the "Madeleine" is a nickname—the church is dedicated to St. Mary Magdalene. Construction began in 1764, but the original architect was replaced with another who wanted to turn the structure into a building "that would shame the Parthenon."

In Napoleon's heyday the church was torn down and reconstructed as "the Temple of Glory," honoring the Grand Army. In 1816 it was made into a church again, although it didn't officially open until 1842. And it almost became the first railway station in Paris.

The temple is ringed with a Corinthian colonnade, its columns holding up an encircling frieze (one of the pediments depicts the Last Judgment). Bas-reliefs on the bronze door represent the Ten Commandments, and in niches along the façade are statues of saints. From the portal you have a panoramic vista down the rue Royale to the Egyptian obelisk on the Place de la Concorde. Inside the church, a trio of skylit domes illuminate the central nave, the gilded globe lanterns, and the inlaid marble floor.

Concerts are staged here at least once a month (tel. 42-65-86-32 for information). Métro: Madeleine.

Boulevard de la Madeleine

The Boulevard de la Madeleine is the most fashionable part of the Grands Boulevards in this era. At no. 11, Marguerite Gautier, heroine of *La Dame aux Camélias* died of consumption. Nowadays, the ground floor is a tea salon and chocolate shop. On the right side, you can purchase boxes of chocolate; on the left, order tea and mouthwatering, calorie-loaded pastries served by waitresses in black uniforms and stiffly starched white aprons.

Boulevard des Capucines

The Boulevard de la Madeleine leads to the Boulevard des Capucines, where, at no. 14, now the Hôtel Scribe, a plaque honors those "pioneers of the cinema," the Lumière brothers, who launched their films on December 28, 1895.

Across the street is the **Museum Cognacq-Jay,** 25 Boulevard des Capucines, 2e (tel. 42-61-94-54), like a specimen of the past preserved under a bell jar. This somewhat esoteric collection was gathered by the late Ernest Cognacq, founder of the Samaritaine department store.

In a town house, the museum is a world of gilt, paintings, tapestries, porcelain, statuary, gouaches, and various renditions of maidens dressing and pursuing domestic activities. Of the French works, those of Boucher, Fragonard, Greuze, Chardin, and Lépicié, pastels by Latour and Perronneau, drawings by Watteau (exhibited in rotation), and busts by Lemoyne are the most important. But there are also portraits by English artists, such as Sir Joshua Reynolds, Sir Thomas Lawrence, and others. Tiepolo's *Banquet of Cleopatra* and Rembrandt's *L'Anesse du Prophète Balaam* (painted when he was only 20) represent the old masters of Europe. A good collection of furniture and decorative objects of the 18th century assembled by Cognacq and Louise Jay have been tastefully arranged in the museum.

Diagonally across the street from the Café de la Paix, the museum is open daily except Monday from 10 a.m. to 5:40 p.m.; admission is 8F ($1.10). Métro: Opéra.

Place de l'Opéra

The Place de l'Opéra is dominated by the Opéra house, described in the following chapter. Also opening onto that square is one of the best-known cafés in Europe, the Café de la Paix, described in the next chapter.

What I will describe in this chapter is the **Opéra Museum,** Place Charles-Garnier, 2e, entered from a side entrance of the Opéra itself. All is nostalgia here: the sets, the sketches, the costumes, the performances from the Opéra's memorable past. Simulated stage sets of some operas produced since 1669 are only part of the attractions. On display are Léger's sketch of *Bolivar,* Utrillo's *Louise,* a portrait of Carlotta Zambelli, one of Wagner by Renoir, and many sketches by Boucher. Fans, masks, busts by Carpeaux, the piano of Massenet, memorabilia of Pavlova and Nijinsky, even a scale model of the Opéra—nothing is forgotten. Both the museum and the more-than-200,000-volume library are open daily except Sunday from 10 a.m. to 5 p.m. for 6F (83¢) admission. Métro: Opéra.

3. More Museums

The greatest museum of Paris, the Louvre, and other important ones such as the Cluny have already been previewed. Here are some others, the first of which is one of the most interesting in Paris.

THE RODIN MUSEUM (HÔTEL BIRON): These days Rodin is acclaimed as the father of modern sculpture, but in a different era his work was labeled obscene. The world's artistic taste changed, and in due course the government of France purchased the gray-stone 18th-century luxury residence in Faubourg St-Germain. The mansion was the studio of Rodin from 1910 till his death in 1917. The rose gardens were restored to their 18th-century splendor, a perfect setting for Rodin's most memorable works.

In the courtyard are three world-famous creations: *The Gate of Hell, The Thinker,* and *The Burghers of Calais.* Rodin's first major public commission, *The Burghers* commemorated the heroism of six burghers of Calais who, in 1347, offered themselves as hostages to Edward III in return for his ending the siege of their port. Perhaps the single best-known work, *The Thinker* in Rodin's own words "thinks with every muscle of his arms, back, and legs, with his clenched fist and gripping toes." Not yet completed at Rodin's death, *The Gate of Hell,* as he put it, is "where I lived for a whole year in Dante's Inferno."

Inside the building, the sculpture, plaster casts, reproductions, originals, and sketches reveal the freshness and vitality of that remarkable man. Many of his works appear to be emerging from marble into life. Everybody is attracted to *The Kiss* (of which one critic wrote, "the passion is timeless"). Upstairs are two different versions of the celebrated and condemned nude of Balzac, his bulky torso rising from a tree trunk (Albert E. Elsen commented on the "glorious bulging" stomach). Included are many versions of his *Monument to Balzac* (a large one stands in the garden), which was Rodin's last major work and which caused a furor when it was first exhibited.

Other significant sculpture includes Rodin's *Prodigal Son* (it literally soars); *The Crouching Woman* (called the "embodiment of despair"); and his *The Age of Bronze,* an 1876 study of a nude man, modeled by a Belgian soldier. (Rodin was accused—falsely—of making a cast from a living model.)

At 77 rue de Varenne, 7e, the museum (tel. 47-05-01-34) is open daily except Tuesday from 10 a.m. to 5:15 p.m. (to 6 p.m. from April 1 to September 30); 15F ($2.07) admission, half price on Sunday. Métro: Varenne.

Digression: At the Hôtel Biron, you'll be on the threshold of what was the most elegant residential district of Paris in the 18th century, the **Faubourg St-Germain.** If you don't have to rush immediately to Napoleon's Tomb, try to explore some of that once-aristocratic district, lying roughly between the Invalides and St-Germain-des-Prés. At one time or another, some of the most celebrated names in France have lived there: Mme Récamier, Lafayette, Chateaubriand, Turgot, Queen Hortense, Mme de Montespan, André Gide, Ingres, Corot, Baudelaire, and Guillaume Apollinaire.

Deserted by fickle fashion, the former mansions are now occupied by foreign embassies or ministries such as the French Ministry of National Education. At 138 rue de Grenelle, Marshall Foch, the supreme Allied commander in World War I, died on March 20, 1929. On the same street, at 59 rue de Grenelle, Alfred de Musset lived from 1824 to 1839, before George Sand lured him away on an amorous adventure. The façade at the poet's residence is the most elegant on the street—note the *Fountain of the Four Seasons,* designed by Bouchardon in 1739. A woman, signifying the City of Paris, is seated on a throne of lions, dominating the figures of the Seine and the Marne at her feet. In niches to each side of her—favorite roosts of Parisian pigeons—are bas-reliefs depicting the four seasons. Autumn is illustrated with cherubs harvesting the grapes from the vineyards.

GEORGES POMPIDOU NATIONAL CENTER FOR ART AND CULTURE: In 1969 George Pompidou, then president of France, decided to create a large cultural center including every form of 20th-century art. The center was finally opened in 1977 on the Plateau Beaubourg, in the midst of a huge, car-free pedestrian district east of the Boulevard de Sebastopol 4e, (tel. 42-77-12-33). The structure, towering over a festive plaza, is the subject of much controversy. Parisians refer to the radical exoskeletal design as "the refinery." The Tinker-Toy-like array of pipes and tubes surrounding the transparent shell are actually functional, serving as casings for the heating, air conditioning, electrical, and telephone systems for the center. The great worm-like tubes crawling at angles up the side of the building contain the escalators that transport visitors from one floor to the next. Inside, no interior walls block one's view. Each floor is one vast room, divided as necessary by movable partitions.

The unique structure has already proved a favorite attraction for Parisian and foreign visitors alike, drawing more viewers each year than Paris's former top sight, the Eiffel Tower. From the top of the center, you can also enjoy one of the best views of the city. The center is made up of four separate attractions:

The **Musée National d'Art Moderne** (National Museum of Modern Art) offers a large collection of 20th-century art. The museum space has recently been redesigned, giving the widest possible scope of modern and contempoary art in an international manner. The uniqueness of the Pompidou Center in cultural life today is shown vividly. The collections include French and American masterpieces. All the current trends of modern art are displayed on two floors (entrance on the fourth floor) in well-lit rooms of varying sizes. From the Fauves up to current abstract and expressionist works, the range is complete.

Featured are such artists as Max Ernst (a sculpture, *The Imbecile),* Kandinsky, Vuillard, Bonnard, Utrillo, Chagall, Dufy, Juan Gris, Léger, Pollock, as well as sketches by Le Corbusier and stained glass by Rouault. Modern sculpture includes works by Alexander Calder, Henry Moore, and Jacob Epstein. A gallery of contemporary artists (Galeries Contemporaines), on the fifth floor, demonstrates the trends in artistic activity today. Special exhibitions and demonstrations are constantly being staged in the Grande Galerie to acquaint the public with the significant works of the 20th century. Guided tours are available.

The center also houses the **Public Information Library** where, for the first time in Paris's history, the public has free access to one million French and foreign books, periodicals, films, records, slides, and microfilms in nearly every area of knowledge.

The **Center for Industrial Design,** covering some 40,000 square feet of space, emphasizes the contributions made in the fields of architecture, visual communications, publishing, and community planning.

The **Institute for Research and Coordination of Acoustics/Music** brings together musicians and composers interested in furthering the cause of music, both contemporary and traditional. Concerts, workshops, and seminars are frequently open to the public.

In addition to its four main departments, the center also offers a children's workshop and library and a "cinémathèque," which tells the history of motion pictures.

The Pompidou Center is open daily except Tuesday. Hours are noon to 10 p.m. on weekdays and 10 a.m. to 10 p.m. on Saturday and Sunday. A day pass, costing 30F ($4.14) grants visitors access to any part of the center, although special exhibits may require an additional admission fee. The Museum of Modern Art, when visited separately, costs 16F ($2.21), with free admission on Sunday. Métro: Rambuteau.

MUSÉE PICASSO: When it opened at the beautifully restored Hôtel Salé (salt mansion), a state-owned property in Le Marais, the press hailed it as a "museum for Picasso's Picassos." And that's what it is. Almost overnight it became—and continues to be—one of the most popular attractions in Paris. The Hôtel Salé is at 5 rue de Thorigny, 3er (tel. 42-71-25-21); Métro: St-Sébastien. It is open daily from 10 a.m. to 5:15 p.m. except Tuesday; on Wednesday, it remains open till 10 p.m. Admission is 20F ($2.75) or half price on Sunday. The greatest Picasso collection in the world, acquired by the state in payment of inheritance taxes totaling 50 million dollars, consists of 203 paintings, 158 sculptures, 16 collages, 19 bas-reliefs, 88 ceramics, and more than 1,500 sketches and 1,600 engravings, along with 30 notebooks. These works are representative of the artist, spanning some 75 years of his life and changing styles.

The range of paintings includes a remarkable self-portrait in 1901 and goes on to embrace such masterpieces as *Le Baiser* ("the kiss") painted at Mougins in 1969. The museum also acquired another masterpiece he did a year later at the same place on the Riviera: it's called *Reclining Nude and the Man with a Guitar.* It's easy to stroll through the handsome museum seeking your own favorite work (mine is a delightfully wicked one, *Jeune Garcon à la Langouste,* "young man with a lobster," painted in Paris in 1941). The Paris museum owns several intriguing studies for *Les Demoiselles d'Avignon,* the painting that launched Cubism. Many of the major masterpieces such as *The Crucifixion* and *Nude in a Red Armchair* should remain on permanent view. However, because the collection is so vast, temporary exhibitions, featuring such items as his studies of the Minotaur, will be held for the public, probably at the rate of two a year. In addition to Picasso's own treasure trove of art, works by other masters from his private collection are displayed, including the contributions of such world-class artists as Cézanne, Rousseau, Braque, and André Derain, as well as Miró. Picasso was fascinated with African masks, and many of these are on view as well.

The collection opened here in 1979 (the artist died in 1973), but the mansion was constructed in 1656 by Aubert de Fontenay who collected the dreaded salt tax in Paris.

MARMOTTAN MUSEUM: A town-house mansion with all the trappings of the First Empire, the Marmottan Museum is one of the many private family collections on display in Paris. Occasionally a lone art historian would venture to 2 rue Louis-Boilly, 16e, on the edge of the Bois de Boulogne, to see what Paul Marmottan donated to the Académie des Beaux-Arts. Hardly anybody else did . . . until 1966, when Michel Monet, son of Claude Monet, died in a car crash, leaving a bequest of his father's art—valued at $10 million—to the little museum. The Académie des Beaux-Arts suddenly found itself heir to more than 130 paintings, watercolors, pastels, and drawings—and a whole lot of Monet-lovers, who can, in one place, trace the evolution of the great man's work.

The gallery owns more than 30 pictures of his house at Giverny, and many of water lilies, his everlasting intrigue. The bequest included his *Willow,* painted in 1918, his *Houses of Parliament,* from 1905, even a portrait Renoir did of Monet when he was 32. The collection has been hailed "one of the great art treasures of the world," and that it is. Ironically, the museum had always owned Monet's *Impression,* from which the movement got its name.

Paul Marmottan's original collection includes fig-leafed nudes, First Empire antiques, assorted objets d'art, bucolic paintings, and crystal chandeliers. Many of the tapestries date from the Renaissance, and you can also see the extensive collection of miniatures donated by Daniel Waldenstein.

The museum is open daily except Monday from 10 a.m. to 6 p.m.; 20F ($2.76) admission. Métro: La-Muette.

MUSEUM OF THE MONUMENTS OF FRANCE: At the Palais de Chaillot,

Place du Trocadéro, 16e (tel. 47-27-35-74), this museum houses moldings of the *grandes oeuvres* of French sculpture, including entire façades and portals, as well as reproductions of the most significant mural paintings up to the 16th century. Reproduced in detail are such landmarks in art as the southern façade of Chartres Cathedral (1220-1225) as well as the western one (1145-1160). The Romanesque and Gothic sculptures can be examined from an intimate perspective; in the original, much of the intricacy is lost or the sculpture too elevated to be appreciated.

Not only will you see some of the sculpture of such cathedrals as Notre-Dame and Reims, but such sights as the 16th-century southern door of the transept of Beauvais Cathedral; that decorative masterpiece, the tomb of François II and of Marguerite de Foix at Nantes; the door to the chapter house of Bourges Cathedral; the 1560 north door of the transept in Rouen's Church of St. Maclou; and the 1535 Hôtel de Bernuy (school for boys) at Toulouse. Notable are the reproductions of the painted pillars at St-Savin-sur-Gartempe at Vienne.

Many of the Romanesque and Gothic mural paintings are reproduced right down to their faded glory (see, for example, the 14th-century dome of the Cathedral of Cahors, the town that was the ancient capital of Quercy). Perhaps the most ghoulish work is from La Brigue Chapel, the most humorous the fork-tailed monsters devouring flesh from the château de Villeneuve-Lembron, Puy-le-Dôme (1515-1517). The monuments museum is open daily except Tuesday, from 9:45 a.m. to 12:30 p.m. and 2 to 5:15 p.m., charging an admission of 12F ($1.66), half price on Sunday. Métro: Trocadéro.

MUSÉE DE L'HOMME: This museum, which deserves to be better known, is devoted to the history of people and their way of life. It is in the Palais de Chaillot (tel. 45-05-70-60) at the Place du Trocadéro, 16e.

In the first gallery as you enter is a case containing the most important exhibit, the Cro-Magnon "Menton man," discovered in 1872 in the Grimaldi grottoes on the French Riviera. Among the replicas are South African and Sahara cave paintings. One long gallery depicts African cultures, with some of the best-known pieces of African art. Then follow Ethiopia, with a beautiful and rare set of church paintings, North Africa, the Middle East, and Europe, with a series of traditional garb displayed. The upstairs galleries are filled with representative artifacts from the Arctic, Asia, Oceania, and the Americas. The North American section contains some of the oldest Plains Indian pieces in existence. Of particular note are the chaman costumes from Siberia, the renewed exhibits dealing with Laos and Cambodia, a complete set of door carvings from New Caledonia, some of the best-known carvings from Polynesia, and pre-Columbian art from South and Central America.

One big room is turned over to temporary exhibitions, dealing with prehistoric or ethnographical themes. A smaller, free-entrance display area has been set up in the hall. A library sells scientific books dealing with the history of man and his cultures. On the third floor, a Photographic Documentation Department (Photothèque) is open to the public.

The museum is open daily except Tuesday, from 9:45 a.m. to 5:15 p.m. for an admission of 15F ($2.07).

CITÉ DES SCIENCES ET DE L'INDUSTRIE: A city of science and industry has risen at La Villette, 30 Avenue Corentin Cariou, 19e (tel. 42-20-27-28). When its core was originally built in the 1960s, it was touted as the most modern slaughterhouse in the world. But when the site was abandoned as a failure in 1974, its echoing vastness and unlikely location on the northern edge of the city presented the French government with a problem. In 1986, the converted premises opened as the world's most expensive ($642 million) science complex, designed "to modernize mentalities" as a first step in the process of modernizing society.

What a visitor sees is a project so ambitious that only a portion was completed by 1986. Eventual plans call for the canals surrounding the complex of buildings to flood portions of a surrounding park. What you'll see today, after picking your way through the still-active construction site, is something akin to a futuristic airplane hangar which only becomes coherent after you ascend the almost interminable escalator to the second floor. There, busts of Plato, Hippocrates, and a double-faced Janus gaze silently at a tube-filled space-age riot of high-tech girders, glass, and lights, something akin to what a layman might think of the interior of an atomic generator. The sheer dimensions of the place are awesome, a challenge to the arrangers of the constantly changing exhibits. Some of the exhibits are couched in an overlay of Gallic trendiness, including seismographic activity as presented in the comic-strip adventures of a jungle explorer. Among others is the silver-skinned Geodesic Dome (called the Géode) which shows the closest thing to 3D cinema in Europe on the inner surfaces of its curved walls. It is a 112-foot-high sphere with a 370-seat theater.

The place is so vast, with so many options, that a single visit gives only an idea of the scope of the as-yet-unfilled project. Even entrance fees and hours may change before your actual visit. However, count on spending 40F ($5.52) for adults, 20F ($2.76) for children. It is open daily except Monday from 2 to 10 p.m., and it lies between the Porte de Pantin and the Porte de la Villette Métro stops.

MARINE MUSEUM (MUSÉE DE LA MARINE): This museum occupies the same address as the two above—Palais de Chaillot, Place du Trocadéro et du 11 Novembre. A lot of it is pomp: gilded galleys and busts of stiff-necked admirals. There's a great number of old ship models, including, for instance, the big galley *La Réale,* the *Royal-Louis,* the rich ivory model *Ville de Dieppe,* the gorgeous *Valmy.* A barge constructed in 1811 for Napoléon I was used to carry another Napoleon (the Third) and his empress, Eugénie, on their first visit to the port of Brest in about 1858. The imperial crown is held up by winged cherubs.

Models of World Wars I and II warships strike a more ominous note, and there are many documents and artifacts concerning merchant fishing and pleasure fleets, oceanography, hydrography, with films illustrating the subjects. Thematic exhibits explain, for instance, ancient wooden shipbuilding, development of scientific instruments, merchant navy, fishing, steam, and sea traditions, and show some souvenirs of explorer Laperouse's wreck in Vanikoro Island in 1788. Important paintings include Joseph Vernet's *The Ports of France* during the 18th century.

The museum is open daily except Tuesday from 10 a.m. to 6 p.m. Admission is 14F ($1.93). For information, telephone 45-53-31-70. Métro: Trocadéro.

PALAIS DE TOKYO: This imposing building, at 13 Avenue du Président-Wilson (tel. 47-23-36-53), was erected on the site of an establishment that used to turn out the Savonnerie carpets. The present structure is a palace constructed for the International Exhibition in 1937. It is not, as its name suggests, a museum of Japanese art. The National Museum of Modern Art used to be here before its transfer to the Pompidou Centre.

Since 1978 the Palais de Tokyo has housed the **Musée d'Art et d'Essai,** which features temporary exhibitions on various themes presenting works from the Louvre and other national museums, and it has one of the finest collections of post-impressionists in Paris. See, for example, Seurat's *The Circus,* started in 1891 but never finished because of his death. There is a large collection of paintings from Gauguin and the School of Pont-Aven, Vuillard, Bonnard, Redon, and Toulouse-Lautrec. There are also photo exhibits.

The Palais de Tokyo is open from 9:45 a.m. to 5:15 p.m. daily except Tuesday, charging 12F ($1.66) admission (half price on Sunday). Métro: Iéna or Alma-Marceau.

MUSÉE D'ART MODERNE DE LA VILLE DE PARIS: Right next door to the Palais de Tokyo, at 11 Avenue du Président-Wilson (tel. 47-23-61-27), this interesting museum displays a permanent collection of paintings and sculpture owned by the City of Paris. In addition, the **M.A.M.** section of the city's modern art museum presents ever-changing temporary exhibitions on individual artists from all over the world or on international art trends. Bordering the Seine, the salons display works by such artists as Chagall, Matisse, Léger, Braque, Picasso, Dufy, Utrillo, Delaunay, Rouault, and Modigliani. See, in particular, Pierre Tal Coat's *Portrait of Gertrude Stein*. Picasso wasn't the only artist to tackle this difficult subject. Other sections in the museum are **ARC**, which shows work of young artists and new trends in contemporary art, and the **Musée des Enfants,** which has exhibitions and shows for children. The Modern is open from 10 a.m. to 5:30 p.m. daily except Monday, charging 9F ($1.24) admission, half price for children and students. It's free on Sunday. On Wednesday it remains open until 8:30 p.m. Métro: Iéna or Alma-Marceau.

GUIMET MUSEUM: Named after its founder and established originally at Lyon, the Guimet was transferred to Paris in 1889. It received in 1931 the collection of the Musée Indochinois du Trocadéro and, after World War II, the Asian collections of the Louvre. Today it is one of the world's richest museums of its genre.

The art ranges from Tibet to Japan to Afghanistan to Nepal to Java to India to China. There are even sculptures from Vietnam. The most interesting displays are on the ground floor, the exhibits encompassing Buddhas, heads of serpentine monsters, funereal figurines. See, for example, antiquities from the temple of Angkor Wat. The Jacques Bacot gallery is devoted to Tibetan art: fascinating scenes of the Grand Lamas entwined with serpents and demons.

On the first floor is the Indian section with the remarkable Mathura Serpent-King (second century A.D.), the Amaravati reliefs. René Grousset, a French art historian, was impressed with the "simple paganism, the innocent pleasure in the nude form." Of a harem group from that school (3rd century), he found its sensuality "refined," its freshness "agreeable." On the same floor, the Rousset collection is to be seen.

On the top floor, the Michael Calmann collection is devoted to vases, statuettes in porcelain, ceramics, and pottery, including the Grandidier collection, that run the gamut of Chinese dynasties—going back six or seven centuries before the birth of Christ and forward to the Ts'ing Dynasty (1644-1911).

Across from the Museum of Modern Art de la Ville de Paris (above), the Guimet is open daily except Tuesday from 9:45 a.m. till noon and 1:30 till 5:15 p.m.; 12F ($1.66) admission. The museum is at 6 Place d'Iéna, 16e, and for information, telephone 47-23-61-65. Métro: Iéna or Alma-Marceau.

MUSÉE DES ARTS DÉCORATIFS: The Museum of Decorative Arts, 107 rue de Rivoli, 1er (tel. 42-60-32-14), is in the northwest wing of the Pavillon de Marsan of the Louvre, offering a treasury of furnishings, fabrics, wallpaper, objets d'art, and other items which add up to well-conceived displays of the style of living followed in other times, ranging from the Middle Ages to the present. The museum was refurbished during the early 1980s, with some striking displays set up which were formerly stowed away. Among these, notable are the art deco boudoir, bath, and bedroom done in the 1920s for couturier Jeanne Lanvin by designer Rateau. This and other decorative art displays from 1900 to 1925, including design work by Gallé, Fréchet, Sue et Mare, and Chareau, are on the first floor, together with collections of contemporary art and a 1900 room.

Displays of decorative art from the Middle Ages to the Renaissance are on the second floor, while rich collections from the 17th, 18th, and 19th centuries occupy the third and fourth floors. You can wander from room to room, getting an idea of the scope and depth of the French style: a 15th-century four-poster, a sword, a rifle, 16th-century musical instruments, diamond-studded walking sticks, exquisite enamelware, Norman glassware, decorative woodwork, and lots of gilt. Elegant salons let you peek at the high life in the First and Second Empires, as well as the Louis XV and Louis XVI periods. The fifth floor contains specialized centers of the museum, such as wallpaper and drawings, and documentary centers detailing fashion, textiles, toys, crafts, and glass trends.

For many people, the sixth floor holds the most interest, holding the prestigious collection of the works of Jean Dubuffet which the artist donated to the museum. A prodigious painter whose style fluctuated amazingly from period to period, Dubuffet once wrote, "I feel a need that every work of art should in the highest degree lift one out of context, provoking a surprise and shock." In that, he succeeds.

The museum also organizes temporary exhibitions. It is open daily except Monday and Tuesday, from 12:30 to 6:30 p.m., Sunday from 11 a.m. to 5 p.m. Admission can range from free to whatever. Métro: Palais-Royal.

PETIT PALAIS: Built by architect Charles Girault, the small palace faces the Grand Palais (housing special exhibitions)—both erected for the 1900 Exhibition.

The Petit Palais, on the Avenue Winston-Churchill (tel. 42-65-12-73), contains works of art belonging to the City of Paris. Most prominent are the Dutuit and Tuck collections. In the Dutuit collection are Egyptian, Greek, and Roman bronzes, 11th-century Byzantine designs, rare ivory statues (the most prominent of which is of a Roman actor), and a series of ancient Greek porcelains. From the Middle Ages are enamels, sculpture, and hand-lettered and -painted manuscripts. A good collection of 17th-century Dutch and Flemish paintings are also on view, with representative artists including Breughel *(Wedding Pageant)*, Rubens, Hobbema, Ruysdaël, and others.

The museum's other major collection was donated by Edward Tuck in 1930. It's composed mainly of decorative artwork of the 18th century, including tapestries, furniture (much gilt), wood-paneled salons, and porcelains, which give a good overview of the esthetic sense of France at the time of the fall of the ancien régime.

The rooms that encircle the interior garden of the museum are dedicated to 19th-century French painting, including a few works by major impressionists before they had the experience to perfect their techniques. In the collection are canvasses by Courbet, Daumier, Corot, Delacroix, Manet, Sisley, Mary Cassatt *(Le Bain)*, Maurice Denis, Odilon Redon, a series of portraits (one of Sarah Bernhardt), and art by Edouard Vuillard and Pierre Bonnard. Not to be missed are sculptures by Rodin, Bourdelle, and Maillol, and creations of what is currently the craze in antique stores, glassworks by Gallé and Lalique.

The museum is open daily except Monday, from 10 a.m. to 5:40 p.m. Admission is 9F ($1.24), unless there's a special exhibition for which the charge is usually 18F ($2.48). It's free on Sunday. Métro: Champs-Elysées.

JACQUEMART-ANDRÉ MUSEUM: This late-19th-century town house was built by Edouard André, who later married Nélie Jacquemart, an artist. Together they formed a collection of rare French 18th-century decorative art and Italian Renaissance works. Mlle André, who died shortly before World War I, willed the building and its contents to the Institut de France. At 158 Boulevard Haussmann, 8e (tel. 45-62-39-94), it is perhaps the best of the little decorative art museums of Paris. The collection can be viewed any day except Monday and Tuesday, from 1:30 to 5:30 p.m. for 10F ($1.38) admission. Closed in August. Métro: Miromesnil or St-Philippe-du-Roule.

You enter through an arcade leading into an enclosed courtyard. Two white lions guard the doorway. Inside are Gobelin tapestries, Houdon busts, Savonnerie carpets—and a rich art collection, including Rembrandt's *The Pilgrim of Emmaüs*. Represented are paintings by Van Dyck, Tiepolo, Rubens, Watteau, Boucher, Carpaccio, and Mantegna *(Virgin and Child)*. Donatello torchères, statuary (including a wingless victory), Slodtz busts, della Robbia terracottas (Ganymede with the eagle), and antiques round out the collection. The salons drip with gilt, and the winding stairway to the top floor is elegant.

MUSÉE CERNUSCHI: Bordering the Parc Monceau, this small museum is devoted to the arts of China. It's another one of those mansions whose owners stuffed them with an art collection, then bequeathed them to the City of Paris. The address—7 Avenue Velásquez—was quite an exclusive one when the town house was built in 1885.

Inside, there is, of course, a bust of Cernuschi—and that is as it should be, a self-perpetuating memorial to a man whose generosity and interest in the East was legend in his day. Now the collections include a fine assortment of Neolithic potteries, as well as bronzes from the 14th century B.C., the most famous perhaps the tiger-shape vase. The jades, ceramics, and funereal figures are exceptional, as are the pieces of Buddhist sculpture. Most admirable is a Bodhisattva originating from Yun-kang (6th century). Rounding out the exhibits are some ancient paintings, the best known of which is *Horses with Grooms*, attributed to Han Kan (8th century, T'ang dynasty). The museum (tel. 45-63-50-75) also houses a good collection of contemporary Chinese painting. The museum may be visited any day except Monday from 10 a.m. to 5:40 p.m.; 9F ($1.24) admission, free on Sunday except for exhibitions. Métro: Monceau or Villiers. Bus 30 or 94.

NISSIM DE CAMONDO MUSEUM: At 63 rue de Monceau (tel. 45-63-26-32), near the Musée Cernuschi, this museum is a jewel box of elegance and refinement, evoking the days of Louis XVI and Marie Antoinette. The pre-World War I town house was donated to the Museum of Decorative Arts by Comte Moïse de Camondo (1860-1935) in memory of his son, Nissim, a French aviator killed in combat in World War I.

Entered through a courtyard, the museum is like the private home of an aristocrat of two centuries ago—richly furnished with needlepoint chairs, tapestries (many from Beauvais or Aubusson), antiques, paintings (the inevitable Guardi scenes of Venice), bas-reliefs, silver, Chinese vases, crystal chandeliers, Sèvres porcelain, and Savonnerie carpets. And, of course, a Houdon bust (in an upstairs bedroom). The Blue Salon, overlooking the Parc Monceau, is impressive. You can wander without a guide through the gilt and oyster-gray salons.

Open all year, the museum may be visited from 10 a.m. to noon and 2 to 5 p.m. for 12F ($1.66) admission. It's closed Monday and Tuesday. Métro: Villiers.

BALZAC MUSEUM: At 47 rue Raynouard, 16e (tel. 42-24-56-38), in the residential district of Passy near the Bois de Boulogne, sits a modest house. Here the great Balzac lived for seven years beginning in 1840. Fleeing there after his possessions and furnishings were seized, Balzac cloaked himself in secrecy (you had to know a password to be ushered into his presence). Should a creditor knock on the Raynouard door, Balzac could always escape through the rue Berton exit.

The museum's most notable memento is the Limoges coffee pot (the novelist's initials are in mulberry pink) that his "screech-owl" kept hot throughout the night as he wrote *La Comédie Humaine* to stall his creditors. Also enshrined here is a cast of Balzac's hands, described by Gautier as the hands of a true prelate.

Although unfurnished, the little house is filled with reproductions of caricatures of Balzac. (A French biographer once wrote: "With his bulky baboon silhouette, his blue suit with gold buttons, his famous cane like a golden crowbar, and his abundant, disheveled hair, Balzac was a sight for caricature.")

The house is built on the slope of a hill, with a small courtyard and garden. The museum is open daily except Tuesday, from 10 a.m. to 5:45 p.m., charging 9F ($1.24) for admission. Métro: Passy or La-Muette.

GRÉVIN MUSEUM: The desire to compare this museum at 10 Boulevard Montmartre, 9e (tel. 47-70-85-05), to Madame Tussaud's of London is almost irresistible. Grévin is the number-one waxworks of Paris. It isn't all blood and gore, and doesn't shock some as Tussaud's might. Presenting a panorama of French history from Charlemagne to the mistress-collecting Napoléon III, it shows memorable moments in a series of tableaux.

Depicted are the consecration of Charles VII in 1429 in the Cathedral of Reims (Joan of Arc, dressed in armor and carrying her standard, stands behind the king); Marguerite de Valois, first wife of Henri IV, meeting on a secret stairway with La Molle, who was soon to be decapitated; Catherine de Medici with the Florentine alchemist Ruggieri; Louis XV and Mozart at the home of the Marquise de Pompadour; and Napoleon on a rock at St. Helena, reviewing his victories and defeats.

Two shows are staged frequently throughout the day. The first, called the "Palais des Mirages," starts off as a sort of Temple of Brahma, and through magically distorting mirrors, changes into an enchanted forest, then a fête at the Alhambra at Granada. A magician is the star of the second show, "Le Cabinet Fantastique"; he entertains children of all ages.

The museum is open from 1 to 7 p.m. daily, the ticket office closing at 6 p.m., but it is open from 10 a.m. to 7 p.m. during French school holidays. It charges 34F ($4.69) for adults and 22F ($3.03) for children under 15. Métro: Montmartre or Richelieu-Drouot.

A subsidiary, the **"new Musée Grévin,"** is in the Forum des Halles at Grand-Balcon-Niveau, 1 rue Pierre Lescot, 1er (tel. 42-61-28-50), one of the world's most modern underground shopping centers situated on the site of the famous Halles, in the heart of Paris. It is a sound-and-light wax museum displaying the Belle Époque at the turn of the century with wax figures of Victor Hugo, Toulouse-Lautrec, Sarah Bernhardt, and other famous persons. The 20 scenes cover the Moulin Rouge and its French cancan, the building of the Eiffel Tower, and other fabulous scenes. The museum is open daily from 10:30 a.m. to 7:30 p.m., with the ticket office closing at 7:15 p.m. The charge is 32F ($4.41) for adults and 20F ($2.76) for children under 15. Métro: Les Halles.

MANUFACTURE NATIONALE DE SÉVRES: Madame de Pompadour loved Sévres porcelain. She urged Louis XV to order more and more of it, thus ensuring its position among the fashionable people of the 18th century. Two centuries later, it is still fashionable.

The Sévres factory, next door to a museum, has been owned by the State of France for more than two centuries. It was founded originally in Vincennes, and moved to Sévres, a riverside suburb of Paris, in 1756. The factory may be visited on Thursday, except holidays and in July and August. The visits are free. The factory's commercial service sells porcelains to the public daily except Sunday and holidays. The museum opens its doors every day except Tuesday, from 9:30 a.m. to noon and 1:30 to 5:15 p.m. for 10F ($1.38) admission, half price on Sunday.

The **Musée National de Ceramique de Sévres** shelters one of the finest collections of faïence and porcelain in the world. Some of it belonged to Madame du Barry, Pompadour's hand-picked successor. You can see the Sévres ware as it looked from the day it was created and as it looks straight from the factory today. On view, for example, is the "Pompadour rose" (which the English insisted on calling the "rose du Barry"), a style much in vogue in the 1750s and 1760s. The painter Boucher made some of the designs used by the factory, as did the sculptor Pajou (he did the bas-reliefs for the Opéra at Versailles). The factory pioneered what became known in porcelain as the Louis Seize style—it's all here, plus lots more, including works from Meissen (archrival of Sèvres). Charging 10F ($1.38) for entrance, it is open from 9:30 a.m. to noon and 1:30 to 5:15 p.m. except Tuesday.

Take the Métro to the end of the Pont de Sèvres line, walk across the Seine to the Left Bank, and you'll be there.

MUSÉE ZADKINE: This museum, at 100 bis rue d'Assas, 6e (tel. 43-26-91-90), near the Luxembourg Gardens and the Boulevard St-Michel, is one of the newest of the museums of Paris. Once it was the private residence of Ossip Zadkine, the sculptor. Now the collection of this famous artist has been turned over to the City of Paris for public viewing. Included are some 300 pieces of sculpture, displayed both within the museum and in the garden, which gives a rural charm to the heart of the city. In addition, many drawings and paintings are also exhibited. Hours are from 10 a.m. to 5:30 p.m. Tuesday to Sunday. Admission is 9F ($1.24). Métro: Luxembourg or Vadim.

4. More Churches

VAL-DE-GRÂCE: According to an old proverb, to understand the French you must like Camembert cheese, the Pont Neuf, and the dome of Val-de-Grâce.

After 23 years of a barren marriage to Louis XIII, Anne of Austria gave birth to a boy who would one day be known as the Sun King. In those days, if monarchs wanted to express gratitude, they built a church or monastery. On April 1, 1645, seven years after his birth, the future Louis XIV laid the first stone of the church. At that time, Mansart was the architect. To him we owe the façade in the Jesuit style. Le Duc, however, designed the dome, and the painter Mignard decorated it with frescoes. Other architects included Le Mercier and Le Muet.

The origins of the church go back even further, to 1050, when a Benedictine monastery was founded on the grounds. In 1619 Marguerite Veni d'Arbouze was appointed abbess by Louis XIII. She petitioned Anne of Austria for a new monastery, as the original one was decaying. Then came Louis XIV's church, which in 1793 was turned into a military hospital and in 1850 an army school.

The church may be visited from 9 a.m. to noon and 2 to 5 p.m. daily, except during services. To reach it, walk up rue du Val-de-Grâce from Boulevard St-Michel. Métro: Luxembourg.

CHURCH OF ST. STEPHEN-ON-THE-MOUNT: Once there was an abbey on this site, founded by Clovis and later dedicated to Ste Geneviéve, the patroness of Paris. Such was the fame of this popular saint that the abbey proved too small to accommodate the pilgrimage crowds. Now part of the Lycée Henri IV, the Tower of Clovis is all that remains from the ancient abbey (you can see the Tower from rue Clovis).

Today, the task of keeping alive the cult of Ste Geneviéve has fallen on the Church of St-Étienne-du-Mont, on Place Ste-Geneviéve, practically adjoining the Panthéon. The interior is in the Gothic style, unusual for a 16th-century church. Construction on the present building began in 1492 and lasted until 1626.

Besides the patroness of Paris, such men as Pascal and Racine were entombed in the church. Incidentally, the tomb of the saint was destroyed during the Revolution. However, the stone on which her coffin rested was discovered later, and the relics were gathered for a place of honor at St. Étienne.

The church possesses a remarkable rood screen, built in the first part of the 16th century. Across the nave, it is unique in Paris—uncharitably called spurious by some, although others have hailed it as a masterpiece. Another treasure is a wood-carved pulpit, held up by a semi-nude Samson who clutches a bone in one hand, having slain the lion at his feet. The fourth chapel on the right (when entering) contains most impressive stained glass from the 16th century. Métro: Monge.

CHURCH OF ST. GERMAIN L'AUXERROIS: Once it was the church for the Palace of the Louvre, drawing an assortment of courtesans, men of art and of law, artisans from the quartier, even royalty. Sharing the Place du Louvre with Perrault's colonnade, the church contains only the foundation stones of its original belfry built in the 11th century. It was greatly enlarged in the 14th century by the addition of side aisles. The little primitive chapel that had stood on the spot eventually gave way to a great and beautiful church, with 260 feet of stained glass, including some rose windows from the Renaissance.

The saddest moment in its history was on August 24, 1572. The unintentional ringing of its bells signaled the St. Bartholomew Massacre, in which the Protestants suffered a blood bath. The churchwardens' pews are outstanding, with intricate carving, based on designs by Le Brun in the 17th century. Behind the pew is a 15th-century triptych and Flemish retable (so badly lit you can hardly appreciate it). The organ was originally ordered by Louis XVI for Sainte Chapelle. In that architectural mélange, many famous men were entombed, including the sculptor Coysevox and Le Vau, the architect. Around the chancel is an intricate 18th-century grille.

5. The Gardens of Paris

We've already walked through the Tuileries. In this section we explore some other oases, beginning with the—

LUXEMBOURG GARDENS: Hemingway told a friend that the Luxembourg Gardens "kept us from starvation." He related that in his poverty-stricken days in Paris, he wheeled a baby carriage (the vehicle was considered luxurious) and child through the gardens because it was known "for the classiness of its pigeons." When the gendarme went across the street for a glass of wine, the writer would eye his victim, preferably a plump one, then lure him with corn . . . "snatch him, wring his neck," then flip him under Bumby's blanket. "We got a little tired of pigeon that year," he confessed, "but they filled many a void."

Before it became a feeding ground for struggling Montparnasse artists of the 1920s, Luxembourg knew greater days. But it's always been associated with artists, although students from the Sorbonne and children predominate nowadays. Watteau came this way, as did Verlaine. Balzac, however, didn't like the gardens at all. In 1905 Gertrude Stein would cross the gardens to catch the Batignolles-Clichy-Odéon omnibus pulled by three gray mares across Paris, to meet Picasso in his studio at Montmartre, where she sat while he painted her portrait.

The gardens are the best on the Left Bank (some say in all of Paris). Marie de Medici, the much-neglected wife and later widow of the roving Henri IV, ordered a palace built on the site in 1612. She planned to live there with her "witch" friend, Leonora Galigaï. A Florentine by birth, the regent wanted to create another Pitti Palace, or so she ordered the architect, Salomon de Brossee. She wasn't entirely successful, although the overall effect is most often described as Italianate.

The queen didn't get to enjoy the palace for very long after it was finished. She was forced into exile by her son, Louis XIII, after it was discovered that she was plotting to overthrow him. Reportedly, she died in Germany in poverty, quite a comedown from that luxury she had once known in the Luxembourg. Incidentally, the 21 paintings she commissioned from Rubens that glorified her life were intended for her palace, although they are now in the Louvre. The palace can't be visited without special permission in advance.

But you don't come to the Luxembourg to visit the palace, not really. The gardens are the attraction. For the most part, they are in the classic French tradition: well groomed and formally laid out, the trees planted in designs. A large water basin in the center is encircled with urns and statuary on pedestals—one honoring Ste Geneviéve, the patroness of Paris, depicted with pigtails reaching to her thighs. Another memorial is dedicated to Stendhal.

Crowds throng through the park on May Day, when Parisians carry their traditional lilies of the valley. Birds sing, and all of Paris (those who didn't go to the country) celebrates the rebirth of spring.

BOIS DE BOULOGNE: One of the greatest and most spectacular parks in Europe, le Bois is often called the main lung of Paris. Horse-drawn carriages traverse it, but you can also take your car through. Many of its hidden pathways, however, must be discovered by walking. If you had a week to spare, you could spend it all in the Bois de Boulogne and still not see everything.

Porte Dauphine is the main entrance, although you can take the Métro to Porte Maillot as well. West of Paris, the park was once a forest kept for royal hunts. In the late 19th century it was in vogue. Carriages containing elegantly attired and coiffured Parisian damsels with their foppish escorts rumbled along the Avenue Foch. Nowadays, it's more likely to attract picnickers from the middle class. (And at night, hookers and muggers are prominent, so be duly warned.)

When Emperor Napoléon III gave the grounds to the City of Paris in 1852, they were developed by Baron Haussmann. Separating Lac Inférieur from Lac Supérieur is the Carrefour des Cascades (you can stroll under its waterfall). The Lower Lake contains two islands connected by a footbridge. From the east bank, you can take a boat to these idyllically situated grounds, perhaps stopping off at the café-restaurant on one of them.

Restaurants in the Bois are numerous, elegant, and expensive. The Pre-Catelan contains a deluxe restaurant of the same name and a Shakespearean theater in a garden said to have been planted with trees mentioned in the bard's plays.

Two racetracks, Longchamp and the Auteuil, are in the park. The annual Grand Prix is run in June at Longchamp (the site of a medieval abbey). The most fashionable people of Paris turn out, the women gowned in their finest haute couture. Directly to the north of Longchamp is Grand Cascade, the artificial waterfall of the Bois de Boulogne.

The Jardin d'Acclimation is for children, with a small zoo, an amusement park, and a narrow-gauge railway. Its major attraction, however, is pedal cars which the *enfants* can drive, following traffic signals. Unlike in the real world, violators are only reprimanded by a policeman, never ticketed.

In the 60-acre Bagatelle Park, the Comte d'Artois (later Charles X) brother-in-law of Marie Antoinette, made a bet with her—he could erect a small palace in less than three months—and won. If you're in Paris in late April, go to the Bagatelle to look at the tulips, if for no other reason. In late May one of the finest and best-known rose collections in all of Europe is in full bloom.

PARC MONCEAU: One widely known American writer once said that all babies in the Parc Monceau were respectable. Having never known one who wasn't, I can only agree with the pundit. At any rate, babies like Parc Monceau. Or at least their mothers and/or nurses are fond of wheeling their carriages through it. Much of the park (Métro: Monceau or Villiers) is ringed with 18th-

and 19th-century mansions, some of them evoking Proust's *Remembrance of Things Past*.

The park was opened to the public in the days of Napoléon III's Second Empire. It was built in 1778 by the Duke of Orléans, or Philippe-Egalité, as he became known. Carmontelle designed the park for the duke, who was considered at the time the richest man in France. "Philip Equality" was noted for his debauchery and his pursuit of pleasure. No ordinary park would do.

Monceau was laid out with an Egyptian-style obelisk, a dungeon of the Middle Ages, a thatched alpine farmhouse, a Chinese pagoda, a Roman temple, an enchanted grotto, various chinoiseries, and of course a waterfall. These fairytale touches have largely disappeared except for a pyramid and an oval-shaped *naumachie* fringed by a colonnade. Many of the former fantasies have been replaced with solid statuary and monuments, one honoring Chopin. In spring, the red tulips and magnolias are worth the air ticket to Paris.

BUTTES-CHAUMONT: In the industrial working-class district of Belleville, immortalized in the songs of Maurice Chevalier, Napoléon III and Baron Haussmann created this park out of a plaster-of-paris quarry. In a sense, they were the harbingers of the ecology movement, as the quarry had been turned into a rubbish dump.

Today, in the northeast of Paris, in the 19th Arrondissement, the 60 acres of parkland center around a rock island and a swan lake. You can take a boat for a tour of the lake, or else climb a mountain. A suspension bridge over the water was once called Suicide Bridge.

Try to avoid the park on Sunday afternoon—unless you love people, lots of them. Métro: Buttes-Chaumont.

6. The Markets of Paris

Paris at times seems a vast open-air market. The most important ones are previewed below, beginning with the—

FLEA MARKET: The French call this world-famed market **Marché aux Puces.** Here, what someone considers junk becomes valuable property in the eyes of others. Some of the merchandise is stolen only the night before. The ragpickers of Paris still come here, although whoever buys their poor merchandise, bits of string and scraps of 1920 cloth, I'll never know. It's estimated that the complex has 2,500 to 3,000 open stalls and shops spread over a four-square-mile area.

The market is open only on Saturday, Sunday, and Monday. To get there by Métro, take the train to Porte de Clignancourt (bus 56 also goes to this point). After leaving the underground station, turn left and cross Boulevard Ney, then walk north on Avenue de la Porte de Clignancourt. You'll pass stalls offering cheap clothing, but I advise you to ignore them and walk on until you see the entrances to the first maze of flea-market stalls on the left. Monday is the traditional day for bargain hunters. Remember to bargain, and that means not paying the second price asked, or even the third. Steals are rare here, because the best buys have been skimmed by dealers. However, someone occasionally turns up with a treasure. Most of the stalls are open from 10 a.m. to 6 p.m., and business is brisk, the total reportedly about $120,000,000 annually for the entire market. About half of this take comes from visitors from other countries.

THE VILLAGE SUISSE: This is a vast Left Bank complex of 200 antique shops and boutiques at 78 Avenue de Suffren, 15e, and 54 Avenue de la Motte Picquet, 15e. Don't go here for bargains. Unlike the Marché aux Puces, everything at the Village Suisse is in an excellent state of repair. Interior decorators of Paris frequent the village's precincts for their wealthy clients, looking for that Louis XVI console. Oil paintings, silver, copper, and pewter, plus antique furniture in all major periods and styles are presented. It is open Thursday through Monday from 10:30 a.m. to 7 p.m. By Métro, get off at the La Motte Picquet underground station, then walk along Avenue de la Motte Picquet until you reach the entrance at no. 54.

THE BIRD MARKET: I don't suggest that you buy anything—this market is one of the *curiosités* of Paris. From the Louvre to the Hôtel-de-Ville, long rows of shops are spread along the Seine, selling both wild and tame birds. Like unset gems, these birds in all the colors of the rainbow huddle in cages. Fantail pigeons, parrots, canaries, parakeets, and many rare birds are sold here. (Sometimes, however, there are complaints that the beautiful colored bird becomes a pale yellow canary after his first bath.) Pet fishes and tortoises are also for sale. On Sunday, birds are sold at the Flower Market, previewed below.

THE FLOWER MARKET: Certainly France has no more colorful market. The **Marché aux Fleurs** is a bouquet treat. Walking along enjoying this feast of scent, you'll encounter stall after stall ablaze with color. Most of the flowers are shipped in from the Riviera, having escaped the perfume factories. The market is on the Île de la Cité, 4e, at Place Louis-Lépine, along the Seine behind the Tribunal de Commerce. It is open weekdays. Métro: Cité.

THE STAMP MARKET: Avid collectors are drawn to nearly two dozen stalls set up on a permanent basis under shade trees below Rond Point, off the Champs-Elysées. Rare stamps and ordinary ones are sold on Thursday, Saturday, and Sunday. Métro: Champs-Élysées.

COUR AUX ANTIQUAIRES: This elegant Right Bank arcade is a complex of miniature shops and art boutiques, each opening onto a courtyard. Nearly two dozen collectors are found here, each one operating independently. Merchandise includes antique lace, tableware, post-impressionist 19th-century paintings, Oriental porcelains, silver pill boxes, jade bottles, modern art, circa 1925 jewelry, 18th-century paintings, and Russian icons. The address is 54 rue du Faubourg St-Honoré, 8e (tel. 47-42-43-99). Métro: Place de la Concorde.

7. A Sightseeing Miscellany

From graveyards to sewers, this grab bag of Parisian "extras" is wide ranging, beginning at:

PÈRE-LACHAISE: When it comes to name-dropping, this cemetery knows no peer. Everybody from Madame Bernhardt to Oscar Wilde (his tomb by Epstein) was buried here. So were Balzac, Delacroix, and Bizet. The body of Colette was taken here in 1954, and in time the little sparrow, Piaf, would follow. The lover of George Sand, Alfred de Musset, the poet, was buried under a weeping willow. Napoleon's marshals, Ney and Masséna, were entombed here, as were Chopin and Molière.

Some tombs are sentimental favorites, the tomb of Jim Morrison, American rock star who died in 1971, reportedly drawing the most visitors. Proust often has a fresh red carnation resting on his grave site. The great Isadora Duncan is reduced to a "pigeon hole" in the Columbarium where bodies have been cremated and then "filed." If you search hard enough, you can find the tombs of those star-crossed lovers, Abélard and Héloïse, the ill-fated lovers of the 12th century. At Père-Lachaise they have found peace at last. Lovers of a different kind can also be found here. One stone is marked Alice B. Toklas on one side, Gertrude Stein on another.

Spreading over more than 40 acres, Père-Lachaise was acquired by the City of Paris in 1804. Nineteenth-century French sculpture abounds, each family trying to outdo the other in ornamentation and cherubic ostentation. Some French Socialists still pay tribute at the Mur des Fédérés, the anonymous grave site of the Communards who were executed on May 28, 1871. Frenchmen who died in the Resistance or in Nazi concentration camps are also honored by the monument.

The cemetery is open from 7:30 a.m. to 6 p.m., spring through autumn (from 8:30 a.m. to 5:30 p.m. otherwise). A guide at the entrance may give you a map outlining some of the well-known grave sites. For information, phone 43 70-70-33. Métro: Père-Lachaise.

LES GOBELINS: The founding father of the dynasty, Jehan Gobelin, came from a family of dyers and clothmakers. In the 15th century he discovered a scarlet dye that was to make him famous. By 1601 Henry IV had become interested, bringing up 200 weavers from Flanders whose full-time occupation was to make tapestries (many now scattered across the museums and residences, both public and private, of Europe). Oddly enough, until then the Gobelin family had not made any tapestries, although the name would become synonymous with that art form.

Colbert, the minister of Louis XIV, purchased the works, and under royal patronage the craftsmen set about executing designs by Le Brun. Closed during the Revolution, the industry was reactivated by Napoleon. It is still going strong at 42 Avenue des Gobelins, 13e (tel. 43-37-12-60). You can visit the factory—the studios of the crafts people, called *ateliers*—on Wednesday and Thursday from 2 to 5:15 p.m., paying 15F ($2.07) for admission. Some of the ancient high-warp looms are still in use. The craftspeople turn out modern tapestries inspired by such artists as Picasso, Léger, Matisse, and Miró. Métro: Gobelins. For information, get in touch with Caisse Nationale des Monuments Historiques, 62 rue Saint-Antoine, 4e (tel. 48-87-24-14).

CITÉ UNIVERSITAIRE: At the border of the Parc Montsouris is an international student community founded in 1922. In an idyllic setting, the students live in houses (often designed by famous architects), which suggest those of their native lands. For example, Le Corbusier did the Swiss House in 1933. The Portuguese House was donated by the Gulbenkian Foundation, the estate left by the Armenian oil tycoon. Donated by John D. Rockefeller, Jr., the Maison Internationale is the largest building, complete with a swimming pool and theater. The most interesting walk is along **Avenue Rockefeller,** where in spring the trees are heavily laden with blossoms, and students can be seen returning to their residences with loaves of French bread under their arms. Métro: Cité Universitaire.

THE CATACOMBS: Every year an estimated 50,000 tourists explore some 1,000 yards of tunnel in these dank Catacombs (tel. 43-22-47-63) to look at some six million skeletons ghoulishly arranged in artistic skull-and-crossbones fashion. It has been called the empire of the dead. First opened to the public in 1810, the Catacombs are now illuminated with overhead electric lights over their entire length.

In the Middle Ages the Catacombs were originally quarries, but in 1785 city officials decided to use them as a burial ground. So the bones of several million persons were moved here from their previous resting places, the overcrowded cemeteries being considered health menaces. In 1830 the prefect of Paris closed the Catacombs to the viewing public, considering them obscene and indecent. He maintained that he could not understand the morbid curiosity of civilized people who wanted to gaze upon the bones of the dead. Later, in World War II, the Catacombs were the headquarters of the French Underground.

The Catacombs are open Tuesday to Friday from 2 to 4 p.m. and Saturday and Sunday from 9 to 11 a.m. and 2 to 4 p.m. Admission is 12F ($1.66) for adults, 6F (83¢) for children. The entrance is at 1 Place Denfert-Rochereau, 14e. Métro: Denfert-Rochereau.

THE SEWERS OF PARIS: Some say Baron Haussmann will be remembered mainly for the vast, complicated network of Paris sewers he erected. The *égouts* of the city, as well as telephone and telegraph pneumatic tubes, are constructed around a quartet of principal tunnels, one 18 feet wide and 15 feet high. It's like an underground city, with the street names clearly labeled. Further, each branch pipe bears the number of the building to which it is connected. These underground passages are truly mammoth, containing pipes bringing in drinking water and compressed air as well as telephone and telegraph lines.

That these sewers have remained such a popular attraction is something of a curiosity. They were made famous by Victor Hugo's *Les Misérables.* "All dripping with slime, his soul filled with a strange light," Jean Valjean in his desperate flight through the sewers of Paris is considered one of the heroes of narrative drama.

Tours begin at Pont de l'Alma on the Left Bank (Métro: Alma-Marceau). A stairway there leads into the bowels of the city. However, you often have to wait in line as much as half an hour. Visits are possible on Monday and Wednesday and on the last Saturday of each month, except for public holidays and the days before and after. Hours are 2 to 5 p.m. A one-hour visit costs 10F ($1.38). *Warning:* Visiting hours are likely to change from those stated, and times and days of opening should be verified with the tourist office before you go there. Telephone 47-05-10-29 for more information. The tour consists of seeing a movie on sewer history, followed by a short tour (ten or 15 minutes). Many visitors don't consider it worth the wait.

8. Paris for Children

Despite the fact that Paris is not really a city geared for the enjoyment of children, there are nevertheless a number of activities in which youngsters can participate.

PARKS AND ZOOS: The definitive children's park in Paris is the **Jardin d'Acclimation,** a 25-acre zoo-cum-amusement park on the northern edge of the Bois de Boulogne, 16e (tel. 46-24-10-82). This is the kind of place popular with the very young and also adults, although teen-agers are not intrigued by it usually. The visit starts with a ride from Porte Maillot to the Jardin entrance, through a stretch of wooded park, on a jaunty, green-and-yellow narrow-gauge train. A one-way fare costs 5F (69¢), plus 5.40F (75¢) for the entrance fee. Inside the gate, there is an easy-to-follow layout map. The park is circular, and if you follow the road in either direction, it will take you all the way around and bring you back to the train at the end.

En route, you will discover a house of mirrors, an archery range, miniature golf, zoo animals, an American-style bowling alley, a puppet theater (on Thursday, Saturday, Sunday, and holidays), a playground, a hurdle-race course, and a mass of junior-scale rides, shooting galleries, and waffle stalls. There are also pony rides, plus boats to sail in on a mill-stirred lagoon. Let Asterix and Obelix be your hosts in a real Gallic village, just like the ones that covered France at the time of the Romans. An outstanding attraction is *La Prévention Routière,* a miniature roadway operated by the Paris police. The youngsters drive through it in small cars equipped to start and stop and are required by two genuine Parisian gendarmes to obey all street signs and light changes.

The Jardin is open daily from 10 a.m. to 6:30 p.m., to 7:30 p.m. on Sunday. Métro: Les Sablons.

There is a modest zoo in the Jardin des Plantes, near the natural history museum (see below), but the best zoo Paris has to offer is in the **Bois de Vincennes,** on the outskirts but quickly reached by the Métro. Open daily from 9 a.m. to 5:30 p.m., to 6 p.m. on Sunday. Admission is 25F ($3.45); children between 4 and 10 pay 15F ($2.07). This modern zoo displays its animals in settings as similar to their natural habitats as possible. The lion has an entire veldt to himself, and you can watch as Barbary sheep leap from ledge to ledge or pose gracefully on a cement mountain reminiscent of Disneyland's Matterhorn, at the foot of which penguins waddle around pools. Métro: Porte Dorée.

The large inner-city parks all have playgrounds with tiny merry-go-rounds and gondola-style swings. If you're staying on the Right Bank, take the children for a stroll through the **Tuileries Garden,** where there are donkey rides, ice-cream stands, and a marionette show. At the circular pond, you can rent a toy sailboat with a prod to keep it moving and controlled. On the Left Bank, equivalent delights exist in the **Luxembourg Gardens.** If you go to the gardens of the **Champ de Mars,** you can combine a donkey ride for the children with a visit to the nearby Eiffel Tower.

PUPPET SHOWS: The puppet and marionette exhibitions in the above-mentioned parks are a great Paris tradition and worth seeing, but the words are in French, which may detract from your child's enjoyment.

Shows are given at the Tuileries Gardens at 3:15 p.m. on Wednesday, Saturday, and Sunday all summer. At the Luxembourg Gardens, puppet productions with sinister plots, set in Gothic castles and Oriental palaces, are presented. Some young critics think the best puppet shows are given in the Champ de Mars. Performance times at both Luxembourg Gardens and the Champ de Mars vary with the day of the week and the production being staged. All are colorful and enthusiastically produced. You may have to whisper the story line to your monolingual offspring as you go along, but when Red Riding Hood pummels the wolf over the head with an umbrella, laughter and understanding will surmount any language block. Prices vary, depending on the extravagance of the production, from 8F ($1.10) to 16F ($2.21).

MUSEUMS: Exhibits in Paris museums are identified in French, so it's best to take children who cannot read that language to museums whose displays are self-explanatory or of interest in themselves. Displays of special interest may be found in the following museums, which are previewed in Part 3 of this chapter.

Musée de l'Homme, Palais de Chaillot, Place du Trocadero et du 11 Novembre, 16e (tel. 47-04-62-10), displays artifacts illustrating the way different peoples around the world live and have lived in the past. **Musée de la Marine,** also in the Palais de Chaillot (tel. 45-55-31-70), features a kaleidoscopic collection of models, maps, figureheads, and whole craft over the centuries. **Musée Grévin,** 10 Boulevard Montmartre, 9e (tel. 47-70-85-05), Paris's leading waxworks, isn't all blood and gore. It contains fascinating looks into French historical lore. Two different shows are given frequently each day. The Grévin has a subsidiary in the Forum des Halles at Grand-Balcon Niveau, 1 rue Pierre Lescot, 1er (tel. 42-61-50), also described in part 3 of this chapter.

If your children are interested in natural history, take them to the **Musée National d'Histoire Naturelle,** 57 rue Cuvier, 5e (tel. 45-87-00-28) in the Jardin des Plantes, which was founded as a scientific research center in 1635. It has spread its exhibits much wider, having today galleries of Paleontology, Anatomy, Mineralogy, and Botany, with massive skeletons of dinosaurs and mastodons among many other collections. The galleries are open daily from 1:30 to 5 p.m., from 10:30 a.m. to 5 p.m. on Sunday. Admission is 14F ($1.93) for adults, half price for children. Within the museum grounds are tropical hothouses containing thousands of species of unusual plant life and a menagerie with small animal life in simulated natural habitats. These are open from 11 a.m. to 1:30 p.m. daily except Tuesday, charging 20F ($2.76) for admission. Métro: Jussieu or Austerlitz.

Budding scientists delight in the **Palais de la Découverte** in the Grand Palais on Avenue Franklin-D.-Roosevelt, 8e (tel. 45-59-16-65) if they know French. Displays, machines to test muscular reactions, and live experiments are combined with lectures on physics, chemistry, and biology experiments, as well as on astronomy, space, geology, genetics, and medicine. There's also a planetarium. The museum is open daily except Monday, from 10 a.m. to 6 p.m. Planetarium shows are held at 11 a.m. and 2, 3, and 4:30 p.m. on weekdays, with an additional show at 5:45 p.m. on Saturday and Sunday. Admission to the museum and planetarium show is 21F ($2.90). Métro: F.-D.-Roosevelt.

AN AFTERNOON ON MONTMARTRE: On Sunday afternoon, whole French families crowd the top of the Butte Montmartre to join in the fiesta atmosphere. Start by taking the Métro to Anvers and walking to the **Funiculaire de Montmartre.** You'll run the gauntlet of several balloon-sellers before you get there. The funicular is a small, silvery cable car that slides you gently up the steep, grassy hillside to Sacré-Coeur on the crest. Once up, follow the crowds to the **Place du Tertre,** where a Sergeant Pepper–style band will usually be blasting away off-key and where you can have the youngsters' pictures sketched by local artists.

Signs lead from the Place to the **Musée de Cire de la Butte Montmartre,** a waxworks previewed in Part 1 of this chapter, under "Montmartre." Before returning to the cable car, take in the views of Paris from the various vantage points and have an ice cream in an outdoor café on the Place. Métro: Abbesses.

MISCELLANY: The **Flea Market** and the **Bird Market,** described above in Part 6, are sure to hold an attraction for children as well as adults. If your child is a stamp collector, don't miss the **Stamp Market,** also previewed in Part 6 of this chapter.

On the Left Bank, go to **Rigadon** (see Left Bank Shops, Part 10 of this chapter), a puppet and doll world, where they can look even if you don't buy.

Another shop for a browsing treat, this time on the Right Bank, is **Au Nain Bleu** (also described in Part 10). Here you can look at a world of playthings such as toy soldiers, stuffed animals—all sorts of things to gladden young hearts.

9. In the Environs

In the suburbs of Paris—reachable by either bus or Métro—are more sightseeing targets, beginning with:

THE BASILICA OF ST. DENIS: In the 12th century, Abbot Suger placed an inscription on the bronze doors of St. Denis: "Marvel not at the gold and expense, but at the craftsmanship of the work." The first Gothic building in France that can be dated precisely, St. Denis was the "spiritual defender of the State" during the reign of Louis VI ("The Fat"). The massive façade, with its crenelated parapet on the top similar to the fortifications of a castle, has a rose window. The stained-glass windows, in stunning colors—mauve, purple, blue, and rose—were restored in the 19th century.

St. Denis, the first bishop of Paris, became the patron saint of the French monarchy. Royal burials began here in the 6th century and continued until the Revolution. The sculptures designed for tombs—some two stories high—span the country's artistic development from the Middle Ages to the Renaissance. You are conducted through the crypt on a guided tour (in French only). François I was entombed at St. Denis. His funeral statue is nude, although he demurely covers himself with his hand. Other kings and queens here include Louis XII and Anne of Brittany, as well as Henri II and Catherine de Medici. However, the Revolutionaries stormed through, smashing many marble faces and dumping royal remains in a lime-filled ditch in the garden. Royal remains were reburied under the main altar during the 19th century.

In the dreary industrial suburb of St. Denis, the basilica is at 22 bis rue Gabriel-Peri (tel. 42-43-05-10; take the Métro to the St. Denis station). It is open from 10 a.m. to 6 p.m. daily; Sunday hours are from 2 to 6:30 p.m. The price of admission is 11F ($1.52), half that on Sunday and holidays.

The next sight can easily be tied in with a visit to St. Denis.

MUSÉE NATIONAL DE LA RENAISSANCE: At a charmingly situated place right outside Paris, heading north on the route to Chantilly, Valéry Giscard d'Estaing, the former French president, inaugurated this museum devoted to works of the Renaissance. Called Le Château d'Ecouen, the castle in the hamlet of Ecouen was constructed between 1538 and 1555 for the high constable, Anne de Montmorency. In 1806 Napoleon assigned the building as a school for daughters of Le Légion d'Honneur. On a promontory in a park-like setting, the château contains an exceptional collection of works from the Renaissance— tapestries, paintings, and objects of art—which betray a heavy Italian influence. See especially the best-known tapestry, *David and Bathsheba,* 245 feet long. The museum (tel. 39-90-04-04) is open daily except Tuesday, from 9:45 a.m. to 12:30 p.m. and 2 to 5:15 p.m., charging an admission of 12F ($1.66), which is lowered to half price on Sunday. To reach the château, take the Métro to the Basilique de St-Denis, then bus 268 to Ezanville, which stops at the imposing museum.

CHÂTEAU DE VINCENNES: It's been called the Versailles of the Middle Ages, and it's had a checkered career. Encircled by the once-great forest, the Bois de Vincennes, the château, like Versailles, was originally a hunting lodge. At the south of the town of Vincennes, the castle was founded by Louis VII ("The Young") in 1164, but it has subsequently been rebuilt many times. What you see today is merely a shell of its former self.

St. Louis (Louis IX) was fond of the castle; it is said that he administered justice while sitting under his favorite oak tree in the forest. Inspired by the Sainte Chapelle in Paris, Charles V ordered a chapel built in 1379. That "citizen of the world," Mazarin, and the mother of Louis XIV directed the completion of two pavilions.

Louis XIV, however, wasn't especially fond of Vincennes, because he had another home in mind. In time the château was to become a porcelain factory, an arsenal under Napoleon, and a supply depot for the Nazis. Now it is being restored by the government. Its most memorable role was that of a prison or dungeon, the most famous prisoner being Mirabeau, the French revolutionist and statesman.

Vincennes is a suburb, about five miles east of Notre-Dame. Take the Métro to the Château de Vincennes. It is open daily, with guided tours. Admission costs 8F ($1.10), dropping to half that on Sunday and holidays.

ST-GERMAIN-EN-LAYE: Gourmet cooks know that béarnaise sauce was invented here, although the town has other distinctions. Only 13 miles northwest of Paris, St-Germain-en-Laye traditionally drew Parisians wishing to escape the summer heat.

Louis XIV lived here, but he was to desert it for Versailles. Still, St-Germain-en-Laye has been the seat of the royal court. The Métro line from Paris will take you directly to the entrance to the **Château Vieux** (tel. 34-51-53-65), standing in the heart of town and dating from the 12th century. Built by François I, the castle is made of brick. Once James II stayed here, enjoying

French hospitality while hoping to regain the throne of England. However, this Stuart king died here. Napoléon III ordered that the château—built on a hill on the left bank of the Seine—be turned into a museum, tracing the history of France from the cave dwellers until the Carolingian era. And so it is today: the **French Museum of National Antiquities,** with displays of tools, stones, even arms and jewelry used or worn by the early settlers of Gaul. The museum is open daily except Tuesday, from 9:45 a.m. to noon and 1:30 to 5:15 p.m., charging an admission of 12F ($1.66).

Of special interest is **Sainte-Chapelle,** built by St. Louis in the 1230s. To visit it, however, you must apply to the custodian.

At the end of the tour, I'd suggest a stroll through Le Nôtre's gardens, open from 7 a.m. till 9:30 p.m. At the world-famed **Terrace,** a panoramic view of Paris unfolds before you. On this terrace Henri IV built the Château Neuf, stashing his brood of illegitimate children there, at the end of the 16th century.

The remains of the castle are now the **Pavillon Henri IV,** 21 rue Thiers (tel. 34-51-62-62), an illustrious hotel. The Comte d'Artois, the brother of Louis XVI, was granted it as a gift. He planned to demolish it; then along came the Revolution. It was partly rebuilt in 1836 and became a hotel of world renown, favored by such writers as Dumas, who wrote *The Three Musketeers* here. Standing at the edge of the belvedere gardens of the old château, it is still elegantly old-fashioned. In a corner chamber the Sun King played fun and games with Mme de Montespan. In memory of them, a room has been set aside as a museum.

The fortunate few who get to spend the night will find 42 handsomely furnished bedrooms, beginning at 500F ($68.95) in a single and going up to 1,500F ($206.85) for an excellent double. You can always order the classic dishes here—carré d'agneau rôti, rognon de veau (veal kidney) dijonnaise, and, of course, pommes soufflées, which were invented here, along with sauce béarnaise, which is just the thing to top your chateaubriand. For a complete meal, expect to spend from 400F ($55.16) to 450F ($62.06) per person.

To go here by public transport, take the RER Métro line (A-1), in the direction of Saint-Germain-en-Laye. The ride lasts half an hour, and you're deposited about a five-minute walk from the pavilion, which is open daily.

10. Shopping in Paris

Perfumes in Paris are almost always cheaper than in the States. And that means all the famed brands: Guerlain, Chanel, Schiaparelli, Jean Patou. Cosmetics bearing French names (Dior, Lancôme) also cost less. Gloves are a fine value.

TAX REFUND: If you've been here less than six months, you are entitled to a refund on the value-added tax (VAT) on purchases made in France to take home —under certain conditions. The *détaxe*, or refund, is allowed on purchases of goods costing more than 1200F ($165.48) in a single store, but it's not automatic. Food, wine, and tobacco don't count, and the refund is only granted on purchases you carry with you out of the country, *not* on merchandise you have shipped home.

Here's what you must do: Show the clerk your passport to prove you're eligible for the refund. You will then be given an export sales document in triplicate (two pink sheets and a green one), which you must sign. You'll also be given an envelope addressed to the store. Go early to your departure point, as there are sometimes queues waiting at the booth marked *détaxe* (refund) at French Customs. If you're traveling by train, go to the *détaxe* area in the station before boarding. You can't get your refund documents processed on the train. The refund booths are outside the passport checkpoints, so you must take care of that business before you proceed with the passport check.

Only the person who signed the documents at the store can present them for the refund. Give the three sheets to the Customs official, who will countersign and hand you back the green copy. Save this in case problems arise about the refund. Give the official the envelope addressed to the store (be sure to put a stamp on the envelope). One of the processed pink copies will be mailed to the store for you. You can either be reimbursed by check sent by mail to your home, or sometimes it is made to a credit-card account. Usually it is by check in convertible French francs. In some cases you may get your refund immediately, paid at an airport bank window.

If you don't receive your tax refund in four months, write to the store, giving the date of purchase and the location where the sheets were given to Customs officials. Include a photocopy of your (green) refund sheet.

SHOPPING HINTS: Do your shopping within the city proper or wait until you fly out to make some of your purchases. In the tax-free shops at Orly and Charles de Gaulle Airports, you will get a minimum discount of 20% on all items and up to 50% off on such things as liquors, cigarettes, and watches. Among the stock on sale: crystal and cutlery, French bonbons, luggage, wines and whiskies, pipes and lighters, filmy lingerie, silk scarves, name perfumes (although the selection is skimpy as to size and variety), knitwear, jewelry, cameras and equipment, French cheeses, and antiques. Remember that what you buy must travel with you, and you are allowed to bring into the States the retail value of $400 in overseas purchases without paying Customs duty.

Shops in general are open from around 9 a.m. to 7 p.m. Small shops take a two-hour lunch break. Most close on Sunday and Monday. The flea market and some other street markets are open Saturday, Sunday, and Monday. That intriguing sign on shop doors reading *Entrée Libre* means you can browse at will. *Soldes* means "Sale." *Soldes Exceptionel* means they're pushing it a bit.

RIGHT BANK SHOPS: Start at the Havre-Caumartin Métro stop to begin your tour of two *Grands Magasins*. On the corner is **Le Printemps,** 64 Boulevard Haussmann, 9e (tel. 42-82-57-87), the city's largest department store. Actually, it consists of three stores connected by bridges on the second and third floors. Go to Brummel for clothing for men, both sports and dress. Printemps de la Maison is mainly for records and books, furniture and houseware, while the Nouveau Magasin sells clothes for women, young people, and children (the ground floor is mainly for perfume, cosmetics, gifts, and Paris handcrafts). Interpreters stationed at the Welcome Room on the main floor will help you claim your discounts, guide you to departments, and aid you in making purchases.

Another of the great department stores of Paris is the **Galeries Lafayette,** 40 Boulevard Haussmann, 9e (tel. 42-82-34-56). Inside most doorways is a Welcome Service telephone to direct you to the merchandise you're interested in. Of the three buildings comprising this department store, Lafayette offers the most exciting merchandise for visitors. On the ground floor are found the perfumes for which Paris is famous, as well as gifts, books, and records. The third floor has an exceptional collection of dresses for women. Incidentally, the top of Galeries Lafayette is open on sunny days. I suggest you take the elevator up there for an exceptional view of Paris. Métro: Chaussée-d'Antin.

After the vastness of these emporiums, you may want to devote your attention to some specialty shops. Up the avenue, at 73 Boulevard Haussmann, 8e, is the century-old **Trousselier** (tel. 42-65-32-23). You'll think at first it's simply a florist shop with some artfully displayed sprays. But look again, or touch—and you'll see that every flower is artificial, shaped in silk and hand-painted by craftspeople who pursue this famous French craft in the workshops in the rear. And what exquisite work! Everything is lifelike in the extreme. One cluster will bear a bud, a full-blown flower, and then one just past its prime and fading at the edges. The prices are worthy of the quality. This recently renewed store has been in the same family for three generations. Madame Trousselier is actually there to welcome you. Métro: Havre-Caumartin.

Then walk back to the rue Tronchet. Before turning down the street, stop in at the corner establishment, **Aux Tortues,** 55 Boulevard Haussmann, 8e, (tel. 42-65-56-74), across from Au Printemps. Offbeat and charming, this is one of the most delightful specialty shops of Paris, offering items unique and unusual made in ivory, *écaille* (tortoiseshell), and semiprecious stones. Look especially for the ivory miniatures. The prices aren't cheap, but then, you wouldn't expect them to be. Métro: Havre-Caumartin.

Turning down the street flanked by young boutiques, you'll arrive at the "youngest" shop of them all, the **Stars Enfantines,** 17 rue Tronchet, 8e (tel. 42-65-32-89), specializing in clothing for children. Price tags are taken off, but in general the merchandise sells for 20% less than its original price. Clothes are usually suitable for children ranging in age from three months to 16 years. Métro: Madeleine.

Along the rue Royale, the street of the legendary Maxim's, you can turn right onto the rue du Faubourg St-Honoré, that platinum strip of the city where the presidential palace shares space with the haute-couture houses of Lanvin and Courrèges.

Lanvin (tel. 42-65-14-40) occupies two buildings at the corner of rue du Faubourg St-Honoré and the rue Boissy-d'Anglas (8e). The shop at 15 rue du Faubourg St-Honoré specializes in men's clothing, with a handsome collection of shirts and ties (the shop will also custom-make men's shirts and suits). I think Lanvin is the most elegant shirtmaker in Paris. The shop at 22 rue du Faubourg St-Honoré is the home of the celebrated haute couture workshops as well as an elegant women's store where *prêt-à-porter* (ready-to-wear) fashions can be purchased. Métro: Concorde.

Hermès, 24 rue du Faubourg St-Honoré, 8e (tel. 42-65-21-60), is a legend, of course. The shop is especially noted for its scarves, made of silk squares printed with antique motifs. Three well-known Hermès fragrances, two for women and one for men, make excellent gift choices. The gloves sold here are without peer, especially those for men in reindeer hide, doeskin, or supple kid. The leather-goods store at Hermès is the best known in Europe. The craftspeople working on the premises turn out the Hermès handbag, an institution that needs no sales pitch on these pages. Métro: Concorde.

Céline, 24 rue François-1er, 8e (tel. 47-20-22-83), is one of the best choices for conservative, well-made clothes that Parisian women say almost never wear out. There's also a selection of elegant shoes and handbags. The store is open from 9:30 a.m. to 1 p.m. and from 2:15 to 6:30 p.m. It is closed Sunday. Métro: F.-D.-Roosevelt.

Of course, there are others—so many others! You can visit **Christian Dior,** world-famous for its custom-made haute couture, at 26-32 Avenue Montaigne, 8e (tel. 47-23-54-44), with a wide selection of both women's and men's ready-to-wear, sportswear, and accessories, including separate salons for shoes and leather goods, furs, children's and junior's clothing, and a variety of gift items, costume jewelry, lighters, pens, among other offerings. Métro: F.-D.-Roosevelt.

The spirit of **Chanel** lives on, and her shop at 31 rue Cambon, 1er (tel. 42-61-54-55), across from the Ritz, is still very much in business. Métro: Concorde. There is also a Chanel Boutique at 42 Avenue Montaigne, 8e (tel. 47-23-74-12). Métro: F.-D.-Roosevelt.

And **Pierre Cardin** boutiques are popping up in every hotel and on every street corner. You can't miss them.

Emilio Pucci, 4 rue de Castiglione, 1er (tel. 42-60-89-42), is the Parisian showcase for this talented and temperamental Italian designer. Across the street from the Inter-Continental Hotel, this boutique carries a full line of accessories for women, all created with special flair. Included in the array are scarves, handbags, hats, belts, even his own perfume. Of course, Pucci enjoys one of the most outstanding reputations in Europe for his blouses and bright silk jersey dresses, some in geometric prints, and show-stopping swim suits. Métro: Tuileries.

Gucci, 350 rue St-Honoré, 1er (tel. 42-96-83-27), is yet another showcase for a fabled Italian designer. Gucci, of course, is noted for his leather goods, including shoes and handbags. This boutique also has an excellent collection of scarves and two-piece ensembles. Its sweaters are especially outstanding. Métro: Tuileries. Other addresses are 27 rue du Faubourg St-Honoré, 8e, and 2 rue du Faubourg St-Honoré, 8e.

Michel Swiss, 16 rue de la Paix, 2e (tel. 42-61-71-71), looks like many of the ultra-chic façades near the Place Vendôme. But once you get inside (there's no storefront window), you'll see that the dozens of luxury perfumes, makeup, leather bags, neckties, and Lacoste shirts and sweaters are discounted 25% if you pay with cash or travelers checks and 20% if you pay with credit cards. The store is two flights above ground level, which is reachable by a small elevator. It might be a good idea to avoid the crowds who pile in here at lunch. It is open from 9 a.m. to 6:30 p.m. every day but Sunday. Métro: Opéra.

Josephine Fisse, 5 rue Clément-Marot, 8e (tel. 47-23-45-27), close to the angle of the Avenue Montaigne, is a super-chic, super-expensive boutique that carries the latest fashions of six of the trendiest designers in France and Italy. It is designed as a hi-tech format, and the attractive saleswomen occasionally dress in leather. The store is open daily except Sunday, from 10 a.m. to 7 p.m. Métro: F.-D.-Roosevelt.

Here's a round-up of other Right Bank shopping establishments you might want to take a peek at:

Museum Reproductions

A boutique at 107 rue de Rivoli, 1er (tel. 42-60-32-14), is connected with the **Musée des Arts Décoratifs,** in the Pavillon de Marsan section of the Louvre, and offers a variety of handsome household goods, some of them exact copies of items in the collection displayed in the museum. The small, austere shop has goods displayed on shelves lining the walls, illuminated by soft lights. Craftspeople have copied such museum pieces as faïence, molded crystal, nouveau jewelry, porcelain boxes, scarves, and other items. The merchandise offered here is of fine workmanship and great beauty. The boutique is at the rear of the Louvre, a block from the Place Vendôme. The shop is open daily from noon to 6 p.m., from 11 a.m. to 5 p.m. on Sunday. There is no charge for admission, and you can find interesting items in low to expensive price ranges. Métro-Louvre.

For Unusual Engravings

Carnavalette, 2 rue des Francs-Bourgeois (tel. 42-72-91-92), off the Place des Vosges, 4e, in the Marais sector, sells unusual one-of-a-kind engravings, plus a large collection of satirical 19th-century magazines and newspapers, whose illustrations many people buy for framing. Métro: St-Paul.

For Perfumes

Freddy of Paris, 10 rue Auber, 9e (tel. 47-42-63-41), near the American Express and the Opéra, offers moderate rates on all name-brand scents, top-fashion handbags, scarves, ties, French umbrellas, Limoges, crystalware, and costume jewelry. His shop is open daily from 9 a.m. to 6 p.m. except Saturday and Sunday. Métro: Opéra or Auber.

For Antiques

Le Louvre des Antiquaires, 2 Place du Palais-Royal, 1er (tel. 42-97-27-00), is the largest antique center in Europe, attracting collectors, browsers, and those interested in everything from Russian icons to 19th-century furniture to art deco. The center stands across from a giant parking lot at the side of the Louvre. Housing some 240 dealers, the showrooms are spread across 2½ acres of well-lit modern salons. The building, a former department store, was erected in 1852, according to Napoleon's plans for the rue de Rivoli. The establishment leads you down an enormous flight of skylit stairs, past a café and reception area, into the inner sanctum where you find the dealers operating from 11 a.m. to 7 p.m. every day except Monday. Métro: Palais-Royal.

China and Crystal

Lalique, 11 rue Royale, 8e (tel. 42-65-33-70), is directed today by the granddaughter of the original founder. Known around the world for its glass sculpture and decorative crystal, the shop sells a wide range of merchandise at prices slightly lower than abroad. Be warned that purchases are limited, and long delays are required. It is open from 9:30 a.m. to 6:30 p.m. every day but Sunday. On Monday and Saturday only, the staff takes a lunch break between noon and 2 p.m. Métro: Concorde.

Au Grand Siècle, 31 rue La Boetie, 8e (tel. 45-36-25-96), is an elegant shop presenting the final word on antiques and reproduction furniture, silver, and crystal, especially Lalique, Waterford, and Swarowsky. A small place, it is nevertheless filled to the brim with every imaginable item, including a splendid collection of lamps and small gifts. Lladro porcelain and Hummel figurines are sold here. No low-priced items are offered, but it is a memorable experience in exquisite taste. It is open Tuesday through Saturday from 9:30 a.m. to 6:30 p.m. Métro: Miromesnil.

Baccarat, 30 rue de Paradis, 10e (tel. 47-70-64-30). Purveyor to the kings and presidents of France since 1764, Baccarat still manufactures crystal that spokespersons say is more than 30% lead, and that commands prices substantially higher outside France. The trip is worth the visit even for visitors not intending to purchase, since there is a museum of the company's most historic models on the premises. It is open daily except Sunday, from 9 a.m. to 6 p.m., on Saturday from 10 a.m. to 12:30 p.m. and 2 to 6 p.m. Métro: Château-d'Eau.

Limoges-Unic, 12 and 58 rue de Paradis, 10e (tel. 47-70-61-49), sells a wide stock of Limoges china, Porcelaine de Paris, Villeroy & Boch, Baccarat, Daum, Lalique, St-Louis, Christofle, and many other items for table decorations. It is open from 9:45 a.m. to 6:30 p.m. every day. It is closed Sunday. Métro: Château-d'Eau-Poissonniere.

For Glassware

The **Amon Gallery** (Galerie d'Amon), 28 rue St-Sulpice, 6e (tel. 43-26-96-60), just off the Luxembourg Gardens and the Church of St. Sulpice, has a permanent exhibition of glass work, with a wide range of items from France and abroad. Madeleine and Jean-Pierre Maffre display items in blown glass, blown engraved glass, molded glass, and paperweights by the top craftsmen in their fields. Métro: Odéon.

For Champagne

La Maison du Champagne, 48 rue des Belles-Feuilles, 16e (tel. 47-27-58-23). If, by the time you read this, the dollar still enjoys a favorable rate of exchange against the French franc, then the famed bubbly of France might be a good buy. The inventory in this shop, with its more than 90 labels, includes some wines dating back to 1909, and some of the cognacs go back as far as the late 19th century. These, of course, are frighteningly expensive, although there's a respectable selection of affordable vintages as well. Charles Delmare is the wine expert who owns this establishment, which, as its name implies, specializes in champagne. It is open from 10 a.m. to 1 p.m. and 3 to 8 p.m. every day but Sunday, Monday, and in August. It will mail your purchases anywhere in the world. Métro: Dauphine or Victor Hugo.

For Chocolates

La Maison du Chocolat, 225 rue du Faubourg St-Honoré, 8e (tel. 42-27-39-44), is the best place in all of Paris to buy chocolates. The restrained decor contains racks and racks of chocolates, priced individually or by the kilo. Each is made from a blend of as many as six different kinds of South American and African chocolates, flavored with just about everything imaginable. Chocolate pastries are sold also. Everything for sale is made in the super-modern facilities in the establishment's cellars before being sent up on an old-fashioned dumbwaiter. Robert Linxe, the owner, maintains hours between 9:30 a.m. and 7 p.m. every day of the week but Sunday, Monday, and in August. Métro: Ternes.

For the Dining Table

Au Bain Marie, 20 rue Hérold, 1er (tel. 42-60-94-55), occupies quarters near the Place des Victoires. It is one of the best choices in town for all kinds of new and antique table and bedroom linen, some of it painstakingly embroidered. Square French pillowcases of heavy linen with initials hand done by nuns are a specialty. They also sell virtually everything that would touch a dining table. If you like to entertain, many of their accessories might also appeal to you. There is, in addition, a wide range of cookbooks from all schools and eras of cuisine. They are open from 10:30 a.m. to 7 p.m. daily except Sunday. Métro: Louvre or Sentier.

Haute Coiffure

Jacques Dessange is a star on the scene, offering unisex hair styling in its several shops in Paris, including those at 37 Avenue F.-D.-Roosevelt, 8e (tel. 43-59-31-31), Métro: F.-D.-Roosevelt; 4 Avenue de la République, 11e (tel. 43-57-07-49), Métro: République; and Tour-Maine-Montparnasse, Centre Commercial, 17 rue de l'Arrivée, 15e (tel. 45-38-72-08), Métro: Montparnasse-Bienvenue.

For Stylish Hats

One of the most distinguished outlets for hats for both men and women in Paris is the chapelier of **E. Motsch,** 42 Avenue George-V, 8e (tel. 47-23-79-22), right off the Champs-Élysées. In this sedate corner store, the staff offers almost every type of headgear, ranging from berets to Scottish tam-o-shanters. The section for women contains some of the most stylish, although conservatively sedate, hats in Paris. Métro: George-V.

Men's Wear

Cerruti has a men's boutique at 27 rue Royale, 8e (tel. 42-65-68-72), Métro: Concorde or Madeleine; as well as two for women, at 15 Place de la Madeleine, 8e (tel. 47-42-10-78) and 39 Avenue Victor-Hugo, 16e (tel. 45-00-32-32). Cerruti is also a good tailor for men, working in Paris since 1967.

Lingerie

Cadolle, 14 rue Cambon, 1er (tel. 42-60-94-94). All of Paris nostalgically remembers the founding mother of this store, Hermine Cadolle, as the person who in 1889 invented the brassière. Today the store is managed by Hermine's great-great- and great-great-great-granddaughters, Alice and Poupie Cadolle. This is the place to go for a made-to-order or a ready-to-wear fit in lingerie. Custom-made whalebone corsets are still available, and the nightgowns range from the demure to the scandalous. It is open from 9:30 a.m. to 1 p.m. and 2 to 6:30 p.m. daily except Sunday. Métro: Concorde.

Gifts for Children

Au Nain Bleu, 406 rue St-Honoré, 8e (tel. 42-60-39-01). Any child you love is expecting a present from Paris, and at the "Blue Dwarf" you'll be bedazzled by the choice. Nor can any adult withstand the temptation to browse through this paradise of playthings. It's a world of toy soldiers, stuffed animals, games, model airplanes, technical toys, model cars, even a "Flower Drum Kit." Puppets come in all shapes, sizes, and costumes. Métro: Concorde.

Gifts

Eiffel Shopping, 9 Avenue de Suffren, 7e (tel. 45-66-55-30), offers you a free glass of cognac while you browse through the designer collection (Dior, St-Laurent, Lanvin, Cartier, Chanel, to name just a few) of handbags, ties, scarves, watches, sunglasses, jewelry, perfumes, Lalique crystal, and much more. This tax-free shopping center, only one block from the Eiffel Tower, offers top-quality merchandise at discount prices, and all the salespeople are bilingual. It is open daily from 9:15 a.m. to 8 p.m. and on Sunday from 11 a.m. to 8 p.m. Métro: Bir Hakeim. A second shop is at the Paris Convention Center, Porte Maillot, Boulevard Gouvion St-Cyr, 17e (tel. 47-58-24-09), two floors above the Air Terminal, close to Concorde Lafayette and Meridien Hotels. Métro: Porte Maillot.

For the Bath

Raymond, 100 rue du Faubourg St-Honoré, 8e (tel. 42-66-69-49), is one of the principal outlets for Porcelaine de Paris. And if you're shopping for what might be the most elegant bathroom fixtures in the world, including basins and faucets fashioned from hand-painted porcelain, they have it here. They'll mail your purchase anywhere. Near the Élysée Palace, the store is open from 9:30 a.m. to 6:30 p.m. Tuesday to Saturday. It is closed on Sunday, Monday, and in August. On Saturday, the staff takes a luncheon break from 12:30 to 2 p.m. Métro: Concorde or Champs-Élysées-Clemenceau.

Bookstores

W. H. Smith & Son, 248 rue de Rivoli, 1er (tel. 42-60-37-97), is the English bookshop in Paris. A wide selection of books, magazines, and newspapers published in the English-speaking world are available. You can even get *The Times* of London, of course. There's a fine selection of maps if you plan to do much touring. Across from the Tuileries Gardens, W. H. Smith also has a combined tea room and restaurant. Métro: Concorde.

Shakespeare and Company, 37 rue de la Bûcherie, 5e (no phone), is the famous bookstore founded by the legendary Sylvia Beach, who was called the "mother confessor to the Lost Generation." Hanging out in this shop in days of yore, you were likely to encounter everybody from Gertrude Stein to Ernest Hemingway to F. Scott Fitzgerald. In more recent decades you might have attended an autograph party for the late diarist, Anaïs Nin. Henry Miller called the store "a wonderland of books." It is not slick like any modern chain, and the history associated with it, the rich traditions, are still maintained by the gruffly warm-hearted owner, George Whitman, who is originally from Boston. It is a unique Paris institution, and it is open seven days a week from 11 a.m. to midnight. Métro: St-Michel.

CUT-RATE SHOPPING: Paris no longer caters just to the well-heeled in its boutiques. Several shops have opened that offer leftover merchandise from some of the better-known fashion houses. Many items are sold 20% to 50% less than their original prices when they were displayed in a store along the Champs-Élysées. Of course, the famous labels have been cut out, but it's still the same clothing. Discount houses tend to be crowded, often bustling, and a bit rushed. At each of the following stores, however, at least one of the employees speaks English.

Le **Mouton à Cinq Pattes,** 8 rue St. Placide, 6e (tel. 45-48-86-26), in the Montparnasse area, offers heavily discounted creations of several well-known women's designers, usually with their labels removed. A few storefronts away, you'll find a similar system for men's clothing, with discounts matching those of its sister store. It's called Annexe, 48 rue St. Placide, 6e (tel. 45-48-82-85). The management has thoughtfully added an outlet for infants' and children's clothes a few steps away at 10 rue St. Placide, 6e (tel. 48-48-86-26), where designer garments for toddlers and preteeners are sold in imaginative combinations at discounted prices. The Métro stop for all these stores is St. Placide.

If you're in the St-Germain-des-Prés area, this same discount chain maintains two outlets in that neighborhood as well. At **Nuage-Rouge,** 26 rue des Canettes, 6e (tel. 43-26-52-32), children's clothes are sold at sometimes heavily discounted prices (Métro: St. Sulpice). The chain's newest store, specializing in clothes for both men and women, is at 19 rue Gregoire des Tours, 6e (tel. 43-29-73-56). Take the Métro to either Mabillon or Odéon. All of these stores are closed all day Sunday and on Monday morning.

Mendès (Saint-Laurent), 65 rue Montmartre, 2e (tel. 42-36-83-32). Many of the fashion-conscious but also budget-conscious women of Paris come here to buy models from the recent collections of Yves Saint-Laurent, Lanvin, and a handful of other well-known designers at discounts that usually average around 50%. There are no dressing rooms, no alterations, and no exchanges or refunds, but that doesn't prevent a batallion of struggling women from buying clothes from the winter collection at reduced prices after the middle of January. Clothes from the summer collection become available after mid-July. All of this activity takes place on two floors of a building at the edge of the garment district. The store is open Monday to Thursday from 9:30 a.m. to 5:30 p.m., Friday and Saturday from 9:30 a.m. to 4:30 p.m. It is closed all day Sunday. Métro: Les Halles.

Au Fil de Laure, 7 rue Sédillot, 7e (tel. 47-05-46-31), near Les Invalides, is a reduced-price outlet for late-model and used clothing from some of the biggest designers in Paris. The attractive and friendly staff members speak English and are happy to answer your questions. There's also a collection of summer clothes sold in the dead of winter at vastly reduced prices, as well as a line of children's apparel. Clothes in stock include models by Saint-Laurent, Dior, Chanel, Givenchy, Burberry's, and Scherrer, as well as many women's accessories. The shop is open daily except Sunday, from 10:30 a.m. to 7 p.m. Métro: École Militaire.

A shop that seems to have a "permanent sale" is **Les Trouvailles,** 55 rue de la Convention, 15e (tel. 45-78-21-95). Here outfits sell at about one-fourth of their original price. You'll find the latest fashions for women and children. Métro: Javel.

At last Paris has a hand-me-down shop, although the merchandise hardly qualifies for "Secondhand Rose." It's **Maxipuces,** 18 rue Cortambert, 16e (tel. 45-03-37-31). Some of the wealthiest women in Paris, and some of the most chicly dressed, bring their high-fashion clothing to this shop. How does an Yves Saint-Laurent hand-stitched evening gown, which originally sold for some 4,500F ($620.55), strike you with a price tag of 1,000F ($137.90)? Your friends back home may be dazzled when you appear at a party in such an original. The shop is closed daily from 1 to 2:30 p.m. and all day Sunday and Monday. Métro: La-Muette.

LEFT BANK SHOPS: Start your Left Bank shopping tour at the historic Place de l'Odéon. On a street branching off from here is **Rigodon,** 13 rue Racine, 6e (tel. 43-29-98-66), a puppet-and-doll world for every child, even for those who are children only at heart, but they're dolls to look at, not to play with. Hanging from its ceiling is one of the most varied and sophisticated collections of puppets in Paris. They come in all characters, sizes, and prices, and include everything from angels to witches on broomsticks to bat women with feather wings. Rigodon makes porcelain dolls. The painting on the faces and the costumes are unique for each model, be it a queen with all her power or the amazon of the hunt. There are marionettes (with strings) from French artisans. The prices of the dolls and marionettes begin at 300F ($48.27) and go to 5,500F ($756.30), to 8,500F ($1,172.15) for one-of-a-kind and animated dolls. You can also walk to the rue de Tournon, 6e, one of the most interesting streets for shopping on the Left Bank. At 13 rue de Tournon is a fashion complex, with stylish boutique items for both men and women at **Micmac St. Tropez** (tel. 43-54-44-99). Métro: Odéon.

After walking back along the rue de Tournon for a while, you can cut onto the rue de Seine, 6e, where art nouveau posters are sold cheek-by-jowl with genuine old masters. You pass along the **Buci street market,** where you can gather the makings of an unforgettable picnic under the shrill guidance of vendors. Métro: Odéon.

The **Galerie Documents,** 53 rue de Seine, 6e (tel. 43-54-50-68), contains one of the most original collections of old posters (from 1870 to 1930) in Paris. Many of them are inexpensive, although you could easily pay 1,200F ($165.48) for an original. Your poster selection will be mailed back home in a tube.

Aux Muses d'Europe, 64 rue de Seine, 6e (tel. 43-26-89-63), sells a collection of antique lace dresses of rare beauty, as well as contemporary clothing (1930s to 1960s) and accessories. With items collected from all over France by the mother-daughter team of Marguerite and Katia Belleville, the shop has appeared in nationwide television broadcasts in Japan and frequently welcomes actresses who need to dress in period costumes. The shop is not large, but the clothing racks stretch up to the ceiling. Ask to see the lace-trimmed baby dresses as well. It is open from 11 a.m. to 7 p.m. every day but Sunday. Métro: Odéon.

If you want a photograph of any Paris scene, old or new, apply at **Roger Viollet,** 6 rue de Seine, 6e (tel. 46-33-35-23), at the foot of the street. Every inch of wall space is lined with green looseleaf notebooks containing archives of photographs, some seven million in all, from every country in the world. The shop has been stockpiling photos since 1880. Métro: Odéon and St-Germain-des-Prés.

At the end of the rue de Seine you can walk along the quais for galleries filled with graphics. On the river side of the street open stalls dispense tourist prints, postcards, secondhand books, and funky antique postcards—but few real bargains or finds.

And **Le Monde en Marche,** 34 rue Dauphine, 6e (tel. 43-26-66-53), has a large assortment of creative playthings, mainly wooden toys, for children at reasonable prices. There are also music boxes for children, as well as little tin animals. Métro: Odéon.

LES HALLES: Now that Les Halles is going through a rebirth, the produce market having moved elsewhere, a growing number of fashionable boutiques have moved in, opening on the side streets. The following is only one of many of these avant-garde boutiques:

Sara Shelburne, 10 rue du Cygne, 1er (tel. 42-33-74-40), is what happens when a law student graduates but switches to couture. This is a ready-made boutique for women, with colorful dresses, separates, hostess gowns, coats, sportswear, knits, and well-styled evening wear. An interesting detail: Sara designs and makes all her fabrics. She will make "on measure" for the same price as ready-to-wear. However, you must allow her a few days. In addition, Sara Shelburne has opened a wedding dress department that attracts people from all over the world.

Chapter VI

PARIS AFTER DARK

**1. Cafés, Bars, and Pubs
2. Wine Bars
3. Spectacles
4. Folk Songs and Chansonniers
5. Supper Clubs
6. Jazz and Discos
7. Opera, Theater, and Music Halls**

IN PARIS, YOU CAN DO almost anything after dark; you can even have the Arc de Triomphe lit just for you. The entertainment is varied, not just at the Lido and the Folies Bergère, where everybody goes, but at little offbeat places such as the *caveaux* of the Left Bank. Visitors are constantly seeking the unusual.

Whether it's a splashy Las Vegas spectacle, "crazy" striptease, Juliette Greco in a supper club, a walk along the Seine, a cellar disco, or a smoky jazz club—Paris offers it.

1. Cafés, Bars, and Pubs

CAFÉS: The hour of the apéritif is a firmly entrenched ritual in Paris. Below are some of the more interesting cafés for your initiation into the custom.

Brasserie Lipp, 151 Boulevard St-Germain, 6e (tel. 45-48-53-91), has been called the "rendezvous for le tout Paris," the city's unofficial Social Register. Picasso and Charles de Gaulle used to patronize this St-Germain-des-Prés landmark, as did Max Ernst, Sartre, André Gide, Man Ray, Simone de Beauvoir, James Joyce, and James Baldwin. The owner, Roger Cazes, said Hemingway was the first man he saw at the 1944 Liberation. Nowadays, sitting on the moleskin banquettes, their faces reflected in the "hall of mirrors," are, perhaps, Françoise Sagan and Catherine Deneuve.

The Lipp doesn't serve Coca-Cola, but it does offer good-tasting Alsatian beer. Right after the Franco-Prussian war of 1870-1871, an Alsatian, Lippman, opened the café, preferring "not to live in Germany."

A restaurant is inside, including an upstairs dining room that never enjoys quite the same vogue as the back room. At the rush hours it's always difficult to get a seat, unless you're known by the management.

Many prefer to visit for breakfast, even as early as 8:30 a.m., ordering the traditional black coffee and croissants. At lunch or dinner, the house specialty is choucroute (sauerkraut), served with pork accompaniments. Some say Lipp serves the best sauerkraut in Paris; others ask, "Who cares?" About three or four plats du jour are offered, costing from 85F ($11.72) to 115F ($15.86). Food is served until 1 a.m. (it's most fashionable to arrive late at night). The café is closed on Monday and in July, 15 days for Christmas, and 15 days for Easter.

In black jackets and white aprons, the waiters keep alive the tradition of fin-de-siècle Paris. May it live forever! Métro: St-Germain-des-Prés.

Café de Flore, 173 Boulevard St-Germain, 6e (tel. 45-48-55-26). In his *A Memoir in the Form of a Novel (Two Sisters)*, Gore Vidal introduces his two main characters thus: "I first saw them at the Café de Flore in the summer of 1948. They were seated side by side at the center of the first row of sidewalk tables, quite outshining Sartre and de Beauvoir, who were holding court nearby." Sartre, the granddaddy of existentialism, was often here during the war years. A key figure in the Resistance, he sat at his table clad in a leather jacket and wearing a beret. He was writing a trilogy: *Les Chemins de la Liberté* ("The Roads to Freedom"). Other famous faces who have frequented the Flore include Camus, Picasso, and Apollinaire.

An espresso costs 13F ($1.79), and domestic beer costs the same. Go anytime before 2 in the morning. Métro: St-Germain-des-Prés.

Deux Magots, 170 Boulevard St-Germain, 6e (tel. 45-48-55-25). Piquant blonds smoke long cigarettes. Women in black leather stroll in looking as if they've stepped right out of 1933 Berlin. An assortment of male clients resemble extras from *Irma la Douce*. Just blink your eyes for a moment and you will have missed a scene. The Deux Magots is now legendary, of course, drawing not only the most sophisticated of the St-Germain-des-Prés set but an abundance of visitors in summer, the latter virtually monopolizing the limited number of sidewalk tables. Waiters rush about, seemingly oblivious to your waiting to place your order or pay the bill.

Inside are two large Oriental statues that give the café its name. Once known as the gathering place of the intellectual elite, Deux Magots drew such illustrious figures as Sartre, Simone de Beauvoir, and Jean Giraudoux. The crystal chandeliers are too brightly lit, but the regular clients are used to the glare. After all, some of them even read newspapers there. Off-season, it's not a lonesome café, as the habitués quickly learn who's who. A coffee costs 13F ($1.79), and domestic beer is the same price. Deux Magots is closed in August. Métro: St-Germain-des-Prés.

Café de la Paix, Place de l'Opéra, 9e (tel. 42-68-12-13), is an institution, staked out as an American enclave ever since the Yankee troops marched down the street in their victory parade after World War I. It is still the most popular café in Paris with U.S. visitors, many of whom sit there reading their mail from the nearby American Express. Legend has it that if your next-door neighbors from Omaha are in Paris, you'll find them if you sit under the familiar green canopy at a sidewalk table long enough. To entertain you in the meantime, there's that stunning view of the Opéra.

The ghosts of the great are here: Émile Zola, Oscar Wilde, Edward VII, de Maupassant, Chevalier, Caruso, Chagall. No one can remember Charles de Gaulle dining here, but a messenger arrived and ordered a "tinned" ham for the general's first supper when he returned to Paris in 1944 at the Liberation. Even Nixon has had a coffee at the Café de la Paix.

You can get the drink your fancy dictates: a whisky for 35F ($4.83) to 46F ($6.34), a Coca-Cola for 18F ($2.48), or café espresso for 12F ($1.66), service included. It's open from 10 a.m. to 1:30 a.m. all year. Métro: Opéra.

Fouquet's, 99 Champs-Élysées, 8e (tel. 47-23-70-60), sits behind a barricade of potted plants at the side of the Champs-Élysées in a pleasant location where even Jacqueline Onassis has been known to stop for coffee. You can select a table outdoors in the sunshine or retreat to the glassed-in elegance of the leather banquettes and rattan furniture. A formal dining room in a separate section serves full meals costing from 200F ($27.58). Most visitors, however, stop by for a glass of wine at 28F ($3.86) or a sandwich at 30F ($4.14). The café has been collecting both anecdotes and a patina since it was founded in 1901. Métro: George V.

La Coupole, 102 Boulevard Montparnasse, 14e (tel. 43-20-14-20). So well known is this Montparnasse café that some visitors stop off here with suitcases for a beer or coffee before beginning the search for a hotel. The clientele is mixed, ranging from attractive artists' models to young men dressed like Rasputin. In 1928 Fraux and Lafon—two waiters at the Café du Dôme—opened La Coupole. At first the Montparnasse regulars resented it, but it is now more of a landmark than any other café. Many of the Dôme's faithful customers were lured away, including Kiki, the prostitute who wrote a memoir with a foreword by Hemingway. The pillars running down the middle of the large room were decorated by artists between the two World Wars.

Open till 2 a.m., La Coupole is a big, bold, and brassy brasserie. At one of its sidewalk tables you can sit and watch the passing scene, ordering a coffee or a cognac VSOP. Actually, you wouldn't think it to look at the place (the dining room resembles that of a railway station), but the food is quite good. Try, for example, such main dishes as sole meunière or a pepper steak. Especially popular are the fresh *belons* (oysters) in season, served with a special sauce. The tables on the right have the white tablecloths and the correspondingly higher tabs. Meals cost from 250F ($34.48). The café is open seven days a week, as is the basement where a band plays for dancing. The "tea dance" is from 4:30 till 7 p.m., the soirée from 9:30 p.m. to 2 a.m. Your minimum is achieved by ordering a drink at 55F ($7.56) in the afternoon, 80F ($11.03) at night. Métro: Raspail.

La Rotonde, 105 Boulevard du Montparnasse, 6e (tel. 43-26-68-84). It's only a memory drawn from the pages of *The Sun Also Rises*. Once patronized by Hemingway, the original Rotonde has faded into history. The new one shares the once-hallowed site with a motion-picture theater. Papa wrote, "No matter what café in Montparnasse you ask a taxi-driver to bring you to from the right bank of the river, they always take you to the Rotonde." Full meals cost from 250F ($34.48). If you have a drink at a table, coffee costs 8F ($1.10), a glass of wine 12F ($1.66), and beer 11.50F ($1.59). Prices if you stand at the bar are 6F (83¢) for coffee, 10F ($1.38) for wine, and 9.50F ($1.31) for beer. Métro: Raspail.

Le Select, 99 Boulevard du Montparnasse, 6e (tel. 42-22-65-27), was also in *The Sun Also Rises*. Hemingway's hero walked past the "sad tables" of the Rotonde to the Select. Physically, the Select is somewhat as it was when it was favored by Jean Cocteau. Le Select basks in its former glory as a literary café, but it continues to flourish. It is beyond fads, seemingly outliving change, based on the eternal truth that a person needs a drink and drinking companions. A coffee goes for 7F (97¢) to 13.50F ($1.86), depending on the size. Wine by the glass begins at 11F ($1.52) and most other alcoholic drinks cost 30F ($4.14) to 45F ($6.21). Salads and sandwiches, warm or cold, begin at around 25F ($3.45). They have 40 different whiskies and some 20 different cocktails here, many of which are rather exotic. Métro: Raspail.

Le Dôme, 108 Boulevard du Montparnasse, 14e (tel. 43-35-25-81), has made a comeback. Redecorated in the belle époque style, it has never been more glamorous. All that remains of Le Dôme of times past are the pictures on the walls. Everybody showed up here at one time or another; today you get a healthy quota of foreign visitors. You can visit just for a coffee, costing from 8F ($1.10), or a full meal in the 225F ($31.03) range. Oysters are sold on the sidewalk under a red awning. Or you can enjoy such classic dishes inside as pot-au-feu, turbot with fresh morels, or bourride provençale. Métro: Raspail.

Rosebud, 11 bis rue Delambre, 14e (tel. 43-26-95-28), perpetuates the memory of Orson Welles's great movie *Citizen Kane*. It also refers to a failed Otto Preminger movie, *Rosebud,* which marked the screen debut of former New York City Mayor John Lindsay. It's an all-night eatery and bar, open till 3 a.m.

Some of the clients appear dressed '20s-style, with headbands and cloches. Others could have modeled for Toulouse-Lautrec. The Rosebud is a combined coffeehouse, bar, and social center. Wine bottles line the walls, the tables are packed tightly together, and you're allowed just to "be"—screened off from the street viewers by discreetly drawn shades. Everybody seemingly knows everybody else.

Popular with the late-night set is a bowl of homemade chili con carne, at 40F ($5.52), although you can order a hamburger at 45F ($6.21). Wine by the glass begins at 20F ($2.76). Métro: Edgar-Quinet.

Café de Cluny, 20 Boulevard St-Michel or 102 Boulevard St-Germain, 5e (tel. 43-26-68-24), is placed strategically at the intersection of these two famous avenues, overlooking the hub of the Left Bank and the Museé de Cluny. One of the main meeting places for visitors and locals alike, this large, bustling oasis attracts a striking proportion of pretty girls—mostly, alas, waiting for their boyfriends. Local beer goes for 15F ($2.07), a glass of wine for 12F ($1.66). Métro: St-Michel.

Le Mandarin, 148 bis Boulevard St-Germain, 6e (tel. 46-33-98-35), is an elegantly decorated corner café thronged with young people of the Left Bank and visitors soaking up the atmosphere of St-Germain-des-Prés. At the brass bar you can order fine wines, certainly a coffee. The bentwood chairs are scattered over several interior raised platforms and eventually spill out onto the sidewalk in warm weather. Decorated with lace-covered hanging lamps, brass trim, and lots of exposed wood, the establishment serves good food as well as wine by the glass for 14F ($1.93). Punch is a specialty, as is onion soup auvergnat. Ice creams and sherbets are also a specialty, with elaborate sundaes priced at around 35F ($4.83). Try a coupe Aphrodite: mint ice cream smothered in melted chocolate sauce. Métro: Odéon or Mabillon.

Café le St-André, 2 rue Danton, 6e (tel. 43-26-56-59), is one of many cafés in the area, although this one is particularly appealing because of the way it opens onto the quiet Place St-André-des-Arts near the traffic-clogged Place St-Michel. Decorated in a reproduction art nouveau style with tulip-shaped lighting fixtures and bentwood chairs, it serves fixed-price meals at 50F ($6.90), as well as sandwiches from 12F ($1.66) and glasses of wine from 12.50F ($1.72). Métro: Odéon.

Café le Départ, 1 Place St-Michel, 5e (tel. 43-54-24-55), is conveniently placed on the banks of the Seine, within view of both the spire of the Sainte Chapelle and the dragon statue of the Place St-Michel. The decor is almost overwhelmingly art nouveau, with wall murals of 19th-century couples courting at the edge of a river, fanciful chandeliers, red-leather banquettes, and bentwood chairs. Beer costs an average of 16F ($2.21), wine is around 12F ($1.66) a glass, and whisky from 28F ($3.86). An array of house cocktails includes a "Saint-Michel" (Polish vodka, grapefruit juice, and cream of banana). Salads, sandwiches, and warm and cold snacks are offered as well, each priced from 12F ($1.66). Métro: St-Michel.

Le Henri IV, 13 Place du Pont-Neuf, 1er (tel. 43-54-27-90). Try to drop in at sunset, ordering an apéritif at this dramatic location—in a 17th-century building opposite the statue of the "Vert Galant" at Pont-Neuf. Your host, Monsieur Cointepas, bottles his own wines, listing some of his prize drinks on a blackboard menu. You might order a special beaujolais or perhaps a glass of Chinon, the latter "tasting more of the earth." If you sit at a table (drinks are cheaper at the bar), you can order a big glass costing from 12F ($1.66) to 23F ($3.17), service included. Snacks, including wild boar pâté, range from 14F ($1.93) to 18F ($2.48). As the owner puts it, it depends on what you spread on your slice of bread. Five farmer's lunches are offered at 43F ($5.93) each. The place is closed Saturday and Sunday and in August, but open otherwise from 11:30 a.m. to 9:30 p.m. Métro: Pont-Neuf.

Ma Bourgogne, 19 Place des Vosges, 4e (tel. 42-78-44-64). As you sit under the arcades here, you'll think you're in an Italian town, perhaps Bologna. The café is most exciting at festival time in the Marais district, but otherwise it slumbers quietly, as it has since the days of Victor Hugo, who used to live on the square. Coffee costs 7.70F ($1.06), a small admission price to pay for the mood and the view. For 16F ($2.21) you can have a glass of Châteauneuf-du-Pape. In summer select one of the rattan tables outside. In winter you may have to hover under the beamed ceiling inside. The café offers a wide selection of hams, pâtés, and sausages, as well as a sauerkraut garnie. Meals cost from 150F ($20.69). Métro: St-Paul or Chemin-Vert.

Bar des Théâtres, 6 Avenue Montaigne, 8e (tel. 47-23-34-63), enjoys a fame throughout Paris that might be more than it deserves, but its location on what is said to be the most expensive residential street in the world contributes to its image. It's across from the Théâtre des Champs-Élysées, and before and after *le spectacle,* the café is almost mobbed with theater-goers who extend the show into the paneled dining room in back. There, meals cost from 150F ($20.69) to 220F ($30.34) and might include saddle of lamb provençale, roast duckling, house-style sauerkraut, salmon, foie gras, strawberry tart, and attractively priced wines. As you approach this establishment from the tree-lined avenue outside, all you see at first is a somewhat hysterical café decorated in a geometrically modern style, with a chic clientele that seems to enjoy the cramped tables and the standard café drinks. It is open from 7:45 a.m. till 1:30 a.m. every day of the week. Métro: F.-D.-Roosevelt.

BARS AND PUBS: Surpassed by the sidewalk cafés, the bars nevertheless enjoy a unique position in Parisian life. The pubs, on the other hand, are currently more in vogue than the cafés—especially if they are in the belle époque style.

Harry's New York Bar, 5 rue Daunou, 2e (tel. 42-61-71-14). The management instructs you how to get here: tell the cab driver, "Sank roo Doe Noo." Otherwise, take the Métro to the Opéra and walk down.

No bar in Europe is better known (a host of imitators was inspired). No bar in Paris is more popular with Americans, Harry's having been made famous by such men as Fitzgerald, William Faulkner, and John Steinbeck. In the 1920s and 1930s it was patronized by Elliot Paul *(The Last Time I Saw Paris),* Gertrude Stein, Ford Madox Ford, and Ring Lardner. It was also an oasis for American newspapermen in Paris and the birthplace of the Bloody Mary and the sidecar.

Opened on Thanksgiving Day 1911, it was operated by the original Harry until his death in 1958. Nowadays the atmosphere of polished wood is kept suitably subdued by a Scot, Andy McElhone, the son of the founder. In 1932 J. H. Cochrane set the world's drinking-speed record here, downing 4.4 pints in 11 seconds. Primo Carnera hung up his gloves at Harry's in 1929, after losing the world's heavyweight championship; they are still there, dangling from a wooden monkey. Perhaps the greatest tribute to Harry's today comes from the fact that the IBF, the International Bar Flies, meets here regularly. A dry martini costs 38F ($5.24) and whiskies range from 40F ($5.52) to 165F ($22.75), the latter price for a 1938 MacAllan single malt Scotch. The downstairs room has been redecorated and fitted with its own wet bar, and a piano player provides music from 10 p.m. to 2 a.m. Métro: Opéra or Pyramides.

Sir Winston Churchill, 5 rue de Presbourg, 16e (tel. 45-00-75-35). A corner of "ye olde" England in Paris. Actually, it's "merely the mock," but the reproduction is good. If the cut-glass mirrors, the Edwardian decor, the plush banquettes, and the dark wood do not convince, the tea from Fortnum & Mason surely will. Winston Red Barrel and Churchill Brown Ale are available on draft. You can even get "the real English breakfast," with orange juice, porridge, eggs, bacon, grilled tomato, toast, butter, and marmalade, plus tea, for 55F ($7.56). The cook prepares a series of English specialties such as roast beef with Yorkshire pudding. Meals cost 175F ($24.13) to 200F ($27.58). An Irish whisky is sold for 30F ($4.14) to 45F ($6.21), depending on whether it's day or night. A beer costs from 9F ($1.24) for a half pint. Métro: Place Charles-de-Gaulle (Étoile).

Pub Renault, 53 Avenue des Champs-Élysées, 8e (tel. 42-56-18-40). Although it borrows the word "pub" from the English, there is no resemblance to that familiar institution. This is a decidedly offbeat place, where, to get your seat in the back, you have to walk through an exhibition hall of Renault cars. While munching a hamburger, you can order the latest vehicle. In addition, there are gifts and gadgets, a boutique of records, and a car-rental office. At the charming café, you sit in a "horseless carriage," ordering a set meal for 175F ($24.13), or just have a drink. The pub is open from 10 a.m. to 2 a.m. Its latest attraction is a video club. Métro: F.-D.-Roosevelt.

Pub Saint-Germain-des-Prés, 17 rue de l'Ancienne-Comédie, 6e (tel. 43-29-38-70), is the only one in the country to offer 23 draft beers and 450 international beers. Leather niches render drinking discreet. The decor consists of gilded mirrors on the walls, hanging gas lamps, and a stuffed parrot in a gilded cage. Also, leather-cushioned handrails are provided for some mysterious purpose—guidance perhaps? You'll need it. There are seven different rooms and 500 seats, which makes the pub the largest in France. The atmosphere is quiet, relaxed, and rather posh, and it's open day and night. Genuine Whitbread beer is sold, and Pimm's No. 1 is featured. You can also order snacks or complete meals here. Drinks start at 10.50F ($1.49), menus at 82F ($11.31). Métro: Odéon.

Le Grand Pub Lady Hamilton, 82 Avenue Marceau, 8e (tel. 47-20-20-40), near the Champs-Élysées, is a charming French version of a British pub. In addition to a wide range of famous beers, you can enjoy tasty dishes at reasonable prices. If you choose to eat on the terrace in summer, you have an excellent view of the Arc de Triomphe. Specialties include onion soup gratinée, snails, filet steak and other meats, mixed salad, hamburger, and many desserts. A complete meal costs about 130F ($17.93). Métro: Étoile.

Le Bar, 10 rue de l'Odéon, 6e (tel. 43-26-66-83), right off the Place de l'Odéon, is one of the most popular Left Bank hangouts for students. It is permanently packed in the evenings with university students who order drinks that range in price from 14F ($1.93). The walls are decorated with posters, and a jukebox makes the joint jump. If you speak French, it might help if you're seeking contacts. But, as one Frenchman remarked, "Everybody at the Odéon speaks English." Métro: Odéon.

La Closerie des Lilas, 171 Boulevard du Montparnasse, 6e (tel. 43-26-70-50). Hemingway, Picasso, Gershwin, and Modigliani all loved the Closerie and, since it's going through a renaissance as one of the hottest bars in Paris, chances are you will too. Even if you don't plan to dine here (see Chapter IV), you can still search out which place along the banquettes or at the well-oiled bar that your favorite Lost Generation artist might have preferred (look for the brass nameplates). Of course, Hemingway would be appalled at the price of a Scotch and soda—50F or $6.90—but beer and coffee are more reasonable. Métro: Port-Royal.

The Grand Hotel Bars

If you want to re-create the elegance of the salons of 18th-century France in a late-20th-century setting, try one of the bars of the grand hotels of Paris. Before the end of your martini, just about anyone might come in (and frequently does). In any event, dress up, talk softly, and be prepared to spend at least 60F ($8.27) to 80F ($11.03) for a drink. You're not paying for the drink but for an ambience unmatched in most places.

The **George V Bar,** 31 Avenue George-V, 8e (tel. 47-23-54-00), is a divinely elegant combination of modern and classical design. All of it is arranged in an attractively symmetrical format of black accents over beige and maroon marble in a design that looks almost like a stage set. The most prominent feature is the massive crystal lighting fixture whose edges pleasingly correspond to the dimensions of the rectangular room. Of course, if there's someone you're trying to avoid, you can always sit among the upholstered couches and Regency-style antiques of the nearby salon. Métro: George-V.

Hôtel de Crillon, 10 Place de la Concorde, 8e (tel. 42-65-24-24). This world-famous watering hole inside this world-famous hotel used to attract some of the most prominent members of the so-called Lost Generation, including Hemingway and Scott and Zelda Fitzgerald. Do you recall that Hemingway's fictional heroine, Brett Ashley, broke her promise to have a rendezvous there with Jake Barnes in *The Sun Also Rises*? Over the years it has also attracted most of the Kennedys, along with Noël Coward and practically every upper-level staff member of the American Embassy. Classified as a historical monument, the hotel was recently refurbished under the watchful eye of fashion designer Sonia Rykiel. The decor of the bar no longer basks in the 1950s glow it did, but has undergone a covering of wood paneling. In the back is a 40-seat restaurant. Métro: Concorde.

Bar Anglais, Hôtel Plaza Athénée, 25 Avenue Montaigne, 8e (tel. 47-23-78-33). On your way through this deluxe citadel you'll pass a chattering Telex machine that carries recent quotes from the world's leading stock exchanges. This is, of course, in case you want to check the value of your investment portfolio. In the rarefied atmosphere of this elegant bar, it seems appropriate to do so. As its name would imply, the bar has a decor that is vintage Anglo-Saxon, although the service is definitely French and the drinks international. On the lower level of the hotel, the bar is open from 11 a.m. to 1:30 a.m. seven days a week. Drinks begin at 45F ($6.21) and go up, depending on what you order. Métro: Alma-Marceau.

Hôtel Bristol Bar, 112 rue du Faubourg St-Honoré, 8e (tel. 42-66-91-45). Looking over a central courtyard covered with latticework and dotted with greenery and well-kept glasses, you can sit in wicker chairs between pink marble columns and thick Oriental rugs. Some distance away (one thing about the Bristol is that it has lots of space), a raised platform has a better view of the Regency-style bar. Specialties are usually mixed by the chief barman, Michel Le Regent, who has developed such prize-winning combinations as a "Crazy Horse cocktail" (strawberries, bananas, scotch, and champagne), or a Pluton (orange juice, pineapple, Pernod, vodka, and strawberries). A pianist adds to the pleasure every evening from 7:30 to midnight. Métro: St-Philippe-du-Roule.

Regency Bar, Hotel Prince de Galles, 8e (tel. 47-23-55-11), under Marriott's restoration, has joined the ranks of the grand hotel bars of Paris. In high-ceilinged splendor, ringed with the amber tones of carefully crafted full-grained paneling, guests sink into their leather-upholstered copies of 18th-century armchairs and enjoy the hot hors d'oeuvres and well-mixed drinks. A live pianist performs most evenings. House drinks include the bourbon-based "White House" and the rum-based "Mississippi." Métro: George V.

Les Drug Stores

In a class by themselves, these so-called Drug Stores are pacesetters of what has become an international craze, combining a coffeehouse, ice-cream soda fountain (serving champagne and caviar, no less), snackbar, cocktail lounge, newsstand, and boutiques offering everything from baby oil to jewelry. When first created, they were denounced by the traditional French as American "vulgarisms," but they are, in fact, uniquely Parisian—totally unrelated to the drugstore usually found in the United States. Sophisticated, stylish, glitteringly avant garde, they offer frenzied activity approaching a world's fair exposition.

The exteriors of the Drug Stores are architecturally traditional, but inside they're another story. The St-Germain-des-Prés branch—the most popular—is imaginatively decorated. Next door to the Brasserie Lipp, at 149 Boulevard St-Germain-des-Prés, 6e (tel. 42-22-92-50), Le Drug Store's boutiques sell everything from mustache cups to hearts of palm. They are open daily till 2 a.m., even on Sunday. A set menu, served all day, costs 100F ($13.79), including drink and service. The most popular item, seemingly, is a hamburger on a toasted bun. Some of the desserts are smothered in enough whipped cream to make them immoral. Métro: St-Germain-des-Prés.

Another Drug Store in Paris, quite similar to the one at St-Germain, is at Publicis Champs-Élysées, 133 Avenue des Champs-Élysées, 8e (tel. 47-23-54-34). Métro: Place Charles-de-Gaulle (Étoile).

2. Wine Bars

Many Parisians now prefer to patronize wine bars instead of their traditional café or bistro. The food is often better, and the ambience more inviting. Wine bars come in a wide range of styles, from old and traditional places to modern "trendy" gathering centers.

Au Franc Pinot, 1 Quai de Bourbon, 4e (tel. 43-29-46-98). At the foot of the Pont-Marie, this is the oldest wine bistro in Paris. It dates from the early 17th century, built on a double tier of vaulted cellars. The establishment was renovated in 1980 by Bernard and Michelle Meyruey, who added an inventory of about two dozen wines that are sold by the glass. These you can consume while standing at the large wooden bar (which is crowned by a large metal rooster), or on one of the bentwood chairs in the warm glow of the stained-glass windows.

If you descend into one of the deepest cellars of Paris, you'll find a cozily intimate restaurant. A set menu is available for lunch or dinner, costing 165F ($22.75), although a more expensive à la carte meal goes for 265F ($36.54). This might include such specialties as lamb with crayfish in a tarragon cream sauce, or terrine of foie gras with fresh duckling from Landes, plus a small selection of other classic French dishes. The last glass of red sancerre, beaujolais, or riesling is consumed at the bar at 11:30 p.m. It is closed every Sunday and Monday. Métro: Pont-Marie.

Willi's Wine Bar, 13 rue des Petits-Champs, 1er (tel. 42-61-05-09). Journalists and stock brokers alike are attracted to this increasingly popular wine bar, in the center of the financial district close to the Bourse. Surprisingly, it is run by two Englishmen, Mark Williamson and Jim Johnston. They offer about 180 different kinds of wine, and each week about a dozen "specials" are featured.

Very crowded at lunchtime, it often settles down to a lower decibel count in the evening, when you can better enjoy the 16th-century beams and the warm, friendly ambience. A blackboard menu informs you of the daily specials, which are likely to include a filet of beef à la ficelle, spinach quiche (gâteau d'omelette aux épinards), duck, and fresh fish dishes, along with a spectacular dessert, the chocolate terrine. The plat du jour will most likely cost 60F ($8.27) to 80F ($11.03), and you can enjoy wines by the glass from 18F ($2.48) to 55F ($7.26). It is closed Saturday evening, Sunday, and in August. Métro: Bourse or Palais-Royal.

Au Sauvignon, 80 rue des Saints-Pères, 7e (tel. 45-48-49-02), is considered the best-known wine bar in Paris, and is it ever minuscule. Narrow and small, it still has a very chic reputation. The owner is from Auvergne, and when he's not polishing his zinc countertop or preparing a plate of charcuterie for a client, he will sell you beaujolais at 6F (83¢) to 12F ($1.66), depending on the size of the glass. It's even more popular these days to order a glass of fresh white sancerre. He also sells wines from Alsace and St. Émilion. The fresh Poilâne bread is ideal with the Auvergne ham, the pâté of the country, or the crottin de Chavignol goat cheese. The place has old ceramic decor along with frescoes by Left Bank artists. If you drop in here for a little wine and a snack, count on spending from

35F ($7.56). It is closed on Sunday, on religious holidays, and for all of August, but open otherwise from 9:15 a.m. to 10:30 p.m. Métro: Sèvres-Babylone.

La Tartine, 24 rue de Rivoli, 4e (tel. 42-72-76-85), is Old Paris. It's like a movie set. Inset mirrors, brass decorative details, a zinc bar, and frosted globe chandeliers form the decor. At any moment you expect to see Tito, Trotsky, or Lenin walk in the door (each of this unholy trio was a former patron). At least 50 wines are offered at reasonable prices, and all categories of wine are served by the glass. A plate of charcuterie will cost from 23F ($3.17), and you can order sandwiches for 10F ($1.38) to 15F ($2.07). At least seven kinds of beaujolais are offered, along with a large selection of bordeaux. The light, white sancerre is more favored than ever. Why not some young goat cheese from the châteaux country? La Tartine is closed on Tuesday and on Wednesday morning, but open otherwise from 7:30 a.m. to 10 p.m. Métro: St-Paul.

Blue Fox Wine Bar, 25 rue Royale (Cité Berryer), 8e (tel. 42-65-08-47), is a creation of Steven Spurrier, who also owns the already-recommended Moulin du Village (see Chapter IV). Adjoining the restaurant he has opened this successful wine bar, supplied by his highly regarded Caves de la Madeleine. A large selection of wines by the glass is sold, along with charcuterie, salads, cheeses, and simple plats du jour. It's an unpretentious place but nevertheless frequented by some of the chicest people of Paris. It's on two levels, with lace curtains and plenty of wood used. At lunch it tends to be overcrowded, as it fills up quickly with the people who staff the shops around the Place de la Madeleine and along the rue Royale. A simple meal and a glass of wine will cost from 120F ($16.55). It is closed Saturday evening and Sunday. Métro: Concorde or Madeleine.

Les Domaines, 56 rue François 1er, 8e (tel. 42-56-15-87). Music and showbiz types often have a rendezvous over a glass of wine here at one of the city's trendiest wine bar restaurants. Vintage wines can be ordered by the glass. The smallest glass of the least expensive wine goes for 14F ($1.93), but you might pay as much as 80F ($11.03) for a large glass of a rarer vintage. The establishment is open for full meals, including breakfast, or just a glass of wine between 8 a.m. and 1 a.m. every day of the week except Sunday.

The ultra-modern decor of designer Philippe Starck includes high-tech combinations of chrome tubing, mottled granite, and space-age simplicity. At lunch and dinner, a fixed-price classic French menu costs 160F ($22.06) per person. A la carte meals, costing from 200F ($27.58), might include a salad of roast kid or else of haddock, spinach, and leeks, a selection of hunter-style terrines, sea trout with sage, and a very interesting assiette de canard, with portions of duck served on the same platter in five different ways. The cheese assortment is excellent. Métro: George-V.

3. Spectacles

According to legend, the first G.I. to reach Paris at the Liberation in 1944 asked for directions to the **Folies Bergère,** 32 rue Richer, 9e (tel. 42-46-77-11). His son does the same today. Even the old man comes back for a second look.

A roving-eyed Frenchman would have to be in his second century to remember when the Folies Bergère began. Apparently, it's here to stay, like Sacré-Coeur and the Eiffel Tower. The affection of Parisians for it has long turned into indifference (but try to get a seat on a July night). Some, however, recall it with sentimentality. Take, for example, the night the "toast of Paris," Josephine Baker, descended the celebrated staircase, tossing bananas into the audience.

Opened in 1886, since the turn of the century the Folies Bergère has stood as the symbol of unadorned female anatomy. Fresh off the boat, Victorians and Edwardians—starved for a glimpse of even an ankle—flocked to the Folies Bergère to get a look at much more. Yet the Folies also dresses its dancers (at least

1,600 costumes at the last revue I saw) in those fabulous showgirl outfits you associate with Hollywood musicals of the 1930s. The creator of the spectacle surely must have inspected more navels than General Eisenhower did troops. Every Folies performer, house rules seemingly dictate, must wear at least eight bushy tails and a nest of towering plumes, that is, those who wear anything at all.

The big musical review begins nightly, except Monday, at 8:45. You can go to the box office anytime between 11 a.m. and 6:30 p.m. for tickets. The orchestra or balcony loge seats are likely to run you around 300F ($41.37), with the *galerie* going for 100F ($13.79). A scale model at the box office shows you locations. Métro: Cadet or rue Montmartre.

Lido Cabaret Normandie, 116 bis Avenue des Champs-Élysées, 8e (tel. 45-63-11-61), is housed in a panoramic room with 1,200 seats, with excellent visibility. This palatial nitery puts on an avalanche of glamour and talent, combined with enough showmanship to make the late Mr. Barnum look like an amateur. The permanent attraction is the Bluebell Girls, a fabulous precision ensemble of long-legged international beauties. The rest of the program changes, but the bill I last saw included a couple on ice skates, two camels, and a real waterfall. And that's only one show, called "Panache."

The dinner-dance at 8:30 nightly costs 500F ($68.95), including half a bottle of champagne. However, you can go solely for "La Revue" (at either 10:45 p.m. or 1 a.m.) and pay a minimum of 300F ($41.37), which also includes the half bottle of champagne, taxes, and service. And if you perch at the bar, you can get two glasses of champagne for 250F ($34.48). If you're a lone man you'll run into thirsty companions at the bar.

Go at least once in a lifetime. Métro: George-V.

Moulin Rouge, Place Blanche, 18e (tel. 46-06-00-19). Sometimes the showgirls are dressed (but not always) in feathers befitting a bird of paradise. At a recent opening a critic put it aptly: "The show must have cost a bundle." Seemingly no expense is spared in this would-be wicked, spectacularly stunning revue. A question arises, "Is it any different from the Lido?" Frankly, not that much. However, the truth admittedly won't stop hordes of visiting firemen from going to both of them.

For the festivities, the minimum charge is 360F ($49.64) per person, that tab including half a bottle of champagne. Should you desire both dinner and the obligatory champagne, the charge is 525F ($72.40) to 600F ($82.74) per person, the quotation including service. The food? Newspaperman Wolf Kaufman put it thus: "The groceries are well served and decently cooked." If you drop in and station yourself at the bar, drinks average around 180F ($24.82) each. Dinner begins at 8 p.m., the show at 10 p.m.

Hollywood studios of yore notwithstanding, the French cancan is danced best here. Renoir and Toulouse-Lautrec, especially the latter, immortalized "The Red Windmill." In his billboards Toulouse-Lautrec captured the dancers as no artist ever did, before or after.

If you're not interested in women displaying their wares, perhaps you'll be titillated by handsome young men in lamé loincloths (considered daring before the age of show-everything). On one recent occasion a nude couple dove into a tank for underwater love. You may be less fortunate and see a ballet, more naughty than Esther Williams—but a ballet, nevertheless.

Footnote: Appearing with Madame de Morny in a mime drama, *The Dream of Egypt,* Colette once performed a prolonged kiss—much to the righteous indignation of the first-nighters. The affair became known as the "Scandal of the Moulin Rouge." Métro: Place Blanche.

Crazy Horse Saloon, 12 Avenue George-V, 8e (tel. 47-23-32-32). Arthur Sainer wrote a review of the Sam Shepard play *Shaved Splits* that would have been appropriate as a description of the show at "Crazy." He called it (the play, that is): "frantic, wondrous, surly, delicious, expansive, cryptic, blatant, elegiac, fatiguing, corrupting, virginal, metaphorical, literal, stupefying, messy, giggly, two-dimensional, corrosive, counter-erotic, spaced out, rhetorical, convulsive, metallic, grubby, pricky, convivial, gyrational, overheated, pop-eyed, flat-eyed, wide-eyed and funky."

That should tell you that Alain Bernardin's stripteasery is no ordinary cabaret. Gypsy Rose Lee told Bernardin, "You have gone beyond Minsky!" It's a French parody of a Far West saloon, which became the first emporium in France where the strippers tossed their G-strings to the winds, throwing up their hands for the big "revelation."

The management invites you to "Be cool! Do it yourself! We dig English like Crazy!" The out-of-towners are crowded in tighter than a powwow at Crazy Horse's tent. Between acts, which make use of rear-screen projections, there are vaudeville-type skits and dancing on the mini-size floor. The first show, lasting less than two hours, goes on at 9 p.m., the second at 11:30 p.m. At the bar, two drinks cost 300F ($41.37) per person, increasing to 450F ($62.06) per person for two drinks at the tables, plus 15% for service. Métro: George-V.

Le Milliardaire, 69 rue Pierre-Charron, 8e (tel. 42-25-25-17). The French have a hard-to-translate word for it: *bruit*. Call it almost anything you like: roar, zip, snap, clatter, bang, crack, ping, rattle, tramp, tread, blare. Regardless, I fully guarantee you'll hear all of these sounds by spending one *soir* at the Milliardaire. Right off the Champs-Élysées, this glamour nook is entered by walking down an arcade and through a saloon-like door. Inside, at 10:30 p.m. and 12:30 a.m., the dancers take it all off, a treat for students of anatomy. The "skin game" is played with professional skill. A rival of the Crazy Horse Saloon, Le Milliardaire boasts a bevy of beauties.

You can watch the show for 300F ($41.37) per person, which includes two drinks at your table, or for 322F ($44.40) per person, including a half bottle of champagne. If you're a lone male, expect some Dry Gulch Gerties to move in to help you share your thirst. Closed Sunday. Métro: F.-D.-Roosevelt.

4. Folk Songs and Chansonniers

FOLK SONGS: In a class by themselves, the following recommendations are sentimental favorites and decidedly offbeat.

Au Lapin Agile, 22 rue des Saules, 18e (tel. 46-06-85-87), is a little cottage near the top of Montmartre. Once known as the Café des Assassins, it was patronized by Picasso and Utrillo. Amateurs and established artists have painted it (see, in particular, *Le Lapin Agile* by Utrillo).

For decades it has been the heartbeat of French folk music. Today poetry reading, folk songs, and sing-alongs continue. Every night except Monday talented performers entertain in a humble atmosphere, with tables and crude banquettes set around the walls. The price of admission and your first drink ranges from 60F ($8.27) for regular customers. The second drink costs 25F ($3.45), however. Evening performances begin at 9:15, ending at 2 a.m. An hour at Au Lapin Agile is a glimpse into the soul of Old Montmartre. Métro: Lamarck.

Au Caveau de la Bolée, 25 rue de l'Hirondelle, 6e (tel. 43-54-62-20), is a cabaret where the action takes place in a cellar built in 1317 as part of the historic Abbey of St-André. In time it was a prison, a breeding ground for the Revolution, and a literary club, drawing such absinthe drinkers as Paul Verlaine and Oscar Wilde. After descending a staircase, you search for a seat in one of the niches of the vaulted cellar—and then the spell begins. Balladeers, poets, and what one observer called "wittytellers, realistic and fancy fellows" are the performers. Often the audience joins in; it's especially popular with Left Bank students who know the "dirty old French songs."

The fixed-price dinner, costing around 200F ($27.58), is served every night except Sunday, at 9 p.m. and is followed by a cabaret show. However, you won't understand the jokes and references made in the show unless your French is extremely good. The cabaret starts at 11 p.m., and if you've already had dinner, you can order a drink for about 70F ($9.65). On Sunday, a jazz show begins at 10 p.m. No dinner is served.

You'll find this establishment, which seats only 24 persons, on a tiny street leading into the western edge of the Place St-Michel. The beginning of the street is down a short flight of steps under a giant archway beneath one of the square's grandiose buildings. Métro: St-Michel.

Caveau des Oubliettes: You enter through a church close, which hardly puts you in the mood for what you're about to see. The address is 1 rue St-Julien-le-Pauvre, 5e (tel. 43-54-94-97), in the Latin Quarter, across from Notre-Dame. Founded in 1920 by Marcel François, the *caveau* is one of the most popular attractions on the after-dark tourist circuit of Paris. It's sheltered in a 14th-century prison, the word *oubliette* meaning a dungeon with a trap door at the top as its only opening: victims were pushed through portholes into the Seine to drown. In costumes of different epochs, singers present *chansons* (love songs)—sentimental or bawdy—of France from the 11th to the 14th centuries. After the show, a guide will conduct you through the museum exhibiting a chastity belt, arms and armor, and thumbscrews. Drinks, including the entrance fee, begin at 70F ($9.65), with service. Hours are 9 p.m. to 2 a.m. Métro: St-Michel.

CHANSONNIERS: The chansonnier (literally "songwriter") is a Parisian institution. *Chansonner* means to lampoon, which gives you some idea of what to expect. The theaters of the chansonniers, especially those on the otherwise tawdry Boulevard de Clichy, provide a nostalgic link with the past. Nightly songs are not only sung but are often created on the spot, depending for their inspiration on "the disaster of the day."

The commentary on the day's events is loaded with satire, as parody holds hands with burlesque in this time-honored Gallic amusement. Wit and ridicule, fanciful and fantastic, make for an extravagant, bombastic revue. At the pinnacle of his power and glory, Charles de Gaulle was the number-one target of the barbs of these pundits, who irreverently pictured him as *le roi soleil* (sun king). Hear the comments of the chansonniers on the "oldest profession," many of whose devotees slink by outside their doors at Clichy.

My favorite places include **Théatre Des Deux Anes,** 100 Boulevard de Clichy, 18e (tel. 46-06-10-26). A sign, "Leave your chewing gum at the door," sets the tone. Down from the Moulin Rouge, the theater charges 140F ($19.31) to 160F ($22.06) for its seats. Performances begin nightly at 9. Closed Wednesday. The box office is open from 11 a.m. to 7 p.m. Métro: Blanche.

I hope these revues survive forever; society needs them.

5. Supper Clubs

Le Toit de Paris, Hilton International Hotel, 18 Avenue de Suffren, 15e (tel. 42-73-92-00). This would be an ideal choice for that first (or last) romantic dinner in Paris. Set in an undeniably romantic location on top of the Hilton, it has a view from the sweeping expanses of its glass windows of one of the world's most unusual panoramas, the Eiffel Tower. The government, it would seem, almost graciously illuminates it for your dining pleasure.

You'll be ushered to your table by an impeccably polite team of well-trained waiters. There you will be offered a selection of delicacies likely to include medallions of lobster with crayfish, six oysters gratinéed on a bed of grated cabbage, and escalope of salmon with green lentils. Other selections are filet of lobster garnished with cèpes, lamb noisettes with a creamy taragon sauce, pan-fried duck, and foie gras in a truffle sauce. The cheese and dessert trays overflow with French specialties. The restaurant is closed on Sunday and in August.

Count on spending from 325F ($44.82) for a meal here. Throughout your dinner, a dance band plays live music which turns the evening into more of a supper club with after-dinner dancing. Métro: Bir Hakeim.

Villa d'Este, 4 rue Arsène-Houssaye, 8e (tel. 43-59-78-44), is a sentimental favorite of mine. That's where I first met and photographed Juliette Greco. "You have made me beautiful," she said upon seeing the photographs. Frankly, in her case that task wasn't difficult. Amália Rodrigues, the great *fadista* of Lisbon, has also appeared there. You get the point: a showcase of some of the finest vocal artists in Europe. Of course, don't go expecting legendary talent such as the women named—but if they were appearing in Paris, the Villa d'Este is likely to be where you'd go to see them.

Right off the Champs-Élysées, this elegant supper club offers—in addition to entertainment—a smooth orchestra for dancing. A four-course dinner served at 8:30 p.m. (typical nightclub cookery) is yours for 300F ($41.37), plus 20% for service, increasing to 360F ($49.64) on weekends. Closed in July and August. Métro: Place Charles-de-Gaulle (Étoile).

6. Jazz and Discos

JAZZ: Paris is the leading jazz center of Europe. From the *caveaux* of the Left Bank to the clubs on the Right, you'll hear that Dixieland or Chicago rhythm. Many of the establishments recommended below combine jazz with rock.

Club St-Germain/Le Bilboquet, 13 rue Saint-Benoit, 6e (tel. 45-48-81-84), enjoyed great fame during its existentialist heyday. It's still around, offering some of the best jazz in Paris. The film *Paris Blues* was shot here. Right in the heart of throbbing St-Germain-des-Prés, it offers both a "jazz restaurant" and a disco.

The basement level is reached via a mirrored stairwell. There, you'll find a sunken, rather small dance floor with pink spotlights, red walls, and black leather banquettes. Open from 11 p.m. till dawn every night of the week, this is the disco part. Called the Club St-Germain, both it and the jazz club charge 80F ($11.03) for a drink.

On the upper level is Le Bilboquet, where you hear all that jazz. A copper ceiling and wooden wall panels surround a sunken bar with brass trim, forgiving lighting, Victorian candelabra, and comfortable seats. On an encircling raised tier, as well as an elevated balcony, you'll find immaculate linens covering the dinner tables. The menu is limited but classic French, specializing in carré agneau, fish, and beef, which might be preceded by a large choice of appetizers, including smoked salmon and terrines. Count on spending from 200F ($27.58) up. The restaurant is open from 7:30 p.m. to 1 a.m., and the bar serves from 8 p.m. to 4 a.m. The music usually begins at 10:45 p.m., ending at 3 a.m. Métro: St-Germain-des-Prés.

Le Patio, Hôtel Méridien, 81 Boulevard Gouvion-St-Cry, 17e (tel. 47-58-12-30), may look like the Palm Court at the Plaza Hotel in New York. But it's a good jazz center, located in the largest hotel in the country, at Porte Maillot. A good jazz band plays here against a backdrop of fountains daily from 10 p.m. to 2 a.m. Just enter from the street, heading for the courtyard in the heart of the hotel. You will be charged no cover, and there isn't even a minimum. However, drinks begin at about 85F ($11.72). Métro: Porte Maillot.

Caveau de la Huchette, 5 rue de la Huchette, 5e (tel. 43-26-65-05), is also popular, especially with a young crowd and jazz lovers, although it was once known by Robespierre and Marat. French jazz musicians reign supreme here, joined sometimes by international and American greats, such as Lionel Hampton, Art Blakely, Wild Bill Davis, and others. Providing you are 18 years of age, you descend a winding stone staircase into a real cellar where you can listen to jazz and jive. The entrance fee is 40F ($5.52) Sunday to Thursday, 50F ($6.90) on Friday and Saturday. However, women students pay only 35F ($4.83), and most drinks begin at 12F ($1.66). The *caveau* is open every day. The fun starts at 9:30 p.m., lasting until 2:30 a.m. On Friday it's open until 3 a.m., till 4 a.m. on Saturday and holiday evenings. Métro: St-Michel.

Trois Mailletz, 56 rue Galande, 5e (tel. 43-54-00-79), used to be the medieval cellar that housed the masons who constructed Notre-Dame. Many of them carved their initials into the walls. Today it is a haven for jazz aficionados of all nationalities, and one of the few places in the district where students don't predominate. Musical celebrities appearing here have included Memphis Slim, Bill Coleman, and Nina Simone. A piano bar is on the upper floor. It is open every day from 5 p.m. and requires no cover charge. The jazz club is on the lower level, and it is open from 8 p.m. to 5 or 6 a.m. every day except Monday and Tuesday. The entrance fee is 25F ($3.45) to 100F ($13.79), depending on the artist. Once inside, drinks cost 35F ($4.83) to 55F ($7.56). Métro: Maubert-Mutualité.

Slow Club, 130 rue de Rivoli, 1er (tel. 42-33-84-30), really isn't. Offering New Orleans Dixieland jazz, it is one of the most popular Right Bank clubs, near the Louvre and Châtelet. The club is open every night except Sunday and Monday (but when those dates fall on holidays, then it's open). The fun starts at 9:30 p.m., lasting until 2:30 a.m. However, on Friday it stays open until 3 a.m., till 4 a.m. on Saturday. The regular entrance fee is 45F ($6.21), except Friday and Saturday when it's 55F ($7.56), with drinks beginning at 10F ($1.38). Métro: Châtelet.

Another Right Bank favorite is **Caméléon,** 57 rue St-André-des-Arts, 6e (tel. 43-26-64-40). You're invited to the downstairs cellar, a combined disco/jazz center and video bar specializing in "cave dancing." Weekdays, there's a 50F ($6.90) entrance charge. A whisky costs upward of 45F ($6.21). Look for the neon-lit chameleon outside. Métro: Odéon.

New Morning, 7-9 rue des Petites-Ecuries, 10e (tel. 45-23-51-41). Perhaps its title derived from the tendency of its clients to remain inside until rays of early sunlight filter into the narrow streets of the garment district surrounding it. Its reputation as the most interesting jazz club in Paris began only after its owner redesigned this high-ceilinged loft to allow jazzmaniacs to dance, talk, flirt, and drink elbow-to-elbow at the stand-up bar. The appropriate dress code is jeans or whatever, and concerts and musical soirées might include a range of practically anything except disco. The only rule here seems to be that there are very few rules. It opens at 9:30 every evening except Sunday. A phone call will verify if a special jazz concert is planned on the night of your visit. Entrance costs 60F ($8.27) after which a drink goes for 25F ($3.45). Métro: Château-d'Eau.

THE DISCOS: The French gave the world the discothèque, but that term is likely to mean anything today, as the recommendations set forth below will reveal.

Le Palace, 8 rue du Faubourg Montmartre, 8e (tel. 42-46-10-87), is the leading disco of Europe. Right in the heart of the Boulevards, it was once a theater, and many of the old trappings still remain. The main hallway is decorated in light brown with large mirrors, and the former foyer on the left (as you enter) is a bar, drawing fashionable Parisians who often finish the evening here after a première at a Right Bank theater. From the bar you can climb to the balcony, which is filled with tables and chairs. Or from the main entrance you can join the disco dancing in the hall, the scene reflected in a wide mirror at the end. There you'll find another bar.

The music is quite loud but of good quality, and you will likely be listening to everybody from Diana Ross to Paul McCartney, from Grace Jones to Pink Floyd. Colored light rays flash around you, and an illuminated mobile rises and falls. A curtain rises, revealing erotic but humorous posters, along with pictures of the great Hollywood film stars. Most of the crowd is young, but all ages patronize the place. There's no entrance fee, although the first drink costs 75F ($10.32). It opens seven nights a week at 11 p.m. for the disco and at 9 p.m. for the adjoining restaurant, whose phone is 45-23-44-62. Meals average 150F ($20.69) per person. Métro: Montmartre.

Le Sept, 7 rue Ste-Anne, 1er (tel. 42-96-25-82). Is disco really dead? Perhaps, although the grande dame of Paris gay bars still makes a major effort to keep it alive. An upstairs bar and restaurant welcomes a crowd that in the 1970s might have approached terminal sophistication and which today has moved on to other pastures. A low-ceilinged dance floor on the lower level used to welcome the most famous celebrities of Gay Paree (and most of Gay Europe as well). Still, if you're gay, Le Sept is a Paris institution which might be worth the 55F ($7.56) price of a drink. In any event, go late. Métro: Palais-Royal or Pyramides.

Riverside Club, 7 rue Grégoire-de-Tours, 6e (tel. 43-54-46-33), is the typical Left Bank cellar disco. Usually this one has a line at the door, an international crowd attracted here not so much by what's happening inside as by the interesting clients likely to show up. It opens at 10 nightly. The entrance fee is 55F ($7.56) from Sunday to Thursday, increasing to 65F ($8.97) on Friday and Saturday. The price of entrance includes a ticket for one free drink. After the first libation, additional ones cost 40F ($5.52) with alcohol, 30F ($4.14) without. Customers dance inside, sometimes *comme des foux* (like lunatics), to the music which ranges from new wave to reggae to punk but never disco. Métro: St-Michel.

LATIN MUSIC: Currently, rue Monsieur-le-Prince in St-Germain-des-Prés, 6e is one of the most popular nightlife streets on the Left Bank. Activity reaches a frenzied pitch on Friday and Saturday nights, when automobiles are parked on the sidewalk and laughter and singing go on until dawn.

A standout on the street is **l'Escale,** 15 rue Monsieur-le-Prince, 6e (tel. 43-54-63-47), which is small and dark, a cozy, intimate ambience enhanced by Latin murals. Latin rhythm is featured. The sound of the gaucho pierces the air. Your first drink costs anywhere from 45F ($6.21), but you can nurse it as long as you like. The club also has a "cave" where you can dance to a Cuban combo. Métro: Odéon.

TRANSVESTITES: **Madame Arthur,** 75 bis rue des Martyrs, 18e (tel. 42-64-48-27). Behind the splashy façade, right off the Place Pigalle, Madame Arthur is no lady. His/her robust, blatant innuendo and humor, with no holds barred, either stuns or amuses.

For years now this club has been one of the leading female-impersonator cabarets in Paris—in the world, really. At the bar your first libation will cost 80F ($11.03), increasing to 120F ($16.55) at a table. Every night Madame Arthur is receiving at 10, although the show begins at 11 p.m. The cabaret shuts down at 3 a.m. Métro: Abbesses.

7. Opera, Theater, and Music Halls

THE OPÉRA: Dominating that frenetic traffic hub the Place de l'Opéra, 9e, l'Opéra (tel. 47-42-57-50) is the largest in the world. Although it consumes more land area than any other theater, it doesn't have as many seats as the theater at Châtelet. The building was designed by a young architect who entered a contest in 1860 in the heyday of Napoléon III's Second Empire. He adorned the façade with marble and sculptures, including *The Dance* by Carpeaux.

At one time or another most of the great, glittering personages of Europe —Henry James, the Divine Sarah—have descended the wide marble steps of the Grand Staircase. In red and gold, the theater or auditorium is sheltered under a dome adorned by Chagall in 1964, the subject of a controversy that continues to this day. Between acts, gravitate to the Grand Foyer, decorated with paintings, sculpture, chandeliers. Any fabulously wealthy king or monarch would feel at home there.

You have to attend a performance to see the inside of this neobaroque splendor. Tickets usually go on sale about one week before the actual performance. The box office is open from 11 a.m. to 6:30 p.m. Tickets range in price from 35F ($4.83) to 400F ($55.16), depending on the type of performance. The Opéra is closed in August and on Sunday night. Métro: Opéra.

For light-opera productions, go to the **Opéra-Comique**, 5 rue Favart, 2e (tel. 42-96-12-20). The most expensive seats cost about 260F ($35.85), although many good ones are offered for 165F ($22.75). The Opéra-Comique is closed in summer, but the box office is open otherwise from 11 a.m. to 6:30 p.m. two weeks before a performance is scheduled. Métro: Richelieu-Drouot.

THEATERS: Paris has five national theaters, including its opera house. Of course, the problem for most visitors is the language. However, for those who speak even high-school French, the theater can be a sparkling attraction in Paris. Perhaps you'll want to spend one night at the **Comédie-Française**, Place du Théâtre-Français, 1er (tel. 42-96-10-20), the First Theater in Paris. The French classics, including works by Racine and Molière, are performed here, as are dramas by the most important among contemporary authors. Prices begin as low as 15F ($2.07), going up to 110F ($15.17). Métro: Palais-Royal.

The **English Theatre of Paris,** 55 rue de Seine, 6e (tel. 43-26-63-51), presents a changing schedule of English-language plays. In a small storefront on a well-known street in the Latin Quarter, it can make for an exciting, offbeat evening. Recent productions include *Sexual Perversity in Chicago, Educating Rita,* Harold Pinter's *The Caretaker,* and shows for children. Métro: Odéon.

Operas, concerts, and ballets are performed at the **Théâtre des Champs-Élysées,** 15 Avenue Montaigne, 8e (tel. 47-23-36-86). National and international orchestras, incidentally, appear here. The box office is open daily except Sunday from 11 a.m. to 5:30 p.m. Métro: Alma-Marceau.

MUSIC HALLS: This institution is still going strong in Paris. Offering popular family entertainment at its best, the **Olympia**, 28 Boulevard des Capucines, 9e (tel. 47-42-25-49), has seen the greats, including Piaf. It still books top entertainers, often venturing into Broadway-type shows. At widely varying prices, 2,000 seats are available in the huge hall, ranging from 80F ($11.03) to 160F ($22.06). Recently Yves Montand appeared here, but you had to book as early as four months in advance to obtain a seat. Expect lots of vaudeville, much of it corny. Shows are presented nightly at 8:30, except on Sunday and Monday. Métro: Opéra or Madeleine.

CONCERTS: The concert-going public is kept busy year round in Paris, with daily offerings taking up full newspaper columns. Organ recitals are featured in the churches (the largest organ is in St. Sulpice); jazz shatters the peace of the city's modern art museum. The best orchestra in France belongs to Radio France, and top-flight concerts with guest conductors are presented in the **Radio France Auditorium,** 116 Avenue Président-Kennedy, 16e (tel. 42-30-36-15). The price of seats depends on who is performing. Métro: Passy.

Chapter VII

THE ÎLE DE FRANCE

1. Versailles
2. Fontainebleau
3. Vaux-le-Vicomte
4. Barbizon
5. Milly-la-Forêt
6. Rambouillet
7. Chartres
8. Illiers
9. Provins
10. Malmaison
11. Senlis
12. Compiègne
13. Chantilly
14. Beauvais
15. Château de Thoiry
16. Giverny

FIRST, VERSAILLES, then Fontainebleau and the Cathedral of Chartres. Those are the places known to international visitors, and those are the meccas that draw the tour buses. Indeed, they are the principal stars in the galaxy of the Île de France—and rightly so. They need no selling from me, but the lesser-known spots in this green belt surrounding Paris do.

Everything recommended in the chapter that follows lies within a one-day trip from Paris. You can, for example, wander through the archeological garden of medieval Senlis in the morning, thrill to the Château of Chantilly in the afternoon, and enjoy the showgirls at the Moulin Rouge in Paris that evening.

Much of the "Island of France" is known to us through the paintings of such artists as Corot, Renoir, Sisley, Degas, Monet, and Cézanne. This ancient land through which Caesar's armies marched is often called the heart of France. Seemingly, it is the dream of every Parisian to have a little rustic cottage or farmhouse in this province. Romanesque ruins, Gothic cathedrals, castles left over from the age of feudalism, châteaux evoking the splendor of the 18th century, great forests such as Fontainebleau or Chantilly, sleepy villages, even an African game reserve—you'll find all of these and more. Besides the attractions, small regional restaurants will introduce you to the provincial cooking of France.

I'll begin the exploration at one of the top-ranking sights in the world—

1. Versailles

Back in *le grand siècle,* all you needed was a sword, a hat, and a bribe for the guard at the gate. Providing you didn't look as if you had smallpox, you'd be admitted to the inner precincts of the palace, there to stroll through glittering salon after dazzling chamber—watching the Sun King at his banqueting table, or else doing something more personal. Louis XIV was indeed the State, and was accorded about as much privacy as an institution.

In 50 years Versailles went from the simple hunting lodge of Louis XIII to a lavish palace, a monument to the age of absolutism. What you see today has been called the greatest living museum of a vanished life on the face of our planet. Conceived in 1661, the construction involved anywhere from 32,000 to 45,000 workmen, some of whom had to drain marshes—often at the cost of their lives—and move forests.

Enraged with jealousy that his finance minister, Fouqunet, could live better at Vaux-le-Vicomte than he did at Fontainebleau, Louis XIV set out to create a palace that would be the awe of Europe. He entrusted Louis Le Vau with the architecture, although Hardouin-Mansart was to play a great role later on. Le Brun decorated the interior. Together these men created grandeur and elegance that were to be copied but never duplicated all over Europe. Versailles became a symbol of pomp, ceremony, and opulence.

To keep an eye on them (and with good reason), Louis XIV summoned the nobles of France to live at his court. There he amused them with constant entertainment and lavish banquets. To some he awarded such tasks as holding his ermine-lined robe. While the French aristocrats played away their lives, often in silly intrigues, the peasants back on the estates were sowing more than grain. They were planting the seeds of the Revolution.

When the Sun King shone no more in 1715, he was succeeded by his great-grandson, Louis XV, who continued the outrageous pomp, although he is said to have predicted the outcome: *"Apres moi, le déluge"* ("After me, the deluge"). His wife, Marie Leczinska, was shocked at the morality, or lack of it, at Versailles. When her husband tired of her, she lived as a nun, while the king's attention wandered to Madame de Pompadour, who was accused of running up a debt for her country far beyond that of a full-scale war. On her death, Madame du Barry replaced her.

Louis XVI, however, found his grandfather's behavior scandalous—in fact, he ordered that the "stairway of indiscretion" be removed. This rather dull, weak king and his queen, Marie Antoinette, were at Versailles when they were notified, on October 6, 1789, that mobs were marching on the palace. As predicted, *le déluge* had arrived.

Napoleon stayed at Versailles, but he never seemed overly fond of it. Perhaps the image of the Sun King burned too strongly in his mind. The Citizen King, Louis-Philippe, who reigned from 1830 to 1848, prevented the destruction of Versailles by converting it into a museum dedicated to the glory of France. To do that, he had to surrender some of his own not-so-hard-earned currency. John D. Rockefeller contributed heavily toward the restoration of Versailles, and work continues to this day.

The six magnificent **Grands Apartments** are in the Louis Quatorze style, taking their names from the allegorical ceiling paintings. The best-known is the Salon of Hercules, painted by François Le Moyne, using Pompadour red and depicting the club-carrying strongman riding in a chariot. Beginning in 1733 the artist worked on that ceiling for three years, completing it in time for his suicide. Louis XV was delighted (by the painting, not the suicide). In one of these apartments, the Salon of Mercury, Louis XIV died in 1715 after one of the longest reigns in history, lasting 72 years.

Visitors pass through the Salon of War, viewing a bas-relief by Coysevox depicting a triumphant Sun King on horseback trampling on his enemies (or victims). Finally, they arrive at the most famous room at Versailles: the **Hall of Mirrors,** 236 feet long. Begun by Mansart in 1678 in the Louis XIV style, it was decorated by Le Brun with 17 large windows matched with corresponding reflecting mirrors. On June 28, 1919, the treaty ending World War I was signed in this corridor. Ironically, the German Empire was also proclaimed there in 1871.

The royal apartments were for show, but Louis XV and Louis XVI retired to the **Petits Apartments** to escape the demands of court etiquette. Louis XV died in his bedchamber in 1774, the victim of smallpox. In a second-floor apartment, which can be visited only with a guide, he stashed away Mme du Barry and earlier Mme de Pompadour. Also shown is the apartment of Mme de Maintenon, who was first the mistress of Louis XIV, later his wife. Attempts are being made, as far as possible, to return the **Queen's Apartments** to their original setting as in the days of Marie Antoinette, when she played her harpsichord in front of specially invited guests.

Her king, Louis XVI, had an impressive **Library,** designed by Gabriel, which was sumptuous enough; but, library or no, the monarch remained dim-witted. Its panels are delicately carved, and the room has been restored and refurnished. The Clock Room contains Passement's astronomical clock, encased in gilded bronze. Twenty years in the making, it was completed in 1753. The clock is supposed to keep time until the year 9999. At the age of seven Mozart played in this room for the court.

Gabriel designed the **Opéra** for Louis XV in 1748, although it wasn't completed until 1770. The bas-reliefs are by Pajou, and bearskin rugs once covered the floor. In its heyday it took 3,000 powerful candles to light the place. The final restoration of the theater was carried out in 1957, replacing Louis-Philippe's attempt at refurbishing.

With gold and white harmony, Hardouin-Mansart built the **Royal Chapel** in 1699, dying before its completion. Louis XVI, when still the dauphin, married Marie Antoinette there. Both were teenagers.

Spread across 250 acres, the **Gardens of Versailles** were laid out by the great landscape artist André le Nôtre. At the peak of their glory, 1,400 fountains spewed forth. *The Buffet* is an exceptional one, having been designed by Mansart. One fountain depicts Apollo in his chariot pulled by four horses, surrounded by tritons emerging from the water to light the world.

Le Nôtre created a Garden of Eden in the Île de France, using ornamental lakes and canals, geometrically designed flower beds, and avenues bordered with statuary. On the mile-long "Grand Canal" Louis XV—imagining he was in Venice—used to take gondola rides with his "favorite," whoever that was.

A long walk across the park will take you to the **Grand Trianon,** in pink-and-white marble, designed by Hardouin-Mansart for Louis XIV in 1687. Traditionally, it's been a place where France has lodged important guests, although De Gaulle wanted to turn it into a weekend retreat for himself. Nixon slept there in the room where Madame de Pompadour died. Queen Victoria did not, failing to show up for an expected visit. Madame de Maintenon—once called "a devil in the guise of a woman"—also slept there, as did Napoléon I. The original furnishings are gone, of course, with mostly Empire pieces there today.

Gabriel, the designer of the Place de la Concorde in Paris, built the **Petit Trianon** in 1768 for Louis XV. Actually, its construction was inspired by Madame de Pompadour, who died before it was readied. So Louis used it for his trysts with Madame du Barry. In time, Marie Antoinette adopted it as her favorite residence. There she could escape the rigid life back at the main palace. Many of the current furnishings, including a few in her rather modest bedroom, belonged to the ill-fated queen. Napoléon I once presented it to his sister Pauline Borghese, but the emperor ungallantly took it back and gave it instead to his new bride, Marie-Louise.

Behind the Petit Trianon is the **Hamlet,** that collection of little thatched farmhouses—complete with a water mill—where Marie Antoinette could pretend she was a shepherdess, tending to her perfumed lambs. Lost in a bucolic world, she was there on the morning the news came from Paris that the Revolution was launched. Nearby is the **Temple of Love,** built in 1775 by Richard Mique, the queen's favorite architect. In the center of its Corinthian colonnade is a reproduction of Bouchardon's Cupid shaping a bow from the club of Hercules.

Between the Grand and the Petit Trianons is the entrance to the **Carriage Museum,** housing coaches from the 18th and 19th centuries—among them one used at the coronation of Charles X, another used at the wedding of Napoléon I to Marie-Louise. One sleigh rests on tortoise runners. (Your ticket to the Petit Trianon will also admit you to see these *voitures.*)

The Grand Apartments, the Royal Chapel, and the Hall of Mirrors can be visited without a guide anytime between 9:45 a.m. and 5 p.m., costing 16F ($2.21) for admission. Other sections of the château may be visited only at specific hours or on special days. Some of these sections are closed temporarily as they undergo restoration. The palace is closed Monday and holidays.

The Grand Trianon is open daily except Monday, from 9:45 a.m. to 5 p.m. Entrance costs 12F ($1.66). The Petit Trianon, which can be visited on the same ticket, is open daily except Monday, from 2 to 5 p.m., costing 8F ($1.10) separately.

A VERSAILLES SPECTACLE: The Tourist Office of Versailles offers a program of evening fireworks and illuminated fountains on several occasions throughout the summer, at 9:30 p.m. on about a half a dozen evenings, which are announced a full season in advance. Those dates usually fall on Saturday and occasionally on Wednesday, although the schedule could easily change from year to year. Spectators sit on bleachers clustered at the Boulevard de la Reine entrance to the Basin of Neptune. The most desirable frontal-view seats cost 75F ($10.32), the seats with a side view going for 55F ($7.56), with standing room on the *promenoir* selling for 35F ($4.83) for adults; free for children under 10.

Called *Le Triomphe de Neptune,* the spectacle includes piped-in music by Rameau and Lulli, with a text written partially by Molière and La Fontaine. Gates open 1½ hours before showtime. Tickets can be purchased in advance at the Office of Tourism in Versailles, 7 rue des Reservoirs (tel. 39-50-36-22), from 9:30 a.m. to 6 p.m., and at ticket agencies in Paris, which usually add a 10% service charge. Two such agencies are Agence E.R. Perrossier, 6 Place de la Madeleine (tel. 42-60-58-31), and Agence des Champs-Élysées Daisy, 78 Avenue des Champs-Élysées (tel. 43-59-24-60). If you've just arrived in Paris, you can always take your chances and purchase tickets an hour ahead of showtime at the ticket booths in the Place des Armes, just in front of the château, where there's ample parking. The show lasts for one hour only.

GETTING THERE: Versailles lies only 13 miles southwest of Paris. If you're driving down (Route N10), you can park your car on the Place des Armes in front of the palace. To reach Versailles without a car, it's not necessary to take a guided tour. Take the Métro to the Pont de Sèvres exit and switch onto bus 171. The trip to Versailles costs 11F ($1.52) and lasts 15 minutes. If you pay with three Métro tickets from your carnet packet, the cost is only 7.50F ($1.03). You'll be let off near the gates of the palace. It's also possible to travel to Versailles on one of the commuter trains leaving every 15 minutes from Paris. The station is connected to the Invalides Métro stop. Go all the way to the Versailles

–Rive Gauche station, turning right when you come out. Eurailpass holders travel free; otherwise, the cost is about 8F ($1.10) one way.

WHERE TO STAY: Trianon-Palace, 1 Boulevard de la Reine (tel. 39-50-34-12), is almost like living at the Grand Trianon. It's a classically designed palace, set in its own five-acre garden bordering those of the Trianons of the Château de Versailles. Its stately old-world charm, its quietness near where Marie Antoinette romped with her perfumed sheep, are pervasive.

In 1919 the hotel was the headquarters of the Versailles Peace Conference. Gathered in the salon were Woodrow Wilson, Lloyd George, and Clemenceau, plus other national leaders from Italy and Belgium. Today the Trianon-Palace graciously serves many visitors who make it their base for exploring Paris, as it's only 25 minutes by car from the Champs-Élysées to the peace of the countryside. The dignified rooms are decorated traditionally, with subdued colors—all harmonious, aided by the discreet use of antiques and many fine reproductions. Many of the bedchambers are decidedly old-fashioned, although a few of them have been renewed in a modernization program. In a single room the rate is 480F ($66.19) to 790F ($108.94), rising to 620F ($85.50) to 1,050F ($144.80) in a double.

For years the hotel's restaurant has been the classic dining choice in Versailles. The dining room is dramatic, with fluted columns, crystal chandeliers, and cane-backed Louis XVI-style chairs. The set menus are quite extensive, at 172F ($23.72) and 240F ($33.10). The food embraces most of the classic French dishes. On one recent occasion I began with an avocado vinaigrette, followed by coquilles St-Jacques bordelaise, lamb chops with a risotto studded with bits of chicken liver, then a selection from the cheese board, and finally, crêpes suzette. A banquet really.

Bellevue Hotel, 12 Avenue de Sceaux (tel. 39-50-13-41), on one of the city's grandest tree-lined avenues, is only a three-minute walk from the entrance to the château. It has an unpretentious corner façade painted white, and a simple lobby area that is mostly modern except for some half-timbered accents and an 18th-century bust. The French-style double rooms rent for 200F ($27.58) to 290F ($39.99), depending on the plumbing. A limited number of triples is available for 315F ($43.44).

Hôtel Le Versailles, 7 rue Sainte-Anne (tel. 39-50-64-65), is on a quiet square just to the side of the frenetic shop-lined street bordering the château. The design includes a slate-covered mansard roof supported by chiseled stone walls and dignified windows set with insulated glass panes. Although the building is only 17 years old, it looks curiously like an outbuilding of the château, an impression you'll quickly lose when you see the modern interior. The lobby contains a futuristic navy-blue and white bar, focused spotlighting, and a receptionist who will sign you into one of 48 bedrooms, each of which contains a private bath and private phone. There's parking on the premises. Singles rent for 260F ($35.85) to 290F ($39.99), while doubles cost 300F ($41.37) to 320F ($48.27).

If you're cutting costs, consider the **Hôtel Richaud,** 16 rue Richaud (tel. 39-50-10-42), on a small street opposite the Versailles Hospital, which was built during Louis XIV's reign. This 39-room hotel has been completely redecorated, with modernized rooms and plumbing. The floors are carpeted, and the decorations are classic but nicely assorted. The furniture has no particular style, but it's comfortable. Prices start at 210F ($28.96) for a double room with a shower, rising to 265F ($36.54) for a room with bath and toilet. Most of the accommodations have TV.

RESTAURANTS: Chances are, you'll be dining at Versailles. The town is well equipped, offering restaurants in all price ranges. I will survey the best in each price range.

Les Trois Marches, 3 rue Colbert (tel. 39-50-13-21). Gérard Vié is, it is generally conceded, the most talented and creative chef entertaining visitors to Versailles these days. He has brought a remarkable culinary experience to his restaurant, and because of that, attracts a discerning clientele who don't mind paying the high prices. If you order à la carte, your tab is likely to range from 430F ($59.30) to 530F ($73.09) per person. Fixed-price meals, however, go from 275F ($37.92) to 375F ($51.71), not including service. The nouvelle cuisine is subtle, often daringly inventive and conceived, the service smooth. Don't go with any preconceived notions about food here, because Monsieur Vié is likely to break down your reserves. In air-conditioned comfort, you can order his specialty, which is canard (duck) de Challans with cider vinegar and honey. For those who want to be more experimental, I suggest, if featured, a raw haddock with pepper, even steak with oysters. From September to May he offers a warm flan made with foie gras and oysters that is heavenly and smooth. Another seasonal specialty in the spring is a crayfish salad with crisp vegetables. Monsier Vié has introduced *grand siècle* music and costumed servants for his *soupers du Roy*. These are certainly interesting, but expensive.

In summer you can order lunch on the terrace, shaded by umbrellas. Otherwise, you are directed into one of several tiny dining rooms, seemingly like a private club. These rooms are part of the restored Hôtel Particulier, dating from the 18th century. The restaurant is closed on Sunday and Monday.

La Boule d'Or, 25 rue du Maréchal-Foch (tel. 39-50-22-97), is the oldest inn in Versailles (1696). Diners are transported back through the centuries. There are two floors, the upper one more formal, with an antique grandfather clock, paneled windows, ceramic-stove fireplaces, damask cloths, Louis XIII-style chairs, a glass case with books of Louis XIII, Louis XIV, and Louis XV, plus pictures by Hobéma, Mignard, and Sorg. The chef, Claude Saillard, specializes in many dishes native to Franche-Comté, a mountainous district south of Alsace, and also in the 17th- and 18th-century style of cooking, which is very important in Versailles.

A set menu is offered at 185F ($25.51). Among the à la carte selections, a well-recommended specialty is le carré d'agneau (loin of lamb) with gratin dauphinois (potatoes thinly sliced and baked with a creamy cheese mixture), but a minimum of two must order it. For dessert, try perhaps a sorbet covered with raspberry liqueur. For a complete meal, expect to spend from 275F ($37.92), not including service. Closed Monday.

Le Potager du Roy, 1 rue du Maréchal-Joffre (tel. 39-50-35-34). Philippe LeTourneur used to work for another Versailles chef, Gérard Vié, before setting up his own attractive restaurant on a busy street corner in a commercial part of town. Set behind a maroon façade, in a simple modern decor of several warmly decorated rooms, he cooks such specialties as a salad of lamb tongues with éminced'endive, mousse of scallops, veal kidneys with mustard sauce, fricassée with two kinds of fish, and roast pigeon with a garlic mousse. Fixed-price meals cost around 95F ($13.10) to 135F ($18.62), service not included. For the money, these are the best-quality meals you can order at Versailles.

2. Fontainebleau

Napoleon called the Palace of Fontainebleau the house of the centuries. Much of French history has taken place within its walls, perhaps no moment more memorable than when Napoléon I stood on the horseshoe-shaped stairway and bade a loving farewell to his army before his departure to Elba and exile. That scene has been the subject of seemingly countless paintings, including Vernet's *Les Adieux* of the emperor.

Napoleon's affection for Fontainebleau (perhaps Versailles carried too many memories of Louis XIV) was understandable. He was following the pattern of a grand parade of French kings in the pre-Versailles days who used Fontainebleau as a resort, hunting in its magnificent forest. Under François I the hunting lodge became a royal palace, much in the Italian Renaissance style that the king so admired and wanted to imitate. The style got botched up, but many artists, including Benvenuto Cellini, came from Italy to work for the French monarch.

Under the patronage of François I, the School of Fontainebleau—led by the painters Rosso Fiorentino and Primaticcio—grew in prestige. These two artists adorned one of the most outstanding rooms at Fontainebleau: the **Gallery of François I,** 210 feet long. (The restorers under Louis-Philippe did not completely succeed in ruining it.) Surrounded by pomp, François I walked the length of his gallery while artisans tried to tempt him with their wares, job seekers asked favors, and heavily scented courtesans tried to lure him away from the Duchess d'Etampes. The stucco-framed panels depict such scenes as Jupiter (portrayed as a bull) carrying off Europa, the *Nymph of Fontainebleau* (with a lecherous dog appearing through the reeds), and the monarch holding a pomegranate, a symbol of unity. However, the frames compete with the pictures. Everywhere is the salamander, symbol of the Chevalier King.

If it is true that François I built Fontainebleau for his mistress, then Henri II, his successor, left a fitting memorial to the woman he loved, Diane de Poitiers. Sometimes called the Gallery of Henri II, the **Ballroom** is in the mannerist style, the second splendid interior of the château. The monograms H & D are interlaced in the decoration. The king didn't believe in keeping his affection for his mistress a secret. At one end of the room is a monumental fireplace supported by two bronze satyrs, made in 1966 (the original ones were melted down in the Revolution). At the opposite side is the salon of the musicians, with sculptured garlands. The ceiling contains octagonal coffering adorned with rosettes. Above the wainscotting is a series of frescoes, painted between 1550 and 1558, depicting such mythological subjects as *The Feast of Bacchus.*

An architectural curiosity is the **Louis XV Staircase,** richly and elegantly adorned. Originally, the ceiling was decorated by Primaticcio for the bedroom of the Duchesse d'Etampes. When an architect was designing the stairway, he simply ripped out her floor and used the bedroom ceiling to cover the stairway. Of the Italian frescoes that were preserved, one depicts the Queen of the Amazons climbing into Alexander's bed.

When Louis XIV ascended to the throne, Fontainebleau was virtually neglected because of his preoccupation with Versailles. However, he wasn't opposed to using the palace for house guests—specifically such unwanted ones as Queen Christina, who had abdicated the throne of Sweden. Apparently thinking she still had "divine right," she ordered one of the most brutal royal murders on record—that of her lover, Monaldeschi, who had ceased to please her.

Although in the main neglected by Louix XIV and his heirs, Fontainebleau found renewed glory—and shame—under Napoléon I. You can wander around much of the palace on your own, but most of the **Napoleonic Rooms** are accessible by guided tour only. Impressive are his throne room and his bedroom (look for his symbol, a bee). You can also see where the emperor signed his abdication (the document exhibited is a copy). The furnishings in the Empress Josephine's apartments and the grand apartments of Napoleon evoke the Imperial heyday.

Minor apartments include those once occupied by Mme de Maintenon, the much-neglected wife of Louis XIV. Another was occupied by Pope Pius VII, who was kept a virtual prisoner by Napoleon; still another by Marie Antoinette. A bed she ordered didn't arrive on time, although the Empress Eugénie, wife of Napoléon III, later slept in it.

The apartments (tel. 64-22-27-40) are open daily except Tuesday, from 9:30 a.m. to 12:30 p.m. and 2 to 5 p.m., charging an admission of 12F ($1.66).

After your long trek through the palace, a visit to the gardens and especially the carp pond is in order, but the gardens are only a prelude to the Forest of Fontainebleau.

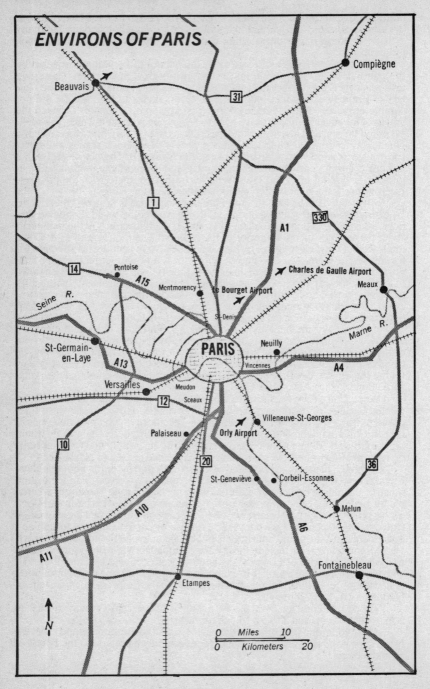

ENVIRONS OF PARIS

GETTING THERE: Fontainebleau is reached by frequent train service from the Gare de Lyon in Paris, a 37-mile journey. Depending on which train you take, the trip lasts from 35 minutes to one hour. The round-trip fare in economy class is about 50F ($6.90). The train station of Fontainebleau is just outside the town in Avon, a suburb of Paris. For the two-mile trip to the château, you can take the town bus, which makes a round trip every 10 to 15 minutes on weekdays (every 30 minutes on Sunday).

WHERE TO STAY: You need not venture far from the château for either a room or a meal.

Hôtel de l'Aigle Noir (The Black Eagle), 27 Place Napoléon-Bonaparte (tel. 64-22-32-65), directly opposite the château, has its own share of dignity and glamour. Once the private home of the Cardinal de Retz, it was built with a formal entrance to its courtyard, through the high, dark, iron grill and pillars crowned by the namesake black eagles. The private mansion was converted into a hotel in 1720. It has recently been completely remodeled, its atmosphere more inviting than ever, making it the uncontested choice for the finest lodgings in Fontainebleau. The 26 bedrooms and four suites have private baths and all the modern conveniences. Each is individually decorated with antiques and pleasantly tasteful colors. Singles range from 850F ($117.22), while doubles cost from 1,050F ($144.80). Units also contain color TV, radio, mini-bar, direct-line phone, double windows, and electric heating. The hotel also has the finest restaurant in town, Le Beauharnais (see my dining recommendations).

Hôtel-Restaurant Legris et Parc, 36 rue du Parc (tel. 64-22-24-24), is my favorite hotel in its price range in Fontainebleau. It's on a narrow street that becomes a tree-lined country lane when it enters the rambling rear lawns of the château a few steps away. Part of the façade is art nouveau, unusual for Fontainebleau, although another wing is much older. The classical-revival lobby contains elegant reproduction furniture, marble floors, an occasional antique, and fabric-covered walls in soothing shades of gold and blue.

The staff, often members of the Legris family, is charming, speaks English, and will usher you to one of the cozy bedrooms, some of which are freshly painted and papered, with even a scattering of 17th-century timbers dating from the original construction of the house. Each of the rooms has a private bath and telephone, and is suitable for either one or two persons. They range in price from 220F ($30.34) to 300F ($41.37). The in-house restaurant is across the courtyard from the lobby, behind a half-timbered rustic-style pavilion set with glass between many of the half-rounded beams. Racine wrote one of his works here, and later Louis XV bought it to lodge his personal corps of bodyguards.

Napoléon, 9 rue Grande (tel. 64-22-20-39), is a classically designed, rather formal hotel lying only a short walk from the château. A coaching inn a century ago, it has turned its carriage yard into a pleasant courtyard, with a flagstone walk, urns of flowers, and lots of shrubbery. The inn is operated by the Verne family, who speak English, as does the staff. Mrs. Verne, in fact, was reared in the States, and Mr. Verne was a chef in America for ten years. The lobby area has lots of Oriental rugs, big arched windows looking out over the street, and a garden-style tea room filling up most of the floor space. An inviting bar off the reception area has an ornate oval ceiling, Louis-Philippe chairs, and a neoclassical fireplace.

The bedrooms, for the most part, are filled with blond reproductions of antiques, the attention centering around the padded and flowered headboards. A double with private bath rents for 365F ($50.33); with shower, 295F ($40.68). Singles range in price from 320F ($44.13) with bath, dropping to 258F ($35.59) with shower. All tariffs include service, taxes, and a continental breakfast. All units have color TV and a mini-bar.

Since the Napoléon is so convenient to the château, many visitors come to the attractively formal pastel-colored dining room for a luncheon. A choice of two set meals is offered for 100F ($13.79) to 175F ($24.13), plus service. You can also order à la carte, paying around 200F ($27.58) per person.

WHERE TO DINE: Le Beauharnais, in Hôtel de l'Aigle Noir, 27 Place Napoléon-Bonaparte (tel. 64-22-32-65). In what had been a former courtyard, this most beautiful restaurant in town has been installed. It is divided into two separate rooms, whose walls are upholstered in gray-blue silk. The decor is filled with Empire furniture and potted palms. Specialties include breast of duckling with salad, ris de veau (sweetbreads) in puff pastry in a nettle-flavored cream sauce, fricassée of chicken with eel, veal with lemon, and breast of pigeon with chives, as well as a changing collection of other dishes, depending on the seasonal produce. Fixed-price meals cost 200F ($27.58) to 275F ($37.92), but if you order à la carte, expect to spend from 375F ($51.71). The restaurant is closed on Sunday night and on Monday as well as in February.

Le Filet de Sole, 5-7 rue du Coq-Gris (tel. 64-22-25-05), is a well-honored little restaurant, just a few minutes' walk from the château. Its neo-Norman façade is difficult to spot on a narrow street deep in the heart of town, but it's well worth the search. A four-course set menu is offered for 185F ($25.51), including service, although you pay extra for wine. To begin, you can choose between a homemade pâté or half a dozen escargots, followed by your main dish, usually the namesake of the restaurant: filets de sole with a lobster sauce. The 225F ($31.03) menu gastronomique is more elaborate, of course, and also includes service. The specialties are filet de sole, lobster bisque, and carré d'agneau (loin of lamb) with parsley, served only for two persons. A mouthwatering crêpes Suzette—quite a concoction—is the preferred dessert, again just for two. The set meals are served from noon to 2 p.m. and 7 to 8:30 p.m. An à la carte menu is offered until 11 nightly. The restaurant is closed Tuesday, Wednesday, and during July.

Le Dauphin, 24–26 Grande-Rue (tel. 64-22-27-04), offers one of the best and most reasonably priced meals in town. In the inner city, near the tourist office, it is a short walk from the château. The decor is that of a country-style tavern, with red-checked curtains and red napery. Specialties include endive in roquefort dressing, steak au poivre flambé in cognac, noisettes of lamb with a tarragon sauce, and confit de canard from Landes with flap mushrooms. Dessert might be either a tarte tatin or a pear sorbet. Fixed-price meals cost 62F ($8.55) on weekdays, going up to 100F ($13.79) on Sunday and holidays. À la carte meals, however, could run as high as 160F ($22.06). The restaurant is closed at the beginning of September and for all of February, and it is regularly closed on Tuesday night and all day Wednesday.

3. Vaux-le-Vicomte

Just north of the Forest of Fontainebleau, a distance of 12 miles, the Château Vaux-le-Vicomte (tel. 60-66-97-09) was built in 1656 by Nicolas Fouquet, Louis XIV's ill-fated minister of finance. To save the reputation of his godfather, Cardinal Mazarin, who had amassed a fabulous fortune while he was Prime Minister, young Louis XIV, inspired by the evil-minded Colbert, decided to lay the responsibility for mismanaging the French Treasury at Fouquet's door and have him arrested and tried. To throw his future victim off the track, Louis expressed a desire to be invited to Vaux. Two weeks later, the king had Fouquet arrested, but not before Louis hired the same artists and architects who had built the château to begin work on the grand task of building Versailles. Visitors today can see the striking similarities between the two monuments to *le grand siècle*.

The view of the château from the main gate gives one an idea of the splendor of 17th-century France. The French columns and pillars echo grandeur. On the south side, a majestic staircase sweeps toward the formal gardens, designed by Le Nôtre. Lined by a border of trees and statues, the gardens are dominated by a copy of the *Farnese Hercules*. The grand canal, flanked by cascading waterfalls, divides the lush greenery.

The interior of the château, now a private residence, is completely furnished and decorated in 17th-century pieces. The great entrance hall leads to 12 state rooms among which is the oval rotunda. Many of the rooms are hung with Gobelin tapestries and decorated with painted ceiling and wall panels by Le Brun with sculpture by Giradon. A tour of the interior also includes the private apartments on the first floor among which was Fouquet's personal suite, and also the huge basement with its wine cellar, the servants' dining room, and the copper-filled kitchen.

A **Carriage Museum** was opened in 1979, lying in the stables of the castle. The carriages are of three different types—country, town, and sports and hunting. The 25 vehicles exhibited are perfectly restored, dating from the 18th and 19th centuries. Vehicles are displayed with mannikin horses and people.

From April 1 to November 1, the château is open daily from 10 a.m. to 6 p.m. In November to March, it's open from 2 to 5 p.m. on Saturday and Sunday. From June to September, candlelight evenings are held every Saturday, when the château can be visited by the light of more than a thousand candles, from 8:30 to 11 p.m. On those evenings, the Écureuil cafeteria and the Carriage Museum stay open until midnight. On the second and last Saturday of each month, the fountains of the 13 main pools play from 2 to 6 p.m.

To visit only the gardens costs 12F ($1.66). A full visit, however, including the Carriage Museum, château, and gardens, costs 40F ($5.52).

The **Restaurant L'Écureuil** lies in the first courtyard. The beautiful decoration follows the style of a 17th-century inn. It's self-service, with meals costing from 100F ($13.79). You can enjoy mixed salads of different types, as well as a grilled steak, followed by cheese of the province (brie) and topped by cakes and homemade fruit tarts. The restaurant is closed from November to April.

4. Barbizon

In the 19th century, the Barbizon School of painting gained world renown. On the edge of the Forest of Fontainebleau, some 35 miles southeast of Paris, the village was a haven and a refuge for such artists as Théodore Rousseau, J. F. Millet, and Corot. Many of these painters could not find acceptance in the conservative salons of Paris.

In Barbizon they turned to nature for inspiration and painted pastoral scenes as they saw them—that is, without nude nymphs and dancing fauns. These artists attracted a school of lesser painters, including Charles Daubigny and Diaz. Charles Jacques, Decamps, Paul Huet, Ziem, Troyon, and many others would follow. Although recognition was delayed, it finally arrived. The School of Barbizon enjoyed the last laugh: the paintings of its adherents hang in the great museums of the world.

Today Barbizon's chic is known far and wide, attracting some of the most fashionable Parisians with its celebrated inns, such as Bas-Bréau, that flank the main street. Some dismiss the village as affected, complaining about its outrageous prices. Like the artists in the past, others bask in Barbizon's sunshine and enjoy its forest-filtered air. Because of the high level of innkeeping, it is popular for gourmet weekends.

Along the street you can visit the ateliers of some of the more noted painters, such as Millet. Inside his studio, now an art gallery, is an etching of *The Man with the Hoe*, as well as some of his original furnishings. Born of a peasant family in Normandy, Millet used to take his sketch pad into the fields during the day. He would return in the late afternoon to add the finishing touches in his studio, which is now open daily except Tuesday till 6 p.m., charging no admission. You can also visit the vine-covered second-floor atelier of Rousseau on the same street, next door to a little chapel.

Finally, l'Auberge du Père Gannes, an ancient inn, has been turned into a gallery open to the public. In its heyday, Millet, Charles Jacques, Corot, Rousseau, Rosa Bonheur, even Delacroix and Ingres used to drop in. The management didn't discriminate: writers too were welcomed. Verlaine came this way, as did Robert Louis Stevenson and George Sand with her effete lover, the poet Alfred de Musset.

FOOD AND LODGING: Among the inns, each of the following is outstanding in its classification.

The Upper Bracket

Bas-Bréau (tel. 60-66-40-05) is one of the great old inns of France. Starting in the 1830s, it sheltered many famous artists when it was known as Monsieur Siron's auberge. Robert Louis Stevenson stayed here, writing his *Forest Notes* in one of the bedrooms. When Napoléon III and his empress stopped by for a day in 1868, purchasing some paintings from the Barbizon School, the inn became known as the Hôtel de l'Exposition.

At the edge of the Forest of Fontainebleau, the hotel is rambling, with vistas of shade trees opening onto courtyards. It's furnished in rich, lustrous provincial antiques and fool-the-eye reproductions. In cooler months, life centers around an open brick fireplace in the living room, with its heavy overhead beams and decorative objects such as a copper lavabo and wooden wine-press tables.

The bedrooms are furnished in part with antiques, many of them collector's pieces. Often clients prefer the rooms in the rear building, which open directly onto semiprivate sun terraces laden with chairs and parasols along with long flower boxes profusely planted with red geraniums. The prices are extremely high, but worth it for those who can afford it. A twin- or double-bedded room peaks at 1,200F ($165.48) to 1,300F ($179.27), a single going for 850F ($117.22). More expensive apartments and bungalows are also available.

Meals in the old-world dining room or in the courtyard range in price from 375F ($51.71) to 500F ($68.95). Specialties include filet de charolais en feuilleté, grouse d'Écosse rôti, and soufflé chaud aux framboises (raspberries). In summer, while surrounded by pink geraniums, guests can enjoy good-tasting fish dishes flavored with herbs from the hotel's own garden, which also has a profusion of flowers and vegetables. Try, especially, Saint-Pierre à l'oseille, a full-flavored white fish firm in texture, served with a tangy-tasting sorrel sauce. I'm especially fond of the petites escalopes de foie gras chaud aux épinards. Fresh spinach leaves are slightly wilted to form a bed for fast-seared slices of fresh duck liver. When the brisk autumn breezes blow, go here for wild game, none finer than the well-known specialty of the house—pâté chaud de grouse (this is a game Scottish grouse pâté that has been wrapped in a pastry puff and coated with a consommé-clear brown sauce). The inn shuts down in early January, reopening in mid-February.

The Middle Bracket

Les Charmettes, 40 Grande-Rue (tel. 60-66-40-21), is an informal châlet-style inn in the center of Barbizon. Enclosed on three sides, its courtyard contains a graveled area for tables (very French) and towering old trees facing the main street. Vines crawl over the rustic inn, sprawling over the front stone-and-iron grill. Simple though it may be, it was the 1948 honeymoon rendezvous of the then Princess Elizabeth and Prince Philip. The 19th-century painter J. K. Bodner also lived there. The interior rooms are styled like a hunting lodge:

beamed walls and ceiling, stuffed moose heads, plus the additional warming touches of lots of paintings and sketches left by artist guests. No one has ever tried to create a chic setting, preferring to keep it home-like. The tariffs for rooms depend on their size and the plumbing. The best doubles with bath cost 200F ($27.58). Singles without bath go for 110F ($15.17), with a service charge added. Three apartments are also rented.

Hôstellerie les Pléiades, 21 Grande-Rue (tel. 60-66-40-25), is run and directed by the town's local historian who, before purchasing the place 30 years ago, worked as a dishwasher near the piers in Boston and later managed several PX operations for American soldiers in Europe. Roger Karampournis, aided by his wife, Yolande, has since gone on to become one of the best-known chefs in the gourmet circle of Barbizon. Excluding the prestigious Bas-Bréau, he runs the finest restaurant in town and also has 18 fully renovated rooms to rent.

The flower-dotted property actually opened as a hotel back in 1914. Roger and Yolande organize many of the frequent conventions, dinner debates, and wedding receptions held in the paneled and timbered public rooms. At my last visit, the lucky winner of a raffle was awarded his weight in wine. The cookery here has flair and style. Expect to spend from 175F ($24.13) to 275F ($37.92) for an elegant repast, and make sure you arrive with a reservation.

The rooms, rented either as singles or doubles, range in price from 280F ($38.61) to 380F ($52.40), depending on the accommodation. Les Pléiades was once inhabited by the painter Daubigny. Weekend stopovers from Paris are encouraged.

The Budget Range

Le Relais, 2 Avenue Charles-de-Gaulle (tel. 60-66-40-28), is seemingly incongruous for ultra-chic Barbizon. But it has its own style—in fact, it is so personal and down-to-earth comfortable that many prefer it to the more prestigious inns. The Relais is a corner tavern, with a provincial dining room centering around a small fireplace. In sunny weather, tables are set out on the rear yard, with a trellis, an arbor, and trees. A set meal costs from 96F ($13.24) and is simple, good, and filling, although served on weekends only. On Sunday you're given a wider choice and can select a 130F ($17.93) menu. For a main course, you are likely to be served veal trotters, chitterling tournedos, or duckling in the fruits of the season. The inn is closed on Tuesday and Wednesday and for the last two weeks in August.

5. Milly-la-Forêt

Jean Cocteau believed that religion and artistic freedom did not necessarily conflict. As if to prove his point, he decorated the interior of the little stone 12th-century **Chapel of St. Blaise** (tel. 64-98-96-68) right outside this little village 12 miles from Fontainebleau. Painted in the closing years of his life (he died in 1963), the chapel formed his own memorial, and his tomb was placed there. The man who flavored the pre-World War II decades in France with his imaginative and daring unconventionality, who traveled far (he once went around the world in three months), made for himself a peaceful, even sleepy resting place.

Inside, the frescoes are secular. One, for example, depicts a wide-eyed and bewhiskered cat, his tail curving upward toward his head, looking haplessly at a beanstalk-like giant flower. Another shows an almond-eyed Christ-like figure wearing a crown of thorns, his mouth a snarl.

In his day Cocteau was considered immoral, but by 1955, following his election to the Académie Française, his reputation was assured. In his *White Paper* he has written candidly about his homosexuality, making the point that he did not want mere toleration. The poet, who was considered avant-garde in the 1920s, got his wish. By today's standards, the opium-smoking *enfant terrible* of another era appears tame.

6. Rambouillet

Pompidou used to go there "for the hunt," as did Louis XVI. Thirty-four miles southwest of Paris, Rambouillet was also visited by Charles de Gaulle, although his grandson actually got more use out of it than did the general. Dating from 1375, the château is surrounded by a park and a great forest. Once it was occupied by the marquise de Rambouillet, before it became a royal abode. It is said that she taught the haut monde of Paris how to talk. To her home she brought a string of poets, painters, and cultured ladies and gentlemen.

François I, the Chevalier King, died at Rambouillet in 1547, having been stricken with a fever at the age of 52. When it was later occupied by the Count of Toulouse, Rambouillet was often visited by Louis XV, who was amused by the nobleman's witty and high-spirited wife. Louis XVI acquired the château for the state, but his wife, Marie Antoinette, was bored with the whole place, calling it "the toad." In her surprisingly modest boudoir are four panels representing the seasons.

Marie-Louise came here in 1814, after leaving Napoleon. She was on her way to Vienna with "the king of Rome." A sad Napoleon slept there shortly before leaving on the long voyage to exile at St. Helena.

In 1830 Charles X, the brother of Louis XVI, abdicated after the July Revolution. After that, Rambouillet became privately owned. At one time it was a fashionable restaurant, attracting Parisians, who could also go for rides in gondolas. Napoléon III, however, returned it to the Crown. In 1897 it was designated as a residence for the presidents of the Republic. Superb woodwork is used throughout, although the furnishings are unprepossessing. The walls are adorned with tapestries, many dating from the era of Louis XV.

The château charges 10F ($1.38) admission. From April 1 to September 30 it is open from 10 a.m. to noon and 2 to 6 p.m. (closes at 5 p.m. off-season). It is closed all day Tuesday and when the president is in residence.

WHERE TO DINE: Relays du Château, 2 Place de la Libération (tel. 34-83-00-49), conveniently lying near the entrance to the château, is best known for its outdoor terrace and well-prepared cuisine. The simple but flavorful specialties include a fricassée of sole with mushrooms, duckling with cherries, a terrine of guinea fowl, and sweetbreads in a mustard sauce. Fixed-price menus cost from 110F ($15.17) to 170F ($23.44), while à la carte dinners range from 300F ($41.37). Meals are served daily except on Sunday night and Tuesday. A handful of simply furnished rooms cost from 120F ($16.55) in a single, 250F ($34.17) in a double, with a continental breakfast included.

7. Chartres

Many observers have felt that the building aspirations of medieval man in France reached their highest expression in the **Cathedral of Chartres.** Down through the centuries it has been known as the "Stone Testament of the Middle Ages." Go there to see its architecture, its sculpture, and—perhaps most important—its stained glass, which gave the world a new and unique color, Chartres blue.

The town of Chartres lies 60 miles southwest from Paris by car, reached by N10. From Paris's Gare Montparnasse, trains run directly to Chartres, the trip taking less than an hour, passing through the sea of wheatfields that characterize Beauce, the granary of France. Suddenly, the massive bulk of Our Lady of Chartres, with its two dissimilar towers, appears above the small gabled houses.

Before entering, stand in awe in front of the royal portal. Reportedly, Rodin sat for hours on the edge of the sidewalk, drinking in the Romanesque sculpture. His opinion: Chartres is the French Acropolis. When a shower descended, a friendly soul offered him an umbrella—which he declined, so transfixed was he by the magic of his precursors.

First, how did it begin? The origins are uncertain; some have suggested that the cathedral grew up over an ancient Druid site, which had later become a Roman temple. As early as the 4th century it was a Christian basilica. A fire in 1194 destroyed most of what had then become a Romanesque cathedral, but it spared the western façade. The cathedral that you see today dates principally from the 13th century, when it was built with the combined efforts and contributions of kings, princes, churchmen, and pilgrims from all over Europe.

One of the greatest of the world's High Gothic cathedrals, it was the first to use flying buttresses. In size, it ranks third in the world, bowing only to St. Peter's in Rome and the Cathedral of Canterbury in Kent, England.

The **Old Tower** (Clocher Vieux) with its 350-foot-high steeple dates from the 12th century. The so-called **New Tower** (Clocher Neuf) is from 1134, although the elaborate ornamental tower was added in 1506 by Jehan de Beauce, following one of the many fires that have swept over the cathedral.

French sculpture in the 12th century broke into full bloom when the western façade or **Royal Portal** was added. A landmark in Romanesque art, the sculptured bodies are elongated, often formalized beyond reality, in their long, flowing robes. But the faces are amazingly (for the time) lifelike, occasionally betraying *Mona Lisa* smiles. In the central tympanum, Christ is shown at the Second Coming, while his descent is depicted on the right, his ascent on the left. Before entering, you should walk around to both the north and south portals, each dating from the 13th century. The bays depict such biblical scenes as the expulsion of Adam and Eve from the Garden of Eden.

Inside is a celebrated **choir screen;** work on it began in the 16th century and lasted until 1714. The niches, 40 in all, contain statues illustrating scenes from the life of the Madonna and Christ—everything from the massacre of the innocents to the coronation of the Virgin.

But few of the rushed visitors ever notice the screen: they're too transfixed by the light from the **stained glass.** Covering an expanse of more than 3,000 square yards, the glass is without peer in the world and is truly mystical. It was spared in both World Wars because of a decision to remove it painstakingly piece by piece.

See the windows in the morning, at noonday, at sunset—whenever and as often as you can. Like a kaleidoscope, they are never the same. Most of the stained glass dates from the 12th and 13th centuries.

It is difficult to single out one panel or window of special merit; however, an exceptional one is the 12th-century *Vierge de la Belle Verrière* ("Our Lady of the Beautiful Window") on the south side. Of course, there are three fiery rose windows, but you couldn't miss those even if you tried.

The nave—the widest in France—still contains its ancient maze. The wooden *Virgin of the Pillar,* to the left of the choir, dates from the 14th century. The crypt was built over a period of two centuries, beginning in the 9th. Enshrined within is *Our Lady of the Crypt,* a 1976 Madonna that replaces one destroyed during the French Revolution. You can visit the crypt from 10:30 to 11 a.m. and 2:30, 3:30, 4:30, and 5:30 p.m. for an admission of 6F (83¢). Apply at La Crypte, 18 Clôtre Notre-Dame (the south portal). Try to get a tour conducted by Malcolm Miller, an Englishman who has spent some three decades studying the cathedral and giving the tours in English. His rare blend of solid scholarship, informative lecture style, wit, enthusiasm, and humor will help your understanding and appreciation of the cathedral. He discusses the history, the architecture, stained glass, and sculpture, providing insight into the purpose and organization of these elements of the great Chartres Cathedral. He usually conducts tours at noon and 2:45 p.m. Monday through Saturday.

After your visit, you can stroll through the episcopal gardens, enjoying yet another view of this most remarkable of French cathedrals. If time remains, you may want to explore the cobbled medieval streets of the **Old Town** (Vieux Quartiers). At the foothill of the cathedral, the lanes contain gabled medieval houses that close in like sheets in the wind. Humped bridges span the Eure River. From the Bouju Bridge, you will see the lofty spires in the background. Try, in particular, to find your way to the rue Chantault, with its colorful façades, often timbered, one dwelling eight centuries old.

HOTELS: Many visitors like Chartres so much they want to stay over. If such is your wish, the following recommendations are suitable.

Grand Monarque, 22 Place des Épars (tel. 37-21-00-72), is the leading hotel of this cathedral city. A classic building enclosing an inner courtyard, it provides quiet, comfortable bedrooms. Recent renovation has improved it considerably, and it still attracts a handsome clientele that enjoys its old-world charm—such as an art nouveau stained-glass skylight or the Louis XV-style chairs in the dining room. The bedrooms offer reproductions of antiques, and most of them have space enough for a sitting area. A double with private bath goes for 455F ($62.75).

Even if you don't stay here, you may want to drop in to dine. A 240F ($33.10) luncheon or dinner is offered, as are more elaborate ones. The chef, Monsieur Jallerat, offers as his specialties filets de sole homardine, canard col vert aux baies de genièvre (wild duck with gingerberries), and fricassée de rognons (kidneys) et de ris de veau (sweetbreads) aux girolles. Pâté de Chartres is another delight, as is the boneless rib of lamb.

Hôtel de la Poste, 3 rue du Général Koenig (tel. 37-21-04-27), offers one of the best hotel values in Chartres, in part because of its convenient location in the center of town across from the main post office and in part because of its soundproof and comfortably furnished bedrooms scattered between a new (mid-1970s) wing and a much older, completely renovated, section. Motorists will appreciate the in-house garage. There is a total of 60 rooms, 38 of which contain a private bath. All of them have wall-to-wall carpeting. Depending on the plumbing, singles cost from 95F ($13.10) to 173F ($23.87) and doubles from 160F ($22.06) to 225F ($31.03). The polite staff will serve you dinner in the attractive dining room at 60F ($8.27) to 108F ($14.89) for a fixed-price meal.

WHERE TO DINE: The finest of the lot in Chartres is **Henri IV,** 31 rue du Soleil d'Or (tel. 37-36-01-55). For years, the "brigade" taught by the late Monsieur Maurice Cazalis, one of the master chefs, has been welcoming gourmet-minded Parisians and foreigners who journey south to the cathedral city. The restaurant occupies the second floor of a small building, about a five-minute walk from the cathedral. Inside, it is modern, with a slight provincial overtone of beamed ceilings, paneled walls, and bay windows with pink geraniums.

Specialties remain in the grand tradition of French cuisine, but the sauces, I suspect, are lighter today. Dishes include turbot with pistachio butter, duck liver with apples, sweetbreads with port wine, and homemade pastries. I recommend the small meringue cakes with nuts, named in honor of George Sand. The standard menu costs 180F ($24.82), with a more elaborate repast being presented for 230F ($31.72). There is an à la carte menu as well. Incidentally, the restaurant has one of the best cartes des vins in France. Don't take my word for that. It is officially recognized as such. Closed Monday night, Tuesday, and for part of February. Downstairs on the ground floor, simpler and less expensive courses are offered.

Normand, 24 Place des Epars (tel. 37-21-04-38), is a Norman-style restaurant on the main square of Chartres, about a ten-minute walk from the cathedral. Owned by Madame Normand, it offers an individualized cuisine and an inviting decor of wooden timbers, plaster walls, heavy beams, wrought-iron lamps, stained-glass windows, and murals depicting scenes from Normandy. Specialties on Madame's à la carte menu include pâté de Chartres, escalope de veau florentine, and côte d'agneau (lamb). You can always get a good grilled steak. The chef prepares excellent pastries as well as a pear Melba. Count on spending 75F ($10.32) to 160F ($22.06) for a complete meal. The restaurant is closed Monday and holidays.

8. Illiers

On the outskirts of this small town, 15 miles from Chartres, the Syndicat d'Initiative has posted a sign: "Illiers, Le Combray de Marcel Proust." Illiers is a real town, but Marcel Proust in his imagination made it world famous as Combray in *A la recherche du temps perdu*.

The taste of a madeleine launched Proust on his immortal recollection. To this day hundreds of his readers from all over the world flock to Illiers to taste a madeleine dipped in limeflower tea in one of the many pastry shops that sell them. Following the Proustian labyrinth, you can explore the gardens, streets, and houses that he so richly wrote about. Young Proust visited Illiers more or less regularly until he was 13 years old. The town is epitomized by its Church of St. Jacques, where Proust as a boy placed hawthorn on the altar.

Some members of the Proust family have lived at Illiers for centuries. Proust's grandfather, François Proust, was born there on the rue de Cheval-Blanc. At 11 Place du Marché, just opposite the church, he ran a small shop where he made candles. His daughter, Elisabeth, married Jules Amiot, who ran another shop, this one at 14 Place du Marché. Down from Paris, young Marcel would visit his aunt at 4 rue du Saint-Esprit, which has now been renamed rue du Docteur-Proust, honoring Marcel's grandfather.

The **Amiot House** is now a museum, charging a 10F ($1.38) entrance fee. In the novel this was the house of "Aunt Léonie." Filled with antimacassars, it is typical of the solid bourgeois comfort of its day. Upstairs you can visit the bedroom where the young Marcel stayed, and today it contains souvenirs of key episodes in the novel. In addition, you can see the room where his aunt spent many years before dying of an illness. It can be visited at 3 and 4 p.m., except on Tuesday.

In the center of town, a sign will guide you to sights that have connections with the great writer.

9. Provins

Feudal Provins, the "city of roses," lies about 50 miles southeast of Paris. It is one of the most interesting tourist destinations in the Île de France. To wander through its medieval streets is to experience France of long ago. Historic, romantic and beautiful, Provins is a town that soared to the pinnacle of its power and prosperity in the Middle Ages, then fell into a slumber after its ruin in the Hundred Years' War. Because of its proximity to Paris, it is surprising that it remains so little known by foreigners.

Once it was the third town of France, after Paris and Rouen, and its Fair of Champagne rivaled those of Troyes. The city is also known for its "Damask Rose," brought back from the Crusades by Thibault IV. The Duke of Lancaster through marriage became the Count of Provins, including the rose in his coat-of-arms. A century and a half later the red rose of Lancaster confronted the white rose of York in the "War of the Roses."

The upper town—*ville-haute*—is perched on a promontory, and the lower town—*ville-basse*—is crossed by two rivers, the Durteint and the Voulzie, an affluent of the Seine.

With its towers and bastions, Provins was surrounded by ramparts in the 13th century, protecting it from the vast plains of Brie. From the Porte St-Jean, you can tour **the ramparts,** which are well preserved.

In the upper town, **Caesar's Tower** (Tour César), (tel. 64-00-16-65), erected on the site of a Roman fort, can be visited from 10 a.m. to noon and 2 to 6 p.m. for an 8F ($1.10) admission. It closes on Sunday morning and at 5 p.m. off-season. Its tower is a belfry to the **Church of St. Quiriace,** built in the 12th and 13th centuries. The church contains a majestic Gothic primitive choir and a modern dome. Joan of Arc stopped off here on her way to Orléans. A short walk away takes you to **Grange-aux-Dimes,** containing three 12th-century rooms, one above the other, housing an archeological museum with some precious stones.

In the Lower Town, the major attraction is the **Hôtel-Dieu,** which was formerly the palace of the comtesses of Champagne. It is visited by those wishing to see its underground passages with graffiti evoking those at Pompeii.

WHERE TO DINE: **La Fontaine,** 10 rue Victor-Arnoul (tel. 64-00-00-10). One of the best restaurants in the district is in a pleasant garden setting ringed with shrubbery in the center of town. Menu specialties are cheerfully served in an attractively rustic dining room, if you don't want to eat outside. They include conservatively nouvelle variations of traditional French, and particularly Burgundian, specialties. These include baby rabbit with mustard sauce, panache of salmon and turbot with sage, chicken in raspberry vinegar, and a wide array of delectably fruited desserts. Fixed-price meals range from 95F ($13.10) to 145F ($20), while à la carte dining costs around 250F ($34.48). The restaurant is usually closed on Thursday, for the first three weeks of February, and for the last two weeks of August. La Fontaine also rents out 13 simply furnished bedrooms for 90F ($12.41) in a single and 140F ($19.31) in a double.

Le Berri, 17 rue Hugues-le-Grand (tel. 64-00-03-86). English-speaking Monsieur Tournefier will welcome you to his pleasant auberge, featuring a very good and filling meal for 96F ($13.24), or more elaborate repasts for 120F ($16.55) You can also order à la carte at a cost of about 160F ($22.06) to 180F ($24.82). The food is in the typical regional style—duck pâté, lamb cooked with green beans, a selection of local cheese, or a tart of the house made with fresh fruit. On the à la carte menu, you can select from more elegant fare, such as tournedos Rossini, even roebuck in season, and quenelles of pike covered with a crayfish sauce. The service is friendly. The restaurant is closed in July and for the first two weeks in January. It is always closed on Monday. Incidentally, the set menus are not featured on Sunday.

10. Malmaison

This old house has had its moments. From his campaign in Egypt, Napoleon wrote to the woman here who "called forth from me the basic forces of nature, impetuosity as volcanic as thunder." The recipient of the letter was his wife Joséphine Tascher de Pagarie, widow of General de Beauharnais. She wasn't exactly mourning his absence—rather, she was flirting with young Hippolyte Charles, who amused her with his jokes. Apparently, however, she changed her mind about the "queer man" she'd married, rushing to meet him on his return from Paris.

Of course, Napoleon wasn't exactly a faithful husband. When he was writing her the letter from Egypt, he was with a mistress. At Malmaison, Marie Walewska, the sensual wife of an aging Polish count, paid Napoleon a short farewell visit in 1815, one year after Joséphine's death, before his departure to St. Helena. She bore the emperor a son in 1810, Alexandre Walewska.

The château—really a country residence far removed from the grandeur of the Tuileries or Compiègne (other Napoleonic residences)—was built in the 17th century, beginning in 1622. It was purchased in 1799 by Joséphine, who had it restored and renewed, fashionably decorating it. She subsequently enlarged the estate (but not the château). In the tenth century Norman invaders landed here and devastated all the countryside around—hence the name, Malmaison, or "bad house." Popular references to Malmaison having been a sanitorium for lepers are unfounded. Today it is filled with mementos and Empire furnishings. The veranda and the council room are obviously inspired by Napoleon's tent from his military campaigns. His study and desk are exhibited in his library. In the basement was the kitchen, and the chimney pipes allowed a system of central heating. Marie-Louise, his second wife, took Napoleon's books with her when she left France. These books from the Tuileries were purchased by an English couple who presented them to the museum at Malmaison. Most of the furnishings were in Malmaison originally, or they came from the Tuileries or St. Cloud. Napoleon always attached a sentimental importance to Malmaison, spending a week there before his departure for St. Helena.

In 1809, following her divorce because of childlessness, Joséphine retired there. She was passionately devoted to her roses until her death in 1814 at the age of 51. The roses in the garden, where swans glide gracefully by, form a fitting memorial to Napoleon's "sweet and incomparable love of my life." A towering tree on the premises is said to have been planted by the wife of the First Consul after one of his victories.

The bed in which Joséphine died is exhibited, and even her toilet kit with such practical items as a toothbrush. A Gerard portrait flatters her. In fact, many of the portraits and sculpture immortalize a Napoleonic deity. See, for example, David's equestrian portrait of the emperor. For more information on Malmaison, telephone 47-49-20-07.

The château, about ten miles west of Paris (three miles northwest of St. Cloud), can be visited every day except Tuesday, from 10 a.m. to noon and 1:30 to 4:30 p.m. for an admission of 16F ($2.21), 8F ($1.10) on Sunday. To reach Malmaison by public transportation from Paris, take the Métro A-1 line from Place Charles-deGaulle to the La Défense stop. There board bus 158A for a six-mile run to the country house.

11. Senlis

An ancient Roman township surrounded by forests, Senlis slumbers quietly today. Barbarians no longer threaten its walls, as they did in the third century. Royalty is gone too, although all the kings of France from Clovis to Louis XIV have either passed through or taken up temporary residence here.

A visit to the northern French town can be tied in with a trek to nearby Chantilly (Paris is 32 miles to the south). Today the core of Vieux Senlis is an archeological garden, attracting visitors from all over the world. But the first target on everybody's list is the journey across cobblestone streets to:

THE CATHEDRAL: Its graceful and elegant 13th-century spire—towering 256 feet—dominates the countryside for miles around. The façade is a study in contrasts: the western side almost severe, the southern portal in the flamboyant Gothic style. A fire swept over the building in 1504, and much rebuilding followed—so the original effect is lost. A 19th-century decorative overlay was applied to the original Gothic structure, which was begun in 1153 to honor Notre-Dame.

Before entering the cathedral, walk around to the western porch to see the sculptures, which enjoy a landmark position in French art. Depicted in stone is an unusual calendar of the seasons, along with scenes showing the ascension of the Virgin and the entombment. The builders of the main portal imitated the work at Chartres.

Inside, the light, airy feeling of Gothic echoes the words of a critic who said it was "designed so that man might realize that he was related to the infinite and the eternal." In the forecourt are memorials to Joan of Arc and Marshal Foch.

A short walk from the cathedral delivers you to the doorway of the:

CHÂTEAU ROYAL: Built on the ruins of a Roman palace, the castle followed the outline of the Gallo-Roman walls, some of the most important in France owing to their state of preservation. Once inhabited by such monarchs as Henri

II and Catherine de Medici, the château—now in ruins—encloses a complex of buildings. It is open every day except Tuesday and Wednesday mornings, from 10 a.m. to noon and 2 to 6 p.m., April 1 to September 30 (otherwise it closes at 5 p.m.). Entrance fee for Château Royal gardens is 5F (69¢), and to the unique **Museum of the Veneri** (Hunting) (tel. 44-53-00-80) it is 9.40F ($1.30). Of the 28 towers originally built, only 16 remain, some well preserved. One ruin houses the King's Chamber, the boudoir of French monarchs since the time of Clovis. Nowadays it's in bad need of restoration, and hopefully funds can be found. Within the complex is the Priory of St. Mauritius, resting under a wooden sloped roof. It not only honors a saint but was founded by one, the French king Louis IX.

FOOD AND LODGING: **Hôstellerie de la Porte Bellon,** 51 rue Bellon (tel. 44-53-03-05), is a combined hotel and restaurant, which together make it my favorite choice in Senlis. The 300-year-old building was a former abbey designed with three floors of simple big windows, white shutters, and flower boxes filled with blue and violet pansies. The ground floor contains a bar area surrounded by provincial French paneling, a bubbling fish tank, and a collection of old pewter. The adjacent restaurant is accented with country-style flowered wallpaper, charmingly rustic accessories, and a massive fireplace. Fixed-price meals are offered for 88F ($12.14) and 140F ($19.31).

Double or single bathless rooms cost from 110F ($15.17), and rooms with bath range between 190F (26.20) to 225F ($31.03), depending on the plumbing and accommodation. The hotel is on a quiet cobblestone street with an adjacent parking lot, about a block from the junction of the main road from Paris to Lille with the rue de Meaux.

Rôtisserie de Formanoir, 17 rue du Châtel (tel. 44-53-15-99), lies on a narrow cobblestone street sloping up to the cathedral. This pleasant and elegant restaurant has a façade of massive stones, wrought-iron grillwork, wooden shutters on either side of big windows, and a cast-iron replica of a bejeweled hand that serves as a door knocker. The building was a convent during the 1500s, but today it's graciously managed by the Bauchart family, who propose menu specialties such as filet of beef with foie gras sauce, salmon blinis, cassolette of snails with tarragon, grilled veal kidneys, and a mixed grill of lamb, veal, chicken, and beef. In winter, there's likely to be a fire blazing in the well-designed antique fireplace. A full meal costs from 240F ($33.10) to 260F ($35.85) on the à la carte offering, although a two-course fixed-price meal is served every day except Sunday for 65F ($8.97). Dessert might consist of one of the establishment's homemade sherbets.

An economical choice for dining is **Le Chalet de Sylvie,** 1 Place de Verdun (tel. 44-53-00-87). A mock timbered-and-stucco structure at a busy intersection, this popular restaurant attracts those seeking drinks (both an American bar and a salon de thé are on the premises). For either luncheon or dinner, it draws the budget-conscious with its set meal for 120F ($16.55). The repast might begin with quiche Lorraine or a terrine de lapin (rabbit), then follow with a grilled entrecôte. Service and beverages are extra.

12. Compiègne

The most famous dance step of all time was photographed in a forest about four miles from the center of town: Hitler's "jig of joy" on June 22, 1940, not only heralded the ultimate humiliation of France but shocked much of the world. At the peak of his power, the Nazi dictator forced the vanquished French to capitulate in the same railway coach where German plenipotentiaries signed the Armistice on November 11, 1918.

The coach was transported to Berlin, where it was exhibited, but an Allied bomb destroyed it in 1943. What you see today is a reproduction in exact detail of the original coach of Marshal Foch, the supreme Allied commander in World War I. It can be visited from 8:30 a.m. to noon and 1 to 6:30 p.m. Three-dimensional slides are projected on the screen, showing scenes from "The Great War." **The Glade,** as it is known, is on the Soissons Road.

But you don't go to Compiègne—which the French call *la ville de l'armistice*—just for memories of war. In the town's heyday, before it became an unwilling host to the Germans in 1870, again in World War I, and finally in 1940, royalty and the two Bonaparte emperors flocked there.

Life at Compiègne centered around the **palace.** It wasn't always a place of pomp. Louis XIV once said: "In Versailles, I live in the style befitting a monarch. In Fontainebleau, more like a prince. At Compiègne, like a peasant." But the Sun King returned again and again.

His successor, Louis XV, set about rebuilding the château, based on plans drawn up by Gabriel. The king died before work was completed, but Louis XVI and Marie Antoinette continued the expansion program. The palace always had special memories for them. Both were teenagers when they first met there on a spring day in 1770. An up-and-coming dauphin, the future king was so embarrassed by the encounter that, it is said, he never once dared look into her face—rather, kept gazing at her feet.

As if Austrian princesses hadn't learned a lesson, another teenage girl, Marie-Louise, arrived at Compiègne to marry a French emperor, Napoléon I. In a dining room visited on a guided tour, Marie-Louise had her first meal with the mighty ruler. Accounts maintain that she was paralyzed with fear of this older man (Napoleon was in his 40s at the time). After dinner, he seduced her, an act that is said to have only increased her fears.

It wasn't until the Second Empire that Compiègne reached its pinnacle of social success. Under Napoléon III and his empress, Eugénie, the autumnal hunting season was the occasion for gala balls and parties—some, according to accounts, lasting ten days without a break. It was the "golden age": women arrived in Worth-designed crinolines and danced to the waltzes of Strauss. Light operas of Offenbach echoed through the chambers and salons. Eugénie fancied herself an actress, performing in the palace theater for her guests.

In the gold and scarlet Empire room, Napoléon I spent many a troubled night. His library, known for its "secret door," the ceiling designed by Girodet, is also on the guided tour. In the Queen's Chamber, the "horn of plenty" bed was used by Marie-Louise. The furniture is by Jacob, the saccharine nude on the ceiling by Girodet.

Dubois decorated the charming Salon of Flowers. The largest room, the Ball Gallery, was adorned by Girodet, the work symbolizing the battles of Napoléon I (sculpture fancifully depicts the emperor and his mother in flowing Grecian robes).

In the park, Napoléon I ordered the gardeners to create a green bower to remind his new queen, Marie-Louise, of the one at Schönbrunn.

The château (tel. 44-40-01-00) is open daily except Tuesday, from 9:30 a.m. to noon and 1:30 to 5 p.m. Admission is 16F ($2.21) weekdays, 8F ($1.10) on Sunday. The same ticket admits you to the other museums in the château.

One wing of the palace houses the **National Automobile and Touristic Museum,** exhibiting about 150 vehicles: everything from chariots familiar to Ben Hur to bicycles to a Citroën "chain-track" vehicle. Also to be seen in Compiègne are the **Musée du Second-Empire,** with its collection of paintings, sculpture, and furniture from that period, including works by Carpeaux; and **Musée du l'Impératrice,** with its souvenirs from the imperial family.

The *picantins* strike the hours at the **Hôtel de Ville,** erected in the early 16th century with a landmark belfry. Nearby is a **Museum of Historical Figurines,** (tel. 44-40-26-00), a unique collection of about 100,000 tin soldiers: everything from a Louis XVI trumpeter to a soldier from World War II. The Battle of Waterloo is depicted. It can be visited from 9 a.m. to noon and 2 to 6 p.m. (closes on

Monday and earlier off-season). Admission is 8.40F ($1.16). At the town square stands a statue of Joan of Arc, who was taken prisoner at Compiègne by the Burgundians on May 23, 1430, before she was turned over to the English.

GETTING THERE: The journey from Paris to this Oise River valley town takes 50 minutes by rail. By car, it's reached on the northern Paris-Lille motorway (E3), a distance of 50 miles. A visit to Compiègne is traditionally tied in with an excursion to Senlis.

FOOD AND LODGING: L'Hôstellerie du Royal-Lieu, 9 rue de Senlis (tel. 44-20-10-24), offers pleasant accommodations and a good restaurant behind a mock-timbered façade on the road to Paris, about 1¼ miles from the center of town. Monsieur and Madame Bonechi maintain this place with an iron-willed discipline, working hard to impose their standards on a well-trained staff. They have carefully decorated 20 rooms in a rambling two-story annex, each in a different style. The accommodations have names such as Madame Pompadour, Madame Butterfly, and La Goulue, although less fanciful units include rooms done in a representative scattering of different "Louis" periods or in Empire.

Both the rooms and the terrace of the rustic restaurant look out over an immaculate garden with tall trees centered around an enormous copper cauldron formerly used for making gruyère cheese and now serving as a flowerpot. Accommodations, each with a private bath, rent for 275F ($37.92) in a double. The three suites go for around 390F ($53.78) apiece. Full meals in the elegantly rustic dining room are served on blue-and-white china and might include a four-fish stew with red butter, a provocative scallops dish with endive, fresh asparagus, filet of beef with morels in cream sauce or with foie gras, and an award-winning cassolette of snails with anise. Dessert soufflés are available if you order them 30 minutes in advance. Fixed-price meals cost 180F ($24.82) and 260F ($35.85), rising to 360F ($49.64) if wine is included.

The leading choice in the center of town is the **Rôtisserie du Chat Qui Tourne**, holding forth under the roof of the **Hôtel de France**, 17 rue Eugène-Floquet (tel. 44-40-02-74). Madame Robert, the proprietor, believes in judicious cooking and careful seasoning, and she prices her table d'hôte menus to appeal to a wide range of budgets. For example, you can order a complete dinner for 100F ($13.79), including some of the house specialties. However, for 225F ($31.03) you can partake of the menu gastronomique. The latter repast is likely to begin with a terrine de canard (duck), follow with a trout meunière, proceed to le poulet rôti (roast chicken) à la broche, and end with dessert. Service and tax are included, but you must add the cost of your drinks. Bargain hunters in food are drawn to her simple 78F ($10.76) menu, which includes an appetizer, a main course, one vegetable, and dessert. It's served only from noon to 2 p.m. and 7:30 to 9 p.m. Of course, there's a choice à la carte menu as well, on which one of my favorite dishes is les rognons aux trois moutardes, kidneys in a sauce made with three different types of mustard.

The old name, "Inn of the Cat that Turns the Spit," dates from 1665. Downstairs is a bar as well as a dining room in the traditional country-inn style.

Madame Robert also rents out some simply furnished but clean and comfortable bedrooms. Depending on the plumbing, singles range from 95F ($13.10) to 195F ($26.89), with doubles priced from 175F ($24.13) to 365F ($50.33).

13. Chantilly

Parisians use this town, 26 miles north of its capital, as a resort retreat from big-city living. Known for its frothy whipped cream and its black lace, it draws the crowds mainly because of its racetrack and its château. The first two Sundays in June are the highlight of the turf season, bringing out such a fashionable crowd that many women go just to see who's wearing what.

The **Château de Chantilly** and the **Musée Condé**—once the seat of the Condé—is idyllically situated on an artificial lake. You approach it along the same forested drive that Louis XIV, along with hundreds of guests, rode for a banquet prepared by Vatel, one of the best-known French chefs. One day, when the fish didn't arrive on time, Vatel committed suicide. The effect of the château is decidedly French Renaissance, with gables and domed towers, but a part of it was rebuilt in the 19th century. It is skirted by a romantic, mysterious-looking forest once filled with stag and boar.

In 1886 the owner of the château, the Duc d'Aumale, left the park and palace to the Institute of France, along with his fabulous art collection and library. Aside from the sumptuous furnishings, the château is a museum, housing works by artists such as Memling, Van Dyck, Botticelli, Poussin, Watteau, Ingres, Delacroix, Corot, Rubens, and Vernet. See especially Raphael's *Madonna of Lorette, Virgin of the House d'Orléans,* and his *Three Graces* (sometimes called the *Three Ages of Woman*). The foremost French painter of the 15th century, Jean Fouquet did a series of about 40 miniatures, and the museum is also rich in Clouet portraits, such as one of Marguerite de France as an *enfant.* In the jewel collection shines the rose diamond that received worldwide attention when it was stolen in 1926. Of the Condé library acquisitions, one is celebrated: an illuminated manuscript from the 15th century illustrating the months of the year, *Les Très Riches Heures du Duc de Berri.*

The petit château was built by Jean Bullant in about 1560 for one of the members of the Montmorency family, a man named Anne. The stables (see below), a hallmark in French 18th-century architecture, were built to house 240 horses with adjacent kennels for 500 hounds. If time remains, try to wander in the garden laid out by Le Nôtre. In the park are a hamlet of rustic cottages and the House of Sylvie, a graceful building constructed in 1604 and rebuilt by the Grand Condé, bearing the nickname of the Duchess of Montmorency, Maria-Felice Orsini. The polygon-shape room was added to house handsome wood paneling of the 18th century which was originally in a hunting lodge in the forest of Dreux.

The château (tel. 44-57-03-62) is open from 10 a.m. to 6 p.m. in summer and from 10:30 a.m. to 5 p.m. off-season, charging 23F ($3.17) for admission. It is closed on Tuesday. Trains leave the Gare du Nord station in Paris, the trip taking about an hour.

The **Musée Vivant du Cheval,** on the rue du Connétable, occupies the restored Grandes Écuries, the stables built between 1719 to 1735 for Louis-Henri, duc de Bourbon and prince de Condé, who occupied the château and estate. Besides being fond of horses, he believed in reincarnation and expected to come back as a horse in a future life. Therefore, he had the stables built fit to house a prince. The stables and an adjoining kennel structure for 500 hounds fell into ruins over a couple of centuries, but they have now been restored as a museum of the living horse, with thoroughbreds housed alongside old breeds of draft horses, Arabs and Hispano-Arabs, and farm horses. Yves Bienaimé, a certified riding instructor who undertook the restoration and establishment of the museum, has exhibitions tracing the history of the horse's association with man, as well as saddles, a blacksmith shop, and displays of equipment for care of the animals. There is also horse-race memorabilia. The museum is open daily except Tuesday, from 1 to 5:30 p.m. Admission is 30F ($4.14).

FOOD AND LODGING: **Hôtel d'Angleterre,** 5 Place Omer-Vallon (tel. 44-57-00-59), is a typical village inn, which lies on a busy, often noisy, street. Unpretentious, it is not without charm if you accept it for what it is. The simple bedrooms are adequately kept and modestly priced. Depending on the plumbing, singles range from a low of 85F ($11.72) to a high of 145F ($20), and doubles begin at 110F ($15.17), going up to 165F ($22.75). You can dine either inside or, on fair-weather days, in the tiny courtyard. The cuisine is good home-cooking. A set meal costs only 85F ($11.72), plus the cost of your beverage. Try the country terrine and the beef bourguignon. Closed between January 5 and February 15.

Le Relais Condé, 42 Avenue du Maréchal-Joffre (tel. 44-57-05-75), is a popular restaurant both for aficionados of the nearby racetrack and for visitors coming only to look at the celebrated château. The site was once a chapel, considerably altered and expanded to serve the gastronomic demands of Etiennette Luck. The cuisine ranges from French traditional to items bordering on La Nouvelle Cuisine. The daily menu might include sweetbreads Condé, gratin of lobster, or salad of smoked breast of duckling with gizzards. The wine list includes vintages from throughout France. Full meals range from 225F ($31.03) to 275F ($37.92), although a fixed-price menu is offered at 175F ($24.13). The restaurant is closed Monday and Tuesday, from mid-January to early February, and from mid-July to early August.

Tipperary, 6 Avenue du Maréchal-Joffre (tel. 49-57-00-48), is one of the leading restaurants. On the ground floor of an old town house, it offers outside café tables. To begin your repast, try the chef's specialty, a terrine de perdreau (young partridge). Other specialties include the chef's omelet, scallops, chateaubriand, sole meunière, and pepper steak. Expect to spend at least 180F ($24.82) for a really good meal.

Les Quatre Saisons de Chantilly, 9 Avenue du Général-Leclerc (tel. 44-57-04-65), is a winning Franco-Danish combination on a major artery on the outskirts of town. Meals are served in a flowered terrace. However, if you decide to dine inside, the decor there is almost like a garden too. Menu items are divided into equal parts of Nordic, Burgundian, and Nouvelle. The marinated herring might be the best way to get your meal going. It might be followed by several kinds of salmon dishes (one smoked and served in a blini), plus a wide range of Danish beers and French wines. The restaurant is enormously popular, and is connected with the famed Flora Danica on the Champs-Élysées in Paris. In Chantilly, fixed-price meals cost 125F ($17.41) on Sunday and holidays, 90F ($12.41) on weekdays. À la carte dinners go for 225F ($31.03) and up. The restaurant is closed Monday and for three weeks in February. It serves dinner otherwise until 10:30 p.m.

ON THE OUTSKIRTS: If you'd like to stay within easy driving distance of Chantilly, you'll find far better accommodations, atmosphere, and food outside of town at the following recommendation:

Chaumontel (Luzarches)

Château de Chaumontel (tel. 44-71-00-30), at Chaumontel, just northeast of Luzarches, 6½ miles from Chantilly, dates from the latter part of the 16th century. Although it has had many aristocratic owners in its long history, it was once the hunting lodge of the Prince de Condé, whose domain was at Chantilly. But by 1960 it had been turned into a hotel, offering 20 bedrooms furnished with a restrained taste and most comfortable. The least expensive doubles (with a toilet only) rent for 150F ($20.69); the cost rises to anywhere from 250F ($34.48) to 300F ($41.37) in a double with complete bath. A few apartments are available, costing two persons 550F ($75.63) to 570F ($78.60).

The dining room is done in the rustic style, and you almost feel as if you're an invited guest at a private country estate rather than a room number. The food is excellent, including a number of specialties such as roast lamb and poached turbot. A meal costs from 150F ($20.69).

There are many strolls you can take on the château's park-like grounds. It is closed from mid-July until the end of August.

14. Beauvais

Beauvais, where Victor Hugo "spent mellow hours," has always been at the crossroads between such points as Paris, Rouen, Reims, and Amiens. Because of that, it has known the ravages of war inflicted by the Normans, the English, the Burgundians, and the Germans. In the 1472 siege by the Burgundians, a girl named Jeanne Hachette (Hatchet) seized the enemy standard by axing its bearer and became the local heroine. In 1918 Marshal Foch directed operations from Beauvais.

The last attack was by the Nazis in June of 1940. However, the town has risen from that disaster, having been rebuilt according to the original plan. Before the war Beauvais was known for its tapestries, the manufacture of which was started by Colbert in 1664. The looms and the artists are now at Gobelins in Paris. However, to honor the old tradition, a **National Tapestry Gallery** was opened next to the cathedral. A workshop with four low-warp looms is tended by weavers here, and exhibitions are regularly changed. The study of all the trends of tapestry making, both ancient and modern, is pursued. And most important, the gallery allows Beauvais to retain its link with its long-standing tradition. The town lies 46 miles northwest from Paris, 50 miles east of Rouen.

Spared from the 1940 bombardment was the:

CATHEDRAL OF ST. PIERRE: In the words of Viollet-le-Duc, this cathedral was "the Parthenon of France." Still uncompleted, it is a masterpiece of Gothic architecture, dating from 1247 when it incorporated part of a Carolingian church. It is said to have the highest Gothic choir in the world, 158 feet under the vault. In fact, the pillars were so tall that the vaulting fell in 1284. After this inauspicious beginning, a stone bell tower was erected that soared more than 500 feet high, the tallest in the world at that time. However, it collapsed in 1573, just four years after it was built.

So many wars and structural collapses did the Beauvais cathedral suffer that only the transept, choir, and a single bay of the nave, plus seven apse chapels, were ever completed. It has been said that the nave of Amiens, the portal at Reims, the towers of Chartres, and the choir at Beauvais would make the greatest cathedral in the world.

The collection of tapestries inside is remarkable, especially the *Acts of the Apostles,* based on original designs by Raphael and woven at Beauvais by 17th-century artisans. Some of the stained glass dates from the 13th century and from the 16th-century School of Le Prince. On the north portal is a remarkable carving, *The Man in the Wheelbarrow.* In the Treasury is a collection of liturgical vestments and goldsmiths' work, and the cloisters are from the 14th century.

The curiosity of the cathedral is an astronomical clock, built in 1864 by August Vérité and said to be the largest in the world. It was based on another celebrated clock, the one at Strasbourg. At certain times of the day it presents a scene from the Last Judgment.

CHURCH OF ST. ÉTIENNE: If time remains, try to visit this nearby church that represents a marriage of Romanesque (nave) and Gothic (choir). Somehow the union manages to come off harmoniously. The bombs of 1940 badly damaged the choir, although it subsequently been repaired. Of the 16th-century stained glass, the most outstanding is the *Tree of Jesus* by Angrand-le-Prince. Goering wanted to own the bearded statue of St. Wilgeforte in the nave, dating from the 16th century. On the façade is a *roue de la fortune* (wheel of fortune) in the rose window of the north transept.

WHERE TO STAY: The **Chenal Hôtel,** 63 Boulevard du Général-de-Gaulle (tel.

44-45-03-55), is the most modern hotel choice in town, with efficient bedrooms that are more individualized than you'd expect. The in-house video offers two programs every night on the color TV in each bedroom. All 29 units have private bath, phone, and mini-bar as well. There's a bar on the premises, but no restaurant. A single ranges from 260F ($35.85) with twins or doubles costing 300F ($41.37) to 310F ($42.75), breakfast not included.

WHERE TO DINE: À La Cotelette, 8 rue des Jacobins (tel. 44-45-04-42), has been considerably upgraded and improved so that now it is considered the best place to dine in town. Claude Layrac, the owner, is filled with pleasant surprises, as he knows how to take many standard French dishes and give them original flair. I haven't tried all the chef's dishes, but I'm fond of many of them, especially the blanquette de lotte (turbot) with watercress. Also madly exciting is the filet de boeuf with peppercorns flambéed with cognac, and the magret of duckling in a mustard sauce. The desserts are distinguished as well. If you order à la carte, expect to pay from 225F ($31.03). However, you'll find two set menus featured-one at 85F ($11.52) and another at 150F ($20.69). This centrally located restaurant offers a pleasant musical ambience, with the decorative touches of a country inn. Closed Sunday night, Monday, and in July.

Crémaillère, 1 rue Gui-Patin (tel. 44-45-03-13). This family-run restaurant, in a charming, rustic-style house, offers excellently prepared regional specialties. Daniel Lemènager is the talented chef de cuisine, and he maintains a consistent quality in the *bonne tradition familiale*. He is assisted by his mother, Renée-Marie. A superb specialty is the chef's trout with peppercorns, served in a sorrel sauce. Try also the tripe cooked in Norman cider. For dessert, you might try the gâteau glacé Maxime (an iced sweet). If you order à la carte, count on spending from 190F ($26.20) per person, although you can select a set menu for 100F ($13.79), a great bargain. Madame Leménager speaks English and always extends a heartfelt welcome to foreign visitors. The restaurant is closed on Tuesday evening and all day Wednesday.

15. Château de Thoiry

What do you do if you're sitting out a storm in a 16th-century château playing Chopin's piano and raindrops keep falling on your head? Well, the Count de La Panouse decided it was time to open his castle to the public and raise some funds to fix the roof. In they trekked that year (1966), asking to see not only the piano but the original manuscripts of two unpublished Chopin waltzes that the American pianist Byron Janis discovered in a broom closet. Much to the count's disappointment, however, the antique furniture, more than 43 handwritten letters of French kings, and the original financial records of France from 1745 to 1750 just didn't lure enough customers.

Then the count's son, Paul, came up with an idea that turned the Château de Thoiry into a tourist attraction that in one year drew more tourists than either the Louvre or Versailles. He turned the grounds into a wild game reserve, populated with elephants, giraffes, zebras, monkeys, rhinoceroses, alligators, hyenas, lions, tigers, kangaroos, bears, and wolves. More than 1,000 animals and birds roam at liberty. The reserve and park cover 300 acres, although the estate is on 1,200 acres.

The park has extensive possibilities for promenades on foot. In the French gardens you can see Asian deer, llamas, Asian sheep, and many types of birds, including flamingos and cranes. In the tiger park a promenade has been designed above the tigers. Visitors can no longer walk in the Monkey Park, but can gaze on these fascinating animals from a bridge above. In addition, in the *caveau* of the château is a vivarium. More gardens may be opened in the near future. Paul and Annabelle de La Panouse are also restoring the 17th-, 18th-, and 19th-century gardens as well as creating new ones.

To see the animal farm, you take a minibus from the parking lot of the château, or else drive your own automobile, providing it isn't a convertible. Is there any danger? Perhaps, although it is slight. Anticipating troubles, the owners carry thousands upon thousands of francs' worth of insurance. However, all that is likely to happen to you is that an elephant might stick his trunk in your window if you leave it open.

The park is most crowded on weekends, but if you want to avoid the crush at these times, visit on Saturday or Sunday morning. The grounds are open daily in summer from 9:45 a.m. to 6 p.m. (to 6:30 p.m. on Sunday). Winter hours are from 10 a.m. to 5 p.m. (to 5:30 p.m. on Sunday). Visitors are charged 49F ($6.76) to visit the château, its museums, and the surrounding park and gardens; 20F ($2.76) for just the château and museums. Prices are lower for children accompanied by adults. However, hours for entering the château are adjustable by demand and are not posted. On the grounds is a fast-food restaurant, a standard menu costing 37F ($5.10). You can take a food basket and have a picnic among the gentler animals.

Drivers should take the Autoroute de l'Ouest toward Dreux, turning at Le Pontel onto Route D11. Tourist-bus passengers enjoy a special group price to and from Thoiry, including visits to the park and château and other attractions. On Saturday such buses leave Porte Maillot at 8:45 a.m. and Porte St-Cloud at 8:55 a.m. On Sunday departures are from Port Maillot at 1:15 p.m. and from Porte St-Cloud at 1:25 p.m. You may call 34-87-40-67 for more information about the bus schedule.

FOOD AND LODGING: Hôtel de l'Étoile (tel. 34-87-40-21). Guests have use of the stone and timber garden-style sitting room in this rustic three-story inn with the rounded canopies set over each of the windows. There's a dolphin-shaped fountain decorating one of the walls and even a pleasant restaurant with lots of masonry trim. The 12 comfortable and colorful bedrooms all contain private bath and cost from 200F ($27.58) in a single, from 300F ($41.37) in a double. Meals in the restaurant range from 100F ($13.79) to 175F ($24.13).

16. Giverny

The house with its pink crushed-brick façade and the gardens where Claude Monet lived for 43 years have been restored and opened to the public. Born in 1840, Monet, the French impressionist painter, was a brilliant innovator, excelling in representing the effects of light at different times of the day. He is most known, of course, for his series of paintings of the Rouen Cathedral and of water lilies.

Leaving Poissy, Monet came to Giverny in 1883. He took a small railway linking Vetheuil to Vernon, discovering the village at a point where the Epte stream joined the nearby Seine. Many celebrities came to his home, Le Pressoir (tel. 32-58-28-21), to visit and to enjoy the company and the good cooking, among them Clemenceau, Cézanne, Rodin, Renoir, Degas, and Sisley. At the death of Monet in 1926, his son, Michel, inherited the house but left it abandoned until it decayed in ruins. The gardens became almost a jungle, inhabited by river rats. In 1966 Michel Monet died, leaving the house to the Beaux Arts Academy. It wasn't until 1977 that Gerald Van der Kemp, who restored Versailles, decided to work on Giverny. Mostly it was restored with gifts from American benefactors, especially Mrs. Lila Acheson Wallace, head of *Reader's Digest,* who contributed $1 million.

Guests can stroll through the garden with its thousands of flowers, including the nymphéas. You cross a Japanese bridge hung with wisteria to a dreamy setting of weeping willows and rhododendrons. Monet's studio barge was installed on the pond.

The museum is open every day except Monday from April 1 to October 31, charging an admission of 25F ($3.45). You can visit just the gardens for 15F ($2.07). Museum hours are 10 a.m. to noon and 2 to 6 p.m., and the gardens are open from 10 a.m. to 6 p.m.

The best way to go to Giverny is to rent a car, taking the Autoroute de l'Ouest (Pont de St-Cloud) toward Rouen. You leave the autoroute at Bonnières, then cross the Seine on the Bonnières Bridge. From there, a direct road with signs will bring you to Giverny. Expect about an hour of driving, and try to avoid weekends. It's also possible to go by rail on the Paris–Rouen line (Paris–St-Lazare) to Vernon station, where taxis are available to take you to Giverny. Another way to get to Giverny is to leave the highway at the Bonnières exit and go in the direction of Vernon. Once in Vernon, cross the bridge over the Seine. On the other side, follow the signs directing you to Giverny or to Gasny (Giverny is before Gasny). This way is easier than going through Bonnières, where there aren't many signs.

WHERE TO DINE: Auberge du Vieux Moulin, 21 Route de Vernon (tel. 32-51-46-15), is the most convenient luncheon stopover for visitors exploring the Monet house. The Boudeau family maintains a series of cozy dining rooms whose walls are covered with original paintings inspired by the impressionists. You can walk here from the museum (about 10 pedestrian minutes) so that leaving your car in the museum parking lot is an attractive option. A simple but fresh traditional French meal costs about 100F ($13.79) per person.

Chapter VIII

THE CHÂTEAU COUNTRY

1. Châteaudun
2. Tours
3. Montbazon
4. Azay-le-Rideau
5. Luynes
6. Villandry
7. Loches
8. Amboise
9. Blois
10. Chaumont
11. Chambord
12. Beaugency
13. Cheverny
14. Valençay
15. Chenonceaux
16. Orléans
17. Sully-sur-Loire
18. Les Bézards
19. Gien
20. Langeais
21. Ussé
22. Chinon
23. Fontevraud-l'Abbaye
24. Saumur
25. Angers
26. Le Mans
27. Loué

THE VAL DE LOIRE is called "The Garden of France." Bordered by vineyards, the winding Loire Valley cuts through the soft contours of the land of castles deep in the heart of France. Along the way are *levées* (dikes), some dating from centuries ago, built to hold back the lazy Loire should it become the turbulent Loire.

Many Crusaders returning to their medieval dungeon-like quarters brought with them the news of the elegance and opulence of the East. Soon enough, they began to rethink their surroundings. Later, word came across the Alps from neighboring Italy of a great artistic flowering, of artists such as Leonardo da Vinci and Michelangelo. And so, in the days of the French Renaissance, when the kings of France built châteaux throughout this valley, the emphasis was on sumptuousness. An era of pomp and circumstance was to reign here until Henri IV moved the court to Paris, marking the decline of the Loire.

The Valley of the Loire has played a major part in the national consciousness. Joan of Arc, the maid of Orléans, came this way looking for her dauphin, finding him at Chinon. Carried around from castle to castle were mistresses, the list now legendary, ranging from Agnès Sorel (the mistress of Charles VII) to Diane du Poitiers (the mistress of Henri II). In his heyday, the Chevalier King brought Leonardo da Vinci from Florence, installing him at Amboise. Catherine de Medici and her "flying squadron" of beauties, Henry III and his handsome minions—the people and the events make a rich tapestry. The Loire has a tale to tell, as even the most cursory visitor to its châteaux discovers. Its sights and curiosities are multifarious, ranging from Renaissance, medieval, and classical châteaux to residences where Balzac wrote or Rabelais lived, to Romanesque and Gothic churches, to Roman ramparts, to such art treasures as the Apocalypse Tapestries. There's even the castle that inspired the fairytale "Sleeping Beauty."

The best way to see the Loire is in your own car, free from tour buses and guides herding you in and out of castles. Attempts to explore the valley in two to three days are doomed. If your schedule can accommodate it, allow at least a week. If you wish, you can stay in one of the big towns, such as Tours, with their wide range of accommodations. But you may prefer to seek out a central yet seemingly isolated village with an old inn where the pace is less frenetic, the food worthy of the finest tables in the Loire, and the price the kind you don't mind paying.

Autumn or spring is ideal, although most of the intriguing son-et-lumière (sound-and-light) programs take place in summer when the châteaux are floodlit. First performed on the banks of the Loire, these pageants have become one of the main attractions of France.

Proceeding directly from Paris via Chartres, the first stopover is at:

1. Châteaudun

Twenty-seven miles south of the cathedral city of Chartres, your first château in the Loire Valley emerges. Austere, foreboding, it rises on a stonebound table over a tributary of the Loire. Looking like an impregnable fortress, it isn't the most "warm-hearted" gateway to the château country, but it's imposing and interesting. Originally it was erected as an important fortress to protect the surrounding countryside from its jealous and restless neighbors. In 911 the Normans went on a rampage in this area and succeeded in burning much of the castle.

The comrade in arms of Joan of Arc, Jean Dunois, called the Bastard of Orléans, rebuilt the chapel and the façade in the 15th century. The donjon, a huge round tower 150 feet high, had been reconstructed in the 12th century. The façade on the right, elaborately ornamented, was the result of a 16th-century restoration.

Although begun in the Middle Ages, the château is a mixture of medieval and Renaissance architecture. The roof is pierced with towering chimneys and large dormers. After a great fire swept over Châteaudun in the 18th century, Hardouin, an architect of Louis XV's, directed what was almost an entire reconstruction of the town, indiscreetly turning over the castle to the homeless, who stripped it of its finery. By 1935 the government had acquired the fortress and a major restoration program was launched. Even today it's not richly furnished, but a collection of tapestries depicting such scenes as the worship of the golden calf now cover the walls. The most admirable architectural features are the two carved staircases.

Inside the Saint-Chapelle, a keep dating from the Middle Ages, is a collection of more than a dozen 15th-century robed statues, including a woman with a sword standing on a man's head.

From April 1 to September 30, hours are 9:30 to 11:45 a.m. and 2 to 6 p.m. From October 1 to March 31, hours are 10 to 11:45 a.m. and 2 to 4 p.m. Admission is 10F ($1.38), half price on Sunday and holidays. For more information, telephone 37-45-22-70.

WHERE TO DINE: Caveau des Fouleurs, 56 rue Fouleries (tel. 37-45-23-72), is what is known as a troglodytic cave, a rough-hewn *caveau* bordering the Loire, complete with a flower garden and a stereo club. The service is friendly and efficient, and the food is the best at Châteaudun. The price is reasonable too, an excellently prepared set meal going for just 90F ($12.41), a more elaborate and copious one for 175F ($24.13). If you dine à la carte, expect to pay 180F ($24.82) and up.

In air-conditioned comfort you can select such classic dishes as grilled veal kidneys and entrecôte with béarnaise sauce. The crab soup here has lots of fresh crab in it, and the trout is served in several ways. The chef specializes in pigeon cooked in an earthenware casserole. The cave makes a fine luncheon stopover if you're driving down from Paris en route to the Loire Valley. The restaurant is closed August 15 to September 1 and February 15 to March 1, as well as on Sunday night and Monday.

WHERE TO STAY: Most visitors press on to the Loire Valley to spend the night. However, if you got a late start from Paris, you'll find a perfectly adequate little hotel in Châteaudun. It's the **Hôtel de Beauce,** 50 rue Jallans (tel. 37-45-14-75), lying on a one-way street. Access is easier if you reach rue Jallans from the outside boulevard. The 24 pleasantly furnished bedrooms, all doubles, range in price from 115F ($15.86) to 210F ($28.96), depending on the plumbing. The modern hotel is well kept, and usually there's someone on the staff who speaks English. The hotel doesn't have a restaurant, and is closed December 15 to January 15 and on Sunday off-season.

Hôtel Saint-Michel, 28 Place du 18-Octobre and 5 rue Pean (tel. 37-45-15-70), is a clean, convenient place to stay right on the main square of the town. The 19 simply furnished rooms are all equipped with hot and cold water basins, and some have showers. Singles pay 95F ($13.10) and doubles 200F ($27.58). The hotel has no restaurant. You can enter the Saint-Michel from the Place du 18-Octobre, to be welcomed by the friendly family in charge.

2. Tours

Although without a major château, the industrial and residential city of Tours is the traditional center for exploring the Loire Valley. At the junction of the Loire and Cher Rivers, it was one of the great pilgrimage sites of Europe in the Middle Ages. The devout en route to Santiago de Compostela in northwest Spain stopped off at Tours to pay homage at the tomb of St. Martin, the Apostle of Gaul, who had been bishop of Tours in the 4th century. One of the most significant conflicts in world history, the Battle of Tours in 732, checked the Arab advance into Gaul.

The townspeople are fond of pointing out that Tours, not Paris, is the logical site for the capital of France. It virtually *was* the capital in June of 1940, when Churchill flew there to meet with Paul Reynaud.

The **Cathedral of St. Gatien,** the chief attraction of Tours, honors an evangelist of the third century. Its façade is in the flamboyant Gothic style, flanked by two towers the bases of which date from the 12th century, although the lanterns are Renaissance. The choir was built in the 13th century, and each century up to and including the 16th produced new additions. Sheltered inside is the handsome 16th-century tomb of the children of Charles VIII. Some of the stained-glass windows, the building's glory, date from the 13th century.

The **Musée des Beaux-Arts de Tours,** 18 Place François-Sicard (tel. 47-05-68-73). An archbishop's palace of the 17th and 18th centuries complete with Louis XVI woodwork and Tours silk-damask hangings, provides the background for this museum of art. Among the foreign acquisitions the most outstanding paintings are Mantegna's *Christ in the Garden of Olives* and *The Resurrection.* Other foreign works are an early Rembrandt *(Flight into Egypt)*, plus canvases by Rubens, Luca Giordano, and Matthäus Günther. The French school is represented by Le Sueur, Boucher, Vernet, Vuillard, Degas *(Calvary)*, Delacroix *(Comedians and Buffoons)*, and Monet. The most important sculpture is by Houdon and Lemoyne. Charging 6F (83¢) for admission, the museum is open daily from 9 a.m. to 12:45 p.m. and 2 to 6 p.m. (closed on Tuesday).

For an introduction to the Loire Valley, visit the **Historial of Touraine Museum** at Château Royal, Quai d'Orléans (tel. 47-61-02-95). Here are 15 scenes and 150 wax figures tracing 1,000 years of Touraine history, including its kings and queens, the sound of Ronsard's poetry, the sights of the beautiful valley with its castles of Azay-le-Rideau, Chambord, and Chenonceau among others, and the great houses such as the Clos-Lucé where Leonardo da Vinci lived for many years. The museum is open from 9 a.m. to 8 p.m. daily from June to September and from 9 a.m. to 12:30 p.m. and 2 to 7 p.m. in winter. Admission is 24F ($3.31) for adults, 14F ($1.93) for children under 15.

HOTELS: In accommodations, the best choices fall in:

The Middle Bracket

Méridien, 292 Avenue de Grammont (tel. 37-28-00-80), is a pleasant modern hotel in the style of the *grand siècle.* It might be called "the Inn of the Three Rivers," as it stands on the banks of the Cher between the Indre and the Loire. Built on the prestigious boulevard of Tours, it lies outside the heart of the city, with plenty of its own grounds, including a French garden and a swimming pool. It's a curious combination of a 20th-century motel in the style of an 18th-century French country home. In the modernized château it is fully air-conditioned, each of its soundproof bedrooms containing a private bath. The rooms are appropriately styled and designed for today's traveler, with a discreet use of good modern furnishings blended with antique reproductions. The colors are bright, and there's a sitting area for breakfast or drinks. In a single the tariff is 385F ($53.09) to 500F ($68.95) nightly, increasing to 450F ($62.06) to 600F ($82.74) in a double. In addition, six apartments, spacious and well appointed, are rented at far higher tariffs. The reception hall is classic, the effect softened by glittering crystal chandeliers and planters of boxwood to keep conversational groupings apart. At the recessed salons the windows are draped in velvet. A rôtisserie, which is closed on Sunday and from the first of November until April 1, is on the premises. On the à la carte menu, dishes made with high-quality ingredients will mean a tab of about 225F ($31.03) per person.

Le Royal, 65 Avenue de Grammont (tel. 47-64-71-78), caters to travelers who want modern facilities without sacrificing tradition. Its lounges as well as its 35 bedrooms are furnished in Louis XV and Louis XVI styles, showing both taste and imagination. Based on size and placement, doubles cost from 320F

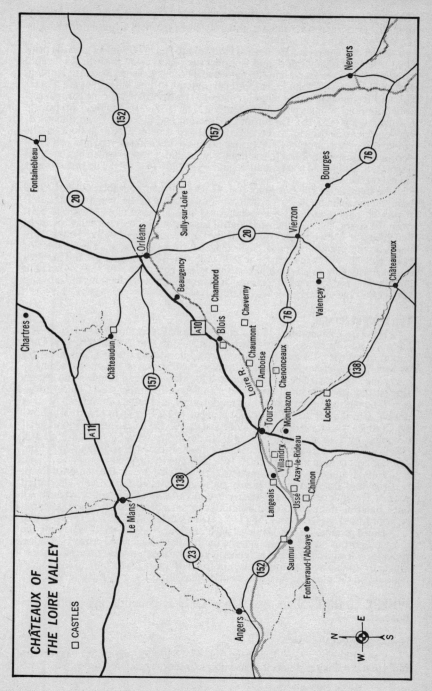

CHÂTEAUX OF
THE LOIRE VALLEY

□ CASTLES

($44.13), and singles go for 275F ($37.92). Each unit has a private bath. Although there is no restaurant, a country-style tavern offers alcoholic drinks. Underground parking is available.

Hôtel de l'Univers, 5 Boulevard Heurteloup (tel. 47-05-37-12), on the principal artery, is highly rated, and is in fact the oldest place in town. In its gold book of signatures you'll find the names of Thomas Edison, Rudyard Kipling, Ernest Hemingway, John D. Rockefeller, and the former kings of Spain, Portugal, and Romania. Rather large, it offers 100 bedrooms with some form of private plumbing. Singles with shower go for 275F ($37.92). Doubles with private bath cost 400F ($55.16). Each room is different and functional with fully tiled, well-equipped bathroom and coordinated color schemes. All the floors in the public rooms are carpeted. The furnishings have been improved, and you'll notice an occasional antique. In the hotel's main dining room, which has been redecorated, you'll find a set menu beginning at 125F ($17.24). The restaurant is closed on Saturday.

Le Central, 21 rue Berthelot (tel. 47-05-46-44), is a suitable, old-fashioned hotel off the main boulevard, within walking distance of the river and cathedral. It provides adequate and comfortable lodgings at reasonable rates. Set back from the street, the aptly named Central has a front and rear garden with lawns and trees. It is owned and operated by the Tremouilles family. Those twin-bedded with private bath cost 320F ($44.13) for two persons. The doubles or twins with showers are cheaper at 280F ($38.61). The bargains are the bathless doubles with concealed wash basins and bidets, going for 170F ($23.44). There are two salons decorated in the French manner with reproductions of 18th- and 19th-century pieces. An enclosed garage is available.

The Budget Range

Hôtel de Châteaudun, 38 rue et Place de la Préfecture (tel. 47-05-79-94), has only one official star in its crown, but it's a rare find in a bustling city. On a corner of a quiet little square, it is painted white with shutters. The hotel is run by Mrs. Troin, who puts herself entirely at the disposal of her guests, seeing to everyone's comfort. She has worked in both Montréal and London and speaks English fluently. Her small sitting room is filled with hand-carved Chinese furniture. The bedrooms are roomy and modernized, and some contain a shower. A double with shower is 118F ($16.27), going up to 145F ($20) in a twin with shower. Doubles with wash basin and bidet cost 91.50F ($12.62), but 135F ($18.62) if occupied by four persons. The one single room available goes for 61.50F ($8.48). What was once a private dining room is now the room in which Mrs. Troin serves continental breakfasts (not included in the rents).

Hôtel Gambetta, 7 rue Gambetta (tel. 47-05-08-35), in the center of town, is a pleasant hotel, offering plenty of space in its conservatively decorated rooms. The quietest units are those clustered around an interior courtyard. All but a handful of the 39 accommodations contain a private bath. The Tassi family, your hosts, charge from 125F ($17.24) in a single, 275F ($37.92) in a double.

Hôtel Armor, 26 bis Boulevard Heurteloup (tel. 47-05-29-60), isn't the most glamorous hotel in town, but the neutral decor of its four dozen bedrooms provides safe and convenient lodgings in a central location near the train station. Single or double accommodations rent for 120F ($16.55) to 280F ($38.61), depending on the plumbing. A continental breakfast is the only meal served.

WHERE TO DINE: Tours offer choices for dining from the upper bracket to budget:

Upper Bracket Viands

Les Tuffeaux, 19 rue Lavoisier (tel. 47-47-19-89), one of the best restaurants in town, invites diners into its antique interior, rendered softer with yards of pastel fabric, for tastes of the gourmet delicacies that are making chef Michel Devaux well known. Specialties include foie gras of duckling, panache of fish in a delicately flavored stock, filet of sole "en habit" accompanied by a purée of freshwater crayfish, a roulade of rabbit served with cabbage leaves, and a range of desserts of which I can heartily recommend iced nougat with raspberry sauce. In the heart of the old city, the restaurant offers full meals for 275F ($37.92) à la carte. These are served every day except Sunday, Monday, and during parts of January and August. Dinner is offered until 9:30 p.m. only.

Rôtisserie Tourangelle, 23 rue du Commerce (tel. 47-05-71-21). In the heart of the modern commercial district, this pleasant restaurant offers a pleasing combination of specialties concocted from regional ingredients and served with local wines. Jacques Arrayet presents tempting specialties which might feature a filet of sandre with a white sabayon, a terrine of shrimp and sandre in lemon-flavored butter, garlic-roasted pigeon served with thyme-flavored honey, or a twin mix of sole and salmon with a shellfish mousse and "white butter." Dessert might be a splendid concoction of pears and essence of raspberry in flaky pastry. Fixed-price menus cost from 150F ($20.69) and 310F ($42.75), with à la carte dinners going for 280F ($38.61) up. The restaurant is closed Sunday night, all day Monday, for two weeks in March, and between Bastille Day and the beginning of August.

The Middle Range

Les Jardins du Castel, 10 rue Groison (tel. 47-41-94-40), provides a monumental outdoor setting in a large and very old private house ringed with garden statuary and the dappled shadows of a century-old tree. Only a single fixed-priced menu is offered at 150F ($20.69). The choice of each course, however, provides a wide selection of various specialties, the creations of Philippe Manoussas. You might enjoy a compote of duckling with baby vegetables, a gratin of oysters with bacon, or a gâteau of mussels and crayfish with freshly made noodles. À la carte meals cost from 200F ($27.58). No food is served Sunday night, Monday, and in January.

La Poivrière, 13-15 rue du Change (tel. 47-20-85-41), will afford you the chance to dine in a building almost as old as many of the châteaux in the Loire Valley. Constructed in the 15th century, the building has the same massive timbers and beams as many of the other old structures that surround it. Menu items, carefully prepared, include roast pigeon with pearl onions, duckling in puff pastry with garlic, and seafood pot-au-feu. There's a 120F ($16.55) fixed-price meal offered at lunchtime only. You can order à la carte every day except Sunday, Monday, and in August, paying from 250F ($34.48) for a complete meal.

Budget Dining

Relais Buré, 1 Place de la Résistance (tel. 47-05-67-74). There's an elegantly comfortable restaurant one floor above ground level, but many guests never venture beyond the street-level brasserie, where late night pub-style dining is somewhat of an institution in Tours. Upstairs, the more elaborate menu offers such specialties as roast filet of lotte with white wine sauce, Lyon-style calves' liver, or a four-fish terrine. In the more traditional restaurant, fixed-priced menus go for 100F ($13.79) and 120F ($16.55). À la carte meals range from 110F ($15.17) and 165F ($22.75). Downstairs, prices are about 20% less. The establishment, at the edge of the old city, serves meals daily except Monday.

CHÂTEAU-LIVING IN THE OUTSKIRTS: Château de Beaulieu, Joué-les-Tours (tel. 47-53-20-26). Secluded and gracious, this 18th-century country estate 4½ miles southwest of Tours will link you to the lifestyle of another era,

even though it has been completely renovated and is a three-star hotel. You'll be captivated by the formal entrance with its graveled drive encircling a bronze fountain of cherubs and urns of flowers. A double curving stairway leads to the reception hall.

Even if you can't stay here, try at least a visit for a meal; but call in advance, as space is limited. Jean-Pierre Lozay is the owner of the hotel, and he is also an excellent chef de cuisine. He offers two tourists menus, one at 155F ($21.38) and another at 200F ($27.58). His special feature is his menu gastronomique at 320F ($44.13), which includes foie gras frais maison. The specialties of the house are cassolette de petits gris frais à la crème d'ail, filet of sole Beaulieu, and giboulée de cerises.

In the beamed-ceilinged dining room classic French windows open onto views of the gardens, complete with two public swimming pools (from July to September) and four tennis courts. In summer the hotel has a terrace with a large grill where clients can select from the best cuts of meat or fish and watch the chef prepare them to their liking. The terrace overlooks the garden.

There are only 19 bedrooms, with mahogany and chestnut pieces, paneled recessed window, fireplaces, and good plumbing. The cost of the rooms ranges from 350F ($48.27) with shower and from 550F ($75.63) for the deluxe chambers with private baths and toilets. For a minimum stay of three days, half-board rates are offered, ranging from 680F ($93.77) to 900F ($124.11) for two persons daily. Beaulieu is open all year long.

The village of Joué-les-Tours is reached by taking the D86 from Tours and then the D207 for Beaulieu.

3. Montbazon

The Indre River winds its way below. Cows graze in the fields. All is quiet now. Once, however, the sound of battle was heard between the forces of the warring counts of Anjou and Blois. In time Henri III made Montbazon a grand duchy, but the Revolution ended that bit of pomposity.

The ruins of a tenth-century **keep**—built by Foulques Nerra, known as the Black Falcon—can be explored from 9 a.m. to noon and 2:30 to 7 p.m. from March to October. These ruins have been restored by William Dudley (architect) and Lilian Whitteker (painter).

Nearby you can visit **Montlouis-sur-Loire,** where the castle of **La Bourdaisière** has been rebuilt since its destruction. Only the stables are authentically 17th century. Lilian Whitteker, the American painter born in Cincinnati, Ohio, in 1881 retired there. She is known for her paintings of flowers. The Franco-American Foundation displays a permanent exhibit of paintings on the grounds.

LIFE IN THE CHÂTEAUX: Le Chateau d'Artigny, Montbazon (tel. 47-26-24-24), is *très grand.* It was built for the perfume king François Coty, who lived and entertained there lavishly. For example, what is now the wine cellar was once a private cold storage for Madame Coty's furs or those of her guests. In the rotunda ballroom an artist did a ceiling painting of the red-caped tycoon and his wife in white surrounded by their family. The proprietor, Mr. Rabier, will tell you about an unfinished chapel, a pavilion half the size of the one at Versailles, and why the kitchen was installed upstairs. (Monsieur Coty's sense of smell was so acute that he enjoyed only the scent of flowers, and he knew that unpleasant cooking odors ascend.) A favorite room, lined with pink marble, was the one-time pastry room. Nowadays, the former private mansion is operated as a deluxe hotel for guests who want country-estate holidays where they can live in grandeur and total comfort. Everybody—just everybody—checks in, from Henry Ford II to Elizabeth Taylor.

Against this background weekend soirées are popular, as well as musical evenings featuring perhaps a violinist. The dignified drawing room and corridors are furnished classically, with fine antiques, gilt torchères, Louis XV-style chairs, and bronze statuary. In typical château style, there are many acres of private parkland, as well as a large formal garden at the front entrance with a round reflection pool. Set among the trees is a flagstone-edged swimming pool. The bedrooms are furnished in various periods, with a generous use of antiques (much Louis XVI and Directoire). It's preferred that you take the half-board rate, at a cost ranging from 600F ($82.74) to 2,000F ($275.80) per person.

The superb cuisine in the paneled and gilt dining room is one of the major reasons for staying here. The least expensive set menu begins at 220F ($30.34). Ordering à la carte, expect to pay from 400F ($55.16) per person. Wines? You name it. Certainly Chinon and Montlouis. The hotel is closed from December 1 to January 10. On Route N10, it lies less than a mile outside Montbazon.

Domaine de la Tortinière, Montbazon (tel. 47-26-00-19), is a picture-postcard château perched high on a hillside overlooking the Vallée de l'Indre. It was built in the belle époque style in 1861, with high peaked towers, baroque gables and windows, and curving, balustraded exterior staircases leading from the rolling lawns to the ivy-covered terraces. The interior furnishings are modest in comparison with the architecture, although quite adequate. Fourteen rooms and seven apartments are offered. In a double or twin-bedded room, the tariff is 550F ($75.63). These units contain complete bathrooms. Apartments are even more expensive—from 750F ($103.43) for two persons. Some of the rooms are in an ivy-covered, petite Renaissance-style pavilion in the garden between cedar trees.

If you can't stay at the château, perhaps you'll consider a meal in the trellis garden. A set menu costs 210F ($28.96), and you can sample such dishes as stuffed sole served with a creamy crayfish sauce, fried filet of duck with a sweet-and-sour sauce and the fresh fruit of the season, and a filet of beef sauté with a delicate foie-gras-and-pepper sauce, garnished with greens. The "domaine" is open from March to November 15. It lies about one mile off the N10 between Tours and Montbazon.

4. Azay-le-Rideau

Its machicolated towers and blue-slate roof pierced with dormers shimmer in the moat, creating a reflection like one in a Monet painting. Then a white swan glides by, rippling the waters. The defensive medieval look is all for show. The Château of Azay was created as a private residence during the Renaissance. A site was selected at an idyllic spot on the banks of the Indre River, about 13 miles southwest of Tours. A previous château that stood there was in ruins. (In fact, the whole village was known as Azay-le-Brûlé or Azay the Burnt. Passing through with his court in 1418, the dauphin, later Charles VII, was insulted by the Burgundians. A whole garrison was killed for this "outrage," the village and its fortress razed.)

Gilles Berthelot, the finance minister of François I, built the château beginning in 1518. Actually, his big-spending wife, Philippa, supervised its construction. Both of them should have known better. So elegant and harmonious, so imposing was the creation that the Chevalier King grew immensely jealous. In time Berthelot fled, the château reverting to the king. François I didn't live there, however, but started the custom of granting it to "friends of the Crown." After a brief residency by Prince Frederick of Prussia in 1870, the château became the property of the state in 1905.

Before entering you can circle the mansion, enjoying its near-perfect proportions. Many critics consider it the crowning achievement of the French Renaissance in Touraine. Architecturally, its most fancifully ornate feature is a great bay enclosing a grand stairway with a straight flight of steps. The Renaissance interior is a virtual museum.

The largest room at Azay, the Banqueting Hall, is adorned with four 17th-century Flemish tapestries representing scenes from the life of Constantine (it took a craftsperson one year to weave just four square feet). In the kitchen is a collection of utensils, including a wooden mold capable of making 45 different designs on cakes. The corner carvings are most unusual: one, for example, shows a dog biting its own ear. In the dining room is a trio of 16th-century Flemish tapestries. The fireplace is only a plaster molding of a chimneypiece made by Rodin for the Château of Montal. The fireplace masterpiece, however, is in a ground-floor bedroom containing a 16th-century four-poster. Over the stone fireplace hovers a salamander, the symbol of François I.

From the second-floor Royal Chamber, look out at the gardens—the scenery described by Balzac in *The Lily of the Valley*. This bedroom, also called the Green Room, is believed to have sheltered not only François I but Louis XIII and Louis XIV. The adjoining Red Chamber—so named because of its damask —contains a portrait gallery, including a *Lady in Red* (erroneously attributed to Titian) and a scene showing Gabrielle d'Estrées (the favorite of Henri IV) in her bath. An odd 17th-century inlaid cabinet with ivory plates represents *The Woes of War*.

Charging 15F ($2.07) for admission, the château is open every day except Tuesday, from 9 a.m. to noon and 2 to 5 p.m. (closes at 4:30 p.m. off-season). For 25F ($3.45) you can attend a son-et-lumière program there on a summer night at 10 and 11.

A MEDIUM-PRICED INN: The **Hôtel du Grand Monarque**, Place de la République (tel. 44-45-40-08), is an old ivy-covered coaching inn dedicated to providing the best local cuisine, along with clean and attractive rooms and personalized service. But it's more than that, of course. The inn has been in the hands of the same family for several generations. Today Monsieur Serge Jacquet runs everything like clockwork. The guest book tells the story. You'll see everybody from the Duke and Duchess of Kent, the president of Turkey, the Queen Mother of England, and "Harry & Bess" who had a "grand luncheon." Calder liked staying here so much that he contributed a large sketch, which hangs in the glass-covered courtyard.

The patio is the hub of life, with its open staircase leading to the antique-furnished bedrooms. A tamed boar runs loose, the rest of the menagerie consisting of peacocks, hens, dogs, cats, and chinchillas. Naturally, animals belonging to guests are also welcome.

The food is especially good, so it's easy to comply with the requirement that in season guests must take half or full board. For half board, the tariff ranges from 235F ($32.41) to 400F ($55.16) in a single, from 220F ($30.34) to 280F ($38.61) per person in a double. The higher tariffs are for accommodations with private baths. A typical meal might include a gratin of sweetbreads flavored with sherry, followed by a fish course such as braised turbot with salmon caviar. A simple meal here costs about 135F ($18.62), although you can easily spend up to 225F ($31.03) or more. The complete cellar places emphasis on the wines of the region. The restaurant is closed from November 15 to March 1; the hotel is open all year.

5. Luynes

A stark 15th-century castle rises on the banks of the Loire on an ancient Gallo-Roman site. Underneath the mountain the local vineyard owners use the caves as storage warehouses. The château was originally built by the Maillé family, but its name was changed when it was acquired by Charles d'Albert de Luynes, whom the king made a duke in 1619. His descendants still own the château today and have not opened it to the public.

LIVING IN A CHÂTEAU: Domaine de Beauvois, Route de Cleré (tel. 47-55-50-

11). Its position is memorable: set up from the Loire in the midst of its own 380 acres of parkland, including a large pond for fishing and canoeing plus a swimming pool. Dating from the 15th century, the hotel reflects the simple, classic château architecture, with its central tower, formal entrance, and a terraced reflection pool. You can climb the tower for a view of the "domaine," taking in the bridle paths and the tennis courts. The drawing room contains a marble fireplace, a chandelier of iron and colored glass, and three tall windows opening onto the reflection pool. The furnishings are eclectic, utilizing antiques, upholstered pieces, and fabric-covered walls.

Depending on one's mood, there are four places at which to dine—an opulent Louis XV room, a rustic Louis XIII room, and the more primitive 15th-century tower room with a stone fireplace. One wing contains a large dining room that can cater up to 100 persons. Typical of the cuisine are crayfish fricassée in Vouvray wine, beuchelle à la Tourangelle (ragoût of kidneys and sweetbread), and Calvados soufflé. If you want to visit for a meal, a set lunch is featured for 140F ($19.31) or a gourmet repast for 320F ($44.13) with a choice of dishes. Dining à la carte is at a price ranging from 340F ($46.89) to 450F ($62.06).

The bedrooms are individually decorated in a highly stylized fashion, with matching fabric on the walls coordinated with the draperies and upholstery. Skillfully made reproductions are mixed discreetly with antiques. Room 12 is on a grand-opera scale, with a ten-foot fireplace and an armoire, and Room 26 has overscale pink hydrangea wallpaper, the same motif reflected in the draperies and bedcover.

Reservations are accepted, but only if a prior deposit has been sent. A double room costs 500F ($68.95) to 1,100F ($151.69), and even more expensive suites are offered. You can also stay at La Closerie, an annex of the château. Half-board terms are obligatory in season, costing 750F ($103.43) to 1,800F ($248.22). Service and taxes are included in all the tariffs. The château, closed from mid-January to mid-March, is 6½ miles from Tours, 2 miles from Luynes, lying off the D49.

6. Villandry

The 16th-century-style gardens of this medieval and Renaissance château are celebrated throughout the Touraine. Forming a trio of superimposed "cloisters," with a water garden on the highest level, they were planned by Dr. Carvallo, founder of La Demeure Historique. The grounds contain 10½ miles of boxwood sculpture, which the gardeners must cut to style in only two weeks in September. Every square of the gardens seems like a mosaic. The borders represent the many faces of love: tender, tragic (with daggers), or crazy, the latter evoked by a labyrinth in the middle that doesn't get you anywhere. Pink tulips and dahlias suggest sweet love; red, tragic; and yellow, unfaithful. Crazy love is symbolized by the use of all colors. The vine arbors, citrus hedges, shady walks —all this keeps six men busy full time. One garden contains all the common French vegetables except the potato, which wasn't known in France in the 16th century (even as late as 1771 the potato was considered "unfit for human consumption," until its virtues were extolled by Parmentier).

You can visit the gardens alone, arriving finally at a terrace from which you can see not only the gardens but a view of the small village and the 12th-century church of Villandry. If you want to visit the château, you'll need a guide. He'll point out the Spanish paintings in the salons, the furnishings in the dining room and gallery. In addition, you'll see an unusual Moorish ceiling with scallop shells. After that, the guide goes with you onto the terrace and explains the symbolical and historical gardens.

Originally a feudal castle stood at Villandry, but in 1532 Jean Lebreton, the chancellor of François I, built the present château, its buildings forming a U surrounded by a two-sided moat. It costs 20F ($2.76) to visit the gardens and go on a guided tour of the château. The château is open only from mid-March to mid-November. The gardens, which can be visited without a guide for 15F ($2.07), are open from 9 a.m. to sunset. Guided tours of the château leave from 9 a.m. to 6:30 p.m. (until 5:30 p.m. off-season). Villandry is 20 miles from Chinon, 11 from Tours, and 5 from Azay-le-Rideau.

FOOD AND LODGING: Le Cheval Rouge (tel. 47-50-02-07), has the best cuisine in town, served with a polite dignity and all the usual flourishes. Specialties include grilled trout with white wine, grilled steak, terrine of foie gras, breast of duckling with morels, many seasonal game dishes, and other traditional favorites, all prepared with flavor and zest. The establishment stands practically in the shadow of the château. The fixed-price meal for 125F ($17.24) represents good value. A la carte meals cost 300F ($41.37) and up. The Dudit family closes its restaurant on Monday in April, May, September, and October, shutting down entirely from November to March. There are some 20 simply furnished bedrooms on the premises, if you'd like to spend the night here. They're priced at 192F ($26.48) in a single, rising to 280F ($38.61) in a double.

7. Loches

Forever linked to the memory of that legendary beauty Agnès Sorel, Loches is the *cité médiévale* of the château country. In the hills on the banks of the Indre River, it is called the city of kings. Known as the acropolis of the Loire, the château and its satellite buildings form a complex called the **Cité Royale.** The House of Anjou, from which the Plantagenets descended, owned the castle from 886 to 1205. The kings of France occupied it from the mid-13th century until the days of Charles IX, the son of Catherine de Medici, who was king from 1560.

The château today is mainly remembered for *la belle des belles* (the beauty of beauties), Agnès Sorel. After much wandering (including a time in Paris) and much abuse, her tomb rests inside the castle today, her velvet cushion guarded by two angels, her feet resting on two rams. In 1777 her tomb was opened, the coffin revealing a set of dentures and some locks of hair, all that remained from what was considered the most dazzling beauty of the 15th century. She had been the maid of honor to Isabelle de Lorraine, but was singled out by the dauphin (Charles VII) for his "favors." She was to have great influence over the king until the day of her mysterious death. Mlle Sorel was the first of a long line of royal mistresses living ostentatiously along with the kings at court. Her successors would be women such as Diane de Poitiers and Madame de Pompadour. The future king, Louis XI, wasn't captivated by Mlle Sorel; he once slapped her in the face and chased her at sword point. Fouquet painted her as the Virgin—one of her breasts completely exposed—but it was a posthumous portrait, its likeness to the actual mistress unknown (the masterpiece is now owned by Antwerp).

The château also contains the oratory of Anne of Brittany, decorated with sculptured ermine tails. One of its most outstanding treasures is a triptych of *The Passion* from the Fouquet School, dating from 1485. Charging 10F ($1.38) for admission, the château is open from 9 a.m. to noon and 2 till 6 p.m. in summer. It closes at 5 p.m. from the first of October until mid-March. However, it is open throughout the day in July and August. The château is closed Wednesday during the off-season and in December and January.

The ancient **keep** *(donjon)* of the Counts d'Anjou can also be visited. The Round Tower of Louis XI contains rooms formerly used for torture. A favorite method of tormenting the victim was to suspend him in an iron cage. The Cardinal Balue was held that way for more than ten years. In the 15th century in the

Martelet, the Duke of Milan, Ludovico Sforza (Ludvico il Moro), its most famous prisoner, painted frescoes on the walls to pass the time. He died at Loches in 1508. The keep (you're admitted with your château ticket) is open from 9:30 a.m. to 12:30 p.m. and from 2:30 to 6:30 p.m. (in winter till 5:30 p.m.). The château and the keep are open between noon and 2 p.m. in July and August. The keep is closed on Thursday in the off-season and in December and January. If visited separately, admission is 10F ($1.38).

Nearby the **Collegiate Church of St. Ours** spans the 10th to the 15th centuries and is an interesting example of Romanesque architecture. The portal is richly decorated with sculptured figures, unfortunately damaged by time and renovations but still attractive. Monumental stone pyramids *(dubes)* surmount the nave. The west door reflects exceptional carving.

Finally, you may want to walk the **ramparts**, enjoying the view of the town, including a 15th-century gate and Renaissance inns.

Loches lies 25 miles southeast of Tours.

FOOD AND LODGING: **Grand Hôtel de France,** 6 rue Picois (tel. 47-59-00-32), is charmingly French, with an inner courtyard where you can dine under parasols. Many of its bedrooms overlook this green domestic scene. There is a petite dining room with soft paneling, crystal, bowls of flowers, and crisscross white-organdy curtains—a welcoming atmosphere. Three set meals are offered, the lowest just 58F ($8); the next, a 70F ($9.65) meal with six courses; and the most expensive, a 95F ($13.10) repast featuring four of the chef's specialties. No food is served Sunday night and Monday at lunchtime from September to the end of June. The restaurant is also closed on Friday night from October to Easter. The hotel is closed for the month from January 15 to February 15. The accommodations are cheap for the area: from 65F ($8.97) to 170F ($23.44) in double rooms with complete bath. Singles begin at 75F ($10.32). Many rooms open onto a courtyard with vine-covered balconies. English is spoken.

Hôtel du Château, 18 rue du Château (tel. 47-59-07-35), is a simple 15th-century inn with a plain façade on a hillside street, just below the medieval town. The house is U-shaped, with a little courtyard and terrace for breakfasting containing a wide pergola of honeysuckle and yellow roses. A circular stone staircase leads to the rooms. The bedrooms are modernized, often with tiled bath and provincial reproductions of antiques. Armoires are substituted for closets. Some rooms are tiny; others are large enough for three. For the better doubles with private bath, the rate is 230F ($31.72) nightly. The bathless singles cost 95F ($13.10). Breakfast under the pergola is included in the room rates. The best feature for last: Madam Robin, the innkeeper, is as natural as homemade bread with stone-ground flour. The hôtel is closed from December 1 to April 1.

Luccotel, rue de Lézards (tel. 47-91-50-50), is a quiet and comfortable hotel on a hill overlooking Loches and the château. It is surrounded by a 2½-acre park. The establishment has 42 rooms, all with bath, toilet, direct-dial phone, TV, and automatic alarm clock. Two of the rooms are suitable for the handicapped. Doubles rent for 180F ($24.82) to 250F ($34.48). The hotel has an excellent restaurant, Le Lézard, which offers a youthful and inventive cuisine in both set and à la carte menus, costing from 75F ($10.32) to 175F ($24.13). A bar and TV lounge invite guests to relax.

George Sand, 39 rue Quintefol (tel. 47-59-39-74), is a tastefully redecorated inner-village inn that dates from the 17th century. Loaded with rustic accoutrements, in a convenient location a few steps from the base of the château, the inn was completely renovated in 1982, when a modern bath was added to each of its 17 bedrooms. Units cost 150F ($20.69) in a single and 320F ($44.13) in a double. The in-house restaurant has a terrace overlooking the Indre, and several of the bedrooms (the quieter ones are in the rear) look over one of the river's tributaries. Monsieur and Madame Fortin, the owners, offer one fixed-price meal for 65F ($8.97) and another for 160F ($22.06). Specialties include a fondue of goat with a confit of leeks, filet of sandre (a river fish) in white butter, and breast of duck George Sand. The hotel is open all year.

8. Amboise

On the banks of the Loire, Amboise is in the center of vineyards known as Touraine-Amboise. Leonardo da Vinci spent his last years in this ancient city. Dominating the town is the **Château of Amboise** (tel. 47-57-00-98), the first in France to reflect the impact of the Italian Renaissance.

A combination of both Gothic and Renaissance, this 15th-century château is mainly associated with Charles VIII, who built it on a rocky spur separating the valleys of the Loire and the Amasse. The only son of Louis XI of France and Charlotte of Savoy, the future Charles VIII was born at Amboise on June 30, 1470. At the age of 25, he returned to France after his Italian campaign. With him he brought artists, designers, and architects from "that land of enchantment." In a sense, he was bringing the Italian Renaissance to France. His workers built the *logis du roi,* the apartments of the king, its façade pierced by large double-mullioned windows and crowned by towering dormers and sculptured canopies. Charles VIII died at Amboise on April 8, 1498, after an accident: he banged his head against the wall. The blow didn't kill him until after he'd witnessed a fête planned that day for his entertainment. At the end of the terrace, near the room of his queen, Anne of Brittany, is a low doorway where it is said the mishap took place.

Later Louise of Savoy and her children lived at Amboise. One of her offspring in 1515 became King François I; the other was Margaret of Navarre. François continued to live at Amboise, making considerable additions to the castle. The château enjoyed its golden hours under the Chevalier King, as he sponsored a number of brilliant festivals, including some that featured contests between wild animals. The most memorable event was the arrival of Charles V in 1539. Preceded by torchbearers, the emperor grandly began to climb up one of the ramps, but a torch ignited a banner in the fabric-draped tower and he was nearly burned alive.

The skyline of Amboise is characterized by two squat towers, the Hurtault and the Minimes, which contain ramps of huge dimensions so that cavaliers on horseback or nobles in horse-drawn chariots could ascend them.

The name Amboise became linked in 1560 with a series of some of the most savage executions in France—executions that followed the Amboise Conspiracy, a Huguenot plot led by a La Renaudie of Brittany. Its aim was to remove François II from the influence of the House of Guise. Decapitations and mass hangings followed, much to the after-dinner amusement of the young François II and his queen, Mary Stuart (later Mary, Queen of Scots). During the 19th century much of Amboise was destroyed, and it was only partially restored later.

You visit first the flamboyant Gothic Chapel of St. Hubert, built on the ramparts in the late 15th century and distinguished by its lace-like tracery. It allegedly contains the remains of da Vinci. Actually the great artist was buried in the castle's Collegiate Church, which was destroyed between 1806 and 1810. During the Second Empire excavations were undertaken on the site of the church, and bones discovered were "identified" as those of Leonardo.

Today the walls of the château are hung with tapestries, the rooms furnished in the style of the époque. From the terraces are panoramic views of the town and of the Loire Valley. The château may be visited daily from 9 a.m. to noon and 2 to 6:30 p.m. (till sunset in winter). Admission is 16F ($2.21) for adults and 8.50F ($1.17) for children 7 to 15 years of age.

Finally, you might visit **Clos-Lucé** (tel. 47-57-62-88), a 15th-century manor house of brick and stone. In what had been an oratory for Anne of Brittany, François I installed "the great master in all forms of art and science," Leonardo da Vinci. Loved and venerated by the Chevalier King, da Vinci lived there for three years, dying at the manor in 1519. (Incidentally, those death-bed paintings depicting Leonardo in the arms of François I are probably symbolic; the king was supposedly out of town when the artist died.) From the window of his bedroom Leonardo liked to look out at the château where François lived. Whenever he was restless, the king would visit Leonardo via an underground tunnel, discovered recently by the Beaux-Arts. Nine days before his death, the artist made a will leaving untold riches of books, drawings, and instruments to his "beloved pupil and faithful companion" Francescoda Metzi. You can visit what is believed to have been the kitchen—the domain of the faithful servant Mathurine, mentioned by da Vinci in his will, to whom he left his cloak of "good black cloth, trimmed with leather."

Inside, the rooms are well furnished, some containing reproductions from the period of the artist. The lower level is reserved for da Vinci's designs, models, and inventions, including his plans for a turbine engine, an airplane, and a parachute. Clos-Lucé is open daily from 9 a.m. to noon and 2 to 6:30 p.m. From the first of June until the end of August it takes no lunch break. Admission is 23F ($3.17), although students pay only 16F ($2.21). There are tours in English.

GETTING THERE: Amboise is 15½ miles from Tours, 22 miles from Blois. In summer, regular bus service connects Amboise with such centers as Tours, Blois, and Chenonceaux.

CHÂTEAU LIVING: The **Château de Pray,** Route de Chargé D751 (tel. 47-57-23-67), provides a genuine introduction to the better half of French life at moderate prices. It is rooted in French history, tracing its origins to Geoffroy de Pray in 1244. Since 1955, however, it has belonged to the Farard family, who have turned it into a paying proposition.

The castle, on a hillside overlooking the Loire, rivals those on the Rhine. It is of a simple but classic design, with tall twin towers on either side and an elaborately formal garden. Antlers and other such hunting trophies hang in the entry hall. The small drawing room is paneled, with a fireplace, fine antiques, old oil paintings, and an adjoining terrace where guests gather for drinks. The best bargain is half board, costing from 350F ($48.27) to 550F ($75.63) per person. As only 16 rooms are available, reservations are imperative. Most Americans like no. 16 the best. Called "Sorbiers," it contains a fine antique four-poster bed with twisted columns, as well as a tiled private bath.

The family has engaged a chef whose meals make dining a pleasure and a treat. He offers 142F ($19.58) to 180F ($24.82) menus, the latter including a fish course. A typical dinner would start with a selection of hors d'oeuvres, follow with grilled Loire salmon with beurre blanc, then roast guinea hen, a fresh salad, a selection of cheese, and a homemade pastry. Excellent Loire wines are available. The dining room has a classic ceiling-high, sloped fireplace where logs burn slowly on nippy nights. The chairs are provincial fruitwood, the dishes and linen are patterned, and most important, the leaded-glass windows open toward the river. Closed from January till February 10.

A MEDIUM-PRICED HOTEL: Novotel, 17 rue des Sablonnieres (tel. 47-57-42-07). Beyond the waters of this modern hotel's swimming pool, you can spot parts of the Loire valley below, as well as a distant château. The more than 80 well-furnished bedrooms contain phone, radio, and private bath, costing from 300F ($41.37) to 350F ($48.27), either single or double occupancy. The format which has proved successful in other members of this nationwide chain works

well here too. Facilities include a good restaurant and tennis courts on the prem
ises.

BUDGET INNS: **Lion d'Or** (Golden Lion), 17 Quai Charles-Guinot (tel. 47-57-
00-23), is a leading hostelry of Amboise. Bearing the stamp of a manor, it has
steep slate roofs and wide windows providing a view of the Loire. The lounges
are less important here, as the emphasis is on the high-ceilinged dining room
with its river view. The owners, Mr. and Mrs. Willieme, run the hotel, and the
cook, Christophe Constantin, reigns in the kitchen. The half-board rate ranges
from 225F ($31.03) to 275F ($37.92) per person. In the dining room, you can
choose one of two different meals, the lower priced at 120F ($16.55), the other
at 185F ($25.51). The 185F meal begins with assiette confite du Val de Loire,
followed by dentelle de Saumon à la ciboulette and pailleté du Chinon, then
épaule d'agneau (lamb) farci and salad, cheese, and, as dessert, fleur de sorbet
au coulis de framboise (raspberries). Specialties include foie gras frais de canard
(duck), coquilles St-Jacques aux endives, médaillon de veau aux champignons,
and sabayon de pêches au champagne. Ordering à la carte will cost about 185F
($25.51) to 275F ($37.92) per person. Closed November 2 to March 15.
    Belle-Vue, 12 Quai Charles-Guinot (tel. 47-57-02-26), is an efficient inn
right at the bridge crossing the Loire. Its façade is uninspired, with lots of functional additions and modernizations, and its interior lounges are very simple.
However, the Belle-Vue does open onto a garden area, which is not only beautiful but restful. Parasol tables are set out on various flagstone terraces around a
free-form swimming pool. A single rents for 150F ($20.69) and a double goes for
230F ($31.72). All rooms are furnished in a modern, convenient style. The hotel
is closed from mid-November to mid-December and in January. It closes Sunday night off-season. The hotel's river-view restaurant, Le Monseigneur, offers
a set menu at 125F ($17.24) weekdays.

THE LEADING RESTAURANT: The **Auberge du Mail,** 32 Quai Général-de-
Gaulle (tel. 47-57-60-39), is a little riverfront restaurant outside the town on the
road to Tours. In the opinion of many discriminating diners, it serves the finest
food in Amboise, even if it is more unpretentious than some of the other establishments. You can park your car across the street under the shade trees, where
a gypsy family is likely to solicit you.
    At the auberge, you can select a table in the inner garden, where you'll find
both the reception area and a pleasant drawing room arranged around an ornamental pond. Then you must decide which of François Le Coz's set menus you
wish to sample. Each one offers tasty fare. The cheapest menu costs 125F
($17.24) and the menu gastronomique goes for 200F ($27.58). Some of the
chef's specialties appear on these menus, but you can order à la carte as well,
paying around 175F ($24.13) to 225F ($31.03), depending on the specialties you
select. The dish that seems to earn the most praise is the filet de chevreuil sauce
grand veneur (roebuck with a currant sauce). If you're very hungry, you might
want to precede the course with the chef's celestines de fruits de mer or the foie
confit au Vouvray. The latter is very much like goose liver, except it isn't (its
ingredients remain a secret of the chef). A simple bottle of Loire wine comple-
ments most meals. The restaurant is open from April 1 to November but closed
on Tuesday night. It also rents out 14 simply furnished rooms, with singles costing from 100F ($13.79); doubles go for 275F ($37.92).

9. Blois

    A wound in battle had earned him the name "Balafré" (Scarface), but he
was quite a ladies' man nonetheless. In fact, on that cold misty morning of De-

cember 23, 1588, the Duke of Guise had just left a warm bed and the arms of one of Catherine de Medici's lovely "flying squadron" girls. His archrival, Henri III, had summoned him. As he made his way to the king's chambers, perhaps he was dreaming of the day when the effeminate little monarch would be overthrown and he, the champion of the Catholics, would become ruler of France.

The king's minions were about. Nothing unusual—Henri was always surrounded with attractive young men these days. Then it happened. The guards moved menacingly toward him with daggers. Wounded, the duke was still strong enough to knock a few down. He made his way toward the door, where more guards awaited him. Staggering back, he fell to the floor in a pool of his own blood. Only then did Henri emerge from behind the curtains. "My God," he is reputed to have exclaimed, "he's taller dead than alive!" The body couldn't be shown: the duke was too popular. Quartered, it was burned in a fireplace in the château. Then Henri's mother, Catherine de Medici, had to be told the "good news."

The murder of the Duke of Guise—one of the most famous assassinations in French history—is only one of the memories of this château, which was begun in the 13th century by the counts of Blois. Charles d'Orléans (son of Louis d'Orléans, assassinated by the Burgundians in 1407), the "poet prince," lived at Blois after his release from 25 years of English captivity. He had married Mary of Cleves and had brought a "court of letters" to Blois. In his 70s, Charles became the father of the future Louis XII, who was to marry Anne of Brittany. Blois was launched in its new role as a royal château. In time it was to be called the second capital of France, and Blois the city of kings. However, Blois became a palace of banishment. Louis XIII for a time got rid of his interfering mother, Marie de Medici, by sending her there; but this plump matron escaped by sliding into the moat on a coat down a mound of dirt left by the builders. Then in 1626 the king sent his conspiring brother, Gaston d'Orléans, there. He stayed.

If you stand in the courtyard of the great château, you'll find it's like an illustrated storybook of French architecture. The Hall of the Estates-General is a beautiful work from the 13th century; the so-called gallery of Charles d'Orléans was actually built by Louis XII in 1498–1501, as was the Louis XII wing. The François I wing is a masterpiece of the French Renaissance; the Gaston d'Orléans wing was built by François Mansart between 1635 and 1637. Of them all, the most remarkable is the François I wing, containing a spiral staircase, with elaborately ornamented balustrades and the king's symbol, the salamander. In the Louis XII wing, seek out paintings by Antoine Caron, court painter to Henri III, depicting the persecution of Thomas More.

Restoration of the interior is continuing, but the royal emblems were destroyed during the Revolution. Note the paneling behind which many people placed secrets, perhaps Catherine de Medici her poisons. The room where the Estates-General met in 1588 is the oldest part of the château, nowadays containing tapestries from the 17th century, some based on cartoons by Rubens, others in the Renaissance style illustrating scenes from the life of Marc Antony.

From March 15 to October 1, the château (tel. 54-74-16-06) is open daily from 9 a.m. to noon and 2 to 6:30 p.m.; from October 1 to March 14, to 5 p.m. From the end of March until mid-April and from June 1 to August 31, it is open without interruption. Admission is 15F ($2.07). A son-et-lumière program is presented in summer at a cost of 20F ($2.76).

GETTING THERE: Usually visited in conjunction with nearby Chambord, Blois lies 35 miles from Orléans, 37 miles from Tours. On the right bank of the Loire, it is the center of the château district. (In 1429 Joan of Arc launched her expeditionary forces from here to oust the English from Orléans.)

FOOD AND LODGING: Hostellerie de la Loire, 8 rue de Lattre-de-Tassigny (tel.

54-74-26-60), is an inn where you can get not only rooms but well-prepared meals. In fact, it's generally conceded that the Loire serves some of the finest food in Blois. The hotel is on a *very* busy street, facing the river. The area is frequented by the motorcycle set at night, and many readers have complained that they got no sleep in the front rooms. Request, if available, a chamber in back. There are 17 rooms in all, a few with private bath renting for 160F ($22.06) for a single, 250F ($34.48) for a double with bath and toilet. A single without bath costs 85F ($11.72). The rooms are basic, but sufficiently comfortable for an overnight stopover.

In the dining room, you're offered meals at various prices. The 100F ($13.79) tourist menu is always generous, and you're not made to feel a criminal for requesting it. A more elaborate meal is featured for 230F ($31.72). Closed from mid-January till mid-February and Sunday all year.

La Péniche, Promenade du Mail (tel. 54-74-37-23). You'll have the chance to experience the waters of the Loire close up as you dine inside this floating barge tied up to one of the right bank's inner-city quays. Painted a dusty rose, the vessel is the domain of Germain Bosque, who will emerge from the kitchens at frequent intervals to inquire about the well-being of his guests. Fish is a specialty. I recommend the paupiette of sandre with salmon mousse, or perhaps you'd prefer a ragoût of snails with cèpes (flap mushrooms). À la carte dinners range from 225F ($31.03) to 260F ($35.85), while a set menu is offered for 140F ($19.31). Open every day, the restaurant serves dinner until 9:30 p.m.

L'Espérance, 189 Quai Ulysse-Besnard (tel. 54-78-09-01), lies about 1¼ miles away on the N152 in the direction of Tours. Dining here is like stepping back a half century into the most traditional ambience to be found in Blois. Monsieur Dutheuil, the owner, skillfully directs an efficient and flavorful kitchen and organizes the team of family-related waitresses who serve you within a sweeping view of the Loire and the hills around it. Menu items include such richly conservative dishes as truffled omelets, tournedos Rossini, la lotte en cocotte, a juicy chicken with morels, a full range of game terrines and pâtés, and crisp roast duckling. À la carte meals cost 300F ($41.37), while set meals range from 130F ($17.93) to 190F ($26.20). The establishment is closed Sunday night, all day Monday, and part of February.

St-Jacques, Place de la Gare (tel. 54-78-04-15), is a little hotel right opposite the railway station. It offers 33 bedrooms with either shower only or shower and toilet. Singles cost 105F ($14.48), with the most expensive doubles peaking at 175F ($24.13). A continental breakfast is the only meal served. St-Jacques is open all year.

Anne de Bretagne, 31 Avenue J-Laigret (tel. 54-78-05-38), is a simple inn a two-minute walk from the railway station, tucked away on a small plaza. It has a gabled front and a pair of large vines of red roses meeting to form an arch. Little red-and-white tables are set out invitingly. The proprietor has been putting up guests from all over the world, and on her desk rests a stack of letters requesting space awaiting an answer. Her inn is scrubbed and waxed clean—no fussiness, no frills, but good value for your money. There's central heating in the nippy months. Doubles with private bath or shower are tabbed at 270F ($37.23). Bathless singles rent for 105F ($14.48). The inn is closed the last two weeks in February.

10. Chaumont

On that long-ago morning when Diane de Poitiers crossed the drawbridge, the château of Chaumont looked grim. Its battlements, its pepper-pot turrets crowning the towers—the whole effect resembled a prison. Henri II, her lover, had died. The king had given her Chenonceaux, which she loved, but Catherine de Medici in her widow's weeds had banished her from her favorite château and shipped her off to Chaumont. Inside, portraits reveal the king's mistress to have truly lived up to her reputation as forever beautiful. Another portrait—that of Catherine de Medici, wife of Henri II, looking like a devout nun—invites unfavorable comparison.

Chaumont (Burning Mount) was built during the reign of Louis XII by Charles d'Amboise. Looking down at the Loire, it is approached by a long walk up from the village through a tree-studded park. The original fortress had been dismantled by Louis XI. In 1560 it was acquired by Catherine de Medici. At one time Madame de Staël, banished from Paris by Napoleon, resided there. Chaumont was privately owned and inhabited until it was acquired by the state in 1938.

Architecturally, the castle spans the intermediate period between the Middle Ages and the Renaissance. Inside, the prize exhibit is a rare collection of medallions by Nini, an Italian artist. A guest of the château for a while, he made medallion portraits of kings, queens, nobles, even Benjamin Franklin who once visited Chaumont.

In the bedroom occupied by Catherine de Medici is a portrait of a witty-looking cardinal who wanted to become the pope (he bears a striking resemblance to Vincent Price). There is also a rare portrait of Catherine, painted when she was young, wearing many jewels, including a ruby later owned by Mary, Queen of Scots. Catherine was superstitious, always keeping her astrologer, Cosimo Ruggieri, at her beck and call. She had him housed in one of the tower bedrooms (a portrait of him remains). It is reported that he foretold the disasters awaiting her sons, including Henri III. In the astrologer's bedroom is a most unusual tapestry depicting Medusa with a flying horse escaping from her head.

From April 1 to September 30 the château (tel. 25-46-98-03) is open from 9 to 11:30 a.m. and 2 to 6 p.m. In the off-season it is open from 9:30 to 11:45 a.m. and 1:45 to 5:45 p.m. Admission to both the château and the stables is 14F ($1.93), the fee lowered to half fare on Sunday and public holidays. It is closed on Tuesday.

FOOD AND LODGING: **Maphôtel Terminus Reine,** Place Général-de-Gaulle (tel. 25-03-66-66), stands right in the heart of town, across from the train station. It's one of the best places to stay within Chaumont, although its accommodations are very simple. Nevertheless, the rooms have been renovated and are well kept. In all, 63 units are rented at a cost of 135F ($18.62) in a single, rising to 320F ($44.13) in a double. The restaurant also serves good food, offering generously portioned meals costing from 100F ($13.79) to 225F ($31.03). The less expensive meal is exceptionally good, and you needn't pay the extra money for the more lavish spread. The restaurant doesn't serve meals on Sunday night from November 1 to Easter. A basement pizzeria offers meals even less expensive until midnight.

11. Chambord

When François I, the Chevalier King, used to say, "Come on up to my place," he meant Chambord, not Fontainebleau or Blois. Construction workers, some 2,000 strong, began to piece together "the pile" in 1519. What emerged after 20 years was the pinnacle of the French Renaissance, the largest château in the Loire Valley. It was ready for the visit of Charles V of Germany, who was welcomed by nymphets in transparent veils gently tossing wildflowers —fresh from the encircling forest of Sologne—in the emperor's path.

In the years that ensued, French monarchs—Henri II and Catherine de Medici, Louis XIII, Henri II—came and went from Chambord, but not one of them developed the affection for it held by François I. The brother of Louis XIII, Gaston d'Orléans, restored the château in part. His daughter, "La Grande Mademoiselle" (Mlle de Montpensier), related in her writings that she used to force her father to run up and down Chambord's famous double spiral staircase after her. Because of its curious structure, he never caught her.

Louis XIV made nine visits there. Molière's *Monsieur de Pourceaugnac* was performed at Chambord for the Sun King. According to a much-repeated theatrical legend, the playwright saved the play by leaping into the orchestra pit, eliciting a hearty roar from the up-to-then stony-faced king. Molière also previewed *Le Bourgeois Gentilhomme* there.

Driven from the throne of Poland, Stanislas Leczinski, the father-in-law of Louis XV, took up residence in 1725, spending eight years at Chambord. Perhaps its most colorful resident, however, was Maurice Saxe, the marshal of France in 1743 and an illegitimate son of Augustus II of Saxony. To Chambord he imported cavalrymen from the West Indies. Ruling with an iron fist (even invoking the death penalty), he apparently applied the standard of brutality to his mistress, Madame Favart. Falling into decay, the château became—at the lowest point in its history—a munitions factory. The state acquired Chambord in 1932.

The château is set in a park of more than 13,000 acres, enclosed within a wall stretching some 20 miles. Looking out one of the windows from one of the 440 rooms, François I is said to have carved on a pane, with a diamond ring, these words: "A woman is a creature of change; to trust her is to play the fool." On seeing the estate, Chateaubriand said Chambord was like "a lady whose hair has been blown by the wind." Its façade is characterized by four monumental towers. The keep contains a spectacular terrace, which the ladies of the court used to stand on to watch the return of their men from the hunt. From that platform you can inspect the dormer windows and the richly decorated chimneys, some characterized by winged horses.

The three-story keep also encloses the already-mentioned corkscrew staircase—superimposed so that one person may descend at one end and another ascend at the other without ever meeting. The apartments of Louis XIV, including his redecorated bedchamber, are also in the keep. A trio of rooms was restored by the government, but not with the original furnishings, of course.

Hours are 9:30 a.m. to noon and 2 to 5 p.m. from January through March and from the first of November through December; from April 1 to the end of September and July until the end of August, visits are possible from 9:30 a.m. to 5 p.m. Admission is 20F ($2.76) in summer, 9F ($1.24) in winter.

A CONVERTED MANOR (BUDGET LIVING): Hôtel du Grand-St-Michel, 103 Place Saint-Michel (tel. 54-20-31-31) is a manor house turned hotel, occupying an enviable position opposite the entrance to Chambord. The front bedrooms, of course, overlook the château, especially handsome when illuminated in the evening. The character of St-Michel is that of a country inn geared to overnight visitors—so don't expect personalized service. The decor is provincial. In summer, meals are served on the terrace under an awning.

The rooms are plain, but well kept and comfortable. A double with private bath rents for 295F ($40.68), but many satisfactory doubles with a minimum of plumbing, such as water basins and bidets, are in the 130F ($17.93) range. There is only one set menu, at 95F ($13.10), which at last inspection offered a lot of the chef's specialties, including civet de marcassin and quenelles de brochet. In season a large choice of game is offered. Expect to pay 170F ($23.44) for the set meal on Sunday, which is more elaborate. Closed from mid-November to December 20. In the off-season the restaurant does not serve on Monday night or Tuesday.

12. Beaugency

The heart of this ancient Loire Valley town is an archeological garden called the **City of the Lords,** named after the counts who enjoyed great power in the Middle Ages. A major event in the history of medieval Europe took place there: the marriage of Eleanor of Aquitaine and Louis VII was dissolved in 1152. These two monarchs had fallen into a bitter dispute during the Second Crusade, and attempts at a reconciliation had failed. The tempestuous Eleanor sought a divorce on the grounds of consanguinity—that is, they were cousins in the fourth degree, such relatives being forbidden to marry according to the rules of the day. This remarkable woman later became queen consort of Henry II of England, bringing southwestern France as her dowry. She was also, of course, the mother of Richard the Lion-Hearted. At a much later date, in 1429, Joan of Arc rid Beaugency of the English.

On the right bank of the Loire, the town boasts a bridge dating from the 14th century. It's unusual in that each of its 26 arches is in a different style.

The 15th-century **Château Dumois,** floodlit at night, contains a folklore museum of the Orléans district. At the Place Dumois, the collection consists of hairpieces, costumes, waistcoats, and antique furnishings, displayed in various salons. For 8F ($1.10) admission, the château may be visited daily except Wednesday, from 9 to 11:30 a.m. and 2 to 6 p.m. (till 4 p.m. in winter). A son-et-lumière program is staged from mid-May to August 30.

Near the château is **St. George's Vault,** a gate of the former castle of the Lords of Beaugency, which opened from the fortress onto the Rû Valley and the lower part of town.

The **Church of Notre-Dame** would have been a good example of Romanesque art of the 12th century if the Gothic hadn't intruded. Originally it was attached to a Benedictine abbey. Nearby is **St. Firmin's Tower,** all that remains of an old church that once stood on the Place St-Firmin. A trio of bells is sheltered in this tower, whose spire rises to a height of 180 feet. From the structure a magnificent view of the river valley unfolds before you. In the archeological garden, the **Hôtel-Dieu** (the old hospital) is one of the oldest buildings in Beaugency, having been erected in the 11th century, its roofing edge in the Romanesque style. **St. Étienne's Church,** built in the 11th century, is one of the oldest churches of France, and **Cesar's Tower** is a good example of 11th-century military art.

FOOD AND LODGING: **Hostellerie de l'Écu de Bretagne,** Place du Martroi (tel. 38-44-67-60), is an oldish, low, sprawling coaching inn, set on a quiet square. There are café tables outside for enjoying beverages, plus an inner courtyard for cars (here horse-drawn coaches used to bring travelers from Paris). You feel the presence of the attentive and proud proprietor, Guy Conan, who keeps his keen eye on the kitchen and dining room. Have a predinner drink in the country tavern, with its provincial tables and Breton carved paneling. Dining in the modernized restaurant is the real reason for staying here. There are three set meals, 90F ($12.41), 110F ($15.17), and 140F ($19.31), the last one being for the gastronomique. Note that the menu is divided into classic and regional dishes. On the à la carte menu, try the lentilles en salade or cul de lapereau (young rabbit) au miel (honey). Especially recommendable is noisette of pork with prunes. Home-made fruit tarts are invariably good.

In regard to rooms, a bathless double goes for 110F ($15.17); doubles with bath range from 220F ($30.34) to 270F ($37.23). The inn is closed from the last week of January through February.

L'Abbaye de Beaugency, 2 Quai de l'Abbaye (tel. 38-44-67-35), is an old building that offers satisfied clients of the limited number of rooms a stunning view of the Loire and the old bridge a short distance away. The large and sunny bedrooms were completely renovated a short time ago, and spacious and modern bathrooms were added. Single rooms cost 410F ($56.54) and doubles 520F ($71.71). The hotel's restaurant charges from 210F ($28.96) to 260F ($35.85) for an à la carte meal, around 165F ($22.75) for a table d'hôte. The restaurant, whose tables share a view of the river and a cold-weather fireplace, is noted for such specialties as coq au vin, filets of sole Beaugency, and seasonal game dishes. Armand Aupetit is the manager.

La Tonnellerie, 12 rue des Eaux-Bleues (tel. 38-44-68-15), is a pleasant old house in Tavers, not quite two miles from Beaugency on Route N152. Guests enjoy the view of the garden, the outdoor pool, and the restaurant, all skillfully maintained by the Aulagnon family. Open from April 30 till October 5, the establishment charges 158F ($21.79) to 210F ($28.96) for meals. Full board, popular with urbanites escaping for a quiet weekend in the country, costs 410F ($56.54) to 500F ($68.95) per person daily. The 24 rooms, without meals, cost 400F ($55.16) in a single, 460F ($63.43) in a double.

La Sologne, Place St-Firmin (tel. 38-44-50-27), set in a distinguished neighborhood in the heart of the old city, is a small family-run hotel with well-maintained but slightly old-fashioned rooms. There's no restaurant, although breakfast is served by Andrée Rogue or one of her assistants. The 16 rooms rent for 100F ($13.79) in a bathless single, for 240F ($33.10) in a double with bath. La Sologne is closed from mid-December to February 1 and every Sunday night between November 1 and March 1.

13. Cheverny

The *haut monde* still comes to the Sologne area for the hunt. It's as if the 17th century never ended. It did, of course, and 20th-century realities such as taxes are *formidable*—hence the château must open some of its rooms for inspection by paying guests. At least that keeps the tax collector at bay and the hounds fed in winter.

Unlike most of the Loire châteaux, Cheverny is inhabited, actually lived in by the descendants of the original owner, the vicomte de Sigalas. Lineage is traced back to Henri Hurault, the son of the chancellor of Henri III and Henri IV, who built the first château in 1634.

This particular ancestor married an 11-year-old girl, Françoise Chabot. When that lady grew up, she developed a passion for page boys that lasted until her husband interrupted her nocturnal activities. After killing her frightened lover, he offered his spouse two choices: she could either swallow poison or else have his sword plunged into her heart. She elected to swallow from the bitter cup. Perhaps to erase the memory, he had the old castle torn down and a new one—the present château—built for his second wife. It attracted many fashionable visitors over the centuries, among them the "Grande Mademoiselle," who compared its beauty to "the Alcine Island or the Apolidor Palace." In a sense the château is "pure"—that is, it was constructed in a short period of time and has remained substantially as it was intended. Designed in the classic Louis XIII style, it contains square pavilions flanking the central pile.

Inside, the antique furnishings, tapestries, rich decorations, and objects of art warm things up considerably. A 17th-century French artist, Jean Mosnier, decorated the fireplace with motifs from the legend of Adonis. In the Guards' Room is a collection of medieval armor resting under a painted ceiling. Also displayed is a Gobelins tapestry depicting *The Abduction of Helen of Troy.* In the king's bedchamber, another Gobelins tapestry traces the *Trials of Ulysses,* such as his landing on the island of Circe. Most impressive, however, is a stone stairway of carved fruit and flowers.

Bypassing a kennel of hounds, you reach the **Salle de Trophées,** a hunting museum with an outstanding collection of antlers—more than 2,000 of them. You needn't spend much time there unless you dig weird headgear. The tree-shaded park of streams and ponds—although offering only a hint of its former glory—is impressive enough.

Floodlit at night, the château (tel. 54-79-96-29) charges an admission fee of 18F ($2.48), half price for children, for a 30-minute guided tour. From June 15 to September 15, it is open from 9 a.m. to 6:30 p.m. At other times of the year, it is usually open from 9:30 a.m. to noon and from 2:15 to 5:30 p.m. A *Fêtes Nocturnes* is staged in summer, costing 35F ($4.83) per person, 15F ($2.07) for children 7 to 14 years old. Cheverny is easily explored by a side-trip jaunt from Blois, eight miles to the northwest.

FOOD AND LODGING: Les Trois Marchands, Place de l'Église (tel. 54-79-96-44). This much-renovated coaching inn has been handed down for generations from father to son, the present proprietor being Jean-Jacques Bricault. Next to a church with a tall thin spire, the "Three Merchants" is three stories high, with awnings, a mansard roof, sidewalk tables, and a glassed-in courtyard. Tables are set under brightly colored umbrellas in the shade of linden trees. There diners are courteously served a fine regional cuisine. Meals are also available in a large tavern-style dining room with beamed ceilings and provincial furnishings. Set meals are offered at 100F ($13.79) and 180F ($24.82). The menu gastronomique at 220F ($30.34) might include a ballotine de canard (duckling) with pistachio nuts, followed by fresh salmon, then quail flambé, plus fresh string beans, a garden salad, a selection from the cheese board, and a homemade pastry. The 100F ($13.79) meal isn't to be ignored either—including, on one recent occasion, a selection of fresh hors d'oeuvres, followed by lapereau (young rabbit) sautéed in a red wine and stock. The cellar offers a good white wine of the house, called Cour-Cheverny.

Madame Bricault is in charge of the rooms and the comfort of the guests. Most of their rooms are traditionally furnished, with padded headboards and provincial chests. Doubles range from 120F ($16.55) to 260F ($35.85), depending on the plumbing: the top price brings a complete bath. The hotel is closed from January 15 to March 1. It is closed on Tuesday from October 1 until March.

Saint-Hubert, rue Nationale (tel. 54-79-96-60), about 800 yards from the château, is a roadside inn built in the old provincial style, with bedroom wings opening onto a courtyard. All is kept refreshingly spic and span. The secret of its success lies in Jean-Claude Pillaut, the chef de cuisine. He provides not only a restful and pleasant stopover but an especially fine cuisine. Three set menus are offered, costing from 200F ($27.58). For the least expensive tab, I recently dined on la terrine de caille en gelée, followed by sandre (a Loire fish) with "white butter," a selection of cheese, and a homemade fruit tart. The most expensive menu is likely to offer lobster or fresh spring asparagus. Game is featured here in season. An overnight stay costs from 240F ($33.10) in a double, service and tax included. The inn is closed from December to January 15 and on Tuesday.

14. Valençay

One of the handsomest Renaissance buildings in the château country, Valençay (tel. 54-00-10-66) was acquired in 1803 by Talleyrand on the orders of Napoleon, who wanted his shrewd minister of foreign affairs to receive dignitaries in great style. During its occupancy by Talleyrand, some of the most important personages in Europe passed under the portal of Valençay. Not all those guests, notably Ferdinand VII of Spain, wanted to visit the château. Driven from his homeland in 1808, the king was housed at Valençay for six years, on orders of Napoleon, as "the guest of Talleyrand."

In 1838 Talleyrand was buried at Valençay, the château passing to his nephew, Louis de Talleyrand-Périgord. Before the Talleyrand ownership, Valençay was built in 1550 by the d'Estampes family on the site of an old feudal castle of the lords of Châlons. The dungeon and the great west tower are of this period, as is the main body of the building; but other wings were added in the 17th and 18th centuries. The effect is grandiose, almost too much so, with domes, chimneys, and turrets.

The interior furnishings are especially rewarding, as the apartments are sumptuously furnished, mostly in the Empire style but with Louis XV and Louis

XVI trappings as well. In the main drawing room is a star-footed table, said to have been the one on which the Final Agreement of the Congress of Vienna was signed in June 1815 (Talleyrand represented France).

Seven private apartments are open to the public. Visits to Valençay usually are the longest of any château in the Loire, lasting 45 minutes. The Museum of Talleyrand that used to stand on the premises is now closed, but some of the collection is displayed in the new rooms of the castle. In the park is a museum of some 60 antique cars (circa 1890–1950). After your visit to the main buildings, you can walk through the zoological garden and deer park. On the grounds are many exotic birds, including flamingos.

To visit the castle, car museum, and park costs 20F ($2.76), but it is only 8F ($1.10) to visit just the park. The château, museum, and park are open mid-March to mid-November from 9 a.m. to noon and 2 to 7 p.m. From mid-November to mid-March, it is possible to visit only the park and the car museum, from 9 a.m. to noon and 2 p.m. to sunset weekends only. The village of Valençay lies 35 miles south of Blois.

FOOD AND LODGING: Hôtel d'Espagne, 9 rue du Château (tel. 54-00-00-02). When you pass through the wide-arched entrance of this former coaching inn, you'll find yourself in an old compound—a U-shaped building encompassing an open flagstone courtyard with trimmed boxwood shrubbery, plus tubs and planters of bright flowers. It's the tiny kingdom of Monsieur and Madame Fourré and their family, who provide an old-world ambience combined with comforts and a first-class kitchen. The kinks in the hotel have long ago been smoothed out, as the Fourré family has been there since 1875. The bedrooms have their own names and individuality. You may, for example, be assigned a chamber decorated in the authentic period of Empire, Louis XV, or Louis XVI. The hotel in reality is a cluster of adjoining buildings, almost like a village in miniature. There are 12 bedrooms, plus six suites. The average double or twin-bedded room rents for 400F ($55.16) to 550F ($75.63).

Meals are provided in the dining room or gardens. The chef's specialties include noisettes of lamb in tarragon and a special dessert, délicieuse au chocolat. If you are selecting the specialties on the à la carte menu, expect to pay from 280F ($38.61) to 330F ($45.51) per person. Set menus begin at 140F ($19.31). The inn is closed from mid-November to mid-March.

If your budget calls for something far less expensive, then your best bet is Le Chêne Vert (The Green Oak), Route Nationale (N760) (tel. 54-00-06-54). It's merely a wayside village café, with outdoor tables, where you can order especially good meals. There is a 50F ($6.90) meal, which on a typical day might include an appetizer of Westphalian ham, followed with beef bourguignon, accompanied by tomatoes in the Provençal style, and ending with cheese and dessert. A better meal, the menu gastronomique, featuring dishes such as terrine, roebuck with a pepper sauce, braised endive, cheese, and dessert, costs 140F ($19.31). Drinks are extra. You may want to cap your luncheon by ordering a glass of framboise. The inn is closed for most of June, on Sunday night, and also on Saturday off-season.

15. Chenonceaux

This chef d'oeuvre of the Renaissance has essentially orbited around the series of famous *dames de Chenonceaux* who have occupied it. Originally the château was owned by the Marqués family, but its members were extravagant beyond their means. Deviously, Thomas Bohier, the comptroller-general of finances in Normandy, began buying up land around the château. Finally, the Marqués family was forced to sell to Bohier, who tore down Chenonceaux, preserving only the keep, and building the rest in the emerging Renaissance style. In that undertaking, he was ably assisted by Catherine Briçonnet, the daughter of a wealthy family from Tours. After her husband died in 1524, Catherine lived for only two more years; at her death François I seized the château.

In 1547 Henri II gave Chenonceaux to his mistress, Diane de Poitiers, who was 20 years his senior. For a time this remarkable woman was virtually the queen of France, in spite of Henri's wife, Catherine de Medici. Apparently Henri's love for Diane continued unabated, even though she was in her 60s when the king died in a jousting tournament in 1559. Critics of Diane de Poitiers accused her of using magic not only to preserve her celebrated beauty but to keep Henri's attentions from waning.

Upon Henri's death, his jealous wife became regent of France. She immediately forced Diane de Poitiers to return the jewelry Henry had given her and to abandon her beloved Chenonceaux in exchange for Chaumont, which she did not want. Catherine added her own touches to the château, building a two-story gallery across the bridge—obviously inspired by her native Florence. The long gallery running along the Cher River contains a black-and-white diamond floor.

It was at Chenonceaux that Catherine received a pair of teenage honeymooners: her son, François II, and his bride, Mary Stuart. Another son, Henri III, sponsored an infamous fête at Chenonceaux. As described by the historian Philippe Erlanger: "Under the trees of this admirable park the King presided over the banquet, dressed as a woman. He wore a gown of pink damask, embroidered with pearls. Emerald, pearl, and diamond pendants distended the lobes of his ears, and diamonds shone in his hair which, like his beard, was dyed with violet powder." After Henri III was assassinated (by Jacques Clément), Chenonceaux was occupied by his widow, Louise de Lorraine. Even though the king had preferred his "curly-haired minions" to her she nevertheless mourned his death for the rest of her life, earning the name *La Reine Blanche* ("White Queen").

In the 18th century, Madame Dupin, the grandmother of George Sand, acquired the château. A lady of the aristocracy, she was the wife of the "farmer-general" of France. She is said to have brought the "talents of the époque" to her château, employing Rousseau as a tutor for her sons. However, when the author of *The Social Contract* declared his undying love for her, she asked him not to return. Rousseau is said to have fallen violently ill, "sick with humiliation."

In the 19th century Madame Pelouse took over the château and began the difficult task of restoring it to its original splendor. That duty is still being admirably carried out by the present owners, the chocolate-making Menier family.

Many of the walls today are covered with Gobelins tapestries, including one depicting a woman pouring water over the back of an angry dragon, another of a three-headed dog and a seven-headed monster. The chapel contains a delicate marble Virgin and Child, plus portraits of Catherine de Medici in her traditional black and white. There's even a portrait of the stern Catherine in the former bedroom of her rival, Diane de Poitiers. But in the Renaissance-style bedchamber of François I, the most interesting portrait is that of Diane de Poitiers as the huntress Diana, complete with a sling of arrows on her back. *The Three Graces* are by Van Loo.

The château (tel. 47-29-90-07) is open daily from 9 a.m. to 7 p.m. mid-March to mid-September. From then until October 31 it closes at 6 p.m., and in November it shuts down at 5 p.m. From December 1 through January 31, it's open from 9 a.m. to noon and 2 to 4 p.m. From February 1 to mid-March, it closes at 5 p.m. Admission is 20F ($2.76).

The history of Chenonceaux is related in 15 tableaux in the **wax museum,** which charges an additional 6F (83¢) admission. Diane de Poitiers, who, among other accomplishments, introduced the artichoke to France, is depicted in three of the tableaux. One shows her in a familiar setting—in her bedroom with Henri II. Another portrays Catherine de Medici tossing out her husband's mistress.

A son-et-lumière spectacle—"In the Old Days of the Dames of

Chenonceaux"—is staged in summer; admission is 20F ($2.76). The village of Chenonceaux is 7½ miles from Amboise, 21 miles from Tours.

FOOD AND LODGING: Hôtel du Bon-Laboureur et du Château (tel. 47-29-90-02). Even though it's on the main road of the village, it suggests a remote country house. The façade and tall chimneys are covered with ivy, and the rear garden has a little guest house, plus formally planted roses. Within sight of the Loire, and within walking distance of the château, the inn is run by a kindly, attractive family whose fine taste is apparent everywhere. Louis-Claude Jeudi ("Mr. Thursday") is not only the owner but the chef de cuisine; Mme Jeudi is in charge of the welfare of their guests.

Founded in 1880, the hotel still maintains the flavor of that era, but fortunately private bathrooms have been added to the well-appointed bedrooms. Doubles, either with private shower or complete bath cost from 400F ($55.16). Singles with bath go for 260F ($35.85).

If weather permits, you can request a table in the courtyard, under a maple tree (perhaps the pink hydrangeas will be in bloom and the red roses clinging to the high stone wall). Inside, the beamed dining room is old world, with a tall grandfather clock, high-backed ladder chairs, and an open cupboard with pewter bottles and regional ceramics. There are two fixed-price menus, the cheaper one costing 115F ($15.86) and including some of the chef's specialties. You're likely to be offered rillettes (highly seasoned ground pork), grilled blood sausage, a round slice of veal with sautéed mushrooms, scalloped potatoes, the salad of the season, and the pastry of the day, perhaps made with fresh strawberries or cherries. The 225F ($31.03) menu gastronomique provides such specialties as quenelles made with crayfish and ris de veau (sweetbreads) seasoned with wine from Porto. The inn is closed from mid-December to mid-February.

Au Gâteau Breton on the N76 (tel. 47-29-90-14), is a refreshing place at which to dine or have tea. In the heart of the village, within walking distance of the château, this little Breton-type inn opens toward its rear sun-terrace dining area. Gravel paths run between little beds of pink geraniums and lilacs, red tables rest under bright canopies and umbrellas, and ivy grows over the walls.

Dining here is most satisfying. Madame Herembert, the wife of the patron, asks, "Have you had enough?" Everything her husband prepares in the kitchen is homemade, and he provides as well a cherry liqueur, a specialty of the region. Their front room is set aside for the selling of his tasty pastries; in cool months meals are served in the rustic rooms in the rear. There are several set menus, the lowest costing 46F ($6.34), and more courses are yours if you order the 60F ($8.27) or 85F ($11.72) meals. They are closed on Tuesday and from mid-November to mid-December.

16. Orléans

Orléans suffered heavy damage in World War II, so those visiting who hope to see how it looked when the Maid of Orléans was there are likely to be disappointed. However, the reconstruction of Orléans has been judiciously planned, and there are many rewarding targets for visitors.

Orléans is the chief town of Loiret, on the Loire, about 80 miles from Paris. Joan of Arc relieved the city in 1429 from the attacks of the Burgundians and the English. That deliverance is celebrated every year on May 8, the anniversary of her victory. An equestrian statue of Joan of Arc stands in the **Place du Martroi,** which was created by Foyatier in 1855.

From that square you can drive down the rue Royale—rebuilt in the 18th-century style—across the **Pont George-V,** erected in 1760. After crossing the bridge you'll have a good view of the town. A simple cross marks the site of the Fort des Tourelles, which Joan of Arc and her men captured.

Back in the heart of town, you can go to the **Cathedral of St. Croix** (tel. 38-66-64-17), begun in 1287 in the High Gothic period, although burned by the Huguenots in 1568. The first stone on the present building was laid by Henri IV in 1601, and work continued on the cathedral until 1829. Inside, the church of the Holy Cross contains an excellent organ from the 17th century, and some magnificent woodwork from the early 18th century in its chancel, the master-piece of Jules Hardouin-Mansart and other artists of Louis XIV. You'll need a guide to tour the chancel and the crypt and to see the treasury with its Byzantine enamels, its goldwork from the 15th and 16th centuries, and its Limoges enam-els. There is no admission fee, but you should tip the guide.

To the northwest of the cathedral, the **Groslot Hôtel,** a Renaissance man-sion, was built from 1550, under Henri II, and embellished in the 19th century. The king, François II, lived in it during the fall of 1560 and died here on Decem-ber 5. He was the first husband of Mary, Queen of Scots. Other kings came here. On a lighter note, it was here that Charles IX met his lovely Marie Touch-et. The statue of Joan of Arc praying (at the foot of the flight of steps) was the work of a daughter of King Louis-Philippe. She was Princess Marie of Orléans. In the garden you can see the remains of the 15th-century chapel of St. Jacques. The Groslot Hôtel was the town hall from 1790 to 1982. In front of it is the new municipal center.

Another church of much interest, lying near the Loire, is the **Church of St. Aignan** (tel. 38-53-05-95), which was consecrated in 1509. The choir and tran-sept remain, but the nave was burned by the Protestants. In a gilded, carved wooden shrine lie the remains of the church's patron saint. The crypt, com-pleted in 1029, is intriguing, containing some decorated capitals. This surely must be one of the earliest vaulted hall-crypts in all of France.

The **Musée des Beaux-Arts** (tel. 38-53-33-22), reopened in 1984, is mainly a picture gallery of French works from the 15th to the 19th centuries. Some of the works once hung in Richelieu's château. Other pieces of art include busts by Pigalle, *St. Sebastian with Lantern* by Georges de La Tour, and a fine array of portraits, including one of Mme de Pompadour, of whom, when she first crossed the Pont George-V, the people of the town remarked: "Our bridge has just borne France's heaviest weight." See also works by Corrège, Le Nain, Phil-ippe de Champaigne, La Hire, Boucher, Watteau, and Gauguin, as well as a salon of pastels by Perronneau. Several foreign works are also displayed, includ-ing a lovely Velásquez. The museum is open from 10 a.m. to noon and 2 to 6 p.m. in summer, charging 10F ($1.38) for admission. It is expected to be closed on Tuesday, but check at the tourist office.

WHERE TO STAY (IN TOWN): Sofitel Orléans, 44-46 Quai Barentin (tel. 38-62-17-39), offers the finest accommodation right in the heart of town, within walking distance of the Place du Martroi with its statue of Joan of Arc. Border-ing the river, the hotel stands at the Pont Joffre. A modern, bandbox structure, it offers 110 well-furnished rooms with all the conveniences. One person pays anywhere from 400F ($55.16) to 465F ($64.12), and two persons are charged from 480F ($66.19) to 560F ($77.22). The Sofitel also has two suites, one re-served for a bride and her groom, another for presidents. The restaurant and bar, Le Vénerie, serves regional specialties, a full table d'hôte menu costing 220F ($30.34), including table wine. The hotel also has a big swimming pool.

Terminus, 40 rue de la République (tel. 38-53-24-64), facing the railway station, is a suitable place to stay in spite of its unromantic-sounding name. The decor of the rooms is ordinary but agreeably comfortable. The service is atten-tive, and the price is reasonable enough—200F ($27.58) in a single, rising to 240F ($33.10) in a double. Incidentally, the hotel is immaculately kept. There is no restaurant, although you can order a continental breakfast.

Less expensive, **St-Martin,** 52 Boulevard A-Martin (tel. 38-62-47-47), is a

22-room hotel on a broad boulevard near the cathedral, yet its rooms aren't too noisy. The hotel is conveniently situated for touring the sights of Orléans or shopping for souvenirs of Joan of Arc. There is no restaurant, yet you will be close to some excellent ones (see below). The rooms are simply furnished but clean. A single rents for 120F ($16.55) to 170F ($23.44), that tariff rising to 195F ($26.89) to 250F ($34.48) in a double. A few of the accommodations contain a private bath.

On the Outskirts

Actually, one of the more comfortable hotels is not in Orléans at all but south of the town (head down the N20). There you'll find **Novotel Orléans La Source,** 2 rue Honoré-de-Balzac (tel. 38-63-04-28). In a beautiful park with a swimming pool, this modern hotel offers such diversions as *pétanque* (French bowling) and table tennis. The decor is tasteful and restrained, providing much comfort, such as air conditioning and color television. A single rents for 330F ($45.51), that rate going up to 350F ($48.27) in a double. On the premises is a grill, offering a set meal for 150F ($20.69) till midnight.

Another possibility if you're a motorist is **Le Beauvoir,** 43 rue du Beauvoir at Olivet, three miles south by the D15 (tel. 38-63-57-57). Here 23 rooms are offered in a large modern building with a garden overlooking the peaceful Loiret. The chambers are well furnished and impeccably maintained, renting for 100F ($13.79) in a single, that rate going up to 250F ($34.48) in the best doubles. The cuisine is excellent, as great care goes into the preparation of every dish. One reader raved about the "tiny tomato roses and strips of carrots" surrounding the main dishes. You get individual attention here. Even if you're not staying over, you can order a complete meal for 75F ($10.32) to 110F ($15.17), although you are likely to spend 150F ($20.69) on the à la carte menu. Closed Sunday night.

THE BEST RESTAURANTS: La Crémaillère, 34 rue N.-D.-de-Recouvrance

(tel. 38-53-49-17). Paul Huyart is perhaps the finest chef in Orléans. He serves food that is memorable, and although many authorities give him ratings, I haven't seen any yet that are high enough. Go here and plan to make an evening of it, savoring every course. His fresh duckling foie gras has a lively flavor. All of his main dishes I've sampled tasted original and imaginative—his ragoût of scallops with oysters (October to April only), his sautéed crayfish with asparagus tips, and his exquisite soup of strawberries with passion fruit. The chef is definitely talented. He calls his pièce de résistance gigot de mer aux gousses d'ail. I suggest a Quincy wine if it fits in with your food order. This spicy, dry white wine is from a village on the Cher River, not far from Bourges, in central France, although it is considered a wine of the Loire Valley. The restaurant shuts down in August and on Sunday night and Monday. Expect to pay 275F ($37.92) and up for a meal.

La Poutrière, 8-10 rue de la Breche (tel. 38-66-02-30), is named after the massive ceiling beams of the farmhouse that it occupies. This restaurant provides a perfect escape into a well-organized and quite beautiful environment set up by Marcel Thomas, a former chef on the ocean liner *France,* and his partner, André Saunier. The menu offers a wide choice of highly detailed dishes, some of which are wild salmon with black pepper in a watercress sauce, calves' brains with lobster sauce, terrine of John Dory, and salmon in puff pastry. Charging 160F ($22.06) to 280F ($38.61) for a meal, the place is closed Sunday night and Monday. Dinner is served, with reservations advisable, until 9:30 p.m.

Les Antiquaires, 2-4 rue au Lin (tel. 38-53-52-35), is in an old mansion on a small street near the river. It is maintained with great style by Michel Pipet. The menu is filled with well-prepared specialties, such as marinated tuna with anise and Loire salmon with parsley butter. The air-conditioned restaurant charges 200F ($27.58) to 240F ($33.10) à la carte. Set meals are offered for 110F ($15.17) to 160F ($22.06). The place is closed Sunday and Monday and in August.

Auberge de la Montespan, route de Blois, out the N152 (tel. 38-88-12-07), lies about a mile from Orléans, its garden and terrace on the Loire. The house is from the era of Louis XIV. The owner is Monsieur Fournier, who carefully selects a staff that shows consideration and most attentive service to each guest. The cuisine is the standard French repertoire, and it is done quite well. Of course, try the Loire salmon, although there are other fish dishes as well. The chef specializes in game pâté. If you want something unusual, he even does a tête de veau (veal head) with a creamy sauce. A set meal costs 135F ($18.62), but is not available on Sunday. If you order à la carte, expect to pay from 250F ($34.48). The restaurant is closed from Christmas until February. In addition, the host offers eight well-furnished rooms with superb views of the Loire. A single rents for 220F ($30.34), that tariff rising to 350F ($48.27) in a double. All of the rooms contain a bath.

At Saint-Jean-de-Braye, **La Grange,** 205 Faubourg Bourgogne, route de Nevers (tel. 38-86-43-36), is an old mill restored in a neorustic style, offering choice grills and special platters. Robert Dupuy is in complete control, welcoming guests to his fine establishment, which has much charm. It lies about two miles east of Orléans on the N60. You can come here to drink fine wine and to contemplate the menu, which is likely to include turbot mousse with watercress, boneless slices of duck with red pepper, sweetbreads with hurtleberries, and veal kidneys in a mustard sauce. The menus range in price from 100F ($13.79) to 150F ($20.69). Ordering à la carte is likely to cost you in the neighborhood of 250F ($34.48) per person. The restaurant is closed during most of August and January, as well as on Sunday and Monday.

17. Sully-sur-Loire

Southeast of Orléans stands the beautiful **Castle of Sully** (tel. 38-35-25-60), where Joan of Arc persuaded Charles VII to go to Reims and proclaim himself king of France. The château is named, however, for the duc de Sully, the minister of Henri IV. The castle was mostly destroyed in World War II, but it has been restored. It was originally constructed in the 14th century, although enlarged after 1602 by Sully. Exiled from Paris, Voltaire spent much time with Sully. A theater was built for Voltaire in which his plays could be performed.

Several apartments in the 14th-century wing of the castle are open to the public. Sully's remains were placed in the oratory. On the second floor an apartment was covered with timberwork, which is considered the finest such work from medieval days. It is so well preserved it is hard to believe that it's actually 600 years old. In the Renaissance pavilion you can see the minister's study and his bedroom. Both rest under painted ceilings. You are conducted through the château on guided tours, which in summer leave from 9 to 11:45 a.m. and 2 to 6 p.m. In the off-season, hours are 10 to 11:45 a.m. and 2 to 5 p.m. (in November it closes at 4:30 p.m., and it is completely closed from the first of December until the end of February). Admission is 12F ($1.66) per person.

FOOD AND LODGING: La Poste, 11 rue Faubourg St-Germain (tel. 38-36-26-22), is a typical French provincial hotel. Don't judge it by its façade, however. Inside it is cozy and comfortable. Its 27 bedrooms, five of which contain private bath, are simply furnished but well kept, costing 100F ($13.79) in a single, 250F ($34.48) in a double. The hotel has a lovely garden. In the pillared dining room the service is informal, the reception most hospitable, and the food good, with lots of local produce used when available. The chef does the usual range of Loire specialties exceedingly well, and the portions are ample, the menu having variety. The least expensive way to dine here is to order the 85F ($11.72) menu, although you could spend 220F ($30.34) if you're ravenously hungry. Closed in February.

Hostellerie Grand Sully, 10 Boulevard Champ-de-Foire (tel. 38-35-27-56), is also suitable if you're stopping over for the night, perhaps en route to Burgundy and the French Alps. It has only a dozen bedrooms, half of which contain private bath. The accommodations are modestly furnished, costing from 100F ($13.79) in a single to a high of 275F ($37.92) in a double. The bar is pleasant, and there is also a garden. Food of good quality is served in the agreeable restaurant, where a set menu is offered for 80F ($11.03), an almost-more-than-you-can-eat one for 200F ($27.58). The inn is better known as a restaurant than as a hotel, and is in fact the finest dining establishment in Sully-sur-Loire. It is closed from December 1 to January 5 and on Wednesday.

18. Les Bézards

This village, at the edge of the Forest of Orléans, is the far eastern extremity of the Loire Valley. It lies on the main route between Paris and Nevers, and is a popular stopping-off point with Parisians, who stay at the following recommendation, exploring the lovely towns of Gien and Briare farther along the Loire.

Auberge des Templiers, N7 at Boismorand (tel. 38-31-80-01), lies to the east of Orléans a distance of 43 miles. The inn was once a stagecoach stop, and even that ancient *relais* was built on the site of an older hospice once belonging to the Knights Templars. The vine-covered auberge appears rustic, but that is a misleading first impression. Inside you'll find a haven of luxury, comfort, and recreation. As you stroll to your room you'll wander through flower gardens, deciding on the annex, the thatched-roofed La Chaumière, or perhaps the handsomely appointed little manor house. The newest accommodations are in a pavilion by the pool. Ask for the tiny tower room if you prefer a snug nest. It's completely round, with old beams. The rooms are furnished with reproductions of antiques. Even the bathrooms are well decorated, with beautiful tiles and wallpaper. Naturally, the price for all this is high: doubles begin at a low of 450F ($62.06), going up to a high of 1,050F ($144.80) for deluxe units. Even more expensive apartments are available. On the grounds is a heated swimming pool, plus tennis courts. Out by the pool the hotel has been known to stage wild-boar barbecues, but not every day.

In the bar with its beamed ceiling you can enjoy an apéritif in front of a hearth with oak logs blazing and the glow soft from the brass chandeliers. Dining is by candlelight, of course. In autumn you are likely to be seated near a Parisian gourmet, drawn here to sample some of Monsieur Dépée's wild-game dishes. A profusion of wild game is to be found in the area, including woodcock and pheasant. Thus in season you can order, perhaps, stuffed young rabbit for dinner. The chef's repertoire isn't confined to game, however. Try the white mousse of liver or veal liver cooked in cider vinegar, and especially the sole à l'orange or young guinea hen with lime. For dessert, perhaps you'll order the soufflé glacé with a whisky-and-honey sauce. It's sinful. Meals are served in the garden in fair weather. A menu classique is offered for 275F ($37.92) and a menu dégustation for 410F ($56.54), both with 12% service charge added. The finest of regional wines, such as sancerre, are stocked here, along with more expensive choices. The auberge, if I can call it that, is closed from mid-January to mid-February.

19. Gien

A town of flowers, known for its porcelain, Gien was heavily bombed in the early months of World War II. But the reconstruction has been skillful, the town planners showing a healthy respect for traditional architectural styles. The town is in red brick that contrasts with the geometric designs and edgings in black brick.

Founded in 1820, the porcelain factory, **Faïencerie de Gien,** is at Place de la Victoire in the western part of Gien, covering about 18 acres. It is open from 9:30 to 11:30 a.m. and 2 to 5 p.m. daily except Sunday and holidays. Telephone 38-67-00-05 for permission to visit.

Stroll along the Loire river promenade with its shade trees, and cross the humpbacked bridge dating from the 15th century for a good view. If you're planning to stay over, avoid the weekends, especially in autumn. French hunters after wild game in the surrounding area (woodcock, pheasant, rabbit) seem to book up all the rooms.

The **Château of Gien,** rebuilt in 1484, once belonged to Anne de Beaujeu, the comtesse of Gien, the eldest daughter of Louis XI. Installed in the castle is an **International Hunting Museum** (tel. 38-67-24-11), which is open daily to the public from Easter until the end of October from 9 a.m. to noon and 2:15 to 6:30 p.m., charging an admission of 12F ($1.66); off-season, it closes an hour earlier. Inside you'll find a collection of weapons, pictures, and prints, all devoted to *la chasse* down through the ages. The most interesting section of the restored castle is the Great Hall, with its paintings by Desportes.

The **Church of St. Joan of Arc** stands nearby on the Place du Château, but it is modern, the design pleasing and harmonious. Only the tower dates from the 15th century, the time of Anne de Beaujeu. After its destruction in 1940, the church was rebuilt in the postwar years in red brick with black geometric designs. Inside the baptistery, the baked-earth capitals, the ceramic statues, and the stained-glass windows should be observed, as well as the uncommon "Way of the Cross" made in the local earthenware works.

FOOD AND LODGING: For a meal or a room, I suggest **Rivage,** 1 Quai Nice (tel. 38-67-20-53), an attractively situated hotel lying right by the river promenade with its shade trees. Sportsmen gravitate here on the weekends, getting a hearty welcome from the patron, Christian Gaillard. He offers a very good set meal (weekdays only) at 80F ($11.03). Otherwise, the menu is 150F ($20.69). Try to get a room overlooking the Loire. The accommodations are pleasantly decorated and most comfortable, costing 90F ($12.41) in a single, 250F ($34.48) in a double. The staff is attentive and friendly.

Hôtel Beau-Site-Restaurant La Poularde, 13 Quai de Nice (tel. 38-67-36-05), is an honest and pleasant *restaurant avec chambres,* serving well-prepared family-style cooking based on old regional recipes. Joel Danthu offers generous portions of such dishes as brochette of Loire Valley fish, several trout dishes, duck with peaches, and many more delicacies. Excellent meals are politely served, costing 75F ($10.32) to 175F ($24.13). Eight simply furnished rooms are rented, with individual plumbing being at a minimum. The charge is 85F ($11.72) in a single, 150F ($20.69) in a double. You can stay here all year except from January 1 to January 15. The restaurant is closed at that same time and also on Sunday night.

20. Langeais

The formidable gray *pile,* a true fortress of the Middle Ages, dominates the town. The façade is foreboding, but once you cross the drawbridge and go inside, the apartments are so richly decorated that the severe effect is softened or forgotten. The castle dates back to the ninth century, when the dreaded Black Falcon erected what was considered the first dungeon in Europe, the ruins of which remain to this day. The present structure was built in 1465 in the reign of Louis XI. That the interior is so well preserved and furnished is due to Jacques

Siegfried, who not only restored it over a period of 20 years but bequeathed it to the Institute of France in 1904.

"She arrived at Langeais carried in a litter decked with gold cloth, dressed in a gown of black trimmed with sable. Her wedding gown of gold cloth was ornamented with 160 sables." The date was December 6, 1491. The marriage of Anne of Brittany to Charles VIII was to be the golden hour of Langeais. Their symbols—scallops, fleurs-de-lis, and ermine—set the motif for the Guard Room. In the Wedding Chamber, where the marriage took place, the walls are decorated with a series of seven tapestries known as the *Valiant Knights*.

At the entrance to Langeais, a large tapestry illustrating the life of Nebuchadnezzar shows him covered with hair and stricken with madness. In a bedchamber known sardonically as "The Crucifixion," the 15th-century black-oak four-poster is reputed to be one of the earliest known. The room takes its odd name from a tapestry of the Virgin and St. John standing on a flower-bedecked ground. In the Monsieur's Room a rare Flemish tapestry depicts such motifs as Virginia snake-root leaves and pheasants on railings, surrounded by a border of fruit. The Chapel Hall was built by joining two stories under a ceiling of Gothic arches. In the Luini Room is a large fresco by that artist, dating from 1522, removed from a chapel on Lake Maggiore, Italy. It represents St. Francis of Assisi and St. Elizabeth of Hungary with Mary and Joseph. The Byzantine Virgin in the drawing room is considered an early work of Cimabue, the Forentine artist. The best for last: the *Tapestry of the Thousand Flowers* in the Drawing Room is like an ageless celebration of spring, a joyous riot of growth, a symbol of life's renewal.

Langeais is open mid-March to mid-September from 9 a.m. to noon and 2 to 6:30 p.m. However, in July and August, because of the peak demand, it does not shut down for lunch. From September 16 to 30 it closes at 6 p.m. For the first two weeks of October it closes at 5:30 p.m. From mid-October to the first of November it closes at 5 p.m., and from November to mid-March it shuts down at 4:30 p.m. It is also closed on Monday. For information, telephone 47-96-72-60. Admission is 16F ($2.21). The town of Langeais lies between Saumur and Tours, the latter a 16-mile drive to the east.

FOOD AND LODGING: Hosten et Restaurant Langeais, 2 rue Gambetta (tel. 47-96-70-63), is a true country inn, with an informal atmosphere—no fancy airs, but excellent food and service. As a restaurant it qualifies as upper bracket, but as a hotel it is in the budget to medium-priced range. The Hosten family bought this 75-year-old hotel in 1948. Madame Hosten takes care of the guest accommodations, and her husband Jean-Jacques reigns in the kitchen (he was trained at the Savoy in London and the Ledoyen on the Champs-Élysées in Paris). The restaurant has accumulated honors for years.

In addition to those in the major dining room, tables are set up in the open courtyard under umbrellas and flowering trees. The least expensive menu is 165F ($22.75), a more elaborate one 275F ($37.92). Monsieur Hosten even proposes a *menu de prestige*, including blanquette de soles et turbots, escalope de saumon a l'oseille (sorrel), terrine chaude de brochets with a sauce Nantua, and le homard (lobster) Cardinal. Desserts are likely to include the classic soufflé au Grand-Marnier and la charlotte au coulis de framboises (raspberries).

A double room with bath costs 300 F ($41.37), but a double with shower is only 220F ($30.34). The inn is closed from mid-June to July 10 and mid-January to February 5, as well as Monday night and Tuesday.

La Duchesse Anne, 10 rue de Tours (tel. 47-96-82-03), is a former coaching inn. The simple white-painted hostelry still possesses its covered central carriage passageway, leading to a courtyard. Garden tables are set out for dining, and cages of singing birds abound; there's even a tank of trout. Regardless of your budget, chances are you'll find a meal here to suit your purse. The cheapest lunch or dinner costs 95F ($13.10) and includes three courses. A 220F ($30.34) dinner offers at least five of the chef's specialties, such as grilled Loire shad with white butter and stuffed mushrooms.

Not all the rooms contain private baths, but they do offer hot and cold running water. Singles rent for 120F ($16.55), and doubles go for 240F ($33.10). The rooms are practical and keynoted by simplicity. The inn is closed October 15 to October 31, on Sunday night, and on Monday off-season.

21. Ussé

At the edge of the hauntingly dark forest of Chinon, the Castle of Ussé was the inspiration behind Perrault's legend of "The Sleeping Beauty" (called in French "Belle au Bois Dormant"). On a hill overlooking the Indre River, it is a virtual forest of steeples, turrets, towers, chimneys, and dormers. Originally conceived as a medieval fortress, it was erected at the dawn of the Renaissance. Two powerful families—Bueil and d'Espinay—lived in the château in the 15th and 16th centuries.

Vauban, the military engineer who in the 17th century designed systems of fortifications for French cities, was a frequent visitor when Ussé was owned by his son-in-law, the Marquis de Valentinay. At one point in its history Mlle d'Ussé ordered royal apartments built for an anticipated visit of Louis XIV that never materialized. In time the château was owned by the Duke of Duras and later by Mme de la Rochejacquelin before coming into its present ownership by the Marquis de Blacas. The terraces, laden with orange trees, were laid out in the 18th century. When the need for a "fortified" château had long since passed, the north wing was demolished, opening up a greater view, as the occupants wished to enjoy the sun and the landscape.

You used to have to settle for a look from the outside, but the marquis has opened a large number of rooms to the public. The guided tour begins in the Renaissance chapel, with its sculptured portal and handsomely designed stalls. Then you are escorted through the royal apartments, furnished with tapestries and antiques, including a four-poster in red damask. One gallery displays an extensive collection of swords and rifles.

The château is open from Easter to September 30 from 9 a.m. to noon and 2 to 7 p.m. (to 6 p.m. October 1 to November), charging 22F ($3.03) for admission. The hamlet of Ussé lies only nine miles from Chinon.

22. Chinon

Remember when Ingrid Bergman as Joan of Arc sought out the dauphin even though he tried to conceal himself among his courtiers? The action in real life took place at Chinon, one of the oldest fortress-châteaux in France. Charles VII, mockingly known as the King of Bourges, centered his government at Chinon from 1429 to 1450. In 1429, with the English besieging Orléans, the maid of Orléans, that "messenger from God," prevailed upon the weak dauphin to give her an army. The rest is history.

The seat of French power stayed at Chinon until the Hundred Years' War ended. It was here that Louis XII in 1498 received Cesare Borgia, the son of the notorious Pope Alexander VI, when he brought permission from Rome to dissolve Louis's marriage to his "deformed" wife. Later he married Anne of Brittany.

On the banks of the Vienne, in the heart of Rabelais country, Chinon retains a medieval atmosphere with its grim feudal ruins. Nineteen miles from Langeais, it consists of winding streets and turreted houses, many built in the 15th and 16th centuries in the heyday of the court. For the best view, drive across the river, turning right onto the Quai Danton. From that vantage point you'll have the best perspective of the town, seeing the castle in relation to the village and the river. The gables and towers make Chinon look like a toy village.

The most typical street is the **rue Voltaire,** lined with 15th- and 16th-century town houses. At no. 44, Richard the Lion-Hearted died on April 6, 1199, after suffering a mortal wound while besieging Chalus in Limousin. In the heart of town, the **Grand Carroi** was the crossroads of the Middle Ages.

The most famous son of Chinon, Rabelais, the great Renaissance writer, walked these streets. He was born at La Devinière, on the D17 near the N751, now the **Musée Rabelais.** It is open mid-March until the end of September from 9 a.m. to noon and 2 to 6 p.m. In the off-season it closes at 5 p.m. It is also closed on Wednesday in the off-season, and is completely shut down in December and January. Admission is 8F ($1.10) per person. Rabelais used his native scenery as background in many of his stories.

The château is three separate strongholds, badly ruined. Some of the grim walls remain, although many of the buildings—including the Great Hall where Joan of Arc sought out the dauphin—have been torn down. Some of the most destructive owners were the heirs of Cardinal Richelieu. Now gone, the **Château de St-Georges** was built by Henry II of England, who died there in 1189. The **Château de Mileu** dates from the 11th to the 15th centuries, containing the keep and the clock tower, where a **Museum of Joan of Arc** has been installed. Separated from the latter by a moat, the **Château du Coudray** contains the Tour du Coudray, where Joan of Arc stayed during her time at Chinon. In the 14th century the Knights Templar were imprisoned there (they are responsible for the graffiti on the walls) before meeting their violent deaths.

The château is open daily except Wednesday, from 9 a.m. to noon and 2 to 6 p.m. (till 5 p.m. in winter), charging 10F ($1.38) for admission. It is closed in December and January. A son-et-lumière program is presented in summer at 25F ($3.45) per person.

FOOD AND LODGING: **Hostellerie Gargantua,** 73 rue Voltaire (tel. 47-93-04-71), stands in a row of ancient buildings almost opposite the house where Richard the Lion-Hearted died. Just a short walk from the river, it's in the old town mansion of a bailiff. Named after Rabelais's amiable giant, the Gargantua features a tiny glass-covered courtyard, complete with tall plants, which is used for al fresco dining in good weather. A winding staircase leads to the simply furnished bedrooms. Guests of the hotel are obligated to take meals, but that is no hardship since the food is so good. The price of the rooms, doubles, ranges from a low of 210F ($28.96) to a high of 475F ($65.50), the latter containing private bath and decorated in Louis XVII style.

Whether you stay here or not, do come for the excellent meals. A not-to-be-missed delicacy is the fluffy omelette Gargamelle. A creamy fondue sauce is just one of its ingredients. A meal with wine costs about 200F ($27.58). The hotel is closed from November 15 to March 15.

Grand Hôtel de la Boule d'Or (Golden Ball), 66 Quai Jeanne d'Arc (tel. 47-93-03-13), is a coaching inn, with the carriage yard now converted into an almost lush dining area. The setting is one of glistening white walls and an overhead arbor and trellis with trailing vines and red roses. White chairs and tables are set out for drinks and meals that range in price from 75F ($10.32) to 175F ($24.13).

Owned by Béatrice Lebrun, the inn has long been a favorite with the English. The front rooms open onto the river, but the quieter ones are at the rear. Full-board prices range from 230F ($31.72) per person. In rooms with shower, one person pays 150F ($20.69), the cost going up to 175F ($24.13) for two. In units with complete bath, the charge is 175F ($24.13) for one person, 250F ($34.48) for two, with breakfast costing extra. Madame Lebrun loves cardinal red, using it whenever possible: front canopies, valances, garden lounge cushions, bed covers, and draperies. The hotel is open every day from April to October, closing Monday off-season. Its annual closing is in December and January.

Au Plaisir Gourmand, 2 rue Parmentier (tel. 47-93-20-48), is a recently established restaurant whose owner, Jean-Claude Rigollet, used to direct the chefs at Les Templiers in Bézards. Having tired of working for someone else, he's launched out on his own, operating an intimate dining room with a limited number of tables in an 18th-century building loaded with charm and historic detailing. Menu items change frequently. You might, depending on the day, select among a salad of warm turnips with foie gras, warm oysters with leeks, steamed chicken with truffles, and fricassée of lotte with lobster butter. À la carte meals cost from 200F ($27.58) to 240F ($33.10), while table d'hôte menus range from 125F ($17.24) to 170F ($23.44). The restaurant is open daily except Sunday night and Monday at lunchtime. Reservations are suggested.

Le Sainte-Maxime, 31 Place du Général-de-Gaulle (tel. 47-93-05-04), is a superior restaurant—really an unexpected discovery in such a provincial town. From its decor, you wouldn't expect such a fine establishment. Set back from the main square, it is much like a tavern. Maurice Sarot is the all-seeing proprietor. His fixed-price meals cater to most budgets: 125F ($17.24) and 175F ($24.13), the latter a superb repast of exquisite quality, but the low-priced meals are also satisfactory. On the à la carte menu you can enjoy his chateaubriand, a recommended specialty. The terrine du chef is a good beginning, and other highly praised dishes include the stuffed escargots and the brochet (pike) in a white-butter sauce. An à la carte dinner will cost about 210F ($28.96) to 250F ($34.48) per person. The restaurant is closed from December 15 to January 10, and on Sunday night.

On the Outskirts

Château de Marçay (tel. 47-93-03-47) stands at Marçay, about 4½ miles from Chinon on the D116. The sumptuous decor of this 15th-century château-fortress, untouched in any of the region's civil wars, is worth the trip. The owners rent out 23 well-furnished bedrooms, plus three apartments for those who want to go truly luxurious. A single costs 575F ($79.29), a double going for 420F ($57.92) to 1,050F ($144.80). Full-board terms are favored, ranging in price from 850F ($117.22) to 1,150F ($158.59) per person.

The château's restaurant employs Sylvain Knecht, who used to work in well-rated restaurants in Talloires and Megève, to maintain the high gastronomic standards of this member of Relais et Châteaux. Specialties include lobster salad with baby spinach, sauerkraut of fish with tarragon, and a saffron-flavored mussel soup. The view from the garden terrace or from the dining room windows is panoramic, and the accessories are elegantly rustic. À la carte meals cost from 280F ($38.61) to 295F ($40.68), and there is also a set menu for 205F ($28.27). Both the hotel and the restaurant are closed from mid-January to mid-March.

23. Fontevraud-l'Abbaye

You're likely to trip over a British colonel muttering, "These tombs should be in Westminster Abbey where they belong!" For in the Romanesque church at Fontevraud-l'Abbaye (tel. 41-51-73-52) the Plantagenet dynasty of the kings of England are buried. Why there? These monarchs, whose male line vanished in 1499, were also the counts of Anjou, and they left instructions that they be buried on their native soil.

Contained within the 12th-century church—with its four Byzantine domes —are the remains of the two English kings or princes, including Henry II of England, the first Plantagenet king (the one who fought with Thomas Becket) and his wife, Eleanor of Aquitaine, perhaps the single most famous woman of the Middle Ages (at one time she was married to Louis VII of France). Her crusading son, Richard the Lion-Hearted, was also entombed here. The Plantagenet line ended with the death of Richard III at the Battle of Market Bosworth in 1485. The last occasion when the matter of returning the tombs of the Plantagenet kings to England was raised was on the eve of the 1867 Universal Exhibition. In a spirit of goodwill, Napoleon III offered the reclining statues to Queen Victoria. This led to a strong protest on the part of Angevin archeologists. The emperor had to write to the queen, begging her to free him from such a rash promise. To save Napoleon from embarrassment, the queen recognized that, after all, it would be contrary to the wishes of the two kings who, as they were dying, expressly requested that their remains be buried in the abbey church of Fontevraud. The tombs fared badly in the Revolution, as mobs invaded the church, desecrating the sarcophagi and scattering their contents on the floor.

More interesting than the tombs, however, is the octagonal Tour d'Evraud, the last remaining Romanesque kitchen in France. Surrounding the tower is a group of apses crowned by conically roofed turrets. A pyramid tops the conglomeration, capped by an open-air lantern tower pierced with lancets.

The abbey was founded in 1099 by Robert d'Arbrissel, who had spent much of his life as a recluse, although he enjoyed a reputation at one time as a sort of Billy Sunday of the Middle Ages. His abbey was like a public-welfare commune, very liberal in its admission policies. One part, for example, was filled with aristocratic ladies, many of them banished from court, including discarded mistresses of kings. The four youngest daughters of Louis XV were educated there as well. Aside from the nuns and monks, there were lepers, and a hospital for the lame and sick who arrived almost daily at the abbey's doorstep. The foundation was controlled by powerful "abbesses" appointed by the king. Under Napoléon I the abbey was converted into a prison and remained so for 160 years. Now the prisoners are gone and the abbey is being restored—actually rebuilt in parts—at great expense to the French government.

In the chapterhouse are some interesting 16th-century frescoes. A cloister dates from the same period, although one section goes back to the 12th century. The refectory is also from the 1500s.

Fontevraud-l'Abbaye lies about ten miles southeast of Saumur, near the confluence of the Loire and Vienne rivers. From April 1 to September 30, visiting hours are 9 a.m. to noon and 2 to 4 p.m. The rest of the year, hours are from 10 a.m. to noon and 2 to 6:30 p.m. Admission is 20F ($2.76) in summer, 9F ($1.24) off-season. To reach the abbey, take Route N147 for about 2½ miles from the village of Montsoreau.

24. Saumur

At a point where the Loire separates to encircle an island, Saumur is set in a region of vineyards. (Do sample some of the local produce, like the Saumur mousseux.) Founded in 1768, its Cavalry School, as well as its riding club, the Black Cadre, are world renowned. Its horsemen are considered among the finest in Europe (to see a rider carry out a *curvet* is to thrill at the training of both man and beast). The townspeople have even installed a **Musée du Cheval**—that is, a museum devoted to the history of the horse down through the ages, complete with stirrups, antique saddles, spurs, and whatever.

The museum is housed in the **Château of Saumur** (tel. 41-51-30-46), towering over the town from a promontory overlooking the Loire. The Poet Prince, René of Anjou, called it "the castle of love." In the famous *Book of Hours* of the duc de Berry at Chantilly, a 15th-century painting shows Saumur as a fairytale castle of bell turrets and gilded weathercocks. But these adornments are largely gone, leaving a rather stark and foreboding fortress.

Under Napoleon the castle became a prison, eventually degenerating into a barracks and munitions depot. The town of Saumur acquired it in 1908 and began the herculean task of restoration. Now one of the most interesting regional museums (devoted to decorative arts) in the Loire has been installed. The galleries grew out of the collection begun by Count Charles Lair. The museum is noted mainly for its ceramics, dating from the 16th through the 18th centuries. A series of 13th-century enamel crucifixes from Limoges is remarkable, and also displayed are illustrated 15th-century manuscripts, polychrome sculpture (some from the 14th century), tapestries, and antique furnishings.

The château is open daily July 1 to September 30 from 9 a.m. to 6:30 p.m. (in the evening from 8:30 to 10:30 p.m. July 1 to August 31), charging 14F ($1.93) for admission. From April 1 to June 30 and October 1 to October 31 it is open from 9 to 11:30 a.m. and 2 to 6 p.m. Finally, from November 1 to March 31 it's open daily except Tuesday from 9:30 to 11:30 a.m. and 2 to 5 p.m.

About six miles east of Saumur, Route N751 will take you to the **Château de Montsoreau,** with its Musée des Goums devoted to Moroccan troops who fought with the Allies in World War II. Immortalized by Dumas in *La Dame de Montsoreau,* the château, even without its museum, would be worthy of a visit. It was constructed in the 15th century in the Gothic style by a member of the private court of Charles VII. A Renaissance stairway was added in the 16th century. The château may be visited daily except Tuesday, from 10 a.m. to noon and 1 to 6 p.m. for a 10F ($1.38) admission. For more information, telephone 41-51-70-25.

FOOD AND LODGING: Le Roi René, 94 Avenue du Général-de-Gaulle (tel. 41-67-45-30), is a dignified hotel on a quiet square looking over the Loire River. It has been completely revamped and much improved, with many comforts added. All the bedrooms are equipped with private bath, color TV, and direct-dial phone, along with double-paned windows. Louis Chapeau is in charge, and he has employed a fine staff. The simplest singles rent for 220F ($30.34), a double costing from 300F ($41.37). The inn also serves good food, with menus costing 85F ($11.72) to 135F ($18.62). The hotel is open all year, but the restaurant is closed at lunchtime Saturday.

Le Gambetta, 12 rue Gambetta (tel. 41-51-11-13), is on a side street in an old town house. A garden out back is used in fair weather. For openers, try the terrine de pâté maison or a dozen snails in garlic butter. Main-dish specialties include tournedos Gambetta, filet steak with pepper flamed with brandy, brochet au beurre blanc, and a matelote d'anguilles (eels). The dessert spectacular is soufflé maison for two. Everything tastes better with the wines of Saumur. For a complete meal, expect to spend from 110F ($15.17) to 150F ($20.69). Closed Sunday night and Monday and from December 20 to January 10.

L'Escargot, 30 rue du Maréchal-Leclerc (tel. 41-51-20-88), is a typical French bistro. Inside are two dining rooms suggesting a mellowed tavern atmosphere. In all, "The Snail" is an ingratiating setting for a tasty meal. The establishment offers two set menus, at 110F ($15.17) and 130F ($17.93), including hors d'oeuvres, a fish and a meat course, plus dessert. Service and drinks are extra. Some of the chef's specialties appear on the fixed-price menus. Special dishes include brochet (pike) in beurre blanc and grilled Loire salmon with a béarnaise sauce. Try also the river fish, sandre, with white butter and sorrel. The restaurant is closed Tuesday night, on Wednesday off-season, and all of November.

A CHÂTEAU-HOTEL ON THE OUTSKIRTS: Hostellerie du Prieuré, Chênehutte-les-Tuffeaux (tel. 41-50-15-31). The waiter serves you heavenly rognons de veau sautés à moutarde (sautéed veal kidneys in a mustard sauce) while you look out at one of the finest views of the Loire—a span of 40 miles—in the château district. The "priory," a Relais et Châteaux, has a steep roof, dormer windows, and a large peaked tower, sitting on a plateau of a 60-acre park.

Dating from the 12th century, it was restored in the 15th. Designed for meditation, it is now turned over to organized recreation, with additional bungalows and a mini-golf course under the trees where monks of old used to stroll. There's even a heated swimming pool. While not rated as a luxury establishment, the hostellerie does offer completely comfortable and gracious living. The tone is set by the Grand Salon, with its ornately carved stone fireplace, clusters of crystal chandeliers, oak furniture, and the fleur-de-lis bar.

The bedrooms are traditional, each one treated differently, utilizing, for example, a few antiques and tufted head- and footboards. The director, Monsieur Doumerc, welcomes half-board guests at prices ranging from 775F ($106.87) to 1,025F ($141.35) per person. Rooms vary considerably as to size and position. The dining room has many windows, allowing everyone a chance to watch the sunset over the Loire. Three fixed-price menus are offered at 260F ($35.85), 330F ($45.51), and 370F ($51.02). The hotel is open from March 5 to January 5. The hostellerie lies about 4 miles west of Saumur on the D751.

25. Angers

Once the capital of Anjou, Angers lies on both banks of the Maine River. Although it suffered extensive damage in World War II, it has been considerably restored. Somehow it blends the charm of the provinces with the suggestion of a sophisticated life. Most often it is used by visitors as headquarters for exploring the châteaux district in the west.

The moated **Château of Angers** was once the home of the counts of Anjou, its origin going back to the ninth century. The notorious "Black Fulk" lived there, and in time the Plantagenets, who became the kings of England. (One of their descendants, Geoffrey the Handsome, married Matilda, the granddaughter of William the Conqueror. Their son, Henry Plantagenet, later Henry II of England, married the legendary Eleanor of Aquitaine after she was divorced by the king of France.)

After the castle was destroyed, it was reconstructed by St. Louis. From 1230 to 1238 the outer walls and 17 massive towers were built—a formidable fortress well prepared to withstand almost any invader. The château was especially favored by the Good King René, in whose reign a brilliant court life flourished until he was forced to surrender Anjou to Louis XI. Louis XIV, in time, turned the château into a prison, dispatching his former finance minister, Fouquet, to a cell there. In the 19th century the castle was again a prison, and in World War II it was used by the Germans as a munitions depot. Allied planes bombed it in 1944.

The castle should be visited if for no other reason than to see the **Apocalypse Tapestries**, considered one of the great masterpieces of art to come down from the Middle Ages. This series of tapestries wasn't always so highly regarded, serving once as a canopy for orange trees to protect the fruit from unfavorable weather conditions and at another time to cover the damaged walls of a church. Based on cartoons by Hennequin of Bruges, they were made by Nicolas Bataille beginning in 1375. Louis I of Anjou had ordered them for the walls of his castle. In the 19th century they were purchased for only a nominal sum.

Seventy-seven pieces of them stretch a distance of 335 feet, the series illustrating the book of Saint John. One scene is called *La Grande Prostituée*. Another shows Babylon invaded by demons; yet another depicts men in combat with a seven-headed dragon or a peace scene with two multiheaded monsters holding up a fleur-de-lis staff. In still another, warriors are riding on the backs of lions.

After seeing the tapestries, you can go on a tour of the fortress, including the courtyard of the nobles, the prison cells, the ramparts, the windmill tower, a 15th-century chapel, and the restored royal apartments. The château is open from around Easter until the end of June from 9:30 a.m. to noon and 2 to 6 p.m.

Beginning in July and lasting through September it is open without interruption from 9:30 a.m. to 6:30 p.m. From October until around Easter it is open from 9:30 a.m. to noon and 2 to 5:30 p.m. Admission is 15F ($2.07).

The **Cathedral of St. Maurice** is from the 12th and 13th centuries, the previous church that stood on this site having been destroyed in a fire. The main tower, however, is from the 16th century, and the statues on the portal represent everybody from the Queen of Sheba to David at the harp. On the tympanum is depicted *Christ Enthroned,* the symbols, such as the lion for St. Mark, representing the Evangelists. Inside, the stained-glass windows from the 12th through the 16th centuries have made the cathedral known throughout Europe. The oldest one illustrates the martyrdom of St. Vincent (the most unusual window is from a later period: ex-St. Christopher with the head of a dog). Once all the Apocalypse Tapestries were exhibited there; now only a few remain. It is said that Henri Gervais, who designed the imposing central altar, did so from his death bed. The 12th-century nave is a landmark in cathedral architecture, a clear, simple, coherent plan that is a work of harmonious beauty and refinement. It is covered with Angevin vaulting.

WHERE TO STAY: Hôtel d'Anjou, 1 Boulevard Foch (tel. 41-88-24-82), is a four-floor hotel standing on the main boulevard of town, next to a large park. Fifty rooms are rented out at prices ranging from 400F ($55.16) for a double, from 295F ($40.68) for a single. You get practical comfort at reasonable prices. The rooms are furnished conventionally, with traditional pieces, pleasant and informal. The manager sees to it that everything is kept spic and span and that guests are welcomed politely and cared for well.

On the premises is one of the better restaurants in town, La Salamandre, which offers both regional specialties and some very good and fresh-tasting fish dishes. Try especially the sole in tomato sauce and filets of duck with spring turnips. Set meals cost 85F ($11.72) to 190F ($26.20), and you'll spend from 200F ($27.58) up by ordering à la carte. The restaurant is closed on Sunday.

Hôtel Concorde, 18 Boulevard Foch (tel. 41-87-37-20), in the commercial center of town, is an attractively pleasant balconied hotel that opened in 1972. The reception area has a high ceiling and tall expanses of exposed stone, while the contemporary bedrooms have all the modern comforts and are done in boldly patterned fabrics. The hotel restaurant is loaded with plants, big windows, and lots of chrome, and serves brasserie-style meals from 100F ($13.79). Room prices are 330F ($45.51) in a single, 420F ($57.92) in a double.

La Croix de Guerre ("Military Cross"), 23 rue Château-Gontier (tel. 41-88-66-59), is a *relais gastronomique.* The rooms are comfortable, and the *patron* is a master of the art of cooking. Right near the Place Leroy, the inn stands on a quiet street and is bedecked with boxes of pink geraniums in summer. In the courtyard are espalier roses. The color-coordinated bedrooms are superior, surprisingly so, with well-designed reproductions of antiques. A single rents for 100F ($13.79), a double costing from 200F ($27.58). Plumbing is minimal. The inn serves only a continental breakfast.

Boule d'Or (The Golden Ball), 27 Boulevard Carnot (tel. 41-43-76-56), has a pleasant small-town country look to it, with umbrellaed tables set out on the sidewalk behind planters of flowers. It provides not only reasonable meals, inn fashion, but some modern bedrooms built L-shaped around a rear courtyard, almost in the style of a motel. To stay there, two persons in a room with bath pay 175F ($24.13); three or four persons, 200F ($27.58). The furnishings are most satisfactory and comfortable. The dining room is pure provincial, with colorful cloths and napery, worn wood, copper pans, and an open Breton cupboard containing ceramic dishes. A standard 90F ($12.41) set menu is offered, although you are likely to spend 150F ($20.69) if you order à la carte. My most recent dinner here began with a rich-tasting pâté (I could have ordered a tempting selection of hors d'oeuvres instead), followed by filet of turbot, then côte de veau (veal), a salad, a choice of cheese, and finally a dessert.

On the Outskirts

Château de la Jaillière, La Chapelle St-Sauveur, at Varades (tel. 40-98-62-54), is a heavily embellished 19th-century château with flowering gardens, expansive lawns, a private tennis court, dozens of marble fireplaces, tapestries, and period furniture. Lying 22 miles west of Angers on Route D6, which intersects the N23 between Angers and Nantes, the château is owned by the Countess d'Anthenaise, who takes a personal interest in the well-being of her guests, offering insights into the region's history with well-prepared dinners at around 175F ($24.13) per person. The accommodations include only three beautifully furnished rooms, each with double beds, a complete bathroom, and carefully maintained antiques. Each unit, with breakfast included, rents for about 500F ($68.95) for two persons. You can stay here from June 1 to October 30, but it must be for at least two nights.

WHERE TO DINE: **Le Toussaint,** 7 rue Toussaint (tel. 41-87-46-20), offers an exceptionally intimate environment for an evening meal. Housed in a rustic building dating from the 1600s, the tables are cleverly illuminated to make practically anyone look terrific. All of this is the perfect backdrop for the imaginative platters that Michel Bignon concocts from regional recipes, adding a creative flourish and frequently signing his name to the top of the plates on which they're served. Menu items might include Loire Valley salmon with mango, steamed crayfish, fondant of duckling with rye bread, soufflé of sole, duckling in Cointreau, ragoût of snails, and a matelote of Loire eels with a local red wine sauce. However, actual food items are changed seasonally. The fixed-price menus represent good value at 156F ($21.51) and 200F ($27.58), while à la carte dinners go for 300F ($41.37). The restaurant is closed Sunday, Monday, and for most of August.

Le Quéré, 9 Place du Relliement (tel. 41-87-64-94). Named for its owner, Brittany-born Paul Le Quéré, this may be the most avant-garde restaurant, in terms of cuisine, in town. Many of the tables are angled toward the view offered by the prominent bay window, illuminating the specialties, which, while based on regional ingredients, are nonetheless original. Examples include ragoût of noodles with shrimp and morels, a gratin of fresh oysters with champagne, salad of pigeon breast, shrimp, and artichokes with hot liver garnish, and turbot in papillote with anchovy butter sauce. Generous table d'hôte menus are available at 150F ($20.69), while à la carte meals cost 275F ($37.92) and up. The place is closed Friday night, all day Saturday, and for most of July.

Le Logis, 17 rue Saint-Laud (tel. 41-87-44-15), tastefully directed by the Guinet family, is a two-level restaurant painted warmly in shades of reds. One of the appetizers is a terrine of John Dory, which attracts repeat customers. Other specialties are filet of lotte in raspberry vinegar, a marmite of well-flavored fish, grilled lobster, or a cassolette of crayfish. Full meals cost 220F ($30.34) to 270F ($37.23) if you order à la carte, or you can enjoy a set menu for 120F ($16.55) or 220F ($30.34). The restaurant is closed Saturday night, Sunday, and from mid-July to mid-August.

Le Petit Saint-Germain, 3 rue Saint-Laud (tel. 41-87-52-67), managed by Jean-Claude Boissinot, borrows heavily from regional recipes and transforms them into nouvelle dishes all its own. The culinary creations served amid the dining room's masses of flowers are not cheap, but diners whose palates are jaded by the standard French specialties will find one of the city's more unusual menus here. Specialties include home-smoked Loire Valley salmon, baby pigeons cooked with rhubarb, calf's head on a bed of artichokes, fricassée of chicken with white wine from the Loire, and an eel stew with fresh plums and wine. À la carte meals cost around 240F ($33.10), while fixed-price menus go for 82F ($11.31) and—perhaps a better value considering what you'll get—120F ($16.55). It is closed every Sunday and Monday, and from mid-August until early September. Dinner is served until 9:30 p.m.

26. Le Mans

Our next stopover lies not in the Loire valley, but on both banks of the Sarthe, a Loire tributary. Halfway between Paris and Nantes, Le Mans was the capital of the counts of Maine in the Middle Ages. But it is more known to the world as the scene of the annual roaring event, the Grand Prix, a 24-hour sportscar race in June on a road circuit three miles south of the city.

If you'd like to explore, the city's most interesting sector is called **Le Vieux Mans,** extending north from the Place de la République, which is the focal point of Le Mans. On a hill overlooking the Sarthe, the **Maison de la Reine Bérengère,** at 11 rue de la Reine Bérengère, dates from the 16th century and contains a lovely courtyard. The house is so named because it is believed to have been erected on the site of a former mansion once owned by Queen Berengaria, wife of Richard the Lion-Hearted.

At the north end of the rue de la Reine Bérengère stands the imposing **Cathedral of St. Julian,** founded by its namesake. Pause on the Place St-Michel to take in a view of the 12th-century doorway of the south porch, the most outstanding architectural feature of the church's façade. In the cathedral's Romanesque nave, dating from the 11th century, is some of the oldest stained glass in France, created in the early part of the 12th century. The legend of St. Julian is traced in the west window. In the transept, seek out the tombs of Charles I of Anjou and of Guillaume Du Bellay, erected during the French Renaissance. The Gothic choir of the 13th century is richly decorated. See the beautiful tapestries above the choir stalls.

The Romans fortified Le Mans in the third century, and on the western edge of the old sector of town you can see remains of these **Roman fortifications,** with ten towers that have survived the 20 sieges the city suffered, including the famous Battle of Le Mans in 1871 with the Germans. Le Mans was the culmination of General Chanzy's retreat into western France after the winter campaign.

A stroll along the Avenue de Paderborn, near the cathedral, will lead to the **Musée de Tesse,** in a park setting. It is open from 9 a.m. to noon and 2 to 6 p.m. The collection offers a large group of paintings, including some Italian primitives, and an enamel plaque made in the 12th century for one of the Plantagenets.

Back on the heartbeat Place de la République, you can go southeast of the square to visit the **Church of La Couture,** part of an abbey founded in the seventh century by St. Bertrand. Its porch with fine statuary is from the 13th century. Inside are some interesting tapestries and pictures, including *Elijah's Dream,* and a beautiful Madonna in white marble, standing opposite the pulpit.

If you're in Le Mans because you're interested in automobiles, you may want to drive out on the D139 to the **Automobile Museum** (tel. 43-72-50-66). It is open from 9 a.m. to noon and 2 to 7 p.m. (till 6 p.m. off-season), charging an admission of 20F ($2.76). There is not space to exhibit all the collection, so the show is changed periodically. However, you're certain to see some of the early vintage automobiles, including some antique Renaults and several racing models.

WHERE TO STAY: Le Moderne, 14 rue Bourg-Belé (tel. 43-24-79-20), is one of the best places to stay at Le Mans, unless you prefer the more modern (and more expensive) chain hotel, the Concorde. At any rate, the Moderne serves the finest cuisine in the city. Go here at any time but in June when race-car fans occupy every table and every bed. Madame Gazonnaud and Monsieur Derboulle are in charge, and they run an attractive, inviting hotel.

They are rightly proud of their food specialties, and do a roaring trade. Two set meals are offered—one for 120F ($16.55), another for 175F ($24.13), both representing good value. To begin your meal, there is no finer selection than the foie gras of the chef. It's velvety smooth and sinfully delicious. If you're ordering à la carte, you'll find that the chef specializes in grilled lobster, but this dish is too expensive for most visitors. More reasonably priced, and another specialty, is chicken cooked with morels. Regional wines include Quincy, Chinon, and Bourgueil. The rooms, 32 in all, are comfortably furnished and of a good standard, costing 220F ($30.34) in a single and 300F ($41.37) in a double.

Chantecler, 50 rue de la Pelouse (tel. 43-24-58-53), is surprisingly quiet, considering its inner-city location near the train station. The modern decor is evident in tastefully redecorated bedrooms, an accommodating bar, and a restaurant. The 36 rooms rent for 155F ($21.38) in a single, 255F ($35.17) in a double.

If you're looking for less expensive accommodations, try the **Central,** 5 Boulevard René-Levasseur (tel. 43-24-08-93). It doesn't have a restaurant, but does offer 55 nicely furnished rooms that are well maintained and comfortable. The charge is 180F ($24.82) in a single, rising to 225F ($31.03) in a double.

WHERE TO DINE: **Le Grenier à Sel,** Place de l'Eperson (tel. 43-23-26-30), is run by a mustachioed chef, André Plunian, who flamboyantly prepares specialties for which gourmets drive for miles around to enjoy. A handwritten menu is radically different from day to day, depending on the availability of ultra-fresh ingredients. Of course, everything depends upon the inspiration of the chef whose restaurant is installed within an antique building formerly used by government tax collectors. A modestly priced set menu is presented for 120F ($16.55); however, most visitors opt for the à la carte offerings, priced from 230F ($31.72) to 280F ($38.61) per meal. Typical dishes would include a fricassée of crayfish with sauterne, baby lamb with new vegetables, and grilled sweetbreads with fresh noodles. Meals are served daily except Sunday and during much of August.

La Renaissance, 114 Avenue du Général-Leclerc (tel. 43-24-98-38), offers a good meal prepared with style. It is directed with efficiency by René Martin. Veal Cordon Bleu is a sure bet. Children are pampered with a special menu at 60F ($8.27), while adults can receive a surprisingly good value meal for 75F ($10.32) and up. It is closed during August, Sunday night, and Monday.

If you've got one day before heading back to Paris, or wherever, I'd suggest two final stopovers in the Sarthe district, of which Le Mans is the capital. The first is at—

27. Loué

In this village, 17½ miles from Le Mans, the **Ricordeau,** 13 rue Libération (tel. 43-88-40-03), is an inn and château, perhaps the finest in the Sarthe district. Gilbert Laurent runs this provincial stopover, which he has transformed into a hotel of charm and character, well worth a detour and a good place at which to relax after an exhausting tour of the châteaux country. In the heart of the village, the hotel offers 19 beautifully furnished rooms, 14 of which contain private bath. The simplest single rents for only 175F ($24.13), but if you want a double with complete bath, expect to pay as much as 400F ($55.16).

Monsieur Laurent enjoys a wide reputation for his French cookery, including such specialties as poulet of Loué (made with cream and morels), turbot in Sancerre with wild mushrooms, and pigeon stuffed with sweetbreads. A set menu costs 180F ($24.82), another even better one going for 230F ($31.72). He also has an interesting wine cellar, with such regional selections featured as Quincy and Bourgueil. The hotel shuts down in January, and the restaurant is closed on Monday night and Tuesday.

The next morning you can plan a visit to—

SOLESMES: A short drive southwest from Loué, lying 29 miles west from Le Mans, Solesmes enjoys world fame for its Gregorian chants. In 1010 a priory was founded here, and it was directly responsible to the abbey of La Couture at Le Mans, which we've already visited. However, the priory was suppressed during the Revolution. In 1830 it became a Benedictine monastery, and seven years later was raised to the rank of an abbey, which lasted until 1901. At St. Peter's Abbey, called Abbaye St-Pierre in French, you can see the Saints of Solesmes, an outstanding collection of carvings in the transepts. But mostly visitors come here hoping to hear the revived Gregorian chants.

Chapter IX

NORMANDY

1. Rouen
2. Jumièges
3. Saint-Wandrille
4. Caudebec-en-Caux
5. Pont-Audemer
6. L'Aigle
7. Orbec
8. Caen
9. Bayeux
10. Port-en-Bessin
11. D-Day Beaches
12. Cherbourg
13. Le Mont St-Michel
14. Pont l'Évêque
15. Cabourg
16. Deauville
17. Trouville
18. Honfleur
19. Le Havre
20. Fécamp
21. Dieppe

TEN CENTURIES HAVE gone by since the Vikings invaded the province of Normandy. The early Scandinavians might have come to ravish the land, but they stayed to cultivate it, bringing their cattle and their women. Of course, they didn't entirely revert from warriors to butter-and-egg men. Rather, they set out on conquests that were to give them England and even Sicily. The Normans produced great soldiers, none more famous than William the Conqueror, who defeated the forces of King Harold at Battle Abbey in 1066. The English and the French continued to do battle on and off for 700 years—a national rivalry that climaxed at the 1815 Battle of Waterloo.

Much of Normandy was later ravaged in the 1944 invasion that began on a June morning when parachutists and airborne troops dropped from the sky at Sainte-Mère-Église and Bénouville-sur-Orne. The largest armada ever assembled was about to begin one of the most momentous sagas in world history, the reconquest of continental Europe from the Nazis. Today, many come to Normandy just to see the D-Day beachheads.

Some of the province evokes a Millet landscape. Cattle graze sleepily in the fields turned a verdant green by the heavy Atlantic rainfall. Wood-framed houses exist side by side with postwar modern buildings that rose out of the ashes of World War II. Miraculously spared from the bombardments heaped on Normandy in the battle are stained-glass windows, sculptured woodwork, and Gothic architecture. Many great buildings, regrettably, were leveled to the ground.

The wide beaches attract those seeking a family holiday, although in August the sands of Deauville draw the most chic Europeans and North Americans. Not far from the banks of the Seine you come upon a tiny hamlet where Monet painted his water lilies. Transatlantic liners pull into Le Havre, the fishermen's nets are set off by a background of cliffs, and yachts clog the harbor. Normandy, like Brittany, seems to look toward the sea. Or so you think until you venture into its heartland and glimpse lush pastures and fragrant apple orchards.

1. Rouen

"We've got one of the greatest cathedrals in Europe, many attractions," the woman at the Tourist Office laments, "but always, always they want to know where *she* was burned alive." *She* is Joan of Arc, and she died "on the Place du Vieux-Marché," answers the woman automatically.

The capital of Normandy, Rouen is the second most important tourist center in the north of France. It is also a hub of industry and commerce, the third-largest port in France. Victor Hugo called it "the city of a hundred spires." Half of it was destroyed in World War II, mostly by Allied bombers, and many Rouennais were killed. In the reconstruction of the old quarters some of the almost forgotten crafts of the Middle Ages were revived.

On the Seine, 84 miles northwest of Paris, the city of Rouen is a good center for exploring much of Normandy. It is rich in historical associations: William the Conqueror died here in 1087, Joan of Arc in 1431.

THE SIGHTS OF ROUEN: This city has its share of formidable attractions, beginning with—

Rouen Cathedral

Most of the world knows Rouen's cathedral, immortalized by Monet in an impressionistic series of paintings depicting the three-portal main front with its galaxy of statues.

The present-day cathedral, a symphony of lace-like stonework, was reconstructed in part after the bombings of World War II. Consecrated in 1063, it was rebuilt after the "great fire" of 1200, the work lasting for centuries. Two soaring towers distinguish it; one, the **Tour de Beurre** (Tower of Butter), was financed by the faithful willing to pay good money in exchange for the privilege of eating butter at Lent. The tower is a masterpiece of the flamboyant Gothic style. Containing a carillon of 56 bells, a three-story lantern tower, built in 1877 and utilizing 740 tons of iron and bronze, rises to a height of almost 500 feet.

Especially interesting in the interior, the **Chapelle de la Vierge** is adorned with the Renaissance tombs of the cardinals d'Amboise as well as Jean de Brézé. Also entombed inside was the "lion" heart of Richard the Lion-Hearted—a token of his affection for the people of Rouen.

The cathedral is closed from noon to 2 p.m. and on Sunday from 1 to 3 p.m. No admission is charged.

Behind the cathedral, the **Archbishop's Palace** was bombed out during the

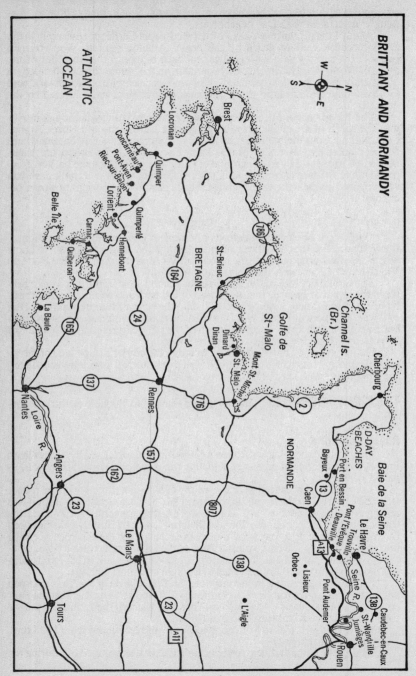

BRITTANY AND NORMANDY

war. Now it stands naked against the sky. The broken arches and rosette windows witnessed the trial of Joan of Arc in 1431. At this same spot her rehabilitation was proclaimed in 1456.

To and Through the Place du Vieux-Marché

A lane running between the cathedral and Place du Vieux-Marché is called **rue du Gros-Horloge** (Street of the Great Clock). Now a traffic-free pedestrian mall, it is named for an ornate gilt Renaissance clock mounted on an arch, Rouen's most popular monument. The arch bridges the street and is connected to a Louis XV sculpted fountain with a bevy of cherubs and a belltower. At night the bells still toll a curfew. Visitors who purchase a ticket at the Beaux-Arts (see below) are entitled to visit the belfry to see the iron clockworks and the bells. Hours are from 10 a.m. to 12:15 p.m. and 2:30 to 5:30 p.m. from Easter to mid-September.

Of course you'll want to visit **Place du Vieux-Marché** (Old Marketplace), marking "the final abode" of Joan of Arc. Tied to a stake, she was burned alive on a pyre set by the English on May 30, 1431. Kissing a cross while she was being chained, she is reported to have called out "Jesus!" as the fire was set. Afterward her ashes were gathered up and tossed into the Seine.

In the center of a monumental complex in the square is a modern church displaying stained-glass windows from St. Vincent. Beside it a bronze cross marks the position of St. Joan's stake.

Nearby at 15 Place de la Pucelle (Square of the Maid), stands the **Hôtel de Bourgtheroulde** (tel. 35-88-42-42), which is Gothic-inspired, although it shows traces of the beginning of the Renaissance. It dates from the 16th century and was built by William the Red (Guillaume le Roux). The inside yard is exceptional. Once in the courtyard, look back at the Gothic building with its octagonal stair tower. The left gallery is entirely Renaissance. A bank uses the hôtel now, and access is free during working hours. On Saturday and Sunday you can visit by ringing a bell and asking for the porter. On the square is a small outdoor market for fresh food.

More Churches

Besides the cathedral, two other Rouen churches seek attention. One is the **Church of St. Maclou,** behind the cathedral. It was built in the florid Gothic style, with a step-gabled porch and handsome cloisters. It is known for the remarkable panels on its doors, dating from the 16th century; my favorite (to the left) is the "Portal of the Fonts." The church was originally constructed in 1200, rebuilt in 1432, and finally consecrated in 1521, although its lantern tower is from the 19th century. It sits on a square of old Norman crooked-timbered buildings. Inside, pictures dating from June 4, 1944, document St. Maclou's destruction.

If you walk from rue de la République to Place du Général-de-Gaulle, you'll be at the **Church of St. Ouen,** the outgrowth of a seventh-century Benedictine abbey. Flanked by four turrets, its 375-foot octagonal lantern tower, in the Gothic style, is called "the ducal crown of Normandy." One of the best-known Gothic buildings in France, the present church represents the work of five centuries. Its nave is of the 15th century, its choir from the 14th (but with 18th-century railings), and its remarkable stained glass from the 14th through the 16th centuries.

On May 23, 1431, Joan of Arc was taken to the cemetery of St. Ouen, where officials sentenced her to be burnt at the stake unless she recanted. An abjuration was signed by her, thus condemning her to life imprisonment; that sentence was later revoked.

Museums

The **Musée des Beaux-Arts,** entered on the Square Verdrel, is one of the most important provincial museums in France, with portraits by David, plus works by Delacroix and Ingres (don't miss his *La Belle Zélie).* One of the most important masterpieces in the museum is a retable by Gérard David called *La Vierge et les Saints (The Virgin and the Saints).* A whole salon is devoted to Géricault, including a portrait he did of Delacroix. Other works are by Veronese, Velásquez, Caravaggio, Rubens, Poussin, Fragonard, Ingres, and Corot. There is a large collection of paintings by Sisley and Monet, including a version of the latter's *Rouen Cathedral.* It is one of his most famous studies. There are also important paintings by Dufy and sculptures by Duchamp-Villon.

The **Musée de la Céramique,** 1 rue Faucon, is in a 17th-century house. One of the greatest treasures here is its Rouen faïence, which pioneered a special red in 1670. The exhibits provide a showcase for the talents of Masseot Abaquesne (1500-1564), considered the premier French craftsman in porcelain. In time his position was usurped by Louis Poterat (1673-1696). As well, an exceptional showcase is devoted to chinoiseries dating from 1699 to 1745.

Le Secq des Tournelles (Wrought Ironworks Museum). Entered from the rue Jacques-Villon, this unique museum is housed in the 15th-century Church of St. Laurent. Its collection ranges from what the press once called "forthright masculine forging to lacy feminine filigree, from Roman keys to the needlepoint balustrade that graced Mme de Pompadour's country mansion." An aristocrat in Paris, Le Secq des Tournelles began the collection in 1870. So passionately was he devoted to it that his wife divorced him, charging alienation of affection. Donated to the city of Rouen, the collection now includes as many as 14,000 pieces.

Some of the pieces date from the days when English ships blocked French ports during the worst days of Napoleon's rule. Many French women—always concerned with fashion—went to their blacksmiths instead of their goldsmiths for sophisticated jewelry fashioned out of iron. These men could even turn out an orthopedic corset. Some of the collection is enlightening (including kitchen utensils dating from the 17th century), others merely amusing (a pair of scissors formed like a sea pelican, its beak making the blades). Removed from the d'Ourscamp Abbey, a 13th-century gate is remarkable for its filigree.

The same 10F ($1.38) ticket admits you to the Beaux-Arts, the ceramics museum, and the wrought-ironworks display. Hours for the three museums are from 10 a.m. to noon and 2 to 6 p.m. They are closed Tuesday and on Wednesday morning and holidays.

Musée Flaubert et d'Histoire de la Médecine, 51 rue de Lecat, was the birthplace of Gustave Flaubert, the French novelist who wrote the masterpiece *Madame Bovary.* His father was the director of Rouen's public hospital. Flaubert was born in the director's quarters of the hospital and spent the first 25 years of his life in the city. The bedroom where Flaubert was born in 1821 is intact. In addition, family furniture and medical paraphernalia are displayed. Only a glass door separated the Flaubert family from the ward filled with moaning patients. Contiguous to the family's billiard room was the dissection ward, where Flaubert would go to peek at the corpses.

Hours are 10 a.m. to noon and 2 to 6 p.m.; closed Sunday, Monday, and holidays. There is no admission charge.

Flaubert fans may want to visit the author's family home at **Croisset,** an industrial suburb of Rouen. The Flaubert pavilion is open from 10 a.m. to noon and 2 to 6 p.m.; closed Thursday, Friday morning, and most holidays. Admission is 5F (69¢) although it's free on Sunday and holidays. At the pavilion Flaubert wrote *Madame Bovary* and *Salammbô.*

The life and tragic martyrdom of Joan of Arc, France's national heroine, are traced at **Le Musée Jeanne d'Arc,** 33 Place du Vieux-Marché (tel. 35-88-02-

70). The museum is on the old market square where Joan was burned to death in 1431. In a vaulted cellar believed to have existed in Joan's era, you can see wax-works depicting the main stages of her life from Domremy, where she was born, to the stake at which she died. The museum is open daily from 9 a.m. to 7 p.m. in summer, from 10 a.m. to noon and 2 to 6 p.m. in winter. Admission is 12F ($1.66) for adults, 6F (83¢) for children.

HOTELS: Finding a room in Rouen can be a bit tricky if you don't have a reservation. In summer, tourists fill up the limited accommodations, and during the rest of the year business travelers often book many hotels solidly, as Rouen is then more an industrial and commercial center than it is a tourist mecca.

Upper Bracket Hotels

Frantel, rue Croix-de-Fer (tel. 35-98-06-98), is an excellent choice for those seeking the most up-to-date modern comforts in a city of antiquity. The location is unbeatable—right at the cathedral of Rouen and the rue du Gros-Horloge. Air-conditioned bedrooms, 121 in all, are well furnished and immaculately kept, costing from 430F ($59.30) in a single, that figure going up to 500F ($68.95) for the best doubles, all with private bath. The bedrooms are models of contemporary functional design. Its restaurant, Le Tournebroche, serves good food as well, set meals costing 110F ($15.17) to 225F ($31.03), although you can spend far more, of course, by ordering à la carte. It is closed Sunday.

Hôtel de Dieppe, Place Bernard-Tissot (tel. 35-71-96-00), has been run by the Guéret family since 1880, and each new generation has modernized the premises somewhat. More recently, two new floors with 15 rooms have been added. Dieppe's essential character, however, remains that of a traditional French inn. In 1977 the fourth generation took over its responsibilities; Jean-Pierre Guéret, ten years with Hilton International, is the general manager. Directly opposite the railway station, it is actually two buildings joined together. All its rooms have bath or shower, plus toilet. The newer rooms are preferable; many have been redecorated as well, and graced with art reproductions and period pieces. Singles range from 275F ($37.92); doubles, 345F ($47.58). In the adjoining rôtisserie, Le Quatre Saisons, you can select a menu for 160F ($22.06). À la carte specialties include duckling à la presse or sole poached in red wine. Prices include tax and service.

Middle-Bracket and Budget Lodgings

Hôtel Le Nord, 91 rue Gros-Horloge (tel. 35-70-41-41). I'd rank this hotel number three in Rouen, after the Frantel and the Dieppe, although it isn't nearly so well equipped as those two. In the center of the commercial district of town, the hotel has 62 rooms, each comfortably furnished and with private facilities. There's no restaurant on the premises, although breakfast is served. A basic single room rents for 162F ($22.34), while the best doubles cost 280F ($38.61).

Le Viking, 21 Quai du Havre (tel. 35-70-34-95), right on the riverbank overlooking the Seine, provides charming views from its front rooms (the traffic can be thunderous at times, however). A completely modern establishment, Le Viking has 35 bedrooms. Accommodations are clean-cut and utilitarian; twin-bedded rooms with private bath or shower cost 230F ($31.72). Bathless singles go for 120F ($16.55), going up to 210F ($28.96) with bath. Breakfast is the only meal served. In July and August, when the pilgrimage to Rouen reaches its zenith, you really should reserve at least two weeks in advance.

Hôtel de Québec, 18-24 rue de Québec (tel. 35-70-09-38), is a neat, modern, brick-built corner hotel, with 38 inexpensive bedrooms. A block from the Seine, within walking distance of the cathedral and some of the city's best restaurants, the hotel is well run and friendly. The bedrooms are small but serviceable, many opening onto a rear courtyard where parking is provided. The tariff for two persons in a room with private bath is 250F ($34.48). Singles without bath cost from 95F ($13.10).

Hôtel de la Cathédrale, 12 rue St-Romain (tel. 35-71-57-95), is a small, 23-room hostelry. Staying here is like being in a private home. The location is choice, behind the cathedral and opposite the Archbishop's Palace where Joan of Arc was tried. The street on which the hotel stands has been restored, the 19th- and 20th-century overlays giving way to the original black-and-white timbered façades. Good, clean, but simply furnished double rooms peak at 250F ($34.48) with a private bath. Singles cost from 125F ($17.24).

La Vieille-Tour, Place de la Haute-Vieille-Tour (tel. 35-70-03-27), is a small (23 rooms) modern hotel on a square, a block from the Seine, within walking distance of the cathedral. In fact, you'll often hear the chimes from your bedroom window. The lobby is tiny, the breakfast lounge small. But many of the bedrooms are spacious, some with two double beds. Furnishings are contemporary. The most desirable accommodations face the square. The cost of a double with complete bath is 235F ($32.41), but less expensive doubles with less plumbing go for 195F ($26.89). Singles begin at a modest 97F ($13.34), going up to 185F ($25.51) with complete bath. You'll pay an additional charge for your croissants, coffee, and jam with Normandy butter for breakfast.

RESTAURANTS: Now it's time to sample the rich Norman cuisine I've been telling you about. I'll begin at—

The Leading Restaurants

La Couronne, 31 Place du Vieux-Marché (tel. 35-71-40-90), is not only the most ancient restaurant in Rouen, dating back to 1345; it lays claim as well to being the oldest *auberge* (inn) in France. Housed in a half-timbered building that looks like a setting for Hansel and Gretel, it stands directly on the square where Joan of Arc was burned at the stake. During World War II a 500-pound bomb exploded in its rear courtyard, but, amazingly, wooden pegs held La Couronne together. The dining rooms, on several floors, are reached by wooden stairs leading around fireplaces.

La Couronne has won fame for its caneton (duckling) rouennais. Many gourmets have compared it in quality to that of La Tour d'Argent in Paris. Certainly the prices are better in Rouen. The duck is roasted (after its neck has been wrung, so as not to lose any blood), then the breast slices are flamed in Calvados before being covered in a blood sauce. The drumsticks are grilled until they are crisp. A superb dish! The seafood couldn't be fresher. Other specialties are the goose liver, lobster, spiny lobster, turbot with orange and honey, barbue au safron, and shellfish. The best desserts are gratin de pommes au Calvados, assiette du gourmet, and assiette de sorbet. Set menus are offered for 108F ($14.89), 175F ($24.13), and 250F ($34.48), wine included. If you order à la carte, your dinner will cost from 325F ($44.82). The restaurant is closed Sunday evening. Last orders are taken at 9:45 p.m.

Bertrand Warin Restaurateur, 7-9 rue de la Pie (tel. 35-89-26-69). You'll have to pass next to the former house of Pierre Corneille to enter the graciously proportioned entranceway of this elegant villa in the inner part of the city. The interior is filled with beautifully ornamented tables, served with good manners by a well-trained staff. Many of the menu items are based on traditional Norman recipes, although a few are more contemporary and seem popular with the well-heeled crowd flocking here to enjoy them. A special treat might be the duckling, prepared as a liver terrine or as a main course. Apple sherbet is a refreshing dessert. The table d'hôte menu costs from 120F ($16.55), while à la carte meals range from 300F ($41.37) to 340F ($46.89). The restaurant is closed Sunday night, Monday, and in August.

Le Beffroy, 15 rue Beffroy (tel. 35-71-55-27). By French standards, this restaurant is more avant garde socially than it is gastronomically, in the sense that the wife, Dorothée l'Hernault, works in the kitchens while her husband, Bernard, directs the service in the heavily beamed dining room. Cuisine choices depend on market availability of the ingredients, although representative specialties are well-prepared versions of sole with poached oysters, blanc de turbot with raspberry butter, Bresse chicken with crayfish, rabbit with anise, terrine of duck with onion jam (that's *confiture d'oignons*), and luscious desserts. Fixed-price menus range from 115F ($15.86) to 180F ($24.82), while an à la carte dinner costs around 275F ($37.92) per person. The restaurant is closed Sunday, Monday, in August, and for part of February. Dinner is served until 9 p.m.

The Middle Bracket

Maison Dufour, 67 rue St-Nicholas (tel. 35-71-90-62), is one of the best preserved of the 17th-century inns of Normandy. In the true Norman style, it's a five-story corner building built of timber and plaster. Inside are several dining rooms, a veritable forest of aged and seasoned beams, and all the trappings necessary for a colorful atmosphere: copper pans and pots, spices, woodcarvings, and engravings. The dishes—prepared and served under the eagle eye of Monsieur Dufour—are so outstanding that it's difficult to single out specialties. Many dishes are based on classic recipes; others are from the nouvelle cuisine repertoire. An always reliable opener is delectable black mussels in a creamy sauce. The filet de sole is the favorite fish entree. An excellent main dish is half a roast Rouen duckling with apples, served to two or more diners. The average meal will run about 250F ($34.48). The restaurant is closed Sunday night and Monday, and takes a vacation in August.

Au Bois Chenu, 23-25 Place de la Pucelle (tel. 35-71-19-54). The proprietor, Michel Barrel, is happy to assist guests who would like to know what to order, as the restaurant offers several set menus ranging in price from 80F ($11.03) to 120F ($16.55). The terrines, including an orange-flavored one of duck, are always fresh and well made, and appetizers are tempting. The menu is likely to undergo seasonal changes, but past favored dishes have included an escalope of fresh salmon in a white-butter sauce, white brill flavored with mustard, roasted veal kidneys, and, in season, roast pheasant flavored with Calvados.

For dessert, you'll be tempted by a plate of the cheese of Normandy or a tart made with the fruit of the season, perhaps strawberries. The restaurant lies a short distance from rue Gros, in the vicinity of the market. The place is intimate and tastefully decorated in a restrained fashion, tables set under hand-hewn Norman beams. The restaurant is closed Tuesday night and Wednesday, and for part of July and August.

Low-Cost Dining

Pascaline, 5 rue de la Poterne (tel. 35-89-67-44), is an informal bistro filled with gatherings of friends who seem to make this a regular rendezvous point. The menu is filled with French puns and unusual illustrations, and it offers a set meal that seems to be one of the best bargains in town, costing around 110F ($15.17). It's served daily. À la carte items include fresh oysters, tenderloin steaks, and duckling fricassée. Desserts here are an ice cream lover's delight.

Brasserie du Vieux Marché, 2 Place du Vieux-Marché (tel. 35-71-59-09), specializes in fruits de mer, or fruits of the sea. The larder must be well stocked, as the chef offers the widest selection of food on his set menus of any kitchen in Rouen. For 75F ($10.32) you can enjoy the simplest meal, beginning with hors d'oeuvres and including a main dish, as well as a choice of cheese or dessert. A second menu goes for 85F ($11.72), and a more elaborate menu at 160F ($22.06) includes some more expensive dishes, such as oysters and steak au poivre. You can also dine à la carte.

Up the Seine 17 miles from Rouen is the town of:

2. Jumièges

Called one of the most beautiful ruins in France, **Jumièges Abbey** (tel. 35-91-84-02) was founded by St. Philbert in the 7th century, although it was rebuilt in the 10th century by Duke Guillaume ("Long Sword"). The abbey church was consecrated in 1067 by the archbishop of Rouen in the presence of William the Conqueror.

One of the architectural wonders of Normandy, Jumièges was seized by the state during the French Revolution. It was later sold to a wood merchant and subsequently vandalized. Salvaged finally in the mid-1800s, it has been turned over to the state. The 100-foot-high nave is complete, and the porch is surrounded by two towers 150 feet high. In summer the hours are 10 a.m. to noon and 2 to 6 p.m. It is closed on Sunday. Admission is 8F ($1.10).

About six miles farther on lies the village of—

3. Saint-Wandrille

The **Abbey of Saint Wandrille** (tel. 35-96-23-11) was founded in 649 by Wandrille, an official of the court of King Dagobert. Wandrille was called an "athlete of God" because of his great spiritual training and influence. In the course of centuries the buildings have suffered from fire, thunder and lightning, and the attacks of men, among whom were the Vikings. That is why nothing survives of the original 7th-century monastery. Ever since 649 monks have lived in the abbey, except for a hundred years or so because of French political troubles.

A monumental blue gate from the 18th century frames the entrance to the monastery. Inside the great courtyard you can see a building housing a factory in which household products, such as wax and polish, are manufactured to help the community make a living. Next to the factory stand the microfilm workroom and several workshops.

The cloisters are from the 14th to the 16th centuries. In the north gallery, a lavabo (wash basin) is a beautiful and unique piece of work from about 1500. The church is well worth even a short visit. A 14th-century barn originally located 30 miles from the abbey was transplanted and reerected in 1967–1969 as the abbey church.

A guided tour is given weekdays at 3 and 4 p.m. (Sunday and holidays at 11:30 a.m. as well), costing 10F ($1.38) for adults, free for children. Products by the monks are on sale.

In the village, the **Auberge Deux-Couronnes** (tel. 35-96-11-44) is an old Norman inn that makes a good luncheon or dinner choice if you're in the hamlet visiting the abbey and listening to Gregorian chants. The daily menus at 70F ($9.65) and 130F ($17.93) are highly commendable. This gem of a restaurant is beautifully run, and the chef does all the Norman specialties well. That means a cuisine of butter, cream, cheese, and cider. But there are other standard French dishes as well. In addition to the good food, you get friendly service. The restaurant is closed in September, and it shuts down also February 3 to February 20, Sunday night, and all day Monday.

4. Caudebec-en-Caux

Set in an amphitheater on the banks of the Seine, this charming little town was nearly destroyed in World War II. At the end of the Ste-Gertrude Valley, it is the scene of the "Mascaret," which is a tidal wave occurring in the estuary of the Seine at the time of the fall and spring equinoxes.

Its Gothic **Church of Notre-Dame**, dating from the early 15th century, was saved from the 1940 fires. Henri IV called the church "the handsomest chapel in my kingdom." Restoration work in the 16th century was carried out by Guillaume Le Tellier. On the west side is a trio of flamboyant doorways, surmounted by a rose window.

Although damaged in the war, the **Maison des Templiers** has been restored, showing it to be an outstanding example of secular architecture from the 13th century. It can be visited on Saturday and Sunday May to September (every day in July and August) from 10 a.m. to noon and 3 to 6 p.m.

FOOD AND LODGING: On a hill, with a view of the Seine, stands the **Manoir de Rétival**, 2 rue St-Clair (tel. 35-96-11-22). Once a hunting lodge, it receives guests in its ten chambers from April to November, charging 190F ($26.20) in a single, 440F ($60.68) in a double. The bedrooms are in the antique style, and some even have fireplaces. In warm weather guests like to sit out on the terrace overlooking the river and the heather-covered plains of Caux. The second-floor salon, to which guests also retreat, is a lovely period piece with an interesting chimney.

Since the manor no longer serves meals other than breakfast, I suggest the **Normandie**, Quai Guilbaud (tel. 35-96-25-11), where the owner offers a simple, well-prepared cuisine in a setting overlooking the Seine. The chef prepares such dishes as grilled fresh sardines, eggplant fritters, fried sand eels, and Norman chicken. Meals range in price from 55F ($7.56), which is an extremely good buy considering the quality and the size, the price going up to 140F ($19.31), the latter more food than the average diner may desire. In addition, the patron of this *restaurant avec chambres* has enlarged his room capacity to 15. The accommodations are simple but adequate in comfort, costing from 132F ($18.20) in a single, the tariff going up to 250F ($34.48) in a double. The inn shuts down on Sunday night, and is also closed in February.

5. Pont-Audemer

The father of William the Conqueror used to storm through this historic town of markets and tanners. A number of old houses still stand on the **rue de la Licorne** (the street of the unicorn). A few visitors pass through to see the **Church of St. Ouen**, dating from the 11th century, with a 1450 façade and Renaissance stained-glass windows. But the real reason foreigners head this way is because of a remarkable old Norman inn, detailed below.

Pont-Audemer is 23 miles northeast of Lisieux and makes a convenient stopover between Deauville and Rouen.

FOOD AND LODGING: Auberge du Vieux Puits (The Inn of the Old Well), 6 rue Notre-Dame-du-Pré (tel. 35-41-01-48), is a dreamy picture-postcard cliché of a mellowed 17th-century Norman inn. You'll recognize it quickly, with its half-timbered façade, small street-floor windows, and third-floor dormers. An L-shaped building, it partially encloses an old garden. Try to schedule at least a night's stopover. Beamed ceilings, half-timbered walls, country chairs, and plain wooden tables mark the interior. Copper and brass pots and pans hang from the beams, and above the fireplace is a pewter collection.

The inn is owned and run by Monsieur and Madame Jacques Foltz. Those interested in the specialties should order à la carte, paying 200F ($27.58) to 240F ($33.10) per person for a complete meal. Especially recommended is the canard aux cerises (duck with cherries), the filet de sole Vieux Puits, and the truite (trout) Bovary au champagne. Many diners prefer to finish their meal with the three classic cheeses of Normandy: camembert, Livarot, and Pont-l'Évêque. For dessert, you can order a thick tart (hopefully strawberries will be in season) smothered in rich Norman cream. Norman cider is most appealing.

Madame Foltz offers eight old-fashioned bedrooms in the main inn, five with private shower and three with a wash basin. With shower, the single rate is 135F ($18.62), between 160F ($22.06) and 290F ($39.99) in a double. With a wash basin, the rate in a room for one or two persons is only 100F ($13.79) a night. The best equipped rooms, six in all, each with private bath, are in a new wing built with timbers and a tile roof. For two, prices are 290F ($39.99) for a large bedded room, 330F ($45.51) in a twin. Guests in these rooms must stay here on half-board terms. The auberge is closed from mid-December to mid-January and the first week of July, plus Monday night and all of Tuesday.

Denise Carel, La Ricardière, Route de Lisieux (tel. 32-41-09-14), offers one of the most charming accommodations in the area, an 18th-century house with a few bedrooms to rent, lying off route D139 on the outskirts of town (follow the road signs in the direction of Lisieux). The house enjoys a secluded setting in a scene typical of the Norman countryside: grazing cows and half-timbered buildings. A mother-daughter operation, the house is warmly furnished and decorated, showing the influence of the daughter's background as an artist. The mother of the household once wrote a guidebook on the history of the area. For a spacious bedroom with private bath, with a good breakfast included, the charge is 275F ($37.92) for two persons.

6. L'Aigle

A good center for touring the upper valley of the Risle, L'Aigle contains **St. Martin's Church** with its 15th-century square tower and another smaller tower dating from the 12th century. In addition, it also has an interesting waxworks—**Musée Juin 44: Bataille de Normandie**, 44 Place Fulbert-de-Beina (tel. 33-24-19-44), with its re-creation of some of the major personalities of that epic battle, including Churchill and Charles de Gaulle. Their voices, recorded at the time, can also be heard. The museum is open from 9 a.m. to noon and from 2 to 6 p.m., charging an admission of 12F ($1.66).

L'Aigle—its denizens are called Aiglons, or little eagles—is a metal-working center, a tradition going back to ancient times. Frankly, the town isn't a major sightseeing attraction. My main reason for recommending it for those touring in Normandy is because of—

The **Hôtel du Dauphin**, Place de la Halle (tel. 33-24-43-12), which has one of the most charmingly decorated interiors of any hotel in Normandy. In grand provincial comfort, Michel Bernard and Jean-Paul Leroi will welcome you to one of their color-coordinated rooms, some of which have the beams exposed. All 30 of their chambers are decorated in a different style, and 18 contain private bath. Depending on the room, singles begin at 187F ($25.79), the tariff rising to 410F ($56.54) and up in a double with private bath. In the handsomely decorated public lounges, you may find such style you won't want to leave the premises. Tea and pastry are a delight in the salon known as "Coin du Feu" with its fireplace. The food at the Dauphin is among the most outstanding in the area, specialties including sole Normande, langouste (lobster) au porto, saumon (salmon) braisé au Pouilly, caneton (duckling) à la bigarade, and homemade ice cream and fruit tarts. If you order à la carte you are likely to pay as much as 220F ($30.34) to 270F ($37.23). However, set meals are offered for as low as 118F ($16.27). The hotel is open all year.

7. Orbec

In a peaceful valley of the Pays d'Auge, near the source of the Orbiquet River, Orbec is a Norman town that has preserved its character. It lies 12½ miles from Lisieux, 22 miles from L'Aigle, and 43 miles from Caen. Although the town has an interesting **Church of Notre-Dame,** from the 15th and 16th centuries, the real reason people come here is to sample the food at—

Au Caneton, 32 rue Grande (tel. 31-32-73-32), a 17th-century Norman house in the rustic style, standing on this principal business artery. You dine in small dark rooms by lamplight reflecting on an illuminated chimney piece. Copper pots hang on the white walls. Joseph Ruaux, a *Diplômé d'Honneur de Grand Palais,* is the chef and owner; he knows the value of classic simplicity and is an expert at seasoning and saucing. As cookery fads come and go, he has maintained his popularity over the years, drawing visitors who come all the way from Paris.

His feuilletté of lobster with spinach is outstanding. After sampling it, I thought my most recent meal could only go downhill. It didn't—far from it. The duckling Ma Pourme is his pièce de résistance. He also does a superb roast leg of duckling cooked in cider vinegar. Of course, this is Calvados country, so one of those mellow mulled drinks with your meal would be in keeping with an age-old tradition. Menus are offered at 210F ($28.96) to 280F ($38.61). À la carte orders run about 270F ($37.23) to 320F ($44.13) per person. It's important to call ahead to reserve a table. The restaurant is closed on Monday night and Tuesday, and in October and February.

8. Caen

On the banks of the Orne, the port city of Caen suffered great damage in the Allied invasion of Normandy in 1944. Nearly three-quarters of the city's buildings, some 10,000 in all, were destroyed, although the twin abbeys founded by William the Conqueror and his "good wife, Matilda," were spared. Eight miles from the English Channel, 150 miles northwest of Paris, the city today is essentially modern, with many broad avenues and new apartment buildings.

William the Conqueror made Caen his seat of government. The son of Robert the Devil and a tanner's daughter, young William had been known as "The Bastard" in the days before he conquered England. He proposed marriage to his cousin Matilda, the daughter of Baldwin V of Flanders. She is said to have told her ladies-in-waiting that she'd "rather take the veil than marry a bastard." However, William galloped on horseback to Flanders, grabbed Matilda by the hair—and she changed her mind. The Papal Council at Reims had prohibited the alliance because of their close kinship, but in 1059 Pope Nicholas II granted dispensation. To show their penance, William and Matilda founded the Abbaye aux Hommes and the Abbaye aux Dames at Caen.

The **Abbaye aux Hommes** (tel. 31-84-81-25), in the Norman Romanesque style of architecture, also includes the **Église St-Étienne,** both entered on the Place Monseigneur-des-Hameaux. During the height of the 1944 battle, denizens of Caen flocked to St-Étienne for protection from the bombardments. Twin Romanesque towers, their spires dating from the 13th century, rise 300 feet into the air (Caen is known as "a city of spires"). Inside, a simple marble slab in front of the high altar commemorates the site of William's tomb. The Huguenots destroyed the tomb in the uprising of 1562, save for a hipbone that was recovered. However, in the French Revolution the last bit of William the Conqueror's dust was scattered to the wind.

For a tour of the abbey ensemble (entrance at no. 5) you must wait to be conducted by a guide. It is open daily from 9 a.m. to noon and 2 to 5 p.m. for 5F (69¢) admission fee. Inside, the hand-carved wooden doors are exceptional, as is an elaborately sculpted wrought-iron staircase. From the cloisters, you get a good view of the two towers of St-Étienne. Part of the former abbey houses municipal offices.

On the opposite side of town, the **Abbaye aux Dames** was founded by Matilda and it embraces the **Church of the Trinité.** Like St-Étienne, its façade is flanked by two Romanesque square towers. Destroyed during the Hundred Years' War, its spires were never rebuilt. Inside, the ribbed vaulting is interesting architecturally. In the 12th-century choir rests the tomb of Queen Matilda. To see the choir, the transept, and the crypt, you must go on a guided tour between 9 a.m. and noon or between 2 and 7 p.m. (till 6 p.m. in winter).

If time remains, you may want to visit the **château**, close to the Relais des Gourmets. There you may enjoy a walk in the castle gardens, from which you can look out over Caen. The citadel is from the 14th and 15th centuries; it was badly damaged in the war. The approach ramp is from the front of the Church of St. Pierre.

HOTELS OF CAEN: The city has no super-expensive lodgings, its hotels falling in the medium-priced and budget range.

Le Relais des Gourmets, 15 rue de Geôle (tel. 31-86-06-01), at the foot of the Château de Guillaume-le-Conquérant, is a charming little four-star hotel. Proprietor Jean Legras-Daragon has been awarded many culinary honors, and you may dine (à la carte, if you wish) in the hotel's little terraced garden. There is also a high-quality restaurant next door, l'Écaille, facing the castle of William the Conqueror. Here Monsieur Legras-Daragon serves excellent seafood, including lobster, oysters, and all the fish of the channel. Meals cost from 175F ($24.13) to 230F ($31.72) at both the restaurants.

Some caged songbirds are among the permanent residents of the hotel. Many pleasant antiques, including a 13th-century closet, and reproductions adorn the lounges and reception area. The 32 bedrooms are of generous size, many with views of the garden or the château walls. The rate for two persons in a double with shower bath is 240F ($33.10), increasing to 380F ($52.40) with a complete bath.

Malherbe, Place Maréchal-Foch (tel. 31-84-40-06), occupies the prime position in the new part of Caen, on a wide, tree-shaded boulevard, opposite a large sports park. It's in the tradition of a business person's hotel, offering 50 rooms at several price levels. Madame Ravel is your gracious hostess. The best twin-bedded rooms with bath are 420F ($57.92); double-bedded rooms with bath are 270F ($37.23). The rooms are comfortable and well furnished. The bar draws many Americans who use Caen as a center for touring the D-Day beaches. The Malherbe was selected by Darryl F. Zanuck for his cast when he was shooting *The Longest Day.*

Hôtel Le Moderne, 116 Boulevard du Maréchal-Leclerc (tel. 31-86-04-23), in the pedestrian zone of the inner city, offers quiet and calm lodging in 56 comfortably up-to-date rooms. The cheapest single costs around 140F ($19.31), while the most expensive double rents for 360F ($49.64). There's a bar on the premises and a good restaurant, Les Quatre Vents (see my restaurant recommendations).

Bristol, 31 rue du 11-Novembre (tel. 31-84-59-76), is modesty itself, a simple hotel in a block of modern apartments and shops a short way from the park. Consider the Bristol more of a stopover hotel than an island of charm. If you want a private bath, expect to pay 260F ($35.85) for a double or twin-bedded room. An even better bet is one of the smaller rooms with a cabinet de toilette, costing just 160F ($22.06) in a single. A continental breakfast is the only meal served.

Hôtel des Quatrans, 17 rue Gémare (tel. 31-86-25-57), is an unremarkable hostelry, suitable only for an overnight stay, yet it is one of the best bargains in Caen. The 26 simply furnished rooms offer only the most basic plumbing. The singles cost 115F ($15.86), while doubles go for 240F ($33.10).

THE FOOD OF CAEN: Caen is famed for its tripe à la mode de Caen. Even if you don't normally like tripe, you might want to give it a try here. Perhaps you'll change your mind. Caen shares nearly all the culinary specialties of Normandy.

Except for many of its chefs who have gone modern, the cooks of Caen rely heavily on the use of cream. Everything, of course, tastes better with the celebrated cheeses of the region, along with that spirited cider, Calvados.

La Bourride, 15-17 rue du Vaugueux (tel. 31-93-50-76), offers the best food in Caen. As the restaurant's name implies, there is indeed a bourride served here, concocted from five kinds of fish, delicately seasoned and watchfully cooked under the expert eye of Michel Bruneau. The restaurant is in a beautiful old house near the château, on a traffic-free street in the center of the oldest part of Caen. The dining room contains thick stone walls pierced with well-proportioned windows and a magnificent Renaissance fireplace. Service, directed by Madame Bruneau, includes tactful advice on an array of prominent wines to accompany any of the following specialties: salmon salad with Nantais butter, crayfish mousse with green peppers, local roast pigeon with apples, a Japanese-inspired fish dish served raw with soy sauce, barbue with peaches, and a papillote of truffles with green cabbage leaves. Desserts are often strongly dependent on fruit and are usually excellent. Set menus are offered for 160F ($22.06) to 320F ($44.13), while à la carte meals cost 310F ($42.75) to 370F ($51.02). The Bruneaus take a much-deserved rest on Sunday and Monday, for ten days in January, and for the last two weeks in August.

Les Quatre Vents, 116 bis Boulevard du Maréchal-Leclerc (tel. 31-86-04-23), is the restaurant connected with the Hôtel Le Moderne. You'll be warmly welcomed by Jacqueline Mabille, who will seat you in the Italian-style dining room, whose walls are decorated with landscape murals. Food items are well prepared and might include seafood salad with basil, lotte with cucumbers and fresh mint, calves' liver with apples, and breast of duckling with raspberries. Table d'hôte menus are offered for between 90F ($12.41) and 190F ($26.20). If you prefer to dine à la carte, expect to spend around 215F ($29.65), perhaps more. Open every day, the restaurant serves dinner until 10 p.m.

Le Dauphin, 29 rue Gémare (tel. 31-86-22-26), is not only one of the outstanding restaurants of Caen but also offers good accommodations. The decor of Robert Chabredier is provincial modern, and he offers meals for 95F ($13.10) to 275F ($37.92). The cookery is imaginative, and there are many interesting sauced dishes and specialties, including a ragoût of small lobster with fresh pasta, sweetbreads forester style, and warm oysters in red butter. His dessert specialty is apple charlotte. Only the freshest of ingredients are used. The restaurant is closed on Saturday and from mid-July until August 12. Its 21 bedrooms are well furnished and maintained, renting for 225F ($31.03) in a single with shower to 330F ($45.51) for the best double with private bath.

Les Échevins, 36 rue Écuyère (tel. 31-86-37-44), offers an intimate environment for intimate dinners, a feeling encouraged by the restaurant's division into two rooms, each containing about 20 seats, both lacquered in shades of black and dusty rose. Patrick Régnier is the chef, assisted in the dining room by his attractive wife. He prepares the kind of dishes he once cooked with flair at an exclusive Paris restaurant, Benoît, before establishing his own domain in Caen.

Menu specialties reveal a rich collection from his repertoire, often augmented by perfectly blended sauces. Examples are the crayfish salad au Noilly, turbot suprême with oysters, and filet of beef with foie gras sauce. Set meals range in price from 140F ($19.31) to 200F ($27.58), while à la carte meals cost around 300F ($41.37). The restaurant is closed Sunday and at lunchtime on Monday, as well as two weeks in July.

LIVING AND DINING ON THE OUTSKIRTS (DELUXE): At Bénouville, 6½

miles northeast of Caen, **Le Manoir d'Hastings,** on the N814 (tel. 31-44-62-34), is a converted priory from the 17th century with an enclosed Norman garden. Its owner, Claude Scaviner, is an advocate of La Nouvelle Cuisine. If in your Norman tour you've tired of cream and Calvados with everything, then head here for a refreshing lighter meal. The chef's creativity is inspired, and he has developed his own style and language with food. He might propose la truffe (truffle) en papillote (wrapped in oil paper and baked) or homard (lobster) de nos côtes au cidre (cider) brut. Monsieur Scaviner makes le bar (bass) so delicately flavored you'll want to kidnap him for your own kitchen. His cider-cooked ham and his Bresse squab herald him as a master of his art. For dessert, I suggest la tarte chaude normande. Three set menus are presented, costing 150F ($20.69), 275F ($37.92), and 350F ($48.27), the latter the price of a menu gourmand, offering seven *petits plats dégustation,* based on the shopping and the inspiration of the season.

The manoir is now a *restaurant avec chambres,* offering 11 handsomely furnished rooms, each lying in a Norman garden. The cost is 500F ($68.95) in a single, going up to 850F ($117.22) in a double, taxes and service included. The manor is closed Sunday night and Monday off-season, and it is also closed from October 1 to October 15 and February 1 to February 15.

If you find living in Caen too bleak, you'll discover the most luxurious trappings at Audrieu, 11 miles from Caen (head out the D94). At Audrieu, the **Relais Château d'Audrieu** (tel. 31-80-21-52) is a beautiful 18th-century château set on its own park grounds. The château has a gracious pair of young owners, Gérard and Irène Livry-Level, who have decorated many of their rooms with antiques. Some of the produce, such as raspberries in summer, come from their own garden. Calla lilies that they also grow are often used to decorate the bedrooms. Here you can enjoy not only the setting and the swimming pool but the excellent specialties of the chef, Alain Cornet, who offers a simplified menu for 150F ($20.69) or an elaborate gourmet repast with five specialties for 350F ($48.27). Try his scallops effiloché with corn salad and ginger, leek and cider fondue with oysters in their shells, or turbot with carrots and parsley cream sauce. For dessert, I suggest his warm royal puff pastry with apple and cinnamon or orange mousse with candied orange. His cuisine is extremely interesting, and customers leave with smiles.

Lovely rooms are rented to guests at rates of 560F ($77.22) to 620F ($85.50) in a single, from 620F ($85.50) to 920F ($126.87) in a double. In all, 30 chambers, including four suites, are available, each furnished with antiques and equipped with private bath. The château is closed each year in December, January, and February. The rest of the year the hotel is open every day. However, the restaurant is closed on Wednesday off-season.

9. Bayeux

The dukes of Normandy sent their sons to this Viking settlement to learn the Norse language. Bayeux has changed a lot since then, but miraculously it was spared from bombardment in the 1944 Allied invasion of Normandy. The first town liberated in France, Bayeux gave De Gaulle an enthusiastic welcome when he arrived there on June 14. Today the sleepy town, 17 miles northwest of Caen, is filled with Norman timbered houses, stone mansions, and cobbled streets.

The **Cathedral of Bayeux** has been called "the Reims of Normandy." It was consecrated in 1077 by Odo, the brother of William the Conqueror. The ruler's son, Beauclerc, partially destroyed it in 1105. Left over from an earlier church, its Romanesque towers rise on the western side, although the central tower is from the 15th century, with an even later topping. Inside, the nave is a fine example of the Norman Romanesque style. Rich in sculptural decorations, the 13th-century choir contains handsome Renaissance stalls. To see the crypt and the chapter house (13th century), apply to the sexton. Incidentally, the crypt was built in the 11th century, then sealed. Its existence remained unknown until it was discovered in 1412.

The **Musée la Tapisserie de la Reine Mathilde,** 6 rue Lambert-Leforestier (tel. 31-92-05-48), contains Matilda's tapestry, the most famous in the world.

The only problem is, the **Bayeaux Tapestry** isn't a tapestry but an embroidery, and it wasn't by Matilda, the wife of William the Conqueror. It was probably commissioned in Kent, the work of unknown Saxon embroiderers between 1066 and 1077. It's a band of linen stretching 231 feet, 20 inches wide, with worsteds of eight colors depicting some 58 scenes. The first recorded mention of the embroidery was in 1476, when it was explained that the tapestry was used to decorate the nave of the Cathedral of Bayeux.

Housed in a structure built for it, the embroidery is behind glass. It tells the story of the conquest of England by William the Conqueror, including scenes such as the coronation of Harold as the Saxon king of England, Harold returning from his journey to Normandy, "the mysterious personage of Aelfgyve," the surrender of Dinan, Harold being told of the apparition of a comet (a portent of misfortune), William the Conqueror in war dress, and the death of Harold. Decorative borders include scenes from *Aesop's Fables*. Men, horses, ships, and weapons—the panorama of history sweeps by.

The embroidery may be viewed from June 1 to September 30 without interruption from 9 a.m. to 7 p.m., at other times usually from 10 a.m. to 12:30 p.m. and 2 to 6 p.m. The admission is 15F ($2.07) for adults. You can rent earphones for 2F (28¢) that give you a running lecture on the embroidery.

The **Musée Memorial de la Bataille de Normandie,** Boulevard Fabian-Ware (tel. 31-92-93-41), stands across from the cemetery of Brittany. This museum deals exclusively with the military and human history of the battle for Normandy. Inside are about 440 feet of window and film displays plus a diorama. Wax dummies of soldiers in their uniforms, along with the tanks and guns used to win the battle, are exhibited. In the peak visiting months of June through August, the museum is open from 9:30 a.m. to 7 p.m. without interruption. On other occasions, hours are 10 a.m. to 12:30 p.m. and 2 to 6:30 p.m. From November to March, it is open only on Saturday and Sunday. Admission is 15F ($2.07) for adults.

FOOD AND LODGING: **Lion d'Or,** 71 rue St-Jean (tel. 31-92-06-90), is like an old French coaching inn, with a large open courtyard and mansard roof. Lush window boxes decorate the façade. You can sleep or dine well here. One meal is required of overnight guests. The hotel has been renovated especially to keep that old-world inn atmosphere, which is both pleasant and comfortable. The rooms are personalized with a lot of warmth; they are set well back from the street, which provides quiet. In all, 30 rooms are offered, 22 with some form of private bath or shower. Depending on your room assignment, rates range from 285F ($39.30) to 420F ($57.92) per person for half board.

The beamed dining room has elegant cloth-covered walls, decorated with painted reproductions of the Bayeux tapestry. Hanging from the beams are ornate but beautifully fashioned curtains, providing more intimacy. Windows look out onto a courtyard replete with palms and pots and baskets of bright-red geraniums. The cookery here is famous. Your meal might include meatloaf, a specialty of the house, or else fresh poached trout with shallot butter, chicken à la Vallée d'Auge flambé (cooked in cider with cream and mushrooms), Normandy cheese, and, to top it off, a sort of meringue cake called Saint-Eve, a specialty of Bayeux. There are lots of excellent wines, plus an attractive bar with a fireplace. Meals begin at 85F ($11.72), going up to 210F ($28.96). The inn is closed from December 20 to January 20.

Hôtel Pacary, 117 rue St-Parrice (tel. 31-92-16-11), is a fairly anonymous modern hotel set in a well-planted park with a pleasant swimming pool. The functionally furnished bedrooms, 65 in all, rent for 230F ($31.72) in a single and 325F ($44.82) in a double. Meals in the restaurant on the premises cost from 65F ($8.97) to 150F ($20.69). You're likely to run into a conference group or social function using one of the large public rooms.

Family Home, 39 rue Général-de-Dais (tel. 31-92-15-22), is a private house, an old presbytery set in the center of Bayeux near the famous cathedral and the museums, on a quiet street leading to the main street, rue St. Malo. In winter, there's usually a fire blazing in more than one of the fireplaces. You'll find five simply furnished double bedrooms, which rent for 70F ($9.65) per person without bath and for 100F ($13.79) per person with a private bath and toilet. A generous breakfast is included in the tariffs. If you wish, you can prepare your own meals in the house's kitchen. Monsieur and Madame Lefevre also serve copious and varied meals to guests at their home for 75F ($10.32), which includes wine and the service charge. The wine served is a smooth Anjou produced by Mme Lefevre's family at its own vineyards.

10. Port-en-Bessin

Those wanting to get away from the popular tourist centers may consider the Port, as it's called locally. In the Calvados section, 5½ miles from Bayeux, it opens onto a harbor enclosed by two half-moon jetties. Try to arrive early in the morning, except Sunday, to see the fish auction.

While there, consider a stopover, either for a room or meal, at **Hôtel de la Marine,** Quai Letourneur, right on the harbor (tel. 31-21-70-08). It's simplicity itself, but that may be what you're seeking. The air-conditioned dining room on the second floor faces the sea. The style is pleasant, with carpeting and rustic furniture. Everything is of good standard without any particular originality. A set meal is offered for 75F ($10.32), including, for example, an appetizer of small shellfish, followed by poulet Vallée d'Auge with curried rice, a blanket of fish, and pastry. Specialties of the chef include a cassolette de homard (lobster) in a Newburg sauce, turbot grillé béarnaise, huitres chaudes normandes, barbue à l'oseille, marmite de poisson, and a mousseline of turbot in a lobster sauce. Service is very good.

A clean and comfortable bedroom overlooking the sea, with either bath or shower and toilet, goes for 95F ($13.10) to 160F ($22.06) in a double.

11. D-Day Beaches

From June 6 to the breakthrough on July 18, "the longest day" was very long indeed. The greatest armada the world had ever known—men, warships, landing craft, tugboats, Jeeps, whatever—had assembled along the southern coast of England in the spring of 1944.

On June 5, at 9:15 p.m., the BBC announced to the French Resistance that the invasion was imminent, signaling the underground to start dynamiting the railways. Before midnight, Allied planes were bombing the Norman coast fortifications. By 1:30 on the morning of June 6, members of the 101st Airborne were parachuting to the ground on German-occupied French soil. At 6:30 a.m. the Americans were landing on the beaches code-named Utah and Omaha. One hour later the British and Canadian forces were making beachheads at Juno, Gold, and Sword.

The Nazis had mocked Churchill's promise in 1943 to liberate France "before the fall of the autumn leaves." When the invasion did come, it was swift, sudden, and a surprise to the formidable "Atlantic wall." Today veterans from Canada, the United States, and Britain walk with their families across the beaches where "Czech hedgehogs," "Belgian grills," pillboxes, and "Rommel asparagus" once stood.

The exploration begins at the modest little seaside resort of **Arromanches-les-Bains,** 6½ miles from Bayeux. In June of 1944 it was a little fishing port, until it was taken by the 50th British Division. Towed across the English Channel, a mammoth prefabricated port known as "Winston" was installed to supply the Allied forces. "Victory could not have been achieved without it," said Eisenhower. The wreckage of that artificial harbor—also known as "Mulberry"—lies right off the beach, *la plage du débarquement*. The **Musée du Débarquement** (tel. 31-22-34-31) has been installed, featuring relief maps, working models, a cinema, and photographs showing such scenes as the opening "Pontoons." A diorama of the landing, with an English commentary, is featured, including showing of the British film *Port Wilson*. Charging 12F ($1.66) for admission, the museum is open mid-April until the end of May from 9 a.m. to noon and 2 to 6:30 p.m. From the end of May until the end of August, hours are 9 a.m. to 6:30 p.m. without interruption. From September 1 to 15, visits are possible from 9 a.m. to noon and 2 to 6:30 p.m.; from 9 a.m. to noon and 2 to 6 p.m. from September 16 to mid-April.

Moving along the coast, you arrive at **Omaha Beach,** where the wreckage of war can still be seen. "Hanging on by their toenails," the men of the 1st and 29th American Divisions occupied the beach that June day. The code-name Omaha became famous throughout the world, although the French up to then had called the beaches St-Laurent, Vierville-sur-Mer, and Colleville. A monument commemorates the heroism of the invaders. Covering some 173 acres, the **Normandy American Cemetery** is filled with crosses and stars of David in Carrara marble. The remains of more than 9,300 American military dead were buried there on territory now owned by the United States, a gift from the French nation. The cemetery is open from 8 a.m. to 6 p.m.

Farther along the coast, the jagged lime cliffs of the **Pointe du Hoc** come into view. A cross honors a group of American Rangers led by Lt.-Col. James Rudder who scaled the cliff using hooks to get at the pillboxes. The scars of war are more visible here than at any other point along the beach.

Much farther along the Cotentin Peninsula is **Utah Beach,** where the 4th U.S. Infantry Division landed at 6:30 a.m. The landing force was nearly two miles south of their intended destination, but, fortunately, Nazi defenses were weak at this point. By midday the infantry had completely cleared the beach. A U.S. monument commemorates their heroism.

Nearby you can visit **Sainte-Mère-Église,** which not too many people had heard of until the night of June 5 and 6 when parachutists were dropped over the town. They were from the 82nd U.S. Airborne Division, under the command of Matthew B. Ridgeway. Members of the 101st U.S. Airborne Division, commanded by Gen. M. B. Taylor, were also involved. Thus little Sainte-Mère-Église became the first town in France to be liberated in the long war against Germany.

In the town is the **Airborne Museum,** Place du 6 Juin, at which you can see many relics. From April to November the Museum is open daily from 9 a.m. to noon and 2 to 7 p.m. (in July and August it stays open all day without a break). From November to April it is open only on Sunday and holidays. The cost is 12F ($1.66) for adults, free to military personnel in uniform. In the town is **Kilometer "O"** on the **Liberty Highway,** marking the first of the milestones the American armies reached on their way to Metz and Bastogne.

FOOD AND LODGING: At Grandcamp-Maisy, near Omaha Beach, you'll find a little fishing village in danger of silting up. In summer, French families turn it into a modest but pleasant seaside resort, which was also heavily visited in 1984 by Americans on the 40th anniversary of the D-Day landings.

I recommend a luncheon stopover, or even an overnight stay, at the **Hôtel Duguesclin** (tel. 31-22-64-22), which is open all year except from mid-January to February 5 and for part of October. This is a typical Norman inn and restaurant. The fish soup there is excellent, and I also endorse the Norman sole if featured on the menu. Everything tastes better with country bread and Norman butter. The cheapest you can dine for here is about 75F ($10.32); however, if you get carried away with the fish selections, expect a tab of 130F ($17.93) or more. The rooms, 26 in all, are simply furnished, a bathless single costing 85F ($11.72). You can have the most expensive double in the house for only 220F ($30.34).

Back at Arromanches-les-Bains, the only place remotely recommendable is the **Hôtel de la Marine** (tel. 31-22-34-19), which does business only from March 1 to mid-November. After you've visited the Musée du Débarquement, you may want to enjoy a simple, straightforward meal here, costing from 65F ($8.97) and featuring "fruits of the sea." Should you wish to stay over, you'll find that the Marine rents out a total of 20 simply furnished bedrooms, costing from 125F ($17.24) in a single and from 200F ($27.58) in a double. The place will serve you just fine if your expectations aren't too high.

12. Cherbourg

At the tip of the Cotentin Peninsula, Cherbourg was the chief supply port for the Allied landings in the invasion of Normandy in 1944. On the English Channel, at the mouth of the Divette River, Cherbourg is the third great naval base of France. Its naval port was begun on orders of Napoléon Bonaparte, and it contains extensive drydocks and shipbuilding yards. Because of its location, 60 miles south of England's Isle of Wight, it was connected by the "Pluto" pipeline under the ocean, supplying fuel from the Isle of Wight to Cherbourg. Today you can take a motorboat trip through the great artificial port.

The history of the battle at Cherbourg—in fact, the story of the Allied landings at Normandy—unfolds at the **Musée de la Libération** (tel. 33-20-14-12), which is reached by a winding road. At the top you'll have a good view of the town and the port. The museum was installed in the Fort du Roule. Photographs show the Germans surrendering, and an armory room displays artillery and equipment, including uniforms of Luftwaffe pilots. That teleguided contraption, a "Goliath," is also shown. One of the most interesting sections is devoted to modern propaganda, including the underground press and a moving Paul Colin poster, *Wounded France Awakes to Liberty*. The French contribution to the Allied victory isn't neglected either. The museum is open April through September from 9 a.m. to noon and 2 to 6 p.m., charging an admission of 5F (69¢). Off-season it is open daily except Tuesday from 9:30 a.m. to noon and 2 to 5:30 p.m.

Back in town, the **Church of La Trinité,** on the south side of the Place Napoléon, was built from 1423 to 1504, and is a fine example of the flamboyant style. It is one of the few historic buildings still left in Cherbourg.

The **Hôtel de Ville de Cherbourg,** or town hall, rue Vastel (tel. 33-44-40-22), possesses the minor **Musée Thomas-Henry,** which is open daily, except Tuesday in summer, charging 5F (69¢) for admission. It has a collection of European paintings, including some Spanish and German ones. A statue of a local painter, Jean-François Millet, stands in the public garden, and inside the museum you can see examples of his work. Look for a panel by Fra Angelico Lippi. Other works are by Poussin, Vernet, and David.

WHERE TO STAY: In bandbox modern, the **Mercure Cherbourg,** Gare Maritime (tel. 33-44-01-11), is the best place to stay in the port. It faces the Port de Plaisance, as well as the Gare Maritime. Your room may open onto a fishing fleet, usually from Britain. The hotel offers 81 well-equipped bedrooms with either private bath or shower. The rates for one person range from 280F ($38.61), and two persons pay from 420F ($57.92). On the premises, Le Chateaubriand faces the sea, featuring good food and specializing in fish dishes. The bar, La Timonerie, also faces the sea and is a scenic place to stop for a drink at sunset, watching the fleet in the harbor.

Le Louvre, 2 rue H-Dunant (tel. 33-53-02-28), isn't a museum but one of the finest bargain accommodations at Cherbourg. It has no restaurant, and is admittedly modest in its appointments, yet it charges only 115F ($15.86) in a single without bath, 262F ($36.13) in the most expensive doubles with private bath. The rooms are comfortable and well maintained, and 33 of the 42 accommodations come equipped with private plumbing. Monsieur and Madame Segonds extend a warm welcome.

WHERE TO DINE: The **Café du Théatre**, Place Général-de-Gaulle (tel. 33-43-01-49), offers excellently prepared grilled lobster in a prawn sauce and other tempting dishes made with "fruits de mer," although the chef also does meat dishes well. Try, in particular, his pepper steak or his mixed grill. A set menu is offered for just 75F ($10.32). If you order à la carte, you can easily spend 140F ($19.31). The cuisine is simple, but the ingredients are fresh, compelling enough reason to visit.

13. Le Mont St-Michel

Considered one of the greatest sightseeing attractions in Europe, Le Mont St-Michel is surrounded by massive walls measuring more than half a mile in circumference. Connected to the shore by a causeway, it crowns a rocky islet at the border between Normandy and Brittany. The rock is 260 feet high.

Le Mont St-Michel is noted for its tides, considered the highest on the continent of Europe, measuring at certain times of the year a 50-foot difference between high and low tide. Unsuspecting tourists wandering across the sands—notorious for their quicksands—can be trapped as the sea rushes toward the Mont at a speed comparable to that of a galloping horse. Every day there are two high tides, varying from 20 to 50 minutes. The **Syndicat d'Initiative, Le Mont Saint Michel** (tel. 33-60-14-30), in the old Guard Room of the Bourgeois at the left of the town gates, will provide you with free tables of the annual tides. About twice a month the granite hilltop is completely surrounded by water, but the causeway leading to it is never under.

Ample parking space is provided. However, if you're going by train, you have to get off at Pontorson, the nearest station, six miles from "the Mont." Here you can make bus connections that will take you to the abbey, which lies 47 miles from Dinan, 30 miles from St-Malo, and 80 miles from Caen. The bus schedules are somewhat erratic, so you may have to take a taxi. To reach the abbey, you have to climb the steep Grande Rue, lined with 15th- and 16th-century houses. Along the way, you may have to fight off souvenir peddlers and Normans hawking their omelet specialties.

Those who make it to the top can begin their exploration of the "Marvel of the West." The **abbey** is open year round: from 9 to 11:30 a.m. and 1:30 to 6 p.m., May 15 to September 15 (off-season, to 4 p.m.), charging 20F ($2.76) for admission, only 10F ($1.38) off-season. You must go on a guided tour, leaving every 15 minutes and lasting 45 minutes. You can enter the abbey gardens afterward. No tours in English are conducted on Friday.

In the 8th century an oratory was founded on the spot by St. Aubert, the bishop of Avranches. It was replaced by a Benedictine monastery, founded in 966 by Richard I, Duke of Normandy. That met with destruction by fire in 1203. Large parts of the abbey were financed by Philip Augustus in the 13th century.

Ramparts encircle the church and its ensemble of buildings, a part of which includes the "Merveille" (Marvel), one of the most important Gothic masterpieces in Europe. One of these, the Salle des Chevaliers, is most graceful. Begun in the 11th century, the abbey church consists of a Romanesque nave and transept, plus a choir in the flamboyant Gothic style. The rectangular refectory is from 1212, the cloisters with their columns of pink granite from 1225.

Three **museums** of Le Mont Saint-Michel relive the history of the site, with scenes of historical reconstitutions and ancient collections (including arms, pictures, sculpture, and clocks), plus a unique collection of 250 models of ancient ships. All three museums can be visited for a combined ticket of 30F ($4.14).

The **Logis Tiphaine** can also be visited for another 6.50F (90¢). It was the home of Tiphaine de Raguenel, spouse of Bertrand Duguesclin, constable of France in the 16th century.

FOOD AND LODGING: Plan to spend at least a night here at one of the town's typically French inns. And be sure to sample—

Mother Poulard's Legendary Omelet

La Mère Poulard (tel. 33-60-14-01) is a gastronomic shrine. It's sacred to those who revere the omelet that the simple village woman Annette Poulard began making at the end of the last century. Her omelet "secret" has been passed on to the operator of the inn today, Bernard Heyraud. Mother Poulard would hold her beaten egg mixture over a hearth fire in a long-handled copper pan. That same tradition exists today among village women wearing the traditional garb. Stacked on a counter are baskets holding hundreds of fresh eggs, which are broken into large bowls to be beaten with large metal whips, turning them into a foamy, frothy mixture.

In truth, it's more of an open-fire soufflé than an omelet. The secret lies partially in the use of the wood, traditional oak. Set meals (including the omelet) are featured, costing 175F ($24.13), 260F ($35.85), and 450F ($62.06), taxes and service included, although your drink is extra.

In the true tradition of a French inn, upper-floor rooms are offered for sleeping. There are 27 in all, renovated and furnished in the typical Norman fashion, and 16 have private bath. For half board, including dinner (the cheapest menu), room, and a continental breakfast, the charge ranges from 300F ($41.37) to 550F ($75.63) per person. In season the manager will ask you to take your meals on the premises (not a hardship). La Mère Poulard is open from April 1 to October 1.

The Budget Inns

Les Terrasses Poulard (tel. 33-60-14-09) is a reconstruction of several old village houses, perched prettily up the hill on the stone city wall. Its entrance is opposite a parish church founded in the 11th century. Two dining rooms provide a panoramic view of the sea, offering meals at several price levels. The least expensive way to dine here is to order a menu at 75F ($10.32). However, if you want more elaborate fare, you'll spend 160F ($22.06) and up. The inn is run by Gustave and Sonia Letertre. Open February to November.

Hôtel du Mouton Blanc (tel. 33-60-14-08) is a village house complex converted into a restaurant on its lower floors, with 26 bedrooms available for overnighters upstairs. Tables are set not only inside, which is decorated in the rustic Norman fashion, but outside on the terrace overlooking the sea. True to the pattern of the restaurants of Le Mont Saint-Michel, the omelet is offered along with fruits de mer (fruits of the sea). Three fixed-priced meals are featured, at 80F ($11.03), 150F ($20.69), and 220F ($30.34). A double room with private bath or shower costs 240F ($33.10), dropping to 100F ($13.79) in a bathless room. The inn is closed from mid-November to mid-February.

A Rustic Norman Farmhouse

If the casinos of Deauville or the tides of Le Mont Saint-Michel have begun to bore you, head for the rustic splendor of **Verte Campagne** (Hostellerie Meredith-Desnos), Hameau Chavalier par Trelly (Manche) (tel. 33-47-65-33), about 30 miles north of Le Mont Saint-Michel. Take Route D7 north from Avranches to Lengronne and follow the signs north from town. A small road winds through groves and orchards bringing you to a white wooden barrier with an old farmhouse just beyond. You are welcomed by friendly dogs, but mainly by Madame Meredith, the gracious lady of the manor. Monsieur Desnos looks after the dining room.

The farmhouse is timbered and entirely renovated, the decoration sumptuous, with antiques and lots of brass utensils. The bar is so cozy you will want to linger. The atmosphere is comfortably formal—a place where you feel you may be expected to dress for dinner, but don't mind doing so. If you're spending the night, ask for the "splurge" double bedroom at 275F ($37.92), offering red carpeting, curtains, bedcover, and vanity—everything in harmony with the pink "Vichy" pattern. Standard doubles cost 175F ($24.13). Based on double occupancy in one of these rooms, the full-board rate is 250F ($34.48) per person. The farmhouse is closed in November and for the first week in February.

14. Pont l'Évêque

Famous for its cheese since the 13th century, Pont l'Évêque, 11 miles from Lisieux, was severely damaged during the liberation of Normandy from the Nazis in 1944. Many discerning French people use it as a special retreat for food and lodging, since they don't like paying the more rarified tariffs at nearby Trouville or Deauville.

If you like the town, you might want to stay over at **Le Lion d'Or**, 8 Place du Calvaire (tel. 31-65-01-55), which is attractive and charming but often heavily booked for what the French call *le weekend*. Under the direction of Jean-Pierre Vaseur, it also serves good food, a set meal costing from 105F ($14.48), although it's easy to spend at least 180F ($24.82). This Lion roars not too far from the railway station. The rooms are modestly furnished, well kept, and comfortable. Expect to pay 140F ($19.31) in a single, 240F ($33.10) in a double. Of the 25 rooms, 15 contain private bath. The hotel shuts down from November 15 to November 25.

Auberge de la Touques, Place de l'Église (tel. 31-64-01-69), offers the chance to dine in typical Norman style on traditional specialties, which include barbue (brill) with apples, terrines of the house, and a well-seasoned duckling. Many dishes are cooked in cream or cider, expertly prepared by chef Dominique Froger. Fixed-price menus cost from 95F ($13.10) to 165F ($22.75), while à la carte meals range from 185F ($25.51) to 250F ($34.48). Closed Monday night, Tuesday, and from mid-November to Christmas.

15. Cabourg

Literary fans will know of this small resort as "Balbec" in *Remembrance of Things Past* by Marcel Proust, who used to spend his summers here. The French writer vividly evoked this "Second Empire" resort as it existed in the belle époque era. Proust found lodgings at the Grand Hotel (see below).

It's still fashionable to stroll along the Boulevard des Anglais, which runs along the sandy beach. The town is preferred by many who shun the so-called carnival atmosphere of Deauville and Trouville, two much larger and better known resorts, which will be previewed shortly.

Those with an interest in history may want to drive over to see **Dives-sur-Mer,** a hamlet that was once far more important than it is today. In 1066 William the Conqueror (who wasn't known as that then) set out from this large port to capture England. Once there, you can visit the former pilgrimage church of Notre-Dame de Dives, dating from the 14th century, although its transept is from the era of William the Conqueror. Take time also to visit Les Halles, the covered market of Dives-sur-Mer, which was originally built in the 15th century.

But for the atmosphere of a sea resort, you'll want to return to the Côte Fleuri and Cabourg, which boasts a casino on the beach.

WHERE TO STAY: Grand Hotel P.L.M., Promenade Marcel-Proust (tel. 31-91-01-79), is considered a still-grand reminder of the opulent days of the late

19th century, when its most famous guest was Proust. The hotel is on the edge of the water, with terraces for outdoor dining in the restaurant, Le Balbec (see my recommendation on where to dine), and dozens of balconies set between the oversize rooms and the open sea. There's no contest—the hotel is still the most luxurious one in town. Many Parisians make trips just to spend a weekend in one of the well-furnished rooms, often carrying copies of *Remembrance of Things Past* in to dinner with them. Receptionists in the marble entrance hall quote rates of 620F ($85.50) in a single, 850F ($117.22) in a double. All accommodations have private bath, phone, and TV.

Hôtel de Paris, 39 Avenue de la Mer (tel. 31-91-31-34), despite its pretentious name, is a small, family-run establishment with comfortably simple, clean rooms, most of them bathless. Units cost from 150F ($20.69) in a single, from 260F ($35.85) in a double. Breakfast is the only meal served.

WHERE TO DINE: Restaurant Le Balbec, Grand Hotel P.L.M., Promenade Marcel-Proust (tel. 31-91-01-79), draws a loyal crowd of regular customers from the surrounding region despite the fact that it's part of the town's grandest hotel. Chef Michel Ruhlman's specialties are served in a turn-of-the-century decor that is sumptuous, with polite service, views of the sea, and immaculate napery. Menu specialties include salade folle aux St-Jacques (scallops) with foie gras, matelote au vieux cidre, and rognons de veau (sweetbreads) au genièvre. Set menus are offered for 160F ($22.06) to 190F ($26.20), while à la carte meals cost from 250F ($34.48) to 400F ($55.16). Le Balbec is open all year.

ON THE OUTSKIRTS: Le Moulin du Pré (tel. 31-78-83-68), Route de Gonneville-en-Auge, is about 4½ miles from the center of Cabourg out Route D513 in the direction of Caen. This hostelry is the personal statement of the Hamchin and Holtz families. The daughter of the Hamchins married a poet named Holtz and remained to operate the establishment. Set inside an old millhouse, the hotel offers ten rooms, four of them with private bath, all decorated in shades of pink, with windows opening onto panoramic views of the verdant countryside. Accommodations rent for 110F ($15.17) in a single and 200F ($27.58) in a double. Meals are prepared by the charming and inventive Jocelyne Holtz and feature such specialties as terrine of suckling pig en gelée, turbot flan with sage, vegetable terrine with foie gras, and an aromatic array of grilled meats. The restaurant serves table d'hôte and à la carte meals for 180F ($24.82) to 290F ($39.99). It is closed from October 1 until mid-March as well as on Sunday night and Monday except in July and August.

16. Deauville

This resort has always been associated with the famous. For example, Coco Chanel began her career here in the summer of 1913, opening a boutique selling tiny hats. The grand ladies of her day paraded by under the weight of fruits and flowers. "How can the mind breathe under those things?" she asked. That isn't the problem today. Bare heads, bare feet, bare virtually anything is de rigueur during the day. However, the briefest bikini-wearers often don evening dress for nocturnal activities, including concerts, ballets, or the casino nightclub where some of the major headliners in all of Europe appear in high season.

Parasols dot the beach, and beauties abound, especially in August. Many bathers just walk up and down the slat boards to see and be seen, dropping in occasionally for an apéritif at **Le Bar du Soleil.** One French countess confided that she diets for three months straight before making her summer appearance on the sands of Deauville. The **Plage Fleurie** is a beach aptly named, studded with bright flowers. The rich, the celebrated flock to Deauville in August, enjoying its golden sands.

The mayor of Deauville frankly conceded to the press, "We are looking for the élite, not the masses." Once the resort of Trouville, built in the days of Louis-Philippe, was the most fashionable place to go—until 1859 when the duc de Morny, a half-brother of Napoléon III, crossed the Touques River and founded Deauville, which quickly replaced the other resort with the fickle arbiters of taste. With its golf courses, its casino, its deluxe hotels, its racing season (two tracks: **La Touques** and **Clairefontaine**), its regattas, its yachting harbor, its polo grounds, its tennis court, whatever, Deauville is a formidable contender for the business of the smart crowd. Although dress, customs, lifestyles, and morality have changed, Deauville has never completely left the Edwardian era in which it reached its zenith.

Launched in the 1920s, the **Casino d'Été,** open from mid-March to mid-September, is the heart of the nighttime complex, complete with the super-expensive, scarlet-flamed **Le New Brummell's** nightclub, as well as the superb but high-priced **Casino Grill Room** and the **Ambassadeurs** restaurant. You pay a 50F ($6.90) fee to enter the casino, but that merely gets you across the threshold. Since 1959 the **Winter Casino** has been open from mid-September to mid-March. Its restaurant-cabaret, **La Malibran,** and **Ciro's,** for lunch only, are right on the beach.

If you don't want to go swimming at the beach, you can visit the $2-million **La Piscine.** Opened to the public in 1966, the Olympic pool is 150 feet long.

Every year for a week in early September, there's a switch from the usually wholly European genteel glamour. It's then that the **film festival** is held honoring only movies made in the United States. During that time, screen notables—actors and actresses, producers, directors, and writers—join and briefly eclipse the high rollers at the casinos and the horse-race and polo crowd. Originated in 1975, the Deauville Film Festival has drawn a wide range of stars, such as Kirk Douglas, Gene Kelly, Lana Turner, Gregory Peck, Rock Hudson, Gloria Swanson, and Shelley Winters, to name a few. No prizes are awarded to the films shown, but oddly, a prize for literature is the only award given.

A TRIO OF DELUXE HOTELS: **Normandy,** rue Mermoz (tel. 31-88-09-21), is the largest of the deluxe hotel coterie that includes the Royal and the Hôtel du Golf, all of which are owned by the casino interests. To me, the Normandy is the most interesting—a block-long structure built to resemble a Norman village, with turrets, gables, and tiny windows peeking out of high-sloping roofs. Opposite the casino, this year-round hotel opens onto a park of trimmed shrubs, beds of red geraniums, tennis courts, and lawns.

The interior is as comfortable as a vast rambling country house. The many reception rooms are furnished in a warm manner. Activity centers around the main rotunda, which is encircled by a colonnade of marble pillars, and the dark-paneled drinking lounge, where in August you might even run into Gunther Sachs and his friends. Bedrooms are furnished with antiques or reasonably good reproductions. The price of a room is determined by its view and its size, a double ranging from 1,130F ($155.83) to 1,550F ($213.75), including breakfast and service. Full-board terms of 450F ($62.06) per person in addition to the room tariff are offered. A complete luncheon or dinner costs about 320F ($44.13). Lunches are served in the dining room and in the open-air restaurant, where you eat under umbrellas.

Royal, Boulevard Eugène-Cornuché (tel. 31-88-16-41), is also impressive. Adjoining the casino, it occupies a key position, fronting a block-wide park between the hotel and the water. High-trimmed yew hedges are arranged to make various terrace levels for lawns and flower beds. The Royal is like a great regal palace, providing grandiose living for big spenders.

Each of its rooms—some mammoth in size—contains a private bath (some have shower, no tub), the price of the accommodations varying widely according to room views. The bedrooms are decorated with period furniture, with matching floral cretonne fabrics, loomed carpets, and (in some) spacious sitting-room areas fronting the ocean. Open from Easter to October, the *grand luxe résidence* charges from 850F ($117.22) for its simplest doubles with shower and toilet all the way to a peak 1,600F ($220.64) for doubles with complete bath and private balcony or terrace. A single begins at 800F ($110.32), going up to 1,570F ($216.50) with complete bath.

Dinner, beginning in price at 250F ($34.48), is served in the elegant, highly stylized dining room with its period chairs, sparkling crystal, and wall of arched mirrored doors. In fair weather, lunch is provided on the terrace or lawn as well. There's also a grill, decorated in leather, where quick meals are served. A private heated swimming pool is reserved for guests of the hotel, and there's a sauna inside the garden where a luncheon buffet is served. Two recreation rooms, one set aside for children, are at your disposal, as well as a TV channel showing a different movie daily. This is an ideal place to spend a holiday *à la française*.

Hôtel du Golf, at New-Golf, 1½ miles from Deauville on the D278 (tel. 31-88-19-01), is for sporting fans. Seemingly transplanted from some eastern U.S. resort area such as the Adirondacks, it is a focal point for golfers. A colossal mock-Norman structure with a beamed façade, this hotel adjoins the grassy golf course and is near the race track and stadium. Open from mid-May through September, it charges 500F ($68.95) in a single, from 750F ($103.43) in a double, plus service. The furnishings are comfortable but set no design pace. Meals are served discreetly in the gracious dining room, where large-paned windows overlook the country setting. Guests gather in the tavern-style drinking lounge, relaxing in armchairs and exchanging golf scores.

MEDIUM-PRICED AND BUDGET HOTELS: P.L.M. Deauville, Boulevard Eugène-Cornuché (tel. 31-88-62-62), offers everything you'd expect from a well-run modern hotel. Behind an angular façade, the bedrooms are comfortable and well equipped, with private baths and balconies, and the location offers easy access to the beaches at Trouville and the entertainment possibilities in Deauville. The hotel is in Port-Deauville, a short distance from Deauville proper. All rooms have phone, TV, and mini-bar. Accommodations rent for 400F ($55.16) in a single, 520F ($71.71) in a double.

Helios Hotel, 10 rue Fossorier (tel. 31-88-28-26). The half-timbering of this hotel's façade was built only a few years ago, but guests often think it's antique. It sits midway between the monumental center of the resort and the beach, behind a flowering courtyard with a swimming pool. Each of its comfortable bedrooms has all the modern conveniences, with singles costing 275F ($37.92), doubles going up to 450F ($62.06). It is closed in January.

La Fresnaye, 81 Avenue de la République (tel. 31-88-09-71), is an upper-class private villa turned hotel. Set back from the busy boulevard about six blocks from the beach, the stone, brick, and timbered building is a crazy quilt of architecture, with towers, cupolas, and bays. At the rear of the house an area is set aside for parking in a tree-shaded garden. Family-owned, La Fresnaye is managed by a gracious woman who speaks English; a bevy of town women are employed as chambermaids and waitresses. Since it was once a private villa, the bedrooms are of various sizes, the most expensive double with private bath costing 480F ($66.19), including a continental breakfast, tax, and service. Bathless singles cost from 160F ($22.06). Breakfast is the only meal offered. On the main floor are a front parlor and a dining room opening onto the rear garden.

Marie-Anne, 142 Avenue de la République (tel. 31-88-35-32), is the private domain of Madeleine Grigaut, who carefully maintains four apartments and 25 rooms, all with private bath, telephone, and radio. The ornate building is in the middle of a charming private garden. There's no restaurant on the premises, but breakfast is included in the room prices of 230F ($31.72) for a single, 400F ($55.16) for a double. The apartments cost 460F ($63.43) to 550F ($75.63) per day for two persons. The hotel is open all year.

Le Continental, 1 rue Désiré-le-Hoc (tel. 31-88-21-06), is a simple and clean hotel good for an overnight stop. All but seven of the 49 rooms contain private bath. The cheapest single rents for 130F ($17.93), while the most expensive double costs around 280F ($38.61). Breakfast is included in the tariffs, although there is no restaurant on the premises. There is, however, a bar. Madame Perrot, the owner, is usually on hand to assist you and direct the staff, but she closes the hotel from mid-November to mid-March.

UPPER-BRACKET RESTAURANTS: **Le Ciro's,** Promenade des Planches (tel. 33-88-18-10). Should you arrive on your yacht, chances are you'll have lunch here. You couldn't get much closer to the water, or be more chic. Ciro's provides the best seafood in Deauville—it's expensive, but worth it. Tables are placed on two levels; both have walls of glass allowing a fine view of the sea. You can make your lobster selection from a tank as you enter.

The kitchen always stocks a wide range of delectable French oysters and mussels. If you want a little bit of everything, ask for the plateau de fruits de mer, which contains not only lobster but the various oysters and clams. The most expensive item on the menu is grilled lobster, but there are many other interesting fish dishes as well, including barbue (brill) cooked in Norman cider. Elaborate beginnings to your repast might be a foie gras of duckling or a lobster salad with truffles. Although King Neptune reigns around here, you can also order such classic French dishes as a grilled filet of beef with a béarnaise sauce or grilled lamb cutlets. Everything is prepared well. The least expensive way to dine here is to order one of the gastronomique menus, costing from 145F ($20). Otherwise, count on spending from 300F ($41.37) and up on the à la carte menu. It is open only for lunch except in July and August when dinner is also served.

Saratoga, 1 Avenue du Général-de-Gaulle (tel. 31-88-24-33). You're more likely to encounter a group of lunching women shoppers here, carefully coiffed and manicured and often accompanied by their dogs, than to see a group of men comparing football scores. That's probably because both the decor and the food items seem aimed at delicate palates and light appetites. These facts don't prevent the Saratoga from doing a brisk business, especially at noon, when the garden is at its best. Linda Porrasse and her husband Jean are the owners, and they present a bouillabaisse made entirely from Channel fish rather than Mediterranean ones, as you might expect. You can also choose freshwater salmon with spinach, foie de volailles with truffle sauce, John Dory with leeks, or seafood salad from among the specialties. À la carte meals cost 200F ($27.58) to 240F ($33.10). The restaurant is closed Monday night, all day Tuesday, and from the first week of January to the first week of February. The restaurant is only a short distance from the casino.

Augusto, 27 rue Désiré-le-Hoc (tel. 31-88-34-49), is an intimate, friendly bistro, where Jean-Claude and Claudine Lebreton maintain high standards for cuisine and service. The restaurant has four dining rooms, one with silk-covered walls and another with a nautically inspired decor. Upstairs are garden-style and Norman rooms. The specialty here is lobster from Brittany. Culinary creations of the Lebretons are raw salmon with green lemon and fresh fruits, fresh homemade foie gras, bisque of fresh lobster, lobster salad with raspberry vinegar, roast quail on toast, and the following lobster dishes: grilled with white butter, à la nage, in corail sauce, with garlic sauce, or broiled the American way. It's priced according to weight and is presented alive and weighed for each diner. Count on spending from 350F ($48.27) for a dinner here. The restaurant is closed on Monday and Tuesday off-season, and in January and February.

MEDIUM-PRICED DINING: **Le Petit Vatel,** 129 Avenue de la République (tel. 31-88-21-56), is a simple place offering good food at reasonable prices. It's a bistro with a bar on one side and dining tables on the other. The tables overflow

onto the sidewalk, in the typical French fashion. The location is central but not chic, on the main boulevard of Deauville, overlooking a park. Open from Easter to October, it offers a set meal for 85F ($11.72), good value considering the quality. A typical menu might include a choice of pâtés, followed by coq au vin, plus a salad or a cheese selection, as well as dessert. A more elaborate meal is presented at 130F ($17.93). Service is an additional 15%.

Chez Miocque (Bar Cintra), 81 rue Eugène-Colas (tel. 31-88-09-52), is a bustling brasserie-café, doing a brisk business at sidewalk café tables. Right in the core of Deauville, Chez Miocque is within sight of the casino, the luxurious Normandy, and the fashionable boutiques. Its owner is known simply as Jack. He's an American from New York City, and he'll welcome you for lunch or dinner, or for only a drink. His average price for a complete dinner (without wine) is about 150F ($20.69) to 200F ($27.58). I recommend his fish of the day, his pepper steak, his sole meunière, followed by a tarte Tantin.

17. Trouville

This resort launched the Côte Fleurie—the "Flower Coast"—at the start of the Second Empire. As the first major seaside resort in France, it was developed during the days of Louis-Philippe, the "Citizen King," and has long been fashionable. It lies just across the Touques River from its more sophisticated (and more expensive) rival, Deauville.

Admittedly, Trouville is old, but like a charming countess it wears its years with a hautiness, covering a wrinkle with a mere blush. Time was when Trouville was the formal resort; nowadays it gives Deauville that privilege, as it is noisier and more fun for some. At least you don't have to keep counting your francs as you do in Deauville.

When the sea bathers have left Trouville's splendid sands to return to Paris or wherever, Trouville lives. Its hardcore resident population of fisherfolk see to that.

On the seafront Promenade des Planches is a large swimming pool, called the Piscine Olympique, and an impressive casino, which, nevertheless, isn't as grand as the one at Deauville.

WHERE TO STAY: The most recommendable accommodations are a modest and inexpensive lot.

One of the bargains of the resort is the little 20-room **Maison Normande**, 4 Place Maréchal-de-Lattre-Tassigny (tel. 31-88-12-25). Its bedrooms aren't bad, although don't expect a lot of fancy plumbing. A basic single rents for 200F ($27.58), a double going for 350F ($48.27). The hotel is closed in December and January.

Carmen, 24 rue Carnot (tel. 31-88-35-43), is a small hotel directed by the Bude family. They maintain a flowering inner courtyard encircled by some of their 15 bedrooms and the simple dining room. All the units have mini-bar and TV, and 12 of them have a complete bath. The charge for a single is 105F ($14.48); for a double, 260F ($35.85). Meals in the hotel's restaurant range in price from 65F ($8.97) to 180F ($24.82) and are served every day except on Tuesday and during most of January.

Les Sablettes, 15 rue Paul-Besson (tel. 31-88-10-66), is a small and unpretentious hotel near the casino, operated by the Pozza family. They charge from 118F ($16.27) for a single and from 210F ($28.96) for a double in their 17 simply furnished units. There's parking on the premises. The hotel is closed from mid-November to the first of February.

WHERE TO DINE: If you want something inexpensive without sacrificing quality, try **La Petite Auberge**, 7 rue Carnot (tel. 31-88-11-07), where I recently enjoyed an excellently prepared meal for 65F ($8.97). However, this fine repast might not be available on *le weekend*. The soupe de poissons was one of the finest I've enjoyed along the flower coast. A seafood au gratin with choice pieces of fish is also recommended. It's possible to spend 150F ($20.69) or more on a Saturday or Sunday. The restaurant is closed from mid-November to mid-January and on Tuesday and Wednesday off-season.

Les Vapeurs, 160 Boulevard Fernand-Moureaux (tel. 31-88-15-24). If the current penchant for 1950s-style decorations remains in fashion, this restaurant will be assured of business for a long time to come. The windows face the port, and in warm weather you can sometimes dine at sidewalk tables. Seafood is the specialty, and a wide range of shrimp, mussels, oysters, and fish is offered, although sauerkraut is also popular here. À la carte meals, prepared by Gérard Bazire, range from 150F ($20.69) to 200F ($27.58). The restaurant is closed Tuesday night and Wednesday, except in the height of summer. It is also shut down for the last two weeks of November and from early January till early February.

18. Honfleur

At the wide mouth of the Seine, opposite Le Havre, the fishing port of Honfleur is one of Normandy's most charming, with plenty of local color. Honfleur is actually 500 years older than Le Havre, dating from the 11th century. Early in the 17th century colonists set out from here to find Québec. The township has long been favored by artists, including, in times gone by, Daubigny and Corot. Monet also found inspiration here, and Baudelaire wrote *Invitation au Voyage* at Honfleur.

From the Place de la Porte-de-Rouen you can begin your tour of the town, which should take about an hour. Stroll along the **Vieux Bassin,** the old harbor, with its fishing boats and tall, slate-roofed, narrow houses. The former governor's house, **Lieutenance,** on the north side of the basin, dates from the 16th century. Nearby is the **Church of Ste. Catherine,** built entirely of timber in the 15th century by shipbuilders. The belfry stands on the other side of the street, and is also built of wood.

The **Musée Eugène-Boudin,** Place Erik Satie (tel. 31-89-16-47), has a good collection of the painters who flocked to this port. The largest collection is of the pastels and paintings of Eugène Boudin, of course. It is open daily except Tuesday, from 10 a.m. to noon and 2 to 6 p.m. March 15 to September 30. The remainder of the year, hours are from 2:30 to 5 p.m. weekdays except Tuesday, from 10 a.m. to noon and 2:30 to 5 Saturday and Sunday. Admission is 8.50F ($1.17).

WHERE TO STAY AND DINE: La Ferme St-Simeon, route Adolphe-Marais (tel. 31-89-23-61), is a 17th-century, three-story house with a wood and slate façade. An old cider press is a focal point in front of this Norman hostelry, and apple trees ringed with red geraniums decorate the lawn. From the back patio, you can see Le Havre and the English Channel. It was the haunting light and shimmering water that drew artists to this hilltop inn, which is said to be the place where impressionism was born in the last third of the 19th century. Boudin dazzled Monet here, and Courbet met Baudelaire.The 10-room inn and its 11-room guest house offer tranquil hospitality provided by Roland Boelen, his wife Michele, their four grown-up children, and a son-in-law, Pierre Arnaud, who is the chef. In the main building are a bar, used for drinks and the serving of breakfast, and a restaurant. The public rooms have terracotta floors, carved wood, and copper and faïence touches. The bedrooms, done mostly in 18th-century style, vary in size, with rents ranging from 900F ($124.11) in a single to 1,400F ($193.06) in a double.

Dining at the inn is an experience, with food being served either in the restaurant, comprising three rooms flowing together, or on the terrace with a view of the Seine estuary and Le Havre. The chef knows how to turn a simple bistro dish into a plate worth remembering. However, if you're feeling fashionably elegant, as most diners do here, you'll request one of the lobster dishes. Both classic and simple dishes are served, the kitchen moving with ease between the two. Try the chausson of lobster, a fricassée of rice and kidneys, or else the sole normande. Meals run from 325F ($44.82) to 375F ($51.71).

The hotel and restaurant are closed from December to the first of February. The restaurant is closed on Wednesday from the first of October to the end of March.

Le Cheval Blanc, 2 Quai des Passagers (tel. 31-89-13-49), is a combined hotel and restaurant in what is said to be one of Honfleur's most desirable privately owned buildings, a portside villa dating from the 1400s. Each of the interior bedrooms offers a view of the port, 12 of them containing private bath. Rooms range from 270F ($37.23) in a single to 370F ($51.02) in a double, with a continental breakfast included.

The restaurant is perhaps the prime reason for an overnight stay. While seated on velvet chairs beneath exposed ceiling beams, you'll enjoy a view of one of the most charming ports in the north of France. Menu specialties are laden with intensely detailed sauces and garnishes, and include cassolette of crayfish, mussels with saffron, and many other dishes adorned with truffles or foie gras. Table d'hôte menus begin at 180F ($24.82), while à la carte meals usually cost more, ranging from 250F ($34.48) to 300F ($41.37). Robert Samson, the owner and chef, usually closes his establishment on Monday and from mid-November to February 1.

Hostellerie Lechat, 3 Place Ste-Catherine (tel. 31-89-23-85). The sharp-eyed owners, M. Gignoux and M. Blais, see that everything is run to perfection. The rooms, although modest, are fine for an overnight stopover at the center of the port. They are 26 in all, 14 of which contain bath, and each is comfortably furnished. A single costs 200F ($24.82), and a double goes for 350F ($48.27). In the restaurant the waitresses serve excellently prepared dishes—eels dieppoise, spit-roasted leg of lamb, and prawns cooked in seawater. The chef also does some superb terrines. A meal will begin at 110F ($15.17). However, you'll spend from 190F ($26.20) if you wish to sample the more elegant selections of *les classiques de la mer.* The restaurant is closed on Wednesday and for lunch Thursday.

L'Absinthe, 10 Quai de la Quarantaine (tel. 31-89-39-00), is known by practically everyone in town as a locale where the decor is beautiful (with exposed stone and heavy ceiling beams about a century and a half old), the portions are extravagant, and the cuisine is well prepared and savory. Chef Antoine Geffrey, who apprenticed for many years at Troisgros, will probably make an appearance in the dining room before the end of your meal. A dinner might consist of veal kidneys with Calvados, rack of lamb with thyme, well-garnished shellfish, lotte with ginger, and attractive desserts. Fixed-price meals range from 120F ($16.55) to 180F ($24.82) while if you choose to order à la carte, you'll pay from 230F ($31.72) to 275F ($37.92). The restaurant is closed Monday night and Tuesday off-season and from November 12 to December 20.

19. Le Havre

France's major Atlantic port, at the mouth of the Seine, Le Havre lay in ruins in 1945, the worst-damaged port at the end of World War II, and the competition was stiff for that distinction. The city had been the target of more than 170 bombings. But the recovery of Le Havre was amazing, and now the largest container ships and oil tankers afloat can dock there easily. You can reach Trouville and Deauville by boat during the summer or you can go across one of Europe's longest suspension bridges, which celebrated its first anniversary in 1960.

A modern city, with tall blocks of apartment houses and large, pleasant squares, Le Havre, unlike some French towns, has radically changed since it was ordered created by François I in the 16th century. There is a lot to see in Le Havre and its environs. It is possible to tour the port by boat in summer. I suggest you go to the **Tourist Office,** Place de l'Hotel de Ville (tel. 35-21-22-88), for information about the different tours you can join.

If you drive out to **Le Heve Lighthouse,** a modern structure, you'll have a good view of the port, the "Flower Coast," and an estuary of the Seine. In summer, lighthouse tours begin at 10 a.m., and (naturally) the guide expects a tip.

The **Church of St. Joseph** is built of reinforced concrete, dominated by a bell tower nearly 350 feet high. It is the tallest building made of reinforced concrete in the country. The vast interior is awesome, with its square pillars supporting a lantern tower. Light pours in through panes of colored glass. A vista of Le Havre unfolds from the top of the tower. Visits are possible from 9 a.m. to noon and 2 to 7 p.m.

For another splendid view, go to the **Fort de Ste-Adresse,** above Ste-Adresse, a suburb of Le Havre. On a clear day, you can see not forever but the Côte de Grace, Honfleur, and the Seine estuary. On a recent summer visit, the entire coast of Calvados could be seen.

The glass and metal **André Malraux Musée des Beaux-Arts,** Boulevard J.-F.-Kennedy (tel. 35-42-33-97), is sophisticated in design, brilliantly showing off a collection that includes works by Raoul Dufy, along with many of the impressionists who were drawn to the north coast, including Monet, Pissarro, Sisley, and Renoir. There is also an outstanding collection of the works of Eugène Boudin, whom we encountered in Honfleur. The museum, charging no admission, is open from 10 a.m. to noon and 2 to 6 p.m. It is closed on Tuesday.

The **Museum of Ancient Le Havre** (Musée de l'Ancien Havre), 1 rue Jerome-Bellarmato (tel. 35-42-27-90), is in a restored 17th-century town house, which can be visited to see its pottery, porcelain, ship models, and engravings and watercolors tracing the history of Le Havre. It is open from 10 a.m. to noon and 2 to 6 p.m. However, it is closed on Monday and Tuesday.

WHERE TO STAY: Le Bordeaux, 147 rue Louis-Brindeau (tel. 35-22-69-44), is the lead hotel even though it doesn't have a restaurant. In the modern style, it is right in the center of the port, near the Bassin du Commerce. Your bedroom window might overlook a yacht belonging to a wealthy Londoner, as many of them seem to. The compact bedrooms, 31 in all, are brightly and pleasantly furnished, and the bathrooms show intelligent planning. Rates are 300F ($41.37) in a single, the cost rising to 510F ($70.33) in a double. Tariffs include a continental breakfast, service, and taxes. Here you get professional, friendly service.

Le Mercure, Chaussée d'Angoulême (tel. 35-21-23-45), a few steps from the ocean, is a member of a nationwide hotel chain. It offers comfort in some 100 air-conditioned rooms, each with private bath, phone, radio, and TV. Well-furnished rooms range in price from 375F ($51.71) in a single to 480F ($66.19) in a double. The hotel's restaurant offers set menus for 130F ($17.93) every day of the year.

Astoria, 13 Cours de la République (tel. 35-25-00-03), is a contemporary hotel across from the train station. It offers clean and comfortable accommodations, all with bath, phone, and TV. Singles rent for 190F ($26.20), and doubles go for 270F ($37.23). A fixed-price meal in the in-house restaurant costs 65F ($8.97), or you can dine à la carte for 155F ($21.38), every day except Friday at noon and on Sunday. Mr. Ternisien is the owner/manager.

WHERE TO DINE: Le Monaco, 16 rue de Paris (tel. 35-42-21-01), attracts the bright young French to its modern precincts, plus a large coterie of English people who seem to visit for the weekend. A sophisticated restaurant, the place offers a menu of variety and interest. The cookery is often excellent, as reflected by braised turbot in Calvados. You might also enjoy the feuilleté of snails cooked in cider or the barbue suprême with sorrel. Fresh salmon is occasionally featured, again served with sorrel, and the roast lamb is always reliable. In keeping with its tradition as a seaport restaurant, the chef is also likely to offer fresh mussels, prawns, and oysters. Menus are priced at 85F ($11.72) and 200F ($27.58). The restaurant also rents out ten compact bedrooms that are pleasantly furnished, catering adequately for short visits at a cost of 110F ($15.17) in a single, 265F ($36.54) in a double. The restaurant is closed on Monday except in July and August, and the hotel shuts down in February and from September 1 to September 15.

La Petite Auberge, 32 rue St-Adresse (tel. 35-46-27-32), has a nice, pleasing ambience that I'm especially fond of. I like the price even better: 87F ($12) for a complete meal. Considering the quality and the portions, this is the best meal for the price at Le Havre. Of course you can dine here more expensively, paying from 260F ($35.85), but it isn't really necessary except perhaps on Saturday night when the cheaper menu is not available. The specialties include a selection of shellfish, turbot cooked in the Norman style, and savory mussels. Try, if featured, the lamb curry or the chef's own special way of doing chicken. The restaurant is closed in August, and on Sunday night and Monday.

20. Fécamp

This cod-fishing port, 27 miles northeast of Le Havre, is where the popular Benedictine liqueur is distilled. At the mouth of the Fécamp River, this town is squeezed between two high cliffs. De Maupassant once lived here, using it as the setting in some of his stories.

According to legend, the "True Blood" of Christ drifted to Fécamp from Palestine in the trunk of a fig tree. That relic is today the precious Treasury in the **Church of La Trinité,** which dates mostly from 1175 to 1225. From its central tower, 210 feet high, you'll have a good view of this seaside resort and the English Channel. The venerated relic of the True Blood is housed in a 16th-century tabernacle. The former abbey church's length of 416 feet almost rivals that of Notre-Dame in Paris, which extends 10 feet more. In the transept is an interesting *Assumption* from the late 15th century, and from the next century there are some splendid carved screens.

The **Musée de la Bénédictine,** 110 rue Alexander-le-Grand (tel. 35-28-00-06), owes its inception to a monk, Vincelli, who distilled the aromatic plants growing along the cliffs. You can tour the distillery, with its Gothic-and Renaissance-style buildings, including the old distilling chamber where the now world-famous liqueur was first produced. It is open from 9:30 to 11:30 a.m. and 2 to 5:30 p.m. daily, charging an admission of 15F ($2.07).

FOOD AND LODGING: Most visitors drive on to Le Havre or Dieppe for the night, although the valiant **Angleterre,** 93 rue de la Plage (tel. 35-28-01-60), will provide you with a snug nest if you're not too demanding. It offers 30 modestly furnished rooms, charging 200F ($27.58) in a single and 250F ($34.48) in a double. The hotel shuts down from November 20 until sometime after Christmas when English people often cross the Channel for a holiday in France.

The best restaurant is **Auberge de la Rouge,** at St-Léonard (tel. 35-28-07-59), one mile south by the D925, which does consistently fine cooking. Try the lobster à l'armoricaine or the sole normande, two very good specialties. A set meal will run 75F ($10.32), although you can easily spend from 200F ($27.58) if you order à la carte. The restaurant is closed Sunday night and Monday.

Another good possibility is **Le Maritime,** 2 Place Nicolas-Selles (tel. 35-28-21-71), which has comfortable chairs and well-appointed tables opening onto a view of the port. Tempting fish dishes and daily changing specialties are features of the enjoyable menu, which is likely to run from 75F ($10.32) to 200F

($27.58). The place has become a favorite locally, its habitués drawn here by cookery that is competent and enthusiastic. The restaurant is open all year.

21. Dieppe

In a valley bordered by steep white cliffs reminiscent of those at Dover (England), Dieppe on the Channel coast has long been popular as a seaside resort, in spite of its pebbly beach. In fact it is one of the oldest seaside resorts in France, as it is the nearest beach to Paris, 104 miles away and easily reached by rail. Dieppe has enjoyed favor with the English too, including Oscar Wilde, many of the British preferring it to their own Brighton in Sussex.

Badly shattered during World War II, Dieppe is now a progressive, modern town, the fourth-largest passenger port in the country. The cross-Channel steamer arrives from Newhaven, near Brighton on England's south coast, dispensing the daily trippers seeking a "holiday on the continent."

One of the safest and deepest harbors in the English Channel, the subject of a daring but unsuccessful Canadian commando raid in 1942, the port of Dieppe is most interesting. The outer port, the **Port de Voyageurs,** is where the Channel ferryboats dock. Under the arcades you can attend a lively fish market. But the fishing port itself, **Port de Pêche,** has more local color. Beyond it lies the commercial harbor, **Port de Commerce,** which does a lively banana trade with the West Indies.

Six streets meet at the Place du Puits-Salés, the heart of Dieppe. From this small square you can walk up the rue St-Jacques to the **Church of St. Jacques** (St. James), founded in the 13th century. Supporting the more modern central tower, the transept is the oldest part of the church. St. Jacques has some lovely portals and is elegantly decorated.

West of the harbor, with its casino and bathing beach, you reach the **Castle of Dieppe,** on a high chalk cliff. The château, dating from 1435, has been much altered over the years. It houses a museum that contains an excellent, even celebrated, collection of Dieppe ivories, plus some medieval and Renaissance sculpture, a large collection of 19th-century European paintings including works by the impressionists, and other souvenirs of the seaport. See also the prints by Georges Braque. Charging 5.50F (76¢) admission, the museum is open every day except Tuesday, from 10 a.m. to noon and 2 to 6 p.m. from June 1 to September 30, from 10 a.m. to noon and 2 to 5 p.m. the remainder of the year.

South of Dieppe stands the **Castle of Miromesnil** (get a map from the tourist office) where De Maupassant was born in 1850. The castle can be visited May 1 until mid-October from 2 to 6 p.m. for an admission of 12F ($1.66). With its souvenirs of the writer, and its chapel, the castle lies near the hamlet of St-Aubin-sur-Scie, which is reached along the D54.

FOOD AND LODGING: The best hotel is **La Présidence,** 1 Boulevard de Verdun (tel. 35-84-31-31), which opens onto the sea, standing right next to the Municipal Casino. It is ultra modern and functional, with well-planned bedrooms and up-to-date baths. The friendly receptionist will book you in here at 225F ($31.03) in a single, the cost rising to 420F ($57.92) in a double. La Présidence has a good grill room, Le Queiros, featuring a simple but effective French cuisine with plenty of fresh oysters and scallops. The chef also does meat dishes well, including that choice beef cut, onglet, which is grilled here, occasionally with shallots. More exotic specialties include a calf's head in vinaigrette sauce and skate in black butter. The least expensive meal goes for 135F ($18.62), and you can spend from 220F ($30.34) by ordering à la carte. The air-conditioned hotel also has a garage.

Bargain hunters may want to seek out the **Windsor,** 18 Boulevard de Verdun (tel. 35-84-15-23), which is also on the beach, on the same boulevard as La

Présidence. Its 46 bedrooms are conservatively modern, agreeably comfortable, definitely of a good standard. However, the singles are small but basically equipped. The hotel also has a good restaurant, where French dishes are prepared with care and excellent fresh ingredients are used whenever possible. Menus go for 85F ($11.72) and 150F ($20.69). The restaurant doesn't serve on Sunday night from October to Easter.

In town, **À La Marmite Dieppoise,** 8 rue St-Jean (tel. 35-84-24-26), has a varied menu and moderate cost—a set meal goes for 90F ($12.41), although it is not available on Friday and Saturday nights when you could easily spend 155F ($21.38). The owner-chef, Jean-Pierre Toussaint, offers, naturally, la marmite dieppoise as his specialty, in honor of the namesake of his restaurant. But you can also dine equally well on mussels marinière, an assiette of fresh seafood, and a fisherman's-style sauerkraut. In this cheerfully decorated place, the service is prompt and friendly. However, it is closed from June 22 to July 5 (this can vary) and on Thursday night, Sunday night, and Monday.

Le Port, 99 Quai Henri IV (tel. 35-84-36-64). Its harborside location is appropriate to the seafood which is this establishment's specialty. Within an elegantly conservative dining room, at one of a handful of tables covered with immaculate linen, you can enjoy some of the freshest fish in town. Menu items include a thick slice of monkfish with fresh fennel, roast shank of rabbit with a mustard sauce, several preparations of mussels, and an array of sole dishes. There's also a limited selection of meat dishes. Fixed-price menus cost between 70F ($9.65) and 110F ($15.17), while à la carte dinners go for between 160F ($22.06) and 210F ($28.96). No meals are served Thursday and during a one-month vacation in December and January.

Chapter X

BRITTANY

1. Nantes
2. La Baule
3. Carnac
4. Quiberon
5. Belle-Île-en-Mer
6. Hennebont
7. Quimperlé
8. Pont-Aven
9. Riec-sur-Belon
10. Concarneau
11. La Forêt-Fouesnant
12. Quimper
13. Locronan
14. Dinan
15. Dinard
16. St-Malo

THE OLD PEOPLE may be fading away, but while they live, so will the past. In the northwestern corner of France, in the ancient province and duchy of Brittany, the Bretons stubbornly hold onto their traditions. True, the young people head for Paris for "a better life," and the men who returned from World War II brought "alarming" new ideas. Nevertheless, deep in the heart of the interior, called l'Argoat, the old folks quietly live in stone farmhouses, with much the same ideas their grandparents had. The older women, at least on special occasions, still can be seen wearing their starched lace headdresses.

The Breton language is still spoken, better understood by the Welsh and the Cornish folk than by the French. Sadly, it may die out altogether, in spite of attempts by folklore groups to keep it alive. In that sense, Brittany is the Wales of France.

Conquered by Caesar in 56 B.C., the land was once called Armorica. However, the Celtic inhabitants of the British Isles, the Britons, crossed the Channel in A.D. 500, fleeing from the invading Angles and Saxons.

The true Bretons—except those whose parents married "foreigners" from Paris—are generally darker and shorter than their compatriots in France. These characteristics reflect their Celtic origin, which still lives on in superstition, folklore, and fairy tales. Breton *pardons* are famous. These are religious festivals, sometimes attracting thousands of pilgrims who turn up in traditional dress.

Nearly every hamlet has its own *pardon*. These observances are major attractions, drawing the French from as far away as Marseille and Scots from

Glasgow. The best-known ones are on May 19 at **Treguier** (honoring St. Yves, who consoled the poor and righted wrongs); on the second Sunday in July at **Locronan** (in the footsteps of St. Ronan); on July 26 at **St-Anne-d'Auray** (honoring the "mothers of Bretons"); and on September 8 at **Le Folgoet** (commemorating *ar foll coat,* or that "idiot of the forest").

Many Bretons consider themselves a nation within a nation. Movements for independence—particularly strong in the 19th century—come and go. Brittany was joined with the crown of France through Anne of Brittany's marriages to Charles VIII and later to Louis XII.

Traditionally, the province is divided into **Haute-Bretagne** and **Basse-Bretagne.** The rocky coastline, some 750 miles long, is studded with promontories, coves, and occasional beaches. Like the prow of a ship, Brittany projects into the sea. Hence, the province gives France its best sailors. The interior, however, is a land of sleepy hamlets, stone-built farms, and moors covered with yellow broom and purple heather. First-time visitors to the craggy peninsula would be better advised to stick to the coastline, where salt-meadow sheep can be seen grazing along pasture land whipped by sea breezes. Those leaving Le Mont Saint-Michel can center at the trio of tourist towns, St-Malo, Dinan, or Dinard. Coming from the château country, visitors can explore the South Brittany coastline.

Assuming you're beginning your exploration after leaving the Loire, your first major stopover will be uncharacteristic of Brittany:

1. Nantes

In western France, Nantes is the largest town of Brittany, although in spirit it seems to belong more to the château country along the Loire. The mouth of the Loire is about 30 miles away, and at Nantes the river divides into several branches. Nantes spreads itself over these Loire islands, but it lies mostly on the north bank. A commercial and industrial city, it is a busy port that suffered great damage in World War II. The city is known for the Edict of Nantes, sponsored by Henri IV in 1598, guaranteeing religious freedom to Protestants (it was later revoked). Many famous people have lived here, from Molière to Madame de Sévigné to Stendhal to Michelet.

The **Cathedral of St. Peter** (Cathédrale St-Pierre) (tel. 40-47-84-64), begun in 1434, wasn't finished until the closing years of the 19th century, yet it remained harmonious architecturally, a rare feat of which few European cathedrals can boast. The façade is characterized by two square towers, but it is the interior that is more impressive. It is 335 feet long. Its pièce de résistance is the Renaissance masterpiece of Michel Colomb—the tomb of François II, Duke of Brittany, and his second wife, Marguerite de Foix. There is yet another impressive work of art, also a tomb, that of General Juchault de Lamoricière, a native of Nantes and a great African campaigner. The work is by the sculptor Paul Dubois, completed in 1879. After a fire totally destroyed the roof in January 1972 (rebuilt in 1975), the interior of the cathedral was completely restored. It attracts by the whiteness of its walls and pillars, contrasting with the rich colors of the new stained-glass windows. The crypt, dating from the 11th century, shelters a museum of religions.

Between the cathedral and the Loire stands the second major sight of Nantes, the **Ducal Château,** once the seat of the dukes of Brittany. It was here that the previously mentioned Edict of Nantes was signed. The castle was founded in either the 9th or 10th century, although François II had it rebuilt in 1466 for Duchess Anne. It is flanked by large towers and a bastion. The Duchesse de Berry was imprisoned here, as was Gilles de Retz, known as "Bluebeard," who confessed to more than 100 murders.

Behind its walls the castle has installed three museums: the **Museum of Decorative Arts** in the Tour du Fer à Cheval (the Horseshoe Tower), the **Museum of the Salorges** (history of Nantes since the 18th century), and the **Museum of Pop-**

ular **Regional Art** in the Grand Gouvernement building (costumes, arts, and crafts, along with wrought-iron works). In the peak visiting months of July and August, the museums are open daily from 10 a.m. to noon and from 2 to 6 p.m. At other times of the year, hours are the same but everything is closed on Tuesday. All three museums can be visited for a 5F (69¢) ticket; free on weekends.

First, the Decorative Arts Museum takes up only one room at present, and it's dedicated to contemporary textile art. Next, the Museum of the Salorges was created by Nantes industrialists in 1928. It offers exhibits on the different aspects of commercial, colonial, and industrial activities of the city since the 18th century, including the slave trade. Ship models are especially interesting, including fishing boats of Brittany. The Museum of Popular Regional Art presents many aspects of costumes, furniture, and handcrafts of the Vendean people. Two rooms are devoted to headdresses and costumes.

If time remains, you might want to visit the **Musée des Beaux-Arts de Nantes,** 10 rue Georges-Clemenceau (tel. 40-74-53-24), east of the Place du Maréchal-Foch. It is one of the most interesting provincial galleries of art in western France, containing an unusually fine collection of sculptures and paintings, accenting the French modern schools. Sculpture and temporary exhibitions are displayed on the ground floor. See Ingres's portrait of Madame de Senonnes, a painting by Courbet, plus works by Delacroix and Georges de la Tour, and *Two Saints* by Bergognone. There are also examples from the Italian school. See also the collection of modern paintings, including works by Kandinsky, Hartung, Poliakoff, and Gorin. The museum is open daily except Tuesday from 10 a.m. to noon and 1 to 5:45 p.m., charging 5F (69¢) for admission.

Of minor interest, the **Palais Dobrée** is a town mansion from the 19th century that was built by an important collector in Nantes, from whom the palace takes its name. It stands alongside the manor of Jean de la Touche from the 15th century, where the bishops of Nantes occasionally lived. Both buildings are museums, containing a varied collection gathered by Monsieur Dobrée, including prehistoric and medieval antiquities, along with Flemish paintings from the 15th century and many ecclesiastical relics. The museum is open daily except Tuesday from 10 a.m. to noon and 2 to 5 p.m., charging 5F (69¢) for admission. The museum is in the vicinity of the Place Graslin, near the attractive Cours Cambronne.

Jules Verne, the French novelist *(Around the World in Eighty Days)*, was born in Nantes in 1828, and literary fans like to seek out his house at 4 rue de Clisson in the Île Feydeau.

HOTELS: Sofitel Nantes, rue Alexandre, Île Beaulieu (tel. 40-47-61-03), stands on an island surrounded by the Loire. Five minutes from the heart of town and the railway station, it offers 100 well-furnished chambers that are a model of efficient hotel planning. In fact, this chain hotel is the best place to stay in town for those seeking the most up-to-date amenities and modernity. Singles pay from 380F ($52.40) to 440F ($60.68); doubles, 440F ($60.68) to 540F ($74.47). All the rooms come with complete modern bath. The restaurant and bar, La Pêcherie, offers a wide choice of seafood and fish dishes, with meals costing 170F ($23.44) to 250F ($34.48). In addition, the hotel has a swimming pool with a lounging terrace, plus tennis courts.

Hôtel Central, 4 rue du Couëdic (tel. 40-20-09-35), is another excellent choice—*très confortable,* as the French say. The hotel has a discreet exterior and offers rooms that are pleasantly and agreeably decorated. In a single, expect to pay 240F ($33.10) to 400F ($55.16); the tariff is 400F ($55.16) in a double. The Central restaurant is a good dining choice. It does well-prepared grills, among other offerings. I recently enjoyed a crayfish bisque and a quiche Nantes style. Such standard international fare is featured as minute steak, veal escalope milanese, and steak tartare, a very popular choice. Menus are priced at 100F ($13.79) and 140F ($19.31).

L'Hôtel, 6 Place de la Duchesse-Anne (tel. 40-29-30-31). Behind the modernized symmetry of its townhouse façade lies a comfortable hotel whose 32 bedrooms benefit from the attention lavished on it by the hardworking owners. It sits across the street from the moat surrounding the Château des Ducs de Bretagne, within easy access of the dining and entertainment facilities of Nantes. A scattering of 19th-century antiques stand in the tile-floored reception area. Nearby are the paneled walls and deep modern sofas and chairs of the sitting room. Each room, containing a private bath, phone, and TV, is uniquely different from its neighbors, outfitted in original colors—sometimes vivid—which complement the bentwood and rattan furnishings. A single goes for 285F ($39.30), a double for 310F ($42.75).

France, 24 rue Crébillon (tel. 40-73-57-91), is right in the center, near the river. It's recommended for a suitable overnight stop, although you may find some of its rooms noisy. Rooms are, for the most part, stylized with reproductions of French antiques or traditional pieces. Rates depend a great deal on the unit you occupy. The most expensive are styled in the Louis XVI-Trianon tradition. In a single, the tariff begins at 255F ($35.17), climbing to 420F ($57.92) for two persons. The bar is pleasantly charming, and a tea salon is more formal. The restaurant is stylishly furnished and serves a top-notch set dinner for 90F ($12.41) and up.

Alternatively, you may prefer the comparable **Graslin,** 1 rue Piron (tel. 40-89-16-09), which doesn't have a restaurant, however. The hotel lies on a steep old street near the harbor. It is utterly unpretentious but, again, suitable for an overnight stop if you're economizing. Singles rent for 115F ($15.86) the cost going up to 200F ($27.58) in a double, a good bargain for Nantes. Only a few of the rooms contain private bath or shower, and these are grabbed up first.

RESTAURANTS: Les Maraîchers, 21 rue Fouré (tel. 40-47-06-51), attracts those seeking lighter fare than the traditional cuisine served in most of the city's leading restaurants. The domain of Serge Pacreau, it offers food of exceptional quality, and locals debate endlessly and needlessly as to which restaurant offers the best cuisine, Coq Hardi or Les Maraîchers. Both are good—they are just different. In a modern atmosphere, you can enjoy near-perfection or perfection in some dishes—steamed scallops, a salad of mussels, the foie gras of the house, grilled lobster, and duckling with turnips (in season). Each dish, even a simple turbot, comes out of the kitchen as an original and imaginatively prepared concoction. Dining à la carte can easily run up your tab to 250F ($34.48) to 325F ($44.82). However, set menus are offered, the cheaper one costing 165F ($22.75). The restaurant is closed at lunchtime on Saturday, and on Sunday, Monday, and in August.

Coq Hardi, 22 allée du Charcot (tel. 40-74-14-25), near the railway station, is known for its bass in the beurre blanc sauce and its canard du muscadet. On a busy promenade near the river, this top-grade restaurant offers you a chance to dine in a refined, modern atmosphere, enjoying well-prepared dishes and formal, polite service. Menus go from 100F ($13.79) up, or at around 215F ($29.65) if you're ordering à la carte. The restaurant closes on Saturday.

Le Nantais, 161 rue des Hauts-Pavés (tel. 40-76-59-54). Many of the citizens of Nantes seem to prefer the big rear dining room, whose entrance passes through the kitchens. Here the food is generously served, well prepared, and savory. The Garnier family, the owners, attract a loyal crowd of regular guests, many of whom, like Monsieur Garnier, are avid cycling fans of the Tour de France. You can dine on such specialties as duckling with muscadet, a wide selection of fish, terrine of eel or terrine of crayfish, and a full array of other temptations. Complete à la carte meals cost 215F ($29.65), while set menus are offered for 88F ($12.14) to 160F ($22.06). The restaurant is open every day except for most of August and February.

In my search for the restaurant that serves the best meal in town at low cost, I found the **Restaurant des Voyageurs,** 16 allée du Commandant-Charcot (tel. 40-74-02-41). Menu items are not the most innovative in the region, but they're well seasoned, well prepared, and generously served. You might choose duckling with green peppercorns, sole with essence of crayfish, or something from the wide array of meat dishes. Fixed-price menus range from 65F ($8.97), while à la carte meals cost from 130F ($17.93). The restaurant is closed for the first two weeks of January.

About five miles east of the city, on Route N751, near Basse-Goulaine, stands an exceptionally good little restaurant, **Mon Rêve** (tel. 40-03-55-50). People of Nantes have been coming to this place for years, knowing they can dine well in a park-like setting with a rose garden. The chef, Gérard Ryngel, and his wife Cecile took over operation of Mon Rêve in 1979 and have given free rein to the talent and inventiveness they showed previously in a four-star restaurant near Nantes. Monsieur Ryngel produces such dishes as the fresh Loire salmon steak, wild duck with Bourjeuil sauce, and light, airy pastries. He also makes the famous beurre blanc (white butter) sauce, a specialty of Brittany. His repertoire is vast, including both regional specialties and those of his own creation. Regional specialties include canard (duckling) cooked with muscadet and a medallion of sandre (zander, a freshwater fish) with the beurre blanc sauce. Those of his own invention include a delectable dish of sweetbreads with crayfish, turbot with lobster, along with a coquilles St-Jacques (scallops) en chemise that deserves a prize. Try also his cul de lapin (rabbit) in muscadet and his aguillettes de filet de boeuf (beef) au Bourgueil. He also proposes a menu gourmand at 208F ($28.68) that is among the most outstanding dinners you are likely to be served in the area. However, if you're rushed, ask for the *déjeuner rapide* at 150F ($20.69), which is surprisingly good. You can spend at least 300F ($41.37) ordering à la carte. The restaurant is closed on Sunday night, Wednesday between October and March, and 15 days in February.

2. La Baule

Founded in the heyday of the Victorian seaside craze back in 1879, **La Baule** remains as fresh and inviting as the Gulf Stream that warms the waters of its wide, five-mile-long, crescent-shaped, white sandy beach—considered by many (and not just hoteliers) as the finest in Europe. It's in a bikini-for-bikini race with Biarritz for supremacy as the most fashionable resort on the Atlantic Coast, occupying a strip known as the Côte d'Amour ("Coast of Love").

That Prince of Gamblers, François André, founded the casino and the major resort hotels, claiming later that a hound tricked him by showing him the beach in fair weather and that La Baule, despite his considerable investment, was a losing proposition. However, his name is forever linked to the success of the resort. The weather is most unpredictable. Pines grow on the dunes. On the outskirts, Easter-egg villas, landscaped with honeysuckle, jasmine, pomegranates, figs, and palms, draw the wealthy chic in season, lasting from the end of June till mid-September. Should you arrive at any other time, you might have La Baule to yourself. The movie stars go to Deauville or Cannes, and La Baule draws more of a middle-class clientele. But the wealthy with quiet money still come here, as the yachts in the harbor testify. Tennis, golf, and sailing are popular along the coast.

Of course, there's the inevitable casino, which often books top talent.

This South Breton resort is still essentially French, drawing only a nominal string of sun-seeking foreigners. It lies 49 miles west of Nantes, the old capital of the dukes of Brittany.

HOTELS: Everything is here, from palatial digs to a simple villa. First—

Deluxe Living
Hermitage, Esplanade François-André (tel. 40-60-37-00), is the regal palace of this beach kingdom. Impressively built seven stories high and studded with red balconies, it occupies a dominant position on the beach. The upper three floors, with green timbers, are a mélange of gables and dormers. Ornate and plush, the interior is in direct contrast to the casual beach. The air-conditioned bedrooms, each with a marble or tile private bath, are furnished with reproductions of English and French antiques. Several rooms have been transformed into the modern style. There is no shabby grandeur here; everything is kept up to a high standard. In July and August, a double room with bath costs 1,800F ($248.22) with a sea view, dropping to 1,400F ($193.06) if it opens onto the garden in the rear. Half-board costs 880F ($121.35) to 2000F ($275.80) per person daily, including service.

The Hermitage offers a choice of three dining places: a beach terrace, a grill, and a main dining room with arched windows, paneled ceilings, and glittering chandeliers. Behind the scenes is a corps of white-hatted chefs turning out top-drawer cuisine. In the restaurant, expect to spend 260F ($35.85) to 300F ($41.37) per person. The main drawing room is conservatively modern. A heated seawater pool is another facility. The Hermitage is open from mid-April to mid-October. Under the same management are an 18-hole golf course and 28 tennis courts.

Castel Marie Louise, Esplanade du Casino (tel. 40-60-20-60), is a Breton manor house providing grand living in a pine-park estate along the oceanfront. Seemingly created as a private, overscale villa for some wealthy person, the stone-built, gabled castle now offers plush living for vacationers all year round except in February. The public rooms, including a salon for drinks, are furnished tastefully in the French provincial style, with mellow fruit woods set against autumnal colors. The wall tapestries depict stylized animals in brown and green. Most of the 28 renovated accommodations on the upper floors come with private balcony; two rooms are in a tower. Furnishings reflect several styles, including Louis XV, Directoire, and rustic. In high season, from July 1 till the end of August, full board ranges from 900F ($124.11) to 1,020F ($140.66) per person. These rates include taxes and service.

The excellent chef is reason enough to stay here; even if you aren't a guest, you may want to stop for a meal. Specialties include lobster and home-smoked salmon. Many diners prefer to begin their meal with Breton oysters, perhaps following with turbot. A set menu is featured for 225F ($31.03), although an à la carte bill will easily reach the 400F ($55.16) mark.

The Middle Bracket
Alexandra, 3 Boulevard René-Dubois (tel. 40-60-30-06), is one of the best of the modern hotels in the center of La Baule. Right on the oceanfront, the Alexandra boasts eight floors of ultramodern bedrooms with all-glass walls opening onto private balconies facing the beach. An open-air terrace with umbrellas and sidewalk tables, plus planters of flowers and greenery, set it off from the coastal road. The ninth-floor solarium is a popular spot for drinks and coffee, and guests sit under parasols. Although the second-floor dining room is exposed through glass to the ocean, and the drinking lounge is *intime* with tufted velour chairs, the bedrooms are the best feature. In July and August, the full-board rate per person is 400F ($55.16) to 460F ($63.43). These rates include service and taxes. The hotel is open from April 1 to September 30.

Bellevue Plage, 27 Boulevard de l'Océan (tel. 40-60-28-55), occupies a prominent yet peaceful position in the center of the shoreline curving around the bay. The decor is contemporary, with a rooftop solarium where many guests gravitate during their stay, plus a garden and a restaurant with a sweeping view of the water. Each of the 34 pleasant bedrooms has its own bath, TV, and phone. Rents range from 350F ($48.27) in a single to 520F ($71.71) in a double. You'll find a beach, sailboats for rent, and access to the spa facilities of the resort right in front of the hotel. Open March 20 to October 10.

The Budget Range

Helios, 7 Boulevard René-Dubois (tel. 40-60-22-38). The welcome is typically French, and the owner speaks English. Facing the sea, this pleasant budget hotel has two glass doors opening into the lobby, whose walls are covered with a Toile de Jouy tapestry. A little sitting corner is furnished with rustic tables and chairs. From the lobby you ascend to the large dining room, whose windows open right onto the water in summer. The walls are covered with the same Toile de Jouy as the lobby. The furniture is Breton-rustic. The bedrooms are furnished without any particular originality but in a functional style, and they're kept clean and comfortable. Doubles with private shower or bath range from 250F ($34.48) to 300F ($41.37). All rooms are for two persons. Depending on the room, the full-board rate ranges from 300F ($41.37) to 350F ($48.27) per person. The hotel is open from April 1 until the end of September.

Hotel Flepen, 145 Avenue de Lattre-De-Tassigny (tel. 40-60-29-30). When the original owners of this villa commissioned its construction, they selected a site within a short walk of the beach. Today, after a transformation into a recently renovated hotel, the establishment attracts beach lovers who congregate on its outdoor terrace and garden. About 60% of the two dozen bedrooms contain a private bath, and each has a phone. Singles begin at 140F ($19.31), with doubles costing 350F ($48.27), breakfast not included. The hotel is closed from mid-October to mid-April.

THE BEST RESTAURANT: L'Espadon (The Swordfish), 2 Avenue de la Plage (tel. 40-60-05-63). Perched atop a tall apartment building complex, the most elegant of La Baule's restaurants overlooks the town and its beaches. The ambience is contemporary chic, the food excellent, the service traditional. Three set meals are offered: a club menu at 85F ($11.72), a tourist one at 150F ($20.69), and a gastronomic repast at 280F ($38.61). À la carte, you might begin with moules (mussels) à la crème, then follow with suprême de St-Pierre soufflé à l'oseille (sorrel) or perhaps grilled bass with fennel or fricassée de homard. I also suggest a casserole of belons (oysters) and duckling julienne. For dessert, try, if in season, the fraises (strawberries) Romanoff. For an à la carte meal here, expect to spend 300F ($41.37) to 350F ($48.27) per person. The restaurant is closed Sunday night and Monday, and in winter.

3. Carnac

In May and June the fields are resplendent with golden broom. Sometimes the good weather at this seaside resort continues into October. But aside from "sea and sail," Carnac, 62 miles southeast of Quimper, is one of the most important centers in the world for seeing evidence of the human race's prehistoric past. For there you'll find the **Field of Megaliths,** the huge stones, numbering in the hundreds, considered the most important prehistoric find in northern France. Their arrangement and placement, however, remain a mystery. At **Carnac Ville,** the museum of prehistory Miln-LeRouzic, is the third such museum in Europe. The collections are from 350,000 B.C. and from the 8th century A.D. The museum is open daily except Tuesday, from 10 a.m. to noon and 2 to 5 p.m., charging 12F ($1.66) for admission.

Even if Carnac didn't possess dolmens, cromlechs, and menhirs, its pine-studded sand dunes would be worth the trip. Protected by the Quiberon Peninsula, **Carnac-Plage** is a family resort.

FOOD AND LODGING: **Tal Ar Mor Novotel,** Avenue l'Atlantique (tel. 97-52-16-66), offers cheerfully decorated rooms, 106 in all, in a modern setting near the ocean. Accommodations are spacious and well furnished, and each has a private bath. Rooms rent for 380F ($52.40) in a single, 460F ($63.43) in a double. Guests have access to a spa facility and an indoor saltwater swimming pool. A restaurant on the premises serves a meal for 120F ($16.55). The hotel is closed in January.

Le Diana, 21 Boulevard de la Plage (tel. 97-52-05-38), on the most popular beach in town, offers a terrace where you can sip drinks and watch the crashing waves. The contemporary bedrooms are fairly spacious, with balconies attached to the units facing the sea. Accommodations cost 350F ($48.27) in a single, 600F ($82.74) in a double. There is a restaurant in the hotel where you can order a meal beginning at 150F ($20.69). You can pay far more, of course, by ordering some of the higher priced fish dishes. The hotel receives guests from the first week of May until the end of September.

Lann Roz, 36 Avenue de la Poste (tel. 97-52-10-48), is built in the Breton manner and surrounded by a private garden of flowers and lawns. Within walking distance of the water, it's a good, inexpensive oasis for budget-minded visitors in search of a sea holiday. Family-owned and operated, Lann Roz is under the wing of Madame Le Calvez, who is friendly and hearty, inviting guests to sunbathe on the wide stone terrace opening off the family-style living room. Also fronting the garden is a typical Breton dining room, where Madame has instructed the cook to keep the meals regional and the portions generous. You don't have to be a guest of the hotel to drop in for a meal, costing from 115F ($15.86) to 240F ($33.10). In high season, half-board terms range from 215F ($29.65) to 335F ($46.20) per person per day. The hotel is closed on Wednesday afternoon and in January.

Ker Ihuel, 59 Boulevard de la Plage (tel. 97-52-11-38), is a modest villa with a white plaster façade, set amid pine trees in a residential area, directly on the coast road. On a raised stone terrace, garden furniture is set out for drinks and sunbathing. Across the road is a strip of dunes and a sandy beach. Sun and the ocean breezes pour into the bedroom windows. The Ker Ihuel is a genial family-run place, attracting the French who like an informal holiday. The interior lounge and dining room are decorated in a provincial Breton style, that theme extending to the bedrooms as well. Some of the rooms contain shower or tub, plus hot and cold running water in the basins, but the toilets are in the corridors. In July and August, the full-board rate ranges from 240F ($33.10) to 275F ($37.92) per person, these tariffs lowered in May, June, and September. The higher price is for an accommodation with private bath. In high season, from June 1 to September 15, a minimum stay of three days is required. The hotel is open from May 1 to September 20.

Les Alignements, 45 rue Cornély (tel. 97-52-06-30), is a 27-room establishment where the mother does the cooking, the father the managing. The front is sober and pleasant enough; the back looks out onto a garden. Inside, everything blends and is clean and efficient. On the second and third floors the rooms have balconies or loggias. Those facing the street have double windows to keep down the noise. For decoration, wall tapestries have been used effectively and fabrics have been color-coordinated. Incidentally, the keys to the rooms are made of brown leather in the shape of fish. Half board, which is required in July and August, ranges from 190F ($26.20) to 220F ($30.34) per person. Two persons are rented rooms from 175F ($24.13) to 230F ($31.72), the higher price for units with complete baths. Nonresidents are welcome to dine here, in a modern room with a rustic touch created by tiles and wooden walls. The price of the set menus ranges from 60F ($8.27) to 120F ($16.55). For the second price, I recently enjoyed Breton oysters followed by grilled crab. The inn is open from May 5 to September 22.

4. Quiberon

A sardine-fishing port, Quiberon is also a noted South Breton resort with a large white sandy beach attracting "family affair" tourists. It's on a peninsula that was once an island, connected to the mainland by what has been called "a narrow tongue of alluvial deposits." Aside from the beach, the best local sight is the rugged Breton fishermen hauling in their sardine catch.

The entire coast—the **Côte Sauvage** (Wild Coast)—is rugged, the ocean breaking with fury onto the reefs, its waves lashing against the jagged rock at the cliff's edge, then surging with a roar into the grottos eating into the shoreline. Fierce northern winds, especially in winter, lash across the sand dunes, shaving the short pines that grow there. On the landward side, however, the beach is calm and relatively protected.

WHERE TO STAY: Sofitel-Quiberon, Pointe de Goulvars (tel. 97-50-20-00), is a blockbuster of a beachside hotel, part of an aggressive chain that doesn't look back, preferring to go all-out in the contemporary mode. The bedrooms have private balconies opening directly onto the sea or the rear plaza. A wall of glass —screened nightly by soft pastel draperies—seemingly brings the outdoors in. In muted colors, the bedrooms are tasteful, and each contains a shiny tile bath. The rates depend on the placement of the accommodation: two persons pay anywhere from 600F ($82.74) to 1,000F ($137.90) for half board. The hotel is closed in January.

Behind its wall of glass, the lounge is sun-drenched, the carpeting picking up the brightness. A chic bar-lounge provides a social center for predinner drinks. If you don't want to swim in the Atlantic, there is a covered Olympic-size pool with an all-glass front facing the sea. The Restaurant Thalassa, overlooking the water, combines a sophisticated modern decor with the best of the viands at the resort. For 200F ($27.58) you can order a complete dinner. On the à la carte menu, costing around 275F ($37.92) to 325F ($44.82), specialties include fines belons (oysters), palourdes farcies (stuffed clams), and barbue (brill) grillée.

Ker Noyal, rue de St-Clement (tel. 97-50-08-41), lies in a well-planned and tended garden a short walk from the beach. It has an intimate country-club atmosphere. Graveled walks are bordered by brilliantly colored flowers, the grounds are studded with pine trees, and white garden furniture is set under pagoda-style parasols. The rooms, in the main building of the older annex, overlook either the sea or the garden—or both. The newer building has sun balconies with wrought-iron furniture. Each comfortable accommodation is tastefully outfitted in contemporary style, kept light and airy. For a room with private bath, in high season the full-board rate peaks at 400F ($55.16) per person, dropping to 340F ($46.89) per person for a bathless room; these tariffs include service and taxes. Meals—a *cuisine soignée*—are served in one of two dining rooms, with a view of a walled-off garden of summer flowers. Set menus are offered for 150F ($20.69) and 175F ($24.13). The hotel is open from March 1 to October 31.

Ty-Briez, 23 Boulevard Chanard (tel. 97-50-09-90), is a stone-built hotel right on the water. Its owner is friendly and gracious. The bedrooms are furnished in a homey, comfortable style, and many open onto sea views. The rate in a single is 130F ($17.93), going up to 260F ($35.85) for the most expensive double with bath. The hotel offers snacks in its crêperie, and there is a bar as well, plus a lounge furnished in the typical Breton style. The hotel is open mid-May to late September.

WHERE TO DINE: Le Relax, 27 Boulevard Castero (tel. 97-50-12-84), offers a pub-style atmosphere with a magnificent view of the bay. Specialties served in the rounded dining room include a generously portioned fixed-price menu, which changes every day, and a short à la carte list specializing in seafood. You might enjoy the John Dory with sage, grilled lobster, or any of the other tasty dishes. Table d'hôte menus range from 60F ($8.27) to 220F ($30.34), or you can order a complete à la carte meal for 180F ($24.82) to 220F ($30.34). The owner opens the establishment from February to mid-November, and closes it on Sunday night and Tuesday, except in July and August.

La Goursen, 10 Quai d l'Océan à Port Maria (tel. 97-50-07-94), might be one of the most charming places in town for a turn-of-the-century bistro, especially since the service is friendly and the fish dishes inviting. Michel Lucas, owner and chef, offers such specialties as filet of bar with mustard sauce, garlic-flavored fish sausages, mariner-style sauerkraut, and John Dory with baby vegetables. For an à la carte meal, you'll pay 170F ($23.44) to 220F ($30.34). The restaurant is closed on Tuesday, except evenings in July and August, and from mid-November till Easter.

Les Pêcheurs, rue Kervozes à Port Maria (tel. 97-52-12-75), is a fish restaurant where owner Roger Boutet performs a skillful cuisine with Breton-style lotte, sole meunière, and for shellfish lovers, a giant platter including just about everything crustacean you can think of, attractively garnished with lemons and seaweed. Set menus range in price from 60F ($8.27) to 90F ($12.41). If you order à la carte, expect to spend around 180F ($24.82) for a complete meal. You can dine until 10 p.m. In summer the restaurant is open daily, but in low season (from mid-September to mid-June) it closes on Monday. It is also closed November 15 to December 20.

5. Belle-Île-en-Mer

From Quiberon, you can take a steamer (several run daily) to **Belle-Île,** the largest island off the coast of southern Brittany. Cars can also be transported. Or you can take a guided tour, "Les Cars Bleus." In season it is necessary to book a day in advance. About ten miles off the coast, the storm-wracked island is dramatically eerie with its rocky cliffs, reef-fringed west coast, its **Grotte de l'Apothicairerie,** and its general sense of isolation and seclusion from the world. Valleys cut through the ravines, wending their way to such small ports as **La Palais,** the point at which you dock.

In the days before he made the Sun King jealous and was overthrown, Fouquet, the finance minister, erected a château on the island, and much later the great actress Sarah Bernhardt enjoyed spending her summers at Belle-Île, occupying a fort. So did Marcel Proust, Flaubert, Manet, and Courbet.

If you're not over on the day tour and would like to stay on the island, exploring it in more depth, you'll find excellent accommodations at—

PORT DE GOULPHAR: One of the most charming spots on the island, attracting thousands of nature-lovers in summer, this port on a narrow inlet is framed by cliffs. It lies on the southern shores of the island, the boats docking at Le Palais on the north.

Castel Clara (tel. 97-31-84-21) is a Relais et Châteaux of warmth and color —bright oranges, reds, rose tones, and forest green. At an enchanting spot, this complex seems to extend to the Côte Sauvage. There are few places along the coast where guests can enjoy such peace along with ideal service and a first-class cuisine. From mid-March to the end of October, the hotel rents out 45 bedrooms, each with private marble bath, TV set, and phone. Under paneled ceilings, the rooms are well furnished, and as you pull back the draperies, you can walk out onto your own wide balcony with a view of the sea. Rates begin at 600F ($82.74) in a single, rising to 850F ($117.22) in a double. Full board costs from 650F ($89.64) per person in summer.

If you're just visiting the island for the day in your car, you'll find good food served here, with menus priced at 120F ($16.55), 180F ($24.82), and 200F

($27.58). However, it will easily cost from 300F ($41.37) if you dine à la carte. The hotel also offers a large terrace with a solarium around a heated seawater swimming pool. The cozy bar is *très intime,* and there's even a playroom for children and a billiard table.

Manoir de Goulphar (tel. 97-31-83-95) is a creamy white building under a blue roof with a round tower. The hotel is built in a traditional style, lying on the Goulphar Harbor, which many have compared to a fjord in Norway. The rocky landscape on the wild coast makes for a tranquil setting for "Le Manoir," which, although modern, looks from a distance like a country estate. A first-class hotel built in the 1970s, it offers 52 stylish bedrooms with private baths, toilets, and sunny balconies opening onto the Atlantic and the harbor at Goulphar. A single costs 270F ($37.23) rising to 420F ($57.92) in a double. Most guests stay here on the board plan, ranging from 340F ($46.89) to 650F ($89.64) per person. The restaurant offers excellent service in a pleasant atmosphere. The dining room opens onto views of the coast, and the public sitting rooms, under paneled ceilings, are semi-luxurious. The hotel receives guests from March 20 to November.

SAUZON: Port de Goulphar has long had a monopoly on the desirable accommodations on the island. But this following recommendation is a serious challenger.

Le Cardinal, à la Pointe du Cardinal (tel. 97-31-61-60), is one of the more attractive modern hotels in the region, dramatically situated amid low-lying heath on a peninsula extending into the glittering ocean. Water-sports lovers will appreciate the facilities available, as well as the view of the harbor. The earth-tone color scheme is relaxing and pleasant, and the air-conditioned bedrooms contain all the modern comforts. The hotel is closed from September 30 until mid-June. Attractively furnished bedrooms cost 160F ($22.06) in a single, 400F ($55.16) in a double. However, half board is required in high season, costing from 300F ($41.37) to 600F ($82.74) per person.

DINING AT BANGOR: In your tour of the island, you might want to plan your day so you can stop off at the following recommendation for a meal:

La Forge, Route de Port-Goulphar (tel. 97-31-51-76), is aptly named, occupying a converted blacksmith's shop. When you dine here, you can easily see that the gracious but strong-willed owner, Odile Mulon, is firmly in charge of the dining room, making sure that customers are well looked after. The room is about as charmingly rustic as any you'll find in Brittany, constructed from blocks of local granite that must have taken many months of work by the stonemasons.

Mme Mulon's husband, Marcel, prepares seafaring specialties such as a corille of mussels and oysters, turbot with a shallot purée, crab with grilled scallops, local lamb, oysters in champagne, and lobsters in puff pastry with anise and basil. A set menu is offered for 100F ($13.79), but many diners opt for the à la carte selection, costing around 250F ($34.48) per person for a complete meal. In high season, you can enjoy your repast either in the main dining room or on the flowered outdoor terrace, served until 10 p.m., until 9 p.m. the rest of the year. The restaurant is closed from mid-November till the end of March.

6. Hennebont

On the outskirts of this once-fortified town split by the Blavet River is one of the most delightful accommodations in all of South Brittany. It lies three miles south of the town, on a private road off N781, and is called the—

Château de Loeguénolé (tel. 97-76-29-04). A hilltop estate of 900 acres overlooking the tree-covered Blavet River valley, it is a stately château owned by the same family for more than 500 years. It's filled with antiques, tapestries, and paintings accumulated over the centuries. Madame de la Sablière doesn't use her family title, wanting to live for today, not in another era. She persuaded her husband that in order to preserve and restore the château they should take in paying guests.

The word has gotten around, and discriminating clients, such as writers, painters, and statesmen, beat a path to her door. The drawing rooms and the petit salons are furnished with old pieces. You ask her about a painting in the corner drawing room. "That is Lafayette; he married my great-grandmother" (or did she say "great-great-"?). "Yes, those are two Vernet paintings, and those tapestries in the dining room are from the 17th century."

The bedchambers vary widely in size and furnishings, the price difference depending not only on that but on the view and position of the room as well. In high season, from July 1 to August 31, the half-board rate per person ranges from 630F ($86.88) to 930F ($128.25), including service and taxes. A bath has been installed in each of the 38 accommodations, with decorative floral sprays and harmonious colors. While the second floor has great old bedrooms, the upper-floor accommodations—the converted maids' rooms—are also charming. Some of the rooms are in a converted Breton cottage.

Even if you can't stay here, it would be wise to call ahead and request a meal in the dining hall, decorated with a room-wide Aubusson tapestry. While sitting on Louis XVI red-velvet and cane chairs, you can order such specialties as filet de boeuf poêle au foie gras frais, suprême de barbue (brill) with cider and leeks, and saumon (salmon) grillé. A set meal is offered for 130F ($17.93) and up, but you can order à la carte for around 350F ($48.27), selecting a fine wine from the cellar. The château is closed from mid-November to February 1.

7. Quimperlé

Built on a hillside, Quimperlé offers a refreshing sojourn into the charm of a former age. Because of its unique situation—where two rivers, l'Isole and l'El-lée, meet to form the Laïta—it is called a paradise for anglers. The salmon and trout are fairly abundant.

In the lower town, the Basse-Ville, is **St-Croix,** a unique Romanesque church with an 11th-century crypt. Its Greek-cross plan is based on that of the Holy Sepulchre in Jerusalem. The hill overhanging the town like a sugarloaf gives it the nickname "Le Mont St-Michel of the land."

About a mile away, the **Carnoët State Forest** is a setting for romantic horse-back riding, with its towering trees re-creating the mood of the legends of the Breton Bluebeard and of St. Maurice, that charmer of birds. Only 6½ miles away you can explore the beaches with their hidden coves, enjoying the adventure of the sea and practicing sailing at the school at **Le Pouldu.**

FOOD AND LODGING: **Hôtel de l'Hermitage,** au Manoir de Kerroch, Route du Pouldu (tel. 98-96-04-66), stands in a garden of about five acres, enclosed by an old stone wall. At the edge of a forest that very likely belonged to the manor at one time, it is 1½ miles from Quimperlé, reached via the D49. You drive along the Laïta River, passing under a Romanesque-style bridge, till you reach a creaky iron gate and a most tranquil setting. The Hermitage is a complex of three buildings, surrounded by rose bushes and cherry trees and with a heated swimming pool. The owners, Martial and Valérie Ancelin, rent 23 bedrooms, one with a full tub-bath, the others with private shower or a simple hot- and cold-water basin. Doubles cost from 255F ($35.17), singles from 230F ($31.72). The rooms come in many shapes and sizes, and the furnishings are mixed antiques, reproductions, and modern. The half-board rate ranges from 250F ($34.48) to 350F ($48.27) per person daily.

Relais du Roc, Route du Pouldu, at Kerroch (tel. 98-96-12-97), lies more than a mile south of Quimperlé on the D94. This restaurant has filled its contemporary premises with antiques and rustic accessories. It offers a seafood menu that includes the obligatory shellfish, lotte with sorrel, many kinds of ocean fish, and a variety of grilled meats. Set meals cost from 80F ($11.03) to 210F ($28.96), with an à la carte repast going for around 250F ($34.48). In high season, the place is open every day, but is closed Monday the rest of the year. It is also shut down from mid-December to mid-January.

8. Pont-Aven

Paul Gauguin loved this village with its little white houses along the gently flowing Aven. In the late 19th century a school of painters followed in his trail, led by Maurice Denis, Sérusier, and Émile Bernard. The colony of artists became known as the School of Pont-Aven.

Before departing for Tahiti, Gauguin painted *The Golden Christ* and *The Beautiful Angela* here. People can admire the crucifix that inspired *The Golden Christ* in the Chapelle de Trémalo, not a mile away from the little town. Every year the Société de Peinture organizes an exhibition of paintings by other members of the School of Pont-Aven, including Sérusier, Bernard, and Delavallée.

Another resident of Pont-Aven was Théodore Botrel, who won his fame composing patriotic French songs during World War I.

Pont-Aven, ten miles south of Concarneau, is quiet and peaceful today, a Breton market village with a good and beautifully situated restaurant, described below.

WHERE TO DINE: Moulin de Rosmadec (tel. 98-06-00-22). When it comes to a charming setting, this 15th-century reconstructed stone mill has no peers in Brittany. Regional meals are served in a two-level dining room, where you're surrounded by antique furniture and decorative accessories. In addition (and this is preferred in good weather), you can enjoy your meal on an "island" terrace while listening to the water from the river churning past. Honeysuckle scents the air, red and pink roses climb the stone wall, and orchids and rhododendrons edge up against the moulin.

The owners, Madame and Monsieur Sébilleau, serve some of the finest viands along the south coast of Brittany. The specialties include truit aux amandes (trout with almonds), homard (lobster) grillé à l'estragon (tarragon), and poulardes farcies (stuffed pullets). Expect to pay from 250F ($34.48) to 320F ($44.13) per person for a good meal. Closed from October 15 to November 15 and in February, and on Wednesday and on Sunday night off-season.

9. Riec-sur-Belon

The flat-shelled oysters found off the shores of this village are, without qualification, the finest in France. In other words, Riec-sur-Belon is not a sightseeing attraction but rather a haven for gastronomes. In this village is one of the finest restaurants in France, described below.

WHERE TO DINE: Chez Mélanie, 2 Place de l'Église (tel. 98-06-91-05). Throughout the war years, Curnonsky, the "Prince of Gastronomes," lived at this inn, eating, drinking, and talking with the legendary Mélanie. Both are gone now, but the tradition of great food is carried on by Germaine Trellu.

Each dining room is furnished with old Breton furniture and decorative accessories. The patina of age and much polishing have given luster to the armoires, the carved chests, the wooden shelves, and a grandfather clock. Contemporary paintings seem to cover every square inch of wall space in the dining rooms and corridors, and the skylit kitchen contains an elaborate collection of copper pots and pans.

From that bustling kitchen 12 specialties are produced, many of which are included on the set menus. It will cost 275F ($37.92) to 325F ($44.82) for a complete meal. Specialties include timbale de fruits de mer, palourdes farcies (stuffed clams), homard (lobster) à la sauce crème, coquilles St-Jacques (scallops), pâté de volaille, huîtres (brown-flesh oysters) extra supérieures du belon, and galette Bretonne.

If you want to stay overnight, reserve in advance. Each of the seven accommodations is furnished in a typical Breton style and is comfortable and decorative enough to tempt you to prolong your visit. A double with bath costs 240F ($33.10). One bathless single is available at 185F ($25.51). The inn is closed from November to February 1, and on Tuesday.

10. Concarneau

Painters love this port, never tiring of capturing on canvas the changes and subtleties of the colorful fishing fleet in the harbor. It's my favorite of the South Breton coastal communities—primarily because it doesn't depend on tourists for its livelihood. In fact its canneries produce nearly three-quarters of all the "tunny" fish consumed in France.

Walk along the quays here, especially in the late evening, and watch the rustic Breton fishermen unloading their catch; enjoy the tang of the sea air, and later join the men for a pint of potent cider in their local taverns. Sometimes their words are unfathomable, but not their friendliness.

Of course all tourists visit Concarneau to explore its **Ville-Close,** an ancient hamlet surrounded by ramparts, some of which date from the 14th century. From the quay, cross the bridge and descend into the isolated citadel world of the old town. Admittedly, the souvenir shops have taken over, but that shouldn't spoil it for you. You can easily spend an hour wandering the narrow, winding alleys, gazing up at the towers, peering at the stone houses, pausing for a moment on a secluded square snug behind monumental granite walls. For a splendid view of the port, walk the ramparts. The cost is 3F (41¢) for adults, half price for children.

Also in the old town is a fishing museum, **Musée de la Pêche,** rue Vauban, Ville-Close (tel. 98-97-10-20), which you can visit from 9:30 a.m. to 8:30 p.m., for an admission of 20F ($2.76), 10F ($1.38) for children. In a 17th-century building, it displays ship models and exhibits tracing the development of the fishing industry.

HOTELS: After sightseeing, repair to one of the nearby beaches of **Les Sables Blancs.** Or check into one of the hotels of this port town and enjoy a relaxing seashore vacation, which might include boating, coastal fishing, tennis, golf, horseback riding, and canoeing.

Upper-Bracket Living

Hôtel La Belle Étoile (Beautiful Star), Plage du Cabellou (tel. 98-97-05-73), is at the Point of Cabellou, a waterside retreat three miles from the center of Concarneau. Mrs. and Miss Raout-Guillou have taken two villas with their own sandy beach, nestling in the bay among the pines and facing the walled city with wide terraces and colorful parasols, and have made them into a haven of comfort, relaxation, and peace in their setting of greenery and flowers. Individualized rooms on the upper floors of the hotel overlook either the harbor or the gardens. They are decorated with good reproductions of English and French antiques. All rooms are centrally heated and have private bath, toilet, and telephone. In high season, obligatory half board ranges from 700F ($96.53) to 900F ($124.11) per person.

There is a combination bar and lounge, plus a tea room for guests. An open-air dining room looking out onto the harbor offers the chef's specialties, including grilled lobster. Nonresidents can enjoy a set meal from 185F ($25.51) up. The hotel is open from March 1 to November 30, and the restaurant serves from Easter until the end of November.

The Budget Range

Grand Hôtel, 1 Avenue Gueguen (tel. 98-97-00-28), is the best choice in the center of this colorful port. Directly on the quay, across from La Ville-Close, the Grand Hôtel overlooks the fishing fleet and the marketplace with its open stalls selling fresh vegetables, fruit, fish, even clothing. The bedrooms have different price levels, depending on the plumbing and the view. A double with twin beds and bath costs 275F ($37.92); a double with hot and cold running water goes for only 135F ($18.62). Open from Easter to October.

WHERE TO DINE: Le Galion, 15 rue Saint-Guénolé, La Ville-Close (tel. 98-97-30-16), may be one of the best examples in Brittany of a country-style inn ringed with granite walls and massive timbers. In the heart of the old city, the cozily rustic dining room has a massive fireplace that in cold weather sends out the warmth customers need to fight off the Atlantic chill. The hosts, who welcome guests into the dining room and prepare the tasty dishes, are proudly Breton and bear a name whose spelling proves it: Gaonac'h.

Specialties served on Le Galion's painted china are such seafaring dishes as barbue (brill) with cabbage and essence of red peppers, fricassée of crayfish with lobster, filet of red mullet with flan in a parsley cream sauce, and grilled bass with cucumbers. Fixed-price menus range from 130F ($17.93) to 265F ($36.54), or you can select from the à la carte offerings for 340F ($46.89) and up. The restaurant is closed Sunday night, Monday, for a week in December, and from February 4 till mid-March.

La Coquille, 1 rue du Moros at Nouveau Port (tel. 98-97-08-52), is a pleasant Breton restaurant from which you can admire the fishing boats used to bring in the catch you may find on your dinner plate. Set directly on the port, La Coquille serves primarily seafood, particularly lobster, which you can see scurrying along the bottom of the large aquarium bubbling against the wall. The small outdoor terrace offers a view of the port during warm weather. Jean-François Le Maître, the owner, offers an inexpensive fixed-price meal for 80F ($11.03) on weekdays. Other set meals cost 150F ($20.69) and 190F ($26.20). A la carte dinners range in price from 215F ($29.65) to 240F ($33.10) and are served daily except Sunday night, Monday, from Christmas to mid-January, and during part of April and May.

Les Sables Blancs, Plage des Sables-Blancs (tel. 98-97-01-39), owned and directed by the Chabrier family, is a seaside restaurant serving standard French specialties, usually on a terrace with a view. You might begin your meal with a helping of crab with mayonnaise or marinated mussels. Table d'hôte meals cost from 75F ($10.32) to 170F ($23.44). You may find the restaurant section swamped with a tour group; if so, I recommend that you postpone your meal here. The Chabriers have a few simple rooms to rent, most with private bath, at 198F ($27.30) for a single, 280F ($38.61) for a double.

If you love crêpes, be sure to visit Noz Ha Deiz (Night and Day), Place St-Guénolé in La Ville-Close. Reached via a bridge and a cobblestone street, the crêperie is in an old building with thick natural stone walls and a fireplace, plus a rough beamed ceiling. The husband-and-wife team, Michel and Josiane Chaze, combine elaborate and rich furnishings, such as a tapestry-covered armchair, with Louis XIII country-crude furniture and copper buckets and pots. Rare paintings by a well-known friend of Gauguin's are also displayed.

The proprietors bring crêpe-making to its highest level. For the set price of 58F ($8), you're given a meal that consists of one buckwheat crêpe with smoked salmon, Breton scallops, crab, and mussels, followed by a crêpe with ham, egg, cheese, tomato, and mushrooms, ending with a crêpe flambée with Grand Marnier. The most appropriate beverage is a 28F ($3.86) pewter jug of cool, locally made cider. The crêperie is open from March till the end of September, generally from 11:30 a.m. to 11 p.m. It's quite wonderful to sit before a 17th-century fireplace savoring a crêpe topped with rich homemade ice cream.

11. La Forêt-Fouesnant

Set in an orchard district of South Brittany, La Forêt-Fouesnant turns out the best cider in the province. One of Brittany's finest manor houses—open to the public for both rooms and meals—lies in the environs of this sleepy village. It's reached by going along the N783 and turning off at the clearly indicated sign, five miles from Concarneau, eight miles from Quimper.

FOOD AND LODGING: Manoir du Stang (tel. 98-56-97-37) is approached via a long, tree-lined avenue. Passing under a stone tower gate, you enter the graveled courtyard leading to the entrance of the ivy-covered, 16th-century manor house. On your right is a formal garden, with walks through beds of pink and red flowers. Raised stone terraces lead to 25 acres of rolling woodland. The Manoir du Stang is the domain of Monsieur and Madame Guy Hubert, who provide gracious living in period drawing rooms, studies, lounges, and dining room liberally furnished with Breton antiques. My favorite salon features Breton paneling, plus a fireplace, chunky crystal, and Louis XIII chairs.

Guests are lodged either in the main building or in the even older annex, the latter with a circular stone staircase. Your bedroom is likely to be furnished with silk fabrics and fine antiques. A maid in starched lacy Breton cap will bring a breakfast tray to your room each morning. Rates depend on the length of your stay, the time of the year, and the plumbing. The top rate in a double is 600F ($82.74); singles pay 340F ($46.89). Most guests stay here on the half-board plan, at a rate ranging from 400F ($55.16) to 550F ($75.63). The manor is open from May 3 to September 20.

Equally beguiling are the meals, the chef's specialties being homard (lobster) grillé à l'estragon (tarragon), mousseline de turbot, côte de boeuf au poivre vert, fruits de mer (seafood), and huîtres (oysters), de la baie de la Forêt-Fouesnant. If you are just stopping over, set meals range in price from 190F ($26.20) to 240F ($33.10).

12. Quimper

This is the town that pottery built. Its faïence decorates tables from Africa to Canada. Skilled artisans have been turning out the Quimper-ware since the 17th century, using bold provincial designs. You can tour one of the factories receiving visitors during your stay at Quimper; inquire at the helpful Office de Tourisme, 6 rue René-Madec (tel. 98-95-28-86).

At the confluence of the Odet and Steir Rivers in southwestern Brittany, Quimper was the medieval capital of Cornouailles. In some quarters it maintains its old-world atmosphere. Charming footbridges span the rivers. At the Place St-Corentin, the **Cathedral of St. Corentin** is the town landmark, characterized by two towers that climb to a height of 250 feet. The cathedral was built between the 13th and 15th centuries. It is considered the oldest example of Gothic architecture in Britanny. The spires weren't added until the 19th. Inside, the 15th-century stained glass is exceptional—well worth a look.

Also on the square is the **Musée des Beaux-Arts**, 40 Place St. Corentin (tel. 98-95-45-20). Its collection of paintings includes works by such major artists as Rubens, Boucher, Fragonard, Oudry, Chasseriau, Corot, and Marquet. There's an exceptionally good exhibition from the northern schools and Pont-Aven school (Bernard, Sérusier, Lacombe, Maufra, Denis, Meyer de Haan). See also the works of artist Eugène Boudin, known for his 19th-century views of

Quimper. Charging 4F (55¢) for admission, the gallery is open daily except Tuesday, from 2 to 6:30 p.m.

WHERE TO STAY: **Griffon,** 131 Route de Bénodet (tel. 98-90-33-33), offers a peaceful setting just outside the city in verdant surroundings that are augmented by a covered and heated swimming pool. The public rooms of this modern hotel are the kind that make you want to linger with a newspaper or just relax and watch the passing scene. The 48 bedrooms are spacious, clean, and comfortable. Each has a private bath, phone, and radio/alarm. A single costs 265F ($36.54), and a double goes for 350F ($48.27). There is a restaurant on the premises, Créach Gwenn, where you can dine modestly if you order the 75F ($10.32) set menu. It is closed Saturday night and again on Sunday in the off-season.

Tour d'Auvergne, 13 rue Réguaires (tel. 98-95-08-70), lies just a short block from the Odet. Even though centrally positioned, it is quiet. It has a modern look to it, with a little salon featuring a wall-size mural, a blow-up of an engraving of a battle scene. Most of the 45 well-furnished double rooms contain private bath and rent for 300F ($41.37) nightly. A bathless single costs 180F ($24.82). One of the principal reasons for staying here is the food, as the kitchen features Breton specialties. Set meals are offered for 75F ($10.32) and 185F ($25.51), the latter a menu gastronomique with expensive shellfish. However, the less expensive menu is invariably good, including on one recent occasion spider crabs with mayonnaise and a saddle of rabbit with mustard sauce. The restaurant is closed on Saturday night and Sunday from October to April 30.

Hôtel Moderne, 21 bis Avenue de la Gare (tel. 98-90-31-71), is an old-fashioned hotel near the train station. It has been renovated so that about half of the 60 rooms have private bath. The simple units rent for 125F ($17.24) in a single, 250F ($34.48) in a double.

The hotel restaurant is attractive, with inviting menu specialties such as crayfish in puff pastry, filet of beef with a five-pepper sauce, duckling with apples, and grilled beefsteak "style Moderne," served for two persons. A sherbet or calorie-laden profiteroles might make a satisfying dessert. There is a set menu on weekdays costing 75F ($10.32), as well as several other fixed-price meals served whenever the restaurant is in operation, costing as much as 92F ($12.69) to 160F ($22.06). For an à la carte dinner, plan to pay as much as 180F ($24.82). Between October and April the kitchen shuts down on Saturday. It takes a vacation from mid-December till mid-January.

WHERE TO DINE: **Le Capucin Gourmand,** 29 rue des Réguaires (tel. 98-95-43-12), is known throughout the town as the kind of place where a resident can get a filling and well-prepared meal without ruining a budget. Your repast might include any of the seafood specialties which are prepared fresh with gusto. Begin, perhaps, with half a dozen oysters, then follow with a pot-au-feu of four kinds of fish, including scallops, oysters, turbot, and sole. Each is cooked individually and then served together with an herb sauce, spinach, and turnips. Other main dishes include a filet of John Dory with mustard sauce, a tender sole meunière, grilled red mullet, or a temptingly aromatic fricassée of crayfish with morels. Fixed-price meals range from 115F ($15.86) to 175F ($24.13), while à la carte dinners cost from 190F ($26.20). The establishment is closed Sunday night and all day Monday.

La Rotonde, 37 Avenue de la France-Libre (tel. 98-95-09-26), is a pleasant and well-managed restaurant that is the personal statement of chef Paul Fevrier. Specialties are a wide array of seafood, which might include seafood salads, grilled, poached, or sautéed fish in delicate sauces, and turbot in a pink butter sauce. Rich, fruity desserts are offered as a suitable finish for your meal. Table d'hôte menus range from 65F ($8.97) to 110F ($15.17), while you will spend around 235F ($32.41) if you choose to order à la carte. The restaurant is closed every Saturday at lunchtime, on Sunday, during part of February, and for a three-week period stretching from June into July.

You'll find good food at the small restaurant **Les Tritons,** 2 rue Haute (tel. 98-90-61-78), run by Marcel Baïer. At his warmly decorated restaurant you get consistently reliable cooking. Some plates are simple although far from ordinary. Try, for example, his duck stew, his stewed anglerfish, or his Breton soup made in an earthenware pot with cabbage. The menu is varied, the service efficient. Fixed-price meals cost 95F ($13.10) and 110F ($15.17), and à la carte orders average around 130F ($17.93) to 160F ($22.06), plus service. The restaurant is closed Monday and in September.

13. Locronan

A gem among Breton villages, Locronan was once known as the City of Weavers, earning its fame in the 17th century when 300 workers labored seven days a week weaving sails for the Royal Navy. Today two weaving concerns continue the tradition, but the village is mostly noted for its old bearded wood-carvers.

The Renaissance core of Locronan, the **Place,** is remarkably preserved, standing virtually intact from the 16th and 17th centuries, with granite houses, old beams, delicate cut stone, and open well. The church on the stone square is from the 15th century, containing an interesting Chapel of Pénity in which is the tomb of St. Ronan, the patron saint of Locronan. The hermit Ronan was driven from Ireland in the fifth century. In penitence he ran four miles every day of his life, 7½ miles on Sunday. Every six years his memory is revived in a **Grand Troménie,** a pageant considered one of the most extraordinary in France. A colorful procession covers the 7½ miles, gathering numerous of the faithful along the way. The neighboring parishes display the relics of their patron saints.

FOOD AND LODGING: **Hostellerie au Fer à Cheval,** Route du Bois-de-Nevet-Locronan (tel. 98-91-70-67). "The Horseshoe" was built in a contemporary style, but it fits in well with the landscape. In the large lounge, bay windows open onto the countryside. The decoration, although modern, preserves some rustic elements, including tile floors and a large fireplace of white stone. The dining room also avoids coldness, using fishnet curtains, "glass balloon" lamps, and a tapestry. Some of the bedrooms have a mezzanine reached by a stairway. The accommodations are quiet and spacious, with large windows opening onto the scenery. The hotel is pleasant, almost deluxe, but with reasonable prices: 175F ($24.13) in a single, from 250F ($27.58) in a double. A meal ranges in price from 65F ($8.97) all the way up to 200F ($27.58) or more.

Manoir des Möllien, Plonevez-Porzay (tel. 98-92-50-40), is a solid stone manor house with a central core dating from the 1600s, although the annexes that contain the bedrooms are more recent. Many city dwellers check into this country-style hotel, which lies almost two miles northwest of Locronan, for the peace and the good cuisine served in this personal domain of Marie-Anne Le Corre. Each of the ten bedrooms has its own panoramic terrace, private bath, and imaginative decor. A single rents for 280F ($38.61), and a double goes for 320F ($44.13). Half-board terms are offered for 280F ($38.61) and 325F ($44.82) per person.

If you want to drop in just for a meal in the massively beamed dining room, you can choose either from the à la carte menu with prices ranging upward from 215F ($29.65) or the fixed-price list with meals costing 75F ($10.32) to 190F ($26.20). Specialties might include a ragoût of lotte in cider vinegar with baby vegetables or fricassée of duckling with celery and cucumbers. The dinner hour ends early here: the last meal is served by 8:30 p.m. The restaurant is closed every Wednesday from October till the end of March. It's open from March 20 to early November and December 22 to January 2.

14. Dinan

Once a stronghold of the dukes of Brittany, Dinan is still one of the best-preserved towns of Brittany. Characterized by houses built on stilts over the sidewalks, this walled town with a once-fortified château lies 19 miles south of St-Malo. Contrasting with the medieval timbered houses are the granite dwellings erected in the 18th century.

For orientation and a panoramic view, head first for the **Jardin Anglais** (English Garden), a terraced garden huddling up to the ramparts. From that vantage point, you can look out over the valley. Spanning the Rance River is a Gothic-style bridge that was damaged in World War II but has been restored.

The most typical street of Dinan is the sloping **rue du Jerzual,** flanked with old buildings, some of which date from the 15th century. The street ends at **La Porte du Jerzual,** an ancient gate. The **rue du Petit-Fours** also contains a number of 15th-century **maisons.**

Dominating the old city's medieval ramparts, the **château** (tel. 96-39-45-20) contains a 14th-century dungeon and a 15th-century tower, both built for military purposes and designed to withstand lengthy sieges. Within the stones you'll see the space for the portcullis and the drawbridge. In the interior, visitors can see an exhibition of the art and architecture of the city, including a collection of locally carved sculpture dating from the 12th to the 15th centuries. The castle is open from 9 a.m. to noon and 2 to 7 p.m. in summer, charging an entrance fee of 5.50F (76¢). In winter the museum might be open for only about an hour in the afternoon, if at all.

The heart of Bertrand du Guesclin, who successfully defended the town when the Duke of Lancaster threatened in 1359, was entombed in a position of honor in the **Basilica Saint-Sauveur.** The church is characterized by its Romanesque portals and its ornamented 16th-century chapels.

FOOD AND LODGING: In Dinan the accommodations are limited but quite good and moderately priced. The food, however, is superb. Many visitors prefer to use Dinan as a base for exploring St-Malo, Dinard, and Le Mont Saint-Michel.

Where to Stay

D'Avaugour, 1 Place du Champs-Clos (tel. 96-39-07-49), is the pet child of Madame Quinton, who has gutted an old building, turning it into the most up-to-date accommodation at Dinan. Small as it is, with just 27 rooms, it is the best hotel in town. All accommodations are with private bath and toilet, costing 350F ($48.27) for two persons. The rooms are furnished with reproductions and occasional contemporary pieces. Half of them overlook the square; the others face the tiny rear garden with its birdcages, large stone fountain, and flower borders. The little front lounge has been treated stylishly, using a lot of natural stone and simple modern furnishings. A very good restaurant, with excellent service and well-prepared food, is in the garden overlooking the ramparts. Monsieur Quinton is the chef. This restaurant, d'Avaugour, is open every day of the year. Another summertime restaurant (which closes on Sunday) has been installed within a former guard's room in a 15th-century tower at the rear of the garden. It specializes in grilled meats prepared on a wood-burning fireplace which was constructed within a large fireplace. Full meals at this place, called La Poudrière, cost from 100F ($13.79).

Le Bretagne, 1 Place Duclos (tel. 96-39-46-15), may be the most popular brasserie in town, usually crowded with passersby and local residents stepping in for a quick glass of wine or a full but informal meal. Fixed-price menus range from 140F ($19.31) to 210F ($28.96) and contain all the standard favorites you'd expect. But mainly the establishment is a hotel, with 46 unpretentious bedrooms upstairs, each with a private bath and phone. A single costs 180F ($24.82), while a double goes for 260F ($35.85).

Marguerite, 29 Place Du-Guesclin (tel. 96-39-47-65), offers renovated bedrooms that are clean and attractive for their price range. Madame Penven, the owner, runs this cozy inn, charging from 240F ($33.10) to 310F ($42.75) in a double. A restaurant on the premises serves satisfying meals for 85F ($11.72) to 230F ($31.72). From October till the end of March the restaurant is closed every Sunday night and all day Monday. It's also closed from mid-December till mid-January.

Where to Dine

La Caravelle, 14 Place Duclos (tel. 96-39-00-11). Jean-Claude Marmion is a dazzling talent who has awakened the sleepy tastebuds of Dinan with his inventive cuisine. He is passionately devoted to the products of the season, fashioning his menu to keep abreast of what is available, good, and fresh on the local markets. Some of his latest specialties include warm oysters with shallots, civet of lobster à la fleur de Bretagne, paupiette de bar fourré with crayfish, a two-fish terrine with peppered mint, steamed turbot with sage, John Dory with green mustard and a red pepper cream sauce, veal kidneys in cider, and several preparations of chilled or warm foie gras. In season Marmion also does the finest game dishes in town, including jugged hare or rabbit. When the first of the spring turnips come in, he prepares a veal filet with these vegetables, often served with an onion compote. A fixed-price meal costs 120F ($16.55). If you order à la carte, however, you can spend as much as 300F ($41.37). The reception, the welcome, and the service are flawless. In fact, this is one of my highest dining recommendations in Brittany.

The establishment also offers rooms for the night in a nearby annex. There are 11 simply furnished bedrooms costing from 90F ($12.41) in a single, from 150F ($20.69) in a double. The establishment is closed on Wednesday except in July, August, and September. It takes a much-needed vacation from mid-October to mid-November.

Mère Pourcel, 3 Place des Merciers (tel. 96-39-03-80), is in the very heart of Old Dinan, transporting you back to the 15th century. In an authentic *maison* of that era, it is filled with old beams and leaded-glass windows. It also enjoys an outstanding reputation for regional food. If you want to order one of the set menus, you will pay either 115F ($15.86) or 215F ($29.65). Most diners, however, seem to prefer the à la carte menu, enjoying such house specialties as a half dozen hot oysters or a pepper steak "Mother Pourcel." You might begin your meal with gratin de langouste à l'armoricaine or a marinade of fresh sardines. A coupe de glace is a specialty of the house. Those who order à la carte are likely to pay from 175F ($24.13) up. It's closed on Monday and from January to March.

Breton Luxury on the Outskirts

Only 12½ miles from Dinan is one of the most charming houses in Brittany, **Manoir du Vaumadeuc,** Pléven par Plancoet (tel. 96-84-46-17), on a country road near Pléven (Route de Lamballe). The vicomtesse de Pontbriand welcomes guests to this manor dating from the 15th century, when it was presented as a dowry gift. Mme de Pontbriand's husband was a colonel in the French army and she traveled widely with him, collecting antiques and objets d'art from all over the world. At the edge of a deep, cool vale, the manor is built of solid Breton granite, its severity softened by the "Vine of the Virgin" blooming across its stones. The entrance is through a Gothic doorway.

Under beamed ceilings, the interior is sumptuously decorated, with tapestries, Louis XV *chauffeuses,* Renaissance chests, wrought-iron chandeliers, and

Brocatel marble. Carvings and doors represent the finest of craftsmanship, as practiced in Brittany in the 15th century. The manor contains seven carved chimneys, all of them different, each a work of regional art.

Only nine bedrooms—each one decorated differently—are rented out, costing 550F ($75.63) in a single, 700F ($96.53) in the most elegant double. Even the bedrooms have fireplaces. The most elegant chamber is no. 6, entered through a large oak door, which opens onto a gallery with a wooden balustrade. Below is a huge room with a big "matrimonial" bed. The Manoir is closed from January 5 until March 15.

15. Dinard

One of the best-known seaside resorts in France, Dinard offers safe, well-sheltered bathing in **La Manche.** Its origins as a resort go back to the heyday of Queen Victoria, when it became popular with the Channel-crossing English, who wanted a continental holiday but one "not too foreign." Dinard offers a trio of beaches, the main one being **Le Grand Plage,** which tends to get crowded in July and August. Another, facing a backdrop of towering cliffs, is **Saint-Enogat.** Still a third, the **Prieuré,** honors a priory that stood nearby in the Middle Ages.

Dinard sits on a rocky promontory at the top of the Rance River, opposite St-Malo. Ferryboats ply between the two resorts. Turn-of-the-century Victorian-Gothic villas, many now converted into hotels, overlook the sea. Gardens and parks abound. Even on rainy days English women, heavily protected from the elements, go for long walks along the promenades, but Dinard is today an attraction for more French and even German tourists, rather than being a stronghold of British and Americans.

From June to September there is *musique et lumière* along the floodlit seafront **Promenade du Clair-de-Lune.** The **New Municipal Casino** in the Palais d'Emeraude is open year round, attracting devotees of roulette, baccarat, and boule. And about five miles from Dinard is the 18-hole golf course at **Saint-Briac,** one of the finest in Brittany.

UPPER-BRACKET HOTELS: Le Grand, 46 Avenue George-V (tel. 99-46-10-28), is Dinard's leading hotel. Open from Easter until October, it commands an excellent view of the harbor. Most of the five floors of this substantial brick structure have balconies and tall French windows. For the most part the bedrooms—some 100, all with bath—are decorated with traditional pieces, including some in the Louis XVI style, with white-painted wood and carnation-red upholstery. The baths are modernized, with tile showers in the tubs. In high season, from June 15 till September 15, the tariffs are 500F ($68.95) in a single, 850F ($117.22) in a double, taxes and service included. Decorated invitingly in autumnal tones, the bar is a popular spot before and after dinner. Good meals, with rather generous portions, are offered in the dignified paneled dining room.

Reine Hortense, 19 rue de la Malouine (tel. 99-46-54-31), is an attractive hotel housed in a 19th-century villa directly on the beach, within sight of the city ramparts. The public salons are glamorously outfitted with luxurious accessories, while the comfortable bedrooms are far more spacious than you'd ever expect. Open from March 25 to November 15, the hotel charges 750F ($103.43) in a single, 940F ($129.63) in a double for its ten bedrooms, each of which has a private bath and telephone. There is no hotel restaurant.

MEDIUM-PRICED HOTELS: Printania, 5 Avenue George-V (tel. 99-46-13-07), is an old-world Breton-style hotel. The antique-jammed sitting room, with its dark carved oak, paneled furniture, old clocks, and provincial chairs, sets the tone. A time-seasoned inn, the Printania draws many repeat guests, among them writers and artists. *Everybody* has stayed here, from England's Edward Heath to Americans such as Sinclair Lewis. The main villa stands eight stories high, providing terraces for garden sunbaths plus a "hothouse" glassed-in veranda with potted palms, Breton cupboards, and ceramic pottery. Dinner at Printania, served by young women in white bibbed aprons and starched headdresses, combines superb cookery with a view of the coastline. On August 15, 1944, the hotel was bombed, but the debris was removed in time for the Allied victory celebration.

The bedrooms are furnished with antiques and Breton decorations; some offer private bath, others hot and cold running water. For a minimum stay of five days in the peak of the season, from July 10 to August 31, one person is charged anywhere from 240F ($33.10) to 320F ($44.13) for full board per day, including service and taxes. The hotel is open from Easter to October.

The **Hotel-Restaurant Emeraude Plage**, 1 Boulevard Albert ler (tel. 99-46-15-79), is a friendly, well-run hotel about 55 yards from the main beach and the town center. Claude Luyer, a native of the area, speaks English and makes guests to his hotel feel welcome. Many of the well-furnished, spacious bedrooms overlook the beach. Rents in the nearly 50 units, some with full bath, are 160F ($22.06) in a single and from 290F ($39.99) to 340F ($46.89) in a double. Madame Luyer is the chef, producing excellent meals. Only dinner is served, costing from 120F ($16.55). The hotel is open from March through September.

Balmoral, 26 rue du Maréchal-Leclerc (tel. 99-46-16-97), is a good medium-priced choice for a stay in Dinard. Most of the 31 home-like rooms contain a private bath as well as a phone. Within walking distance of the beaches, the hotel charges 205F ($28.27) in a single, 290F ($39.99) in a double. The Scottish-inspired hotel has no restaurant, but there is a warmly inviting communal TV room and bar. The location is central, a short walk from the casino. The Balmoral is open from March 1 to November 15.

BUDGET ACCOMMODATIONS: Les Dunes, 5 rue Georges-Clemenceau (tel. 99-46-12-72), puts you in the center of Dinard life. Its façade is inviting, with cut fieldstone, elaborate white trim, tall French windows, and balustraded balconies. On the front terrace, garden furniture rests under parasols. High on a cliff away from the water, the hotel is closed from mid-September to April. The bedrooms have a fresh seaside-holiday look, with white curtains and comfortable furnishings. The dining room and lounge overlook the front garden terrace. There are 30 rooms in all, 17 of which have private facilities. Singles cost from 150F ($20.69), with doubles going for 300F ($41.37). It's customary for guests to have their meals at the hotel, with menus costing from 75F ($10.32) to 125F ($17.24).

Hotel Climat de France, 14 rue des Genêts, La Millière (tel. 99-46-69-55), lies about two miles southeast of the city. However, many visitors prefer its rural setting and quiet location. In a pleasantly efficient locale of about two dozen bedrooms, with an adjacent restaurant, the establishment is adequate for a relaxing overnight stopover. Accommodations contain a private bath and radio/alarm, renting for 230F ($31.72) in a single, 275F ($37.92) in a double, breakfast not included. Half board costs from 180F ($24.82) to 315F ($43.44) per person. To get there, follow the D114.

WHERE TO DINE: Altair, 18 Boulevard Féart (tel. 99-46-13-58), is a small, intimate restaurant operated by Patrick Leménager in a somewhat old-fashioned building. You can enjoy such specialties as a full array of seafood including a boudin de fruits de mer Nantua, foie gras in puff pastry André Guillot, mussel flan with artichokes, shellfish salad, sole with a confit of leeks, or filet of beef André Guillot with raspberry vinegar. Fixed-price menus range from 75F ($10.32) to 210F ($28.96). If you choose to dine à la carte, expect to pay from 210F ($28.96). The restaurant is closed Wednesday and from mid-December till mid-January. In warm weather, you may prefer to eat outdoors on the terrace.

The Altair also rents bedrooms, a single going for 110F ($15.17) and a double costing 210F ($28.96). Half-board is required in July and August, when you'll pay from 132F ($18.20) to 180F ($24.82) per person, depending on the accommodation.

Le Petit Robinson, 38 rue de la Gougeonnais (tel. 99-46-14-82), lies almost two miles southeast of Dinard off Route D114 in the hamlet of La Richardais. It is a tastefully decorated restaurant in a seaside villa. The cuisine is conservative and well presented, offering all the standard meat and fish specialties of France, as well as a collection of unusual dishes such as a terrine of rouget with lime and cocoa, curry of sweetbreads with lardoons and mussels, a cassolette of snails with avocado, and crayfish with velouté of shrimp. Table d'hôte meals cost 75F ($10.32) to 135F ($18.62). If you prefer to order à la carte, expect to spend from 170F ($23.44) to 215F ($29.65). The restaurant is closed Tuesday night off-season, Wednesday at lunchtime in July and August, and from mid-November to mid-December.

16. St-Malo

Built on a granite rock in the English Channel, St-Malo is joined to the mainland by a causeway. Dinard is eight miles away. Popular with the English, especially those from the Channel Islands, it makes a modest claim as a bathing resort.

For the best view of the bay and the offshore islets at the mouth of the Rance, you can walk along the **ramparts** that date from the Middle Ages. These walls were built over a period of centuries, some parts of them going back to the 14th. However, they were mainly rebuilt in the 17th century, then vastly restored in the 19th. You can begin your tour at the 15th-century **Gate of St. Vincent.**

At the harbor you can book tours for the **Channel Islands.** Hydrofoils leave for the English island of Jersey. A round-trip passport, of course, is necessary.

At low tide you can walk to the **Île du Grand Bé** to the northwest, site of the lonely tomb of Chateaubriand, "deserted by others and completely surrounded by storms." The tomb—marked by a cross—is simple, unlike the man it honors, but the view of the Emerald Coast makes up for it. It's about a 25-minute stroll.

Called the "Bastille of the West," the **St-Malo Castle,** (tel. 99-56-41-36) and its towers shelter a historic museum with souvenirs of Duguay-Trouin (1673–1736) and Surcouf (1773–1827), the most famous of the St-Malo privateers. The **Museum of St-Malo** is in the donjon. You can visit except on Tuesday, from 9:30 a.m. to noon and 2 to 6 p.m., paying a 5F (69¢) admission. Guided tours are available.

The museum also contains memorabilia of the celebrated native sons of St-Malo. The most famous, of course, was Chateaubriand, the romantic French writer and statesman who created the melancholy hero. However, as well known (even better by Canadians) was Jacques Cartier, the French explorer and navigator who discovered the St. Lawrence River in 1536, thus establishing a French claim. He named the country Canada. The third great son was the morbid Lamennais, the French priest and philosophical and political writer who was born in St-Malo, the son of a ship owner. In 1834 he wrote *Paroles d'un Croyant (Words from a Believer),* which was widely circulated throughout Europe.

The **Galerie Qui Qu'en Groigne,** at Tour Qui Qu'en Groigne, is a wax museum installed in a tower. Historic scenes are re-created, along with effigies of the celebrities of St-Malo. It is open April to September, charging 18F ($2.48) admission.

After the castle and ramparts tour, you'll hopefully have time to explore the cobbled plazas, the flagstone courtyards, the narrow streets, the fish market, the cathedral with a 12th-century nave, and the tall gabled houses. One of the most important of the Breton *pardons* is held at St-Malo in February: the **Pardon of the Newfoundland Fishing Fleet.**

In the resort of St-Servan, adjoining St-Malo, you can visit the **Musée International du Long-Cours Cap-Hornier** in the Tour Solidor, a tower built in 1382, commanding the Rance estuary. Here a history of voyages around the world by way of Cape Horn is depicted in exhibits from the 16th century up to the 20th. Maps, manuscripts, ship models, and nautical instruments are on display. Guided visits are conducted in summer at 10:30 and 11 a.m. and 2, 2:30, 3:30, 4, 5, and 5:30 p.m. for an admission of 5F (69¢).

WHERE TO STAY: The **Central,** 6 Grande Rue (tel. 99-40-87-70), is the leading hotel, and it has been entirely renovated. On a street near the harbor, it is provincial but in a sophisticated way. Most of the remodeled rooms contain private bath. The furnishings are contemporary, but originality shows in the color coordination. Doubles cost 520F ($71.71). Singles pay 300F ($41.37). Full board ranges from 420F ($57.92) to 520F ($71.71) per person, depending on the plumbing. Before dinner you can have a drink in a bar with an *ambience sympathique.* One of the best reasons for staying here is the food. Two set meals are proposed—one at 125F ($17.24), the menu gastronomique at 225F ($31.03). A delicious fish soup and grilled red mullets with anchovy butter are often featured. I'm most enthusiastic about the plentiful seafood platter. Especially delectable is the barbue pochée with white butter. Closed in January.

Elisabeth, 2 rue des Cordiers (tel. 99-56-24-98), contains only 17 rooms, each with private bath and phone. The hotel is well furnished and fairly modern inside, but the architect carefully maintained its 16th-century façade. There's a view of the port from many of the comfortable bedrooms, which rent for 260F ($35.85) in a single, 380F ($52.40) in a double. Breakfast is the only meal served.

Bristol Union, 4 Place de la Poissonnerie (tel. 99-40-83-36), is a comfortable hotel in a desirable setting on the interior of the ancient walls. Accommodations vary widely in quality. About two-thirds of the 28 bedrooms have private bath, and all contain a telephone. Singles rent for 162F ($22.34) and doubles for 250F ($34.48). The hotel, which is run by Michel Férard, is closed from November 15 until February 1.

WHERE TO EAT: À la Duchesse Anne, 5 Place Guy-La-Chambre (tel. 99-40-85-33), is beguilingly built into the ramparts, right near the château. The atmosphere is mellow, with a white-and-gold-paneled ceiling and brown walls. In the summer tables are placed under a large canopy and hydrangea abounds in wall vases. Try the fish specialties here. The fish soup made with hunks of freshly caught seafood, harmoniously spiced and cooked in an iron pot, is excellent. Alternatively, you can sample six oysters from Cancale. As a main dish, you may select grilled turbot with white butter or a pepper steak. Desserts are equally tempting. Expect to spend from 200F ($27.58) for a meal. The restaurant is closed in December, January, and on Wednesday.

Restaurant de la Place, 12 rue des Cordiers (tel. 99-40-85-74). Chances are, you won't find this little bistro-type place in any other guide. But for those who just can't afford the higher-priced viands served at the Duchesse Anne, this little place is a viable alternative. A meal of fresh seafood is likely to cost only 105F ($14.48) per person, plus the cost of your drink. You dine upstairs, and count yourself lucky if you get a table by the window. The restaurant has a cozy Breton atmosphere, and the staff is friendly and accommodating, usually eager to please. You might begin with a selection of local clams (not like those on Cape Cod) and follow with a big dish of savory mussels perfectly cooked. Meat dishes also appear on the menu, but you'll fare better by ordering the sole. A selection of local cheeses or a rich creamy dessert will round things off nicely.

Chapter XI

REIMS AND THE CHAMPAGNE COUNTRY

**1. Épernay
2. Condé-en-Brie
3. Reims
4. Fère-en-Tardenois
5. Château-Thierry
6. La Ferté-sous-Jouarre**

IN ABOUT THREE DAYS a visitor traveling from Paris on the N3—the Autoroute de l'Est—can encompass a world of old cathedrals, battlefields, fantastic food, and some of France's most famous vineyards, topping the exploration with a heady glass of champagne.

On the "champagne trail," you can go first to the wine-producing center of Épernay, and then on to Reims, which lies some 90 miles to the northeast of Paris. After visiting Reims and its cathedral, you can leave on Route 31 east, heading in the direction of Verdun.

Old Roman roads criss-crossed Champagne, and the region has always stood in the pathway of invaders. The clashes here have gone on for two millennia. Even today, names such as Reims evoke ghastly memories of some of the worst fighting of World War I.

1. Épernay

On the left bank of the Marne, Épernay rivals Reims as a center for champagne. With only one-sixth of Reims's population, Épernay produces nearly as much champagne as does its larger sister.

Although the town is a rather pedestrian modern one, Épernay has an estimated 200 miles or more of cellars and tunnels, a veritable rabbit warren, for storing champagne. These caves are vast vaults cut in the chalk rock on which the town is built. Represented in Épernay are such champagne companies as Moët et Chandon (the largest), Pol Roger, Mercier, and de Castellane.

The **Moët et Chandon Champagne Cellars,** 18 Avenue de Champagne, (tel. 26-54-71-11), offer guided tours in English, an expert member of the staff giving you a detailed description of the process of champagne-making. There you can see the *remueurs* at work, twisting each bottle a quarter-turn. At the end of the tour each visitor is given a glass of bubbly. The cellars are open daily from April 1 until October 31 from 10 a.m. to noon and 2 to 5 p.m. From November 2 until March 31 they are open at the same hours weekdays, but closed Saturday, Sunday, and French public holidays.

Seventeen miles from Reims, Épernay has been either destroyed or burned nearly two dozen times as it lay in the path of invading armies, particularly the Germans. Therefore, few of its old buildings are left. However, try to visit the Avenue de Champagne, with its neoclassic villas and Victorian town houses, a curiosity at least.

The **Musée du Vin de Champagne,** 13 Avenue de Champagne (tel. 26-51-49-91), is open Wednesday to Saturday (also on Monday) from 9 a.m. to noon and 2 to 6 p.m.; on Sunday and holidays, hours are from 10 a.m. to noon and 2 to 5 p.m. Admission is 5F (69¢).

By doubling back on the N51 you can also visit the **Abbaye d'Hautvillers,** just north of Épernay, containing the tomb of Dom Pérignon. A blind monk, Pérignon was the cellar-master at the abbey from 1670 to 1715, when he died. He is credited with inventing the process for turning the still wines of the region into the sparkling temptation known as champagne. Of course, one of the most expensive bottles of that bubbly carries the monk's name to this day. Upon drinking champagne for the first time, Pérignon is reported to have said, "I am drinking stars!"

The gracious old abbey has been rebuilt several times since it was founded in the 12th century. When the monks were evicted during the French Revolution, the abbey was purchased by the Moët family. However, it is once more a working church and can be visited at any time of the day. A representative of the Moët company can arrange for you to see the beautiful interior gardens with their incomparable view of the champagne vineyards and the Marne Valley. The river was extolled in verse by La Fontaine and glorified by Corot in his landscapes.

FOOD AND LODGING: If you're staying over, the best hotel—certainly the most scenically positioned—is called, appropriately, **Royal Champagne** (tel. 26-51-11-51). It lies some four miles from Épernay in the hamlet of Champillon, in the direction of Reims, on the N51. The château-inn offers 25 handsomely furnished bedrooms in its posting house, which dates from the 18th century. Windows open onto views of the champagne vineyards. Singles begin at 420F ($57.92), going up to 850F ($117.22) in a double. The food is exceptional. Specialties include poached eggs "vigneronne," plus a soup made with freshwater crayfish, which is subtly and delicately flavored and contains (as a surprise) cucumber. As a main dish, you might select little triangular-shaped slices of a white, flaky, delicate-tasting pike-perch, well flavored with herbs. A set meal will cost about 225F ($31.03). Expect to spend around 350F ($48.27) to 420F ($57.92) for a complete meal if you order à la carte.

In Épernay, the preferred choice for both food and lodgings is the hotel-restaurant **Les Berceaux,** 13 rue Berceaux (tel. 26-51-28-84), where Monsieur Luc Maillard is the owner and chef de cuisine (his wife is English). In comfortable, pleasant surroundings, you'll be given one of two dozen bedrooms, all with private bathroom, costing around 240F ($31.20) in a single, 400F ($55.16) in a double.

But where Monsieur Maillard really excels is in his Champenois cookery, among the best in the area. The portions, incidentally, are prodigious, so plan to make an evening meal here an event, and, if you can afford it, everything should be washed down with tremendous libations of champagne. The restaurant has an aquarium with live lobsters and crayfish on display from which you can make a selection if you wish. One specialty is turbot au champagne, or you can have sole au Berceaux and pâté de foie gras of the house. Set meals cost from 140F ($19.31) to 280F ($38.61), although you are more likely to spend about 280F

($38.61) to 320F ($44.13) if you order from the à la carte menu. The dining room is closed on Sunday evening and in February.

The Maillards have initiated a Piano Wine Bar in the hotel, with a bistro-type restaurant where customers can eat more cheaply and quickly than in the main restaurant. People who have a passion for wine-tasting can come here to sample good French wines by the glass, without having to buy a whole bottle. Plans are to add wines from other countries to the stock. Staff members at Les Berceaux speak English and can arrange visits to the champagne houses in the area for you.

For the budget, I'd recommend the more recently opened **Hôtel St-Pierre,** 14 Avenue Paul-Chandon (tel. 26-54-40-80), a continuation of rue St-Thibault. There you can rent pleasantly furnished rooms—only 15 in all—at a cost of 102F ($14.07) for two persons in a room with shower. Even cheaper are the bedrooms with hot and cold running water and a bidet, only 65F ($8.97) for two nightly. The owners are most helpful and friendly, and often extend themselves to make your stay a good one. They shut down from August 18 to September 8 for a well-deserved summer vacation. There is no restaurant.

Restaurant Jean-Burin, 8 Place Mendès-France (tel. 26-51-66-69), is an enormous restaurant decorated luxuriously in the grand 1890s style. The cuisine, served to you by a battery of busy waiters, provides such delicacies as a gigot of stuffed chicken, mousse made from a combination of lotte and mussels, a caillette of chicken livers, a delectable stuffed cabbage, filet of sole with shrimp, and smoked salmon crêpes. It costs 220F ($30.34) to dine here à la carte, or you can choose a set menu for 90F ($12.41) or 110F ($15.17). The restaurant is closed in January and on Monday in November and December and from February to Easter.

From Épernay, you can take the following most popular excursion.

2. Condé-en-Brie

The **Castle of Condé,** lying to the west of Épernay and popularly known as the "De Sade Château," is a very ancient place. The first castle was constructed by Enguerrand of Coucy at the end of the 12th century, probably on the ruins of a Gallo-Roman fortress. A part of the old keep is still to be seen, especially two big rooms with great chimneys and thick walls. The castle was entirely rebuilt at the beginning of the 16th century by the Cardinal of Bourbon, a member of the French royal family, in the Renaissance style. His nephew, Louis of Bourbon, who was the leader of the Protestant party in France and the uncle of the future King Henry IV, called himself "Prince of Condé," probably because he had many fond childhood memories of the place and liked to go there to hunt.

The castle was heavily damaged at the beginning of the 18th century and again rebuilt by a private secretary of King Louis XIV, John Francis Leriget, Marquis de La Faye. He called in the Italian architect Servandoni, who gave to the structure its present appearance. Servandoni invited the fashionable painters of the time to decorate the castle, among them Lemoyne and his disciple, Boucher, Watteau, Lancret, and Jean Baptiste Oudry. All these artists left paintings or frescoes that are still to be seen. Servandoni himself decorated the biggest room of the edifice, making it a sort of theater hall for music and entertainment. The present castle is an exceptional ensemble of the 18th century, through its paintings, woodwork, chimneys, and so-called Versailles floor.

The castle was inherited in 1814 by the Count of Sade and remained the property of the Sade family until 1983. The family name was besmirched perhaps forever by the infamous Marquis de Sade, who was at the time an innovator in literary style but whose sexual practices as described in his writings led to the word *sadism.* The present Count of Sade has devoted his life to the restoration of the castle and to clearing the name of the marquis. To this end he established a museum in the old home place honoring the Marquis de Sade.

The present owner, Monsieur Pasté de Rochefort, is not quite a stranger to the castle. His ancestor, Captain Pasté, was one of the two captains of the private guard of the first Prince of Condé in the 16th century and was therefore present in the castle on many occasions. Monsieur de Rochefort says he will continue the work of the Sade family and restore the parts of the castle that are still damaged.

You can visit the castle from 10 a.m. to noon and 2:30 to 6:30 p.m. in July and August. Otherwise, visits are by appointment only, arranged by phoning 26-82-42-25. Admission is 20F ($2.76) per person. Guided tours in English are available by advance notification.

3. Reims

Reims (pronounced Rans) is an ancient city. French kings came there to be crowned. Joan of Arc escorted Charles VII there in 1429, kissing the feet of the silly man.

Aside from its historical monuments (of which there are many), Reims is visited chiefly because it is the center of a wine-growing district that gives the world a bubbly with which to make toasts. The champagne bottled in this district, of course, is said to be "the lightest and most subtle in flavor of the world's wines." Those planning more than a quick one-day trip can linger in the region, exploring the vineyards and wine cellars, the Gothic monuments, the World War battlefields. Trains leave from Gare de l'Est in Paris, the journey taking about an hour and a half, the distance some 102 miles northeast of the French capital.

On May 7, 1945, the Germans surrendered to General Eisenhower at the **Salle de Guerre,** 10 rue Franklin-Roosevelt, a brick building near the railroad tracks, once a little schoolhouse. The walls of the room are lined with maps of the rail routes, exactly as they were on the day of surrender. It may be visited daily except Tuesday, from 10 a.m. to noon and 2 to 6 p.m. (it is closed, however, from mid-November to mid-March). There is no admission charge.

SEEING THE SIGHTS: Reims is dominated by the **Cathedral of Notre-Dame.** One of the most famous cathedrals in the world, the pointed Gothic edifice at Reims has suffered more bombardments than most fortresses. After World War I, it was restored largely with U.S. contributions. Mercifully, it rode out World War II relatively free. Built on the site of a church burned to the ground in 1211, it was intended as a sanctuary where French kings would be anointed. St. Rémi, the bishop of Reims, had baptized Clovis, the pagan king of the Franks, there in 496. Laden with statuettes, its three portals on the western façade are spectacular. The central portal, dedicated to the Virgin, is surmounted by a rose window. The right portal portrays the Apocalypse and the Last Judgment; the left, Martyrs and Saints. At the northern door of the western façade is the smiling angel. Lit by lancet windows, the nave is immense, with many bays. In summer the cathedral is decorated with a series of 17 tapestries, dating from the 16th century and illustrating scenes from the life of the Virgin. The choir is majestic. The cathedral is at Place du Cardinal-Luçon.

In the palace beside the cathedral is the treasury, containing a 12th-century chalice used for the communion of French monarchs and a talisman said to have been worn around the neck of Charlemagne and to contain a relic of the True Cross. Admission is 9F ($1.24). Hours are from 10 a.m. to noon and 2 to 6 p.m. (till 5 p.m. in winter). For information, phone 26-47-49-37.

The **Church of St. Rémi,** at 53 rue St-Simon, is unfavorably compared to the cathedral; nevertheless, it is an outstanding achievement. Once a Benedictine abbey church, it contains a grand Romanesque nave leading to the choir. Not only the nave but the transepts, one of the towers, and the aisles also date from the 11th century. The portal of the south transept is in the flamboyant style of the early 16th century. Decorating the apse is stained glass, some from the 13th century.

Framed by a shell of stonework is the reconstructed tomb of St. Rémi, elaborately carved with figures and columns in the Renaissance style. The former abbey, rebuilt in the 18th century, has been turned into a historical and lapidary **museum,** open daily except Tuesday from 10 a.m. to noon and 2 to 6 p.m. There is no fee for admission. In the cloister is a Gallo-Roman sarcophagus said to be that of the consul Jovin, who died in 412. There is also a collection of medieval sculpture, mostly Romanesque.

Musée Saint-Denis: Housed in the 18th-century buildings belonging to the old abbey of St. Denis, this fine provincial art gallery is at 8 rue Chanzy (tel. 26-47-28-44). In the Salle Monthelon are more than a dozen portraits of German princes of the Reformation by both "the Elder" and "the Younger" Cranach. The museum has owned this remarkable collection since it first opened in 1795. In the same hall, the Toiles Peintes (light painting on rough linen) date from the 15th and 16th centuries, depicting such scenes as the *Passion du Christ* and *Vengeance du Christ.*

In the Salles Diancourt and Jamot-Neveux are paintings and fine furniture from the 17th and 18th centuries. There are paintings by Van Moll, the Le Nain brothers, Le Brun, Poussin, Mignard, Ph. de Champaigne, and Boucher. In the next room is an excellent series of Corot's tree-shaded walks. The museum also exhibits in four salons paintings by David, Delacroix, Millet, Courbet, Daumier, Gericault, Jongkind, Lepine, Pissarro, Sisley, Monet, Renoir, Gauguin, Bonnard, Matisse, Dufy, Vuillard, Marquet, Puy, Vieira da Silva, and Sima. The hours are from 10:30 a.m. to noon and 2 to 6 p.m. Admission is 10F ($1.38). Closed on Tuesday.

Open year round, the **champagne houses** are most interesting at the autumnal grape harvest. Many are immense, extending for ten miles through chalky deposits. In some of these cellars the populace hid out during the German siege of 1914, many people living there for the length of the war. Even a daily paper was published, the harbinger of the underground press. Many have compared these caves to subterranean towns.

After the harvest, the wine is stored in vats. It takes four to five years before it appears in a bottle on your table. While in the chalk caves, a second fermentation of the wine takes place. The wine-growers wait until the sparkle has taken, as they say, before removing the bottles to racks or pulpits. For about three months a turner is paid just to move them a fraction every day, which is a process of bringing down impurities on the cork. After aging for a few years, the wines are mixed with a *dosage,* the amount determining the dryness. All these methods take place in the caves, which, incidentally, may be 100 feet deep and are at a constant temperature of 50° Fahrenheit.

Among the most visited cellars are those found under the Gothic-style buildings and spacious gardens of the **House of Pommery,** 5 Place Général-Gouraud (tel. 26-05-05-01). A magnificent 116-step stairway leads to a maze of galleries dug into the chalk, more than 11 miles in length and about 100 feet below ground level, where the temperature remains constant in summer and winter. Various stages of champagne making are shown to visitors in their tour of the premises. The House of Pommery welcomes visitors daily from 9 to 11 a.m. and 2 to 5 p.m. A slide show in English is given at the end of the tour.

Frankly, the Pommery cave has generally impressed readers as offering the best tour. However, if you develop *cave* fever, you can visit the houses of some other famous champagne makers, including **Taittinger,** 9 Place St. Nicaise (tel. 26-85-45-35), whose spooky underground caverns once formed part of the crypt of an abbey, and **Piper-Heidsieck,** 51 Boul. Henri-Vasnier (tel. 26-85-01-94), where you can explore the cellars in an electric train. Regrettably, free samples aren't given out at any of the champagne houses anymore.

HOTELS: If a day just isn't enough, you can stay overnight or dine at one of the following.

La Paix, 9 rue Buirette (tel. 26-40-04-08), contends for a premier position. Inside and out, it has been remodeled into a modern hotel. The restaurant is a brasserie-taverne, which proposes some excellent dishes including sauerkrauts, fish, grillades, oysters, and seafood. Decorated in a contemporary style, 105 bedrooms are spread across eight floors. Good strong colors are used throughout, and the beds are springy yet soft. Some of the units overlook a garden with a swimming pool and a chapel. The cost for two persons in a double or twin ranges from 270F ($37.23) to 335F ($46.20), including service and taxes. Singles range from 245F ($33.79) to 295F ($40.68). The restaurant is open daily from noon to midnight. Monsieur Renardias, the owner-manager, will aid you on a champagne cave tour.

Frantel/Les Ombrages, 31 rue Paul-Doumier (tel. 26-88-53-54), is a high-quality member of a national hotel chain with a good reputation. It stands near the entrance to the autoroute, so motorists should have little trouble finding it. The modern decor consists, among other things, of ample bedrooms with all the modern conveniences, such as air conditioning, and often with views of a nearby waterway dotted with river barges. The units cost 300F ($41.37) in a single, 420F ($57.92) in a double. The wood-trimmed restaurant, Les Ombrages, serves dinner every night till 10, offering standard French specialties. You can dine table d'hôte for 75F ($10.32) and 165F ($22.75). If you prefer to choose from the à la carte menu, expect to pay 215F ($29.65) to 240F ($33.10) for a full dinner. The restaurant is closed Saturday for lunch and on Sunday.

Grand Hôtel du Nord, 75 Place Drouet-d'Erlon (tel. 26-47-39-03), provides an efficient, clean, and comfortable accommodation right in the heart of the city. An older building, entirely renovated, it contains small lounges on most bedroom floors where you can have breakfast. The bedrooms are adequate and modestly furnished. Doubles range from 215F ($29.65) with shower and toilet to 285F ($39.30) with complete bath. A continental breakfast is extra. The rates include service and taxes.

Grand Hôtel Continental, 93 Place Drouet-d'Erlon (tel. 26-40-39-35), is on the formal park opposite the railway station. It's a long, low corner building with a mansard roof. In addition to old reception lounges with near-antiques, there are two attractive dining rooms, each with a traditional French look. The rate for two persons in a room with private bath is 280F ($38.61). A single with shower and toilet costs 200F ($27.58).

WHERE TO DINE: **Boyer-Les Crayères,** 64 Boulevard Henry-Vasnier (tel. 26-82-80-80), is one of the great restaurants—also a château hotel—in eastern France. It is an elegant, refined choice for either dining or overnighting. Gérard Boyer is considered one of the world's most outstanding chefs. He was approached by Pommery, the champagne firm, to head the kitchens of their luxuriously refurbished, turn-of-the-century château (formerly owned by the Polignac family), where Pommery's most influential customers are housed, fêted, and fed in a style befitting 18th-century royalty.

The interior is as rich as anything you'll find in France, decorated with 18-foot ceilings, burnished paneling, potted palms, and elegant accessories. The château is set in a verdant 14-acre private park, a tranquil oasis surrounded by one of the leading industrial cities of northern France. The park has its own helicopter pad for debarkation of many of the guests. After you pass through the curved and beveled glass doors into the marble entrance area (where a prominent photograph of Gérard and his father hangs just behind the receptionist), you'll quickly be aware that you are in an unusual setting. Sixteen individually styled bedrooms are available for rent when a champagne mogul is not in residence. You can occupy a single for 1,000F ($137.90) to 1,200F ($165.48), depending on the view. For a double, you'll pay 950F ($131.01) to 1,250F ($172.38).

Many guests make the point of their overnight stay a meal in the restaurant. A masterpiece is the salade du Père-Maurice, made with green beans, artichoke hearts, lemon, foie gras, truffles, and lobster. Other outstanding dishes are nage de sole with crayfish, filet de boeuf au Bisseuil et à la moelle (marrow), pigeon-neau (squab) rôti à l'ail et au persil, and étuvée of Breton lobster with sauterne. Normally you bypass an omelet in a top restaurant, but not here: Boyer offers an omelette aux queues d'écrivisses for two persons, made with crayfish and a creamy sauce that appears to be hollandaise but isn't. The most outstanding dessert is les délices de Marjorie. The wine list specializes in champagne—more than 60 varieties, although Pommery is still the house brand. You dine à la carte for a cost ranging from 350F ($48.27) to 400F ($55.16), paying extra for wine and service. The restaurant is closed Monday and for lunch on Tuesday.

At Châlons-sur-Vesle, six miles west of the city on the N31, **Assiette Champenoise** (tel. 26-49-34-94) is a typical country auberge with untypical food. The chef, Jean-Pierre, produces some award-winning specialties, and I highly recommend a lunchtime stopover if you're touring in the area. The food is cooked with great care and affection. You will spend about 300F ($41.37) to 400F ($55.16) for a complete meal. Specialties include a scallop dish and a plate of three different types of poultry. I also recommend the poisson Bouzy rouge. The wine list naturally offers champagne and some excellent bottles of Bouzy made from black grapes. The restaurant is closed for Sunday dinner and on Wednesday, and shuts down in February.

Restaurant Le Florence, 43 Boulevard Foch (tel. 26-47-12-70), one of the outstanding restaurants of town, stands across a busy boulevard and a park from the train station. It is run by Jean-Pierre Maillot. The building was once an elegant town house built of gray stone, with carved satyrs' heads leering out across the trees. Le Florence offers the best food available in the center of the city. Service is superb, and the grandly formal decor serves as a good foil for the frequently changed menus, which may offer such dishes (inspired by La Nouvelle Cuisine) as crayfish salad, suprême of duckling, braised turbot in champagne sauce, and Bresse pigeon in terrine. Desserts include caramelized pears in puff pastry—an elegant afterthought. Table d'hôte menus begin at around 180F ($24.82), and an à la carte dinner will cost from 325F ($44.82) up. Meals are served until 9:30 p.m. The restaurant is closed on Sunday night, Monday, and for about three weeks in August.

Le Vigneron, Place Paul-Jamot (tel. 26-47-00-71), is a bistro-style restaurant dedicated to the fine arts of champagne memorabilia and good food. The interior of this 17th-century house is filled with old champagne posters, vineyard tools, antique champagne barrels, and other rustic accessories. The food that accompanies the dozens of available brands of champagne consists of such well-prepared items as baked duckling in champagne sauce, garlic sausages (andouillette) with champagne, and champagne-flavored sorbets. À la carte meals cost from 210F ($28.96) and are served every day except Saturday at noon, on Sunday, for three weeks in midsummer, and for two weeks around Christmas. This restaurant-musée, run by Hervé Liegent, is located behind the cathedral.

A Salon de Thé

Les Spécialitiés Rémoises, Place du Cardinal-Luçon (tel. 26-47-64-32), offers the chance to sip tea, coffee, or champagne and to admire the façade of one of the world's most celebrated cathedrals. This is actually a champagne and pastry shop with an adjoining tea room. More than 30 brands of the famous vintage are sold in the vestibule behind the blue façade set with oversize windows. The interior has charming waitresses, a forest-green decor (including the folding chairs), and old champagne posters. Coffee costs from 8F ($1.10), and champagne by the glass goes for 18F ($2.48) and up. The establishment is open from 9:30 a.m. till 7 p.m. every day,except Thursday.

4. Fère-en-Tardenois

For the most superb restaurant in the champagne area—in fact, one of France's greatest—head for Fère-en-Tardenois, 29 miles from Reims. You take the N31 northwest of the cathedral city, passing through Fismes, then turning southwest onto the N367. At a point a mile and a half north of this hamlet lie the ruins of the Château de Fère, a fortified castle dating from the 12th century. There is, as well, a Renaissance viaduct erected in 1560.

Near the colorful ruins stands the **Hostellerie du Château,** out the D967, route Forestière (tel. 23-82-21-13). If it's summer, begin your elegant repast in the sunny garden, sipping the apéritif of the house, a glass of champagne to which the juice of freshly crushed raspberries has been added. Then the serious business begins, and the cuisine here is very serious indeed.

The owners of the restored 16th-century château, the Blot family, oversee every detail, turning out imaginative and original dishes. Of course, the turbot cooked in champagne may be familiar, but not perhaps the freshwater bass, bar de ligne au beurre de truffe. Other specialties are foie chaud à la croque au sel and dégustation des trois mignons (the *trois,* or three, meats used are beef, lamb, and veal).

For all of this, however, expect to pay from 260F ($35.85) to 380F ($52.40) for a set menu, although you can order à la carte as well. The desserts are mouthwatering, but I always skip them and settle happily instead for a boulette d'Avesnes, which is a cone-shaped cheese flecked with herbs and crushed peppercorns, then coated with paprika.

If you'd like, you can reserve a room and spend the night. The family offers 20 guest rooms, all beautifully decorated in shades of burgundy and pink with touches of red, costing from 520F ($71.71) for one of the smaller doubles to 620F ($85.50) for a larger double. Two persons housed in an apartment or suite pay from 850F ($117.22) to 1,300F ($179.27). There are no singles. The château is closed in January and February.

EN ROUTE TO PARIS: If after your tour of the champagne country you have a full day, you can return to Paris leisurely, exploring battlefields and sampling the gastronomy along the way.

After leaving our last stopover at Fère-en-Tardenois, head southwest on the N367 to—

5. Château-Thierry

On the right bank of the Marne, 56 miles from Paris, Château-Thierry is where Jean de La Fontaine, the French poet and fabulist, was born in a 16th-century maison, which is still open to the public on certain days. The **Musée Jean de La Fontaine,** 12 rue Jean-de-la-Fontaine (tel. 23-69-05-60), contains a small collection of his mementos, including some original editions. An industrial town, Château-Thierry contains the ruins of a castle crowning a hilltop which is believed to have been built for the Frankish king, Thierry IV.

Château-Thierry is primarily known in history because it was the farthest point reached by the German offensive in the summer of 1918. Under heavy bombardment, French forces were aided by the Second and Third Divisions of the American Expeditionary Force. At a point a mile west of the town are the battlefields of the Marne. Here thousands of Allied soldiers who died fighting in World War I were buried. Atop the hotly contested Hill 204 a monument stands honoring the American troops who lost their lives.

Those interested in this sad chapter in history may want to continue for a distance of two miles to—

BELLEAU WOOD: Known in French as Bois de Belleau, "The Battle of Belleau Wood" marked the second clash between American and German troops in World War I. The battlesite lies five miles northwest of Château-Thierry. After a struggle that lasted for two weeks of bitter fighting, the woods were finally taken by the Second Division of the U.S. Expeditionary Force under Maj.-Gen. Omar Bundy. Although the Germans suffered many losses, and some 1,650 prisoners were taken, the U.S. casualties were appalling. Nearly 7,585 men and 285 officers were wounded, killed, or missing in action. This battle demonstrated the bravery of the U.S. soldier in modern warfare.

In 1923 the battleground was dedicated as a permanent memorial to the men who gave their lives there. The American cemetery contains 2,288 graves. You'll also see a chapel that was damaged in World War II fighting. Discarded weapons, now rusting, can still be seen along the scorched road—a gruesome sight. For far happier touring in the area, follow the N3 along the Marne to—

6. La Ferté-sous-Jouarre

At the hamlet of Jouarre, you can visit a Benedictine abbey dating from the 12th century and explore one of the oldest crypts in France, going back to the 7th century.

At the **Musée de la Tour de l'Abbaye,** 6 rue Montmorin (tel. 60-22-06-11), medievalists will appreciate the documents preserved here, referring to the history of the Royal Abbey of Jouarre. In its Merovingian crypt, stones evoke the 7th century. There's also a collection of prehistoric artifacts, remnants of the Roman occupation, and a handful of sculptural fragments.

From the abbey, it is a drive of about a mile and a half back to La Ferté-sous-Jouarre, where Parisian gastronomes flock on the weekend to dine at the **Auberge de Condé,** 1 Avenue de Montmirail (tel. 60-22-00-07), one of the most exceptional of the restaurants in what is sometimes called "the ring around Paris."

The appointments aren't luxurious—in fact, the inn is decidedly old-fashioned, but also intimate, with lots of provincial character. It serves delectable dishes and regional specialties worthy of its two-star rating. The Tingaud family welcomes you, inviting you to partake of the cuisine of Émile Tingaud, beginning with feuilleté de truffes et foie gras. After that bit of elegance, you might order either sweetbreads "des gourmets" or filets de sole Vincent-Bourrel. Try also the poulet briarde of Monsieur Tingaud. He poaches this Bresse chicken in a rich stock, and then makes a sauce of cream, butter, and the grainy moutarde de Meaux, for which the region is known. The platter is served alongside the tender baby carrots of Crécy. The cookery is traditional, classical, and of grand quality, accompanied by the finest of champagne. For a complete meal, expect to pay 220F ($30.34) to 300F ($41.37) if you order from one of the set meals. However, diners preferring the à la carte menu might easily spend 400F ($48.27) or even more. The inn is closed on Monday night, Tuesday, and in February.

The Tingaud family also runs **Le Relais,** 4 Avenue Franklin-Roosevelt (tel. 60-22-02-03), which is more modest—and so are its prices. The meals here are well prepared, and the service is polite and friendly. Although the cuisine in no way matches that of the Auberge de Condé, it is nevertheless satisfying. Featured dishes include salmon in muscadet, thin slices of sole in sauce, rabbit in a mustard sauce, and chicken liver salad. Set menus cost from 65F ($8.97) to 120F ($16.55), with à la carte tabs going for 180F ($24.82) to 220F ($30.34). The restaurant shuts down on Wednesday night and Thursday as well as on public holidays.

After dining here, take the Autoroute de l'Est back to Paris, a distance of 42 miles.

Chapter XII

THE ARDENNES AND THE NORTH

1. The Ardennes
2. Amiens
3. St-Quentin
4. Laon
5. Arras
6. Lille
7. Dunkerque
8. Calais
9. Boulogne-sur-Mer
10. Le Touquet-Paris-Plage

MANY MOTORISTS seemingly speed through the north of France, heading south for Paris or more attractive destinations on the French Riviera. However, the region of the north, right on the edge of industrial Europe, also has immense stretches of calm and restful countryside and such cathedral cities as Amiens. Hugging the Belgian border, the terrain is usually low lying, with mills, canals, and factories. From such a landscape came the great artist Henri Matisse.

If you're traveling through the region from July through September, you may want to stop off at one of the Channel beach resorts, such as the most sophisticated, Le Touquet-Paris-Plage. But anytime of the year port aficionados will want to explore a trio of major ones—Dunkerque, Calais, and Boulogne—which, although badly destroyed in World War II, still have much to offer.

For those who have more time, a day or two spent driving through the Ardennes can be a rewarding adventure. Although its name still conjures up modern warfare—in the "Battle of the Bulge" an American general internationalized the term "Nuts!"—the region is one of lakes and an almost impenetrable forest, which gives it a unique character. It is crossed only by a few narrow roads running through gorges. In the section are little villages, such as Fossé, which have harmony and beauty, places of simple charm. However, I'll highlight the two most important centers—at Charleville-Mézières and Sedan.

1. The Ardennes

Little explored by most North Americans, the Ardennes in northern France—bounded by Belgium—is heavily forested. Nature-lovers seek it out. It also attracts lovers of French poetry, as it was the land of Rimbaud. Victor Hugo, George Sand, and Alexandre Dumas wrote of its beauty.

In spite of its terrain, the Ardennes has been the scene of much bitter fighting. In the Franco-German War, Napoléon III surrendered at Sedan in 1870. In World War I the Americans and Germans bitterly fought in the Argonne. Again in World War II the German breakthrough near Sedan came in the spring of 1940 in the Battle of France. The last offensive action of the Germans occurred in the Ardennes, as they made a short-lived penetration there in December 1944.

There are two chief centers for motorists planning to explore the Ardennes.

CHARLEVILLE-MÉZIÈRES: Sister towns separated by the Meuse, these twins

now make a single agglomeration. Arthur Rimbaud was born at Charleville in 1854 at 12 rue Thiers. From 1869 to 1875 he lived at no. 7 on the Quai Rimbaud, now named in his honor. He composed "Le Bâteau ivre" near the old moulin still standing over the Meuse. This poem is hailed as the pioneer of the symbolist movement in French literature. Although the brilliant youth didn't fare very well in Charleville when he lived there (the son of a captain in the French army who later abandoned his family), the town in 1901 unveiled a statue to their by-then favorite son.

At the centenary of his birth, in 1954, the **Musée Municipal,** Vieux-Moulin, Quai Rimbaud (tel. 24-33-31-64), devoted a room to Rimbaud. Souvenirs of the great poet include a piece of his luggage, some drawings, even business papers relating to his long exile in Abyssinia, plus rare editions of his poems and letters, along with some portraits. The museum is open daily, except Sunday morning and Monday, from 10 a.m. to noon and 2 to 6 p.m. Admission is 4F (55¢).

Charleville, founded in 1606 by Charles de Gonzague, is noted for its admirable **Place Ducale.** This is a large rectangular square bounded by brick pavilions, uniform in design, evoking the Place des Vosges in Paris.

Food and Lodging

Charleville or Mézières is recommended as an overnight stopover only. **Le Clèves,** 37 rue Clèves (tel. 24-33-10-75), is a suitable hostelry. It lies in the vicinity of the rail station, as do most of the inns of the town. Basically furnished rooms, 49 in all, are clean and reasonable in price, costing 225F ($31.03) in a single, rising to 350F ($48.27) in a double. The hotel's restaurant serves very good and filling set menus at 75F ($10.32) and 120F ($16.55).

Restaurant La Cigogne, 40 rue Dubois-Crance (tel. 24-33-25-39), is a solidly constructed restaurant behind a stone façade, scattered over two rooms, one with massive oak chairs and heavy ceiling beams. Robert Tabouret, the owner and chef, skillfully prepares a pâté of trout in brioche, terrine of foie gras, poached turbot with hollandaise, a traditional dish of sweetbreads, a terrine of wild game, and duck breast Norman style. Set menus cost 75F ($10.32) and 105F ($14.48). If you choose to order à la carte, expect to pay from 160F ($22.06) to 235F ($32.41) for a complete meal.

Just 12½ miles south of the town is—

SEDAN: This frontier town, just outside the Luxembourg border, is a manufac-

turing center for woolen goods. It was the birthplace of the vicomte de Turrenne in 1611, the popular and heroic French military leader who fought in the Thirty Years' War. The Meuse also flows through this ancient fortress town at the foot of the Ardennes.

Sedan's **Château-Fort** (tel. 24-29-03-28), from the 15th and 16th centuries the largest in Europe, can be visited April 1 to September from 10 a.m. to 6 p.m. for an admission of 15F ($2.07). In October its hours are 1:30 to 5:30 p.m. Otherwise, it's closed the rest of the year.

However, Napoléon III didn't surrender to the Prussians here, but at the Château de Bellevue, out the N64. At the capitulation of the French army on September 2, 1870, he turned over his sword to the Germans.

Food and Lodging

If you're touring in the Ardennes, it would be wise to make Sedan a luncheon stopover, as it has the best restaurant in the area. Its hotels are meager.

Au Bon Vieux Temps, 1-3 Place Halle (tel. 24-29-03-70), is near the Château-Fort. Mme Leterme and her son will feed you very well indeed on such dishes as river fish molded and served with spinach, turbot suprême with sorrel, or minced veal kidneys with Bouzy. The featured wines are Bouzy and Cahors. Expect to pay from 175F ($24.13) to 275F ($37.92) if you order à la carte. Set menus are cheaper, ranging from 60F ($8.27) to 185F ($25.51). The restaurant is closed on Sunday night, Monday, and in February.

L'Europe, 5 Place de la Gare (tel. 24-27-18-71). All the rooms of this traditional hotel are well maintained and clean, but only about half of them contain a private bath. Simply furnished units range from 115F ($15.86) for a single to 215F ($29.65) for a double. A routine restaurant serves good fixed-price meals for 50F ($6.90) and up. The restaurant is closed Sunday and from Christmas till mid-January.

2. Amiens

Due north of Paris about 75 miles, Amiens has one of the finest Gothic cathedrals in France. On the Somme River, a major textile center since medieval days, Amiens was the ancient capital of Picardy. Its old town—a jumble of narrow streets criss-crossed by canals—is worth exploring, although it is very run-down and seedy.

The **Cathedral of Notre-Dame** was begun in 1220 to the plans of Robert de Luzarches and completed about 1270. Two unequal towers were added later. It is 469 feet long, the largest church in France.

Surely the Amiens cathedral is the crowning example of French Gothic architecture. In John Ruskin's rhapsodical *Bible of Amiens,* which Proust translated into French, he extolled the door arches. The three portals of the west front are lavishly decorated, important examples of Gothic cathedral sculpture. The portals are surmounted by two galleries. The upper one contains 22 statues of kings, and the large rose window is from the 16th century.

In the interior are beautifully carved stalls and a flamboyant choir screen. These stalls with some 3,500 figures were made by local artisans in the early 16th century, and they are the loveliest in all of France. The interior is held up by 126 slender pillars, perhaps the zenith of the High Gothic in the north of France. The cathedral, like St. Paul's in London, somehow managed to escape destruction in World War II, and the architecture of Europe is richer for that.

Guided tours can be organized for individuals or parties by applying two or three weeks in advance, either to the Rector, 28 rue Robert de Luzarches (tel. 22-91-44-56), F-80000 Amiens, or to the Tourist Information Office, rue Jean-Catelas, F-80000 Amiens. There is usually no charge for these tours, but contributions are accepted by the guides.

The **Musée de la Picardie,** 48 rue de la République (tel. 22-91-36-44), contains classical sculpture, even Egyptian pieces, as well as a large collection of paintings, particularly from the European schools of the 18th century. There is a Gothic gallery, plus a Renaissance salon. Works on display feature Rodin, Fragonard, Quentin de la Tour, Tiepolo, and Guardi, even a Salvador Dali and a

Cézanne. The museum can be visited daily except Monday, from 10 a.m. to 12:30 p.m. and 2 to 6 p.m.; from 10 a.m. to noon and 2 to 6 p.m. on Sunday.

Finally, you may want to explore the **Hortillonages,** the market gardens east of Amiens that produce fruit and vegetables and are irrigated by little arms the Somme sends in. In the Saint-Leu quarter, you'll see a water market of boats carrying produce from these little truck gardens. Barge excursions often leave from near the Pont de Beauvillé.

WHERE TO STAY: Grand Hôtel de l'Univers, 2 rue Noyon (tel. 22-91-52-51), is the leading choice, lying 150 yards from the railway station in the business heart of town, within a short walk of the cathedral. The Best Western hotel is more than 100 years old, but it has been completely renovated, with double-glazed windows to keep out the noise. Its 41 rooms come in modern Nordic styling, or with reproductions of more traditional French pieces. Rooms with private bath and shower, along with mini-bar and color TV, range in price from 185F ($25.51) in a basic single to a high of 375F ($51.71) for the best doubles. There is an elevator and an American bar, but no restaurant. English is spoken.

Nord-Sud, 11 rue Gresset (tel. 22-91-59-03), in the center of town, is a simple but comfortable hotel supplemented by a brasserie-style restaurant and an adjoining tea room. Most of its 26 rooms have a private bath. They range from singles at 120F ($16.55) to doubles at 240F ($33.10). Denise Duquenne, the owner/manager, organizes fixed-price menus in the dining room for 75F ($10.32) and 130F ($17.93).

Ibis, 4 rue de Maréchal-de-Lattre-de-Tassigny (tel. 22-92-57-33). If you're in a hurry and want a quick meal in an unpretentious, modern setting, you might head for this member of a nationwide chain near the cathedral. À la carte meals cost from 100F ($13.79) to 130F ($17.93). Simple overnight accommodations are offered as well, all with private bath, at prices ranging from 210F ($28.96) in a single to 240F ($33.10) in a double. Ibis is open every day.

WHERE TO DINE: Joséphine, 20 rue Sire-Firmin-Leroux (tel. 22-91-47-38), is a country-style restaurant outfitted with intimate lighting (there's a lamp at each table), imaginative colors displayed on the fabric hung on the walls, and a kind of rustic charm, all supervised by Bertrand Charpentier, the owner. Menu specialties include salmon tartare with chives, veal kidneys flambé, pâté of duckling, and an attractive salad of breast of duck. You can dine à la carte for around 230F ($31.72), or you may prefer one of the fixed-price menus at 90F ($12.41) to 115F ($15.86). Dinner is served till 9 p.m. daily except Sunday night, Monday, and in August.

Le Mermoz, 7 rue Jean-Mermoz (tel. 22-91-50-63), receives fresh products very early almost every morning by truck from Rungis, near Paris, to ensure that its customers are served the best possible viands. Patrick Letellier and chef J.-L. Dufour welcome guests into the carefully planned interior, which contains an upper level, offering specialties such as juicy duckling, lobster pâté, paupiettes of seafood and lobster, and stuffed mussels. You can dine table d'hôte for 110F ($15.17) to 150F ($20.69), or you may prefer to select from the à la carte menu, a complete meal costing from 210F ($28.96) to 260F ($35.85). Closed Saturday, Sunday night, and mid-July to mid-August.

3. St-Quentin

A manufacturing town, 45 miles due east of Amiens, St-Quentin was largely destroyed in World War I, as it lay in the heat of battle for months. The Germans occupied it from the summer of 1914 to the fall of 1918. Now completely rebuilt, the town still has a number of interesting treasures. Once St-Quentin was assigned as the dowry of Mary, Queen of Scots.

On the right bank of the Somme, the hub of the town is the Place de l'Hôtel-de-Ville with a monument erected in 1896 commemorating the Battle of 1557, when Philip II of Spain staged a siege here that threatened Paris. The ornate Gothic façade of the **Hôtel de Ville**, with its curious sculptures, is from 1509, but its origins go back to 1331. It was only slightly damaged in World War II.

To the northeast of the square stands the great collegiate **Church of St. Quentin,** a Gothic building dating from the 12th through the 15th centuries. Damaged in World War I, it was restored and reopened in 1920. The church has large double transepts and a choir screen from the 14th century. Under the choir is an 11th-century crypt housing the tomb of the 3rd-century martyr Saint Quentin, and two of his fellow martyrs.

Also to the north of town hall square, at 28 rue Antoine Lécuyer, is the **Musée Antoine Lécuyer** (tel. 23-64-72-44) containing an admirable collection of the pastels of Quentin de la Tour (1704–1788). It also has an outstanding collection of other paintings and of sculpture. It is open daily except Tuesday, from 10 a.m. to noon and 2 to 5 p.m. (on Saturday until 6 p.m. and on Sunday only in the afternoon). Admission is 4F (55¢).

If you're a Matisse fan and you're in the area, you may want to drive to **Le Cateau,** 25 miles from St-Quentin. The man considered the most important French painter of the 20th century was born in this village in the final hours of 1869. The **Musée Matisse du Cateau,** Palais Fénelon (tel. 27-84-13-15), was reorganized in 1982 and placed within the 18th-century walls of this palace. It includes works of Matisse donated by his family, including designs, engravings, sculptures, illustrated books, and studies for the chapel at Vence on the French Riviera. The museum also includes 26 paintings and sculptures by Auguste Herbin (1882–1960) and five paintings by Geneviève Claisse. It is open in summer from Wednesday through Saturday from 10 a.m. to noon and from 2 to 6 p.m. (on Sunday, from 10 a.m. to 12:30 p.m. and from 2:30 to 6 p.m.). In winter, it keeps the same Sunday hours but closes at 5 p.m. otherwise. The normal tariff is 5.20F (73¢) but that is raised during special exhibitions.

FOOD AND LODGING: **Grand Hôtel et Restaurant Le Président,** 6 rue Dachery (tel. 23-62-69-77), is the premier hotel of St-Quentin, modern and comfortable. The rooms are well furnished and maintained, costing from 240F ($33.10) in a single, from 320F ($44.13) in a double. The hotel is capably managed, and attention is paid to comfort and constant improvement.

The surprise of the provincial hotel is its restaurant, Le Président, which has a young chef, Raymond Brochard, who practices La Nouvelle Cuisine with skill and imagination. His menus at 150F ($20.69) and 250F ($34.48) with taxes and service included, the latter served on Sunday, are remarkable in their versatility. Try his salad of crayfish with avocado, his filet of roast lamb with fresh thyme, or his sweetbreads prepared in an original way. He even takes the standard turbot and sole, giving these *poissons* an original twist. He also does an array of special desserts, depending on the fresh fruits of the season. There is an impressive wine list as well. If you order à la carte, expect to pay from 325F ($44.82). The restaurant is closed Sunday night, Monday, and for three weeks in August.

For more traditional French cookery, try **Au Petit Chef,** 31 rue Émile-Zola (tel. 23-62-28-51), which is in the medium-priced range. Specialties here include sweetbreads, stuffed trout champagne, veal kidneys liègoise, and braised ham nivernais. Near the Hôtel de Ville, the restaurant has menus at 60F ($8.27), 100F ($13.79), and 150F ($20.69). It is closed Friday night, Sunday, and from mid-August to September.

4. Laon

This is arguably the single most intriguing town to explore in the north. Its location is 28 miles from our last stopover in St-Quentin. The capital of the Département of Aisne, Laon has had a long, turbulent history, which, frankly, had to do with its remarkable site, perched on an isolated ridge that rises 328 feet above the plain and the Ardon River.

The Romans early in life saw its strategic value and had it fortified. Laon in time was besieged by Vandals, Burgundians, Franks, whomever. German troops entered in 1870. The Germans came again in the summer of 1914, holding it until the end of World War I. The town is still surrounded by medieval ramparts.

If you arrive at the rail station, lying to the north, you can take (only if you're in good health) a stairway to the town gate, but it's a long climb of hundreds of steps.

Most visitors want to head first to the famed **Cathédrale de Notre-Dame,** which has suffered much war damage over the years, notably in 1870 when an engineer set off a powder magazine as the German troops entered the town. The cathedral escaped relatively unharmed in World War I, however. It stands on the same spot where an ancient basilica once stood until it was destroyed by fire in 1111. The structure has six towers, four of which are complete. Huge figures of oxen are depicted on the façade. Inside you'll find stained glass, some panels dating from the 13th century, along with an 18th-century choir grill.

The town has also the Church of St. Martin from the mid-12th century. The **Musée Archéologique Municipal,** 23 rue Georges-Ermant (tel. 23-23-22-05), is an archeological museum. It has 1,700 artifacts from Greece, Rome, Egypt, Cyprus, and Asia Minor, as well as a collection of medieval French painting and sculpture. But mostly it is the *haute ville,* taken as a whole, that forms an enduring, too-little-visited attraction.

FOOD AND LODGING: Angleterre, 10 Boulevard de Lyon (tel. 23-23-04-62), offers a comfortable collection of accommodations whose quality tends to vary from room to room, depending on how recently it was renovated. About half of them have a private bath, and all contain a phone. They rent for 135F ($18.62) in a single, 240F ($33.10) in a double. The hotel's restaurant serves meals for 70F ($9.65) to 130F ($17.93) daily except Saturday at noon.

Hôtel de la Bannière de France, 11 rue Franklin-Roosevelt (tel. 23-23-21-44), is a long-established hotel, dating back to 1685. This building in the upper reaches of the old part of town close to the ancient cathedral served as a relay station for the postal service. Today its rustically provincial dining room is well maintained by Paul Lefèvre, who, with chef Dominique Havot, offers such dishes as salmon with anise, lamb with tarragon, the salade royale (prawns, scallops, and foie gras), and veal kidneys with Bouzy wine. Set menus cost from 80F ($11.03) to 200F ($27.58), and à la carte meals go for around 240F ($33.10). The restaurant is open daily (with dinner service until 9:30 p.m.) except from a few days before Christmas till January 20. There are 18 homelike bedrooms, mostly with private bath, renting for 115F ($15.86) in a single, 300F ($41.37) in a double.

Chateaubriand, 7 Place St-Julien (tel. 23-20-46-77), offers good food in a simple setting in the upper part of the village. Richard Minks reigns in the kitchen, producing such specialties as breast of duck in raspberry vinegar, veal kidneys, savory meats, and even couscous and paella. Fixed-price menus are offered for 50F ($6.90), 80F ($11.03), and 110F ($15.17), while you'll pay from 180F ($24.82) if you prefer to dine à la carte. The restaurant is open daily except Monday and is closed from mid-August to mid-September.

5. Arras

Despite massive damage in two World Wars, Arras, lying between Lille and Amiens, retains some of the appearance of an ancient Flemish trading town with its squares and gabled houses. This is particularly evident in the center of town around the two arcaded and linked squares, **Grand'Place** and **Place des Héros.**

On the Place des Héros, the Gothic-style **Hôtel de Ville** and its belfry were celebrated when first built in the 16th century. Badly damaged in World War I, the town hall was restored, only to be attacked in World War II. Now again restored, the building and its belfry—245 feet high—can be visited from 9 a.m. to noon and 2 to 5 p.m. The Hôtel de Ville closes at noon on Sunday and on Monday afternoon.

To the northwest of the town hall, the vast **cathedral** was built in the neo-classic style. Inside are two interesting triptychs. The cathedral is entered on the rue des Teinturiers. On the south side is the **Abbey of St. Vaast** (tel. 21-71-26-43), which has had a long, turbulent history but is now a museum, open daily except Tuesday, from 10 a.m. to noon and 2 to 5:30 p.m., charging 4F (55¢) for admission. Sculptures line its small cloister, and works of art are displayed in its large cloister, including an exceptional collection of porcelain, French paintings, and tapestries.

The town has had many associations with famous people. Robespierre was born in a house that can be seen on the rue des Rapporteurs. At 2 impasse de l'Elvoye, rue d'Amiens, is the house where Verlaine stayed after he was imprisoned in Belgium. He once came to Arras with Rimbaud. Both were arrested by police after they pretended to have committed a crime.

The Battle of Arras was the name given to operations against the Germans by British forces in the spring of 1917. Arras has some important war monuments, mainly to the north of the town. A memorial was erected to unknown soldiers who died on the battlefields of Artois in 1914 and 1915, and a British military cemetery and memorial to 200 local patriots executed in World War II were also built.

In the 15th century Arras was a major center for tapestry weavers. In some museums of Europe, Arras is still synonymous with tapestry.

FOOD AND LODGING: Univers, 3 Place Croix-Rouge (tel. 21-71-34-01), is an elegant hotel built in a monastery of the 18th century. Right in the heart of town, it makes for an enchanting stopover. The cloistered interior opens onto a garden. The rooms are handsomely furnished and well maintained, a safe haven for traditionalists who have had too much of the industrialism of the north. Thirty-six rooms of generous size are rented out, and 26 of these contain a private bath. The rate charged is 160F ($22.06) in a single, rising to 320F ($44.13) in a double. Everything here is run with quiet efficiency. You can also dine in the hotel's restaurant, where a set menu goes for 75F ($10.32).

L'Ambassadeur, Place Foch (tel. 21-23-29-80), is another of those *buffet gares* or railway station restaurants, but in France these places often serve the best food, a throwback to an older, more elegant tradition. In well-appointed, comfortable, Louis XIV-style surroundings, you can peruse the menu at leisure, watching for such dishes as a suprême of turbot with red pepper or duckling cooked in cider, perhaps hamhock with leeks. Weekly menus are featured at 100F ($13.79) rising to 160F ($22.06). Closed Sunday night.

If you want something less institutional, many people of Arras consider dining at **Le Chanzy,** 8 rue Chanzy (tel. 21-71-02-02), to be the finest cuisine experience to be had in their town. Robert Troy is in charge, turning out an array of dishes that have earned for him an outstanding local reputation: lobster with scallops, trout, sweetbreads, turbot, and fish filets served in almost every way imaginable—cooked with wine, marinated, with port, with cream, with champagne, you name it. Like its rival, the restaurant stands in the railway station area. The decor was described by one diner as a "1930s S.S. *France.*" Set menus cost 85F ($11.72) and 145F ($20), although you'll spend some 240F ($33.10) ordering à la carte. Monsieur Troy also rents out 19 simply furnished bedrooms, seven of which contain a private bath. Singles cost 100F ($13.79), rising to 240F ($33.10) for the best doubles.

6. Lille

Near the Belgian frontier, Lille is the largest city in French Flanders and is famous for its breweries. One of the world's major textile centers, it is industrial, known for its spinning and weaving. In World War I the Germans occupied it from October 1914 until October 1918. German officers at the time often came to Lille on leave, enjoying a holiday since the city wasn't shelled by the Allies.

Once Lille was the capital of the counts of Flanders, but with the Treaty of Utrecht in 1713, it became a French possession. A few of its medieval buildings remain, and the most elegant part of the old town is the district of St-André, to the north, but essentially Lille is a busy, modern city, with office blocks and wide boulevards.

Public gardens surround the pentagonal **Citadel,** one of Vauban's finest works. It lies west of town and contains barracks and an arsenal.

The **Musée des Beaux-Arts,** Place de la République (tel. 20-57-01-84), is one of the finest art museums of France. One of its most celebrated exhibitions is the wax head of a young girl from the 17th century. Although there is much fine sculpture, the picture galleries are more interesting. Rubens, represented by such works as his *Descent from the Cross,* leads the Flemish masters. Van Dyck's portrait of Marie de Medici is on display. A host of Italian painters have works here, everybody from Botticelli to Veronese, and the Spanish school has turned out too—El Greco, Ribera, Goya.

Of course, more salons are filled with the works of French painters—Watteau's *View of Lille,* La Hyre, a David look at Napoleon, Corot, Monet, Renoir, Sisley, Courbet, even contemporary works, Dufy's *People of the Comédie-Française,* Léger, and a tapestry by Picasso *(Jacqueline,* from 1964). The museum, which also has an outstanding exhibit of Dutch paintings, is open from 9:30 a.m. to 12:30 p.m. and 2 to 6 p.m., charging 5F (69¢) for admission. It is closed on Tuesday and on certain religious and public holidays.

WHERE TO STAY: **Carlton,** 3 rue de Paris (tel. 20-55-24-11), near the railway station, is not only in the center of the city, but also offers bedrooms with some style and occasional charm. The hotel has been renovated with some sensitivity as to the comfort of guests. Some 65 bedrooms are rented out, costing 350F ($48.27) in a single, 480F ($66.19) in a double. There is no restaurant.

If you'd prefer it, the **Holiday Inn,** l'Aéroport de Lille-Lesquin (tel. 20-97-92-02), about five miles from the city center, is just what you'd expect. Consistently good rooms with plumbing as you like it cost from 350F ($48.27) in a single to 420F ($57.92) in a double. The hotel has an indoor swimming pool and a sauna, and will even serve a children's menu in the American style. A set meal at its fast-food Angus goes for a minimum of 100F ($13.79), or you can dine more leisurely in the Grill La Flamme, where you are likely to pay 160F ($22.06) and up for a dinner.

The **Royal,** 2 Boulevard Carnot (tel. 20-51-05-11) is another one of the city's major hotels, central and comfortable. Here you'll be housed in one of its 102 bedrooms, all of which come with mini-bar where you serve yourself. All the modern amenities are here, including direct-dial telephones. The rooms are well furnished, costing 300F ($41.37) in a single, that tariff rising to 420F ($57.92) in a double. The hotel, like its rival the Carlton, does not have a restaurant, but there is an air-conditioned bar.

Le Strasbourg, 7 rue Jean-Roisin (tel. 20-57-05-46), was built in grander days, but this centrally located hotel has been completely modernized. Its 46 comfortable bedrooms each contain a phone, and nearly all have some form of private bath cr shower. The cost is 100F ($13.79) in a single, going up to 250F

($34.48) in a double, breakfast not included. You'll find the hotel behind the Grand'Place.

WHERE TO DINE: À l'Huîtrière, 3 rue des Chats-Bossus (tel. 20-55-43-41), stands on the "street of hunchback cats" and offers the finest products of the sea in grand quality. This premier seafood restaurant of Lille is run by its patron, Jean Proye. The oysters from England are amazingly fresh tasting. The catch of the day always inspires the chef to turn out a spectacular fish dish. You usually can't go wrong by ordering this *plat du jour*. But the chef's repertoire includes many other temptations as well, such as filet de St-Pierre aux quatre légumes (John Dory fish with four vegetables), coquilles St-Jacques à la Bercy (scallops in a sauce made of white wine, parsley, shallots, and cream), fricassée de homard à la crème de laitue (stewed lobster in a lettuce sauce), blanc de turbotin à la moutarde (fileted turbot roasted in a mustard sauce), and rognon et ris de veau sautés en beuchelle (veal kidneys and sweetbreads with a port wine sauce and mushrooms). The bill of fare changes four times a year, according to the season. Average prices for a meal are 325F ($44.82) to 375F ($51.71) per person, including wine and service. The Huîtrière has a plentiful wine cellar. Jean Proye was once honored with the title of Wine-Butler of France. The restaurant is closed on Sunday night, holidays, and from July 22 to September 1.

Before entering the restaurant, you go through one of the most beautiful fish shops in France, built in 1928, where all kinds of seafood is sold, as well as other edibles such as Bresse poultry, Pauillac lamb, goose liver pâté, and cooked dishes.

Le Flambard, 79 rue d'Angleterre (tel. 20-51-00-06), the domain of Robert Bardot (no relation to BB), occupies the loveliest setting for its cuisine, a beautiful 17th-century house, which has survived from "Vieux Lille." However, the cookery is not traditional but is inventive, creative, and always skillfully prepared. Only the freshest ingredients are used in his concoctions, which include sole with crayfish tails and leeks, chicken fricassée with stuffed spring turnips, and sole and turbot Savarin. If you can afford it, you might begin your meal with foie gras d'oie pressé. For all this, expect to pay 400F ($55.16) to 450F ($62.06) à la carte, or you can order one of the table d'hôte meals at 200F ($27.58) and up. The restaurant is closed in August and on Sunday night and Monday.

Le Compostelle, 4 rue St-Étienne (tel. 20-54-02-49), was once an ancient Flemish inn sheltering pilgrims setting out on that long, treacherous journey across France and Spain to Santiago de Compostela in northwestern Iberia. Nowadays the cuisine has undergone a remarkable transformation under the guiding hand of Maxime Barrois, who offers such dishes as foie gras of duckling, turbot with honey and orange sauce, and salmon marinated in citrus, along with excellent cheeses of the region and an array of tempting desserts. Well-conceived menus are offered at 115F ($15.86) and 160F ($22.06), and you can also dine à la carte for 275F ($37.92) to 325F ($44.82). The restaurant is closed on Sunday night.

If you're seeking something simpler, try Alcide, 5 rue Débris-St-Étienne (tel. 20-55-06-61), a little charmer that serves one of the best meals for the price I was able to find in the city. It is a maison run in the old Lille tradition. You can dine here for just 65F ($8.97), a tasty and filling repast, enjoying the standard French repertoire of dishes, including loup flambé with whisky and trout with sorrel. The place is run by Jean-Claude Ovaert, who closes on Friday night, Saturday, Sunday night, and in July.

À la Bascule, 12 rue de Cambrai (tel. 20-52-44-55). If you prefer to eat in a more rustic ambience than the modern one set up on the ground floor of this northern-style French restaurant, you can head up the stairs to the upper dining room. Owner Roger Aubin offers frequently changing choices, which could include the following specialties: quenelles thermidor on a skewer, duckling with pears, Flemish-style chicken, and one of my favorite appetizers, leek tart. Jean-

Luc Leriche, the chef, creates the savory recipes and serves generous portions. Fixed-price menus range from 100F ($13.79) to 135F ($18.62), while à la carte meals cost from 160F ($22.06) to 225F ($31.03). Food is served to a loyal clientele daily except Saturday night, Sunday, and in August.

7. Dunkerque

On the coast of the North Sea only nine miles from the Belgian frontier, Dunkerque (Dunkirk in English) captured the attention of the world from May 26 to June 3, 1940. In a heroic evacuation, a British expeditionary force of 233,000 men and some 112,500 Allied troops were taken across the Strait of Dover to England just before the port was occupied by the Germans. These men were transported in every conceivable craft—motorboats, yachts, even fishing boats.

Dunkerque was nearly destroyed in that war, and it was the last French town to be liberated by the Allies, May 10, 1945. Rebuilt, Dunkerque today is the third port of France. There is daily train-ferry service to Dover.

The heart of town is the Place Jean-Bart, where the major thoroughfares converge. There stands a David d'Angers statue of Admiral Jean Bart, the noted seafarer who was born in Dunkerque in 1650.

The harbor is impressive, with its lock gates, docks, and cranes, as well as several miles of quays. It can be visited in season by a boat embarking from Place du Minck. Boat schedules vary according to the season, the trip taking about one hour.

The **Musée des Beaux-Arts,** Place du Général-de-Gaulle (tel. 28-66-21-57), east of the Gothic church of St-Éloi, contains an interesting collection of Italian, Flemish, and French paintings, including a Van Dyck, Magnasco's *Adoration of the Magi,* and Cranach's *The Resurrection of Lazarus,* plus works by Corot and Vernet. The museum is open from 10 a.m. to noon and 3 to 6 p.m. daily except Tuesday, charging an admission of 5F (69¢).

Dunkerque also has another art museum worthy of your attention. It's the **Musée d'Art Contemporain,** lying off the rue des Bains (tel. 28-65-21-65). The modern collection is filled with lithographs, paintings, and sculptures, and the building is so avant-garde that it, too, attracts attention, like a frame competing with the picture it holds. For 5F (69¢), the collection can be viewed from 10 a.m. to 7 p.m. daily except Tuesday.

FOOD AND LODGING: **Frantel,** 2 rue Jean-Jaurès (tel. 28-65-97-22), is a modern chain hotel, one of the best in the port, near the Bassin du Commerce. It attracts many weekend excursionists who come over from England. Well-equipped bedrooms have private baths, and the rate is 275F ($37.92) to 350F ($48.27) in a single, rising to 310F ($42.75) to 375F ($51.71) in a double. The hotel has a number of amenities, including mini-bars, radios, TV, electric razor sockets, laundry and dry cleaning, safes, a currency exchange, and automatic morning calls.

Europ Hôtel, 13 rue de Leughenaer (tel. 28-66-29-07), is a large, modern hotel where the spacious bedrooms are equipped with many comforts. Well-furnished rooms cost 220F ($30.34) in a single, 350F ($48.27) in a double. All units contain private bath, TV, phone, and radio alarm. There's an informal grill-style restaurant with a self-service hors d'oeuvres table on the premises for quick meals, plus an elegant brasserie, Le Mareyeur, specializing in fish and crustaceans. In the brasserie, full meals range from 100F ($13.79) to 200F ($27.58). The complex also contains a bar suitable for unwinding after a long day.

Hôtel Borel, 6 rue l'Hermitte (tel. 28-66-51-80), is a high-quality, family-run hotel with a view of the port from a few of the 36 bedrooms. There is no restaurant on the premises, but the accommodations, functionally furnished, are clean, comfortable, and well situated. Each room has a private bath, TV, phone, and mini-bar. The charge is from 260F ($35.85) in a single to 320F ($44.13) in a double.

Outside of hotel dining, the best restaurant, believe it or not, is at the railway station, a *buffet gare* known as **Richelieu,** Place de la Gare (tel. 28-66-52-13). You're faced with a choice of either a brasserie or a restaurant. Choose the former if you're in a hurry, the latter if you want an elegant French meal and have plenty of time between trains or boats. The cookery is superb, and the service is excellent and thoughtful. Here you can enjoy some of the chef's specialties, including turbot in a creamy hollandaise sauce, filet of sole "le waterzoi," and veal kidneys flambé. Expect to pay 220F ($30.34) to 275F ($37.92) ordering à la carte. Closed Sunday night.

Motorists might want to leave Dunkerque altogether and head for **La Meunerie,** at Téteghem, about four miles east on the N40 and a switch off onto the D204. The address is 174 rue Pierres (tel. 28-26-14-30). Installed in an old mill, this restaurant in the rustic style treats you to the savory viands of Jean-Pierre Delbé. At an immaculately appointed table, you can dine well on his pot-au-feu harvested from the North Sea or his fried sole, duckling foie gras, or assorted cold meats served with several different types of mushrooms, or even his duckling "de Challans." The dishes are skillfully prepared, and some intriguing combinations of flavors reveal Monsieur Delbé to be a chef of some potential. However, you must pay for this. Menus begin at 180F ($24.82), and à la carte diners can easily run up their tab to 350F ($48.27). The restaurant is closed on Sunday night and Monday.

8. Calais

This is the closest Channel port to England, a distance of 21 miles to the "white cliffs" of Dover. The bombs of World War II destroyed most of Vieux Calais, the old town with its citadel of 1560. In its place, a new quarter was built on an island bordered by the harbor basins and a canal. To the south lies the larger quarter of St-Pierre, an industrial area with its tulle and lace factories.

Originally a fishing village, Calais is today the second most important passenger port in France. It is, of course, in front-ranking position for passenger traffic with England. Several daily cross-Channel sea services operate, not only to Dover but to Folkestone as well, taking both passengers and automobiles.

In history, England's Edward III had reduced the seaport to famine in 1346, until the six burghers of Calais turned themselves over as hostages, an event commemorated by Auguste Rodin's world-renowned monument. The monument stands in the center of town, the Place du Soldat-Inconnu, with its Hôtel de Ville, a town hall built in the Flemish-Renaissance style.

FOOD AND LODGING: The **Meurice,** 5 rue E-Roche (tel. 21-34-57-03), is the best, a comfortable hotel in the center of town. Some of its bedrooms open onto a view of Richelieu Park. The rooms are well furnished and maintained, and there is an interior garden in which you can rest up between Channel crossings. In a single, the tariff is from 200F ($27.58), rising to 245F ($33.79) in a double. The hotel also has a restaurant, La Diligence.

George V, 36 rue Royale (tel. 21-97-68-00), is conveniently located in the center of town, near one of the most popular beaches. This well-restored hotel is engagingly directed by the Beauvalot family. Only a handful of the approximately four dozen bedrooms don't have their own private bath, and each contains a TV, radio/alarm, and phone. Accommodations cost from 120F ($16.55) in a single and from 290F ($39.99) in a double. The in-house restaurant serves fixed-priced menus at 85F ($11.72) and 170F ($23.44). The hotel is open all year, but the restaurant doesn't serve Saturday lunch and is closed all day Sunday.

At **Le Channel,** 3 Boulevard de la Résistance (tel. 21-34-42-30), the Crespo family dedicates most of its time to maintaining a well-organized restaurant where clients dine happily on fish specialties. In summer this rustic place is so popular that reservations are almost a must. Specialties include braised salmon in champagne sauce, duck casserole, a seafood platter, and a brochette of snails. Set menus begin at 65F ($8.97), going up to 225F ($31.03). À la carte orders cost from 220F ($30.34). Le Channel is open daily except Sunday night, Tuesday, and for six weeks beginning December 15.

La Sole Meunière, 1 Boulevard de la Résistance (tel. 21-34-43-01), is a good choice, offering an impressive array of fish and fresh shellfish at reasonable prices. Set menus cost 70F ($9.65) and 98F ($13.51), rising to 200F ($27.58) if you order more elaborately. The restaurant is closed on Monday, and also on Sunday night off-season.

9. Boulogne-sur-Mer

By ship and hovercraft the English for years have been streaking over to Boulogne, less than two hours away, to savor a bit of the continent. On the English Channel, Boulogne is about 30 miles from Dover and Folkestone. One of France's busiest commercial ports, it boasts a modern fishing fleet, with many vessels in active pursuit of herring and mackerel.

Boulogne started as a Roman city from which Julius Caesar and his men sailed in 800 boats to conquer England. In 1803 Napoleon had the same plan, but Admiral Nelson had a different idea. American bombers after D-Day destroyed Caligula's Tower, which celebrated Caesar's role in developing Boulogne as an important Channel port. However, Napoleon's thwarted dream is still commemorated in a **Column of the Grande Armée,** rising 174 feet over Boulogne. A statue of the French emperor tops the column, which lies about 1¼ miles out the N1. It can be visited daily from 9:30 a.m. to noon and 1:30 to 6 p.m. (until 4 p.m. off-season) for an admission of 5F (69¢). It is closed on Tuesday in October.

In World War II Boulogne was one of the most bombed and damaged cities along the English Channel, but it has been impressively rebuilt. The port's old or upper town, **Haute Ville,** is worth exploring, as it is enclosed by 13th-century ramparts and four gateways that miraculously escaped the bombs of 20th-century war. The **Hôtel de Ville** was constructed in the upper town in 1734, but its 155-foot-high belfry is from the 13th and 17th centuries. The old citadel has a certain medieval charm, and it was known to both Charles Dickens and Sir Arthur Conan Doyle, who each lived in Boulogne for a short time.

The town has memorials to both Gen. John J. Pershing, who landed here as the head of the American Expeditionary Force of World War I, and the late President John F. Kennedy.

The principal church of Boulogne is the **Basilica of Notre-Dame,** built in 1827–1866 in the neoclassic style, with a dome. It has an 11th-century crypt, all that is left from the original church that stood on this spot. The crypt is open Monday, Wednesday, and Saturday from 9 to 11:30 a.m. and from 2 to 6 p.m. (on Tuesday and Sunday in the afternoon only). Admission is 6F (83¢).

In addition, the port has some good beaches nearby and even boasts a casino, offering an indoor swimming pool and mini-golf.

FOOD AND LODGING: The **Métropole,** 51 rue Thiers (tel. 21-31-54-30), is considered the best hotel in Boulogne, although it is far from luxurious. Right in the center of the port, it has fairly new equipment and is run by efficient methods. At least 21 of its 27 rooms contain a private bath. The cost is 150F ($20.69) in a single, rising to 240F ($33.10) for the best double with private bath. The hotel doesn't have a restaurant, but remains open all year.

Ibis, Boulevard Diderot (tel. 21-30-12-40), a member of a nationwide hotel chain, stands near the port, the train station, and the ferryboat dock. The 80 simple rooms all have private bath, and some contain TV. Accommodations cost 210F ($28.96) in a single, rising to 260F ($35.85) in a double, and all are comfortable and functional. An informal restaurant on the premises serves meals for 95F ($13.10) and up.

La Matelote, 80 Boulevard Saint-Beuve (tel. 21-30-17-97), is the best restaurant in Boulogne. Tony Lestienne knows how to prepare warm salmon salads (which many residents prefer above anything else on the menu), and other specialties include oyster and winkle soup, duckling in raspberry vinegar, turbot cooked in a court-bouillon, and delectable grilled crayfish. My preferred dessert is a form of sugared apple tart with apricot essence, named for the chef. Meals in the sunny and modern dining room cost from 270F ($37.23) on the à la carte but only 160F ($22.06) on the set menu. The restaurant is closed Sunday night, Tuesday, and the last two weeks of June.

La Liègeoise, 10 rue Monsigny (tel. 21-31-61-15), offers one of the most frequently changed menus in town, usually based on whatever is available at the local markets. Alain Delpierre is the creative force behind the cuisine here, using the training he received at one of Lille's best restaurants before coming to impress Boulogne with his cookery. Near the best-known theater in town, the restaurant serves specialties that have included braised barbue (brill) in mustard sauce, cucumber soup Boulogne style, salmon salad, foie gras of duckling, and turbot stuffed with mussels. Set meals cost from 100F ($13.79) to 240F ($33.10), and dinner is served nightly except Friday and on Sunday night until 9:30.

Hôtel de la Plage, 124 Boulevard Saint-Beuve (tel. 21-31-45-35), is a well-known restaurant with a scattering of bedrooms, each simply furnished, that rent for 115F ($15.86) in a single and 150F ($20.69) in a double. It also offers bargain meals, nicely prepared by chef Delance and served in the rustic dining room. Specialties include a wide range of traditionally prepared fish dishes, many made with local crustaceans. Full meals cost a reasonable 75F ($10.32) to 150F ($20.69). The restaurant is closed Monday off-season and from mid-December till the end of January.

You can drive—some walk it—to Wimereux, about 3½ miles north of Boulogne along the CD940. There on the beach, the **Atlantic,** sur la Digue (tel. 21-32-41-01), is an excellent restaurant, which offers you a choice of elaborately prepared dishes, but not so elaborate that the natural taste has been destroyed. I recently started a meal with an omelet made with fresh crab, then followed with trout and sea bass in the beurre blanc sauce so acclaimed in the Loire Valley. The chef also does a superb turbot pâté in gelatin and a lobster salad with truffles and celeriac. Of course only the best-tasting sole and lobster are sold here. A set menu is offered at 160F ($22.06), and there is also a *grande carte* of the day. In addition, the Hamiots rent out 11 simply furnished rooms overlooking the beach. Most of these contain private plumbing. Rooms, either for one or two persons, rent for 220F ($30.34), all with complete bath. They are closed Sunday night and Monday from October to March and in February.

10. Le Touquet-Paris-Plage

Stretched out along the English Channel are many French resort towns, in all shapes and sizes and of distinctively different character. The most fashionable and the best equipped of all these is Le Touquet-Paris-Plage, just south of Boulogne about 20 miles. Its airport provides car-ferry service to Lydd, near Hythe, in England in about 20 minutes. In addition to a very good golf course, the resort has a glittering casino, the **Casino de la Plage,** and a sandy beach that stretches for about 1½ miles. There is, as well, a racetrack near the Canache River. All this helps to explain why Le Touquet-Paris-Plage was known as "the playground of kings" in the days before World War II.

WHERE TO STAY: The **Westminster,** Avenue du Verger (tel. 21-05-19-66), is a

145-room palace in the antique style, which has long been a favorite of British aristocracy. It stands in a park-like setting not too far from the casino, where everybody here seems to go at night. The deluxe hotel has a well-run restaurant where set menus begin at 165F ($22.75). Rooms are beautifully maintained and well kept, luxuriously provided with amenities. Views open onto the forest or a small estuary of the Canache. It charges 420F ($57.92) in a single, that tariff rising to 720F ($99.29) in a double. The hotel is closed from November 15 to mid-March.

More in keeping with the budget of most readers, the **Côte d'Opale,** 99 Boulevard Dr-Jules-Pouget (tel. 21-05-08-11), is a little 28-room charmer, opening right onto the beach and having the added attraction of a flower-filled terrace. From mid-March to mid-November guests—mainly French and English but a lot of them from Belgium too—occupy these rooms, beginning the season with the first breath of spring air and stretching it until the cold winds whip in from the North Sea. The rooms are simple and comfortable, as are the prices—from 160F ($22.06) in a single to a high of 340F ($46.89) in a double. The hotel also serves good food, with meals costing from 120F ($16.55).

A long-standing bargain oasis is the simple **Hôtel La Plage,** Boulevard de la Mer (tel. 21-05-03-22). Directly on the water, all of its 26 rooms have telephone, TV, and views of the waves. About two-thirds of the units also contain private bath. Accommodations range from singles for 150F ($20.69) to doubles for 260F ($35.85). The Champenoise family closes the hotel from mid-November to mid-March.

WHERE TO DINE: The best place to dine—and there is little dispute about this —is **Flavio-Club de la Forêt,** Avenue du Verger (tel. 21-05-10-22), near the casino and the previously recommended Westminster Hotel, whose guests seem to occupy every table at certain times of the season. The cuisine of Guy Delmotte is particularly fine, and he has awakened staid English tastebuds with some daringly inventive dishes from the repertoire of La Nouvelle Cuisine. In elegance and style, you can select from a menu offering such dishes as steamed fresh salmon, a bass served with crispy vegetables, a lobster salad flavored with basil, and a savory stew of red mullet with cucumbers. His mousseline of lobster and salmon is available from mid-May to mid-October, and his grilled lobster with tarragon butter is expensively toothsome. He is also known for his excellent foie gras made with livers from Les Landes in southwest France. For dessert, try the salad of strawberries and rhubarb with Bouzy from the champagne country, which is spectacularly good. Menus are 215F ($29.65), 250F ($34.48), and 370F ($51.02), the latter for the menu homard (lobster). The restaurant is closed from November to mid-March.

You'll find more reasonable dining at **Le Chalut,** 7 Boulevard Dr-Jules-Pouget (tel. 21-05-22-55), whose comfortable dining room extends into a covered terrace ideal for warm-weather meals. The best value here is the 110F ($15.17) fixed-price menu, which might include salmon sausages, bass in puff pastry, and a full array of other fish delicacies. Bernard Dupont closes his restaurant Tuesday night, Wednesday, and from early January until early February.

Chapter XIII

ALSACE-LORRAINE AND THE VOSGES

1. Verdun
2. Metz
3. Nancy
4. Lunéville and Baccarat
5. Domrémy-la-Pucelle
6. Strasbourg
7. La Wantzenau
8. Illhaeusern
9. Colmar
10. The Wine Road of Alsace
11. The Crest Road
12. Mulhouse

OLD GERMANS STILL SPEAK OF IT as "the lost provinces," a reference to Alsace-Lorraine, whose ancient capitals are Strasbourg and Nancy. Alsace, for example, has been called "the least French of French provinces," perhaps more reminiscent of the Black Forest facing it across the Rhine.

This territory has been much disputed by Germany and France. In fact it became German from 1870 until after World War I, and again, it was ruled by Hitler from 1940 to 1944. But now both of the old provinces are happily back under French control, although they are somewhat independent, remembering the days when they ruled themselves.

In the Vosges you can follow the Crest Road or skirt along the foothills, visiting the wine towns of Alsace.

In its old cities and cathedrals, the castle-dotted landscape evokes memories of a great past, and in battle monuments or scars, sometimes of military glory or defeat. Lorraine is Joan of Arc country too, and many of its towns still suggest their heritage from the Middle Ages.

1. Verdun

At this garrison town in eastern France Maréchal Pétain said, "They shall not pass!"—and they didn't. Verdun, where the Allies held out against a massive assault by the German army in World War I, evokes tin-helmeted soldiers in *All Quiet on the Western Front.* In the closing years of World War I an estimated 600,000 to 800,000 French and German soldiers died battling over a few miles of territory.

Today stone houses clustered on narrow, cobblestone streets give Verdun a medieval appearance. It lies on the muddy Meuse between Paris and the Rhine. Two monuments commemorate these tragic events: Rodin's *Defense* and Boucher's *To Victory and the Dead.*

A tour of the battlefields is called **Circuit des Forts,** covering the main fortifications. On the right bank of the Meuse, this is a good 20-mile run, taking in **Fort Vaux,** where Raynal staged his heroic defense after sending his last message by carrier pigeon. After passing a vast French cemetery of 16,000 graves, an endless field of crosses, you arrive at the **Ossuaire de Douaumont.** Here, the bones of those killed in battle—literally blown to bits—were embedded. Nearby at the mostly underground **Fort de Douaumont** the "hell of Verdun" was unleashed. From the roof you can look out at a vast field of corroded tops of "pillboxes." Then on to the **Trench of Bayonets.** Bayonets of French soldiers instantly entombed by a shellburst form this unique memorial.

The other tour, the **Circuit Rive Gauche,** is about a 60-mile run and takes in the **Hill of Montfaucon,** where the Americans have erected a memorial tower, and the **American Cemetery at Romagne,** with some 15,000 graves.

For information on how to make these tours, go to the **Office de Tourisme,** Place Nation (tel. 29-84-18-85).

FOOD AND LODGING: Le Coq Hardi, 8 Avenue de la Victoire (tel. 29-86-00-68). Veterans will perhaps be interested in the two deactivated bombshells from World War I that flank the entrance to the elegant dining room of this country-style inn. The establishment is actually composed of four 18th-century houses joined together near the banks of the river in the center of town. This is my favorite hotel in Verdun, outfitted with enough exposed stone to have kept masons busy for years. There's even a well-proportioned Renaissance-style fireplace crowned with a sculpture of a salamander (the preferred symbol of François I), plus a scattering of ancient church pews and other antiques.

The dining room, which serves the best food in town, is crowned with timbers and a painted ceiling, along with Louis XIII chairs in needlepoint upholstery. Menu specialties include a salade Coq Hardi with green mustard and pine nuts, duck from Challons with raspberry vinegar, coeur de charolais with marrow, stuffed cabbage with turbot, a cassolette of snails in champagne, and foie gras from Landes. Full meals cost from 165F ($22.75) to 300F ($41.37) and are served daily except Wednesday. If you care to stay overnight, bathless rooms cost 135F ($18.62) in a single, 200F ($27.58) in a double. Units with bath or shower rent for 215F ($29.65) to 250F ($34.48) in a single and 265F ($36.54) to 330F ($45.51) in a double, with a continental breakfast included in all tariffs.

Hôtel Bellevue, 1 Rond-point du Maréchal-de-Lattre-de-Tassigny (tel. 29-84-39-41), across from the botanical gardens, is a family-run hotel with a wrought-iron and glass canopy covering the formal entrance. A small cherub carving adorns a side courtyard, which is separated from the street by a row of severely pruned trees. The hotel's restaurant is known for its wine cellar, with some vintages dating from the 19th century. Only dinner is served, usually costing around 115F ($15.86) and up. The hotel and restaurant are both open every year from April 1 to mid-October. Single rooms begin at 135F ($18.62); the best double in the house costs 400F ($55.16).

Hôtel de la Poste et Restaurant Pergola, 8 Avenue Douaumont (tel. 29-86-03-90), is a member of the Fédération Nationale des Logis de France, a nonprofit national association of hotelkeepers. Members receive financial support from the government, providing they preserve the regional characteristics of an establishment. At Hôtel de la Poste, accommodations contain spacious closets, writing tables, and in some cases a sofa in the bedrooms. A young woman, after my most recent check-in, arrived with a bottle of Vittel water and a bucket of ice. The room was pleasantly kept and well equipped. The least expensive single was priced at 95F ($13.10), the costlier doubles at 200F ($27.58). A continental breakfast is served in the bedrooms, on order. The Pergola restaurant offers fine dining, a multicourse meal costing from 75F ($10.32), although a more "gastronomique" dinner goes for 160F ($22.06). The hotel is closed from January 20 to February 20.

2. Metz

Metz has had many faces. Caesar called it one of the great towns of Gaul. In time it became an important Roman city and later the cradle and heart of the Carolingian empire, until it stood alone as an independent republic before it was annexed to France. The Germans took the town in 1870, and it was ceded to them the following year, becoming the capital of Lorraine. However, it reverted to France in 1918.

It lies in a valley where the waters of the Moselle meet those of the Seille, forming several islands. In spite of much war damage, Metz still contains many quaint old streets, alleys, and houses. It has ten city gates still existing, two of them interesting. The **Porte des Allemands** on the eastern side of town is a castellated structure from 1445, and the **Porte Serpenoise** on the south is flanked by turrets belonging to old ramparts that once encircled Metz.

At the southwestern edge of the city is a beautiful terrace, known as the **Esplanade,** which commands a view of the Moselle Valley. It's a fashionable place for promenading as in olden days, following in the footsteps of the poet Paul Verlaine, who was born here.

The **Cathédrale Saint-Étienne,** with its two tall spires, is among the greatest in France. Begun in 1240, it was finished in 1516 in yellow sandstone. Along with those at Amiens and Beauvais, its 140-foot-tall nave is a daring example of high-soaring Gothic art. In fact, with its slender columns and flying buttresses the cathedral belongs to the "decadence" of the Gothic style.

Go here to see its magnificent stained-glass windows, some by Marc Chagall, others from the 13th century. Perhaps you'll arrive on a clear day and can appreciate why the edifice has been called "the very apotheosis of light." The crypt can be visited from 10 a.m. to noon and 2 to 6 p.m. (to 5 p.m. off-season). Admission is 5F (69/). Apply to the sacristan to see the treasury, which contains what is reputed to be the cloak of Charlemagne, with its Byzantine embroidery and incrustation.

Next to the cathedral, the **Musée d'Art et d'Histoire,** 2 rue du Haut-Poirier (tel. 87-75-10-18), part of which is housed in the old Roman baths, has a splendid Gallo-Roman collection. See, in particular, a cluster of funereal and votive sculpture which was unearthed in the foundations of the building. The other part of the complex is occupied by the **Musée des Beaux-Arts,** which has some impressive medieval series of Dutch masters of the 17th century and some fine French portraits, including Nattier's *Young Woman,* plus works by Delacroix and Corot. Both museums, costing 6F (83¢) for admission, are open from 10 a.m. to noon and 2 to 6 p.m. (to 5 p.m. off-season). They are closed on Tuesday.

The **Church of St-Pierre-aux-Nonnains** is said to be the oldest church in France, with one wall dating from the 4th century. Records say that the original church was incorporated into a Benedictine abbey in the 7th century. The best-preserved section is the 10th-century nave, which has been restored. Archeological excavations have uncovered the foundations of a 4th-century building to one side, which might have been used as a baptistery or more likely (the experts are uncertain) as a private bath during the last days of the Roman Empire. On the Boulevard Poincaré or via the Esplanade, the church might be locked to visitors, in which case someone from the **Office de Tourisme,** Place d'Armes (tel. 87-75-65-21), will arrange to have it opened.

HOTELS: **Sofitel Metz,** Place des Paraiges (tel. 87-74-57-27), is in the modern bandbox style, but it has a lot of comforts, amenities, and facilities, such as a swimming pool inside that will warm your heart more than the severe façade. The rooms, 94 in all, are absolutely first class. There are even three suites—one reserved for honeymooners, the other two for any presidents who might be passing through Metz. Singles cost from 400F ($55.16), and doubles are rented for 510F ($70.33). At Le Café de Metz simple meals are served, and the service is rapid, but at Le Rabelais you can linger long over your wine, enjoying the regional specialties of Lorraine. Of course you'll pay more for the experience, a complete meal costing 145F ($20) to 250F ($34.48).

Hotel Royal Concorde, 23 Avenue Foch (tel. 87-66-81-11). Its stone façade looks like a mixture of Romanesque and art nouveau, which is probably the impression its architects wanted to achieve when they designed it in 1906. It sits across a wide boulevard from the train station in the heart of town. Most of the bedrooms have been streamlined and modernized into a neutrally contemporary format. However, several offer copies of cambriole-legged beds and armchairs, with flocked wallpaper and warmly monochromatic deluxe accessories. The 75 bedrooms rent for 340F ($46.89) in a single, 500F ($68.95) in a double. There's a bar with exposed stonework and a beamed ceiling in the basement, along with sitting rooms adorned with beamed ceilings and copies of Louis XIII furnishings. The Royal Restaurant in an art deco style offers dinners from 175F ($24.13), and the Caveau prepares regional meals costing from 110F ($15.17).

Le Métropole, 5 Place du Général-de-Gaulle (tel. 87-66-26-22). Built in the grandest turn-of-the-century tradition, in a location opposite the train station, this hotel offers about 80 bedrooms. Some are more up to date than others, but each, however, is still comfortable and some have a kind of nostalgic warmth. Rooms are reasonably priced at 110F ($15.17) in a single, 160F ($22.06) in a double, breakfast not included. The in-house restaurant has managed to capitalize on its age, offering a belle époque ambience with weekend piano music and an inexpensive fixed-priced menu at 80F ($11.03). À la carte meals range from 150F ($20.69) to 210F ($28.98). The hotel is open throughout the year, but no meals are served on Saturday at lunchtime.

RESTAURANTS: La Dinanderie, 2 rue de Paris (tel. 87-30-14-40), is a sophisticated restaurant where Claude Piergiorgi concocts a savory collection of intensely detailed specialties which include ravioli with crayfish, filet of red mullet in vinaigrette, filet of beef with marrow, and foie gras. The restaurant serves a 120F ($16.55) fixed-price lunch during the week, but at dinner and on Saturday meals cost 220F ($30.34) to 270F ($27.23). It's closed on Sunday, Monday, and in August.

À la Ville de Lyon, 7 rue des Piques (tel. 87-36-07-01), in the medieval section of town, lies on a street with a medieval name midway between the cathedral and the Préfecture of Police. It's rare that restaurant lovers can eat in a former chapel with an ogival ceiling that's classified by the French government as a historic monument. The basement level is exactly that. The upper level, more recent, is tastefully decorated with paintings and rustic artifacts that serve as an appropriate backdrop for the well-prepared regional specialties. You can dine table d'hôte at prices ranging from 120F ($16.55) (only at lunchtime) to 175F ($24.13). If you prefer to order à la carte, expect to pay 190F ($26.20) to 240F ($33.10). The restaurant is open daily except Sunday night, Monday, and in August.

3. Nancy

In the northeastern corner of France, about 230 miles from Paris, Nancy was the capital of old Lorraine. On the Muerthe River, it is serenely beautiful, with a historical tradition, a cuisine, and an architecture all its own. It was once the rival of Paris as a center for art nouveau. Nancy has a kind of triple face: the medieval alleys and towers around the old Ducal Palace where Charles II received Joan of Arc, the golden gates and frivolous fountains of the rococo period, and the constantly spreading modern sections with their widely known university and industry.

SEEING THE CITY: Its heartbeat, however, is the **Place Stanislas,** to which you may want to head first. It was named for Stanislas Leczinski, the last of the dukes of Lorraine, the ex-king of Poland, and the father-in-law of Louis XV. Stanislas turned Nancy into one of the palatial cities of Europe. The square stands between the two major sectors of the city—the **Ville-Vieille** in the northwest, with its narrow, winding streets, and the **Ville-Neuve** in the southeast, dating from the 16th and 18th centuries when the streets were made broad and straight.

Imposing buildings rise on all sides of the Place Stanislas, which was laid out in 1752-1760 to the designs of Emmanuel Héré. The ironwork gates of the square are magnificent. The grilles stand at each of the four corners, and two enclose fountains, the Neptune and the Amphitrite.

The most imposing building on the square is the **Hôtel de Ville.** See its magnificent inner staircase and the 80-foot-long, forged-iron balustrade with a handrail in a single piece, the masterpiece of Jean Lamour, who designed the screens and fountains of the square.

On the eastern side, the **Musée des Beaux-Arts,** 3 Place Stanislas, in an 18th-century building (tel. 83-37-65-01), contains one of Manet's most remarkable portraits, plus works by Delacroix, Dufy, Utrilo, Bonnard, Modigliani, Lucas of Leyden, and Boucher. Perugino, Caravaggio, Ribera, and Tintoretto represent the Italian schools, Rubens the Dutch masters. The collection is enriched by crystal from the Daum brothers, including their multicolored vases and lamps. See also the paintings by Claude Gellée, who changed his name to Lorrain. The museum is open daily except Tuesday, from 10 a.m. to noon and 2 to 6 p.m., charging 10F ($1.38) for admission.

The **Arc de Triomphe,** constructed in 1754–1756 by Stanislas to honor Louis XV, brings you to the long rectangular **Place de la Carrière,** a beautiful, tree-lined promenade leading to the **Palais du Gouvernement,** built in 1760.

This building adjoins the already-mentioned **Ducal Palace,** built in 1502 in the Gothic style with flamboyant balconies. The much-restored palace contains the **Musée Lorrain,** 64 Grande Rue (tel. 83-32-18-74), one of the great museums of France. To wander through its salons and galleries is to go back into 2,000 years of European history. On the first floor is an entire room devoted to the work of Jacques Callot, the noted engraver, born in Nancy in 1592. Excellent tapestries decorate the Galerie des Cerfs. On display is the flag of Henri II, the first French flag known. The gallery owns a comprehensive collection of the masterpieces of Lorraine art in the 17th century when the duchy was at the zenith of its prestige as a center of art and culture. Other works include three fine pictures by Georges de la Tour, and displays exhibit wrought ironwork, antiques, chinaware, glassware, and costumes. There is also a room of Jewish history in eastern France as well as a pharmacy display. This well-run museum is open daily except Tuesday, from 10 a.m. to noon and 2 to 5 p.m., charging 15F ($2.07) for admission.

Alongside the Ducal Palace stands the **Church of the Cordeliers,** with its round chapel based on a design for the Medici in Florence. Here are the burial monuments of the dukes of Lorraine. The two most notable are those of René II (1509) by Mansuy Gauvain and the duke's second wife, Philippa of Gueldres by Ligier Richier. The sarcophagi of the dukes of the baroque period are found in the octagonal ducal chapel from 1607. The Cordeliers can be visited from 10 a.m. to noon and 2 to 5 p.m. (to 6 p.m. on Sunday) for an admission of 6F (83¢). The convent houses the **Musée d'Arts et Traditions Populaires,** with its collection of antiques, porcelain, and reconstructed interiors of regional maisons.

The **Musée de l'École de Nancy,** 38 rue Sergent-Blandan (tel. 83-40-14-86), attracts art nouveau devotees from all over the world. It may be visited daily except Tuesday. From April 1 to September 30 its hours are 10 a.m. to noon and 2 to 6 p.m. Otherwise, visits are possible from 10 a.m. to noon and 2 to 5 p.m. Admission is 10F ($1.38). Here you can see the turn-of-the-century work of the famed Émile Gallé, whose American counterpart was Louis Comfort Tiffany. Gallé was the most outstanding star of what became known as the "Nancy style." A stunning art nouveau house was appropriately selected for the displays of *l'École de Nancy*. The curves, as reflected by, say, a dining room on display, became known as "sinuous." See, in particular, Gallé's celebrated "Dawn and Dusk" bed. My favorite exhibit is Gallé's much photographed and reproduced "mushroom lamp." Another outstanding artist on display is Eugène Vallin.

Finally, a short walk leads to the **Porte de la Craffe,** the oldest building in Nancy, dating from 1360. The interior was a prison during the Revolution and may be visited daily except Tuesday July to mid-September from 10 a.m. to noon and 2 to 6 p.m. for an admission of 6F (83¢).

WHERE TO STAY: Grand Hôtel de la Reine, 2 Place Stanislas (tel. 83-35-03-01), is an 18th-century mansion standing on a square of incomparable beauty. It is now a Relais et Châteaux run by Jean Aubert. This is an exceptional residence, renting out 54 bedchambers furnished for the most part in the classic French style, with draped testers over the beds, Venetian-style chandeliers, and gilt-framed mirrors—an oasis of comfort and taste. In a single the rate is 500F ($68.95). Doubles cost from 810F ($111.70). Children up to 12 years old can stay free if they share their parents' room. The bathrooms at the hotel are tile and have been completely modernized. The salons are decorated with antique wainscoting, and the grand stairway is monumental.

The restaurant of the hotel, the Stanislas, serves both classic dishes and La Nouvelle Cuisine, and the waiters are formal and considerate. Meals cost 180F ($24.82) to 230F ($31.72). I recently enjoyed such dishes as a "spaghetti" of vegetables and cucumbers, a panache of four-different fish, marmite en croûte, and for dessert, quenelles of mousse with a caramel sauce.

Frantel, 11 rue Raymond-Poincaré (tel. 83-35-61-01), is a modern hotel with a garage, air conditioning, and streamlined comfort. Functional and efficient, it serves both business people and tourists. The bedrooms and private baths are first class, fully equipped, and maintained in a sparkling condition. Prices are from 355F ($48.96) in a single, rising to 500F ($68.95) in a double. The hotel's restaurant, La Toison d'Or, offers *la bonne cuisine,* for which you'll have to pay 140F ($19.31) to 320F ($44.13) if you partake of the food. Although the Frantel is a chain hotel, its restaurant ignores that standardized fact, creating excellently prepared and well-conceived dishes, such as young rabbit in gelatin with small yellow plums, a pot-au-feu made with burbot, and a civet of lamb with wild rice. The restaurant is closed from mid-July through September, and for Saturday lunch and on Sunday. However, Le Thiers, a grill room on the ground floor, is open every day from 11 a.m. to 11 p.m.

Less expensive, the **Albert 1er-Astoria,** 3 rue Armée-Patton (tel. 83-40-31-24), is centrally located, near the railway station. For such a reasonably priced hotel, it is well equipped, with an interior garden, a solarium, and a sauna, although there is no restaurant. Well placed, the curiously named hotel has an English bar, L'Astor. The hotel is run in a businesslike manner, and the bedrooms are soberly furnished, with built-in units. Rates are 180F ($24.82) in a single, 300F ($41.37) in a double.

Hôtel Choley, 28 rue Gustave-Simon (tel. 83-32-31-98), is an unusual hotel that probably should be sought out above more expensive places in Nancy. This is the domain of an Alsatian family whose ancestors escaped to Lorraine in 1875 rather than live in German-occupied territory. Today the third generation of the Choley family lives in this early-18th-century building, which they have transformed into a kind of rustic museum of the folk arts.

Each of the 25 bedrooms (whose access is flanked with the brass lions of an ornate billiard table partially rescued from World War II bombings) is different, often graced with turn-of-the-century antiques, fresh wallpaper, and thick timbers. Single rooms with running water rent for around 120F ($16.55), and doubles cost 200F ($27.58) to 250F ($34.48).

A collection of old musical instruments flanks the stone fireplace in the public room, and the hotel's restaurant is centered around a magnificent pair of sideboards by a Nancy cabinetmaker, Majorelle, whose works are considered among the most valuable of their period, circa 1900. The well-prepared cuisine, described by the Choleys as family style, is served on the nine dining room tables. Set menus cost 135F ($18.62) and 175F ($24.13). There's a parking lot about 150 feet from the hotel.

WHERE TO DINE: **La Capuchin Gourmand,** 31 rue Gambetta (tel. 83-35-26-98), stands near the Place Stanislas. Here you enjoy the excellent quality food of Gérard Veissiére, *le patron-cuisinier*. In his old house, fine regional cookery is practiced with art and flair. His restaurant usually tops the list of every food connoisseur visiting Nancy. In homage to the city's long standing as a capital of art nouveau, the restaurant integrates Gallé and Daum glass with Louis Majorelle furniture. You can, of course, order the classic quiche Lorraine here, and many do, but don't overlook the sole cooked with vermouth, the duck soup with lentils, the fresh foie gras, or the pigeon casserole, certainly not the pêche mignon du Capuchin. The featured wine is Gris de Toul. The service is of the highest standard. Menus are offered at 150F ($20.69) and 300F ($41.37), with à la carte orders averaging around 350F ($48.27) to 400F ($55.16). The restaurant is closed on Sunday night, Monday, and from August 1 to August 15.

La Gentilhommière, 29 rue des Maréchaux (tel. 83-32-26-44). The father of Victor Hugo lived in this classic mansion which is now a restaurant. Oriental rugs practically touch one another, and everything rests under a timbered wood ceiling with dark wood antiques. Two large arched windows set with tinted glass look out over a small street near the arch at the Place Stanislas. The place is run by Mme Bouillier, whose food, some say, is the finest in Nancy, where the competition for that honor is stiff. Specialties and menus are likely to change, but perhaps you'll be served beef with roquefort, veal kidney in a mustard sauce, noisettes of roebuck with three purées, scallops in red butter served on a bed of endive, and sea bass with artichokes. If you're visiting from autumn through spring, you can request the délice de sole Hugo and the tepid salad of salmon with chives. Again, the featured wine is Gris de Toul. This restaurant is a meeting place for the prosperous people of Nancy, who believe that dining takes plenty of time. A menu is offered at 175F ($24.13), and you'll spend from 250F ($34.48) ordering à la carte. After May, you can take meals on a shaded terrace. The restaurant is closed on weekends and in August.

If you find the home-cooking of Lorraine too heavy for you, head for **Le Gastrolâtre,** 39 rue des Maréchaux (tel. 83-35-07-97), behind a simple brown storefront façade. One French food critic called the cuisine here *diététique*, but I wouldn't go that far. Patrick Tanesy has excited Nancy with his nouvelle cuisine dishes such as a snail fricassée with morels and hash, salmon steaks with a rhubarb compote, sea bass with fennel, veal kidneys and sweetbreads with cucumbers, and pullet with frog legs. The list is long and tempting, and he's always coming up with something new and different to delight. Set menus cost 140F ($19.31) to 275F ($37.92), but expect to spend 240F ($33.10) to 300F ($41.37) on the à la carte. The restaurant is closed on Sunday and Monday.

Café Foy, 1 Place Stanislas (tel. 83-32-21-44), is the most prominent café in town, lying in a Regency-style room with ornate ceilings, crystal chandeliers, marble- and brass-trimmed floors, and enormous sunny windows looking out over the celebrated square. In summer the outdoor tables offer the best view possible of the elegantly symmetrical square. The clientele off-season is blue-collar and surprisingly informal in such a grand setting, although in summer when the tourists come, violin and cello music can sometimes be heard in the background. A café crème here costs 15F ($2.07). If you're interested in more than a drink, the Restaurant Le Foy upstairs is reachable by a separate staircase opening directly onto the square. A tourist menu in the restaurant costs 120F ($16.55).

4. Lunéville and Baccarat

If chandeliers and decanters, along with wine glasses, evoke glamor and glitter for you and you've come this deep into Lorraine, you might spend one of the most enjoyable days of your trip to eastern France by visiting Lunéville and Baccarat.

LUNÉVILLE: Lying some 21 miles from Nancy, Lunéville was a walled town in medieval days. After a decline brought on by war, plague, and famine, it rose again under the dukes of Léopold and Stanislas.

Lunéville contains factories that produce some of France's best-known porcelain, painted in patterns easily recognizable for their vivid colors and whimsical designs. For many years in the early 18th century this town was the preferred residence of Léopold, the duke of Lorraine who admired Louis XIV so much (and perhaps to flatter the Sun King) that he erected a **château** that in some ways, particularly the chapel, is a replica of the one at Versailles.

Le Parc des Bosquets, stretching out behind the château, was originally designed for Léopold and later embellished by Stanislas. Today the park follows much of the original 18th-century layout, although many of the basins and fountains have been filled in.

A **museum** (tel. 83-73-18-27), rich in old porcelain, drawings, and paintings, as well as various military weapons, is open daily except Tuesday, from 10 a.m. to noon and 2 to 6 p.m. (to 5 p.m. in winter), costing 5F (69¢) for admission.

There's also a baroque church whose construction ended around 1750, **Église St-Jacques.** It contains a 15th-century pietà of polychrome stone and wood panels carved into Régence detailings.

On a more recent note, automobile buffs will enjoy the more than 200 antique two- or three-wheeled vehicles, a few of which were designed with engines, displayed in the **Musée de la Moto et du Vélo** (tel. 83-74-10-56), just opposite the château. Admission costs 12F ($1.66). You can visit daily except Monday and selected holidays, from 9 a.m. to noon and 2 to 6 p.m.

You'll find shops everywhere selling modern examples of the famed dinnerware, which, if you can pack it properly, can become a treasured souvenir of your visit.

Food and Lodging

Château d'Adomenil (tel. 83-74-04-81) lies about 2½ miles south of Lunéville at nearby Rehainviller. It is set in 16 lovely acres of parkland, the grounds containing a 17th-century wine press. Bedrooms cost 350F ($48.27) to 550F ($75.63), but most people visit just for the food, usually having a predinner drink in a salon with oak beams. The waiter will serve you miniature versions of quiche Lorraine. The patron, Michel Million, one of the most outstanding chefs in the province, will often help you in menu selections, perhaps suggesting such delectable fare as quail wrapped in cabbage leaves. You'll enjoy your repast seated in a comfortable armchair in the discreetly opulent, elegantly conservative dining room of the 19th-century château, with a view of spacious lawns dotted with reflecting pools and peacocks.

Monsieur Million creates superb concoctions, for example, a salad of frogs' legs with peppered mint, lobster in court-bouillon with saffron, filet of lamb en croûte with thyme, filet of John Dory with rhubarb, and pigeon stuffed with chanterelles (mushrooms). His wife, Bernadette, greets guests cheerfully and sees that they receive impeccable service. There is both terrace and indoor dining, but the limited number of tables almost demands that you make a reservation. An à la carte meal costs around 380F ($52.40), and set menus range from 175F ($24.13) to 350F ($48.27). The château is closed Sunday night, Monday, and from the last week in January to the last week in February.

Voltaire, 8 Avenue Voltaire (tel. 83-74-07-09), is a pleasant hotel with a garden, lying just outside the city on the road to Strasbourg. Jean-Marie Pothier, the owner, maintains a well-regarded restaurant and ten simply furnished rooms with private bath. These cost from 125F ($17.24) in a single to 175F ($24.13) in a double. Meals range from 75F ($10.32) to 170F ($23.44). They're served daily except Sunday night and Monday.

BACCARAT: Baccarat crystal has made this small village world famous. A glass company was founded here in 1764, called La Verrerie Sainte-Anne. However, in 1817 it made the big switch from glass to crystal, and it has since been known as the Compagnie des Cristalleries de Baccarat. There is a Baccarat shop on the square near the museum. It is housed in a futuristic rectangular building where the walls are made, appropriately, almost entirely of glass. It's loaded with crystal.

After that, you may want to visit the **Musée du Cristal** (tel. 83-75-10-01), which has audio-visual presentations demonstrating crystal blowing. You learn how lead, potassium, and silica combine to form a glittering piece of crystal. The museum also displays some of the factory's oldest and most noteworthy pieces. From mid-June until July 14 the museum is open from 2 to 6:30 p.m. From July 15 to mid-September hours are 10 a.m. to noon and 2 to 6:30 p.m. It is open only on Saturday and Sunday from May 1 to June 14, and every day from September 15 to 30. It is also open on Sunday in April and from October 1 to 15.

Food and Lodging
Renaissance, 31 rue des Cristalleries (tel. 83-75-11-31), is a pleasant hotel in which Madame Colin offers 19 simple but well-maintained rooms. Singles begin at 85F ($11.72), doubles going for 175F ($24.13). An inexpensive restaurant on the premises serves well-prepared meals for 62F ($8.55) to 160F ($22.06) daily except Friday off-season and in February.

5. Domrémy-la-Pucelle

A pilgrimage center attracting flocks of tourists from all over the world, Domrémy is a simple hamlet that would be overlooked by visitors except for one event: Joan of Arc was born here in 1412. Here she saw the visions and heard the voices that led her to play out her historic role as the heroine of France. The Lorraine village lies 6½ miles from Neufchâteau, 35½ miles from Nancy.

A residence traditionally considered the Arc family house, near the church, is known as the **Maison Natale de Jeanne d'Arc** (tel. 29-94-13-19) and can be visited April 1 to September 15 from 8 a.m. to 12:30 p.m. and 1:30 to 7 p.m. for an admission of 5F (69¢). Off-season it is open from 9 a.m. to noon and 2 to 5 p.m. It is closed on Tuesday from mid-October to the end of March. The *chambre natale* in this simple stone cottage is as bleak as the January morning on which the maid was born. Beside the house is a small museum relating the epic of Joan of Arc in film.

Only the tower remains of the church where Joan was baptized. However, above the village, on a slope of the Bois-Chenu, the **Basilique du Bois-Chenu** was commenced in 1881 and consecrated in 1926. The tree that in spring was "lovely as a lily" and believed to be haunted by "faery ladies" no longer exists.

FOOD AND LODGING: There are two suitable inns if you're looking for a room or food.

La Basilique, at Bois-Chenu (tel. 29-06-93-53), lies less than a mile from the village by way of the D53. It offers a good set meal at 90F ($12.41) and a gargantuan one at 250F ($34.48). The chef specializes in regional dishes. This modest inn rents out 28 rooms, seven of which contain a private bath, charging 115F ($15.86) in a single, 200F ($27.58) in a double. It is closed in January, on Sunday night, and on Monday off-season.

If the hotel's dining room is too crowded, try **La Pucelle** (tel. 29-06-95-72), facing the house of Joan of Arc. It is known for its superb Lorraine pâté, which is the best I've ever sampled. A generous, filling meal can be ordered for only 75F ($10.32), an even better one costing 115F ($15.86). This place rents out 12 rooms, half of which contain a private bath, charging a single person 115F ($15.86) and two persons 150F ($20.69). La Pucelle is closed from January 1 to February 15 and on Monday off-season.

6. Strasbourg

Capital of Alsace, Strasbourg is one of France's greatest cities. It is also the capital of pâté de foie gras. It was in Strasbourg that Rouget de Lisle first sang the "Marseillaise." In June of every year the artistic life of Strasbourg reaches its zenith at the **International Music Festival** held at the cathedral, the Palais de la Musique et des Congrès, and in the courtyard of the Château des Rohan.

Strasbourg is not only a great university city, the seat of the Council of Europe, but one of France's most important ports, lying two miles west of the Rhine. In addition to hosting the Council of Europe, Strasbourg is also the meeting place of the European Parliament, which convenes at the **Palais de l'-Europe.**

Visits by motor launch and a number of Rhine excursions are offered from here. Go to the Office de Tourisme, 10 Place Gutenberg (tel. 83-35-03-00) for the most up-to-date data on these excursions, whose schedules vary depending on the season and the number of passengers interested.

Despite war damage, much remains of old Strasbourg. It still has covered bridges and the old towers of its former fortifications, and many 15th- and 17th-century dwellings with painted wooden fronts and carved beams.

In 1871 Strasbourg became German and was made the capital of the imperial territory of Alsace-Lorraine, reverting back to France in 1918. Germans continue to invade it, but today's visitors are friendly ones, pouring over the border on the weekends to sample the fine food, wine, and beer of Alsace.

One street alone illustrates Strasbourg's identity crisis. A century ago it was called the Avenue Napoléon. In 1871 it became the Kaiser Wilhelmstrasse, turning into the Boulevard de la République in 1918. In 1940 it underwent another change, becoming Adolf Hitler Strasse, before ending up as the Avenue du Général-de-Gaulle in 1945.

THE SIGHTS: The traffic hub of Strasbourg is the **Place Kléber,** which dates from the 15th century. Sit here with a tankard of Alsatian beer and slowly get to know Strasbourg. Eventually everybody seems to cross this square. The bronze statue in the center is of J. B. Kléber, born in Strasbourg in 1753. He became one of Napoleon's most noted generals, and was buried under this monument. Apparently his presence offended the Nazis, who removed the statue in 1940.

However, this Alsatian bronze was restored to its proper place in 1945 at the liberation.

From Kléber Square, you can take the rue des Grandes-Arcades to the **Place Gutenberg**, one of the oldest squares of Strasbourg. It was formerly a *marché aux herbes*. The statue in the center is by David d'Angers, dated 1840. It is of Gutenberg, who perfected his printing press in Strasbourg in the winter of 1436-1437. The former town hall, now the **Hôtel du Commerce**, was built in 1582, and is considered one of the most significant Renaissance buildings in all of Alsace.

With this small orientation, you can now make your way along the rue Mercière to the Place de la Cathédrale to see the crowning glory of Strasbourg.

The **Strasbourg Cathedral**, which inspired the poetry of Goethe, was built on the site of a Romanesque church of 1015. Today it stands proudly, one of the largest churches of Christianity, one of the most outstanding examples of Gothic, representing a harmonious transition from the Romanesque. Construction began on it in 1176. The pyramidal tower in rose-colored stone was completed in 1439, and is the tallest such one dating from medieval times, soaring to a height of 472 feet. You can ascend the tower from 8:30 a.m. to 7 p.m. in July and August. From April to June and in September the hours are 9 a.m. to 6:30 p.m.; in March and October, 9 a.m. to 5:30 p.m.; and from November through February, 9 a.m. to 4:30 p.m. Because of certain structural problems and renovations, visitors are allowed only to climb 329 steps to the platform for a panoramic view. Climbing all the way to the spire is forbidden. To make the climb will cost 6F (83¢).

On the main façade, four large counterforts divide the front into three vertical parts and two horizontal galleries. Note the great rose window, which looks like real stone lace. The façade is rich in sculptural decoration. On the portal of the south transept, the "Coronation and Death" of the Virgin in one of the two tympana is considered one of the finest such medieval works. In the north transept, see also the face of St. Lawrence Chapel, a stunning achievement of the late-Gothic German style.

A Romanesque crypt lies under the chancel, which is covered with a square of stonework. The stained-glass window in the center is the work of Max Ingrand. The nave is vast and majestic, with windows depicting emperors and kings on the north aisle. Five chapels are grouped around the transept, including one built in 1500 in the flamboyant Gothic style. In the south transept stands the Angel Pillar, illustrating the Last Judgment, with angels lowering their trumpets.

The astronomical clock was built between 1547 and 1574. However, it stopped working during the Revolution, and from 1838 to 1842 the mechanism was replaced. The clock is wound once a week. People flock to see its 12:30 p.m. show of allegorical figures. The clock can also be inspected; tickets at 4F (55¢) are on sale daily in the south portal at 11:30 a.m., and visits are allowed between 12:30 and 12:45 p.m. On Sunday Apollo appears driving his sun horses; on Thursday you see Jupiter and his eagle, and so on. The main body of the clock has a planetarium according to Copernicus.

From mid-April until the end of September you can view a son-et-lumière show at the cathedral. In July and August there are conducted tours of the cathedral at 10:15 a.m., 2:30 p.m. and again at 3:30 p.m. every day except Saturday.

On the south side of the cathedral, at the Place du Château, the **Château des Rohan**, built from 1732 to 1742, is an architectural example of supreme elegance and perfect proportions. It is considered one of the crowning design achievements in eastern France in the 18th century, and is noted in particular for its façades and its beautiful rococo interior decoration. On the first floor is a fine-arts museum, with works by Rubens, Rembrandt, Van Dyck, El Greco, Goya, Watteau *(The Copper Cleaners),* Renoir, and Monet. There is as well a museum devoted to decorative arts, including ceramics and the cock of the first astronomical clock of the cathedral. The museum, charging an admission of 5.30F (73¢), is open April 1 to October 1 from 10 a.m. to noon and 2 to 6 p.m. Off-season, its hours are from 2 to 6 p.m. only.

On the southwest corner of the Place du Château, at no. 3, the **Musée de l'Oeuvre Notre-Dame** (tel. 88-32-06-39) is located in a collection of ancient houses with wooden galleries. Inside is a museum illustrating art of the Middle Ages and the Renaissance in Strasbourg and surrounding Alsace. The original building dates from 1347, although there have been many later additions. Some of the pieces of art were formerly displayed in the cathedral, where copies have been substituted. The most celebrated prize is a stained-glass head of Christ from a window said to have originally been at Wissembourg, dating from about 1070, one of the oldest known. There is also a stained-glass window depicting an emperor from about 1200. The medieval sculpture is of much interest, as are the works from the Strasbourg goldsmiths from the 16th through the 17th centuries. The museum's winding staircase and interior are in the pure Renaissance style. The 13th-century hall contains the loveliest sculptures from the cathedral, including the wise and foolish virgins from 1280. Hours and admission are the same as for the Château des Rohan.

The **Musée Alsacien,** 23 Quai St-Nicholas (tel. 88-32-48-95), has been installed in three mansions dating from the 16th and 17th centuries. It is like a living textbook of the folklore and customs of Alsace, containing arts, crafts, and tools of the old province. It keeps the same hours as the museums described above, charging a 3.70F (51¢) admission.

The **Church of St. Thomas,** built between 1230 and 1330, is peculiar in that it has five naves. A Protestant church, it is the most interesting one in Strasbourg after the cathedral. It contains the mausoleum of Maréchal de Saxe, a masterpiece of French art by Pigalle, dating from 1777. The church lies along rue St-Thomas, near the Bridge of St. Thomas.

La Petite France, a long walk from the church down the colorful rue des Dentelles, is the most interesting quarter of Strasbourg. Its houses from the 16th century are mirrored in the waters of the Ill. In "Little France," old roofs with gray tiles have sheltered families for ages, and the crossbeamed façades with their roughly carved rafters are in the typical Alsatian style. Of exceptional interest is the rue du Bain-aux-Plantes. An island in the middle of the river is cut by four canals. For a view, walk along the rue des Moulins, branching off from the rue du Bain-aux-Plantes.

RIVER CRUISES: One of the most romantic ways to spend your time in Strasbourg is to take an excursion on the Ill River, leaving from the Château des Rohan. These depart on a large scale from April to October. The fare is about 30F ($4.14) for adults and 15F ($2.07) for children. It's also possible to take night excursions on the illuminated Ill, also departing from the Château des Rohan near the cathedral. The cost is about the same.

Those with more time may want to take excursions on the Rhine, with a crossing of the Strasbourg lock. These cruises on a 300-passenger ship leave from the Promenade Dauphine, a short trip taking about four hours and costing about 50F ($6.90) for adults and around half fare for children. Meals are served on board, and there is bar service.

Longer excursions along the Rhine can also be booked. Information is provided by the **Strasbourg Port Authority,** 25 rue de la Nuée-Bleue (tel. 88-32-49-15).

HOTELS: Strasbourg has a wide range of hotels in several price brackets. Because of its popularity in summer, many of these fill up quickly—so it's best to arrive with a reservation. I'll lead off with—

The Deluxe Leader

Hilton International Strasbourg, Avenue Herrenschmidt (tel. 88-37-10-10). Hilton's statement of the ultimate in comfort and convenience in this sophisticated city rises seven glassy stories above a university complex within a five-minute drive of the center of town. Impressively designed by a local architect, and containing every convenience and luxury that Hilton is known for, the hotel quickly became a landmark for the residents of Strasbourg after it opened in 1981. In fact the eating and drinking facilities have quickly made this one of the most desirable watering holes in town.

Five kinds of Iberian marble were used in the decor, much of it chosen for its resemblance to the ruddy sandstone used in the construction of the city's famous cathedral, whose spire is visible from the windows of many of the richly contemporary bedrooms. Each of these is outfitted with tasteful artwork, highly livable colors, and spacious, marble-trimmed bathrooms. If you're a sports enthusiast, from the windows of your sunny bedroom you can sometimes witness as many as six or seven tennis and soccer teams hard at play. Each of the bedrooms contains color TV, in-house movies, direct-dial phone, a radio with classical music, a mini-bar, air conditioning, and all the extra services you'd expect in a deluxe hotel. Room rates range from 550F ($75.63) to 650F ($89.64) in a single and from 600F ($82.74) to 700F ($96.53) in a double, service and taxes included.

Clients have included Jerry Lewis and King Hussein of Jordan, both of whom seemed to enjoy the leather-upholstered comfort of the Bugatti Bar, where live music and weekly radio broadcasts make this a center of social life in Strasbourg. The opening of this bar coincided with the 100th birthday of Ettore Bugatti, whose Alsatian factories produced some of the world's most valued antique cars and in honor of whom the paneled walls are highlighted with memorabilia that automobile buffs find fascinating.

The hotel's clientele is among the most international in Europe, so English is a widely accepted second language by the guests, as well as by the 160 members of the well-trained staff efficiently directed by Jean-Claude Noël, one of the Hilton chain's top managers. On the premises are a sauna, a health club, a first-class restaurant (see my dining recommendations), massage facilities, and an impressive array of interpretive and secretarial facilities, along with a security system. There is also the moderately priced Le Jardin, which offers a breakfast buffet as well as well-prepared and presented meals. In summer the terrace seats around 60 people; it's open from Easter until normally around the end of September, depending on the weather.

To get here, take the Strasbourg-Centre exit from the autoroute, following signs to the Wacken, Palais des Congrès, and the Palais de l'Europe. Keep an eye out for the smoked-glass and aluminum façade capped with the Hilton logo. Public buses 6, 16, and 26 make frequent runs from the old city.

The Upper Bracket

Sofitel Strasbourg, Place St-Pierre-le-Jeune (tel. 88-32-99-30), is a contemporary, 180-bedroom hotel in the city center. It stands on a stately, tree-shaded square next to one of the city's oldest churches. From the garage basement there is direct elevator access to all floors, where you'll find such amenities as soundproof windows, three-speed air conditioning, and wall-to-wall carpeting. The atmosphere, the architecture, the furnishings—French traditional combined with modern—are light and airy. Of course, you could be living in southern California instead of the old city of Strasbourg. Singles range in price from 510F ($70.33), and doubles peak at 800F ($110.32). Once you get past the marble lobby, the lounges and the bar, Le Thomann, are warm and inviting. Its restaurant, Le Saint-Pierre, opens onto the little plaza with beds of seasonal flowers. The food is in the international style. Thus you are likely to be offered Valencian paella for two, sauerkraut alsacienne, roast lamb flavored with the herbs of Provence, and a zander suprême with Riesling. An à la carte meal will cost from 200F ($27.58) up.

The Middle Bracket

Terminus Gruber, 10 Place de la Gare (tel. 88-32-87-00). One of the leading modern hotels of Strasbourg, built at the railway station, the Terminus Gruber has a streamlined façade that doesn't suggest the warmth and tradition of its interior. The bedrooms are comfortably furnished in a somewhat dated but still pleasing French fashion. Baths are tile and immaculately maintained. In all, 80 rooms with bath or shower are rented at rates ranging from 240F ($33.10) to 550F ($75.63) in a single, the latter with private salon. Doubles are priced from 275F ($37.92) to 620F ($85.50). The hotel offers two restaurants—Le Salon des Aubussons, which seems primarily a meeting place for Strasbourg business people at lunch, and the more inviting La Cour de Rosemont, which is a luxuriously appointed restaurant for dinner. The latter restaurant has very good food, including such specialties of Alsace as snails and choucroute garnie (sauerkraut with pork products). In season the chef specializes in game dishes, such as roast pheasant. His fish dishes, such as a turbot soufflé, are sometimes artistic statements. Menus go for up to 150F ($27.58), plus service, and an à la carte dinner here averages around 220F ($30.34). Incidentally, the hotel also has a Brasserie Terminus-Gruber, serving a very good set meal for just 85F ($11.72).

Hôtel Monopole-Métropole, 16 rue Kuhn (tel. 88-32-11-94), is housed in an old-fashioned red brick and stone building covered with turn-of-the-century detailing. On a quiet street corner near the train station, the hotel contains a modernized lobby with a scattering of antiques, among them a 17th-century carved armoire and a bronze statue of a night watchman illuminating the path up the paneled stairwell. An extension of the salon displays oil portraits of 18th-century Alsatian personalities and glass cases filled with pewter tankards and brass candlesticks. If you opt for breakfast at the hotel (not included in the room rates), you'll have it in the high-ceilinged and spacious Alsatian-style dining room. The 98 bedrooms are surprisingly different, many with Louis-Philippe antiques, high ceilings, and an old-world kind of grace. Singles cost 250F ($34.48), and doubles go for 375F ($51.71). No meals are served other than breakfast. Léon and Monique Siegel are the proprietors. Members of their family have owned this establishment since 1919.

France, 20 rue Jeu-des-Enfants (tel. 88-32-37-12), stands in the vicinity of the railway station and the center of town. Each chamber has its entry hall for luggage, as well as an all-tile bath with a stall shower. The beds are soft, and the fruitwood and Formica furnishings slick and practical. Accommodations also have velvet-covered armchairs and carpeting in rich colors. Singles cost 300F ($41.37), the double rate rising to 430F ($59.30). Breakfast is enjoyed in a room where a window wall opens onto a view of the plaza. The hotel is color-happy, relying a great deal on autumnal tones. The lounges are less skillfully decorated than the bedrooms, although pleasant.

The Budget Range

Vendôme, 9 Place de la Gare (tel. 88-32-45-23), shelters Eurailpass holders and others, enjoying a central position opposite the railway station. The 39-room hotel occupies a fairly new building, offering rooms of comfort and style. Everything is modern, and there is a private bath or shower in each chamber. Furnishings are either provincial or in contemporary lines. Singles rent for 165F ($22.75) to 190F ($26.20), depending on the plumbing, that tariff rising to 210F ($28.96) to 250F ($34.48) in a double. All the rooms have TV and direct-dial phone, and there is a comfortable lounge-bar. Breakfast is the only meal served.

Gutenberg, 31 rue des Serruriers (tel. 88-32-17-15), stands near the Place Gutenberg. Madame Lette welcomes you to her 1745 mansion, which offers a warm atmosphere with plenty of old furniture and pictures. There are no singles, but doubles start at 104F ($14.34) with hot and cold running water. With shower, the cost is 180F ($24.82), rising to 210F ($28.96) with complete bath.

Hotel des Princes, 33 rue Geiler, at the Conseil de l'Europe (tel. 88-61-55-19), rates only two stars from the government, but it's one of the best values in town. Singles cost 240F ($33.10) with doubles going for 290F ($39.99). In general, accommodations are spacious and well kept. Management is friendly and cooperative. The location is in a fairly peaceful area, lying about a 15-minute walk from the heart of the city. A continental breakfast is the only meal served.

FOR ALSATIAN FARE: Au Crocodile, 10 rue de l'Outre (tel. 88-32-13-02). This is a beautiful old restaurant where patrons go to taste the grande cuisine of É-mile Jung. His food is generally more inventive, often more daring in concept, than the traditional restaurants of Strasbourg. On a summer day the golden light that pours down through yellow skylights might illuminate a boned quail that has been stuffed with foie gras, then braised slowly in goosefat and chilled in a meat gelatin. You might start your meal with a remarkable flan of watercress and frogs' legs or the celebrated endive salad with hot goose liver. You might even order stuffed roast suckling pig here, or sausages that evoke memories of the smoked German würst. Then there are turbot with thin strips of vegetables, timbale of sole and lobster, crayfish in tarragon gelatin—always something interesting and probably some dishes you've never sampled before. Another grand specialty is a filet of beef en croûte. Naturally, you get the finest wines Alsace has to offer. Expect to pay 380F ($52.40) to 440F ($60.68) if ordering à la carte. The restaurant is closed from July 8 to August 6, and on Sunday and Monday.

La Maison du Boeuf, Hilton International Strasbourg, Avenue Herren-schmidt (tel. 88-37-10-10), is the deluxe restaurant contained within the aluminum and glass walls of the most luxurious hotel in Alsace. You'll pass through the skylit marble-covered lobby before entering the brass-trimmed doors leading to this elegant belle époque-style restaurant. Winner of a nationwide award for its wine list, the establishment has spared no expense in making this one of the best restaurants in Strasbourg. While sitting on comfortable peacock-blue chairs in a room accented with scarlet carpeting, dark paneling, and etched glass, you'll be served an array of tempting delicacies from the kitchen of Chef Dominique Michou.

Specialties include a pleasing mix of Alsatian and international dishes, including a mousseline of mullet with an essence of leeks, a panache of three different fish (including smoked salmon), fresh asparagus with a truffled vinaigrette sauce, fresh scallops with a saffron-flavored lettuce purée, exquisite American beef grilled with *gros sel*, breast of pigeon served with small stuffed cabbage, and a beignet of foie gras with sweet-and-sour sauce. The salmon is smoked personally by the chef, who claims to never allow anyone to watch him for fear of giving away his secret. Full meals range from 225F ($31.03) to 275F ($37.92). It is open for lunch and dinner daily except Saturday at lunchtime. Reservations are suggested. The maison is closed in August and one week in February.

Maison Kammerzell, 16 Place de la Cathédrale (tel. 88-32-42-14), is not only one of the best restaurants in Strasbourg but a sightseeing attraction in its own right. Dating from 1467, and facing the cathedral, it is an Alsatian gingerbread house reminiscent of Hansel and Gretel. Its carved wooden framework is from the Renaissance period, and a cheese dealer known as Martin Braun built the three overhanging stories in 1589. It is richly decorated, and nowadays it is a shrine of gastronomy. Paul Schloesser is the owner, and his cuisine is exciting and varied.

If you've never ordered it, I suggest la choucroute formidable (two persons are required). This is the great specialty of Alsace, prepared with goosefat, Riesling wine, and juniper berries, and served with pork products such as Strasbourg sausages, pork cutlets, and smoked breast of pork. Two recent dishes I enjoyed here were a cassolette of snails with mushrooms "from the forest," along with a ballotine of duck and regional quetsch plums. Other specialties include noisette of hare with wild berries, jugged hare with fresh noodles, coq au Riesling, calves' kidneys in wine vinegar, and stewed beef with horseradish mustard. Menus are priced at 150F ($20.69) and 170F ($23.44), and you can also order à la carte at a cost of around 260F ($35.85). The restaurant is closed on Wednesday.

La Maison des Tanneurs, 42 rue du Bain-aux-Plantes (tel. 88-32-79-70), is a timbered building established in 1572, standing on one of the most typical of the old streets of the quarter known as Petite France. Its dining terrace opens onto the canal. The decor is very warm, with many flowers and well-selected Alsatian antiques. In this characteristic sector, you dine very well on some of the outstanding specialties of the Alsatian kitchen. Sometimes the restaurant is called "La maison de la choucroute." Naturally, sauerkraut is the specialty, accompanied by a formidable array of pork products, although two persons must order the dish. But the chef knows how to do other dishes equally well, including the classic opener, if you're feeling extravagant: a parfait of foie gras with fresh truffles. Main dishes I recommend include crayfish tails à la nage, or poulet—known as coq au Riesling—cooked in white wine and served with noodles. If ordering à la carte, expect to pay around 200F ($27.58) to 240F ($33.10). The restaurant is closed on Sunday and Monday and takes a holiday June 26 to July 9 and from December 22 to January 23.

Valentin-Sorg, 6 Place Homme-de-Fer (tel. 88-32-12-16), has long been a favorite dining room of mine, even when it stood on a street known as "the old winemarket street." But it long ago was transferred to the 14th (top) floor of a building called "the Tower," standing on the "Square of the Iron Man." Many would patronize it if only for the view. Fortunately, it not only offers a panoramic vista but is one of the finest restaurants in the city, often ranked as number two or three. Here you can order the classic dishes of the French menu—sole Pyramide, sweetbreads Demidoff, frogs' legs with Riesling, tournedos Rossini, duck in orange sauce, even beef Wellington (24-hour notice), which sounds strangely heretical in France. Menus are offered at 140F ($19.31) and 220F ($30.34). The restaurant is closed Sunday night, Tuesday, and from mid-August until September 1 and from mid-February until March 1.

Buerehiesel, 4 parc de l'Orangerie (tel. 88-61-62-26), is also known as "Chez Westermann." It is distinguished for two reasons—La Nouvelle Cuisine of Antoine Westermann and the setting in the Orangerie, which is a beautiful park, at the end of the allée de la Robertsau, near the Council of Europe. The park was planned by the landscape artist Le Nôtre and was offered to the Empress Joséphine. In such a distinguished setting, you can enjoy the admirable specialties of the inventive chef—a terrine of sweetbreads with foie gras, sole and lobster à la nage (cooked in court-bouillon and flavored with herbs), salmis de pigeon au Bourgogne, zander with noodles, steamed spring chicken with cabbage. Set meals begin at 225F ($31.03), and à la carte orders average between 340F ($46.89) to 400F ($55.16). The restaurant is closed on Tuesday night and Wednesday, 15 days in August, and for parts of January and February.

Brasserie de l'Ancienne Douane, 6 rue de la Douane (tel. 88-32-42-19), is housed in a monumental stone building on the banks of the River Ill. From the outside, along a street in the oldest part of town, you'll see only the arcades of the lower floor and the forbiddingly small windows of the simple façade. Inside, however, the view opens onto a scene known to everyone in Strasbourg as an inviting, noisy, spacious, and high-ceilinged room where service is efficient and rapid, and the food is plentiful and savory. The rooms are somewhat formal, with Teutonic-style chairs and heavily timbered ceilings, but you can be sure that if the musicians from the city orchestra, the athletes from the local football team, or the Strasbourg equivalent of the Jaycees are celebrating something, they'll eventually end up here.

Among the *specialités Alsaciennes* are the well-known "sauerkraut of the Customs officers" and the foie gras of Strasbourg. Chicken in Riesling with Alsatian noodles, onion pie, veal escalope filled with ham and cheese, and ham knuckle with potato salad and horseradish are also popular dishes. You can eat here for 130F ($17.93) to 170F ($23.44). The brasserie is open every day.

Taverne de l'Ancienne Douane, 6 rue de la Douane (tel. 88-32-42-19), is housed in the same building as the Brasserie de l'Ancienne Douane (see above) and serves basically the same menu at the same prices. The main difference between the two establishments is that the *taverne* is closed Tuesday night and Wednesday and that it contains only about 30 or 40 seats, as opposed to the hundreds who can flock into the brasserie. The tavern offers a limited number of tables set up on a parapet stretching over the waters of the Ill, which is perfect for a quiet and secluded lunch on a warm day—if you can get a table.

L'Arsenal, 11 rue de l'Abreuvoir (tel. 88-35-03-69). You'll eat in a warmly paneled typically Alsatian ambience if you stop for a meal in this pleasant restaurant operated by two Schneider brothers. The building is historic, and a few of the diners on the benches next to yours might be members of the European Parliament. The food combines Alsatian recipes with more recent inventions. The *carte* changes every few weeks, but on any occasion it might include sauerkraut with smoked fish, pike mousse in cabbage leaves, goose with white cabbage, and refreshingly light sherbets for dessert. A la carte meals cost around 210F ($28.96), while fixed-price meals go for 150F ($20.69). Reservations are important. Dinner is served until midnight daily except on weekends. The restaurant is closed the last two weeks in January and from mid-July to mid-August.

Pfifferbriader, 9 Place du Marché-aux-Cochon-de-Lait (tel. 88-32-15-43), behind the cathedral and close to Ill Quay, offers fast-food service in the popular tavern style. Look for the popular plat du jour. There is a 50F ($6.90) set menu and a tourist menu at 70F ($9.65). A la carte orders will cost from 90F ($12.41) to 110F ($15.17) for the average repast. Many working Strasbourgers come here to enjoy their lunch break.

7. La Wantzenau

Instead of dining in Strasbourg, many motorists prefer to head north for 7½ miles to the village of La Wantzenau, which has very good restaurants and lots of regional specialties. Go northeast on the N68 if you'd like to follow their example.

There the **Zimmer,** 23 rue des Héros (tel. 88-96-62-08), serves the famous chicken dish of the village—poussin à La Wantzenau. Gastronomes drive over from Germany just to sample it. Under the watchful eye of Marie-Reine Zimmer, excellent regional specialties in large portions are served—matelote with Riesling, salmon stewed with mushrooms, and breast of duck with vegetables. Menus are offered at 100F ($13.79) to 180F ($24.82), with à la carte selections peaking at around 220F ($30.34). Featured wines include Pinot Noir and Edelzquicker. The restaurant is closed on Sunday night and Monday and takes a vacation in August.

Au Moulin, 25 Route de Strasbourg (tel. 88-96-20-01), is another favorite; it is set in a flower garden. A large house, it feeds diners well in a traditional setting. Not only is the cookery exceptional, but the wine is also rewarding, including Riesling, Pinot Noir, and Tokay. German diners from across the border come here with their list of dishes to order—such specialties as foie gras frais maison, matelote with white wine, poussin (pullet) Mère Clauss, omelet with fines herbes, and carré d'Agneau (loin of lamb with ribs). Menus cost 140F ($19.31) and 200F ($27.58). The restaurant, run by Charles Clauss, is closed on Sunday night and on Thursday, and in July.

The old mill, opposite the restaurant, has been transformed into a comfortable and very quiet hotel, decorated with taste. The 20 rooms have either private bath or shower, along with alarm clock, radio, and direct-dial phone. Two persons are housed for anywhere from 200F ($27.58) to 280F ($38.61), with a continental breakfast costing extra. The managers are the two daughters of Monsieur Clauss, Béatrice Wolff and Andrée Dametti.

Finally, **À la Barrière,** 3 Route de Strasbourg (tel. 88-96-20-23), is on many a connoisseur's short list. It is urbanely run by Gilbert Aeby, who sees that wines and food are carefully served, although not in an ostentatious way. The chef likes nothing better than producing regional cooking for hungry diners. His foie gras with truffles adds an elegant touch, followed by his barbue (brill) suprême. In hunting season, he also offers roast pheasant and roebuck. Fish dishes are also recommended, especially the turbot served with a creamy hollandaise sauce and the salmon steaks with sorrel. Zander cooked in Riesling is also good. The least expensive meal goes for 175F ($24.13), but you will more likely spend 230F ($31.72) ordering à la carte. The restaurant is closed on Wednesday night and Thursday and takes a vacation from August 15 to September 5.

8. Illhaeusern

Gourmets from all over the world flock to this sleepy village, 11 miles north from Colmar, for one important reason—**L'Auberge de l'Ill,** Route de Collonges (tel. 89-71-83-23). The Haeberlin brothers have a total commitment to food. They combine the finest quality Alsatian specialties with La Nouvelle Cuisine and other classic offerings. They do this so well that their restaurant is one of the greatest in France. In this small village east of Route N83, the brothers Haeberlin serve unforgettable meals in an elegant setting under the willows of the riverbank. The scene could have been painted by Watteau. It used to be the Haeberlins' family farmhouse, and it is furnished with antiques and highly polished silver holloware. In the beautiful flower-filled garden of the inn you can take your apéritif or coffee and brandy at a table under the weeping willows, watching the quiet-flowing Ill go by.

Jean-Pierre, a talented painter, is in charge in the dining room. He knows it well, considering he designed it for dining perfection. Paintings, some by Bernard Buffet, decorate the walls. Paul is in charge in the kitchen. Once the Haeberlin women did the cooking in the family, and Paul first learned cuisine from his mother and aunt. Soon he was taking dishes of Alsatian origin and making them into grande cuisine, as represented by matelote au Riesling or eel stewed in Riesling wine. "Cooking is an art, and all art is patience," you are reminded; and some dishes require a 24-hour notice. Paul also came up with new and inventive ways to serve foie gras. His dishes have perfect harmony. Jean-Pierre comes up with names for the new ones, such as turbot de l'Ill, for the river that flows through the hamlet. After frying, the turbot is surrounded by a cream sauce made with lobster, chopped tarragon, tomatoes, and almond-size pieces of cucumber. Another unusual dish is a mousse of pike surrounding a core of boned frogs' legs, all served in a velvety sauce atop a bed of spinach.

The partridge, pheasant, and duckling are hardly better anywhere in Europe, and the in-season-only main dishes are flavored deliciously. Sometimes braised slices of pheasant and partridge are served together with their dressing, the inevitable chestnuts, but also a rainbow of woodsy wild mushrooms. They are served with very light, almost airy Breton cornmeal pancakes, which come as a surprise. Of course, a winey game sauce is also used. The salmon soufflé in a velvety smooth white sauce is surely unequaled in all of France and in fact is celebrated. A pale pink slice of salmon is peaked with a pike soufflé. This delicate concoction is glazed under a cream and Riesling sauce, spiced with just a dab of fresh tomato concassé. For an appetizer I suggest a salade de lapereau, if featured—filets of baby hare with slivered artichoke hearts. Morels are served with this dish. The cheese selection is impressive. The local rye bread, sliced paper-thin, is studded with walnuts and served along with the array of cheese. The sorbets, particularly the pale grapefruit, literally melt in your mouth.

Of course, reservations are imperative. Set meals cost from 275F ($37.92) to 420F ($57.92). A la carte can climb to 450F ($62.06). The restaurant is closed on Monday night and Tuesday, and for one week in July and February.

9. Colmar

One of the most attractive towns in Alsace, Colmar is filled with many old medieval and early Renaissance buildings, with half-timbered structures, sculptured gables, and gracious loggias. Little gardens and wash houses surround many of the old homes. Its old quarter looks more German than French, filled as it is with streets of unexpected twists and turns. As a gateway to the Rhine country, Colmar is a major stopover south from Strasbourg, 44 miles away. On the Ill River, Colmar is the third-largest town in Alsace, lying near the vine-covered slopes of the southern Vosges.

Its major attraction is the **Musée d'Unterlinden** (Under the Linden Trees), Place d'Unterlinden (tel. 89-41-89-23), one of the most visited and most famous of all French provincial museums. The museum is housed in a former Dominican convent built in 1232. The convent was the chief seat of Rhenish mysticism in the 14th and 15th centuries. Converted to a museum around 1850, it has been a treasure house of art and history of Alsace ever since.

The jewel of its collection is a celebrated immense altar screen with folding, two-sided wing pieces. It was designed that way to show first the Crucifixion, then the Incarnation, framed by the Annunciation and the Resurrection. The carved altar screen depicts St. Anthony visiting the hermit St. Paul. It also reveals the Temptation of St. Anthony, the most soothing and beguiling part of the work, which has some ghastly scenes of misshapen birds, weird monsters, and loathsome animals. The demon of the plague, for example, is depicted with a swollen belly and purple skin, his body blotched with boils, a diabolical grin spread across his horrible face. He stands on webbed feet, his hands rotting stumps reaching out to seize the hermit's breviary. One of the most exciting works in the history of German art, the *Issenheim Altarpiece* was created by the Würzburg-born Matthias Grünewald (1460–1528), called "the most furious of realists." His colors glow, his fantasy overwhelms you.

The museum has other attractions as well, including the magnificent altarpiece of Jean d'Orlier by Martin Schongauer from around 1470. Also displayed are other works of artists from the 14th to the 15th centuries who were painting in Colmar. In religious art, the former convent has a large collection of wood-carvings and stained glass from the 14th to the 18th centuries, plus some lapidary collections of the Gallo-Roman period, including funereal slabs. Its armory collection includes ancient arms from the Romanesque to the Renaissance periods, featuring halberds and crossbows. Charging 15F ($2.07) for admission for adults, 7F (97¢) for students, the museum is open daily from 9 a.m. to noon and 2 to 5 p.m. between November 1 and March 31, to 6 p.m. from April 1 to October 31. In the off-season it is closed on Tuesday.

St. Martin's Church (Église St-Martin), in the heart of old Colmar, is a collegiate church begun in 1230 on the site of a Romanesque church. It has a notable choir erected by William of Marburg in 1350. The church is crowned by a steeple rising to a height of 232 feet. About two blocks away, opening onto the Place des Dominicains, is the **Église des Dominicains,** which contains one of the most celebrated artistic treasures of Colmar, Martin Schongauer's painting *Virgin of the Rosebush,* all gold, red, and white, with fluttering birds. Look for it in the choir. Visiting hours are from 10 a.m. to 6 p.m. However, it is shut down from November to March. Admission is 5F (65¢).

One of the most beautiful houses in Colmar is the **Maison Pfister,** 11 rue des Marchands (tel. 89-41-33-61), a civic building erected in 1537 with wooden balconies. It stands at the corner of the rue Mercière. On the ground floor is a wine boutique (wineshop) which presents a comprehensive range of all wines of France. The shop is owned by a major Alsace wine grower, Mure, proprietor of the vineyard Clos St-Landelin.

If you take St. Peter's Bridge over the Lauch River, you'll have an excellent view of Old Colmar and can explore the section known as **Petite Venice** because it is riddled with canals.

With all the attention focused on the Statue of Liberty in New York these days, interest has revived in Auguste Bartholdi, who was born in Colmar in 1834. This sculptor enjoys world fame as the creator of the Statue of Liberty. **Musée Bartholdi,** 30 rue des Marchands (tel. 89-41-90-60), is a small memento-filled museum of the artist, containing some modest sculptures, but nothing on the scale of his major achievement of course. The museum supplements its exhibits with displays tracing the history of Colmar. Visiting hours are 10 a.m. to noon and 2 to 6 p.m. daily from April 1 to October 31. From November 1 to March 31, the museum is open only on Saturday and Sunday from 10 a.m. to noon and 2 to 5 p.m. Admission is 6F (83¢).

While in Colmar, you can visit the offices of the **CIVA (Alsace Wine Committee),** Maison du Vin d'Alsace, 12 Avenue de la Foire aux Vins (tel. 84-41-06-21), for information about free tours of wineries in the district. The office is usually open weekdays from 9 a.m. to 5 p.m. Arrangements should be made as far in advance as possible.

HOTELS: The **Terminus-Bristol,** 7 Place de la Gare (tel. 89-23-59-59), has been the traditional leader. Behind a red sandstone façade, it contains within its precincts one of the finest restaurants and bars in Colmar, the Rendez-vous de Chasse, which is recommended separately as a dining choice. Right at the busy railway station, this hotel rents out 70 bedrooms, all done in a wide-ranging French styling using both sleek modern and provincial 18th-century-type pieces. Rooms come equipped with private bath and toilet. The single rate is 300F ($41.37), rising to 820F ($113.08) in a double.

La Fecht, 1 rue de la Fecht (tel. 89-41-34-08), is conveniently set at the edge of the old city. Its garden and outdoor terrace add a breath of fresh air. Albeit small, its nearly 40 bedrooms are well designed, each outfitted with phone, radio/alarm, and TV. Accommodations cost between 150F ($20.69) in a single, rising to 280F ($38.61) in a double, breakfast not included. The in-house restaurant serves well-prepared meals, a table d'hôte ranging from 60F ($8.27) to 225F ($31.03). The hotel is open throughout the year, but the restaurant is closed on Sunday night and Monday.

Hostellerie Le Maréchal, 4-5 Place des Six-Montagnes-Noires (tel. 89-41-60-32), is the pleasing result of what happens when three 16th-century houses are joined together into one labyrinthine hotel. The Lauch River is visible from the rear windows, as are rows of narrow, half-timbered canalside houses. You'll climb a wide staircase to reach your room; if it's in the east wing, it might be half-timbered, slope-ceilinged, fairly small, and rustically simple. The friendly manager offers single rooms for 140F ($19.31). Doubles cost from 275F ($37.92). When Gilbert Bomo set up this hostelry in 1972, he created a winter restaurant with a welcoming fireplace. In summer the restaurant is moved to another part of the complex, one with a water view. You can feast on such specialties as stuffed quail, good beef and veal dishes, and lamb cooked provençale style, accompanied by Tokay and Alsatian wines. Set menus cost from 80F ($11.03) to 180F ($24.82).

Hôtel Turenne, 10 Route de Bâle (tel. 89-41-12-26), is a modern hotel with pointed roofs and wooden shutters. The furniture is in classic wood of good quality, and the rooms have a warm, inviting atmosphere. No singles are available, but doubles—no baths, only toilets—rent for 200F ($27.58), increasing to 220F ($30.34) with complete bath. A continental breakfast is extra. In the evening, you can relax in the lounge which has damask linen upholstery.

RESTAURANTS: Maison des Têtes, 19 rue des Têtes (tel. 89-24-43-43), is in a building that dates from 1609. Now a Colmar monument, this wine restaurant got its name from the sculptured heads in its stone façade. The entrance is through a covered cobblestone driveway and open courtyard with what must surely be the oldest grapevine in France. Two dining rooms contain time-aged wood paneling on the walls and the beamed ceiling. Art nouveau lighting fixtures are clusters of glass grapes. Stained-glass and leaded windows, an elaborate hand-carved wooden clock, a free-standing stove with decorative tiles combine to give the "House of Heads" the atmosphere of a cozy Black Forest inn. The food is excellent, including the traditional foie gras with truffles and the special sauerkraut with pork products. If you're there in the right season you can enjoy roebuck served with morels. Fresh trout is braised in Riesling wine, as is the Rhine salmon. Young chicken is flavored with a tarragon sauce, and there is a crayfish dish in the style of the chef. The meals here are monumental, and the Alsatian wines are superb. Menus are offered at 100F ($13.79) and 225F ($31.03). A la carte diners pay in the neighborhood of 200F ($27.58) to 220F ($30.34). The restaurant is closed Sunday night and Monday, and from the end of January to mid-February.

Schillinger, 16 rue Stanislas (tel. 89-41-43-17), is what the French call a *belle maison*, with Louis XVI-style decor. Jean Schillinger is a chef of considerable talent. His cookery is now even better than it was, and dish after dish reflects his enthusiastic professionalism. Try, for example, his foie gras frais maison, his foie d'oie chaud au vinaigre, and his duckling in lemon sauce (served only to two persons). Menus are offered at 160F ($22.06) to 300F ($41.37), and the average à la carte order costs from 300F ($41.37), plus 12% service. The restaurant is closed on Sunday night and Monday, and from July 6 to August 5.

Au Fer Rouge, 52 Grand Rue (tel. 89-41-37-24), is a black-and-white-timbered storybook building. A gable opens onto a small cobblestone square. The windows are stained and bottle glass—shuttered, with outside boxes overflowing in summer with geraniums. There are two levels for dining, each with aged oak beams with carved trim. Many brass and copper kitchen implements hang from the beams. In such a traditional setting, Patrick Fulgraff, the owner, has departed from the typical Alsatian fare of sauerkraut and foie gras. His cuisine is more inventive, in the style of the legendary Paul Bocuse of Lyons or Monsieur Peyrot's Vivarious in Paris.

Specialties include noisettes of lamb with tarragon, quail with shredded cabbage and truffles, filet of beef with marrow, wild duck cooked in its own juice, and for dessert, perhaps apples and cinnamon in puff pastry. The food selections are wisely balanced to give variety, and the staff has been well chosen to provide good service. Three menus are offered, costing 190F ($26.20), 270F ($37.23), and 310F ($42.75). The restaurant shuts down on Sunday night and Monday, and takes a vacation from late July to early August and early January to the end of the month.

Rendez-vous de Chasse, 7 Place de la Gare (tel. 89-41-10-10), is in the previously recommended Hotel Terminus-Bristol at the railway station. This hunter-style restaurant is popular with the local residents, especially at Sunday lunch when entire families take up the tables. The style is modified Louis XIII. In season roebuck is featured, although throughout the year you are likely to get such delectable concoctions as côte de boeuf with a shallot confit, Bresse pigeon with lobster, and a ragoût of sweetbreads and veal kidneys. Sorbets depend on the best fruits of the season. In colder weather you can enjoy the baronial fireplace as you contemplate your dessert, perhaps vacherin glacé à l'Alsacienne. Meals cost from 230F ($31.72) to 285F ($39.30). The restaurant is closed from January 2 to January 15.

On the Fringe

For those who'd like to stay or dine on the outskirts, I recommend l'-**Auberge du Pére Floranc,** with its annex, le Pavillon, 9 rue Herzog, at Wettolsheim, three miles out by way of roads N417 and D1 bis (tel. 89-41-39-14). At this idyllic spot you can eat and dine very well, enjoying Edelzwicker wine along with Riesling. René Floranc provides a first-class cuisine with many specialties, including a terrine of foie gras and a cassolette of snails with those flap mushrooms that is classic cookery at its finest. Quail is also featured in season. Another highly rated dish is stuffed pike en croûte, as well as a tender tournedos. One touch I like—his cake is named after Albert Schweitzer, who was born nearby. Service is friendly and polite. Menus are offered at 100F ($13.79) and 300F ($41.37). The decor of the bedrooms is in a grand French style, making for an engaging and rewarding stopover in the Pavillon, the annex of the auberge. The cost is 90F ($12.41) in a single, rising to 225F ($31.03) for the best double rooms with private bath. The inn is closed on Sunday night off-season, on Monday, from mid-July to August and from mid-November to early December.

10. The Wine Road of Alsace

From Strasbourg, motorists heading south to the sights of Colmar, 42 miles away, can take the N83, a direct route. However, if you've got the time, the famous wine road of Alsace is one of the most rewarding sightseeing targets in eastern France. For some 60 miles the road goes through charming villages, many of which are illuminated on summer nights for your viewing pleasure. Along the way are country inns if you'd like to stop and sample some of the wine, perhaps take a leisurely lunch or dinner or a room for the night. The wine road runs along the foothills of the Vosges. Medieval towers and feudal ruins evoke the pageantry of a faded time.

Of course, the slopes are covered with vines, as there are an estimated 50,000 acres of vineyards along this road, sometimes reaching a height of 1,450 feet. Some 30,000 families earn their living tending the grapes. The best time to go is for the vintage in September and October.

Riesling is the king of Alsatian wine, with its exquisitely perfumed bouquet. Other wines include Chasselas, Knipperle, Sylvaner, Pinot Blanc (one of the oldest of Alsatian wines), Muscat (a dry fruit wine), Pinot Auxerrois, Pinot Gris, Traminer, and Gewürztraminer.

The traditional route starts at—

MARLENHEIM: This agreeable wine town—noted for its Vorlauf red wine—lies 13 miles due west of Strasbourg on the N4. You might want to visit it even if you can't take the complete route, as it offers an excellent inn, **Hostellerie du Cerf,** 30 rue du Général-de-Gaulle (tel. 88-87-73-73), where Robert Husser, the patron, will feed you with such specialties as fresh foie gras, a cassolette of lobster, a ballotine of quail (in season only) with sweetbreads, scallops and oysters cooked in court-bouillon and flavored with herbs, roast turbot served with small strips of vegetables, or a trout with sorrel. The selection of pastries and sorbets is praiseworthy, and certainly the wine list of Alsatian vintages is commendable. Menus are priced at 160F ($22.06), 230F ($31.72), and 320F ($44.13). The inn is closed in February and on Monday and Tuesday. It also rents out 19 pleasantly furnished rooms, charging 200F ($27.58) in a single, 270F ($37.23) in a double.

WANGEN: One of the many jewels along the route, Wangen contains narrow, twisting streets. A city gate is crowned by a tower. It's one of the most typical of the Alsatian wine towns. The road from Wangen winds down to—

MOLSHEIM: This is one of the ten free cities of Alsace, called the "Decapolis." It retains its old ramparts and has a Gothic and Renaissance church built in 1614–1619, plus a large fountain. Its Alte Metzig, or town hall, was erected by the Guild of Butchers and is a most interesting sight, with its turret, gargoyles, loggia, and a belfry housing a clock with allegorical figures striking the hour.

ROSHEIM: Nestled behind medieval fortifications, this old wine-growing town —another of the ten free Alsatian cities of the empire—has a Romanesque house of the 12th century and the Church of Sts. Peter and Paul, also Romanesque, from two centuries later, which is dominated by an octagonal tower. Medieval walls and gate towers evoke its past.

OBERNAI: The patron saint of Alsace, Obernai, was born here. With its old timbered houses and colorful marketplace, the Place du Marché, it is one of the most interesting stopovers along the wine route. Its walls are partially preserved. The Place de l'Étoile is decked out in flowers, and the Hôtel de Ville of 1523 has a delightful loggia (inside you can view the council chamber). An old watchtower, the Tour de la Chapelle, is from the 13th and 16th centuries. The town's six-pail fountain is one of the most spectacular in Alsace.

If you'd like to stop for a meal or even an overnight stay, I recommend **Le Parc,** 169 rue du Général-Gouraud (tel. 88-95-50-08), which is surrounded by a park, the inspiration for the name. The establishment contains three different dining rooms, each in a different style yet all richly decorated as a perfect setting for the well-planned cuisine. The fresh food depends on what is available in the local markets and might include lotte with mushrooms, duckling with apples and cèpes (flap mushrooms), a salad of foie gras, salmon in red wine sauce, and rich fruit desserts. Meals range from 300F ($41.37), although a relatively inexpensive table d'hôte menu is sometimes offered at lunch for 110F ($15.17). On the premises, the owner, Marc Wucher, has about 50 rooms for rent, all spacious and well furnished. Additional facilities include a California-style hot tub, a sauna, and a fitness center. Accommodations range in price from 240F ($33.10) in a single to 335F ($46.20) in a double. In high season, half board is required, priced from 300F ($41.37) to 400F ($55.16) per person. The dining rooms are closed Sunday night and Monday, and the entire operation shuts down the last two weeks in November and from about June 23 to July 7.

BARR: The grapes for some of the finest Alsatian wines, Sylvaner and Gewürztraminer, are harvested here. The castles of Landsberg and Andlau stand high above the town. Barr has many pleasant old timbered houses and a charming Place de l'Hôtel-de-Ville with a town hall from 1640.

MITTELBERGHEIM: Perched like a stork on a housetop, this is a charming village. Its Place de l'Hôtel-de-Ville is bordered with houses in the Renaissance style.

The town has an excellent inn, **Winstub Gilg,** 1 Route du Vin (tel. 88-08-91-37). Georges Gilg, its oldtime chef, attracts a loyal following of the habitués from Strasbourg who are drawn to his rustic Alsatian auberge. He specializes in the products of the region, including an onion tart. Naturally, the formidable sauerkraut is among his hearty offerings, as is a more delicate foie gras en brioche. My most recent dish was one of the most enjoyable along the entire wine road: a pike-perch soufflé with chervil. Other main-dish specialties include stewed kidneys and sweetbreads, duck with oranges in the Nantaise fashion, and a joint of beef in a Black Pinot wine sauce. If at least five persons are in your party, the chef will prepare his Alsatian special, called baeckeoffe, with three different meats. In the shooting season he is likely to offer roast pheasant with grapes, perhaps young wild boar chops or venison with cranberry sauce and fresh mushrooms. Expect to spend 140F ($19.31) to 260F ($35.85) for a meal here. Monsieur Gilg also rents out 11 simply furnished rooms, charging 135F ($18.62) for a single, 160F ($22.06) for a double. The inn is closed Tuesday night and Wednesday, and from late June to early July, and early January to early February.

ANDLAU: This garden-like summer resort was once the site of a famous abbey dating from 887, founded by the disgraced wife of the emperor, Charles the Fat. It has now faded into history, but a church remains which dates from the 12th century. In the tympanum are noteworthy Romanesque carvings.

A pleasant place to eat in Andlau is **Au Boeuf Rouge,** 6 rue du Dr-Stoltz (tel. 88-08-96-26), the popular restaurant which the André Kieffer family transformed from what had been a 16th-century relay station for the postal services. You can eat either in the rustically decorated ground-floor dining room or climb a flight of stairs for what the local dialect calls a *winstub.* Menu specialties are well prepared and classic. You'll be offered homemade terrines, game cock, fresh trout, a wide array of meats, and if you're in the mood for it, a tempting selection from the dessert cart. Full meals range from 210F ($28.96) to 250F ($34.48), or there are fixed-price menus for 83F ($11.47) to 190F ($26.20). The restaurant is closed Wednesday night and Thursday, and from shortly after Christmas until February 1.

DAMBACH: In the midst of its well-known vineyards, Dambach is one of the delights of the wine route. Its timbered houses are gabled with galleries, and many contain oriels. Wrought-iron shop signs still tell you if a place is a bakery or a butcher. The town has ramparts and three fortified gates. A short drive from the town leads to the Saint Sebastian chapel, with a 15th-century ossuary.

Going through Chatenois, you reach—

SÉLESTAT: This was once a free city, a center of the Renaissance, and the seat of a great school. Its **Bibliothèque Humaniste** (tel. 88-92-03-24) contains a rare collection of manuscripts, including Sainte-Foy's *Book of Miracles*. This library is open in the morning from Monday through Saturday from 9 a.m. to noon; afternoon hours are from Monday through Friday, 2 to 5 p.m. Admission is 6F (83¢). One of its most interesting Renaissance buildings is called **Maison de Stephan Ziegler.** The Gothic **Church of St. George** contains some fine stained glass and a stone pulpit which was gilded and painted. Finally, see the **Church of Ste. Foy,** built of red sandstone from the Vosges in the Romanesque style in the 12th century. Towered battlements enclose the town.

La Couronne, 45 rue de Sélestat (tel. 88-85-32-22), in the hamlet of Baldenheim, about 5½ miles east of Sélestat, is a good place to stop for a meal. The rustically pleasant restaurant is directed by Marcel Trébis, who is assisted by chef Daniel Rubiné. The various rooms of this place, each filled with flowered patterns, are linked to one another railroad style. Specialties have been influenced by the chef's apprenticeship at Fleury, a well-known restaurant in Lyon. They include flan of chicken livers with crayfish, suprême of sole in white wine, tournedos with marrow sauce, veal kidneys with mustard sauce, and frogs' legs in puff pastry with Riesling. Set menus cost 90F ($12.41) to 200F ($27.58), while the à la carte meals range from 260F ($35.85) to 300F ($41.37). These are served every day except Sunday night and Monday at lunchtime. To get here, take the D21 east from Sélestat, and when the road forks, take the right-hand turn, the D209.

From Sélestat, you can make an excursion to—

HAUT-KOENIGSBOURG CASTLE: Standing 2,500 feet up on an isolated peak, this 15th-century castle—the largest in Alsace—treats you to an eagle's-nest view. From its platforms, a panoramic view of the Vosges unfolds. It once belonged to the Hohenstaufens. During the Thirty Years' War the Swedes dismantled the château, but it was rebuilt in 1901 after it was presented as a gift to Kaiser Wilhelm II. In March and October the castle can be visited from 9 a.m. to noon and 1 to 5 p.m. From April 1 to September 30 it is open to 6 p.m. From November 1 until the end of February hours run to 4 p.m. Admission is 12F ($1.66). For more information, telephone 89-92-11-46.

Descending again, the trail picks up and leads to—

BERGHEIM: Renowned for its wines, this town has kept part of its 15th-century fortifications. There are many timbered Alsatian houses and a Gothic church.

RIBEAUVILLÉ: In September a fair is held here known as the "Day of the Strolling Fiddlers." At the foot of vine-clad hills, the town is charming, with old shop signs, pierced balconies, turrets, and flower-decorated houses. See its Renaissance fountain and its Hôtel-de-Ville which has a collection of Alsatian tankards known as "hanaps." Of interest also is the Tour des Bouchders, a "butchers' tower" of the 13th and 16th centuries. The town is also noted for its Riesling and Traminer wines.

In Ribeauvillé, **Clos St-Vincent,** Route de Bergheim (tel. 89-73-67-65), is a Relais et Château, one of the most elegant dining and lodging choices along the Alsatian wine road. Bertrand Chapotin sells more here than his lovely view of the Haut-Rhin landscape in a vineyard setting. His food is exceptional—hot duck liver with nuts, turbot with sorrel, roebuck (in season only) in a hot sauce, veal kidneys in Pinot Noir. Of course, the wines are smooth, especially the Riesling and Gewürztraminer which everybody seems to order. A complete meal here costs 230F ($31.72) to 300F ($41.37). The restaurant is closed Tuesday and Wednesday, and takes a vacation from mid-November to March. Very comfortable and handsomely appointed rooms—only eight in all—are rented out to lucky guests who can snare one: 510F ($70.33) in a single, rising to 700F ($96.53) in a double, with breakfast, taxes, and service included. Encircled by the Trimbach vineyards, the inn offers units with either private terrace or balcony. In summer, roses bloom in profusion.

RIQUEWIHR: This town, surrounded by some of the finest vineyards in Alsace, appears much as it did in the 16th century. With its well-preserved walls and towers, its great wine presses and old wells, it is one of the most rewarding targets along the route. The town has many houses in the Gothic and Renaissance styles, with wooden balconies, voluted gables, and elaborately carved doors and windows. Its most interesting houses are the Maison Liebrich, built in 1535; the Maison Preiss-Zimmer, from 1686; and Maison Kiener, from 1574. If possible, try to peer into some of the galleried courtyards, where centuries virtually have stopped. The High Gate of Dolder, straddling an arch through which you can pass, is from 1291. Nearby, the pentagonal Tower of Thieves (sometimes called "the robbers' tower") contains a torture chamber. The château, from 1539, offers a minor museum devoted to the history of Alsace.

For an overnight stay, you might try **Le Riquewihr,** Route de Ribeauvillé (tel. 89-47-83-13). There's a late-night bar in this establishment, but it has no restaurant. That doesn't seem to prevent the recently constructed bedrooms, each with a view over the vineyards just outside of town, from doing a brisk business, especially in summer. Each of the 49 rooms is individually decorated and contains a private bath, TV, radio alarm, and phone. Accommodations range from 160F ($22.06) in a single to 280F ($38.61) in a double. It's open all year.

A good place to dine is the **Auberge du Schoenenbourg,** 2 rue de la Piscine (tel. 89-47-92-28), where meals are served in a garden setting completely surrounded by vineyards at the edge of the village. The cuisine of François Kiener offers a delectable array of tantalizingly prepared dishes—foie gras maison you expect, but salmon soufflé with sabayon truffles is an elegant touch. Perhaps you'll order the panache of fish with sorrel or a medallion of beef with a tomato coulis. For a side order, I suggest the hearts of lettuce with a creamy roquefort dressing, followed by crème caramel with orange. Meals range in price from 210F ($28.96) to 270F ($37.23). The restaurant is closed Wednesday night and Thursday, and for all of January until around February 14.

KIENTZHEIM: Known for its wine, Kientzheim is one of the three colorful towns to explore in this valley of vineyards, ranking along with Kaysersberg and Ammerschwihr. Two castles, timber-framed houses, and walls that date from the Middle Ages make it an appealing choice for a visit. After you have passed through, it is just a short drive to—

KAYSERSBERG: Once a Free City of the empire, Kaysersberg lies at the mouth of the Weiss Valley, built between two vine-covered slopes and crowned by a feudal castle that was ruined in the Thirty Years' War. Kaysersberg rivals Riquewihr as one of the most colorful towns along the wine route.

Nestled in a valley between two low hills, the town stretches snake-like along either side of a rushing stream. From one of the many ornately carved bridges, you can see the city's medieval fortifications stretching along the top of one of the nearby hills. Many of the houses are from the Gothic and Renaissance eras, and most of them have prominent half-timbering, lots of wrought-iron accents, small leaded windows, and multiple designs carved into the reddish sandstone that seems to have been the principal building material.

In the cafés you'll hear a confusing combination of French and Alsatian. The language spoken is usually determined by the age of the speaker, the older ones remaining faithful to the dialect spoken by their grandfathers.

Dr. Albert Schweitzer was born in this pleasant town in 1875. His house stands near the fortified bridge over the Weiss. You can visit the cultural center Albert Schweitzer from June to October from 10 a.m. to noon and 2 to 6 p.m.

In Kaysersberg, **Chambard,** 9-13 rue du Général-de-Gaulle (tel. 89-47-10-17), is the domain of a chef of unusual versatility and imagination, Pierre Irrmann. His restaurant, with an adjoining hotel, is at the bottom of the main street of town, a thoroughfare lined with half-timbered houses, each of which seems to be at least 300 years old. You'll recognize the establishment—the finest in town—by the gilded wrought-iron sign hanging above the cobblestones. Inside you'll find a renovated (1984) but rustically antique ambience of exposed stone and polished wood, as well as a cuisine that uses products of the region with such finesse that it's well worth planning your wine route tour to include a stop at this exceptional restaurant. Naturally, Riesling and Tokay are the wines to order with the repast. Tokay, incidentally, was brought to France from Hungary by a captain of the imperial forces who fought the Turks on the *puszta* and later introduced the grape to Alsace.

Try Monsieur Irrmann's foie gras, his turbot in ginger, the Bresse chicken sautéed with crayfish tails, chicken sautéed with Riesling, or the heart of artichoke filled with goose liver. For dessert, I suggest the mousse Chambard. Service is supervised by the owner's charmingly efficient wife, Marie-Madeleine. Full meals cost 140F ($19.31) to 320F ($44.13) for table d'hôte, around 340F ($46.89) for an à la carte feast.

If you decide to spend the night, the Chambard offers an annex which was constructed in 1981 to match the other buildings on the street. Separated from the restaurant by a stone wall and an antique winepress, the hotel has a massive Renaissance fireplace transported from another building. Its 18 rooms rent for 380F ($52.40) double occupancy, and two suites are offered for 500F ($68.95). The hotel is closed from the end of November till December 10 and for the first three weeks of March. The restaurant is also closed then, as well as on Sunday night and Monday.

Le Lion d'Or, rue Général-de-Gaulle (tel. 89-47-11-16), presents an exceptionally beautiful decor conveniently situated on the cobblestone main street of town. A carved lion's head is set into the oak door leading into the restaurant, where beamed ceilings, stone detailing, brass chandeliers, and the room's focal point, a massive fireplace, are grouped attractively. The building dates from 1521 and is freshened with flowered or immaculately white napery, depending on which of the several rooms you choose. If you eat at one of the outdoor tables, you'll have a view of one of the prettiest streets of Alsace. Full meals cost 100F ($13.79) to 200F ($27.58) and are served daily except Tuesday night and Wednesday, and from January 15 to March 5.

ROUFFACH: One vineyard worth exploring is **Clos St-Landelin,** Route du Vin (Carrefour RN 83/Route de Soultzmatt), lying 10½ miles south of Colmar. For information, call 89-49-62-19. Here the vines grow on little hills at the foot of the Vosges. Rouffach is sheltered by one of the highest of the Vosges mountains, the Grand Ballon, which stops the winds that bring rain. That makes for a dry climate and a special grape. Since 1630 the Muré family has owned the vineyards. Nowadays it's a brother-sister team, René and Reine-Thérèse Muré. In their cellar is the oldest wine press in Alsace, dating from the 13th century. They welcome visitors, and English is spoken.

Finally, to cap the wine road tour, as you move near the outskirts of Colmar—

AMMERSCHWIHR: Once an old Free City of the empire, it was almost completely destroyed in 1944 in World War II battles, but has been reconstructed in the traditional style. Motorists stop off here in increasing numbers to drink the wine, especially Käferkopf. A trio of gate towers, a 16th-century parish church, and remains of its early fortifications evoke yesterday.

The best news for last. The most superb restaurant I've ever found along the Alsatian wine route is here—**Aux Armes de France,** 1 Grande-Rue (tel. 89-47-10-12). In a lovely flower-filled setting, Pierre Gaertner receives the finest gourmets of France and Germany, who know of his superlative cuisine. He trained under the legendary Fernand Point. If you go here for lunch, you may spend the afternoon, and you can even book one of the eight rooms with bath and toilet if you'd like to stay for dinner too. The rate is 220F ($30.34) in a single, rising to 300F ($41.37) in a double, plus service.

The patron runs an immensely popular concern with enthusiasm and expertise. The cuisine, for such a small town, is definitely sophisticated, so much so it comes as a bit of a surprise. Of course, be prepared to spend fairly lavishly, but, then again, you won't need to dine until the third day after taking a meal here. If you can afford it, I suggest the fresh foie gras served in its own gold aspic. One gourmet wrote, "It is truly brushed with angels' wings." Main dishes include a wide repertoire of the classic cuisine with imaginative variations: roebuck (in season) in a hot sauce, sole cooked with vermouth, lobster fricassée with cream and deliciously expensive truffles, sole with hazelnuts, beef cooked in Pinot Rouge, a ragoût of kidneys with sweetbreads laced with Calvados, and soufflés and crêpes to stagger the imagination. Menus are priced at 175F ($24.13) to 350F ($48.27), plus service. The restaurant is closed on Wednesday and Thursday night, and it takes a vacation from January 5 to January 30.

A charming little place to stay, if you don't want to press on to Colmar, is the **Arbre Vert,** 7 rue des Cigognes (tel. 89-47-12-23), which has a delightful interior decoration. Near an old fountain, it is warm and inviting, welcoming you to one of its dozen bedrooms at a low rate of 100F ($13.79) in a single, 200F ($27.58) in a double. The inn also serves very good Alsatian specialties. Meals cost 100F ($13.79) to 200F ($27.58). The inn shuts down on Tuesday, and from November 20 to December 10 and February until March 25.

11. The Crest Road

From Basel to Mainz, a distance of some 150 miles, the Vosges mountain range stretches along the west side of the Rhine Valley. It bears many similarities to the Black Forest of Germany. Many German and French families spend their entire summer vacation exploring the Vosges. However, those with less time may want to settle back for a quick look at these ancient mountains that once formed the boundary between France and Germany.

The Vosges are filled with tall hardwood and fir, and traversed by a network of narrow, twisting roads with hairpin curves. Deep in these mountain forests is the closest that France comes to having a wilderness.

You can penetrate the mountains by heading due west from Strasbourg. But one of the more interesting routes is picked up from Colmar. From that ancient Alsatian town, you can explore some of the highest of the southern Vosges with their remarkable beauty. The **Route des Crêtes,** or the crest road, begins at **Col du Bonhomme,** to the west of Colmar. The road was devised by the French High Command in World War I to carry supplies over the mountainous front. From Col du Bonhomme you can strike out along this magnificent road, once the object of such bitter fighting but today a series of panoramic vistas, including one of the Black Forest.

At **Col de la Schlucht** you will have risen a distance of 4,905 feet. Schlucht is both a winter and a summer resort, and it is considered one of the best-known beauty spots of the Vosges, with a panoramic vista unfolding of the Valley of Munster and the slopes of Hohneck. As you skirt along the edge of this splendid, glacier-carved valley, you'll be in the midst of a land of pine groves with a necklace of lakes. You may want to turn off the main road and go exploring in several directions, the scenery is that tempting. But if you're still on the crest road, you can circle **Hohneck,** which is one of the highest peaks of the Vosges, rising 5,300 feet, dominating the Wildenstein Dam of the Bresse winter sports station.

At **Markstein** you'll come into another pleasant summer and winter resort. From there, you can take the N430, then the D10 to **Munster,** where the savory cheese is made. You go via the **Petit-Ballon,** a landscape of forest and mountain meadows with lots of grazing cows.

Finally, at **Grand-Ballon** you will have reached the highest point you can go by road in the Vosges, 4,662 feet. From there you can get out of your car and go for a walk. If it's a clear day, you'll be able to see the Jura, the French Alps beyond, and can gaze upon a panoramic vista of the Black Forest.

FOOD AND LODGING AT MUNSTER: La Cigogne, 4 Place du Marché (tel. 89-77-32-27), offers a spacious dining room and a rustic Alsatian decor to the loyal clients who enjoy an exceptional table d'hôte menu costing only 70F ($9.65). For the price, considering the quality, this may be one of the best meals in the Vosges. Ordering à la carte and tasting some of the more elaborate specialties, such as duckling in green peppercorns or beef Wellington, can run the tab up to 190F ($26.20). The Pultar family also rents out ten simply furnished rooms for 100F ($13.79) in a single, from 200F ($27.58) in a double. The restaurant is closed Sunday night and Monday.

You might choose to stay at **Au Chêne Voltaire** (tel. 89-77-31-74), in the hamlet of Luttenbach, less than two miles out on the D10. This inn is designed chalet style in the midst of an isolated section of the forest. The modern bedrooms are in a separate building from the rustically inviting restaurant. Unfortunately, you can't dine here unless you're a resident of the hotel. The 19 rooms, 13 with bath, rent for 100F ($13.79) in a single, for 155F ($21.38) in a double. Half-board rates range from 120F ($16.55) to 150F ($20.69) per person. The place is closed for the first two weeks in March and from mid-November to mid-December.

12. Mulhouse

Called Mülhausen by the Germans, this industrial city is topped in size only by Strasbourg in Alsace. Between the Vosges and the Black Forest, it lies about 56 miles south of Strasbourg, but only some 21 miles northwest of Basel if you're taking the train from Switzerland. On the same Ill River that flows through Strasbourg, it is the capital of an arrondissement in the département of Haut-Rhin.

If Mulhouse has an identity problem, it is to be forgiven. From 1308 until 1515 it was a free imperial city, but in 1648 it was added to the Swiss confederation. It remained with Switzerland until 1798 when it joined France. However, from 1871 to 1918 it was under German control. It is a totally bilingual city; both German and French are spoken today.

For a look at the old town, head for the marketplace, called Place de la Réunion. The town hall, the **Hôtel de Ville,** dates from the 16th century, and is the much-photographed, most interesting structure in town. Its walls are frescoed, and it has a covered outside stairway, an example of the so-called Rhenish-Renaissance style.

Those with time to explore will find some interesting museums in Mulhouse.

THE CHIEF SIGHTS: Musée de l'Automobile, 192 Avenue de Colmar (tel. 89-42-29-17), is for the traveler who appreciates fine machinery and antique cars. When it was established, it united under one roof the noteworthy collections of the Schlumpf brothers, who during the course of their lifetimes had accumulated more than 400 vintage cars, covering the most important keystones of the European automobile industry. Many of these cars, most of which are in working order, are glistening mementos of eras when courtesans and grand duchesses disembarked from their finely engineered vehicles assisted by entire retinues of servants.

The inventory runs all the way from the steam-powered Jacquot (1878) to custom-made Ferraris, more than 100 Bugattis, including two of the most expensive of those models ever made, Rolls-Royces, and many more. The combined total should stun any aficionado of the automobile industry. The museum is open daily except Tuesday, from 10 a.m. to 6 p.m. weekdays. Entrance costs 27F ($3.72).

Musée Français du Chemin de Fer, 2 rue Alfred-Glehn (tel. 89-42-25-67), assembles on about a half-dozen covered railroad tracks a noteworthy collection of train engines and cars. Included are a cutaway section of a steam engine, with diagrams explaining how it works, as well as historic steam-powered trains that include the car used by Napoléon III's aides-de-camp in 1856. The interior decor is by Viollet-le-Duc. On the premises is also a collection of fire engines and pumps, some of them made from wood and dating from the 18th century. Admission is 25F ($3.45). The museum is open daily from 9 a.m. to 6 p.m. April to September, from 10 a.m. to 5 p.m. off-season.

Musée de l'Impression sur Étoffes, 3 rue de Bonnes-Gens (tel. 89-45-51-20), also is worth a visit. More than ten million swatches of cloth are contained within the archives of this museum, tracing the development of printed fabrics from the middle of the 18th century. On the second floor you'll find preserved the machines that once were used to print cloth, as well as a collection of old clothing, cloth, and wallpaper from Alsace and the rest of France. Also included are designs from the Far East and Persia. The museum is open from 10 a.m. to noon and 2 to 6 p.m. The printing machines are demonstrated every Monday and Wednesday at 2:30 p.m. in July and August. The museum is closed on Tuesday. Admission is 18F ($2.48).

WHERE TO STAY: **Frantel,** 4 Place Charles-de-Gaulle (tel. 89-46-01-23), is a comfortable modern hotel, part of a nationwide chain, near the train station in the center of town. The rooms, about 100, all have private bath, soundproofing, TV, radio alarm, phone, and mini-bar. They range in price from 360F ($49.64) in a single to 415F ($57.23) in a double. Children under 12 stay free sharing a room with their parents. There's a bar on the premises as well as a restaurant, L'Alsace Frantel, which attracts an active clientele from Mulhouse residents who come for the good food. The modern dining room serves such specialties as turbot with basil, pot-au-feu of duckling, and rillettes of salmon. Full meals range from 75F ($10.32) to 265F ($36.54) and are served daily except Saturday at lunch and Sunday.

Bourse, 14 rue de la Bourse (tel. 89-56-18-44), offers 50 quiet rooms in a convenient location near the stock exchange, train station, and the Place de la République. Bathrooms are usually modern, even if the decor of the rooms ranges from old-fashioned to contemporary. Each of the units has a TV, phone, and private bath, and about half of them look out over a peaceful inner courtyard. Accommodations are priced at 250F ($34.48) in a single, 340F ($46.89) in a double. The hotel is closed from just before Christmas until early January.

Salvator, 29 Passage Central, Centre Europe (tel. 89-45-28-32), is a surprisingly peaceful hotel in the center of the town's entertainment district, near the Musée de l'Automobile. About three-quarters of the 40-odd rooms contain private bath, TV, and phone. They rent for 130F ($17.93) in a single, 215F ($29.65) in a room for two.

WHERE TO DINE: **Guillaume Tell,** 1 rue Guillaume-Tell (tel. 89-45-21-58), is known both for its 17th-century architecture and for the fine quality of its food. This pleasant restaurant is the personal statement of Raymond Ostermann. Menu specialties include everything from the traditional repertoire of Alsatian cuisine, such as noisette of roebuck in season, filet mignon with morels, turbot in champagne sauce, and sauerkraut St-Hubert, made with pheasant whenever it's in season. Set menus range from 50F ($6.90) to 175F ($24.13), while à la carte meals cost from 250F ($34.48) up. The restaurant is open daily except Tuesday night, Wednesday, and from mid-July to August 8.

Le Relais de la Tour, 3 Boulevard de l'Europe (tel. 89-45-12-14), is panoramically situated on the 31st floor of the slowly rotating **Tour de l'Europe,** which encompasses everything from the Vosges to the Jura to the Black Forest of Germany. The chef prepares specialties that a complete rotation of the tower (72 minutes) will hardly allow enough time to savor. You might try the quail stuffed with foie gras mousse, a gratin of seafood, and veal in the Zurich style. Menus begin at a modest 90F ($12.41), going to 220F ($30.34) and above if you order à la carte.

Le Belvédère, 80 Avenue de la Première-Division-Blindée (tel. 89-44-18-79). If you order one of this restaurant's fish specialties, it will probably arrive with a ceremonious lifting by the waiter of the silver bonnet that shelters its oversize plate. The intimacy is enhanced by the immaculate napery and the candlelight, which dimly illuminates the verdant plants scattered throughout the dining room. There is also a fireplace. Menu items include a three-fish platter in Riesling, a stew of mussels in puff pastry, a filet of pike-perch in a parsley cream sauce, and when available, a well-prepared sole meunière or amandine. During the week a table d'hôte meal is offered for 100F ($13.79). The rest of the time, repasts range in price from 130F ($17.93) to 200F ($27.58). The restaurant is closed every Monday night, Tuesday, and from the end of July to mid-August. The Harréus family are the hardworking owners.

Chapter XIV

THE FRENCH ALPS

1. Évian-les-Bains
2. Morzine-Avoriaz
3. Flaine
4. Chamonix-Mont Blanc
5. Megève
6. Albertville
7. Annecy
8. Talloires
9. Aix-les-Bains
10. Chambéry
11. Grenoble
12. Courchevel

NO PART OF FRANCE is more dramatically scenic than the Alps. The western ramparts of the Alps and their foothills is a majestic section of grandeur. From the Mediterranean to the Rhine in the north, they stretch along the southeastern flank of France.

The skiing here has no equal in Europe, not even in Switzerland. Some of the resorts are legendary, including Chamonix-Mont Blanc, the historic capital of alpine skiing, with its 12-mile Vallée Blanc run. Mont Blanc, of course, is the highest mountain in Europe, rising 15,780 snowy feet.

Most of my recommendations will fall in the area known as Savoy, taking in the French lake district, including the largest alpine lake, which the French share with Switzerland. The French call it Lac Léman, but it is known as Lake Geneva in English.

1. Évian-les-Bains

On the château-dotted southern shore of Lac Léman, 26 miles from the city of Geneva, Évian-les-Bains is a spa and tourist resort, one of the leading ones of eastern France. Its lakeside promenade lined with trees and sweeping lawns has been fashionable since the 19th century. In the 16th century Évian was ruled by Switzerland, but it passed to France in 1860.

In the 18th century the waters of Évian—still and tasteless—became famous, and the first spa buildings were erected there in 1839. Bottled Évian is one of the great French table waters, considered beneficial for everything from baby's formula to gout, arthritis, and salt-free diets.

In the center of town is the Hôtel de Ville and the **Casino Royal,** patronized heavily by the Swiss from across the lake. The casino, charging a 45F ($6.21) entrance fee to its gaming rooms, offers blackjack, baccarat, and roulette, among other games, and has floor shows two or three nights a week from June to mid-September, the price depending on the attraction featured. The cost of entrance is usually lowered the rest of the week when music is played for dancing.

In addition to its spa buildings, Évian offers an imposing **Ville des Congrès,** or convention hall, earning for the resort the title of "city of conventions."

In summer the **Nautical Center** is a popular attraction. It lies right on the lake, and has a 328-foot pool with a diving stage, a solarium, restaurant, bar, and children's paddling pool.

The major excursion in Évian is a boat trip on Lake Geneva. The boats of the **Compagnie Générale de Navigation** ply between landing stages on the lake. You can go to the Office de Tourisme, Place d'Allinges (tel. 50-75-04-26), and pick up a schedule of tariffs and hours. You're given a choice of trips, including night cruises in summer. Those who want to see it all can tour both the Haut-Lac and the Grand-Lac. The quickest and most heavily booked of all trips is the crossing from Évian to Ouchy-Lausanne, Switzerland, on the north side.

Crescent-shaped Lake Geneva is the largest lake in Central Europe. In the 18th century the name of Lac Léman was revived. Taking in an area of approximately 225 square miles, the lake is formed by the Rhône, and it is noted for its unusual blueness, almost a transparent look the farther one gets from the muddy Rhône.

A CHOICE OF HOTELS: **Hôtel de la Verniaz et Ses Chalets,** Avenue Verniaz (tel. 50-75-04-90), is the most glamorous and sophisticated place to stay at Évian, attracting a host of celebrated people that have included, in times gone by, the Aga Khan and Elizabeth Taylor. Up from the lake, the well-known country house stands on a hillside, allowing a panoramic view of woods, waters, and the Alps on the horizon. It is perhaps the most self-contained establishment in the area, and is beautifully run and managed by Yanou and John Verdier.

The central building is in the rustic style, with balconies, beams, and plaster or stone construction. The guest rooms are either here in the main house or in one of the separate chalets, such as "Le Cyclamen," which has its own garden and total privacy if you can afford it. The personable owners are delighted when honeymooners check into one of their chalets. The least expensive single in the main building goes for 380F ($52.40), rising to 500F ($68.95), although you'll spend as much as 500F ($68.95) to 875F ($120.66) for a large twin-bedded chamber with a complete private bath. The five chalets range in price from 900F ($124.11) to 1,900F ($262.01). On park-like grounds you'll find a trout and crayfish pool, a tennis court, some 20 horses for riding, and a heated swimming pool. The hotel also serves some of the best food at the spa (see my dining recommendations). It is closed in December and January.

Royal Hôtel, Plateau des Mateirons (tel. 50-75-14-00), was created for guests who want to live with a touch of splendor. There is dignity, serenity, and ample opportunity for feasting the eyes in this deluxe establishment with top-grade facilities. Set back from the resort and the center of town, and surrounded by a large park, the angular façade of this imposing turn-of-the-century building offers a panoramic view of the lake and the Swiss Alps. The interior contains imposingly proportioned public rooms with vaulted and embellished ceilings, elegant furnishings, extensive French- and Italian-style murals, and in some cases, richly grained paneling. A heated private swimming pool is accessible by elevator from all the rooms, and guests enjoy the hotel gym, exercise programs, and the wide array of sports facilities, including golf, tennis, and archery.

Within the walls of this place you'll find five different restaurants. The most elaborate and best rated is the Café Royal, done in a sumptuous decor that includes frescoes and murals by a well-known artist, Gustave Jaulmes. The menus change here practically every day, with André Crispino, the award-winning chef, concocting such dishes as cassolette of crayfish, lakefish with port, and seafood pot-au-feu. A table d'hôte meal costs around 275F ($37.92).

Each of the rooms has its own balcony or loggia. Rates depend on what kind of arrangement you check in on. On my last visit that included nine separate tariffs, ranging from tennis to golf to "super dietetic." Only to give you an idea of the prices charged, expect to spend from 1,200F ($165.48) daily in a single and from 1,800F ($248.22) in a double, plus meals. If you're considering staying here, ask for one of the package rates, which will be more beneficial financially. The hotel is open from mid-February to mid-December.

Les Cygnes, Grande-Rive (tel. 50-75-01-01), is one of the best bargains at the spa, although it's away from the center. It's a Norman-style villa opening onto a lake port, and it's characterized by dormer windows, a conically shaped tower, a decorative beam-and-plaster façade, a mansard roof, and an entrance courtyard surrounded by abundant flowers and shrubs. All this, plus a waterside terrace with a grape arbor and a boat pier extending into the lake, makes for a delightful holiday escape and evokes another era.

The hotel is family run, and it's a homey place at which to stay, anchoring in for a few days and using it as a base from which to explore Lake Geneva. The bedrooms are pleasant but decidedly old-fashioned, as they should be. A single rents for 200F ($27.58), that tariff rising to 275F ($37.92) in a double. The good-size dining room, with its beamed ceiling and high-backed ladder chairs, always seems ready to serve a meal. On my latest rounds there, I enjoyed a homemade soup, followed by oeuf (egg) poêle, then a veal escalope fried in butter with an accompaniment of fresh vegetables, ending with pears in syrup. Visitors not staying at the hotel are welcome to drop in for a meal, costing 115F ($15.86) and up. Or if you're staying at the hotel, you may want to take full board, ranging in price from 220F ($30.34) to 270F ($37.23) per person. The hotel is open only from June to mid-September.

One of the best and most scenic places to stay in the environs is at **Les Prés Fleuris,** on Route Thollon, 4½ miles from Évian (tel. 50-75-29-14). It's a casual, white-painted, attractive little villa with a lakeside location, and it's open from mid-March to late October. There are only 12 bedrooms, but each is sumptuously furnished with antiques or reproductions. The rates range from 640F ($88.26) to 1,020F ($140.66) for two persons. For guests there is a comfortable sitting room with big, soft armchairs, and many vases of fresh flowers are placed about in summer. Glass walls capitalize on the view. Checkered tablecloths and white wrought-iron chairs are set under the trees for meals in fair weather. The food served by Monsieur and Madame Demonceau-Frossard is exceptional. Full board costs 700F ($96.53) to 1,000F ($137.90) per person daily, but a minimum stay of three days is required for those terms. A set menu is featured at 200F ($27.58), or you may select from the à la carte offerings, costing from 300F ($41.37).

WHERE TO DINE: Chez Lapierre, au Casino (tel. 50-75-03-78), is the most elegantly appointed restaurant in Évian. Since there's an entrance leading directly to it from the street, diners can avoid passing through the gaming sections if they prefer not to be tempted to risk what they otherwise could have used to pay the price of a dinner. In this case that's around 400F ($55.16) and more per person for à la carte and 250F ($34.48) for the fixed-price menu.

This is perhaps the ultimate experience in the region of "dining as entertainment." The service is exceptionally formal. Only dinner is served, since the restaurant is closed at lunchtime. The chef, Roger Michelet, blends classic and modern dishes, as reflected by the sautéed beef with flap mushrooms from the

Limousin area, a salad of fresh vegetables, crayfish, and fresh truffles, sautéed frogs' legs with scallops, and trout en papillote. Dessert could be an iced soufflé of raspberries. Dinner is served until 1:30 a.m.

Bourgogne, 73 rue Nationale (tel. 50-75-01-05), is a charming inn with many appealing decorative touches, located near the Congress Hall. Come here if you want a delectable meal, irreproachable service, an attractive setting, and excellent wine. Main dishes include le filet de boeuf au poivre (pepper steak) and la crépinette de truite cooked with champagne and le ris de veau (sweetbreads). I also suggest le carré d'agneau (lamb) à la Provençale. The chef also does the omble-chcvalier (char), a fish somewhat like a trout that comes from the deep lakes of Savoy. Another specialty is crêpes Bourgogne, requiring at least two diners. Regional wines featured are Crépy and Roussette. Bourgogne offers the best set meal in Évian, costing 120F ($16.55), although the menu gastronomique runs as high as 200F ($27.58) and includes not only oysters or foie gras but a cassolette of crayfish, followed by a filet of beef with a béarnaise sauce. If you order à la carte, you will more likely pay 250F ($34.48). The inn also offers eight well-furnished and comfortable bedrooms, costing 380F ($52.40) for two persons. The restaurant is closed from November to just before Christmas, Monday lunch in July and August, and Tuesday night and Wednesday off-season.

Hôtel de la Verniaz et Ses Chalets, Avenue Verniaz (tel. 50-75-04-90), recommended previously as a hotel, serves an exceptional cuisine as well. The main dining room is a warm setting with provincial chairs and an open fireplace. Even more engaging is the rustic Rôtisserie, where tables are placed to catch the warmth of the wood-burning fir set in a raised brick fireplace. Olive wood is used in roasting, or else vine branches. When weather permits, white garden furniture is set on a graveled terrace under fringed umbrellas. Before a meal here, guests gravitate in the late afternoon to Le Bar, luxuriously rustic with its wooden tower and ceiling decorated with an alpine brass horn made into a chandelier. This is the center for whisky tasters in the area, as at least 150 scotch whiskies are available. Even the bagpipe clan meets here. Specialties of the restaurant include crayfish with dill, truite saumonée au champagne, a foie gras frais de canard maison, and the finest of spit-roasted game, poultry, and meat. Regional wines featured are Crépy and Roussette. A set meal is offered for 180F ($24.82), although you are more likely to spend 300F ($41.37) if you order à la carte. The restaurant is closed in December and January.

Da Bouttau, Quai Charles-Besson (tel. 50-75-02-44), was originally founded in Nice in 1860, but it has been a good two-fork restaurant happily ensconced in Évian for many years. In fair weather you can request a dining table outside. Even though in the Alps, Da Bouttau retains its Mediterranean provincial decor with an elaborate use of copper pots. Not all those pots are used for decoration, however. The proprietor, Yves Ramillon, serves some of the best food at the spa. In honor of its past, Da Bouttau still specializes in dishes from Provence. Right near the casino, the restaurant fronts the lake. A set meal is offered for 100F ($13.79), and it is excellent, featuring on one recent occasion a salade niçoise followed by poule niçoise, then osso buco, cheese, and dessert. Another more elaborate repast goes for 180F ($24.82). On the à la carte menu, you can order such specialties as a Mediterranean bouillabaisse or grilled loup, even a most interesting chicken-and-crayfish dish. An à la carte meal can cost from 220F ($30.34). The restaurant is closed from mid-January to March and on Monday night and Tuesday in winter.

2. Morzine-Avoriaz

The tourist capital of the Haut-Chablais district, Morzine stands in the middle of foothills and forest. The most northerly of the French alpine resorts, it offers such attractions as sleighrides and beautiful pine forests, as well as ice shows and more than a dozen cabarets. For years it was known as a summer resort, but now its acclaim as a winter ski center seems to have overshadowed that previous reputation.

Like Samoëns, Morzine was noted in the 19th century for its fraternities of artisans, particularly masons. When winter came, these artisans used to wander about the countryside, taking their skills with them.

Based in Morzine, you can visit **Lac de Montriond,** at an altitude of 3,490 feet. A tour of this famous and beautiful lake takes about two hours for an 18-mile journey.

One of the most modern and sophisticated ski centers of Europe has been developed at **Avoriaz,** towering over Morzine. Even if you don't want to stay in one of its hotels, you may want to take a cable car up for a look and perhaps a meal.

By cable car or bubble car you can also go to **Le Pléney,** at 5,367 feet, enjoying a view from its belvedere looking out on Mont Blanc. Through the Dranse Gap a vista of Lake Geneva unfolds.

WHERE TO STAY: Le Dahu (tel. 50-79-11-12) is a four-story modern structure, built on the side of a hill so as to offer panoramic views. Its white plaster façade is relieved by wooden balconies and picture windows opening onto the village and alpine range. Although sleekly contemporary, the hotel has some old-fashioned warming touches, such as stone fireplaces around which guests gather to talk after a session on the slopes in winter. In summer the wide terraces become the social center, as guests gather for sunbathing and refreshments. There is also a shady lawn with flower gardens. Meals are served in a provincial-style dining room with reed-seated chairs and oxen-yoke chandeliers. The bedrooms are up to date, and many have been given home-like touches. All of them contain private bath or shower. The charges range from 215F ($29.65) in a single to 385F ($53.09) in a double. The full-board plan goes from 345F ($47.58) to 450F ($62.06) per person. The hotel is open from June 30 to August 31 and from mid-December to Easter.

Le Carlina (tel. 50-79-01-03), a Mapote / Best Western hotel, is an informal village chalet which, in spite of its modesty, has maintained a high respect among its skiing habitués. Its interior is rustic, with several lounges—from the library to the inglenook parlor—containing open fireplaces, plus an abundance of cozy conversation nooks. The decor accent is alpine, with beamed ceilings and flagstone floors. While not fashion-setting, its bedrooms are pleasantly decorated and most comfortable, costing 320F ($44.13) in a single and from 380F ($52.40) in a double. All rooms come with private bath. In summer there is a refreshment terrace with umbrella tables on the street level. In evening, life gravitates around the Carlina Club where you can either dance or join in the folk music. The cuisine is most agreeable, as is the polite, friendly service. The least expensive set meal, and it's a heartily recommendable one, costs 125F ($17.24). However, you can stay here on the full-board plan, going from 350F ($48.27) to 480F ($66.19) per person. Le Carlina is open from late June to September and from mid-December to mid-April.

Chamois d'Or (tel. 50-79-13-78) offers one of the best bargains at this increasingly popular resort. An overscale pine chalet, it has a façade of wooden trim and balconies—and one season, from December 20 to April 10. In winter skiers check in, sitting snugly in front of an open fire, meeting friends and drinking hot grog when not on the slopes. All rooms have private bath and toilet and are furnished in a semi-rustic style. No single rooms are available. Half board ranges in price from 200F ($27.58) to 230F ($31.72) per person daily. The inn also serves one of the best meals at the winter resort, several tempting courses for 85F ($11.72).

AT AVORIAZ: Hôtel des Dromonts, Avoriaz 1800 (tel. 50-74-08-11), stands on the crest of an Alp, an avant-garde complex that reigns unchallenged as the chicest alpine retreat in France. A bizarre architectural wonder, it spreads out to include luxurious apartment villas, a cluster of boutiques, restaurants, a nightclub, and of course elaborate playtime facilities. The architectural theme evokes cliff-dwelling days with beehive balconies. Natural shingles cover the façade, and both the public and private rooms are oddly shaped. Long, winding ramps lead you through space over intimate fireplace nooks, past boutiques and drinking bars as well as restaurants. Every possible facility is here for *le weekend*—Le Solarium, La Taverne, Le Drugstore, Le Roc-Club Disco. Your bedroom will probably be in an explosive modern design with a liberal use made of natural wood and bright colors, even "futuristic" furniture. The crowd attracted to these premises is usually youthful and brimming with energy. Ski runs and lifts are right at the door. Expect to pay from 685F ($94.46) to 720F ($99.29) per person for full board. The highest prices are charged at Christmas, Easter, and in February. The hotel is open from mid-December to mid-April.

Les Hauts Forts, Avoriaz 1800 (tel. 50-74-09-11), does a sister act with Des Dromonts. With the same bizarre architecture, it offers almost as much for your money as Les Dromonts, although its tariffs are lower. Bedrooms are furnished in an avant-garde style and often are irregularly shaped. Fifty bedrooms are rented out. In high season, two persons are charged from 520F ($71.71) to 640F ($88.26) for a room, although in certain off-season periods the rate is lowered to 430F ($59.30) to 500F ($68.95). Singles occupying a double are charged 50% more. The hotel receives guests from mid-December to April 15. Facilities include a cinema, many recreational facilities, a solarium, a gallery of boutiques, and, again, ski lifts virtually at your door. There's also a good restaurant, serving a meal for 160F ($22.06) to 300F ($41.37) in case you're just visiting the Alphigh resort from Morzine. You can enjoy nouvelle cuisine meals.

3. Flaine

Flaine enjoys a superb location, about 30 miles from both Morzine and Megève. Flaine boasts deep powder snow from November through April. The chalets of Flaine, at 5,412 feet, are above the valley of the Arve and the Carroz-d'Araches.

From its cable-car station, inaugurated in 1969, you are whisked up to Les Grandes Platières. There you can admire the Désert de Platé and look out on a magnificent view of Mont Blanc. Skiers have a choice of downward trails—a thrilling descent in a four-minute run on the Diamant Noir ski trail or a 60-minute run via the Serpentine trail.

WHERE TO STAY: Totem (tel. 50-90-80-64) operates only in winter, taking advantage of the blankets of snow which enhance the view from its rows of bay windows. This comfortable, concrete-walled hotel is the preferred favorite of seekers of a romantic sojourn in the mountains. Each of its more than 50 bedrooms contains its own bath and phone (most have TV as well). Accommodations range from 290F ($39.99) in a single to 460F ($63.43) in a double, with breakfast included. Full-board rates, the preferred way of booking in here, go from 400F ($55.16) to 510F ($70.33) per person daily. An indoor swimming pool and tennis courts are within easy access. The cozy dining room is the setting for excellently prepared meals, including such dishes as grilled John Dory with essence of shrimp, sweetbreads in puff pastry, roast duck, and thick grilled slices of freshwater salmon. Service is friendly and elegant, with fixed-price menus costing 180F ($24.82). À la carte orders go from 300F ($41.37). The hotel opens 10 days before Christmas and closes in mid-April.

Gradins Gris (tel. 50-90-81-10) is another excellent choice. Fifty-one contemporary rooms come equipped with telephone, private bath and all the modern conveniences. For these you pay 310F ($42.75) in a single and from 400F

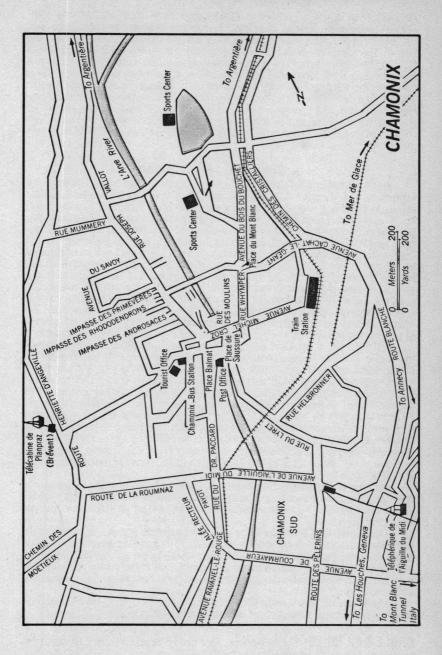

CHAMONIX

To Argentière

Sports Center

L'Arve River

VALLOT

RUE MUMMERY

RUE JOSEPH

Sports Center

AVENUE DU BOIS DU BOUCHET

Place du Mont Blanc

CHEMIN DES CRISTALLIERS

AVENUE CACHAT-LE-GÉANT

To Mer de Glace

Meters
Yards
200
200
0
0

DU SAVOY

AVENUE

IMPASSE DES PRIMEVÈRES

IMPASSE DES RHODODENDRONS

IMPASSE DES ANDROSACES

RUE DES MOULINS

RUE WHYMPER

AVENUE MICHEL

Train Station

ROUTE BLANCHE

RUE CROZ

Tourist Office

Place Balmat

Place de Saussure

Post Office

Chamonix Bus Station

Post Office

RUE HELBRONNER

RUE DU LYRET

To Annecy

HENRIETTE D'ANGEVILLE

Télécabine de Planpraz (Brévent)

ROUTE

DR. PACCARD

AVENUE DE L'AIGUILLE DU MIDI

ROUTE DE LA ROUMNAZ

ALLÉE RECTEUR PAYOT

RUE DU PAYOT

CHAMONIX SUD

Téléphérique de l'Aiguille du Midi

CHEMIN DES MOETIEUX

AVENUE RAVANEL-LE-ROUGE

AVENUE DE COURMAYEUR

ROUTE DES PÈLERINS

To Les Houches, Geneva

To Mont Blanc Tunnel Italy

($55.16) in a double. Full-board plans range from 450F ($62.06) to 550F ($75.63) per person nightly. The hotel receives guests from mid-December until the end of April. The rooms open either onto the spruce forest or onto the Forum, the center of life in Flaine, as in ancient times. Marcel Breuer's passion for diamond-shaped panels is particularly noticeable on a moonlit night, as you stand looking at the façade of Les Gradins Gris. After a day on the slopes, skiers return to the warmth of Breuer's fireplace in the lounge. In the Salon-Cimaise you'll find a coffee table with a relief by Roy Adzak, canapes by Agnoli, armchairs by Aalto, and tapestries by Albers. From the Salon-Cimaise you can go out onto the sun terrace or head for the main dining room, which offers a superb cuisine. Motorists in the area might want to drop in to enjoy its 225F ($31.03) set meal, a very good value.

4. Chamonix–Mont Blanc

At an altitude of 3,422 feet, Chamonix, opening onto Mont Blanc, is the historic capital of alpine skiing. Chamonix, the site of the first winter Olympic games in 1924, lies huddled in a valley almost at the junction of France, Italy, and Switzerland. Dedicated skiers all over the world know of its ten-mile **Vallée Blanche** run, considered one of the most rugged in Europe, certainly the longest. Daredevils also flock here for mountain climbing and hang-gliding.

A charming, old-fashioned mountain town, Chamonix has a most thrilling backdrop—**Mont Blanc,** Europe's highest mountain, rising to a peak of 15,780 feet. When two Englishmen, Windham and Pococke, first visited Chamonix in 1740, they were thrilled at its location, and later wrote a travel book making the village known around the world. When their guide was published, it was believed that no human foot had yet trod on Mont Blanc. In the summer of 1786 Jacques Balmat became the first man to climb the mountain. In the old quarter of town a memorial to this brave pioneer stands in front of the village church.

With the opening of that seven-mile miracle **Mont Blanc Tunnel,** Chamonix became a major stage on one of the busiest highways in Europe. The tunnel provides the easiest way to go through the mountains to Italy by literally going *under* those mountains. Motorists now stop at Chamonix even if they aren't interested in winter skiing or summer mountain climbing. Toll rates for the tunnel depend on the distance between the axles of the vehicle being taken through. Most visitors will be interested in either one-way or round-trip passage, since they won't be interested in a ten-passage ticket, for which rates are slightly cheaper. One-way passage for most cars is either 90F ($12.41) or 115F ($15.86), while one-way passage for most motorcycles is 60F ($8.27). Round-trip passage for most cars is either 110F ($15.17) or 145F ($20), while for most motorcycles it's 75F ($10.32).

Because of its exceptional equipment, Chamonix is one of the major sports resorts of Europe, attracting a sophisticated international crowd. It has 13 chair lifts, 28 surface lifts, 7 gondolas, and 7 cable cars, all facilities available for just one ski-lift pass.

The **Casino de Chamonix** is the hub of its nightlife activity. It's open daily from 4 p.m. to 4 a.m. A passport is required. You can also dine at the Casino's **Le Royal** restaurant (tel. 50-53-07-65), where meals begin at 250F ($34.48). Teas and dinner dances are offered in the grill room, and at the tables you can play such games as roulette, boule, and chemin de fer. In the casino club, live shows are presented.

The **Office du Tourisme** at the Place de l'Église (tel. 50-53-00-24) will provide information on all aspects of the attractions of Chamonix.

CABLE-CAR RIDES: The belvederes that can be reached from Chamonix by cable cars or mountain railways are famous.

In the heart of town you can board a cable car heading for the Aiguille du

Midi and on to Italy, a harrowing journey. The first stage of the trip, a nine-minute run to the **Plan des Aiguilles** at an altitude of 7,544 feet, isn't so alarming. But the second stage, to an altitude of 12,602 feet, the **Aiguille du Midi** station, may make your heart sink, especially when the car rises 2,000 feet between towers.

At the summit you are 1,110 yards from the peak of Mont Blanc. From the belvedere you have a commanding view of the Aiguilles of Chamonix and the Vallée Blanche, the largest glacier in Europe (9.3 miles long and 3.7 miles wide). You also have a panoramic view for 125 miles of the Jura and the French, Swiss, and Italian Alps.

You leave the tram station along a chasm-spanning narrow bridge leading to the third cable car and the glacial fields that lie beyond. Or you can end your journey at Aiguille du Midi, returning to Chamonix. Generally the cable cars operate all year. Summer departures are from 6 a.m. to 5 p.m., leaving at least every half hour. In winter the hours are from 8 a.m. to 4 p.m., leaving every hour. The round-trip fare to the Aiguille du Midi station is about 90F ($12.41). The return fare from Chamonix to Pointe Helbronner is 145F ($20). For information about other cable-car rides and fares, call the **Société Touristique du Mont-Blanc** at 50-53-30-80.

For the final lap of the trip you go across high mountains and pass jagged needles of rock and ice bathed in a dazzling light. The final trip to **Pointe Helbronner** in Italy—at an altitude of 11,355 feet—requires a passport if you wish to leave the station and descend on two more cable cars to the village of Courmayeur. From there you can go to nearby Entrèves to dine at **La Maison de Filippo**, called a "chalet of gluttony," the Chamonix visitor's favorite restaurant across the border in Italy. The round trip from Chamonix to Pointe Helbronner is 150F ($20.69). After all that, you may swear off cable cars for life. However, another aerial cableway takes you up to **Brévent** at an altitude of 8,284 feet. From here you'll have a first-rate view (frontal) of Mont Blanc and the Aiguilles de Chamonix. The trip takes about 1½ hours round trip. Cable cars operate all year except from November 1 to December 15, beginning at 8 a.m., shutting down at 5 p.m. In summer, departures are at least every half hour. The price of a round-trip ticket is 50F ($6.90).

A final aerial goal might be to **Le Montenvers,** at an altitude of 6,276 feet. Here, from the belvedere at the end of the cable-car run, you'll have a view of the celebrated **Mer de Glace,** or sea of ice, which is four miles long. The **Aiguille du Dru** is a rock climb notorious for its difficulty. The trip takes 1½ hours, including a return by rail. Departures are from 8 a.m. until 6 p.m. in summer or 4:30 p.m. in winter. The round-trip fare is 45F ($6.21).

As a curiosity, you can visit a cave hollowed out of the Mer de Glace. A cable car connects it with the upper resort of Montenvers, the trip taking just three minutes. The fare is 10F ($1.38). To enter the cave costs an additional 10F ($1.38). There is, as well, a small zoo containing such animals as bison, nutria, beaver, and marten. The zoo may be visited June 15 to October 5 from 9 a.m. to 7 p.m. for a 10F ($1.38) admission.

Reader Jeffrey Stanton of Marina del Rey, California, reports: "This third leg of the journey was acclaimed an engineering triumph when it was built in the early 1960s. Its three miles of cables are supported in only two intermediate places. Because support towers can't be placed on a glacier, one of the two intermediate supports is another cable attached to two adjacent peaks. The cars—traveling in threes to facilitate loading—at an altitude of 600 feet above the chasm-scarred glaciers, pass stupendous mountain vistas on the flank of Mont Blanc. On the Italian side, you can watch skiers on the snowfields even in summer."

WHERE TO STAY: Mapotel Alpina, 79 Avenue du Mont-Blanc (tel. 50-53-47-77). Prominently situated in the center of town, this contemporary hotel looks like a collection of cement and glass cubes stacked on top of one another. The decor is functional and trendy. A chic ski crowd can be seen in the early evening, lounging on the colonial-style furniture. The compact bedrooms each contain private bath, phone, big windows, color TV, and mini-bar. Depending on the season and the exposure (rooms with a view of Mont Blanc cost more), singles rent for 300F ($41.37) to 450F ($62.06), and doubles cost 325F ($44.82) to 480F ($66.19). The hotel is closed from October to mid-December and from mid-April to mid-May.

Hôtel Mont-Blanc et Restaurant Le Matafan, Place de l'Église (tel. 50-53-05-64), enjoys a setting in tranquil gardens, with its own swimming pool and tennis courts. It also has one of the finest dining rooms at the resort. The seven-story, overscale villa has shuttered windows and balconies, plus a double-decker sun terrace, looking due south onto the Aiguille du Midi and the Mont-Blanc massif. The Morand family owners close the hotel from October 15 through December 15 but are open otherwise, charging from 600F ($82.74) in a single, 920F ($126.87) in a double, including full board. The rooms have been completely renovated and furnished in a rustic style, with pine paneling. Each has its own private bath and telephone.

Food is served in the impressive main dining room, featuring a circular raised fireplace with a wood-faced hood. Separated from the main dining room is the cozy restaurant-bar, Le Matafan, a favorite summer or winter rendezvous for ski teachers, mountain guides, and tourists. A specialty is mountain lake fish. The set meal on one recent occasion featured smoked salmon, followed by grilled tournedos with béarnaise sauce, plus a salad and a selection from the cheese board, climaxed by dessert. Set menus range from 180F ($24.82) to 220F ($30.34).

L'Auberge du Bois Prin, aux Moussoux (tel. 50-53-33-51). *Bois prin* means kindling wood, and you'll certainly be able to gather lots of it in the hills that surround this isolated 11-room guest house. It was built in 1976 by the Carrier family, who still maintain the attractive wood-lined interior, the garden, the encircling stone terraces, the cut-out balconies, and the flagstone roofs. Some of the upper bedrooms are in a charming antique style, with upholstered headboards and views of the Chamonix Valley and Mont Blanc. Depending on the season, room rents start at 480F ($66.19) for singles, 760F ($104.80) in a double. All accommodations have private bath, and triples or quads are available as well. The popular hotel restaurant serves both lunch and dinner. The entire establishment shuts down from early May to early June and mid-October to mid-December.

Hôtel Albert 1er et de Milan, 119 impasse Montenvert (tel. 50-53-05-09), is an expanded mountain chalet run by Mr. and Mrs. Marcel Carrier. Set in the center of the resort, it is surrounded by its own informal flower gardens and a tennis court. From every window there is a view. Even the vision-clear dining windows provide panoramas of Mont Blanc. In winter clients meet for convivial gatherings around the open fireplace. The rooms are of decent size, many opening onto balconies, and they are traditionally furnished with reproductions in classic French styles. In all, 32 rooms are rented out at rates ranging from 290F ($39.99) in a single to a peak 500F ($68.95) in a double. Full-board terms are 330F ($45.51) to 415F ($57.23) per person daily. The hotel is closed from mid-April to mid-May and from early October to late November. Even if you aren't a guest, you may want to call for a table at dinner, as the food is among the best served in Chamonix, a meal costing from 130F ($17.93) to 320F ($44.13). Specialties include a terrine de saumon (salmon) sauce corail, ris de veau (sweetbreads) with crayfish, and an escalope with morels.

Au Bon Coin, 80 Avenue de l'Aiguille-du-Midi (tel. 50-53-15-67), is the inexpensive little domain of René Moggino, who gives you a gracious welcome. The two-star hotel has much modern comfort and clean, well-kept rooms, often with views of the surrounding mountainside. Autumnal colors predominate. The chambers also contain private baths and terraces where you can soak up the sun, even in winter. Au Bon Coin is chalet style, charging 180F ($24.82) in a single and from 220F ($30.34) in a double, including a continental breakfast. The situation is tranquil, and the owner provides private parking as well as a garden. The hotel is open from July 1 until October 1 and from December 20 to April 20.

Les Gentianes at Le Lavancher (tel. 50-54-01-31) is a wood and stucco chalet near the top of one of Chamonix's most scenic suburbs. A car is practically essential unless a visitor wants to feel completely isolated from everything, which some of the clientele here seem to enjoy. Monsieur Ragon, the owner, set up 14 rooms here in 1965. Some of the sunny, clean, and simple units offer a good view of Mont Blanc. With half board figured in, the per-person rates range from 220F ($30.34) to 275F ($37.92), depending on the accommodation. It is open from June to mid-September, mid-December to early January, and late January to mid-April.

WHERE TO DINE: Since most guests dine at their hotels, Chamonix has few outstanding independent restaurants, with the following exception.

La Tartiffle, rue des Moulins (tel. 50-53-20-02). Nelly duFour, a nonskiing, blue-eyed grandmother, is one of Chamonix's rare entrepreneurs who takes the business of maintaining ancient Savoyard customs seriously. Many of the dishes served in her three-level restaurant are based on 18th-century mountain recipes, which she researched just before setting up shop on the site of an inner-village barn that she tore down and rebuilt to her own taste. The items marked in red on the menu are Savoyard, and you'll find among them a cheese fondue with polenta (which is excellent), potée savoyarde aux charcuterie du pays, and a Savoyard omelet, made with an assortment of cheeses from the region. Meals range from 105F ($14.48) to 175F ($24.13).

The centuries-old poem associated with the name of the restaurant reflects the region's mountain independence. *Tartiffle* means potato in dialect. As the poem goes, "I would prefer to be free rather than to eat the government's potatoes." The restaurant is closed from May to mid-June and October to mid-December.

5. Megève

Called a *cité verte,* Megève is famous as a summer resort set in pine forests, foothills, and mountain streams. But it's even better known as a charming cosmopolitan town, referred to as a *capitale du ski.* The old village with its turreted houses gathered around the church, dating from the 17th century, suggests what Megève looked like at the turn of the century. However, after 1920 the new town came along, attracting people who like to go to the mountains just for fun and not just those fanatical about skiing, although they come in hordes too. Megève was made popular by the Baroness de Rothschild.

Tennis, horseback riding, and cable railways add to the attractions. There are wide views of the Mont Blanc area from the top of each ski lift. The range of amusements includes a casino, nightclubs, discos, dancing, and shows. At the foot of Mont Blanc, Megève is actually one of the best equipped of the French winter sports resorts, a social center of international status.

In the environs you can take a chair hoist to **Mont d'Arbois,** at an altitude of 6,000 feet. Here a magnificent panorama unfolds, including not only Mont Blanc but the Fis and Aravis massifs. Cable service is from July 1 to September 15 at every half hour, beginning at 9 a.m. and ending at 7 p.m. To reach the station take the Route du Mont d'Arbois from the center of the resort, going past the golf course.

From 2 p.m. to 6 a.m. the center of the old village is closed to traffic, except the pedestrian variety and sledges. You can shop at leisure (some 200 tradespeople await your service, ranging from a cobbler to an antique dealer, along with many boutiques).

The **Ski School** (tel. 50-21-00-97) is one of the foremost in Europe, with 184 monitors as well as 32 children's instructors. Collective courses include the complete French skiing method, as well as alpine skiing and ski touring.

Much improvement has been made in recent years in sports facilities, including the skiing area of Le Jaillet, now linked with Combloux by the latest type of six-seater telecabine, carrying 1,800 passengers per hour, or the Essertons chair lift serving challenging trails, or the Prés chair lift between Le Jaillet and Le Christomet. The Rocharbois cable car now links Rochebrune and Mont d'-Arbois mountains. A high-capacity gondola connects Megève and Mont d'-Arbois.

The **Megève Relais des Sports et des Congrès** (Sports Palace and Assembly Hall) (tel. 50-21-15-71) is for ice sports, swimming, tennis, meetings, and often shows and gala festivals. It's a complex of two swimming pools with solarium, saunas, an Olympic-size skating rink, a curling track, a body-building room, a dance salon, bar, restaurant, gymnasium, tennis courts, auditorium, conference rooms, and exhibition gallery.

WHERE TO STAY: Megève has several accommodations, ranging from deluxe to budget:

A Deluxe Choice

Hôtel Mont Blanc, Place de l'Église (tel. 50-21-20-02). Clients from as far away as Paris scheme to get a room here during high season. Built in 1970, this is the elegant number-one choice in town, in the village center near the church. Its elaborate chalet balconies are recognizable from a distance, while the warmly patterned interior offers comfortable, velvet-covered chairs amid Oriental rugs, modern sculptures, attractive accessories, and small-scale charm.

The 60 bedrooms are extremely well furnished and soundproofed, with private baths, balconies, and all the modern conveniences. Half-board rates range from 1,050F ($144.80) to 1,400F ($193.06) per person. Suites, of course, cost even more. The hotel's garage will keep your car warm. The hotel restaurant, Les Enfants Terribles, is covered separately below.

The Medium-Priced Range

Castel-Champlat (tel. 50-21-25-49) is a white five-story corner building on a street corner in the heart of the resort. It has a rustically modern decor of oak trim and travertine floors and is surprisingly simple, yet such singers and stars as Petula Clark and Bardot have stayed there. Owned for some 35 years by the Morand family, this is a turn-of-the-century building that was radically renovated in the 1950s. It is closed from April 15 to July 20. The establishment offers only 19 rooms, along with a bar and restaurant. Summer rates in a double range from 300F ($41.37) to 350F ($48.27). These same doubles with bath can go as high as 500F ($68.95) in winter. The establishment maintains an annex with six apartments a short distance from the funicular, Le Chamois, for skiers about to attempt the slopes of Mont d'Arbois / Rochbrune.

Coin du Feu, Route de Rochebrune (tel. 50-21-04-94), is one of the best of the middle-bracket hotels, built in the modern grand-chalet style. It offers a lot of amenities, including an American bar and table tennis. Connections are easily made to the Rochebrune cable car. Rooms are well furnished and beautifully maintained, and the hotel is most comfortable. Only 33 rooms are available, and the cost is 500F ($68.95) in a single, 520F ($71.71) to 600F ($82.74) in a double. At night you can order good regional meals. The hotel is open from mid-December to early April and from July to early September.

Au Vieux Moulin (tel. 50-21-22-29) was named after an old mill that doesn't exist anymore, but the establishment that replaced it is a four-story stucco and wood-trimmed building with green shutters, separated from the street by a tiny pool, a lawn, and wrought-iron gates. The 33 rooms and the lobby with its coffered ceilings and black slate floors are maintained with great care by the Marchionini family, the owners. The attractively simple bedrooms, with half board, rent for 350F ($48.27) to 400F ($55.16) per person in high season. The hotel has a swimming pool and a terrace. It's open from mid-May to mid-September and mid-December to mid-April.

A Budget Inn

Perce Neige, Route de Rochebrune (tel. 50-21-22-13), blends in well with the local scene, complete with alpine-green shutters and sun-seeking balconies. Inside, the owner has attempted a more cosmopolitan style with modern furnishings. There are a total of 20 pleasantly furnished bedrooms. You can stay here on the full-board plan at a rate going from 220F ($30.34) to 250F ($34.48) per person nightly. If you're dining only, a set meal costs 75F ($10.32). The hotel is open from July to mid-September and from mid-December to early April.

WHERE TO DINE: **Au Capucin Gourmand,** rue du Crêt-du-Midi (tel. 50-21-01-98), is a rustically decorated, mountain-style restaurant owned by Guy Barbin, formerly of Bise in Talloires. Service is supervised by Barbin's attractive wife, who usually foresees virtually any request a diner may have. Specialties include Savoyard dishes, along with a blanquette of crayfish tails, fresh salmon in ginger, roast lamb, and a spicy form of Bresse pigeon. Fixed-price menus cost from 145F ($20) but are served only at lunchtime on weekdays. À la carte meals cost from 275F ($37.92) up. Dinner is served till 9:15 p.m. In summer you can dine outdoors on the open terrace if you wish. In low season the restaurant is closed Monday. It also shuts down from early April till late June and from November 1 to December 15.

Les Enfants Terribles, Hôtel du Mont-Blanc, Place de l'Église (tel. 50-21-20-02), is the acclaimed restaurant with the adjoining bar where Jean Cocteau painted the wall frescoes that gave the place its name. The bar might be considered one of the prime rendezvous points of the *enfants terribles* who posture for one another during their vacations in Megève, although the well-decorated restaurant serves a highly refined menu to a faithful crowd. Menu items are often prepared with expensive extras such as truffles, foie gras, and fine wines. Try, for example, the steak Enfants Terribles. Chef Laïb prepares a classic cuisine. Locally inspired dishes are also popular. Dinner is served daily until midnight either indoors or on a covered terrace during warm weather. Set menus range from 170F ($23.44) to 240F ($33.10), or you can enjoy an à la carte selection for around 300F ($41.37) or more. Closed mid-April to late May and September to late October.

Le Prieuré, Place de l'Église (tel. 50-21-01-79). Menu specialties in this Savoy-style tavern include the full scope of local fare, plus several dishes from outside the region. Examples are alpine-style dried beef as an appetizer, omble (lake fish) with sorrel, a wide selection of beef and veal plates, and savory filets of perch. You are served by a battery of polite waitresses who work hard to see that you are well taken care of, either in the dining room or on the terrace in warm weather. A fixed-price menu is offered for around 150F ($20.69), with your tab going up to 210F ($28.96) to 250F ($34.48) if you prefer to use the à la carte list. The restaurant is open daily except Monday, from early September until just before Christmas, and from Easter until July.

6. Albertville

It would be easy to miss the center of Albertville if a motorist isn't paying attention. The road leading up to it runs alongside a river for miles before the town limits, and the trees practically block the view from the main road. It is one of the gourmet centers of the Savoy.

The origins of the town date from centuries ago, with a city called Conflans, whose confines are surrounded by the modern settlement of Albertville. Within its narrow streets, where traffic is prohibited in high season, lie a church, a Grande Place with an 18th-century fountain, a collection of medieval buildings occupied by artisans and craftspeople, and a municipal museum, **Musée des Conflans** (tel. 79-32-57-42), which is contained within the Maison Rouge. This displays old utensils, local carvings, prehistoric mementos, and furniture. The Maison Rouge was a 13th-century convent later transformed into a military arsenal. In June, July, August, and September, it's open from 10 a.m. till noon and 2 to 7 p.m. From Easter till May 31 it's open only in the afternoon. Admission is 7F (97¢).

FOOD AND LODGING: Hôtel Million, 8 Place de la Liberté (tel. 79-32-25-15), was established in 1790 by an ancestor of Philippe Million, the current owner and chef whose cuisine did much to put Albertville on the gastronomic map. The operation is contained within a white-walled building with strong horizontal lines, gables, and a position on a flagstone-covered square set back from the main artery running through town. The spacious public rooms include an elegant salon and a peach-colored dining room whose staff offers a proper genteel welcome. Each of the 29 bedrooms contains a private bath and lots of well-ordered space. They rent for 250F ($34.48) in a single to 350F ($48.27) for a double.

The richly decorated restaurant offers fixed-price menus at anywhere from 150F ($20.69) to 420F ($57.92). The reputation of chef Million has attracted what has become almost a cult following throughout the region. He prepares such specialties as petals of pigeon in a goose-liver gelée, red snapper and prawns with an orange vinaigrette, scallops with roasted shallots, ravioli in a lobster nage, duck with watercress and turnips, apricots with a pistachio coulis, and caramel feuillantine. There's a pleasant outdoor terrace for summer dining.

The hotel is closed from late April to mid-May and from late September to early October. The restaurant is closed Monday, except at night from mid-July to the first of September. It is also closed Sunday night all year.

Chez Uginet, 8 Place Charles-Albert (tel. 79-32-00-50), is directed by Alain and Nicole Rayé, who prepare delicate combinations of food that merit a stop in Albertville for at least one meal. In a stone building high on a bank above the river, connected to the quiet road with a long causeway, the restaurant contains a discreet and elegant decor. The 60 seats have held a varied collection of diners, including, one day last winter, 12 European ski champions who came in for dinner together. You'll be able to communicate with Nicole in English, if you wish. She'll probably advise you to order one of the house specialties, which might, on any given day, be Brittany lobster; soup of scallops with essence of sea urchins; sweetbreads with truffles; a "mosaic" of foie gras, duckling, and vegetables; a soup of crayfish with ginger; and an unusual blend of pralines and pears, with essence of strawberries for dessert.

Menus range from 150F ($20.69) to 340F ($46.89). There's a terrace with a view of the rushing river where you can enjoy a leisurely warm-weather dinner. The Rayés close their restaurant on Tuesday, for two weeks between late June and early July, and from mid-November to early December.

7. Annecy

On Lac d'Annecy, the jewel of the Savoy Alps, the resort of Annecy makes the best excursion base for touring Haute-Savoie. The former capital of the counts of Geneva, Annecy opens onto one of the best views of lakes and mountains in the French Alps.

The resort is dominated by **Château d'Annecy,** its Queen's Tower dating from the 12th century. It was in this castle that the counts of Geneva took refuge in the 13th century. You can go up to the castle and look out upon the town's roofs and belfries. The museum is open daily except Tuesday from 10 a.m. to noon and 2 to 6 p.m., charging 6F (83¢) for admission. Students and children are admitted at half price.

Canals cut through the old part of town, **Annecy-le-Vieux,** and because of this Annecy has been called "the Venice of the Alps." You can explore the arcaded streets of the old town where Jean-Jacques Rousseau arrived in 1728, sent there in the hope that the charismatic Mme de Warens could save his soul from heresy. On the Place J-J-Rousseau, the house where the madame once lived has disappeared, but not her memory. There is a little monument with Rousseau's bust in the courtyard.

After exploring Annecy, I suggest a visit to **Les Gorges du Fier,** six miles from Annecy, a 12-minute run by train from the Lovagny station (the Aix-les-Bains line). You can also go to the **Office de Tourisme,** 1 rue Jean-Jaurès (tel. 50-45-00-33), and get the latest schedule of daily motorcoach trips offered. This striking gorge is considered one of the most interesting sights in the French Alps. A gangway takes visitors through a winding gully, varying from 10 to 30 feet wide. The gully was cut by the torrent through the rock and over breathtaking depths. You'll hear the roar of the river at the bottom. Emerging from this labyrinth, you are greeted by a huge expanse of boulders—a "sea of rocks." The gorge is open from Easter to October, the tour taking less than an hour and costing 15F ($2.07). It remains open from 9 a.m. to 6 p.m. (till 7 p.m. in July and August).

In the area, you can also visit the 14th-century **Château de Montrottier** at Lovagny (tel. 50-46-23-02). From its tower a view of Mont Blanc unfolds. The château contains pottery, Oriental costumes, armor, tapestries, and antiques, as well as some bronze bas-reliefs by Peter and Hans Vischer of Nürnberg, their art dating from the 15th century. The castle is open daily from Easter to mid-October from 9 a.m. to noon and 2 to 6 p.m., charging 15F ($2.07) for admission. You're shown through on a conducted tour.

Of course, one of the most interesting excursions is a tour of **Lac d'Annecy.** These tours are available from Easter until the end of September. In July and August there are at least 12 steamers leaving from Annecy. It's best to take a combined ticket, costing 75F ($10.32) and allowing visitors to cruise the lake and take a cable car—called a téléphérique—to **Mont Veyrier.** In seven minutes you take a 2,600-foot jump to the top of the mountain at 4,280 feet. From the mountain's rocky slopes, a panoramic view unfolds—considered one of the most beautiful belvederes in the French Alps. If you're planning to tour the mountain, allow another hour in your schedule.

WHERE TO STAY: Hôtel des Trésoms et de la Forêt, 3 Boulevard de la Corniche (tel. 50-51-43-84), is the best place to stay in Annecy, certainly the most tranquil and scenically positioned of all the hotels near the town. It's actually more of an attractive private villa than a hotel—set in its own three acres of a promontory overlooking Lac d'Annecy, the Alps, and the town. The hotel is a substantial villa, painted white with cherry-red shutters. Try to get a lake-view room if possible. However, all the accommodations are pleasant and attractively furnished, costing from 265F ($36.54) in a single, from 450F ($62.06) in a double with complete private bath. The rooms have a Swiss cleanliness. The wines of the region are gently handled and reasonably priced. The food is traditional and wholly reliable. If you're touring in the area, you can call up and reserve a table, ordering a complete meal from 185F ($25.51) to 225F ($31.03). The hotel is open only from April 1 until the end of October.

Hôtel La Réserve, 21 Avenue d'Albigny (tel. 50-23-50-24). Set across the road with a view of the ducks and swans paddling across the lake, this red-shuttered Beaux Arts villa is crafted from stucco and stone. The Eigenmann family is technically of Swiss citizenship despite owning this hotel for the past quarter of a century. The simple interior is sunny, marble trimmed, and graced with ornate ceilings. The upstairs contains 12 bedrooms, which rent for 280F ($38.61) in a single, 320F ($44.13) in a double. All have private bath or shower, color TV, and a lot of high-ceilinged, old-fashioned charm. The Réserve's restaurant has big windows, fresh flowers, flowered Limoges porcelain, and good food. You might have a meal of duckling with cherries, veal kidneys with tarragon, tournedos with morels, escalope of fresh salmon with lemon and olive oil, or a fera (fish from the lake) grenobloise. You'll pay 140F ($19.31) to 180F ($24.82) for a set menu. Full board costs from 380F ($52.40) to 440F ($60.68) per person, depending on the accommodation. Both the hotel and the restaurant are open daily except for the period just before Christmas to late January and for the last week in June and the first week in July.

At Chavoires, three miles from Annecy, Le Pavillon de L'Ermitage (tel. 50-60-11-09) is another charming candidate for lakeside tranquility seekers, although the villa is in the environs. A long, distinguished-looking, white-painted villa, it is set right on the water, in the midst of vineyards. It even has its own boat landing. The rooms are comfortable and well furnished, but most guests come here to enjoy the food. Maurice Tuccinardi competes with the Auberge de Savoie (recommended below) in his cuisine. His dining room offers lakeside views, and in summer guests can eat out on the terrace under a cool, leafy arbor. Three menus are featured at 160F ($22.06), 210F ($28.96), and 280F ($38.61). If you order à la carte, expect a bill ranging from 275F ($37.92). Specialties include omble chevalier (char), a fish somewhat like a trout found in the deep lakes of Savoy. It is prepared like salmon trout. Other main dishes are a soufflé de brochet (pike) and poularde de Bresse. Incidentally, I highly recommend the latter offering, because chicken from the ancient part of France known as Bresse has been eulogized by many gourmets, its praise sung in verse by many poets. The hotel contains only a dozen bedrooms, and these rent for 280F ($38.61) in a single, rising to a peak 420F ($57.92) in a double with private bath. The Pavillon is open from March till the first of November.

Bargain seekers may also be drawn to the Super Panorama (tel. 50-45-34-86), on the route du Semnoz, about 1½ miles from the heart of Annecy. With a name like that, this simple little inn had better have a view to sell, and it does. Admirably situated, the hotel opens onto a splendid vista of lake and mountain. You can sit out on the terrace enjoying it, or take a promenade in many directions. The hotel rents out only five bedrooms, which are modestly furnished. In season, half board is obligatory, at a rate of 220F ($30.34) per person daily. This is one of the best values offered at this lakeside resort, considering that the alpine food is good and hearty and the portions of generous size. The hotel is closed from January 5 to mid-February and on Tuesday.

WHERE TO DINE: One of the best restaurants in Annecy—and this has been true since I first dined there back in 1959—is the Hôtel de Savoie, 1 Place St-François (tel. 50-45-03-05). Many of the townspeople prefer this restaurant as a luncheon rendezvous, although I gravitate to it in the evening when it is quieter. The setting is rustic, the cookery exceptional in a robust, regional sense. The atmosphere is informal, and such local wines as Crépy and Roussette are served at reasonable prices. To begin your meal, I recommend a terrine of pike served with a beurre neige, roughly translated as "snow butter." The chef is at his most skillful when preparing a saddle of lamb served with a game sauce. His most noteworthy dessert is a soufflé glacé aux noisettes. If featured, his tarragon chicken and his crayfish bordelaise are highly recommendable. Expect to pay from 160F ($22.06) to 250F ($34.48) for a complete meal. The restaurant shuts down from June 15 to July 15, on Tuesday night from October to June, and on Wednesday night year round.

Le Belvédère, a mile out Route du Semnoz (tel. 50-45-04-90). Born in La Rochelle, the patron, Jean-Louis Aubeneau, grew up with the sound of the ocean in his ear and fish on the table every night. Although he has long since moved to the Alps, he carries his heritage of the sea with him, offering the finest seafood cookery in all of Annecy, inventing dishes of his own instead of relying on classic methods of preparation. Call for a table at lunch or dinner, and you'll also get a good view of the lake. I recommend his pot-au-feu of the ocean, a marvelous meal, or perhaps his turbot sautéed with three different kinds of pepper. He also makes a soup of scallops with little strips of vegetables cut in the julienne fashion that is filled with flavor, and his masterful touch is reflected in his stuffed brill with red mullet mousse and a caviar-laced sauce to add the proper zest. Menus are offered at 160F ($22.06), 200F ($27.58), and 275F ($37.92). Monsieur Aubeneau also rents 11 simply furnished rooms which have beautiful views of the lake. Full board is obligatory in season, costing 235F ($32.41) to 260F ($35.85) per person. The hotel is only open from May 1 to September 30. The restaurant is closed on Sunday night and Monday, as well as in November and for 15 days in April.

8. Talloires

Eight miles from Annecy is my preferred spot on Lake Annecy, the charmingly situated village of Talloires. Chalk cliffs surround a pleasant bay. At the lower end a wooden promontory encloses a small port. An 18-hole golf course and water sports such as skiing, boating, swimming, and fishing make this a favorite spot with French holiday makers.

Talloires is a gourmet citadel, containing one of France's great restaurants, the Auberge du Père Bise, and a Benedictine abbey founded here in the 11th century but now transformed into a deluxe hotel. First, the restaurant, in case you're just motoring through.

Auberge du Père Bise (tel. 50-60-72-01) is an elegant chalet restaurant in a private park at an enchanting spot on the lake. One food critic called its viands "gastronomic fantasies." It's a joyous recommendation for those who can afford the steep tariffs. Long before the automobile became popular, the Swiss came down from Geneva to dine with Père Bise, who opened his auberge at the turn of the century. Of course he's gone now, but the heirs, Monsieur and Madame François Bise, carry on in his great tradition, having inherited his secret recipes. You enter through a little tile reception lounge directly onto the spectacular kitchen with its glistening copper pots and pans. The kitchen area is almost the same size as the generous dining room, with its sparkling silverware and bowls of fresh flowers. But in fair weather guests overlook even so tempting a setting and head instead for the vine-covered pergola with its view of the lake.

The chef specializes in omble chevalier, that most delicate of fish which tastes somewhat like a cross between a trout and a salmon. It appears at least four times on the menu—braised in port, with a Nantua sauce, a Vermeille sauce, and even as an entrée (meunière or with hollandaise) if you don't want to order it as a main course. Main dishes that have enraptured such guests as the late Duke of Windsor include braised pullet in a tarragon sauce, carré de présalé au feu de bois (for two persons—that is, young lamb, most delicate, which had been fattened in meadows along the alpine lakes and cooked over a wood fire). Seasonal dishes include braised pullet with fresh morels of the type Madame du Barry personally selected for Louis XV, roebuck Grand Veneur, roasted woodcock, and jugged hare. Another specialty—*sur commande*—is volaille Souvaroff, chicken filled with foie gras and truffles, sprinkled with a quality cognac, and baked in a casserole after being sealed with dough.

Whenever one of the Rothschilds drops in, he or she naturally orders the soufflé Rothschild Grand-Marnier, named in their honor, although Bardot preferred the strawberries with a heavenly selection of petits-fours. The wine cellar is among the finest in France. For a regional choice, order either the Apremont or Seyssel. Menus range from 450F ($62.06) to 550F ($75.63), which is about the same as if you'd ordered à la carte. The restaurant is closed for lunch on Wednesday, all day Tuesday from February through April, and from mid-October until the end of December.

The auberge rents out bedrooms in either the main building or an annex, which might be an old house with a garden. The single rate is 600F ($82.74), with doubles paying 1,200F ($165.48). Even more expensive are apartments, costing from 1,400F ($193.06) to 2,800F ($386.12) for two persons.

Le Cottage (tel. 50-60-71-10). The brother of Père Bise, Georges Bise, founded this establishment around 1920. Nowadays his son, Fernand Bise, carries on, maintaining the high tradition. Monsieur Georges once entertained Sir Winston Churchill here. After World War I the chef cooked a banquet for President Briand, converting a spinach-hater into a spinach devotee. If you want to know what tempted that president of long ago, you can still order épinards en branches Georges-Bise here. At his terraced restaurant, the chef also specializes in the previously mentioned omble chevalier, that delicate salmon-like fish that is prepared in at least four different ways at Le Cottage. Specialties include a mousse of chicken livers, wild young duck plain roasted with fresh green pepper, and a warm strawberry soufflé. Menus are priced at 180F ($24.82), 240F ($33.10), and 320F ($44.13). If you order à la carte, count on spending from 300F ($41.37).

The Cottage also offers 34 rooms, elegantly furnished and most comfortable, in traditional French styling. The rooms rent for 550F ($75.63) in a single to a high of 800F ($110.32) in one of the luxuriously appointed double rooms with complete private bath. The Cottage receives guests from mid-March to mid-October.

Nearby, the old Benedictine abbey is now **Hôtel de l'Abbaye** (tel. 50-67-40-88), a Relais et Châteaux that has entertained many an internationally known guest, including Walter Cronkite and "Baby Doc" Duvalier who fled there in 1986 after his abdication as dictator of Haiti. The abbey has been turned into one of the most exceptional character hotels in France. The building was reconstructed in the 17th century. With its own landing stage, the hotel is secluded. Used as a rest camp for the army in World War II, it was turned into a hotel again in 1945. In a former age, monks used to store wine in a cellar that is now a bar, an example of the changing times around here.

The entrance to the abbey is through an iron gateway. You stroll along shaded walks, bypassing formal French gardens. The hotel is richly outfitted with beamed ceilings, antique portraits, thick walls, modern deep leather chairs, and richly carved balustrades. The great corridors lead to converted bedchambers—no two alike—where the atmosphere of the past has been carefully preserved, although the niceties of today (telephones, private baths) have been installed. Along this lofty hall are suspended wooden balconies leading to a second level of bedrooms. The furnishings are distinguished. Hopefully, you'll get a chamber with a frescoed ceiling. There are 31 rooms in all, renting for 600F ($82.74) in a double. In season, half board (obligatory) ranges from 550F ($75.63) to 750F ($103.43) per person daily, taxes and service included. The dining room with its large wooden chandeliers was the monks' dining hall. In summer guests can also dine outside under the shade trees, enjoying a view of the lake. Lovers eventually find a secluded spot by the old moss-covered stone well. The abbey is closed from mid-December to mid-January.

Villa des Fleurs (tel. 50-60-71-14) is an attractive *restaurant avec chambres* that should be better known. The proprietors, Marie-France and Charles Jaegler, personally transformed the 1905 structure after they moved to Talloires from the Vosges some 12 years ago. Many of the attached rooms look out on the heavily pruned plane and linden trees of the rear garden. The friendly and hard-working Jaeglers produce good meals, which might include veal kidneys, giant prawns in whisky sauce, a salade landaise with foie gras, and filet of fera, which lives only in the lake at the bottom of the hotel's garden and in Lake Geneva. The food is generously and perfectly served in a big-windowed dining room with a view of the water. Fixed-price menus cost 140F ($19.31), 195F ($26.89), and 275F ($37.92). If you want to spend the night, the seven bedrooms are outfitted with modern private baths and rustic Victorian era decor. Single or double rooms rent for 320F ($44.13) each. They're at the top of a green-carpeted winding stair, and the only drawback is that there is no elevator. This is my favorite establishment in its price range in Talloires.

9. Aix-les-Bains

Forty-five miles north from Grenoble, Aix-les-Bains is the most fashionable spa of eastern France and one of the largest. Its hot springs, which offered comfort to the Romans, are said to be useful in the treatment of rheumatism. The spa is well equipped for visitors, containing flower gardens, a casino (the Palais de Savoie), a race course, a golf course, and a lake, Lac du Bourget, with a bathing beach.

It was at Aix-les-Bains that Lamartine, the French poet (author of *Poetic Meditations*), met the doctor's wife, Julie Desherettes, the "Elvire" of his early poems and the inspiration for his most famous piece, "Le Lac," composed in the autumn of 1817. His "Elvire" died in December of that year, and romantic French schoolgirls have been weeping ever since. Balzac also described the lake in his novel *Peau de Chagrin*.

Les Thermes Nationaux d'Aix-les-Bains (tel. 79-35-38-50) are open all year long. The New Baths were launched in 1934 and later expanded and renovated in 1972, which completed the structure begun in 1857 by Victor Emmanuel II. To visit, go to the caretaker at the entrance opposite the Hôtel de Ville, which is the former château of the marquises of Aix in the 16th century. Before you enter the baths you can visit the thermal caves. Once inside, you can see vestiges of the Roman baths. The baths are open from April till the end of October daily, except Sunday and holidays, beginning at 3 p.m. Admission is 3F (41¢).

Also in the center of the spa are two other Roman remains—a **Temple of Diana,** a square building, and the **Arch of Campanus,** a triumphal arch 30 feet high.

The spa's most interesting museum is the **Musée du Docteur-Faure,** Boulevard des Côtes (tel. 79-61-06-57), where you'll find a modern art collection, including watercolors by Rodin plus works by Degas, Corot, and Cézanne. It is open in summer daily except Tuesday, from 10 a.m. to noon and 2 to 6 p.m., charging an admission of 5F (69¢). In winter it is open until 4 p.m. every day except Monday and Tuesday.

You can take a bus ride from Aix to the small town of Revard at an altitude of 5,080 feet, where you'll be rewarded with a panoramic view of Mont Blanc.

Regular steamer service takes you on a four-hour boat ride on **Lac du Bourget,** a beautiful trip. For information about departure times (which change seasonally), consult the **Office de Tourisme,** Place M-Mollard (tel. 79-35-05-92). Boats depart from the landing stage at Grand Port.

The **Abbaye Royale de Hautecombe** can also be visited on a boat trip, with two to five steamers leaving every day from Easter until September 30. To board a boat, go also to the landing stage at Grand Port. The price is 25F ($3.45), the trip takes 2½ hours. The abbey, which has been called the Saint-Denis of Savoy, is the mausoleum of the princes of the House of Savoy. It stands on a promontory jutting out into the lake. It is open to the public from 10:30 a.m. to noon and 2 to 6 p.m. The church was rebuilt in the 19th century in what is called the "Troubadour Gothic" style. If you'd like, you are permitted to attend mass in Gregorian chant on Sunday at 9:15 a.m. and on weekdays at 9:30 a.m. Vespers are at 6 p.m. in summer, at 5 p.m. in winter. There are no organized visits on Monday.

Visitors can also look at a monastic exposition close to the landing stage of the abbey in a 12th-century Cistercian barn. For more information, call 79-54-26-12.

WHERE TO STAY: Hôtel Ariana, Avenue de Marlioz (tel. 79-88-08-00), is the most up-to-date hotel in town, catering to a spa-oriented clientele who enjoy taking quiet walks through the surrounding park. The hotel was built in 1983 next to the baths of the Marlioz Institute, on the outskirts of town. The stylized glass and loggia-dotted exterior opens into a modernized art deco interior highlighted by repeating curves, contrasting shades of metal, wood, and fabrics, and plenty of white marble and carpeting. Tunnel-like glass walkways connect it to the therapeutic outbuildings. Depending on the season, half board ranges from 275F ($37.92) to 620F ($85.50) per person, based on double occupancy. All accommodations contain private bath, loggia, radio, color TV, and phone.

Hostellerie le Manoir, 37 rue Georges-1er (tel. 79-61-44-00), in the Parc du Splendide-Royal, is an old building with a rustic decoration that has the look of a country house in bygone times. Within walking distance of the thermal center, it is pervaded with charm. Pathways weave in and about the old-world gardens in which outdoor furniture has been placed under shade trees. Guests order breakfast or dinner, weather permitting, on an attractive terrace bordering the garden. Most of the public rooms, as well as the bedrooms, open onto terraces and flowering shrubbery. The white-stucco hotel with its shutters has an overhanging roof. The interior furnishings are traditional, with a sprinkling of antiques. The dining hall has large wooden beams, a tall, open fireplace, and a center that opens onto a wooden mezzanine. Here a good cuisine is served, costing 120F ($16.55) to 190F ($26.20) for a set menu. I've enjoyed smoked salmon, trout cooked in vermouth, peppersteak, gnocchi, and a mouthwatering strawberry tart. The chef also does an excellent pâté de campagne.

The bedrooms are well furnished, with chintz draperies and provincial pieces. Each has its own private bath and telephone. The rate is 250F ($34.48) in a single, peaking at 375F ($51.71) in a double. You can ask for full-board rates, going for anywhere from 260F ($35.85) to 420F ($57.92) per person. The manor shuts down from Christmas to late January.

WHERE TO DINE: One of the best restaurants, Lille, le Grand Port (tel. 79-35-04-22), stands near the landing stages where you can get steamers for tours of Lac du Bourget. It is also possible to secure an accommodation here, as the inn rents out 18 simply furnished rooms at prices that begin at 235F ($32.41) in a single, going up to 260F ($35.85) in the best double. The hotel is closed January 1 to March 1 and on Wednesday.

But most guests go here for the superb cuisine. The food, under the direction of Georges Lille, is rich and quite subtle. The chef's preferred dish is ombre chevalier (char), a fish somewhat like a trout found in the deep lakes of Savoy. Here it's made all the more elegant as it's cooked in champagne. I also recommend the chicken "Mère Lille," and, in season only, a raspberry soufflé which is the best I've ever enjoyed anywhere. Featured wines are Gamay and Roussette.

In season you can dine out on the large shaded terrace. Menus are priced from a relatively modest 120F ($16.55), going up to 290F ($39.99). If you order à la carte, expect to spend from 250F ($34.48) to 300F ($41.37) per person.

Davat, also at Grand Port (tel. 79-35-09-63), is not only another leading restaurant but also an excellent and modestly priced place at which to stay in beautiful surroundings. Its chief attraction is its lovely flower garden with potted plants and singing birds. Again, its bedrooms, 20 in all, are simply furnished, costing from 240F ($33.10) in a single to 320F ($44.13) in a double. Guests at the Davat are allowed to take the full-board terms, ranging from 320F ($44.13) per person. The cooking is robust, the drinking of regional wines most pleasurable, and the service is warm and gracious. If you're visiting only for a meal, you'll find one of the best set menus at the spa, costing only 110F ($15.17), although you could easily spend as much as 250F ($34.48). The hotel and restaurant are closed from November 1 to late March. No food is served on Tuesday.

10. Chambéry

This town, 31 miles south from Annecy, used to be the capital of an ancient sovereign state, the Duchy of Savoy. It is not as important a resort as most of the other alpine or lake centers previously considered, yet with its handsome streets, good food, and château, it has much to lure visitors. Everywhere you look are reminders of the 15th and 16th centuries.

The residence of the former dukes, **Château des Ducs de Savoie,** towering over the city, is best visited on a guided tour. The château was founded in 1232, then rebuilt in the 15th century. Its Sainte-Chapelle contained the Holy Shroud for most of the 16th century, until its removal to Turin in Italy. The chapel is in the Gothic style, construction having begun in 1408. If you're willing to climb nearly 200 steps, you will have a panoramic vista from the top of Round Tower. The underground chambers, which used to be barracks, can also be explored. Charging 18F ($2.48) for admission, the château is open daily except Sunday morning, from 10:30 a.m. to noon and 2 to 5 p.m. from mid-June to mid-September.

From the château, you can take the **rue de Boigne,** the most characteristic street in Chambéry, lined with porticoes, which will lead you to the **Fontaine des Éléphants,** erected in memory of General de Boigne (1751-1830), a native son, who left to his hometown some of the fortune he acquired in India.

In the environs you can visit **Les Charmettes,** (tel. 79-33-44-48), the handsome 17th-century country house where Jean-Jacques Rousseau lived with Madame de Warens between 1738 and 1740. The property lies 1¼ miles southeast of Chambéry. Head out the rue de la République which becomes the rue J-J-Rousseau. The bedroom of Rousseau contains his original furniture, and in the drawing room you can see Mme de Warens's clavichord. You can wander in the beautiful garden, where the madame tended her beehives, and from the terrace take in a view of the Chambéry valley. Rousseau praised the country house in his *Confessions.* You can visit here daily except Tuesday, from 10 a.m. to noon and 2 to 6 p.m. Admission is 4F (55¢).

WHERE TO STAY: Ducs de Savoie Le Grand Hôtel, 6 Place de la Gare (tel. 79-69-54-54), stands right at the railway station, a four-star international hotel of charm and dignity. Rooms are furnished with French traditional pieces. Singles are rented with shower or complete bath at rates ranging from 260F ($35.85) and doubles with private bath at 540F ($74.47). The public rooms of Le Grand are inviting, especially the disco and the Bar Américain. The hotel's restaurant, La Vanoise, serves some of the finest food in Chambéry. Menus are offered at 120F ($16.55), 180F ($24.82), and 270F ($37.23). You can take meals in summer on the terrace outside under shade trees. The restaurant is closed Sunday.

Hôtel Résidence le France, 22 Faubourg Reclus (tel. 79-33-51-18), is modern, built with balconies for its 48 streamlined and well furnished bedrooms, renting for 210F ($28.96) in a single with bath, that tariff rising to 320F ($44.13) in a double with bath. All rooms are soundproofed and air-conditioned, and taxes and service are included in the rates. Breakfast is the only meal served. The hotel has a contemporary lobby, with seats clustered around a small bar.

Hôtel des Princes, 4 rue de Boigne (tel. 79-33-45-36), is a good bargain, right in the heart of Chambéry. Its rooms are modestly appointed but clean and immaculately kept. A double with bath costs 350F ($48.27), a single going for 225F ($31.03). Some family rooms are available.

If you have a car, you might want to stay at a little charmer outside of town, **Aux Pervenches** (tel. 79-33-34-26), at Charmettes, 1¼ miles southeast by the D4. The host and chef at this stone chalet-style inn rents out 13 bedrooms at rates ranging from 85F ($11.72) in a single to 150F ($20.69) in a double. Rooms are furnished in the typical style of a French inn, with flowery wallpaper and simple furniture. The house, open all year, stands near the Rousseau home. A good set meal is offered for 82F ($11.31), or you can order à la carte, paying from 140F ($19.31). The restaurant is warm and inviting, as an alpine dining room should be. The inn is closed from mid-August to early September and in February. The restaurant is closed Sunday night and Wednesday.

WHERE TO DINE: The best restaurant—and few critics dispute this—is **Roubatcheff,** 6 rue du Théâtre (tel. 79-33-24-91). At this charming place, which attracts the social and industrial elite of Chambéry, the dining room and kitchen are run by Jean-Philippe Roubatcheff. The restaurant is attractive, warm, and inviting, everything carefully chosen to form a backdrop for dining.

An imaginative French menu offers some dishes of nouvelle cuisine origin and some surprising Russian specialties—one does not encounter Russian dishes too often in French provincial cities. Nevertheless, Monsieur Roubatcheff specializes in blinis with smoked salmon. He also offers lamb shashlik. The chef shines even brighter with stuffed mussels that taste so fresh they must have been flown in from Brittany, pasty of wild duck, turbot with truffles, fresh salmon with mushroom sauce, and young guinea fowl cooked in raspberry vinegar. Menus are offered at 140F ($19.31), 200F ($27.58), and 320F ($44.13), with à la carte orders averaging around 300F ($41.37). The restaurant is closed on Sunday night and Monday, and from mid-June to mid-July.

If you want to dine less elegantly, and far less expensively, **La Chaumière** (Thatched Hut), 14 rue Denfert-Rochereau (tel. 79-33-16-26), serves the best fixed-price dinner in town, costing only 75F ($10.32). Quality products are used, chef Alain Boisson is skilled at doing simple French dishes, and the service is efficient and polite. Coq au vin and andouillette are the specialties. You won't go away hungry—or broke. However, the restaurant is closed one week in early March, two weeks in August, on Wednesday off-season, on Sunday, and on Saturday night from June to August.

11. Grenoble

The ancient capital of Dauphiné, this city is a major target for those exploring the heart of the French Alps. As the commercial, intellectual, and tourist center of the alpine area, it is a logical stopping-off place for motorists traveling between the Riviera and Geneva. It is a sports capital in both winter and summer. It attracts many foreign students, as its university has the largest summer-sessions program in Europe. The university occupies a modern campus on the outskirts of the city, and many buildings erected for the 1968 Olympics have been put to creative uses.

For orientation, you might head for the **Place Grenette,** which is a lively square made all the more so with beautiful alpine flowers in late spring and early summer. Everybody at some point in a busy day seems to stop off at this traffic-free mall, enjoying a drink or a cup of espresso. Pastel-colored sidewalk chairs are placed around table medallions.

This square enjoys many associations with Stendhal, who was born Henri Beyle at Grenoble in 1783 and went on to write such masterpieces as *The Red and the Black* and *The Charterhouse of Parma.* It was here that Antoine Berthet, the supposed original role model for Stendhal's Julien Sorel, was executed for attempted murder in 1827.

Having soaked up enough atmosphere, you may want to do more exploring. I suggest a ride on the **Téléférique de la Bastille.** These high-swinging cable cars run about every 12 minutes, taking you over the Isère River from 8:30 a.m. to midnight from the Quai St-Stéphane-Jay. A round trip costs 10F ($1.38). From the belvedere where you land you'll have a panoramic view of the city and the surrounding mountains. If you want to walk, you can return on foot. Signs point the way to the Parc de la Bastille and the Parc Guy-Pape, leading eventually to the **Jardin des Dauphins,** which is open in summer from 9 a.m. to 7:30 p.m. daily.

If you prefer, from the Belvédère de Grenoble you can take the **Télésiège Bastille-Mont-Jalla** for an even loftier view of the environs. To board the car in Grenoble, head for the Gare de Départ on the Quai St-Stéphane-Jay, facing the Jardin de Ville.

The next major sight is the **Musée des Beaux-Arts,** Place de Verdun (tel. 76-54-09-82), one of the best art galleries in provincial France. The collection, however, is hardly provincial. After World War I its director managed to secure a fabulous collection of modern art, and this exhibition was subsequently expanded. Today you can see Matisse's *Intérieur aux Aubergines,* Léger's *Le Remorqueur,* a Delauney, a Bonnard, a Klee, a Max Ernst, or a Gonzalez. Contemporary works include a 1968 Martial Raysse right up to Jean Dubuffet's *Mire G. 137: Kowloon,* 1983. Upstairs, you encounter more familiar masters such as Gustave Doré, Boudin, Monet, Gauguin, Matisse, Rouault, and some works by Fantin-Latour (1836-1904), the Grenoblois painter. On that floor, you will see a fine Egyptian collection. The gallery has some excellent works by Veronese, Tintoretto, Philippe de Champaigne, Le Lorrain, and Georges de la Tour. Here also you can see the well-known *Saint Grégoire Entouré de Saints* by Rubens. The museum is open from 12:30 to 7 p.m. daily except Tuesday. Admission is 8F ($1.10).

If you have time, I recommend a visit to the **Musée Dauphinois,** rue Maurice-Gignoux (tel. 76-87-66-77), which lies across the Isère in the Sainte-Marie-d'en-Haut section. Here a collection of ethnographical and historical mementos of Dauphiné have been assembled, including some beautiful bronzes. It's a cavalcade of folk arts and crafts. The museum is open daily except Tuesday, from 10 a.m. to noon and 2 to 6 p.m. Admission is 8F ($1.10).

Finally, Grenoble has a dazzling **Maison de la Culture,** designed by the architect A. Wogenscky. At the **Office du Tourisme,** 14 rue République (tel. 76-54-34-36), you can pick up a calendar listing the events of the month, everything from an exhibition of the impressionists to cinema showings, orchestral concerts, or perhaps a dance troupe from Tunisia. The cultural center is open daily except Monday, from 11 a.m. to 6 p.m. (to 7 p.m. on Sunday). Constructed in 1968, the center lies in the new quarter of Malherbe. It is closed for part of August.

WHERE TO STAY: Park Hôtel, 10 Place Paul-Mistral (tel. 76-87-29-11), is the leading modern hotel of Grenoble. A bright place, it has contemporary styling in its lounges and bedrooms, which are well kept and comfortably furnished with many amenities. The interior is tastefully classic, its furnishings a medley of both new and old. Discreet colors and black accents are used. The staff, dressed in gray flannel, is polite and helpful. The Taverne di Ripaille, open from noon to midnight, is an attractive rendezvous, luring Grenoblois and an international clientele. Singles rent for 520F ($71.71), a double costing 850F ($117.22). Varied room arrangements are offered (double beds, twins, whatever), but all of them are equipped with either shower or complete bath. Rooms are soundproofed, a necessity in traffic-busy Grenoble, and they're also air-conditioned.

Hôtel Lesdiguières, 122 Cours de la Libération (tel. 76-96-55-36), is named after the Renaissance lord of Grenoble who, under Henri IV, fortified and embellished the city. This facility serves as a training ground for the local hotel school. Everyone—including the receptionist, the bellboys, and the restaurant staff—will be fresh-faced members of the most recent graduating class, and other than an occasional seizure of shyness, all of them do just fine.

The hotel is contained on a spacious lawn at the edge of the city. The imposing premises are fashioned from gray-brown stucco with white trim and brick accents. Inside, the sunny public rooms are filled with Louis XIII chairs, Oriental rugs, and elegant accessories. Set menus in the dining room cost 145F ($20) and 170F ($23.44), with a slightly more expensive à la carte meal offered in the evening only. The elevator will take you to one of the 36 well-furnished bedrooms, each containing a private bath or shower. Singles range from 200F ($36.54), to 265F ($27.58) while doubles cost from 255F ($35.17) to 320F ($44.13). The hotel shuts down from December 20 to January 4 and for all of August.

Hôtel d'Angleterre, 5 Place Victor-Hugo (tel. 76-87-37-21). Behind a classic façade, this traditional-appearing hotel, with its tall, graceful windows and wrought-iron balconies, has a sparkling contemporary interior, a reflection of a good designer at work. The hotel opens onto a pleasant square with huge chestnut trees in the center of Grenoble. The salons, with wood-grained walls and ceilings, have tropical plantings and trim, stylish furnishings. Most of the bedrooms are equally modish, with telephones, radios, TV, soundproofing, and dressing tables. On the fifth floor the units have huge old beams, a French alpine flavor with provincial furnishings. The single rate is 240F ($33.10) to 320F ($44.13), rising to 400F ($55.16) in a double. Only breakfast is served.

Stendhal, 5 rue Docteur-Mazet (tel. 76-46-21-44), is favored for its location (a block from the river) and its low prices. It has an old-fashioned French character, its pink and gray façade contrasting pleasantly with the other buildings. You stay here for the convenience and comfort of the rooms, although it looks slightly tattered. Thirty-eight bedrooms are well kept, the beds soft, and the furnishings in basic modern, with a backdrop of busy wallpaper designs. The rooms opening onto the courtyard are less noisy. Singles rent for 125F ($17.24) with water basins, and you'll pay 260F ($35.85) in a double with a private bath. Breakfast, brought to your room, is the only meal served.

Hotel Belalp, 8 Avenue Victor-Hugo (tel. 76-96-10-27). This tastefully contemporary hotel offers many sunny and well-maintained accommodations priced at 180F ($24.82) in a single, rising to 240F ($33.10) in a double. Each unit has its own private bathroom and television. The hotel sits one floor above ground level in a combination apartment/office building. There's no restaurant on the premises, but you can order drinks in a tiny bar. The location is in the suburb of Seyssinet, a mile from the center of town, along the N531. It is closed in August.

WHERE TO DINE: Poularde Bressane, 12 Place Paul-Mistral (tel. 76-87-08-90), enjoys an elegant modern setting for its superb cuisine. This place is run by Jean-Charles Piccinini, who may have an Italian ancestry as reflected by some of his specialties. In honor of the restaurant's namesake, the kitchen must offer poularde Bressane as its main specialty, and it does so agreeably well. This is a favorite dish with the urban business people, all prosperous looking, who frequent this establishment at lunch. I've known this restaurant for many years —even when it was at another location—and in the late 1970s I noticed its menus undergoing a dramatic transformation, reflecting a trend toward lighter cooking and subtler sauces. Its steamed sea bass is a case in point. The chef's fish pâté is superb, as is his red mullet flavored with basil. Try also the barbue with fresh asparagus, fresh salmon in a parsley cream sauce, and filet of sea bass with pink peppercorns. Of course, none of these actual items may be available, as the menu is very much that of a cuisine du marché—that is, based on the shopping in the market that day. Menus are offered at 150F ($20.69) to 190F ($26.20). You'll spend from 300F ($41.37) ordering à la carte. The restaurant is closed Saturday at lunchtime, Sunday, and in August.

Auberge Bressane, 38 ter. rue Beaublache (tel. 76-87-64-29), is run by its remarkable chef, Roger Décher, and is not to be confused with the previous recommendation, despite the similarity of names. Here the fortunate Dauphiné goes to dine on some outstanding regional cookery, as well as on classic dishes, enjoying such local wines as Crépy and Gamay. The most ordered dish is poulet de Bresse cooked with vinegar, although many seem to prefer the loin of lamb au Brouilly. In spring the chef offers a superb dish, a gratin of crayfish. For dessert, the pineapple soufflé may tempt you. Menus are offered at 175F ($24.13) and 225F ($31.03). The dining room is delightfully gracious, as is the service. The restaurant is closed Sunday.

Rabelais, 55 Avenue Alsace-Lorraine (tel. 76-46-03-44), serves the finest low-cost meal in Grenoble, in my opinion. A modern corner restaurant, it is next door to the Hôtel de la Gare. The least expensive menu, offered for just 55F ($7.56), is filling and well prepared, using fresh ingredients skillfully handled. For this price I recently enjoyed celeriac cut in the julienne style, served with a rémoulade sauce, followed by a côte de porc lyonnaise, potatoes, fresh peas, and then dessert. If you're flush you can also order more expensive menus with costlier ingredients at 120F ($16.55) and 160F ($22.06), the latter probably more than you'd want to eat, especially at lunchtime. The food is in the typical French fashion, and I mean that as a compliment, featuring tournedos Rabelais, a croustade of fruits de mer (seafood), a ballotine de canard (duckling), and the popular pepper steak. The Rabelais closes in August and on Friday night and Saturday.

In the Environs

At Varces, eight miles into the environs of Grenoble, **L'Escale,** Place de la République (tel. 76-72-80-19), is a honey of a place run by René Brunet, who not only serves better food than you'll find in Grenoble, but also rents out seven choice, chalet-type rooms plus five other units in a pleasant garden setting, charging 320F ($44.13) in a single, 620F ($85.50) in a double.

Monsieur Brunet seems to be in love with food, and his affection is contagious. Go here only if you have an afternoon or an evening to spend, so that you can savor every course. Always remember to reserve a table, as chef Brunet's popularity is soaring. The artist in the kitchen seems to have taken full advantage of the produce in this rich region of Dauphiné, set between the Alps and the Rhône Valley. He is likely to dazzle you with his coulibiac de saumon en croûte, cassolette of crayfish with morels, young duckling with mint and prunes, escalope of foie gras with truffles and small noodles, rascasse (a Mediterranean fish used in bouillabaisse) cooked in court-bouillon, and fresh salmon in velouté sauce with Sancerre, that pale, fresh wine that comes from a hill town in the Upper Loire. Menus are offered at 150F ($20.69) and 450F ($62.06), or you can order à la carte. The restaurant is closed Sunday night all year and Monday from mid-October to mid-March.

Chavant (tel. 76-25-15-14) lies in Bresson, a little more than 4½ miles south of Grenoble on the D5 and the D264. Follow the signs to Ebyens. This is an old farmhouse in the hills, owned and managed by an endless collection of members of the Chavant family. It contains eight well-decorated bedrooms, many with 19th-century antiques, and a well-known restaurant where you are likely to encounter good food. Jean-Pierre Chavant, the chef, worked for a period in New Orleans. His specialties include lotte with fennel sauce; escargots maison; quail stuffed with foie gras, truffles, morels, and madeira sauce; and pear cake with fresh raspberry sauce. There's likely to be a fire burning in the Louis XIII fireplace in the antique-filled salon, which might contribute to a relaxing evening.

Rooms cost from 360F ($49.64) for a single to 600F ($84.12) in a double, while meals range from 225F ($31.03) to 360F ($49.64). Dinner is served until 9:30 nightly. Closed on Wednesday and from Christmas to New Year's. In warm weather, a beautiful garden with flowers, trees, wicker chairs, and fuschia and pink napery welcomes guests into the sunshine.

A SIDE TRIP TO CHARTREUSE: A monk invented champagne, and monks have created some of the famous wines and liqueurs, but the Carthusians did not actually invent Chartreuse, the liqueur named for them. However, they are generally credited with having done so. Today they are the custodians of the ultra-secret formula of Chartreuse, which is exported around the world (the United States is the number-one foreign market). The formula was given to the Carthusians in 1605 by Marshal d'Estrées. It was an elixir involving the distillation of 130 herbs, and it was believed to have been originated by an anonymous alchemist.

Eventually the formula found its way to **La Grande Chartreuse** (or charterhouse), which was founded in 1084, about 20 miles north of Grenoble. The monastery was destroyed and rebuilt many times, the present buildings dating from 1688. The French Revolution broke up monastic orders, but somehow the monks still held onto their formula, returning to Grenoble in 1816 with the restoration of the monarchy. However, they were expelled from France again in 1903 during a period of anticlericalism. They took their recipe with them to their monastery at Tarragona in Spain where they continued making their liqueurs. They returned to La Grande Chartreuse again in 1940, shortly before the German attack on France.

The monastery is no longer open to the public, but you are allowed to visit the **Musée Cartusien** at La Correrie (tel. 76-88-60-45), in a building dating from the 15th century and standing at the head of the valley. The museum can be visited April to October from 9 a.m. to noon and 2 to 6:30 p.m. for an admission of 9F ($1.24). In this unusual museum you get a glimpse of what life is like for one of the monks, who for the most part maintain silence. The music you hear in the background is the monks chanting. The museum lies about 1½ miles from the monastery. It is closed Sunday.

For most visitors, even more interesting than the museum is a visit to **Voiron**, about 20 miles away, where the secret formula for the "Elixir of Long Life" is used at this distillery to make the famed Chartreuse. The distillery lies on the main street of town, and free visits are possible from 8 to 11:30 a.m. and 2 to 6:30 p.m. daily. Dressed in chartreuse green, a hostess will show you around, letting you view the copper stills and then taking you to the cellar, which is filled with gargantuan casks made of oak. The liqueur matures in these casks for several years. At the end of the tour you are given a free drink of the yellow Chartreuse or the fiery green one, or one of the new Chartreuse products. You can also purchase bottles at a shop on the premises. It is said that only three monks and the Father Procurator have access to the formula.

Before you head out into the Massif de la Chartreuse, in which the monastery and distillery lie, arm yourself with a good, detailed map from the tourist office in Grenoble.

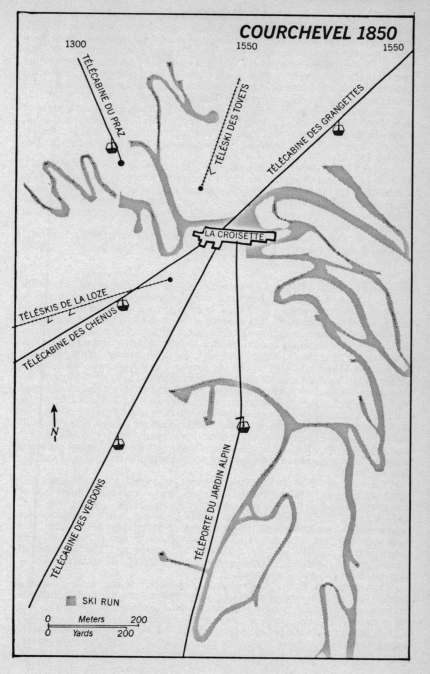

COURCHEVEL 1850

1300   1550   1550

TÉLÉCABINE DU PRAZ

TÉLÉSKI DES TOVETS

TÉLÉCABINE DES GRANGETTES

LA CROISETTE

TÉLÉSKIS DE LA LOZE

TÉLÉCABINE DES CHENUS

N

TÉLÉCABINE DES VERDONS

TÉLÉPORTE DU JARDIN ALPIN

■ SKI RUN

0   Meters   200
0   Yards   200

12. Courchevel

The most modern ski resort in France, Courchevel is colorful and intriguing, a winter sports resort of international status attracting a sophisticated clientele. This startlingly ultramodern ski metropolis is considered the most efficient one in Europe. Right after World War II it was one of the least known of the resorts in the alpine valleys. Now it is a model of town planning, with its villa, chalets, hotels, and a church in avant-garde architecture spread over the slopes amid the firs. In summer it is a popular residential center.

The terrain ranges from beautifully kept wide trails to immense areas of varied ground, both above and below the tree line for "off-trail" skiing. In all, there are 86 marked ski runs, including one reserved for bobsleds and the 14-mile run from La Saulire to Brides. The winter skiing season extends from December 1 to April 30.

In ascending order of altitudes, the resorts are Saint-Bon (3,850 feet), Le Praz (4,260 feet), Courchevel-1550 (5,090 feet), Moriond, also called Courchevel-1650 (5,413 feet), and most important, Courchevel-1850 (6,070 feet), the latter the pilot resort of the community and the heart of the chair-hoist network. From Courchevel-1850, you can take a cable car to the summit of Saulire, the trip lasting 1½ hours.

The various resorts along the slopes have an abundance of hotels in all categories. I'll supply only a rundown on some personal favorites in a wide range of prices.

AT COURCHEVEL-1850: Le Byblos des Neiges, Le Jardin Alpin (tel. 79-08-12-12), is one of the most glamorous and imaginatively decorated hotels in town, filled with a fanciful mix of rusticity and sophistication, attracting a clientele from all over the world. The exterior is designed like a giant chalet, whose overhanging eaves and jutting balconies are well suited to an alpine climate. Inside, some 70 luxurious bedrooms offer country elegance and warmth. Only guests taking their meals here are accepted, and the full-board rate ranges from 750F ($103.43) to 1,000F ($137.90) per person. On the premises are a sauna, steam room, a gym, piano bar, and two restaurants. The more famous of the two dining spots, Les Arches, is ringed with wood paneling and crisscrossed with heavy ceiling beams. Rooms are warmed with open fireplaces. Chef Serge Champion offers such specialties as lobster with a fondue of endive, along with well-prepared grilled meats and fish. Fixed-priced meals cost between 260F ($35.85) and 360F ($49.64), with à la carte dinners going between 420F ($57.92) and 480F ($66.19). Reservations are most important for nonresidents, and the hotel and its restaurants are closed between the end of April and until just before Christmas.

Carlina (tel. 79-08-00-30) is favored by many, not only for its attractive situation but because its restaurant, Noël Pâques, offers some of the finest food at the resort. The restaurant is also exceedingly comfortable. Menus cost 210F ($28.96) to 250F ($34.48). The hotel offers 53 rooms, where pleasant color schemes blend smoothly with the clean lines of contemporary furniture. The bedrooms are neat, practically laid out, and relaxing in decor. The half-board terms go from 680F ($93.77) to 1,300F ($179.27) per person. The hotel is open from Christmas to Easter. On the premises are a disco and a hairdresser. Overflow guests are housed in an annex.

L'Annapurna, Route Altiport (tel. 79-08-04-60), is another leading contender. In a modern style, it offers four-star comfort, including such facilities as an enclosed swimming pool, a gymnastics center, a physiotherapy center, and three saunas. The bedrooms are models of contemporary functional design, with utilitarian units and practical furniture. They have their own immaculately kept private bath and are fitted with radio, color TV, video, and telephone. From December 20 to April 15 half-board guests are accepted, at a rate of

1,300F ($179.27) per person. The restaurant is successful in its treatment of both local and national dishes. Here you can enjoy a meal full of flavor even if you aren't a guest of the hotel, paying 275F ($37.92). There's also a piano bar.

Hôtel Pralong 2000, Route Altiport (tel. 79-08-24-82), is a first-class hotel where grand comfort is the keynote. Skiers get a friendly welcome here between December 20 and April 15. As a guest, you'll have direct access to the ski trails. The hotel is an outstanding showcase for the craft of the modern hotelier, brilliantly designed with faultless decor and operated with clockwork efficiency. Rooms are of functional and uniform design with many built-in conveniences. In its 72 streamlined chambers, only full-board guests are accepted at rates ranging from 530F ($73.09) to 1,100F ($151.69) per person. The main dining room, in case you're not a guest of the hotel, serves a set meal for 250F ($34.48) or 300F ($41.37). For dinner, I suggest La Paral, where you can dine on an excellent cuisine. Specialties include turbot with morels, sautéed veal kidneys, and one of the finest apple tarts you're likely to taste in the Alps. Featured wines are Gamay and Mondeuse.

Much less expensive, the **Caravelle,** au Jardin Alpin (tel. 79-08-02-42), enjoys a tranquil setting, facing a backdrop of the summit of La Saulire. It offers 50 recently restored and well-furnished rooms, an indoor swimming pool, Jacuzzi, sauna, solarium, the only squash court in Courchevel, a fitness room, a musculation room, and table tennis. It accepts half-board guests only, charging them from 500F ($68.95) to 650F ($89.64) per person. Lunch is served on the sunny terrasse, a set meal costing 80F ($11.03). The hotel is open from December 10 to April 15.

Its neighbor, **Airelles,** au Jardin Alpin (tel. 79-08-02-11), is another good bet. All the rooms are built for comfort, and you can enjoy good cookery, a set meal costing 160F ($22.06). The cuisine, under the direction of Jean Bouvachon, is superb. The bedrooms, 44 in all, are well equipped with modern conveniences, costing from 500F ($68.95) in a single to 575F ($79.29) in a double. Full-board terms range from 400F ($55.16) to 620F ($85.50) per person. Après-ski life takes place in the bar-salon. The hotel is open from mid-December to mid-April.

Finally, an even better bargain is found at the small **Dahu** (tel. 79-08-01-18), where 28 pleasant rooms are offered. From December 15 to April 30 guests are received with courtesy and consideration at this friendly establishment. A double with private bath goes from 400F ($55.16). The full-board terms are from 460F ($63.43) per person. An excellently prepared set meal goes for 130F ($17.93). The fish dishes are especially good, complemented with satisfying sauces.

Chapter XV

BURGUNDY AND MORVAN

1. Chablis
2. Auxerre
3. Joigny
4. Vézelay
5. Avallon
6. Planchez
7. Château-Chinon
8. Autun
9. Beaune
10. Chagny
11. Bouilland
12. Gevrey-Chambertin
13. Dijon
14. Montbard
15. Saulieu
16. Aubigney

VINEYARD CASTLES and ancient churches make La Province de Bourgogne in eastern France the land of the good life for those who savor food and drink. Once, Burgundy was as powerful as La Belle France herself, its dukes spreading their might across Europe.

The famed Valois dukes ruled Burgundy from 1363 to 1477. The splendor of their court became known throughout Europe. To maintain its shaky independence, Burgundy faced many struggles, notably under the leadership of Charles the Bold, who seemed in perpetual conflict with Louis XI. When Charles died in 1477, Louis XI invaded the duchy. The duchy became annexed to the French crown, albeit reluctantly.

Even so, the Habsburgs still maintained their claims to Burgundy. But after its reunion with France, Burgundy was still to know no peace, as it suffered many more upheavals, such as its ravaging in the Franco-Spanish wars beginning in 1636. Peace came in 1678.

At the time of the French Revolution, Burgundy disappeared as a political entity when it was subdivided into the départements of France, Yonne, Saône-et-Loire, and Côte-d'Or.

The dukes of Burgundy are but a dim memory now, but they left a legacy of vintage red and white wines to please and excite the palate. The six major wine-growing regions of Burgundy are Chablis, Côte de Nuits, Côte de Beaune, Côte de Chalon, the Mâconnais, and the Nivernais.

1. Chablis

A celebrated wine-making village lying 12 miles from Auxerre, Chablis is the gateway to northern Burgundy and the capital of the vineyards of Basse Bourgogne. It is surrounded by about 20 wine villages, many of them clustered along the banks of the Serein River which flows through the town.

Chablis is not much of a tourist village, at least in the sense of having many attractions, yet its fame is so great that visitors flock there anyway. In the 16th century the region was especially prosperous, producing wines for much of what was then called France.

Incidentally, if you taste new chablis in any of the wine cellars, it is likely to be very acidic and raw. The professionals taste the wine, then spit it out.

The ideal time to go is in October, when tractors loaded with grapes freshly picked ride through the streets of the town. After aging, the wine begins to take on a delicate aroma around March of the following year.

Many wine makers in the village will allow you to visit their premises. They'll explain that the vine which produces the wine is from the chardonnay family, which locals call Beaunois. Many Parisians flock to the village to buy their chablis directly from the producer. Chablis, of course, is the most famous of all white burgundies. The finest chablis is called Grand Cru, and is produced in seven rigidly defined areas, all of them clustered on the right bank of the Serein.

Among the sightseeing attractions of the town, the 12th-century Church of St. Martin is visited, as is the Romanesque former parish Church of St. Pierre.

FOOD AND LODGING: **Hostellerie des Clos,** rue Jules Rathier (tel. 86-42-10-63). One of the newest restaurants in town lies, with its adjacent hotel, within a very old chapel and manorial house. Michel Vignaud is the enterprising owner whose cuisine follows a fine line between traditional favorites and innovative creative statements of his own. Each course of the fixed-price menu comes with a glass of local wine best suited to bring out the flavor in the food. Specialties include terrine of sandre, veal kidneys with grapes, and grilled crayfish in walnut oil. Fixed-price menus range from 125F ($17.24) to 300F ($41.37), with à la carte costing from 290F ($39.99) and 350F ($48.27). The 26 air-conditioned bedrooms contain private bath, phone, and radio-alarm. They rent for 230F ($31.72) in a single, 340F ($46.89) in a double. Both the hotel and its restaurant are closed Wednesday night, every Thursday until just before dinner, and in January.

Auberge du Bief, 2 Avenue de Chablis, Ligny-le-Châtel (tel. 86-47-43-42), is a pleasant country inn surrounded by gardens and a terrace. It's almost seven miles north of Chablis on the D91. Chef and owner Serge Baffet maintains an elegant dining room replete with pink napery, big windows, and silver candelabra. Specialties include sweetbreads and veal kidneys with pasta, a terrine of eel and sole with two kinds of butter, and a full range of rich desserts, wheeled to your table on a cart. Table d'hôte menus range from 105F ($14.48) to 155F ($21.38), or if you prefer to dine à la carte, you can expect to spend from 190F ($26.20) to 265F ($36.54). The restaurant is closed Monday night, Tuesday at lunchtime, and for about two weeks in October.

L'Étoile, 4 rue des Moulins (tel. 86-42-10-50), serves regional meals which, naturally, might be accompanied by a local chablis. Food items include a fondue of chicken, chitterling sausages, and meats, with full meals priced between 75F

($10.32) and 200F ($27.58). Fifteen simple bedrooms are available upstairs, only about half of which contain private bath or shower. Units rent for 100F ($13.79) to 200F ($27.58). The establishment is closed Monday, Tuesday night, and from mid-December through January.

2. Auxerre

This old town was founded by the Gauls and enlarged by the Romans. On a hill overlooking the Yonne River, it is the capital of Lower Burgundy and the center of vineyards, some of which produce chablis.

Joan of Arc spent several days here in 1429. Napoleon met Marshal Ney here on March 17, 1815, on the former emperor's return from Elba. King Louis XVIII had sent Ney to stop Napoleon. Instead, Ney embraced him and turned his army against the king. For that gesture, Ney was later shot in Paris.

Pay a visit to the **Cathédrale St-Étienne,** built during the 13th century but not completed until the 16th. It is a good example of the flamboyant Gothic style. The front is remarkable, with its sculptured portals. Inside, the stained glass is famous, some of it the original from the 13th century. In the crypt, all that remains of the Romanesque church that stood on this site, you can see frescoes from the 11th century.

Auxerre used to be a gastronomic relay on the road between Paris and Lyon, but the Autoroute du Soleil has mostly ended that. However, shops display interesting regional specialties, including chocolate snails filled with almond praliné, chocolate truffles with rum-soaked grapes, and garlic sausage baked in brioche, even sourdough bread from wood-fired ovens.

FOOD AND LODGING: Le Maxime Hôtel, 2 Quai de Marine (tel. 86-52-14-19). The 19th-century building that houses this hotel used to be a warehouse for the salt that was sold to the butchers and bakers of the town. Now a family-run hotel, it contains a conservatively bourgeois decor, an elevator, and attractively decorated bedrooms, many with views of the river or of the old city. Breakfast is served in the room or else the salon/reading room marked by Oriental rugs, polished paneling, and pervading silence. Madame Fortune and her son Pascal, who is the chef in the family-run dining room a few steps away, are the owners. The 25 cozy rooms rent for 275F ($37.92) to 420F ($57.92) for a double room.

Le Normandie, 41 Boulevard Vauban (tel. 86-52-57-80), is an imposing 19th-century hotel which, despite its convenient position in the center of town, is surprisingly quiet. There's no restaurant, although guests may relax in the pleasant garden and take breakfast on the terrace. All 50 of the rooms have TV, outside phone, bath, and antique furnishings. The price in a double is 220F ($30.34) to 260F ($35.58). There is a garage on the premises.

Le Maxime, 5 Quai de la Maxime (tel. 86-52-14-19). Some of the stone walls of this restaurant date from the 13th century, which contributes to the obvious and deserved pride the staff shows in making this restaurant a drawing card. Run by the hotel previously recommended, the dining room sits on the bank of the river, welcoming guests as they admire the big-beamed ceiling, massive wrought-iron chandelier, paneling carved with regional designs, and enormous exposed grill sheltered by a row of hanging copper pots. Three of the charming and genteel waitresses have worked here for almost 30 years and seem as involved with the well-being of the guests as they were the first day they came to work.

The restaurant offers such specialties as grilled lamb and grilled mutton chops, coquelet on a spit for two persons, a whole trout meunière or "au bleu," and a full array of meats. The terrine du chef comes with many condiments. You can enjoy a set meal for 110F ($15.17) or 200F ($27.58). If you choose to order à la carte, expect to pay slightly more. Members of the Maxime Fortune family have owned this restaurant since 1945, and today one of the sons, Pascal, produces the excellent cuisine. Maxime is open every day, except for Saturday lunch, Thursday, and in February.

Le Jardin Gourmand, 56 Boulevard Vauban (tel. 86-51-53-52), is the popular restaurant where everyone in town has dined at least once—and probably will again. The freshly imaginative decor is a pleasing combination of Louis XVI and a flowering garden. Pierre Boussereau is the experienced chef who prepares *La Nouvelle Cuisine du marché,* allowing the impeccably fresh ingredients to speak for themselves. His wife Sylvie, the gracious hostess, will recommend such specialties as a nage of scallops with pleurotes, a ragoût of shrimp, young rabbit with sweetbreads and acacia honey, turbot in raspberry vinegar, freshly made chèvre in puff pastry, and ragoût of lamb with eggplant. In warm weather, food is served in the garden or on the terrace. Fixed-price menus range from 135F ($18.62) to 300F ($41.37), while à la carte meals cost from 280F ($38.61) to 325F ($44.82). The restaurant is closed Monday all year, Sunday evening in off-season, the last two weeks in August and the first week in September, and the last two weeks in December.

La Petite Auberge, 2 Place Passeur, in Vaux (tel. 86-53-80-08), is an intimately small, rustically decorated restaurant whose windows look out over a view of the river. Jean-Luc Barnabet, the chef and owner, prepares such dishes as roasted crayfish with an essence of tomatoes, pigeon with garlic, avocados in puff pastry, and a host of other specialties that combine fresh ingredients with lightened forms of traditional Burgundian cooking. Dessert might be a gratin de fruits, with fresh fruits grilled and served in a sabayon. The restaurant charges from 120F ($16.55) to 200F ($27.58) for table d'hôte meals, from 265F ($36.54) for à la carte repasts.

You'll find the *auberge* at Vaux, about 3¾ miles southeast of Auxerre on the D163. When you arrive, Marie Barnabet, the chef's wife, will probably greet you at the door. The place is closed Sunday night, Monday, certain holidays, from December 24 to January 15, and the first two weeks in July.

3. Joigny

The most notable event that ever happened in Joigny was a revolt by the townspeople against their feudal lord, Guy de la Trémoille, in 1438. After attacking his château, they kidnapped him and killed him with blows from the mallets used at that time as vintners' tools. To this day the coat-of-arms for the city contains a depiction of a mallet, and the people of Joigny have ever since been called *les Maillotins.*

Today, visitors appreciate the many winding, narrow streets leading to the Église St-Thibault, completed in the early 1500s, unusual because of its asymmetrical interior, and the Église St-Jean.

The town's celebrated restaurant—and the reason to visit Joigny—is considered one of the finest dining establishments in all of Europe. It's **À la Côte St-Jacques,** 14 Faubourg de Paris (tel. 86-62-09-70), lying at the edge of town on the N6 highway leading to Sens. Michel Lorain is the mustachioed and vigorous entrepreneur who, with his wife Jacqueline (a noted sommelière in her own right) and his son, Jean-Michel, transformed his family's 300-year-old house into one of the most luxurious Relais et Châteaux in the region. Jean-Michel returned many years ago from an apprenticeship at one of the best restaurants in Switzerland, Chez Girardet, adding new life to the cuisine.

Most visitors come for a cuisine which produces nationwide publicity. On an outdoor terrace where you can hear birds singing in the nearby garden, or in one of a pair of monochromatically elegant, very modern dining rooms, you can enjoy such specialties as carp en gelée with spinach buds, a cassolette of morels and frogs' legs accompanied by tender asparagus shoots, salmon with a caviar cream sauce, duckling with lentils and new onions, and a crayfish gazpacho with zucchini. The selection of desserts is stupendous. Fixed-price menus cost 190F

($26.20) to 420F ($57.92), while à la carte dinners average around 550F ($75.63).

If you decide to spend the night, you can select one of the 18 elegantly upholstered bedrooms in the main building. These are priced from 350F ($48.27) in a single up to 1,400F ($193.06) for a sumptuous double. A cluster of private houses across the highway was recently acquired by the Lorains who, at great expense, radically upgraded them into super-elegant apartments, priced at between 1,400F ($193.06) to 2,100F ($289.59) for two persons. An underground tunnel paved with medieval flagstones and lined with statues links these two very sophisticated decors into one coherent and well-managed unit. Most accommodations benefit from views of the countryside and the nearby river from their balconies. A heated swimming pool is on the premises. The hotel and its restaurant are closed between early January and mid-February.

4. Vézelay

For many this is the high point of their trip through Burgundy and Morvan. Because it contained what was believed to be the tomb of St. Mary Magdalene, that "beloved and pardoned sinner," it was once one of the great pilgrimage sites of the Christian world.

On a hill 360 feet above the surrounding countryside, the town is characterized by its ramparts and its old houses with sculptured doorways, corbelled staircases, and mullioned windows. The site of Vézelay was originally an abbey, founded by Girart de Roussillon, a count of Burgundy (troubadours were fond of singing of his exploits). It was consecrated in 878 by Pope John VIII.

On March 31, 1146, Saint Bernard preached the Second Crusade there; in 1190 the town was the rendezvous point for the Third Crusade, drawing such personages as Richard the Lion-Hearted and King Philippe-Auguste of France. Later, Saint Louis of France came here several times on pilgrimages.

Park outside the town hall and walk through the medieval streets past flower-filled gardens. After about a quarter of a mile of climbing streets, you reach the **Basilique Ste-Madeleine** (tel. 86-33-24-36). The largest and most famous Romanesque church in France, this basilica is only ten yards shorter than Notre-Dame de Paris. The façade was rebuilt by Viollet-le-Duc, who restored Notre-Dame. You enter the narthex, a vestibule of large dimensions, about 4,000 square feet. Look through the main door for a tremendous view of Burgundian-Romanesque glory. The high nave is built in white and beige chalk stones. It is full of light, and each capital shows a different sculpture. It's possible to visit the Carolingian crypt, where the tomb of Mary Magdalene formerly rested (today it contains some of her relics). From the narthex you can ascend the tower, in July and August only, at 4F (55¢), for a view of the old town and the hilly landscapes.

Afterward, you can end your walk by going alongside the ancient walls and back to the Place du Champ-de-Foire at the lower end of town.

If you're dining or staying over, the preferred choices follow.

FOOD AND LODGING: **Poste et Lion d'Or** (tel. 86-33-21-23) is a local monument, the former *poste relay*, built at a time when owners had the materials and room to construct expansively and grandly. The present patron, René Danguy, has masterfully restored the inn to its former glory, and as someone observed, "it smells of good times of another era." You feel you're being welcomed at a first-class place, although the tariffs are comparable to those at a modest Parisian hotel. Singles cost from 230F ($31.72) Doubles are priced at 610F ($84.12) for a room with bath. Service and taxes are included, but a continental breakfast is extra. The food is exceptionally good. I especially like the escargots (snails) de Bourgogne in chablis and the stuffed trout (truite farcie) with herbs. Menus cost 220F ($30.34) to 275F ($37.92), and if you order à la carte, expect to pay from

250F ($34.48) to 300F ($41.37), the latter a Pantagruelian meal. It is open from Easter until November.

Relais du Morvan (tel. 86-33-25-33) is a simple hotel and restaurant directed by Antoine Lopez and his wife Nicole. You'll see it at the bottom of the hill near the public parking lots as you first drive into the village. The colorful dining room has several walls of exposed stone, heavy ceiling beams, and a Louis XIII fireplace that usually burns brightly throughout the winter. The restaurant serves set four-course meals costing 80F ($11.03) to 175F ($24.13). Homemade ice creams and pastries are tasty desserts. Nine compact bedrooms are rented out. All have shower and sink, but toilet facilities are in the hallways. Singles cost 110F ($15.17), with doubles ranging from 160F ($22.06) to 185F ($25.51). The place is closed Tuesday night, Wednesday, and in January.

On the Outskirts

L'Espérance, St-Père sous Vézelay (tel. 86-33-20-45), has become one of the most celebrated restaurants of Burgundy. Although its fast fame may have come as a shock to Marc and Françoise Meneau, who began their business with what had been a family bakery just over a dozen years ago, it wasn't really surprising to the satisfied diners who wouldn't think of coming to Vézelay without stopping here. Customers have included ex-President Nixon, Madame Chou En-lai, and a gaggle of show-biz-oriented Parisians.

The complex is at the bottom of the hill on which the Romanesque church of Vézelay appears as a symbol of the Middle Ages. Inside, however, a contrast is immediately evident from the flower-rimmed Plexiglass columns, which double as ventilation and add a note of hi-tech modernism to the carefully planned antique decor. Attractive blond Françoise Meneau helped in decorating the exquisitely appointed public rooms and the 25 marble and monochromatic bedrooms, which are elegant and intensely stylized. There are also five luxury suites. Doubles begin at 600F ($82.74), but suites for two cost from 2,000F ($275.80). The dining room's craftsmanship resulted in slabs of flagstones with Oriental rugs and high windows providing illumination and overlooking a garden where ducks paddle around.

On the menu you may see such items as green olives stuffed with truffles and then covered with an essence of truffles, warm sautéed foie gras with a galette of corn, fish consommé à la crème de caviar, crayfish with wild mushrooms, baked crayfish with concentrated essence of fennel, filet of veal in horseradish sauce with cornbread, and wild duckling roasted with bay leaves. Full dinners range from 400F ($55.16) to 500F ($68.95). The restaurant is closed on Tuesday and at lunchtime on Wednesday.

5. Avallon

This old fortified town is shielded behind its ancient ramparts, upon which you can stroll. A medieval atmosphere still permeates the town, and you'll find many 15th- and 16th-century houses. At the town gate on the Grande-Rue is a **clock tower** from 1460. The Romanesque **Church of St. Lazarus** dates from the 12th century and has two interesting doorways. The church is said to have received the head of St. Lazarus in 1000. This turned Avallon into a pilgrimage site. Today Avallon is used as a base for excursions to the north of the Massif du Morvan. But it is mainly visited because it is a gastronomic highlight of Burgundy, as reflected by the following recommendations.

FOOD AND LODGING: **Hostellerie de la Poste,** 13 Place Vauban (tel. 86-34-06-12). Napoleon slept here some time ago, and if you stop in for a meal or for the night, you'll see artifacts that haven't changed much since then. The entire hostelry, set on either side of a stone courtyard accessible only by passing under an arch leading in from the street, is filled with old iron fireplace implements, marble mantelpieces, hunting trophies, rifles, tapestries, and antiques. You can rent a room here for 325F ($44.82) to 650F ($89.64) in a double. If you prefer a bungalow, the charge will be 1,000F ($137.90) for two persons.

The restaurant serves, at deluxe prices, some of the most acclaimed food in France. This is a tradition maintained today by René and Catherine Hure. Specialties include a combination of chicken, kidneys, and sweetbreads in puff pastry with truffle sauce, cassolette of shrimp, duckling with mushroom fricassée, magenta of bass with saffron, and saddle of roast venison in season. Set menus range from 200F ($27.58) to 360F ($49.64), service included. If you choose to dine à la carte (service not included), you'll pay 480F ($66.19) to 600F ($82.74). Dinner is served until 9:30 p.m. daily except from mid-November to mid-March. In summer, tables with pink napery are set up in the charming courtyard.

Equally enchanting—and also expensive—is the **Moulin des Ruats,** Vallée du Cousin (tel. 86-34-07-14), a Relais et Châteaux two miles outside of town, reached by taking the D247. On the banks of the Cousin, this country inn in the valley offers serene and elegant dining under the direction of Yves and Geneviève Luciani. Dining here is a delight because you can combine the pleasures of good food with attractive surroundings. In pleasant weather the terrace overlooking the stream is a favorite spot for diners. As might be expected, freshwater fish is a specialty at the inn, with the honors going to truite au bleu beurre blanc crème du Major Thompson, a stream trout tossed live into a broth of onions, vinegar, carrots, and cayenne, and then served with a white butter sauce made with shallots and cream. Named for a character in a novel by Pierre Daninos (who has been a favorite customer), the trout is only one of three fish—pike and salmon are the other two—cooked in this way.

Chicken is another popular dish at the Moulin des Ruats, and it is cooked in a variety of ways, including the traditional coq au vin. But the sensational dish here is the fondue de volaille à la crème des Ruats—a boned chicken breast sautéed in butter, flamed with cognac, and then simmered in the best chablis. After the wines are reduced to their essence, cream and mushrooms are added to create the sauce. Another specialty is quail from the Dombes. Although the menu lists a variety of desserts, you should try the homemade fruit tarts. These are custom-made after your order, requiring half an hour's wait. Your choice is assembled, popped into the oven, and delivered to your table sizzling. In addition to the excellent menu, the hostellerie offers a fine wine list, plus a number of unusual after-dinner liqueurs. A complete meal usually costs 175F ($24.13) to 230F ($31.72).

If you wish to spend the night, you can get a double room with bath for 320F ($44.13), a double without bath for a low of 180F ($24.82). The Moulin is open from March through October.

Le Moulin des Templiers, Vallée du Cousin-Pontaubert (tel. 86-34-10-80). The route to this country house set at the edge of the river will take you along the N457 in the direction of Pontaubert, about 2½ miles west of the center of Avallon. The setting is in the midst of an almost primeval forest. The bedrooms are small but selectively furnished in a rural style that agrees well with the country environs. Marie-Françoise Hilmoine, the dignified and genteel hostess, will bring breakfast to your room in the morning. No other meals are served. Open from April until November, the hotel charges around 140F ($19.31) for a single with a private shower, from 250F ($34.48) for a double with bath or shower.

Restaurant Le Morvan, 7 Route de Paris (N6) (tel. 86-34-18-20), is a rustic inn on the edge of town, with many of its tables opening onto a view of a verdant park. Menu specials, prepared by the chef, Jean Breton, may be filet of smoked duckling, veal scallop with ris de veau (sweetbreads) and sorrel, a timbale of snails with chablis, and excellent terrines, many of which are supplied by Breton to Fauchon in Paris. Fixed-price menus range from 120F ($16.55) **to** 190F

($26.20), while à la carte meals usually cost about 220F ($30.34). The restaurant is closed Monday. In low season lunch is served, but the doors are closed for dinner daily except on Saturday night. It is also closed the last two weeks of November and for three weeks in January. To get there from the center of town, follow the signs to the N6 in the direction of Auxerre.

6. Planchez

Some people call this village the world capital of Christmas trees because of the forests surrounding it. The Nazis burned down nearly three-quarters of Planchez in reprisals against the French Resistance Movement. But that sad memory is blotted out today. From here you can take a road to **Lac des Settons,** a scenic spot of nearly 850 acres along the Cure River Valley. Its dam dates from 1861.

Back at Planchez, I have the following recommendation:

FOOD AND LODGING: **Le Relais de Lacs,** Place de la Poste (tel. 86-78-41-68), is another one of France's owner-run inns where you get a good night's sleep, excellent food, and moderate tariffs. The hotel stands on the only square in the hamlet, next to the pocket-size post office. The windows are small, and hanging baskets of flowers are placed outside to welcome travelers. Inside, the setting is in the typical bistro style. Adjoining the drinking area is a rustic dining room with small tables around a fireplace. Set menus go for 62F ($8.55) to 230F ($31.72). À la carte meals cost 160F ($22.06) to 220F ($30.34). I recently enjoyed an appetizer of the cold cuts of Morvan, then sole en papillottes, followed by beef filet en croûte, fresh mushrooms, a salad, a selection of cheese, and a sherbet. The wine list is impressive, and a lot of great bottles at reasonable prices are available.

The owner, François Dumarais, rents out 36 bedrooms, 22 with bath. The chambers are more homey than impressive, but all is kept immaculate. Toilets and baths are in the corridors. Singles begin at 85F ($13.10), doubles peaking at 190F ($26.20). Breakfast (not included in the rates) is a pleasant surprise, with lots of coffee, plenty of local butter, homemade toasted bread, and pots of homemade jam, and orange juice. The restaurant is closed on Wednesday off-season, from mid-November to mid-December, and from early January to mid-February.

From Planchez, the D17 will bring you to the **Barrage de Pannessière Chaumard,** the great dam of the Yonne. Turn around and join the N444 to—

7. Château-Chinon

This scenic town was a natural fortress, looking out over the plains of Morvan and Nivernais. Once it was a feudal castle, and it's seen many battles. You can climb to the **Panorama du Calvaire** at 2,000 feet, once the site of a Gallic settlement. The overall panorama is remarkable from this vantage point. You look over not only the town but the Morvan mountains in the distance. In clear weather you may even see westward to the Loire Valley and south to the summit of **Haut Folin** (3,000 feet). Finally, if you have a car, take the **Promenade du Château** running along the side of the hill and making a circuit of the slate-roofed town.

FOOD AND LODGING: **Au Vieux Morvan,** Place de la Mairie (tel. 86-85-05-01), is a pleasant country-style inn where you can get good local cooking and a bed for the night. The location is central, and the dining room opens onto a panoramic view of the Valley of the Yonne. This inn was once a favorite retreat of French President François Mitterand. A very good meal is offered for only 65F ($8.97), but gourmets and/or gourmands may opt for the hefty 175F ($24.13) repast. The latter is likely to include hors d'oeuvres, filet de lotte (angle-fish) à l'Américaine, pintade (guinea-fowl) rôtie, and cheese or ice cream. There are 23 simply furnished bedrooms with varied plumbing. Singles begin at 68F ($9.38), and the most expensive doubles are 190F ($26.20). A continental breakfast is extra. The inn is closed from November 12 to January.

You leave Château-Chinon by the N78, heading toward Autun. At the town of **Arleuf,** take the D500 on your right, a narrow and rough road through a large, dark forest. At a fork, turn right to **Glux.** After Glux, follow the arrows to **Mont Beuvray** via the D18. You reach the summit through the D274, a narrow, winding, one-way road. After two miles of climbing, you're at **Oppidum of Bibracte,** capital of the Eduens, a Gallic tribe. At this altitude of 2,800 feet, Chief Vercingetorix back in A.D. 52 organized the Gauls to fight Caesar's legions. From this summit the view is splendid over Autun and Mont St-Vincent. If the weather is clear, you can see the Jura and snowy Mont Blanc. All around are oaks and beeches, some of them more than 1,000 years old. After leaving Mont Beuvray by the D274, you'll come to **St-Léger-sous-Beuvray.** There you can head to Autun via the D3.

8. Autun

Deep in burgundy wine country, Autun is one of the oldest towns in France, lying some 30 miles west of Beaune. In the days of the Roman Empire it was often called "the other Rome." Some of the Roman relics still stand, including the remains of a theater, the **Théâtre Romain,** the largest in Gaul, holding some 15,000 spectators. It was nearly 500 feet in diameter. Outside the town you can see the quadrangular tower of the **Temple of Janus** rising incongruously 80 feet on the plain.

Once, Autun was an important link on the road from Lyon to Boulogne, as reflected by the **Porte d'Arroux,** with two large archways used now for cars, and two smaller ones for pedestrians. It's in the northwest section, rising 55 feet. Also exceptional is the **Porte St-André,** or St. Andrew's Gate, about a quarter of a mile northwest of the Roman theater. Rising 65 feet high, it too has four doorways, and is surmounted by a gallery of ten arcades.

The crowning achievement of Autun, however, is the **Cathédrale St-Lazare,** standing on the highest point in Autun, built in 1120 to house the relics of St. Lazarus. On the façade, the tympanum in the central portal depicts the Last Judgment; it is one of the triumphs of Romanesque sculpture. Some of the stone carvings are by Gislebertus, one of the few artists at that time who signed their names to their works. Inside, a painting by Ingres depicts the martyrdom of St. Symphorien, who was killed in Autun. In summer you can climb the tower and from there enjoy a good view over the town.

The **Musée Rolin,** 3 rue des Bancs (tel. 85-52-09-76), is installed in a 15th-century *maison* built for Nicolas Rolin, who became a celebrated lawyer in his day (born in 1380). An easy walk from the cathedral, the museum displays a fine collection of Burgundian Romanesque sculptures, as well as paintings and archeological mementos. From the original Rolin collection are exhibited the *Nativity* by the Maître de Moulins, along with a statue that's a masterpiece of 15th-century work, *Our Lady of Autun.* From March 16 to September 30 it is open from 9:30 a.m. to noon and 2 to 6:30 p.m. From October 1 to November 15 it is open from 10 a.m. to noon and 2 to 5 p.m., from November 16 to December 31 to 4 p.m. On Sunday throughout the year, hours are 2:30 to 5 p.m. It is closed on Tuesday, and charges 7F (97¢) for admission.

FOOD AND LODGING: **Hôtel St-Louis,** with **Restaurant La Rotonde,** 6 rue de l'Arbalète (tel. 85-52-21-03), is an old posting inn built in 1696 on the main Paris-Nice road. Napoleon slept there twice, once with his wife Joséphine, on January 10, 1802, and again on March 15, 1815, upon his return from the island of Elba on his victorious march to Paris. If you want to have the feeling of the period, ask for the Napoleonic chamber, relatively inexpensive at 275F ($37.92) per night. Inside are two canopied mahogany beds and an Empire fireplace. A more "republican" double with bath rents for 260F ($35.85) and you can get even more republican in a double with shower at 245F ($33.79). Most of the bedrooms have rustic furniture and floral wallpaper, and some contain brass beds. Owner Monsieur Barra provides an imperial reception to guests, either in the American bar or the rococo reception lounge. His dining-room and the furnishings are Empire, with large bay windows overlooking the courtyard (once the stables). Waiters in black and white serve good meals, set menus costing 120F ($16.55) to 185F ($25.51). The restaurant is closed for Tuesday lunch, and the hotel takes a long vacation from November 15 to March 1.

Hostellerie du Vieux Moulin, Porte Arroux (tel. 85-52-10-90), is a good bargain both for meals and for lodging. The hostellerie has a rich, warm, and inviting ambience, what the French call *cadre rustique*. There are 18 simple but clean rooms, ranging in price from 100F ($13.79) in a bathless single up to 240F ($33.10) for the most expensive doubles with private bath. In summer you can sit out at a table overlooking the garden and a tiny millstream nearby. Most guests are content to order the 120F ($16.55) meal, although a huge 205F ($28.27) gastronomique special is featured. Dominique Tarel is the chef de cuisine. The restaurant at the inn is by far the finest in Autun. The inn is closed on Sunday night and Monday, and takes a winter vacation from December 10 to March 1.

Leave Autun on the N73. After six miles, turn left onto the D326 toward **Sully.** There you can admire the **Château de Sully,** although you can't go inside. This Renaissance residence was known as the Fontainebleau of Burgundy.

Leave Sully by taking the D26 until you cross the N73. Turn left toward Nolay and go through this small village. Three miles past Nolay, you'll reach **La Rochepot** with its magnificent castle. It is a medieval-style fortress with an aisle built during the Renaissance. The attraction is open from Palm Sunday to November 1 daily except Tuesday, from 10 a.m. to noon and 2 to 6 p.m. Admission is 8F ($1.10).

After La Rochepot, head toward **Beaune,** first on the N6, then on the N74. When you're on the N74 you're on the wine road, passing through some of the best-known burgundy vineyards, including Chassagne Montrachet, Puligny-Montrachet, Meursault, Auxey Duresses, Volnay, and Pommard.

9. Beaune

This is the capital of the burgundy wine country and is also one of the best-preserved medieval cities in the district, with a girdle of ramparts. Its history goes back more than 2,000 years. Twenty-four miles south of Dijon, Beaune was a Gallic sanctuary, later a Roman town. Until the 14th century it was the residence of the dukes of Burgundy. When the last duke, Charles the Bold, died in 1447, Beaune was annexed to the crown of France.

Its **Musée de l'Hôtel-Dieu de Beaune,** Avenue Guiaone-de-Salins (tel. 80-24-75-75), is a perfectly preserved 15th-century hospice which remains a working hospital—one of the world's richest, since its own vineyards produce such renowned wines as Aloxe-Corton and Meursault. (On the third Sunday of November the wines are auctioned.) This Gothic masterpiece has a multicolored tile roof, and it shelters treasures of Flemish-Burgundian art. In the *chambre des pauvres* (room of the poor) you can admire painted, broken-barrel-style, timbered vaulting. Most of the furnishings are authentic. In the museum the masterpiece is a 1443 polyptych of the *Last Judgment* by Roger van der Weyden. In summer it is open from 9 a.m. to 6 p.m.; off-season it closes for lunch from noon to 2 p.m. The charge is 12.50F ($1.72) for adults, half price for children.

North of Hôtel-Dieu, **Collégiale Notre-Dame** was begun in 1120, in the style of Burgundian Romanesque. In the sanctuary of this church are displayed some remarkable tapestries illustrating scenes from the life of Mary. They may be viewed from Easter to Christmas.

In the former mansion of the dukes of Burgundy the **Musée du Vin de Bourgogne,** rue d'Enfer (tel. 80-22-08-19), has been installed. The history of the burgundy vineyards is presented. In viewing the tools and history of wine making, you get to trace the Burgundian way of life over the years. The rooms in which the collection—tools, objets d'art, documents—is presented date from the 15th and 16th centuries. A collection of wine presses is displayed in a press house from the 14th century. Admission is 5F (69¢) for adults and 3F (41¢) for children.

Musée des Beaux-Arts et Musée Marey, Hôtel de Ville (tel. 80-22-20-80). The Fine Arts Museum of Beaune contains a rich Gallo-Roman archeological section from the district, including funereal stones and other statuary along with pottery. The main gallery of paintings houses works from the 16th to the 19th centuries, including Flemish primitives. Sculptures from the Middle Ages and the Renaissance are also displayed. A larger part of the museum honors the Beaune physiologist Étienne Jules Marey (1830–1904), who discovered the principles of the cinema long before 1895. The museum is open daily except Tuesday, from 9 a.m. to noon and 2 to 5:30 p.m. from Easter until November. To visit these museums, you can use the same ticket you purchased to visit the museums previously described.

WHERE TO STAY: Hôtel de la Poste, 3 Boulevard Clemenceau (tel. 80-22-08-11), has been in the Chevillot family for 75 years. Although its members have improved everything, they have kept the original rustic style. The reception hall is spacious, with many nooks for lounging. The style of the bedrooms is personalized; some beds are made of brass while others are padded. In all, 25 bedrooms are rented, plus four apartments. The cost in a single is 680F ($93.77), going up to 850F ($117.22) in the most expensive double. Menu specialties include crayfish in cream and duckling au poivre vert. If you dine à la carte, expect to spend from 300F ($41.37) to 350F ($48.27). The hotel is closed from mid-November to April.

Hôtel de Bourgogne, Avenue du Général-de-Gaulle (tel. 80-22-22-00), offers 120 very comfortable bedrooms at 215F ($29.65) for a single, 250F ($34.48) for a double. The hotel belongs to the hotel owners' association of Beaune. It stands just outside the walls, about a quarter of a mile from the old city. The furnishings are up-to-date, and the style is very inviting. You can also eat in the hotel in an elaborate dining room where prices begin at 100F ($13.79) for a set meal. The reception is very courteous and helpful. Closed from early January to early February and from Sunday noon to Tuesday morning each week from December to mid-March.

Hostellerie de Bretonnière, 43 Faubourg Bretonnière (tel. 80-22-15-77), is the best bargain in town. Entered through a courtyard, it is well run, offering clean, comfortable, and quiet rooms, 22 in all. The rate is only 105F ($14.48) in a single, rising to 220F ($30.34) in a double. There is no restaurant, but a continental breakfast is served.

WHERE TO DINE: Auberge St-Vincent, Place de Halle (tel. 80-22-42-34), is in a 17th-century house conveniently opposite Les Hospices in the center of town. The luxurious interior seems appropriate for the elegant dishes overseen by Lucette Laurent. The cuisine is obviously inspired by Burgundian tradition, but newer influences can be seen in the sophisticated *cuisine du marché* and other dishes, such as a ragoût of crayfish with small vegetables, veal kidneys Burgundy style, and a magnificent breast of duckling. Table d'hôte menus range from 120F ($16.55) to 190F ($26.20), and à la carte meals cost around 240F ($33.10). In low season, the restaurant is closed Sunday and all of December. The rest of the year, dinner is served nightly until 10 p.m.

Relais de Saulx, 6 rue Louis-Véry (tel. 80-22-01-35), offers one of the most beautiful dining rooms in town, crossed with heavy timbers and luxuriously decorated with good paintings and yards of warm velvet. Chef Monnoir prepares a sophisticated combination of traditional bourguignonne cuisine and up-to-date adaptations such as a filet of sea perch with cream sauce heavily laced with local red wine, a warm terrine of monkfish and crayfish with a crustacean-flavored butter sauce, noisette of baby lamb with cider vinegar and honey, and a carefully prepared dessert trolley. Attractive fixed-price menus are priced between 85F ($11.72) and 180F ($24.82). A menu dégustation is offered for around 250F ($34.48) per person. The restaurant, on a narrow street behind the Hospices, is closed Sunday night, Monday, holidays, from mid-February to mid-March, and for about a week at the end of August.

From Beaune you might consider the following detour, before picking up the Burgundian wine trail again.

10. Chagny

Eleven miles southwest of Beaune, Chagny is a busy, bustling commercial and industrial town. Its major antiquity is a church with a Romanesque tower dating from the 12th century. Although it wouldn't be included in an average sightseeing tour of Burgundy, gourmets flock here from all over the world to sample the viands in the following establishment:

FOOD AND LODGING: **Lameloise,** 36 Place d'Armes (tel. 85-87-08-85), is a *relais gourmand,* a hotel and restaurant in an ancient Burgundian *maison* that sets about the best table in the entire province where the competition is really tough. The cuisine of Jean and Jacques Lameloise, father and son, is inspired. These men are passionately devoted to good food and wine. One pleased diner told me, and I concur, "With the Lameloise family, food is truly raised to an art." The service and decor are impeccable. If I gave out stars, I'd award Lameloise three, making it one of the premier tables of France. Their salad of fresh green beans and crayfish might sound ordinary, but it is extraordinary. The kitchen also does a feuilleté of sweetbreads that is delicately flavored. Sweetbreads are employed again in something else on the menu, a salad with crayfish. Other specialties include a blanquette of salmon with pearl onions and aiguillettes of duckling with fresh figs. From the ancient cellars emerge some of the finest in wines. Try, in particular, Rully and Chassagne-Montrachet. Meals are in the 400F ($55.16) to 500F ($68.95) range.

The establishment also rents out beautifully furnished and comfortable rooms, costing from 300F ($41.37) in the simplest single to a high of 700F ($96.53) for the best doubles with private bath. The restaurant is closed Thursday for lunch and on Wednesday, and from early December to early January.

Les Capucines, 30 Route de Chalon (tel. 85-87-08-17), is a pleasant hotel and restaurant within the thick walls of an old stone house set in a park at the edge of the city. All but three of the 15 rooms contain private bath. Accommodations range from 145F ($20) in a single to 275F ($37.92) in a double. Meals go from 120F ($16.55) to 265F ($36.54) and are served in the attractive restaurant daily except Sunday night and Monday at lunch in low season. In high season you can eat lunch and/or dine daily.

Auberge du Camp Romain, Chassey-le-Camp (tel. 85-87-09-91), is about as secluded and peaceful a spot as you could hope for—a perfect destination for a drive through the countryside. When you get here, you'll be able to view the pottery studio that fills a small part of the large-scale premises. The hotel is fairly modern. Jean-Louis Dressinval will offer you directions over the phone if you want to rent one of his 25 rooms, which range in price from 102F ($14.07) in a basic single to 300F ($41.37) in the best double. The in-house restaurant, which is closed Wednesday from October to March and for the six weeks following New Year's, serves well-prepared, fixed-price meals for 85F ($11.72) to 150F ($20.69). To get here, follow first the D974 and then the D109 for about 3¾ miles west of Chagny.

Leaving Beaune on the D2, the most colorful route is to—

11. Bouilland

The drive to this village takes you through one of the most famous white-wine roads of Burgundy, along the narrow valley of the Rhoin. Soon Bouilland, circled by wooded hills, comes into view. Its church is 900 years old and in re-markably good shape. Here in this secluded oasis you may wish to follow your gastronomic nose to the following recommendation.

FOOD AND LODGING: Hostellerie du Vieux Moulin (tel. 80-21-51-16) has won respect for its owner and chef de cuisine, Monsieur Jean-Pierre Silva, who has turned this small inn at the edge of the village into an excellent place for dining. He sets one of the best tables in Burgundy. The dining room, overlooking a mill and the Rhoin, is comfortable, with stone floors, tapestry-covered seats, and Burgundy-style furniture. In the sumptuous dining room, you might begin with a fish mousse served with two sauces or a feuilleté of snails with a tomato cream sauce. The oyster flan is velvety and outstanding. The menu usually offers a se-lection of about five fish dishes nightly, including a ragoût of scallops served with the fresh vegetables of the season. Among the main courses I suggest the noiset-tes d'agneau (lamb) served with a purée of shallots. If you're here in the right season I'd endorse the noisettes de chevreuil (roebuck) Saint-Hubert. After a salad of the season made with the freshest of greens, and an order of cheese (perhaps), you are then fortified to face the table of desserts. After that, the staff may have to carry you out. An à la carte meal costs from 300F ($41.37) up. Three set menus, costing from 150F ($20.69) to 285F ($39.30) are offered. The most expensive is a surprise composed on the spot by the chef, with many tiny courses, each made from the freshest ingredients available from the market.

The hotel maintains eight rooms in the main house, as well as five more luxurious accommodations in an outlying annex. In the main building, single or double rooms with full bath cost from 250F ($34.48), while a trio of rooms less fully equipped cost from 150F ($20.69) to 200F ($27.58), depending on the plumbing. In the annex, double rooms cost 450F ($62.06) to 700F ($96.53). The entire operation closes from mid-December to the end of January. The restau-rant is closed every Wednesday and at lunchtime on Thursday.

THE WINE ROUTE TO DIJON: Back on the N74, the road takes you through the wine district en route to Dijon.

Along the way you'll pass through **Aloxe-Corton,** where the Emperor Charlemagne once owned vineyards. The Corton-Charlemagne is still a famous white burgundy. **Comblanchien** is known for a white stone quarried from neigh-boring cliffs. At **Nuits-St-Georges** a wine is produced that enjoyed great renown during the reign of Louis XIV.

The next village is **Vougeot,** whose vineyards produce an excellent red wine. Here you can visit the **Château du Clos de Vougeot** (tel. 80-62-86-09), a Renais-sance building associated with the Brotherhood of the Knights of Tastevin, known for its promotion of the wines of Burgundy. Surrounding the château is one of the most celebrated vineyards of France. You can explore the great 12th-century cellar. Hours are from 9 to 7 p.m. July 1 to September 15.

Leave the N74 for the D122. This will take you through **Chambolle Mus-**

igny, a spot of great scenic beauty, then to **Morey St-Denis** and **Gevrey-Chambertin,** marking the beginning of the Côte de Nuits wine district.

12. Gevrey-Chambertin

This town eight miles south of Dijon was immortalized by the writer Gaston Roupnel. Typical of the villages of the Côte d'Or, Gevrey added Chambertin to its name, which is the name of its most famous vineyard. In the village stands **Le Château de Gevrey-Chambertin,** constructed at a high point of the village around the 10th century by the lords of Vergy. The thick-walled castle was in disrepair by the 13th century, but it was restored and expanded by the powerful order of the monks of Cluny, who retained the corkscrew staircases whose unevenly spaced steps, now polished slick by the passage of thousands of feet, sometimes prove difficult to negotiate. The great hall is impressive, with exposed ceiling beams. The guardsmen's room in the watchtower and the collections of aging wines in the vaulted cellars are part of the château's charm. Between April 15 and November 15, guided tours are given (in French), lasting about 30 minutes. Hours are from 10 a.m. to noon and 2 (2:30 on Sunday) to 6 p.m. In winter, tours are given from 10:30 a.m. to noon and 2:30 to 6:30 p.m. The château is closed on Sunday morning, Christmas, New Year's Day, Easter, and All Saints' Day. Tours cost around 12F ($1.66). The village church with its Romanesque doorway dates from the 14th century.

FOOD AND LODGING: La Rôtisserie du Chambertin, rue Chambertin (tel. 80-34-33-20). You would think that the owner of this unusual restaurant intentionally hid it to keep people from going there, so inconspicuous is it. The only indication is an unmarked door in the open courtyard with a menu posted next to it. However, the world finds its way to her door, as Céline Menneveau is considered one of the most outstanding woman chefs in the country. You enter through a museum devoted to the history of barrel making (the owner's great-grandfather was the town cooper on this very spot), then pass beneath the vaults dating from the 11th century, and finally arrive in a modern, almost psychedelically lit room. The electronic decor is offset by several traditional pieces, creating a warm, friendly atmosphere in which to sample the cuisine.

As the name suggests, the restaurant specializes in grilled and spit-roasted meats, but grilled sole and turbot are also on the menu. For an appetizer I suggest tourte de pigeon (pigeon pie) or terrine de foie de volaille truffé (chicken liver pâté with truffles), both excellently prepared by Mme Menneveau. One of her most superb dishes is ravioli stuffed with truffles and served with a sauce made of fresh lemon and tarragon, along with fresh mushrooms and cream.

In spite of the variety on the menu, I recommend passing everything by to order the spit-roasted ham. This whole, fresh ham has been marinated for several days in white wine, then basted for hours with its own marinade as it slowly turns on the rôtisserie. Accompanying this—and most main dishes—are fresh spinach and potatoes au gratin. After such a heavy meal, you may prefer to nibble on some of the cheeses, but if you crave a sweet finale, you'll be overwhelmed by the velvety-smooth chocolate cake.

Above all, don't neglect the inn's wines. Chambertin has been called "the wine for moments of great decision." Perhaps that is why Napoleon always took it on his campaigns—even to Moscow. Although the wine list is not extensive, it includes the best of recent vintages. A complete meal, including wine and service, is likely to cost 300F ($41.37) to 350F ($48.27). The restaurant is closed on Sunday night and Monday, and from late July to late August.

Les Millésimes, 25 rue de l'Église and rue de Meixville (tel. 80-51-84-24). Jean and Monique Sangoy, who once lived with their children in Argentina, have now opened one of the most outstanding restaurants in the area. You enter the courtyard of what used to be a warehouse for the fermentation of local wines by passing under an iron archway announcing the name of the place. Monique Sangoy will welcome you, sometimes assisted by one of the family's attractive daughters. Meals are eaten under the stone vaulting in one of the cellars, attractively lit with small table lamps. Jean Sangoy, with the help of his sons, prepares the cuisine, offers tours through the well-stocked wine cellars, and proposes such recipes as oysters au gratin with sherry, poultry stuffed with truffles, sea bass en croûte, sweetbreads braised with Noilly, and a homemade foie gras that melts in your mouth. Full meals with wine usually range from 280F ($38.61) to 320F ($44.13). They're served daily except Tuesday, Wednesday at lunch, and from early January to mid-February.

If you're staying over, I recommend the **Hôtel les-Grands-Crus** (tel. 80-34-34-15), a 24-room charmer near a tiny château that traces its origins back to the 12th century. Opened in 1977, the hotel is run by Monsieur and Madame Pierre Mortet, helpful hosts who speak English. Your bedroom window opens onto views of the vineyards of Burgundy and of a church going back to the 12th century. Prices begin at 240F ($33.10) in a single, going up to 320F ($44.13) in a double with bath. Rooms contain telephone and TV, and some of the furniture is in the Louis XV style. The hotel does not have a restaurant, but serves a continental breakfast. In addition, guests can enjoy the fine wines of Burgundy. Grands-Crus shuts down from December 10 to February 15 and on Sunday from November 15 to March 1.

Les Terroirs, 28 Route de Dijon (tel. 80-34-30-76). You wouldn't know it from the outside, but this is one of the warmest and most attractively decorated places in the area. It's also a bargain. It rents out a total of 15 bedrooms, with prices beginning at 225F ($31.03) in a single, rising to 325F ($44.82) in a double. There is an inviting bar, but a continental breakfast is the only meal served. The hotel is closed from November 22 to January 10.

At Brochon, you're at the boundary between the Côte de Nuits district and the Côte de Dijon. Farther on, at **Fixin** you can stop to visit **Parc Noisot** for a view of the environs of Dijon. **Marsannay-la-Côte,** next, produces a rosé wine from black grapes. At **Chenove,** the vineyards were once owned by Autun monks and the dukes of Burgundy. Finally, you reach—

13. Dijon

Dijon is known overseas mainly for its mustard. In the center of the Côte d'Or, it is the ancient capital of Burgundy. Here good food is accompanied by great wine. Between meals you can enjoy Dijon's art and architecture.

The remains of the former palace of the dukes of Burgundy (**Ancien Palais des Ducs de Bourgogne**) has been turned into the **Musée des Beaux-Arts** (Fine Arts Museum), Place de la Sainte-Chapelle (tel. 80-30-31-11), which is open from 10 a.m. to 6 p.m. except on Tuesday. Entrance is 8F ($1.10). One of the oldest and richest museums in France, it contains exceptional sculpture, ducal kitchens from the mid-1400s (with great chimneypieces), a representative collection of European paintings from the 14th through the 19th centuries, and modern French paintings and sculptures. Take special note of the Salle des Gardes, built by Philip the Good. It was the banqueting hall of the old palace. The grave of Philip the Bold was built between 1385 and 1411 and is one of the best in France. A reclining figure rests on a slab of black marble, surrounded by 41 mourners.

A mile from the center of town on the N5 stands **Chartreuse de Champmol,** the Carthusian monastery built by Philip the Bold as a burial place; it is now a mental hospital. Much was destroyed during the Revolution, but you can see the Moses Fountain in the gardens designed by Sluter at the end of the 14th century. The Gothic entrance is superb.

Major churches to visit in Dijon include the **Cathédrale St-Bénigne,** a 13th-century abbey church in the Burgundian-Gothic style; the **Église St-Michel,** in the Renaissance style; and the **Église Notre-Dame,** built in the 13th century in the Burgundian-Gothic style with a façade decorated partly with gargoyles. On the Jaquemart clock, the hour is struck by a mechanical family.

WHERE TO STAY: Hôtel de la Cloche, 14 Place Darcy (tel. 80-30-12-32), rises grandly like an adapted version of an 18th-century château in the commercial center of town. It is in fact a historic monument whose origins date back to the 15th century. Today visitors can revel in the sophisticated decor of the interior, which was done as recently as 1982. The lobby benefits from the sunlight streaming in from a nearby park and a pinkish-beige color scheme enhanced by dozens of Oriental rugs and pink and gray marble floor. The lobby-level bar is one of the most elegantly posh places in town to have a drink. Its leather and black accents complement the exposed brass and wood tones, and a view of the garden is shared by an adjoining glassed-in tea room. The comfortable bedrooms range in price from 350F ($48.27) to 420F ($57.92) in singles, while doubles cost from 400F ($55.16) to 480F ($66.19).

The hotel's in-house restaurant is named after its very famous chef, Jean-Pierre Billoux. Within a very grand decor which fills both the ground floor and stone-walled cellar of the hotel, you can enjoy the dishes which have put this hotel on the gastronomic map of Burgundy. Mr. Billoux prepares such mouth-watering specialties as hot pâté en croûte, a fine-textured consommé of pike-perch with leeks, quenelles of red snapper, roast wild duck stuffed with foie gras, terrine of pigeon with garlic, fricassée of local snails with garlic, and imaginatively elegant desserts. Fixed-price menus cost between 230F ($31.72) and 360F ($49.64), while à la carte dinners are priced between 400F ($55.16) and 550F ($75.63). Reservations are suggested for meals served daily except Sunday night and all day Monday.

Hostellerie du Chapeau Rouge, 5 rue Michelet (tel. 80-30-28-10), is a Dijonnais landmark, partly because of its desirable site on a quiet street just behind the cathedral and partly because of its celebrated restaurant (see below). The hotel, a member of the nationwide Mapotel chain, is filled with 19th-century antiques, even in the bedrooms, warm colors, and all the modern comforts. You'll appreciate the skylit salon, formerly the courtyard of the 15th-century building. Today it looks like the rattan- and plant-filled atrium of an expensive Florida residence. Each of the 33 rooms contains a private bath and phone. A single rents for 260F ($35.85), that price peaking at 510F ($70.33) in a double.

Hôtel Ibis-Central, 3 Place Grangier (tel. 80-30-44-00), is prominently situated on a busy downtown square in the center of town across from the main post office. It's a clean, attractively priced hotel with pleasantly renovated decor. You can stay in a single room for 200F ($28.96) to 215F ($29.65); a double will cost from 255F ($35.17).

WHERE TO DINE: La Toison d'Or, 18 rue Ste-Anne (tel. 80-30-73-52), offers meals that are gastronomic experiences you will probably never forget. Some of the best cuisine available in a region famous for great food is combined with esthetic pleasure here. The restaurant is at the end of a large stone courtyard, accessible from a quiet street in the old part of town. Inside, the decor is elegantly rustic. Someone will offer you—in English—a tour of the adjoining wine museum and the medieval buildings next door. The premises are part of a 15th-century house which, with its sculpted inner courtyard, was connected to the adjoining 17th-century building. Your guide, depending on the day, might be Madame Barboso, the attractive blond wife of the chef. Her tour will include a grisly depiction of medieval slayings, Carolingian tortures, and a look at the 1,001 accessories that go into the local history of wine making.

Three menus are offered, one at 115F ($15.86), another at 128F ($17.65), and the third at 170F ($23.44). In the half-timbered ambience of stone walls, Oriental rugs, high ceilings, and Louis XIII chairs, you'll enjoy such specialties as feuilleté of trout with a sorrel-flavored sabayon, duck livers and sweetbreads sautéed in a spinach salad, incredibly smooth foie gras, a half-cooked filet of salmon in a delightful bitter sauce, and filet of duckling doused in liver sauce with grated truffles. À la carte meals range from 300F ($41.37) up. The wine list is staggeringly extensive, and many of the vintages are surprisingly moderately priced. The restaurant is closed for lunch on Saturday, all day Sunday, and for about two weeks in August.

La Chouette, 1 rue de la Chouette (tel. 80-30-18-10). Parts of the building date from the 15th century yet the cuisine is totally up-to-date at this family-run restaurant directed by chef Breuil. In one of the city's most delightful old-fashioned sections, the house presents a chipped façade to the quiet cobblestone street. Inside are leaded-glass windows, lots of exposed wood, pink and white lace napery, and a heavily beamed ceiling. Menu specialties include veal kidneys with a thyme-flavored cream sauce, a filet of beef, Bresse pigeon in a garlic cream sauce, filet of sole in a leek sauce, curried monkfish with eggplant, and a full array of other imaginative dishes where the strongly flavored sauces are often as delectable as the main ingredients. A simple set meal is offered for around 95F ($13.10), although more elaborate ones can range as high as 260F ($35.85). À la carte dinners begin at 275F ($37.92) and can go much higher. Meals are served every day except Monday night, Tuesday, and in January.

Le Rallye, 39 rue Chabot-Charny (tel. 80-67-11-55), could not possibly have a more traditional setting, in a stone building on a busy street in the heart of the old city. Owners Roger and Yvette Roncin prepare such specialties as turbot with a fondue of leeks, chicken from Bresse steamed with thyme, leeks in puff pastry with cream sauce, veal liver in raspberry vinegar, mignon of pork with plums, and rabbit with fresh noodles. If you can get a table, you'll see that the interior contains a heavily beamed ceiling, expansive yellowish walls, and old-fashioned furniture. The table d'hôte menus range from 85F ($11.72) to 170F ($23.44), while ordering à la carte can cost 200F ($27.58) and up. Food is served daily except Sunday, Monday for lunch, holidays, from mid-February to early March, and about the last two weeks in July.

Hostellerie du Chapeau Rouge, 5 rue Michelet (tel. 80-30-28-10), has for years benefitted from the happy collaboration of chef Ernest Jung (now in his 60s and a former recipient of the prestigious *Meilleur Ouvrier de France* award) and owner Robert Mornand. On a quiet street just behind the cathedral, the establishment looks like a stone-walled country inn with plain wooden shutters and a surprisingly modern interior decor. The tortoise-shell walls, masses of flowers, warm colors, and sparkling silver candelabra serve as the attractive setting for the imaginative platters prepared by chef Jung with the assistance of a team of much younger helpers. On the menu you'll find filet of beef in a truffle sauce, aiguillettes of duckling in pink peppercorns, suprême of pigeon with chicory, a ragoût of sweetbreads with chicken wings, and mignon of veal in a green pepper and cream sauce. A tempting dessert, which you order at the beginning of your meal, might be the tarte soufflée with warm apples. Meals cost from 275F ($37.92) to 325F ($44.82). The restaurant is closed from just before Christmas until early January.

TOURING NOTES: You can leave Dijon on the N5, heading toward **Paris.**

For a few miles you run on a new road in the **Vallée de l'Ouche,** alongside the Burgundy Canal. The scenery is severe, with large fields spreading over the hills. At **Pont de Pany** keep going on the N5 toward **Sombernon.** After Aubigny, on your left lies the artificial lake of **Grosbois.** The scenery is typical of agricultural France, with isolated farms, woods, and pastures.

You pass through **Vitteaux** and just before the next village, **Posanges,** stands a magnificent feudal château. You can't visit it, but it's worth a picture.

Continue on the N5 for a few miles after Posanges until you come to a railroad crossing. There on your left is another old castle, now part of a farm.

The next village you reach is **Pouillenay.** Turn right there onto the D9, heading toward **Flavigny-sur-Ozerain.** Park your car outside the walls and walk through the old streets. This once-fortified town is filled with decaying grandeur.

You leave Flavigny on the D29, crossing the D6 and turning left on the small D103 toward **Alise-Ste-Reine.** This was the site of the camp of Alésia. In 52 B.C. Caesar overcame Gallic forces here. Millet sculpted a statue of the leader of the Gauls, Vercingetorix. Visitors can explore the excavated ruins of a Roman-Gallic town and visit the **Musée Alésia** (tel. 80-96-10-95) from 9 a.m. to 7 p.m. from July 1 to September 15. Off-season hours are 10 a.m. to 6 p.m. However, it is closed from November to March. Admission is 12F ($1.66) per person. Alise-Ste-Reine honors a Christian girl who was decapitated for refusing to marry a Roman governor, Olibrius. As late as the 17th century, a fountain at the site of the beheading was said to have curative powers.

After Alise-Ste-Reine you can head back toward the village of **Les Laumes,** a railroad center. Before entering the village, make a U-turn to the right, taking the N454 to **Baigneux-les-Juifs.** After the village of **Grésigny** there is a farm-fortress surrounded by water on your left.

One mile farther on, turn right toward the **Château de Bussy Rabutin.** Roger de Rabutin was the cousin of letter-writing Madame de Sévigné. He also wrote, ridiculing the foibles of the court of Louis XIV. For this he had to spend six years in the Bastille. The façade of his former château is characterized by two round towers. The château, miraculously, has survived mostly intact, including the interior decoration ordered by the count. The gardens and park are attributed to Le Nôtre. It is open April 1 to September 30 from 9 a.m. to noon and 2 to 6 p.m. During the rest of the year it receives visitors from 10 a.m. to noon and 2 to 5 p.m. It is closed on Tuesday, and admission is 10F ($1.39).

Going back to Grésigny, turn right before the farm-fortress, then left. Outside the village, turn right again toward **Menetreux Le Pitois.** You're now off the main road and into some real country.

Once back on the N5, head on to **Montbard.** After six miles you reach the village of **Marmagne.** There you can turn right on the D32 toward the **Abbey of Fontenay** (tel. 80-92-15-00). Isolated in a small valley, Fontenay is one of the most unspoiled examples of a 12th-century Cistercian abbey. The abbey was once a paper mill but it's not been restored. The church, from 1139, is one of the oldest Cistercian churches in the country. The cloisters are especially elegant. Open from 9 a.m. to noon and 2 to 6:30 p.m., the abbey charges an admission fee of 20F ($2.76).

14. Montbard

On the Burgundy Canal, this busy port was the birthplace of Comte George Louis Leclerc de Buffon, born there in 1707. The French naturalist was the author of the monumental *Histoire Naturelle,* published in 1749–1804 in 44 volumes. In spite of his international fame, he remained simple in his tastes, preferring to live in Montbard rather than Paris.

Buffon died in Paris in 1788, and he was buried in Montbard in a small chapel next to the **Church of St. Urse.** The **Parc Buffon** was laid out by the great master. You can visit **Tour St-Louis,** where mementos of Buffon are displayed; it is open from 10 a.m. to noon and 3 to 6 p.m. except Wednesday. Buffon's study, **Cabinet de Travail de Buffon,** where he wrote his many volumes, is also open to the public.

FOOD AND LODGING: Hôtel de l'Écu, 7 rue Auguste-Carré (tel. 80-92-11-66), is a sure bet for an excellent meal and a comfortable bed in this part of Burgundy. Owner Bernard Coupat maintains the rustically 18th-century-style dining rooms in apple-pie order, serving such dishes as meurette of beef and a full range of local specialties, which might, when you visit, include breast of duckling beaunoise, coq au vin, or Burgundian snails. Set menus range in price from 75F ($10.32), served only on weekdays, to 210F ($28.96). Children's menus are available as well. If you'd like to stay here overnight or longer, the cost for full board, depending on the season, ranges from 250F ($34.48) to 300F ($41.37) per person. The establishment is closed Saturday and from mid-November to March. To reach it, if you're driving on the A6, exit at Bierre-les-Semur and continue about 15½ miles through the rolling countryside.

Le Saint-Rémy, 2 Route de Dijon, Saint-Rémy (tel. 80-92-13-44), offers the possibility of relaxing Burgundian style in an attractive rustic setting. Meals are skillfully prepared by the owner, Jean Clara. Specialties include eggs en meurette, escargots, a full range of beef and veal dishes, and sweetbreads in mustard sauce. Set meals range in price from 100F ($13.79) to 160F ($22.06) and are served daily except Monday and at night except Saturday and Sunday. The place is closed from just before Christmas to late in January.

ON THE ROAD: Leaving Montbard, cross the Burgundy Canal and take the N80 toward Semur-en-Auxois. A few miles away from the city on the right stand the impressive ruins of the feudal Château de Montfont. In Semur you can visit Église Notre-Dame, rebuilt in the 13th and 14th centuries. You can also spend an hour or so touring the ramparts of the old château there.

The N80 carries you toward Saulieu. At the crossroads with the N70, turn left toward the ruins of Thil, a collegiate church founded in the 14th century. The ruins of the 12th-century château nearby can't be visited without a guide. It was built on the site of a Roman oppidum, and some of the walls date back to the 9th century. The panorama over the countryside is pleasant.

At the village of Precy-sous-Thil, join the N80. The road passes through a forest. After ten miles, you reach—

15. Saulieu

Although the town is fairly interesting, its gastronomy has given this small place international fame. On the boundaries of Morvan and Auxois, the town has enjoyed a reputation for cooking since the 17th century. Even Madame de Sévigné praised it in her letters. So did Rabelais.

The main sight is Basilique St-Andoche on the Place de la Fontaine, which has some interesting decorated capitals. In the art museum, Musée François Pompon, Place de la Fontaine (tel. 80-64-09-22), you can see many works by François Pompon, the well-known sculptor of animals. His bull, considered his masterpiece, stands on a plaza off the N6 at the entrance to Saulieu.

FOOD AND LODGING: Hôtel de la Côte d'Or, 2 rue d'Argentine (tel. 80-64-07-66). Chef Alexandre Dumaine long ago made this hotel world famous. He is long gone, but today, following a string of chef-owners, Bernard Loiseau works hard to maintain the standards. He is one of the most creative and inventive chefs in Burgundy today. The former stagecoach stopover serves one of the finest cuisines in France, even in Europe for that matter. The cooking is less traditional than in times past, but fans of the "new cuisine" will prefer it, as the emphasis is less on sauce and more on herbs. Specialties are based on the season. All the great burgundies are on the wine list. The food is strictly from farm and garden—no tricks, nothing frozen. Lunch costs from 230F ($31.72), dinner from 400F ($55.16).

If you want to stay overnight, if you've had a little too much burgundy, you'll find recently renovated accommodations. Your bed will be comfortable, although it's likely to be 200 years old. The style of the rooms range from Empire to Louis XV, an accumulation of several generations of innkeepers. Fifteen accommodations with private bath or shower are rented, costing from 250F ($34.48) for two persons, rising to 700F ($96.53), plus 15% service. In addition, two persons can rent one of nine apartments in an annex decorated in a contemporary style. Rates range from 850F ($117.22) to 1,500F ($206.85), plus service. The inn is closed for Wednesday lunch and on Tuesday from November to the end of March, as well as shutting down entirely from mid-November to early December and for the first two weeks in March.

Hotel de la Poste, 1 rue Grillot (tel. 80-64-05-67). Its 17th-century walls were originally built as a postal relay station. The Virlouvet family completely renovated its interior. Their comfortably upholstered and air-conditioned bedrooms contain private bath, a phone, and sometimes a view of a flowering courtyard. Singles or doubles rent for between 225F ($31.03) and 330F ($45.51), breakfast not included. The belle époque dining room is open to nonresidents interested in a conservatively well-prepared meal. Specialties include escalope of sea perch with baby vegetables, shrimp with saffron and asparagus tips, filet of Charolais beef with a marrow sauce, kidneys in a sauce of aged mustard, and terrine of rascasse. Fixed-price meals begin at 120F ($16.55) but could cost twice as much on the à la carte.

16. Aubigney

This little hamlet, about 9 miles from Gray and some 27 miles from Dijon, would have little to recommend if it weren't for the following establishment, whose hospitality and good food make it worthy of a trip there. It is especially ideal for motorists who would prefer to stay away from the tourist centers such as Dijon. Aubigney lies in the southwestern corner of the département of Haute-Saône.

FOOD AND LODGING: **Auberge du Vieux Moulin** (tel. 84-31-21-16), offers a calming and beautiful ambience in a centuries-old building, under the skillful direction of Louise Mirbey and her daughter Elisabeth. Under the tiled hip roof lies a property that has been in the Mirbey family since the end of the 18th century and that used to serve as a mill for grinding wheat and then for sawing timbers.

Today you'll find elegantly maintained antiques, immaculate napery, gilt-rimmed mirrors, and sparkling table settings. Both of the genteel owners are active members of the Association des Restauratrices Cuisinières, a nationwide organization of female chefs that meets regularly to promote the role of women within the male-dominated bastion of French cuisine. In fact, Elisabeth, with two other cuisinières, was the first woman to prepare a meal within the Élysée Palace, at which President Mitterand dined with Françoise Sagan on Elisabeth's preferred dessert, crêpes de la chandeleur en aumonière à la crème de Grand Marnier.

Specialties include sweetbreads house style, shrimp in champagne sauce, morels with cream sauce, and rabbit in wine sauce. The homemade desserts are feathery light and make savory endings to full meals. Fixed-price meals range from 130F ($17.93) to 320F ($44.13), while à la carte costs around 250F ($34.48). Technically, the "old mill" is open for meals every day, but it's important to call ahead for reservations if you plan to dine or to overnight in one of the seven bedrooms. This especially applies from December till the end of February, although in summer the loyal local clientele usually assures that there will be other diners joining you. Accommodations range from 220F ($30.34) in a single to 330F ($45.51) in a double.

Chapter XVI

THE VALLEY OF
THE RHÔNE

1. Bourg-en-Bresse
2. The Beaujolais Country
3. Lyon
4. Pérouges
5. Roanne
6. Vienne
7. Condrieu
8. Valence
9. Montélimar

LE RHÔNE, just as mighty as the Saône is peaceful, is celebrated for the excellence of its table. These two great rivers form a part of the French countryside that is often glimpsed only briefly by motorists rushing south to the Riviera on the thundering Mediterranean Express. But this land of mountains and rivers, linked by a good road network, invites more exploration than that; it is the home of the beaujolais country; France's gastronomic center, Lyon; Roman ruins, charming villages, and castles.

It was from the Valley of the Rhône that Greek art and Roman architecture made their way to the Loire Valley, the château country, and finally to Paris. The district abounds in pleasant old inns and good restaurants, offering a regional cuisine that is among the finest in the world.

I'll start our exploration in the north, which is really the southern part of Burgundy, ending our itinerary in the northern sector of Provence.

1. Bourg-en-Bresse

The ancient capital of Bresse, this farming and business center lies on the border between Burgundy and the Jura, 21 miles from Mâcon, 38 miles north of Lyon. It is considered a gastronomic center in the region.

Art lovers are attracted to its **Church of Brou,** with magnificent tombs, one of France's greatest artistic heritages. In the flamboyant Gothic style, the church was built between 1506 and 1532 by Margaret of Austria, the ill-fated daughter of the Emperor Maximilian. Over the ornate Renaissance doorway the tympanum depicts Margaret and her "handsome duke," Philibert, who died when he caught cold on a hunting expedition. The initials of Philibert (sometimes known as "the Fair") and Margaret are linked by love-knots.

Inside, the nave and its double aisles are admirable. Look for a rood screen which is ornately decorated with basket-handle arching. To tour the choir you'll need the services of a guide. Rich in decorative detail, the choir stalls, 74 in all, were made out of oak, the work completed in just two years by the local craftsmen. One detail shows a fat monk spanking a little boy who is on his knees, his naked rear exposed.

The tombs form the church's greatest treasure. In Carrara marble, the statues are of Philibert, who died in 1504, and of Margaret of Austria, who remained faithful to his memory until her own death in 1530. Another tomb is that of Margaret of Bourbon, the grandmother of François I, who died in 1483. See also the stained-glass windows, inspired by a Dürer engraving, and a retable depicting *The Seven Joys of the Madonna*.

From April 1 to September 30 the church can be visited from 8:30 a.m. to noon and 2 to 6:30 p.m. During the rest of the year hours are 10 a.m. to noon and 2 to 6:30 p.m. Admission is 8F ($1.10) weekdays, half price on Sunday.

If time remains, see the **Church of Notre-Dame,** begun in 1505 and containing some finely carved stalls dating from the 16th century. There are some 15th-century houses on the rue du Palais and the rue Gambetta, if you'd like to wander around town.

Many people from Lyon who have seen the tombs drive north from their city just to dine at the following recommendation.

WHERE TO DINE: **Auberge Bressane,** 166 Boulevard de Brou (tel. 74-22-22-68). This ancient part of France is known around the world for the excellence of its capon and roasting chickens. Bresse poultry is considered the best in France, and it has been eulogized by all the "peers of the table." Therefore in its ancient capital it is fitting and proper that the chef, Jean-Pierre Vullin, specialize in the succulent volaille de Bresse, served with cream and morels when in season. The chicken is bathed in milk, giving it a pearly color. Of course the chef, presiding over his old, rustic *maison*, knows how to do other dishes equally well. You may enjoy a gâteau of chicken liver, pike quenelles with a Nantua sauce, frogs' legs with fines herbes, a gâteau of crayfish tails, or sea bass flavored with fresh basil. You can accompany any or all of these with regional wines such as Seyssel and Montagnieu. Set menus are offered at 150F ($16.55), 200F ($27.58), and 320F ($44.13). A la carte dinners range from 275F ($37.92) to 350F ($48.27). Service is extra. The restaurant is closed Monday night, Tuesday, and from late November to mid-December. The auberge is across from the Church of Brou.

Hotel Restaurant du Mail, Route de Trévoux (46 Avenue du Mail) (tel. 74-21-00-26), is one of the most popular restaurants in the region. If you drop in on a weekend, especially on Sunday at noon, you're likely to see everyone and his or her country cousin enjoying the conservative specialties, which include, for example, sautéed frogs' legs, roast Bresse chicken, warm salad of sea bass (loup), and tartly fruited desserts. Roger Charolles, the chef, directs the operation in what has become an unchanging but sure-bet institution. Fixed-price menus range from 90F ($12.41) to 200F ($27.58), while à la carte dinners cost from 215F ($29.65) to 240F ($33.10). The establishment closes its doors Sunday night, Monday, the first two weeks in June, and from just before Christmas till mid-January. A handful of simple rooms, 11 in all, are available for 120F ($16.55) in a single and 255F ($35.17) in a double.

If you'd like to spend less money, you'll find very good food at **Au Chalet de Brou,** Boulevard de Brou (tel. 74-22-26-28), which is also in the restaurant cluster facing the Church of Brou. The chef offers tasty poultry dishes among his specialties. Regional products and fresh ingredients are emphasized. A set meal begins at 75F ($10.32), and others go for 95F ($13.10) and 190F ($26.20). The restaurant is closed Thursday night, Friday, from June 1 to June 15, and from just before Christmas to mid-January.

WHERE TO STAY: **Hotel du Prieuré,** 49 Boulevard de Brou (tel. 74-22-44-60). One of the newest hotels in town rises like a modernized villa within a large and well-kept garden, a few steps from the intricate stonework of the Church of Brou. Inside, an array of contrasting fabrics and designs in the plushly uphol- stered sitting room is accented with an occasional potted palm. The 14 bed- rooms are sunny, conservative, and comfortably furnished, each soundproofed and, for the most part, with a private terrace or balcony. The staff members do their best to make visitors feel at home. Singles cost 300F ($41.37); doubles, 520F ($71.71).

Le Logis de Brou, 132 Boulevard de Brou (tel. 74-22-11-55), stands in the vicinity of the church. It has 30 rooms to rent, 18 of which contain private bath. Units are comfortably furnished, somewhat dated, costing 146F ($20.13) in a single, the price going up to 280F ($38.61) in a double. There's a charming little salon with a fireside, but no restaurant—which will free you to sample the viands at the establishments already recommended.

2. The Beaujolais Country

The vineyards of Beaujolais start about 25 miles north of Lyon. This wine- producing region is small—only 40 miles long and less than 10 miles wide—yet it is one of the most famous areas in the nation and has become increasingly known throughout the world because of the "beaujolais craze" that began in Paris some 25 years ago. The United States is now one of the three big world markets for beaujolais. In an average year this tiny region produces some 30 million gallons of the wine, more than 130,000,000 bottles.

Léon Daudet once wrote, "Lyon has three rivers, the Rhône, the Saône, and the Beaujolais." Unlike the wine road of Alsace, the beaujolais country does not have a clearly defined route. Motorists seem to branch off in many directions, stopping at whatever point or wine cellar intrigues or amuses them. I can't think of a way to improve on that system.

However, in the capital of beaujolais, **Villefranche,** it would be wise to go to the **Office du Tourisme,** 7 rue de la Paix (tel. 74-68-05-18), not far from the market place. There you can pick up a booklet on the beaujolais country con- taining a map of the region and giving many itineraries. The booklet lists some 30 villages and the wine-tasting cellars open to the public.

In Le Beaujolais—the countryside, not the wine—you'll find a colorful part of France: not only vineyards on sunlit hillsides but pleasant golden cot- tages where the vine growers live, as well as historic houses and castles. It has been called the "Land of the Golden Stones."

If you want specific sites to visit, I suggest the monastery, Le Prieuré, at **Salles,** the church and the Romanesque cloister built in the 11th and 12th centur- ies out of mellow golden stones, plus **Le Chapitre des Chanoinesses,** the chapter house of the canonesses erected in the 18th century. The tour through the com- plex takes about 1½ hours. The site is open in July and August from 10:30 a.m. to noon and 2:30 to 5:30 p.m., charging an admission of 4F (55¢). If the guide isn't there and for other months of the year, telephone 74-67-51-81 or 74-67-57- 39. Salles lies northwest of Villefranche. Before you reach it, you might want to stop first at—

Saint-Julien-sous-Montmelas, 6½ miles northwest of Villefranche. This charming village was the home of Claude Bernard, the father of physiology, who was born there in 1813. The small stone house in which he lived—now the **Musée Claude-Bernard** (tel. 74-67-51-44)—contains mementos of the great scholar, including instruments and books that belonged to him. The museum is open every day except Monday, from 9 a.m. to noon and 2 to 6 p.m., charging an admission of 6F (83¢).

Most people don't come to the beaujolais country to visit specific sites but rather to drink the wine. There are some 180 châteaux scattered throughout this part of France. At many of these a wine devotee can stop and sample the beau- jolais or buy bottles of it.

One of the friendliest and most inviting of these châteaux is the **Domaine de Bois-France,** just beyond Jarnioux. There you are invited to enter a large, deep room. One side of this cellar is lined with huge barrels of beaujolais; their spigots are decorated in summer with wildflowers, a nice touch. Tables and chairs are placed in front of the barrels, and you can select a seat for enjoying your beaujolais-tasting adventure. You can also enter another long, narrow room down a flight of steps. This cellar has a vaulted stone ceiling supported by pillars. The air is pungent with the aroma of beaujolais. In the deep cellar you'll find a vine grower in an indigo-blue apron ready to hand you samples. You can drink as many vintages as you like, or as much as you can hold. But the man in the apron is keeping count. At the end of your spree he'll present you with a bill. You can also buy bottles of beaujolais here.

Juliénas is a village that produces a full-bodied, robust wine. In this village people go to the **Cellier dans l'Ancien Église,** the old church cellar, to sip the wine. A statue of Bacchus with some scantily clad and tipsy girlfriends looks on from what used to be the altar.

At **Chenas,** three miles south of Juliénas, you might want to schedule a luncheon stopover. A popular eating place, one of the best dining rooms in the beaujolais country, is **Robin,** aux Deschamps (tel. 85-36-72-67). Daniel Robin is an excellent cuisinier, having worked with the great Alain Chapel. He does superb regional dishes, including a Bresse chicken cooked in beaujolais and some of the finest andouillette (chitterling sausage) I've ever sampled, or if you prefer, you can dine more elegantly on foie gras of duckling. His gratin of crayfish and his Charolais bourguignon have drawn the praise of gastronomes. At his lovely old house you can enjoy a meal for 145F ($20) to 280F ($38.61). Naturally, you can order the best of beaujolais. The restaurant is closed on Wednesday and at night except on Saturday. Vacation time is from the end of July through the first week in August and from mid-February to mid-March.

Heading south, you reach **Villié-Morgon,** which produces one of the greatest of beaujolais wines. In the basement of the Hôtel de Ville, in a village-owned park, the **Caveau de Morgon** (tel. 74-04-20-99) is open daily from 9 a.m. to noon and 2 to 7 p.m., charging no admission.

If you'd like another dining choice in the beaujolais country, I suggest driving south from Villié-Morgon to the junction with the D37. Head due east to—

Belleville-sur-Saône. There **Le Beaujolais,** 40 rue du Maréchal-Foch (tel. 74-66-05-31), run by Mesdames Dalmaz and Boutorine, is one of the leading restaurants in the whole district, some say the very best. Diners enjoy a rustic medieval ambience and the cuisine of the beaujolais country, which is likely to feature andouillette (chitterling sausage) with beaujolais, frogs' legs sautéed with fines herbes, crayfish in a cream sauce, coq au vin that is rich and tasty, and rosette lyonnaise, a large, dry sausage. In this provincial setting the service is polite and considerate—in all, a friendly stopover. Menus are offered at 75F ($10.32), 120F ($16.55), and 150F ($20.69). The restaurant is closed Tuesday night, Wednesday, and for most of December.

Or as an alternative you can continue for an 11-mile run to Chatillon-sur-Chalaronne, where you'll find a charming inn, **Au Chevalier Norbert,** Avenue C-Desormes (tel. 74-55-02-22), run by Mr. and Mrs. Villon (he is the chef de cuisine). Their rooms are well furnished and comfortable. Depending on the room assignment and the plumbing, doubles begin at 215F ($29.65), going up to 435F ($59.99), the latter with twin beds and a dressing room. You are always able to order a good dinner here, except on Monday when the restaurant is closed. Their simplest menu, at 125F ($17.24), is called their business bill of fare. Other menus are offered, including a 185F ($25.51) "greedy bill of fare." For gourmets with gargantuan appetites, there is always the "toasting bill of fare," at 285F ($39.30).

3. Lyon

At the junction of the turbulent Rhône and the tranquil Saône, a crossroads of Western Europe, Lyon is the third-largest city in France. It is a leader in book publishing and banking and is the world's silk capital. It is also the gastronomic capital of France. Some of the most highly rated restaurants in the country, including Paul Bocuse (about which more below), are found in and around Lyon. Such dishes as Lyon sausage, quenelles (fish balls), and tripe lyonnaise enjoy international renown. The region's succulent Bresse poultry is the best in France.

Forty-five minutes by plane and less than four hours by train from Paris, 319 miles away, Lyon makes a good stopover en route to the Alps or the Riviera. There are two train stations in Lyon. If you're arriving from the north, don't get off at the first station, Gare Part-Dieu. Continue on to Gare Perrache, where you can begin sightseeing.

Founded in 43 B.C., the city became known as Lugdunum, capital of Gaul, a cornerstone of the Roman Empire. Although its fortunes declined with those of Rome, it revived during the French Renaissance.

A seat of learning, Lyon has a university that is second only to the Sorbonne of Paris. Incidentally, the university has a veterinary school founded in 1762, the oldest in the world.

SEEING THE CITY: A good beginning for your tour of Lyon is the **Place Bellecour,** one of the largest and most charming squares in France. A handsome equestrian statue of Louis XIV looks out upon the encircling 18th-century buildings. Going down rue Victor-Hugo, south of the square, you reach the **Basilique Romane de St-Martin-d'Ainay,** the oldest church in Lyon, dating from 1107.

Nearby are two of the city's most important museums. The first, at 30 rue de la Charité, is the **Musée des Arts-Décoratifs** (tel. 78-37-15-05), in the Lacroix-Laval mansion built by Souffiot in 1739 (he was the architect of the Panthéon in Paris). It contains furniture and objets d'art, mostly from the 17th and 18th centuries, although the medieval and Renaissance periods are also represented—a little bit of everything, from ivory-decorated rifles to fourposters in red velvet. It is open from 10 a.m. to noon and 2 to 5:30 p.m. except Monday, charging 11F ($1.52) for admission. Your ticket entitles you to visit not only the Museum of Decorative Arts but the even more interesting **Musée Historique des Tissus,** next door at 34 rue de la Charité (tel. 78-37-15-05), which keeps the same hours. In the 1730 Palace of Villeroy, the museum, one of the most unusual attractions of Lyon, contains a priceless collection of fabrics from all over the world and spanning 2,000 years—a woven record of civilization. Some of the finest fabric made in Lyon from the 17th century to the present day is displayed. The textiles embroidered with religious motifs in the 15th and 16th centuries are noteworthy, as are the 17th-century Persian carpets.

Back at the Place Bellecour, head north along rue de l'Hôtel-de-Ville, which leads to the **Place des Terreaux.** Dominating this square of buildings is the **Hôtel de Ville,** one of the most beautiful town halls in Europe, dating from 1746. The outside is dark and rather severe, but the inside is brilliant and friendly to visitors, just like the people of Lyon.

On the south side of the square stands the **Palais des Arts** (also called the Palace of St. Pierre), a former Benedictine abbey, with an outstanding collection of paintings and sculpture displayed in its **Musée des Beaux-Arts,** 20 Place des Terreaux (tel. 78-28-07-66). Built between 1659 and 1685 in the Italian baroque style, the palace is open from 10:45 a.m. to 6 p.m. daily except on Tuesday, charging no admission. First, you step into the most charming courtyard in Lyon, graced with statuary, chirping birds, and shady trees. On the ground floor is a large sculpture collection. Some of the Oriental porcelain displays humorous motifs. The parade of art history passes by: Etruscan, Egyptian, Phoenician, Sumerian. See in particular Perugino's altarpiece. The top floor is devoted to more contemporary art, with works by Dufy, Léger, Picasso, Matisse, Braque, Bonnard, Sisley, Manet, Monet, Degas, Van Gogh, Rodin, and especially Gauguin.

Nearby at 13 rue de la Poulaillerie, the **Musée de l'Imprimerie et de la Banque** (tel. 78-37-65-98) is housed in a 15th-century mansion that was the Hôtel de Ville of Lyon in the 17th century. It is devoted to mementos of Lyon's position in the world of printing and banking. Printing exhibits include a page of a Gutenberg Bible, 17th- to 20th-century presses, manuscripts, 16th- and 18th-century woodcuts, and many engravings. This is one of the most important printing museums in Europe, ranking with those at Mainz and Antwerp. It has a collection of books dating from "all epochs," including incunabula, books printed before Easter 1500. It also contains the first book printed in Lyons, as well as the first book printed in French. The exhibits continue until you reach the birth of the modern press. The banking section depicts Lyonnais banking in the 16th century, right up to the present. In addition to this general sweep of Lyon banks, you can see such details as the quotation of industrial shares in 1875. The museum is open daily from 9:30 a.m. to noon and 2 to 6 p.m. except on Monday and Tuesday. Admission is free.

Vieux Lyon

From the Place Bellecour cross the Pont Bonaparte to the right bank of the Saône. You'll be in Vieux Lyon, one of France's leading tourist attractions, the result of massive urban renewal. Covering about a square mile, Old Lyon contains one of the finest collections of medieval and Renaissance buildings in Europe. Many of these houses were built five stories high by thriving merchants to show off their newly acquired wealth. After years as a slum, the area is now fashionable, attracting antique dealers, artisans, weavers, sculptors, and painters, who never seem to tire of scenes along the characteristic **rue du Boeuf,** one of the best streets for walking and exploring.

Greeting you first, however, is the **Primatiale St-Jean,** 70 rue Saint-Jean (tel. 78-42-11-04), a cathedral built between the 12th and 15th centuries. Its apse is a masterpiece of Lyonnais Romanesque. Exceptional stained-glass windows are from the 12th to the 15th centuries. Seek out in particular the flamboyant Gothic chapel of the Bourbons. On the front portals are medallions depicting the signs of the zodiac, the story of creation, and the life of St. John which number among the finest examples of French medieval sculpture. The cathedral's 16th-century Swiss astronomical clock is intricate and beautiful; it announces the hour at noon, 2 p.m., and 3 p.m. grandly, with a rooster crowing and angels heralding the event. Incidentally, the axis of the cathedral curves slightly to suggest the curve of Christ's body on the cross. In the cathedral on the right, you can enter the treasury where rare pieces are exhibited, including jewels and precious Lyonnais silk. This room can be visited in the afternoon daily except Tuesday. Admission is 8F ($1.10) for adults, 5F (69¢) for children and students.

South of the cathedral is **Manécenterie,** noted for its Romanesque façade from the 12th century. The boys who sang in the medieval choir at the church were housed there, making it the oldest residence in Lyon.

North of the cathedral is the major sector of Old Lyon, where restoration is proceeding financed in part by the French government. It is a true *musée vivant,* or living museum, with narrow streets, courtyards, spiral stairs, hanging gardens, and soaring towers. The most outstanding of these courtyards is the overhanging gallery of the **Hôtel Buillioud,** built in 1536 for a bureaucrat by Philibert Delorme, who designed the Tuileries Palace in Paris.

On the rue de Gadagne (no. 10) stands the **Hôtel de Gadagne,** an early 16th-century residence. Rabelais described its rich decor. It now houses the **Musée Historique de Lyon** (tel. 78-42-03-61), with interesting Romanesque sculptures on the ground floor. Other exhibits include 18th-century Lyon furniture and pottery, Nevers ceramics, a pewter collection, and numerous paintings and engravings of Lyon vistas. It is open from 10:45 a.m. to 6 p.m. except Tuesday. No admission is charged. In the same building is the **Musée de la Marionette** (same phone), which has three puppets by Laurent Mourguet, creator of Guignol, the best known of all French marionette characters, as well as marionettes coming from other regions of France (Amiens, Lille, Aix-en-Provence, and others), plus important collections from around the world (Italy, Belgium, Turkey, Indonesia, and Russia). It keeps the same hours as the history museum.

While still in Vieux Lyon, try to visit the 16th-century **Maison Thomassin,** Place du Change, a mansion with exceptional Gothic arcades; the 16th-century **Hôtel du Chamarier,** 37 rue Saint-Jean, where the Marquise de Sévigné lived; and finally, the **Church of St. Paul,** with its octagonal lantern tower from the 12th century. The church has been rebuilt, but it traces its history back to the 6th century.

Rising to the west of Vieux Lyon on a hill on the west bank of the Saône is—

Fourvière Hill and Basilica

This richly wooded hill, on which numerous convents, colleges, hospitals, two Roman theaters, and a superb Gallo-Roman museum have been established, affords a panoramic vista of Lyon, with its many bridges across two rivers, the rooftops of the medieval town, and in clear weather, a view of the surrounding countryside extending to the snow-capped Alps. Enthroned on its summit is the 19th-century **Basilica of Our Lady of Fourvière** (Basilique Notre-Dame de Fourvière) (tel. 78-25-51-82), fortress-like with its four octagonal towers and crenelated walls. Its interior is covered with richly colored mosaics. Adjoining is an ancient chapel, dating from the 12th to the 18th centuries. The belfry is surmounted by a gilded statue of the Virgin.

The Gardens of the Rosary extend on the hillside between the basilica and the 13th-century Cathedral of St. Jean. They are open between 8 a.m. and 6 p.m. and provide a pleasant walk. A vast shelter for up to 200 pilgrims is found here. An elevator takes visitors to the top of the towers. Two funiculars serve the hill. The round-trip fare is 8F ($1.10).

In a park south of the basilica are the excavated **Théâtres Romains,** a Roman theater and odeum at 6 rue de l'Antiquaille. The theater is the most ancient in France, built by order of Augustus Caesar in 15 B.C., and greatly expanded during the reign of Hadrian. It had a curtain which was raised and lowered during performances. The odeum, which was reserved for musical performances, apparently was once sumptuously decorated. Its orchestra floor, for example, contains mosaics of such materials as brightly colored marble and porphyry. The third remaining building in the sanctuary was dedicated in A.D. 160 to the goddess Cybele, or Sibella, whose cult originated in Asia Minor. All that remains are the foundations, although they almost seem to dominate the theater (175 feet by 284 feet). An altar dedicated to a bull cult and a monumental statue in marble of the goddess are exhibited in the **Musée de la Civilisation Gallo-Romaine,** 17 rue Cléberg (tel. 78-25-94-68), which is a few steps from the archeological site. From March to October the site is open from 9 a.m. to noon and 2 to 6 p.m. daily except Sunday morning. You can visit with a guide on Sunday and holidays between 3 and 6 p.m. Admission is free. Performances are given at both theaters in summer.

Croix-Rousse

North of Lyon's downtown district lies **Colline de la Croix-Rousse,** crowned by the baroque church of **St-Bruno-des-Chartreux.** This sector has been the center of the French silk industry since the 15th century. Until fairly recently the old houses along the hill were still inhabited by weavers who both lived and worked there. You can visit a workshop at **Musée des Canutes,** 10-12 rue d'Ivry (tel. 78-28-62-04), where weavers work at their age-old craft. Lyon is famed for its renewed silk industry. The museum is open from 8:30 a.m. to noon and 2 to 6:30 p.m. daily except Sunday. Admission is 4F (55¢).

The area is distinguished by its *traboules*—rather long and dimly lit passageways running under the Gothic vaulting of the houses. Often they extend from one building to another and even from one street to another.

On the Outskirts

Built on the slope of Croix-Rousse, near **Condate,** a Gallic village at the confluence of the Rhône and Saône Rivers, stands the **Arena of the Three Gauls,** a partly excavated amphitheater. It's known to have existed several centuries before the Romans arrived. Delegates from 60 tribes from all over Gaul met here in the earliest known example of a French parliamentary system—in fact, it is sometimes referred to as the world's first parliament. For this reason the 2,000th anniversary of France, its bimillennium, will be celebrated in Lyon in 1989.

Across the Rhône, the 290-acre **Parc de la Tête** is the setting for a son-et-lumière program from June to October. Surrounded by a wealthy residential quarter, the park has a lake, illuminated fountains, a fine little zoo, and a botanical garden with greenhouses. Its rose garden, with some 100,000 plants, is unique.

In the tiny village of **Hauteville** near Lyon stands one of the strangest pieces of architecture in the world, representing the lifelong avocation of a French postman, Ferdinand Cheval. It is a palace of fantasy in a high-walled garden. One is reminded of Simon Rodia, who built the unique Watts Tower in Los Angeles. During his lifetime Monsieur Cheval was ridiculed by his neighbors as a "crackpot," but his palace has been declared a national monument. The work was finished in 1912, when Cheval was 76 years old; he died in 1925. The north end of the façade is in a massive rococo style. The turreted tower rises 35 feet, and the entire building is 85 feet long. The elaborate sculptural decorations include animals, such as leopards, and artifacts, such as Roman vases.

At **Rochetaillée-Saône,** seven miles north of Lyon on La Route Nationale 433, the **Musée Français de l'Automobile "Henri Malartre"** is installed in the historic **Château de Rochetaillée** (tel. 78-22-18-80). One of the earliest cars exhibited is an 1898 Peugeot. A 1908 Berliet, a 1900 Renault, and such later models as a 1938 Lancia-Astura delight as well. The château is surrounded by a large park. From March 15 to September 14 the museum is open from 8 a.m. to noon and 2 to 7 p.m., the rest of the year to 6 p.m. The admission is 15F ($2.07).

HOTELS: Lyon has never been as renowned for its hotels as for its restaurants; however, there are many worthy candidates.

The Upper Bracket

Sofitel Lyon, Quai Gailleton (tel. 78-42-72-50), is the leading hotel in Lyon, with a patio containing tropical plants and a panoramic restaurant, Le Sofi-Shop, where set meals start at 115F ($15.86). Another restaurant, Les Trois Dômes, is located upstairs on the eighth floor; a repast there starts at 425F ($58.61). Opening onto the Rhône, it also tempts with its views of Vieux Lyon. The bar, Le Frégoli, is a favorite predinner rendezvous. The 200 combination bed-sitting rooms all have warm decorative themes in autumnal colors, along with picture windows, television, radio, direct-dial phone, and individually controlled air conditioning and heating. Singles rent for 720F ($99.29); doubles peak at 1,050F ($144.80).

Frantel, 129 rue Servient (tel. 78-62-94-12), is said to be the tallest hotel in Europe, as it is situated inside the cylindrical glass-walled tower shared by the Crédit Lyonnais bank. The seven-story lobby is ringed with an atrium-like series of corridors leading to the functionally furnished but comfortable bedrooms. Each of these contains a dramatically tiled modern bath and well-coordinated accessories. The 242 rooms rent for 500F ($68.95) in a single, for 650F ($89.64) in a double. One of the hotel's restaurants, L'Arc-en-Ciel, lies on the tower's 30th floor, offering well-prepared specialties and a panoramic view, all for 210F ($28.96) to 285F ($39.30) for a meal. The restaurant is closed all day Sunday, lunchtime Monday, and from mid-July to August 31. La Ripaille grill room serves meals from 125F ($17.24) and is closed Friday night and Saturday. The hotel is in a part of town known as La Part-Dieu Nord.

Le Grand Hôtel Concorde, 11 rue Grolée (tel. 78-42-56-11), was built near the river at the end of the 19th century. Its elegant cream-and-beige exterior conceals an interior that was almost completely renovated in 1982 into a conservative style which uses rich colors, Oriental rugs, and marble accents. Each of the 150 well-furnished rooms contains a mini-bar, TV, phone, air conditioning, and private bath. Prices range from 420F ($57.92) in a single to 700F ($96.53) in a double.

Hôtel Terminus (Terminus Perrache), 12 Cours de Verdun (tel. 78-37-58-11), as its name suggests, lies near the Perrache train station. The hotel offers some of the best rooms in Lyon. These are outfitted with plush fabrics and inviting colors, and open onto hallways graced with Oriental runners, 19th-century furniture, and painted jardinières. The hotel bar, which serves unusually large drinks, is more modern than the other sections, and a recently restored restaurant is near the front entrance. Be warned that the rooms facing the street may be noisy at night, although the management has taken pains to soundproof them. Singles rent for 400F ($55.16), while doubles cost 660F ($91.01).

The Middle Bracket

Hôtel Carlton, 4 rue Jussieu (tel. 78-42-56-21), is an elegant, high-ceilinged hotel near the Rhône. The lobby has a coffered blue-gray and gold ceiling and a wrought-iron elevator set between the limestone curves of the grand staircase. Pleasantly furnished singles rent for 260F ($35.85) to 330F ($45.51), while doubles peak at 440F ($60.68).

Hôtel des Artistes, 18 Place Célestins (tel. 78-42-04-88), is a little gem. Right in the city center, it's home base for many singers, actors, and revue artists who appear in the theater across the square. Autographed photographs are kept under glass at the reception desk. The rooms have varied plumbing and are priced accordingly, singles averaging around 260F ($35.85), doubles peaking at 340F ($46.89). The furnishings are modern, and all is clean and comfortable.

The Budget Range

Hôtel La Résidence, 18 rue Victor-Hugo (tel. 78-42-63-28), is one of my favorite budget hotels in Lyon. At the corner of a pedestrian zone, the ornate 19th-century façade is painted in two shades of yellow. The English-speaking management will offer you a room with bath priced at 190F ($26.20) to 200F ($30.34) either single or double. Two singles with shower are priced at only 155F ($21.38) apiece. There's no bar on the premises, but drinks can be served in the green-and-white-trimmed marble lobby if you want them.

Bayard, 23 Place Bellecour (tel. 78-37-39-64), opposite the Lyon Tourist Office, is a remake of an old town house, opening directly onto the landmark

Place Bellecour midway between the two rivers. Don't be put off by the entrance, which is down a narrow hallway on the second floor. Inside, you'll find special accommodations, each with a different name, price, and decor, ranging from rustic to Louis XIV to Directoire to "grandmère." Singles rent for 160F ($22.06), doubles for 210F ($28.96). Parking is available.

Grand Hôtel des Terreaux, 16 rue Lanterne (tel. 78-27-04-10), is an appealing choice, lying within the historic and artistic quarter of Lyon. The old-style façade has been renovated, as have the modernized rooms. Rates are from 210F ($28.96) to 230F ($31.72) in a single, the latter with bath, and from 250F ($34.48) to 275F ($37.92) in a double, depending on the plumbing. Bargain specials are the units for three persons, costing from 290F ($39.99) to 320F ($44.13). Spread on five floors, reached by elevator, the rooms are clean, comfortable, and quiet. Some are decorated in the Louis XV style. Within a 15-minute walk of the hotel are several famous restaurants, along with *bouchons* which specialize in a typical à la lyonnaise cookery.

Grand Hôtel des Étrangers, 5 rue Stella (tel. 78-42-01-55), offers simple and uncluttered rooms at relatively inexpensive prices. Conveniently located in the center of town, it is a six-story white building with wrought-iron window guards. The modernized interior contains a bar area with leatherette chairs, while the rooms usually have phone, TV, and refrigerator. Depending on the plumbing, singles cost 240F ($33.10) to 310F ($42.75), while doubles range from 300F ($41.37) to 375F ($51.71), with breakfast included.

WHERE TO DINE: Even though I've labeled these starred restaurants upper bracket (and they most assuredly are that), a diner of moderate means can often eat at one of these citadels of cuisine by ordering their most reasonably priced set menu. For example, one such set menu recently began with an escalope of foie gras with mushrooms "from the woods" and went on to other delectable dishes.

The food in Lyon, as already noted, is among the finest in the world, as exemplified by the following recommendation.

The Upper Bracket

Paul Bocuse, Pont de Collonges (tel. 78-22-01-40). The man is the most famous contemporary chef in the world. His restaurant—one of the greatest in France—is on the banks of the Saône at Collonges-au-Mont-d'Or, more than 5½ miles north of Lyon on Route N433. Monsieur Bocuse is also one of the great Gallic ambassadors. Once called an enfant terrible, he's been known to dance on the tables at the end of the evening and even toss champagne glasses in the air. He specializes in regional produce and cookery. He was the leading exponent of La Nouvelle Cuisine but once told the press he considers that innovative cookery "a joke." He seems to have returned to dishes familiar to him long ago. That is, when he's in Lyon. Because he's such a renowned chef, he's often away on tours.

Most repasts at his luxuriously appointed establishment begin with a Burgundian apéritif, Kir (champagne and a crème de cassis or black currant liqueur, or even a touch of raspberry liqueur). My favorite main course, which I invariably have when I pass through the area, is an impeccably constructed loup en croûte. This is a sea bass on a bed of tarragon and other herbs and stuffed with lobster mousse. It's then baked in a pastry shell symbolically decorated to represent the fish inside. It is served with a light tomato-and-cream sauce Choron ladled over it. But Monsieur Bocuse does many other dishes well too. For openers, try his warm pâté of game birds bécassines served with truffles, or his terrines of foie gras and squab. The fruit sorbets are among the best I've ever had, particularly the strawberry. For a complete meal, expect to pay at least 550F ($75.63) and up, which may turn out to be one of the best investments you've ever made. Set meals are offered for 290F ($39.99), 375F ($51.71), and 420F ($57.92), plus service. The restaurant is open all year round.

Although Paul Bocuse is my admitted favorite, Lyon has many great restaurants, which is why I always spend several days there on my journeys through France.

I always venture out for at least one meal at **Alain Chapel** (tel. 78-91-82-02) in the hamlet of Mionnay, 12½ miles north of Lyon. This Relais Gourmand is one of the great restaurants of France. A stylish place with a flower-garden setting, it at first evokes an Iberian parador. But once you enter you'll be treated to some of the finest food the Lyon district has to offer, in a three-star restaurant. Monsieur Chapel is one of the premier cuisiniers of the world. He even knows how to take a calf's ear and make it interesting (by breading it and stuffing it with sweetbreads). But you can find far more temptations on the menu than that.

I recommend, as an appetizer, the gâteau de foies blondes, for which the chef is celebrated. This is a hot mousse of chicken livers and marrow, pale gold in color, which has been covered with a pink Nantua sauce. Perhaps you'd prefer instead a velvety-smooth eel pâté in a puff pastry with two butter sauces. (Be warned: Monsieur Chapel's specialties change, depending on the shopping or the season, and some of the items recommended may not be available during your visit.) Yet another seasonal offering is a pan-fried skillet of fresh mushrooms that grow in the woods. His poulette de Bresse en vessie is incomparable. This is a truffled chicken poached and sewn into a pig's bladder (to retain its juices), baked and served with a cream sauce with a bit of foie gras. Accompanying it are discreetly chosen vegetables of the season, often turnips or parsnips or carrots cooked *al dente*.

I could go on and on—a lobster salad with truffles and breast of squab, a trinity of salads (including mushrooms of the woods and violet artichokes flavored with fresh chervil from the garden), foie gras with crayfish tails, a hot pâté of young rabbit. To dine here will cost around 450F ($62.06) to 600F ($82.74), but it may be one of the most memorable meals of your life. The restaurant is closed Monday, Tuesday at lunchtime, and from early January to early February. Gastronomes are fond of booking one of the establishment's beautifully furnished bedrooms, only 13 in all, costing 600F ($82.74) for a standard double, 800F ($110.32) for a deluxe superior twin.

Roger Roucou (also called La Mère Guy), 35 Quai J-J-Rousseau (tel. 78-51-65-37), at La Mulatière, is considered the most famous traditional restaurant in Lyon. An elegant domain, it is on the right bank of the Saône, offering superb cookery. Unlike Bocuse, Roger Roucou is likely to be on the premises, painstakingly supervising every platter that emerges from his kitchen. La Nouvelle Cuisine seems to hold little interest for him. His cookery reflects the time-tested recipes of Escoffier and others, along with his own masterful touch. Dining in La Salle Louis XV, you are likely to be presented with an array of dishes that might include foie gras de canard (duckling) au poivre vert, truffles périgourdine, sole soufflé Escoffier, one of the finest Bresse hens I've ever tasted, and turbot with champagne. Not only is the cookery refined, so is the service. Everything is backed up by a reasonably priced wine cellar.

For such a deluxe restaurant, you can dine here reasonably well by sticking to one of the set menus, the cheapest of which is priced at 180F ($24.82). Other, more elaborate menus cost 260F ($35.85) and 320F ($44.13). Of course, if truffles or foie gras tempted you to go à la carte, you could be faced with a tab of 400F ($55.16) and up. This opulent and bourgeois restaurant is closed Sunday night, Monday, and in August.

La Tour Rose, 16 rue du Boeuf (tel. 78-37-25-90), stands in Vieux Lyon, near the Palais de Justice. Its chef, Philippe Chavent, has been called a culinary genius. Still a young man, he opened this elegant restaurant in a historic 17th-century building with a pink tower and hanging gardens for al fresco dining. The restaurant, a huge vaulted room, has soft lighting and an tranquil decor. Monsieur Chavent creates a light cuisine as tasty as it is pleasing to the eye. Main dishes are likely to depend on the season. You might begin your meal with a sea urchin bisque or, in warmer weather, a potato salad whose smooth dressing is dotted with caviar. Other favorites are the cold fish salad with diced tomatoes and julienne cucumbers (nage de poissons), pigeon pot-au-feu, chicken fricassée, and filets of red mullet with curry sauce. A house specialty is duck with figs. Many of the desserts are not complicated, but great care goes into the selection of ingredients. A set lunch costs from 175F ($24.13), and for dinner you are likely to spend from 400F ($55.16) to 450F ($62.06) or much more. Always call far ahead for a reservation. The restaurant is closed on Sunday.

Pierre Orsi, 4 Place Kléber (tel. 78-89-57-68). There's a delicacy about this restaurant that extends to the pink napery, the dusty-rose-colored decor, the long dresses of the waitresses (designed in flowered materials by Laura Ashley), and the intensely detailed accessories. The bouquets of flowers scattered throughout the dining room elicit almost as much attention as do the menu specialties. Pierre Orsi rises before dawn each day to select the freshest ingredients for the day's menus, which could include lotte and daurade cooked with fresh basil, perfectly prepared veal kidneys, raw salmon marinated in lime juice, Bresse pigeon with garlic, lobster and wild mushrooms in puff pastry, and wild duckling with rice.

Pierre Orsi usually circulates among the guests in the dining room after a meal, and his wife, Geneviève, couldn't be more charming as she supervises the service. On weekdays, a fixed-price meal is offered for 180F ($24.82). A la carte costs around 380F ($52.40). From September till the end of April the restaurant is closed Saturday at lunchtime. The place shuts down Sunday all year and takes a vacation for the entire month of August.

Nandron, 26 Quai Jean-Moulin (tel. 78-42-10-26), is a salon and restaurant (air-conditioned on the second floor) that opens onto the river, near Pont Lafayette. Gérard Nandron is a chef of considerable talent who knows how to do both simple and complex dishes that are virtually flawless. His sauces are light and well balanced, and he uses fresh local ingredients whenever possible. Specialties include the Bresse chicken cooked in tarragon vinegar, quenelle de brochet à la lyonnaise, blanquette de volaille de Bresse, braised sweetbreads with mussels, and veal liver in mustard sauce—all excellently prepared regional specialties. Some of his newer, more challenging fare, however, follows the nouvelle cuisine trend: a vegetable pâté with tomato mousse, sole or turbot simmered in court-bouillon with herbs, fresh mushrooms "of the woods," and raw salmon with citron. Set menus are offered at 240F ($33.10) and 300F ($41.37), plus service. On the à la carte selection, expect to pay from 350F ($48.27). The service is friendly, the waiters most helpful, and English is spoken. Nandron is closed Friday night, Saturday, and from late July to late August.

Vettard, 7 Place Bellecour (tel. 78-42-07-59), stands on a large open square bordered by plane trees. It adjoins the Café Neuf-Glacier. Jean Vettard is a man of grand talent who knows how to turn out a superb regional cuisine in a gastronomic capital where standards are high. No dish is more typical here than pike quenelles with a Nantua sauce made with bits of crayfish or his pan-fried tournedos. But this chef is also an inventor and is constantly adding new dishes to his menu. These might include a mignon de veau poêlé with a vegetable coulis, loup (sea bass) raidi with olive oil and sherry vinegar, or blancs de poularde à la creme de muscat with leeks. For dessert, he proposes a "table des desserts," giving one a large choice. Set menus are offered at 240F ($33.10) and 340F ($46.89), plus 12% extra for service. He also has an outstanding choice of wines, including some regional ones such as Pouilly-Fuissé, Beaujolais Villages, Côte du Rhône, and Saint-Joseph. The restaurant is closed on Sunday, on Saturday night from May to September and for most of August.

Daniel et Denise, 2 rue Tupin (tel. 78-37-49-98). In this case, Daniel refers to Daniel Leron, winner of the coveted *Meilleur Ouvrier de France* award in 1976, an honor given for culinary craftsmanship. Menu specialties in this conservatively decorated downtown restaurant include a gratin of crayfish tails, terrine of lobster, sweetbreads with wild mushrooms in puff pastry, soufflé of turbot, and filet of baby lamb en croûte. Set menus cost 140F ($19.31) and 215F ($29.65). À la carte meals range from 275F ($37.92) to 325F ($44.82), and all are served daily except Sunday, Monday at lunchtime, and in August.

La Mère Brazier, 12 rue Royale (tel. 78-28-15-49), in the vicinity of Pont Morand, has grown from a 1921 lunchtime rendezvous for silk workers in Lyon to a citadel of good food attracting gastronomes from all over the world. The restaurant is presided over by the daughter-in-law and one of the granddaughters of the founding mother, Mme Brazier. They are Carmine and Jacotte Brazier. Unmistakably Gallic with simple decor and wood paneling, it is an attractive setting for a long, leisurely lunch or an outstanding supper. Here you can order some excellently prepared regional dishes, accompanied by such local wines as Mâcon, Juliénas, Morgon, and Chiroubles. Perhaps you'll begin with artichoke hearts stuffed with foie gras, or maybe the smoked Nordic salmon. Main-dish specialties are volaille demi-deuil (boiled chicken with truffles under the skin, served with vegetables, rice, and bouillon), and superbly smooth quenelles de brochet (pike). More extravagant fare includes lobster Belle Aurore or à la nage. Not only is the food admirable, the service is solicitous. Fixed-priced meals are offered at 180F ($24.82) and 200F ($27.58), plus service. On the à la carte menu, expect to pay from 300F ($41.37). The restaurant is closed at noon on Saturday, on Sunday, and in August.

Léon de Lyon, 1 rue Pléney (tel. 78-28-11-33), has a typically Lyonnais atmosphere. It lies on a somewhat hidden but colorful street, well worth the effort to locate. Downstairs is a restaurant and bar in the style of Old Lyon, but you can also dine upstairs. Hydrangeas are planted above the entrance in summer. The atmosphere may be traditional and typical, but the food certainly isn't. When I first visited this place some 25 years ago it was a family dining room where guests tucked their napkins under their chins. Now its owner, Jean-Paul Lacombe, has been called a daring challenger to the top chefs of Lyon.

His cuisine is most inventive. Some of his Lyonnais customers claim he serves the finest food within the city proper and ranks right after Paul Bocuse and Alain Chapel in the environs. Monsieur Lacombe does a regional cuisine, based on the products of the season. Therefore you might be eating oysters accompanied by a Pouilly-Fuissé, the dry white burgundy, or enjoying his pike quenelles or his entrecôte marchand de vin, or, in season, his snails bubbling in butter. As part of his standard repertoire he offers coq au vin beaujolais, la poularde Mère Léon aux morilles (à la crème), and filets de sole aux nouilles (noodles). Newer and more challenging fare includes a terrine of sweetbreads with spinach, a feuilleté of scallops, and even a quenelle of hare with a purée of turnips, a culinary first for me. In season he also offers those flap mushrooms known as cèpes. His sorbets made with fresh fruits are rewarding desserts. In the center of Lyon, the restaurant offers menus at 175F ($24.13) and 320F ($44.13). Expect to pay from 300F ($41.37) if you order à la carte. It is closed on Sunday and for lunch on Monday.

The Middle Bracket

Le Quatre Saisons, 15 rue de Sully (tel. 78-13-76-07). Lucien Bertoli worked as Paul Bocuse's maître d' for more than a decade, a fact which in anyone's eyes adds a note of grace to this establishment. An excellent restaurant, the "four seasons" is known for its impeccable service and friendly welcome. Mr. Bertoli and his charming wife serve an imaginative cuisine based on the availability of produce in the marketplace that day. After being seated at one of the skillfully decorated tables, you can order such dishes as scallops in puff pastry, red snapper with fennel, a succulent version of roast duck, and sweetbreads with an oyster and foie gras sauce. The best value here is a fixed-price menu at 180F ($24.82). À la carte costs much more. The establishment is closed for either lunch or dinner on Saturday, depending on the season, all day Sunday, and in August.

Les Fantasques, 53 rue de la Bourse (tel. 78-37-36-58). As you enter, an array of the freshest fish available in Lyon will be spread out in an impressive display near the entrance. In an elegantly conservative decor, within the shadow of the Lyon stock exchange, Mr. and Mrs. Gervais offer a tempting fixed-price menu at 165F ($22.75); à la carte is more expensive. Specialties of the establishment include a savory lobster terrine, a bouillabaisse which aficionados claim is as good as (maybe better than) many along the Riviera, daurade in fennel sauce, and a filet of sole with a delectable garlic mayonnaise. Meals are served daily except Sunday, and reservations are necessary.

Chez Gervais, 42 rue Pierre-Corneille (tel. 78-52-19-13). The classic cuisine of this well-established restaurant is served in a fancifully lacquered decor of gray and pink, where tables are scattered over two nicely decorated floors. Your dining experience includes a friendly welcome and a copious choice of well-prepared specialties, including warm seasonal asparagus in three sauces, stuffed turbot in a champagne sauce, a gratin of crayfish tails, veal kidneys with white port sauce, and a fricassée of chicken with aged vinegar. Gervais Lescuyer is the owner and chef, and he is aided in the dining room by his charming wife. Fixed-price menus start at 185F ($25.51), with à la carte orders costing more. The establishment is closed all day Sunday throughout the year, all day Saturday between May and October, and in July.

The Budget Range

Tante Alice, 22 rue Remparts-d'Ainay (tel. 78-37-49-83), has the flavor of a country inn. Up front is an old-fashioned bar and in back is a bistro. The cuisine is rich, and many of the specialties are featured on the set menus at 75F ($10.32) and 150F ($20.69). The traditional beginning is quenelle de brochet maison. For a main course, I'm especially fond of filet de sole Aunt Alice. (My Aunt Alice could never make a sole that good.) The restaurant is closed Friday night, Saturday, and from mid-July to late August.

La Tassée, 20 rue Charité (tel. 78-37-02-35). Go here if you're seeking a real Lyonnais atmosphere, the kind of bistro of legend that made Lyon celebrated for its cuisine. The chef here isn't interested in a lot of fancy show or frills. Instead he believes in serving good food and plenty of it, at prices most people can afford. The Lyonnais believe in eating, and workers often take a break at 10 a.m. for a *mâchon*. Perhaps its equivalent would be a coffee break in American offices or an "elevenses" in London. La Tassée serves a *mâchon* that is quite large. From the kitchen emerge hot sausages, salads, and herb-flavored cheese, among other offerings.

On my most recent visit I arrived at the bar just as the beaujolais nouveau had come in. It is a thin, sharp wine, bearing little resemblance to the real beaujolais with its uncomplicated taste and flowery bouquet. The wine is served in a shallow metal cup known as a *tastevin*. As its name indicates, it is used by wine tasters. So intrigued was I with the place that I returned for dinner, which I found most soul-satisfying. Huge portions are served, and you might be offered anything from strips of tripe with onions to game or perhaps sole. A set meal begins at 90F ($12.41), a very good value. A more elegant repast costs 140F ($19.31) or 175F ($24.13). The restaurant is closed on Sunday.

Chez Raymond, 21 rue des Rancy (tel. 78-60-58-67). Lyon's reputation for food, it is generally conceded, is based not so much on haute cuisine as on good home-cookery done by the revered *mères lyonnaises*. An enterprising mother-daughter team, Josette and Joëlle Chovet, carry on that tradition at this intimate dining room. Full meals cost from 140F ($19.31) and 185F ($25.51), and are served daily except Saturday, Sunday, and in August. Reservations are suggested for meals which might include such time-honored favorites as breast of duckling with green peppercorns, civet of hare, monkfish in a chive sauce, veal kidneys in a succulent sauce, and crayfish Raymond. Each of the desserts is made on the premises.

Auberge Rabelais, 39 rue Saint-Jean (tel. 78-37-07-43), is good and inexpensive, a winning choice in Le Vieux Lyon. It's fairly new but with an old look. You can enjoy meals at 80F ($11.03), 110F ($15.17), and 130F ($17.93). Specialties include quenelles de brochet, scallops with saffron, chicken cooked with fruits, and a thick steak known as pavé Rabelais. The chef also serves a hearty salade niçoise, which you might want to order if you're there for lunch. The restaurant is closed on Sunday and for Monday lunch.

Chevallier, 40 rue Sergent-Blandan, off rue Terme (tel. 78-28-19-83), is on a cobblestone street where horse chestnuts bloom in spring. It's a short walk from Place Sathonay, one of the oldest and most characteristic of Lyon's squares. The setting is simple, although many refined touches such as stemmed glassware are used. An exceptionally good meal is offered here for 85F ($11.72), one of the finest bargains in the city. A more elaborate repast goes for 115F ($15.86), and à la carte dinners range from 160F ($22.06). It is served from noon to 1:30 p.m. and 7 to 9 p.m. The restaurant, run by Mr. Torrent and Mr. Devaux, is closed Tuesday, Wednesday, and all of September and February.

4. Pérouges

The Middle Ages live on. Saved from demolition by a courageous mayor in 1909 and preserved by the government, this village of craftspeople often attracts movie crews; *The Three Musketeers* and *Monsieur Vincent* were filmed here. The town sits on what has been called an "isolated throne," atop a hill some 22 miles northeast of Lyon off Route 84, near Meximieux.

Follow rue du Prince, once the main business street, to **Place du Tilleul** and the Ostellerie du Vieux Pérouges, a fine regional restaurant (described below) in a 13th-century house. In the center of the square is a **Tree of Liberty** planted in 1792 to honor the Revolution. Nearby stands the **Musée de Vieux Pérouges** (tel. 74-61-00-88), displaying such artifacts as hand-looms. It is open from 10 a.m. to noon and 2 to 6 p.m., charging 10F ($1.38) for admission. It is closed on Wednesday. In the village's heyday in the 13th century weaving was the principal industry, and linen merchants sold their wares in the Gothic gallery.

The whole village is a living museum, so wander at leisure. The finest house is on the rue du Prince: it's the **House of the Princes of Savoy.** You can visit its watchtower. Also ask to be shown the garden planted with "flowers of love." In the eastern sector of the **rue des Rondes** are many stone houses of former hand weavers. The stone hooks on the façades were for newly woven pieces of linen.

FOOD AND LODGING: Ostellerie du Vieux Pérouges, rue du Prince (tel. 74-61-61-00-88), is one of the treasures of France, a handsome and lavishly restored group of 13th-century timbered buildings. The proprietor, Georges Thibaut, runs a museum-caliber inn furnished with polished antiques, Norman cupboards with pewter plates, iron lanterns hanging from medieval beams, glistening refectory dining tables, stone fireplaces, and wide plank floors. The restaurant is run in association with **Le Manoir,** where overnight guests are accommodated at rates ranging from 600F ($82.74) to 740F ($102.05) in a double. The annex is cheaper: 420F ($57.92) for a double room.

The food is exceptional, especially when it's served with the local wine, Montagnieu, a sparkling drink that's been compared to Asti-Spumante. Set meals range in price from 140F ($19.31) to 280F ($38.61). Specialties include terrine truffée Brillat-Savarin, écrevisses (crayfish) pérougiennes, and a dessert, galette pérougienne à la crème (a type of crêpe). After dinner, ask for a liqueur made from a recipe from the Middle Ages and called Ypocras, "the liqueur of the gods." It's unique. The inn is closed Thursday at lunch and on Wednesday.

5. Roanne

On the left bank of the Loire, this is an industrial town which is often visited from Lyon, 54 miles away, or Vichy, 44 miles away, because it contains one of France's greatest three-star restaurants, previewed below. Roanne was an ancient station on the Roman road from Lyon to the sea.

Located in a beautiful neoclassic mansion built at the end of the 18th century by the architect de Lavoipierre, the **Musée Joseph Déchelette,** 22 rue Anatole-France (tel. 77-71-47-41), offers an exceptional display of Italian and French earthenware from the 16th, 17th, and 18th centuries, as well as earthenware produced in Roanne from the 16th to the 19th centuries. Important collections of prehistoric, protohistoric, and Gallo-Roman archeology are displayed, and there is an excellent selection of ancient paintings. When the resettling of collections is completed, this will be one of the most important privately endowed museums in this part of France. The museum is open from 10 a.m. to noon and 2 to 6 p.m. daily except Tuesday. Admission is free.

The major church, **St-Étienne,** dates from the 13th and 14th centuries with overhauls in the 19th century.

FOOD AND LODGING: The **Hôtel des Frères-Troisgros,** Place de la Gare (tel. 77-71-66-97), is the magnet referred to earlier. A railway-station hotel, this French mecca is one of the great dining rooms of France. The restaurant of Pierre Troisgros has certainly earned a place in French gastronomic lore.

For an appetizer alone, you might be presented with a mousse of grives (a juniper-scented pâté of larks), or perhaps warm oysters in butter "in the style of Julia," or thin escalopes of salmon in a sorrel sauce. The celebrated opener, however, is the mosaic pâté of mixed vegetables with truffles, a delectable dining experience. I also like the mussel soup flavored with saffron. Among the main dishes, legs of duck served au vinaigre, a panache of fish, thyme-scented chops of a ewe, Charolais beef with marrow in a red-wine sauce, and a superb-tasting squab are recommendable. You might follow with an interesting assortment of cheese, or request a praline soufflé. The petits-fours with candied citrus peel may make you linger longer than you intended.

Set menus are in the 220F ($30.34) to 400F ($55.16) range—quite steep—but then, you're paying for an acclaimed cuisine, beautiful service, and quality dishes excellently and creatively prepared. Service and wine are extra. À lla carte tabs range from 450F ($62.06). The restaurant is closed two weeks in August, in January, and on Tuesday and Wednesday for lunch. The hotel also rents out 18 rooms, which do not match the style of the restaurant; they cost from 450F ($62.06) in a single to a high of 600F ($82.74) in a double. Six apartments are also rented.

At Coteau

Artaud Hôtel Restaurant, 133 Avenue de la Libération (tel. 77-68-46-44), is one of several restaurants in the satellite village of Le Coteau, nearly two miles from the center of Roanne on the N7. In an elegant, recently redecorated dining room, Nicole and Alain Artaud offer classic or nouvelle cuisine. Among the dishes are a salad of lotte with saffron, a salad of fried foie gras with strips of smoked breast of duckling, beef from the local farms, and all sorts of sweets. A variety of French wines is stocked. Menus cost from 85F ($11.72) to 225F ($31.03), and you get a choice of a number of different dishes. The restaurant is closed on Sunday. You can also stay in the hotel in comfortable and modern rooms, paying 175F ($24.13) in a single and 320F ($44.13) in a double.

Auberge Costelloise, 2 Avenue de la Libération (tel. 77-68-12-71). Many local restaurateurs might find proximity to Troisgros threatening, but chef Daniel Alex and his wife seem to enjoy filling the vacuum of what might be needed in the region, that is, an attractive restaurant with attractive cuisine at attractive prices. Many of the restaurant's oil paintings are illuminated by spotlights showing off their best points. Food items can be chosen from a sort of "fixed-price à la carte menu," which changes every week. You might find a gâteau of chicken livers with essence of shrimp for your enjoyment, or perhaps filet of sole with a confit of leeks, a pavé of Charolais bordelaise, and a full array of other unusual dishes. You can order fine vintages of Burgundian wines by the pitcher if you wish. Meals range from 95F ($13.10) to 200F ($27.58), and they are served daily except from mid-July until late August, in February, and Sunday and Monday all year. The restaurant is in Coteau, a Roanne satellite village.

6. Vienne

Of course, every gourmet knows of Vienne because it contains one of the world's greatest restaurants (see below). But even if you can't afford to partake of the haute cuisine at that deluxe citadel, you may want to visit Vienne for its sights. About 17 miles south from Lyon, on the left bank of the Rhône, it is a wine center, the most southern of the Burgundian towns.

A Roman colony founded by Caesar in about 47 B.C., Vienne contains many embellishments from its past making it a true *ville romaine et médiévale*. Near the center of town on Place du Palais stands the **Temple d'Auguste et de Livie,** inviting comparisons with the Maison Carrée at Nîmes. It was ordered built by Claudius, and was turned into a temple of reason at the time of the Revolution. Another outstanding monument is **La Pyramide du Cirque,** a small pyramid that was part of the Roman circus. Rising 52 feet high, it rests on a portico with four arches and is sometimes known as the tomb of Pilate.

Take rue Clémentine to the **Cathédrale Saint-Maurice,** dating from the 12th century, although it wasn't completed until the 15th. It has three aisles but no transepts. Its west front is built in the flamboyant Gothic style, and inside are many fine Romanesque sculptures.

In the southern part of town near the river stands the **Church of St. Pierre,** at Place Saint-Pierre, a landmark that traces its origins to the 5th century, making it one of the oldest medieval churches in France. It contains a **Musée Lapidaire** (tel. 74-85-20-35) displaying architectural fragments and sculptures found in local excavations.

A large **Théâtre Romain** has been excavated at the foot of **Mont Pipet,** east of town. Theatrical spectacles were staged here for an audience of thousands. Visiting hours April 1 to October 15 are 9 a.m. to noon and 2 to 6:30 p.m., except on Monday and Tuesday. For the rest of the year hours are 10 a.m. to noon and 2 to 5 p.m. (from 1:30 to 5:30 p.m. on Sunday). The tariff is 12F ($1.66), which also entitles you to visit most of the major attractions of the city.

WHERE TO DINE: La Pyramide, 14 Boulevard Fernand-Point (tel. 74-53-01-96). Fernand Point, world-renowned chef who made this into one of the world's greatest restaurants, is dead, but his octagenarian widow maintains the tradition he established by greeting you at the door and by encouraging the imaginative talents of chef Guy Thivard. Many of the staff members have been here so long —some as long as 50 years—that they vividly remember the days when Fernand ruled the establishment as a precursor to the kinds of lighter cuisine that later swept through France. Menu specialties, featured in the time-honored format of the fixed-price meal, include foie gras, pigeon en gelée, turbot in champagne, a cassolette of sweetbreads, and truffled Bresse chicken. Prices for a full meal can range from 350F ($48.27) to 600F ($82.74). These are served daily except

Monday night, Tuesday, and in February. Seating is in the air-conditioned, silk-draped interior, or if you prefer, you may dine on the garden terrace.

Magnard, 45 Cours Brillier (tel. 74-85-10-43), is a high-quality restaurant that takes quite seriously the traditions it endeavors to maintain. Menu specialties, prepared by chef Pierre Janonat, include a filet of turbot with mussels, tournedos with a morel-flavored cream sauce, and chicken with shrimp. À la carte meals range from 220F ($30.34) to 250F ($34.48), while set menus cost 95F ($13.10) to 180F ($24.82), plus service. These are served daily except Tuesday night, Wednesday, for parts of February, and for two weeks in August.

Le Bec Fin, 7 Place Saint-Maurice (tel. 74-85-76-72). The best-prepared and most generously served fixed-price meals in town are available within the rustic walls of this friendly restaurant near the cathedral. À la carte specialties are somewhat more sophisticated, and you may be offered salads laced with all the delicacies of the region (foie gras, smoked duckling, and the like), breast of duckling with a truffled sauce, filet of turbot, and lotte with saffron. The set menus range from 70F ($9.65) to 180F ($24.82), service not included. The restaurant is closed Sunday night, Monday, from mid-January to early February, and for two weeks near the end of August.

7. Condrieu

Just 11 miles from Vienne, this Rhône-side hamlet is a favorite stopover point for in-the-know Parisians driving from Paris to Avignon. There you'll find one of the choicest spots along the Rhône.

It's the **Hostellerie Beau-Rivage,** 2 rue de Beau-Rivage (tel. 74-59-52-24). Although the Rhône may be somewhat industrial around these parts, you soon forget that because of the captivating charm of this establishment. At this sylvan retreat, covered with a Virginia creeper, the fast-flowing river passes by as you view it from a dining terrace with its weeping willow. A Relais et Châteaux, the inn offers chambers decorated in the antique style. One of them, if you can snare it, is a former apartment, with lots of space and a decor in the Renaissance style. The other rooms are of good size, decorated in an old-fashioned way, with singles costing 250F ($34.48) and doubles going for 500F ($68.95).

The cuisine of Paulette Castaing, one of the grand women chefs of Lyon, is exceptional and respectful of tradition. Try her tarragon chicken cooked in a pig's bladder (to seal its juices), her terrine of young rabbit, her smoked salmon blinis, her lobster bisque, stuffed quail, matelote of eels, or her fry of small red mullets, perhaps her mousseline of lobster with chervil. Everything is washed down with one of the Côtes du Rhône wines. Menus are offered at 200F ($27.58) and 280F ($38.61), with à la carte dinners costing 325F ($44.82) to 375F ($51.71). The place is closed from January 5 to mid-February.

8. Valence

Valence stands on the left bank of the Rhône, between Lyon and Avignon. A former Roman colony, it later became the capital of the Duchy of Valentinois, which was set up by Louis XII in 1493 for Cesare Borgia.

The most interesting sight in Valence is the **Cathédrale St-Apollinaire,** consecrated by Urban II in 1095, although it certainly has been much restored since that long-ago time. Built in the Auvergnat-Romanesque style, the cathedral stands on the Place des Clercs in the center of town. The choir contains the tomb of Pope Pius VI, who died here a prisoner at the end of the 18th century.

Adjoining the cathedral is the **Musée Municipal,** 4 Place des Ormeaux (tel. 75-43-93-00), noted for its nearly 100 red-chalk drawings by Hubert Robert done in the 18th century. It also has a number of Greco-Roman artifacts. On Monday, Tuesday, Thursday, and Friday, it is open from 2 to 6 p.m., and on Wednesday, Saturday, and Sunday its hours are from 9 a.m. to noon and 2 to 6 p.m. Entrance is 5F (69¢).

On the north side of the square, on the Grand-Rue, you'll pass the **Maison des Têtes**, built in 1532 with sculptured heads of Homer, Hippocrates, Aristotle, and other Greeks.

WHERE TO DINE: **Restaurant Pic**, 285 Avenue Victor-Hugo (tel. 75-44-15-32), is worth the drive down from Paris. It is perhaps the least known of the great three-star restaurants of France but one of the best. Not only is the cookery exceptional, the wine list is most rewarding, featuring such regional selections as Hermitage and St-Péray as well as Côtes du Rhône. The restaurant was begun a generation ago by Jacques Pic's father. It was known only to the snugly bourgeois merchants and prosperous farmers from nearby, until word of its great cuisine spread to Paris. Then it was placed on every gourmet's list of stopovers between Lyon and Avignon.

The villa, with a flower-garden courtyard, is charming. In the dining room big tables and ample chairs invite you to spend a long time dining. First, you have to face a dazzling choice of appetizers—a ballotine of squab, pâté de foie gras en croûte, an émincé of duck flecked with truffles and a slice of fresh duck liver, or a corn salad with truffles. Notable also are the delicate breasts of small game birds. For a main course I always gravitate to the filet of sea bass served in a velvety velouté and crowned by caviar. Do not overlook, however, the chicken cooked in a pig's bladder, the filet of sole in champagne, or the lamb stew seasoned with basil (it also includes nuggets ofSsweetbreads and kidneys for added flavor). In season, I suggest one of the chef's masterpieces—noisettes of venison that are tender and served in a wine-dark sauce light as chiffon. His sweetbreads flavored with saffron and his mint-flavored veal kidneys are sublime—as are the warm welcome and impeccable service. The cheese selection is exceptional, everything accompanied by rye bread studded with walnuts. The desserts are a rapturous experience, from the grapefruit sorbet to the cold orange soufflé.

Set meals cost from 220F ($30.34) to 450F ($62.06), service included. Ordering à la carte usually costs from 500F ($68.95). The restaurant is closed on Sunday night, Wednesday, and in August, much to the disappointment of the mass migration from Paris that descends on Pic on its way down to the Riviera. For serious gastronomes, the Pic rents out two double rooms at the rate of 375F ($51.71) per night, plus two apartments, each one suitable for two persons, costing from 650F ($89.64). Always reserve as far in advance as possible.

If the rarefied prices at Pic are not for you, I'd suggest dining at the simple but good **Chaumont**, 79 Avenue Sadi-Carnot (tel. 75-43-10-12), where André Margier will give you a fine meal for just 55F ($7.56). The food is prepared in ways that are familiar—tender country ham, sole cooked in butter, a rich coq au vin, artichokes with potatoes, a fine selection of cheese, and some very filling desserts. More expensive menus are offered, at 65F ($8.97), 105F ($14.48), and 120F ($16.55). If you like the place, you might ask to book one of his modestly furnished rooms, 11 in all, renting for 95F ($13.10) in a single to 150F ($20.69) in a double, which is the best bargain accommodation I was able to find in Valence.

WHERE TO STAY: **Hôtel 2000**, Avenue de Romans (N92) (tel. 75-43-73-01), has the best accommodations in town, its quiet, beautifully kept chambers done in a modern style. However, there are only 31 rooms, which are likely to be booked on a summer night by motorists heading south. If you plan to stay over, call in advance. Rates are 275F ($37.92) in a single, rising to 420F ($57.92) in a double. Units come with radio and mini-bar, and on the premises are a sauna and a solarium, even a flower garden where you can take breakfast.

If that hotel is full, I suggest the **Novotel**, 217 Avenue Provence (tel. 75-42-20-15), on the N7 in the southern part of town. It has far more rooms, 107 in all, furnished with style and taste, going for 300F ($41.37) in a single, 340F ($46.89) in a double. There is also an American bar, plus a restaurant and swimming pool to make your stopover here even more tempting.

If you're seeking a better bargain, try the little 26-room **Hôtel de l'Europe,** 15 Avenue Felix-Fauré (tel. 75-43-02-16), which doesn't have a restaurant but rents out rooms in the Provençal style that are comfortable and agreeable. So is the cost—from 115F ($15.86) in a single to 240F ($33.10) in a double. The motoring French are fond of this one.

9. Montélimar

If you've been following the Rhône trail south from Valence, you have now reached Provence. For your gateway to this enchanting land, I suggest this ancient Provençal town, standing on the Roubion, a river that runs 2½ miles east of the Rhône. Montélimar lies on the historic route between Paris and Arles. It is famous for its nougat, which is a splendid almond confection. You can purchase nougat in one of the local shops, or visit the factory where it's made.

But don't plan to visit the 12th-century fortress château, as it is used as a prison. However, there are remains of the ramparts that once encircled the town, and four old gates dating from the 14th, 15th, and 16th centuries.

FOOD AND LODGING: Relais de l'Empéreur, 1 Place Marx-Dormoy (tel. 75-01-29-00), stands just five minutes from the autoroute, and it is well worth your stopping off that busy motorway, either for one of the finest meals in the region or for a charmingly restful overnight sleep. Roger Latry invites you to his dining room, decorated in the Napoleonic style, where you'll be presented with his array of specialties, perhaps a terrine of lark de la Drôme, chicken tarragon, wild duck (in season), maigret of duckling, a suprême of guinea-fowl with morels, salmon in a sorrel sauce, or herb-flavored lamb. The food is remarkable, the service grand, and the reception fit for an emperor, as the name of the restaurant suggests. For dessert, try his selection of sorbets.

A set menu costs 190F ($26.20), and you can count on spending from 250F ($34.48) to 300F ($41.37) if you order à la carte. The restaurant is closed from mid-November to just before Christmas. Its 40 rooms are beautifully decorated in either the Napoleonic campaign style or "Malmaison," costing 330F ($45.51) in a single, 550F ($75.63) in a double.

Budget seekers may gravitate to the **Hôtel Beausoleil,** 14 Boulevard Pêcher (tel. 75-01-19-80), except when it is closed for two weeks in August. Otherwise, it is a small, 16-room villa which is immaculately kept and well maintained. Rooms come with a variety of plumbing, a simple single with hot and cold running water and a bidet renting for 115F ($15.86); the best double with bath costs 220F ($30.34). Breakfast is the only meal served. There is no elevator, but an electric dumbwaiter will transport your baggage upstairs.

Chapter XVII

THE MASSIF CENTRAL

1. Bourges
2. Nohant (St-Chartier)
3. Vichy
4. Clermont-Ferrand
5. Le Puy
6. Aubusson
7. Limoges
8. Aurillac

IN YOUR RACE SOUTH to Biarritz or through the Rhône Valley to the Riviera, you will have to penetrate the Massif Central, the rugged agricultural heartland of France. The most discerning, who have ventured into this region, have often returned with tales of ancient cities, lovely valleys, and a provincial cuisine that makes one dream of going there to savor the delicacies and specialties.

With its rolling farmland and highly individualistic people, its châteaux and manor houses (in many of which you can stay and dine), and its isolated countryside, this is the most unspoiled and untainted part of France—your chance to see and be part of a life all too rapidly fading. This is a large, varied territory, containing the capital of the old province of Auvergne, Clermont-Ferrand, and also the old capital of Limousin, Limoges.

From the spa at Vichy to the volcanic *puys* of Auvergne, there is much of interest to the visitor and much to learn about the art of good living. We'll begin in the George Sand country in the old province of Berry, then proceed to Auvergne and motor west to Limousin.

1. Bourges

Once the capital of Aquitaine, Bourges lies in the geographical heart of France 95 miles northwest of Vichy, 175 miles northwest from Lyon. It can easily be visited from Orléans at the end of your eastern trek through the Loire Valley. The commercial and industrial center of Berry, this regional capital is still off the beaten path for much tourism, even though it has a rich medieval past still very much in evidence today. Its history goes back far beyond the Middle Ages. Caesar called it one of the most beautiful places in Gaul. Joan of Arc spent the winter of 1429–1430 here.

On the summit of a hill, dominating the town, the **Cathédrale St-Étienne** is one of the most beautiful Gothic cathedrals of France. It was begun at the end of the 12th century and completed half a century later. Subsequent additions have been made, however. Flanked by two asymmetrical towers, it has five magnificent doorways, including one depicting episodes in the life of St. Stephen, to whom the cathedral is dedicated. In harmonious splendor, with a high vaulted roof, the cathedral has five aisles and is remarkably long, 407 feet deep, one of the largest Gothic cathedrals in the country.

Mostly, the Bourges cathedral is distinguished for its stained-glass windows, among the finest in France. In rich blues and deep ruby reds, many of these windows were made between 1215 and 1225. One scene, *A Meal in the House of Simon,* is vividly colored, showing Jesus lecturing before Simon on the forgiveness of sins as Mary Magdalene repents at his feet.

To climb the north tower for a view of the cathedral and Bourges, you must obtain a ticket from the custodian, costing 15F ($2.07). The same ticket allows you to explore the crypt. Dating from the 12th century, it is the largest in France. Its best-known tomb, that of the Duke of Berry, was built between 1422 and 1438, topped by a white marble figure of the duke. However, the recumbent figure is the only part of the original tomb that has survived. The cathedral is open from 8 a.m. to noon and 2 to 6:30 p.m., but the crypt cannot be visited on Sunday.

Guided tours are conducted through the **Palais Jacques-Coeur,** on rue Jacques-Coeur (tel. 48-24-06-87), from 9 to 11:15 a.m. and 2 to 5:15 p.m. in summer, from 10 to 11:15 a.m. and 2 to 4:15 p.m. in winter. It is closed on Tuesday. Admission is 8F ($1.10). These four main buildings around a central court were erected about 1450 by the finance minister and banker Jacques Coeur, who had amassed a fortune. It is considered one of the greatest secular Gothic buildings in France. However, Monsieur Coeur never really got to enjoy the palace much. After a trial by a jury of his debtors, he was tossed into prison by the weak Charles VII and died there in 1456. His original furnishings no longer remain, but the decoration and wealth of detail inside the palace form a remarkable and rare view of how opulent life could be in the 15th century if money were no object. In the dining hall is a monumental chimneypiece, and in the great hall are sculptures from the 15th and 16th centuries.

The Hôtel Cujas, an elegant structure built around 1515 for a wealthy Florentine merchant, now contains the **Musée du Berry,** 4 rue des Arènes (tel. 48-70-41-92), which can be visited from 10 to 11:30 a.m. and 2 to 5:30 p.m. It is closed on Tuesday, otherwise charging an admission of 6.50F (90¢). The museum displays a large collection of prehistoric and Gallo-Roman artifacts. One salon has some interesting funeral sculpture. Paintings are also displayed, including a collection of the works of the Bourges artist Jean Boucher.

The Renaissance mansion, **Hôtel Lallemant,** rue Bourbonnoux (tel. 48-70-19-32), is open to the public daily except Tuesday from 10:15 to 11:15 a.m. and 2:15 to either 3:15 or 4:15 p.m. Admission is 6.50F (90¢). Standing to the north of the cathedral and built for a rich textile merchant, it has been transformed into a museum of decorative art. Its galleries are like a textbook of the colorful history of Bourges, and displays are mounted of china, objects of art, and ceramics. There is also a large exhibit of antique furniture.

You may want to wander through the **Jardins de l'Archevêché,** the archbishop's gardens which Le Nôtre is credited with having laid out in the 17th century. In these gardens you'll have a good view of the eastern side of the cathedral.

If time remains, the older parts of Bourges are worth exploring. As you walk along cobblestone streets you'll see many remains of the Middle Ages and the Renaissance, even some Roman ramparts and 13th-century fortifications that have been preserved.

FOOD AND LODGING: Although Bourges has a number of modest hotels, it is not a major stopover point for tourists, most of whom seem to visit for lunch and then take off to other destinations. However, the city does have an exceptional restaurant, **Jacques-Coeur,** 3 Place Jacques-Coeur (tel. 48-70-12-72), facing the Palais Jacques-Coeur. François Bernard serves a traditional cuisine and does so exceedingly well. Against the backdrop of a medieval decor, he prepares such specialties as veal kidneys berrichonne, fresh frogs' legs sautéed with herbs, scallops (available from spring to October), a head of veal with a highly seasoned white sauce, and beef stew à la mode. The desserts are all homemade and tempting, and service is politely efficient. You can dine for 220F ($30.34) to 280F ($38.61) by ordering à la carte. Wines featured are Quincy and Menetou-Salon. The restaurant is closed Saturday, Sunday night, and from mid-July to mid-August.

Christina, 5 rue Halle (tel. 48-70-56-50), has comfortable rooms, furnished in part with some stylish pieces. In all, 76 rooms are for rent, 51 containing private bath. The single rate is 200F ($27.85), rising to 240F ($33.10) in a double. The hotel has no restaurant, but offers breakfast.

Hostellerie du Grand Argentier, 9 rue Parerie (tel. 48-70-84-31), is an unpretentious family-style restaurant with parts of its decor dating from the 15th century. The generously portioned meals range from 85F ($11.52) to 130F ($17.93). Simply furnished rooms are available for anywhere from 220F ($30.34) in a single to 270F ($37.23) in a double. The restaurant is closed Sunday night and Monday, and from just before Christmas till February.

2. Nohant (St-Chartier)

George Sand was the pen name of Amandine Lucile Aurore Dupin, Baronne Dudevant, the French novelist born in 1804. Her memory is forever connected to this little Berry hamlet near the Indre Valley, four miles north of La Châtre, 10 miles from Ardentes, and 19 miles from Châteauroux.

In her early life she wrote bucolic tales of peasants, but she also penned romantic novels in which she maintained that women were entitled to a freedom equal to men. Among 80 novels, some of her best known were *François le Champi* and *La Mare au Diable.* She was also known for her love affairs, her most notorious being with Alfred de Musset, who journeyed with her to Venice, and Chopin, who went with her to Majorca. At the time of her death in Nohant in 1876, George Sand had become a legend.

It was at the **Château of Nohant** (tel. 54-31-06-04) that George Sand learned the ways and thoughts of the peasants. It was to this same château that in time she would invite some of the intellectual and artistic elite of Europe—Flaubert, Balzac, Delacroix, Liszt, and Théophile Gautier. The château is an 18th-century mansion that has been turned into a museum, housing the mementos of George Sand and her admirers and friends. You can see the boudoir where she wrote *Indiana,* the novel published when she was 28 years old. You can also visit her private bedchamber and study. At Nohant, George Sand staged theatricals for her guests, dramatizing several of her novels, not very successfully, according to reports. Sometimes today, fêtes romantiques de Nohant are staged, with an impressive list of musical performers, perhaps in some way recapturing the glory that the château knew in its heyday.

The tour through the mansion takes about half an hour, and it is open from the first of April until the end of September from 9 to 11:45 a.m. and 2 to 6 p.m. Its off-season hours are 10 to 11:45 a.m. and 2 to 4 p.m. It is closed on Tuesday. Admission is 12F ($1.66).

FOOD AND LODGING: If you'd like to stay over in Nohant, I suggest a simple inn, **La Petite Fadette** (tel. 54-31-01-48). The food here is quite good, a set meal costing 85F ($11.72), or for 130F ($17.93) you can dine very well indeed à la carte. Fifteen simply furnished rooms are rented out to literary fans who come to pay their respects to George Sand. Singles are charged 110F ($15.17), and the most expensive doubles cost 160F ($22.06). The inn is closed from January 3 to February 3, from July 1 to September 15, and on Tuesday.

Within walking distance of Nohant and its George Sand Museum is the hamlet of St-Chartier and the **Château de la Vallée Bleue,** Route Verneuil (tel. 54-31-01-91). This house was built by Dr. Pestel, who wanted to be close to his patient, George Sand, at whose nearby château he was a frequent guest. The two châteaux are separated only by fields and trees. To his own home, Vallée Bleue, he invited such guests as Musset, Delacroix, Flaubert, Chopin, and Liszt, whose names have been given to the rooms. The doctor's former home is architecturally graceful in a ten-acre park with a 400-year-old oak among the many trees.

The château's owners, Mr. and Mrs. Gerard Gasquet, are professional hoteliers and restaurateurs who have been in the business for nearly a quarter of a century. Only 15 rooms are rented to guests, at rates beginning at 125F ($17.24) in a single, rising to 250F ($34.48) in a double. The food, prepared by Mr. Gasquet, is served in one of the two dining rooms, where Mrs. Gasquet will take your order. Excellent regional specialties are offered, done in what is known as cuisine actuelle (halfway between nouvelle cuisine and classical cuisine, with an accent on the presentation). You might choose sweetbread salad with vinegar of wild berries, snails in a pastry crust berrichonne, filet of sole Vallée Bleue with lobster sauce and mushroom sauce, chicken George Sand with a crawfish sauce, and for dessert the hazelnut charlotte with chocolate sauce. Two set menus cost 100F ($13.79) and 160F ($22.06), or you can order à la carte. The hotel is open all year except in January, and the restaurant serves lunch and dinner daily except on Wednesday in winter.

3. Vichy

This world-renowned spa on the north edge of Auvergne, noted for its sparkling waters, looks much as it did a century ago when the princes and industrial barons filled its rococo casino. From 1861 Napoléon III was a frequent visitor, doing much to add to the spa's fame throughout Europe. However, by the 1980s the clients and their tastes have changed. In recent years Vichy has begun a major step in sprucing up its hotels and modernizing its baths. In that, it has been successful. It not only caters to the elderly, called the *curistes,* but it is a modern city for health and relaxation, aided in no small part by the Perrier craze that has swept not only Europe but North America and other countries.

The Perrier Company has a contract to bottle Vichy water for sale elsewhere, and it also runs the city's major attractions. The chief spa of France, Vichy lies on the Allier River, 227 miles from Paris and 108 miles westnorthwest of Lyon. In World War II Vichy was the seat of the collaborationist government under Marshal Pétain. But no one here seems to want to talk about the years 1940 to 1944.

Gardens separate the town from the Allier. The spa waters are said to alleviate liver and stomach ailments. Vichy is a sports and recreation center, with a casino, theaters, regattas, horse racing, and golf.

A promenade with covered walks, the **Parc des Sources,** is the center of the spa's fashionable life. At night it is brilliantly illuminated. Le Grand Casino, the Hall des Sources, the Galerie Napoléon, and the Grand Établissement Thermal (the largest treatment center of its kind in Europe) are found here. The baths can be visited on Wednesday, Thursday, and Saturday from 3 to 4:30 p.m. from June until the end of August. Admission is 4F (55¢).

WHERE TO STAY: Pavillon Sévigné, 10 Place Sévigné (tel. 70-32-16-22). The letter-writing Marquise de Sévigné stayed here when she was in Vichy for "the cure." Of course the hotel, built in the époque of Louis XIII, has been transformed since Madame's day. She contributed much to the resort's 17th-century popularity—"The countryside alone could cure me," she said. Of course, she admitted that Vichy was a bore—"But that is the cure." For those who enjoy gracious, old-style living, the Pavillon near the thermal spa now offers 37 interestingly and individually decorated bedrooms, all with private bath. In season you can stay here on the half-board plan at a rate ranging from 500F ($68.95) to 700F ($96.53) per person. The hotel is open year round.

Aletti Thermal Palace, 3 Place Joseph-Aletti (tel. 70-31-78-77), is the undisputed palace hotel of town, containing all the grandly proportioned vistas and elegant accessories you'd expect. It's open only from early May till the end of September, during which it charges from 400F ($55.16) in a single to 520F ($71.71) in a double. Many of the rooms have balconies looking over the forested park, plus handsomely crafted furniture.

Hotel Albert 1er, Avenue du Prés-Doumer (tel. 70-31-81-10), offers attractively decorated bedrooms in a turn-of-the-century building that looks out over a quiet street and a pleasant garden. Each of the rooms contains a mini-bar, and most of them have private bath. They cost between 160F ($22.06) in a single and 360F ($49.64) in a double. The hotel is open all year.

Hôtel Chambord, 84 rue de Paris (tel. 70-31-22-88), is a pleasantly renovated hotel conveniently situated near the train station. Most of the bedrooms contain private bath, although about six of them do not. Prices range from 140F ($19.31) in a bathless single to 220F ($30.34) in the best double. The hotel's restaurant serves meals for 75F ($10.32) to 200F ($27.58) daily except Monday and from June 20 to early July. The restaurant is closed Saturday and also on Sunday off-season.

WHERE TO DINE: **La Grillade Strauss,** 5 Place Joseph-Aletti (tel. 70-98-56-74). Some of the best food at the spa is served at a three-story 19th-century villa where Napoléon III lived for part of the time between 1861 and 1862. Gina and Gérard Boucher and their chef, Didier Cadiet, prepare a well-balanced cuisine where fixed-price menus cost between 140F ($19.31) and 215F ($29.65). Menu specialties include a vegetable terrine with chive sauce, crayfish and scallops in a salad mixed with mangoes, homemade foie gras, paupiettes of sole with saffron flavoring and mussels, stingray with salmon caviar and broccoli, and an émincé of calves' liver with a bacon-flavored cream sauce. In winter, the establishment is closed Sunday night and all day Monday; otherwise, it's open every day in season.

Le Violon d'Ingres, 5 rue du Casino (tel. 70-98-97-70), may be in one of the dreariest parts of Vichy but is nonetheless sought out by restaurant patrons from throughout the region. The intimate dining room is elegantly outfitted with the kinds of accessories that make it even more personal—flowers, fine porcelain, and expensive accessories. Jacques Muller, the chef, prepares such specialties as a terrine of turbot in essence of freshly picked tomatoes, suprême of guinea-fowl with whisky sauce, a warm salad of breast of pigeon served with goose liver and quail eggs, and breast of duckling with peaches. Set menus cost 180F ($24.82) to 240F ($33.10), and à la carte repasts go for 280F ($38.61) to 375F ($51.71). The violin stops its music on Tuesday and from January 2 to March.

4. Clermont-Ferrand

The ancient capital of Auvergne, this old double city in south-central France has looked down on a long parade of history. On the small Tiretaine River, it lies 112 miles west of Lyon and was created in 1731 by a merger of two towns, Clermont and Montferrand. It is surrounded by hills, and in the distance lies one of the great attractions of Auvergne, Puy-de-Dôme, the volcanic mountain I'll describe farther on.

To begin your tour, head for the center of Clermont, the bustling **Place de Jaude,** where you can sample a glass of regional wine at a café under the shade of a catalpa tree before taking the rue du 11-Novembre, branching off from the main plaza. This street leads to the **rue des Gras,** the most colorful and interesting artery of Clermont.

The **Musée de Ranquet,** 1 Petite rue Saint-Pierre (tel. 73-37-38-63), is housed in the Maison des Architects, a Renaissance landmark. This museum contains Gallo-Roman artifacts as well as a series of exhibits showing regional furniture and workaday objects, including regional pottery from the 18th century. Perhaps most interesting, the museum owns a duet of "arithmetical machines" which belonged to Pascal, the only two of their kind said to exist outside of private collections in France. There's also a room filled with memorabilia devoted to France's hero of the battle of Marengo, General Desaix. The museum is open between 10 a.m. and noon and from 2 to 5 p.m. between October and April; in summer it stays open until 6 p.m. It is closed Monday and on Sunday morning.

The **Musée Bargoin,** 45 rue de Ballainvilliers (tel. 73-91-37-31), is also of interest. It has a wide range of exhibits, including some prehistoric objects, along with wooden carvings and bronzes of the Gallo-Roman era. It also has some interesting stained-glass windows, plus a wide range of paintings, including works by Armand Guillaumin, Joseph Vernet, Carle van Loo, Gustave Doré, and Buffet. The Flemish, French, and Italian masters range from the 17th to the 19th centuries, and there are contemporary artists as well. It keeps the same hours as the museum outlined above.

Built of dark volcanic stone, the **Cathédrale Notre-Dame** is one of the great Gothic churches of central France, dating primarily from the 13th and 14th centuries. It witnessed later additions in the 19th century. Inside, its most outstanding feature is the series of stained-glass windows from the 13th and 14th centuries.

After leaving the cathedral, you can explore **Vieux Clermont,** a small surrounding sector that contains many old houses of the 16th and 18th centuries, notably the **Maison de Savaron,** constructed in 1513 at 3 rue des Chaussetiers. It has a beautiful courtyard and a staircase tower.

One of the finest examples of the Auvergnat Romanesque style of architecture is the **Église Notre-Dame-du-Port,** dating from the 11th and 12th centuries and rising in the northeastern part of town. It has four radiating chapels, and its transept is surmounted by an octagonal tower. The building is made of lava from volcanic deposits in the region. The crypt holds a 17th-century "black Madonna."

Between the two churches stands the Renaissance Fontaine d'Amboise, ordered built on the Place de la Poterne, its pyramid supporting a statue of Hercules. Nearby is the Square Pascal, commemorating the fact that Blaise Pascal was born here in 1623 in a house on the already-mentioned rue des Gras. Regrettably, the house was demolished in 1958, but a statue in the square honors the native son, the author of *Pensées*.

About 1⅛ miles northeast of town is the shrunken and somnolent **Montferrand,** once socially elegant and wealthy. It contains many ancient houses with beautiful courtyards, including one dedicated to an elephant, another to Adam and Eve. Many of these Gothic and Renaissance houses are in excellent states of preservation. The most notable *maisons* are on the rue Jules-Guesde, where you'll find the Hôtel Fontreyde at no. 28 and the Hôtel de Lignat at no. 18.

After leaving town, you can drive for about 11 miles before you come to that volcanic mountain, **Puy-de-Dôme,** jutting up 4,800 feet. It is considered the oldest volcano in France. Once the Gauls erected a shrine at its peak, but the Romans replaced it with a temple dedicated to Mercury. In the 19th century the foundations of this temple were discovered and the ruins dug out. Pascal came here to illustrate his theory of the barometric pressure of air. From the mountain's summit, a panoramic view of this whole part of France—much of it of volcanic origin—unfolds. On a clear day you can see all the way to Mont Blanc in the east. To get to the mountain, you must take a toll road.

WHERE TO STAY: Frantel, 82 Boulevard Gergovia (tel. 73-93-05-75), is modern and central, standing near the Jardin Lecoqu, the loveliest gardens in Clermont. Rooms are well furnished and immaculately maintained, renting for 365F ($50.33) in a single, that tariff rising to 450F ($62.06) in a double. Its restaurant, La Rétirade, serves a set dinner nightly for 185F ($25.51) and up. Closed Saturday for lunch and all day Sunday.

Its rival is **P.L.M. Arverne**, 16 Place Delille (tel. 73-91-92-06), still central and modern but much smaller. It lies near the basilica of Notre-Dame-du-Port. Accommodations are as good as you'd expect in this first-class hotel where everything works, including the plumbing. Singles rent for 320F ($44.13), and two persons are charged 425F ($58.61). The hotel is run by a pleasant staff who will direct you to the restaurant Gergovie, which offers a set dinner for 110F ($15.17). It too is closed Saturday for lunch and again on Sunday, when this twin town gets very sleepy indeed.

Gallieni, 51 rue Bonnabaud (tel. 73-93-59-69), is in the same bracket, and its restaurant Le Charade, offers some of the best cuisine in town. The rooms, 80 in all, are furnished in a modern style with much comfort, at a cost of 165F ($22.75) in a single, rising to 320F ($44.13) in a double. Expect to spend from 150F ($20.69) if you elect to dine here. The restaurant is closed Saturday.

WHERE TO DINE: Le Clavé, 10-12 rue St-Adjutor (tel. 73-36-46-30). The room which contains this restaurant is modern, as are the geometric patterns covering the lacquered chairs. Nonetheless, a nostalgic charm derives from the scattering of antiques, some gilded, which fill the nooks of crannies of the blue and white dining room. Likewise, the menu offers a choice of both traditional and modern specialties, each prepared with fresh ingredients and dedicated skill. Your meal might include a time-tested foie gras en terrine or an unusual warm chiffonnade of crustaceans. If you prefer fish, you might try that old Mediterranean favorite, rascasse bonne femme or a filet of Atlantic perch, grilled and served with fennel and "white butter." Beef might be a pavé of beef with a foie gras sauce or a more daring breast of duckling cooked with raspberry vinegar. Desserts are wheeled to your table on a trolley, and they depend on the inspiration of the chef, Jean-Claude Gérard, who once worked for Maxim's in Paris. Fixed-priced menus are offered for between 130F ($17.93) and 275F ($37.92), with à la carte dinners costing from 250F ($34.48). Meals are served daily except Saturday at lunchtime and all day Sunday in summer.

La Table d'Hôte, 42 rue Fontgiève (tel. 73-30-95-23). Its sophisticated decor might be more at home in Paris than the Auvergne, but that is only one of the advantages which have made this establishment the hot new restaurant in town. In a pink and black decor, including potted flowers, you can enjoy seasonal specialties from a short but changing menu. Examples of chef Roland Flourens's cuisine include a super-fresh selection of the fish of the day, perhaps a sea perch with a lime sabayon. He also serves a skillfully edited platter of mixed fish in a white butter sauce. To begin your meal, perhaps you'll try a homemade foie gras with a garnish of turnips en confit, terminating with a hot soufflé perfumed with violets. A fixed-price menu goes for 135F ($18.62), another for 260F ($35.85), with à la carte dinners costing from 280F ($38.61). The restaurant is closed every Saturday at lunch and on Sunday evening.

5. Le Puy

The site of Le Puy has been called one of the most extraordinary sights of France. The steep volcanic spires left from geological activities that ended millennia ago were capped with Romanesque churches, a cathedral, and a collection of medieval houses which rise sinuously from the plain below. The history of Le Puy is centered around the cult of the Virgin Mary, which prompted the construction of many of the city's churches.

The sightseeing attractions of Le Puy include the Romanesque **Cathédrale Notre-Dame,** which used to house many of the pilgrims heading toward Santiago de Compostela in Spain. Marked by a vivid Oriental and Byzantine influence, it's worth a visit. The adjoining cloisters are open from 9 a.m. till noon and 2 to 6 p.m. daily except Tuesday. Admission is 10F ($1.37). Some of the carved capitals date from the Carolingian era, and many experts cite the geometric wall patterns as something derived from Arab influences. The same ticket admits you to the adjoining **Chapelle des Reliques et Trésor d'Art Religieux,** which contains fabrics and gold and silver objects from the church treasury, as well as an unusual enameled chalice from the 12th century. The hours are the same as for the cloisters (see above).

If you don't mind climbing one of the volcanic chimneys for a panoramic view of the town and the surrounding region, head for the **Rocher Corneille** anytime from 10 a.m. to 5 p.m. October to March, from 9 a.m. to 6 p.m. mid-March to the end of April, from 9 a.m. to 7 p.m. May 1 to the end of June and during September, and from 9 a.m. to 8 p.m. in the height of summer. It's closed in December and January except on Sunday afternoon and during school holidays. It is also closed on Tuesday from November 1 to March 15. Admission is 5.50F (76¢). Once you get there, you'll see a huge statue of the Virgin Mary, erected and paid for by national fundraising in 1860. Cast in solid iron melted down from the hundreds of cannons seized at the battle of Sebastopol, it weighs 110 tons. You can climb an interior stairwell to reach an observation platform set into the Virgin's crown.

Another unusual attraction is the **Chapelle St-Michel-d'Aiguilhe,** atop the Rocher St-Michel. It's a very long climb up rocky stairs to reach this place, but when you get there, you'll be struck by the Oriental influences in the floor plan, the arabesques, and the mosaics crafted from black stone. On view are some 12th-century murals and an 11th-century wooden depiction of Christ. It may be visited daily in season from 9 a.m. to noon and 2 to 7 p.m. Closes earlier off-season. Admission is 3.50F (48¢).

If you appreciate handcrafts, you'll enjoy the **Musée Crozatier,** Jardin Henry Vinay (tel. 71-09-38-90), which displays a full collection of lace, some of which dates from the 16th century. Also on view are a collection of carved architectural embellishments from the Romanesque era and paintings from the 14th to the 18th centuries. Open from 10 a.m. to noon and 2 to 6 p.m. (from October 1 to the end of April, closing is at 4 p.m.), it's closed in February and on Tuesday. Admission is 6.40F (88¢).

WHERE TO STAY: Hôtel Chris'tel / Restaurant Chavagnac, 15 Boulevard Alexandre-Clair (tel. 71-02-24-44), offers comfortable rooms in a good location in a contemporary building. Each of the 30 rooms has a TV, private bath, writing desk, easy chair, and full length windows which open onto a balcony. The cost begins at 215F ($29.65) in a single, rising to 260F ($35.85) in a double. The hotel has a pleasant staff, and an inviting dining room serving an excellent cuisine, a full meal costing from 90F ($12.41). The restaurant is closed for lunch on Friday and Saturday and takes a vacation from mid-December to mid-January. The location of the hotel, about 12 minutes from the center of town, is a five-minute walk from the Jardin Henry Vinay.

WHERE TO DINE: Le Bateau Ivre, 5 rue Portail-d'Avignon (tel. 71-09-67-20), offers an intimate dining room inside a pretty house with lots of rustic detailing. Monsieur and Madame Datessen cook and supervise the dining room, offering such specialties as stuffed crab, salmon with sorrel, sweetbreads with cèpes, and a full array of other well-prepared French dishes. Open every day except Sunday, Monday, and most of July, the restaurant charges around 85F ($11.72) for a set menu, 130F ($17.93) and 180F ($24.82) for an à la carte meal.

6. Aubusson

Deep in France is the "ville de la tapisserie." In the narrow Creuse Valley, this little market town enjoys world renown for its carpets and tapestries.

It is 59 miles northwest of Clermont-Ferrand by road, some 60 miles east of Limoges. The unspoiled town is characterized by clock towers, bridges, peaked roofs, and turrets—all of which formed the inspiration of the painter Gromaire's widely reproduced cartoon *View of Aubusson.* Against the gray granite, rainbow-hued skeins of wool hang from the windows. Ateliers, the workshops of the craftspeople, are spread throughout the town. Many are open to the public (inquire at the door).

The origin of the industry is unknown. Some credit the Arabs who settled here in 732. Others think the craft came from Flanders in the Middle Ages. For years the favorite subject was *The Lady and the Unicorn,* the original of which was discovered in the nearby Château de Boussac. Many tapestry reproductions of 18th-century painters such as Boucher and Watteau have also been made. Since World War II, designs by such painters as Picasso, Matisse, and Braque have been stressed. In summer you can attend a special exhibition of tapestries and carpets at the **Hôtel de Ville.**

The **Musée de la Tapisserie,** Centre Culturel Jean Lurçat, Avenue des Lissiers (tel. 55-66-03-36), contains exhibits related to the 20th-century rebirth of the Aubusson carpet-weaving industry.

La Maison du Vieux Tapissier, rue Vieille (tel. 55-66-32-12), exhibits old carpets, and also displays a reconstruction of what an old carpet-weaving studio looked like.

FOOD AND LODGING: **Hôtel de France,** 6 rue Déportés-Politiques (tel. 55-66-10-22), offers comfortable, pleasantly furnished rooms that peak at 280F ($38.61) for two persons. The least expensive singles cost 160F ($22.06). The food is quite good, especially fresh river trout in season and tender, white veal. Also in season, fraises des bois (wild strawberries) make a succulent finish to any repast. The selection from the Limousin cheese tray is delectable. Meals begin at 75F ($10.32), going up to 210F ($28.96). The restaurant is closed Sunday night and Monday from September to the end of April.

7. Limoges

The ancient capital of Limousin, Limoges is a town in west-central France famous for its exquisite porcelain and enamel works, the latter a medieval industry revived in the 19th century. Rising on the right bank of the Vienne, the town historically has had two parts, the Cité, its narrow streets and old maisons occupying the lower slope, and the town proper at the summit.

If you'd like to see an enameler or a porcelain factory, go to the local office of the Syndicat d'Initiative (tourist office) on the Boulevard de Fleurus (tel. 55-34-46-87), which will supply you with a list of workshops to visit. Or instead go directly to the famous **Haviland factory,** Place David-Haviland (tel. 55-79-20-18), from 9 a.m. to noon and 2 to 5 p.m. Monday through Friday. Since 1842 this company has been exporting to the United States and elsewhere, and their customers have included everyone from Ulysses S. Grant to the late Shah of Iran. An American, incidentally, founded the Haviland firm. Over the years the company has used the designs of such artists as Gauguin and Dali.

Unfortunately, you can't buy pottery at the Haviland firm. But you can find an outlet by going to the **Prestige de Limoges,** 2-13 Boulevard Louis-Blanc (tel. 55-34-58-61). It sells only Limoges porcelain "worthy of carrying that distinguished appellation," as well as crystal and table accessories. Prices seem competitive and attractive—certainly cheaper than you might find in Paris. It is open Tuesday to Saturday from 10 a.m. to 6 p.m., and will ship your purchases overseas.

The **Musée National Adrien-Dubouche,** 8 bis Place Winston Churchill, displays a beautiful collection of Limoges china. In its porcelain collection the museum is second in France, bowing only to Sèvres. Its galleries trace the entire history of chinaware, including not only that in Europe but in Japan and China as well. Entire dinner sets of noted figures are here. The main gallery also contains contemporary Limoges ware. Charging 15F ($2.07) for admission, 8F ($1.10) on Sunday (free for children under 18), the museum is open daily except Tuesday and holidays, from 10 a.m. to noon and 1:30 to 5 p.m. The location is at the park, Place du Champ-de-Fiore.

The **Cathédrale St-Étienne** at the Place de la Cathédale was begun in 1273, but it took many years to complete. The choir, for example, was finished in 1327, but work was going on in the nave until almost 1890. The cathedral is the only one in the old province of Limousin to be built entirely in the Gothic style. The main entrance is through St. John's Portal (Portal St-Jean), which has some beautiful carved wooden doors from the 16th century. The portal was constructed at the flowering peak of the flamboyant Gothic style. The entrance is surmounted by a rose window. Inside, the nave appears so harmonious it is hard to imagine that its construction took six centuries. The rood screen is of interest, built in 1533 in the ornate style of the Italian Renaissance. The cathedral also contains some admirable bishops' tombs from the 14th to the 16th centuries.

Adjoining the cathedral, the old archbishops' palace has been turned into the **Musée Municipal,** Place de la Cathédrale (tel. 55-33-70-10), which is open from 10 a.m. to noon and 2 to 5 p.m. daily except Tuesday and holidays. In summer its hours are 10 a.m. to noon and 2 to 6 p.m. including Tuesday. The 18th-century building, elegant in line, has an outstanding collection of Limoges enamels dating from the 12th century, as well as some enamel paintings by Léonard Limousin, who was born in 1505 in Limoges and went on to win world acclaim and the favor of four monarchs. When Renoir painted porcelain in Limoges in his early years, he did a portrait of Madame Le Coeur which can also be viewed. Admission is free. The museum stands in the **Jardins de l'Évêché,** which offer a view of the Vienne and the Bridge of St. Stephen from the 13th century.

Another church of interest, **Église St-Michel-des-Lions,** was launched in the 14th century and work continued in the 15th and 16th centuries. The church has some late Gothic stained glass, plus relics of St. Martial, including his head.

WHERE TO STAY: The **Frantel,** Place de la République (tel. 55-34-65-30), is the town's leading hotel, an island of modernity in a place of antiquity. Its location is convenient, right in the center of Limoges. Motorists will find a large municipal parking lot nearby. The Frantel offers 75 well-equipped and modish rooms in the chain-hotel style. You don't get luxury, but you do get comfort and convenience at a cost of 350F ($48.27) in a single, rising to 425F ($58.61) in a double. The hotel's major restaurant, Le Renoir, is named for a famous former resident of Limoges. It is also one of the town's leading places to dine, attracting the prosperous porcelain manufacturers of today. The chef, Lucien Moreau, prepares a cuisine that is original and audacious. On any given night you might be served a brochette of snails with white cheese, perhaps a delicate fricassée of burbot with strips of spring turnips, or slices of grilled tender duckling cooked in wine, certainly beef in cahors and sweetbreads with morels. Desserts aren't neglected either. Monsieur is most inventive in that department. Menus are offered at 70F ($9.65) to 165F ($22.75). You will spend around 200F ($27.58) to 165F ($22.75) ordering à la carte. The restaurant shuts down on Saturday and Sunday.

Mapotel Luk, 29 Place Jourdan (tel. 55-33-44-00), is a medium-size, first-class hotel considered the challenger to the Frantel. It is also in the center, often attracting business people from America, even Japan, in town to deal with the manufacturers. The equipment and furnishings in the rooms are in top-notch condition, and the chambers are generous in size, costing from 300F ($41.37) in a single to 425F ($58.61) in a double. Facilities include private baths and telephones, and the maid service is good. A special feature of the hotel is the Taverne Alsacienne on the first floor, featuring specialties of that region; a set meal costs from 85F ($11.52).

Le Richelieu, 40 Avenue Baudin (tel. 55-34-22-82), is just south of the town center, on the main route to Périgueux. The hotel is small, more like an inn, with 27 modestly furnished bedrooms that have the distinct advantage of having soundproof windows so you can get a decent night's sleep. Prices are in keeping with the size and location—125F ($17.24) in a single, 225F ($31.03) in a double. Breakfast is the only meal served.

Caravelle, 21 rue Armand-Barbès (tel. 55-77-75-29), just north of the city center, a long block from the wooded Champ-de-Juillet, is a highly recommendable modern hotel designed so that it can stay young for many years to come. It possesses a tranquil atmosphere and a friendly staff. The rooms are simply furnished, costing 175F ($24.13) in a single, 240F ($33.10) in a double. There is no restaurant, but breakfast can be brought to your room.

WHERE TO DINE: Le Trou Normand, 1 rue François-Chénieux (tel. 55-77-53-24). The reference to the north of France is perhaps a private joke on the part of the owner, viewed by his patrons as a salty entrepreneur whose specialty is the preparation of elegant fish dishes. You'll be greeted by his charming wife, Madame Metais, who might recommend one of the day's specialties. These are likely to include turbot with saffron, perch with fresh mushrooms, a crayfish salad, or one of several preparations of salmon, which might be followed by a fresh fruit sorbet or a delicate pastry. A la carte meals cost from 280F ($38.61) and are served daily except Sunday and Monday and from mid-July to mid-August.

Cantaut, 10 rue Rafilhoux (tel. 55-33-34-68). As you dine here, you'll be able to admire the masonry of the Romanesque vaulting above your head. The establishment is housed in one of the oldest buildings of the old part of town, in a room that requires a descent down a flight of stairs. Patrice Cantaut, originally from Provence, produces a sophisticated cuisine that frequently reflects adoption of new ideas. Full meals range in price from 115F ($15.86) to 280F ($38.61). Specialties include terrine of lobster and fish, gourmand de volaille with madeira, and sumptuous desserts whose recipes stem from the chef's days as a pastry maker. The restaurant is closed every Sunday from May till September.

LIVING IN THE ENVIRONS: Within an easy drive of Limoges are some of the most desirable living choices (good food, too) in the heartland of France. I'll share my favorites, beginning with—

At Saint-Martin-du-Fault

La Chapelle Saint-Martin (tel. 55-75-80-17) is the choicest place to stay in the environs of Limoges, if you enjoy a turn-of-the-century style of living and superb food in the tradition of the Relais et Châteaux chain. The location is seven miles northeast from Limoges, via the N147 and the D35. The hotel—and I hesitate to call it that—is graciously situated in a private park with two ponds attracting seasonal fowl. You couldn't find a more peaceful retreat in "Greater Limoges" where the atmosphere is as sophisticated and enchanting. Your host, Monsieur Dudognon, closes his place Monday and in January and February, but at other times he accepts guests in one of his nine individually decorated bedrooms, which are most tasteful. You must write or call well in advance. Charges range from 380F ($52.40) in a single to 520F ($71.71) in a double. The food is excellent, the ingredients selected with care, and the dishes prepared with flair, in the traditional style of the classic French cuisine. Expect to pay from 235F ($32.41) for a memorable repast.

At Nieuil

The **Château de Nieuil,** less than a mile from Nieuil on the Route de Fontafie à gauche (tel. 45-71-36-38), was the first château-hotel created in the country. It opened back in 1937 when Monsieur and Madame Fougerat started to welcome paying guests. Today it is still in the same family, with Jean-Michel and Luce Bodinaud in charge. On its large, estate-like grounds, the château at first suggests a building and a setting in the Loire Valley. The garden, beautifully maintained, is the pride of its owners. The château dates from the 16th century, but it was much restored in the 19th century. Only 11 beautifully appointed rooms are rented out, all of which overlook the garden. Singles pay 450F ($62.06) the rate rising to 750F ($103.43) in a double. The half-board tariff ranges from 550F ($75.63) to 1,000F ($137.90) per person daily. The cuisine is excellent, using regional produce whenever possible. Therefore you might be served a burbot in a sorrel sauce, a mousseline of salmon with vegetables cut julienne, and veal liver flavored with onions and lime. There is a swimming pool, plus tennis. The château receives guests from mid-April to mid-November.

8. Aurillac

Residents of Aurillac, the capital of Cantal, are proud of the fact that the first French pope came from a 9th-century abbey on the premises of what is today the commercial center of upper Auvergne. Known to Christendom as Sylvester II, his prepapal name was Gerbert. His name, of course, changed after he was named pope in time for the millennium in A.D. 999.

Gerbert is said to have introduced the pendulum-weighted clock, the navigational astrolabe, an improved musical organ, and arabic numerals into Western Europe. All of this happened after he abandoned the limited confines of 10th-century Aurillac and went to study at the Arabic universities of Spain. Later, Aurillac became a center for the study of alchemy.

During the 16th century the wars of religion attracted hundreds of Protestants into the confines of the city. The Catholic authorities ordered a general massacre of the Protestants, who were later avenged.

In the 18th century Colbert, the brilliant finance minister, encouraged lace, goldsmithing, and crafts industries in Aurillac, a few vestiges of which survive today.

The **Château St-Étienne** houses a 13th-century dungeon and a Maison des Volcans in one of the castle's wings. This contains geological specimens and audio-visual presentations on rocks, crystals, and minerals. From July to mid-September it's open daily except Sunday, from 10 a.m. till noon and 3 to 7 p.m. The rest of the year it's open daily except Sunday, from 9 a.m. to noon and 2 to 6 p.m. Admission is 9F ($1.24).

Other than possessing a rich history, Aurillac doesn't have too much to offer, although it's used as a base to explore the **Monts du Cantal.** This is one of the richest regions in France for the exploration of the unusual geological formations in which the area abounds.

FOOD AND LODGING: La Thomasse, rue du Dr-Mallet (tel. 71-48-26-47), is a pleasantly functional hotel—the best in town—set above the city in a tranquil park. The approximately two dozen well-furnished rooms cost 280F ($38.61) in a single to 390F ($53.78) in a double. You'll be near the public swimming pool and the city tennis courts if you want to exercise between sightseeing expedi-

456 DOLLARWISE GUIDE TO FRANCE

tions. Jacques Berthomieux, the owner, keeps this well-run establishment open year round, serving only breakfast.

Grand Hôtel de Bordeaux, 2 Avenue de la République (tel. 71-48-01-84), is one of the best bargains in town, attracting those seeking good, comfortable rooms, of which there are 37 in all. The trendily decorated bar here is one of the most popular places in town. The bedrooms are fairly spacious, and all have been modernized and contain a phone and mini-bar. Many have TV, and about 75% of them have a private bath. Accommodations, depending on the grandeur and the plumbing, range in price from 220F ($30.34) in a single to 310F ($42.75) in a double. The hotel is closed from just before Christmas till mid-January. You'll recognize the building by its white walls and white shutters across the street from the Palais de Justice in the center of town, and by its Mapotel and Best Western signs out front.

Le Crémaillère, Route Tulle (tel. 71-48-10-70), lies about two miles from town at Les Quatre Chemins. Several years after the oldest son of this family-run business went to Paris to apprentice himself at two well-known restaurants in the capital, he returned to make a good establishment even better. This restaurant is the personal statement of the Gibert family, who, with justifiable pride, attract some of the best-heeled clients in the region. The intimate interior is classically decorated in soothing tones of beige, and the cuisine is courteously served with a finesse that seems to make the food taste even better. In warm weather you can eat on the outdoor terrace. Specialties change frequently, although the fixed-price menu at 165F ($22.75) includes some of the best of them. Your meal might include fricassée of crayfish with spices, a salad of Auvergnat-style bleu cheese, baby cabbage stuffed with crayfish, escalope of warm foie gras of duckling with apples, and raw sauerkraut salad with smoked salmon. A cheaper set menu is offered for 85F ($11.72), while à la carte meals usually average around 210F ($28.96). The restaurant is closed Sunday and from September 1 to June 30.

À la Reine Margot, 19 rue Guy-de-Veyre (tel. 71-48-26-46), is a rustically outfitted restaurant where the skillful owner and chef, Georges Dagiral, works almost incessantly to assure a savory stopover. Menu specialties include generous portions of roast beef platters, croustade of sweetbreads, or sweetbreads with flap mushrooms, Auvergnat-style ham, pepper steak, and other country-style dishes. Set-price menus are available at 75F ($10.32), 95F ($13.10), and 130F ($17.93). The restaurant is closed on Monday.

Chapter XVIII

THE PÉRIGORD-DORDOGNE REGION

1. Périgueux
2. Lascaux (Montignac)
3. Les Eyzies-de-Tayac
4. Beynac-et-Cazenac
5. Brive-la-Gaillarde (Varetz)
6. Sarlat-la-Canéda
7. Rocamadour
8. Cahors
9. Montauban

GASTRONOMES SEEKING FOIE GRAS AND TRUFFLES and nature lovers have always sought out the Périgord and Dordogne region of France. In this chapter we'll look at some old capitals of old provinces (long ago subdivided into départements of France). Périgueux, to begin our tour, was the capital of the old province of Périgord. After following the trail of the Cro-Magnon people, we will visit Cahors, the ancient capital of Quercy, to be followed by Montauban, the city of the painter Ingres.

But in Périgord and the Dordogne it is not the towns themselves that hold the fascination, but the unspoiled countryside, a rich, fertile region of much undiscovered charm and antique character. In some villages the Middle Ages seem to live on. It is said that there are no discoveries to be made in France, but you can defy the experts and make many discoveries for yourself if you give yourself adequate time to visit a region too often neglected by the North American.

Between the province of Limousin and the deep valleys of the Aquitaine (from which came Eleanor, the most famous woman of the Middle Ages), lies Périgord. More than 40% of it is still covered with woodland.

The Dordogne, an inland département of southwestern France, is a land of crystalline and limestone rocks. Fine medieval castles rise abruptly on the hilltops, remembering a grander day.

Once these lands were called "the undiscovered provinces," but for the French at least, that is a dated reference today. In summer the major towns seem overrun with tour buses, but in the villages off the beaten track the bucolic life still holds forth.

1. Périgueux

Gastronomes speak of it as a "city of foie gras and truffles." Throughout France you'll see dishes appearing on menus with the appendage of *à la Périgourdine*. That means a garnish of truffles, the tastiest fungus nature ever provided. Foie gras is sometimes added as well.

Capital of the old province of Périgord, Périgueux stands on the Isle River about 70 miles east-northeast of Bordeaux and some 63 miles south and slightly west of Limoges. In addition to its food products, the region is known for its Roman ruins and medieval churches. The city is divided into three separate sections: the old Roman town or Cité, the medieval town on the slope of the hill, and to the west, the modern town.

In the medieval quarter, known as Le Puy St-Front, the **Cathédrale St-Front** was built from 1125 to 1150, the last of the Aquitanian domed churches. Dedicated to St. Fronto, a local bishop, it is one of the largest churches in southwest France. A major reconstruction took place in the 19th century, work continuing until the dawn of the 20th. Its four-story bell tower rises nearly 200 feet, overlooking the marketplace. It is surmounted by a cone-shaped spire. With its five white domes and colonnaded turrets, it evokes memories of Constantinople. The interior, somewhat bare, is built on the plan of a Greek cross, unusual for France. Hearty visitors can apply to the sacristan (tip expected) for a tour of the roof. On this tour, you can walk between the domes and turrets, looking out over **Vieux Périgueux** with its old houses running down to the Isle.

The other remarkable church—this one lying in the Cité area—is the **Église St-Étienne-de-la-Cité** (St. Stephen's in the City), a cathedral until 1669 when it lost its position to St-Front. The church was built in the 12th century, but it has been much mutilated since then. It contains a 12th-century bishop's tomb and a fine carved wooden reredos of the 17th century, depicting the Assumption of the Madonna.

Built on the site of an Augustinian monastery, the **Musée de Périgord,** 22 Cours Tourny (tel. 53-53-16-42), contains an exceptional collection of prehistoric relics as well as sculptures, Gallo-Roman mosaics, and a lapidary collection. Many of the artifacts were taken from "digs" in the Périgord region, which is rich in prehistoric remains. Charging a 5F (69¢) admission, the museum is open from 10 a.m. to noon and 2 to 6 p.m. (to 5 p.m. off-season). It is closed on Tuesday.

The **Tour de Vésone** rises nearly 85 feet in the air beyond the railway station. It was the cella of a Roman temple dedicated to the goddess Vesuna, and it is all that remains to conjure up images of ancient rites.

The **Arènes,** a vast, elliptical amphitheater that once held as many as 22,000 spectators, is another reminder of the days when Périgueux was a Roman town. Now in ruins, the amphitheater had a diameter of 1,312 feet and dates from the 3rd or even the 2nd century.

Near the arena are the remains of the **Château Barrière,** which was built in either the 11th or the 12th century on Roman foundations.

WHERE TO STAY: **Domino,** 21 Place Francheville (tel. 53-08-25-80), is a conservative and pleasant hotel directed by Madame Curelly. Some of the slightly old-fashioned bedrooms look out over a vine-covered interior courtyard, which might provide a pleasant area for a midafternoon rest. Rooms range from 190F ($26.20) in a simple single to 400F ($55.16) in the best-equipped double. Half board is required in the hotel's restaurant during high season. This ranges, depending on the accommodation, from 265F ($36.54) to 340F ($46.89) per person. Many of the 50-some rooms contain color TV and private bath.

Hôtel Bristol, 37 rue Antoine-Gadaud (tel. 53-08-75-90), is a quiet hotel in the center of town. There's no restaurant, but breakfast is served. The welcome you'll receive from the staff is genuinely cheerful. Rates range from 170F ($23.44) in a single to 280F ($38.61) in a double. Most of the accommodations contain private bath and color TV.

L'Écluse, Route de Limoges (tel. 53-06-00-04), lies 5½ miles from Périgueux, reached on the N21 which takes you to the hamlet of Antonne-et-Trigonant. It's worth the drive to sleep peacefully here. L'Écluse is a solid stone building on a tranquil river. The internal atmosphere is that of stylish country modern. Even the bedrooms have a rustic theme, but not crude, each chamber evoking a scene of French country life, as do the public rooms. There are 50 bedrooms, each with private bath. The rate in a single is 200F ($27.58), rising to 300F ($41.37) in a double. In high season, half board is required, costing from 230F ($31.72) to 420F ($57.92) per person daily. Closed Saturday off-season.

WHERE TO DINE: **L'Oison,** 31 rue Saint-Front (tel. 53-09-84-02). It's said in Périgueux that the talented young chef of this restaurant, Régis Chiorozas, can do more with fresh ingredients and air than anyone else in town. That might account for the exquisite lightness of his *nouvelle cuisine du marché,* examples of which include a salad of crayfish with passion fruit-flavored butter, jambonnette of chicken with a fumet of truffles, panache of fish, viennoise of John Dory with artichoke hearts, and sublime desserts. All of these are served amid the rust-colored wall hangings of this former warehouse that, since it opened in 1982, has become the preferred dining spot of this city's well-heeled gourmets and a regular meeting place for the local civic leaders. Table d'hôte menus range from 100F ($13.79) to 240F ($33.10), while à la carte meals cost 300F ($41.72) and up. Dinner is served till 10 p.m. daily except Sunday night, Monday, and from mid-February till mid-March.

Le Vieux Pavé, 4 rue de la Sagesse (tel. 53-08-53-97). René Maurence maintains this second-floor restaurant, which is decorated in a medieval style and lies on one of the narrowest streets of the old town. The stone walls of the building date from the 1300s. The cuisine offers attractively updated versions of traditional regional dishes, using very fresh ingredients. You might select a juicy pavé of beef with a truffle sauce, a maigret of duckling, or whatever else the local market had for sale on the day of your visit. Fixed-priced menus range from 125F ($17.24) to 180F ($24.82), with à la carte meals going from 180F ($24.82) to 230F ($31.72). The restaurant is open daily all year except on Sunday.

La Flambée, 2 rue Montaigne (tel. 53-53-23-06), is the kind of restaurant where you'll be greeted cordially, fed well, made to feel comfortable, and charged for a very satisfactory dining experience. The Thevenet family, the owners, prepare a rich cuisine of fresh local ingredients and plenty of experienced attention. Foie gras in several different forms is a specialty here, and is frequently used generously among the main courses. Maigret of duck and a wide choice of succulently grilled fresh fish are other popular choices, as well as tournedos Rossini and lobster from the in-house aquarium. A fixed-priced menu is offered for 110F ($15.17), while à la carte dinners range from 210F ($28.96) to 250F ($34.48). The restaurant is closed Sunday.

2. Lascaux (Montignac)

The **Caves at Lascaux,** near the Vézère River town of Montignac in the Dordogne region of southwestern France, contain the most beautiful and most famous cave paintings in the world. If you were not among the fortunate thousands who got to view the actual paintings before 1963, you may be permanently out of luck. The cave drawings have been closed to the general public to prevent deterioration, but a replica gives you a clear picture of the remarkable paintings. They were discovered in 1940 by four boys looking for a dog and were opened to the public in 1948, quickly becoming one of France's major tourist attractions, drawing 125,000 visitors annually. However, it became evident that the hordes of tourists had caused atmospheric changes in the caves, endangering the paintings. Scientists went to work to halt the deterioration, known as "the green sickness."

Visits to **Lascaux I** are by invitation only, and people in certain professions, including those involved in museums, science, and journalism, are qualified to visit, providing they obtain permission months in advance. If you think you might qualify, you can write to: Conservateur de la Grotte, Boîte Postale 52, Périgueux 24002, France.

A short walk downhill from the caves leads to **Lascaux II** (tel. 53-51-95-03), which is an impressive reproduction in cement and molded above ground. The 131-foot long reproduction displays some 100 paintings so that visitors will at least have some idea of what the "Sistine Chapel of prehistory" looked like. Here you can see majestic bulls, wild boars, stags, "Chinese horses," and life-like deer, all depicted by Stone Age hunters from 15,000 to 20,000 years ago. Admission is 15F ($2.07) and hours are from 10 a.m. to noon and from 2 to 4 p.m. daily except Monday. The "cave" is completely closed from the first week of January until February 3.

With the same ticket you can also visit a museum devoted to the cave art. It's at **Le Thot**, lying 4½ miles from Montignac along the D706. The museum is open from 9:30 a.m. to 9:30 p.m. in summer. Off-season, its hours are from 10 a.m. to noon and from 2 to 5 p.m. It stays open until 6 p.m. on Sunday, and is closed all day Monday. After a visit here, you can walk out on the terrace for a view of the Valley of the Vézère and the hills of Lascaux.

Before the closed-down grotto of Lascaux, a narrow surfaced road branches off to the right. It goes through a woodland setting for about half a mile until it reaches the prehistoric site of **Régourdou**. This site, discovered only in 1954, produced such finds as a jawbone and other artifacts. It can be visited April 1 until the end of September from 9 a.m. to noon and 2 to 6 p.m. for a 10F ($1.38) admission. Off-season it is open from 10 to 11:30 a.m. and 2 to 4 p.m.

FOOD AND LODGING: The traditional choice is **Soleil d'Or,** 14 rue du 4-September (tel. 53-51-80-22), an old mansion with a beautiful garden, which offers both bedrooms and apartments. In one of the comfortable bedrooms the cost is 180F ($24.82) in a single, rising to 325F ($44.82) in a double. Ten apartments are also rented at a rate of 350F ($48.27) to 700F ($96.53) for two persons. In season, it's necessary for guests to stay here on the half-board plan, paying from 200F ($27.58) to 275F ($37.92) per person daily. The hotel offers an excellent set menu at 85F ($11.72). Other meals are offered at 120F ($16.55) and 240F ($33.10). Specialties include a terrine of fresh foie gras, duck steak with honey, and escalopes with fresh foie gras. The patron is Alain Benedetti. The service is polite and friendly but a little rushed in summer. The hostellerie, which has been completely transformed and upgraded, also has a swimming pool, a tea salon, and a pub. The inn is closed the first three weeks in March and from early November to the end of December.

Château de Puy Robert, Route 65 (tel. 53-51-89-24). In 1986, Monsieur and Madame Albert Parveaux, hoteliers whose success was already evident in one of France's alpine ski resorts, bought and renovated a 19th-century château, turning it into an elegant hotel and restaurant. The windows of its extremely comfortable accommodations look out over the caves of Lascaux, the valley of the Vézère, and the establishment's small but heated swimming pool. Each unit is handsomely furnished, costing 350F ($48.27) in a single, 750F ($103.43) in a double. There are only 12 rooms, so reservations are important. They also rent three apartments at 1,000F ($137.90) for two persons. Philippe Lecourt is the sophisticated chef whose cuisine presents the best of super-fresh local ingredients in an imaginative format with creative touches. Specialties change with the season. Meals range in price from 175F ($24.13) to 275F ($37.92). The hotel, found about two miles outside of town, is open from June 1 to mid-October.

3. Les Eyzies-de-Tayac

When prehistoric skeletons were unearthed in 1868, the market town of Les Eyzies was launched as an archeologist's dream. This area in the Dordogne Valley was found to be one of the richest in the world in ancient sites and deposits. Little by little, more and more caves were discovered in the region. In some of these caves our early ancestors had made primitive drawings going back some 30,000 years, the most beautiful and most famous, of course, being at Lascaux. Many caves around Les Eyzies are open to the public.

For orientation purposes, pay a visit to the **Musée National de Préhistoire** (tel. 53-06-97-03), which is installed in a fortress castle dating from the 11th and 12th centuries and once inhabited by the barons of Beynac. The fortress was installed in a cliff towering over Les Eyzies. On the terrace is a rather unflattering statue of Neanderthal man that was the work of the sculptor Dardé in 1930. The prehistoric artifacts on display were all discovered in the area. One building displays a reconstructed Magdalenian tomb of a woman containing her skeleton. Charging 8F ($1.10) for admission, the museum is open daily except Tuesday, from 9:30 a.m. to noon and 2 to 6 p.m. (to 5 p.m. off-season).

Even if your time is limited, I suggest that you see at least one cave in the area. The most interesting is called **Grotte du Grand-Roc** (the Cave of the Big Rock) (tel. 53-06-96-76). It is open from 9 a.m. to noon and 2 to 6 p.m. from late March to the end of June and mid-September to the first of November. In high season, from July 1 to mid-September, hours are from 9 a.m. to 6:30 p.m. Entrance fees are 18F ($2.48) for adults, 9F ($1.24) for children. From the cave entrance, you wander into a tunnel of stalagmites and stalactites. The caves lie just northwest of the market town on the left bank of the Vézère (signs point the way on the D47).

The **Grotte de Font-de-Gaume,** (tel. 53-06-97-48) will also admit a small number of visitors daily (my group contained only 12 people, including two professors from the U.S.). This cave has not only been around for a long time, but it's been on the grand tour since back when the guardians weren't as protective as they are today. Therefore some of those markings you see were not from the Magdalenian Ages, but from British students on a holiday back in the 18th century. Here bison, reindeer, and horses, along with other animals, reveal the skill of the artists of prehistoric times. Of course, this cave does not have paintings as well preserved as those at Lascaux. Warning: Unless you show up very early or in off-season, it may be impossible to get a ticket to look at these remarkable drawings. In season, the demand far exceeds the supply of tickets. Hours are 9 to 11 a.m. and 2 to 5 p.m. from the first of May until the end of September. Off-season, hours are 10 to 11 a.m. and 2 to 3 p.m. The caves are closed on Tuesday. Admission is 20F ($2.76).

Heading out the D47 will take you to the **Grotte des Combarelles** (tel. 53-06-97-72), which has guided tours. Admission is 20F ($2.76). It is closed on Tuesday. Discovered at the turn of the century, this cave has many drawings of animals, including musk oxen, horses, bison, and aurochs. In other words, it's a gallery of Magdalenian art. It keeps the same hours as the Grotte de Font-de-Gaume just recommended.

There are many other caves in the area to visit, but if you linger you might as well stay over and become an amateur archeologist.

FOOD AND LODGING: **Cro-Magnon,** Route de Périgueux (tel. 53-06-97-06), has winning qualities—a lovely, spacious garden with a swimming pool and a shaded dining terrace. The bedrooms are not only attractive and warmly decorated, but they capture some echoes of the past while including the necessary modern amenities. The owner Jacques Leyssales, and his chef Alain Guillois, work together to produce exceptionally good food. Even if you're not staying here you may want to sample one of the menus at 115F ($15.86) or 150F ($20.69). For 250F ($34.48) you get a gastronomic repast. Specialties include a terrine of fresh foie gras, mousseline of lobster, stuffed trout with fines herbs, baked truffles, and aiguillettes of duckling with asparagus points and cucumbers. From the Cro-Magnon caves come not paintings but such wines as Caillevet and Clos-de-Gamot. In season, only half-board guests are accepted, at rates ranging from 360F ($49.64) to 750F ($103.43) per person. The hotel receives guests from late April to mid-October.

Le Centenaire (tel. 53-06-97-18) provides the double magic of its owners, Mr. and Mrs. Scholly, and their talented, creative chef, Roland Mazère. The hotel is charming, owing to extensive and intelligent renovation and decorating. It contains 25 bedrooms individually and pleasantly furnished, each with private bath and the usual amenities. The rate is 300F ($41.37) in a single, rising to 350F ($48.27) in a double. The hotel has a heated outdoor swimming pool, a health club, and a shopping gallery. Even if you don't stay here, you can dine, ordering one of the menus at 160F ($22.06), 260F ($35.85), or 360F ($49.64). You'll pay from 320F ($44.13) if you order à la carte. The cuisine is in the lighter, more modern French style, with such dishes as fresh foie gras in a terrine, a brochette of fresh salmon (only from May to September), noisettes d'agneau (lamb), young hare with a purée of onions, a ragoût of sweetbreads, brains, crayfish, and a variety of mushrooms known as mousseron, and lobster with truffles. Service is friendly and efficient. In all, this is a rewarding stopover for both rooms and meals. The inn is open only from mid-April to November 5.

Centre, Place de la Mairie (tel. 53-06-97-13), is better for the budget, enjoying a rustic setting and the serenity of its garden at the edge of the river. Gérard Brun will house you most comfortably in one of his provincial bedrooms, which he rents at rates beginning at 210F ($28.96) per person for half board. The patrón's cooking is unusually fine, and the good news is that he serves probably the best fixed-price meals in town, considering cost and quality, going for 75F ($10.32), 100F ($13.79), 160F ($22.06), and 240F ($33.10). Specialties are aiguillettes of duck with cèpes (flap mushrooms), assiette périgourdine, ragoût of seafood, pot-au-feu of fish, prawns, and soufflé aux noix. In season, you can enjoy meals on a shaded terrace. The inn is closed from mid-November to March.

Les Glycines, Route de Périgueux (D47) (tel. 53-06-97-07), presents solid regional cookery, comfortable accommodations, and dozens of charming touches. These include an outdoor veranda with a protective grape arbor where you'll be served drinks while listening to the birds singing. Monsieur and Madame Henri Mercat are the hard-working owners of this four-acre garden setting. Their 25 well-furnished bedrooms rent for 230F ($31.72) in a single, 350F ($48.27) in a double, breakfast not included. Half board costs between 230F ($31.72) and 320F ($44.13) per person, depending on the accommodation. Specialties in the restaurant include such time-honored favorites as an émincé of goose en confit. Fixed-priced menus are available for 110F ($15.17) and 250F ($34.48), and the hotel is closed between October and April.

4. Beynac-et-Cazenac

Rising from the summit of a rocky plateau, the **Château of Beynac** dominates the village at its feet. From its terraces a panoramic view of the Dordogne Valley unfolds. The most agile can reach it by foot. Others prefer to take the road, which circles around for about a mile and a half before coming to the castle. The keep is from the 13th century. The aristocracy of Périgord used to assemble in the Grand Hall, with its ogival vaulting. In the oratory are some

Gothic frescoes of *The Last Supper*—not da Vinci, but interesting nevertheless. Although the castle is a curiosity, it is really the view that makes it worth the climb. Charging 9F ($1.24) for admission, the château is open from July 1 to September 30 from 9:30 a.m. to noon and 2 to 7 p.m. From March 1 until the end of June and from October 1 to November 5, it is open from 10 a.m. to noon and 2:30 to 6 p.m.

FOOD AND LODGING: Hôtel Bonnet (tel. 53-29-50-01) has been a secret address the English took with them to the Dordogne for decades. It was even known to Henry Miller. Now this old family-run hotel is becoming better known, which should please Renée Bonnet. If you don't mind the noise from the traffic, try to get a front room with a river view. The chambers are pleasantly furnished and most comfortable, costing from 150F ($20.69) in a single to a high of 225F ($31.03) in a double. Guests are accepted from late March to mid-October. The atmosphere is casual and relaxed around here (frankly, there isn't much to do, and that's what the guests seem to prefer). There is a salon where cards and games are sometimes played, and there's also a bar.

By all means try to stop for a meal here if you're motoring through the Dordogne. On a large, creeper-covered terrace, you can take your meals above the river after you've had a stroll in the garden. I recently started with crudités and was amazed at the appetizing array of delectable dishes presented to me: those large flap mushrooms sautéed with garlic and herbs, celeriac cut julienne and served with a velvety rémoulade sauce, quenelles with a Nantua sauce laced with truffles, hearts of palm, a salad of lentils and shallots, mussels in heavy cream, a bright-green artichoke in a vinaigrette sauce, plus marinated beets, green and red peppers, eggplant ratatouille, and cauliflower. It seemed endless. If you can make it, you might proceed by ordering the trout from the Dordogne River, which is broiled in country butter and covered with slivered walnuts. The chef does quail on a bed of grapes poached in red wine, and the roquefort cheese served here is superb. Set menus are offered at 88F ($12.14) and 170F ($23.44). Half-board terms range from 250F ($34.48) to 280F ($38.61) per person.

5. Brive-la-Gaillarde (Varetz)

Three of the old provinces of France—Limousin, Quercy, and Périgord—met near here. At the crossroads, Brive the "bold" is an inviting town, with its memories of the renowned French novelist Colette, who lived nearby when she was the wife of Henri de Jouvenel (see Castel-Novel, below). An important gastronomic center, Brive is a land of fine fruits, truffles, vegetables, and liqueurs, and in some of its shops you can buy a uniquely flavored local mustard cherished by gastronomes.

If you want to know anything about Brive, go to the Musée Ernest-Rupin, 18 rue Docteur-Massenat (tel. 55-75-90-15), right in the center of town. In a lovely Louis XIII mansion, this provincial museum is eclectic, containing everything from artifacts from prehistoric digs to Gothic sculpture to mementos of Brive's celebrated native sons. It is open from 10 a.m. to noon and 2 to 6 p.m. (to 5 p.m. off-season), charging an admission of 5F (69¢). It's closed Sunday.

Nearby is the Église St-Martin, which is a hodgepodge of architectural styles, with a Romanesque transept and aisles from the 14th century.

If you have a car, I suggest that you head south of Brive on the D38 until you reach the "red village" of Collonges. This tiny hamlet contains petite mansions built of dark-red stone, including one corbelled house from the 16th century dedicated to the Siren. The church nearby is Romanesque, built in the 11th and 12th centuries, with a belfry in the Limousin style.

After leaving Collonges, you can continue south, passing the Puy Rouge, until you reach Meyssac, which is also built of red sandstone, known as "Collonges clay." The people of the village make a pottery out of this clay. The village is charming, with wooden buildings, some with porch roofs, and antique towers.

From Meyssac, you can take the D14 which becomes the D96 until you reach the intersection with the D20. Take the D20, which becomes the D8, leading north to Brive again. On the way back, you might like to stop at the tiny village of **Turenne,** its old houses giving you a sleepy look at long-ago provincial France.

From there, continue along the D8, passing through Nazareth, until you connect with the D158 leading to **Noailles.** On a hillside, the Noailles church with its Limousin-style bell tower dominates the rolling green countryside. From Noailles, it is just a short drive back into Brive.

FOOD AND LODGING: La Truffe Noire, 22 Boulevard Anatole-France (tel. 55-74-35-32), lies in the heart of the city, within walking distance of the major sights. At this hotel, you can get a well-furnished bedroom that is fairly well protected from traffic noise. The place is sweetly old-fashioned, offering 35 bedrooms at rates ranging from 170F ($23.44) in a single to 300F ($41.37) in a double. The "Black Truffle" also has a restaurant, offering set meals at 90F ($12.41) to 130F ($17.93).

La Crémaillère, 53 Avenue de Paris (tel. 55-74-32-47). Charles Reynal is winning increasing acclaim as a chef of versatility and inventiveness. He knows how to take regional products and create award-winning dishes from them. Specialties are egg in a coddler with a purée of truffles and morels, puff pastry of leeks and goose liver, flan of flap mushrooms with a sauce of morels, sliced filet of duck with cassis berry sauce, farci of cabbage with sweetbreads, warm puff pastry with red fruits, and puff pastry with marinated prunes and plum liqueur. The restaurant is reasonably priced, offering set menus for 80F ($11.03), 150F ($20.69), and 200F ($27.58). A la carte dinners average around 220F ($30.34). Happily, the chef also rents out a dozen comfortable and well-furnished bedrooms for 140F ($19.31) in a single, 230F ($31.72) in a double. The place is closed in February, the last two weeks of July, and on Sunday night and Monday all year.

At Varetz

Château de Castel-Novel (tel. 55-85-00-01). This isolated old château set on 25 acres of grounds still exudes the spirit of Colette, who often lived here when she was the wife of Henri de Jouvenel (a man who regarded himself as a "connoisseur of women"). The French novelist drew the political and literary luminaries of her day to Varetz. The château, once owned by the Viscount of Limoges, is reached by going out the D152 for 6½ miles. It is open only from May 5 to October 20, and reservations for either rooms or meals are always necessary because of the château's special qualities and limited capacity, only 23 bedrooms. Ten new rooms are in an annex, La Métairie. On a broad plateau, dominating the Valley of the Vézère, the château is now the domain of Albert Parveaux. Its towers, which once sheltered the lords of Aubusson, come into view first. Inside, Colette's library has been turned into a charming salon, and the old stables have been converted into a banqueting hall. Two persons can stay here for as little as 300F ($41.37) in the annex, 500F ($68.95) in the château. There are five apartments as well, costing from 1,350F ($186.17) for two persons, if you're interested in honeymooning here. A swimming pool and tennis courts add to the attractions of the place.

The cuisine has been notably improved and made exciting under chef Jean-Pierre Faucher. He prepares such temptations as three fish in a roquefort cream sauce, duckling stuffed with sorrel, a ragoût of foie gras and truffles, and a salad made with cèpes (flap mushrooms) and gizzards. To dine here costs from 320F ($44.13). Of course, there are wines of Cahors.

6. Sarlat-la-Canéda

The capital of "Black Périgord" (or Périgord Noir in French) is a town from the Middle Ages, beautifully preserved. Most writers who visit it always report that it's a "living museum." The townspeople have worked for the past two decades to restore their age-old houses, mostly built of ochre stone, which close in like sheets in the wind along narrow, winding cobblestone streets, which are lit by lanterns.

Old Sarlat, called Vieille Ville, has a main street, rue de la République, which is very commercial and not of tourist interest. But don't judge Sarlat by that. Its history goes back to Gallo-Roman times. It's had a town charter since 1298, and at the time of Charlemagne it was an ecclesiastical center of some note. Its fame reached a zenith in the 14th century, when it was known in France as a bustling center of artisans, painters, and students.

The **Office de Tourisme** at the Place de la Liberté (tel. 53-59-27-67) will give you a map, detailing the most outstanding attractions, and you can take it from there. Allow about two hours (without stopovers) for a complete tour.

The **cathedral** is a major attraction. As early as 1317 it was an episcopal seat, losing that distinction in 1790. It stands on the Place du Peyrou, which is a good starting point for your tour. The church has a Romanesque bell tower, but most of the structure is from the 16th and 17th centuries. Much of the interior is in the late Gothic style.

Nearby stands the **Maison de la Boétie,** a charming Renaissance house, the finest in Sarlat, which dates from 1525 and was once inhabited by the town's most famous son, Étienne de La Boétie, who was born five years after the house was completed. A criminal magistrate, he had a close, lifelong friendship with Montaigne. Montaigne was at La Boétie's bedside when he died in 1563, and that death inspired Montaigne's essay on "Friendship." The house is studded with mullioned windows and has a painted gable.

The town has, naturally, an architectural curiosity called **Lanterne des Morts,** or lantern to the dead. A 12th-century tower, characterized by a tall cone-shaped roof, it is supposedly the oldest structure in Sarlat. Its appearance has been compared to that of a beehive.

For the most part you will not need to seek out more than the obligatory landmarks. All of Sarlat makes for an interesting tour. You can even allow yourself to get lost, as you'll invariably wind up back at the Place de la Liberté, the heart of town.

The best time to arrive would be for the Saturday-morning market at the **Place des Oies** (geese). Or perhaps you'll be able to attend an open-air performance in August at the Sarlat festival (rooms are impossible to find at that time).

FOOD AND LODGING: La Madeleine, 1 Place de la Petite-Rigaudie (tel. 53-59-12-40), is often referred to as the "grande dame" of the city's hotels. It's in a solidly constructed, charmingly no-nonsense kind of building in the center of town. The 22 bedrooms are for the most part spacious, with many conveniences. Prices range from 240F ($33.10) in a single to 325F ($44.82) in a double, with half board (required in high season) costing from 280F ($38.61) to 340F ($46.89) per person. The old-world dining room is supervised by the chef who is also the owner, Philippe Melot. Specializing in the traditional rich dishes that the abundance of local ingredients seems to encourage, he cooks dishes such as ragoût of duckling with red wine, foie gras, sweetbreads with morels, and flavorful sauces rich with truffles, cèpes, and wild mushrooms. Fixed-price menus range from 85F ($11.72) to 210F ($28.96), but you'll pay from 275F ($37.92) up if you order à la carte. Dinner is served either indoors or on the outdoor terrace every night till 9, except from mid-November to mid-March when the owners take a vacation.

Hotel St. Albert, 10 Place Pasteur (tel. 53-59-35-98), is a well-known establishment, owned for generations by the Garrigou family, who still impose a warmhearted but traditional tinge to the way they manage it. It sits near the post office on a square a few steps from the entrance to the old city. Inside, the conservatively modern decor includes a handful of regional accessories and a pleasant neutral collection of streamlined furniture. Single or doubles rent from 130F ($17.93) to 210F ($28.96). If you're looking for a bit more luxury, you can walk around the corner to the other hotel owned by the Garrigou family. It's **La Salamandre,** rue Abbé Surguier (tel. 53-59-35-98), a former distillery where 21 additional bedrooms and a handful of duplex apartments cost from 220F ($30.34) and 280F ($38.61) in a single or double.

The main allure of the enterprise lies within the restaurant of the St. Albert. The menu blends in no way to what the owners consider faddish cuisine. They seem to celebrate a series of robust and sumptuously conservative platters like grandmère used to make. There's an honest adherence to Périgourdine authenticity, using very fresh ingredients in such specialties as stuffed cabbage, poule au pot, truffle soufflé, five different preparations of homemade foie gras (with or without truffles), and a succulent grilled and garnished breast of duckling. Juicy beef and lamb dishes are also featured. A tempting series of fixed-price menus cost 140F ($19.31) and 240F ($33.10). À la carte dinners average 185F ($25.51). The hotels are open all year, and the restaurant closes Sunday night, as well as all day Monday off-season.

Hostellerie Marcel, 8 Avenue de Selves (tel. 53-59-21-98), offers a flexible collection of fixed-price menus ranging from 55F ($7.56) to 165F ($22.75). All are well prepared by Marcel Clérot, who has become popular in town for his shish kebab with sorrel, sweetbreads Périgueux, stuffed goose neck, confit of duckling, and an unusual collection of tasty desserts. The cheapest set menus are not offered on weekends. The restaurant is closed from mid-November till the end of January and on Monday except during the summer.

Rossignol, Boulevard Henri-Ariet (tel. 53-59-03-20), is on a busy artery just at the edge of the city limits. You'll find it on the upper floor of an ancient building at the end of the rue Fénelon, housed inside an old but renovated family-run property. In warm weather, guests enjoy dining on an outdoor terrace. René Rossignol is the owner, and his son Jacques is the chef de cuisine. The menu includes such fish dishes as sole filet with hazelnuts, as well as good meat specialties. Table d'hôte menus are priced from 65F ($8.97) to 70F ($9.65) and from 104F ($14.34) to 200F ($27.58). Dinner ends relatively early here, the last orders being taken at around 8:30 p.m. The establishment is closed Monday and for two weeks in March and two weeks in November.

On the Outskirts

Hostellerie de Meysset, Route des Eyzies (tel. 53-59-08-23), is in a forested park about half a mile west of Sarlat, in a large country house on top of a hill overlooking the surrounding scene. The cuisine, in the capable hands of Gérard Lasserre, is composed of an unusual blend of regional recipes with a modern twist. Specialties include duck liver with a coulis of truffles or breast of duckling in a sauce made with flap mushrooms, perhaps stuffed pigeon. Meals, which are served every day except on Monday and in October, range from 155F ($21.38) to 250F ($34.48), depending on what you order. About 30 spacious and conservatively furnished rooms and apartments are offered for overnighters, renting for 300F ($41.37) in a single to 380F ($52.40) in a double. In high season, half board is required, costing from 360F ($49.64) to 580F ($79.98) per person.

Hotel La Hoirie, at La Canéda (tel. 53-59-05-62), about 1¼ miles from Sarlat, lies within an old-fashioned and charming house ringed with a flowering garden. A fire within the massive hearth is likely to greet you in the beamed and stone-walled salon. Members of the Sainneville de Vienne family will serve drinks if you request them. There's a rectangular swimming pool set into the lawn outside. The 15 comfortable accommodations are priced at 250F ($34.48) in a single, 370F ($51.02) for the best doubles. Each is equipped with a private bath. The establishment, built originally as a hunting lodge, is open only from mid-March to mid-November.

7. Rocamadour

The Middle Ages seem to live on here as they do in Sarlat. After all, Rocamadour reached the zenith of its fame and prosperity in the 13th century. Make an effort to see it even if it's out of your way—34 miles from Brive, 39 miles from Cahors. The setting is striking, one of the most unusual in Europe. Towers, old buildings, and oratories rise in stages up the side of a cliff on the right slope of the usually dry gorge of Alzou. The gravity-defying village, with its single street (lined with souvenir shops), is boldly constructed. It is seen at its best when approached from the road coming in from the tiny village of L'Hospitalet. Once in Rocamadour, you can take a flight of steps from the lower town to the churches halfway up the cliff. The less agile would be advised to take the elevator instead, at a cost of 10F ($1.38) for a round-trip ticket.

The entrance to the village is through the Porte de Figuier (Fig Tree Gate), through which many of the most illustrious Europeans of the 13th century passed. One of the oldest places of pilgrimage in France, Rocamadour became famous as a cult center of the black Madonna. The village was supposedly founded by Zacchaeus who entertained Christ at Jericho. He is claimed to have come to Rocamadour with a small black wooden statue of the Virgin, although some authorities have suggested that this statue was actually carved in the 9th century.

At the Place de la Carreta is the entrance to the **Grand Escalier** (stairway) leading to the ecclesiastical center at the top, a climb of 216 steps. Even today, pilgrims make this difficult journey on their knees in penance. If you make it, you'll arrive at the **Parvis des Églises**, Place St-Amadour, with its seven chapels. Guided tours of the chapels are conducted June 1 to September 15 from 9 a.m. to 6 p.m.

The **Musée-Trésor** can be visited July 1 to August 31 from 9 a.m. to 6:30 p.m.; April through June and from the first of September to the end of October from 9 a.m. to noon and 2 to 6 p.m. The admission charged is 8F ($1.10). Among other treasures is a gold chalice presented by Pope Pius II.

Against the cliff, the **Basilica of St. Savior** was built in the Romanesque-Gothic style from the 11th to the 13th centuries. It is decorated with paintings and inscriptions, recalling visits of celebrated persons, including Philippe the Handsome.

In the **Chapelle Miraculeuse**, the "holy of holies," the mysterious St. Amadour (believed to be the publican, Zacchaeus) is said to have carved out an oratory in the rock. Hanging from the roof of this chapel is one of the oldest clocks known, dating from the 4th century. Above the altar is the venerated statue of the Madonna.

The **Chapel of St. Michael** was built in the Romanesque style and is sheltered by an overhanging rock. Inside are two frescoes that are rich in coloring, dating (perhaps) from the 12th century.

Above the door leading to the **Chapelle Notre-Dame** is a large iron sword that, according to legend, belonged to Roland.

Built on a cliff spur and now inhabited by chaplains, the **château** was medieval before its restoration. It was originally built for the defense of the holy sanctuaries but was unable to keep out the pillaging hordes over the centuries. The château is only of minor interest, but the view from its ramparts is spectacular. It is open July 1 until the end of August from 9 a.m. to 7 p.m. Otherwise, its off-season hours are 9 a.m. to noon and 1:30 to 6 p.m. Admission is 5F (69¢).

FOOD AND LODGING: **Mapotel Beau-Site et Notre-Dame,** rue Roland-le-Preux (tel. 65-33-63-08). The stone walls which give this hotel so much character were built in the 15th century by a commander of the Order of Malta. Today, the views from the rear terrace encompass a sweeping look at the Val d'Alzou. A cavernous fireplace, big enough to roast an ox, fills part of the heavily beamed reception area. Other parts of the hotel have been outfitted with a trendy collection of modern globe lights and pseudo-medieval touches. The hotel offers 55 comfortable bedrooms in its main building and in an annex. They are priced between 170F ($23.44) in a single and 250F ($34.48) in a double. Both the hotel and its restaurant are closed between mid-November and late March. The restaurant serves a flavorful and regionally inspired cuisine prepared by members of the Menot family, who have owned the place for many generations. Specialties include sautéed lamb with mustard flowers served with an eggplant flan, duckmeat salad, raw marinated salmon with green peppercorns, a combination of sea bass with crayfish tails in an anise-flavored butter sauce, and a dessert soufflé of caramelized walnuts. Fixed-price menus cost between 75F ($10.32) and 180F ($24.82). À la carte dinners average 250F ($34.48).

    Château de Roumégouse (tel. 65-33-63-81) is a château-inn at Roumégouse, out the N681, 2½ miles southeast of Rocamadour. This château, from the 15th century, is set in a five-acre wooded parkland, and it attracts those who prefer to be away from the souvenir-laden tourist bustle of Rocamadour. Terraces overlook the Causse. A private, almost home-like quality prevails here, as the place rents out only 11 bedchambers, each one different architecturally and decoratively. Singles cost 300F ($41.37), that tariff going up to 650F ($89.64) in a double. You dine in a lovely old hall with a well-preserved atmosphere. Menus cost 120F ($16.55), 183F ($25.24), and 260F ($35.85). The restaurant is closed on Tuesday at lunchtime and from December to the end of March.

    Sainte-Marie, Place des Senahles (tel. 65-33-63-07), is the personal statement of its owner, who has created an enchanting little 22-room place at which to stay. There is an old-world sense to this maison, providing chambers of special comfort and charm. Rates are 150F ($20.69) in a single, rising to 225F ($31.03) in a double. Guests are received from late March to November. Good meals are provided, with menus costing 55F ($7.56) and 165F ($22.75). There is an unusually fine view from the terrace of Sainte-Marie.

8. Cahors

    The ancient capital of Quercy, Cahors was a thriving university city in the Middle Ages, and many antiquities of its illustrious past life still remain. However, Cahors is known today mainly for its almost-legendary red wine that is made principally from the Malbec grapes grown in vineyards around this old city, 55 miles north of Toulouse in central France. Firm but not harsh, Cahors is considered one of the most deeply colored of fine French wines.

    The town lies on a rocky peninsula almost entirely surrounded by a loop of the Lot River. It grew up near a sacred spring, which, incidentally, still supplies the city with water. At the source of the spring, the **Fontaine des Chartreux** stands by the side of the **Pont Valentré** (also called the Pont du Diable), a bridge with a trio of towers, a magnificent example of medieval defensive design erected between 1308 and 1380, then much restored in the 19th century. The pont, the first medieval fortified bridge in France, is the most colorful site in Cahors, with its crenellated parapets, its battlements, and its seven pointed arches. The central tower can be visited by the public July 1 to August 31 from 10 a.m. to noon and 3 to 7 p.m. for 7F (97¢) admission.

    Dominating the old town, the **Cathédrale St-Étienne** was built in 1119 but reconstructed in part between 1285 and 1500. It appears to be a fortress and was the first cathedral in the country to have cupolas, giving it a Romanesque-Byzantine look. One of the most remarkable features is its finely sculptured north portal, a Romanesque door carved about 1135 in the Languedoc style. Adjoining the cathedral are the remains of a Gothic cloister from the latter part of the 15th century.

Cahors is a starting point for an excursion to the **Célé and Lot Valleys,** a long, colorful journey that many French people are fond of taking in the summer, a round trip of about 125 miles, lasting some two days if you have plenty of time for sightseeing. The Office of Tourisme, Place Briand (tel. 65-35-09-56), provides maps giving itineraries.

FOOD AND LODGING: **Wilson,** 72 Boulevard du Président-Wilson (tel. 65-35-41-80), is an attractively designed, modern hotel conveniently situated in the center of the city. Each of the spacious bedrooms contains a private bath, telephone, radio/alarm, TV, and mini-bar. Renovated in 1982, the hotel charges from 250F ($34.48) in a single to 415F ($57.23) in a double. There's a parking lot nearby.

France, 252 Avenue Jean-Jaurès (tel. 65-35-16-76), provides the best rooms in the town center, from its perch right at the railway station. It offers 79 well-furnished chambers, costing 225F ($31.03) in a single, 250F ($34.48) in a double. Each room is satisfactorily equipped, and the maids provide good service. Breakfast is the only meal served.

La Taverne, 42 rue Jean-Baptiste Delpech (tel. 65-35-28-66), offers an outstanding local cuisine and many regional specialties in a rustic decor. Patrick Lannes runs a fine place with the aid of his chef, Serge Guillevet. If you've never tried the cuisine of Quercy, you can do so here, ordering from menus costing 110F ($15.17), 150F ($20.69), and 230F ($31.72). Some award-winning specialties include truffles in puff pastry, a magnificent scallop dish, rabbit stew, tournedos with foie gras, a salad of truffles, and duckling with cèpes (flap mushrooms). The restaurant is closed Sunday night and Monday.

AN EXCURSION TO GROTTE DU PECH-MERLE: Discovered in 1922, this prehistoric cave near Cabrerets some 21 miles east of Cahors, was once used for ancient religious rites. Wall paintings and carvings were found in it. You're allowed to explore the cave, from Easter to the end of September from 9 a.m. to noon and 2:30 to 6 p.m.; in October, tours leave at 10 and 11 a.m. and at 3 and 4:30 p.m. Adults pay 28F ($3.86); children, 15F ($2.07). Some two miles of chambers and galleries are open to the public, who wander where prehistoric people did some 20,000 years ago, leaving petrified footprints to show for it. Aurignacian Age art includes drawings of mammoths and bison. One cave is called the picture gallery, as it is decorated with the outlines of two horses.

9. Montauban

Some 31 miles north of Toulouse, this pink-brick capital of the Tarn-et-Garonne is the city of the painter Ingres and the sculptor Bourdelle.

Montauban, on the right bank of the Tarn, is one of the most ancient of the fortified towns of southwest France. It is still dominated by the fortified **Church of St. James.** The town was the headquarters of the Huguenot rebellion in 1621. The most scenic view of Montauban is at the 14th-century brick bridge, **Pont-Vieux,** which connects the town to its satellite of **Villebourbon.** The bridge is divided by seven arches.

An admirer of Raphael and a student of David, Jean Auguste Dominique Ingres was born in 1780 in Montauban, the son of an ornamental sculptor and painter who was not well-to-do. The father recognized his son's artistic abilities early and encouraged him greatly. Ingres lived for a part of his life in Italy, seek-

470 DOLLARWISE GUIDE TO FRANCE

ing inspiration in classical motifs. He was noted especially for his nudes and historical paintings, all of which are today considered fine examples of neoclassicism. One of his first exhibitions of portraits in 1806 met with ridicule, but later generations have been more appreciative.

Although the Louvre in Paris owns many Ingres masterpieces, upon his death in 1867 the artist bequeathed to Montauban more than two dozen paintings and some 4,000 drawings. These are displayed at the **Musée Ingres**, 19 rue de la Mairie (tel. 63-63-18-04), in a 17th-century bishops' palace built on the site of two previous castles, one of which had been inhabited by the counts of Toulouse. The museum is open from 10 a.m. to noon and 2 to 6 p.m. except Monday, charging 4.50F (62¢) for admission. One painting in the collection is *Christ and the Doctors*, painted when Ingres was 82. The *Dream of Ossian* was intended for Napoleon's bedroom in Rome. On the ground floor are works by Bourdelle (1860–1929), who was heavily influenced by Rodin. Two busts Bourdelle did, of Ingres and of Rodin, are particularly outstanding.

For a final look at a masterpiece by Ingres, head for the **Cathédrale Notre-Dame**, a classical building framed by two square towers. In the north transept is the painting the church commissioned, *Vow of Louis XIII*.

FOOD AND LODGING: **Mapotel Ingres,** 10 Avenue Mayenne (tel. 63-63-36-01), occupies a convenient setting close to the railway station. Its contemporary exterior shelters about 30 comfortably efficient bedrooms, some of which overlook a well-tended rear garden. Each contains air conditioning and a private bath, as well as a TV with about two dozen channels. Accommodations cost from 340F ($46.89) in a single, 500F ($68.95) in a double. Breakfast is the only meal served.

Hôtel du Midi, 12 rue Notre-Dame (tel. 63-63-17-23), lies in the heart of the most historic part of town, just opposite the cathedral. This pleasantly renovated old house contains four separate dining areas ranging from a vaulted antique style to warmly contemporary, complete with a fireplace for winter days. The decor sometimes includes painted interior ceilings. On Sunday and holidays the fixed-price menus range upward from 180F ($24.82), although during the week they're cheaper, ranging from 75F ($10.32). Your meal might include bass with red butter, sauté of veal with leeks, maigret de canard à l'ancienne, confit of goose, and a tasty collection of hors d'oeuvres from the buffet table. If you need a place to spend the night, the hotel offers some 50 well-furnished rooms, most of which contain private bath and color TV. Rooms cost from 120F ($16.55) in a single to 330F ($45.51) in a double.

Hostellerie les Coulandrières, Route de Castelsarrasin (tel. 63-03-18-09), lies two miles west of the center of Montauban. Hostelleries have their own charm and warmth, and this one is especially good, located as it is on three acres of parkland. Joëlle and Jean Castell have provided a swimming pool and a volleyball court, even a place for bowling and mini-golf. The lounges and dining room are traditionally furnished, and there are 21 pleasantly comfortable and well-equipped bedrooms, renting for 320F ($44.13) in a single, 330F ($45.51) in a double. Half-board guests are accepted at a rate of 300F ($41.37) to 600F ($82.74) per person nightly. The inn is closed Sunday night and in April.

Delmas, 10 rue Michelet (tel. 63-63-03-74). Near the Place Nationale on a popular street in the old part of town, this traditional establishment contains a delicatessen on the ground floor and a contemporary dining room upstairs. Specialties include a caper-flavored version of foie gras, veal kidneys with mustard sauce, flap mushrooms à la bordelaise, chicken with morels, and turbot with leeks. The restaurant, which serves meals except Sunday night, Monday, and in August, charges from 65F ($8.97) for a set meal weekdays, 145F ($20) on Sunday. À la carte dinners cost from 200F ($27.58).

Chapter XIX

BORDEAUX AND THE ATLANTIC COAST

**1. Bordeaux
2. The Wine Country
3. Angoulême
4. Cognac
5. Saintes
6. La Rochelle
7. Poitiers**

FROM THE HISTORIC PORT of La Rochelle to the bordeaux wine district, the southwest of France is too briefly glimpsed by the motorist rushing from Paris to Spain. But the area is becoming better known for its Atlantic beaches, its medieval and Renaissance ruins, its Romanesque and Gothic churches, its vineyards and charming old inns that still practice a splendid regional cuisine.

In our journey through this most intriguing part of France we will not stay entirely on the coastline, visiting such cities as Bordeaux and La Rochelle as the title of the chapter suggests, but will dip inland for a glass of cognac and trips to such nearby art cities as Poitiers and Angoulême.

Allow at least a week for this journey—just enough time to sample the wine, savor the gastronomic specialties, and see at least some of the major sights of this ancient region over which the French and English fought so bitterly for so many years.

1. Bordeaux

The great port city of Bordeaux, on the Garonne River, the capital city of Aquitaine, struck Victor Hugo as "Versailles, with Antwerp added." As the center of the most important wine-producing area in the world, Bordeaux attracts many visitors to the offices of wine exporters here, most of whom welcome guests. (For a trip through the bordeaux wine country, refer to the next section.)

If you'd like to know more about bordeaux wine, and have time for a tour, go to the **Maison du Vin** (House of Wine), 1 Cours du 30-Juillet (tel. 56-52-82-82), lying near the **Office de Tourisme,** 12 Cours 30-Juillet (tel. 56-44-28-41), just off the Esplanade des Quinconces. Members of the staff will give you maps showing the most popular wine routes. In addition to your own private car, you might consider other methods of transportation: houseboat, bus, or horse-drawn caravan.

Bordeaux is a city of warehouses, factories, mansions, and exploding suburbs, as well as wide quays five miles long. Now the fifth-largest city of France, Bordeaux was for 300 years a British possession, and even today it is called the most un-French of French cities, although the same has been said of Strasbourg.

Your tour can begin at the **Place de la Comédie**, which lies at the very heart of this venerated old city, a busy traffic hub that was a Roman temple in olden days. On this square one of the great theaters of France, the **Grand Théâtre**, was built between 1773 and 1780. A colonnade of 12 columns graces its façade. Surmounted on these are statues of goddesses and the Muses. Apply to the porter if you'd like to visit the richly decorated interior, a harmonious setting of elegance and refinement.

From here you can walk to the **Esplanade des Quinconces** to the north, which was laid out between 1818 and 1828, the largest square of its kind in Europe, covering nearly 30 acres. A smaller but lovelier square is the **Place de la Bourse,** bounded by quays opening onto the Garonne. It was laid out between 1728 and 1755, with a fountain of the Three Graces at its center. Flanking the square are the Custom House and the Stock Exchange.

The finest church in Bordeaux is the **Cathédrale St-André,** standing in the south of the old town. It lacks only 20 feet of being as long as Notre-Dame in Paris. At the 13th-century Porte Royale or "royal door" the sculptures are admirable. See also the sculptures on the North Door, dating from the 14th century. Separate from the rest of the church is the Tour Pey Berland, a belfry begun in the 15th century and rising 155 feet high.

Bordeaux also has another church with a separate belfry. It's the **Basilique St-Michel** with its adjoining **Tour St-Michel.** The belfry of the church is the tallest tower in the south of France. Rising 374 feet, it was erected in 1472. Once it was possible to climb the 228 steps for a panoramic view of the port. But you'll have to settle for a view of the tower only from the ground, as the problems of safety and insurance have proved insurmountable. For information about the church, or the other four major churches of Bordeaux, you can telephone the Presbytère (tel. 56-52-50-32), but only if you speak a little French.

Bordeaux has yet another interesting church, the **Église St-Seurin,** whose most ancient sections, such as its crypt, date from the 5th century. See the porch, which was left over from an earlier church. It has some capitals from the Romanesque era.

The **Musée des Beaux-Arts,** 20 Cours d'Albret (Jardin du Palais Rohan) (tel. 56-90-91-60), has an outstanding collection of art ranging from the 15th through the 20th centuries. Works by Perugin, Titian, Rubens, Veronese, Delacroix, Gros, Redon, Marquet, and Lhote are displayed. The museum is open daily except Tuesday, from 10 a.m. to noon and 2 to 6 p.m. It closes at 5 p.m. off-season. Admission is 10F ($1.38) per person.

The **Pont de Pierre,** with 17 arches, stretches 1,594 feet across the Garonne and is considered one of the most beautiful bridges in France. Ordered built by Napoléon I in 1813, the bridge can be crossed on foot for a fine view of the quays and the port.

And for an even better view, I suggest a **tour of the port,** which lasts for about 1½ hours and encompasses a float up the river and all around the harbor. It departs from the Embarcadères des Quinconces, on the Quai Louis XVIII in the center of town, every weekday at 2:30 or 3 p.m. between April and October, and costs 35F ($4.83).

On most weekends during the same time period, a tour embarks from the same place and covers the estuary and a few of the vineyards, including Blaye, Libourne, and Cadillac. The tour, which doesn't include lunch, costs 80F ($11.03) and lasts for an entire day. Exact departure times for these tours, as well as for an occasional nighttime floating concert, are available from the Office of Tourism or at the boat captain's office near the Quai (tel. 56-32-32-50). Any tour can be canceled at any time without warning, "for reasons of security."

There's also a floating restaurant, the **Alienor,** member of the Grands Bateaux d'Aquitaine, 27 Quai de Queyries (tel. 56-86-50-65), which offers the possibility of a floating lunch or dinner on the Garonne. The fixed-price meal ranging from 160F ($22.06) to 269F ($37.10) can accompany trips lasting from a few hours to a full afternoon, with stopovers in Blaye, Cadillac, Bourg-sur-Gironde, or Libourne. For information, get in touch with the office.

WHERE TO STAY: **Frantel,** 5 rue Robert-Lateulade (tel. 56-90-92-37), is a luxurious hotel of distilled sophistication and personalized decoration standing near the Place Gambetta in the heart of town, which was the old Place Dauphine in the era of Louis XV. In a setting of such antiquity, the most up-to-date contemporary comfort provides a contrast. The staff is friendly and helpful, and the maid service is efficient. In a single the tariff is 420F ($57.92), rising to 580F ($79.98) in a double. If you'd like to make an evening of it, I suggest dining at Le Mériadeck, the hotel's main restaurant, one of the finest in Bordeaux. Expect to spend from 250F ($20.69) to 300F ($41.37).

Grand Hôtel de Bordeaux, Place de la Comédie (tel. 56-90-93-44). Some residents believe that this hotel's elaborately carved white stone façade is one of the most beautiful in Bordeaux. Whether that's true or not, a stay at this hotel generally means a good solid kind of bourgeois comfort. The location on this heartbeat square is shared with the Grand Théâtre. The conservatively decorated bedrooms offer quiet and calm behind soundproof windows, and each contains air conditioning, TV, full bath, and phone. Single or double rooms range from 370F ($51.02) to 520F ($71.71).

Sofitel Bordeaux-le-Lac, Zone Hôtelière du Lac (tel. 56-50-90-14), lies north of town near the Pont d'Aquitaine, in the vicinity of its chain-fellow and rival, the Aquitania. It is close to the lake and the Palais des Expositions, and it attracts a large clientele of international business people. Its 100 bedrooms with private bath are warmly decorated, color coordinated, containing no distracting frills, although all the required facilities are provided. In a single the rate ranges from 445F ($61.37); in a double or twin, from 520F ($71.71). To relax tired muscles, there is a heated swimming pool with a terrace and a refreshment bar. For dining, you'll find regional specialties and other dishes offered at La Pinasse, where a meal will cost in the neighborhood of 210F ($28.96).

Le Majestic, 2 rue de Condé (tel. 56-52-60-44), is very recommendable if you're more traditional-minded and want an oasis of comfort right in the heart of the city, near the Grand Théâtre. Modernization for creature comforts has not disturbed its antique qualities. All of its 50 bedrooms contain private bath. Rates are 225F ($31.03) in a single, rising to 325F ($44.82) in a double. The hotel does not have a restaurant, but serves breakfast.

Français, 12 rue du Temple (tel. 56-48-10-35), is liked by travelers who want to be in an old part of Bordeaux, away from noise and traffic. Here you'll find, surprisingly enough, peace and a good night's sleep. Lying behind a graceful and classic façade with balconies, the hotel has been considerably upgraded in recent years. In a single with shower, it charges from 175F ($24.13), the cost rising to 300F ($41.37) in a comparable double. Breakfast is the only meal served.

Etche Ona, 11 rue Mautrec (tel. 56-44-36-49), is small but tranquil and central, and one of the best bargain accommodations I've been able to find in Bordeaux. It lies within walking distance of many of the city's major attractions, including the Grand Théâtre, the Cathédrale St-André, the Place de Bourse, and the quays. The rooms, 35 in all, are nicely furnished, costing from 110F ($15.17) in a single, to 250F ($34.48) in a double; some of the rooms have private baths. Breakfast is the only meal served.

Hotel Atlantic, 69 rue Eugène Leroy (tel. 56-92-92-22), is small, only 36 rooms, but centrally located for those desiring to be near the train station, Gare St-Jean. Rated only two stars, it has a friendly, welcoming staff, some of whom speak English. Most of the rooms are tasteful and comfortable and are well lit with adequate storage space. Singles begin at 175F ($24.13), going up to 265F ($36.54) in a double. A continental breakfast is the only meal served.

Hotel des Pyrénées, 12 rue St. Rémi (tel. 56-81-66-58), is a bargain oasis for Bordeaux. The location is about a five-minute taxi ride from the central rail station. The hotel is well run, with many spacious rooms, a total of 19. Rated only two stars by the government, it rents only doubles, the rates depending on the plumbing. The cheapest has a toilet, the more expensive a complete bath. Tariffs for two persons go from 125F ($17.24) to 200F ($27.58). A continental breakfast is the only meal served, and the hotel closes from August 15 until the end of the month.

WHERE TO DINE: Dubern/Christian Clément, 42 Allées de Tourny (tel. 56-48-03-44). This famous restaurant was always considered a favorite in Bordeaux, both for its lushly carved paneling and the seriousness with which it prepared Bordelais food. Its reputation was greatly enhanced in 1986 when it joined forces with what, until then, had been viewed as its most potent competitor in Bordeaux, Christian Clément. Today, platters made famous by Mr. Clément in his other restaurant are served in a setting more worthy of his exalted culinary skill. He's known for his imaginative, frequently changing adaptations of classic cuisine, always based on a carefully selected foundation of super-fresh ingredients.

Complemented by Dubern's superb collection of wines, you can enjoy, as for example, a consommé with crayfish, oysters, and spinach, perhaps milk-fed lamb with shallots, medallions of veal with ginger, crêpes stuffed with foie gras, or else cabbage filled with fresh salmon. For an appetizer, perhaps fresh oysters will intrigue you. They come in a lime-flavored sabayon sauce wrapped in leaves of Swiss chard. The elaborate desserts are likely to include a peach sabayon with bordeaux. Reservations are vital, and a fixed-price menu is offered at 260F ($35.85). Ordering à la carte will more likely cost from 310F ($42.75) to 390F ($53.78). The restaurant is closed on Sunday.

Clavel, 44 rue Charles-Domercq (tel. 56-92-91-52). The Barcelona-born chef who breathes life into this softly illuminated restaurant is credited as being one of the most proficient chefs of Bordeaux. Francis Garcia spent most of his youth working with his parents at the Château Margaux where the Greek owners encouraged him to become a chef. Apprenticeships at some of the most prestigious restaurants of the region preceded his acquisition of the plant-filled, mirror-ringed Clavel which now offers some of the most delectable food in town. Aided in the dining room by his wife, Géraldine, he serves such tempting specialties as roast of veal with capers, truffle flan with essence of morels, old-fashioned roast hare with vegetable crêpes, a gratin of lobster, perhaps a gratin of oysters laced with foie gras, and a superb collection of desserts. Fixed-priced menus cost from 260F ($35.85). For cuisine prepared in the kitchen of the master, but considerably less expensive, you should consider a meal at Mr. Garcia's adjacent Bistro du Clavel, where a fixed-price menu, with a different glass of wine included with each course, costs only 170F ($23.44). Both establishments are closed Sunday and Monday, for three weeks in July, and for two weeks in February.

Le Saint-James, Place Camille-Hosteins (tel. 56-20-52-19), lies in the small town of Bouliac, right outside Bordeaux. Its chef de cuisine is Jean Marie Amat. Even chefs on vacation decide to drop in to see why this fellow-professional generates such admiration and enthusiasm among his loyal habitués. When he serves his sautéed lobster with a tarragon-flavored mousseline, you begin to understand. Perhaps you'll sample his eggplant terrine flavored with cumin, or his beautifully conceived salad of artichoke hearts with foie gras. From May to October he offers small baked lobsters. One of his finest dishes is a pullet with a broth of truffles. Monsieur Amat is perhaps best known for his duck. Around that noble bird he builds an entire dinner, complete with bouillon made from the duck. He takes its skin and makes it crisp, which also makes for good eating. He grills the legs, and the tender breast is sliced and served with a sauce that has been thickened with blood. Other recommendable specialties include sea perch or bass with a thyme-flavored cream sauce, glazed and grilled duckling, squab with a caramel glaze, and a blanquette de veau with fresh kidney beans. An elegant meal here will run from 340F ($46.89) to 400F ($55.16) if you order à la carte. If you stick to one of the set menus at 120F ($16.55), 235F ($32.41), or 310F ($42.75), you'll fare very well indeed. The restaurant is open all year. In fair weather guests can dine on the terrace, its gardens sweeping toward the Garonne in the distance.

La Tupina, 6 rue de la Porte de la Monnaie (tel. 56-91-56-37), is small and cozy, the very special statement of one of Bordeaux's most talented young chefs, Jean-Pierre Xiradakis. His cookery is inspired, and duck is his specialty. For example, your meal might begin with croûtons that have been spread with duck rillettes, a most savory concoction. Shredded duck preserved in its own fat is another dish that allows Monsieur Xiradakis's talents to show themselves at advantage. His salads often use giblets, skin, and livers from his prized ducks. Of course, he doesn't ignore the classic regional specialties such as truffles and foie gras; a recent potato salad sampled here contained slices of the black truffles of the Périgord region. His foie gras often comes steamed en papillote. Try, if featured, his veal ragoût, which is made with leeks and carrots, or his tripe of veal in a well-seasoned stock. He also keeps a good wine cellar. Expect to pay 160F ($22.06) to 200F ($27.58) for a meal here. The restaurant is closed Sunday at lunchtime.

Chez Le Chef, 57 rue Huguerie (tel. 56-81-67-07), is an excellent little restaurant where you can dine in a garden setting right in the heart of Bordeaux. Denis Ocio is the director, owner, and chef de cuisine. He offers one of the best set meals in the city, charging 95F ($13.10), as he insists on using the freshest of produce and quality meats, along with fine regional wines of the Bordeaux district. The cookery is both traditional and nouvelle. You can order more intricate set menus for 130F ($17.93) and 200F ($27.58). The restaurant is closed in October, as well as on Sunday night and Monday.

Le Vieux Bordeaux, 27 rue de Buhan (tel. 56-52-94-36), is one of the best established restaurants in town, a virtual neighborhood institution. In a decor of vermilion walls, exposed wood, and almost incongruous modern accents, you can enjoy such specialties as a pavé of fresh salmon served with warm oysters, roasted sweetbreads, turbot with a buttered truffle sauce, hare with onions, and a gratin of lobster with fresh noodles. A fixed-price menu is offered at 110F ($15.17), another for 160F ($22.06). À la carte costs from 230F ($31.72) per person. No meals are served Saturday at lunch and all day Sunday.

La Forge, 8 rue du Chai-des-Farines (tel. 56-81-40-96), is a kind of neighborhood bistro where Jean-Michel Pouts, a former chef on the ocean liner *France,* prepares specialties such as brochette of pork with gruyère and savory grilled meats. La Forge offers well-prepared meals every day except Sunday, Monday, and from mid-August to mid-September. Set menus cost 75F ($10.32), 95F ($13.10), and 150F ($20.69), while à la carte meals go for 150F ($20.69) and up.

2. The Wine Country

Bordeaux is one of the capitals of French gastronomy. Many consider the district the equal of Lyon. Dugléré, born here, became one of the great men of classical French cookery.

The major wine districts of Bordeaux are **Graves, Médoc, Sauternes, Entre-deux-Mers, Libourne, Blaye, and Bourg.**

North of the city of Bordeaux, the Garonne River joins the Dordogne. This forms the Gironde, a broad estuary comprising the heart of the bordeaux wine country. More than 100,000 vineyards produce some 70 million gallons of wine a year. Some of these are among the greatest red wines in the world. The white wines are lesser known.

Some of the more famous vineyards are pleased to welcome visitors, providing they don't arrive at the busy harvest time. However, most of them are not likely to have a permanent staff to welcome you. In other words, don't just show up on the doorstep. You must call first or check with local tourist offices about appropriate times for visits.

The most serious visitor will write to **International Wine Tours,** 12 Place de la Bourse, 33076 Bordeaux Cedex, France (tel. 56-90-91-28), for information about wine tours.

MÉDOC: The Médoc, an undulating plain covered with vineyards, is one of the most visited regions in Southwest France. Its borders are marked by Bordeaux and the Pointe de Grave. In the Haut-Médoc, the history of growing grapes to make wine dates from the era of Louis XIV. Throughout the region are many isolated châteaux producing grapes. Only a handful of these châteaux, however, are worthy of your time and attention. The most visited château, of course, is that of Mouton-Rothschild, said to be an attraction in Southwest France second only to Lourdes, in spite of the red tape involved in visiting it.

Before heading out on this wine road, make sure you have a detailed map from the tourist office in Bordeaux, since the "trail" is not well marked and you could get lost. Head in the direction of Pauillac on D2e, the wine road, called the *Route des Grands-Crus.*

In the Haut-Médoc, the soil is not especially fertile but absorbs much heat during the day. To benefit from this, the vines are clipped close to the ground. The French zealously regulate the cultivation of the vineyards and the making of the wine. Less than 10% of the wines from the region are called bordeaux. These are invariably red, including such famous labels as Châteaux Margaux, Château Latour, Châteaux Mouton, and Château Lafite. Most of these celebrated labels are from grapes grown some 3,000 feet from the Gironde River.

Lying near the village of Margaux on the D2 road is the Château Margaux, built in the Empire style in the early years of the 19th century and frequently called the Versailles of the Médoc. The château gardens have swans that were contributed by Queen Elizabeth II. Visits to the estate are allowed between 9 a.m. and 12:30 p.m. and 2 to 5:30 p.m. on weekdays except in August and the harvest period. Appointments are made by letter or by phoning 56-88-70-28. The estate covers more than 650 acres of which some 187 produce Château Margaux and Pavillon Rouge du Château Margaux. Almost 30 acres are devoted to the production of Pavillon Blanc du Château Margaux. You can also see the exterior of the château, but it is inhabited privately, and there are no tours of the inside. You are allowed to wander through the English gardens, however.

Some ten miles beyond Margaux will take you to St-Julien, where nearly all foreign visitors head for the **Château de Beychevelle.** Again, you should arrange this appointment through the already-mentioned Maison du Vin in Bordeaux (you can also call on your own; the number is 56-59-05-14). The duc d'Épernon ordered this château built in 1757. As the Grand Admiral of France, he commanded all ships passing in front of the edifice to dip their sails. The name of the château means "lowered sails." If you've made prior arrangements, you can visit from 9 a.m. to noon and 2 to 6 p.m. on weekdays. On Saturday, hours are only from 9 a.m. to noon.

At Pauillac you'll find a port with deep water which services the vessels that carry the region's renowned vintages. In this district of "first growths," you'll find the famous names of Lafite-Rothschild, Mouton-Rothschild, and Latour.

Literally thousands of visitors head for the **Château Mouton-Rothschild,** one of the many homes of the Baron Philippe de Rothschild. During her lifetime, his American-born wife Pauline helped restore this château and contributed greatly to making it so outstanding. In terms of things to see, there is no château in the Médoc capable of competing with it. The wine from this place was classified as *premier cru* in 1973. Before that, it was labeled a "second growth." Providing you made an appointment by calling 56-59-22-22, you can visit the cellars from 9 to 11:30 a.m. and 2 to 5 p.m. It is closed on weekends, holidays, and in August. You're ushered into a welcoming room that is beautifully furnished with some of the Rothschild collection of sculpture and paintings. A 16th-century tapestry depicts the harvesting of the grape. An adjoining museum, in former wine cellars known as *chai,* contains art from many eras, much of it related to the cultivation of the vineyards. You can also see goldsmiths' work from the 15th and 16th centuries. Look, in particular, at a collection of modern art, including a statue by the American sculptor Lippold.

The next château of importance (and it's nearby) is **Château Lafite** (tel. 56-59-01-74). To reach it, continue along the D2. If arrangements have been made in advance, guided tours are possible from 9 to 11 a.m. and 3 to 5 p.m. Count on spending at least an hour here. The château is closed on weekends, holidays, and from mid-September to the end of November (these dates vary). The vinothèque contains many vintage bottles, such several dating from 1797. Surrounded by cedars, the château was purchased in 1868 by the Rothschilds.

FOOD AND LODGING IN MÉDOC: Several villages in Médoc and Haut-Médoc offer inns suitable for a meal or an overnight stay. My recommendations follow.

At Esconac-Cambes

Hostellerie à la Varenne, Route D10 (tel. 56-21-31-15), was built as a dignified and stately mansion in 1930. But over the years it's become an inn, housing guests not only in its main building but in a row of joined bungalows. The accommodations open onto a garden and the impressive river. In summer, chairs and tables are set out on a wide terrace where wine is sampled. The owner, Maryse Naronian, handles her guests well, supervising the cleaning of the attractive, tidy rooms, pouring bordeaux wine in the tavern, or serving in the more formal dining room. The cottage bedrooms have tile baths. A room, either single or double, with bath rents from 275F ($37.92); however, a double or single with shower costs only 160F ($22.06). A set meal goes for 95F ($13.10) including a simple wine from the area. The super-gastronomic repast costs 200F ($27.58). À la carte suggestions include hors d'oeuvres, terrine du chef, trout with almonds, lampreys bordelaise, and duck à l'orange. The restaurant is closed Sunday night.

At Lesparre-Médoc

La Mare aux Grenouilles (tel. 56-41-03-46). Here you'll find unquestionably the best food in this popular stopover point, and it's the most reasonable in price. The setting isn't special, and the wine list isn't as impressive as you might expect, but the food and the reception are just fine. You can dine very well here for only 110F ($15.17). The restaurant is closed on Monday from the first of October until the first of March.

LIBOURNE: This is a sizable market town with a railway connection. At the junction of the Dordogne and Isle Rivers, Libourne is considered roughly the center of the St-Émilion, Pomerol, and Fronsac wine districts. In the town, a large colonnaded square still contains some houses from the 16th century, including the **Hôtel de Ville.** In addition, you can explore the remains of 13th-century **ramparts.**

In the center of town the **Office de Tourisme,** Place Surchamp (tel. 57-51-15-04), will give you complete information on how to visit the bordeaux vineyards.

FOOD AND LODGING: **Hôtel Loubat,** 32 rue Chanzy (tel. 57-51-17-58), stands across from the railroad station plaza and has an exterior that warms the heart at once. Although it suggests a small country inn, some provincial decorator has given its interior a "new look" by using reproductions of French country pieces intermixed with semimodern. Nevertheless, it's the leading hotel in town, offering 45 rooms at rates that are quite reasonable. A double costs 300F ($41.37) and a single goes for 120F ($16.55). Best of all is the 110F ($15.17) set meal, including the wine of the region (but not the 15% service charge). There is as well an impressive à la carte menu, which could mean a check of 250F ($34.48). The chef's specialties include turbot cooked in champagne, duckling with mushrooms, and sweetbreads with crayfish. Off the dining room is a summer garden used primarily for wine tasting, a favorite gathering place for foreign buyers. Monique and Jacques Douté are your friendly, helpful proprietors, and they have a fine reputation in the town for their outstanding food specialties and cellar of bordeaux wine. The place is open all year.

Gare Hôtel, 43 rue Chanzy (tel. 57-51-06-86), is exactly that—a hotel at the railway station. That may not sound attractive, but the station is small, and there is a pleasant parking plaza separating the hotel from the terminus. The hotel is neat, with ten bedrooms, plus an inviting combination dining-and-drinking lounge on the street floor. In a double the price is 150F ($20.69), with shower and water basin. The food is abundant, and two set meals are featured, one at 65F ($8.97), another at 100F ($13.79). In the evenings and late afternoons, it's pleasant to order wine at one of the sidewalk tables. The restaurant is closed Sunday, and the hotel shuts down in November.

Le Landais, 15-17 rue des Treilles (tel. 57-74-07-40). The dozens of local vintners who crowd into this country-style restaurant often overflow into the adjoining garden during warm weather. The owners skillfully prepare such specialties as duckling, eels with parsley, and an array of beef and veal dishes. Full meals, some priced as low as 45F ($6.21), can range as high as 120F ($16.55). Lunch and dinner are served daily until 10 p.m.

ST-ÉMILION: This wine-growing district is world renowned. It is also an archeological gem of the Middle Ages, standing on a limestone rock where a warren of cellars has been dug out. The wine of St-Émilion was called "Wine of Honor," and British sovereigns nicknamed it "King of Wines." Saint-Émilion is about 24 miles east of Bordeaux. The most popular vineyard in the area, and the one most receptive to receiving visitors, is the **Château Pavie.** It is run by the Valette family. If you wish to visit it, you must call 75-24-72-02 to make an appointment.

Named for an eighth-century Breton saint, a former baker who became a monk, St-Émilion is surrounded by vineyards. It enjoys a dramatic location, lying on a limestone plateau looking out onto the Valley of the Dordogne. The town, made of a golden stone for the most part, is known for its macaroons.

The heart of the city is the Place du Marché, between the two hills on which St-Émilion lies. An old acacia tree marks the center. It's busy on market days, quiet at other times. Ancient tradition is still maintained in the town by the existence of La Jurade. Dressed in silk hats and scarlet robes edged with ermine, these judges sample the vintages of each vintner to see which output is worthy of being labeled "St-Émilion, appellation contrôlée."

The **Église Monolithe** is considered the most important underground church in France. This cave church is about 37 feet high, 67 feet wide, and nearly 125 feet long. It was carved out of limestone rock by the Benedictines, the work taking place between the 9th and 12th centuries. The façade is marked with three bay windows from the 16th century. A 14th-century portal depicts the Last Judgment and the resurrection of the dead sculpted into the rock.

Close at hand is the grotto where it is believed that St. Émilion lived the quiet life of meditation and contemplation which eventually led to his canonization. Called the **Chapelle de la Trinité,** it is a rare structure in the southwest of France. The chapel dates from the 13th century, and below it is a grotto which is said to contain the bed of St. Émilion, on stone. You can also view a spring of water surrounded by a 16th-century balustrade. In the cave near the chapels are galleries containing catacombs chiseled into the rock.

Finally, you may want to view the **Château du Roi.** The castle was founded by Henry III of the Plantagenet line in the 13th century. Until 1608 it served as the town hall. From the top of the dungeon one gets a view of St-Émilion. On a clear day you can see the Valley of the Dordogne.

The **Office de Tourisme,** Place des Créneaux (tel. 57-24-72-03), organizes guided tours of the main monuments of the medieval city every day. The charge is 16F ($2.21) per person. The tour includes the Hermitage (St-Émilion's grotto), the Trinity Chapel, the catacombs, and the Église Monolithe. Cassettes cost another 15F ($2.07).

FOOD AND LODGING: **Hostellerie de Plaisance,** Place du Clocher (tel. 57-24-72-32), is the choice *restaurant avec chambres* of this little medieval town, and it blends in easily with the antiquity all about. Many of its bedrooms open onto stone monuments and towers. The rooms have been tastefully styled, with full knowledge that some of the most sophisticated wine tasters and buyers in the world will be sleeping in them. The smaller singles with private bath rent for 350F ($48.27), although the most luxurious doubles cost 550F ($75.63). These have sun terraces where you can enjoy breakfast, viewing the old village buildings and nearby vineyards. Three excellent set meals are offered, featuring wines of the region. The costs are 94F ($12.96), 136F ($18.75), and 170F ($23.44), service included. Free parking is available in the courtyard.

Logis de la Cadène, Place Marché-au-Bois (tel. 57-24-71-40), is a modest inn near the Office of Tourism. The Logis offers a typical inn experience, including moderately priced regional fare. The two popularly priced set meals include the local wine. The least expensive dinner is 60F ($8.27). If you want a wider selection, you can order the 80F ($11.03) set dinner. A gastronomic repast, including the best wines of the house, will cost about 140F ($19.31). The Logis is closed Monday all year, from mid-June until the end of that month, and September 1 to 15.

WINE TOURS: The **Syndicat Viticole,** rue Gaudet (tel. 57-24-72-17), provides excellent tours of the bordeaux wine area. In addition, you can pick up a list of all the nearby vineyard châteaux. In this region even a small vineyard with a tiny cottage is called a château. But there are many great ones, including some of architectural interest.

3. Angoulême

On a hill between the Charente and Aguienne Rivers, Angoulême lies 72 miles north of Bordeaux. It can easily be visited on the same day as Cognac. A

"Balzac town," Angoulême first saw the novelist in 1831 when he came here and much admired his host's wife, Zulma Carraud.

The hub of the town is the Place de l'Hôtel-de-Ville, with its **Town Hall** erected in 1858–1866 on the site of the old palace of the dukes of Angoulême, where Marguérite de Navarre, sister of François I, was born. All that remains of the ducal palace are the Tower of Valois from the 15th century and the Tower of Lusignan from the 13th century.

The **Cathédrale St-Pierre** was begun in 1128, and it suffered much restoration in the 19th century. Flanked by two towers, its façade has a total of 75 statues—each in a separate niche—representing the Last Judgment. This church is one of the most startling examples of the Romanesque-Byzantine style in the country. Some of its restoration was questionable, however. The architect, Abadie (the designer of Sacré-Coeur in Paris), tore down the north tower, then rebuilt it with the original materials in the same style. In the interior you can wander under a four-domed ceiling.

Adjoining the cathedral is the former Bishops' Palace, which has been turned into the **Musée Municipal,** 1 rue Friedland (tel. 45-95-07-69), with an interesting collection of European paintings, mainly from the 17th through the 19th centuries. The most interesting exhibits in the museum are the African art and ethnological collections as well as some of original comics. It is open daily except Tuesday, from 10 a.m. to noon and 2 to 6 p.m. (from 10 a.m. to 6 p.m. in July and August). Admission is free.

Finally, you can take the **Promenade des Remparts,** boulevards laid down on the site of the town walls. Going along, you'll have a superb view of the valley almost 250 feet below.

FOOD AND LODGING: **France,** 1 Place Halles (tel. 45-95-47-95), is an old hotel with a well-tended flower garden, lying close to the encircling Promenade des Remparts. The bedrooms here, 61 in all, are nicely furnished in a traditional manner, and 44 of them contain private bath. Singles pay 230F ($31.72), and two persons are charged 360F ($49.64) in a room with private bath. Half-board rates are offered at 250F ($34.48) to 300F ($41.37) per person in a double room. The hotel has a small but good menu of traditional French dishes. If you'd like to drop in to dine, you'll find meals priced at 150F ($20.69), or you can dine à la carte. The restaurant is closed from just before Christmas to early January, Saturday, and at lunchtime on Sunday.

For the most luxurious accommodations you'll have to drive to Asnières-sur-Nouère, 5½ miles away. **Le Moulin du Maine-Brun** (tel. 45-96-92-62) is reached by heading out the N141. When you arrive at La Vigerie (the sign will indicate that you've gone about 5 miles from Angoulême), you turn to your right. This is an old mill, set in the Charente countryside, which has been converted into a distinguished and comfortable inn on the road from Paris to Spain. The Ménager family, who made this their private home until 1964 when they started receiving paying guests, are antique collectors. With flawless taste and an eye for authenticity, they set about furnishing this hotel, where no two bedrooms are alike. Under the beams of the old mill they have added Napoleonic beds, a Louis XIV bar, Charles X pieces, whatever. At night guests gather around a cozy fireplace or enjoy candlelit dinners. The old water mill is now the main house, and guest rooms have been added in a pavilion overlooking the millstream and the gardens. The hotel is surrounded by 12 acres of beautiful grounds. The double rate is 500F ($68.95). All that cardinal-purple velvet costs money, as does lounging around a swimming pool in this part of the country.

The cuisine is exceptional at this Relais et Châteaux. In season, it is obligatory to take the half-board rate, costing 1,025F ($141.35) for two persons daily. If you're visiting just for a meal, you'll find menus at 180F ($24.82) and 270F ($37.23). If you order à la carte, expect to spend from 260F ($35.85). Specialties include a pike mousse with an asparagus sabayon, an omelet with small snails, fresh duckling foie gras with old cognac, a feuilleté of mussels with Pineau des Charentes, lobster suprême with tarragon, a côte de boeuf Charentaise, and some of the finest trout I've ever tasted. Monsieur Ménager is justly proud of his wine cellars, which contain some of the finest bordeaux and rare cognacs. The vegetables for your meals are grown on the family's own farmland. They even have their own special cognac du Maine-Brun and their own cheese, which is mild and white. The Moulin is closed from November 1 to mid-December.

La Chamade, 13 rampe d'Aguesseau (tel. 45-38-41-33), looks in many ways like a mixture of a lighthearted bistro with a dose of summer garden thrown in for color. Hanging chandeliers, expansive murals, and table lamps add to the ambience set up by the owner, Phillipe Lafforgue. Many diners claim that it's the best restaurant in the city. Specialties are ultra-fresh dishes such as warm oysters and foie gras in puff pastry, pigeon with cabbage in sherry, raw salmon with essence of oysters, and scallops in peach liquor. Fixed-price menus cost 145F ($20), while à la carte meals go for 250F ($34.48). The establishment is open every day except Monday at lunchtime, on Sunday, the first three weeks of August, and for about a week in February.

4. Cognac

Cognac, 23 miles west of Angoulême and about 70 miles southeast of La Rochelle, is a center for making brandy that has ennobled the tables of history. It's worth a detour to stop off here to visit one of the château warehouses of the great cognac bottlers. Martell, Hennessey, and Otard welcome visits from the public, and will even give you a free drink at the end of the tour. If you'd like to visit a distillery, go to its main office during regular business hours and make your request. The staffs are generally receptive, and you will see some brandies that have aged for as long as 50 or even 100 years. You can ask about guided tours at the **Office de Tourisme,** 16 rue du XIV Juillet (tel. 45-82-10-71).

François I was born in the town's ancient, now dilapidated château in the center. It dates from the 15th and 16th centuries and was a former residence of the House of Valois. It is now a cognac warehouse.

Cognac has two beautiful parks which should be visited: the **Parc François 1er** and the **Park de l'Hôtel-de-Ville.** The Romanesque-Gothic **Church of St. Léger** is from the 12th century, its bell tower from the 15th century.

FOOD AND LODGING: **Moderne,** 24 rue Élisée-Mousnier (tel. 45-82-19-53), opening onto the Place Sous-Préfecture, is a modest 40-room inn in the center of town. Rooms are comfortably although simply furnished, and the welcome by Monsieur and Madame Michel Blomme is polite and friendly. A single rents for 152F ($20.96) and a double goes for 250F ($34.48). Rooms contain private bath, toilet, and phone. The hotel doesn't have a restaurant, but serves a continental breakfast. There is a garage if you're driving. Closed mid-December to mid-January.

Logis de Beaulieu, N141 direction Saintes (tel. 45-82-30-50), is a handsome manor house with an excellent location in the hamlet of St-Laurent-de-Cognac, three miles from the center of Cognac. The logis is a high-ceilinged, generously proportioned villa with a tile roof, angled bay windows, and heavy shutters. The reception area contains a baronial staircase of polished wood curving past an ascending collection of stained-glass windows.

The logis stands in a large park dotted with old trees, with enjoyable views and verdant shrubs. The attractive owner, Danielle Biancheri, offers boating, a volleyball court, and 21 pleasantly furnished bedrooms, 12 of which have private bath. The cheapest singles rent for 115F ($15.86), while doubles cost as much as 450F ($62.06). The hotel also serves well-prepared meals produced by George Biancheri, holder of a Grand Coron d'Or award of French gastronomy. On view is a prized collection of old cognacs. Fixed-price menus cost 115F

($15.86), 120F ($16.55), and 200F ($27.58). Half board ranges from 260F ($35.85) to 350F ($48.27) per person. The hotel is closed from mid-December till just after New Year's.

Les Pigeons Blancs (The White Pigeons), 110 rue Jules-Brisson (tel. 45-82-16-36), was a relay station for the postal service in the 17th century and has been attractively transformed into a popular restaurant. It is a Tachet family affair, as you are welcomed by Catherine, Jacques, and Jean-Michel. Specialties, prepared by Jacques-Henri Tachet, include fresh salmon with sorrel, savory beef dishes, and a gratinée of two kinds of fish (rascasse and John Dory), lightly seasoned and delicately flavored. Fixed-price menus range from 100F ($13.79) to 180F ($24.82). If you choose to dine à la carte, expect to spend from 260F ($35.85). Six rooms are available if you wish to spend the night here, costing 180F ($24.82) for a single, 290F ($39.99) for a double. Closing is on Sunday and for the first two weeks in January.

On the Outskirts

Moulin de Cierzac, Route de Barbezieux, Saint-Fort-sur-le-Né (tel. 45-83-01-32). At the southern periphery of the village, this three-story stone house has white shutters, strong horizontal lines, and lots of character. A stream runs beside the foundations of this former mill house whose origins date from the 17th century. The rustic dining room has windows that open onto a view of the park. Specialties include steamed lobster in orange butter and filet of lamb in a garlic cream sauce. A table d'hôte meal costs 110F ($15.17); à la carte, 280F ($38.61) to 320F ($44.13). If you want to stay overnight, ten pleasantly furnished rooms are available, five with private bath, costing from 250F ($34.48) in a single to 420F ($57.92) in a double. The establishment is closed Monday in low season and for the month of January.

5. Saintes

The much-battered monuments of this town on the bank of the Charente River demonstrate just about every civilization since the Roman occupation, which made it the capital of Southwest France. Today, on the tree-lined streets bordered with shops, you're likely to enjoy an unusual stopover.

The ancient Roman city was called Mediolanum Santonus, and was the place to which the Latin poet Ausone came to die at about the same time that Saint Eutrope began to Christianize the town. This latter action led to repeated attacks by barbarians. During the Middle Ages the Plantagenet rulers covered the city with religious monuments, many of which were visited by the pilgrims wending their way down to Santiago de Compostela in Spain.

During the 18th century and continuing into the 19th, the city witnessed the construction of many of its neoclassical buildings, such as the national theater and mansions erected by nobles as well as brigands. Saintes also holds the honor of being the birthplace of the 16th-century inventor of enameling, Bernard Palissy (1510–1590).

Major attractions include the **Abbaye aux Dames,** founded in 1047 by Geoffroi Martel, Count of Anjou. It became a convent, attracting women from the finest families in France. Daughters of the nobility, among whom was the future Marquise de Montespan, were educated here. After the Revolution, so great was the hatred of the local people that the church was transformed into a dress shop. In 1942, after 20 years of restoration from the ravages of a more secular age, the church was reconsecrated. The style is Romanesque, although sections date from the 18th century. A festival of ancient music takes place here every summer.

Arc de Germanicus, on the Esplanade André-Malraux near the tourist office, was built in A.D. 19 of local limestone. In 1842 it was moved from a position near the end of a Roman bridge the authorities were demolishing to a new location on the right bank of the Charente. It's dedicated to Germanicus and Tiberius.

The **Cathedral of St. Pierre** was built on Roman foundations in the 12th century and greatly expanded in a flamboyant Gothic style in the 15th century under the direction of three bishops, all members of the aristocratic Rochechouart family. Parts were destroyed by the Calvinists in 1568, then rebuilt. The enormous organs date from the 16th and 17th centuries.

The **Old City** is an area of winding streets and a distinctly medieval flavor, stretching around the Cathedral of St. Pierre.

Eglise St-Eutrope is considered one of the most important monuments in all of Southwest France, despite the alterations to the nave that a misdirected series of architects performed in 1803. It was built in the 1400s by Louis XI, who revered St. Eutrope as his favorite holy man, believing the saint had cured him of a disease. The vast crypt is only half buried underground because of the slope of the land, and it's more a subterranean church than a crypt. The sarcophagus, said to contain the remains of St. Eutrope, dates from the 4th century. There's a very deep well, nearly 150 feet, in the crypt as well as several Roman-era baptismal fonts.

The **Arena** is accessible from the rues St-Eutrope and Lacurie. To visit it, ring the bell for the custodian. Built at the beginning of the 1st century A.D., it is one of the oldest remaining Roman amphitheaters in the world, although it is medium-size in comparison to others. Many of the seats are covered today with wild shrubs and greenery. In its heyday it could hold 20,000 spectators. A fountain has been built halfway up the slope of one of the sides, marking the spot where a disciple of St. Eutrope was beheaded.

Musée Dupuy-Mestreau is installed in an 18th-century palace with many rich architectural details of that period, as well as furniture, more than 200 rare postage stamps of the region, re-creations of centuries-old regional costumes, painted porcelains, 13th-century weapons, and a re-creation of an aristocratic 18th-century bedroom. Guided tours are conducted from spring to fall from 2:30 to 4:30 p.m. In July and August, additional visits are offered at 3, 3:30, 4, and 5 p.m. It is closed Monday and on holidays, plus October 15 to April 15. Admission is 15F ($2.07).

FOOD AND LODGING: Le Relais du Bois St-Georges, rue de Royan (tel. 46-93-50-99). Several buildings comprise this hotel and restaurant at the edge of town in a verdant park with a heated, covered swimming pool and a small lake with ducks and swans. Some of the comfortably modern rooms are furnished with antiques, and some have a private terrace. Prices for the two dozen units range from 220F ($30.34) to 380F ($52.40) in a single to 400F ($55.16) to 480F ($66.19) in a double. Half board costs from 365F ($50.33) to 400F ($55.16) per person, depending on the accommodation. The restaurant section is part of what used to be an old farmhouse. The rustic dining room has been renovated so that most of an entire wall opens onto a view of the park. The chef prepares the savory specialties, which include marinated tournedos, filet of bar, and terrine of sliced duck. A fixed-price menu is served for 110F ($15.17), although an à la carte meal costs from 200F ($27.58). The restaurant is closed Monday at lunchtime.

Hotel Commerce Mancini, rue des Messageries (tel. 46-93-06-61), is a combined hotel and restaurant in the center of town, near the main post office. Robert Baty is the energetic entrepreneur whose Renaissance-style dining room, run by his son, François, attracts many of the area's most prosperous business people every day at lunch. Specialties include a frequently changing collection of dishes such as filet of raw bass marinated in fresh mint, émincé of duck breast with an essence of raspberries, turbot braised in St-Émilion, liver of duckling in gelatin, and well-prepared veal dishes. Set menus range from 80F ($11.03) to 275F ($37.92), and an à la carte meal goes from 250F ($34.48). The restaurant is closed Saturday and from just before Christmas until February. Quiet and well-furnished bedrooms, all with private bath, are also offered, ranging from 220F ($30.34) in a single to 320F ($44.13) in a double. The hotel has the same vacation times as the restaurant, except that it receives guests on Saturday most of the year.

Brasserie Louis, 116 Avenue Gambetta (tel. 46-74-05-91), is a pleasant eating place inside the Hôtel Avenue, directed by the Claude Huret family. Set menus cost from 72F ($9.93) to 120F ($16.55). The restaurant is closed Monday in off-season. If you need a room for the night, the hotel charges 125F ($17.24) in a single, 200F ($27.58), in a double for its 15 rooms, most of which have private bath, phone, and access to a pleasant garden.

At St-Georges-des-Côteaux

La Vieille Forge (tel. 46-92-98-30) is about 3¾ miles northwest of town on the N137. As its name would imply, it used to be a forge for a local blacksmith, although today instead of beating plowshares the staff is more likely to be beating egg whites for the local specialties, which are worth the trip to the forge. Table d'hôte menus are available from 75F ($10.32). If you order à la carte, you are likely to pay from 120F ($16.55). If you're not in a hurry, you can enjoy a pleasant afternoon. Closed Monday night.

6. La Rochelle

Once known as the French Geneva, La Rochelle is a historic port, formerly the stronghold of the Huguenots. From the port sailed the founders of Montréal and many others who helped to colonize Canada. On the Atlantic coast, the city lies 90 miles southeast of Nantes on the railway line to Bordeaux. From the 14th to the 16th centuries it enjoyed its heyday as one of France's great maritime cities.

As a hotbed of Protestant factions, it armed privateers to prey on Catholic vessels. But it was eventually besieged by Catholic troops. Two strongmen led the fight—Cardinal Richelieu (with, of course, his Musketeers) and Jean Guiton, formerly an admiral and then mayor of the city. Richelieu proceeded to blockade the port. Although La Rochelle bravely resisted, on October 30, 1628, Richelieu entered the city. From the almost 30,000 citizens of the proud city, he found only 5,000 survivors.

La Rochelle became the principal port between France and the colony of Canada, but the loss of Canada by France ruined its Atlantic trade.

SEEING THE CITY: There are now two different aspects of La Rochelle, the old and untouched town inside the Vauban defenses and the modern and industrial suburbs. Its fortifications have a circuit of 3½ miles with a total of seven gates.

The oldest tower is the **Tower of St. Nicholas,** dating from 1384. From the top you can enjoy a view over the town and the islands in the bay, **Ré** and **Oléron.** The tower is open from 9:30 a.m. to 12:30 p.m. and 2:30 to 6:30 p.m. in season (2 to 5 p.m. off-season), charging 15F ($2.07) for admission.

Opposite St-Nicholas is the **Tour de la Chaine,** a sister tower from which was anchored a large chain that closed the harbor at night. It too dates from the 14th century.

The **Tour de la Lanterne,** once a lighthouse, keeps the same hours as St-Nicholas. If you wish to visit both towers, you can buy a combined ticket for 20F ($2.76). It was built in the 15th century and was used mainly as a jail. The La Rochelle sergeants were imprisoned there in the 19th century.

The town with its arch-covered streets will please the walker. The port is still a bustling fishing harbor and one of the greatest sailing centers in Western Europe. Try to schedule a visit in time to attend a fish auction at the harbor. The best streets for strolling are **rue du Palais, rue Chaudrier,** and **rue des Merciers** with its ancient wooden houses. On the latter street, seek out in particular the houses at nos. 17, 8, 5, and 3.

You may also want to visit the **Maison Henri II,** rue des Augustins, which was built in the mid-16th century. The **Hôtel de Ville** on rue Gargoulleau is also interesting architecturally. It is open from Easter until the end of September from 9:30 to 11 a.m. and 2:30 to 5 p.m. (it closes Saturday at noon). During the rest of the year, it can be visited only from 2:30 to 4 p.m. (closes Saturday at noon). During the rest of the year, it can be visited only from 2:30 to 4 p.m. (closes Saturday and Sunday). Admission is 4F (55¢).

Museum Lafaille, 28 rue Albert 1er (tel. 46-41-18-25), is housed in a handsome 18th-century building surrounded with a flowering garden. The place has kept its original paneling. Clement de Lafaille, a former comptroller of war, collected an oceanographic and mineral collection that has been augmented since he donated it to the city. Rare shellfish are included in the collection, as are an idol from Easter Island, an embalmed giraffe given to Charles X (the first such specimen to be seen in France), and a parade boat encrusted with gems that was presented as a gift from the King of Siam to Napoléon III. The museum is open from 10 a.m. to noon and 2 to 6 p.m. (to 5 p.m. from mid-September to mid-June). It also shuts down on Sunday morning, on Monday, and on holidays. Admission is 5F (69¢).

Musée des Beaux-Arts, 28 rue Gargoulleau (tel. 46-41-16-27), occupies an episcopal palace that was built in the mid-18th century. Contained within are examples of French painting from the 17th to the 19th centuries, with works by Eustache Le Sueur and Brossard de Beaulieu, along with Corot and Fromentin. Some 20th-century art is by Maillol and Lagar. The museum is open from 10 a.m. to noon and 2 to 6 p.m. (to 5 p.m. from mid-September to mid-June). Admission is 5F (69¢), and the ticket is also good for entrance to the Musée d'Orbigny-Bernon (see below).

Musée d'Orbigny-Bernon, 2 rue Saint-Côme (tel. 46-41-18-83), has accumulated what the curators consider the most important artifacts relating both to the history of La Rochelle and to the history of ceramics. Included are the religious implements Richelieu used when he celebrated the first mass after the reconquest of the town from the Protestants in 1628, as well as painted porcelain from many points throughout France. For entrance hours and prices, see the Musée des Beaux-Arts (above).

One of La Rochelle's newest museums is called the **Musée du Nouveau-Monde,** Hôtel Fleuriau, 10 rue Fleuriau (tel. 46-41-46-50), and it traces the port's 300-year-old history with the New World. It begins with exhibits relating to the discovery of the Mississippi Delta in 1682 by LaSalle and goes on to the settling of the territory of Louisiana. Other exhibits trace French settlements in Guadeloupe and Martinique and other islands of the West Indies. The museum is open daily except Tuesday from 10:30 a.m. to 6:30 p.m., charging an admission of 6F (83¢).

Outside La Rochelle you may want to visit the commercial port at **La Pallice,** three miles to the east. The Germans erected large submarine bases there in World War II, some of which can still be seen. The port was heavily bombarded by the Allies. Buses to La Pallice are available at the railway station in La Rochelle, but you may prefer a round-trip by ferry.

A toll bridge leads to the resort island of **Oléron,** 4 miles wide and 20 miles long. It is covered with beaches, dunes, and pines. The bridge is at Marennes, some 35 miles south from La Rochelle. The round-trip fare is 50F ($6.90) for a motor car.

WHERE TO STAY: Hotel Les Brises, Chemin de la Digne-Richelieu (tel. 46-43-89-37), is one of the most tranquil and scenically located hotels at La Rochelle. Its box-shaped, balconied façade occupies a seafront position behind a sturdy retaining wall and a parasol-shaded patio. The hotel sits opposite the new port

(Port des Minimes) within view of a soaring 19th-century column dedicated to the Virgin. Each of the 46 immaculate bedrooms is neatly arranged with lots of exposed wood furniture, and each also has a private bath. Rates are 250F ($34.48) in a single, 475F ($65.50) in a double. A covered parking garage is on the premises.

France-Angleterre, 22 rue Gargoulleau (tel. 46-41-34-66), provides 76 attractively decorated bedrooms for guests and also operates one of the port's most acclaimed restaurants, Le Richelieu. The establishment is in the center of town, a stroll from the old port or Parc Charruyer. The hotel provides private baths and very satisfactory furnishings, and there is an emphasis on cleanliness and order. Singles are rented at 288F ($39.72); doubles go for 406F ($55.99). Many of the rooms overlook a beautiful courtyard garden, and a garage is also available. At Le Richelieu the menu offers highly commendable seafood dishes, including a terrine of pike with scallops, pike steamed with seaweed and served with a velvety-smooth beurre blanc, a feuilleté of lobster with a watercress mousse, a pot-au-feu of the sea, and turbot with small vegetables. Service is friendly, not rushed, and even the side dishes are cooked to perfection. À la carte orders average 260F ($35.85). Le Richelieu is closed on Sunday and at lunchtime Monday.

Hôtel François I, 13 rue Bazoges (tel. 46-41-28-46), is a nice, private hotel run with a lot of taste and kindness. You have the feeling of living two centuries ago. Nevertheless, the rooms are pleasantly furnished and the plumbing is quite modern. Service is efficient as well. The price range of the 34 rooms goes from 150F ($20.69) in a single, from 220F ($30.34) in a double. Breakfast is the only meal served.

WHERE TO DINE: **Richard Coutanceau,** Plage de la Concurrence (tel. 46-41-48-19). Within a rose-colored dining room whose mirrors reflect a bay-windowed view of the water, you'll enjoy a delectable cuisine. Considered a recently arrived but shining star on the city's restaurant scene, the establishment owes its success to the rigorously applied inspiration of owner/chef Richard Coutanceau and his graciously efficient wife. The elegant table settings are the perfect foil for a "modernized" cuisine that might include super-fresh shellfish plucked from nearby waters, curried turbot, roast pigeon with a fumet of St. Émilion (served with a fricassée of crayfish), and, to finish it off, a light textured dessert, perhaps a gratin of fresh fruits with pistachios. Fixed-priced menus cost from 180F ($24.82) to 350F ($48.27). À la carte meals average 280F ($38.61). The restaurant is closed every Sunday and also on Monday night.

La Marmite, 14 rue Saint-Jean-du-Pérot (tel. 46-41-17-03), is the personal statement of chef Louis Marsin and is becoming better known all the time. The decor is somewhat of a mix between a tavern and a café, with one of the corners reserved for a small salon which might be the perfect place for a before-dinner apéritif. Many of the specialties lean toward the modern French recipes the chef learned in his many apprenticeships throughout the country. They include escalope of turbot with fresh tomatoes, lotte in muscadet, fresh salmon with sorrel, and lobster with sauterne. Every day except Wednesday and from mid-January to early February, the restaurant serves à la carte meals at prices ranging from 220F ($30.34) to 290F ($39.99). Tables d'hôte begin at 150F ($20.69).

Chez Serge, 46 Cours des Dames (tel. 46-41-18-80), is an attractively informal brasserie within a distinguished-looking house facing the harbor. As its location implies, seafood is the specialty, often winningly prepared by owner/chef Serge Coulon. You might begin with a delectable pâté of crayfish and continue with an escalope of turbot with fresh tomato sauce. You might also try the excellent fish soup. Fixed-price menus cost 110F ($15.17) and 160F ($22.06), and à la carte dinners average 240F ($33.10). The restaurant is open every day.

Les Quatre Sergents, 49 rue Saint-Jean (tel. 46-41-35-80), is a nostalgically decorated garden restaurant whose ceiling is composed of a turn-of-the-century glass canopy streaming with sunlight. The site is in the center of town near the port, which makes dining on the ragoût of seafood especially appropriate considering your proximity to the water. Other specialties are turbot duxelle and a wide array of regional dishes. Open daily except Sunday night and Monday, the restaurant charges 65F ($8.97) to 150F ($27.58) for fixed-price menus, 180F ($24.82) to 240F ($33.10) for à la carte meals.

7. Poitiers

This city, the ancient capital of Poitou, the northern part of Aquitaine, is filled with history and memories. Everybody has passed through here from England's Black Prince to Joan of Arc to Richard the Lion-Hearted.

Some 200 miles southwest of Paris on the rail line to Bordeaux, Poitiers stands on a hill overlooking the Clain and Boivre Rivers. It was this very strategic location that tempted so many conquerors. Charles Martel proved the savior of Christendom by chasing out the Moslems in 732 and perhaps altering the course of European civilization. Poitiers was the chief city of Eleanor of Aquitaine, who discarded her pious French husband, Louis VII, in favor of England's Henry II.

For those interested in antiquity, this is one of the most fascinating towns in France. That battle we learned about in the history books was fought on September 19, 1356, between the armies of Edward the Black Prince and those of King John of France. It was one of the three great English victories of the Hundred Years' War, distinguished by the use of the longbow in the skilled hands of English archers.

In the eastern sector of Poitiers the twin-towered **Cathedral of St. Pierre** was begun in 1162 by Henry II of England and Eleanor of Aquitaine on the ruins of a Roman basilica. It was completed much later, but it has always been undistinguished architecturally. However, the interior, which is 295 feet long, contains some admirable stained glass from the early 13th century.

From the cathedral you can walk to the **Baptistère St-Jean,** which is considered the most ancient Christian monument in France. It was built as a baptistery in the first half of the 4th century on Roman foundations, then extended in the 7th century. Opening onto the rue Jean-Jaurès, this monument contains frescoes from the 11th to the 14th centuries and a collection of funerary sculpture. It is open all year daily except Tuesday. From April 1 until September 30, hours are from 10:30 a.m. to 12:30 p.m. and from 3 to 6 p.m. Off-season, it is open only from 2:30 to 4:30 p.m. Admission is 6F (83¢).

A favorite place of pilgrimage in times gone by, the 11th-century **Église Ste-Radegonde,** in the eastern section of Poitiers, commemorates the patroness of Poitiers. In its crypt is her black marble sarcophagus. Radegonde, who died in 587, was the consort of Clotaire, king of the Franks.

Notre-Dame-la-Grande is from the late 11th century, built in the Romanesque-Byzantine style and considered one of the most richly decorated churches in the country. See especially its west front, dating from the mid-12th century. Surrounded by an open-air market, the façade, carved like an ivory casket, is characterized by pine-cone-shaped towers. Carvings on the doorway represent biblical scenes.

From the Place du Maréchal-Leclerc, in the center of town, you can take the rue Carnot to the Romanesque church of **St-Hilaire-le-Grand,** dating from the 11th and 12th centuries. The church, after much destruction, was restored in the 19th century.

The **Église-de-Montierneuf** was begun in 1077 by William VI, Duke of Aquitaine, who is now buried within its precincts. Once attached to a Benedictine monastery, the church was much restored during the Gothic and Baroque eras. After he proclaimed the First Crusade, Urban II in 1006 consecrated the choir.

The **Palais de Justice** incorporates the 14th-century keep and some other parts of a ducal palace that stood here. It was here that Joan of Arc was questioned by the doctors of the university who composed the French Court of Parliament, and also here that Richard the Lion-Hearted was proclaimed Count of Poitou and Duke of Anjou in 1170. It is open to the public daily except Sunday, from 9 a.m. to noon and 2 to 6 p.m.

The **Musée St-Croix** (tel. 49-41-07-53), entered from the rue St-Simplicien, was built on the site of the old abbey of St-Croix from which it takes its name. The museum has a fine arts section devoted mainly to painting, especially Flemish art from the 15th and 16th centuries and Dutch paintings from the 16th to the 18th centuries. Several works by Bonnard, Sisley, and Oudot are displayed from the 19th and 20th centuries, along with a bronze, *The Three Graces,* by Maillol. A separate archeological section concerns the history of Poitou, dating from prehistoric times through the Gallo-Roman era, the Renaissance, and up to the end of the 19th century. Open from 10 a.m. to noon and 2 to 6 p.m., the museum is closed Tuesday and holidays. Entrance is free.

WHERE TO STAY: The **France,** 28 rue Carnot (tel. 49-41-32-01), is almost semi-luxurious, a place where the food equals the excellence of the setting. In the attractive garden is a covered terrace where you can take your morning coffee and croissants before plunging into the historic sights of Poitiers. The hotel has been superbly transformed, and is now the choice place to stay in this venerated old city. The attractively furnished rooms overlooking the gardens are especially restful. All the bedrooms, however, have fine furnishings and accessories. Seventy-five of the 86 bedrooms come with private bath. Singles cost 350F ($48.27), and two persons pay 700F ($96.53). The hotel also has a good restaurant, offering meals at 120F ($16.55) and 140F ($19.31). The chef specializes in regional cookery, and does so exceedingly well—grills "from the woods," tender beef, saffron-flavored scallops, and blood sausage. The hotel and restaurant are open all year.

Le Chalet de Venise, 6 rue de Square (tel. 49-88-45-07), at Saint-Benoit, is a little discovery, a ten-room inn near a small church in a pleasant location for those who don't want to be right in the heart of town. Each chamber has a distinct personality, and the hotel and the restaurant with its glowing fireplace are warmly furnished, relying heavily on autumnal colors. Guests can also enjoy a shaded, graveled terrace, taking drinks at the tables that have been invitingly set out. Take the D88 south for 2½ miles from Poitiers, or Route A10, exiting at no. 20, Poitiers Sud. The chalet is surrounded by trees and shrubbery and opens onto the water. Prices are reasonable, and the bedrooms, although simply furnished, are comfortable and immaculately kept, costing 130F ($17.93) in a single, from 190F ($26.20) in a double. Seven rooms contain private shower, and the rest come with complete bath. Personally, although you may disagree, I found the food among the best served in the Poitiers area. Dieters may find the portions overly large. Set menus are offered for 75F ($10.32) and 140F ($19.31), and for many of the specialties of Poitou you'll have to order à la carte. The inn is closed on Sunday night, Monday, and during the entire month of January.

Hotel du Plat d'Étain, 7 rue Plat-d'Étain (tel. 49-41-04-80), is one of the best hotel bargains in Poitiers. Several readers have commented on the unusual warmth of the staff. The location is along the side of a very narrow alleyway barely wide enough for a single car. The location is also a few steps from the Place du Maréchal Leclerc, which makes sightseeing and restaurant-hopping easy. The 26 simple bedrooms are reasonably priced at 65F ($8.97) in a single, 160F ($22.06) in a double, not including breakfast.

WHERE TO DINE: **Maxime,** 4 rue Saint-Nicholas (tel. 49-41-09-55), is conveniently located in the center of town. This rustically decorated haven attracts a wide cross-section of the residents of Poitiers. Specialties include seafood prepared in many different ways by Bernard Renault. Perhaps you'll enjoy a gratin of Atlantic fish, sole with cabbage, piccata of lotte with anise, or one of the many other offerings. Set menus range from 85F ($11.72) to 160F ($22.06), while an à la carte meal costs around 240F ($33.10). Dinner is served until 11 p.m. every day.

Aux Armes d'Obernai, 19 rue Arthur-Ranc (tel. 49-41-16-33), is a small Alsatian restaurant in the center of town near the central post office. Everything is well prepared by Denise Hussar, who is assisted by her husband Louis. Specialties include lamb with thyme leaves, mignon of veal with honey and lemon, and sole with crayfish and a fondue of leeks. Fixed-price menus range in price from 75F ($10.32) to 175F ($24.13), and an à la carte meal will cost from 210F ($28.96). The restaurant is closed Sunday night, all day Monday, from mid-February until early March, and for the first two weeks in September.

Restaurant Pierre Benoist, Croutelle (tel. 49-57-11-52). This establishment had been a working farm until Pierre Benoist, aided by his wife, adapted it to the particular demands of their top quality cuisine. Many visitors find the outdoor terrace hard to resist, particularly because of its view over the wooded hillsides of the valley of the Clain. A few of the dishes reflect regional tradition—for example, a rump of billygoat with green garlic. However, the main reason for visiting is to enjoy the light-textured specialties, including perhaps a terrine of scallops with vouvray, stuffed and steamed chicken with baby vegetables, foie gras in a clear-colored aspic with pine nuts, or brochette of shrimp in almond-flavored butter. To finish, a selection of fruited dessert soufflés is presented. Full meals, served daily except Sunday night and Monday, cost between 250F ($34.48) and 300F ($41.37) on the à la carte menu. A fixed-price menu costs only 170F ($23.44). The Benoists take a well-deserved vacation for two weeks in April and two weeks in August. The location is in the farming hamlet of Croutelle, about 4½ miles southwest of Poitiers on the N10.

Chapter XX

THE BASQUE COUNTRY AND THE PYRÉNÉES

1. Bayonne
2. Biarritz
3. St-Jean-de-Luz
4. Pau
5. Eugénie-les-Bains
6. Lourdes
7. Cauterets
8. Ax-les-Thermes
9. Perpignan

THE CHIEF TOURIST INTEREST in the Basque country, a land rich in folklore and old customs, is confined to a small corner of southwestern France, near the Spanish frontier. There you can visit the Basque capital at Bayonne and explore the coastal resorts, chic Biarritz and St-Jean-de-Luz. In the Roman arena at Bayonne in July and August you can see a real Spanish bullfight. The typical costume of the Basque—beret and cummerbund—isn't as plentiful as it once was, but still evident.

Stretching the length of the Spanish frontier, the vast Pyrenean region of France is a land of glaciers, wild summits, thermal baths, subterranean grottoes and caverns, winter sports centers, and trout-filled mountain streams. Pau is a good base for excursions in the western Pyrénées; and Lourdes, of course, is the major religious pilgrimage center in all of France.

We'll begin in the west, working our way east across the mountain range to Perpignan.

1. Bayonne

The leading port and pleasure-yacht basin of the Côte Basque, Bayonne is a cathedral city and capital of the Pays Basque. It is characterized by narrow streets, quays, and ramparts. Enlivening the local scene are bullfights, pelota games (jai alai), and street dancing at annual fiestas. The town is divided by the Nive and Adour Rivers. While here you may want to buy some of Bayonne's chocolate at one of the arcaded shops along **rue du Port-Neuf,** later enjoying a coffee at one of the cafés along **Place de la Liberté,** the hub of town.

Grand Bayonne, the old town, is within the ramparts of Vauban's fortifications, lying on the left bank of the Nive. This part of town is dominated by the **Cathédrale Ste-Marie,** one of the most outstanding in the southwestern part of the country, dating from the early 13th century. A Gothic building, it is characterized by two towers, one built as late as the 19th century. Incredibly beautiful, it is distinguished by its stained-glass windows in the nave. Many niches along the walls contain elaborate sarcophagi. From the 13th-century cloister you have a view of the remarkable architecture of the cathedral.

Nearby stands the **Château-Vieux,** built on the original Roman walls. Such prisoners as du Guesclin were held here in one of the towers waiting for their ransom money to be raised.

Across the river is **Petit Bayonne,** the museum district. Here the **Musée Basque,** 1 rue Marengo (tel. 59-59-08-98), at the foot of a Nive-spanning bridge, is one of the finest regional museums in France. Certainly it's the best museum for understanding the original and highly imaginative Basque people. Regional costumes, many reserved for dancing, and scale models of Basque architecture, both French and Spanish, fill the precincts, along with prints, paintings, and sketches (the latter depicting such customs as bull-baiting). In one room is a replica of a large country kitchen. Downstairs on a stone floor are displayed implements used in boating, trapping, tilling the soil, and other activities. Many exhibits are related to Basque maritime exploits. Ancient tombstones prepare the way for your visit to a chapel and sacristy. The museum is open July 1 to September 30 from 10 a.m. to noon and 2:30 to 6:30 p.m., charging an admission of 6F (83¢). From October 1 until the end of June its hours are 10 a.m. to noon and 2:30 to 5:30 p.m.

The top floor is most unusual, a tiny **Musée de la Pelote,** separate from the Basque Museum, with illustrations from this popular Basque game, including examples of the *chistera,* the wicker bat used. Models of costumes are exhibited, along with photographs of famous players. The museum keeps the same hours as the Musée Basque.

The other important museum is the **Musée Bonnat,** 5 rue Jacques-Lafitte (tel. 59-59-08-52), containing a collection of artwork the painter Léon Bonnat donated to the city, including his own. Bonnat was especially fond of portraits, often of ladies in elegant 1890s dresses. In his own *Jacob Wrestling with the Angel,* the angel is so delicate and effete it's really no contest. Far greater painters whose works are represented include Degas, David, Goya, Ingres, Daubigny, Rubens, Piero della Francesca, Van Dyck, Rembrandt, Tiepolo, El Greco, Ribera, Murillo, Constable, even Leonardo da Vinci. The museum is open from 10 a.m. to noon and 4 to 8 p.m. June 15 to September 10, charging 6F (83¢) for admission. On Saturday and Sunday the rest of the year it is open from 10 a.m. to noon and 3 to 7 p.m. It is also open on Friday until 10 p.m. It is closed on Tuesday, however.

WHERE TO STAY: The **Agora,** Avenue Jean-Rostand (tel. 59-63-30-90), is a comfortable hotel housed in an angular modern building. Many of the well-furnished bedrooms look out over old trees and the river. The pleasant accommodations cost from 255F ($35.17) in a single to 300F ($41.37) in a double. You might enjoy a drink on the bar terrace stretching toward the river or a meal in the hotel's restaurant, La Grande Assiette, where you'll pay 90F ($12.41) to 140F ($19.31). Food is served every day.

Au Capagorry, 14 rue Thiers (tel. 59-25-48-22), rises town-house fashion amid an interconnected row of intricately carved stone-fronted buildings about two blocks from the cathedral. Many restaurants are within an easy walk, as the hotel has no dining room. Inside, a cozily contrasting series of patterned wallpapers adds gaiety and warmth. There's an in-house bar, plus 48 comfortable bedrooms, decorated both in traditional or conservatively modern styles. Each has its own bath and phone. Mr. and Mrs. Paris, the owners, charge from 160F ($22.06) to 270F ($37.23) in a single, 230F ($31.72) to 340F ($46.89) in a double.

Aux Deux Rivières, 21 rue Thiers (tel. 59-59-14-61), is a calm and quiet hotel despite its central location in town. Most of the approximately 60 simply furnished bedrooms contain private bath. Rentals range from 155F ($21.38) in a single to 330F ($45.51) in a double.

On the outskirts of Bayonne you'll find a whole different world at the **Mendi Alde,** Route de Cambo-les-Bains (tel. 59-63-58-44), 1½ miles outside of town on the D932. This little nine-room hotel is for budgeters, charging only 125F ($17.24) in a single, 220F ($30.34) in a double. There is no restaurant, but a continental breakfast is served. The bedchambers are simply furnished, and the hotel is well kept, doing a thriving family business in summer. Boule and table tennis are also offered.

WHERE TO DINE: La Tanière, 53 Avenue du Capitaine-Resplandy (tel. 59-25-53-42), has some of the best seafood in the port. Monsieur and Madame Gérard Villanova have decorated the restaurant in a Louis XIII style, and in such a setting you'll be offered feuilleté de sole au champagne, an assortment of fish with vegetables, and filet of veal with foie gras. Service is friendly and polite. A set menu costs 140F ($19.31), and you'll spend around 180F ($24.82) if you order à la carte. The restaurant is closed Monday evening and all day Tuesday except during the busy tourist months of July and August. It takes a vacation from mid-June to early July.

Beluga, 15 rue des Tonneliers (tel. 59-25-52-13). Jean-Claude Géudon is the most creative chef in Bayonne. In a charming quarter of the old city, Petit-Bayonne, between the Adour and the Nive, he opened this restaurant, serving an array of specialties to tempt the most fastidious of diners. These include foie gras de canard (duckling), escalope de bar, and, a masterful dish, his émincé de boeuf flavored with mustard. You might also try his aiguillette of duckling. For dessert, his soupe d'orange à la menthe fraîche is superb, as is his charlotte au chocolat. There is a fine wine list as well. Meals are offered at 250F ($34.48) à la carte, 120F ($16.55) table d'hôte. The restaurant is closed on Sunday and in January.

For really authentic Basque cookery, head for **Euzkalduna,** 61 rue Pannecau (tel. 59-59-28-02). I have only the highest commendation for the regional cuisine of Madame Aguirre. Her fish soup is excellently prepared. I've enjoyed it on at least three different occasions, and it always tasted different but good, its ingredients depending on the catch of the day. She also prepares superb mussels in vinaigrette, plus an array of other Basque dishes, including omelets. Meals begin at 130F ($17.93) and go up, depending on what you order. The restaurant is closed Sunday night, Monday, the first two weeks in June, and from mid-October to early November.

2. Biarritz

One of the most famous seaside resorts in the world, Biarritz in southwest France was once a simple fishing village near the Spanish border. Favored by the Empress Eugénie, the Atlantic village soon attracted her husband, Napoléon III, who launched it on the road to fashion. Later Queen Victoria showed up, and her son Edward VII visited more than once. Today it is busy from July to September, quietly settling down for the rest of the year. Frankly, I prefer it in June, when the prices are lowered, the flowers are in bloom—especially the spectacular hydrangea—and there's space on the beach. Surfboarding is most popular here, drawing many Stateside youths.

On the fringe of the Basque country, Biarritz has good wide sandy bathing beaches (the surf can be dangerous at times on the Grand Plage). Cliff walks, forming a grand promenade planted with tamarisks, are one of the most enduring attractions of Biarritz. The most dramatic point is **Rocher de la Vièrge** (Rock of the Virgin), connected to the shore by a footbridge. Enclosed by jetties, **Port des Pêcheurs** (Port of the Fishermen) is yet another scenic spot.

ACCOMMODATIONS: Biarritz offers a wide choice of places to stay in all price ranges.

A Deluxe Choice

Hôtel du Palais, Avenue de l'Impératrice (tel. 59-24-09-40), is and has been the playground for the international elite of this century. Originally it was built in 1854 by Napoléon III as an imposing residence for his Empress Eugénie so that she wouldn't get homesick for nearby Spain. He picked the most commanding position on the beach, in view of the rocks and rugged shoreline. It's a true palace, with grand halls and staircases, marble columns, and art nouveau trappings. Edward VII of England stayed here in 1906 and 1910; Alfonso XIII (the last king of Spain) in 1909; the Duke of Windsor in the 1940s; and Haile Selassie in 1956.

Guests are especially attracted to the free-form swimming pool on the lower terrace, with its encircling umbrellas and pads for sunbathing. At night, excellently prepared meals are served dramatically in the classic columned dining room, softly lit by glittering crystal chandeliers. Of course, there are elaborately furnished suites, but even the average bedrooms are decorated with style, employing period furnishings, silk draperies, marquetry, and bronze hardware. Open from Easter till November, the hotel charges its highest prices from July till September 15: from 1,000F ($137.90) in a single, from 1,700F ($234.43) in a double. To be given board rates you must stay a minimum of three days. Room tariffs are based primarily on the view and the size of the room.

A Château-Hotel

Château de Brindos, Lac de Brindos (tel. 59-23-17-68), is the most romantic stopover on the Côte Basque for those heading for Spain. Once you've arrived here, you may change your mind and never make it to San Sebastián. In the vicinity of the airport, the Château de Brindos lies about 1½ miles from Biarritz. Set on its own park grounds, it even has a private lake. Inside, the decoration of both the public rooms and the 16 bedrooms is in period styles, imaginatively conceived and beautifully executed. Guests gather in comfortable armchairs around the large stone fireplace, and take regional specialties in the hotel's dining hall. For the pinnacle of Basque charm and comfort, you pay dearly—from 850F ($117.22) in a single to 1,050F ($144.80) for the best double rooms. The rooms in the annex do not overlook the lake. The cuisine is superb, including a soup of foie gras, a mousseline of turbot in caviar sauce, duckling with small vegetables, and sea bass grilled with fennel. If you'd like to drive out there to dine, always call for a reservation. You'll average around 250F ($34.48) to 300F ($41.37) on the à la carte menu. The hotel shuts down only between January 10 and March 1.

The Upper Bracket

Eurotel, 19 Avenue de la Perspective (tel. 59-24-32-33), is an upper-bracket hotel for the dollarwise traveler who wants all the modern luxuries and amenities without the belle époque trappings that usually fatten the tab. Although not on the beach, its position is even more striking—perched on top of the cliff, away from the center of town, with panoramic views from every window.

The design concept of the 12-story structure is enlightened, with the rooms extending out beyond sliding glass doors onto a private open-air loggia. The soft sofas are turned into beds at night, converting back to sofas during the day. You can ask for a streamlined, completely equipped kitchenette with a stove and refrigerator. The baths have showers, decorative tiles, and all sorts of gadgets to make life more convenient. In addition, the rooms are air-conditioned and soundproof. The hotel charges its highest rates between June 1 and September 30. The rooms are priced according to facilities, the least expensive with a large bed, the costliest with a loggia and twin beds. Two people pay a high of 750F ($103.43), including taxes and service. Singles cost from 460F ($63.43). There are two bars and one snackbar, as well as a bar on the tenth floor of the building affording the most spectacular view in all Biarritz. Set meals cost from 180F ($24.82), not including wine.

Hôtel Miramar, Avenue de l'Impératrice (tel. 59-24-85-20), is about the most modern structure in a neighborhood surrounded by 19th-century buildings. The conservative and tasteful bedrooms open onto a view of the sea and the cliffs that define its borders. On the premises you'll find a saltwater swimming pool, piano bar, gymnasium, sauna, solarium, beauty center, hairdresser, and an adjoining spa facility. The bedrooms, each of which has its own bath, telephone, TV, and mini-bar, cost from 650F ($89.64) in a single to 1,500F ($206.85) in a double.

The hotel's restaurant, Relais Miramar, has caught on with the *beau monde* who frequent Biarritz in summer. Set beside the pool, the establishment offers outdoor dining or shelter in the rustically modern interior. The cuisine is executed by an ex-chef at one of Paris's best restaurants, André Gaüzere, who creates light-textured specialties such as a salad of apples, truffles, breast of duckling, foie gras, a rouelle of bass and lobster with tarragon butter, and a dessert of apples in puff pastry with green-apple sorbet. Open every day for lunch and for dinner until 9:30 p.m., the relais charges 250F ($34.48) for a fixed-price menu, 400F ($55.16) for à la carte meals.

Château du Clair de Lune, 48 Avenue Alan Seeger (tel. 59-23-45-96). Aficionados of French literature might be drawn to this place because it was lavishly praised by poet Alan Seeger in 1916 as the most magnificent place in town. It is still going strong. Constructed at the turn of the century, it has been modernized and updated into a well-upholstered series of 10 accommodations, whose windows overlook a garden filled with exotic trees and shrubs. There's no restaurant on the premises, and the establishment is open all year. Each of the bedrooms has its own private bath and phone, with singles or doubles costing from 340F ($46.89) to 450F ($62.06). An apartment is rented at 620F ($85.50) to two persons.

The Middle Bracket

Plaza, Avenue Édouard-VII (tel. 59-24-74-00), combines a vaguely art deco decor with modern conveniences in a desirable position near the casino in the center of town. Many of the large bedrooms have a private terrace. In high season meals are served in a formally classic dining hall, while in low season they move to a less formal pub. The 60 bedrooms all contain private bath, TV, radio/alarm, phone, and mini-bar. Accommodations rent for 320F ($44.13) in a single to 525F ($72.40) in a double. Meals cost around 130F ($17.93) for a fixed-price menu.

Hôtel Regina and Golf, 52 Avenue de l'Impératrice (tel. 59-24-09-60), is a small 19th-century villa set in a residential part of town, midway between the ocean and the golf course. The comfortable bedrooms, 48 in all, usually have views of the water. Those with kitchenette cost slightly more per day than regular bedrooms, which range from around 400F ($55.16) in a single to 460F ($63.43) in a double. Each of the units has a phone, mini-bar, and private bath. There's an interior garden on the premises, and if you want to go exploring, a lighthouse is on a plateau a short distance away.

Hôtel Windsor, Grande Plage (tel. 59-24-08-52), is a well-managed modern hotel whose rooms look out over the ocean. The clean and functional bedrooms go for 220F ($30.34) in a single and 400F ($55.16) in a double. Half board costs from 360F ($49.64) to 750F ($103.43) per person depending on the accommodation and the season. Open from late March to early November.

Hôtel Carlina, Boulevard Prince-de-Galles (tel. 59-23-03-86), is a well-recommended hotel whose rooms offer an exceptional view of the Pyrénées and the Atlantic Ocean. Most of the popular water sports are offered, including windsurfing. On the premises is a terrace bar and a solarium. The well-furnished rooms rent for 520F ($71.71) in a single and 620F ($85.50) in a double. The hotel is closed from early November to April 1.

El Mirador, 10 Place Ste-Eugénie (tel. 59-24-14-91), enjoys a dreamy position right on the most favored square of Biarritz, set near the edge of a cliff overlooking the sea. Most of its 27 rooms have not only a sea view but also a private bath. The accommodations are quite nice, with a homey mixture of modern furniture and traditional pieces. Since the hotel owns what is considered one of the best restaurants in the resort, the Rôtisserie du Coq Hardi (see below), it's wise to take half board at El Mirador. Including service and taxes, the half-board tariff is 400F ($55.16) to 700F ($96.53) per person, lower off-season. The place is closed from the end of October to Easter.

The Budget Range

Hôtel du Port-Vieux, 43 rue Mazagran (tel. 59-24-02-84), is warmly recommended, especially for those who desire *chambres sans pension*. You're free to travel for your lunch and dinner, perhaps to sample the fish restaurants of St-Jean-de-Luz or the Basque cuisine in Spain's San Sebastián. In high season (July 10 to September 15) you pay 205F ($28.27) for the best double rooms, with twin beds and a shower and water basin, that tab including a continental breakfast, service, and taxes. Bathless doubles drop in price to only 170F ($23.44). The "Old Port" is neat as can be. It is open from the first of March to the end of November.

Océan, 9 Place Ste-Eugénie (tel. 59-24-03-27), right in the heart of restaurant row, is an older, six-story, white-painted corner building next to a church, on the ocean end of the park. It's rated highly for convenience, cleanliness, and good food. The bedrooms vary considerably in size, but each is comfortable and well tended by a bevy of scrubbing and polishing maids. The view from some of the rooms is memorable, overlooking the plaza and the sea beyond. Full board is 450F ($62.06) per person. For just a room, it is 450F ($62.06) for two. The hotel is closed from mid-November to late March. You can dine at the sidewalk tables under a canopy.

Palacito, 1 rue Gambetta (tel. 59-24-04-89), is a small and unpretentious hotel which makes few claims other than to provide decent housing at a fair price. Only 4 of the 28 bedrooms contain private bath. Rooms range from 120F ($16.55) in a single to 190F ($26.20) in a double.

Washington Hotel, 34 rue Mazagran (tel. 59-24-10-80). Two of the most attractive aspects of this pleasant hotel are the indoor/outdoor dining room which brings the odor of flowers into the other rooms and the cultivated charm of its owner, Madame Marcé. Born in America, she moved to France when she was 12 and today handles the day-to-day business of running her hotel with gracious bilingual skill. Depending on the plumbing, a twin-bedded room costs 120F ($16.55) to 230F ($31.72), breakfast not included.

DELUXE DINING: Café de Paris, 5 Place Bellevue (tel. 59-24-19-53), is one of the greatest restaurants along the Basque Coast. Across from the casino, it sits on a charming belvedere overlooking the sea. Pierre Laporte brings elegance both to the setting and to the cuisine. Here you get not only haute cuisine, but on

occasions haute couture. While sitting under the potted palms, you can—just for openers—get started with truffes (truffles) au vin de champagne. After years of serving traditional French cookery, the chef now specializes in the new cuisine. Specialties include a fish soup that is most savory, followed perhaps by a vegetable pâté with a mousse made of flap mushrooms. Duckling with lime is one of the featured main dishes, as is squab with hurtleberries. If it's offered, order the tart made with fresh asparagus. Smoked fresh salmon is very good here, as is the brochette of lobster. For a fine finish, try the different types of sorbet with sauterne. Of course, none of these dishes may be available at the time of your visit, because the menu undergoes constant change. But you get the idea of the type of elegant cuisine offered. Expect to pay from 380F ($52.40) to 420F ($57.92) for a complete meal. The restaurant is closed in March and on Monday off-season.

OTHER DINING SELECTIONS: Rôtisserie du Coq Hardi (Bold Rooster), 10 Place Ste-Eugénie (tel. 59-24-13-81), occupies the ground floor of El Mirador Hôtel. Its tables are arranged to let guests enjoy the view at the edge of the ocean walk. The chef features excellently prepared specialties, many of them appearing on the set menus. Three out of four dishes served here are true creations. Try moules (mussels) poulettes or the Bayonne ham. The coquilles St-Jacques is yet another seafood favorite. Main dishes include the specialty, côte de boeuf à la broche, served only for two. Cèpes (flap mushrooms) bordelais are another good offering. Easily recommendable are the poulet de grain à la broche and escalope de veau Mirador. Anticipate an à la carte bill ranging from 275F ($37.92) to 325F ($44.82). Set menus cost 120F ($16.55) to 150F ($20.69). Closed from the end of October to Easter.

L'Alambic, 5 Place Bellevue (tel. 59-24-53-41), offers a lighthearted decor and a trendily sophisticated ambience for late-night meals and brasserie food. You'll find this place amid a gaggle of younger persons in a spot adjoining the Café de Paris. The menu includes dishes such as hamburgers and steaks, as well as chicken in cream sauce, sautéed veal liver lyonnaise style, and pipérade with eggs, plus an array of salads. Dinner is served till 11 p.m. and costs 120F ($16.55) to 200F ($27.58). The restaurant is open every day in high season, closed Monday in low season, and takes a vacation in March.

Alta Mar, 2 rue Gardères (tel. 59-24-13-00). The interior of this establishment near the casino is, as its name (High Seas) implies, decorated like the interior of a boat. The attractively simple cuisine includes specialties such as seafood marmite, duckling with lime juice, and salade landaise dotted with foie gras. Fixed-price menus range from 60F ($8.27) to 230F ($31.72), while à la carte meals cost around 200F ($27.58). The place is closed every Wednesday and from November 1 to mid-December.

AFTER DARK: Nightlife in Biarritz revolves around the **Casino Bellevue,** which opens July 1, closing September 15. You must bring your passport to enter.

Otherwise, you can patronize the **Municipal Casino,** which is open all year (4 p.m. till 2 a.m.). It lets you in providing you have a passport and are more than 21 years of age. Within the building is a club offering music for dancing.

3. St-Jean-de-Luz

This Basque country tuna-fishing port and beach resort is the goal of many a person's pipedream. About ten miles south of Biarritz moving toward the Spanish frontier, St-Jean-de-Luz lies at the mouth of the Nivelle.

In its principal church, the 13th-century Église St-Jean-Baptiste, Louis XIV and the Spanish infanta, Marie-Thérèse, were married in 1660. The interior is among the most handsomely decorated of all Basque churches, with painted wooden panels. Surmounting the altar is a statue-studded gilded retable.

At the harbor, the brick and stone **Maison de l'Infante,** a mansion in the Louis XIII style, sheltered the Spanish princess. The Sun King, meanwhile, dreamed of another woman at the **Château Lohobiague,** on the Place Louis-XIV, the center of the old port.

Many narrow streets flanked by old houses provide interesting strolls in this port town. If possible, try to attend a fish auction. Livening up the resort are pelota, fandangos, and a celebration beginning on June 24 called **Toro del Fuego.** Highlight of the festivities is when a snorting papier-mâché bull is carried through town. The townspeople literally dance in the streets.

HOTELS: L'Hôtel de Chantaco, Golf de Chantaco (tel. 59-26-14-76), a mile from the center of St-Jean-de-Luz out the D918. This Basque mansion, run by Monsieur et Madame Pierre Larramendy, is surrounded by an 18-hole golf course and parklands and lies just a mile from the ocean. There are 24 bedrooms, each with complete bath, each luxuriously furnished and equipped. It seems more like a country palace, with Moorish arches, a side patio garden, and an interior that has been skillfully decorated with taste and restraint. The reception hall has two stone fireplaces, a wrought-iron gallery, and high-backed tapestry-covered chairs. The drawing room is handsomely furnished and inviting. There is a refectory table where you can write your letters by the light of two silver candelabra. Breakfast is served in a patio with wisteria-covered arches. As you bite into your croissant, you listen to the sound of water splashing in a fountain. Rates are 450F ($62.06) in a single, rising to 700F ($96.53) in a double. The hotel's restaurant, El Patio, serves a high-quality regional cuisine. Try the filets of sole Chantaco and the gâteau Basque. It's better to stay here on the half-board plan, ranging from 600F ($89.64) to 750F ($103.43) per person in high season, including service. The hotel is open from April to October.

Hôtel Madison, 25 Boulevard Thiers (tel. 59-26-35-02), is a conservatively decorated and attractively comfortable hotel with many old-fashioned details. Near the casino and not far from the beach, the hotel offers a handful of apartments and about two dozen tastefully furnished rooms priced from 230F ($31.72) in a single and 265F ($36.54) in a double. Each of them has a private bath, and a television set can be brought to your room on request. A Basque-style bar, tea room, and terrace are among the facilities. The location is between the beach and the casino. The Madison is open all year long.

Hôtel de la Plage, 33 rue Garat (tel. 59-51-03-44), is well located right by the beach. It is warmly furnished in the Basque style. Everything is kept immaculate, and the welcome is friendly. There are only 30 rooms. A single with toilet and bidet costs from 150F ($20.69). Two persons pay from 300F ($41.37) in units containing shower or complete bath. The cost of full board is another 300F ($41.37) per person daily. For a four-course dinner, you pay 100F ($13.79). The inn is open from Easter to mid-October.

Villa Bel-Air, Promenade Jacques-Thibaud (tel. 59-26-04-86), near the casino, is a 16-room hotel offering clean and well-furnished rooms facing the beach. Most of the units have private bath. Prices range from 155F ($21.38) in a single to 265F ($36.54) in a double. Half board in the hotel's restaurant costs 180F ($24.82) to 260F ($35.85) per person. A fixed-price menu is offered for 75F ($10.32). Monsieur Pees-Ramirez opens his restaurant only for dinner. Meals are served every day from June to October. There is a snackbar on the terrace at lunchtime in July and August. The hotel shuts down from mid-November to late March.

Le Prado, Place de la Pergola (tel. 59-51-03-71), is a simple hotel whose outdoor terrace was built to feature a view of the ocean. About two-thirds of the approximately 40 rooms contain private bath and telephone. Accommodations range in price from singles for 180F ($24.82) to doubles for 235F ($32.41). There's a restaurant on the premises.

La Fayette, 20 rue de la République (tel. 59-26-17-74), is an old-fashioned but comfortable hotel near the Place Louis-XIV. Marie Colombet, the owner, charges from 175F ($24.13) in a single, 225F ($31.03) in a double. All but one of the units have private bath, and each contains its own phone. Half board ranges from 200F ($27.58) per person. The hotel also runs one of the best restaurants in town, Kayola. It features a cuisine of the sea, such as a casserole of scallops of lotte, but it does other regional fare equally as well, including grilled duck. A set menu begins at 65F ($8.97), a superb bargain. The hotel is closed in January.

RESTAURANTS: **Léonie,** 6 rue Garat (tel. 59-26-37-10). You'll have plenty of details to admire in this rustic restaurant, and many of the structural beams are visible from the well-decorated tables that are scattered over the ground floor and a raised balcony. A la carte meals offer good value, costing 180F ($24.82) to 220F ($30.34). Dishes might include aiguillette of duckling with pears, paupiette of sole with crayfish, seafood salad, and a well-stocked dessert cart. André Etchenic is your host, opening his restaurant every day except Monday. He is shut down the first two weeks of February.

Auberge Kaiku, 17 rue de la République (tel. 59-26-13-20), is the best restaurant in town, one centered around the personalities of its Basque owners, Émile and Jeanne Ourdanabia. The building dates from 1460 and is said to be the oldest house in town. That claim is easy to believe after a quick inspection of the impeccable dining rooms with their hand-hewn ceiling beams and carefully chiseled masonry. You'll find this place on a narrow street just off the Place Louis-XIV, in the center of the village. Menu specialties are a combination of lightened nouvelle cuisine techniques with regional ingredients and traditions. You might enjoy the John Dory with fresh mint, grilled shrimp, filet of beef with essence of truffles, duckling in honey, and sole with flap mushrooms. Reservations are important here, since the number of tables is limited. Full à la carte meals begin at 200F ($27.58) but could go much higher. During low season the establishment is closed on Wednesday and from mid-November till just before Christmas.

At **La Taverne Basque,** 5 rue de la République (tel. 59-26-01-26), the wine that accompanies your generously portioned and well-prepared meal might easily be a Spanish red. Madame Sarthou is the owner, catering to a loyal clientele which at one time or another has included practically everyone in town. A fixed-price menu represents good value for around 70F ($9.65), another at 125F ($17.24), although an à la carte meal begins at 180F ($24.82). You might enjoy fresh oysters, mussels in broth, grilled sardines, or an aiguillette of duckling with apples, ending with a flaky dessert pastry. The establishment is open every day in July and August, while the rest of the year it shuts down Tuesday night and all day Wednesday. Dinner is served till 10 p.m.

La Vieille Auberge, 22 rue Tourasse (tel. 59-26-19-61), is a Basque-style tavern specializing in fish. Monsieur and Madame Grand offer three set menus: 70F ($9.65), 96F ($13.24), and 100F ($13.79), the last a gargantuan repast. Their recipes, for the most part, are both Basque and Landaise, and each dish tastes better when accompanied by the *vin du pays,* or wine of the country. The tavern is closed from November 11 to March 22 and on Wednesday.

Le Petit Grill Basque, 4 rue St-Jacques (tel. 59-26-03-53), is a small auberge with a low ceiling and many small round tables covered with fresh napkins. Set meals, each featuring Basque specialties, are offered at 80F ($11.03) and 120F ($16.55), the latter, with four courses, most highly recommendable. The restaurant is closed from just before Christmas to mid-January, for two weeks in May, and on Friday year round.

Ramuntcho, 24 rue Garat (tel. 59-26-03-89), is a typical Spanish Basque-style restaurant with lots of beams and wooden tables. In this tavern setting, you can order a three-course meal, a simple one at 55F ($7.56) or a more elaborate one at 110F ($15.17), with fish specialties. The restaurant is closed on Monday and from October 1 to Easter.

4. Pau

High above the banks of the Gave de Pau River, the all-year resort of Pau is a good halting point in your trek through the Pyrénées. The town was once the residence of the kings of Navarre. The British discovered it back in the early 19th century, launching such innovative practices as fox hunting, a custom which has lingered.

Even if you're just passing through, go along the **Boulevard des Pyrénées,** an esplanade erected on orders of Napoléon I. You'll have what is perhaps the most famous panoramic view in the Pyrénées. After seeing the white-capped peaks of the Anie and Midi-de-Bigorre, Lamartine, the poet, said, "The land-view at Pau is, like the sea-view at Naples, the finest in the world."

At the western end stands the **Château de Pau,** 2 rue de Château (tel. 59-27-36-22), dating from the 12th century and still steeped in the Renaissance spirit of the bold Margaret of Navarre, who wrote the bawdy *Heptaméron* at 60. This collection of tales amused her brother, François I. The castle, however, has seen many builders and many tenants. Louis XV ordered the bridge that connects the castle to the town, while the great staircase hall inside was commissioned by Margaret herself. Louis-Philippe had all the apartments redecorated around 1840. Inside are many souvenirs, including a crib made of a single tortoise shell for Henry of Navarre, who was born here. There is a splendid array of Flemish and Gobelins tapestries. The great rectangular tower, Tour de Gaston Phoebus, is from the 14th century. The castle is open daily from 9 to 11:45 a.m. and 2 to 5:45 p.m. in summer (off-season from 9:30 to 11:45 a.m. and 2 to 4:45 p.m.), charging an admission of 10F ($1.38).

On the château's third floor a **Musée Régional** contains ethnographical collections of Béarn, the old name of the country of which Pau was the capital. Keeping the same hours, it charges an admission of 4F (55¢).

The **Musée des Beaux-Arts,** rue Mathieu-Lalanne (tel. 59-27-33-02), displays a collection of European paintings, including Spanish, Flemish, Dutch, English, and French masters, such as El Greco, Zurbarán, Degas, and Boudin. Hours are daily except Tuesday from 10 a.m. to noon and 2 to 6 p.m. Admission is free.

Finally, you may want to walk through the beautiful **Parc National,** the gardens (or what is left of them) that used to surround the château in the 16th century.

WHERE TO STAY: Hôtel Continental, 2 rue du Maréchal-Foch (tel. 59-27-69-31), is from all points the leading hotel of Pau. In the center of town, convenient for local sights and shopping, it has undergone an extensive modernization program, including soundproofing of its windows. All of its 110 bedrooms have been equipped with private bath and stylishly decorated. Each has its own private bar and TV, and the hotel garage may be used free. A single rents for 280F ($38.61), rising to 400F ($55.16) in a double. The hotel also employs a brilliant chef who attracts not just guests but lots of nonresidents too to the Continental's restaurant, Le Conti. Both the staff and the food they serve are outstanding, the cuisine going beyond professional showmanship, including such specialties as scallop pâté, fresh foie gras with prunes, a smooth, tender, tasty chicken suprême, and a pipérade that is as superb as any you'll be served in the Basque country. You are likely to spend from 220F ($30.34) ordering à la carte. The restaurant remains open all year.

Hôtel Paris, 80 rue Émile-Garet (tel. 59-27-34-39), offers about 40 rooms, each of which has a private bath, radio/alarm, color TV, mini-bar, and telephone. It's near the post office. The recently renovated bedrooms cost from 260F ($35.85) in a single to 370F ($51.02) in a double. Those units facing the interior courtyard tend to be the quietest.

Hôtel Roncevaux, 25 rue Louis-Barthou (tel. 59-27-08-44), offers around

40 well-maintained and soundproof bedrooms, all but two of which contain private bath, direct-dial phone, color TV, and video. A single costs 250F ($34.48), a double going for 360F ($49.64).

Hôtel-Restaurant Corona, 71 Avenue du Général-Leclerc (tel. 59-30-64-77), provides good value for the money, in a modern decor. The restaurant offers menu specialties often based on regional recipes. You might enjoy the duckling, the pipérade, the veal, or any of the well-prepared desserts. Fixed-price menus cost 75F ($10.32) to 200F ($27.58), although the cheaper ones are available only on weekdays. The restaurant is closed Saturday and the first two weeks in November. Some 20 simply furnished rooms are available, most with private bath, costing 100F ($13.79) in a single and 215F ($29.65) in a double.

Le Postillon, Place de Verdun (tel. 59-32-49-15). The perfume from the masses of flowers in the enclosed courtyard sometimes enters through the windows of this cozy hotel's 27 bedrooms. About two-thirds of the pleasingly decorated accommodations contain private bath, while the rest have shared facilities in the hallways. Prices range from 90F ($12.41) in a single to 170F ($23.44) in a double, breakfast not included. Only breakfast is served, but there is a choice of restaurants nearby.

WHERE TO DINE: Chez Pierre, 16 rue Louis-Barthou (tel. 59-27-76-86) Raymond Casau is among the finest cuisiniers in Béarn, where, according to *Larousse Gastronomique,* "the art of cookery has never ceased to be honored and practiced." The restaurant is in a restored house dating from the mid-19th century. You have a choice of dining downstairs where there are only eight tables and some paintings in a hunting motif, or else upstairs where you'll find a trio of tiny salons. His specialties include sole with white mushrooms and small new cucumbers, and fresh salmon braised with Jurançon, a rather sweet, golden Pyrenean wine, celebrated in history and legend and much loved by Henri IV. The cassoulet with white beans at Pierre is a dish worthy of an award. The cuisiniers take natural products of the region and use them creatively. For example, the lamb comes from the Ossau valley and has been called "as tender as a strawberry." In air-conditioned comfort, you can enjoy splendid service and a rewarding cuisine, with most dinners ranging in price from 250F ($27.58) to 320F ($48.27). The restaurant takes a vacation in February. It is also closed Sunday.

Patrick Jourdan, 14 rue Latapie (tel. 59-27-68-70). Your table in this modern bistro will probably be partially screened off by a row of verdant plants. The cuisine is among the best in town, consisting of rich dishes based on regional applications of foie gras, first-rate meats, and the freshest possible vegetables. You might enjoy an émincé of sweetbreads with foie gras and noodles, one of the elaborate salads, roast pigeon with cabbage, duck liver with apples, sole fourrée Patrick, and a host of savory desserts. À la carte meals range from 275F ($37.92), with fixed-price menus offered for 210F ($28.96) to 250F ($27.58), plus service. The restaurant is open daily except Saturday at lunchtime and Sunday. It is closed for the last two weeks in August.

Au Fin Gourmet, 24 Avenue Gaston-Lacoste (tel. 59-27-47-71), across from the train station, is ably directed by the Clément Ithuriague family. Two of the sons, both in their mid-20s, are responsible for the cuisine and service, which are handled admirably. On a table covered with immaculate napery, you'll be served such specialties as maigret of duckling, braised stuffed trout, escargots, foie gras, grilled salmon, and tasty desserts. During the week a set menu is offered at 80F ($11.03). On weekends, a more elaborate fixed-price meal ranges from 110F ($15.17). An à la carte dinner can average around 250F ($27.58). In warm weather, you can eat on the terrace surrounded by flowering plants. The family closes the restaurant for the first two weeks of January, the last two weeks of June, and on Monday.

Hostellerie de Canastel, 2 Avenue Rausky, Route d'Oloron (tel. 59-06-13-

40), lies in the hamlet of Jurançon, for which the wine is named. It is reached by going south on the N134 for about a mile. This is an inn-style hotel where the atmosphere is delightful, the food superior. The owner has installed a swimming pool for the enjoyment of guests. The hostelry is an overhanging roadside place, yet it is private enough. The owner has provided many comforts and conveniences in the attractively furnished rooms, for which the charge is 240F ($33.10) in a single, 300F ($41.37) in a double. You'll be served breakfast on the terrace if you wish. If you dine here, you'll find menus at 130F ($17.93) and 180F ($24.82). The restaurant is closed Sunday night year round and on Monday off-season.

5. Eugénie-les-Bains

A century ago the Empress Eugénie came here to "take the cure." Now some of the most discerning people in the world are following in her footsteps, but for a slightly different attraction. In the Landes section of France, in the foothills of the Pyrénées, about 33 miles from Pau, this spa village is better known today than it ever was because of—

Les Prés et les Sources d'Eugénie (tel. 58-51-19-01), the creation of Michel Guérard, the now-famous master chef whose cuisine minceur started a revolution in French cooking in the early 1970s. In this gracefully fashionable country hotel and restaurant, M Guérard practices his art assisted by a staff of 16 chefs. Dieters may choose from a tasty variety on the minceur menu, but gourmets are not ignored here, either. The "grand menu gourmand" draws devoted fans from all over the world.

When you first enter the cheerfully decorated restaurant operated by Michel and his wife, Christine, you may want to select your dessert before you decide on the rest of the meal because all pastries are cooked to order. Then you may settle into an appetizer such as eggs scrambled with chives and caviar or a delicate cream-of-crayfish soup. Seafood is plentiful, as indicated by an array of entrees that include whiting in white-wine sauce and mullet steamed with seaweed and oysters. Grilled breast of duck in cream sauce and braised rabbit are choice game dishes. One of the house favorites is the pot-au-feu, as good here as it was in Monsieur Guérard's former restaurant in Paris. If you wish to stick to the minceur cuisine, you may select tender lamb steamed with fennel or a number of fresh fish dishes. The vegetables are always fresh and in season, often chosen personally by Monsieur Guérard from the local farms. Desserts—most of these are non-minceur—include a tasty coffee cream or a puff-pastry apple tart. Prices for meals range from 400F ($55.16) to 600F ($82.74), really a "big splurge," but a worthy investment to true lovers of good food.

The establishment also offers 28 guest rooms, each individually decorated and all contributing to the fairytale-like atmosphere. Room rates range from 900F ($124.11) for a double per night. Both the hotel and restaurant are open from mid-March to mid-November.

6. Lourdes

Muslims turn to Mecca, Hindus to the waters of the Ganges; but for Catholics Lourdes is the world's most beloved shrine. Nestled in a valley in the southwestern part of the Hautes-Pyrénées, it is the scene of pilgrims gathering from all over the world. Nail down your hotel reservation in overcrowded August.

On February 11, 1858, the Virgin is believed by the Roman Catholic world to have revealed herself to a poor shepherd girl, Bernadette Soubirous. Eighteen such apparitions were reported. Bernadette, subject of the film *Song of Bernadette,* died in a convent in 1879. She was beatified in 1925, then canonized in 1933.

Her apparitions literally put Lourdes on the map. The town has subsequently attracted millions of visitors from all over the world, the illustrious and the poverty-stricken. Many of the truly devout are often disheartened at the tawdry commercialism that hangs over Lourdes today. And some holiday-seekers are acutely disturbed by the human desperation of victims of various afflictions spending their hard-earned savings of a lifetime seeking a "miracle," then having to return home without a cure. However, the church has recognized many "cures" which took place after patients bathed in the springs, labeling them "true miracles."

THE SIGHTS OF LOURDES: From July 1 to September 20, tourists and pilgrims on a short visit can join the **Day Pilgrims,** a pilgrimage conducted in English that gathers at 9 a.m. at the statue of the Crowned Virgin for a prayer meeting in the meadow facing the Grotto. Parts of these services include a 9:30 a.m. Stations of the Cross and a mass at 11:15 a.m. In the afternoon, assembling at the same spot at 2:30 p.m., pilgrims are taken on an explanatory visit to the Sanctuaries or places associated with Bernadette. At 4:30 there is a Procession of the Blessed Eucharist, starting from the Grotto. The 9 p.m. Marian celebration, rosary, and torchlight procession, all start from the Grotto as well. For more information about this dramatic tour, apply to the information center under the right-hand ramp when you're going toward the Grotto.

In the Sanctuaries there are hostesses to welcome you all year at the **Office de Touristes et Isolés,** under the ramp on the right when you face the basilica. Hours are 9 a.m. to noon and 2 to 6 p.m. The hostesses present the *Story of Lourdes and of Bernadette,* told with slides. The free slide show (in English) runs about 15 minutes.

At the **Grotto of Massabielle** the Virgin is said to have appeared 18 times to Bernadette between February 11 and July 16, 1858. This venerated site is accessible to pilgrims both day and night, and a Holy Mass is celebrated there every day.

The Statue of Our Lady depicts the Virgin in the posture she is said to have taken and in the place she reputedly appeared when she made herself known to Bernadette, saying to her in Pyrenean dialect, "I am the Immaculate Conception."

At the back of the Grotto, on the left of the altar, is the **Miraculous Spring** that reportedly welled up on February 25, 1858, during the ninth apparition, when Bernadette scraped the earth as instructed. The Virgin is said to have commanded her, "Go and drink at the spring and wash there." The water from this spring is collected in several big reservoirs, from which one can drink it.

Other Sanctuaries associated with St. Bernadette include the crypt, the first chapel built on top of the Grotto, the Basilica of the Immaculate Conception, the Rosary Basilica, and the underground Basilica of St. Pius X. In town, there are the house where Bernadette lived, the Cachot, the baptismal font in the parish church, and the hospital chapel where she made her first communion.

The **Upper Basilica,** at Place du Rosaire, was built in the 13th-century ogival style, but it was not consecrated until 1876. It contains one nave split into five equal bays. Lining its interior are votive tablets. On the west side of the square is the **Rosary Basilica,** with two small towers. It was built in 1889 in the Roman-Byzantine style and holds up to 4,000 persons. Inside, 15 chapels are dedicated to the "mysteries of the rosary."

The oval-shaped **Basilica of Pius X** was consecrated in 1958. An enormous underground chamber covered by a concrete roof, it is 660 feet long and 270 feet wide, holding as many as 20,000 pilgrims. After St. Peter's in Rome, it is the world's largest church.

Nearby, the **Musée Bernadette** (tel. 62-94-13-15) contains scenes representing the life of the saint. It is open from 9 a.m. till noon and 2 to 6 p.m. The true Bernadette devotee will also seek out the **Moulin de Boly,** rue Bernadette-Soubirous (tel. 62-94-23-53), where the saint was born January 7, 1844, the daughter of a miller. Her former home is open Easter through October from 8 a.m. till 7:30 p.m. This was actually her mother's house. Bernadette's father, François Soubirous, had his family home in another mill, **Moulin Lacadé,** also on rue Bernadette-Soubirous. Visiting hours are 9 a.m. till noon and 2 to 7 p.m. None of these attractions charges admission.

You can visit the impressive wax museum, **Musée Grévin,** 67 rue de la Grotte (tel. 62-94-33-74), where displays retrace not only Bernadette's life but also the life of Christ. There is a reproduction of Leonardo da Vinci's *The Last Supper.* This museum is in the center of Lourdes. It is open daily April to November from 9 a.m. to noon and 1:30 to 7 p.m. Admission is 18F ($2.48) for adults, 8F ($1.10) for children under 15.

Crowning the resort is the castle, **Château-Fort de Lourdes.** From the terrace, a handsome vista spreads before you (take the elevator from below). An excellent example of medieval military architecture, the castle contains the **Musée Pyrénéen** (tel. 62-94-02-04), with its collection of handicrafts and costumes from this mountain region. There's a collection of dolls in nuns' habits. In the courtyard are scale models of different styles of regional architecture, including Spanish. Both the château and museum may be visited from 9 to 11 a.m. and 2 to 6 p.m. from April 1 to mid-October. Otherwise, it closes at 5 p.m. off-season and is shut on Tuesday in winter. Admission is 13F ($1.79).

EXPLORING THE PYRÉNÉES: Lourdes is one of the finest bases for exploring the Pyrénées. You can take tours into the snow-capped mountains across the border into Spain or go horseback-riding near **Lac de Lourdes,** two miles northwest of the town.

The **Office de Tourisme** at Place du Champ-Commun (tel. 62-94-15-64) in Lourdes will pinpoint particular highlights on a map. Outstanding ones include **Bagnères-de-Bigorre,** a renowned thermal spa; **Pic du Jer,** for a magnificent vista; **Béout,** for a panoramic view and an underground cave where prehistoric implements have been found (reached by cableway); **Pibeste,** for another sweeping vista of the Pyrénées; the **Caves of Medous,** an underground river with stalactites; and the **Heights of Gavarnie,** at 4,500 feet, one of France's great natural wonders, requiring a full day.

HOTELS: **Grand Hôtel de la Grotte,** 66-68 rue de la Grotte (tel. 62-94-58-87), is a traditional favorite, decorated in typical upper-bourgeois French taste. The hotel, built in 1872, lies only five minutes from the sanctuaries. Open from Easter to mid-October, it offers 83 well-furnished rooms, charging from 360F ($49.64) in a single to 500F ($68.95) for the best twin. Depending on the room, the compulsory full-board tariff ranges from 375F ($51.71) to 610F ($84.12) per person per day.

Galilée et Windsor, 10 Avenue Peyramale (tel. 62-94-21-55), has a traditional façade, although it's modernized inside, often with plastic furnishings. Air-conditioned, the hotel offers pleasant rooms in flowery chintz. All have private bath and toilet. The hotel charges from 330F ($45.51) in a single and from 380F ($52.40) in a double. The full-board rate ranges from 280F ($38.61) to 380F ($52.40) per person. Guests are received from the end of March to mid-October.

Panorama, 13 rue Sainte-Marie (tel. 62-94-33-04), is also a good hotel, lying close to the Grotto. The carpeted bedrooms contain typically modern and functional furniture and there is a pleasant dining room, plus a spacious and comfortable lounge. The management prefers guests to take the full-board arrangement, which costs 300F ($41.37) to 325F ($44.82) per person, including service. English is spoken. The hotel is open from the end of March to October 31.

Notre-Dame de France, 8 Avenue Peyramale (tel. 62-94-91-45), next to the

Windsor, is another good budget hotel, clean and simple, offering a total of 74 units, each with a minimum of furnishings although they contain either private bath or shower as well as toilet. In high season, the full-board rate runs from 225F ($31.03) to 300F ($41.37) per person. The hotel is open from Easter until early October.

Auberge Provençale, 4 rue Baron-Duprat (tel. 62-94-31-34), is in the heart of Lourdes. It lies only a short walk from the shrines, and it's close to the home of St. Bernadette, the parish church, and the old fortified castle. The staff at the front desk speak English, and I've found them helpful in calling taxis and making advance reservations for your next night's stopover. Rooms are somewhat small, but suitable nevertheless. For 380F ($52.40) you're given a double room with shower and toilet. The hotel also runs a medium-priced dining facility, La Bella Napoli, a pizzeria, which offers specialties from both Italy and Provence. Meals cost 75F ($10.32) to 110F ($15.17). Quite near the hotel is a large car park.

RESTAURANTS: Some of the best food is at the **Taverne de Bigorre et Albert,** 21 Place du Champ-Commun (tel. 62-94-78-45). There you'll pay 130F ($17.93) for the gastronomic menu and 94F ($12.96) for the tourist menu. Try the tournedos with flap mushrooms. The tavern is closed in January and on Monday. The Albert is also one of the best budget hotels at Lourdes, offering a total of 27 comfortably furnished bedrooms at a rate of 180F ($24.82) in a single, rising to 195F ($26.89) in a double.

L'Ermitage, Place Mgr-Laurence (tel. 62-94-08-42), is decorated almost like an English club, with lots of exposed wood and well-planned detailing. Daniel Chaubon, the chef, turns out such specialties as a curried mussel flan, confit of duckling, braised salmon in Jurançon, a wine praised by Henry IV of France, along with filet of beef braised in madeira. Fixed-price menus cost 80F ($11.03). An à la carte meal will range in price from 180F ($24.82). The owner closes the establishment from mid-October to May 1.

7. Cauterets

The souvenir peddling and the aggressive commercial atmosphere of Lourdes offends many visitors. If you are among them, I suggest that you strike out for the mountains. One sylvan retreat, 18½ miles south from Lourdes, is Cauterets. The site of a dozen curative thermal springs, this little hamlet composed mainly of hotels has been famous since Margaret of Navarre, arriving with her court, put it on the map. Even George Sand and Victor Hugo came this way, seeking cures for various ailments. The local folk will tell you, "You can be cured of whatever ails you at Cauterets, and that means everything."

Cauterets is also a center for touring some of the most majestic sights of the Pyrénées. The most popular tour is to the **Pont d'Espagne** and the **Lac de Gaube,** south of Cauterets. The road goes along for about ten miles to the Pont d'Espagne. After that, only the hearty continue on foot. The **Cascade du Pont-d'Espagne** is considered the most dazzling of the waterfalls in and around Cauterets. If you're willing to walk for about an hour, you can take the path that leads to the Lac de Gaube. This lake occupies a magnificent setting, extolled by such visitors as Chateaubriand and Vigny. It has been used to illustrate almost every guide written about the Pyrénées since the Romantic period.

FOOD AND LODGING: **Les Trois Pics,** 12 Boulevard Leclerc (tel. 62-92-53-64). Whether you're a hill climber, an experienced rock climber, or simply someone who likes to relax in a country place in front of an open fire in the evening, this might be the hotel for you. Its modern façade is set against the Pyrénées, and it has all the amenities you need for a comfortable sojourn. Most of the rooms have private bath, and some have a balcony overlooking the Pyrénées. They rent for 220F ($30.34) in a single and 310F ($42.75) in a double, with fixed-price meals offered in the dining room for 95F ($13.10) and 180F ($24.82). Fondue dinners are held on some evenings. The hotel closes from late April to early June and from early November to just before Christmas.

Bellevue et George V, Place de la Gare (tel. 62-92-50-21), is one of the best buys at the resort. Rated two stars by the government, it lies close to the rail station at the foot of the téléférique. A family-run place, it is most inviting with an attractive lounge and a fine dining room where you can order complete dinners featuring a regional cuisine. A Basque cake, for example, is served warm from the oven. Meals begin at a modest 75F ($10.32). In all, 41 rooms are rented, many quite spacious and opening onto views of the Pyrénées. Singles or doubles go for 250F ($34.48) a night. The hotel is open from June 1 until the end of September and from December 20 to April 20.

If you'd like to be truly remote, I suggest that you journey to **La Fruitière,** four miles from Cauterets along the N21C. There you'll find a petite inn, **Hostellerie La Fruitière** (tel. 62-92-52-04). The "Fruit Shop" is only a simple inn, renting out eight bedrooms for 105F ($14.48) in a single and 140F ($19.31) in a double. Fixed-price meals, costing 60F ($8.27) to 115F ($15.86), are served daily except Sunday to all customers. Sunday evening dinner is reserved for residents of the hotel only. The food is very good, with an emphasis on regional dishes such as confit, game, mushrooms from the forest, as well as trout and salmon caught in local streams. Set apart from all the commercialization, the inn is most tranquil, decorated in an amusingly rustic style with antlers, open stone fireplaces, pitchforks, and blacked-beamed ceilings. It lies on a paved road, although in the midst of a national forest. From the inn there are many walks through woodlands, along lanes, and up hills. It is open only from May 20 until October 1. No food is served on Sunday night.

8. Ax-les-Thermes

In the Valley of the Ariege, Ax is at the same time a thermal spa, a summer retreat, and a winter sports station. Some 80 springs feed it, supplying three spas: le Couloubret, le Modèle, and le Teich. Saint Louis ordered the construction of the **Bassin des Ladres,** which serves as a public washing spot. Originally its purpose was to care for leprous soldiers who returned from the Crusades. The 19th-century Hôpital St-Louis, built in 1846, is a thermal bath dating from the grand days of spas.

Several outings are possible through the Pyrénées' rocky masses, with splendid views on many sides of gushing springs, mountainous rivers, and craggy peaks. Many visitors might also want to go to Andorra, that tiny principality in the Pyrénées. There is daily bus service in summer from Toulouse to Barcelona, via Ax-les-Thermes and Andorra.

FOOD AND LODGING: **Mapotel Royal Thermal,** Esplanade le Couloubret (tel. 61-64-22-51). Most of the bedrooms inside this comfortable modern hotel have a private balcony or terrace, with views over the mountains. About a dozen apartments are available, and double rooms rent for 180F ($24.82) to 330F ($45.51). Full board is offered for 250F ($27.58) to 300F ($41.37) per person.

Roy René, 11 Avenue Dr-Gomma (tel. 61-64-22-28), offers a recently constructed series of attractively furnished rooms. About two-thirds of the units have modern baths, and all of them represent good value for the money. They range in price from 170F ($23.44) in a double. If you want to include meals in the country-style restaurant, full board ranges from 220F ($30.34) to 280F ($38.61) per person. If you just want to drop in for a meal, set menus cost 60F ($8.27) to 145F ($20). The establishment is closed from the end of October to February 1.

Hôtel-Restaurant la Lauzeraie, Avenue Delcassé (tel. 61-64-20-70), is a pleasant retreat that will welcome you with a good bed and a fine meal after a day of touring in the Pyrénées. It's also a good bargain: a single with hot and cold running water begins at 85F ($11.72), a double costing 150F ($20.69), with a shower bath and toilet. Regional specialties are often served in the dining room, costing from 45F ($6.21) to 115F ($15.86), the price for a gargantuan repast.

Le Chalet, Avenue Adolphe-Turrel (tel. 61-64-24-31), is a comfortable hotel across the street from the park surrounding one of the town's spa facilities. Each of the ten bedrooms has its own balcony, private bath, and telephone, and they rent for 180F ($24.82) in a single, 225F ($31.03) in a double. Full board costs 200F ($27.58) to 235F ($32.41) per person. If you just want to stop for a meal, fixed-price menus are available for 60F ($8.27) and 120F ($16.55). The establishment is closed from mid-November until just before Christmas and also in January.

9. Perpignan

At Perpignan you may think you've already crossed the border into Spain. Actually, Perpignan was once the second city of Catalonia, ranking after Barcelona. Even earlier it was the capital of that curiosity, the kingdom of Majorca. But when the Roussillon—the French part of Catalonia—was finally partitioned off, Perpignan became French forever, authenticated by the Treaty of the Pyrénées in 1659. However, Catalan is still spoken, especially among the country people. There is much traffic between Perpignan and Barcelona.

Perpignan derives its name from the legend of Père Pinya, a plowman who is said to have followed the Tet River down the mountain to the site of the town today, where he started cultivating the fertile soil, with the river carrying out its promise to water the fields.

Among the chief things to see, the Castillet is a machicolated and crenellated building of red brick. It's a combination of a gateway and fortress, dating from the 14th century. If you ask the keeper, you can climb the tower for a good view of the town. The second-best-known building is the Loge de Mer, a sort of maritime stock exchange erected in 1397, which was enlarged in the 16th century. With its arcaded court, it is rather Venetian in style.

The Cathédrale St-Jean dates from the 14th and 15th centuries. The cathedral has an admirable nave and some interesting 17th-century retables. Leaving by way of the south side of the door, you'll find a chapel on the left containing the Dévot Christ, a magnificent woodcarving depicting a Jesus contorted with pain and suffering, his head, crowned with thorns, drooping on his chest.

At the top of the town, the Spanish citadel encloses the Palais des Rois de Majorque, or the palace of the kings of Majorca. This structure from the 13th and 14th centuries has been restored by the government. It is built around a court which is encircled by arcades. You can see the old throne room with its large fireplaces, and a square tower with a double gallery. From the tower there is a fine view of the Pyrénées. The former palace can be visited daily except Tuesday, from 9:30 a.m. to noon and 2 to 6 p.m. for 8F ($1.10) admission.

If you'd like to take an excursion, you can visit Thuir, where Byrrh, the apéritif with a red-wine base, is made. The cellars, among the largest in Europe, can be viewed from 8:30 to 11:45 a.m. and 2:30 to 5:45 p.m. weekdays only. Thuir lies ten miles southwest of Perpignan.

WHERE TO STAY: The Park Hôtel, 18 Boulevard Jean-Bourrat (tel. 68-35-14-14), is favored by most travelers heading for Spain's Costa Brava. Certainly its position is desirable, facing the Jardins de la Ville with their bird sanctuary. Rooms are well furnished and handsomely maintained, and there is an air of professionalism about the place. Singles begin at 200F ($27.58), rising to 310F ($42.75) in a double. The rooms have a nice ambience, are fully equipped, and most of them overlook the gardens. The hotel also runs a good restaurant, Chapon Fin, offering set menus at 95F ($13.10) and 200F ($27.58). The restaurant is closed on Sunday and for the last three weeks in August. There's parking for 20 cars in the basement.

La Loge, Place de la Loge (tel. 68-34-54-84), is a beguiling little hotel of only 29 bedrooms. Although modern, it has a charmingly tasteful interior. The location is right in the heart of town, near not only the Loge de Mer, from which it takes its name, but the Castillet as well. It is also near a canal outlet of the Tet. More than half the attractively furnished bedrooms contain a private toilet. Singles begin at 140F ($19.31), rising to 265F ($36.54) in a double. A continental breakfast is the only meal served.

Athéna, 1 rue Queya-Marché-République (tel. 68-34-37-63), lies in the old part of town, handy for all sights, just a short stroll from the cathedral. Even though it is centrally located, the hotel is in a tranquil zone. The building dates from the 14th century and has been considerably modernized and updated. Now, 28 of its 38 bedrooms come with private bath. Singles rent for 115F ($15.86); doubles, 200F ($27.58) with bath. There is no restaurant, but a continental breakfast is offered.

WHERE TO DINE: The **François Villon,** 1 rue du Four St-Jean (tel. 68-51-18-43), is installed in an authentic Catalonian house dating from the 14th century, with vaults, a special bread oven, and rustic decorations. The cuisine is heavily influenced by France's gastronomic center, Lyon. The menu is subject to change, depending on the availability of products and the season. So the chances are it will be fresh and skillfully prepared by the young chef, Pierre Charreton. His specialties made with local products and regional wines include foie gras mi-cuit au Banyuls, ris d'agneau (sweetbreads) au Mas Amiel, and truffes du Roussillon. Many of your fellow diners are likely to be from Barcelona, as François Villon is known by discerning visitors from that Catalonian port city. Monsieur Charreton offers a unique meal at 150F ($20.69), including a large choice of regional produce. If you order à la carte, expect to spend 250F ($34.48) to 320F ($4.13) per person. The restaurant is closed on Sunday, Monday, and from mid-July to mid-August.

Le Supion, 71 Avenue du Maréchal-Leclerc (tel. 68-34-53-42). The position of this dignified restaurant near the vegetable markets almost assures the impeccable freshness of many of the ingredients used in chef Michel Belcour's cuisine. Menu specialties include sea bass with sautéed zucchini, le carré d'agneau (lamb) vigneronne, turbot with raspberries, and a wide choice of rich desserts. Three set menus are offered: a tourist meal at 108F ($14.89), a dégustation menu at 168F ($23.17), and a gastronomique repast at 250F ($34.48). The restaurant is open all year.

L'Apéro, 40 rue de la Fusterie (tel. 68-51-21-14), is one of the best restaurants in town. It's attractively decorated in a turn-of-the-century style that will probably remind you of an informal bistro, but chef and owner Ange Garcia's cuisine could be accepted in the most formal restaurant in the region. Specialties include aiguillette of duckling in bitter orange sauce, foie gras in pepper-flavored caramel, lamb sweetbreads in puff pastry, and many other light-textured concoctions. Meals range in price from 140F ($19.31) to 180F ($24.82). The restaurant is closed Monday all day and Tuesday at lunch.

Chapter XXI

LANGUEDOC AND THE CAMARGUE

1. Auch
2. Toulouse
3. Albi
4. Cordes
5. Castres
6. Narbonne
7. Montpellier
8. Carcassonne
9. Nîmes
10. Aigues-Mortes

LANGUEDOC, one of the great old provinces of southern France, is a loosely defined area encompassing such cities as Nîmes, Toulouse, and Carcassonne. It's one of the leading wine-producing areas of France, and is fabled for its art treasures.

The Camargue is a marshy delta lying between two arms of the Rhône. South of Arles, this is cattle country. The strong wild black bulls are bred here for the arenas of Arles and Nîmes. The small white horses, most graceful animals, were said to have been brought to the Camargue by the Saracens. They are ridden by *gardians*, French cowboys, who can usually be seen in black widebrimmed hats. The whitewashed houses, the plaited-straw roofs, the pink flamingos who inhabit the muddy marshes, the vast plains, the endless stretches of sandbars—all this qualifies as Exotic France.

1. Auch

On the west bank of the Gers, in the heart of the ancient duchy of Gascony, of which it was the capital, the town of Auch in southwestern France is divided by an upper and lower quarter, each connected by several flights of steps. In the old part of town the narrow streets are called *pousterles*.

These streets center on the **Place Salinis,** from which there is a good view of the Pyrénées. Branching off from here, the **Escalier Monumental** leads down to the river, a monumental descent of 232 steps.

On the north of the square stands the **Cathédrale Ste-Marie,** built from the 15th to the 17th centuries, one of the handsomest Gothic churches in the south of France. It has 113 Renaissance choir stalls made of carved oak, and a custodian will let you in for a look in exchange for 4F (55¢). The stained-glass windows, also from the Renaissance era, are impressive. Its 17th-century organ was considered one of the finest in the world at the time of Louis XIV.

Next to the cathedral stands an 18th-century archbishop's palace with a 14th-century bell tower, the **Tour d'Armagnac,** which was once a prison.

FOOD AND LODGING: Hôtel de France, Place de la Libération (tel. 62-05-00-44). If you could spend only one night in a sleepy provincial town, sampling the regional cuisine, I'd suggest you make it André Daguin's Hôtel de France. In the center of town, close to the cathedral, the hotel has been renovated, with a modern restaurant, a cozy bar, and two lounges. There are only 30 bedrooms, but each has been given a semi-luxurious treatment, and you'll revel in the comforts. Singles begin at 400F ($55.16), regular doubles renting for 500F ($68.95). If you want to spread your family out in a suite, the charge is 600F ($82.74) to 750F ($103.43).

The restaurant is exceptional. Monsieur Daguin and his son Arnaud constantly astonish with their culinary feats, many of which are La Nouvelle Cuisine selections. Your meal might start with a thinly sliced Gascon ham. Among main-dish specialties, you might select small cuts of lamb (taken from the choicest part) with crayfish tails, lou maigret (a grilled breast of duck with a delicate flavor), fresh liver with vegetables, a brochette of salmon with foie gras, and a heavenly concoction of chicken breast with mussels. For dessert, you might be offered several flavors of homemade ice cream, divinely light pastries, or small side dishes of sweets belle époque. Menus are offered at 275F ($27.92) and 375F ($51.71), with à la carte orders averaging 325F ($44.82) to 400F ($55.16). The inn is closed in January, on Sunday night, and on Monday off-season.

2. Toulouse

The old capital of Languedoc, France's fourth-largest city, *La Ville Rose* is cosmopolitan in flavor. The major city of the southwest, it is the gateway to the Pyrénées. A distinctive landscape of gardens and squares, it is especially noted for its red brick buildings.

Built on both sides of the Garonne River at a wide bend, Toulouse is an artistic and cultural center. It's had a stormy history, playing many roles—once it was the capital of the Visigoths and later the center of the counts of Toulouse.

It lies 60 miles west of Carcassonne, but a long 443 miles southwest of Paris, although easily reachable by air.

SEEING THE SIGHTS: The city's major monument is the **Basilica of St. Sernin,** Place St-Sernin. Consecrated in 1096, it is the largest and finest Romanesque church extant. One of its most outstanding features is the Porte Miègeville, opening onto the south aisle and decorated with 12th-century sculptures. The door opening into the south transept is called Porte des Comtes, and its capitals depict the story of Lazarus. Nearby are the tombs of the counts of Toulouse. Entering by the main west door, you can see the double side aisles, giving the church five naves, an unusual feature in Romanesque architecture. An upper cloister forms a passageway around the interior. Look for the Romanesque capitals surmounting the columns. In the axis of the basilica, 11th-century bas-reliefs depict "Christ in his Majesty." The ambulatory leads to the crypt (ask the custodian for permission to enter), containing the relics of 128 saints, plus a thorn said to be from the Crown of Thorns. In the ambulatory, the old baroque retables and shrine have been recently reset and the preservation of the relics in the crypt artistically remade. The relics are those of the Apostles and the first bishops of Toulouse. The ambulatory and crypt may be visited from 10 a.m. to

5:30 p.m. July to September except on Sunday morning. A charge of 6F (83¢) is made. The basilica may be visited daily except during offices.

Opposite St-Sernin is the **Musée St-Raymond,** Place Saint-Sernin (tel. 61-22-21-85), housed in a college reconstructed in 1523. It contains one of the finest collections of Imperial busts outside Rome. Open from 10 a.m. to noon and 2 to 6 p.m. (until 5 p.m. off-season), it charges 2F (28¢) for admission. It is closed Tuesday and Sunday at noon.

Another important museum is the **Musée des Augustins,** rue de Metz (tel. 61-22-21-82). In its 14th-century cloisters is the most important collection of Romanesque capitals in the world. The sculptures or carvings are magnificent, and there are some fine examples of early Christian sarcophagi. On the upper floors is a large painting collection, with works by Murillo, Toulouse-Lautrec, Guardi, Gérard, Delacroix, Rubens, and Ingres. The museum also contains several portraits by Antoine Rivalz (1667–1735), a home-grown artist of surprising talent. Open from 10 a.m. to noon and 2 to 6 p.m., it charges 2F (28¢) for admission. Closed Tuesday.

The other major ecclesiastical building is the **Cathédrale St-Étienne,** at the east end of the rue de Metz. It has a bastardized look (probably because it was built between the 11th and 17th centuries). The rectangular bell tower is from the 16th century. It has a unique ogival nave to which a Gothic-style choir has been added.

One final church worthy of attention is **Jacobins,** in Old Toulouse, west of the Place du Capitole along the rue Lakanal. A Gothic brick church, it dates from the 13th century. The convent, daring in its architecture, has been restored and forms the largest block of buildings in France in use as a monastery.

In civic architecture, the **Capitole,** Place du Capitole, is outstanding. Built in 1753, it houses the Hôtel de Ville, or city hall, plus a theater in its right wing. It is open from 8:30 a.m. to 5 p.m. except on Saturday afternoon, Sunday, and holidays. Entrance is free on Wednesday; otherwise, you pay 1F (14¢).

Toulouse has a number of fine old mansions. More than 50 survive, most of them dating from the Renaissance when Toulouse was one of the richest cities of Europe. The finest is **Hôtel d'Assézat,** on the rue de Metz. It contains a 16th-century courtyard. The mansion houses the Académie des Jeux-Floraux, which since 1323 has presented flowers made of wrought metal to poets.

After all that sightseeing activity, head for the oval-shaped **Place Wilson,** a 19th-century square sheltering the most fashionable cafés of Toulouse.

HOTELS: **Le Concorde,** 16 Boulevard Bonrepos (tel. 61-62-48-60), has a touch of the deluxe—but just a touch. Opposite the Canal du Midi, it stands at the Gare Matabiau, the railway station. Rooms are functional and practical, and there are 100 of them, each containing private bath, television, and radio. They're also air-conditioned. Rates are 350F ($48.27) in a single, rising to 510F ($70.33) in a double. There is also a garage for your car. On the premises, the Rôtisserie de l'Écluse provides good food with fast, efficient service, offering menus for 105F ($14.48) and 170F ($23.44). The restaurant is closed on Sunday and in August.

Frantel Wilson, 7 rue Labéda (tel. 61-21-21-75), is a favorite with the commercial traveler. It doesn't have a restaurant, but there is a piano bar. The hotel places emphasis on attractive, air-conditioned, and soundproof accommodations. The interior design of the bedrooms is contemporary, and you'll have many conveniences, including a mini-bar for your beverages (you report what you drank to the desk clerk when you go to pay the bill). Other amenities include color TV, video, radio, and a device to awaken you automatically. Rates charged are 510F ($70.33) in a single, 585F ($80.67) in a double. Frantel Wilson is in the center of Toulouse, and there is a garage for your car.

Grand Hôtel de l'Opéra, 1 Place du Capitole (tel. 61-21-64-60), is one of the finest accommodations available in the city. The high-ceilinged bedrooms were renovated to incorporate many modern comforts, the units offer splendid views of the swimming pool inside an interior garden and the Place du Capitole. There's a restaurant on the premises and a luxurious bar area where you might enjoy relaxing for a while before retiring. Each of the rooms contains a private bath, telephone, TV, and a radio/alarm. Rooms range in price from 380F ($52.40) in a single up to 1,200F ($165.48) for the most luxurious double.

Sofitel, Toulouse Aéroport de Blagnac (tel. 61-71-11-25), is one of the simpler versions of this chain hotel, not unlike a motel. It lies about a mile by car from the entrance to the airport, about a ten-minute drive into the center of Toulouse. Half of its bedrooms are twins, and all the accommodations are "climate controlled" and soundproof. There is a liberal use of solid color combinations in the bedroom decor, and the theme is cheerful, with many amenities. Singles pay from 500F ($68.95); doubles, from 700F ($96.53). There is a restaurant, Le Caouec, serving haute cuisine and regional specialties, meals ranging from 150F ($20.69) to 220F ($30.34). Especially nice are the indoor heated swimming pool, the sauna, and the tennis courts.

Those wanting to escape Toulouse moderne can head for **La Flânerie,** Route de Lacroix-Falgarde (tel. 61-73-39-12), at Vieille-Toulouse, 5½ miles south by way of the D4. It's so peaceful a place it's worth the drive. The ancient residence stands in its own six-acre garden overlooking the Garonne. The room furnishings have been well selected, setting a high style level. Some of the bedchambers are outfitted with rich, tasteful antiques, including canopy-tester beds, fine marquetry desks, and bronze lighting fixtures—most elegant. However, there are only 12 chambers, so reservations are important. Singles cost from 175F ($24.13), the rate rising to 380F ($52.40) in a double. A continental breakfast is available, and you can also obtain a light supper if requested in advance.

d'Occitaine, 5 rue Labéda (tel. 61-21-15-92), is a hotel school. Maybe because the staff is young, everybody seems to try harder. I've received the best service here of any place in the city. The 17 rooms are well furnished and handsomely maintained, costing from 200F ($27.58) in a single, from 320F ($44.13) in a double. However, the hotel shuts down for school vacations, usually from the end of June until the first of October. Even if you don't stay here, I recommend its fixed-price menu for 125F ($17.24). The restaurant is closed Saturday night and Sunday.

Nearby is the **Royal,** 6 rue Labéda (tel. 61-23-38-70), which is done in a sophisticated style using wrought iron and tiles. It is one of the most agreeable of the small hotels of Toulouse, with a pleasant inner courtyard and a helpful staff. Rooms here are attractively comfortable, costing 240F ($33.10) to 300F ($41.37) in a single, 280F ($38.61) to 350F ($48.27) in a double or twin. There's no restaurant, a continental breakfast being the only meal available.

La Caravelle Hôtel, 62 rue Raymond IV (tel. 61-62-70-65), is a seven-story balconied place with awnings above each of its big glass windows. In the center of town just across from the Matabiau train station, the hotel offers a modern series of geometrically decorated public rooms which include a bar. Each of the sunny bedrooms is equipped with Scandinavian contemporary furniture, a mini-bar, private bath, radio, TV, individually controlled air conditioning, and an automatic masseur. Singles cost 360F ($49.64), that tariff rising to 490F ($67.57) in a double, including service, tax, and breakfast.

Hôtel Raymond IV, 16 rue Raymond IV (tel. 61-62-89-41). Its location on a very quiet street close to the center of town is one of this place's most potent attractions. An antique building, it contains 41 pleasantly decorated rooms, renting for 250F ($34.48) in a single, 330F ($45.51) in a double, including breakfast. Each unit contains a private bath, phone, and TV, and accommodations are well kept.

RESTAURANTS: **Vanel,** 22 rue Maurice-Fonvielle (tel. 61-21-51-82). Lucien Vanel stirs the magic of his craft, turning out scrumptious fare. The patronage is heavily Gallic, and the restaurant is nearly always full—so you'll need a reservation. He gives new meaning and discovers new taste sensations in regional dishes, adding constantly to his own rapidly growing repertoire. His braised sea bass with lettuce is every bit as good (or better) than the seaweed style made famous by Michel Guérard. An endless variety of quality meats and produce, skillfully and creatively prepared, are presented for your selection: marinated duck maigret (from the school of La Nouvelle Cuisine), a cassoulet of snails with nuts, a fricassée of pigs' feet (it may sound unappetizing, but it's delicious), a pâté of pike with eel, a duckling ragoût with sweetbreads. The wine list is imaginative with many interesting selections, including Cahors and Côtes de Duras, and the service is impeccable. Expect to pay from 260F ($35.85) to 300F ($41.37) for a meal. The restaurant is closed on Sunday, Monday for lunch, and in August.

Darroze, 19 rue Castellane (tel. 61-62-34-70). In the center of the city, a short walk from the Place Wilson, this attractive restaurant is decorated in a dignified Louis XV style whose sobriety seems strangely at odds with the kind of joy Pierre Darroze puts into his cooking. His chief assistant is his charming daughter-in-law, Vivianne, who seems to work so well with her septuagenarian mentor that you'll hardly be aware of the 40 years difference in their ages. Menu specialties are based on regional recipes and the freshest possible ingredients. They include salads with truffles and fresh foie gras, jambonnette of duckling confit peasant style, duckling cooked in madeira, foie gras with apples, and wild salmon marinated with coriander. The wine list is staggeringly complete, including more than 300 brands purchased directly from the vineyards, as well as some 40 kinds of armagnac. Four-course fixed-price menus are offered from 130F ($17.93) to 265F ($36.54), with full à la carte meals going for 240F ($33.10) to 300F ($41.37). The Darrozes take a much-deserved rest Saturday at lunchtime and Sunday.

Le Belvédère, 11 Boulevard Recollets (tel. 61-52-63-73), offers a panoramic view of the Garonne and Old Toulouse from its eighth-floor precincts. Under the careful eye of its patron, this exceptional restaurant serves an array of local specialties, including the typical cassoulet au confit and a confit en ratatouille. Set meals are offered for 135F ($18.62). The restaurant is closed on Sunday and in August.

Le Cahuzac, 21 rue Perchepinte (tel. 61-53-11-15). Considering the richness of the decor of this restaurant, it seems appropriate that it's in the antique-sellers district of the old city. The charming owner of this place is Martine Manavit. She has filled her rustic house with painted still-lifes, light-grained wooden furniture, and so many impeccably groomed touches that you'd almost think you were entering a movie set. Menu items to tempt you are likely to be a full range of Gascon specialties, such as sautéed chicken with a confit of garlic, cheese salad, confit with truffles, soup with truffles, and a wide range of flavorful meat dishes. Good-value set menus are offered for 92F ($12.69), 155F ($21.38), and 200F ($27.58). If you prefer to select à la carte, expect to pay 160F ($22.06) to 200F ($27.58) for a full meal here. The restaurant is closed Sunday, Monday at lunchtime, and for all of August.

Le Cassoulet, 40 rue Peyrolières (tel. 61-22-18-99), takes its name from a shell-bean stew originating in Languedoc. The dish is prepared with goose, pork, or mutton. Each is good-tasting, hearty fare. At this restaurant you can order à la carte at a cost of 110F ($15.17) to 150F ($20.69). The proprietor, J. Vincent Bonnamy, does many outstanding dishes in addition to the cassoulet (served here with confit d'oie). For example, a delectable appetizer is a mousse made with corn and mussels. Try also his maigret de canard (duckling) with eggplant. For dessert, his sorbets change with the season, as each is made with fresh fruit. The restaurant is closed the first ten days in January and on Monday.

On the Outskirts

Hôtel de Diane, 3 Route de Saint-Simon or 296 Chemin de Tucaut (tel. 61-07-59-52). The most tranquil retreat in the environs of Toulouse lies about five miles out the D23. This is a hotel/restaurant complex surrounded by a park in which are found an outdoor pool, a turn-of-the-century villa with well-decorated bedrooms, and a rustically modern building housing the restaurant, Saint-Simon. The villa's 35 rooms are priced at 300F ($41.37) in a single, 420F ($57.92) in a double. They usually have wide windows looking out onto the well-manicured grounds and the tennis courts beyond. Patricia and Michel Chagnon, the owners, have affiliated their establishment with the Mapotel and the Best Western hotel chains. They've even hired a tennis pro for anyone wanting to improve his or her game.

The restaurant offers the choice of meals in the garden or inside the imaginatively decorated dining room. The fixed-price menu seems to offer the best value for the money, costing 130F ($17.93). For this, you get the "chariot" of hors d'oeuvres and specialties. The dishes may include foie de canard with oysters in puff pastry, a tartare of fish with raspberry-flavored vinegar, and monkfish with shrimp. If you want to order à la carte, expect to spend around 300F ($41.37). Except on Sunday, the restaurant serves lunch and dinner daily until 9:30 p.m.

3. Albi

The "red city" (for the color of the building stone) of Albi, 47 miles northeast of Toulouse, straddles both banks of the Tarn River, and is dominated by its brooding, fortified **Cathédrale Ste-Cécile,** dating from 1282 and lying near the Place du Vigan, the medieval center of town. After viewing the cathedral, one writer claimed that if it were in Italy, "the French would spend a day in the train to go and see it and that stupendous view." Fortified with ramparts and parapets outside, and containing transepts or aisles inside, it was built by local bishops during a struggle for power with the counts of Toulouse. Inside, look at the 16th-century rood screen. It's exceptional.

Opposite the northern side of the cathedral is the Archbishop's Palace, or **Palais de la Berbie,** another fortified structure dating from the late 13th century. Inside, the **Musée Toulouse-Lautrec** (tel. 63-54-14-09) contains the world's most important collection of that artist's paintings, more than 600 specimens of his work. His family bequeathed the works remaining in his studio. Toulouse-Lautrec was born at Albi on November 24, 1864. Crippled in childhood, his legs permanently deformed, he lived in Paris most of his life and produced posters and sketches of characters in music halls and circuses. His satiric portraits of the demimonde at the turn of the century were both amusing and affectionate. The museum also owns paintings by Degas, Bonnard, Vuillard, Matisse, Dufy, Utrillo, and Rouault. From June 15 to September 30 it is open daily from 9 a.m. to noon and 2 to 6 p.m. Off-season it is open from 10 a.m. to noon and 2 to 5 p.m. It is closed on Tuesday. Admission is 10F ($1.38).

Maison Natale de Toulouse-Lautrec, Hôtel du Bosc (tel. 63-54-21-81), lies in an ancient, narrow street in the oldest part of Old Albi. The mansion belongs today to the artist's great-nephews of the du Vignaud de Villefort family. It was partially built into the 14th-century fortifications that used to encircle the city. The house is open to the public, but it is still inhabited. During his childhood, young Henri, who sprang from an artistic family, did his first artwork here. The salons are on view, as are many valuable household objects. There is also a private collection of paintings, drawings, and watercolors by Toulouse-Lautrec. The house is open daily mid-June to mid-September from 9:30 a.m. to 1 p.m.

and from 2:30 to 7 p.m. Admission is 15F ($2.07). Guided tours in English are available.

FOOD AND LODGING: **Hostellerie St-Antoine,** 17 rue Saint-Antoine (tel. 63-54-04-04), converted from a 250-year-old inn, has been owned by the same family for five generations. Madame Rieux, a talented and inventive interior decorator, dipped heavily into the Toulouse-Lautrec palette when designing this hotel. Her grandfather was a close friend of the painter and was given a few of his paintings, sketches, and prints. Some of these are placed in various spots in the lounge, which opens onto a rear garden with fig trees and flagstone paths. Her sons, Jacques and Jean-Francois, run the hotel today. The atmosphere evokes a private country estate. The bedrooms have been delightfully decorated, with a sophisticated use of color, good reproductions, and occasional antiques. A single with shower rents for 350F ($48.27), increasing to 500F ($68.95) with bath. Doubles are 450F ($62.06) with shower, rising to 600F ($82.74) with bath. Three set menus are offered, at 150F ($20.69), 200F ($27.58), and 270F ($37.23).

La Réserve, Route de Cordes à Fonviane (tel. 63-60-79-79), is a country-club villa on the outskirts of Albi, managed by Jeanine and Hélène Rieux. It is built in the Mediterranean style, with a swimming pool and fine garden where you can dine. Step-terraces lead to the banks of the Tarn River. The upper-story bedrooms have sun terraces and French doors. Half of the accommodations are decorated in a light and cheery modern way, the other in Empire with top-grade reproductions. The colors are coordinated, and the decorative accessories are imaginative. The baths are a delight. Prices run from 400F ($55.16) to 500F ($68.95) in a single, 500F ($68.95) to 700F ($96.53) for the best doubles. Set menus cost from 150F ($20.69) to 275F ($37.92). On the à la carte menu, specialties include pâté de grives (thrush), carré d'agneau (lamb) aux cèpes (flap mushrooms), and tournedos Périgueux. A meal ordered à la carte is likely to run about 250F ($34.48). Guests are received only from April to October.

Hôtel Chiffre, 50 rue Séré-de-Rivières (tel. 63-54-04-60), in the center of town, is a well-maintained establishment that has been directed by members of the Chiffre family since 1918. Some of the fancifully decorated bedrooms open onto a quiet inner courtyard. They cost between 250F ($34.48) in a single and 350F ($48.27) in a double. The in-house restaurant is sought out by many residents of Toulouse for its set menu costing 130F ($17.93), which is a virtual feast. If you order à la carte, it will cost around 200F ($27.58). Specialties include daube Albi style, snails or roquefort in puff pastry, breast of duckling, and a wide array of savory local meat dishes. Dessert might be an ice cream dish called a coupe Lautrec. No meals are served on Sunday between the first of November and the end of March. Half-board plans are also available.

Francis Cardaillac, Marsac-sur-Tarn (tel. 63-55-41-90). In a setting amid the cascading vines of the sun-baked hills of the Tarn Valley, owner-chef Francis Cardaillac, with an engaging charm, maintains high standards within his kitchens as well as in the well-established gardens surrounding his establishment. He prides himself on introducing to the world a modernized version of the gastronomic treats of the Tarn. A wine-tasting bar with a piano is on the premises, as well as an informal brasserie and a heated swimming pool.

The most alluring area is the main dining room and an adjoining terrace where you can enjoy fresh specialties, including such listings as stuffed mussels, snails with chopped mushrooms, calves' liver with a purée of radishes, a foie gras of duckling with apples, asparagus flan, and boneless lamb with a sorrel sauce. There is also a voluptuous selection of desserts. A fixed-price bargain menu costs 135F ($18.62), or you can spend as much as 350F ($48.27) on the à la carte. Meals are served daily except Sunday night and Monday. The restaurant is found along the RN88 in the hamlet of Marsac-sur-Tarn, 6½ miles west of Albi (the RN88 is sometimes known as the "Route St-Affrique"). If you phone ahead for a table, you'll find hand-written nametags identifying your flower-laden spot for the evening.

4. Cordes

The site is remarkable, like an eagle's nest on a hilltop, opening onto the valley of the Cérou 15 miles from Albi. The name Cordes is derived from the textile and leather industries that thrived here during the 13th and 14th centuries. It became a fortified Protestant refuge during the wars of religion.

In the 14th century when the town's troubles eased, artisans working with linen and leather prospered. It also became known throughout France for its brilliantly colored silks. In the 15th century, however, plagues and religious massacres reduced the city to a minor role. A brief renaissance occurred in the 19th century when automatic weaving machines were introduced.

Today Cordes is an arts-and-crafts city, and many of the ancient houses on the narrow streets contain artisans plying their skills—blacksmiths, enamelers, graphics artists, weavers, engravers, sculptors, and painters. You park outside, then go under an arch leading to the old town.

Often called "the city of a hundred Gothic arches," Cordes contains numerous old houses built of pink sandstone. Many of the doors and windows are fashioned of pointed (broken) arches which still retain their 13th- and 14th-century grace. Some of the best-preserved ones line the Grande-Rue, also called the rue Droite.

Among the sightseeing attractions, the **Musée Charles-Portal** is named after the archivist of the Tarn region and an avid historian of Cordes. It contains everyday artifacts of the textile industry of long ago, old farming measures, samples of local embroidery, a reconstructed peasant home interior, and other medieval memorabilia of Cordes.

Maison du Grand Fauconnier (House of the Falcon Master) gets its name because of the falcons carved into the stonework of the roofline. A grandly proportioned staircase leads to the Musée Yves-Brayer (tel. 63-56-00-40), which is open all year, on demand from the Secretariat of the Town Hall, between 8:30 a.m. and noon and 1:30 to 6 p.m. Monday to Friday. From April to November, it is also open on Sunday and national holidays from 2 to 6 p.m., and during the high season, July and August, it can be visited daily from 10 a.m. to noon and 2 to 6 p.m. Admission is 3F (41¢) for adults, 1F (14¢) for children. Yves Brayer came to Cordes in 1940 and became a well-known figure. Watching Cordes fall gradually into decay, he renewed interest in its restoration. Within the museum are exhibited a variety of masterworks from a variety of craftsmen, including designs, textiles, and paintings.

Église St-Michel dates from the 13th century, although many alterations have been performed since then. The view from the top of the tower encompasses much of the surrounding area. For access to the tower, you pay 2F (28¢). Much of the lateral design of the side chapels probably comes from the cathedral at Albi. The organ dates from 1830. Before being shipped here, it was in Notre-Dame de Paris. In case the church is closed, ask at the *tabac* (tobacco shop) across the street from the front entrance.

FOOD AND LODGING: Maison du Grand Écuyer, rue Voltaire (tel. 63-56-01-03). Much of the focus of this establishment lies inside the restaurant, whose premises are classified as a national historic monument. Chef Yves Thuriès began his career as a pastry maker, eventually graduating into the kinds of well-prepared platters that have made his restaurant an almost mandatory stop during a visit to Cordes. Specialties include three confits of lobster, a salad of red mullet with fondue of vegetables, and noisette of lamb in an orange sauce. You can be assured that, because of Monsieur Thuriès's background, the dessert selection is about the grandest and most overwhelming in this part of France. À la carte meals cost 250F ($34.48) to 300F ($41.37), while table d'hôte menus are priced between 140F ($19.31) and 280F ($38.61).

The hotel section is in the former hunting lodge of Raymond VII, Count of Toulouse. Today you can stay in one of the antique-studded bedrooms for 270F ($37.23) in a single, 500F ($68.95) in a double. All the units have exquisitely remodeled private baths. The most desired room honors a former guest, Albert Camus, and contains a four-poster bed and a fireplace. The restaurant is closed on Monday off-season and both the hotel and restaurant shut down from the end of October to April.

Le Parc, Les Cabannes (tel. 63-56-02-59), lies about a mile west of the center of town, on the Route de St-Antonin, the D600. This century-old stone house offers generously portioned meals either under the arch of the garden's trees or inside the paneled dining room. If you arrive in winter, there's likely to be a fire burning under the elegantly proportioned mantelpiece, but regardless of the season, the well-prepared specialties may tempt you to return for a follow-up visit. The cuisine includes homemade foie gras, duckling, poularde occitane, matelote of eels with dried flap mushrooms, and rabbit with cabbage leaves. Claude Izard is the amiable director, charging 70F ($9.65) to 175F ($24.13) for a set menu and around 200F ($27.58) for à la carte meals. Food is served daily except Sunday night and Monday during low season and for the first six weeks after New Year's. People like to go to bed early here, so the last dinner is offered at 8 p.m. If you want to spend the night, about a dozen rooms are offered, ranging in price from 160F ($22.06) in a single to 200F ($27.58) in a double.

5. Castres

Built on the bank of the Agout River, Castres, 27 miles from Albi, is the point of origin of trips to the Sidobre, the mountains of Lacaune, and the Black Mountains. Today the wool industry, whose origins go back to the 14th century, has made Castres one of the two most important wool-producing areas of France. The town was formerly a Roman military installation. A Benedictine monastery was founded here in the 9th century, and the town fell under the counts of Albi in the 10th century. During the wars of religion, it was Protestant.

Jean Jaurès, leader of the unified socialist party in France, was born here in 1859. Along with Émila Zola, he defended Dreyfus in the celebrated trial. He was assassinated in Paris in 1914.

Musée Goya, Hôtel de Ville (tel. 63-59-62-63), is housed in the former archbishop's palace, designed by Mansart in 1669, which also serves as the Hôtel de Ville. Some of the spacious public rooms, whose ceilings are supported with a frieze of the archbishops' coats-of-arms, include 16th-century tapestries and the works of Spanish painters from the 15th through the 17th centuries. Most notable, of course, are the paintings of Francisco de Goya y Lucientes, all of which were donated to the town in 1892 by the Castres-born artist Marcel Briguiboul. *Les Caprices* is a study of figures erected shortly after the illness that left Goya deaf. Filling much of an entire room, it is peopled with highly symbolic images of the demons and monsters.

A few rooms of the palace are reserved for the **Musée Jean-Jaurès,** (same phone as above), including photos, documents, and newspaper articles. See, in particular, an issue of *L'Aurore,* containing Zola's famous *J'accuse* article from the Dreyfus case. The gardens surrounding the palace were designed by Le Nôtre. Charging 5F (69¢) for admission, both of these museums may be visited in summer daily from 9 a.m. to noon and from 2 to 6 p.m. Off-season, the museums are closed on Tuesday, and they shut down at 5 p.m. in winter.

Cathédrale St-Benoît was built on the site of the 9th-century Benedictine abbey by the architect Caillau in 1677. The baroque structure was never completed according to its original plans. The painting at the far end of the church above the altar was executed by Gabriel Briard in the 18th century.

FOOD AND LODGING: If you'd like to spend the night, you'll find good comfort at **Grand Hôtel,** 11 rue de la Libération (tel. 63-59-00-30), which is the best of the moderately priced rooming establishments in town. It is run by Madame Fabre, who also manages La Caravelle, the best restaurant in town. The Grand offers 40 well-furnished rooms costing from 130F ($17.93) for its least expensive single, rising to 275F ($37.92) for the best double with private bath. Breakfast is extra. The hotel shuts down from December 15 to January 15.

For dining, the already-mentioned **La Caravelle,** 150 Avenue de Roque-courbe (tel. 63-59-27-72), is the outstanding choice. Madame Fabre carries on in the tradition of her late husband, one of the outstanding chefs of the region. Her expertise is reflected both in the running and the cuisine of this fine restaurant. Near the river, you can enjoy your repast on a flower-filled terrace, selecting from a set menu of 130F ($17.93) which I've always found perfectly adequate, or else ordering a more elaborate repast at 275F ($37.92). Taxes and service are included. The restaurant is closed on Saturday but open otherwise anytime between June 15 and September 15.

6. Narbonne

A medieval city, 37 miles east of Carcassonne, Narbonne was a port to rival Marseille in Roman times, its "galleys laden with riches." It was the first town outside Italy to be colonized by the Romans. But the Mediterranean, now five miles away, left it high and dry. For that very reason it's an intriguing old place to visit, steeped as it is with antiquity.

The **Cathédrale St-Just** was begun in 1272, but it was never finished. It consists now only of a transept and a choir, 130 feet high, built in the bold Gothic style of the north of France. At each end of the transept the towers, 194 feet high, are from 1480. There is an impressive collection of Flemish tapestries. The cloisters are from the 14th and 15th centuries. They connect the cathedral with the—

Archbishop's Palace, which has the façade of a fortified palace, with a trio of towers from the 13th and 14th centuries. The Old Palace on the right is from the 12th century and the so-called New Palace on the left from the 14th century. The neo-Gothic **Hôtel de Ville,** part of the complex, was constructed by Viollet-le-Duc in 1845–1850.

In the **Palais Neuf** (New Palace), the archbishops of Narbonne lived rather elegantly, I gather. These former apartments are reached by climbing 88 steps up the monumentally impressive Louis XIII staircase. It is said that the old archbishops were hauled up the stairs on mules. Today these apartments have been converted into museums.

Musée Archéologique shows prehistoric artifacts, Bronze Age tools, 14th-century frescoes, and Greco-Roman amphorae. Several of the sarcophagi date from the 3rd century, and some of the mosaics are of pagan origin.

Musée d'Art et d'Histoire is three floors above street level in the former private apartments of the archbishops. These are the rooms in which Louis XII stayed during his siege of Perpignan. The coffered ceilings are enhanced with panels depicting the nine Muses. A Roman mosaic floor is displayed, as are 17th-century portraits. There's a collection of antique porcelain, enamels, and a portrait bust of Louis XIV.

Donjon Gilles-Aycelin offers an idea of the strength of the church leaders of Narbonne during an era in which they competed with military leaders. Dating from the end of the 13th century, it has an observation platform high above the ground, with a view of the cathedral, the surrounding plain, and the Pyrénées.

The museums are open from May 15 until the end of September from 10 a.m. to noon and from 2 to 6 p.m. (close at 5 p.m. off-season). They are also closed on Monday off-season. Admission is 5F (69¢). For the latest details, on the attractions of Narbonne, go to the **Office de Tourisme,** Place R-Salengro (tel. 68-65-15-60). This office is closed Sunday in the off-season.

If you'd like to see Roman artifacts, you can at the **Musée Lapidaire,** which occupies the precincts of the disused 13th-century Church of Lamourguier. It keeps the same hours as the other museums. The location is on the Boulevard Dr-Ferroult. Broken sculptures, Roman inscriptions, relics of medieval buildings—this special collection is considered one of the largest such exhibits in France and one of the most important, but it would take an archeologist to make sense out of a lot of it as it is haphazardly arranged.

The early Gothic **Church of St. Paul Serge** was built on the site of a 4th-century necropolis. Inside, it has an elegantly decorated choir with fine Renaissance woodcarving, and it also possesses some ancient Christian sarcophagi. The chancel from 1229 is admirable. The north door leads to the **Paleo-Christian Cemetery,** part of an early Christian burial ground.

FOOD AND LODGING: La Résidence, 6 rue de 1er-Mai (tel. 68-32-19-41), is my preferred choice of a hotel in Narbonne, lying within a few minutes of the Cathedral of St. Just and the Archbishop's Palace. It is most comfortable, decorated with a collection of antiques. All of its 26 bedrooms contain a private bath, and the rate in a single is 225F ($31.03), rising to 320F ($44.13) in a double. The atmosphere will charm lovers of antiquity. The hotel doesn't have a restaurant but offers breakfast. It does have a sauna.

Mapotel du Languedoc, 22 Boulevard Gambetta (tel. 68-65-14-74), has been modernized. It offers 43 well-equipped and refreshened bedrooms, 29 of them with private bath. Singles go for 130F ($17.93) without bath, rising to 325F ($44.82) in a double with bath. The hotel stands a short distance from the Canal de la Rhône. Its restaurant serves regional specialties, and nonresidents are welcomed for dinner, with menus priced from 75F ($10.32) to 170F ($23.44). The food is in the typical Languedoc style, and you'll be able to sample grilled salmon with anchovy butter, fresh sole, tender lamb cooked with beans, veal liver provençale, and sautéed chicken chasseur. The restaurant is closed on Friday night and Saturday off-season and takes a vacation in January.

Le Réverbère, 4 Place des Jacobins (tel. 68-32-29-18). You'll dine in an intensely cultivated backdrop of Louis XIV paneling, "reverberating" crystal, hand-painted porcelain, and about a thousand subtle details that make this the most superior restaurant in town. Menu items are the carefully organized passion of chef Claude Giraud (a devotee of Michel Guérard) and could include a velouté of foie gras en croûte, a saddle of lamb harlequin style in puff pastry, bonbons of foie gras in a sweet-and-sour honey sauce, a mousse of violet artichokes, and a range of tempting desserts. One of the most attractive offerings is the 165F ($22.75) *menu découvert,* where eight delicately seasoned courses follow one another in an almost awesome parade of culinary skill. À la carte meals range upward from 325F ($44.82). Service is not included in the tariffs. The establishment is closed Sunday night, all day Monday, and in February.

7. Montpellier

The capital of Mediterranean Languedoc, this ancient university city 31 miles southwest of Nîmes is still renowned for its medical school, founded in the 13th century. Nostradamus qualified as a doctor here, and even Rabelais studied at the school. Petrarch also came to Montpellier in 1317, staying for seven years. At a much later time, Paul Valéry met André Gide in the **Jardin des Plantes,** and you might well begin your tour there, as it is the oldest such garden in

France, dating from the 15th and 16th centuries. Reached from the Boulevard Henri-IV, this botanical garden, filled with exotic plants, was opened in 1593.

Nearby is the **Cathedral of St. Pierre**, on the Place St-Pierre, which was founded in 1364. Once the church of a Benedictine monastery, the cathedral suffered badly in religious wars. (After 1795 the monastery was occupied by the medical school.) The cathedral today has a somewhat bleak west front with two towers and a canopied porch.

Called "the Oxford of France," Montpellier is a city of young people, as you'll notice if you sit at a café opening onto the heartbeat **Place de la Comédie,** admiring the Théâtre, the 18th-century Fountain of the Three Graces, or whatever else amuses you. It is the living room of Montpellier, the meeting place of students from all over the world who study here.

The **Musée Fabre,** 13 rue Montpelliéret (tel. 67-66-06-34), is one of the great provincial art galleries of France. Occupying the former Hôtel de Massilian, where Molière once played a season, the museum is named after a pupil of David's who turned over his valuable collection of paintings to Montpellier to form the nucleus of this collection. Fabre's own works are exhibited, but he is hardly the star of his own show. Other works include a good collection of Veronese paintings, especially his *Mystic Marriage of St. Catherine.* There's even a Houdon bust of Benjamin Franklin. The collection of old masters is impressive, but modern painting is also shown, including works by Utrillo and an early Matisse. There is a large number of pictures by Courbet and Delacroix. See, in particular, Courbet's celebrated self-portrait, *The Gentleman with the Pipe.* The gallery is open daily from 9 a.m. to noon and 2 to 5:30 p.m. except Monday, charging no admission.

Before leaving town, everybody takes a stroll along the 17th-century **Promenade du Peyrou,** a terraced park with views of the Cévennes and the Mediterranean. This is a broad esplanade constructed at the loftiest point of Montpellier. Opposite the entrance is an Arch of Triumph, erected in 1691 to celebrate the victories of Louis XIV. In the center of the promenade is an equestrian statue of Louis XIV, and at the end, the Château d'Eau, a monument to 18th-century classicism, a pavilion with Corinthian columns. Water is brought here by a conduit, nearly nine miles long, and an aqueduct. Montpellier was quite popular with British visitors in the 19th century, who strolled along this promenade admiring the splendid terraces and the neoclassic hotels adorned with wrought-iron balconies, a charming sight.

HOTELS: Métropole, 3 rue Clos-René (tel. 67-58-11-22), provides the most superior accommodation in Montpellier. In the heart of the city, it offers 92 bedrooms that are agreeably decorated and well fitted out. All rooms contain TV, mini-bar, and private bath or shower. Ask for a chamber overlooking the unusual interior garden, as such accommodations have a pleasant outlook and are quieter. The rooms are beautifully maintained by the polite, efficient staff. Singles pay 500F ($68.95), the rate rising to 1,100F ($151.69) for the best double. The hotel's gastronomic restaurant, La Closerie, franchised by the well-known chef, Gaston Lenotre, offers attractive French dishes. Try, for instance, a truffles soup or a goose-livered beef filet, and, of course, the excellent desserts of Lenotre. À la carte orders average 325F ($44.82).

Demeure des Brousses, Route de Vauguières (tel. 67-65-77-66), is reached by going less than two miles out the D172E. This 18th-century country house stands in an impressive park. There are 19 bedrooms for rent, each beautifully furnished and containing a private bath. The hotel has been discreetly and tastefully converted, its public and private rooms agreeably decorated. The selection of furniture and decorative objects provides the intimate atmosphere of a gracious home. Room rates are 280F ($38.61) in a single, 450F ($62.06) in a double. The country house is not far from the sea, about a ten-minute drive from the heart of Montpellier. It is open from late March to early April and late April to the first week of October.

Noailles, 2 rue Écoles-Centrales (tel. 67-60-49-80), is an attractive 17th-century building in the old part of Montpellier. You feel connected to the past here. The Noailles stands almost next to the church, Notre-Dame des Tables, and the esplanade with its small lake and rows of plane trees. The bedrooms, 30 of them, rent for 200F ($27.58) in a single, 310F ($42.75) in a double. The rooms are well-furnished and handsomely kept. Breakfast is brought to your chamber if you wish, although no other meals are served.

Hôtel George-V, 42 Avenue St-Lazare (tel. 67-72-35-91), is a well-managed hotel at the edge of a park on the northern edge of the city. There's a bar on the premises, reserved for the hotel's clientele, and about 40 contemporary bedrooms, each with a private bath, phone, and TV. A single rents for 285F ($39.30), a double for 375F ($51.71), including breakfast.

Les Arceaux, 33-35 Boulevard des Arceaux (tel. 67-92-61-76), is a modest little 15-bedroom hotel that is a preferred budget oasis in Montpellier. Its location is excellent, right off the renowned Promenade du Peyrou. Rooms are pleasantly furnished, costing 190F ($26.20) in a single, 240F ($33.10) in a double. Breakfast is the only meal served. Guests enjoy resting on the shady terrace adjoining the hotel.

RESTAURANTS: Réserve Rimbaud, 820 Avenue St-Maur (tel. 67-72-52-53), has a terrace overlooking the water, lying in the Quartier des Aubes. Dining is gracious and elegant here. If you can't get a terrace table overlooking the Lez, or if the weather is bad, then your meals will be served in the harmonious dining room, which is warmly decorated. Top-quality meat, seasonal seafood from the Mediterranean, local game, and fresh vegetables are expertly handled. Trained by his father, a distinguished chef, Jean Tarrit has a culinary reputation of his own, expressing his personal creativity in the kitchen. The results are dishes delicately conceived. Specialties include salmon cooked with sorrel and duckling with green pepper kernels. The cost for a meal here is in the 220F ($30.34) to 360F ($49.64) range. A set meal is offered for 195F ($26.89). The restaurant is closed on Sunday night and Monday, and shuts down the first two weeks in January.

Le Chandelier, 3 rue Leenhardt (tel. 67-92-61-62). The comfortably decorated house which contains this elegant restaurant sits in a not-so-chic street near the train station. That detail seems to prod the long-established partnership of chef Jean-Marc Forest and maître'd Gilbert Furlan into ever greater heights of gastronomic success. At round tables decorated with flowers and elegant porcelain, you can enjoy the day's array of super-fresh specialties. These change frequently, but might include mousse of smoked eel with mint-flavored mussels, sweetbreads of lamb with crayfish in a vinaigrette sauce, veal kidneys in basil, a mosaic of hare with foie gras, and breast of duckling with shallots "en confit." A fixed-price bargain meal is offered at 110F ($15.17), another for 220F ($30.34). À la carte repasts cost from 280F ($38.61) and 340F ($46.89). Reservations are necessary, and meals are served except on Sunday, Monday, during a week's vacation in January, and for three weeks in August.

L'Olivier, 12 rue Aristide-Olivier (tel. 67-92-86-28). A Breton family maintains this small restaurant a short distance from the train station. The surrounding neighborhood isn't the most glamorous in town, but the well-prepared specialties seem to make a visit worth the trip. The limited number of menu items include fresh salmon with oysters, fricassée of lamb with thyme, warm terrine of monkfish, salad of lamb sweetbreads with extract of truffles, and sea bass with vegetables. The welcome you receive is warmhearted and sincere. Set menus are offered for 100F ($13.79) to 145F ($20), while à la carte meals usually cost around 220F ($30.34) for a complete repast. The restaurant is closed every Sunday and Monday. It is also closed from late July to late August.

8. Carcassonne

Evoking bold knights, fair damsels, and troubadours, the greatest fortress city of Europe rises against a background of snow-capped Pyrénées. Floodlit at night, it captures fairytale magic, but back in its heyday in the Middle Ages, all wasn't so romantic. Shattering the peace and quiet were battering rams, grapnels, a mobile tower (inspired by the Trojan horse), quicklime, catapults, flaming arrows, and the mangonel.

Carcassonne, 57 miles southeast of Toulouse, consists of two towns, the **Ville Basse** ("Lower City") and the medieval **Cité**. The former has little interest, but the latter is among the major attractions in France, the goal of many a pilgrim. The fortifications consist of the inner and outer walls, a double line of ramparts.

The inner rampart was built by the Visigoths in the 5th century. Clovis, the king of the Franks, attacked in 506, but he failed. The Saracens overcame the city in 728, until Pepin the Short (father of Charlemagne) drove them out in 752. During a long siege by Charlemagne the populace of the walled city was starving and near surrender until a woman named Dame Carcas came up with an idea. According to legend, she gathered up the last remaining bit of grain, fed it to a sow, then tossed the pig over the ramparts. It is said to have burst, scattering the grain. The Franks concluded that Carcassonne must have unlimited food supplies and ended their seige.

The walls were further fortified by the viscounts of Trencavel in the 12th century and by Louis IX and Philip the Bold in the following century. However, by the mid-17th century Carcassonne's position as a strategic frontier fort was over. The ramparts decayed. In the 19th century the builders of the lower town began to remove the stone for use as material in new construction. But interest in the Middle Ages revived, and the French government ordered Viollet-le-Duc (who restored Notre-Dame in Paris) to repair and where necessary rebuild the walls. Reconstruction continued until recently.

Enclosed within the walls is a small populace. The **Cathedral of St. Nazaire** dates from the 11th and 12th centuries, containing some beautiful stained-glass windows and a pair of rose medallions. The nave is in the Romanesque style, but the choir and transept are Gothic. The organ, one of the oldest in southwest France, is from the 16th century. The tomb of Bishop Radulph is well preserved, dating from A.D. 1266.

WHERE TO STAY: Hôtel de la Cité, Place de l'Église (tel. 68-25-03-34), is the prestigious ivy-covered inn of Carcassonne, built within the city walls, adjoining the cathedral. Many of the accommodations open onto the ramparts and a garden. An adaptation of a church palace, the inn maintains the same medieval architectural heritage of thick stone walls and leaded Gothic windows. You enter into a long Gothic corridor-gallery leading to the lounge and dining room, the latter in strong colors with gilt fleurs-de-lis on the walls. Logs burn in the ceiling-high fireplace on nippy nights. A small Louis XV-style salon is an inviting spot, with antiques and red-and-cream tapestry panels. The bedrooms feature either antiques or reproductions. The price range varies along with the plumbing and the view. For the best doubles with private bath, you pay from 800F ($110.32), or if you're saving money, you are charged 700F ($96.53) for a double with a shower. Singles, with either bath or shower, range in price from 600F ($82.74). You can order a continental breakfast at the hotel or enjoy other meals costing from 175F ($24.13) to 320F ($44.13). The place is open from mid-April to mid-October.

Hôtel La Vicomte, 18 rue Camille Saint-Saens (tel. 68-71-45-45). The view from the windows of this recently designed building encompasses one side of the fortifications surrounding Carcassonne, as well as the parking lot flanking them. From the nearby Porte Narbonnaise, the hotel looks like a sprawling and interconnected series of Mediterranean houses, each with a red tile roof and a belt of greenery. Inside, you'll find 63 comfortable, modern bedrooms, containing conservative furnishings, air conditioning, color TV, radio, and telephone, as well as a personal safe. Singles cost from 340F ($46.89), doubles from 600F ($82.74). There's a swimming pool on the premises, plus a cooperative staff willing to advise guests about tours through the ancient city.

Hôtel Terminus, 2 Avenue du Maréchal-Joffre (tel. 68-25-25-00), is an old-style, very grand hotel whose furnishings by now have reached the age where they can be called antiques. Near the train station, the hotel maintains more than 100 spacious rooms, each of which offers views over the mountains, the Old City, or the river. About 70% of the bedrooms contain a private bath. Room prices quoted in the dignified reception area range from 165F ($22.75) in a single to 320F ($44.13) in a double. The hotel's restaurant, Relais de l'Écluse, offers good meals in a setting of grandeur that sometimes causes it to be filled just with sightseers. If it isn't too crowded, you might enjoy one of the table d'hôte menus at 65F ($8.97), 87F ($12), and 117F ($16.13). If you prefer to order à la carte, expect to pay around 195F ($26.89) for a full meal.

Hôtel du Donjon, 2 rue Comte-Roger (tel. 68-71-08-80), is well positioned, a little hotel big on charm—the best choice for a moderately priced accommodation in Carcassonne. It even has a garden. Built in the style of the old Cité, it lies behind a honey-colored stone exterior studded with windows containing iron bars. The interior is a jewel, reflecting the taste and sophistication of its owner, Madame Christine Pujol, who loves to collect antiques. Rather elaborate Louis XIV-style furniture graces the reception lounges, decorated with gilt-encrusted and tapestry-covered chairs. A new wing containing a block of rooms has been added, but in a medieval architectural style, and the older rooms have been renewed. All of the 30 units now contain a bath or shower along with a direct-dial phone. Doubles range in price from 220F ($30.34) to 320F ($44.13). A continental breakfast is served, and you can enjoy dinner in a rustic setting for 150F ($20.69). The hotel is closed from January 4 until the first of February.

Montségur, 1 Avenue Bunau-Varilla (Route de Pamiers) (tel. 68-25-31-41), is a stately old town house in the Lower City, resting under a mansard roof with dormers. The front garden is screened from the street by trees and a high wrought-iron fence. Monsieur and Madame Lucien Faugeras have furnished the hotel with antiques or reasonably good reproductions, avoiding that institutional look. Modern amenities include air conditioning and an elevator. The bedrooms are cheaper than you'd imagine from the looks of the place. A few doubles with shower go for as little as 300F ($41.37), although they range upward to 350F ($48.27) in a twin-bedded room with bath. A continental breakfast is available, and you can take your other meals at the highly recommended (see below) Le Languedoc restaurant nearby. Closed December 15 to January 15.

Hôtel du Pont-Vieux, 32 rue Trivalle (tel. 68-25-24-99). The central location —a few steps from the Pont Vieux and the medieval section of town—is the most attractive aspect of this 15-room hotel. All but one of the rooms contain a private bath, and each has a phone. Accommodations range in price from 165F ($22.75) in a single to 190F ($26.20) in a double. Vincent Bravo-Pierot is your host.

WHERE TO DINE: Logis de Trencavel, 286 Avenue du Général-Leclerc (tel. 68-71-09-53), is where the distinguished restaurateur Jean-Claude Rodriguez is the star of his own show. He has done what many chefs dream about— discovered an attractive inn where he can produce his specialties and have enough room to serve his guests properly. Just outside Carcassonne he has created this auberge, designed in the Languedoc style. An old stucco villa with a tile roof, the establishment is set back from the roadway and surrounded by its own garden, blossoming with petunias and geraniums. A raftered reception lounge, with dark beams and an open wood fireplace, leads to 12 bedrooms. Half board, required in high season, ranges in price from 280F ($38.61) to 400F ($55.16).

I hope you'll meet this lover of good food: his enthusiasm is unbounded, and he enjoys being appreciated. For 120F ($16.55), he offers a fixed-price luncheon or dinner. Other set menus are priced at 170F ($23.44) and 200F ($27.58). On the à la carte menu, you might begin your meal with a salad of gizzards and artichokes. Most first-time visitors ask for the cassoulet de Carcassonne, the region's most popular dish. The chef's dish is said to be the best in town. You might also prefer sea bass with a scallop-based mousseline or sole in tarragon, perhaps turbot with a fondue of small vegetables. Another well-known specialty is the confit d'oie carcassonnaise, which is goose meat delicately cooked in its own fat and kept in earthenware pots. Ordering à la carte is likely to run your tab up to 240F ($33.10). The restaurant is closed on Wednesday and from January 10 to February 10.

Le Languedoc, 32 allée d'Iéna (tel. 68-25-22-17), is the pride of Monsieur Lucien Faugeras and his son Didier, who also own the previously recommended 19th-century hotel, Montségur. Both are excellent chefs and have created a warm Languedoc atmosphere as a proper setting for their culinary repertoire. The inviting ambience is achieved by rough plaster walls, a beamed ceiling, an open brick fireplace, and provincial cloths draped over peasant tables. It's a real country tavern. You can order two set meals—a fine one for 100F ($13.79) and even more elaborate ones for 150F ($20.69) and 200F ($27.58), including service. His house specialty is le cassoulet au confit de canard (the world-famed stew made with duck cooked in its own fat). The paella valenciana is superb, but the pièce de résistance is tournedos Rossini, served with foie gras truffé (truffles, the Marquis de Cussy's "subterranean empress") and madeira sauce. A smooth dessert is the crêpes flambées Languedoc. If you order à la carte, expect to pay from 225F ($31.03). In summer you can dine out on a pleasant patio. The restaurant is closed Sunday night, Monday, from June 18 to July 3, and from mid-December to mid-January.

Auberge du Pont-Levis, La Cité (tel. 68-25-55-23), stands along a stone-paved street near the Porte Narbonnaise in the oldest part of the city. You can dine either in a Louis XIII dining room one floor above street level or on an outdoor terrace ringed with flowers. Henri Pautard, the owner and chef, is aided by his wife, Andrée. They serve generous portions of such well-flavored specialties as roast pigeon in a garlic sauce, filet of sole with a velouté of lobster, filet of sea bass with cabbage and smoked salmon, and a hearty cassoulet. Fixed-price menus cost between 120F ($16.55) and 260F ($35.85), while à la carte meals go from 280F ($38.61). The restaurant is closed on Sunday night and all day Monday.

9. Nîmes

Nîmes, the ancient Nemausus, is one of the finest places in the world for wandering among Roman relics. A busy industrial city today, about 27 miles southwest of Avignon, it is the gateway to the Rhône Valley and to Provence.

THE SIGHTS: Pride of Nîmes is the **Maison Carrée,** Place de la Comédie, built during the reign of Augustus. On a raised platform with tall Corinthian columns, it is one of the most beautiful and certainly one of the best-preserved Roman temples of Europe. It inspired the builders of the Madeleine in Paris, as well as Thomas Jefferson. The temple houses the **Musée des Antiques** (tel. 66-67-25-57), displaying antique works of art found at Nîmes, including Roman statues, bronzes, and mosaics. The *Venus of Nîmes,* with one arm missing, is one of the featured exhibits. Also exceptional are a bronze head and a statue of Apollo, plus a sumptuous exhibition, the "Frieze of Eagles."

The elliptically shaped **Amphitheater,** Place des Arènes, a twin to the one at Arles, is far more complete than the Colosseum of Rome. It is two stories high, consists of 60 arcades each, and was built of huge stones fitted together without mortar. One of the best preserved of the arenas existing from ancient times, it held more than 20,000 spectators who came to see gladiatorial combats and wolf or boar hunts. It's in good enough condition today to be used for bull-fights.

The **Jardin de la Fontaine,** at the end of the Quai de la Fontaine, was laid out in the 18th century, using the ruins of a Roman shrine. It was planted with rows of chestnuts and elms, adorned with statuary and urns, and intersected by grottos and canals—one of the most beautiful gardens of France. Adjoining the garden is the ruined **Temple of Diana** and the remains of some Roman baths. Over the park towers **Mont Cavalier,** surmounted by the **Tour Magne,** the city's oldest Roman monument, which you can climb for a panoramic view.

Nîmes also has a number of museums. My favorite is the **Musée des Beaux-Arts,** rue Cité-Foulc (tel. 66-67-25-57), containing paintings by Van Loo, Vernet, Watteau, Rubens, Canaletto, and some Rodin busts. Seek out in particular G. B. Moroni's fascinating *La Calomnie d'Apelle.* There's an interesting Gallo-Roman mosaic as well.

You might also visit the **Musée du Vieux Nîmes,** Place de la Cathédrale (tel. 66-36-00-64), housed in an episcopal palace from the 1600s. The museum is rich in antiques, including some pieces from the 17th century, and there are two salons relating to bullfighting, both in the Spanish and in the Provençal styles.

Finally, the Boulevard Amiral-Courbet leads to the **Porte d'Arles,** the remains of a Roman city gate erected during the reign of Augustus.

To visit the Roman monuments, you can buy one comprehensive ticket costing 20F ($2.76). The monuments are open from 9 a.m. to noon and 2 to 7 p.m. (till 5 p.m. off-season). The Amphitheater stays open in June, July, and August from 8:30 a.m. till 7:30 p.m. The museums are open from 9 a.m. till noon and 2 to 7 p.m. (2 to 5 p.m. off-season). In the off-season the monuments shut down on Tuesday.

Outside the City

The **Pont du Gard** is a Roman bridge spanning the Gard River. Its huge stones were fitted together without mortar, and it has stood the test of time. Consisting of three tiers of arches, it dates from about 19 B.C. Take Route N86.

About ten miles farther on lies **Uzès,** a historic city, the "Premier Duchy of France." Standing on a hill, it is full of narrow streets and the former mansions of aristocrats which encircle the **Duché** (tel. 66-22-18-96), a château with a Renaissance façade. The Duché dates from the 11th century, and can be visited from Palm Sunday to September 20. Hours are 9:30 a.m. to noon and 2 to 7 p.m. Off-season, visits are possible from 10 a.m. to noon and 2:30 to 5 p.m. It is closed on Monday except in summer. Admission is 18F ($2.48). The **Cathedral of St. Théodorit,** built mainly in the 17th century, is distinguished by its 12th-century **Fenestrelle,** a circular six-story bell tower with many windows. This campanile is unique in Mediterranean France.

HOTELS: Nîmes offers good accommodations in all price ranges.

The Upper Bracket

Impérator, Place Aristide-Briand (tel. 66-21-90-30), leads all others. It's near the city center and the Roman monuments, opposite Jardins de la Fontaine. The hotel's rear gardens are enticing. You can order lunch here, enjoying the private park, later walking along the graveled paths under shade trees. Bedrooms vary somewhat in character. The best have skillfully reproduced Provençal pieces. Most of them are old-fashioned in a pleasant way. Half of them have been renewed in a traditional way to preserve their character. Singles cost 300F ($41.37), the tariff rising to 550F ($75.63) in a double, including a continental breakfast. All rooms come with private bath or shower, plus toilet. Prices include taxes and service. The hotel is closed from January 15 to February 15.

Mercure Nîmes (formerly Sofitel Nîmes), Chemin de l'Hostellerie, Boulevard Périphérique Sud (tel. 66-84-14-55), lies outside the city proper, yet it is only about a five-minute drive from the arena and the Maison Carrée. It has a contemporary design, allowing for air-conditioning and soundproofing as well as private baths and attractively built-in furnishings. In all, 100 bedrooms are offered costing 320F ($44.13) to 380F ($52.40) either single or double and 550F ($75.63) for a suite. Taxes and service are included in the tariffs. Adjoining the hotel is a swimming pool area, a sun terrace, and a tennis court. The restaurant, Le Mazet, serves grills and specialties.

The Middle Bracket

Le Louvre, 2 Square de la Couronne (tel. 66-67-22-75), is near the arenas in a beautifully preserved and rustically decorated 17th-century villa. The hotel and restaurant are the property of Ruffino Hugette. Some of the well-equipped and air-conditioned bedrooms look out over an interior courtyard dotted with chairs and plants, while others have a view of the fountain in the plaza at the front. Room prices are 135F ($18.62) in a single, 300F ($41.37) in a double. Michel Eve, the chef, is known for his sauces, which cover specialties such as suckling lamb with cèpes (flap mushrooms), civet of lobster, and mussels in puff pastry with zucchini. Set menus are offered for 62F ($8.55) to 180F ($24.82), while à la carte meals cost around 250F ($34.58). The hotel and restaurant are open all year long.

Le Cheval Blanc, Place des Arènes (tel. 66-67-20-03), lies behind a stark façade directly opposite the arena. You enter a classical and large reception hall furnished with Provençal pieces. The dining room is impressive, with fine furniture plus plenty of silver and crystal. Most of the bedrooms are soundproof, and a few have air conditioning and television. The furniture is mainly Directoire, with assorted murals and tapestries. The baths are tile, the walls covered with special matching paper. A single with shower is 220F ($30.34), rising to 300F ($41.37) in a double with a complete bath.

Carrière, 6 rue Grizot (tel. 66-67-24-89), has been modernized. The furnishings are functional, not stylish. A single with shower costs 160F ($22.06). Doubles, all with bath, go for 280F ($38.61). The restaurant, with light-wood tables and chairs, provides set menus—the cheapest one at 55F ($7.56), the most expensive one at 115F ($15.86).

The Budget Range

Hôtel l'Amphithéâtre, 4 rue des Arènes (tel. 66-67-28-51), stands on a narrow, quiet street just behind the Arènes. It offers 21 rooms, which are furnished either with antiques or modern pieces. Every room has its own color scheme, with matching carpeting, bedcovers, and curtains. Two-thirds of the rooms contain private bath. A single with private bath or shower is priced from 85F ($11.72) to 130F ($17.93). A double with a complete bath goes for 145F ($20) to 175F ($24.13). Families, especially those traveling with children, may want to rent a room for three or four with complete bath at 200F ($27.58).

Menant, 22 Boulevard de l'Amiral-Courbet (tel. 66-67-22-85), is on one of the main boulevards, about 300 yards from the Maison Carrée. It's a little corner hotel, offering moderately priced, comfortably furnished rooms. The decor is modern, and the plumbing has been much improved in recent years. The simplest singles rent for 85F ($11.72). Doubles with private bath go for 210F ($28.96). You can order breakfast, the only meal served.

RESTAURANTS: Au Chapon Fin, 3 rue Château-Fadaise (tel. 66-67-34-73), is a tavern-style restaurant about two blocks from the arena, opening onto a little square behind St. Paul's Church. It's nicely decorated, with beamed ceilings, pictures on the walls, small lamps, and a white-and-black stone floor. The owner's wife comes from Alsace, which explains the many Alsatian specialties on the menu. On the à la carte menu you can order such dishes as a salmon mousse, foie gras d'oie-truffé d'Alsace, and a confit d'oie. The most outstanding of the chef's specialties, in my opinion, are filet de St-Pierre aux morilles (morel, a variety of mushroom), and entrecôte périgourdine. Each day a plat du jour is featured. On my most recent rounds, I was treated to a lapin (rabbit) provençal with gratin dauphinois (sliced potatoes, baked with egg, cheese, and milk). The cost? Only 90F ($12.41). The proprietor makes his own confit d'oie from geese direct from Alsace. Another set meal goes for 130F ($17.93) and a gargantuan repast for 220F ($30.34), and each offers a wide choice. Closed on Tuesday.

San Francisco, 33 rue Roussy (tel. 66-21-00-80), is the creative statement of a duet of young Frenchmen who vastly appreciated the time they spent in America. Jean-Marie Lagrange (who trained for several years as a butcher) and his partner, Michel Hermet, serve juicy steaks, chops, and filets in an informally pleasant decor guaranteed to make a visitor feel at home. Your meal might begin with a shrimp-stuffed avocado or a tender salad of grapefruit and crayfish segments. Full à la carte meals cost 135F ($18.62) to 170F ($23.44), and are served daily except Tuesday. On weekends, the establishment is open until late but closes at lunchtime. Annual vacation is for two weeks in February and two weeks in August. The location is in the center of town near Place de la Couronne.

Restaurant Nicolas, 1 rue Poise (tel. 66-67-50-47), is about as local a restaurant as you'll find. It's usually filled with the regular customers of the family running it. Part of its popularity stems from the attractive prices charged for the specialties, which include a bourride known all over town and a wide array of fish and meat dishes. Fixed-price menus are offered for 82F ($11.31) and up, while à la carte meals begin at 150F ($20.69). The place is closed Monday, the first two weeks of July, and from just before Christmas to the middle of the first week in the New Year.

10. Aigues-Mortes

South of Nîmes you can explore a lot of the Camargue country by car. The most rewarding target in this curious landscape is Aigues-Mortes, the city of the "dead waters." In the middle of dismal swamps and melancholy lagoons, Aigues-Mortes is the most perfectly preserved walled town in France. Four miles from the sea, it stands on four navigable canals. Once Louis IX and his crusaders set forth from Aigues-Mortes, then a thriving port, the first in France to be built on the Mediterranean. The walls, which still enclose the town, were constructed between 1272 and 1300. The **Tour de Constance** is a model castle of the Middle Ages, its stones looking out on the marshes today, perhaps recalling the former greatness of the port. If you don't mind the climb of some 50 or more steps, a wide panoramic view unfolds once you're at the top. The ramparts are open in summer from 9 a.m. to noon and 2 to 6:30 p.m. Off-season hours are 10 a.m. to noon and 2 to 5 p.m. Admission is 21F ($2.90).

FOOD AND LODGING: Hostellerie Remparts, 6 Place d'Armes (tel. 66-51-82-77), is an ancient inn where the cookery is noteworthy for its regional dishes, the atmosphere in the lounge is colorful, and the bedrooms are warm, inviting, and most comfortable. Each of the traditionally furnished bedchambers comes with its accompanying private bath, and you'll pay 300F ($41.37) in a single, that tariff going up to 450F ($62.06) in a double. As there are only 19 rooms, you must reserve well in advance. The food is excellent, set menus going for 120F

($16.55), although à la carte dining bills come to an average of 160F ($22.06). Specialties include aiguillettes de canard (duckling), gigot de mer aux herbes de Provence, and salade gourmande au foie gras frais. The inn, which stands at the foot of the Tower of Constance, doesn't serve meals on Monday off-season and is closed entirely in November, for the first half of December, and in January.

St-Louis, 10 rue de l'Amiral-Courbet (tel. 66-53-72-68), is a small inn near Place St-Louis. There are 23 bedrooms, attractively furnished and containing private baths. Rooms, rented either as a single or a double, run in price from 210F ($28.96) to 250F ($34.48). Even though it is modest, the amenities and facilities are more than adequate, and you can not only sleep well here but dine well too. Menus cost from 100F ($13.79) to 190F ($26.20). The cooking is regional. The restaurant is closed on Wednesday off-season, and the inn is closed from January 1 to March 1.

Camargue, 19 rue de la République (tel. 66-53-86-88), is the scene of whatever nighttime activities there are in "the city of dead waters." Downstairs is a charming and elegant restaurant with a patio in an old house. There the owner offers some excellent meats done to perfection on an open-air grill, and local dishes including game. Guests dine under brightly lit fig trees in season. A set meal costs 130F ($17.93) and is a good one, hearty, satisfying, and filling. The restaurant is closed from early January to early February and on Monday in the off-season.

Chapter XXII

PROVENCE

1. Îles d'Hyères
2. Toulon
3. Marseille
4. Aix-en-Provence
5. Vauvenargues
6. Arles
7. Fontvieille
8. Les Baux
9. St-Rémy-de-Provence
10. Avignon
11. Gordes
12. Orange
13. Châteauneuf-du-Pape

PROVENCE, IN SOUTHEAST France, has been called a bridge between the past and present. Yesterday blends with today in a quiet, often melancholy way.

The Greeks and Romans founded cities here, complete with Hellenic theaters, Roman baths, amphitheaters, and triumphal arches. Medieval man erected Romanesque fortresses and Gothic cathedrals. By the 19th century the light and landscapes of Provence were attracting such illustrious painters as Cézanne and Van Gogh.

Despite changes over the years, withered black cypresses and dark-haired, hazel-eyed Provençal people remain. And the howling laughter of the mistral will forever be heard through broad-leaved plane trees.

Provence has its own language and its own customs. Naturally it has its own wines, ranging from elegant Châteauneuf-du-Pape to vins de pays, and its own dishes, such as ratatouille and bouillabaisse.

A part of Provence, the glittering Côte d'Azur, will be dealt with in the chapter on the French Riviera. Provence is bounded on the north by the Dauphiné, on the west by the Rhône, on the east by the Alps, and on the south by the Mediterranean.

1. Îles d'Hyères

Lying off the Riviera in the Mediterranean is a little group of islands enclosing the southern boundary of the Hyères anchorage, from south of Le Lavandou westward to south of Hyères. During the Renaissance, they were called the Îles d'Or from a golden glow sometimes given off by the rocks in the sunlight. The tranquil islands today give no reflection of the periods of attacks by pirates and Turkish galleys, British fleet activity, and landing of Allied troops during World War II.

The islands are reached by a short boat trip from the mainland, with all vehicles left behind. There is no vehicular traffic on the islands, except for bicycles and other means needed for necessary municipal activities. The two largest Îles d'Hyères are national parks dedicated to the preservation of the flora and fauna of the land and the sea world. They are Île de Porquerolles and Île de Port-Cros. The islands are usually warmer in winter and cooler in summer than the Riviera mainland, with most hotels being open from mid-April to the end of September. Restaurants operate on longer schedules.

ÎLE DE PORQUEROLLES: This is the largest and westernmost of the Îles d'Hyères, with a rugged south coast, the north strand being made up of sandy beaches bordered by heather, scented myrtles, and pine trees. The island is about 5 miles long and 1¼ miles wide.

You can get here by ferryboat from many of the seaports along the Côte d'Azur. From **La Tour Fondue** on the Giens peninsula, departures are every half hour in high season, with five crossings per day in the off-season. The crossing takes 15 minutes and costs 42F ($5.79). For information, call 94-58-21-81 in La Tour Fondue. From **Cavalaire** there are two or three weekly crossings between June and September. Round-trip fare is 68F ($9.38). Call 94-64-08-04 in Cavalaire for information. From the **Port de la Plage d'Hyères,** there are six daily crossings, each taking 30 minutes. Round-trip passage is 48F ($6.62). For information, call 94-57-44-07 in Hyères. Crossings are made from **Le Lavandou** from June 10 to September 1 daily, taking one hour. The charge is 68F ($9.38) for a round trip. Phone 94-71-01-02 in Le Lavandou. Between mid-June and October 1, two or three daily trips are made from **Toulon,** each taking one hour. The fare for a round-trip is 65F ($8.97). Information is available from the Service Maritime Touristique Varois, quai Stalingrad in Toulon (tel. 94-92-96-82).

Food and Lodging

Mas du Langoustier (tel. 94-58-30-09) is a resort hotel on the western tip of the island, overlooking a lovely bay ringed with pine trees. It's about 2¼ miles from the port, set in a large park complete with tennis courts. The Mas has guests picked up at the jetty in a covered wagon and transported along a bumpy road to the resort, transformed from an old farm. Even in its farm days, it had notable guests, including Georges Simenon and Jean Giraudoux. During World War II, it was for a short time headquarters for the U.S. Army and Gen. George Patton. Only full-board guests are accepted, for rates ranging from 400F ($55.16) to 550F ($75.63) per person daily. If you just drop in for a meal, expect to pay from 150F ($20.69). Try the loup (sea bass) with Noilly Prat in puff pastry for a taste treat. The house wine is an agreeable island rosé, probably from the very vineyards you passed on your ride to the Mas. You can drink and dine on the hotel's terraces. Tranquility is the watchword at the Mas. It's open from May 1 to September 30.

If you prefer to stay right in the bustling (for the île) village of Porquerolles, I suggest **Le Relais de la Poste** (tel. 94-58-30-26), on the Place des Armes, a little square with a church, trees, café tables, and a boules ground. The pleasant little hotel offers 30 rooms, 19 of them with private plumbing. They are decorated in Provençal style, with loggias. The charge for bed and breakfast is from 275F ($37.92) in a single and from 420F ($57.92) in a double. The hotel has a good restaurant and a crêperie.

ÎLE DE PORT-CROS: Lush subtropical vegetation reminiscent of an island in the Caribbean makes this little dot of land in the Mediterranean a green paradise, 3 miles long and 1¼ miles wide.

To get here, you can take a ferry from three Cote d'Azur ports. From **Le Lavandou,** between Easter and October 20, there are from 2 to 12 daily crossings, with only 3 trips per week in low season. The voyage takes 50 minutes and costs 55F ($7.56). For information, call Cie Maritime des Vedettes "Îles d'Or" at 94-71-01-02 in Le Lavandou. Between June 10 and September 15, there's one crossing per day from **Cavalaire,** taking an hour and five minutes, costing 55F ($7.56). Call Cie Maritime des Vedettes "Îles d'Or" in Cavalaire at 94-64-08-04. From one to four crossings per day are made from **Port de la Plage d'Hyères,** requiring one hour and 15 minutes and costing 65F ($8.97). For information in Port d'Hyères, call Transports Maritimes et Terrestres du Littoral Varois (tel. 94-57-44-07).

Food and Lodging

Le Manoir (tel. 94-05-90-52) is an 18th-century mansion set in a park back from the port. From a seat on its lofty terrace, you can look far down into the azure-colored bay of Port-Cros, shaded by the fronds of the bamboo, eucalyptus, and oleander flourishing here. Only full-board guests are accepted in the 22 rooms, at rates ranging from 500F ($68.95) to 600F ($82.75) per person daily. The hotel has comfortable, snug nooks and crannies, lots of open fireplaces, and attractive, sometimes antique, furniture. The kitchen prepares an unpretentious, super-fresh array of well-conceived dishes for up to 20 diners at a time. You can enjoy a lobster and fish terrine, several kinds of temptingly seasoned meats, and fresh local fish with baby vegetables. The goat cheese comes from the region, and the dessert mousses are worth the calories. The Buffet family charges around 180F ($24.82) for a fixed-price meal. Dinner is served until 9 p.m. Both the hotel and its restaurant are open only from Easter to October.

ÎLE DU LEVANT: Another of the Îles d'Hyères, this one is 5 miles by three-quarters of a mile, mostly a long, narrow ridge. Monks once used this island as a granary and garden, but now it is occupied mostly by ruins and abandoned houses, except for the village of Heliopolis where nudists congregate in summer. The French Navy also has installations on the island. Some ferries from Le Lavandou and Cavalaire make stops here en route to Port-Cros.

2. Toulon

This fortress and modern town is the principal naval base of France, the headquarters of the Mediterranean fleet, lying 42 miles east of Marseille. A beautiful harbor, it is surrounded by hills and crowned by forts. The place is protected on the east by a large breakwater and on the west by the great peninsula of **Cap Sicié.** Projecting from Sicié is **Cap Cépet.** Separated by the breakwater, the outer roads are known as the **Grande Rade** and the inner roads are called **Petite Rade.** On the outskirts is a winter resort colony.

In Vieux Toulon, lying between the harbor and the Boulevard de Strasbourg (the main axis of town), there are many remains of the port's former days before it developed along more modern lines. Visit the **Poissonerie,** the typical Provençal-style covered market, which is busy and bustling in the morning with fishmongers and buyers. Another colorful market is called simply **Marché,** and it spills over onto the narrow streets around the Cours Lafayette. Go in the morning, when it is at its peak.

Also in old Toulon, the **Cathédrale Ste-Marie-Majeure** (St. Mary Major) was built in the Romanesque style in the 11th and 12th centuries, then much expanded in the 17th century. Its badly lit nave is Gothic, and the belfry and façade are from a much later period, the 18th century.

In contrast to the cathedral, tall modern buildings now line the **Quai Stalin-**

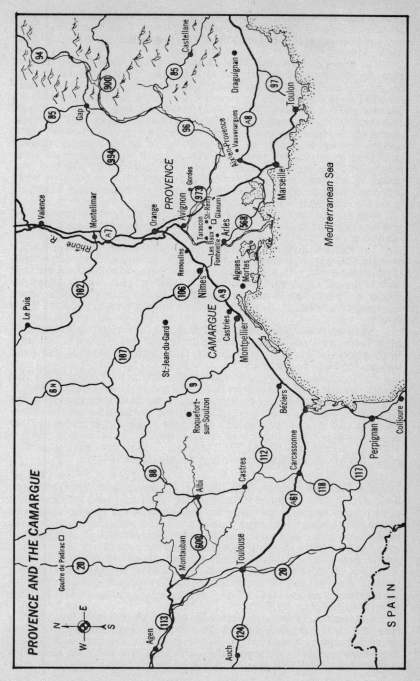

PROVENCE AND THE CAMARGUE

grad, which opens onto the Vieille d'Arse. On the Place Puget, look for the *atlantes* or caryatids, figures of men used as columns. These interesting figures support a balcony at the Hôtel de Ville and are also included in the façade of the naval museum.

The **Musée de la Marine,** Place Monsenergue (tel. 94-02-02-01), contains many figureheads and ship models and is open from 10 a.m. to noon and 1:30 to 6 p.m. daily except Tuesday and holidays, charging adults 14F ($1.93) and children 7F (97¢) for admission. An annex of the museum has been installed in the **Tour Royale,** Pointe de la Mître (tel. 94-24-91-00), built by Louis XII in the early 16th century. The seven circular pillboxes dug into the rock are now exhibition rooms which present figureheads, telamons which formerly adorned vessels, and the guns which armor them. There is a very old, heavy, decorated Chinese gun in one room. The first French navy bathyscaphe is exhibited on the tower esplanade. From June to September, hours are daily from 10 a.m. to 6 p.m. except Monday and holidays. From mid-September to the end of May, hours are from 1 to 6 p.m., although the only open days from November to March are in the Christmas and New Year's holiday season.

You can also tour the **Arsenal Maritime,** where guided excursions of the graving-docks and quays are conducted, leaving between 9 and 11 a.m. and between 2 and 4:30 p.m. Naturally, you tip the guide.

The **Musée de Toulon,** 20 Boulevard du Général-Leclerc (tel. 94-93-15-54), contains both old and contemporary works. The collection begins with a painting of a 13th-century Byzantine cross and continues on to embrace the works of such artists as Fragonard, David, Vuillard, and Van Loo. Also displayed are Egyptian, Greek, and Roman antiquities, and relics from prehistoric times. Charging no admission, the museum is open from 10 a.m. to noon and 2 to 6 p.m.

An hour or two before sunset, I'd suggest a drive along **La Corniche du Mont Faron,** a splendid boulevard along the lower slopes of Mont Faron. From this highway you'll have views of the busy port, the town, the cliffs, and in the distance the blue Mediterranean.

Earlier in the day you could board a funicular near the Frantel Hôtel. This téléphérique or cable car operates between 9 and 11:45 a.m. and 2:15 to 6:15 p.m., costing 25F ($3.45) per person for the ride up. In addition to enjoying the view once you get to the top, you can also visit the **Memorial National du Débarquement,** (tel. 94-93-41-01), which is open June to September from 9 to 11:45 a.m. and 2 to 6:45 p.m. The rest of the year hours are 9 to 11:30 a.m. and 2 to 5:45 p.m. Admission is 13F ($1.79). The museum documents, among other exhibits, the Allied landings in Provence in the summer of 1944.

WHERE TO STAY: **Frantel,** Tour Blanche, Boulevard du Amiral-Vence (tel. 94-24-41-57), is the best hotel at the naval port, even though it's 1½ miles north of the center, standing at the foot of the already-mentioned cable car that carries passengers up Mont Faron. Here you get excellent accommodations, with all the modern comforts you'd want. The rooms are nicely furnished, both the bedrooms and the public salons, and there are attractive gardens with terraces and a swimming pool. One hundred streamlined accommodations are rented, costing 320F ($44.13) to 390F ($53.78) in a single, 370F ($51.02) to 440F ($60.68) in a double. The hotel also offers a restaurant, Le Tour Blanche, with a panoramic view, serving a set meal for 150F ($20.69) and up. The restaurant is closed for lunch both Saturday and Sunday.

La Corniche, 1 Littoral Frédéric-Mistral at Le Mourillon (tel. 94-41-39-53), is an attractive hotel just opposite the Port St-Louis. On the premises you'll find an interior garden dotted with towering evergreens and about two dozen rooms, each with its own bath, telephone, and TV. A single costs from 240F ($33.10); a double, from 350F ($48.27). Set menus in the restaurant range from 105F

($14.48) to 180F ($24.82). The hotel is open all year, although the restaurant is closed Sunday night, Monday, and from mid-January to March.

The **Maritima,** 9 rue Gimelli (tel. 94-92-39-33), lies only a short walk from the railway station and a few minutes from Jardin Alexandre-1ᵉʳ. Its 50 rooms are modestly furnished but well kept and comfortable, costing 85F ($11.72) in a single, 200F ($27.58) in a double. There's no restaurant, but you can order breakfast.

WHERE TO DINE: **Le Dauphin,** 21 bis rue Jean-Jaurès (tel. 94-93-12-07), serves the best food in Toulon. Alain Biles is an advocate of La Nouvelle Cuisine. For years he worked at some of the most prestigious restaurants in Paris, including Lasserre, Lucas Carton, and Jacques Cagna. He believes in using only the freshest products of any given season. Each day he offers a set menu of four courses, costing 200F ($27.58), and it is also a good idea to look over his *suggestions du jour*. These latter dishes depend upon his inspiration of the moment. The menu, backed up by a well-selected wine cellar, is rich and varied, the dishes depending on the creative cookery of Monsieur Biles. He always has a selection of fish, such as scallops, filets of red mullet (often flavored with thyme, basil, and a fondue of tomatoes), salmon, and poissons du jour. His meat selections range from duck breast to pigeon to a filet of beef often served with foie gras. The restaurant is closed Saturday for lunch, on Sunday, in July, and again in February.

Le Lutrin, 8 Littoral Frédéric-Mistral (tel. 94-42-43-43). If there's a celebrity in Toulon, chances are he or she will dine here in the evening. The restaurant is in a converted 19th-century villa that architectural purists call Napoléon III. It overlooks the ocean traffic at Le Mourrillon, southeast of the center of Toulon. In fair weather, guests dine in the garden, or they can retreat inside to the elegantly furnished dining room. Bernard Chaté prepares such specialties as papillote of rascasse (that's translated as a hogfish), and pigeon in truffle juice, along with salmon and turbot dishes. A table d'hôte menu is offered for 105F ($14.48), while à la carte meals cost 150F ($20.69) to 250F ($34.48), not counting a selection from the excellent wine list. Meals are served every day but Saturday.

Madeleine, 7 rue des Tombades (tel. 94-92-67-85), offers the best set menu in town, at 80F ($11.03), or you can order à la carte, a meal starting at 200F ($27.58). The owners, the Belloumeau family, take great pride in their cuisine, yet they refuse to raise their prices. Because of that, they nearly always have a full house. Their restaurant occupies a building dating from the 13th century, just a few steps from the cathedral. You get not just Provençal dishes but also Bordelaise specialties and other cuisine derived from regions throughout France. Featured selections include escalope of fresh salmon with a champagne sabayon, cassoulet of stuffed goose neck, crab bisque, confit of veal kidneys, duckling à la mousseline de foies, and tournedos béarnaise. The establishment's Provençal-style dining room is closed Tuesday night, Wednesday, and in June.

3. Marseille

Bustling Marseille is the second city of France in size but the premier port of the country. A crossroads of world traffic, the city is ancient, founded by Greeks from the city of Phocaea, near present-day Izmir, Turkey, in the 6th century B.C. The city is a place of unique sounds, smells, and sights. It has seen wars and much destruction, but trade has always been its raison d'être.

Perhaps its most common association is with the national anthem of France, "La Marseillaise." During the Revolution, 500 volunteers marched to Paris, singing this rousing song along the way. The rest is history.

Many visitors never bother to visit the museums, preferring to absorb the unique spirit of the city as reflected on its busy streets and at its sidewalk cafés, particularly those along the main street, **Canebière.** The street, lined with hotels, shops, and restaurants, is filled with sailors of every nation and a wide range of foreigners, especially Algerians. It winds down to **Vieux-Port,** dominated by the massive neoclassic forts of **St-Jean** and **St-Nicholas.** The port is filled with fishing craft and yachts, and is ringed with seafood restaurants offering that specialty of Marseille, bouillabaisse. The Nazis blew up the old quarter in 1943, destroying the narrow streets and subterranean passages (and the houses of prostitution).

Motorists can continue along to the **Corniche Président-J-F-Kennedy,** a promenade running for about three miles along the sea. You pass villas and gardens along the way, and have a good view of the Mediterranean as well. To the north, the **Port Moderne,** the "gateway to the East," is man-made. Its construction began in 1844, and a century later the Germans destroyed it. Motorboat trips are conducted along the docks.

From **Quai des Belges** at Vieux-Port you can take one of the motorboats on a 20-minute ride to **Château d'If,** the round trip costing 25F ($3.45). Boats leave about every 15 minutes. On the sparsely vegetated island, François I built a fortress to defend Marseille, the place later housing a state prison that sheltered such illustrious guests as Mirabeau. Carvings by Huguenot prisoners can still be seen inside some of the cells. Alexandre Dumas used the château as a setting for *The Count of Monte Cristo,* although the adventure he invented never took place here. Its most famous association—that with the legendary *Man in the Iron Mask*—is also apocryphal. It is open in summer from 8 a.m. to noon and 1:30 to dusk. Off-season, that is, from October to May, it closes at 4 p.m.

A futuristic touch for Marseille is the 17-story **Cité Radieuse,** Boulevard Michelet, an avant-garde housing development and a landmark in modern architecture designed by the late Le Corbusier, the Swiss architect who introduced influential concepts in functional architecture. Built between 1947 and 1952, and also known as Unité d'Habitation, it is considered the first structure of its kind. Its flawed units have been much criticized, but they are credited with ushering in city planning in France.

MUSEUMS, CHURCHES, AND VIEWS: The **Palais Longchamp,** Place Bernex, was built in the era of the Second Empire. With its spectacular fountain and colonnade, it is one of the most scenic oases in Marseille. In back is a **Jardin Zoologique** with an exceptional collection of birds. Housed in a northern wing of the palace is the **Musée des Beaux-Arts** (tel. 91-62-21-17), displaying a vast array of paintings, both foreign and domestic, from the 14th through the 20th centuries. The ground floor exhibits paintings by Monticelli (a 19th-century artist), including his *Les Flamants,* plus works of other lesser-known Provençal artists. Some 80 sculptures and objects of art, all African, were recently bequeathed to the museum and are displayed in a special room on the ground floor. The museum also shows works by Corot, Millet, Vuillard, Ingres, David, Courbet, Perugino, Philippe de Champaigne *(The Ascension),* Puget *(The Baptism of Clovis),* and Rubens *(Wild Boar Hunt).* Interesting Dufy cubist landscapes plus a collection of other charming works by that artist are also on display, as is a gallery of sculpture by Pierre Puget (1620–1694). One salon on the second floor is devoted entirely to the works of Honoré Daumier, the French caricaturist and painter who was born in Marseille in 1808. Displayed are satiric lithographs and 36 bronzes of the series known as *The Parliamentarians.* The museum is open from 10 a.m. to noon and 2 to 6 p.m. (closed Tuesday and on Wednesday morning). Admission is 6F (83¢), free on Sunday morning. Students are admitted free at all times.

Nearby is the **Musée Grobet-Ladabié,** 140 Boulevard Longchamp (tel. 91-62-21-82), housed in a mansion and containing what was once a private collection, bequeathed to the city in 1923. It possesses exquisite Louis XV and Louis XVI furniture, as well as an outstanding collection of medieval Burgundian and

Provençal sculpture, including capitals from Notre-Dame-des-Doms at Avignon. A music salon displays antique violins, bagpipes, and guitars, plus a letter from Beethoven. Paintings on view are by Monticelli, Corot, and Daubigny. Other exhibits include 17th-century Gobelins tapestries, 15th-century German and Flemish paintings, and 17th-century faïence. The museum is open from 10 a.m. to noon and 2 to 6:30 p.m. (closed Tuesday and on Wednesday morning). Admission: 5F (69¢). Students are admitted free.

At the **Musée Cantini,** 19 rue Grignan (tel. 91-54-77-75), the temporary exhibitions and works of contemporary art often exceed the permanent collection. Housed in what was once a private mansion of the 17th century, this museum is devoted mainly to the most outstanding examples of Marseille and Moustiers pottery, including a superb fountain by Leroy and works by Veuve Perrin, who often used fish in his motifs. Opening onto a beautiful courtyard, the museum may be visited from 10 a.m. to noon and 2 to 6:30 p.m. for an entrance fee of 5F (69¢). Closed Tuesday and on Wednesday morning.

Musée du Vieux-Marseille (tel. 91-90-80-28), in the Maison Diamantée, rue de la Prison, near the Town Hall, is a historical and folklore museum known for its collection of *santons,* little statuettes made of colored clay representing characters associated with the Nativity. They are traditionally made by a few families living in the outskirts, the models and molds passed down from generation to generation. The *santons* appear at a traditional fair in December in Marseille. Other exhibits include furniture, pottery, old maps and engravings, 19th-century paintings by Provençal artists, antique costumes, a scale model of Marseille in 1848, and a costume room. The museum is open from 10 a.m. to noon and 2 to 6:30 p.m., for an admission fee of 5F (69¢). Closed Tuesday and on Wednesday morning.

Musée des Docks Romains du Lacydon, Place Vivaux (tel. 91-73-21-60), is devoted to the remains of the Roman docks unearthed in the old quarter of town. Some discoveries came to light as a result of the German bombings of the port in World War II. There is an outstanding collection of urns (photos show how undersea divers rescued them), plus fragments of Roman statuary and pottery. Open from 10 a.m. to noon and 2 to 6 p.m. (closes an hour earlier off-season), it charges an admission of 5F (69¢). Closed Tuesday and on Wednesday morning.

The **Musée d'Histoire de Marseille,** Centre Bourse, Square Belsunce (tel. 91-90-42-42), is an unusual museum, and one of the city's newest. You're allowed to wander through an archeological garden where excavations are still going on, as scholars attempt to learn more about the ancient town of Massalia, which was founded by Greek sailors. Of course, many of the exhibits, such as old coins and fragments of pottery, only suggest their former glory. To help you more fully realize the era, you're aided by audio-visual exhibits, and the museum has a free exhibition room and a library as well. You can also see what's left of a boat that was dug up on the site. Visitors are received daily from 10 a.m. to 7 p.m. except on Sunday and Monday, and pay 3F (41¢) for the privilege.

For a city as ancient as Marseille, antique ecclesiastical monuments are few. However, the seemingly fortified **Basilique St-Victor** has a crypt that dates from the 5th century, when the church and abbey were founded by St. Cassianus. The crypt, which also reflects work done in the 10th and 11th centuries, may be visited from 10 to 11 a.m. and 3 to 6 p.m. (on Sunday from 3 to 6 p.m. only). Admission is 5F (69¢). With its battlemented towers, the present church is from the 11th century. It's reached by going out the Quai de Rive-Neuve (near the Gare du Vieux-Port).

There are two cathedrals on Place de la Major, near Old Marseille. Their domes and cupolas may remind you of Istanbul. The **Ancienne Cathédrale de la Major** dates chiefly from the 12th century, having been built on the ruins of a Temple of Diana. In its left aisle is the Chapel of St. Lazare, in the early Renaissance style. Nearby is a Lucca della Robbia bas-relief. The newer edifice, **Cathédrale de la Major**, was one of the largest churches built in Europe in the 19th century, some 450 feet long. Its interior is adorned with mosaic floors and red-and-white marble banners, and the exterior is in a bastardized Romanesque/Byzantine style.

The landmark **Basilique de Notre-Dame de la Garde**, Place du Colonel-Edon, crowns a limestone rock overlooking the southern side of Vieux-Port. It was built in the Romanesque/Byzantine style popular in the 19th century, and was topped by a 30-foot-high gilded statue of the Virgin. The pilgrimage to this sanctuary dates from 1214. Visitors come here not so much for the church as for the panoramic vista—best seen at sunset—from its terrace. Spread out before you are the city, the islands, and the sea. About 700 feet below, on the same hill, near where tour buses park, is a World War II tank, the *Jeanne d'Arc*, destroyed by a German shell on this very spot during the battle of Liberation of Marseilles, August 25, 1944. Motorists can drive to the site, and pedestrians can take bus 60, which runs every half hour from Vieux-Port. A restaurant here serves from 7 a.m. to 8 p.m. in summer.

Another vantage point for those seeking a panoramic view is **Parc du Pharo**, a promontory facing the entrance to Vieux-Port. You stand on a terrace overlooking **Château du Pharo**, built by Napoléon III for his empress, Eugénie. Fort Saint-Jean and the old and new cathedrals can be seen clearly.

HOTELS: In general expect a poor lot. I'll deal with the exceptions, beginning in—

The Upper Bracket

Résidence Le Petit Nice, Corniche Kennedy/Anse de Maldormé (tel. 91-52-14-39), is considered among the best hotels and restaurants in Marseille. This has been a family-run enterprise since Jean-Paul Passédat and his elegant wife (who is still a visible presence on the premises) joined two suburban villas together in 1917. They're concealed behind a wrought-iron gate and a high wall. In fact the narrow approach to the establishment will take you past what looks like a row of totally private villas perched just above the rough seas, in a secluded area below the busy street that parallels the beach. There are 18 bedrooms, either in the main building or in an annex, which look out over the coastline and the statue-dotted garden with its P-shaped swimming pool. Rents range from 720F ($99.29) in a single to 1,100F ($151.69) in a double.

The restaurant of the hotel has provided a setting for the talents of Jean-Paul Passédat and Gerald, his son, whose imaginative culinary successes are served in a beautifully furnished dining room whose curved windows encompass a sweeping view of the Marseillaise shore and the rocky islands off its coast. Menu specialties include such items as royal daurade with a confit of eggplant, vinaigrette of rascasse (hogfish), sea devil with saffron and garlic, and many other gustatory triumphs. Table d'hôte menus are offered for 250F ($34.48) to 330F ($45.51), plus service, while à la carte meals cost 440F ($60.68) to 520F ($71.71). They're served every day except Monday until 10 p.m. From early October to the end of March the restaurant is also closed on Tuesday at lunchtime. Both the hotel and the restaurant are closed from January 1 to February 8.

Sofitel Marseille Vieux-Port, 36 Boulevard Charles-Livon (tel. 91-52-90-19), lies in a strategic position at the old port, all of its 219 bedrooms overlooking this active and colorful harbor. The hotel, at the Palais du Pharo, is the most outstanding choice for overnighting in the center of Marseille. It wisely takes advantage of its memorable location. All of its well-furnished bedrooms are individually air-conditioned and soundproof, providing streamlined comfort and such amenities as TV, radio, direct-dial telephone, and of course, a well-equipped private bath. Many of the modern chambers have private balconies where you can order breakfast at a garden table under a sun umbrella, with a view of the sea. Singles range in price from 435F ($59.99) to 650F ($89.64); doubles, from 550F ($75.63) to 1,000F ($137.90). The hotel has two restaurants: Les Trois Forts, which has an ambitious menu and a panoramic situation, charging from 220F ($30.34) for a meal; and Le Jardin, with an open terrace overlooking the sea and near the pool, where a good menu is presented for 130F ($17.93). There's a rather spacious piano bar, La Dérade, although you might prefer the other "bar panoramique," l'Astrolabe, which serves drinks.

Frantel, Centre Bourse, rue Neuve-St-Martin (tel. 91-91-91-29), one of the most modern hotels in town, resembles an enormous bronze cube looking out over the Greco-Roman ruins of the Jardin des Vestiges, a two-minute walk from the old port. It's in a spot adjoining a collection of about 70 boutiques called the Centre Bourse and contains both a formal and an informal restaurant and a black- and peach-colored bar where many of Marseille's shoppers drop in for a drink. A member of the English-speaking staff will offer single rooms for 480F ($66.19) to 530F ($73.09), and double rooms are available for 545F ($75.16) to 600F ($82.74). Each of the 200 units is soundproof and air-conditioned, and contains TV, radio, private bath, phone, mini-bar, and TV.

Hôtel Concorde-Palm Beach, 2 Promenade de la Plage (tel. 91-76-20-00), is a sprawling modern hotel complex set at the edge of the sea about a mile and a half east of the center of town. Popular with commercial travelers, it draws large numbers of professional clients (a doctors' convention when I last stayed here). One of the most sophisticated hotels in Marseille, and also one of the best, it tries to combine a seaside hotel and its resort facilities with a big-city hotel and its concomitant amenities. The interior is a tasteful blend of big windows, soothing autumn colors, expansive terraces, and unusual accessories that include covered aquariums set in front of leather couches. On the premises you'll find a sauna, a gym, an outdoor pool, and 145 slickly modern bedrooms done in a sort of international-modern style. Ideally, try for a bedroom with a balcony opening onto the sea. Singles are priced at 500F ($68.95) and doubles at 520F ($71.71). Meals in the grill room, Les Voiliers, start at a modest 120F ($16.55). Dinner at La Réserve is more elegant, with meals ranging upward from 180F ($24.82).

The Middle Bracket

Le Grand Hôtel Noailles, 66 La Canebière (tel. 91-54-91-48), has for years been one of the port's leading hotels. In its renovated bedchambers you have a choice of modern or traditional styles. The main lounge is tasteful, with ornate bas-relief walls, a draped Campagne ceiling, and Louis XV–style furniture. The wood-paneled bar, Le Samoa, with its Windsor chairs, old prints, and guns, seems more English. Twins with bath in the new section peak at 500F ($68.95). A single costs 300F ($41.37). The hotel's restaurant, Via Veneto, serves both a continental cuisine and Mediterranean specialties.

Le Concorde Prado, 11 Avenue de Mazargues (tel. 91-76-51-11), is the pacesetter in hotel design in Marseille. Created in the '70s, it is located away from the harbor in the newer section. Zippy bronze elevators take you to six floors of gadget-mad accommodations. Beside your bed is a master electronic-control panel. Bedrooms are often done in vivid plaids. You have a choice of rooms overlooking the busy street or else the garden with its reflection ponds. Singles go for 475F ($65.50); doubles are 520F ($71.71).

P.L.M. Beauvau, 4 rue Beauvau (tel. 91-54-91-00), is right at the old port, a most convenient hotel for tourists. This traditional hotel, under chain ownership, overlooks the Vieux-Port. It has an American bar and an excellent restaurant, which is run independently of the hotel. The lobby pays allegiance to Provence, but emphasis is on the good-size rooms, renting for 500F ($68.95) in a single, increasing to 620F ($85.50) in a double.

The Budget Range

La Résidence du Vieux-Port, 18 Quai du Port (tel. 91-91-91-22). This modern nine-story hotel is highly recommended to those who want to be directly on the port, in the center of Marseille's waterfront life. The entrance to the reception area is flanked by a pair of stone lions, which set the tone for the antiques and old sculpture scattered across the stone floor. Part of the decor includes four serpentine baroque columns serving as a room divider for one of the many secluded seating areas. A café and a breakfast room are on the second floor, while a well-designed bar occupies a separate room behind the lobby. If, however, you prefer to read your newspaper or drink your apéritif in privacy, you'll find many attractive nooks and crannies throughout the ground floor. Many of the 52 bedrooms have views over the old port, which will please you if you're a romantic. Most of the units contain private bath, although a few bathless rooms are offered for 110F ($15.17) in a single and 130F ($17.93) in a double. Rooms with complete private bath cost 230F ($31.72) in a single, 260F ($35.85) in a double.

Grand Hôtel Genève, 3 bis rue de la Reine-Élisabeth (tel. 91-90-51-42), provides a great deal of style and comfort for the francs charged. It's not far from the old port, and even though it doesn't have a restaurant, all of its bedchambers have accompanying private bath. Singles rent for 150F ($20.69), and doubles go for 320F ($44.13). There is a radio and individual refreshment bar in each bedroom. The attendant downstairs will direct you to a nearby public garage if you're driving.

La Résidence Bompard, 2 rue des Flots-Bleus (tel. 91-52-10-93), sits on a cliff at the outskirts of Marseille, a ten-minute drive along the coastal road, Corniche Président-J-F-Kennedy. A group of bungalow buildings with kitchenettes surround a large courtyard and garden. A Lebanese family welcomes guests, charging them 275F ($37.92) in a single, 325F ($44.82) in a double. All rooms have TV. The Bompard is best for motorists seeking a tranquil retreat.

RESTAURANTS: At restaurants in Marseille you'll eat some of the best seafood in Europe.

The Upper Bracket

Jambon de Parme, 67 rue La-Palud (tel. 91-54-37-98), is the leading Italian restaurant in Marseille. In fact, it's the leading restaurant, period. The cuisine of Lucien Giravalli is both classic and original. The wine list is extensive, the atmosphere exquisite, the decor a Louis XVI style, although complemented by framed engravings of Italian towns. The fried scampi and the homemade ravioli are as good as any you'd find in the homeland. The veal kidneys in a marsala sauce are exceptional. Or perhaps you'll try tortellini in a smooth cream sauce or filets of capon cooked with champagne. The soup with truffles is a masterpiece, and the sweetbreads with cream is yet another skillfully prepared dish. Naturally, there is ham from Parma. Expect to pay 250F ($34.48) to 325F ($44.82) for a memorable meal. The restaurant is closed on Sunday night and Monday, and from mid-July to mid-August.

Calypso, 3 rue des Catalans (tel. 91-52-64-00), is a fish restaurant right on the water where the old port meets the sea. Guests go here not only for the cuisine of Antoine Visciano but to watch ships and sunsets. The two featured main dishes are bouillabaisse and bourride provençale—both served here with lobster, which increases the price tremendously. You might, as an alternative, order fish soup first, then follow with loup (Mediterranean sea bass) with fennel. The homemade pastries are excellent. Expect to pay at least 320F ($44.13) to 350F ($48.27) for a complete meal. Closed Sunday, Monday, and in August.

Michel–Brasserie des Catalans, 6 rue Catalans (tel. 91-52-64-22), serves absolutely the finest bouillabaisse in Marseille, if you don't mind the shellacked lobsters and starfish on the walls. The Visciano family who run this place will also tempt you with their bourride, another type of fish stew with an aïoli sauce. This is one of the best oldtime restaurants in the port city, serving about everything that creeps and crawls through the Mediterranean. There are few mysterious sauces and fancy dishes. Rather, the culinary emphasis is on the flavor of the seafood. Spices are added discreetly. A meal averages around 320F ($44.13) to 350F ($48.27). The location is agreeable too, at one side of the old port, just beyond the Parc du Pharo. The restaurant is closed on Tuesday, Wednesday, and in July.

The Middle Bracket

Au Pescadou, 19 Place Castellane (tel. 91-78-36-01), is one of the finest restaurants in Marseille, specializing in *fruits de mer et de poissons,* although it's nowhere near the harbor. Rather, it's on a circular traffic hub in the downtown section close to the freeway to Nice. Overlooking a fountain and an obelisk, it can be identified by its open oyster stands on the sidewalk. Nearly all forms of crustaceans, including many indigenous only to Mediterranean waters, are here. It's hard to imagine fish fresher than that served by Barthélémy Mennella. A savory opener might be mussels stuffed with almonds. But for the greatest variety of tidbits, order the "hors d'oeuvres of the fisherman." Main-dish specialties include bouillabaisse de Marseille and gigot de lotte (a monkfish stewed slowly in a cream sauce with fresh vegetables). Try also the coquilles St-Jacques aux morilles (scallops cooked in a mushroom sauce). The cheapest way to dine here is to order one of the set menus, costing 140F ($19.31) or 155F ($21.38). If you order à la carte, expect to spend from 250F ($34.48) up, depending on the fish you select. The restaurant is closed in July and August, and on Sunday night.

The Budget Range

Chez Angèle, 50 rue Caisserie (tel. 91-90-63-35). Marseille is filled with cheap eating places, none of which is very recommendable. A local friend guided me to this little selection, which is most worthwhile if you're watching your francs. It's small, with a typically bistro ambience. Many of the regular customers may have already grabbed all the best tables when you get there, but give it a try anyway. Cookery is both Provençal and Italian, although the decor is more like something you'd expect to find in the hills outside Marseille. Alain Minassian, the owner and chef, doesn't mind if his clients only order a pizza. However, the menu includes well-prepared varieties of ravioli, tagliatelle, osso buco, escargots provençals, and Marseille-style tripe. Fixed-price menus cost 80F ($11.03), while à la carte meals average 120F ($16.55). The place is closed Sunday night and Monday.

Le Gréphan, 18 rue Rodolphe-Pollack (tel. 91-54-08-13), is a simple and likable restaurant where owner René Chanel works hard to create a relaxing ambience as well as specialties such as eggplant parmesan, terrine of trout, and savory meat dishes. Fixed-price menus are offered for 90F ($12.41) and 130F ($17.93), while à la carte meals cost more. The restaurant is closed Saturday, Sunday, for two weeks in February, and in August.

Cousin-Cousine, 102 Courts Julien (tel. 91-48-14-50). The primitive paintings which decorate the walls of this restaurant were as carefully chosen as the ingredients which go into the cuisine. Jean-Luc Sellam is the owner / chef, and each day he concocts his fresh specialties from whatever he found in the city's marketplaces to his liking. You might enjoy such lighthearted and modernized dishes as bouillabaisse of codfish, a stew of duckling with cabbage, and a mouthwatering salad of crayfish and asparagus. Many guests order the 110F ($15.17) fixed-priced menu which represents one of the better values in the neighborhood. There's an outdoor terrace perfect for warm weather dining. No meals are served Sunday and Monday, and during the first two weeks of October and the last two weeks of February.

Living on the Outskirts

At **Gémenos,** 14½ miles from Marseille, the **Relais de la Magdeleine** (tel. 42-82-20-05) is a fine country mansion at the foot of the Sainte-Baume mountain range. Surrounded by park and woodland, the hotel lies near the spot where Mary Magdalene is believed to have ended her days. (Her grotto has long been the site of veneration.) The *relais* offers 20 rooms with bath, costing from 375F ($51.71) to 600F ($82.74) for two persons. The inn has fine architectural details and appropriate furnishings. Over the fireplace in the entry hall is an old carving of the Virgin and Child, and throughout the mansion are portraits and scenic paintings. The drawing room has fine antiques. The rooms are appealingly furnished in a personal way. The *relais* also serves good meals, costing from 175F ($24.13), including such regional dishes as lamb cooked with the herbs of Provence and filet of sole Beau Manoir. There is a good-size swimming pool. Tennis is available 10 minutes away; golf, 20 minutes; and you can be at a bathing beach in 15 minutes. The inn is open from mid-March until the end of October.

4. Aix-en-Provence

The celebrated son of this old capital city of Provence, Paul Cézanne, immortalized the countryside nearby. Just as he saw it, Montagne Sainte-Victoire still looms over the town, although a string of high-rises has now cropped up on the landscape. The most charming center in all of Provence, the faded university town was once a seat of aristocracy, its streets walked by counts and kings. Aix still contains much of the atmosphere acquired in the 17th and 18th centuries before losing its prestige to Marseille, 20 miles to the south. The highlight of the season is its annual **music festival,** one of the best on the continent.

Its **Cours Mirabeau,** the main street, is one of the most beautiful in Europe. Plane trees stretch their leafy branches across the top to shade it from the hot Provençal sun like an umbrella, filtering the light into shadows that play on the rococo fountains below. On one side are shops and sidewalk cafés, on the other richly embellished sandstone hôtels (mansions) from the 17th and 18th centuries. Honoring Mirabeau, the French revolutionist and statesman, the street begins at the 1860 landmark fountain on **Place de la Libération.**

The **cathedral,** on Place de l'Université, is dedicated to Christ under the title Saint Sauveur, that is, Holy Savior or Redeemer. Its Baptistery dates from the 4th and 5th centuries, but the architectural complex as a whole has seen many additions. The cathedral contains a brilliant triptych, *The Burning Bush*, a work of Nicolas Froment in the 15th century. One side depicts the Virgin and Child, the other Good King René and his second wife, Jeanne de Laval.

You might also visit the **Chapelle Penitents-Bleus,** 2 bis rue du Bon-Pasteur. This 16th-century chapel was built in honor of St. Joseph on the ancient Roman/Aurelian road linking Rome and Spain. The chapel was restored by Herbert Maza, founder and former president of the Institute for American Universities.

Nearby in a former archbishop's palace is the **Musée des Tapisseries,** 28 Place des Martyrs-de-la-Résistance (tel. 42-23-09-91). Lining its white and gilded walls are tapestries made at the old factory at Beauvais de Natoire-le-Prince. Berain designed a fanciful and charming series of six, rich in amusing details, depicting such scenes as musicians and Bacchanalian revelry. Charging 12F ($1.66) admission, the museum is open from 9:30 a.m. to noon and 2:30 to 6 p.m. in summer, to 5 p.m. in winter. It is closed Tuesday and in January.

Up the rue Cardinale is the **Museum of Beaux-Arts,** Place Saint-Jean-de-Malte (tel. 42-38-14-70), also called Musée Granet-Palais-de-Malte. The museum owns mainly sketches, not a very typical collection of the great artist's work. Matisse contributed a nude in 1941. Housed in the former center of the Knights of Malta, the fine-arts gallery contains work by Van Dyck, Van Loo, portraits by Pierre and François Puget, Rigaud, Monticelli, and (the most interesting of all) a *Jupiter and Thetis* by Ingres. Ingres also did an 1807 portrait of the museum's namesake, François Marius Granet (1775–1849), showing him to be remarkably handsome. Granet's own works abound, along with engravings, prints, paintings, and watercolors by Cézanne. Yet another salon contains Celto-Ligurian statuary discovered at the Roman town of Entremont, plus archeological discoveries that are Egyptian, Grecian, and Etruscan. Hours are 10 a.m. till noon and 2 to 6 p.m. Admission costs 12F ($1.66). Closed Tuesday and in January.

Outside town, at 9 Avenue Paul-Cézanne, is the **Atelier de Cézanne** (tel. 42-21-06-53), the studio of the painter who is considered the major forerunner of cubism. Surrounded by a wall, the house was restored by American admirers. Repaired again in 1970, it remains much as Cézanne left it in 1906, "his coat hanging on the wall, his easel with an unfinished picture waiting for a touch of the master's brush," as Thomas R. Parker wrote. The atelier may be visited from 10 a.m. to noon and 2 to 5 p.m. daily except Tuesday and holidays. From June to September, it remains open till 6 p.m. Admission is 6F (83¢).

Even more recommended than a visit to Cézanne's studio, and much more than the Musée Granet's Cézanne mementos, is a walk along the **Route de Cézanne,** the D17, which winds eastward through the Provençal countryside toward the Sainte-Victoire. From the east end of the Cours Mirabeau, take rue du Maréchal-Joffre across Boulevard Carnot to Boulevard des Poilus, which becomes Avenue des Écoles-Militaires and finally the D17. The stretch between Aix and the hamlet of Le Tholonet is full of twists and turns where Cézanne often set up his easel to paint Although it is a longish hike (3½ miles), it is possible to do it at a leisurely pace by starting early in the morning. Le Tholonet has a café or two where you can rest and refresh yourself while waiting for one of the frequent buses back to Aix.

READER'S FOOTNOTE TO HISTORY: "The 17th and 18th centuries have indeed left a permanent stamp on the architecture and atmosphere of Aix, somewhat obscuring its earlier Roman and medieval history. Founded in 122 B.C. by a Roman general, Caius Sextius Calvinus, who named it Aquae Sextiae in his own honor, Aix was successively a Roman military outpost and then civilian colony, administrative capital of a province of the later Roman Empire, seat of an archdiocese, official residence of the medieval counts of Provence and thus its political capital. Even after Provence's union with France, Aix remained, until the French Revolution, a judicial and administrative headquarters. Aix's composite history is best reflected in its cathedral and in the City Hall bell tower just down the street: both incorporate architectural elements spanning the centuries from the Roman era to the 17th century. The cathedral's small and charming Romanesque cloister provides a tranquil oasis to visit." (Patricia Hagan, New Haven, Conn.).

Upper-Bracket Living

Paul Cézanne, 40 Avenue Victor-Hugo (tel. 42-26-34-73). The modest façade on a street of sycamores hardly prepares you for such a distinguished interior. Created by its director-proprietor, Georges Delorme, it is a special and tasteful world. Using antiques from his own house, he made every room distinguished. Your accommodation might have mahogany Victorian furniture, Louis XVI–style chairs, marble-topped fruitwood chests, gilt mirrors, and oil paintings. Handmade and hand-painted tiles make the baths consistently attractive. Singles with bath cost 400F ($55.16); doubles with bath cost 750F ($103.43). A recently built new floor is reserved for the most attractive deluxe rooms and suites of the hotel. A small breakfast room opens onto a rear courtyard. The lounge seems more like a private sitting room than the lobby of a hotel.

Hôtel P.L.M. Le Pigonnet, Avenue du Pigonnet par route de Marseille (tel. 42-59-02-90), at the edge of town, is a Provençal villa surrounded by verdant gardens. Behind the salmon-pink façade is an interior with provincial furnishings, either antiques or reproductions. There are 50 rooms, all with private bath or shower. Singles cost 500F ($68.95), with doubles going for 600F ($82.74). In the garden, you can have your breakfast set on a table under the colonnaded veranda overlooking the courtyard reflection pool. There is also a swimming pool. You can dine in summer under the deep shade trees or else at the hotel's restaurant, Le Patio, which offers both a table d'hôte and an à la carte menu, costing from 160F ($22.06) to 200F ($27.58).

The Middle Bracket

Negre Coste Hôtel, 33 Cours Mirabeau (tel. 42-27-74-22). This hotel is so popular with the dozens of musicians who flock to Aix for the summer music festivals that it's usually difficult to get a room at any price. Popularity like that is well deserved at this elegantly white-shuttered building with the 18th-century carvings around each of the window frames. The entrance is flanked with flowers cascading from a pair of jardinières, whose formal lines set the tone for the wide interior staircase, the marble portrait busts, and the huge Provençal armoire decorating the public rooms.

The bedrooms are high ceilinged and contain interesting antiques, plus views from the upper floors over the Cours Mirabeau or the old city. The rear bedrooms are quieter, but you'll find that those facing the front are somewhat protected from the noise by the buffer zone created by the plane trees that line the street. Bedrooms, suitable for one or two persons, range in price from 320F ($44.13) to 420F ($57.92), depending on the accommodation. All units have private bath. An in-house garage costs around 30F ($4.14) per night.

Hotel des Augustins, 3 rue de la Masse (tel. 42-27-28-59), was converted from the old Grands Augustins Convent, which was built in the 12th century. The reception desk is in a chapel. In the beautifully restored setting, the ribbed vault ceilings, stained-glass windows, dressed stone walls, and terracotta floors set off the Louis XIII furnishings. The ground floor is graced with oil paintings and watercolors in the lounge. The 30 spacious, soundproof bedrooms all have private bath, color TV, phone, drink cabinet, and automatic alarm-call facilities. Two of the units have private terraces. Singles cost from 310F ($42.75) to 440F ($60.68), doubles from 350F ($48.27) to 610F ($84.12), twins from 410F ($56.54) to 560F ($77.22), and triples from 490F ($67.57) to 690F ($95.15). The hotel has a private garage on the other side of the famous Place de la Rotonde, where you can rent a space for your car.

Résidence Rotonde, 15 Avenue Belges (tel. 42-26-29-88), is a contemporary hotel right in the heart of town. It has gone to considerable trouble to create a streamlined accommodation in which all is bright and cheerful. Occupying part of a residential building, it has an open spiral cantilevered staircase, with lots of molded plastic and chrome furniture. Doubles with twin beds and a complete bath are 300F ($41.37). Singles rent for 165F ($22.75). Tax and service are included in these prices, but breakfast is extra. The rooms are jazzy, with ornate patterned wallpaper, balloon lamps, Nordic-style beds, and, novelty of novelties, a wardrobe set on a revolving pole. There is no restaurant—just the red-and-gold breakfast room.

The Budget Range

Hôtel La Caravelle, 29 Boulevard du Roi-René (tel. 42-62-53-05). There's a bas-relief of a three-masted caravelle on the stucco façade of this conservatively furnished hotel a three-minute walk from the heartbeat of Cours Mirabeau. Since 1985, Mr. and Mrs. André Negre have maintained this beige structure, with its attractive bedrooms done in muted colors. The price of single rooms begins at 150F ($20.69), with doubles going for 200F ($27.58) to 250F ($34.48), depending on the accommodation. If you wish to take breakfast here, you will be served in the stone-floored lobby.

Hôtel La France, 63 rue Espariat (tel. 42-27-90-15), is conveniently situated in a 19th-century building at the Place des Augustins, around the corner from the Cours Mirabeau. You'll recognize it by its glass and wrought-iron canopy extending over the flagstone-covered square on which it sits. This five-story, two-star hotel offers tastefully modern bedrooms in a friendly setting, although streetside exposures can be noisy. The price of a room depends on the plumbing. Two persons pay 148F ($20.41) to 250F ($34.48), the latter with two beds and a complete private bath.

Hôtel Cardinal, 24 rue Cardinale (tel. 42-38-32-30), is a well-run 21-bedroom hotel that is one of the best bargains at Aix-en-Provence. Mrs. Chambaud and her daughter, Frédérique, will welcome you to their well-maintained hotel, furnished in part with antiques and other traditional pieces. Accommodations have either a large bed or twin beds, and the tariffs range from 180F ($24.82) to 240F ($33.10) a night. Breakfast, which costs extra, is the only meal served.

WHERE TO DINE: Les Caves Henri-IV, 32 rue Espariat (tel. 42-27-86-39), offers well-upholstered comfort in the depths of a 16th-century, air-conditioned cellar in the center of the oldest part of town. The frequently changing repertoire of La Nouvelle Cuisine comes from the sophisticated kitchens of chef Jean-Marc Banzo. Menu specialties, served below the vaulted stone ceilings that have been judiciously strengthened with modern concrete ribs, include sea bass with leeks, medallion of lotte with flan of eggplant and lime sabayon, veal kidneys with a confit of shallots, a mosaic of vegetables with purée of perfumed tomatoes, stuffed rabbit, and sea bass served with a mignonette of pepper on a bed of barely poached spinach. Fixed-price menus range from 155F ($21.38) at lunch. À la carte meals range from 250F ($34.48) and up. Monsieur Banzo closes his restaurant Sunday, Monday, and for part of August.

La Vendôme, 2 bis Avenue Napoléon Bonaparte (tel. 42-26-01-00). In the heart of Aix, near the most extravagant fountain in town, this might be the most elegant and sophisticated place to dine in all the city. You'll find a 1930s-style villa sheltered from the traffic around it by a wall and a gaily lit courtyard filled with urns, statues, flowers, a fountain, and cast-iron garden lamps. After passing through the wrought-iron gate, you'll choose a table either under the towering plane trees or inside the airy dining room. Specialties include filet of charolais, medallions of veal with basil, roast lamb arlésien, chateaubriand for two, filet of sole with grapefruit, pistou soup, poivrade of beef, and cassoulet of crab with morels. Table d'hôte menus are offered at 190F ($26.20) and 275F ($37.92), while à la carte meals range from 250F ($34.48) to 300F ($41.37). The establishment is closed Tuesday night as well as Wednesday except in July and August.

Restaurant de l'Abbaye des Cordeliers, 21 rue Lieutaud (tel. 42-27-29-47). Some 16 years ago, members of the Arzéno family set up what was to become a chic restaurant inside the walls of an 11th-century cloister. You'll be impressed with the thick stone walls, the stucco accents, the high timbered ceilings, and the rows of copper pots adding a rustic overtone to the savory cuisine. I personally prefer the inner of the two rooms, although there's room for an additional 20 tables in the garden in summer, when the seating capacity practically doubles. Fixed-price menus are offered at 105F ($14.48) and 160F ($22.06), or if you prefer to order à la carte, expect to spend 200F ($27.58) to 250F ($34.48), depending on which of the specialties you choose. These might include young rabbit with mushrooms, stewed boar with polenta, roast thrush on toast, deviled snails, mushroom brouillade, and truffled scallops. The menu is in English. The restaurant closes every year from October to November. In winter it closes Monday night and Tuesday and in summer Tuesday and Wednesday at lunchtime.

La Rotonde, 2A Place Jeanne-d'Arc (tel. 42-26-01-95), enjoys the most central position in the heart of Aix-en-Provence. It is a white-shuttered villa with a canopy over its garden terrace. Its tables are placed to give the diners a view of the fountain in the middle of the roundabout. The chef offers a number of excellently prepared appetizers, followed by regional specialties and many inventive new dishes, all under the direction of Pierre-Paul Alfonsi, who has brought new life to this once-staid establishment. He's fond of fish, as reflected by his menu, which is likely to include fresh oysters, followed by a fricassée of sole with a garlic confit. Monkfish, daurade, and sea bass appear with regularity on the menu. But you can also order excellent meat dishes, including beef with shallots, chicken suprême with artichokes and a watercress sabayon, and the main specialty, shoulder of lamb provençal with gratin dauphinois and garlic tomatoes (there's a 30-minute wait for this superb dish). Menus begin modestly at 140F ($19.31). To dine à la carte costs 170F ($23.44) to 225F ($31.03). The restaurant is open all year.

If you're seeking something less expensive, try the **Brasserie Royale,** 17 Cours Mirabeau (tel. 42-26-01-63), renovated in the modern style. Right on this plane-tree-lined boulevard, it is brassy and animated, invariably crowded at mealtimes. With not the least bit of pretense, it dispenses excellent regional cooking at moderate prices. There is an interior dining room, but most habitués gravitate to the glass-enclosed section on the sidewalk under the canopy. Informality reigns, the bustling waiters offering you set dinners for 65F ($8.97) and 95F ($13.10), plus service. You're served such hearty fare as tripe provençale, daube provençale (one of my favorite dishes here), and bourride provençale.

The chef is known for his plats du jour, which on my latest rounds included such dishes as lapin (rabbit) chasseur, paella, osso buco, and couscous. If you're dining light, you might enjoy one of four different kinds of omelets. Wines of Provence come by the half or full bottle. The brasserie is also a *glacier,* and if you visit in the afternoon you can enjoy about 16 different ice-cream specialties, as well as milkshakes or Irish coffee.

FOOD AND LODGING IN THE ENVIRONS: Mas de la Bertrande, in Beaurecueil (tel. 42-28-90-09). Aix has witnessed the transformation of one of its most peaceful and regenerative hotels in the past few years since it was taken over and renamed in 1982. About 4½ miles outside of town, near the hamlet of Beaurecueil, Pierre Bertrand has created a charming three-star hotel set against a stunning backdrop that looks almost like a canvas by Cézanne, at the foot of the Montagne Sainte-Victoire. The operation is housed in a former stable, attractively outfitted with rustic ceiling beams, a country-style fireplace, plushly upholstered furniture, and as sensitive and genuinely concerned a staff as you'll find anywhere in the south of France.

The cuisine is one of the primary reasons for a stopover here, particularly since the vivacious and hardworking chef, Elisabeth Gagnaire, is considered a minor celebrity in the closely knit community of women chefs throughout France. Born in Paris, her parents were both involved in the hotel and restaurant business long before Elisabeth decided to break into the largely male-dominated world of French gastronomy. Her personal specialties, served either on the outdoor terrace or in the pink and wood-toned indoor dining room, both of which are ringed with flowers, might be preceded by the house hors d'oeuvres, called les amusades d'Elisabeth. Then you may select from rillettes of fresh salmon with tomato sabayon and garden perfumes, poached-egg blinis with asparagus tips, salade printanière of quail with foie gras, a mosaic of sole and wild salmon with pink butter, lamb with zucchini and thyme blossoms, or émincé of duckling in honey sauce. The cheese board is richly laden with varieties from throughout France, and the dessert trolley will make you wish you could come back for another gustatory experience. Meals are fixed-price extravaganzas, priced around 190F ($26.20). A copious *menu gourmand* is offered for 260F ($35.85), and an à la carte repast averages around 200F ($27.58) and up.

Best of all about this place, clients seem to be received more as friends than as business arrangements. The hotel organizes group activities, will loan you a bicycle, and will usher you to the swimming pool ringed with cypresses. Half board in one of the eight bedrooms is offered for 700F ($96.53) per couple. Rooms, either single or double, cost 340F ($46.89) without a meal plan included. The restaurant is closed Sunday night and Monday, but the hotel remains open all week long. The entire establishment closes every year for two weeks in February.

At Meyrargues, ten miles from Aix-en-Provence, the **Château de Meyrargues** (tel. 42-57-50-32) provides historical and architectural fascination, as well as a semi-luxurious accommodation in a 12th-century château that was converted into a hostelry in 1952. It is considered one of France's oldest fortified sites, having been a Celtic outpost in 600 B.C. The entrance is imposing, with a reflection pool and twin high stone towers flanking a sweeping, curved, balustraded set of steps. From its terraces and rooms you can enjoy a panoramic view of the Valley of the Durance. Once the lords of Les Baux lived here, but now it is an award-winning holiday retreat. So far the owner, Jeanne Drouillet, has restored only 14 bedchambers, which vary in size, view, and decoration, although all of them are handsomely furnished, in keeping with the tradition of the château. You'll pay from 350F ($48.27) in a single, from 400F ($55.16) in a double. In high season, half board costs 450F ($62.06) to 525F ($72.40) per person daily. In fair weather meals are served on a terrace. The château is closed from November 1 to February 1, and the restaurant is closed on Sunday night and on Monday. Otherwise, nonresidents can order meals in the 175F ($24.13) to 300F ($41.37) range.

5. Vauvenargues

In forbidding hill country ten miles east of Aix-en-Provence the body of Pablo Picasso is buried. Here in this village of mainly retired persons, the artist, who died at 91, painted his *Luncheon on the Grass* and did a portrait in red and black of his wife, the former Jacqueline Roque.

The ocher stone walls of the turreted **château** date from the 14th century, and the buildings in the square style are from the 16th and 17th centuries. On top of the Louis XIII porch is the coat-of-arms of the Vauvenargues family, who were the owners from 1790 until 1947. The castle was purchased by antique dealers, who sold all the furnishings. Picasso acquired it in 1958 and lived here between 1959 and 1961. Visitors aren't allowed inside, but they can see some of his sculptures in the castle park.

FOOD AND LODGING: About the only place to stay is **Au Moulin de Provence** (tel. 42-24-93-11), which offers only a dozen rooms, renting for 130F ($17.93) for the lone single, 220F ($30.34) in a double room with shower and toilet. However, the most expensive doubles, those with complete bath, go for 250F ($34.48). The place is furnished in an intimate, homelike manner. It also serves a good meal for 110F ($15.17) and a menu dégustation for 220F ($30.34). The English-speaking host, Magdeleine Yemenidjian, is always pleased to take care of North Americans. Closed October 31 to March 15.

6. Arles

It's been called "the soul of Provence." Art lovers, archeologists, and historians are attracted to this town on the Rhône. Many of its scenes, painted so luminously by Van Gogh in his declining years, remain to delight. The great Dutch painter left Paris for Arles in 1888. It was in that same year that he cut off part of his left ear. But he was to paint some of his most celebrated works in the Provençal town, including *Starry Night, The Bridge at Arles, Sunflowers,* and *L'Arlésienne.*

The Greeks are said to have founded Arles in the 6th century B.C. Julius Caesar established a Roman colony here in 46 B.C. Under Roman rule Arles prospered. Constantine the Great named it the second capital in his empire in A.D. 306, when it was known as "the little Rome of the Gauls." It wasn't until 1481 that Arles, 55 miles northwest of Marseille by road, was incorporated into France.

SEEING THE SIGHTS: The town is full of monuments from Roman times. It's best to go to the **Office de Tourisme,** Esplanade des Lices (tel. 90-96-29-35), and purchase a comprehensive ticket called a *Billet Globale* for 20F ($2.76), allowing you to visit all the major sights. All the museums (except Museon Arlaten) are open from 8:30 a.m. to noon and 2 to 7 p.m., May 1 to September 30. In spring and autumn they close at 5:30 p.m., at 4:30 p.m. in winter.

The general vicinity of the old Roman forum is now occupied by the **Place du Forum,** shaded by plane trees. Once Van Gogh's *Café du Nuit* stood on this square. Two columns in the Corinthian style and pediment fragments from a temple can be viewed at the corner of the Hôtel Nord-Pinus.

South of this square lies the **Place de la République,** the principal plaza of Arles. A blue porphyry obelisk some 50 feet high dominates this square. On the north is the impressive **Hôtel de Ville,** the town hall from 1673, built to Mansart's plans. It is surmounted by a Renaissance belfry.

On the east side of the square is the **Church of St. Trophime,** noted for its 12th-century portal, one of the finest achievements of the southern Romanesque style. In the pediment the figure of Christ is surrounded by the symbols of the Evangelists. Frederick Barbarossa was crowned king of Arles on this site in 1178. The cloister is built in both the Gothic and Romanesque styles and is noted for its medieval carvings. The church is open free from 8 a.m. to 7 p.m. The cloister hours are 9 to 11:30 a.m. and 2 to 4:30 p.m. Admission is 7F (97¢).

Opposite the main portal is the **Musée Lapidaire d'Art Païen,** Place de la République (tel. 90-96-37-68), housed in the **Church of St. Anne,** dating from 1602. It contains a museum of Roman sarcophagi, a collection of Roman relics, including four large mosaics and a colossal statue of Augustus, plus Etruscan pottery, altars, and prehistoric finds.

The **Musée Lapidaire d'Art Chrétien** (tel. 90-96-37-68), entered on the rue Balze, is considered one of the finest lapidary museums in Europe. Displayed in the chapel of a Jesuit college dating from 1654 is a collection of marble sarcophagi from the 4th and 5th centuries. Many are intricately designed but headless. Some of them depict scenes from the life of Christ. A charming but badly mutilated tombstone depicts children gathering olives. Some fragments of medieval sculpture from the Abbey of Montmajour are also on view. A complete set of coins struck at Arles and dating from the days of Constantine the Great (313–314) are a notable exhibit.

Adjoining but entered at 42 rue de la République is the **Museon Arlaten** (tel. 91-96-08-23), the name written in the old Provençal style. It was founded by Frédéric Mistral, the Provençal poet and leader of a movement to establish modern Provençal as a literary language. The museum was founded with the money he received with his Nobel Prize for literature in 1904. As a setting he selected the former Hôtel Laval-Castellane of the 16th century. Collections illustrate the everyday life of Provence. In reality it's a folklore museum, with regional costumes, portraits, fans, furniture (much of it black walnut), dolls, a salon of music, and one room devoted entirely to mementos of Mistral. Among its curiosities is a letter (in French, no less) from Theodore Roosevelt to Mistral, bearing a letterhead from the "Maison Blanche" in Washington, D.C. The museum is open daily except Monday, from 9 a.m. till noon and 2 to 6 p.m., charging 5.50F (76¢) for admission. From October to February its morning hours are the same, but its afternoon hours are 2 to 4 (2 to 5 in March).

The two great classical monuments of Arles are the **Roman Theater** and the **Amphitheater.** Little remains of the original theater, as it was later used as a quarry. It dates from the 1st century A.D. and was begun by Augustus. Only two marble Corinthian columns remain. Now rebuilt, the theater is the setting for an annual drama festival in July. Incidentally, the *Venus of Arles* was discovered here in 1651. The theater is open daily from 8:30 a.m. till noon and 2 to 7 p.m. (closes earlier off-season). Take the rue de la Calade from the town hall. Nearby, the Amphitheater, or arena, was built in the 1st century A.D., seating almost 25,000 spectators screaming for blood. When aficionados gather for to-the-death bullfights here in summer, history seems to repeat itself. The arena is a huge, colonnaded, oval-shaped structure. The government warns you to visit the old monument at your own risk. Three towers remain (scale one for the view) from medieval times, when the amphitheater was turned into a fortress. Hours are from 9 a.m. till noon and 2 to 6 p.m. daily.

Perhaps the most memorable sight in Arles is **Alyscamps,** once a necropolis established by the Romans, converted into a Christian burial ground in the 4th century. As the latter it became a setting for legends in epic poetry in medieval times. Today it's long and leafy, lined with poplars as well as what remains of the sarcophagi. Arlésiens escape here to enjoy a respite from the heat.

Another ancient monument is the **Baths of Constantine,** near the banks of the Rhône. The thermae are all that remain of a once-grand imperial palace. It's been stripped till just the walls remain. Entrance is on rue Dominique-Maisto. Visiting hours are the same as at the Amphitheater.

Nearby, with an entrance at 10 rue du Grand-Prieuré, is the **Musée Réattu** (tel. 90-96-37-68), containing the collection of Jacques Réattu (1760–1833), a local painter. His private collection was donated to form the museum, but it's been updated by more recent works, including etchings and drawings by Picasso, some depicting bullfighting scenes. Other works are by Gauguin, Dufy, Utrillo, and Léger. The Arras tapestries from the 16th century are distinguished. One entire salon is devoted to Henri Rousseau. The museum is in the former Commandery of the Order of Malta from the 15th century.

WHERE TO STAY: Jules César, Boulevard des Lices (tel. 90-93-43-20), in the center of Arles, was a Carmelite convent in the 17th century. But it's been skillfully adapted, emerging as a stately, gracious country-town hotel. In spite of the noisy neighborhood, most of the rooms are quiet, as they face the unspoiled cloister. The decoration is luxurious, as most of the rooms are furnished with antique Provençal pieces. The owner, Michel Albagnac, attends auctions throughout the countryside, always adding new pieces to complete the harmony. Prices range from 360F ($49.64) in a single to as high as 800F ($110.32) in a double. You wake up in the morning to enjoy the scent of roses, the songs of the birds.

The hotel's restaurant, Lou Marquès, is the best in Arles. Tables for al fresco dining are on the front terrace. The food is extremely fresh. On the à la carte menu, I recommend bourride à la Provençale, baudroie (an extremely ugly angelfish or frogfish that's simply delicious) à l'aïgo, and Arles lamb. The restaurant charges 175F ($24.13) to 300F ($41.37) for an average repast.

Hôtel d'Arlatan, 26 rue du Sauvage (tel. 90-93-56-46), was created from the former residence of the counts d'Arlatan de Beaumont. It's been managed by the same family since 1920. The hotel was built in the 15th century on the ruins of an old palace ordered by Constantine. You can still admire a wall dating from the 4th century. The rooms are furnished with authentic Provençal antiques, the walls covered with tapestries in the Louis XV and Louis XVI styles. Try to get a bedroom overlooking the garden with its palms, pond, and climbing vines. Rooms are available with hot and cold running water or complete private bath. Singles go for 185F ($25.51) to 260F ($35.85); doubles, 380F ($52.40) to 435F ($59.99). A continental breakfast is extra.

Calendal, 22 Place Pomme (tel. 90-96-11-89), stands on a quiet square not far from the arena. Behind the building is a shadowy garden with laurels. You're welcomed by Monsieur Rainaud. The rooms are furnished in the Provençal style, some of the pieces authentic antiques. Flowery wallpaper is popular here. Most of the accommodations have a view of the garden with its ivy-covered trees. All rooms are equipped with shower and toilet, the singles costing 140F ($19.31), and the doubles, 240F ($33.10). A continental breakfast is extra. In the lobby are a few showcases containing stuffed birds.

Mas de la Chapelle, Petite Route de Tarascon (tel. 90-93-23-15). Originally built as a chapel, and later expanded into a comfortable house in the 16th century, this elegant hotel is flanked with nearly symmetrical wings extending outward from a Romanesque center. The rounded archway of its entrance is reflected in the still waters of a nearby pool, beside which a flowering arbor protects garden chairs from the sun. Inside, beamed ceilings, exposed stone, and a massive fireplace capped with a neoclassical frieze and Louis XIII furnishings create the kind of setting where a visitor could lose track of the present. The hotel is surrounded by a six-acre park in which are set three tennis courts, two swimming pools, and flowers. Mme Estienne offers seven bedrooms, each well furnished, containing a private bath and phone. She prefers guests to stay on the half-board plan, costing from 280F ($38.61) to 480F ($66.19) per person. Guests who phone for a table can enjoy à la carte meals from 210F ($28.96) to 280F ($38.61). The establishment is closed in February.

Hôtel du Cloître, 18 rue de Cloître (tel. 90-96-29-50), is right in the St. Trophime cloister—hence its name. It's a modest rural hotel, with rustic rooms facing the yard. A single with shower and toilet rents for 170F ($23.44). Doubles with complete plumbing, either shower or bath, along with toilet, cost from 275F ($37.92).

WHERE TO DINE: Le Vaccarès, Place du Forum, 9 rue Favorin (tel. 90-96-06-17), offers some of the finest food in Arles in an upper-floor dining room reeking of southern French elegance. Bernard Dumas, the hardworking chef, bases many of his inventive recipes on old dishes from around Provence. He mixes unusual items together in a straightforward combination that has won the gastronomic hearts in the region. Specialties include sauté of lamb with pistou, suçarello of mussels with herbs, sea-devil soup, sandre à la poutargue, steamed loup, and émincé of beef with Châteauneuf. Fixed-price meals are offered for 165F ($22.75), but if you choose to dine à la carte, you can expect to pay 220F ($30.24) to 260F ($35.85). The restaurant is closed Sunday, Monday, the last two weeks of June, and from just before Christmas to mid-January.

Le Tambourin, 65 rue Amadée-Richot (tel. 90-96-13-32), offers an attractive environment and friendly service with menu specialties that include Provençal-style trout, onion soup, coquilles St-Jacques, filet of daurade, and fish soup. Raymond Durand is the owner, assisted by his wife, Denise. Set menus range from 70F ($9.65) to 105F ($14.48), while à la carte meals begin at 210F ($28.96). The restaurant is open daily except in January and February.

Hostellerie des Arènes, 62 rue du Refuge (tel. 90-96-13-05), close to the

Arenas, offers Provençal-style meals whose well-prepared specialties include seafood in puff pastry, braised duckling laced with green peppercorns, brochette of mussels with tartar sauce, and veal marengo. In warm weather, meals are served outside on the terrace. The combined owner and chef, Maurice Naval, charges 60F ($8.27) to 95F ($13.10) for table d'hôte menus, with wines priced inexpensively by the carafe or by the bottle. The restaurant is closed Wednesday all year long and Tuesday night every week except in summer. It also shuts down the last ten days of June and from mid-December till the end of January.

7. Fontvieille

Just 6½ miles from Arles, this sleepy little town in the foothills of the Alpilles enjoys associations with the 19th-century novelist Alphonse Daudet. Writing his first novel at the age of 14, this handsome young man in time became a member of the inner circle of the fashionable bohemian literary figures of his day. In 1884 he published the novel *Sappho*. He later became a patron of the young Marcel Proust. Daudet died in 1897, his health having been undermined by venereal disease.

On top of a small hill stands the mill that provided the title for Daudet's *Lettres de Mon Moulin*. The mill has been restored and turned into the **Musée Alphonse Daudet** (tel. 90-97-60-78), with memorabilia of the novelist in the basement. It is open daily from 9 a.m. to noon and 1 to 7 p.m., charging an admission of 6F (83¢). In the off-season it is open only from 2 to 6 p.m.

FOOD AND LODGING: **La Régalido,** rue Frédéric-Mistral (tel. 90-97-73-67), is a member of the Relais et Châteaux. A charming auberge, it is like a Provençal manor, tastefully decorated by the Michel family. It was converted from a 17th-century olive mill. Only 13 rooms are offered, at prices ranging from 400F ($55.16) in a single to 850F ($117.22) in the most expensive double. Staying here is somewhat like being the guest in a private home of a very fine and friendly family. Bedrooms are named after spices and herbs that grow in the region. In the dining room you're impressed by the flower arrangements from Madame Michel's garden, which is studded with umbrella trees and magnolias.

The Michel son, Jean-Pierre, is a maître-cuisinier, following in the footsteps of his father, who was one of the leading chefs of France. The young chef specializes in the following dishes: gratin de moules aux épinards (tender Mediterranean mussels with spinach), pièce d'agneau en casserole et à l'ail (lamb delicately flavored with garlic and herbs), and canard farci au poivre vert (stuffed duckling with green peppercorns). A meal will cost anywhere from 280F ($38.61) to 320F ($44.13).

The inn shuts down from November 30 to January 15, and the restaurant doesn't serve on Monday or lunch on Tuesday.

8. Les Baux

Cardinal de Richelieu called this village a nesting place for eagles. In its lonely position high on a windswept plateau overlooking the southern flank of the Alpilles, Les Baux is a mere ghost of its former self. Once it was the citadel of the powerful seigneurs of Les Baux, who ruled with an iron fist and sent their conquering armies as far as Albania. The town lies just 50 miles north of Marseille and the Mediterranean, nestling in a valley surrounded by mysterious, shadowy rock formations. Hewn out of rock, Les Baux became a mighty fortress. In medieval times troubadours from all over Europe came this way. Here they recited Western Europe's earliest known vernacular poetry.

Eventually, the notorious "Scourge of Provence" ruled Les Baux, sending his men throughout the land to kidnap people. If no one would pay ransom for one of his victims, the poor wretch was forced to walk a gangplank to death over the cliff's edge.

Fed up with the rebellions against Louis XIII in 1632, Richelieu commanded his armies to destroy Les Baux. Today the castle and ramparts are a mere shell, although remains of great Renaissance mansions are to be seen. The population of Les Baux, which once numbered in the thousands, is reduced to only a few hardy souls who endure the fierce sun of summer and the harsh winds of winter.

FOOD AND LODGING: In this unlikely setting you come upon some of the finest hotels and restaurants in all of France.

The Medium-Priced Range

Auberge de la Benvengudo, Vallon de l'Arcoule, Route d'Arles (tel. 90-54-32-54), is a tastefully converted 19th-century farmhouse surrounded with sculptured shrubbery, towering trees, vine-filled urns, and parasol pines. Many of the antiques filling the attractively decorated interior are museum pieces dating from the 18th century and would delight any antique lover with their rich patinas. Daniel and Marise Beaupied are the friendly owners and operators, assisted by their children. They happily extend a *benvengudo* ("welcome" in Provençale) promised by the name of their auberge. Extra benefits of a stopover here include a swimming pool, an expansive flagstone-covered terrace, and unusual accessories, which feature a 19th-century copper still formerly used for making potent eaux-de-vie. You'll see the still in one of the stone-walled and timbered salons.

Daniel creates the savory cuisine, offering such specialties as mousse of loup with crayfish, gigot of lamb, gratin of crayfish tails, and tarte aux citron. Before the end of your stay, you will be shown the enormous stacks of vine and olive wood used to grill the variety of juicy meats served in the pink-accented dining room. Fixed-price menus are offered at 145F ($20) and 180F ($24.82).

The annex contains attractive modern bedrooms with antique four-poster beds, large bathrooms, terraces, and views of either the garden or the village, whose rocky buildings are about a mile away. The hotel and restaurant are closed from November 1 till the end of January. The 20 rooms cost 400F ($55.16) in a double.

Bautezar, rue Frédéric Mistral (tel. 90-97-32-09). You reach this hotel by going down some steps, arriving in a large vaulted dining room with a medieval touch. The furniture is in the rustic Provençal style. The walls of white stone are decorated with cloth tapestries. At the end of the dining room is a terrace with a view of Val d'Enfer. The rooms, containing private bath, are carefully decorated in the Louis XVI style. A double, depending on its view, ranges from 250F ($33.34) to 320F ($44.13). The food is also good, a set meal costing 115F ($15.86) to 180F ($24.82). It is closed from January to mid-March and on Monday.

La Riboto de Taven, Val d'Enfer (tel. 90-97-34-23), is an inviting farmhouse set at the base of a series of wind-carved cliffs, just outside the medieval section of town. You'll pass through a manicured garden which is in sharp contrast to the rocks which surround it, before arriving at the stone interior of this property owned by two generations of the Novi family. Christine and her husband, Philippe Theme, are the English-speaking daughter and son-in-law of the charming founders. They will be eager to explain the origins of the 1835 house, its huge millstone that serves as one of the garden's dining tables, and the 9th-century Provençal fairytale whose main character gave her name to the establishment.

In winter you'll enjoy an apéritif in a slope-roofed, timbered room with a vast fireplace, a Provençal crédence, and Louis XIII furniture that's so elegant you'd never know the place was originally designed as a sleeping area for lambs which grazed around the walls of the property. In summer you'll probably want to sit at the beautifully laid tables outdoors. An outstanding table d'hôte menu is offered for 235F ($32.41), which could include terrine of hare, mousse of sea bass with extract of lobster, warm oysters in puff pastry, noisettes of truffled lamb in a garlic purée, cheese, and homemade desserts. If you're interested in an à la carte meal—which will average from 300F ($41.37) up—you might enjoy the gratin of Breton lobster, aiguillettes of duckling with honey and fresh whortleberries, and suprême of chicken with morels. The establishment is closed Sunday night in low season, Monday throughout the year, and from January 10 to February 20.

The Budget Range

Hostellerie de la Reine-Jeanne, Grand-Rue (tel. 90-97-32-06), is the best bargain at Les Baux. You enter a typical provincial French bistro where you're welcomed by Alain Guilbard, standing behind a bar of waxed wood. The inn is immaculate, the atmosphere warm. In the bedrooms, everything has been carefully considered with the guest's comfort in mind. Three of the rooms have their own terraces with a view of the valley. The most expensive room—the blue room at 230F ($31.72)—is beamed, its walls covered with a flower paper in shades of blue. Less expensive doubles go for 180F ($24.82). Two set menus cost 85F ($11.72) and 130F ($17.93). The inn is closed from the end of November until the first of February and on Tuesday from mid-October to mid-March. Between April and October, only guests desiring full board are accepted.

9. St-Rémy-de-Provence

Nostradamus, the French physician and astrologer whose reputation is enjoying great vogue today, was born here in 1503. In 1922 Gertrude Stein and Alice B. Toklas found St-Rémy after "wandering around everywhere a bit," Ms. Stein wrote to Cocteau. But mainly St-Rémy, eight miles north of Les Baux, is associated with Van Gogh. He commited himself to an asylum here in 1889 after cutting off his ear. Between moods of despair, he painted such works as *Olive Trees* and *Cypresses*.

The cloisters he made famous in his paintings can be visited today at the ancient **Monastery of St-Paul-de-Mausolée,** dating from the 12th century. Now a psychiatric establishment, the former monastery lies east of the D5 highway, a short drive north of Glanum (see below). The cell in which this genius was confined is closed to the public, but it's still worth a visit to explore the Romanesque chapel and cloisters with their circular arches and columns, which have beautifully carved capitals. The cloisters are open from 8 a.m. to 7 p.m. (to 6 p.m. off-season). On your way to the church you'll see a bust of Van Gogh. Incidentally, Dr. Albert Schweitzer was "detained" here in World War I.

A mile south of St-Rémy, along the D5, is **Glanum** (tel. 90-92-23-79), a Gallo-Roman city (follow the road signs to "Les Antiques"). Its historical monuments include an **Arc Municipal,** a triumphal arch dating from the time of Julius Caesar, and a cenotaph called the **Mausolée des Jules.** Garlanded with sculptured fruits and flowers, the arch dates from 20 B.C. and is the oldest in Provence. It is also decorated with bas-reliefs representing chained prisoners. The mausoleum was raised to honor the grandsons of Augustus and is the only monument of its type to have survived. In the area are entire streets and the foundations of private residences from the 1st-century A.D. town. Some remains are from an even earlier Gallo-Greek town dating from the 2nd century B.C. Costing 20F ($2.76) for admission, the excavations are open from the first of April until the end of September from 9 a.m. to noon and 2 to 6 p.m. Otherwise, hours are 10 a.m. to noon and 2 to 5 p.m. The excavations are closed on Tuesday in summer, and both Tuesday and Wednesday in winter.

In the center of St-Rémy, **Le Musée Archéologique,** Hôtel de Sade, rue du Parage (tel. 90-92-13-07), displays finds, both sculptures and bronzes, excavated at Glanum. It is open daily except Tuesday from April to September.

FOOD AND LODGING: Château de Roussan (tel. 90-92-11-63). As the owner of this exquisitely proportioned château said to me during my last visit, "After the war, we had to make some hard decisions." The sorrow he understandably felt at having to turn the seat of his family's history into a hotel isn't visible today, as Pierre Pichon, the charming director (and a member of the family) welcomes guests into the sumptuous architecture that made this kind of house the envy of Europe when it was built.

You'll pass beneath a soaring archway of century-old trees leading up to the neoclassical façade, which was constructed of softly colored local stone in 1701. The history of the place is far older than that, however, since its most famous resident, the Renaissance psychic Nostradamus, lived in a rustic outbuilding a few steps from the front door. As you wander around the grounds you'll feel you're going back through the centuries, particularly when you reach the baroque sculptures lining the surprisingly deep rectangular basin fed by a constantly flowing stream.

The château was transformed into a hotel in 1954 when the owners (the most aristocratic of whom still live in partial isolation in the oldest wing of the building) needed funds to rebuild the place after it and the outlying 18th-century greenhouses were pillaged and then devastated by the Nazi occupation. Today the place is carefully maintained, "thanks to tourism." To be honest, this isn't the most glamorous or the most slickly furnished of the château-hotels in the region, but its almost overwhelming sense of nostalgia, along with the bittersweet grace of an establishment that has "seen it all," makes it my favorite.

The 12 "bedrooms of character" rent for 360F ($49.64) to 500F ($68.95) either single or double occupancy between March 20 and October 20. There's no restaurant on the premises, but an optional breakfast is served in a richly vaulted kitchen where, as a grandfather clock slowly ticks, you'll feel you've wandered back in time.

Hôtel Château des Alpilles, Ancienne Route du Grès (tel. 90-92-03-33), is the choicest and most sophisticated address in town, the kind of place a world-weary Parisian would feel at home in. The philosophy that motivated Françoise Bon when she converted it in 1980 was to create a "house for paying friends."

The house is nothing less than the Empire-style château which, after its construction in 1827 by the Pichot family, housed Chateaubriand and a host of other French luminaries. To reach it, you pass beneath the 300-year-old trees that surround the dignified and rigidly symmetrical neoclassical exterior. The carefully decorated rooms have combined the best of an antique framework with plush upholsteries, rich carpeting, and vibrantly sophisticated colors. Bedrooms are exceptionally spacious and filled with elegantly whimsical accessories, such as a pair of porcelain panthers flanking one of the carved mantelpieces. During the renovations, Madame Bon installed an elevator at great expense, although if you're like me, you'll prefer to descend by the massively graceful stone stairwell at least once during your stay.

Each of the rooms has a travertine-trimmed private bath, huge windows overlooking the trees outside, and 19th-century antiques. If you decide to visit the outdoor swimming pool, you might be greeted by Mme Bon's Yorkshire terriers before they run off to play under one of the property's giant magnolias. There's also a sauna, plus two tennis courts, and a lunchtime grill beside the pool serving salads, sandwiches, and steaks. The 15 double bedrooms rent for 500F ($68.95) to 650F ($89.64) for the most sumptuously decorated. The hotel is open from mid-March to mid-November and from just before Christmas to early January.

Vallon de Valrugues (Hôtel Pratelli), Chemin de Canto Cigalo (tel. 90-92-

04-40), is a Mediterranean-style hotel east of town, surrounded by a flowered park. The buff-colored building, pierced with arches, was built by three members of the Pratelli family in 1969. They furnished it with a combination of antiques and conservative reproductions and constructed a swimming pool surrounded with statues. The marble-covered interior with the heavy ceiling beams was designed to be almost an extension of the garden à la Provençale. Many of the 24 rooms have a private terrace or loggia and rent for 360F ($49.64) in a single, for 410F ($56.54) to 550F ($75.63) in a double, the latter for an apartment. There are tennis courts on the premises, but no restaurant. Cold meals, however, are served around the pool on request. The hotel is open from March 1 to the first of November.

Les Antiques, 15 Avenue Pasteur (tel. 90-92-03-02), is a great 19th-century villa which has been in the same Provençal family for 165 years. This medium-priced hotel run by Gilbert Mistral-Bernard is in a beautiful seven-acre park with a swimming pool. A magnificent reception lounge, with marble floors and tapestries on the walls, opens onto several salons. Everything is rich and stylish; the furnishings are pure Napoléon III. In summer guests have breakfast in what used to be the Orangerie. The rooms are handsomely furnished, usually in pastels or a delicate rose. Some of the accommodations are in a private pavilion in the modern style, with direct access to the garden. Double rooms cost from 350F ($48.27). The only meal served is breakfast. Guests are lodged at the villa from mid-March until the end of October.

Bar/Hotel/Restaurant des Arts, 32 Boulevard Victor-Hugo (tel. 90-92-13-41). If the bohemian life is still alive and well and living at St-Rémy, you'll probably find it at this old-style café and restaurant on the east side of town. Madame Nicole Caritoux is the owner. Even if you plan to have dinner, you'll be tempted to linger in the bar, which is the first room you enter from the street. There you'll find thick wooden tables, simple chairs, a slightly faded decor, and a most unusual collection of people. If you intend to have dinner, don't keep your plans to yourself but tell the English-speaking woman behind the dining room door that you'd like a table. Depending on the traffic, you might wait for up to 45 minutes, although once you enter, you'll find it was worth it. Since the family who owns the place have been in business here since 1947, they've had the chance to collect dozens of original paintings. These, coupled with the pine paneling and the masses of copper pots, combine to form a decor as elegant and sophisticated as the bar area is rough and smoke-stained.

The arrangement is labyrinthine, but once you're seated, you can study the menu. This lists such specialties as rabbit terrine, entrecôte aux cèpes, steak au poivre with champagne, tournedos with madeira and mushrooms, duckling in orange sauce, frogs' legs Provençal, four different kinds of omelets, and trout served three ways. By special order, the chef will serve crayfish, lobster, and game dishes. Fixed-price menus are offered for 55F ($7.56) and 100F ($13.79); the cheaper ones aren't offered on weekends. À la carte meals range between 120F ($16.55) and 150F ($20.69). Food is served every day except Wednesday. If you want to spend the night, the rooms upstairs are pleasantly decorated, some in Provençal style. They're placed among rustic ceiling beams and exposed timbers. The most basic singles begin at 115F ($15.86), the tariff going up to 200F ($27.58) in a double.

Le Jardin de Frédéric, 8 Boulevard Gambetta (tel. 90-92-27-76), is a popular bistro set inside a small villa close to the center of town. The pleasant setting is a backdrop for specialties whose preparation is supervised by its family owners. These might include rabbit with plums, terrine de canard, onion tart, gigot with roquefort, and poached turbot with sorrel. Fixed-price menus cost 90F ($12.41) and 130F ($17.93). À la carte menus average 210F ($28.96). In summer you'll probably want to dine on one of the tables set out in front of the house. The restaurant is closed Tuesday and from November 1 until just before Christmas.

10. Avignon

In the 14th century Avignon was the capital of Christendom; the popes lived here during what the Romans called "the Babylonian Captivity." The legacy left by that "court of splendor and magnificence" makes Avignon even today one of the most interesting and beautiful of Europe's cities of the Middle Ages. It lies 66 miles northwest of Marseille.

SEEING THE SIGHTS: Even more famous than the papal residency is the ditty *"Sur le pont d'Avignon, l'on y danse, l'on y danse,"* echoing through every French nursery and around the world. Ironically, **Pont St-Bénézet** was too narrow for the *danse* of the rhyme. It was all you could do to pass, much less dance. Spanning the Rhône and connecting Avignon with Villeneuve-lès-Avignon, the bridge is now only a fragmented ruin. It may be visited from 9 a.m. to noon and 2 to 7 p.m., till 6 p.m. off-season, for an admission of 6.50F (90¢). According to legend, the bridge was inspired by a vision a shepherd boy had while tending his flock in the field. His name was Bénézet. Actually, the bridge was built between 1117 and 1185, and it suffered various disasters from that time on. Finally, in 1669, half of the bridge toppled into the river. Leading citizens have—as yet unsuccessfully—tried to get the government to repair it. St. Nicholas Chapel stands on one of the piers. It is a two-story structure, one designed in the Romanesque style, the other in the Gothic.

Dominating the city is the **Le Palais des Papes,** Place du Palais des Papes (tel. 90-86-03-32). In 1309 a sick man, nearing the end of his life, arrived in Avignon. His name was Clement V, and he was the leader of the Christian world. Lodged as a guest of the Dominicans, he died in the spring of 1314 and was succeeded by John XXII. The new pope, unlike the popes of Rome, lived modestly in the Episcopal Palace. When Benedict XII took over, he greatly enlarged and rebuilt the old palace. Clement VI, who followed, built an even more elaborate extension called the New Palace. After Innocent VI and Urban V, Pope Gregory XI did no building. Inspired by Catherine of Siena, he was intent upon returning the papacy to Rome, and he succeeded. In all, seven popes had reigned at Avignon. Under them art and culture flourished, as did vice. Prostitutes blatantly went about peddling their wares in front of fat cardinals, rich merchants were robbed, and innocent pilgrims from the hinterlands were brutally tricked and swindled.

From 1378, during the Great Schism, one pope ruled in Avignon, another in Rome. The reign of the pope and the "antipope" continued, one following the other, until both rulers were dismissed by the election of Martin V in 1417. Rome continued to rule Avignon until it was joined to France at the time of the French Revolution.

The ramparts (still standing) around Avignon were built in the 14th century, and are characterized by their machicolated battlements, turrets, and old gates. Olga Carlisle called them "squat and very thick, like huge children's blocks placed there according to a playful up-and-down design."

The fortress Palais des Papes stands on a hill. You are shown through the palace on a guided tour, usually lasting 50 minutes. From October 1 until March 31 visits begin at 9, 10, and 11 a.m. and 2, 3, and 4 p.m. From the first of April until the end of June, visits are more frequent between 9 and 11:30 a.m. and 2 to 5:30 p.m. More frequent visits depart during the busy period from July 1 to September 30: from 9 a.m. to 6 p.m. There are no guided visits from noon to 2 p.m. You can, however, go on your own.

The long tour of the papal palace is somewhat monotonous, as the rooms, for the most part, have long been stripped of their finery. The exception is **St. John's Chapel,** which is known for its beautiful frescoes attributed to the school of Matteo Giovanetti and painted between 1345 and 1348. These frescoes present scenes from the life of St. John the Baptist and St. John the Evangelist. St.

Martial's Chapel, however, was painted by Giovanetti himself. It is on the eastern wall, above St. John's Chapel. The Giovanetti frescoes depict the miracles of St. Martial, the patron saint of Limousin province.

The **Grand Tinel** or banquet hall is about 135 feet long and 30 feet wide. The pope's table stood on the southern side. The bedroom of the pope is on the first floor of the Tour des Anges. Its walls are entirely decorated in tempera with wide foliage on which birds and squirrels perch. Birdcages are painted in the recesses of the windows. In a secular vein, the **Stag Room**—the study of Clement VI—was frescoed in 1343 with hunting scenes. Added under the same Clément VI, who had a taste for grandeur, the **Great Audience Hall** contains frescoes of the prophets, also attributed to Giovanetti and painted in 1352.

Nearby is the **Cathedral of Notre-Dame,** dating from the 12th century and containing the flamboyant Gothic tomb of John XXII, who died at the age of 90. Benedict XII is also buried there. Crowning the top is a gilded statue of the Virgin from the 19th century. From the cathedral, you can enter the **Promenade du Rocher des Doms,** strolling through its garden and enjoying the view across the Rhône to Villeneuve-lès-Avignon.

The **Musée du Petit Palais,** Place du Palais des Papes (tel. 90-86-44-58), is housed in a palace dating from the 14th and 15th centuries. It contains an important collection of paintings from the Italian schools from the 13th through the 16th centuries, including works from Florence, Venice, Siena, and Lombardy. In addition, salons display paintings done in Avignon in the 15th century. Several galleries are devoted to Roman and Gothic sculptures from Avignon. The museum is open from 9:15 a.m. to noon and 2 to 6:15 p.m., charging 13F ($1.79) for admission. It is closed on Tuesday.

The **Calvet Museum,** 67 rue Joseph-Vernet (tel. 90-86-33-84), is housed in an 18th-century mansion with a courtyard praised by Stendhal. It shelters a collection of prehistoric stoneware, Greek marbles, and many paintings. My favorite oil is by Brueghel (the Elder), *Le Cortège Nuptial (The Bridal Procession).* Look for Bosch's *Adoration of the Magi* as well. Other works of art are by Vasari, Mignard, Joseph Vernet, David, Manet, Delacroix, Daumier, Vuillard, Rouault, Renoir, Sisley, Cézanne, Dufy, Utrillo (his *Lapin Agile),* Toulouse-Lautrec, and Seurat. A good collection of contemporary painting, including works by Modigliani and Vasarely, is also displayed. The museum is open from 10 a.m. to noon and 2 to 6 p.m., charging 12F ($1.66) for admission. Closed Tuesday.

An annex of the Musée Calvet, the **Musée Lapidaire** is entered at 18 rue de la République (tel. 90-86-33-84). In a Jesuit church dating from the 17th century it displays a fine and important collection of sculptures from the Gallo-Roman time through the Gothic era. It is open from 10 a.m. to noon and 2 to 6 p.m. There is no charge for admission. The museum is closed on Tuesday.

The modern world is impinging on Avignon, but across the Rhône at **Villeneuve-lès-Avignon** the Middle Ages slumber on. When the popes lived in exile at Avignon, wealthy cardinals built palaces or *livrées* across the river. Many visitors prefer to live or dine there rather than in Avignon (see my recommendations set forth below).

However, even if you're staying at Avignon or just passing through, you'll want to visit Villeneuve, especially to see its Carthusian monastery, **Chartreuse du Val de Bénédiction,** rue de la République, in the heart of town. The largest charterhouse in France, it is open daily from 9 a.m. to noon and 2 to 6 p.m. from the first of April until the end of September. From October 1 to March 30 hours are 10 a.m. to noon and 2 to 5 p.m. Admission is 15F ($2.07) if you wish to visit its museum. Inside, a remarkable *Coronation of the Virgin* by Enguerrand Charonton is enshrined. Painted in 1453, the masterpiece contains a fringed bottom that is Bosch-like in its horror, representing the denizens of hell.

Crowning the town is **Fort St-André,** founded in 1360 by Jean-le-Bon to serve as a symbol of might to the pontifical powers across the river. The Abbey of St. André, now owned privately, was installed in the 18th century. You can visit the formal garden encircling the mansion. The mood here is tranquil, with an aviary of fantail pigeons, a rose-trellis colonnade, fountains, and flowers. Charging 10F ($1.38) for admission, the grounds are open April 1 to September 30 from 9 a.m. to noon and 2 to 6:30 p.m., October 1 to March 31 from 10 a.m. to noon and 2 to 5 p.m.

Try to visit the **Church of Notre-Dame,** founded in 1333 by Cardinal Arnaud de Via, in the center of the hamlet. Its proudest possession is a 14th-century *Virgin of Ivory,* considered one of the great French art treasures.

UPPER-BRACKET LIVING IN AVIGNON: Hôtel d'Europe, 12 Place Grillon (tel. 90-82-66-92), was built originally in 1580 as a palace for the Marquis of Gravezon, but it has been a hotel since 1799. You enter through a courtyard, where tables are set in warmer months. The interior has a remarkable collection of antiques. Whether you go into the grand hall or any of the salons, you'll find tastefully arranged antiques and decorative accessories, such as Aubusson tapestries, Empire consoles, gilt-framed paintings, and an especially fine assortment of Directoire pieces. Equally impressive is the restaurant, La Vieille Fontaine, with its fine fireplace, although the courtyard is more festive. The restaurant is one of the most distinguished in Avignon. The highest quality of ingredients is used in the superb meals. The cuisine is classical, costing 175F ($24.13) to 320F ($44.13). The bedrooms are also tasteful, with handsome decorations and period furnishings. Most of the doubles, with a large bed and a full bath, rent for 670F ($92.39) to 750F ($103.43), although a few "Directoire doubles" with shower go for 420F ($57.92).

Sofitel Avignon, Route de Carpentras, Avignon Nord (Autoroute 7) (tel. 90-31-16-43), lies on the N542, about an eight-minute drive from the Palais des Papes on the *voie expresse.* The position allows for more expansive living. Surrounding the hotel is a swimming pool with a little refreshment bar, plus tennis courts. The 98 bedrooms, half of which are twins, are attractively conceived, with basic built-in units, private bath, air conditioning, and soundproofing. Singles cost 360F ($49.64); doubles, 550F ($75.63).

For meals, Le Majoral serves either regional specialties or fast food, at prices ranging from 125F ($17.24) to 220F ($30.34). Adjoining is an attractive bar, Le Fustier.

At the foot of the Popes' Palace, the most prominent place in Avignon, the **Hôtel Cité-des-Papes,** 1 rue Jean-Vilar (tel. 90-86-22-45), offers you modern comfort in pleasant and restful surroundings, just 20 yards from the biggest parking lot of the city and very close to the New Congress Palace. Built in 1975, the hotel contains 63 rooms, each with bath and toilet, radio, mini-bar, and TV. The prices run from 270F ($37.23) in a single to 320F ($44.13) for the most expensive double. Breakfast is the only meal served.

THE BUDGET HOTELS: Le Midi, 55 rue de la République (tel. 90-82-15-56), boasts a slick modern front and glassed-in lobby. The remodeling has been gradual, but successful. Half of the accommodations have been furnished in a contemporary mode, the others with reproductions of provincial pieces. All are neat and clean, appropriate for an overnight stay, and all contain a complete bath or shower. The most expensive doubles, with private bath, rent for 300F ($68.95) and singles for 225F ($31.03) including service and tax. A continental breakfast is the only meal served.

Hôtel d'Angleterre, 29 Boulevard Raspail (tel. 90-86-34-31). The entry opens onto a large lobby with a tile floor. From the lobby, you go into a little sitting room where the walls are covered with rose-and-gray tapestry. The hotel has no particular originality, although all is clean and pleasant. There is a comfortable living room next to the breakfast room. The walls of the bedrooms are covered with florid paper, and the furniture is in the functional style. The baths are tile, the colors harmonized with those of the bedrooms. The hotel has 37 rooms, 32 of which contain a private bath or shower. A single rents for 178F ($24.55), and a double goes for 280F ($38.61).

THE BEST RESTAURANTS: Hiély, 5 rue de la République (tel. 90-86-17-07), is one of the finest restaurants in Provence. It has a long and devoted following of gourmets. A few years ago, *Holiday* magazine honored it as one of the best restaurants in Europe. For my tastebuds, it has remained so, consistently adhering to an excellent cuisine. The 240F ($33.10) menu is most impressive. To begin your repast you can try one of four specialties, including la petite marmite du pêcheur, a savory fish soup ringed with black mussels, for an additional cost. Main-dish specialties include pintadeau (young guinea-hen) de ferme aux pêches. The pièce de résistance is l'agneau des Alpilles grillé (Alpine lamb) sur feu de bois, also a supplement. Wines in a carafe include Tavel rosé or Châteauneuf-du-Pape. Closed Monday off-season, Tuesday all year, and from mid-June to early July.

Brunel, 46 rue de la Balance (tel. 90-85-24-83), in the most historic heart of Avignon, is managed and maintained by a capable team of young chefs and dining room staff, many of whom are members of the Brunel family. The elegantly modern, air-conditioned dining room is usually filled with flowers, whose perfume seems to enhance the savory odors coming from such specialties as warm curried oysters, warm pâté de canard, lambs' brains with caramelized lemon, and breast of duckling with apples. Desserts are excellent, since one of the Brunel brothers spends most of his time making them. No one will mind if you order one of the well-chosen house wines by the carafe. At lunchtime a fixed-price menu is offered for 200F ($27.58), although at dinner only à la carte meals are served, averaging around 290F ($39.99). The family closes its restaurant on Sunday and Monday off-season, for three weeks in August, and from mid-February to early March.

Auberge de France, 28 Place Horloge (tel. 90-82-58-86), is known for its cuisine, among the finest served in Avignon. The location is adjacent to the Palais des Papes, and there is a parking area nearby for your car. Tassan Primo serves a honey of a cuisine—stuffed mussels, Scottish salmon en papillote, and his pièce de résistance, which he calls Poragneu Coumtadino (stuffed pork and truffles and a roast leg of lamb). His dessert spectacular is a charlotte with nuts and honey. Regional wines featured include Châteauneuf-du-Pape and Beaumes de Venise. A menu is offered for 220F ($30.34), and you will most likely spend the same ordering à la carte. The restaurant is closed on Wednesday night and Thursday, from mid-June to early July, and from mid-January to the first of February.

Les Trois Clefs, 26 rue des Trois-Faucons (tel. 90-86-51-53), is an attractively decorated and attractively priced restaurant directed by Laurent and Martine Mergnac. Their intimate dining room, just behind the city ramparts and the Lapidary Museum, is decorated with lacquered paneling, lots of flowers, and yards of well-chosen fabrics. Menu items depend on what's available in the market that day, and might include hot foie gras of duckling in an herb-flavored sauce, brioche of eggs with truffles, and suprême of guinea fowl with crayfish. Fixed-price menus range from 110F ($15.17) to 220F ($30.34), while à la carte meals average 250F ($34.48). The air-conditioned restaurant is closed every Sunday.

La Fourchette, 7 rue Racine (tel. 90-82-56-01), is an enlightened bistro, run by Robert Hiély, where you can get creative cookery at a moderate price. There are two dining rooms, one like a summer house, with walls of glass, the other more of a tavern, with oak beams, burlap-covered walls, and hanging converted oil lamps. Creating the ambience are ladderback chairs, checked tablecloths, baskets of fresh cherries (in season), wooden kegs, ceramic jugs, copper urns of trailing plants, cages of birds, even a doll's buggy. For just 90F ($12.41) you can have this sample menu: (1) le flan d'épinard et aubergine aux tomates; (2) le foie d'agneau grillé (grilled lamb liver) with raisin sauce; (3) crêpe de pommes de terre; and (4) a superb dessert, orange pelée à vig purée de framboises (raspberries). The restaurant is closed Saturday, Sunday, June 15 to June 20, and the last two weeks in January.

FOOD AND LODGING IN VILLENEUVE: Le Prieuré, Place du Chapître (tel. 90-25-18-20), dates back to 1322 when it was built by a wealthy cardinal—a nephew of the pope—as a palace, or *livrée*. During its checkered career it was everything from a private school to a boarding house for artists, until it was taken over in 1943 by Roger J. Mille, who turned it into an inn, installing modern amenities. Today his son Jacques not only continues the traditions but also makes improvements. The rooms are graced with an eclectic group of antiques and accessories, covering a wide range of French decor and history, with harmoniously coordinated fabrics. There are 26 rooms and nine suites, all with bath. The least expensive room is a single for 380F ($52.40), and a suite for three or four persons will run as high as 1,500F ($206.85). Regular double rooms with private bath range in price from 550F ($75.63) to 1,000F ($137.90). Another smaller house on the grounds was converted to provide more rooms, all with private bath.

Country-estate living rooms open one into the other, with lavishly rich furnishings. The rooms are off a maze of gardens overgrown with trees and seasonal flowers. You dine in front of a huge stone fireplace in the Great Hall or on the flagstone terrace. Meals are good but expensive, a set menu priced at 250F ($34.48). The specialty is sole au plat Pétrarque, named after the Italian poet who spent so much time lambasting the papacy. Le Prieuré is closed from early November to early March.

La Magnaneraie Hostellerie, 37 rue Camp-Bataille (tel. 90-25-11-11), offers a hard-to-find combination—a superb cuisine and attractive rooms. Monsieur and Madame Prayal have brought their homemaking and culinary skills to a full flowering. This 15th-century villa (which once served as a wine-tasting center for owners of the surrounding vineyards) was totally renovated and furnished with antiques and reproductions. In the high season, March 1 till the end of October, half board is required (and desired, as the chef-owner has been awarded at least eight medals for his cookery). Based on double occupancy, the charge for half board ranges from 450F ($62.06) to 850F ($117.22) per person daily. The big news is that Monsieur Prayal includes many of the specialties from his repertoire on his set menus. For nonresidents he offers set meals from 145F ($20) to 200F ($27.58). If you dine à la carte, expect to pay from 250F ($34.48) per person. Each bedroom has its own personality, although I prefer no. 10 with its terrace balcony and bed on a dais, or no. 19, on the top floor, with its view of the old walls of the town. Some lucky couple might also win no. 22, a lovely room in the garden. The oldest rooms in the house, with heavy beamed ceilings, are on the ground floor. Many American guests have arrived for a stay of only one night and have remained for days, enjoying the good food, the friendly atmosphere, and the restful retreat enhanced by the rear garden, tennis court, and swimming pool. La Magnaneraie is highly recommendable.

Villeneuve's budget offering is the Hôtel de l'Atelier, 5 rue de la Foire (tel. 90-25-01-84), a 16th-century village house that has preserved much of its original style. A tiny, two-story, all-purpose central lounge is dominated by a walk-in stone fireplace. In the sun-pocket rear garden, potted orange and fig trees grow, the cook picking the first figs to serve with the morning meal. The inn offers only 19 bedrooms, costing from 140F ($19.31) to 230F ($31.72) in a double with either a shower or private bath. The accommodations are furnished informally, and are certainly comfortable, tidy, and immaculate. In the old bourgeois dining room, a continental breakfast is the only meal served. The inn is closed from December to February.

LIVING ON THE OUTSKIRTS: At Noves, 8½ miles from Avignon, the **Auberge de Noves,** out the D28 (tel. 90-94-19-21), is an elegant Relais et Châteaux run by the Lalleman family, who offer 19 modern and attractively decorated rooms, each with a complete bathroom. On its own hilltop park, it seems a cross between a Riviera villa and a Beverly Hills movie-star mansion of the '20s. When Monsieur and Madame Lalleman purchased it in 1950, it was a religious retreat. Very painstakingly they set about transforming it into one of the finest luxury country estates in Provence. Their bedchambers are furnished with period pieces, and each room has been individually conceived. Views are exceptional, and a few units have their own sun terrace. A single costs 380F ($52.40), and this will be a small room in the wing of the inn. For two persons, a twin-bedded room peaks at 1,950F ($268.91). A 15% service charge is added to all tariffs. Breakfast is extra. In high season, two persons can stay here on the half-board plan (obligatory) at a cost going from 850F ($117.22) to 1,850F ($255.12) daily. It is imperative to make reservations as far in advance as possible. The food is among the best served in the province, including such gastronomic specialties as herb-flavored filet d'agneau (lamb), a chicken-liver mousse, superb sole, veal kidneys Printanier, and rabbit in a mustard sauce. From the first-class wine cellar come such selections as Châteauneuf-du-Pape and Lirac. During the day, guests enjoy the tennis courts and swimming pool. The auberge is closed in January and February. The restaurant does not serve lunch on Wednesday.

At Pontet, three miles north on the N7, the **Hostellerie de Cassagne,** Route de Vedène (D62) (tel. 90-31-04-18), might be your best bet for food and lodging in the Avignon area. It's an enchanting little rustic-style Provence inn with only 14 bedrooms. A double or twin-bedded room ranges in price from 350F ($48.27) to 380F ($52.40); half board is from 820F ($113.08) to 900F ($124.11) for two persons. The bedchambers have a country look and are provided with all the necessities. The rooms overlook a park with a swimming pool and adjacent tennis courts. The cuisine here is exceptionally good. You take your meals in a rustic dining room, or at a table in the garden. The owner, Gallon J. Michel, features such dishes as coquilles St-Jacques and petits légumes, loup or turbot, and deviled lamb. Meals go for 140F ($19.31) to 310F ($42.75) and up if you'd like to visit just to dine. However, call first for a reservation. The restaurant is open all year.

11. Gordes

Past typical Provençal vegetation, the winding road leads to Gordes. All around are stone huts called *bories*. These windowless, beehive-shaped stone dwellings continue to puzzle archeologists. Some have suggested that they predate Christ, while others maintain they were built as recently as the 16th century, possibly by residents fleeing from the plague. The **Borie Village** has opened about two miles outside Gordes. Head out the D15, going right beyond a fork at the D2. A sign will indicate that you make a right-hand turn. The road will be unsurfaced. You must park your car and walk for about 45 minutes to reach this museum where several dwellings have been furnished with primitive tools, including some pottery excavated on the site. Hours are 9 a.m. to dusk from the first of February until mid-November. In deepest winter, hours are only 10 a.m. to dusk on Saturday and Sunday. Admission is 12F ($1.66). Gordes is 25 miles from Avignon and 40 miles from the airport at Marseille.

The **Château de Gordes** dominating the town was erected in the 11th century, then later rebuilt during the first half of the 16th. In the Renaissance style, the charteau was really a fortress with round towers in each of its four corners. A crenellated roof is supported by the north walls. To visit, check with the guard on the right inside the yard. It is open daily except Tuesday from 10 a.m. to noon and 2 to 6 p.m., charging an admission of 10F ($1.38).

The **Musée Vasarely** (tel. 90-72-02-89) is in the Château de Gordes. The painter Victor Vasarely is one of the founding fathers of kinetic art. He has a house nearby, and has leased the château from the village for 35 years for a rental of 1F a year. On the first floor are tapestries in brilliant colors. Betraying a surrealist influence, older works are on the third floor. In all, the château houses 1,500 paintings. The museum is open daily except Tuesday from 10 a.m. to noon and 2 to 6 p.m. Admission is 10F ($1.38).

In the neighborhood of Gordes is **Vénasque,** seven miles southeast of Carpentras on the way to Orange. In this village a bapistery dates from the 6th century.

Even closer to Gordes is **Sénanque,** on the D15 and D177. The **Abbey de Sénanque** (tel. 90-72-02-05) is one of the three Cistercian abbeys of Provence. It was in use as an abbey until 1969. The abbey has had a rough time of it since it was founded in 1148. The bishop of Ménerbes had it ravaged in the 16th century, leading to its abandonment. However, the monks came back in the 19th century. When it ceased to be used as an abbey, the property became a cultural endowment center, still owned by the Cistercians. Major permanent exhibitions are an architectural itinerary through Sénanque and one on Sahara of the Nomads, Desert and Man. As you walk around and explore, it is easy to understand why Thomas Merton found peace here some 30 years ago. The abbey is open daily from 10 a.m. to 7 p.m. in July and August and from 10 a.m. to 1 p.m. and 2 to 7 p.m. September, April, May, and June. From October to the end of March, hours are 10 a.m. to noon and 2 to 6 p.m. Admission is 18F ($2.48) for adults, 5F (69¢) for children. Medieval music and Gregorian chant are still performed here from mid-July to mid-August.

FOOD AND LODGING: **Domaine de l'Enclos,** Route de Sénanque (tel. 90-72-08-22), is the most charming hotel in the region. It sits on a six-acre plot of flowering terrain a short distance above the center of town, opposite a view of the nearby mountains of Provence. There are only ten accommodations on the entire property, each within a thick-walled cottage of local stone, surrounded by a manicured garden. The cottages offer an elegantly rustic decor, the perfect spot for a romantic weekend. Depending upon the choice of cottage, doubles cost between 450F ($62.06) and 1,350F ($186.17). Most guests stay here on the half-board plan, going for 800F ($110.32) to 1,600F ($220.64) per person daily. A pool and tennis court offer distraction.

A superb cuisine is served in the panoramic dining room. There, Philippe Grangier concocts a delectable array of regionally inspired dishes with a creative twist. Specialties change frequently, based both on the availability of ingredients and the inspiration of the young and rising chef. Nonresidents who call for a reservation can enjoy a meal here, perhaps sampling such dishes as grilled salmon with a fennel-flavored butter. Fixed-price menus cost from 160F ($22.06) to 200F ($27.58), with à la carte meals averaging 340F ($46.89). The hotel is open from mid-March to mid-November.

La Mayanelle, rue Combe (tel. 90-72-00-28), is a stone patrician mansion tracing its origins back to the 12th century. It is owned by Monsieur Mayard, who welcomes guests to one of his ten beautifully furnished and accessorized bedchambers, for which he charges 190F ($26.20) for single occupancy, 330F ($45.51) in a double. It's preferable that you take the half-board rate, ranging from 310F ($42.75) to 540F ($74.47) per person. In the vaulted dining room, with its high ceilings, you'll be served such regional specialties as roast guinea fowl, duck with olives, lamb flavored with the herbs of Provence, grilled salmon, and homemade fruit tarts. If you're visiting only for a meal, you'll find menus at 110F ($15.17) to 210F ($28.96). The entry with its informal terrace, weeping willow, open stone staircase, arched windows, and flower planters makes for an inviting welcome. The small mansion, which overlooks the rolling hills of Vaucluse, is closed for dining on Monday night and Tuesday, and takes a vacation from January 2 to March 1.

Les Bories (tel. 90-72-00-51) is about 1½ miles outside Gordes (take D177). It takes its name from those dried stone constructions called *bories*. In this countryside of antiquity, Les Bories blends in with its background, providing a kind of rustic luxury. Near the inn stands the Abbey of Sénanque which dates from the 12th century. Gabriel Rousselet is the chef-owner, and he relies on his spontaneous inspiration in the planning of meals. Although he's a classic cook, he likes innovative dishes as well. He always uses fresh products which he personally selects. His specialties include a croustade of guinea fowl, an omelet with truffles, an orange soufflé, and nougat ice cream. Meals cost from 200F ($27.58) to 300F ($41.37). There are only three bedrooms with private bath, which are rented for 300F ($41.37) in a single, 450F ($62.06) in a double. In fair weather you can dine on a covered terrace with a view. The inn is closed on Wednesday and in December.

12. Orange

Overlooking the Valley of the Rhône, Orange tempts visitors with: (1) the third-largest triumphal arch extant in Europe, and (2) the best preserved Roman theater in Europe. Of the latter, Louis XIV, who toyed with the idea of moving it to Versailles, said: "It is the finest wall in my kingdom."

In the southern part of town, the theater, **le Théâtre Antique,** Place des Frères-Mounet, dates from the days of Hadrian. Built against a hill, it once seated 8,000 spectators in tiered seats divided into three different sections (classes weren't allowed to mix). It is nearly 350 feet long and 125 feet high. Carefully restored, the theater is noted for its fine acoustics, and is used today for outdoor entertainment. In season it is open from 9 a.m. to noon and 2 to 5:30 p.m., charging an admission of 10F ($1.38). At the end of July, a drama, dance, and music festival takes place here, called **Les Choregies d'Orange.** To reach its bureau of information or to inquire about ticket sales, telephone 90-34-15-52 or 90-34-24-24.

To the west of the theater once stood one of the biggest temples in Gaul which, combined with a gymnasium and the theater, formed one of the greatest buildings in the empire. Across the street at Place des Frères-Mounet, the **Musée de la Ville,** Place du Théâtre-Antique (tel. 90-34-10-06), displays fragments excavated in the arena. Your ticket to the ancient theater will also admit you here.

Even older than the theater is the **Arch of Triumph,** on the Avenue de l'Arc-de-Triomphe, which shows some decay but is still fairly well preserved. Built to honor the conquering legions of Caesar, it rises 72 feet and is nearly 70 feet wide. It's composed of a trio of arches held up by Corinthian columns. The sculptural decorations are well preserved. In the Middle Ages it was used as a dungeon for prisoners.

Orange gets its name from the days when it was a dependency of the Dutch House of Orange-Nassau. It lies about 75 miles northwest of Marseille (Avignon is about 16 miles to the south). Before leaving Orange, head for the hilltop park, the **Colline Saint-Eutrope,** for a view of the surrounding valley with its mulberry plantations.

FOOD AND LODGING: **Hôtel Louvre et Terminus,** 89 Avenue Frédéric-Mistral (tel. 90-34-10-08), is a conservatively decorated hotel, the best in town, whose comfort is enhanced with an outdoor terrace ringed with flowers. The Domarle family are the owners, charging from 175F ($24.13) in a single, up to 325F ($44.82) in a double. All but two of the accommodations contain full private bath. The hotel is closed from mid-December to mid-January.

Euromotel, 80 Route de Caderousse (tel. 90-34-24-10), is a comfortably furnished modern hotel outside the edge of the city. Its 100 rooms are arranged around a series of gardens, the largest of which contains an outdoor swimming pool. Each well-furnished unit has its own private bath and phone. Rates range from 280F ($38.61) in a single up to 310F ($42.75) in a double. Fixed-price meals in the adjoining restaurant cost from 85F ($11.72) to 200F ($27.58). The hotel is open all year.

Hôtel Arène, Place de Langes (tel. 90-34-10-95), overlooks a quiet square with plane trees. The rooms are warm, comfortable, and well furnished, with rich tapestries and attractive bedcovers. The top price of 250F ($34.48) is for a double with bath; for a double with shower and toilet the tab is 210F ($28.96). The restaurant is one of the best in town. The owners catered to Queen Juliana when she visited. But even if you're not from the House of Orange, you'll still get a royal welcome from the owners, Monsieur and Madame Gérard Coutel. The restaurant, done in a turn-of-the-century theme, is independent of the hotel. For apéritif time, you are entertained with piano music. Traditional Provençal food is served for around 90F ($12.41) for a set menu, or you can order à la carte.

Le Pigraillet, Colline Saint-Eutrope (tel. 90-34-44-25), is a sensitively directed villa which contains a swimming pool in a pine forest and a popular restaurant that in summer stretches onto an outdoor terrace. Two fixed-price menus are offered, each one featuring well-prepared specialties. The menus cost from 120F ($16.55) to 170F ($23.44), and are served every day except Sunday night and Monday, and from early January to mid-February.

On the Outskirts

At Rochegude, 6½ miles from Orange, the **Château de Rochegude** (tel. 75-04-81-88) is a magnificent turreted castle, now a Relais et Châteaux, standing in its own 37 acres of parkland. It goes back to the 11th century, and throughout the centuries it has been added to by its distinguished owners, which have ranged from the pope to the dauphin. Constructed of stone at the edge of a hill, it is surrounded by the Rhône vineyards. Because of its location in Provence, it is spread out, not drawn in protectively as it might be if it were in Normandy. There are several sunny terraces for refreshments.

The present owners, Messieurs Galibert and Chabert, have brought in many 20th-century innovations, although touches of antiquity survive, including a Roman dungeon. The furnishings and decor throughout the hotel are outstanding. Each of the 25 bedrooms is done in a period, such as Napoléon III and Louis XVI. Some rooms have tapestries, some are mirrored, and others are richly adorned with gilt, crystal, and fine carpeting. The bathrooms are deluxe as well. Singles begin at 360F ($49.64), and doubles cost 1,100F ($151.69). Special features include a marble swimming pool that would have pleased Nero and a tennis court. Reservations are necessary. The château is open from mid-March until the end of October.

I've left the best for last—the food, which is exceptional, as is the service. You can enjoy meals in the stately dining room, surrounded by pots of flowering plants. Specialties include thin ravioli stuffed with cheese, red barbet fish filets on tomatoes and garlic, tournedos with truffles, and delectable desserts. A special feature is a barbecue by the swimming pool where guests prefer to take their meals on sunny days. Perhaps you'd like to stop for a meal. Prices range from 300F ($41.57) to 380F ($52.40).

Hostellerie Le Beffroi, rue de l'Évêché (tel. 90-36-04-71), is at Vaison-la-Romaine, 15 miles northeast of Orange. It is a 16th-century hotel with ochre walls, soft-red shutters, and much of the detailing that came from the original building. Across from the chiseled fountain in the Haute-Ville sector, the hotel is most charming. The interior is freshly wallpapered with country rustic flower designs that enhance the heavy ceiling beams and the plaster detailing above some of the fireplaces. The bedrooms are filled with 19th-century antiques and an intense attention to detail. To get to the hotel, you'll have to wind your car through the cobblestone streets of the old town. The hotel maintains a limited number of parking spaces. There's a garden with a view of the town where you can order breakfast. The 20 rooms range from a simple single with a minimum of plumbing for 120F ($16.55) to a double with bath for 330F ($45.51). Menus range from 100F ($13.79) to 165F ($22.75). No lunch is ever served Tuesday nor are any meals on Monday in the off-season. The hotel is open from mid-March to mid-November.

13. Châteauneuf-du-Pape

When French popes in the 14th century held forth at Avignon, Châteauneuf-du-Pape was built as their Castelgandolfo, or country seat. The "new castle of the pope" is now in ruins, lying about 12 miles north of Avignon, near the north border of Provence, just south of Orange. Although the castle built during the term of Pope John XXII is in ruins, its name is borne today by some of the world's finest red wines as well as a scarce but elegant white wine. The pope who had the castle built also had acres and acres of vineyards planted, thereby initiating the wine industry which bears its name. Little except a magnificent view remains of the castle, but the cellars have been restored and are used as headquarters of the local wine society, Échansonnerie des Papes.

In the vicinity, there are 14 wineries which can be visited and their wines tasted. A map in the Place de la Fontaine, the main square of the little village of Châteauneuf-du-Pape which lies below the castle ruins, shows how to find these wineries.

The museum of the **Caves du Père Anselm** in the village contains a wine press from the 16th century, plows from the 17th and 18th centuries, wine makers' tools, and barrel-making equipment, as well as a tasting cellar. The museum is open from 9 a.m. to noon and 2 to 6 p.m.

FOOD AND LODGING: Another castle, smaller than the Châteauneuf-du-Pape but built on the same lines, lying almost 2 miles outside the village, has been converted into the **Hostellerie Château des Fines Roches** (tel. 90-83-70-23), named for the 19th-century château. The château was named for the smooth rocks of the vineyard soil. The hostelry has only seven bedrooms, handsomely furnished with some antiques and all with bath, TV, and mini-bar. Singles cost from 320F ($44.13) and doubles from 475F ($65.50).

The restaurant of the establishment is its pièce de résistance. Jean-Pierre and Philippe Estevenin, who learned the business from their father, prepare a tempting array of fresh specialties based on the most attractive ingredients in the local markets. Menu specialties are included in fixed-price meals, with additional culinary delights tagged on as supplements. Your meal might include tournedos with truffles, an *assiette dégustation,* filets of red mullet with rosemary, aiguillette of duckling with peaches, or fisherman's salad with olive oil and lime juice. Desserts from the trolley include a flavorful and noteworthy grape-flavored sorbet. An impressive and reasonable wine list is offered, including local vintages which are so popular they are totally consumed here and cannot be found elsewhere.

Dinner, costing from 195F ($26.89), is served until 9 p.m. nightly except Sunday night and all day Monday. Seating is limited, so it's recommended that you make reservations. The hotel is open from March through December. You'll find the Fines Roches on the D17 going south toward Avignon.

Chapter XXIII

THE FRENCH RIVIERA

1. Menton
2. Roquebrune and Cap Martin
3. Monaco
4. Eze and La Turbie
5. Beaulieu
6. St-Jean and Cap Ferrat
7. Villefranche
8. Nice
9. St-Paul-de-Vence
10. Vence
11. Cagnes-sur-Mer
12. Biot
13. Antibes and Cap d'Antibes
14. Juan-les-Pins
15. Golfe-Juan and Vallauris
16. Mougins
17. Grasse
18. Cannes
19. La Napoule-Plage
20. St-Tropez

IT'S BEEN CALLED the world's most exciting stretch of beach. The towns, ports, and hamlets of the Riviera are best approached as if on a safari, going from chic St-Tropez in the west to sleepy Menton at the Italian frontier, climbing into the hill towns such as St-Paul-de-Vence when you tire of the sands.

Every habitué has a favorite oasis and will try to convince you of its merits. Some say "Nice is passé." Others maintain that "Cannes is queen." Still others shun both resorts in favor of Juan-les-Pins, and yet another discriminating crowd would winter only at St-Jean / Cap Ferrat. If you have a large bankroll you may prefer Cap d'Antibes, but if money is short you may find companions at the old port of Villefranche. Truth is, there is no best resort. Each place along the Riviera—Beaulieu by the sea or eagle's-nest Eze—offers its unique flavor and special merits. It's a question of taste, and the French Riviera—Stephen

Liégeard's "Côte d'Azur" (Azure Coast)—is famous or infamous for catering to every taste.

The coast is steep and rocky in the main, but it's studded with harbors, ports, gambling casinos, and beach resorts. It's a sun-drenched land, with olive groves and vineyards, where if you're Harold Robbins, you can afford a villa. Cactus, eucalyptus, bougainvillea, lemons, almonds, mimosa, wild anemones, oranges, roses, and laurel grow in abundance, at the foot of the last spurs of the alpine chain.

A trail of modern artists attracted to the brilliant light and the setting of the Côte d'Azur have left a rich heritage: Matisse in his chapel at Vence, Cocteau at Menton and Villefranche, Picasso at Antibes (and seemingly everywhere else), Léger at Biot, Renoir at Cagnes, and Bonnard at Le Cannet. The best collection of all is at the Maeght Foundation at St-Paul-de-Vence.

The Riviera's high season used to be winter and spring. Fashion dictated that no one went in the summer. However, with changing tastes, July and August have long been the most crowded months, and reservations are imperative. In summer the average temperature is 75° Fahrenheit. In winter the temperature averages around 49° Fahrenheit, particularly in January, when Nice experiences its coldest weather.

In hotels the choice is perhaps the most varied in the world, ranging from a belle époque palace to a stone house in a grape-grower's vineyard in the hills.

The **Corniches of the Riviera,** as depicted in countless films, stretch from Nice to Menton. The Alps drop into the Mediterranean, and roads were carved along the way. The lower road, about 20 miles long, is called the **Corniche Inférieure.** Along this road you'll reach the port of Villefranche, the Cap Ferrat peninsula, Beaulieu, and Cap Martin.

Built between World War I and the beginning of World War II, the Middle Road, or **Moyenne Corniche,** 19 miles long, also runs from Nice to Menton. Winding in and out of tunnels and through mountains, it is spectacular. The highlight of the trip is at mountaintop Eze.

Finally, the **Grande Corniche**—the most spectacular of the roads from Nice to Menton—was ordered built on the ancient Aurelian Way by Napoleon in 1806. La Turbie and Le Vistaëro are the principal targets along the 20-mile stretch which reaches an altitude of more than 1,600 feet at Col d'Eze.

In this chapter we'll explore the Riviera beginning in Menton and ending in St-Tropez.

1. Menton

It's Italianate more than French. Right at the border of Italy, Menton marks the eastern frontier of the Côte d'Azur. Its climate, incidentally, is considered the warmest on the Mediterranean coast, a reputation that attracts a large, rather elderly British colony throughout the winter. Menton experiences a foggy day every ten years, or so they say. And it doesn't have one puddle of posh the way Cannes or Juan-les-Pins does. For that reason, it is sought out and widely praised by its habitués, many of whom are complaining that more and more visitors are discovering Menton's charms every year.

According to a local legend, Eve was the first to experience Menton's glorious climate. Expelled from the Garden of Eden along with Adam, she tucked a lemon in her bosom, planting it at Menton because it reminded her of her former stamping ground. The lemons still grow in profusion here, and the fruit of that tree is given a position of honor at the Lemon Festival in February. Actually, the oldest Menton visitor may have arrived 30,000 years ago. He's still around—or at least his skull is—in the Municipal Museum (see below).

Don't be misled by all those "palace-hotels" studding the hills. No longer open to the public, they have been divided and sold as private flats. Many of these turn-of-the-century structures were erected to accommodate elderly Europeans, mainly English and German, who arrived carrying a book written by one Dr. Bennett in which he extolled the joys of living at Menton.

The town used to belong to Monaco, five miles to the west. The Corniches de la Riviera will take you from Nice to Menton, a distance of 21 miles. On the Golfe de la Paix ("Gulf of Peace"), Menton sits on a rocky promontory, dividing the bay into two parts. The fishermen's town, the older part with narrow streets, is in the east; the tourist zone and residential belt is in the west.

Jean Cocteau liked this resort, and today there is a **Musée Jean-Cocteau, le Bastion** (tel. 93-57-72-30), at the harbor near Quai Bonaparte, in a 17th-century fort near the harbor. The museum contains the death portrait of Cocteau sketched by MacAvoy, as well as MacAvoy's portrait of Cocteau in a better day. Some of the artist's memorabilia are here—stunning charcoals and watercolors, ceramics, signed letters, and 21 brightly colored pastels. Two Aubusson tapestries based on cartoons by Cocteau are also on display. The museum is open from 9 a.m. to noon and 2 to 6 p.m. except Monday and Tuesday. Admission is 4F (55¢).

Cocteau decorated the **Salle des Mariages** at the **Hôtel de Ville,** rue de la République, which is open daily except Saturday and Sunday, from 9 a.m. to noon and 2 to 6 p.m. For 5F (69¢) you'll be admitted. The frescoes are allegorical, and depict, among other things, the legend of Orpheus and Eurydice.

The **Municipal Museum,** rue Lorédan-Larchey (tel. 93-35-84-64), contains the head of the Grimaldi man, found in 1884 in the Baoussé-Rousse caves. In addition, it has an interesting archeological and folkloric collection. The museum is closed on Monday and Tuesday. From June 15 to September 15 hours are 10 a.m. to noon and 3 to 6 p.m. Otherwise, its hours are from 2 to 5:30 p.m.

The **Palais Carnolès,** 3 Avenue de la Madone (tel. 93-35-49-71), contains a collection of 14th-, 16th-, and 17th-century paintings from Italy, Flanders, Holland, and the French schools, as well as an exhibition of modern paintings, including works by Dufy, Valadon, Derain, and Leprin—all of which were acquired by a British subject, Wakefield-Mori. Acquisitions of modern art are also displayed biannually. The museum is open daily except Monday and Tuesday from 10 a.m. to noon and 3 to 6 p.m. (2:30 to 5:30 p.m. in winter). Admission is free.

HOTELS: Menton offers quite acceptable lodgings at prices far lower than you'd pay at nearby Monte Carlo.

Hotel Princess et Richmond, 32 Avenue du Général-de-Gaulle (tel. 93-35-80-20), at the edge of the sea, stands near an intricately carved slate-roof chapel a short distance from the commercial center. Its vivid blue and white façade is graced with fluttering awnings and flanked with a sun-flooded terrace planted with flowers. The owner, Mr. Caravelli, who can often be seen in the marble-floored lobby, rents out 45 comfortable bedrooms, with fine, conservatively styled furnishings and private balconies. Each accommodation is soundproof, with air conditioning, a mini-bar, phone, and TV hookup. All units are suitable for either one or two persons. Depending on the exposure, the room itself, and the season, rates range from 250F ($34.48) to 350F ($48.27). Drinks are served on the roof's panoramic terrace, where a view of the curving shoreline can be enjoyed.

Hotel Chambord, 6 Avenue Boyer (tel. 93-35-94-19), occupies a desirable position on the main square of town, next to the gingerbread-laden façade of the casino. It is a clean and angular hotel faced with rows of metallic balconies and awnings. You'll find a colorful array of streamlined modern rooms, each with a private bath, costing 110F ($15.17) in a single, from 340F ($46.89) to 375F ($51.71) in a double. Breakfast is the only meal served.

Le Napoléon, 29 Porte de France (tel. 93-35-89-50), is built on a palm-tree-shaded avenue, and it has its own free-form swimming pool, set in a small gar-

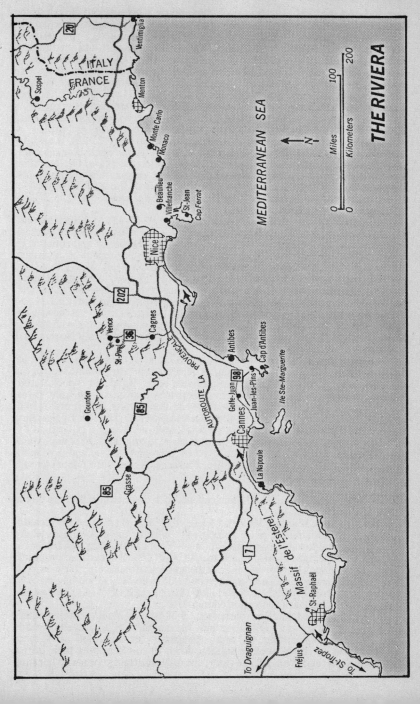

THE RIVIERA

MEDITERRANEAN SEA

Miles
Kilometers
100   200

N

ITALY
FRANCE
Ventimiglia
Sospel
Menton
Monte Carlo
Monaco
Beaulieu
Villefranche
St-Jean
Cap Ferrat
Nice
202
Vence
36
Cagnes
St-Paul
Gourdon
85
85
Grasse
AUTOROUTE LA PROVENÇALE
Antibes
Cap d'Antibes
Golfe-Juan
98
Juan-les-Pins
Ile Ste-Marguerite
Cannes
La Napoule
7
Massif de l'Esterel
St-Raphaël
To Draguignan
Fréjus
To St-Tropez
20

den and stone terrace. Guests unpack, slip into their bikinis, and jump into the pool. Afterward, they meet on the rooftop terrace, enjoying meals in an air-conditioned restaurant, entirely refurbished and redecorated. Furnished with 18th-century English and Italian pieces, the main lounge, with a bar at one side, is really like a large living room. The bedrooms—40 in all, each with bath and balcony—are decorated in vivid colors contrasting with mahogany pieces. All the sea-view rooms are air-conditioned, with a clear view over the water and the old town. The half-board rate ranges from 425F ($58.61) to 780F ($107.56) per person, the latter price for the sea-view units. If you are just stopping by, a luncheon or dinner in the panoramic restaurant on the sixth floor costs from 150F ($20.69). The hotel is closed from November 1 to mid-December.

Hôtel Méditerranée, 5 rue de la République (tel. 93-28-25-25), is a white-and salmon-colored, eight-story hotel whose 90 rooms each contain bath, phone, radio, and mini-bar, along with TV and video reception. On the premises is a raised terrace with a view of the sea, chaise longues, and potted plants. The hotel opened in 1982, about three short blocks from the sea. The attractively decorated bedrooms rent for 320F ($44.13) in a single and 350F ($48.27) in a double. Children under 4 stay free.

Viking, 2 Avenue du Général-de-Gaulle (tel. 93-57-95-85), brings contemporary Scandinavian comfort and style to the Côte d'Azur. Under Swedish management, the hotel is set back one street from the beach and contains its own small swimming pool. The rooms are designed to take maximum advantage of the sun and air, most of the accommodations having tall, wide glass doors opening onto a private balcony. In season, from mid-June to mid-September, the hotel charges from 390F ($53.78) in a double, from 340F ($46.89) in a single, with a continental breakfast costing extra. In addition, studios with kitchen and refrigerator are available, housing from one to four persons (seven days minimum). On the sixth floor is a sun terrace, and there's a massage unit with a sauna as well, reflecting the Viking's Scandinavian ties. The hotel closes November 1 to January 1.

Le Dauphin, 28 Avenue du Général-de-Gaulle (tel. 93-35-76-37), was totally rebuilt in 1967. Just off the beach, its balconies open toward the sea. Of the 30 soundproof hotel rooms, 25 contain private bath. The decor is uncluttered, with stark-white walls, floral draperies, picture windows, and in some cases, Louis XVI-style chairs and beds. A sea-view double with full bath rents for 340F ($46.89). But in a bathless single, the price is only 175F ($24.13). In glistening marble, with gray carpeting, the entry hall is inviting. More popular than the drinking lounge is the raised front terrace overlooking the sea, which comes complete with garden furniture, a fringed canopy, and stone planters of marigolds, geraniums, and birds of paradise. The hotel is closed from late October until just before Christmas.

RESTAURANTS: French and Italian cuisine, with emphasis on fish, are on the bill of fare in Menton.

Rocamadour, 1 Square Victoria (tel. 93-35-76-04), is an especially pleasant restaurant overlooking the port. You dine at tables set under a canopy, where colored lights are turned on at night, adding a bit of gaiety. The chef, Monsieur Ducas, offers meals at 110F ($15.17) to 150F ($20.69). You can also order à la carte, sampling such tasty dishes as grilled scampi, sole meunière, foie gras, confit de canard, maigret de canard, and soupe de poisson. Depending on your choice of a main dish, expect to spend 120F ($16.55) to 250F ($34.48) for a complete meal. The restaurant is closed Monday.

Chez Diana, 31 Quai Bonaparte (tel. 93-35-94-64), is a little dining oddity along the port. It's run by Diana Archer, the daughter of a Lancashire textile magnate, who, according to one newspaper account, led a "grand-Guignolesque life story" before settling down to this charming little bistro. When she's not telling you her life story, she may entertain guests with her singing voice, honoring Gershwin, Brel, and Piaf. She also plays the guitar. But this is not just a house of entertainment or amusement. The kitchen also turns out good food, including savory spaghetti and scampi dishes, along with excellent beef (a few English concoctions), and pizzas as well in honor of Italy just across the border. Set menus cost 60F ($8.27) and 95F ($13.10), and you can also dine à la carte. The place closes on Wednesday in the off-season.

La Calanque (The Creek), 13 Square Victoria (tel. 93-35-83-15), is the best for the budget along the port. Tables are set out under shade trees in the fair weather—within full view of the yachts moored in the harbor. Here, in pleasant and colorful surroundings, you can order a complete meal for 95F ($13.10). On the à la carte selections, you can allow your tastebuds to wander back and forth across the French and Italian borders, but you may end up paying 165F ($22.75) or more. The spaghetti napolitaine, tripe niçoise, soupe de poissons, and fresh sardines (very savory—grilled on charcoal) are recommended. A specialty of the house is the bouillabaisse. If the weather forbids al fresco dining, find a table inside, where it's pleasantly decorated in the style of a provincial inn, with pine paneling, beamed ceilings, and gourds hanging from the rafters. It is closed Tuesday night and Wednesday, and in November.

2. Roquebrune and Cap Martin

Roquebrune, along the Grande Corniche, is a charming little mountain-perched village, with vaulted streets. The only one of its kind, the **Château de Roquebrune** (tel. 93-35-07-22) was originally a 10th-century Carolingian castle. The present structure dates in part from the 13th century. Characterized by two square towers, it contains a historical museum. From the towers, you'll have a spectacular view along the coast to Monaco. The castle gates are open every day from 9 a.m. to noon and 2 to 7 p.m. during July and August. In June and September hours are 9:30 a.m. to noon and 2 to 6 p.m.; in winter, 10 a.m. to noon and 2 to 5 p.m. The château is closed on Friday. Admission is 8F ($1.10) for adults, 4F (55¢) for children under 14.

Three miles west of Menton, Cap Martin is a satellite of the larger resort. It has long been associated with the wealthy and the famous, ever since the Empress Eugénie wintered here in the 19th century. In time, the resort was honored by the presence of Sir Winston Churchill. Don't go there thinking you'll find a wide, sandy beach. You'll encounter plenty of rocks, against a backdrop of pine and olive trees.

WHERE TO STAY: Some excellent selections are to be found, beginning with the most expensive.

Vistaëro, Grande Corniche, Route Nationale 7 (tel. 93-35-01-50). For years, stopping here at least for a drink has been one of the major thrills in driving along the Grande Corniche. This spectacular hotel and *restaurant panoramique* stands like the figurehead of a ship on the outer ridge of the mountains, running parallel to the coast. Featured in many a Riviera espionage or jewel-theft flick, the "airplane view" of Monaco is spectacular. Equally imposing is the design of the Vistaëro. Interlocked by steel girders into the rocks, three levels are cantilevered out into space so that every room seems to float on cloud nine.

Descending to the lower lounges and rooms, you reach a large reflection pool, edged with rows of subtropical plants and flowers. Ocean-view dining rooms open off that. Even if you don't sleep here, consider a deluxe luncheon or dinner. With that view, the food could be mediocre and people would still come. Actually, it's on a high level—expensive, but worth it. Set menus are offered for 190F ($26.20), 300F ($41.37), and 350F ($48.27). On the à la carte, costing around 300F ($41.37), you may prefer to begin your meal with a lobster mousse or perhaps smoked salmon. Fish and meat specialties include sole Vistaëro and carré d'agneau aux herbes (loin of lamb, flavored with herbs, roasted on a spit). An orange tart makes a good dessert. Even if you can't take a meal, stop at the club-like drinking lounge and terrace, selecting a bamboo chair.

To balance the avant-garde architecture, the director decided to furnish the hotel with traditional pieces. For example, the dining room has classical 18th-century-style chairs. The lounge areas—several of them on different levels—contain Oriental rugs, antique bronze torchiers, and strong colors. The bedrooms are individually conceived, each with a vibrant personality, be it in bamboo, plaid, or floral. Every room has a bath, and of course, a view. For half board, in season, one person pays 1,050F ($144.80) to 1,900F ($262.01). The crowning glory of the hotel is its swimming pool, seemingly jutting into space. It's a supreme holiday retreat. The hotel is open only from April to November.

Hôtel Victoria et de la Plage, 7 Promenade du Cap (tel. 93-35-65-90), is a rectangular building constructed in the mid-'60s, but which has been operated by the François Chauffour family since 1980. The hotel is set behind a semi-tropical garden and yellow awnings across the street from the sea. If you have a drink at the bar, decorated with a sweeping mural of the Alps, you'll probably be greeted by the family dog. The 30 well-furnished bedrooms are available from the first of February until the end of October, and each contains a private bath, color TV, and an individual safe. A single costs 220F ($30.34) to 310F ($42.75), a double runs 400F ($55.16) to 500F ($68.95).

WHERE TO DINE: Hippocampe, 44 Avenue Winston-Churchill (tel. 93-35-81-91), is the best restaurant along the seafront. Lodged almost below the coastal road, occupying a garden shelf on the sea, it offers a full view of the bay and even the Italian coastline. Made safe by a thick stone wall, a terrace is shaded by five crooked pine trees. The "Sea Horse" is a garden house of stone and glass, persuasively attractive with its tile roof and scarlet and pink potted geraniums. The host, Jack Teyssier, offers two set meals costing 132F ($18.20) and 250F ($34.48). À la carte specialties include filets de sole en brioche and coq au vin. The terrine of salmon in a basil sauce and the duck with peaches are guaranteed crowd-pleasers. The restaurant is closed in January, May, and October, and on Monday. Out of season, only lunch is served. However, in season, both lunch and dinner are served daily except Thursday and Sunday.

Au Grand Inquisiteur, 18 rue du Château (tel. 93-35-05-37), is a culinary find. It's a miniature restaurant in a two-room cellar (actually an old converted sheep pen) near the top of the medieval mountaintop village of Roquebrune. On the steep, winding road to the château, it is made of rough-cut stone, with large oak beams. Every nook is crammed with bric-a-brac, pewter plates, copper utensils, an old painting of a knight, and a wrought-iron torchère. Taped music contributes to the 16th-century atmosphere. The restaurant is run by a French couple. The husband has been a professional cook since he was 14 years old, and his English-speaking wife reigns in the dining room. In summer—that is, from May until mid-October—they are open for dinner only. Otherwise, they are open for both lunch and dinner. The restaurant is closed on Monday, from early November to Christmas, and for two weeks in mid-January. The cookery depends on the season, as they rely on fresh produce. For example, in summer they offer squash blossoms stuffed with morels. For dinner a menu is offered for 120F ($16.55), or you can order à la carte, paying around 190F ($26.20).

3. Monaco

The outspoken Katharine Hepburn once called it "a pimple on the chin of the south of France." She wasn't referring to the principality's lack of beauty but rather to the preposterous idea of having a little country, a feudal anomaly, taking up some of the choicest coastline along the Riviera. Hemmed in by France on three sides and facing the Mediterranean, Monaco staunchly maintains its independence. Even Charles de Gaulle couldn't force Prince Rainier to do away with his tax-free policy. As almost everybody in an overburdened world knows by now, the Monégasques do not pay taxes. Part of their country's revenue comes from tourism and gambling.

Monaco, or rather its capital of Monte Carlo, has for a century been a symbol of glamor. Its legend was further enhanced by the marriage in 1956 of the world's most eligible bachelor, Prince Rainier, to an American film star, Grace Kelly. She met the prince when she attended the Cannes Film Festival to promote the Hitchcock movie she made with Cary Grant, *To Catch a Thief.* A daughter, Caroline, was born to the royal couple in 1957; a son, Albert, in 1958; and finally a second daughter, Stephanie, in 1965. The Monégasques welcomed the birth of Caroline but went wild at the birth of Albert, a male heir. According to a treaty drawn up in 1918, Monaco would become an autonomous state under French protection should the ruling dynasty become extinct.

At the time of writing, there is speculation that Prince Rainier will turn his tiny realm over to his son Albert, following the tragic accidental death of Princess Grace. Her sports car plunged over a cliff, killing her instantly, and the Monégasques still mourn her death.

Monaco became a property of the Grimaldi clan, a Genoese family, as early as 1297. With shifting loyalties, it has maintained something resembling independence ever since. In a fit of impatience, the French annexed it in 1793, but the ruling family recovered it in 1814, although the prince at the time couldn't bear to tear himself away from the pleasures of Paris for "dreary old Monaco."

The second-smallest state in Europe (Vatican City is the tiniest), Monaco consists of the old town, **Monaco-Ville,** sitting on a promontory, the Rock, 200 feet high—the seat of the royal palace and the government building, as well as the Oceanographic Museum (see below). On the west of the bay, **La Condamine,** the home of the Monégasques, is at the foot of the old town, forming its harbor and port sector.

Up from the port (walking is steep in Monaco) is **Monte Carlo,** once the playground of European royalty and still the center for the wintering wealthy, the setting for the casino and its gardens and the deluxe hotels, such as the Hôtel de Paris. The fourth part of Monaco, **Fontvieille,** is an industrial suburb, surprisingly neat; but this entire principality is kept tidy.

Ironically, **Monte-Carlo Beach** (about which more below), at the far frontier, is on French soil. It attracts a chic, well-heeled crowd, including movie stars in bikinis so perishable they would disappear should they get wet. The resort consists of a freshwater swimming pool, an artificial beach, and a sea-bathing establishment.

No one—just no one—used to go to Monaco in the summer. That has totally changed now—in fact, July and August tend to be so crowded that it's hard to get a room. Further, with the decline of royalty and multimillionaires, Monaco is developing a broader base of tourism (you can live there inexpensively, as you'll see from some of my restaurant and hotel recommendations). But it is misleading to suggest that you can live there cheaply. The Monégasques very frankly court the affluent visitor. You can also lose your shirt. "Suicide Terrace" at the casino, although not used as frequently as in the old days, is still a real temptation to many who have foolishly gambled away family fortunes.

Life still focuses around the **casino,** which has been the subject of countless legends and the setting for many films. High drama is played to the fullest here. Depending on the era, you might have seen Mata Hari shooting a tsarist colonel with a jewel-encrusted revolver when he tried to slip his hand inside her brassiere to discover her secrets—military, not mammillary. Before his death, King

Farouk, known as "The Swine," used to devour as many as eight roast guinea hens and 50 oysters before losing thousands of dollars at the table. *Chacun à son goût.*

Nine miles east of Nice, Monaco reaches its zenith of excitement at its annual **Rallye** and its **Grand Prix** in May.

SEEING THE SIGHTS: In summer, most visitors—many of whom come over from Nice just for the day—want to see the Italian-style home of Monaco's royal family, **Les Grands Appartements du Palais** (tel. 93-30-18-31). Visitors are shown the Throne Room and are allowed to see some of the royal family's art collection, including works by Brueghel and Holbein. Visiting hours are from 9:30 a.m. to 6:30 p.m. form mid-June until the end of September; otherwise, from 10 a.m. to 5 p.m. Admission is 20F ($2.76) per person. The ideal time to arrive is 11:55 a.m. to watch the changing of the guard. It's a brief (ten-minute) show. The palace was originally built in the 13th century, and part of it dates from the Renaissance era.

A major attraction of Monaco is the **Oceanographic Museum and Aquarium** (tel. 93-30-15-14), founded by Prince Albert, the great-grandfather of the present prince. In the main rotunda is a statue of Albert in his favorite costume —that of a sea captain. Displayed are specimens he collected during 30 years of expeditions aboard his oceanographic boats. The Aquarium—one of the finest in Europe—contains more than 90 tanks.

In the zoology room is exhibited Prince Albert's collection. Some of the exotic life he brought up were unknown species before he captured them. You'll see models of the oceanographic ships, aboard which the prince directed his scientific cruises from 1885 to 1914. Prince Albert's last cruises were on board the *Hirondelle II.* The most important part of its laboratory has been preserved and reconstituted as closely as possible. The cupboards contain all the equipment and documentation necessary for a scientific expedition.

On the main floor are skeletons of such specimens as a giant whale that drifted ashore at Pietra Ligure in September 1896, which is believed to have been the same that was harpooned by the prince in May of that year. The skeleton is remarkable for its healed fractures sustained when a vessel struck the animal drifting asleep on the surface. On the first floor, in the physical oceanography room, is an exhibition devoted to the "Discovery of the Ocean." In addition, underwater movies are continuously shown in the lecture room. The museum and aquarium are open daily in July and August from 9 a.m. to 9 p.m.; in June and September, from 9 a.m. to 7 p.m.; and from October to May, 9:30 a.m. to 7 p.m. The entrance fee is 40F ($5.52) for adults, 20F ($2.76) for children 6 to 16.

The **Palace Museum,** more formally known as the Musée du Palais Princier (Souvenirs Napoléoniens et Collection d'Archives), contains a collection of mementos of Napoleon and of Monaco itself. When the palace is closed—that is, when the prince is in residence—this museum is the only part of the palace open to the public. It is open daily from June 15 to October 15 from 9:30 a.m. to 6:30 p.m.; from mid-October to mid-June it is open daily except Monday, from 10:30 a.m. to 12:30 p.m. and from 2 to 5 p.m. Its annual closing is from the end of October until the second week of December. Admission is 10F ($1.38) for adults, 5F (69¢) for children.

You might also want to visit, especially if you have children with you, the **Historial des Princes de Monaco,** a waxworks museum at 27 rue Basse (tel. 93-30-39-05). It is open daily from July to September from 9:30 a.m. to 7:30 p.m.; from February to June, from 9:30 a.m. to 6:30 p.m.; and from October to January, 10:30 a.m. to 5:30 p.m. Admission is 14F ($1.93) for adults, 7F (97¢) for children.

Again, if you have children you may want to take them to the **National Museum** (Musée National), 17 Avenue Princesse Grace (tel. 93-30-91-26), featuring "automatons and dolls of yesterday," along with sculptures in the rose garden. In a villa designed by Charles Garnier, this museum is said to house one of the world's greatest collections of mechanical toys and dolls. See especially the Neapolitan crib from the 18th century, containing some 300 figures. This collection was assembled by Madame de Galea and presented to the principality in 1958. It stemmed from the habit in the 18th and 19th centuries of displaying new fashions on doll models. It is open daily from 10 a.m. to 12:15 p.m. and 2:30 to 6:30 p.m., charging adults 22F ($3.03), and children 5 to 15, 12F ($1.66).

You may also want to visit the **Jardin Exotique** (Exotic Garden), Boulevard du Jardin Exotique (tel. 93-30-33-65), built on the side of a rock and known for its collection of cacti. The gardens were begun by Prince Albert I, who was both a naturalist and a scientist. He spotted some succulents growing in the palace gardens. Knowing that these plants were normally found only in Central America or Africa, he created the garden from them. You can also explore the **Grottoes** in this garden, as well as a **Museum of Prehistoric Anthropology.** They are open daily, including Sunday, from 9 a.m. to 7 p.m.; closes at 6 p.m. off-season. Admission is 24F ($3.31) for adults, 12F ($1.66) for children 6 to 14. From here, the view of the principality is splendid.

HOTELS: In accommodations, the attention focuses on—

Deluxe Living

Hôtel de Paris, Place du Casino (tel. 93-50-80-80), is a Rolls-Royce-and-caviar experience in a prime position, right on the main plaza of Monte Carlo, opposite the casino. It opened in 1865. The ornate façade of the Paris sets the mood, with its marble pillars and nude mermaids rising from the top of the arched entrance doors. In the impressive reception lounge, an art nouveau rose window at the peak of the dome is said to make any woman appear attractive. It casts a glow over the hand-loomed carpeting, potted plants, classic pillars, and patent leather banquettes. At least two dozen movie companies have used this lobby as a background. Constantly being overhauled, the high-style bedrooms are kept fresh by frequent painting, and their furnishings are well tended to by a smoothly trained maintenance staff. High-season tariffs are charged at Christmas, New Year's, Easter, and in May, July, and August. A double with bath ranges in price from 1,500F ($206.85) to 1,700F ($234.43) for two persons. Singles begin at 1,300F ($179.27).

The ornateness is dazzling, with marble pillars, statues lining the wall, crystal chandeliers, sumptuous carpets, Louis XVI chairs, and a wall-size fin-de-siècle mural. To support this ambience, an orchestra softly plays Chopin. The food is superb—appropriate to the memory of Escoffier, who helped organize the kitchens and planned the menus. The evening usually begins in the bar, which combines a paneled ceiling with a baroque gilt bas-relief carving. On top of the Hôtel de Paris, the Grill Room with a sliding roof is vaguely styled in the Louis XIV period, with wrought-iron lanterns and carved woods. While you receive the best service possible, you can watch the arrival and departure of the world's greatest yachts. In back of the distinguished cuisine served at the hotel is a collection of 130,000 bottles of rare and fine wines kept in a dungeon chiseled out of the rocks, a honeycomb of passageways with racked bottles. In the Grill Room, a complete meal can be enjoyed at a price ranging from 500F ($68.95).

Other facilities available include a Bar Américain, boutiques, a beauty parlor, and an underground passageway leading to an indoor swimming pool, "Des Terrasses," perhaps the most spectacular on the coast. Winter winds don't matter, as it's protected, the curving heated pool carved out of a cliffside. A protective glass wall overlooks the yacht-filled harbor. In fair weather the wall can be opened onto an open-air terrace, with umbrella tables and sundeck chairs, set in the midst of palms. There is an authentic Finnish sauna, constructed with natural pine from the north and shaped slatted shelves on which to lie. Massages are available as well.

Hermitage, Square Beaumarchais (tel. 93-50-67-31). Picture yourself sitting in a wicker armchair, being served drinks in a belle époque rotunda under an ornate stained-glass dome with an encircling wrought-iron balcony of trailing ivy. Such is the setting of the Hermitage. There is no better example of turn-of-the-century architecture in all of Monaco. The "palace" was the creation of Jean Marquet (the same man who gave the world marquetry, work inlaid with different pieces of variously colored fine wood).

Just a few minutes from the casino, clinging to the edge of a cliff top, this hotel provides views of the harbor of yachts and the royal palace. The trappings are appropriate for the period, including large brass beds and decoratively framed doors opening onto balconies. The rates are adjusted according to the season. High season is Christmas, New Year's, Easter, July, and August. A double with bath ranges from 1,200F ($165.48) to 1,500F ($206.85). Singles begin at 1,000F ($137.90), going up to 1,300F ($179.27). The hotel's splendidly styled dining room, La Belle Époque, has marbled Corinthian columns, potted palms, paneled walls, and glittering chandeliers. A set meal is offered for 250F ($34.48), and most à la carte orders average 400F ($55.16) to 500F ($68.95). The Bar Scorpion, opened by Princess Grace in 1970, is a chic rendezvous spot. It becomes a piano bar at night.

The Upper Bracket

Loews Monte Carlo, Avenue des Spélugues (tel. 93-50-65-00), is a glistening, glittering voluptuous piece of Las Vegas transplanted with a French accent onto one of the most valuable pieces of real estate along the Côte d'Azur. Considered revolutionary ever since it was completed in 1975, it is now an integral part of Monégasque life. Loews sank the building's pylons deep into the Mediterranean seabottom at the base of a steep hill whose flattened top is the geographical heartbeat of Monte Carlo. The hotel has the most intense concentration of restaurants, bars, and nightclubs in Monaco. Even Prince Albert and Princess Stephanie show up for regular workouts in the seventh-floor health club. Many celebrities are attracted to the hotel, including Walter Cronkite and Peter Ustinov.

The cavernous casino, with its slot-machine "annex" on the seventh floor, presents all the ringing, whirring, clicking, blinking hubbub any gambler could ask for. The drinking facilities include a sun-flooded Tahitian-style lobby bar, with a dimly reflective ceiling and a view of the water. There's also the more intimate Jockey Club, where waiters wear full hunting regalia of dress pinks and white gloves. A pampas-style restaurant, L'Argentin, serves South American–style grilled meats and succulent fish. There is also a formal, gourmet-class restaurant, Le Foie Gras, for cozy suppers. The informal, warmly nautical enclave, Le Café de la Mer, is for breakfasts, snacks, and lighter meals. Near the rooftop, Le Pistou re-creates the flavors and textures of a Provençal inn. The show also has a regular cabaret, with bejeweled and feather-clad beauties, who during the day are likely to be seen enjoying the topless bathing facilities near the hotel's rooftop swimming pool.

The 650 bedrooms in this entertainment extravaganza are tastefully comfortable and plushly upholstered in an array of summertime shades, suggesting Palm Beach airiness. Everything is enhanced by the sweeping panoramic views. Each room has a color TV that can pick up even Atlanta-based news broadcasts. Singles cost from 1,200F ($165.48) to 1,700F ($234.43), doubles from 1,300F ($179.27) to 1,800F ($248.22) daily. Tennis, golf, deep-sea fishing, sailing, and scuba-diving are some of the sports that can be arranged at the Monte Carlo Country Club and the Monte Carlo Yacht Club.

Monte Carlo Beach Hôtel, Roquebrune-Cap Martin (tel. 93-78-21-40), lies not in Monaco but back in France at Roquebrune-Cap Martin. Originally constructed in 1928, for years it was known as the "Old Beach Hotel" until the Société des Bains de Mer decided that was too unglamorous a title for such a luxury retreat. Tons of money later, it emerged with a new name and vastly improved rooms and facilities. The most pampered guest always asks for the most beautiful accommodation in the house, the spacious circular unit that lies above the lobby. Eva Peron stayed here in 1947 during her infamous tour of Europe. Before she died, Princess Grace came here almost every day, paddling around the pool. The Olympic pool is open for a fee to members of the community who seem to have conspired to make this a rendezvous point for the richest and best-looking people along the Côte d'Azur. You'll recognize the hotel by the curved ochre façade whose outer edge follows the line of the rocky coast. Depending on the season, singles range from 1,200F ($165.48) to 1,350F ($186.17), while doubles cost 1,500F ($206.85) to 1,800F ($248.22). Taxes are included, but not the 15% service. It is open from late March to mid-October.

Hôtel Mirabeau, 1-3 Avenue Princesse-Grace (tel. 93-25-45-45). To enter this attractive hotel set at the edge of the water, you'll have to pass through a travertine-covered courtyard filled with plants. The location is just to the side of the Monte Carlo Casino, which makes the swimming pool, the terraces, and the well-furnished bedrooms (each with private bath) especially convenient. On the premises is a graceful restaurant, La Coupole, capped with a glass canopy, as well as an accommodating bar area. You'll recognize this hotel by its very tall format, which towers over the access roads and the green areas around it. Depending on the season, doubles rent for 900F ($124.11) to 1,250F ($172.38), while singles cost 700F ($96.53) to 1,000F ($137.90). The in-house garage (which you'll be grateful for in the traffic-clogged south of France) costs 60F ($8.27) per day.

The Middle Bracket

Balmoral, 12 Avenue de la Costa (tel. 93-50-62-37), was built in 1898 by the grandfather of the present owner, Jacques Ferreyrolles, when Monte Carlo was rising to its heights. Some of the niceties of that era are still respected at the Balmoral. Its position is cliff-hugging, halfway between the casino and the Royal Palace, directly overlooking the yachting harbor. The street entrance makes the building seem low, but from the waterfront you can count eight floors of bedrooms and lounges with sea views. In the little lounge, many family antiques remain, although subtle additions have been made over the years.

The bedrooms remain consistent in theme with the public rooms—home-like, immaculate, and quiet. So inviting is the Balmoral that guests are likely to extend their stays (perhaps taking advantage of lower tariffs). A double room with bath or shower ranges in price from 425F ($58.61) to 525F ($72.40); a single with bath or shower, from 280F ($38.61) to 380F ($52.40). Many rooms contain TV and air conditioning.

Hôtel du Louvre, 16 Boulevard des Moulins (tel. 93-50-65-25), is built in the style of a traditional grand mansion. The furniture, in the main, is antique. Rooms are comfortable and carpeted, the colors in harmony. Each accommodation is different. Higher tariffs are charged for rooms facing the sea. Singles begin at 500F ($68.95), and doubles cost from 620F ($85.50).

Hôtel Alexandra, 33 Boulevard Princesse-Charlotte (tel. 93-50-63-13), is a 55-room belle époque hotel in the center of the business district. Set on a busy street corner, its 19th-century design includes a rounded high-ceilinged lobby with an elegantly neutral color scheme. A member of the Larouquie family will offer bathless rooms for 220F ($30.34) in a double and for 180F ($24.82) in a single. Units with full private bath cost 350F ($48.27) in a single and 420F ($57.92) in a double. Rooms with shower but without a private toilet rent for 290F ($39.99) in a single and 340F ($46.89) in a double, breakfast not included.

The Budget Range

Olympia, 17 bis Boulevard du Général-Leclerc, Beausoleil (tel. 93-78-12-70), a long haul from the main action, is one of the few reasonably priced hotels in Monaco. The lounge is inviting, as is a small but warm bar. Each of the bedrooms has a different flowery wallpaper and comfortable wood furniture. The third- and fourth-floor rooms provide a view of the sea. Singles with hot and cold running water cost from 75F ($10.32). Doubles peak at 180F ($24.82). Service and taxes are included.

RESTAURANTS: Monaco boasts many fine restaurants, most of which charge very high prices. I'll start with—

The Leading Restaurants

Dominique Le Stanc, 18 Boulevard des Moulins (tel. 93-50-63-37). The discreet luxury and superb viands of this place have made it a rendezvous of the rich and famous. In a pale-blue and turquoise dining room, decorated with a riveting collection of antique children's toys, you can sample the cuisine of Dominique Le Stanc. He is from the Vosges mountains in Eastern France, and with his charming wife, Danièle, they have become two of the hottest young restaurateurs along a coastline jammed with culinary competition. A reasonable fixed-price menu is presented at 200F ($27.58), but chances are you'll pay 500F ($68.95) ordering à la carte. Specialties include a variety of open ravioli stuffed with basil, asparagus tips, crayfish tails, artichoke hearts, and parsley, along with an escalope of red snapper served with a black olive purée and a compote of fresh tomatoes, perhaps salmon with morels, or lobster with zucchini, truffles, and thyme, followed by an array of subtly aromatic desserts. Reservations are essential, and meals are served daily except Sunday and Monday, a week in February, and three weeks in November. This is clearly the best dining choice in Monte Carlo today.

Rampoldi, 3 Avenue des Spélugues (tel. 93-30-70-65), is one of the leading independent restaurants, serving some of the finest cuisine in Monte Carlo. The classic French and Italian viands are dispensed in a compatible setting, at the edge of the Casino Gardens. The restaurant is run by Luciano Disaro, who for some 20 years worked with Régine. This is the eating club of "the great," but its tabs are not dazzlingly high. Most guests pay from 300F ($41.37). To begin your repast, try the soupe de poissons, a specialty. The fish dishes are universally good. Try the lobster salad or the ravioli with crayfish. Main dishes are likely to include lamb curry, two kinds of sole, or perhaps the regional dish of Lombardy, osso buco. A soufflé au Grand Marnier for two might be the proper finish for a meal.

Le Bec Rouge, 11 Avenue de Grande-Bretagne (tel. 93-30-74-91). The sympathetic owner, Roger-Claude Roux, has raised his comfortably decorated restaurant to a favorite of nearby residents, who sometimes come close to filling the lovely open-air terrace. If it's too hot, guests retreat to the air-conditioned comfort of the dining room. There, they enjoy specialties such as fresh foie gras, a suprême of turbot, mussel soup, a pot-au-feu of fish, a terrine of sea bass, and roast duckling, perhaps a bavaroise of salmon. Dining à la carte will cost 320F ($44.13) per person. The restaurant is open daily except in January.

Le Foie Gras, Loews Monte Carlo, Avenue des Spélugues (tel. 93-50-65-00), serves exquisitely prepared French food in a rich turn-of-the-century decor of silver candelabra, dark colors attractively contrasting with white napery, potted palms, and rigidly disciplined service. Specialties include an array of dishes made with the delicately flavored foie gras, from which the restaurant takes its name, as well as calves' kidneys as prepared by the master mustard makers of Dijon, filet of John Dory cooked over a steam of anchovy brine, or boned breast of duckling au Cherry Marnier prepared at your table. À la carte meals cost around 500F ($68.95). The restaurant is open only in the evening from 7:30 to midnight every day. Reservations are suggested.

The Middle Bracket

Quick Silver, 1 Avenue Président-Kennedy, in La Condamine (tel. 93-50-69-39), is a portside restaurant built under the highway. It is especially noted for its well-prepared dishes served at its sidewalk tables under an arbor. Michel Henry offers a varied set menu at 100F ($13.79), including soup, pasta, or a terrine, plus a fish or meat course. A savory Mediterranean cuisine is presented, with emphasis on fish dishes. A much more elaborate menu at 165F ($22.75) is also presented, including on one recent occasion a soupe de poissons (fish) with roche, followed by a gratin of crayfish in Nantua sauce, plus lamb cutlets grilled with herbs, topped by a tart made with fresh fruit of the season, the tariff including service and taxes. A gourmet repast is offered for 250F ($34.48), and you can also order à la carte. He is closed in January and on Tuesday.

Sam's Palace, Palais de la Scala, 1 Avenue Henri-Dunant (tel. 93-50-89-33). There had to be such a place in Monte Carlo, a friendly restaurant / bar attracting those who prefer such dishes as Texas-style chili con carne, good steaks, a super-hamburger, and french fries. Sam's is a gratifying stopover during lunch, but in the evening it almost turns into a social club, it's so informal. The average tab comes to 170F ($23.44), unless you stick to the set menu at 90F ($12.41). You can also order good, big drinks at the American-style bar.

Pizzeria Monégasque, 4 rue Terrazzani (tel. 93-30-16-38). In many ways this luxurious pizzeria with vaulted ceilings is considered the melting pot of Monte Carlo. Almost anyone might arrive, perhaps in a Bentley, maybe on a bicycle. The owner has grown accustomed to seeing all the follies and vanities of town pass beneath his door, serving pizzas, fish, and grilled meats to anyone who shows up. The establishment is open only at night. It is closed Sunday and Monday. À la carte meals range from 150F ($20.69) to 195F ($26.89).

The Budget Range

If the prices of the citadels of luxury have frightened you, and if you consider the Monte Carlo Sporting Club and the Hôtel de Paris better suited for the purse of Gunther Sachs, then you may need to know about an unprepossessing street in Monaco known as the **rue de la Turbie.** Not all the Monégasques are rich, as a stroll along this narrow, crescent-shaped street of budget restaurants will convince you. The government labels these restaurants "no class" (that is, unclassified, falling into no particular category). The best of the lot follows.

De La Roya, 21 rue de la Turbie (tel. 93-30-99-96), will give you a filling and tasty meal for only 65F ($8.97). This fixed-price dinner might include a rich and juicy beef bourguignon. If you want to splurge a bit, you can order a more elaborate repast for just 80F ($11.03). The specialty of the house is Spanish paella, but it must be ordered 24 hours in advance.

The Major Refueling Stop

Café de Paris, Place du Casino (tel. 93-50-57-75). If you frequent the Café de la Paix or Deux Magots in Paris, you'll gravitate to their counterpart in Monte Carlo. Everyone seems to end up here at least once a day. Directly opposite the casino and the Hôtel de Paris, the Café de Paris provides a front-row seat to the never-ending spectacle in the "living room" of Monte Carlo. Inside the café you can gamble on the slot machine. There's even a bowling alley and a glorified *le drug store*. The café attracts a well-dressed and affluent-looking crowd which switches from one language to another with apparent ease. You can stop in for only a coffee or a drink, or you can order set menus at 125F ($17.24) and 130F ($17.93), with à la carte dinners costing from 175F ($24.13).

DAYTIME SWIMMING: On French soil, **Monte-Carlo Beach** adjoins the Monte-Carlo Beach Hôtel. Opening March 30 for the summer season, the beach club becomes an integral part of the social life of Monaco. The entrance fee is 45F ($6.21) in April and May and from September 17 to October 15, 75F ($10.32) from June 1 to September 16. Besides the artificial beach, there are two pools, one for children.

Leaving Monte-Carlo Beach to the international set, the Monégasques frequent the **Stade Nautique Rainier-III,** Quai Albert-Ier (tel. 93-30-44-67), at La Condamine. Dramatically built to overlook the yacht-clogged harbor, it is a stupendous pool, a gift from the prince to his loyal subjects. But you don't have to have a passport to swim here. Rather, you pay an entrance fee of 15F ($2.07) in summer. The pool is open in spring and fall from 9 a.m. to 6 p.m.; in July and August, from 9 a.m. until midnight.

MONTE CARLO AFTER DARK: The Russian grand dukes came here at the turn of the century to break the bank at Monte Carlo. However, that legendary honor went to Charley Wells from London's East End, "The Man Who Broke the Bank at Monte Carlo," winning $200,000 in one night. He didn't really have a "system," however, and he died in poverty. A speculator, François Blanc, made the **Monte Carlo Casino,** Place du Casino (tel. 93-50-69-31), the most famous in the world, attracting in time Sarah Bernhardt, Mata Hari, Farouk, and Aly Khan (Onassis used to own a part-interest). The architect of the Paris Opéra, Charles Garnier, built the oldest part of the casino, and it remains a fascinating, extravagant example of period architecture. The nostalgia for the past has faded. The new grand dukes are fast-moving international businessmen on short-term vacations. Baccarat, roulette, and chemin-de-fer are the most popular games, although you can play "le craps" and blackjack as well. As a sign of the changing times, the casino interests have opened a so-called American Room, featuring some 150 slot machines, along with roulette, blackjack, and craps. The gambling rooms are open daily from 10 a.m. You must carry your passport with you and be at least 21 years of age. The private rooms—for serious gamblers only—charge an admission of 50F ($6.90).

The foremost winter establishment, under the same ownership, is the **Cabaret** in the **Casino Gardens.** Its mode of decoration is self-styled as "Georges Reinhard 1880." You can dance to the sounds of a smooth orchestra. A good cabaret is featured, sometimes with ballet numbers. It is open from mid-September until the end of June, but is closed Tuesday. From 9 p.m. you can enjoy dinner at a cost of 275F ($37.92). Drinks, ordered separately, begin at 160F ($22.06). For reservations, telephone 93-50-80-80.

In the **Salle Garnier** of the casino, concerts are held periodically, and full information about them is available at the Tourist Office. The music is usually classical, featuring the Orchèstre National de l'Opéra de Monte-Carlo.

The casino also contains the **Opéra de Monte-Carlo,** whose patron is Prince Rainier himself. This world-famed opera house, opened in 1879 by Sarah Bernhardt, presents a winter and spring repertoire which traditionally includes such greats as Puccini, Mozart, and Verdi. The opera house has had a celebrated history. The famed Ballets Russes de Monte-Carlo were created here by Diaghilev. The national orchestra and ballet company of Monaco appear here. Tickets may be hard to come by. Your best bet is to ask the concierge of your hotel. You can make inquiries about tickets on your own at the Atrium du Casino (tel. 93-50-76-54), which is open daily except Monday from 10 a.m. to 12:30 p.m. and 2 to 5 p.m. Tickets generally range in price from 100F ($13.79) to 250F ($34.48).

Loews Casino, at Loews Monte-Carlo, Avenue des Spélugues (tel. 93-50-65-00), offers a huge room adjoining the lobby that is filled with the one-armed bandits (slot machines) so prevalent in Las Vegas. It features blackjack, craps, and American roulette. It's open from 4 p.m. till at least 4 a.m., and slot machines operate till 5 a.m. Additional slot machines are available on the roof if you want to continue gambling with a wider view of the sea.

Le Folie Russe, Loews Monte-Carlo, Avenue des Spélugues (tel. 93-50-65-00), is Monte Carlo's answer to the Las Vegas-type revues to which it bears an amazing resemblance, especially in its use of topless dancers. This is a dinner/dance cabaret combination. Many viewers like its shows much more than those staged at the cabaret of the Monte Carlo casino. Vaudeville-style acts are thrown in to ease the "monotony" of all those nude dancers. There's a dinner/dance beginning at 8:30 p.m. and a floor show at 11 p.m., with no show or dinner on Monday. Dinner and the show usually cost around 400F ($55.16) per person.

Le Jockey Club, Loews Monte-Carlo, Avenue des Spélugues (tel. 93-50-65-00), is an elegantly appointed English bar with a sculptured wild-cherry wood ceiling and original paintings of Vincennes by the Parisian painter, André Brasilier. A swallowtail-coated maître d' will welcome you from 11 a.m. to midnight. A drink costs around 50F ($6.90).

The New Gregory's After Dark, Les Allées Lumières, Park Palace (tel. 93-50-42-85), is my favorite nightclub in Monte Carlo. It's a lot more fun and doesn't have the pretense of some of the other clubs, especially Jimmy'z or Chez Régine, where you are not likely to get in unless you have a yacht the size of Jupiter anchored in the harbor.

Gregory's is a piano bar, disco, and *club privé,* run by the most fascinating character in Monte Carlo, Gregory Seguin, ex-singer, ex-movie star, ex-whatever. His friends call him "The Baron." Born in Kiev, son of a Russian baroness who escaped the October Revolution, he tramped around the world for a quarter of a century. First he sang in St-Germain-des-Prés, making enough money to cross the Atlantic to New York. He dreamed of making it to Hollywood, but ended up as a miner in the Dakotas. His club lies only moments from the Hôtel de Paris and the Monte Carlo casino. It opens at noon, and the action continues until dawn. He has a game room, plus a large video screen where he projects current hits. He personally greets every guest, and you are made to feel at home here. And he still hasn't forgotten how to perform. Drinks cost around 65F ($8.97).

Other independent nightclubs in Monte Carlo include **L'X club,** 13 Avenue des Spélugues (tel. 93-30-70-55), which used to be owned by Gregory. Open all year, the club is still a popular nighttime target. Its doors open at 11 p.m. Count on spending from 45F ($6.21) for a drink.

The Living Room, 7 Avenue des Spélugues (tel. 93-50-80-31), right nearby, is another popular rendezvous, with drinks beginning at 50F ($6.90). It is a piano bar and *club privé* with a dance floor.

4. Eze and La Turbie

Reached via the Moyenne (Middle) Corniche, Eze occupies an eagle's-nest perch where once medieval villagers were safe from Corsairs raiding the coast and capturing the young girls for harem duty or the strong men for slaves. You park your car in the little square below, then scale the narrow medieval maze to the top, the streets becoming steps. Ancient stone houses, often occupied by artisans who have restored them to their natural beauty, line the way.

At the top is an old château, set in the cactus-filled Jardin Exotique. It is open in summer from 8 a.m. until nightfall. From the first of October until June 14 it's open from 9 a.m. to dusk. Admission is 6F (83¢).

After Eze, a road leads to La Turbie, on the Upper Corniche. At the highest point along the Grand Corniche, 1,500 feet above sea level, stands Emperor Augustus' **Trophy of the Alps.** At the base of the Tête de Chien (Head of a Dog), it was erected in 6 B.C. The monument—restored with funds donated by Edward Tuck—was erected by the Roman Senate to celebrate the subjugation of the people of the French Alps. You can visit the **Musée du Trophée des Alps** (tel. 93-41-10-11) from the first of April until the end of September from 9 a.m. to 7 p.m., when admission is 8F ($1.10). From the first of October until the end of March, hours are 9 a.m. to 5 p.m. and admission is 5F (69¢). At night, from June to September, the Trophy is floodlit, a striking sight along the Upper Corniche. From the terraces, there's a panoramic view of Monaco.

FOOD AND LODGING: **Hostellerie du Château de la Chèvre d'Or,** rue du Barri in Eze-Village (tel. 93-41-12-12), is a miniature retreat not unlike a luxuriously converted monastery. On the side of the stone medieval village, off the Moyenne Corniche, the Hostellerie is a well-preserved complex of village houses on many levels, all with views of the coastline. The owner, Bruno Ingold, has had the interior of the "Golden Goat" flawlessly decorated to maintain its old character, yet has seen to it that it is most comfortable in today's terms. Heavy beams and French and Italian antiques are used throughout. Even if you don't arrive for a meal or a room, try to stop in for a drink in the bar-lounge, with its picture-window views. French doors open onto a terraced swimming pool.

The food is most worthy, living up to the traditions of "Old France." You can begin with foie gras frais de canard (duckling), followed with carré d'agneau (loin of lamb) aux arômes de Provence, or oysters with champagne. For a bit of festivity, try the fricassée of lobster with small vegetables, followed by the soufflé chaud aux framboises (raspberries). Only nine bedrooms and apartments are offered, each with private bath. Some open onto terraces. Singles range in price from 750F ($103.43), with doubles going for 1,200F ($165.48) to 1,600F ($220.64), plus 15% service added to all tariffs. Take time out to enjoy the old ivy-covered wall, the Norman arches of the towers and the colonnades. Closed Wednesday in off-season and from mid-November to mid-February.

At one of the most dramatic points along the Côte d'Azur between Nice and Monte Carlo, Le Cap Estel is a rocky promontory jutting out into the azure sea. Just two miles from Beaulieu, the following hotel is reached along the Lower Corniche.

Le Cap Estel, Eze-Bord-de-Mer (tel. 93-01-50-44), is a successful reincarnation of a turn-of-the-century seacoast villa built for a princess. Now it is transformed into a luxurious hotel run by Robert Squarciafichi, where you can live and dine in style. Below the coastal road, Le Cap Estel is on five acres of terraced, landscaped gardens reached by a sweeping staircase. At the point where the waves dash against the rocks, a covered, heated swimming pool projects out like the bow of a ship. Exotic birds are kept in cages; mauve petunias add color; and the reflection pool is graced with a spraying fountain, lit by colored lights at night when cocktail parties are in progress under a banyan tree.

Because of its situation, all of the rooms overlook the sea, each near a terrace and each with a private bath. There are 35 bedrooms and 10 deluxe apartments. Only board guests are accepted, those who are willing to pay 1,200F ($165.48) to 1,500F ($206.85) per person daily for full board. In the public rooms, modern furnishings rather than antiques have been used. Guests can dine either inside, on an open-air terrace, or under the trees, where umbrella tables have been placed. Occasional barbecues and chicken-on-the-spit dinners are featured. The hotel is closed from November 1 to February 1.

Hôtel Cap-Roux, Eze-Plage, Basse Corniche (tel. 93-01-51-23), is an older traditional hotel, offering a terrace with a view of the sea, a garden, and parking space for cars. It's a colorful place, with standard but convenient furnishings. Two persons in a room with bath pay 275F ($37.92). Singles can stay here for 225F ($31.03).

Auberge Le Soleil, Avenue de la Liberté, at Eze-Bord-de-Mer (tel. 93-01-51-46), is a pink stucco villa a few steps to the side of the Basse-Corniche. The interior is appealing, filled with bentwood rattan chairs, autumnal colors, exposed brick, and lots of warm brass detailing. There's a quiet terrace in back.

The hotel was established when Henri Portanier-Konieczny came from Poland via Alsace to marry his wife Jeanine. The 11 simply furnished bedrooms rent for 200F ($27.85) for two persons. A half-board plan is available at 200F ($27.85) per person. The establishment is closed from mid-November until mid-December. Its list of ice creams is surprisingly lengthy, and the well-prepared meals include fish, terrines, meats, and shellfish. A meal costs 65F ($8.97) to 150F ($20.69).

5. Beaulieu

Protected from the cold north winds that blow down from the Alps, Beaulieu-sur-Mer is often referred to as *La Petite Afrique*. Like Menton, it enjoys the mildest climate along the Côte d'Azur, and is especially popular with the wintering wealthy, including in days gone by James Gordon Bennett, the founder and editor of the New York *Herald* (he sent Stanley to find Livingstone). Originally, the English visitors staked it out, after an industrialist from that country founded a hotel here between the rock-studded slopes and the sea. The **Beaulieu Casino** fronts **La Baie des Fourmis,** the beautiful gardens attracting the evening promenade crowd.

The **Villa Kérylos,** rue Gustave-Eiffel (tel. 93-01-01-44) is a replica of an ancient Greek residence. It was painstakingly designed and built by an archeologist, Theodore Reinach (1860-1928). Inside, the cabinets are filled with a collection of Greek figurines and ceramics. But most interesting is the reconstructed Greek furniture, much of which would be extremely modish and fashionable today. One curious mosaic depicts the slaying of the minotaur and provides its own labyrinth (if you trace the path, expect to stay for weeks). The villa is open daily, except Monday and during the month of November, from 3 to 7 p.m. in July and August, from 2 to 6 p.m. September through June. Admission is 28F ($3.86).

Graced with lush vegetation, including oranges, lemons, bananas, as well as palms, Beaulieu lies between Nice (six miles away) and Monte Carlo (seven miles away). The golf course of Mont Agel is ten miles from the resort.

FOOD AND LODGING: Beaulieu offers choices in all price ranges. I'll begin with a super-expensive deluxe choice by the sea that has contributed greatly to the international fame of Beaulieu.

La Réserve, 5 Boulevard du Maréchal-Leclerc (tel. 93-01-00-01), has risen to stellar heights along the Côte d'Azur, richly deserving its reputation as one of the Riviera's most famous oases. Right on the Mediterranean, it is a pink-and-white palace, offering drama in its scope and refined atmosphere. A number of the public lounges open onto a courtyard, with urns of cascading flowers, bordered grass, and bamboo chairs. The social life centers around the main drawing room, with its harmonious oyster-white sofas and patterned floors—much like the grand living room of a country estate. In Louis XIV–style chairs, guests sit under a Pompeian ceiling in the drinking lounge, discussing their latest adventures (or lack of them!).

The hotel has been rebuilt in stages, hence its bedrooms range widely in size and character. All 50 are deluxe, distinctly different in style, including one with richly embossed white-and-gilt furniture, elaborately carved headboards and chests, chalk-white fabrics, and bronze and crystal lighting fixtures. The baths are equally stylish, with double sinks. Of course, all the bedrooms are air-conditioned, and each has a beautiful view, either of the mountains or the sea. In high season, from July 1 to October 31, you pay anywhere from 1,500F ($206.85) in a twin-bedded room, plus 15% for service. Singles during that peak period go for anywhere from 850F ($117.22), plus service. From May to September, half board is compulsory, costing 820F ($113.08) to 2,300F ($317.17) per person.

The cuisine is world renowned (La Réserve won its acclaim as a "rendezvous of queens and kings" when it was founded as a restaurant by the Lottier family in 1894). The dining room is consistent in design and general aura with the rest of the hotel, providing a quiet, restful ambience, with its coved frescoed ceiling, parquet floors, provincial armchairs, crystal chandeliers, and arched picture windows opening onto the Mediterranean. Specialties include lobster "Roy George," bass Réserve, a crêpe of the "fruits of the sea," and a dreamy soufflé of fresh raspberries.

Built into a huge stone terrace overlooking the water is a swimming pool, heated from October until May. Other facilities include a private harbor for yachts, submarine fishing gear, sauna, and thalassotherapy. The hotel is closed from December 1 until January 9.

Le Métropole, 15 Boulevard du Maréchal-Leclerc (tel. 93-01-00-08), is a fin-de-siècle private villa whose premises offer about the most graciously appointed luxury living along the Côte d'Azur. It's classified as a Relais et Châteaux. The owners, among them Jean Badrutt, have constructed a large swimming pool at the edge of the rocky coastline and surrounded it with flagstones, palm trees, and parasols. An elegant and refined form of cuisine is served on a covered terrace behind a screen of flowers, amid immaculate napery and excellent service. Another part of the grounds contains a manicured grassy area so flat it looks like a putting green on a golf course. The glamorously furnished bedrooms, with half board included, rent for 1,075F ($148.24) to 1,600F ($220.64) per person. Prices vary widely with the season and the exposure of the room. The hotel does not accept credit cards. Closed from November 1 to just before Christmas.

Hôtel Don Gregorio, 3-5 Boulevard Maréchal-Joffre (tel. 93-01-12-15), is an angular modern hotel conveniently located a short walk from the train station. From the top floors you can see St-Jean Cap Ferrat. The bedrooms are attractively functional, containing modern baths whose tiles are arranged in gray, blue, and white geometric patterns. There is a small swimming pool in back, plus a parking lot nearby. Many of the clients come from England, even though the establishment is owned by a U.S.-based chain. Double rooms (which are rented as singles at the same price) cost 500F ($68.95). There's a phone, radio, and TV connection in each unit.

Hôtel Le Havre Bleu, 29 Boulevard du Maréchal-Joffre (tel. 93-01-01-40), has one of the prettiest facades of any inexpensive hotel in town. Its setting is almost idyllic, housed inside what used to be a private Victorian-style villa with vivid blue shutters and lots of gingerbread. There's a garden in front dotted with flowering urns, and arched ornate windows which, while not looking directly out onto the water, at least encompass enough greenery to make you feel you're in the country. The bedrooms of this establishment have been stripped of most of their turn-of-the-century embellishments, but they are impeccably clean and functionally simple. Rooms each have private bath, and tariffs range from 200F ($27.58) to 240F ($33.10), either single or double occupancy. The hotel is open from February 1 to October 31.

Hôtel Sélect, 1 Montée des Myrtes (tel. 93-01-05-42), is a simple, very French hotel in a 19th-century building near the train station. It faces a small park with fountains and trees. As you climb the curving stone steps leading to the upper-floor reception area, you'll pass a Roman-style bust in the lattice-covered entryway. Rooms are functional, renting for 100F ($13.79) in a bathless double and 127F ($17.51) to 170F ($23.44) in a double with bath. The hotel is closed every year from mid-October to mid-December.

La Pignatelle, 10 rue de Quincenet (tel. 93-01-03-37). Who would think that in such a super-expensive resort there would exist this excellent little Niçois bistro? But the locals have to eat somewhere, and not all visitors (in fact, most visitors) can't afford the high prices of La Réserve and Métropole. This restaurant is the most popular dining room in town, and it's usually crowded. Right in the center of Beaulieu, it has a small dining room with a garden. Family run, it offers set menus at 65F ($8.97), 88F ($12.14), and 140F ($19.31). Specialties include the inevitable salade niçoise, soup de poissons (fish), a cassolette of mussels, fresh lobster and daurade, and three kinds of sole, along with scampi provençal and tripe niçoise. The decoration is in the rustic style, and service is until 9:30 p.m. The restaurant is closed on Wednesday and from mid-October to mid-November.

6. St-Jean and Cap Ferrat

It has been labeled Paradise Found. Of all the oases along the Côte d'Azur, no place has the snob appeal of Cap Ferrat. It is a nine-mile promontory sprinkled with luxurious villas, outlined by sheltered bays, beaches, and coves. Vegetation is lush. In the port of St-Jean, the harbor democratically accommodates both yachts and fishing boats.

Somerset Maugham once lived at Cap Ferrat, quite grandly, receiving friends and confiding to them such tidbits as that he hadn't read *Of Human Bondage* since it was published or (in later years) that he longed for death. Leopold II of Belgium once had a villa here (now taken over by the owner of Grand Marnier). Today Brazilian millionaires as well as movie stars (Gregory Peck) own villas along the pine-studded peninsula.

The **Musée Île-de-France,** Avenue Denis-Séméria (tel. 93-01-33-09), affords you a chance to visit one of the most legendary villas along the Côte d'Azur. It was built in the Italianate style by the Baroness Ephrussi, a Rothschild. She died in 1934, leaving the building and its magnificent gardens to the Institut de France on behalf of the Académie des Beaux-Arts. According to her reputation, "she pinched everything from all Europe." The wealth of her collection is preserved: 18th-century furniture; Tiepolo ceilings; Savonnerie carpets; screens and panels from the Far East; tapestries from the factories of Gobelins, Aubusson, and Beauvais; original drawings by Fragonard; canvases by Renoir, Sisley, and Boucher; and rare Sèvres porcelain. Covering 12 acres, the gardens contain fragments of statuary from churches, monasteries, and torn-down palaces. One entire section is planted with cacti. The museum and its gardens are open every day, except Monday and in November, from 2 to 6 p.m. September 1 to June 30, from 3 to 7 p.m. July 1 to August 31. The gardens are also open in the morning from 9 a.m. to noon. Admission is 25F ($3.45) for the museum and gardens, 10F ($1.38) for the gardens only.

FOOD AND LODGING: There's no lack of fine—and expensive—accommodations at Cap Ferrat, but some moderately priced suggestions are included in my list as well.

The Upper Bracket

La Voile d'Or (Golden Sail), Avenue Mermoz (tel. 93-01-13-13), is a brilliant tour de force. It's compressed luxury, run on a personal and intimate scale. An antique collector turned hôtelier, Jean Lorenzi had the good sense to turn over not only the design of the building but also that of its interior to his architect. The location is at the edge of the little fishing port and yacht harbor, on a plateau with a panoramic view of the coast. Living at La Voile d'Or is like being a guest at a house party. The bedrooms, the lounges, and the restaurant open onto terraces, with lawns, flagstones, and gnarled olive and orange trees. On the edge of the upper terrace is a swimming pool, where you feel you're almost in the Mediterranean. Partial tribute goes to English-speaking Mme Lorenzi, a lovely woman from the Netherlands. She's equally comfortable inviting Danny Kaye to "make yourself at home" in the kitchen as welcoming Sam Spiegel ashore when he arrives on his luxurious yacht.

The bedrooms—50 air-conditioned ones in all—are unique. Each has its own decorative theme, utilizing hand-painted reproductions of antiques, gilt carved headboards, baroque paneled doors, parquet floors, antique clocks, paintings, and baths that are a hallmark of luxury. Open March through October, the hotel experiences three seasons, the accommodations priced according to whether the rooms open onto the yacht harbor (more expensive) or the sea and garden. From July to September, half board (required) is 750F ($103.43) to 2,700F ($372.33) per person, based on double occupancy.

Guests gather on the canopied outer terrace for luncheons. In the evening they dine in the more formal and stately room with Spanish armchairs and white wrought-iron chandeliers. Dining is festive, the menu sophisticated, offering regional specialties, plus a few international dishes as well as the classic French cuisine. Richly decorated, the drawing room is most attractive, using hand-loomed fabric-covered sofas and armchairs, Iberian tables, Italian chests, and oil paintings. Most intimate is a little drinking bar, with Wedgwood-blue paneling and antique mirroring. Guests make it their club room: introductions seem hardly necessary.

Grand Hôtel du Cap-Ferrat, Boulevard du Général-de-Gaulle (tel. 93-01-04-54). One of the best features of this turn-of-the-century palace is its location, set at the tip of the peninsula in the midst of a 12-acre garden of semitropical trees and carefully clipped lawns. The establishment's towering white facade is gently angled to enclose the best section of the garden in a kind of embrace, offering views from the elaborately flowering terrace over the sea. Parts of the exterior are pierced with open loggias and big arched windows, whose views look down to the hotel's indoor/outdoor restaurant where the *cuisine du marché* is richly accented with selections from the local markets. These might include a salad of warm foie gras and chanterelles, nage of crayfish and lobster, or breast of duckling with honey and cider vinegar. A la carte meals cost 400F ($55.16) to 475F ($65.50). Many of the diners are residents of the hotel, opting for the half-board plan, ranging from 850F ($117.22) to 2,200F ($303.38) per person.

The beach is accessible via funicular from the main building. There is also a pool, plus an American-style bar opening onto the garden. Tennis courts attract the athletic. You'll find the conservatively modern bedrooms to be most comfortable. Each contains a private bath, a dressing room, air conditioning, and TV. Depending on various factors, rooms range from 900F ($124.11) for a single to 2,300F ($317.17) for two persons. The hotel is owned by an American corporation that seems committed to maintaining its high standards. It is open from late April to the end of September.

The Middle and Budget Bracket

Les Tourterelles, Avenue Denis-Séméria (tel. 93-01-33-31), is a small hillside apartment house where you can live economically, independent of a hotel staff. It is a three-floor building, surrounded by a small garden, reached via a narrow lane with roses and geraniums. Guests gather to sunbathe in the garden and swim in the pool. The big news is the living space you get: a private sun terrace, a living room, a dining area, a twin-bedded room, a private tile bath with shower, and a complete kitchen with all the necessary equipment to prepare a meal. Each apartment is named after a painter and contains reproductions of the artist's work—Rousseau, Utrillo, Gauguin, Degas. Most apartments accommodate from one to three persons, the rates remaining the same, varying only according to the time of year. From October to June two persons pay from 400F ($55.16) per day, and from June to October that increases to 550F ($75.63) per day, with a stay of one week required.

Brise Marine, Avenue Mermoz (tel. 93-01-30-73), is a bargain paradise for so chic a situation. On a hillside terrace, it is a three-story villa with a front and rear terrace. It's up from the road behind a stone balustrade, with statues and urns of pink geraniums. A long rose arbor, beds of subtropical flowers, palms, and pines provide an attractive setting. The atmosphere is casual and informal. Guests either have breakfast in the beamed lounge or under the rose trellis. There is a little corner bar for afternoon drinks. A restaurant on the premises provides dinner only, costing from 100F ($13.79) per person. In comfortably furnished and immaculately kept bedrooms, a single can stay for 320F ($44.13); two persons are charged 420F ($57.92) in a double. The hotel is open from February 1 until the end of October.

Hôtel Panoramic, Avenue Albert-1ᵉʳ (tel. 93-01-06-62), was built in 1958 with a red tile roof and with much style and glamor. The attractively worldly owner, Christiane Maiffret, maintains the airy glass-lined interior as a place to welcome her friends, many of whom are paying guests. You'll reach the establishment by passing over a raised bridge lined with colorful pansies. At the reception desk, the friendly staff will quote you prices for the 20 well-furnished bedrooms ranging from 420F ($57.92) to 520F ($71.71) in a double. Breakfast is included in the price. All units have a sweeping view over the water and the forested hillside leading down to it. The establishment is open from February 1 until the end of October.

Claire Logis, Avenue Centrale (tel. 93-01-31-01), is a rare find among the various hotels of Cap Ferrat. It was established in 1950 in what had been a 19th-century villa surrounded with about two acres of semitropical gardens. The pleasant bedrooms are scattered over three buildings within the confines of the rock-bordered garden. The most famous client of this place was Général de Gaulle, who lived in a room called "Strélitzias" (Bird of Paradise) during many of his respites from the French capital. If you're lucky enough to get his former room, you'll quickly notice the English campaign chests and the chrome-plated hot-water heater in the oversize bathroom.

Each of the villa's 16 rooms is named after a flower, with the most romantic, and the biggest, located in the main building. They're priced between 250F ($34.48) and 360F ($49.64) in a double, with a continental breakfast included. The rooms in the outlying annex are the most modern, while the relatively isolated room above the garage is the most spacious of all. The hotel is closed from mid-November to mid-December.

WHERE TO DINE: Le Petit Trianon, 1 Boulevard du Général-de-Gaulle (tel. 93-01-31-68), is in the upper reaches of the town, near the Hôtel Panoramic. It is accented with canopies and filled with the kind of furniture you'd find in an expensive home in Florida. The upholstery is vivid and appropriately flowery, and the sophisticated table settings are placed outdoors in a small garden. Luc Brouchet is the experienced owner (40 years at his craft), and he serves a fanciful series of specialties, including chicken with crayfish, guinea-fowl with morels, grilled lobster, vegetable terrine, and mousseline of rascasse (hogfish). A fixed-price menu is offered for 200F ($27.58), while an à la carte dinner costs from 275F ($37.92). Meals are served till 9 p.m. every day except Wednesday night, all day Thursday, and from mid-October to mid-February.

Le Provençale, 2 Avenue Denis-Séméria (tel. 93-01-30-15). At night you'll be able to see the lights of nearby Eze from the windows of this intimate restaurant set high above the village. Within a Provence-style dining room, you can enjoy the cuisine of the Lafontan family. Their specialties include raw marinated salmon with olive oil and anise, filets of John Dory with mushrooms, and bourride provençale. Full à la carte dinners cost 275F ($37.92) to 340F ($46.89), with a fixed-price menu going for 180F ($24.82). No food is served on Tuesday and from mid-November to New Year's.

7. Villefranche

According to legend, Hercules opened his arms and Villefranche was born. It sits on a big blue bay that looks like a gigantic bowl, large enough to attract

U.S. Sixth Fleet cruisers and destroyers. Quietly slumbering otherwise, Villefranche takes on the appearance of an exciting Mediterranean port when the fleet's in. Four miles from Nice, it is the first town reached along the Lower Corniche.

Once popular with such writers as Katherine Mansfield and Aldous Huxley, it is still a haven for artists, many of whom take over the little houses—reached by narrow alleyways—that climb the hillside. The **rue Obscure** is vaulted, one of the strangest streets in France (to get to it, take the rue de l'Église). In spirit it belongs more to a North African casbah. People live in tiny houses on this street, totally protected from the elements. Occasionally, however, there's an open space, allowing for a tiny courtyard.

One artist who came to Villefranche left a memorial. His name was Jean Cocteau, and he decorated the 14th-century Romanesque **Chapel of St-Pierre,** presenting it to "the fishermen of Villefranche in homage to the Prince of Apostles, the patron of fishermen." One panel pays homage to the gypsies of the Saintes-Maries-de-la-Mer. In the apse is a depiction of the Miracle of St. Peter walking on the water, not knowing that he's supported by an angel. On the left side of the narthex Cocteau honored the young women of Villefranche in their regional costumes. The chapel is open from 9 a.m. to noon and 2 to 6 p.m. Admission is 5F (69¢).

HOTELS: Versailles, Boulevard Princesse-Grace-du-Monaco (tel. 93-01-89-56), is a hill-clinging, sunpocket hotel, where you can swim in a pool surrounded by a mosaic-tile terrace, palms, and bright flowers. Set back several blocks from the harbor, and outside the main part of town, it gives you a perspective of the entire coastal area. Constructed in the 1960s, it offers bedrooms with picture windows, so every room has a view. The tariffs vary according to the season. In high season you'll pay from 320F ($44.13) in a single, 550F ($75.63) in a double, including service and taxes. The high season is Christmas and April 1 to September 30. Otherwise, tariffs are reduced. Guests congregate on the roof terrace. You can have breakfast here, or even lunch under an umbrella. In the panoramic dining room, decorated in Mediterranean blue, set luncheons or dinners are offered for 175F ($24.13) to 250F ($34.48). The hotel is closed from mid-October to just before Christmas.

Welcome, 1 Quai Courbet (tel. 93-55-27-27), involves you instantly in Mediterranean port life. It was a favorite of Jean Cocteau. Within hailing distance of the fishing and motor boats, it is a six-floor, villa-style hotel with shutters and balconies. The sidewalk café—set under a canopy—is the focal point of town life, serving coffee at any time of the day or night. The lounge and restaurant, St-Pierre, have an open fireplace, thick arches, hand-hewn beams, and fruitwood furniture. The bedrooms are good looking, 35 in all, 30 with private bath. The steepest tariffs are charged in high season (Easter, as well as July through September). For half board, the rate ranges from 400F ($55.16) to 500F ($68.95) per person. A set menu is featured at 150F ($20.96). Once Pope Paul III embarked from this site with Charles V, but nowadays the departures are much more casual, usually on a fishing expedition. The hotel shuts down from early November until December 20.

Hôtel Vauban, 11 Avenue du Général-de-Gaulle (tel. 93-80-71-20), close to the citadel and the old port, is the most charming hotel in town. The establishment is directed by the kindly Madame Castaig, from the Landes region of western France, who established it 15 years ago after remodeling an older, more rundown hotel. The Italianate façade opens into an elegantly formal interior filled with bronze busts, Louis XV-style furniture, and red-and-white flocked wallpaper. Many of the carefully furnished bedrooms have lace accents, reproduction 18th-century furniture, and crystal chandeliers. Even the entrance is flanked with statues of cherubs holding globe lights with overflowing jardinières. Doubles rent for 400F ($55.13) while singles cost 225F ($31.03). There are only a dozen rooms in the hotel, which closes from November 15 till February 15.

RESTAURANTS: Le Massoury, Avenue Léopold-II (tel. 93-01-03-66), is the domain of Pierre Seibt, who used to direct the staff at Lasserre in Paris. He personally supervises the preparation of the house specialties of homemade fresh duck liver, young rabbit cooked in white wine sauce with onions and flavored with thyme (served cold), scallop of turbot with orange sauce and zucchini soufflé, oxtail braised in red wine, breast of duckling with fresh mint sauce, and bitter chocolate cake with orange salad. All of these dishes are served with perfect professionalism on what might be the most dramatically beautiful terrace in town, attached to a Mediterranean-style villa dotted with paintings. Fixed-price menus range from 200F ($27.85) to 310F ($42.75), while à la carte meals cost from 380F ($52.40). The restaurant is closed all day Wednesday throughout the year, except from June until September when dinner is offered on Wednesday night. The restaurant shuts down from mid-November to mid-December.

La Mére Germaine, Quai Corbet (tel. 93-80-71-39), is one of the best of a string of restaurants directly on the port. It's popular with U.S. Navy officers, who have discovered the bouillabaisse made here from tasty morsels of freshly caught fish, and mixed in a caldron with savory spice. On the à la carte menu you'll discover grilled loup (bass) with three herbs and a salade niçoise. Other main dishes worth recommending are the sole Tante Marie (stuffed with mashed mushrooms) and the beef filet with three different peppers. If two or more are dining, you can order the carré d'agneau (lamb). Meals begin at 275F ($37.92) and go up. Plan to relax over a long lunch while watching the fishermen repair their nets. The restaurant is open daily from May to October, otherwise closing on Wednesday. From mid-November until just before Christmas, it shuts down entirely.

La Méditerranée, Avenue Sadi-Carnot (tel. 93-80-78-56), is a modern restaurant, in the lower level of the Zig-Zag apartment house, with an all-glass façade, permitting guests to enjoy a stunning view. Every local as well as many visiting residents from Nice know about the 110F ($15.17) fixed-price meal offered here. For that price, you're likely to get mussels marinières or trout with almonds, finishing with a pâtisserie maison for dessert. More expensive menus are offered at 160F ($22.06). The restaurant is closed Wednesday and from July 1 to July 15.

8. Nice

The Victorian upper class and tsarist aristocrats loved Nice in the 19th century, but it is solidly middle class today. In fact, of all the major resorts of France, from Deauville to Biarritz to Cannes, Nice is the least expensive. It is also the best excursion center on the Riviera, especially if you're dependent on public transportation. For example, you can go to San Remo, the queen of the Italian Riviera, returning to Nice by nightfall. From the Nice Airport, the second largest in France, you can travel by bus along the entire coast to such other resorts as Juan-les-Pins and Cannes.

Nice is the capital of the Riviera, the largest city between Genoa and Marseille (also one of the most ancient, having been founded by the Greeks, who called it "Nike," or victory). Because of its brilliant sunshine and relaxed living, artists and writers have been attracted to Nice for years. Among them were Matisse, Dumas, Nietzsche, Apollinaire, Flaubert, Victor Hugo, Guy de Maupassant, George Sand, Stendhal, Chateaubriand, and Mistral.

In 1822 the orange crop at Nice was bad and the workers faced a lean time. The English residents put them to work building the **Promenade des Anglais,** which today remains a wide boulevard fronting the bay and split by "islands" of palms and flowers, stretching for a distance of about four miles. Fronting the beach are rows of grand cafés, the Musée Masséna, villas, and hotels—some good, others decaying.

Crossing this boulevard in the briefest of bikinis are some of the most attractive people in the world, who come all the way from Israel or Minnesota. They're heading for the beach—"on the rocks," as it is called here. Tough on tender feet, the beach at Nice is shingled, one of the least attractive (and least publicized) aspects of the cosmopolitan resort city. Many bathhouses provide mattresses for a charge.

In the east, the promenade becomes the **Quai des États-Unis,** the original boulevard, lined today with some of the best restaurants in Nice, each of which specializes in bouillabaisse. Rising sharply on a rock is the **château,** the spot where the dukes of Savoy built their castle, which was torn down in 1706. The steep hill has been turned into a garden of pines and exotic flowers. To reach the château, you can take an elevator, a round-trip ticket costing 5F (69¢). The park is open until 8 p.m. from May 1 to August 31, closing at 7 p.m. off-season. Actually, many prefer to take the elevator up, then walk down.

At the north end of Castle Hill is the famous old graveyard of Nice, which is visited primarily for its lavishly sculpted monuments that form their own enduring art statement. It is the largest one in France and the fourth largest in Europe. To reach it, you can take a small canopied "toy train," which will take you to the Bar du Donjon where you can enjoy a drink or a meal.

In the **Tour Bellanda** is the **Naval Museum** (Musée Naval), Parc du Château (tel. 93-80-47-61), sitting on "The Rock," receiving guests from 10 a.m. to 12:30 p.m. and 2:30 to 7 p.m. daily except Tuesday. Off-season, it closes at 5 p.m. and is closed entirely from November 15 to December 15. The tower sits on a precariously perched belvedere overlooking the beach, the bay, the old town, and even the terraces of some of the nearby villas. Of the museum's old battle prints, one depicts the exploits of Caterina Segurana, the Joan of Arc of the Niçois. During the 1543 siege by Barbarossa, she ran along the ramparts, raising her skirts and showing her shapely bottom to the Turks as a sign of contempt, although the soldiers were reported to have been more excited than insulted.

Continuing east from the Rock one reaches the **harbor,** where the restaurants are even cheaper and the bouillabaisse just as good. While sitting here over an apéritif at a sidewalk café, you can watch the boats depart for Corsica (perhaps take one yourself). The port was excavated between 1750 and 1830. Since that time an outer harbor—protected by two jetties—has also been created.

The "authentic" Niçois live in **Vieille Ville,** the old town, beginning at the foot of the Rock. Under sienna-tiled roofs, many of the Italianate façades suggest 17th-century Genoese palaces. The old town is a maze of narrow streets, teeming with local life and studded with the least expensive restaurants in Nice. Buy an onion pizza *(la pissaladière)* from one of the local vendors. Many of the old buildings are painted a faded Roman gold, and their banners are multicolored laundry flapping in the sea breezes.

While there, try to visit the **Marché aux Fleurs,** the flower market at Cours Saleya. The vendors start setting up their stalls at noon. The market opens between 2 and 4 p.m. A flamboyant array of carnations, violets, jonquils, roses, and birds of paradise is wheeled in on carts.

The center of Nice is the **Place Masséna,** with its pink buildings in the 17th-century Genoese style and a **Fontaine du Soleil** (Fountain of the Sun) by Janoit, dating from 1956. The **Municipal Casino,** now closed, was built in 1883. Stretching from the main square to the promenade is the **Jardin Albert-Ier,** with an open-air terrace and a **Triton Fountain.** With its palms and exotic flowers, it is the most relaxing oasis at the resort.

At certain times of the year, Nice is caught up in frenzied carnival activities. The **Nice Carnival** draws visitors from all over Europe and North America to this ancient spectacle. The **Mardi Gras of the Riviera** begins 12 days before Shrove Tuesday, celebrating the return of spring with parades, floats *(corsi)*, masked balls *(veglioni)*, confetti, and battles in which pretty girls toss flowers, and only the most wicked throw rotten eggs instead of carnations. Climaxing the event is a fireworks display on Shrove Tuesday, lighting up the Bay of Angels. King Carnival goes up in flames on his pyre, but rises from the ashes the following spring.

THE MUSEUMS OF NICE: If the pebbles of the beach are too sharp for your tender toes, you can escape into some of the finest museums along the entire Riviera. As of this writing, the museums of the city of Nice do not charge admission. Fronting the promenade is:

The Masséna Museum

This fabulous villa at 65 rue de France (tel. 93-88-11-34) was built in 1900 in the style of the First Empire as a private residence for Victor Masséna, the Prince of Essling and grandson of Napoleon's marshal. The city of Nice has converted it into a museum of local history and regional art. Next door to the deluxe Negresco Hotel, it is open daily except Monday and holidays from 10 a.m. to noon and 3 to 6 p.m. in summer. Winter (that is, October 1 to April 30) hours are 10 a.m. to noon and 2 to 5 p.m.

On the ground floor is a remarkable First Empire drawing room, completely furnished in the opulent taste of that era, with mahogany-veneer pieces and ormolu mounts. Of course there's the representation of Napoleon as a Roman Caesar and a bust by Canova of Marshal Masséna.

The collection of Niçois primitives is notable, including works attributed to the painters of the 15th century, Bréa and Durandi. In addition to the Niçois primitives there are also examples of the Italian, Spanish, and Flemish schools. There are art galleries devoted to the history of Nice and the memories of Masséna and Garibaldi. Yet another gallery is reserved for a display of views of Nice during the 19th century. Folklore and the ethnographia of the County of Nice are presented in three other galleries, together with examples of the history of "the Carnival" in Nice. It should also be noted that the museum contains an excellent collection of arms and armor, as well as ceramics and jewelry.

Musée des Beaux-Arts Jules-Chéret

More distantly located at 33 Avenue des Baumettes (tel. 93-44-50-72), on the western fringe of the city, this fine-arts museum is open from the first of May until the end of September from 10 a.m. to noon and 2 to 6 p.m. From the first of October until the end of April hours are 10 a.m. to noon and 2 to 5 p.m. The museum was named in honor of Jules Chéret, a contemporary of Toulouse-Lautrec; he died in Nice, leaving a series of posters and drawings as well as paintings. In a way he was the inventor, before Toulouse-Lautrec, of modern poster art.

The museum is visited mainly for its outstanding gallery devoted to a dynasty of painters, the Van Loo family of Dutch descent. One of its best-known members, Carle Van Loo, was born in Nice in 1705. He was Louis XV's *Premier Peintre*.

European schools of the 17th, 18th, and 19th centuries are also represented, as are masterpieces by Fragonard, Hubert Robert, and Natoire. A wide panorama of the French masters of the 19th century includes Guérin, Besnard, Blanche, Cabanel, B. Constant, Flameng, and Marie Bashkirtseff and her friends. The gallery of sculptures includes works by J-B. Carpeaux and Rodin.

A fine collection of pre-impressionists is displayed, along with impressionists Boudin, Renoir, Monet, Guillaumin, and Sisley. Paintings by Vuillard, Marquet, Bonnard, Laurencin, Lebasque, and Camoin round out the collection. Important works of Raoul Dufy (28 paintings, 15 aquarelles, 87 drawings, 46 engravings, along with ceramics and tapestry) and Kees Van Dongen *(Chimera* and *The Tango)* may be seen. Four huge canvases by Léopold Sauvage (1928), ceramics by Picasso, and glassworks by Marinot are also displayed. The symbolist movement is represented by the fantastic world of G. A. Mossa, first curator of the museum.

Villa des Arènes

In the once-aristocratic hilltop quarter of **Cimiez,** Queen Victoria would spend her winters at the Hôtel Excelsior, bringing half the court of England with her. Founded by the Romans, who called it Cemenelum, Cimiez was the capital of their province of the Maritime Alps. To reach this suburb, take bus 15 at the Place Masséna, the ride costing 7F (97¢). Recent excavations uncovered the ruins of a Roman town, and you can wander among the diggings. The arena was big enough to hold at least 5,000 spectators, who watched contests between gladiators and wild beasts shipped in from Africa.

The **Cimiez Convent** (Monastère de Cimiez), Place de Monastère (tel. 93-81-00-04), embraces a church that owns three of the most important works from the primitive painting school of Nice by the Bréa brothers. See the carved and gilded wooden main altarpiece. In the sacristy, frescoes are of a most peculiar style, with symbolic and esoteric pictures. Most of these works are in the sacristy, and many other works can only be seen on guided tours, which take place daily at 10 a.m., 11 a.m., and 3, 4, and 5 p.m. except on Sunday.

Open more recently in a restored part of the convent, the **Musée Franciscain** is decorated with 17th-century frescoes. A trip through its precincts has been called "historical and spiritual." Some 350 documents and works of art are displayed, and a monk's cell has been re-created. See also the 17th-century chapel. Hours are daily except Sunday from 10 a.m. to noon and 3 to 6 p.m., and no admission is charged.

In the little Italianate gardens you can get a magnificent view of Nice and the Bay of Angels. Matisse and Dufy are buried in the cemetery.

An 18th-century mansion, surrounded by gardens, houses the **Museum of Archeology** (Musée d'Archéologie) 165 Avenue des Arènes-de-Cimiez (tel. 93-81-59-57), displaying in an attractive presentation artifacts removed from the diggings. The fragments of Roman sarcophagi are intriguing. Upstairs is the **Matisse Museum** (tel. 93-81-59-57), honoring the great artist who elected to spend the last years of his life at Nice, dying here in 1954. Even in his final years he continued to develop his technique of bright color and flattened perspective. Seeing his nude sketches today, you wonder how early critics could denounce them as "the female animal in all her shame and horror." The *Flowers and Fruits* models he did for the Matisse Chapel at Vence are displayed here, as well as an example of his stained glass. See also the collection of the artist's furniture, which he frequently painted.

Both the archeological museum and the Matisse Museum keep the same hours. They are open from the first of October until the end of April from 10 a.m. to noon and 2 to 5 p.m. From the first of May until the end of September hours are 10 a.m. to noon and from 2:30 to 6:30 p.m. The museums are closed at noon on Sunday and all day Monday, and the annual closing is in November.

Chagall Museum (Musée National Message Biblique Marc-Chagall)

In the hills of Cimiez above Nice, the single-story museum is devoted to Marc Chagall's treatment of biblical themes. The handsome museum is surrounded by shallow pools and a garden planted with thyme, lavender, and olive trees.

Born in Russia in 1887, Chagall became a French citizen in 1937. The artist and his wife donated the works—considered the most important collection of Chagall ever assembled—to the French state in 1966 and 1972. Displayed are 450 of his oil paintings, gouaches, drawings, pastels, lithographs, sculptures, ceramics, a mosaic, three stained-glass windows, and a tapestry. A splendid concert room was especially decorated by Chagall with outstanding stained-glass windows. Temporary exhibitions are organized each summer about great periods and artists of all times. Special lectures in the rooms are available both in French and English (for appointments, call 93-81-75-75). The advantages to its members include such things as signed posters by Chagall and the like.

The museum is on Avenue du Docteur-Ménard. It is open daily except Tuesday, from 10 a.m. to 7 p.m. July 1 to September 30, from 10 a.m. to 12:30 p.m. and 2 to 5:30 p.m. October 1 to June 30. The entrance fee is 15F ($2.07), half price on Sunday.

A Museum of Naïve Art

The **Musée International d'Art Naïf Anatole-Jakovsky** (tel. 93-71-78-33) is the newest museum to open in Nice. Sheltered in the beautifully restored Château Sainte-Hélène, on the Avenue Val-Marie in the Fabron district, the collection was once owned by the namesake of the museum, for years one of the world's leading art critics. His donation of some 600 drawings and canvases was turned over to the institution and opened to the public. Artists from more than two dozen countries are represented in the exhibition, which ranges from primitive painting up to the most contemporary of 20th-century works. Charging no admission, the gallery is open from 10 a.m. to noon and 2 to 6 p.m. daily except Monday and holidays.

A Baroque Palace

Palais Lascaris, 15 rue Droite (tel. 93-62-05-54), is intimately linked to the Lascaris-Vintimille family, whose recorded history predates the year 1261. The baroque palace, largely constructed in the 17th-century, contains elaborately detailed ornaments. An intensive restoration undertaken by the city of Nice in 1946 brought back its original beauty. The most elaborate floor is the *étage noble,* which still retains many of its 18th-century panels and plaster embellishments. On the premises is a circa-1738 pharmacy, complete with many of the original porcelain accessories. Classified as a historic monument, the palace is open free from 9:30 a.m. to noon and 2:30 to 6 p.m. It is closed only on Monday, but it shuts down for all of November. Guided tours of Old Nice leave from this building at 10 a.m. and again at 3 p.m. on Wednesday, Thursday, Saturday and Sunday.

A Russian Orthodox Cathedral

The **Cathédrale Orthodoxe Russe** on the Boulevard du Tzarewitch was ordered built by none other than Czar Nicholas. It dates from the glorious belle époque era when some of the Romanovs and their entourage turned Nice and parts of the Riviera into a stomping ground. Everyone from grand dukes to ballerinas walked the promenade, their activities getting a disdainful eye from the staid Victorians. The church is richly ornamented and decorated, with icons included. You'll easily spot the church from afar because of its collection of ornate onion domes. Charging 8F ($1.10) for admission, it is open from 9 a.m. to noon and 2:30 to 6 p.m. Off-season, it is open at 9:30 a.m., closing at 5 p.m. On Sunday its visiting hours are 2:30 to 6 p.m.

READER'S SIGHTSEEING TIP: "For a nice trip and the most beautiful spot I found in France, go to a little town called **Carros.** Take a bus from the Gare Routière (main terminal). The bus goes out past the airport, turns, and heads up the river past the industrial section. On the opposite side of the river and up a 4,000-foot mountain is this 11th-century castle/village, with a French château. There is a small restaurant and store. Some families have lived in the same houses for up to ten generations. The view one way is about 20 miles out into the Mediterranean and the other way is of the Italian Alps" (G. Wayne Lawhorn, Hanover, Va.).

HOTELS: Nice has something to please every pocketbook, beginning with—

The Leading Deluxe Hotel

Negresco, 37 Promenade des Anglais (tel. 93-88-39-51), is one of the super-glamorous belle époque hotels strung along the French Riviera. When Jeanne Augier took over the hotel, wiseacres predicted she'd assumed a "white elephant," or what the French call a "pink elephant." However, she has triumphed, showing what taste and imagination—not to mention money—can do. The Negresco, named after its pre-World War I founder, who died without a franc in Paris in 1920, draws two reactions: (1) some say the original glamour has been restored; (2) others maintain that even in its heyday the Negresco wasn't as good as it is today. The deluxe hotel was built right on the seafront, in the "French château" style, with a mansard roof and a domed tower. Under a dome of stained glass, the rotunda is encircled by columns and decorated with an elaborate hand-woven carpet on which Louis XVI-style chairs are arranged in color groups of royal purple, carnation red, and Versailles gold.

Inspired by the châteaux and museums of France, the decorators of the bedrooms scoured Europe, gathering antiques, tapestries and paintings, and objects of art to lend prestige and drama. Some of the bedrooms have personality themes, such as the Louis XIV chamber, with its green-velvet bed set under a brocaded rose tester. The "Chambre Impératrice Joséphine 1810" regally recreates the Empire bedroom, with a huge rosewood "swan bed" set in a fleur-de-lis draped recess. At the foot and bottom stand two bronze torchiers. The Napoléon III bedroom, with swagged walls and a half-crowned canopy in pink, resting on a leopard-skin carpet, is ultra-feminine. Not only are the rooms extravagantly furnished, but the staff completes the scene by wearing 18th-century costumes. You're greeted at the door by a porter in black boots, a royal-blue and scarlet cape, gold braid, and a red-plumed hat.

Two seasons spin around this hotel, the costliest time to visit being from March 20 to October 1. Rooms range from a minimum of 1,200F ($165.48) in a single to a high of 1,800F ($248.22) in the best, most sumptuously decorated doubles. The most expensive rooms, of course, open onto the Mediterranean. The featured restaurant is the Chantecler (see my dining recommendations).

The Upper Bracket

Splendid-Sofitel, 50 Boulevard Victor-Hugo (tel. 93-88-69-54), is the best of the modern hotels of Nice, built on the corner of a wide boulevard lined with large shade trees. The beach with its promenade is just four blocks away. On the eighth and ninth floors is an open-air swimming pool, surrounded by a deck with parasol tables, a loggia bar for poolside drinks, a sauna, a sunbathing deck, even a wading pool for children. It's a celestial experience to swim there, with a panoramic view of the city, the sea, and the surrounding hills.

The four-star chain hotel is well conceived, with a clean-cut yet not cold decor. Balancing the contemporary architecture are autumnal colors and warmly grained wood paneling. Likewise, the bedrooms are soothingly balanced in style, with the walls of daffodil yellow, white candlewick counterpane, and classic headboards set against paneling of rare imported wood. Every room contains a sparkling tile bath with shower, a radio with five programs of piped-in-music, a television outlet, direct-dial telephone, a hair-dryer, and air conditioning. In addition, most of them open onto a balcony or good-size terrace. There's a slight variation in price, due to room placement and size. Doubles range from 700F ($96.53) to 850F ($117.22), and singles go for 550F ($75.63) to 650F ($89.64). Board is not obligatory, and à la carte meals are available in the Grill Room and Coffeeshop.

The entire hotel was newly built and furnished in 1964, created on the site of the 1883 Splendid, which had been the residence of the king of Wurtemberg. Since 1910 it has been under the control of the same family, who have wisely seen fit to keep their attentive staff, many of whom have been with the hotel for years. Added for guests are a hairdresser, money exchange office, a garage, and boutiques.

Hotel Beach Regency, 223 Promenade des Anglais (tel. 93-83-91-55). Its streamlined design is set alongside the major beachside thoroughfare of Nice. This hotel is probably the most alluring modern palace in town, not dissimilar to the kind of travertine-sheathed hotel you'd expect to find along the Copacabana in Rio. A discreet portico leads into the sun-flooded, elegantly simple lobby. Visitors enjoy a well-decorated lobby bar, whose black lacquer, octagonal floor plan, and high-tech pin lights form a sophisticated oasis for soft piano music. On the premises is a swimming pool with its own bar, plus an array of boutiques, a beauty salon, a sauna and fitness center, and an underground parking garage. The 335 modern accommodations cost between 700F ($96.53) and 1,150F ($144.80) in a single, from 800F ($110.32) to 1,350F ($186.17) in a double, depending on the season and the accommodation.

Hotel Méridien, 1 Promenade des Anglais (tel. 93-82-25-25), occupies one of the most desirable positions in Nice, at the angle of the resort's famous seaside promenade and a flowering park, Le Jardin Albert-1er. The hotel rises in a metallic design of aluminum balconies and strong horizontal lines. A pair of escalators carry visitors to the upstairs reception area. In the marble-floored lobby, futuristic fountains bathe a handful of statues in shimmering light. One of my favorite spots is the plushly upholstered piano bar which, through large sheets of glass, provides a view of the water. An adjacent charmingly elegant restaurant is filled with a polite staff, serving an excellent cuisine. Each of the 314 comfortably modern bedrooms contains a color TV with in-house movies and a well-maintained private bath. Depending on the season and the view, a single or double rents for between 800F ($110.32) and 1,550F ($213.75). A health center on the fourth floor offers spa and hydrotherapy treatments. A rooftop pool and sundeck are a potent lure.

The Middle Bracket

Westminster Concorde, 27 Promenade des Anglais (tel. 93-88-29-44), stands proudly along this famous seaside promenade, a reminder of the grandest belle époque era of Nice. Its elaborate façade was recently restored to its former grandeur, and many renovations were made. The surfside bedrooms were upgraded into a comfortably contemporary format of soundproof windows and well-upholstered furniture. Each unit contains a private bath, phone, TV, and mini-bar. Prices are usually determined by the view, with singles costing 550F ($75.63) to 750F ($103.43), doubles, 750F ($103.43) to 950F ($131.01). Dining and drinking facilities include plant-ringed terraces positioned so that guests can view the water and the Farniente restaurant where a fixed-price luncheon or dinner goes for 190F ($26.20). Despite the modernization this landmark has undergone, its welcome and service are still old-fashioned.

The **Gounod Sofitel,** 3 rue Gounod (tel. 93-88-26-20), a few minutes from the sea, has been taken over by the Sofitel Splendid next door. It has been entirely modernized, and although it retains its old Niçois exterior, with ornate balconies and domed roof, the inside is new. The attractive lobby and adjoining lounge are festive, with Boussac cloth on the walls, old prints, and copper pots with flowers. All the bedrooms are entirely renovated, with modern tile bathrooms or showers, toilets, piped-in-music, TV, mini-bars, and air conditioning. Most rooms are quiet, overlooking the gardens of private homes on both sides. The rates are 420F ($57.92) to 480F ($66.19), including a continental breakfast, service, and taxes, for a twin-bedded room, and 320F ($44.13) to 360F ($49.64) for a single. All units have a direct-dial telephone, and guests can dial a United States number direct from their rooms if they wish.

Guests at the Gounod can enjoy the amenities of the Sofitel next door: swimming pool, sauna, panoramic bar, and beauty parlor. The staff of the Gounod was trained at the Sofitel.

Grand Hôtel Aston, 12 Avenue Félix Faure (tel. 93-80-62-52). Most of its rooms overlook the splashing fountains of the city's showcase, the Espace Masséna, a few blocks from the water. The elegantly detailed 19th-century façade, as well as the interior, was radically renovated. The hotel is now one of the most alluring in its price bracket. Each accommodation has its own mini-bar, TV, radio, phone, and tile bath, sometimes with a double sink. In high season, doubles cost 660F ($91.01), singles, 550F ($75.63). In low season, doubles go for 370F ($51.02), singles, 300F ($41.37), with a continental breakfast included. The plant-filled rooftop terrace, which on certain summer evenings offers dance music and a bar, has a sweeping panorama of the coastline.

West-End, 31 Promenade des Anglais (tel. 93-88-79-91). Time has been kind to this old-fashioned, stately hotel, strongly holding onto its glamorous position on the waterfront. Most of the rooms look out onto the front garden, with its tall date palms, flowers, shrubbery, and a splashing fountain. The entrance is formal but small, with a fine 19th-century tapestry behind the desk, and (to your left) a petit reception salon. With its baronial fireplace and paneled walls, the bar seems to belong in a château. The special advantage of the West-End is its wide range of rates for accommodations, the most expensive with tall French windows opening onto tiny balconies, fronting the sea, the cheapest facing the rear garden. The prices quoted include a continental breakfast, taxes, and a service charge. Double rooms with bath range in price from 325F ($44.82) to 650F ($89.64), and singles go from 280F ($38.61) to 475F ($65.50). Most of the room furnishings are of Provençal style. No meals are served at the West-End, but you'll be near some of the better restaurants of Nice. The hotel has a fitness center with a sauna and solarium.

Busby, 36-38 rue du Maréchal-Joffre (tel. 93-88-19-41), should please those desiring a centrally positioned hotel with a touch of quiet elegance, plus all the modern amenities. Totally renovated, the hotel kept its old Niçois façade, with balconies and shutters at its tall windows. It's on a corner, allowing for more outside bedrooms. The bar is a cozy spot. The long dining room is divided by butterscotch marble columns and decorated with gilded pier-glass mirrors and ladderback fruitwood chairs with rush seats. The bedrooms, dignified yet colorful, might contain a pair of mahogany twin beds set in a red recess and flanked by two white-and-gold wardrobes. In a room with private bath, the rate for two persons is 450F ($62.06), for one, 350F ($48.27). All tariffs include a continental breakfast, service, and taxes. The restaurant is open only from December 15 until the end of May. Meals (lunch or dinner) cost from 100F ($13.79).

Windsor, 11 rue Dalpozzo (tel. 93-88-59-35), right in the heart of Nice, a short walk from the Promenade des Anglais, seems more like a stone villa than a hotel. In the moderately priced bracket, it's a charmer, with about 60 rooms, all excellently kept and containing color TV, radio, and mini-bar. Many of its tall French windows open onto a verdant rear garden with a swimming pool, where guests congregate on the graveled terrace, pleasantly surrounded by coconut date palms and pots of red geraniums. The drawing room, with a blue-and-white coffered ceiling, chestnut-paneled walls, a raised fireplace, and armchairs, is small enough to be intimate. The bedrooms contain private bath or shower. The owner, Mr. Redolfi-Strizzot, charges 420F ($57.92) in a double with complete bath, this tariff including service, taxes, and a continental breakfast. Singles with shower or bath go from 270F ($37.23) to 380F ($52.40). A sauna is available.

La Pérouse, 11 Quai Rauba-Capeu (tel. 93-62-34-63), was once a prison on a rock, but it's been reconstructed and is now a unique Riviera hotel. This little cliff-hanging establishment overlooking the sea is entered through a lower-level lobby, where an elevator takes you up to a handsome setting with gardens and a pool. La Pérouse is built right into the gardens of an ancient château-fort. The hotel is like an old Provençal home, with low ceilings, white walls, and antiques. All is silent, and the atmosphere is near-luxurious. Most of the rooms have a loggia overlooking the bay. Depending on the situation of the room, singles range from 330F ($45.51) to 530F ($73.09); doubles, from 450F ($62.06) to 850F ($117.22). Breakfast is included in these rates. Accommodations have either private shower or bath.

Victoria, 33 Boulevard Victor-Hugo (tel. 93-88-39-60), is part of the Mapotel chain, about five blocks from the seafront facing one of the major boulevards of Nice. The façade is classic, with balconies and shutters on the wide French windows. Best of all is the quiet, rather casually kept rear garden and lawn studded with peach, fig, and palm trees. The interior furnishings are of good standard. A living room opens onto the garden. The whole hotel is decorated with style. The immaculately kept bedrooms are of good size, with bath or shower, direct-dial telephone, color TV, mini-bar, and soundproof windows. Doubles with shower or bath cost 420F ($57.92) to 480F ($66.19).

The Budget Range

Georges, 3 rue Henri-Cordier (tel. 93-86-23-41), is a real discovery. Nestled on a ledge in a tucked-away corner of Nice, it is only an 18-room hotel, furnished in a personal way, employing an instinctive high taste level. Although they had never run a hotel before, Monsieur and Madame Raymond Vidal are doing wonders with this one, adding little touches where many a hotelier would have compromised or cheated. The building, of course, is streamlined and contemporary, but the furnishings employ provincial or perhaps Louis XVI reproductions. An attractive reading room has been added, and there is sunbathing on the third floor. Double wardrobes, twin beds, rich brass hardware, lush towels, and fine bedspreads are used throughout. Picture windows with filmy draperies let in the Mediterranean sun. The accommodations come with private bath, the cheaper doubles costing 225F ($31.03), the upper-floor units going for 340F ($46.89). Service and taxes are included in the rates. All rooms have color TV. Down the street is the major hotel school of Provence. The students could learn from the Vidals.

Saint-Georges, 7 Avenue Georges-Clemenceau (tel. 93-88-79-21), stands on a quiet street about a five-minute walk from the railway station and beaches. Centrally located, it has an ornate façade with architectural details of the last century, typical of many buildings still standing in Nice. Rare for the center of town, there is a restful evergreen garden behind the hotel where meals are served in summer. Inside, the managers, Monsieur and Madame Boiral, have refurbished the hotel in the modern style. Fabric on the wall makes for a colorful decor, and each unit has been equipped with a private shower or bath. A double or twin-bedded room ranges in price from 260F ($35.85) daily, including a continental breakfast, service, and tax. A triple room costs from 340F ($46.89). The managers are especially fond of Americans, providing a warm welcome.

Hôtel des Cigognes, 16 rue Maccarani (tel. 93-88-65-02), is opposite a church near the center of practically everything in Nice, including the train station, a seven-minute walk away. This is one of the prettiest and most tastefully ornate buildings in town. It dates from the 19th-century and was completely renovated in 1983 into a beautifully detailed mixture of antique and slickly but conservatively modern. Within the peach-colored walls of the lobby you'll find brass chandeliers, light-gray carpeting, a richly embellished elevator rising within a wrought-iron cage, and an Italianate reception desk. An attractively friendly member of the staff will check you in for 280F ($38.61) in a single, 310F ($42.75) in a double, and 400F ($55.16) in a triple. Each contains a private bath and phone, and many of them have a TV. This is an excellent hotel choice in a city where it's sometimes hard to find worthwhile medium-priced accommodations. The hotel is owned by a Dutch man and his French wife, who between them speak an assortment of languages. There's a parking garage just down the street.

Locarno, 4 Avenue des Baumettes (tel. 93-96-28-00), is better suited for motorists who don't mind its somewhat out-of-the-way location in Les Baumettes, about an eight-minute ride from the center. Entirely renovated and redecorated, the Locarno offers air conditioning. It is about 50 yards from the sea. The style is French modern, and each of the 48 well-furnished bedrooms contains a bath or shower plus a toilet, as well as a radio and automatic "wake-up" service. All units have TV. Doubles with complete bath rent for 300F ($41.37) to 350F ($48.27). Singles go, on the average, for 240F ($33.10), and all tariffs include a continental breakfast. The exterior is inviting as well, with shutters and arched windows opening onto small balconies. To use the garage of the hotel, an additional charge is imposed.

Flots d'Azur, 101 Promenade des Anglais (tel. 93-86-51-25), is an inexpensive place directly on the sea, not too long a walk from the more elaborate and costlier promenade hotels of Nice. It's a prim, three-story square villa, set back from the street with two coconut trees on either side of the entry. Seemingly, every bedroom of this villa-turned-hotel has a good view, as well as sea breezes. There's a small sitting room and sun terrace in front. The accommodations vary widely in size and decor, a double room with private bath costing 240F ($33.10), but only 210F ($28.96) with a shower. Singles go from 185F ($25.51) to 200F ($27.58), depending on the plumbing. The quotations include service and tax. A continental breakfast is served on the front terrace.

Villa Eden, 99 bis Promenade des Anglais (tel. 93-86-53-70), is a 19th-century villa right on the seafront, previously owned by a Russian countess. Tall palms lead to the entrance to the rear garden, with its 18-foot-high hedges of ivy and red roses. Among parasol tables and bright geraniums, guests gather here in garden chairs. Owned by the Prone family, the Eden offers individualized accommodations. The living room—much like that in a private home—contains a charming collection of antiques, including Empire armchairs covered in harmonious gold. Opening onto the rear garden, the dining room is treated more in a provincial manner. As is to be expected in this converted villa, the bedrooms vary greatly in size, although all have a liberal sprinkling of old furniture, attractive and comfortable. Only breakfast is offered. Prices depend on the plumbing and the beds. Two persons pay as little as 145F ($20) in a room with a double bed and wash basin all the way up to 280F ($38.61) for twin beds with a shower and toilet, breakfast included.

Magnan, Square du Général-Ferrié (tel. 93-86-76-00), is a simple, modern hotel, about a ten-minute bus ride into the heart of town but only a minute or so from the Promenade des Anglais and the bay. A guest can put on his or her bathing suit in the room, then walk to the sea in a beach robe. A six-story building, the Magnan is reached through an entry of marble and glass, with a pair of potted shrubs at the front door. If possible, try to book an upper-floor accommodation, as the view of the Mediterranean will be better from your balcony. A room with shower costs 225F ($31.03) for two persons, 300F ($41.37) for three. However, a twin-bedded room with complete bath goes for 300F ($41.37) to 325F ($44.82) for two persons, from 400F ($55.16) to 430F ($59.30) for three guests.

Suisse, 15 Quai Rauba-Capeu (tel. 93-62-33-00), is unusually positioned, in the old town near the sea, just below the château. Up a flight of steps, it is seemingly interlocked with an old tower. The rooms are furnished in a modified modern style. Strong colors are used throughout. A seafront double with bath costs only 230F ($31.72).

Hôtel Excelsior, 19 Avenue Durante (tel. 93-88-18-05). Its ornate corbels and chiseled stone pediments rise grandly a few steps from the railway station. Inside, its pleasantly modernized decor fills an updated version of a 19th-century hotel. Today, there's a reflecting pool in the large lobby, and antiques have given way to comfortably upholstered armchairs. The beach is a 20-minute walk from the hotel through the residential and commercial core of Nice. The cozy, high-ceilinged bedrooms rent for 140F ($19.31) in a single, 200F ($27.58) to 320F ($44.13) in a double, depending on the plumbing and the accommodation. Breakfast is included in the price.

Hôtel Durante, 16 Avenue Durante (tel. 93-88-84-40), probably shows its best aspects during the annual film festival in nearby Cannes. Then, producers, actors, and directors of all genres check into the establishment's 17 bedrooms, many of which face a quiet interior courtyard. The owner, Mme Dufaure de Citres, dispenses both charm and information about local cinematic events. Several of her rooms have a kitchenette, providing a kind of apartment setting for guests who sometimes check in for lengthy stays. Singles cost 175F ($24.13), doubles, 275F ($37.92).

Little Palace, 9 Avenue Baquis (tel. 93-88-70-49), is for those who yearn for a personalized, old-fashioned atmosphere. This private little world is the domain of Monsieur and Madame Loridan, who are totally Gallic, maintaining the best traditions of another era. Their sitting rooms look as if they were their very own. You expect to see their family in the parlor. The furnishings are a collection of Spanish chairs, Flemish tapestry-framed needlepoint, library tables with pots of ferns, and Chinese lamps with fringed shades. Even the reception desk reminds you of an old inn, with spindles of receipts and an elaborate book for allotting rooms. Doubles with bath or shower range in price from 210F ($28.96), bathless accommodations costing 145F ($20), and all these tariffs include service and taxes. The Little Palace is open all year except for the month of November.

Le Panorama, 38 rue Segurane (tel. 93-55-29-36), is operated by Madame Sornas on the second floor of a building overlooking the port, close to the beach. The furnishings are clean and modern, and the little hotel has a personal touch. Two persons pay only 150F ($20.69) for a room with hot and cold running water and a kitchenette furnished with pots and pans. Four persons get a great bargain for 250F ($34.48) in a large room with shower, toilet, and kitchenette, although some cheaper doubles with less facilities go for 160F ($22.06). The German philosopher Nietzsche once lived here.

Prior, 5 rue d'Alsace-Lorraine (tel. 93-88-20-24), is an immaculately kept small hotel run by pleasant people, Monsieur and Madame Reverdy. Near the train station, the Prior has a lounge and doors decorated in plaids; the stairs and floors are of marble. Most of the rooms have antique furnishings, with chintz bedcoverings and curtains, some with sink and bidet, others with shower, and some with complete bath. Depending on the plumbing, two persons are charged from 115F ($15.86) to 180F ($24.82).

Hôtel Ann Margaret, 1 Avenue Saint Joseph (tel. 93-96-15-70), is a good hotel in its two-star category. Near the city center, the train station, and the beach, the hotel has its own swimming pool, garden, and place for private parking. Several of the 30 comfortable bedrooms have a complete bath. Singles cost from 75F ($10.32) without bath to 140F ($19.31) with shower and toilet. Doubles range in price from 105F ($14.48) to 200F ($27.58), depending on the plumbing.

Central Hôtel, 10 rue de Suisse (tel. 93-88-85-08), is the domain of Madame Cornacchini, a gracious hostess who receives customers as if they were guests in her own home. Her rooms are spacious, light, and airy, and are attractively furnished. Two persons pay 95F ($13.10) nightly. In a room suitable for three guests, the rate goes up to 135F ($18.62). All these tariffs include a petit déjeuner. The location is on an attractive square, within walking distance of the railway station.

RESTAURANTS: This city will feed you Italian food, Niçois dishes, even specialties from Lyon and Périgord, and of course, bouillabaisse. Some of its local restaurants charge the lowest tariffs on the Riviera.

The Leading Restaurants

Chantecler, Hôtel Negresco, 37 Promenade des Anglais (tel. 93-93-88-39). Of all the great palace hotels of France (and there are many), none has a chef to equal young Jacques Maximin. That's a big statement, but the growing fame of this talented genius in the kitchen merits such high praise. He's in lofty company as one of the leading chefs in all of France, and many food critics have predicted that he will one day overtake the fame of Paul Bocuse of Lyon.

All this praise seems to float over the head of Monsieur Maximin, who seems as if he'd rather be supervising his kitchen instead of receiving awards, stars, or toques. A *Meilleur Ouvrier de France,* this young man was given virtual carte blanche in the kitchens at the Negresco by Madame Jeanne Augier. She seemed to have been responsible for the elegant decor, with its red-velvet upholstered chairs, crystal chandeliers, and walls in 17th-century percale. Maximin creates his own decor with platters of food artistically arranged and brilliantly prepared. His dishes seem to depend on his inspiration for the day and especially what he found in the Nicean markets (he accepts only the freshest ingredients).

One menu might be devoted to lobster in various forms, ranging from a bisque to a salad to fricassée. His small squash stuffed with black truffles is about the most elegant version you'll ever taste of this noble vegetable. His pigeon salad with mushroom mousse is sublime, as is his fresh salmon from Scotland. He is likely to stuff ravioli with everything from lobster to scallops. Desserts are spectacular, or at least my latest one—wild strawberries flavored with Grand Marnier and served in a crème-brûlée—was outstanding in every way. À la carte meals cost from 540F ($74.47) to 650F ($89.64), and fixed-price menus are offered for 320F ($44.13), 340F ($46.89), and 500F ($68.95). Reservations are necessary. The restaurant is open daily except in November.

La Poularde (Chez Lucullus), 9 rue Gustave-Deloye (tel. 93-85-22-90), is the domain of Monsieur Normand, who rules with a velvet fist over this Provençal inn, dedicated to serving his guests the finest viands in the city. The patron insists on using only the best vegetables, meats, and fish from the local markets, and he doesn't believe in compromise. Even on my most hurried visits to Nice I try to have at least two meals at La Poularde. What to order? Everything is good, although you might consider the tasty Niçois hors d'oeuvres as a starter. Some of the best main dishes are rouget (red mullet) à la sauvage, capilotade de poularde (pullet) paysanne, loup grillé (grilled bass) with fennel, and châteaubriand for two. The pastry of the house is usually moist and creamy. Count on spending 320F ($44.13) to 350F ($48.27) per person to dine à la carte. Set meals cost 160F ($22.06) to 220F ($30.34). The doors are shut every Wednesday and from mid-July to mid-August.

Girelle Royale, 41 Quai des États-Unis (tel. 93-62-30-04), enjoys the most acclaim of all the restaurants on this promenade bordering the sea. Torchères at night draw attention to its second-floor panoramic deluxe dining room. The 160F ($22.06), plus 15% service, dinner includes a fish or a meat course, such as scampi in tartar sauce or grilled alpine lamb with delicately scented herbs. You might also order the filets of sole in the white wine or a grenadin de veau (veal). The gastronomic menu at 225F ($31.03) is dazzling, offering a choice of the chef's specialties, including *la véritable bouillabaisse,* turbotin de mer farci, or rognon de veau (veal kidneys) au safran (saffron). After 10:30 p.m. you can select only from the à la carte menu. A meal here on a moonlit Mediterranean night is an experience not easily forgotten. The restaurant is open every day from April 1 to September 30, closed on Wednesday during the winter months.

Rôtisserie St-Pancrace, 493 Route de Pessicart, St-Pancrace (tel. 93-84-43-69), was built many years ago, about 3½ miles outside Nice, as a luxurious hunting lodge. Today, it's a spot where dedicated gastronomes get away from the congestion of Nice for a meal in the country. These are served in good weather on a flowering terrace whose view encompasses a rock garden, a lawn, and the countryside of Provence, sloping down to a river valley far below. The staff is one of the best assets of this place. The second-generation owner, Daniel Teillas, is aided by sommelier Antoine Lucciano (whom some critics have named as the best along the Côte d'Azur). Of course, everything depends on chef Jean-Pierre Robert who makes dining here a memorable experience. The modernized and creative cuisine changes with the availability of ingredients, but might include a moussaka with fresh noodles, roast sea bass with marinated tomatoes, ravioli with truffled foie gras, bavarois of shrimp in an anise-flavored sauce, and pot-au-feu with truffles. For all this quality, the bill is not too high: 250F ($34.48) to 350F ($48.27) per person. A fixed-price menu is slightly cheaper.

It's best to phone ahead for a reservation. No meals are served Monday except in July and August when the restaurant is open every day. Annual vacation lasts for a month some time between January and February. To get here, follow the Boulevard de Cessole from Nice, heading north until you reach the hamlet of St-Pancrace.

Moderately Priced Dining

L'Esquinade, 5 Quai des Deux-Emmanuels (tel. 93-89-59-36), on the far side of the harbor near the car-ferry, is rustic. The view of the harbor, the wooden water wheel, the bright tablecloths, the rough plaster walls, and the chandeliers with sheaves of oats and corn make it somewhat of a stage setting, a romanticized *moulin.* The waiters in regional costumes bring dishes to the canopied front—past goldfish tanks—from the large grill at the rear of the restaurant. The chef's specialties include tournedos poêle au roquefort and loup (sea bass) en chemise with a Mondesir sauce. Sorbets round out most repasts. A complete meal will cost 275F ($37.92) to 325F ($44.82). Closed Sunday night and Monday, and from mid-November to late December.

St-Moritz, 5 rue du Congrès (tel. 93-88-54-90), is only a short walk from the Promenade des Anglais, down the street from the American Express and behind the Palais de la Méditerranée. One American journalist wrote: "If I were 22, possessed of plenty of money, and had a movie starlet to beau around (three preposterous postulates), I would dine at the St. Moritz every night." In this mock-chalet setting, celebrities from Cannes often drop in, enjoying the setting with lighting that makes everybody (well, nearly) look glamorous.

But it's the food that wins in the long run. The patrons, Messrs Martial and Marchiani, grow their own herbs in a garden, using them for sauces as well as broiled or grilled dishes. For example, they make a superb sauce verte with freshly cut chives, tarragon, chervil, basil, mint, and marjoram. The bouillabaisse—one of the most savory I've ever sampled in Nice—is superb. Other interesting dishes include a gratin of sole in a champagne sauce with truffles or a maigret de canard (duckling) with green peppercorns. Set menus are offered for 120F ($16.55) to 130F ($17.93). However, if you order à la carte, expect to spend 300F ($41.37) to 380F ($52.40). The restaurant is closed on Thursday and in January.

Barale, 39 rue Beaumont (tel. 93-89-17-94), is presided over by Catherine-Hélène Barale, who believes in preserving a "Nissarda" cuisine—a unique Riviera blend of Italian and French. Her charmingly rustic restaurant, a museum-like assemblage of antiques including kitchen utensils, is bustling and usually stuffed with hungry diners who know they can obtain some of their most memorable Côte d'Azur meals here. Madame Barale was born here, and she's learned the family secrets well. Her wares are listed on a blackboard menu hung with garlic pigtails. Her menu depends on her whim—or shopping—on any particular day. However, she nearly always sells squares of the Nice pizza called pissaladière and, of course, the classic salade niçoise. For a second course you might be served gnocchi or green lasagne. For a main dish you are likely to be offered pieche—poached veal stuffed with fresh Swiss chard, cheese, ham, eggs, and rice. It's superb. A fresh fruit tart rounds out most meals. Expect to pay from 180F ($24.82), which will include a bottle of the house's red wine. Only dinner is served. The restaurant is closed on Sunday, and reservations are imperative. Madame Barale is particular about whom she will feed and not feed. If she likes the crowd on any given evening, she might stage an informal cabaret act, telling her witty stories when her work in the kitchen is finished.

Don Camillo, 5 rue Ponchettes (tel. 93-85-67-95), set back from the coastal road near the foot of the château and the Naval Museum, is run like a country inn. The dining room is long and narrow, with a decorative clutter of paintings and colorful plates set in niches. A still-life table displays wines, elaborately prepared foodstuff, and desserts. The restaurant is simple but pleasant, serving what is generally considered the tastiest Italian food in Nice. The fettuccine is excellent. Main-course selections include osso buco, the Milanese specialty, saltimbocca alla romana, and the risotto with fruits of the sea. Some prefer the ravioli maison, others the tripe maison. For dessert, a smooth choice is zabaglione with sherry, offered for two persons. Meals cost from 130F ($17.93) to 220F ($30.34). Closed Sunday and in July.

Restaurant Le Grand Pavois Chez Michel, 11 rue Meyerbeer (tel. 93-88-77-72). Nestled under the forecourt of a cream-colored art deco apartment building near the water, this elegant restaurant has voile curtains partially concealing the huge glass windows facing the street. The decor's nautical theme is enhanced by the presence in the vestibule of a brass-trimmed ship's steering wheel. As you'd expect, this is primarily a seafood restaurant, serving specialties such as fish soup, salad niçoise, Dutch sole filet for two persons, grilled sea bass flambéed with cognac and fennel, grilled lobster, and bouillabaisse. Dessert might consist of a fresh fruit salad. Full meals, which are served every day except Monday and from the first of July to mid-August, range from 150F ($20.69) to 225F ($31.03).

Chez les Pêcheurs, 18 Quai des Docks (tel. 93-89-59-61). The menu for this romantically situated tavern-style restaurant is encased in an ocean liner's brass porthole attached to the façade. The establishment is captained by Roger and Jean-Michel Barbate, who maintain the heavy ceiling beams, the green and white tablecloths, and the multipaned wood-and-glass doors in shipshape condition. The establishment is set directly on the old harbor, at the end of a long string of less desirable restaurants, with a view looking out over the château and the dozens of fishing boats in front of it. Full meals range from 175F ($24.13) to 250F ($34.48). Your meal might consist of bourride provençale, bouillabaisse, fish soup, sea bass with tarragon, grilled lobster, turbot, daurade, and scampi. The restaurant is closed from November 1 to mid-December, on Tuesday night from mid-December until the end of April, and on Thursday lunch from May 1 until the end of October, and on Wednesday all year.

Rive Droit, 22 Avenue de St-Jean-Baptiste (tel. 93-62-16-72), in the center of town, has a duet of spacious and airy rooms with high ceilings. The standup bar sometimes gets crowded in the late afternoon. The dining room is filled with tints of brown and peach and exposed wood, and decorated with 1900s-style bentwood chairs and modern Italian paintings. The menu is lengthy and tempting. An array of pasta dishes is offered, along with several Niçois specialties.

These include beignets of eggplant, daube provençale with house gnocchi, bavette of beef with shallots, fisherman's soup, and spaghetti with shellfish, along with duckling foie gras, Provence lamb, and crabmeat and avocado salads. Full meals cost from 160F ($22.06), and the staff shuts down on Sunday.

The Budget Range

Taverne Alsacienne, 49 rue Hôtel-des-Postes (tel. 93-62-24-04), is one of the best brasseries in Nice. It is furnished in a typically Alsatian manner, with dark oak paneling, scrubbed wooden tables, and bowls of fresh flowers. And of course there's plenty of good-tasting beer. The chef's larder is well stocked. The set meal at 85F ($11.72), plus service merely gives you a preview. Other more elaborate menus are priced at 100F ($13.79) and at 110F ($15.17). The choucroute spéciale (sauerkraut) is most rewarding if your appetite is large. River trout has always been a favorite on Alsatian menus, and it's served here meunière. Try also the boeuf bourguignon. Food is served until 11 p.m. in case your pension didn't feed you well at 7.

La Nissarda, 17 rue Gubernatis (tel. 93-85-26-29), draws a steady stream of local diners who appreciate the Italian and Niçoise specialties which the owner-chef Albert Muraglia prepares so temptingly. The establishment lies on a tree-shaded square in the heart of the city. You enter the dining room by passing through a bar in front where you may want to enjoy an apéritif. Tripe niçoise is a specialty, and many guests opt for several other of Mr. Muraglia's favorite dishes, including tagliatelle with basil sauce, fettuccine made with two kinds of shellfish, and a succulent ravioli which he perfected during a sojourn several years ago in New York. You can also order a gigot of lamb. A single fixed-price menu at 80F ($11.03) is good value and is cheerfully served by the comfortably bilingual Mme Muraglia. No meals are offered on Wednesday.

Restaurant du Liban, 6 rue du Congrès (tel. 93-87-11-45), was the first and is now the best established Lebanese restaurant in Nice. Its elegant interior contains green and white lacquered walls, Middle Eastern touches, and an occasional presence of an Arabic woman who dances for the amusement of the guests. The menu includes such specialties as tabouli, hummus, falafel, Oriental salad, and baba gannoush, any of which could be ordered as an appetizer. Main courses feature a mixed grill, brochettes of juicy lamb, and chicken. A honey-sweet baklava is a savory dessert, and full meals cost from 175F ($24.13).

Restaurant l'Estocaficada, 2 rue de l'Hôtel-de-Ville (tel. 93-80-21-64). If you don't know what *estocaficada* means, it's Provençal talk for stockfish. And if you don't know that that is the ugliest fish in Europe, there's a dried-out example of one hanging amid a collection of gourds from the ceiling rafters of this typically local restaurant in Old Nice. A place like this could only be directed by a family whose world revolves around the neighborhood, the food, and the clientele who are habitués. The food is simple and robust. Many of its raw ingredients are depicted in the aquatic scenes painted in crudely vivid colors under the false arches of the ground-floor decor. There are only ten tables in the restaurant, yet even that seems to tax the capacity of the tiny kitchen in back, out of which emerge such dishes as fish soup, tomates provençales, bouillabaisse, loup with fennel, grilled sardines, and sole meunière. Fixed-price menus are offered for 50F ($6.90) and 75F ($10.32), while à la carte meals cost around 120F ($16.55), with wine included. The restaurant is open for lunch and dinner every day except Saturday.

Le Saëtone, 8 rue d'Alsace-Lorraine (tel. 93-87-17-95), offers one of the best bargains in town. For just 50F ($6.90) you can enjoy a well-prepared four-course meal, beginning with hors d'oeuvres, then half a roast chicken, a salad, and crème caramel. This price includes service. For 75F ($10.32) you can order five plates. This miniature restaurant contains only two sidewalk tables, and is decorated in a rustic style, using wrought iron and natural woods. It is closed on Wednesday, and from mid-November to mid-December.

L'Étoile, 3 rue de Belgique (tel. 93-87-35-74), also offers one of the best bargains in town. Here you can order a three-course menu (and that includes wine) for only 55F ($7.56). I most recently enjoyed fisherman's soup, followed by roast beef with pommes frites, then an apple tart. The menu offers family-style cooking, with a wide choice of appetizers, meats, and sauces, along with desserts.

NICE AFTER DARK: Paradise Club, 27 Promenade des Anglais (tel. 93-88-29-44), is a club on the lower level of the Westminster Concorde Hôtel. On the fashionable boulevard running alongside the sea, the entrance to the hotel is flanked with two sleeping lions carved from stone. The club is closed most days, but when it's open it's most popular. For lonely vacationers hoping to meet Mr. or Ms Adequate, there is a series of 4 p.m. tea dances every Monday, Saturday, and Sunday, when drinks cost 60F ($8.27). Evening dances are held at 10:30 only on Friday night, at which time drinks cost 75F ($10.32), and on Saturday when drinks cost 85F ($11.72).

Le Relais American Bar, Hôtel Negresco, 37 Promenade des Anglais (tel. 93-88-39-51). Toward the end of her life Lillie Langtry, the actress/companion of King Edward VII, used to sit silently in this place, swathed in veils, speaking to no one. Today you're likely to see at least one of the chic clients wearing a veil, but it will probably to be to accent, rather than hide, her features. The establishment is the most beautiful bar in Nice, filled with quadruplicate white columns supporting the oxblood-colored ceiling, Oriental carpets, English-style paneling, Italianate chairs, and very large tapestries. A piano might be playing noncommittally at the far end of the cavernous room, where a white-jacketed waiter will bring you cocktails with salted peanuts for 60F ($8.27) to 80F ($11.03) apiece.

Pam-Pam Masséna Rhumerie, Place Masséna (tel. 93-80-21-60). A series of art deco, Polynesian, and Gothic architectural details support the overhang of the porch above the café tables of this eclectic combination of styles, music, and drinks. In the heart of Nice, this frequently crowded nightspot often hosts live musical groups playing everything from Latin to Caribbean reggae to popular French tunes for an audience that often includes collections of gaily colored parakeets in ornate cages. Music usually begins in the evening at 9:45. Drinks include a full range of exotic fruited concoctions, many of which begin at 50F ($6.90).

Charlot, 8 rue St-François-de-Paul (tel. 93-62-29-42), is the oldest gay bar in Nice, more than 75 years of age, catering to a mostly male clientele. There's a long bar area, plus another cozy nook for dancing. Most of the youngish guests arrive after 11 p.m., although the bar opens at 9:30 p.m. It is closed on Monday. The establishment charges 25F ($3.45) for a beer, around 50F ($6.90) for a mixed drink. There is no cover charge.

AN EXCURSION TO LEVENS: Levens is an attractive residential town guarding the Vallée de la Vésubie. At a point 15 miles from Nice on the D19, it is at an altitude of 1,800 feet. Excursionists come this way to see some of the most beautiful spots in the mountains.

A trip to the Saut des Français (Frenchmen's Leap) is recommended. It's at the exit from the village of Duranus. French Republican soldiers in 1793 were tossed over this belvedere by Barbets, guerrilla bands from Nice. The fall—without a parachute—was some 1,200 feet down to the Vésubie. At another 15 miles you'll come upon La Madone d'Utelle, at an altitude of 3,900 feet. Here a panoramic view of the Maritime Alps unfolds.

Malausséna, Place de l'Hôtel-de-Ville (tel. 93-79-70-06), stands right in the center of the village. A three-story hotel, it offers clean, comfortable rooms, a dozen in all. For full board the charge ranges from 200F ($27.58) to 250F

($34.48) per person. The plumbing in most of the bedrooms is quite luxurious. Although the inn is fairly simple, the welcome is definitely first class. The food is excellent, although this is not the place to patronize if you're on a diet. Two set meals are offered: a substantial dinner costing from 85F ($11.72) and a huge repast for 160F ($22.06). The inn shuts down from November 1 to December 10.

9. St-Paul-de-Vence

Of all the perched villages of the Riviera, St-Paul-de-Vence is the best known. It was popularized in the 1920s when many noted artists lived there, occupying the little 16th-century houses that flank the narrow cobblestone streets. The hill town was originally built to protect its inhabitants from Saracens raiding the coast. The feudal hamlet grew up on a bastion of rock, almost blending into it. Its ramparts (allow about 30 minutes to encircle them) overlook a peaceful setting of flowers and olive and orange trees. As you make your way through the warren of streets you'll pass endless souvenir shops, a charming old fountain carved in the form of an urn, and a Gothic church from the 13th century. St-Paul lies 17 miles from Cannes, 19 miles from Nice, and 3 miles from Vence.

THE MAEGHT FOUNDATION: The most important attraction of St-Paul lies outside the walls at **Fondation Maeght** (tel. 93-32-81-63). It's one of the most modern art museums in all of Europe. On the slope of a hill in pine-studded woods, the Maeght Foundation is like a Shangri-la. Not only is the architecture daringly avant-garde, but the building houses one of the finest collections of contemporary art on the Riviera. Nature and the creations of men and women blend harmoniously in this unique achievement of the architect José Luís Sert. Its white concrete arcs give the impression of a giant pagoda.

A stark Calder rises like some futuristic monster on the grassy lawns. In a courtyard, the elongated bronze works of Giacometti (one of the finest collections of his works in the world) form a surrealistic garden, creating a hallucinatory mood. Sculpture is also displayed inside, but it's at its best in a naturalistic setting of surrounding terraces and gardens. The museum is built on several levels, its many glass walls providing an indoor-outdoor vista.

The foundation, a gift "to the people" from Aimé and Marguerite Maeght, also provides a showcase for new talent. Exhibitions are always changing. Everywhere you look, you see 20th-century art: mosaics by Chagall and Braque, Miró ceramics in the "labyrinth," and Ubac and Braque stained glass in the chapel. Bonnard, Kandinsky, Léger, Matisse, Barbara Hepworth, and many other artists are well represented.

There are a library, a cinema, a cafeteria, and lounges. In one showroom you can buy original lithographs by such artists as Chagall and Giacometti and limited-edition prints. Admission costs 20F ($2.76), with students paying 15F ($2.07). In season, the museum is open daily including Sunday and holidays from 10 a.m. to 7 p.m. From October 1 through May 30 the hours are 10 a.m. to 12:30 p.m. and 2:30 till 6 p.m. For certain temporary exhibitions, the admission may range from 20F ($2.76) to 25F ($3.45).

FOOD AND LODGING: The best choices in St-Paul-de-Vence are the following:

The Upper Bracket

Le Mas d'Artigny (tel. 93-32-84-54), Route de la Colle et des Hauts de St.-Paul, is like a sprawling Provençale homestead, lying about two miles from St. Paul, at the end of a winding road lined with pines and laurels. The waters of a blue tile swimming pool extend under a cantilevered public area in a way that seems to expand the spaciously sun-flooded lobby into the hills outside. There's a Caribbean-style cluster of plants, giving a tropical note to a descending stone staircase. On easels within the stone lobby is a constantly changing exhibition of art. Of course, there's also a bar and restaurant. Former French president, Giscard d'Estaing, and Germany's Helmut Kohl are two of the illustrious former guests of this Relais et Châteaux.

Each of the comfortably large bedrooms, decorated conservatively modern, has its own terrace or balcony, air conditioning, mini-bar, and phone. Fifteen private apartments are placed end to end on a slope below the establishment's main pool. Each apartment is isolated from its neighbor with a thick hedge, behind which is a small private pool. A trio of private villas, each with its own fireplace, pool, and between five and eight bedrooms, are concealed somewhere on the verdant 16-acre property. Depending on the season and the accommodation, a single or double rents for 400F ($60.68) to 1,250F ($172.38). Apartments cost from 1,200F ($165.48) to 2,000F ($275.80) for two persons.

La Colombe D'Or (The Golden Dove), l Place du Général-de-Gaulle (tel. 98-32-80-02), is a nugget of graceful antiquity. At the edge of this attractive old hamlet, the Renaissance-style villa lies behind tall stone walls, encircling a voluptuous Roman garden and terrace as well as a swimming pool. The proprietors bring an eclectic awareness of fine contemporary paintings to this old inn. It's almost like visiting a museum of contemporary art. You see—just hanging, unguarded—works by Chagall, Rouault, Dufy, Braque, Picasso, and Miró. According to what is now a Riviera legend, many of the paintings were left by artists in the '20s who "painted for their supper." Once featured in a Jean Seberg movie, the flock of snow-white doves hovering about turn "golden" at sunset. Staying here is like being a member of a private club. The bedrooms, 17 in all, are consistently well planned, with very fine antiques and brightly colored tile baths. Half board costs 850F ($117.22) to 1,150F ($158.59) per person.

Even if you can't stay here (reservations are imperative), you may want to have a meal. Most informal is the jungle-like dining patio, with its tables set under umbrellas in the midst of ferns, geraniums, and pink flowering vines growing over trelliswork. Inside, there's a stately pair of dining rooms, with an elaborately carved Renaissance fireplace and provincial chairs. The average à la carte tab begins at 250F ($34.48). A meal I recently ordered included a wide selection of hors d'oeuvres, trout meunière, tender loin of lamb, a salad, and a soufflé Grand-Marnier. Enjoy an after-dinner drink before the fireplace in the lower "pit lounge." The hotel is closed from November to December 15.

Other Selections

Orangers, Chemin des Fumerates, Route de la Colle (D107) (tel. 93-32-80-95), is a villa near the road on a hillside terrace less than a mile from the heart of the village. It is drenched with the scent of roses, oranges, and lemons. The main lounge is impeccably decorated with original oil paintings and lithographs by Picasso, Rousseau, Bernard Buffet, and Rouault. You are treated like a house guest, accommodated in a bedroom lavishly decorated with antiques and Oriental carpets and opening onto a superior view. On the adjoining sun terraces are banana trees, flower beds, and climbing geraniums. Madame Biancheri has created a lovely living oasis. Two persons are charged from 360F ($49.64) to 420F ($57.92). Some units are apartments, costing from 540F ($74.47) for two persons, plus a supplement of 70F ($9.65) per extra guest.

There's a restaurant a few steps away, **Les Oliviers,** Route de la Colle (tel. 93-32-80-13), directed by J. M. Petit, who serves meals in a tavern-style room or on a wide shaded terrace under the leaves of ancient olive trees. Specialties include a conventional but well-prepared blend of fish, meats, and grills. The restaurant is fairly expensive, charging 300F ($41.37) to 400F ($55.16) for a full à la carte meal. It is closed from the first of December until the end of February.

Auberge Le Hameau, 528 Route de la Colle (tel. 93-32-80-24), stands on the outskirts of St-Paul-de-Vence, on the road to Colle at Hauts-de-St-Paul. It is a holiday retreat, a hilltop villa with views of the surrounding hills and valleys. It was conceived by a tasteful architect and designer who provided comfort in a romantic Mediterranean setting. Most of the bedrooms, only 16 in all, overlook the vine-trellised courtyard. There is also an expansive sun terrace with stone planters of fruit trees and flowering shrubs. With white-washed walls and beamed ceilings, the bedrooms come in various shapes and sizes, a single with shower renting for 180F ($24.82), a double for 320F ($44.13). The provincial furnishings are just right for the setting, and the tile baths are completely modern. The hotel staff takes a holiday from November to February 1.

Hotel Climat de France, Les Fumerates (tel. 93-32-94-24), lies at the top of a steep driveway and maintains a house-party atmosphere in its low-slung arrangement of tile-roof townhouses fringing the edges of a rectangular swimming pool. From one of the chaise longues, you can survey the countryside around you. Each accommodation has its own kitchenette, and guests can also use the restaurant near the main entrance's reception desk. Units contain their own awning-shading balcony or poolside terrace. The 19 studio apartments, housing two persons, cost from 320F ($44.13) to 365F ($50.33), while a quartet of units without kitchenette go for 220F ($30.34) for two persons. The year-round hotel, which belongs to a nationwide chain, is managed by Corinne and Dominque Carot.

10. Vence

Travel up into the hills 15 miles northwest of Nice—across country studded with cypresses, olive trees, and pines, where bright flowers, especially carnations, roses, and oleanders, grow in profusion—and Venice comes into view. Outside the town, along Boulevard Paul-André, two old olive presses carry on with their age-old duties. But the charm lies in the **Vieille Ville** (Old Town). Visitors invariably have themselves photographed on **Place du Peyra** in front of the urn-shaped **Vieille Fontaine** (Old Fountain), a background shot in several motion pictures. The 15th-century **square tower** is also a curiosity.

If you're wearing the right kind of shoes, the narrow, steep streets of the old town are worth exploring. Dating from the 10th century, the **cathedral** on Place Godeau is unremarkable except for some 15th-century Gothic choir stalls. But if it's the right day of the week, most visitors quickly pass through the narrow gates of this once-fortified walled town to where the sun shines more brightly, at the—

MATISSE CHAPEL: It was a beautiful golden autumn along the Côte d'Azur. The great Henri Matisse was 77 years old, and after a turbulent personal search, he set out to create his masterpiece, or to quote the artist, "the culmination of a whole life dedicated to the search for truth." Just outside Vence, Matisse created a Chapel of the Rosary for the Dominican nuns of Monteils. From the front you might find it unremarkable and pass it by—until you spot a 40-foot crescent-adorned cross rising from a blue-tile roof.

Matisse wrote: "What I have done in the chapel is to create a religious space . . . in an enclosed area of very reduced proportions and to give it, solely by the play of colors and lines, the dimensions of infinity." The light picks up the subtle coloring in the simply rendered leaf forms and abstract patterns: sapphire-blue, aquamarine, and lemon-yellow. In black-and-white ceramics, St. Dominic is depicted in only a few lines. The most remarkable design is in the black-and-white-tile Stations of the Cross with Matisse's self-styled "tormented and passionate" figures. The bishop of Nice came to bless the chapel in the late spring of 1951. The artist's work was completed. He died three years later.

The chapel is open only on Tuesday and Thursday, from 10 to 11:30 a.m.

and 2:30 to 5:30 p.m. (tel. 93-58-03-26). Admission is free but offerings are welcome.

DELUXE CHÂTEAU LIVING: Le Château du Domaine St-Martin, Route de Coursegoules (tel. 93-58-02-02), two miles outside of Vence, is romantically positioned in a 35-acre park on the crest of a high hill. Built in 1936 on the grounds where the "Golden Goat treasury" was reputedly buried, the country house is a rambling hacienda with spacious courtyards and terraces—an idyllic retreat. When the present owners, the Geneve family, purchased the estate, they had to sign a bill of sale agreeing to share the treasure, if found, with the assignees. Since there were only 15 twin-bedded rooms in the main building, a complex of tile-roofed villas was built in the surrounding terraced gardens, set in the midst of age-old olive trees. On one terrace where the sun beats down strongest, a kidney-shaped swimming pool was installed, surrounded by a flagstone terrace.

You can walk through the gardens on winding walks lined with tall cypresses, past the crumbling chapel ruins and flowering orange trees. Tall arched windows let in the coastal sunlight in the hand-tiled loggia, a gracious gallery with such successfully coordinated antiques as eight-foot-high torchères, Louis XVI armchairs, and gilt mirrors. Equally well furnished, the main drawing room opens onto the sea, making for a private-seeming retreat that has attracted such guests as Truman, Isaac Stern, and Adenauer. One statesman called the château "the anteroom of paradise."

The bedrooms have been equipped with fine furnishings and private baths. A twin-bedded room costs 2,000F ($275.80), and apartment villas cost 2,800F ($386.12) to 3,200F ($441.28) for two persons. The hotel is closed from mid-November through February. Not to be ignored is the cuisine, served in a glassed-in restaurant opening onto a fantastic view of the coastline. Even if you aren't staying here, you can enjoy the food, a set meal costing from 350F ($48.27), plus 15% for service. You can spend as much as 450F ($62.06), ordering à la carte.

A MIDDLE-BRACKET HOTEL: Le Floréal, Avenue Rhin-et-Danube (tel. 93-58-64-40), on the new road to Grasse, is a pleasant, comfortable hotel with a view of the mountains and the sea. Many of the rooms look out on the large swimming pool in the well-kept garden, where orange trees and mimosa add fragrance to the mild breezes. The 43 units have private bath, phone, radio, and TV. Singles cost 350F ($48.27) and doubles 390F ($53.78). The hotel has air-conditioned lounges and a bar, as well as parking space. It's closed in November.

BUDGET LIVING AND DINING: Auberge des Seigneurs (Inn of the Noblemen), Place du Frêne (tel. 93-58-04-24), is an authentic village inn where you'll experience the France of another century. A stone hostelry in the old part of town, the inn is shaded by one of the largest trees on the Côte d'Azur, giving the plaza its name of "Ash Square." Fascinating decorative objects and antiques are placed everywhere. Inside is a long wooden dining table, in view of an open fireplace with a row of hanging copper pots and pans. Corner cupboards, ladderback chairs, wooden casks of flowers, dark beams, an open spit for roasting and grilling—all this is but a background to the superb food, "the cuisine of François I." Meals are offered at 130F ($17.93) and 150F ($20.69). If you stay the night, you'll pay 230F ($31.72) for a double room with a private shower, 210F ($20.96) in a single. The inn is closed Sunday night off-season, Monday, and from mid-October to December 1.

La Farigoule, 15 rue Henri-Isnard (tel. 93-58-01-27), serves regional cooking in a setting of well-preserved, crooked old beams and antique furnishings, including a Welsh cupboard, a collection of dolls, and a grandfather clock. In summer it's best to dine in the rear garden under a rose arbor. Meals are grilled on an open fire. The patronne, Georgette Gastaud, keeps things humming and doesn't even get flustered when a long line forms on Sunday afternoon. There are two set meals offered; the cheaper one, 75F ($10.32), includes soupe aux poissons (fish soup), truite (trout) meunière, a vegetable, and cheese or dessert. You pay extra for service and your beverage. The 90F ($12.41) menu, however, is far more enticing. On my latest rounds I ordered asparagus vinaigrette, mussels marinières, a tender rabbit with seasonal vegetables, plus cheese and dessert, with drinks and service extra. The restaurant is closed from mid-November to mid-December.

On the Outskirts: La Gaude

Hostellerie Hermitage (tel. 93-24-40-05) is the kind of crow's-nest villa that artists have been occupying along this hilly coast for more than half a century. In the heart of the artists' belt, the inn is lodged on the brow of a hilly ridge surrounded by terraces of tall cypresses. A graveled area with a reflection pool is edged by flower beds, and climbing over the walls of the villa are magenta and orange bougainvillea. Opening onto a solarium, the dining room is splashed with color. However, many diners prefer tables set under umbrellas on a small terrace. As for the food, it's worth the expedition up here, even if you aren't staying over. Specialties include paillardines (veal scallops) à la sauge, fricassée de poulet (chicken) à l'estragon, and chaussons de morilles. The inn offers ten bedrooms, a few with private bath. Doubles cost from 250F ($34.48). There are two set menus, one at 100F ($13.79) and a much larger and better one at 180F ($24.82). The dining room is closed on Friday except at night in July and August.

How to get there? First of all, a car is imperative. From the coastal road between Antibes and Cagnes, take the D18 leading to St-Jeannet. The inn is about a 15-minute drive from Vence.

11. Cagnes-sur-Mer

Between Nice and Antibes, Cagnes-sur-Mer, like the Roman god Janus, shows two faces. Its hilltop town, **Le Haut-de-Cagnes,** is one of the most charming spots on the Riviera. Its seafront **Cros-de-Cagnes** is an old fishing port and a rapidly developing beach resort. Its racecourse is considered one of the finest in France. In the "hinterlands" of Nice, Le Haut-de-Cagnes "crowns the top of a blue-cypressed hill like a village in an Italian Renaissance painting," to quote Naomi Barry. For years the town has attracted the French literati (Simone de Beauvoir wrote *Les Mandarins* here) and a colony of painters (Renoir made it famous, selecting it as "the place where I want to paint until the last day of my life").

In a setting of orange groves and fields of carnations, the upper village consists of narrow cobblestone streets with houses dating from the 17th and 18th centuries. You can drive your car to the top, the **Place du Château,** where you can enjoy the view, have lunch, drink an apéritif in a sidewalk café, and pay a visit to:

CHÂTEAU MUSÉE: Once a stronghold of the Middle Ages, the fortress on the Place Grimaldi at Haut-de-Cagnes was built by Rainier Grimaldi in 1301. He was a lord of Monaco and a French admiral (a portrait inside shows what he looked like, and charts reveal how the defenses were organized). In the early 17th century the dank castle was converted into a more gracious Louis XIII château. The historical monument, owned by the town of Cagnes-sur-Mer, consists of both a **Musée de l'Olivier** (Museum of the Olive Tree) and a **Musée d'Art Moderne Méditerranéen.** The ethnographical museum shows the steps involved in the cultivation and processing of the olive. The modern-art gallery displays work by Kisling, Carzou, Dufy, Cocteau, and Seyssaud, among other painters, along with temporary exhibitions. In one salon is an interesting fresco depicting *La Chute de Phaeton* in trompe l'oeil by Carlone, an Italian. From the tower you get a spectacular view of the Côte d'Azur.

The museum is open daily except Tuesday, from 10 a.m. to noon and 2 to 6 p.m. from June 15 to September 30, to 5 p.m. from October 1 to June 14, and is closed entirely from October 15 to November 15. Admission is 3F (41¢). Each year from July to September the International Festival of Painting takes place, with the official participation of 40 nations. For information, call 93-20-85-57.

FOOD AND LODGING: In accommodations and restaurants, Cagnes-sur-Mer offers you a big choice: you can either stay and dine in Le Haut-de-Cagnes, the hilltop town, or else on the water at Cros-de-Cagnes. Much depends on your personal taste. You can also find food and lodgings nearby at La Colle-sur-Loup. We'll begin at:

Le Haut-de-Cagnes

Le Cagnard, rue du Pontis-Long (tel. 93-20-73-22), is an 18th-century inn which has long attracted outstanding members of the French literary and art worlds, such as Simone de Beauvoir, Renoir, Chagall, Soutine, and Modigliani, who came to dine or to lodge here. At the cusp of the ramparts of this medieval feudal hamlet, a scattering of village houses have been joined to form the handsome hostelry. A vaulted dining room covered with subtle frescoes, a vine-draped terrace, and 19 bedrooms were created from the once-private dwellings. The bedrooms as well as the salons were furnished elegantly and with authority by Madame Barel, the owner, using many family antiques and decorative accessories: fruitwood provincial chests, armoires, Louis XV–style chairs, and copper lavabos, plus a few "other era" paintings mixed with some modern works from the Côte d'Azur school. Staying overnight is a treat worth the trouble of a reservation. Behind painted doors, opening off the well-preserved stone steps and corridors, each bedchamber has its own style, sometimes in duplex form and sometimes with a private terrace and views over the countryside. Each, however, contains provincial antiques, plush and impeccably clean upholstery, and lots of sun-flooded, thick-walled charm. Singles cost from 350F ($48.27 and doubles from 550F ($75.63).

Fixed-price meals, including many of the chef's specialties, are offered for 260F ($35.85) to 300F ($41.37), and a menu dégustation, 380F ($52.40), is worth making the trip for. On the à la carte menu, don't miss some of the hot hors d'oeuvres, including such little tidbits as a prune stuffed with foie gras (goose liver) and wrapped in bacon. The meat specialty is Sisteron lamb (carré d'agneau), spit-roasted with Provençal herbs, served only for two persons. A côte de boeuf is good and tender. The extravagantly prepared dessert pièce de résistance is mousseline de glace aux charmeuses de bois. If you order à la carte, your tab is likely to range from 450F ($62.06) to 600F ($82.74). After dinner, join the other guests for coffee in the little salon if it's a cool night or on the ramparts terrace if the weather is balmy. Le Cagnard is closed from the first of November to mid-December.

Le Grimaldi, 6 Place du Château (tel. 93-20-60-24), enjoys the prime position on the main square. Guests dine on the front terrace under bright umbrellas, enjoying the cookery of the chef de cuisine, Monsieur Perrouty. Two set meals are offered, the least expensive one going for 85F ($11.72), which might begin with a salade niçoise, followed with lapin (rabbit) chasseur, potatoes, and salad, then a selection of cheese or fruit. For 145F ($20), you can order a more elaborate menu featuring more expensive dishes, such as escargots (snails) à la Bourgogne. These fixed-price meals include service and beverage. Other main dishes include mussels in the style of Provence and trout with almonds. In addition, six simply furnished rooms, suitable for either single or double occupancy, are rented at a cost of 125F ($17.24) a night. These units contain only a wash basin and bidet. The inn is closed on Tuesday in low season, but open seven days a week in July and August. It is closed from early January to early February.

Josy-Jo, 8 Place du Planastel (tel. 93-20-68-76). Sheltered behind masses of vines and flowers on the main road leading up to the château, this is the best independent restaurant outside of the hotels of Cagnes-sur-Mer. It used to house the studios of both Modigliani and Soutine who, during their poorest days, lived and painted within the thick stone walls which are today contentedly occupied by the charming Bandecchi family. Their cuisine is cheerfully served. It's unfrilled, fresh, and excellent. You can enjoy a brochette of gigot of lamb with kidneys, four succulent varieties of steak, calves' liver, a homemade terrine of foie gras of duckling, an array of salads, and Irish coffee. Full meals cost from 250F ($34.48) and 275F ($37.92). Meats are roasted over an open grill flaming with Portuguese charcoal; other dishes are prepared in the modern kitchens which Georges Bandecchi carefully conceals behind an art-lined dining room. No meals are served on Sunday, during the first ten days of July, and for a month beginning just before Christmas.

Cros-de-Cagnes

Hôtel de la Serre, 22 Boulevard de la Plage (tel. 93-20-10-54), is set across the seaside highway from the beach, behind an art deco façade painted in fiesta colors of ochre and russet. A red-tile roof covers a huge-windowed extension shaded with voile curtains. When it was built in 1940, it was one of the first hotels along this section of the coast. Today members of the Savournin-Fayssat family rent 26 attractive bedrooms, each of which has a private bath and most of which contain a terrace with sea views. Only five of the six accommodations have their own toilet. Shared facilities are in the hallways. Closed between October 1 and December 1, the hotel charges 135F ($18.62) to 180F ($24.82) in either a single or double, depending on the plumbing. Triples cost 190F ($26.20).

La Réserve (Chez Loulou), 91 Boulevard de le Plage (tel. 93-31-00-17), occupies a three-story, 19th-century building whose elaborate façade sits across the busy street from the sea. The large glass extension which juts out into the sidewalk contains provincial chairs and tables which spill over into a pleasant interior ringed with exposed stone and a handful of plants. A 180F ($24.82) fixed-price menu is offered, but most guests order à la carte, paying from 320F ($44.13) per person. Loulou Bertho and his staff have become known for the freshness and types of the fish served here. The fresh grilled fish is certainly worth a detour. You might also enjoy portions of smoked Norwegian salmon, fresh crayfish, a soup of rockfish (in season), house-style aiguillettes of duckling in gelatin, and a limited offering of succulent beef dishes. Surprisingly for the Riviera, the restaurant is closed during the peak visiting months of July and August, but remains open for the rest of the year except on Saturday night and all day Sunday.

La Colle-sur-Loup

Hostellerie de l'Abbaye, Avenue Libération (tel. 93-32-66-77), is a charming hotel housed in a former abbey whose chiseled stone walls, excellent cuisine and 10th-century chapel will plunge you into what might be one of the most unusual hotel stopovers along the Côte d'Azur. The façade rises broodingly over an area filled with old trees, just off the D6 between Grasse and Cagnes-sur-Mer. Meals are served either in the garden near the fountain or in the timbered dining room seated on Louis XIII–style chairs. One of the salon's vaulted ceilings used to shelter the abbey's horses, but today the erstwhile stable is comfortably furnished with a fireplace and wrought-iron chandeliers. If you want just a room for the night, the 15 beautifully furnished units cost from 500F ($68.95) in a single and 650F ($89.64) in a double. Menus are available for 210F ($28.96) to 280F ($38.61) apiece. A heated swimming pool is set into the garden.

SIGHTS IN THE ENVIRONS: On the outskirts are two museums honoring famous Frenchmen.

Les Collettes (tel. 93-20-61-07) has been restored to what it was when the great Renoir lived there, from 1908 until his death in 1919. Here at his *maison* he turned to sculpture, even though he was crippled by arthritis and had to be helped in and out of a wheelchair. Assistants aided in his work, and he also continued to paint with a brush tied to his paralyzed hand. One of his last paintings, *Rest After Bathing,* completed the year he died, is owned by the Louvre.

The house was built in 1907 in a setting of olive trees and an orange grove. In the entrance hall is a bust of Madame Renoir. You can explore the drawing and dining rooms on your own before going upstairs to the artist's bedroom. In his atelier are his wheelchair, and his easel and brushes. From the terrace of Madame Renoir's bedroom is a stunning view of Cap d'Antibes and Le Haut-de-Cagnes. The museum owns only two paintings, but it has nine sculptures. On a wall hangs a photograph of one of Renoir's sons, Pierre, as he appeared in the 1932 film *Madame Bovary.* Inaugurated in the summer of 1960, the museum is open daily except Tuesday, from 2 to 6 p.m. (till 5 p.m. in winter), charging 3F (41¢) for admission. Closed from October 15 to November 15.

In the charming little hamlet of **Villeneuve-Loubet** in the Alps-Maritimes, Auguste Escoffier was born in 1846. Later he was to earn the appellation "the king of chefs and the chef of kings." His career began in 1859 at the age of 12. He was to work until his retirement from London's Carlton in 1921, although he lived until the age of 89, dying in 1935 at Monte Carlo. In the 1890s in London, as chef of the Savoy, he became world famous. In 1959 a museum was created in Escoffier's honor at Villeneuve-Loubet, housed in the Foundation Escoffier, rue Escoffier (tel. 93-20-80-51). A culinary center dedicated to the art of cookery, the museum is international, preserving mementos from the 14th to the 20th centuries from great chefs and gastronomes, including many sugar creations by French pastry cooks. Known as **Le Musée de l'Art Culinaire,** it contains memorabilia of Escoffier's life. Charging adults 10F ($1.38) and children 5F (69¢) for admission, the museum is open from 10 a.m. to noon and 2 to 5 p.m. except Monday and bank holidays. It is closed in November.

12. Biot

Biot is known for its ceramics and pottery and its memories of Léger. Originally settled by Gallo-Romans, it has had a long history. But its fame rests on the earthenware jars it shipped to Phoenicia, making it famous around the Mediterranean. Somehow the potters still managed to turn out their ancient craft, in spite of all the pillaging and destruction that has swept across Biot over the centuries.

In the late '40s glassmaking, especially a bubble-flecked glass known as *verre rustique,* became another local industry. Just stroll along the main shopping street of town, and you'll see many stores displaying this product, in such brilliant colors as cobalt and emerald. The town is also known for its carnations and roses, and these are often sold on the town's arcaded square. But most of them are flown to the capitals of northern Europe. However, in addition to the glass, pottery, and ceramics, most visitors pass through Biot heading for the—

Musée National Fernand-Léger (tel. 93-33-42-20). Cranes, acrobats, scaffolding, railroad signals, buxom nudes, casings, and crankshafts—all these subjects occupied the mind of Fernand Léger (1881–1955). At the place where he chose to work till the day he died, his widow, Madame Nadia Léger, assembled the greatest collection of his art in a museum in this little town four miles from Antibes. From his first cubist paintings, he was ironically called a "Tubist" rather than a "Cubist."

The stone-and-marble façade of the museum is enhanced by Léger's mosaic and ceramic mural. On the grounds is a polychrome ceramic sculpture, *Le Jardin d'Enfant*. Inside, on two floors, you can wander through gallery after gallery of geometrical forms in pure, flat colors. The collection embraces gouaches, paintings, ceramics, tapestries, and sculptures, showing the development of the artist from 1905 until his death. Perhaps the most unusual work depicts a Léger *Mona Lisa* contemplating a set of monumental keys, a wide-mouth fish dangling at an angle over her head.

One critic wrote that "Léger has been attacked by several varieties of 'humanists' for 'dehumanizing' art by mechanizing his figures; but has he not at the same time helped to humanize the machine by integrating it in the painting?" Living in the United States, mainly in New York, during World War II, Léger gloried in "the bad taste, one of the valuable raw materials of the country."

The museum, inaugurated in 1960, is open daily except Tuesday, from 10 a.m. to noon and 2 to 6 p.m., closing at 5 p.m. off-season; it charges 17F ($2.34) for admission.

WHERE TO DINE: Café de la Poste, rue St-Sébastien (tel. 93-65-06-46). The unprepossessing entrance area of this restaurant is furnished like many other bars in the region, outfitted with a zinc countertop, several pinball machines, and a crowd of local residents talking about football scores and the lottery. Once you pass a screen of engraved glass, however, you'll be in what looks like another world. Bernard Peters offers such specialties as zucchini blossoms Niçoise style, red mullet with smoked anchovies, sea bass in herb butter, and noisettes of lamb in a garlic purée. Part of the beauty of his platters stems from his apprenticeship with Roger Vergé at Moulin de Mougins. These dishes are served in a decor where the restored wall murals show the cancan in a turn-of-the-century cabaret, along with mahogany antiques, bentwood chairs, and globe lights. The establishment is closed on Thursday and in November and December. Menus cost 140F ($19.31) and 190F ($26.20), with à la carte orders averaging 250F ($34.48).

Les Terrailleurs, Route du Chemin-Neuf (tel. 93-65-01-59). You might prefer the well-decorated interior if you think the noise of the passing cars would spoil a terrace meal for you. The setting is nothing less than a vaulted 16th-century studio that used to produce clay pots and ceramics. Today the specialties coming from the ovens are far more succulent, including such items as aiguillettes of John Dory with a confit of onions and tomato-flavored butter, breast of duckling with raspberry vinegar, émincé of lamb with tomatoes and mushrooms, and zucchini soufflé with an essence of tomatoes. Meals are served daily except Tuesday and in November. Menus range from 110F ($15.17) to 180F ($24.82).

13. Antibes and Cap d'Antibes

On the other side of the Bay of Angels, across from Nice, sits the ancient, once-fortified port of Antibes. Thirteen miles from Nice by road, it is an old Mediterranean town whose quiet charm is perhaps unequaled along the Côte d'Azur. Jutting out into the sea, it contains a little harbor filled with pleasure yachts and fishing boats. Its potential as a flower-growing center—mainly roses and carnations—is best reflected in the marketplace. If you're staying over in the evening, you can watch fishermen playing the popular Riviera game of *boule*. The Bonaparte family was there in 1794, and it is said that the future princesses stole artichokes and figs from the nearby farms.

On the ramparts stands the **Château d'Antibes,** now turned into the **Picasso**

Museum (tel. 93-33-67-67), housing one of the greatest single Picasso collections. Once it was the home of the princes of Antibes of the de Grasse family, who ruled the city from 1385 to 1608. But Picasso, lodged in a small hotel room at Golfe-Juan after his bitter war years in Paris, needed more space to work. The museum director at Antibes—in one of the smartest moves he ever made—invited the great Spaniard to work and live at the museum. Picasso did, and when he left for better pastures, he gave the museum all the work he'd done at Antibes that year. And what a prolific 1946 it was, a year of goats and centaurs. Some two dozen paintings, nearly 80 pieces of ceramics, some 44 drawings, as well as 32 lithographs, 11 oils on paper, two pieces of sculpture, and five tapestries are on display. In addition, a gallery of contemporary art exhibits works by Léger, Miró, Ernst, de Stael, and Calder, among other modern artists. In contrast, antiquity is reflected in the display of Ligurian, Greek, and Roman artifacts. Charging 15F ($2.07) for admission, the museum is open from 10 a.m. to noon and 3 to 7 p.m. (till 6 p.m. off-season).

Spiritually, Antibes is totally divorced from the celebrated **Cap d'Antibes,** a peninsula studded with the villas and swimming pools of the wealthy. Long a playground of the rich, particularly in the 1920s, it was depicted in *Tender Is the Night,* with F. Scott Fitzgerald's hero, Dick Diver, seen in an atmosphere of "old villas rotted like water lilies among the massed pines." Photographs of film stars lounging at the Eden Roc have enlivened many a Sunday supplement.

Although one doesn't usually think of visiting a museum at Cap d'Antibes, there is in fact the **Musée Naval et Napoléonien,** Batterie du Grillon (tel. 93-61-45-32). An ancient military tower, it houses an interesting collection of Napoleonic memorabilia, naval models, paintings, and army mementos. A toy-soldier collection depicts various uniforms worn by the men, including one used by Napoleon in the Marengo campaign. A wall painting in wood shows Napoleon's entrance into Grenoble; another tableau depicts his disembarkation at Golfe-Juan on March 1, 1815. In contrast to Canova's Greek-god image of Napoleon, a miniature pendant by Barrault reveals the Corsican general as he really looked, with pudgy cheeks and a receding hairline. In the rotunda in the rear is one of the many hats worn by the emperor. You can climb to the top of the tower for a view of the coast that is worth the price of admission, including a wide sweep of Juan-les-Pins and the harbor studded with sailboats. The museum is open daily, except Tuesday and the month of November, from 10 a.m. to noon and 3 to 7 p.m. (off-season, September 2 to October 31 and December 16 to May 31, it's open from 10 a.m. to noon and 2 to 5); admission is 12F ($1.66).

FOOD AND LODGING: The best choices in all price ranges for meals and accommodations follow:

Deluxe Living and Dining

Hôtel du Cap-d'Antibes, Boulevard Kennedy (tel. 93-61-39-01). Around its swimming pool built in the rugged rocks next to the lapping waves of the Mediterranean lie what Fitzgerald called "the notable and fashionable people." The celebrities change with the years, but have included Lloyd George, Anatole France, Bernard Shaw, Somerset Maugham, Chaplin, Fairbanks, Gable, Bogart, Orson Welles, Marlene Dietrich, Johnny Carson, Mary Pickford, Sophia Loren, Picasso, Chagall, Gary Cooper, and the Ford, Kennedy, and Du Pont families. Set in the midst of splendid acres of gardens is the palatial hotel, a monument to a bygone era, inaugurated in 1870. The interior is like a great country estate, with spacious, well-decorated public rooms, marble fireplaces, scenic paneling, crystal chandeliers, and clusters of velvet-tufted armchairs.

All bedrooms are air-conditioned, with private bath and deluxe accessories, the period furnishings ranging from regal to merely sumptuous. Double rooms peak at 2,300F ($317.17), and singles go for 1,300F ($179.27), plus 15%

for service. The hotel is open between April and the end of October. In the peak of the season, guests can dine in the seafront pavilion, the world-famous Eden Rock, its all-glass windows fronting on the Mediterranean. Venetian chandeliers, Louis XV–style chairs, and toile draperies form a dramatic setting. Luncheons are served on the outer terrace, under umbrellas and an arbor. At noon there is a selection of ten hors d'oeuvres to get you started. At dinner, three specialties include bouillabaisse, lobster thermidor, and sea bass with fennel. Expect to pay 380F ($52.40) to 500F ($68.95) if you dine here.

Medium Bracket and Budget

Hôtel Royal, Boulevard du Maréchal-Leclerc (tel. 93-34-03-09), is the best place to stay in the city of Antibes. It was built around 80 years ago in a position just across the road from a sheltering rocky spit edged with private boats. It's the oldest hotel in Antibes, boasting a clientele that has included Bing Crosby and Graham Greene. The Royal maintains its own private beach, a café terrace in front of the red-shuttered façade, and an English-style bar area just off the lobby area. Each of the 43 rooms contains its own private bath, and there are two restaurants on the premises, including the prestigious Le Dauphin. Half-board prices, depending on the season, range from 300F ($41.37) to 375F ($51.71) per person, based on double occupancy. In high season no singles are available, while in low season singles pay a supplement of 100F ($13.79) for half board. The hotel is open from February 1 to October 31.

Auberge de la Gardiole, Chemin de la Garoupe (tel. 93-61-35-03), is run like a glorified country inn by Anne Marie Arama in a delightful, personal way. She knows all about food, supervising its buying at the markets and its preparation. She also directs the service in the dining room and oversees the 20 bedrooms. The auberge is a large villa, spilling out into the surrounding gardens and pergola. Set in a district of largely private estates, it welcomes guests into an all-purpose, high-beamed room where tables are set up for meals when the weather is nippy. It's cheerful, with colored cloths and (on cooler nights) a fire burning on a raised brick hearth, and hanging pots and pans. In fair weather you can dine under a trellis covered with a wisteria vine.

Bedrooms, on the upper floors of the inn and in the little buildings placed in the garden, offer simplicity and charm, with provincial furnishings and good strong colors. In high season, half-board rates range from 270F ($37.23) to 320F ($44.13) per person, depending on the plumbing. Guests are accepted between Easter and October 1. The cuisine is skillfully prepared. Two fixed-price meals await nonresidents: 110F ($15.17) to 160F ($22.06). You pay extra for your drink, but service is included.

Motel Axa, Boulevard Garoupe (tel. 93-61-36-51), is a villa-hotel-apartment house built in the Mediterranean style, with a tile roof, private balconies, arches, and shuttered windows. Set back on a private lane in the center of the cape, it is surrounded by its own grounds and a freshwater swimming pool, along with a tennis court amid gnarled olive trees and a rock garden. It is highly recommended because it gives you an apartment for the same price you'd pay for a bedroom elsewhere. The rates are uncomplicated: 500F ($68.95) to 550F ($75.63) for two persons, including a continental breakfast. In all, the hotel offers 20 rooms, each handsomely equipped and appointed. There is as well a shady garden, and under a pine tree you can find tranquility on the Riviera.

Beau Site, 141 Boulevard Kennedy (tel. 93-61-53-43), is a three-story villa surrounded by eucalyptus trees, pines, and palms. Off the main road, with a low wall of flower urns and wrought-iron gates, it is a tile-roofed, white-stucco structure with heavy shutters. Although not on the beach, it has its own rustic charm; the interior is like a country auberge with oak beams and antiques. Only breakfast is served, and a double room rents for 300F ($41.37) nightly. The villa receives guests from late March to late September.

Deluxe Dining

La Bonne Auberge, Quartier la Brague, Route N7, 2½ miles from Antibes (tel. 93-33-36-65), is a special event. One of the most famous restaurants along the Côte d'Azur, it is a salmon-pink villa along the coastal highway with an impressive crescent-shaped driveway entrance. Covered with ivy, it is fronted by a long row of arbors and arches. The interior is like what "back-lot" MGM used to be, with pink walls, deep arches, black oak beams, carved provincial sideboards, and wrought-iron lanterns casting flickering lights. But most important of all is the proud chef, who provides a cuisine that has won acclaim from visitors from every continent.

Under the direction of Jo and Philippe Rostang, the restaurant turns out a nouvelle cuisine that is ranked among the best along the Riviera. The specialties here are so beautifully prepared that it is hard to recommend specific dishes. Nevertheless, you are likely to be tempted by such pleasurable dishes as fricassée of St-Pierre made with leeks and truffles, mousseline of red mullet with red caviar, crayfish salad, duckling with a compote of pears, foie gras with celeriac, and a peach soufflé that is one of life's enchantments. The service and reception are grand. Ordering à la carte will run in the neighborhood of 350F ($48.27) to 500F ($68.95). Featured wines are Château-Vignelaure and Bellet. The restaurant closes from mid-November to mid-December, the first week in March, and on Monday at lunchtime in July and August.

Upper Bracket Dining

Les Vieux Murs (Taverne Provence), Avenue de l'Admiral-de-Grasse (tel. 93-34-06-73), is a provincial tavern, charmingly located on the ramparts off Antibes with a few outside tables. It produces fine food at a price, especially if you succumb to the delectable house specialty, lobster thermidor. The interior is rustic, a colorful setting for such good seafood. Three highly recommendable dishes include fish soup, rognons de veau à la crème (veal kidneys in a cream sauce), and filet de sole in a champagne sauce, served only for two. A complete meal ranges in price from 220F ($30.34) to 300F ($41.37). The patron makes certain that only the best of fish—and the freshest—is bought at the early-morning market. The restaurant is closed on Wednesday, and its annual closing is from mid-November to just before Christmas.

Le Caméo, Place Nationale (tel. 93-34-24-17), stands in the heart of Antibes, in an elegant 19th-century Provençal villa on a historic square ringed with large trees. This is the best-known inn in the center, the kind of place where local residents gather every afternoon and evening in the bar, perhaps later taking a meal in the adjacent home-style dining room. There, in a slightly cluttered but very clean ambience, the main focus is on the colorful, genteel, and smiling waitresses who perform impeccable service punctuated with solicitous queries about how you enjoyed this course or that. Amid the immaculate napery, bouquets of flowers, and crowded tables, you'll enjoy a cuisine that could include local fish, stuffed mussels, fish soup, aïoli garni, and fried scampi. Fixed-price menus are offered between 95F ($13.10) and 120F ($16.55). If you want to spend the night, pleasantly furnished bedrooms, all of which contain a private bath, are rented for 180F ($24.82) in a single and 240F ($33.10) in a double. The restaurant is closed Sunday night and Tuesday.

ANTIBES AFTER DARK: La Siesta, Pont de la Rivière "Brague" (tel. 93-33-31-31), is a kind of beach club with a dual personality. When entering, you'll see a sign posted giving the requirements for admission: *"L'élégance et la bonne éducation!"* Really an amusement center, La Siesta isn't very sleepy. In the daytime you can spend many sunny hours lounging on the graveled beach or going for a dip in the pool. Meals are available under adjustable umbrellas set around a large reflection pool with overscale lily-pad floats. The use of the beach club facilities costs 65F ($8.97), and snacks are available. At night attention focuses on the disco (at one event, 6,500 showed up) and drinking lounge. You pay 75F ($10.32) for your first drink. The location is about 2½ miles north of Antibes, and hours are 10 a.m. to 4:30 a.m. from June to around the middle of September.

14. Juan-les-Pins

This suburb of Antibes is a controversial resort, drawing highly mixed reactions. Frank Jay Gould developed it in the 1920s and lived there in his own villa. In those days people flocked to "John of the Pines" to escape the "crassness" of nearby Cannes. In the 1930s Juan-les-Pins was drawing a chic crowd of the wintering wealthy of Europe. Today the resort is popular with the better-heeled young Europeans. Maybe their parents aren't rich anymore, but—to judge from the money spent—these attractive young people are high-salaried at least. Activities reach frenzied heights at the July jazz festival.

Juan-les-Pins is often called a honky-tonk town or the Coney Island of the Riviera. Anyone who calls it that hasn't seen Coney Island in a long time. One writer referred to it as "a pop-art Monte Carlo, with eye-popping nude shows, burlesque, and bikini exhibitionists on its nudist-strewn beaches." Perhaps that description is too enticing or provocative for what is such an obviously middle-class resort.

As a nightlife center it is a major contender along the Riviera, attracting many of the resort-hoppers after dark. Many revelers stay up all night in the smoky jazz joints, then sleep it off the next day on the beach. The casino in the center of town offers cabaret entertainment, sometimes till daylight breaks. Then skin-diving and waterskiing predominate. The pines sweep right down to the coast and the sandy beach, which, incidentally, is excellent. Trouble is, you'll need a bulldozer to remove some bronze bodies in July and August if you'd like a spot just for yourself.

ACCOMMODATIONS: From the out-of-reach to the affordable, Juan-les-Pins has them all. I'll begin with—

The Upper Bracket

Belles-Rives, Boulevard Baudoin (tel. 93-61-02-79), at the edge of the resort, is in an enviable position, with its formal entrance on the coastal road, its seaside façade fronting the bay. The lower terraces are devoted to garden-style dining rooms and a waterside aquatic club with a snack-lounge and a jetty extending out into the water. You'll find facilities for boating, waterskiing, sailing, fishing, plus plenty of room to swim. There's also a private sandy beach. Dinners are served on the terrace with a panoramic view of the bay, especially romantic when the lights begin to twinkle at night. The interior is rather subdued, as are the bedrooms; prices depend on the season and the view. Half board is required from May 15 to September 15. At that time the daily half-board rate with bath or shower and air conditioning ranges from 980F ($135.14) to 1,390F ($191.68) per person, with balcony, sea view, breakfast, and dinner. The hotel is open from late March to early October.

Juana, Avenue Gallice (tel. 93-61-08-70), is separated from the sea by park-like grounds studded with cypresses and flower beds. The flowers are changed in the front garden three times a year (hopefully, you'll arrive when the pink and purple petunias are in bloom). The Juana has been owned and managed by the Barache family for three generations. Bedrooms are individually designed and decorated, varying greatly in price, size, and view. Rents range from 740F ($102.05) to 1,050F ($144.80) in a single and from 1,250F ($172.38) to 2,000F ($275.80) in a double, taxes and breakfast included. Half board carries a supplement of 320F ($44.13) per person.

The cuisine is under the management of Monsieur Alain Ducasse, former head chef of the Moulin de Mougins which won top gastronomy awards for his work. The restaurant, La Terrasse, consistently wins acclaim and is reviewed separately.

On the grounds, in a setting of shady palms, are umbrella tables. Right across the park is the private swimming club, where, if you're a hotel guest, you can rent your own "parasol and pad" on the sandy beach at reduced rates. The hotel also has a heated outdoor swimming pool with a solarium and a pool house containing a bar. The Juana receives guests from mid-March to the end of October.

The Middle Bracket

Le Passy, 15 Avenue Louis-Gallet (tel. 93-61-11-09), is a centrally positioned 36-room hotel. One side opens onto a small garden with palm trees and a wide flagstone terrace, the other fronts the sea and coastal boulevard. Generally, furnishings are Nordic modern; all the rooms have private bath (the newer ones have their own little balcony). There are three seasons, the highest tariffs charged between June 15 and September 15, when singles cost from 300F ($141.37); doubles, from 500F ($68.95).

Pré Catelan, 22 Avenue Lauriers (tel. 93-61-05-11), is a substantial villa in a residential area just a few minutes stroll from the town park and the sea. It has the kind of garden a northern European dreams about: rock terraces, towering palm, lemon, and orange trees, large pots of pink geraniums, and trimmed hedges with nooks and crannies for outdoor furniture where you can sneak away for a discreet rendezvous. The atmosphere is casual. The half-board rate ranges from 300F ($41.37) to 400F ($55.16) per person daily, the more expensive rooms including a private terrace. The hotel is open all year, but the restaurant closes from October 15 to March 15.

Hôtel des Mimosas, rue Pauline (tel. 93-61-04-16), is an elegant 1870s-style villa sprawling across the top of a hill in the midst of a verdant tropical garden, five minutes from the center of town. A swimming pool is set, California style, amid huge palm trees. Michel and Raymonde Sauret completely redesigned the interior after they purchased it in 1976. The architect who worked with them studied in the United States, and the result is a slickly contemporary blend of hi-tech with a vaguely Italian kind of sumptuousness. Ten of the hotel's 36 rooms have a private terrace, and all of them have a private bath. There is an unusual high-ceilinged sense of style that seems perfect for summertime living, especially with the masses of exposed terracotta tile and the vivid mix of antique with modern. There's a bar, but no restaurant. Depending on the season and the accommodation, the rate for two persons ranges from 320F ($44.13) to 450F ($62.06), while the tariff for three guests can go as high as 500F ($68.95). The hotel is often fully booked during the peak of summer. It is open March through October.

The Budget Range

Cecil, rue Jonnart (tel. 93-61-05-12), is only 50 yards from the beach. The owner-chef, Monsieur Courtois, provides a very friendly welcome and good meals. The house is well kept, with beige corridors and many antiques in the rooms. The tapestries are in the Provençal style. In summer guests eat on a patio. You stay here on the obligatory half-board plan, paying 220F ($30.34). The Cecil is open from January 15 to October 15.

DINING: La Terrasse, Hôtel Juana, Avenue Gallice (tel. 93-61-20-37), is not only the most outstanding restaurant in Juan-les-Pins, but it is one of the gourmet citadels along the Côte d'Azur. Its much-awarded chef, Alain Ducasse, is a current "darling" of the French food press. Monsieur Ducasse learned his lessons well, in the schools of Chapel, Guérard, Lenôtre, and Vergé. But he has long broken from those "old masters" and charted his own course on the turbulent waters of La Nouvelle Cuisine. A daring chef of imagination, he runs his dining room with extreme skill, paying careful attention to every detail—from the first shopping for the freshest of produce in the markets that morning to the most meticulous place setting. He knows that any aspect, such as careless service, can spoil a great meal, and his aim is perfection.

The ideal place to dine in summer is the outdoor terrace, drawing a lively, sophisticated crowd of young people. His specialties depend on his inspiration. Many were originally Provençal dishes that have been given a modern twist and a new interpretation. Dishes that have won praise in the past include lamb filet mignon in Sisteron, the crayfish salad, and the stuffed young rabbit. If you're not a guest of the hotel, make sure you have a reservation before showing up. Count on spending from 420F ($57.92) to 500F ($68.95) per person. The restaurant is closed for lunch in July and August.

Bijou-Plage, Promenade du Soleil (tel. 93-61-39-07), at the edge of Juan-les-Pins on the coastal road to Cannes, is where you can order bouillabaisse du pêcheur. It'll be made with freshly caught seafood, spiced just right and filling enough to make an entire meal. Decorated in a nautical style, the restaurant is right on the beach—a proper setting for its cuisine. À la carte, such delectable dishes are featured as local grilled fish. A tarte maison rounds out most meals. Expect to spend from 200F ($27.58) to 250F ($34.48) per person. The restaurant is closed from October 10 to December 20 and on Monday evening from December 20 to June 15.

Le Perroquet (The Parrot), Avenue Gallice (tel. 93-61-02-20), is a tavern-like restaurant overlooking the central park. Not unlike a brasserie, it offers one of the most economical and best-prepared meals in the resort town. For 105F ($14.48), you can get a complete five-course luncheon or dinner, with service included. This fixed-price meal often features a choice of such dishes as rabbit in a white wine sauce or osso buco, the Lombard specialty. The restaurant is closed from November 1 to mid-December and on Wednesday.

JUAN-LES-PINS AFTER DARK: Pam Pam Rhumerie, 137 Boulevard Wilson (tel. 93-61-11-05). Stepping into this verdantly furnished rumhouse is like entering a communal village hut in Polynesia. The place is filled with rattan furniture (even the tables have wicker tops and cast-iron bases), South American carvings, hundreds of plants, tropical fabrics, and parakeets occasionally squawking from their roosts. The long bar area is illuminated by spotlights set into South Seas drums, while throughout it all you can hear reggae, Brazilian, or rock music from live groups. The drink list probably includes the most exotic collection along the southern coast of France. Most concoctions are priced from 45F ($6.21). A wide selection of ice creams are laced with tropical liqueurs. The establishment is open every day except from November through February. Music usually plays off and on from 2 p.m. till 4 a.m.

15. Golfe-Juan and Vallauris

From his exile in Elba, Napoleon and 800 men landed at Golfe-Juan in 1815 to begin his Hundred Days. In time Golfe-Juan was to be favored by the American navy, but primarily it is a family beach resort, well sheltered by protective hills planted with orange trees. Just three miles from Cannes, it contains one notable restaurant, Tétou (see below). A short road leads to Vallauris, once merely a stopover along the Riviera, until Picasso made it and its potters famous.

Its ceramics and souvenirs—many the color of rich burgundy—line the streets of Vallauris. Frankly, most of the shops display tasteless ware. One notable exception is **Madoura** (tel. 93-63-74-93), where Alain Ramié, the son of two friends of the late artist, has the only shop licensed to sell reproductions of Picasso's works. The master knew and admired the work of the Ramié family for a long time, ever since he ventured into this small Provençal town after World War II and occupied an unattractive little villa known as "The Woman from Wales." Madoura is open from 9:30 a.m. to 12:30 p.m. and 2:30 to 6 p.m. Some Picasso reproductions are limited to 25 copies, others to as many as 500.

Half the members of the world press clustered one day around the central square where Picasso's statue **Homme et Mouton** *(Man and Sheep)* stands. But they weren't admiring it. Everybody was there to take pictures of a couple getting married: Aly Khan and Rita Hayworth. The council of Vallauris had intended to ensconce this statue in a museum, but Picasso insisted that it remain on the square "where the children could climb over it and the dogs water it unhindered."

At the Place de la Libération stands a chapel of rough stone shaped like a Quonset hut, a horizontal half cylinder. It is now the **Musée National Picasso, Chapelle du Château,** Place de la Libération (tel. 93-58-18-05). Picasso decorated the chapel with two paintings: *La Paix (Peace)* and *La Guerre (War)*. The paintings tug the viewer in two directions—toward love and peace on the one hand, toward violence and conflict on the other. In 1970 a house painter gained illegal entrance to the museum one night and substituted one of his own designs, after whitewashing a portion of the Picasso original. When the aging master ventured out to inspect the damage, he said, "Not bad at all." The National Museum of Vallauris is open from 10 a.m. to noon and 2 to 6 p.m. (off-season, until 5 p.m.), charging 8F ($1.10) for admission, 4F (55¢) for students.

DINING: Tétou, Avenue des Frères Roustand, sur la Plage (tel. 93-63-71-16), fulfills one's fantasy of finding a white beach cottage right on the water where one can get a savory bouillabaisse. The bouillabaisse, usually served for two, is not only delicately spiced but each succulent chunk of fish can be tasted individually. On the à la carte menu, one of the best buys is poissons du pays (sea bass), accompanied by tomates provençales. The soupe de poissons (fish soup) makes a good opener, followed by an excellently prepared sole meunière. After all that seafood, you might enjoy a special powdered and chewy croissant accompanied by grandmother's succulent jams (only in winter). Also featured are homemade raspberry and strawberry tarts in summer. Expect to pay from 380F ($52.40) for a complete meal. The restaurant is closed from mid-October to just before Christmas, the first three weeks in March, and on Wednesday.

16. Mougins

Crowning a hill, this once-fortified town provides a viable choice for those who want to be near the excitement of Cannes but not in the midst of it. The international resort is just five miles away, but spiritually it is a continent away from the quiet life as lived at Mougins. The wealthy set from Cannes, however, has discovered its golfing potential. Picasso knew its possibilities for living. No wonder artists love the rugged, sun-drenched hills covered with gnarled olive trees. In the little valleys, gentle streams flow by. Mougins is the answer to those who fell the Riviera is overrun, overspoiled, and overbuilt.

DELUXE LIVING AND DINING: Le Moulin de Mougins, Notre-Dame de Vie (tel. 93-75-78-24), was a 16th century olive-oil mill. Now it coddles guests in comfort and serves one of the finest and most imaginative cuisines in France. On entering, you pass the ten-foot-wide stone oil vat, complete with a wooden turnscrew and a grinding wheel. Roger Vergé took over the mill in 1969, making it his own culinary kingdom. The "maître cuisinier de France" provides an idyllic setting for a fine meal: thick stone arches, rough old beams, ladderback chairs, Spanish paintings, and open cupboards with copper and painted china.

One day I asked him to list what he considered his best dishes. My pencils wore down after he cited 30. My favored viands include le poupeton de truffe au fumet de champignons, les filets de rougets (red mullet) de roche en barigoule d'artichaut, noisettes d'agneau (lamb) de sisteron with eggplant cake in a thyme-flavored sauce, and a terrine de fruits du temps en crème d'amand avec la glace aux fleurs de lavande. His particular forte is fish from the Mediterranean. Each morning he buys directly from the local fishermen. If you dine here, expect to pay anywhere from 600F ($82.74) per person. Of course, the price depends a great deal on the wine you select. Monsieur Vergé has a lot of fantastic, even historic bottles. But there is also a good local wine selection at humane prices. Advance reservations are recommended.

The old mill offers six beautifully decorated apartments, each a honeymoon lair, with provincial beds, Louis XVI-style chairs and chests, bay windows with white ruffled curtains, and matching flowered toile coverings for furniture and beds. Doubles range from 800F ($110.32) to 1,500F ($206.85), the latter for a suite with terrace. The inn is closed from mid-November to just before Christmas, and mid-February to late March. The restaurant shuts down on Monday and at lunchtime on Thursday.

OTHER FOOD AND LODGING SELECTIONS: Las Mas Candille, Boulevard

Rebuffel (tel. 93-90-00-85), is a 200-year-old Provençal farmhouse renovated in 1982 and turned into the best hotel at Mougins. The public rooms contain many 19th-century furnishings. The dining room has elegant stone detailing and a massive fireplace with a timbered mantelpiece. The establishment maintains both a summer and a winter dining room, with warm-weather meals served upon request on the sun terrace, whose view encompasses most of the valley. In Provençal, *candille* means candle, and you'll see lots of them burning in the large candelabra in the dining room and on the terrace, where menu specialties include zucchini blossoms in a basil-flavored butter sauce, a salad of foie gras and truffles, veal kidneys en cocotte, and other temptations on a menu surprise. Fixed-price menus cost 240F ($33.10) and 280F ($38.61), while à la carte meals average 400F ($55.16). In summer, closed Tuesday for lunch; otherwise, closed Wednesday for lunch, Tuesday, and from mid-November to December 28. Reserve ahead. The attractively furnished bedrooms have private bath, phone, and often a terrace opening onto the garden. Singles range from 600F ($82.74), while doubles cost from 820F ($113.08).

Le Clos des Boyères, 89 Chemin de la Chappelle, Notre-Dame de Vie (tel. 93-90-01-58), is a family villa in a tranquil setting where you can hear the birds chirping and smell the pines. On the side of a tree-covered hill, it is surrounded by a lawn, with a swimming pool on a lower terrace. The rambling entry driveway is edged by lawns and trees. The inn is especially recommended for families with children, as there is room to romp and play. The furnishings are pleasant, informal, and "countrified." Each of the 35 bedrooms has its own bath and telephone. Three sets of rates are charged, the most expensive applying in July and August, when two persons pay 950F ($131.01) and one person is charged 550F ($75.63), including half board, service, and taxes. The hotel is open from February to the end of October, and the restaurant shuts down on Wednesday.

L'Amandier de Mougins, Place du Commandant-Lamy (tel. 93-90-00-91). Its illustrious founder was none other than the world-famous Roger Vergé, whose nearby Moulin de Mougins is described earlier. Originally intended as a simple hideaway for family-style dining, Mr. Vergé and his wife Denise, according to insiders, couldn't resist creating an almost overwhelmingly charming oasis of vaulted ceilings, glowing antiques, and masses of flowers. Perhaps the cuisine and welcome won't parallel Mr. Vergé's first love, his Moulin, but the clientele of L'Amandier is rapidly growing. Fixed-priced menus cost 280F ($38.61), with à la carte meals averaging 450F ($62.06) and 520F ($71.71). It's not cheap by any standard, but nonetheless reasonable for its recipes, flavors, and aromas inspired by the culinary guru of the Côte d'Azur. The actual chef is Francis Chauveau. Specialties include filet of red snapper with rosemary butter, sea bass with a basil-flavored butter sauce, succulent roast lamb, aiguillettes of salmon and John Dory with a lime sauce, a bouquet of sweetbreads with crayfish and chive sauce, and such desserts as a gratin of apricots and almonds. No meals are served on Wednesday, Saturday at lunch, and during all of January and most of February. Reservations are strongly suggested.

Le Relais à Mougins, Place de la Mairie (tel. 93-90-03-47), is one of the best restaurants in the village. It is housed in a beautifully proportioned Provençal building. The façade curves around one of the most perfect village squares in Provence, dotted with three graceful fountains and immaculately maintained flowering shrubs. The interior of the restaurant would please any mason with its exposed stone, although most clients prefer the outdoor terrace whose canopy is sheltered by a severely pruned chestnut tree. André Surmain, the owner, supervises the preparation of a menu inspired by a desire for lightness and creativity. Specialties include chicken suprême with wild mushrooms, filet mignon of duckling from Landes, braised rabbit with pearl onions, and unusual preparations of sea urchins, plus oysters in puff pastry with a mousseline of spinach. Hubert Avilès, the chef, studied under some of the greatest chefs of France. Two set menus are offered at 180F ($24.82) (lunch only) and 215F ($29.65). In the evening, the more elaborate menu goes up to 500F ($68.95) on the à la carte. The establishment is closed during November and on Sunday night and Monday except in July and August.

Hôtel de France, Place du Lamy (tel. 93-90-00-01), stands in the center of the village, a thick-walled hotel, owned by Bernard Lefèvre, that's a welcome budget oasis in super-expensive Mougins. It is one of the oldest houses in the village, containing eight simple bedrooms which may or may not be quiet at night, depending on the season and the number of celebrants on the street outside. Doubles range from 200F ($27.58). The dining room is a village institution. Its walls are interrupted with a large central arch supported by a screw from a wine press. A fixed-price menu is offered for 150F ($20.69) and might include many Provençal specialties. No meals are served on Sunday night, on Monday off-season, and in January.

17. Grasse

Grasse boasts the most beautiful fragrance of any town on the Riviera. Go there to visit the perfume factories. One of the best known, the **Parfumerie Fragonard,** 20 Boulevard Fragonard (tel. 93-36-44-65), is named after the French painter of the 18th century. It is open daily, including Sunday and holidays, from 8:30 a.m. to 6:30 p.m. There is a guided tour by an English-speaking young woman; you'll see "the soul of flowers" extracted. After the tour, you can explore the museum of perfumery, displaying bottles and vases that trace the industry back to ancient times.

Since the 19th century Grasse—10½ miles from Cannes—has been the world's perfume capital, set in the midst of jasmine and roses. Once it was famed as a resort, attracting such widely diverse personages as Queen Victoria and Pauline Borghese.

Of particular interest is the **Musée d'Art et d'Histoire de Provence,** 2 rue Mirabeau (tel. 93-36-01-61), housed in the **Hôtel de Clapiers-Cabris,** constructed in 1771 by Louise de Mirabeau, the Marquise de Cabris and sister of Mirabeau. The museum is rich in paintings, four-poster beds, marquetry, ceramics, brasses, kitchenware, pottery, urns, even archeological finds from the area. Visitors are welcomed from 10 a.m. to noon and 2 to 6 p.m. in summer for an admission of 9F ($1.24), which also entitles you to visit the Villa Fragonard (see below). In winter the afternoon hours are 2 to 5 p.m.; it is closed Saturday, Sunday, and in November; open the first and last Sunday of each month. Entrance is free on Wednesday and Sunday.

Nearby is the **Villa Fragonard,** 23 Boulevard Fragonard (tel. 93-36-02-71). Here are displayed the paintings of Jean-Honoré Fragonard, born at Grasse in 1732, and those of Marguerite Gérard and Alexandre and Théophile Fragonard, sister-in-law, son, and grandson of Jean-Honoré Fragonard. The grand staircase was decorated by Alexandre. The museum is open from 10 a.m. to noon and 2 to 6 p.m. in summer; in winter, afternoon hours are 2 to 5 p.m. It is closed Saturday, Sunday, and in November, with open house on the first and last Sunday of each month. Admission is the same as at the Musée d'Art et d'Histoire de Provence.

FOOD AND LODGING: **Hotel Napoléon,** 6 Avenue Thiers (tel. 93-36-05-87), is a very plain but clean hotel which has bargain rooms at 90F ($12.41) in a single, 160F ($22.06) in a double. Most of the clientele, however, visit for the food, served in generous quantity and with few airs of pretension. While seated on an outdoor terrace or in one of a pair of dining rooms, you can enjoy carafes or bottles of the local wines. Specialties include tripe in the style of Provence (a regional dish of local codfish), along with a selection of meat and fresh fish. Fixed-price menus at 62F ($8.55) are offered weekdays, the price rising by 15F ($2.07) on weekends and holidays. A la carte dinners cost 90F ($12.41) to 160F ($22.06). The restaurant (but not the hotel) is closed every Saturday between mid-November and mid-March.

18. Cannes

When Coco Chanel went there and got a suntan, returning to Paris bronzed, she startled ladies of society. Nonetheless they quickly began copying her, abandoning their heretofore fashionable peach complexions. Today the bronzed bodies—in the briefest of bikinis—that line the sandy beaches of this chic resort continue the late fashion designer's long-ago example.

Popular with celebrities, Cannes is at its most frenzied during the **International Film Festival** at the **Palais des Festivals** on the Promenade de la Croisette. Held in either April or May, it attracts not only film stars but those with similar aspirations. On the seafront boulevards flashbulbs pop as the starlets emerge—usually wearing what women will be wearing in 1990. International regattas, galas, *concours d'élégance,* even a Mimosa Festival in February—something is always happening at Cannes, except in November, which is traditionally a dead month.

Sixteen miles southwest of Nice, Cannes is sheltered by hills. For many it consists of only one street, the **Promenade de la Croisette,** curving along the coast and split by islands of palms and flowers. It is said that the Prince of Wales (before he became Edward VII) contributed to its original cost. But he was a Johnny-come-lately to Cannes. Setting out for Nice in 1834, Lord Brougham, a lord chancellor of England, was turned away because of an outbreak of cholera. He landed at Cannes and liked it so much he decided to build a villa there. Returning every winter until his death in 1868, he proselytized it in London, drawing a long line of British visitors. In the 1890s Cannes became popular with Russian grand dukes (it is said that more caviar was consumed there than in all of Moscow). One French writer claimed that when the Russians returned as refugees in the 1920s, they were given the garbage-collection franchise.

A port of call for cruise liners, the seafront of Cannes is lined with hotels, apartment houses, and chic boutiques. Many of the bigger hotels, some dating from the 19th century, claim part of the beaches for the private use of their guests. But there are public areas.

Above the harbor, the **old town** of Cannes sits on the hill of Suquet. There rises the high **Lords' Tower,** dating from the 12th century. Nearby is the **Musée de la Castre,** Château de la Castre, Le Suquet (tel. 93-68-91-82), housing a museum of fine arts, plus an ethnography section (Peruvian and Mayan pottery, objects of daily use from the Pacific islands, sculpture and ceramics from Southeast Asia), as well as a gallery of ancient civilizations of the Mediterranean, ranging from Roman to Egyptian to Greek to Etruscan to Cypriot artifacts. Charging 3F (41¢) for admission, the museum is open in July, August, and September from 10 a.m. to noon and 3 to 7 p.m., October to March to 5 p.m., and April to June to 6 p.m. On Sunday and Wednesday entrance is free. The museum is closed in November and on Tuesday.

ÎLES DE LÉRINS: Floodlit at night, the Lérins Islands stare across the bay at Cannes, forming the most interesting excursion from the port. From the harbor at Cannes a boat leaves frequently, taking 15 minutes to reach **Île Ste-Marguerite,** 30 minutes to **Île St-Honorat.** For information about departures, telephone 93-39-24-53. The trip to Île Ste-Marguerite costs 20F ($2.76); to St-Honorat, 25F ($2.07).

The first island is named after St. Honorat's sister, St. Marguerite, who once lived there with a group of nuns in the 5th century. Today the island is a youth center, whose members are dedicated to the restoration of the fort when they aren't practicing sailing and diving. From the dock where the boat lands, you can stroll along the island (signs point the way) to the **Fort de l'Île,** built by Spanish troops from 1635 to 1637 above a Roman town from the 1st century B.C., where *The Man in the Iron Mask* was held prisoner.

One of the perplexing mysteries of French history concerns the identity of the man who wore the *masque du fer.* A prisoner of Louis XIV, he arrived at Ste-Marguerite in 1698. Dumas fanned the legend that he was a brother of Louis XIV, and it has even been suggested that his son (by a mysterious woman) went to Corsica and "founded" the Bonaparte family. However, it is most often ventured that the prisoner was a manservant of the superintendent, Fouquet, named Eustache Dauger. At any rate, he died at the Bastille in Paris in 1703.

You can visit his cell at Ste-Marguerite, in which every visitor seemingly has written his or her name. As you stand listening to the sound of the sea, you realize what a forlorn outpost this was.

The **Musée de la Mer,** Fort Royal (tel. 93-39-98-98), traces the history of the island, displaying artifacts of Ligurian, Roman, and Arab civilizations, plus the remains discovered by excavations. These include paintings, mosaics, and ceramics. The museum is open June to September from 10 a.m. to noon and 2 to 6 p.m. (off-season, to 5 p.m.). It is closed in November and December, and charges an admission of 8F ($1.10).

Note: Hours can vary, depending on the arrival of the boats.

Île St-Honorat, only a mile long, is even lonelier. St. Honorat founded a monastery there in the 5th century. Since the 1860s the Cistercians have owned the ecclesiastical complex, consisting of both an old fortified monastery and a contemporary one. You can spend the entire day wandering through the pine forests on the west side of the island, the other part being reserved for prayers in silence.

HOTELS: Putting aside contemplation of such accommodations as prisons and monasteries, turn your thoughts to—

The Leading Deluxe Hotels

Carlton Hôtel, 58 Boulevard de la Croisette (tel. 93-68-91-68). Cynics say that one of the most amusing sights in Cannes is the view from under the vaguely art deco and very grand porte cochère of the Carlton. There you'll see vehicles of every description pulling up to deposit the huge amounts of baggage and the vast numbers of well-heeled guests who have made this one of the most colorful (but not always the most exclusive) hotels in Cannes. Anecdotes about the Carlton abound throughout France. There's the true story of the Saudi family who, in flowing robes and with an English nurse, unloaded their personal supply of watermelons from the top of their van in front of the horrified eyes of the still-not-jaded staff.

Then there's the value system within the French capital that holds a café chair on the Carlton's terrace as something worth almost as much as an invitation to the Élysée Palace. And finally, scattered throughout the western hemisphere is a gaggle of demi-mondaines who, one way or another, began their adulthood as breathless 20-year-olds near the elaborately detailed reception desk of the Carlton. The hotel has become such a part of the heartbeat of Cannes that to ignore it would be to miss the spirit of the resort. Both the format and the legend of the hotel are very, very grand. The twin gray domes at either end of the impressively sprawling façade are often the first to be recognized by the various kinds of starlets planning the nuances of their grand entrances, grand exits, and grand scenes within the hotel's public and private rooms.

Shortly after its construction in 1912 the Carlton attracted the most prominent names in the social registers of Europe, including members of royal families. These were followed decades later by the most important personalities of the cinematic era. Today the property accepts both industrial conventions and tour groups, and is counted as one of the properties of Intercontinental Hotels. Nonetheless, during high season, and especially during the film festival, the grandly ornate public rooms still appear filled with all the voyeuristic and exhibitionistic fervor that seems so much a part of the Riviera, even though it's probably a bit more concentrated at the Carlton. The decor of the two indoor bars and the two indoor restaurants is as glamorously gilded, frescoed, and upholstered as you'd expect. My favorite spot is the Restaurant Bar de la Plage, set right on the sands of the beach.

Prices vary according to the exposure of a bedroom, that is, the least expensive face an interior courtyard, while the costliest look out on the sea. Between the two extremes are many rooms on the sides of the hotel. In low season, singles range from 460F ($63.43) to 910F ($125.49), rising in high season to 850F ($117.22) to 1,460F ($201.33). Doubles in the off-season cost from 610F ($84.12) to 1,040F ($143.42), going upward to 1,075F ($148.24) to 1,670F ($230.29) in peak season.

Majestic, Boulevard de la Croisette (tel. 93-68-91-00), is getting livid looks from the traditional leader, the Carlton. Built many decades ago, the Majestic, in the eyes of the many, now reigns supreme, befitting its name. Constructed around an overscale front patio with a lush swimming pool, the hotel opens directly on the esplanade and the sea. Under tall palms and flowering orange and fig trees, it welcomes a cult of some of the chicest suntans in Europe. Inside, the setting is one of glistening marble, clusters of "dripping" crystal chandeliers, tapestries, seasoned antiques and reproductions, salons with Oriental carpets, Louis XV silk furniture, potted palms, a bar with an equestrian theme, and attentive service. Dining is special in the formal hall, with Louis XVI-style chairs spaciously placed around circular tables, against a backdrop of tall columns and draperies opening onto the courtyard greenery.

The bedrooms are all furnished with a blending of antiques and reproductions, offset by Oriental rugs, marble tables, high-fashion covers and bolsters to the beds, and (in many) a black-marble bath with gold fixtures. Renovated deluxe bedrooms for two persons peak at 1,700F ($234.43), facing the sea, with air conditioning. Singles go from 1,550F ($213.75). Underground parking is available. The director is to be congratulated for turning the Majestic into one of the showplaces of the Côte d'Azur. It is closed from late October to mid-December.

Upper-Bracket Living

Hotel Martinez-Concorde, 73 Boulevard de la Croisette (tel. 93-68-91-91). When this landmark art deco hotel was built in the 1930s, it rivaled anything else along the coast in sheer size. The years weren't kind to this elegant place, which closed and reopened more than once in its lifetime, eventually falling the victim of dust, neglect, and disrepair. In 1982, however, the Concorde chain (whose board of directors includes Jean Taittinger of champagne fame) elevated the 421 bedrooms, the soaring entrance hall, and the duet of restaurants to a formula as luxurious as when it first opened.

It occupies a prime position on the waterfront of Cannes, and has its own private beach with a water-skiing school and a cluster of cabañas. Guests can also enjoy a glistening octagonal swimming pool whose tile edges are ringed with beach paraphernalia. The air-conditioned bedrooms are decked out in bold colors and conservative modern furniture. Rooms cost from 750F ($103.43) in a single up to 2,100F ($289.59) for the most expensive double. The main restaurant, La Palme d'Or, the finest in Cannes, is reviewed separately. The poolside restaurant, l'Orangerie, serves fixed-price menus in an ambience of azure and white lattices. Emphasis is on light, low-calorie meals, costing from 210F ($28.96). The hotel is closed from mid-November to January 23.

Hôtel Gray-d'Albion, 38 rue des Serbes (tel. 93-68-54-54), is the smallest of the major palaces of Cannes. It contains 200 pastel-colored rooms, each outfitted with all the luxury that a modern hotel can offer. Some critics consider the Gray-d'Albion among the most luxurious hotels in France. It's between the Croisette and the popular shopping street, rue d'Antibes. Some of the in-house restaurants, as well as a disco, are described in the following sections. Each of the rooms is air-conditioned and well appointed, with handsome bathroom, color TV, video, phone, mini-bar, and private balcony. In high season, the rate in a single or double room ranges from 1,200F ($165.48) to 1,600F ($220.64). In low season, these same tariffs are from 600F ($82.74) to 980F ($135.14). Suites are the most expensive, of course. The hotel is open all year.

Hôtel Montfleury, 25 Avenue Beauséjour (tel. 93-68-91-50), seems far away from the crush in the center of Cannes, even though it's only a short, but winding, drive to get there. The modern palace is set amid a ten-acre park which it shares with an up-to-date sports complex. The magnificent curved swimming pool is covered with a sliding roof and surrounded by palms. Included in the facilities are tennis courts (many lit for nighttime playing), a wintertime ice-skating rink, and a volleyball court. There are also a sauna, massage facilities, and a gymnasium, plus two restaurants. The comfortable bedrooms are stylishly filled with all the modern conveniences. These include air conditioning, mini-bar, TV, radio, phone, and private terrace. In high season, the single rate ranges from 650F ($89.64) to 700F ($96.53), the double from 750F ($103.43) to 800F ($110.32). In low season, singles cost from 450F ($62.06) to 510F ($70.33), and doubles go for 510F ($70.33) to 590F ($81.36). Closed from late November until January 3.

Le Grand Hôtel, 45 Boulevard de la Croisette (tel. 93-38-15-45), has a garden with tall date palms and a lawn sweeping right down to the waterfront esplanade. A splendid structure of glass and marble, it is part of a complex of adjoining apartment-house wings and encircling boutiques. Eleven floors of bedrooms—each with wall-to-wall picture windows—open onto tile terraces, extending the living space. Vibrant colors are used throughout: sea-blue, olive, sunburst-red, and banana-gold. The baths are lined with colored checkerboard tiles, with matching towels and rows of decorative bottles. The hotel charges its highest tariffs from March 15 to October 15. A double with a sea view costs 1,500F ($206.85). Singles go for 710F ($97.91). The main lounge sets the style level, with "island" clusters of plastic chairs and tables, sofas, and armchairs against a backdrop of an antique Oriental folding paneled screen.

Sofitel Méditerranée, 2 Boulevard Jean-Hibert (tel. 93-99-22-75), is the prime favorite of the international yachting set. It stands directly on the harbor, with surrounding balconies and an open-air rooftop swimming pool. It's a remake of an older hotel, and much ingenuity went into bringing a sense of lightness and brightness to its interior. Against the muted tone inside, color was added to give warmth. From July 1 through August, a single room costs 820F ($113.08) to 980F ($135.14); doubles are 1,030F ($142.04) to 1,200F ($165.48) for a room with a continental breakfast and service included. The more expensive rooms contain balconies fronting the sea and yacht harbor. Good food is served in the dining room in a setting of wood paneling and frosted globe lamps. The hotel is closed from late November to just before Christmas.

The Middle Bracket

Hôtel Splendid, allée de la Liberté (4 and 6 rue Félix-Faure) (tel. 93-99-53-11), built in 1884, is one of the oldest hotels in Cannes. Its 64 rooms are concealed behind an ornate white façade with white-painted wrought-iron accents twisted into sinuous forms which look out onto the old port and the park that borders its edge. The interior design has been changed to eliminate all but a small reception area on the ground floor. Even so, this is a good, conservative hotel, a favorite of academicians, politicians, actors, and musicians. The comfortable bedrooms rent for 400F ($55.16) to 550F ($75.63) for a room with a *grand lit* (double bed) and 600F ($82.74) to 700F ($96.53) for a double room with two beds. Breakfast is included.

Hôtel le Fouquet's, 2 Rond-Point Duboys-d'Angers (tel. 93-38-75-81), is a modern and comfortable hotel set several blocks away from the beach. The establishment is built on a circular street surrounded by several other hotels. Each of the attractively airy units is decorated in shades of dusty rose, containing a mini-bar, a sun-drenched terrace, a private bath, a spacious dressing room, air conditioning, and color TV. In high season, singles range from 750F ($103.43), while doubles cost from 1,300F ($179.27).

Victoria, Rond-Point Duboys-d'Angers (tel. 93-99-36-36), is a stylish modern hotel built right in the heart of Cannes. Completely air-conditioned, it offers accommodations with bath and refrigerator. Nearly half its bedrooms have a balcony overlooking the small park and the hotel's swimming pool. Despite the name, the rooms are more French than English, with coordinated colors and a judicious use of period reproductions. Bedspreads of silk (most often pink) and padded headboards evoke a boudoir quality. The lodgings facing the park cost a little more and are well worth it. Singles peak at 400F ($55.16) and doubles at 620F ($85.50). The more expensive chambers have a terrace. After a day on the beach, guests congregate in the paneled bar, sinking comfortably into the leather couches and armchairs. From this vantage point it's easy to imagine you're back in Buckinghamshire, England. The hotel is closed from mid-November to mid-January.

Canberra, 120 rue d'Antibes (tel. 93-38-20-70), shares ownership with its sister, the Victoria, across the way. However, the atmosphere at the Canberra is mellower, as it's a remake of an older hotel. The overall effect is a mixture of modern and traditional. Limited parking is available in the hotel's small garden. All the air-conditioned rooms come equipped with bath or shower. Singles cost 300F ($41.37), and doubles rent for 510F ($70.33). Rates include service and taxes. You can enjoy a continental breakfast on a canopy-covered front veranda. There is a modest reception bar and lounge. The hotel is open all year.

The Budget Range

Le Saint-Yves, 49 Boulevard d'Alsace (tel. 93-38-65-29), is a genuine old villa classified as a historical monument, set back from the busy coastal boulevard by a front garden and a grove of palm trees. It's only a five-minute stroll from the seafront, although the garden of the villa is so enjoyable that many guests spend a good part of their day there. English-speaking Marylène Camplo owns the villa, part of which she has converted into private apartments that can be rented by the week or by the month. However, she has kept eight rooms, each with private bath or shower, to rent to transient guests. For two persons in a room with private bath she charges from 340F ($46.89) and 380F ($52.40), which includes breakfast (fresh croissants, country butter, and good jam). The bedrooms differ in size and are pleasantly furnished, mainly with odds and ends. Parking is free.

Wagram, 140 rue d'Antibes (tel. 93-94-55-53), is a friendly oasis. It's owned by Monsieur Biscarre, who is assisted by an English-speaking daughter, a brother, and a sister-in-law. Like a string quartet, they provide a harmonious setting for a successful stay at Cannes. The Wagram is on a busy coastal boulevard, about a five-minute walk from the seafront. Away from the traffic, breakfast in the rear garden is an ideal way to start your day. The interior is most comfortable although no style-setter, with lots of plastic-covered furniture. Open all year, the hotel requires that you take all your meals here in July and August, when two persons in a room with bath are charged 850F ($117.22) for full board. Off-season, half board costs 660F ($91.01) for two.

Athénée, 6 rue Lecerf (tel. 93-38-69-54), is a five-story hotel with 16 bedrooms, most with private bath. It's geared for travelers who seek comfortable, inexpensive bedrooms and don't require lounges (there's only a pocketwatch reception lobby). On a quiet business street about four short blocks from the seafront, it provides only breakfast. An American film distributor who stays there at least once a year writes of the courtesy and good treatment he's always received, maintaining that the Athénée gives what "some of its competitors only claim: very good breakfast and clean, comfortable rooms." For the most expensive double with twin beds, expect to pay 500F ($68.95). Singles begin at 275F ($37.92), and a continental breakfast is extra. The hotel closes from November to mid-January.

Mondial, 77 rue d'Antibes and 1 rue Teïsseire (tel. 93-39-28-70), is a moderately modern six-floor hotel on a business street, with stores on its lower floor. The hotel is about a three-minute walk from the beach, and three-quarters of its rooms have a view of the water, the others overlooking the mountains and an avenue. Its soft Devonshire-cream façade is studded with a few small balconies. The attractive bedrooms are the draw here, with matching fabric on the beds and at the windows, sliding mirror doors for wardrobes, direct-dial phones, and compact tile baths. The highest rates are charged in July and August, when the most expensive doubles, with breakfast, rent for 425F ($58.61). However, during the rest of the year two persons pay anywhere from 275F ($37.92) to 385F ($53.09), a good bargain for Cannes. It is closed in November.

De La Poste, 31 rue Bivouac-Napoléon (tel. 93-39-22-58), in the very heart of Cannes, is a modernized but modest little hotel opposite the post office. For its low rates, it offers many conveniences. There is no lobby, only a reception desk with an open staircase. The bedrooms are plain and uncluttered, often with colored candlewick bedspreads set against knotty-pine dado. Spidery shaped chairs and flowery cretonne draperies complete the decor. In high season, doubles with shower bath cost 280F ($38.61). Singles are rented at 175F ($24.13).

Hôtel de France, 85 rue d'Antibes (tel. 93-39-23-34), only two blocks from the sea, is right in the center of town. The rooms are large and clean, and although the furnishings generate little enthusiasm, the welcome is hearty. Doubles range from 280F ($38.61) to 375F ($51.71); singles 230F ($31.72) to 340F ($46.89). Units are equipped with bath or shower, as well as color TV, radio, direct-dial phone, and air conditioning. Tariffs include a continental breakfast, service, and taxes. Rates are reduced off-season. On top of the hotel is an open-air terrace for sunbathing.

Toboso, allée des Oliviers (tel. 93-38-20-05), is a little away from the center, but it's a nice, home-like residence offering tranquility. Formerly a private family villa, it has been slowly and carefully transformed into a small but comfortable hotel. The former family salon is now the main lounge. If you feel romantic, you can use the concert piano to play Chopin. Dancers at the neighboring Rosella Hightower School often frequent the establishment. The 14 rooms have a personal touch. No singles are available; however, doubles range from 275F ($37.92) to 450F ($62.06), the latter with private bath, toilet, and kitchen. Families will be interested to know that some units are large enough for six persons. Most of the rooms have windows facing the gardens, and some have a terrace on which you can sunbathe.

Hotel Roches Fleuries, 92 rue Georges-Clemenceau (tel. 93-39-28-78). Set high on a well-planted hillside above a busy intersection, this family-run hotel provides a pleasant oasis from the traffic below. You'll climb up a long flight of brick-lined steps, past a garden of cactus, palmettos, and flowering vines to reach the cream- and lime-colored façade. Designed as a private villa in the 1930s, the hotel contains 24 simple rooms, each of which is well maintained by Robert and Thérèse Lentz, both of whom speak English. There's an outdoor bar area just outside the front door, and café tables are scattered throughout the various levels of the garden. Bathless rooms, each appropriate for one to two persons, rent for 90F ($12.41) to 125F ($17.24), while units with full bath cost 200F ($27.58) to 220F ($30.34). Accommodations with shower and sink, but without a toilet, cost 190F ($26.20). Motorists will find parking at the rear of the hotel, which is closed from November 15 until right after Christmas.

RESTAURANTS: Cannes seems to have no end of excellent restaurants in all price ranges. First—

Upper-Bracket Dining

La Palme d'Or, Hotel Martinez, 73 Boulevard de la Croisette (tel. 93-84-10-24). When this hotel was renovated by members of the champagne-based Taittinger family, one of their primary concerns was to establish a restaurant rivaling anything else in Cannes. The result was an art deco marvel whose view overlooks both the swimming pool and the sandy expanse of La Croisette. In a room ringed with light-grained paneling and movie posters of the golden years of Hollywood, you can enjoy sublime specialties prepared by Alsatian-born chef Christian Willer.

His experience at some of the greatest temples of French gastronomy have helped him concoct such dishes as a warm foie gras with a fondue of rhubarb, a nage of sole with Bellet wine, a slightly warm salad of monkfish with a hint of pepper, and salmon served with a caviar cream sauce. Many diners find it hard to pass by a bouillon of lobster with basil and fresh vegetables or else a palate-cleansing sorbet flavored with white cheese. Service is close to impeccable. Fixed-priced menus costs 270F ($37.23) and 470F ($64.81), with à la carte meals averaging 500F ($68.95) to 650F ($89.64). The restaurant is open every day, and reservations are vital.

Royal Gray Restaurant, Hôtel Gray-d'Albion, 38 rue des Serbes (tel. 93-48-54-54). After only a few years on the job, chef Jacques Chibois has seen this elegant place firmly entrenched in a position at the top of haute cuisine in Cannes. The decor is suitable to such culinary excellence: it's furnished with all the belle époque detailings in a room where the colorist went wild with his imaginative uses of warmly tinted shades of peach, oxblood, maroon, and ochre. Mr. Chibois is a faithful follower of Michel Guérard, which a gourmet might recognize in such menu specialties as crayfish salad with orange-flavored vinaigrette, basil, and baby spinach; fricassée of lobster; pigeon cooked en papillote; suprême of chicken with crayfish; stuffed eggplant with morels; and supréme of daurade. Dessert is usually an award-winning concoction prepared by a specially recruited pastry chef, Marius Guénard.

Like the hotel that encases it, the restaurant was built in 1980, and has already been renovated and upgraded. No meals are served Sunday night in low season or on Monday throughout the year. The restaurant is also closed in February until the middle of March. Fixed-price menus are offered for 180F ($24.82) (at lunchtime only) and at 290F ($39.99). A menu dégustation, exhibiting many of the chef's culinary skills, is presented at 360F ($49.64). These prices do not include the 15% service charge.

Gaston-Gastounette, 7 Quai St-Pierre (tel. 93-39-47-92), is the best restaurant at the old port, offering vivid views of the marina from the sidewalk tables set on its front terrace. The terrace is separated from the sidewalk by a row of verdant shrubs that pleasantly accent the stucco façade with the wide oak moldings around the big windows. Inside, on tables covered with pink napery, you'll be served such specialties as bouillabaisse, breast of duckling in a garlic cream sauce, grilled sea bass with herbs, fish soup, stuffed mussels, flambéed veal kidneys, pistou soup with fresh basil, scallops provençal, and such fish platters as turbot, sole, and daurade. Sorbet, after all that savory Mediterranean food, is an appropriate dessert. Fixed-price menus are offered at 170F ($23.44), with à la carte meals costing from 240F ($33.10) to 280F ($38.61). The restaurant is closed for the first three weeks of January. It also shuts down one day a week from the first week of November to February.

Le Festival, 55 Boulevard de la Croisette (tel. 93-38-04-81). Against the South of Pago-Pago decor, many of the screen idols and sex kittens go here to drink and dine, the former taking place outside at the sidewalk tables, the latter inside. Whatever your sexual persuasion, you'll meet some interesting people and some characters you'd rather not ("I can't abide the idea of going to Switzerland, really"). Specialties include bouillabaisse with lobster, pepper steak, and loup (bass) au golfe flambé au fenouil (fennel). The traditional opener is soupe de poissons (fish) with rouille, and the smoothest finish is a peach Melba —invented by Escoffier. You can order a terrine of quail with a confit of onion and a mixed-fish grill. Set meals begin at 200F ($27.58). Most à la carte dinners cost from 250F ($34.48). The restaurant is closed from the end of November until the day after Christmas.

La Reine Pédauque, 6 rue du Maréchal-Joffre (tel. 93-39-40-91). Set back from the water on a somewhat commercial street, the restaurant becomes divorced from its surroundings once you step inside. Within is a rustic setting and a staff devoted to the preparation and serving of quality cuisine. Two set meals are offered, one at 160F ($22.06), another at 280F ($38.61), the latter containing many specialties. First, a selection of hot canapés is set before you. From the hors d'oeuvres cart you can have, among other tidbits, the Niçois version of caviar (black olives ground into an appetizer). On the à la carte menu, it is recommended that you try the light, delicate mousseline de bécasse (woodcock) Robert-Dorange, as well as le terrine et la galantine de canard (duck) en croûte. Try also the filet d'agneau (lamb) aux aromates de Provence. The cherries jubilee make for a spectacular finish. Expect to spend from 300F ($41.37) if you order à la carte. Set menus cost 160F ($22.06) and 280F ($38.61). The restaurant is closed on Monday and for the first three weeks in December.

La Voile au Vent, 17 Quai St-Pierre (tel. 93-39-27-84). Right on the port, this restaurant enjoys one of the most romantic situations in Cannes. Under the sharp eye and firm hand of Monsieur Ducrot, the chef specializes in a classic French cuisine, with an emphasis on seafood dishes. You can dine inside or outside at sidewalk tables. The classic fisherman's bouillabaisse is served, but there are many other specialties as well. Especially good main courses are carré d'agneau (lamb) à la moutarde for two, a seafood salad, filet of St-Pierre (a fish) on black noodles, and a suprême of sea bass in a cream sauce with sea urchins. Desserts include crêpes suzette. An average meal here will cost 180F ($24.82) to

260F ($35.85). The restaurant is closed from November 1 till Christmas, and on Thursday.

Blue Bar, Palais des Festivals, Boulevard de la Croisette (tel. 93-39-03-04). On any given night in season you're likely to spot at least four young women who look like BB in days of yore. Small and intimate, this restaurant attracts a chic crowd, mostly young people. While you can dine indoors, the sidewalk tables under umbrellas are infinitely preferred if the weather is right (which it is most of the time). The chef generally sticks to the classic French dishes, with Provençal overtones. Although the repertoire appears limited, it is exceedingly good. The fish soup is a favorite opener, but many Cannois diners begin their meal with a salade niçoise. The steak with freshly crushed peppercorns is a recommendable meat course, and the filets de sole bonne femme should please fish fanciers. To end your meal, try the rich but light chocolate mousse. Meals cost around 300F ($41.37). A service charge is added. Closed late in June to early in July.

La Mère Besson, 13 rue des Frères-Pradignac (tel. 93-39-59-24). Mère Besson is long gone from this favorite restaurant, but her culinary traditions are carried on by her family. At no place in Cannes can you get such a typical Provençal cuisine. All the recommendable specialties are prepared here with consummate skill. A different Provençal dish is featured every day of the week. On my most recent stopover, the delectable offering was estouffade provençale —beef braised with red wine and a rich country stock flavored with garlic, onions, herbs, and mushrooms. Specialties include soupe au pistou and soupe de poissons. Every Wednesday you can order Lou Piech. This is a Niçois name for a veal brisket that has been stuffed with white-stemmed vegetables, peas, ham, eggs, rice, grated cheese, and herbs. The meat is cooked in salted water with vinegar, carrots, and onions, like a stockpot, then served with a thick tomato sauce known as *coulis*. Your tab is likely to be about 200F ($27.58) to 240F ($33.10). The restaurant is closed for lunch and on Sunday.

The Medium-Priced Range

Romanens "La Grande aux Belles," 5 rue Notre-Dame (tel. 93-39-35-16). The atmosphere of this theatricalized restaurant threatens to overshadow the cuisine, but the chef manages to triumph. From hay (just plain hay) to cowbells to drippy candles to carved wooden animals to stirrups to red tablecloths, the cozy ambience goes crazy. A set dinner is offered for 85F ($11.72), another for 110F ($15.17), and a most elaborate one at 200F ($27.58). The most expensive fixed-price meal includes, for example, a médaillon de langouste thermidor, canard (duckling) with olives, pommes soufflées, followed by cheese and a parfait. Some of the cooking is over an open hearth. The restaurant is closed from mid-November to mid-December.

Budget Restaurants

Au Mal Assis, 15 Quai St-Pierre (tel. 93-39-13-38), is my unqualified economy dining choice at the port, enjoying the same vantage point as its more expensive rivals. It is especially recommendable for its 75F ($10.32) set dinner (offered weekdays), which includes some of the chef's specialties. For that price, you're likely to get moules (mussels) provençales, followed by a bouchée aux fruits de mer with freshly done french fries, and finally a selection of fruit or cheese. The chef's specialty is bourride provençale (a fish stew with slices of bread). A 15% service charge is added. Meals are served from noon to 1:45 p.m. and 7 to 9:30 p.m. If you go early, you can grab one of the sidewalk tables. It is closed from October 10 until just before Christmas.

Au Bec Fin, 12 rue du 24-Août (tel. 93-38-35-86), is a simple bistro-style restaurant offering especially good meals. On a street halfway between the railway station and the beach, it has little in the way of decor, relying on wainscoting and nautical wallpaper. Sometimes red carnations are brought in from the near-by fields to brighten your table. In the warmer months the place is kept humming with revolving fans overhead. Most popular is the 80F ($11.03) fixed-price luncheon or dinner, which gives you a wide selection. A first course might include salade niçoise, the house specialty; then caneton (duckling) with cèpes (flap mushrooms), plus a choice of vegetables and dessert. Another set meal begins at 100F ($13.79) and includes more elaborate selections. The restaurant is closed on Saturday night and Sunday.

La Coquille, 65 rue Félix-Faure (tel. 93-39-26-33), in the old town, set back from the port, is the best in a string of budget restaurants on this street. In fact it's among the best for the budget in Cannes, if you're seeking good seafood such as sea bream, red snapper, sole, turbot, or bouillabaisse. La Coquille also offers a fine choice of veal, beef, and lamb dishes. The restaurant has won acclaim for its 75F ($10.32) set menu, which might comprise soupe de poissons aux croûtons à rouille, followed by dorade (sea bream) du golfe grillée au fenouil (fennel), as well as spaghetti or a salad. Service is included, and your drink is extra, of course. The quality is always good, and the fish is always fresh. This meal is served only on weekends; on Sunday other tables d'hôte cost 95F ($13.10) and 135F ($18.62). The restaurant is closed from November 26 to mid-December.

Restaurant du Lyonnais Provençal, 8 bis rue des Frères-Pradignac (tel. 93-39-26-65), blends two cuisines, that of Lyon and that of Provence. Run by Monsieur Gobet, it's a country-style auberge with colored cloths and terrazzo floors, offering good-quality meals at low prices. A complete four-plate dinner is only 52F ($7.17); a more elaborate repast is 75F ($10.32). The cooking is very tasty. For the lower tab you're given a large selection, such as soupe au pistou (vegetable soup flavored with basil, a Côte d'Azur specialty), steak tartare, or Neopolitan spaghetti, plus cheese and dessert. This economy restaurant is only a short walk from the Promenade de la Croisette.

Le Monaco, 15 rue du 24-Août (tel. 93-38-37-76), is a working person's favorite, near the railway station. It is invariably crowded but always cheap. Food is prepared in a likable ambience and served on red and white bistro tablecloths. The kitchen offers generous portions of osso buco with sauerkraut, grilled sardines, spaghetti bolognese, trout with almonds, minestrone with basil, and many other treats, including paella and couscous, both of which are very popular. A four-course fixed-price menu is offered for 70F ($9.65), while a five-course table d'hôte is priced at 95F ($13.10). The establishment serves lunch and dinner every night except Sunday until 10. It is closed from the first of November to mid-December.

CANNES AFTER DARK: Le Casino (tel. 93-38-12-11) is on the Boulevard de la Croisette, next to the Festival and Conference Center. You can have lunch or dinner in the Bistingo, facing the sea, or dance in the Galaxy, the up-to-date nightclub overlooking the old harbor. If you wish to enter the gambling room, you must present your passport and pay 210F ($28.96) for admission, which is good for eight days. Le Casino is closed in summer.

In summer, from June 1 to October 31, when Le Casino closes, the **Palm Beach Casino** handles the heaviest gambling volume in France. Handsomely positioned at the Pointe de la Croisette (tel. 93-43-91-12), it is one of the leading French casinos and a powerful force in the Cannes summer scene. The Palm Beach is a glamorous nighttime rendezvous, charging a 55F ($7.56) admission to its air-conditioned salons, which open at 7 p.m. daily and include all French and American games. It is also a dining and entertainment complex, the major action centering around the **Terrasse du Masque de Fer** (Iron Mask Terrace). Here you'll pay 360F ($49.64) for dinner, plus the cost of drinks and service. Dinner is served in the open air. Two orchestras play for dancing. Toward the end of dinner, ballet and cabaret are featured. Every week, gala evenings take place, with special decorations, well-known show business personalities, and fireworks. (Actually, you can arrive at the Palm Beach beginning at 10 a.m.) You can also dance from 11 p.m. till dawn at **Jackpot,** a private, air-conditioned disco.

Whisky à Go-Go, 115 Avenue de Lérins (tel. 93-43-20-63), is the favored spot if you're young—or think you are. Facing the Palm Beach Casino, it seems more a nightclub than a disco. You sit in comfortable armchairs in this two-level establishment, watching the action. Seating 700, Whisky is the biggest such club on the French Riviera, and guests are treated to a light show with colored lasers, smoke, and fog. From her glassed-in cage, a disc jockey spins the latest. Changing color patterns are projected on the mirrored back wall. Waiters bring you your drink, at 85F ($11.72) and up.

Studio Circus, 48 Boulevard de la République (tel. 93-38-32-98), is all the rage. It opens at 11:30 p.m., charging from 85F ($11.72) for a drink. A spring and summer place, it is very trendy. Wear your chicest apparel. The place is liberated and very frenetic, catering to a varied group.

Jane's Piano Bar/Disco, Hôtel Gray-d'Albion, 38 rue des Serbes (tel. 93-68-54-54), offers a sophisticated ambience of colored lights, warm colors, and an occasional live singer. In the piano bar section, drinks cost 80F ($11.03) apiece. In the restaurant section, fixed-price menus, served from 8 p.m. to 2 a.m., go for 155F ($21.38). Disco action begins at 11 p.m.

Finally, **Club La Chunga,** 72 Boulevard de la Croisette (tel. 93-94-11-29), is a restaurant and international piano bar, with a typical South American trio. The panoramic terrace makes it especially appealing in summer as an elegant Côte d'Azur rendezvous for show business people. It offers meals beginning at 200F ($27.58). A scotch costs 65F ($8.97).

19. La Napoule-Plage

On the Golfe de la Napoule with its sandy beaches stands this secluded resort, once an obscure fishing village. In 1919 it was Shangri-la to an eccentric American sculptor, the son of a New York banker, and his architect wife. Fleeing from the "charlatans" of America, who he felt had profiteered in World War I, Henry Clews emphasized the fairytale existence of his new home—now the **Henry Clews Museum**—by inscribing over the entrance, "Once upon a time."

Taking over the ruins of a medieval château, the Clewses set about the mammoth task of rebuilding. The sculptor, who has been described as "the greatest America has ever produced," covered the capitals and lintels with the grotesque menagerie of his own private world, revealing a tortured (some have said perverse) mind. Scorpions, pelicans, gnomes, monkeys, lizards—no subject seemingly was taboo to him. Striking back at the critics who "didn't understand my work," he pictured them as blind. His women were often distorted and shrunken by age—his *Cat Woman* in particular, with drooping breasts revealing "feminine vice." This sculpture depicts a suffragette as he saw her marching on Fifth Avenue and expresses his view of feminism. The artist was preoccupied with old age in both men and women, and greatly admired chivalry and dignity in man as represented by Don Quixote—whom he likened to himself.

Clews died in Switzerland in 1937, and his body was returned to La Napoule-Plage for burial. Before her death in 1959, Mrs. Clews opened their château to the public ("Castle of weird images opens!" hailed the press). The castle (tel. 93-49-95-05) is open daily except Tuesday from 3 to 5 p.m. It is also closed for about 21 days in December. Admission is 12F ($1.66).

WHERE TO STAY: **Loews La Napoule Hôtel** (tel. 93-49-90-00) stands impressively at the inner curve of a stone-rimmed spit of land near a man-made harbor. As you approach it from Cannes, it rises starkly visible from about five miles away across the flat expanse of beachfront. This establishment offers about as strong a flavor of Las Vegas as you'll find in France outside of Monaco. It was the first hotel in France to build an in-house casino, and the last establishment (just after the building codes changed) to be allowed to set a casino directly on the beach. This, coupled with one of the most recently constructed hotel formats on the Côte d'Azur (they opened in 1983), makes it a major contender in the competitive world of Riviera palace hotels.

The physical plant is dramatically contemporary, filled with plush touches, warm shades of tangerine and brass, and lots of marble. The directors have imported the kind of entertainment that mingles nudity with music, feathers, glitter, plumes, and a Nevada-style choreography, making for a glamorous extravaganza. There's a full range of sports as well, including a large heated freshwater swimming pool and a 27-hole golf course. Tennis courts are on the premises as well. Although the hotel has been well received by everyone who has stayed in it, it's too young to have gathered a guest list of publicly recognized names. However, that is rapidly changing since the 1985 visit of the King of Qatar who, with his retinue, occupied a floor of the hotel for several months, paying eventually a bill of more than a million dollars.

Most of the attractively modern bedrooms are angled toward a view of the sea and are outfitted with 24-hour room service, modern baths, air conditioning, hair dryers, phones, and recently released in-house movies. Singles or doubles range in high season from 1,300F ($179.27) to 1,800F ($248.22), with sharp off-season reductions. Half board in La Brasserie is another 300F ($41.37) per person. VAT is extra, but service is included. The more formal of the hotel's restaurants, Chez Loulou, offers carefully prepared cuisine which competes with the best restaurants of La Napoule and nearby Cannes. A la carte meals cost around 480F ($66.19) and are served by a charmingly professional staff. Diners have an air-conditioned view of the illuminated swimming pool.

Ermitage du Riou (tel. 93-49-95-56) is housed in a building that looks like a South American hacienda. Built in 1952, it angles around a central rounded tower, all of it encased in peach-colored stucco with maroon shutters. There's a small egg-shaped pool in the semitropical garden, and the entire premises is surrounded by a wall. Some of the rooms have views over the golf course and the river. Double occupancy rates with half board included range from 1,050F ($144.80) to 1,400F ($193.06) for two persons. All accommodations have private bath, refrigerator, and self-dial phone. The more expensive units contain a balcony or terrace, air conditioning, a safe, and color TV. The hotel is closed from November 4 until right before Christmas.

La Calanque (tel. 93-49-95-11). The foundations of this charming hotel date from the Roman Empire, when an aristocrat built his villa here. Today the far more recent hotel (circa 1942) is owned by extended members of the Rolland family. A major feature is a garden-style indoor and outdoor restaurant. The hotel looks a lot like a hacienda, with pink stucco walls, brown shutters, and a big illuminated terrace filled with summertime diners. To register here, you'll have to pass through the dining room to the bar area in the rear, near the fireplace. There, you'll be quoted full-board rates of 220F ($30.34) to 275F ($37.92) per person, based on double occupancy. Double rooms without meals cost 230F ($31.72) per room, depending on the plumbing. Although the leafy plane trees in front cut out much of the noise from the street, you'll still find the quietest units in the rear. The hotel's restaurant and 18 rooms are closed from mid-October to mid-March.

WHERE TO DINE: L'Oasis, rue Honoré-Carle (tel. 93-49-95-52), is the domain of the Outhier family, who have turned it into one of the greatest restaurants along the Riviera. It is a true oasis of gourmet food, attracting many visitors from Cannes (reservations are imperative). Set back from the waterfront, it is not easy to find but worth the search, even if you have to drive all the way over from Nice. Louis Outhier, a well-established chef, makes ordering easy. He lists set meals, each containing specialties. À la carte specialties include loup en croûte (bass in a pastry shell) for a minimum of three diners, and turbot braisé au champagne, requiring a minimum of two. Another excellent dish is foie de canard (duck liver). Everything is backed up by an excellent wine list. Expect to pay 550F ($75.63) to 650F ($89.64) if you order à la carte. However, set menus are offered at 375F ($51.71) and 400F ($55.16). The restaurant is housed in a small villa with a palm garden. It's closed from the first of November until mid-December, and on Monday night and Tuesday.

20. St-Tropez

Lasciviousness is rampant in this carnival town, but a true Tropezian resents the fact that the port has such a bad reputation. "We can be classy too," insisted one native. Creative people in the lively arts along with ordinary folk create a volatile mixture. One observer said that St-Tropez "has replaced Naples for those who accept the principle of dying after seeing it. It is a unique fate for a place to have made its reputation on the certainty of happiness."

St-Tropez was greatly popularized by Bardot in *And God Created Woman,* but it's been known for a long time. Colette lived here for many years. Even the late diarist Anaïs Nin, confidante of Henry Miller, posed for a little cheesecake on the beach here in 1939 in a Dorothy Lamour bathing suit. Composer Ned Rorem bought a canary-yellow shirt at Vachon, to go, as related in his famous diary, with "my golden legs in khaki shorts, my tan sandals, and my orange hair." Earlier, St-Tropez was known to Guy de Maupassant, Signac, Matisse, and Bonnard.

Artists, composers, novelists, and the film colony are attracted to St-Tropez in summer. Trailing them is a line of humanity unmatched anywhere else on the Riviera for sheer flamboyance. Some of the most fashionable yachts bringing the chicest people anchor here in summer, disappearing long before the dreaded mistral of winter.

Near the harbor is the **Musée de l'Annonciade,** at the Place Georges-Grammont (tel. 94-97-04-01), installed in the former chapel of the Annonciade. It is open daily except Tuesday, from 10 a.m. to noon and 3 to 7 p.m. (the afternoon hours are 2 to 6 p.m. in winter), charging an admission of 9.30F ($1.28). As a legacy from the artists who loved St-Tropez, the museum shelters one of the finest modern-art collections on the Riviera. Many of the artists, including Paul Signac, depicted the port of St-Tropez. Opened in 1955, the collection includes such works as Kees Van Dongen's yellow-faced *Woman of the Balustrade,* and paintings and sculpture by Bonnard, Matisse, Rouault, Braque, Vuillard, Dufy, Utrillo, Seurat, Dunoyer de Segonzac, Vlaminck, Derain, Despiau, and Maillol. It is closed in November.

On the outskirts of St-Tropez, at a distance of two miles, **Port Grimaud** makes for an interesting outing. If you approach the village at dusk when it is softly bathed in Riviera pastels (much like Portofino, Italy), it will look like some old hamlet, perhaps from the 16th century. But this is a mirage. Port Grimaud is the dream-fulfillment of its promoter, François Spoerry, who carved it out of marshland and dug canals. Flanking these canals, fingers of land extend from the main square to the sea. The homes are Provençal style, many with Italianate window arches. The owners of boats can anchor right at their doorsteps. One newspaper called the port "the most magnificent fake since Disneyland." One of its promoters has described it as "a village as it would have been if architects did not exist."

HOTELS: For such a famous resort, St-Tropez has a shocking lack of hotel rooms. If you're arriving in July and August without a reservation, you'd better not entertain hopes of spending the night—unless, of course, you're good at meeting "countesses."

Deluxe Living and Dining

Byblos, Avenue Paul-Signac (tel. 94-97-00-04). Its builder spent $3 million to create what he told the press was "an antihotel, a place like home." In that he succeeded—providing "home" has salons removed intact from Beirut palaces and 3000 B.C. Phoenician gold statues valued at that time at $50,000. Set apart from the other hotels, up on a hill from the harbor, this deluxe establishment resembles a village complex from a bird's-eye view—complete with intimate patios and courtyards, plus a "high-fashion" swimming pool. Inside, the hotel's decorator created a seductive retreat, filling salon after salon with antiques and rare decorative objects, many brought from Lebanon, including polychrome carved woodwork on the walls, marquetry floors, a Persian-rug ceiling, and nooks for objects of art.

Every bedroom maintains a unique character. In one, for example, there is a fireplace with a raised hearth, paneled blue-and-gold doors, rustic beams, and a bed recess on a dais. There is a total of 110 rooms and apartments, including Le Hameau which is composed of ten individual duplex apartments built around a small courtyard with an outdoor spa. Prices vary according to the season. From mid-May until around the end of September, a single rents for 1,500F ($206.85), a double going for 1,600F ($220.64) to 2,000F ($275.80), with apartments and suites costing more, of course. In off-season, a single goes for 850F ($117.22), a double for 1,050F ($144.80) to 1,400F ($193.06). Every room has a fashionably styled private bath. Your bedroom window may have a balcony overlooking the inner courtyard or else open onto a stepped-down terrace of flowers. Four bars provide varied and dramatic settings for drinks; and dining is still another treat. The grill room, La Braiserie, is complemented by an independent gastronomic restaurant, Le Chabichou. Later in the evening you can dance on a circular floor surrounded by bas-relief columns in the hotel's nightclub. The hotel is closed from November 1 to April 12.

Résidence de la Pinède, Plage de la Bouillabaisse (tel. 94-97-04-24), rises within a forest of pines between the Gulf of St. Tropez and the busy (but unheard) traffic of one of the village's crowded access roads. From some angles, the hotel appears like a repetitive series of stucco-covered towers linked with terracotta balconies. Inside, a spacious kind of airiness permeates the beamed dining room and the pseudo–Louis XVI, very comfortable bedrooms. Most of the guests spend their time on the terrace, ringing the curved swimming pool, on the adjacent beach, or in one of the hotel's two indoor/outdoor restaurants.

The establishment was founded in 1952, designed around an existing tower once used to store olives. Audrey Hepburn, Raquel Welch, and Pierre Salinger have all stayed here. Today, Nicole and Jean-Claude Delion offer 40 bedrooms, each with radio, TV, air conditioning, and private bath. They open onto views of the sea or of a semitropical garden. Open between March and October, the establishment charges 1,600F ($220.64) to 2,400F ($330.96) for two persons, double occupancy, with half board included, depending on the season.

The Upper Bracket

Le Yaca, Boulevard d'Aumale (tel. 94-97-11-79), was built in 1722 as the first hotel in St-Tropez. In 1927 Colette lived here, and before that a collection of pre-impressionist painters, the most prominent of whom was Paul Signac. From the unpretentious façade off a narrow street in the old part of town, the hotel opens into a high-ceilinged reception area looking onto an inner courtyard filled with flowers and a flagstone-covered swimming pool. Many of the simple rooms look out over the quiet interior of the hotel. My favorite units are on the upper floor, with handmade terracotta floor tiles and massive ceiling timbers. Open from mid-April to mid-October, the hotel charges from 650F ($89.64) to 1,050F ($144.80) in a double room in high season. An additional person is lodged in the same room for 240F ($33.10).

Mas de Chastelas (tel. 94-56-09-11) is one of the most charming addresses in the environs, lying some 2 miles from the center of St-Tropez (arm yourself with a map). Open from April until the end of September, it is an old Provençal pink stucco house with white shutters and an outdoor plant-ringed pool. It has become a celebrity favorite, attracting leaders from the fashion and show-business worlds of Paris. Run by Gérard Racine, it was once a silkworm-raising house. Today, converted into a hotel, it stands in a park-like setting about six minutes from the harbor. Lunch is only for residents, but if you call for a reservation you can enjoy dinner here for 260F ($35.85). Jean-Louis Vosgien is the chef, turning out such specialties as red mullet in red wine sauce, and ravioli stuffed with fish and served with a saffron and sea urchin cream sauce. The desserts are richly tempting. The hotel rents out 21 rooms, ranging in price from 520F ($71.71) in a single and 900F ($124.11) in a double, plus ten apartments more expensively priced.

Hôtel La Maison Blanc, Place des Lices (tel. 94-97-52-66). This 19th-century villa whose walls, as its name would imply, are white, stood empty for ten years before Jean-Claude Rieu and Jacques Chiron (a decorator and an architect) renovated it into the most carefully planned interior in St-Tropez. It's furnished with art deco chairs, Oriental rugs, tastefully rich colors (including peach, salmon, soft grays, and white), and the kind of knickknacks usually found only in private homes. A wrought-iron and wooden staircase curves gracefully up to the intensely individualized bedrooms, each of which has marble accents in its super-modern bath, and the kind of slickly professional mixture of antique with modern. Each of the accommodations is air-conditioned, and one on the top floor is a rustically timbered duplex. A waiter will bring you drinks in the bar, in your room, or in the garden, which is separated from the square by a wall, and which many consider more authentically Provençal than any other in St-Tropez. Prices for the eight rooms vary with the accommodation, ranging from 780F ($107.56) to 1,150F ($158.59) for two persons, service not included. Open all year.

The Middle Bracket

La Ponche, Place du Rèvelin (tel. 94-97-02-53), is a cluster of remodeled fishermen's houses, opening on one side onto a little plaza fronting a tiny sandy beach where a club atmosphere prevails. In a secluded and relatively unknown but central part of St-Tropez, it attracts many interesting clients.

Most of the accommodations are small but charmingly furnished. Doubles overlooking the sea cost 360F ($49.64) to 410F ($56.54); doubles with terrace go for as much as 500F ($68.95) to 640F ($88.26). Across the little plaza (which in the evening becomes a social center) are a few highly individualized apartments fronting the little beach. A central glassed-in lounge in the main building is furnished with antiques and original paintings. Two dining rooms have been decorated with 18th-century antiques and original paintings. The food is rather "new cuisine," although grilled fish from the Mediterranean has always been featured. Specialties are stuffed fish and savory bouillabaisse. The hotel is open from April 1 to October 1.

Hôtel La Tartane, Route des Salins (tel. 94-97-21-23), is set on its own grounds about midway between the center of St-Tropez and the Plage des Salins, about a four-minute drive from each if there's no traffic. There's a stone-rimmed pool set into the garden, an attractively furnished series of public rooms with heavily timbered ceilings and often with terracotta floor tiles, and 12 well-furnished bungalows centered around the pool. Facilities include a Jacuzzi. Accommodations cost 550F ($75.63) for two persons. Breakfasts are elaborate and attractive, and lunch is offered between 1 and 3 p.m. (no dinner). The hotel is open from mid-March to early November.

Sube, 15 Quai Suffren (tel. 94-97-30-04), could be your first choice if you want to be dead center, right on the port. Directly over a popular coffeehouse, it is entered through an arcade of shops. There's a two-story-high beamed lounge with an all-glass front, letting you enjoy your morning coffee while watching the harbor activity. A ten-foot-high fireplace, a wall torchère, and provincial chairs drawn together provide the decorations. The bedrooms are overly small and decorated in a provincial style (the skill of navigating in the closed quarters of a yacht will be invaluable here). The beds are soft, and the maids keep everything neat and tidy. Two persons in a room with a patio pay 500F ($68.95). Simple singles begin at 150F ($20.69). These tariffs include a continental breakfast, service, and taxes. The hotel is open from March 1 to November.

Hôtel Ermitage, Avenue Paul-Signac (tel. 94-97-52-33), is an elongated white-walled three-story hotel with green shutters, a red tile roof, an elegantly appointed interior, and a sun terrace. The 30 rooms rent for 275F ($37.92) in a single and 380F ($52.40) in a double. Only breakfast is served. It's closed from early November to early December.

The Budget Range

Coste, Port du Pilon (tel. 94-97-00-64), is on the outskirts of St-Tropez across the coastal road from the sea. Ignore the severe motel-like façade. Behind it is a large courtyard with an old garden of orange trees, palms laden with ivy, flowering oleander, terracotta pots of cacti and geraniums, and of course, olive trees. Garden furniture is scattered informally, and guests can relax with a view of the sea. At the front, two tiers of bedrooms with iron-railing balconies—almost New Orleans style—are balanced on strong, square pilings. The older building (circa 1950) at the rear was once the private villa of the owner, Monsieur Coste. Between June 15 and September 15 he rents double rooms with bath for 250F ($34.48), charging only 180F ($24.82) for bathless doubles in the older villa. Served in the garden, breakfast is extra. It is open from March 15 to November 1.

Lou Cagnard, Avenue Paul-Roussel, Route de Ramatuelle (tel. 94-97-04-24), is a pleasant place at which to stay, tranquil enough if you get a rear room overlooking the garden. A remake of an old house on a village road, it's somewhat like a roadside inn, with a tile roof and green shutters. Madame Rul doesn't speak a word of English, but somehow she manages to cope with her North American guests. The tariffs include taxes and service, but a continental breakfast is extra. A double-bedded room without bath goes for 150F ($20.69), the tariff increasing to 280F ($38.61) in a double with complete bath. The hotel is closed from November 15 till right before Christmas.

Hôtel les Capucines, Le Treizain (tel. 94-56-05-46), is a complex of three stucco buildings with red tile roofs and lots of Mediterranean flavor. They're grouped around a swimming pool with a Jacuzzi in a sunny area surrounded by pine trees about a mile away from the center of St-Tropez. The main salon has a dramatically high beamed ceiling and a large brick fireplace, while the simple bedrooms sometimes look out large French doors into the garden. Each of them contains a private bath, phone, air conditioning, private terrace, and a country theme of heavy furniture and exposed wood accented with stucco. Doubles range from 340F ($46.89) to 600F ($82.74), depending on the plumbing and the season. Views from parts of the premises encompass parts of the Bay of St-Tropez.

RESTAURANTS: The range is from *très chic* to affordable.

Upper-Bracket Dining

Chabichou, Avenue Foch (tel. 94-54-80-00), is clearly the best dining choice at the resort. It's beneath the Byblos Hotel but has a separate entrance on the Avenue Foch. It's a spacious format of Hellenistic frescoes, mosaics, and shades of blue and white which play down the massive structural columns supporting the building upstairs. A bubbling aquarium separates the activity in the kitchens from the dining room which, in summer, is extended with a popular terrace stretching onto the sidewalk toward the busy traffic.

The owner and chef, Michel Rochedy, was known as the best chef at a cluster of French ski resorts, notably Courchevel, before deserting the Alps for the sun of Provence. His well-researched specialties include a combination of fresh morels and asparagus meunière, a salad of crayfish marinara, grilled turbot with eggplant, and roast hare with aged vinegar and honey, along with a suprême of grilled pigeon. Most reasonable are the fixed-price menus at 220F ($30.34) and 320F ($44.13). À la carte repasts average 550F ($75.63). The restaurant is open daily between mid-May and early October.

Leï Mouscardins, sur le Port (tel. 94-97-01-53), has been loaded with culinary honors. At the extreme end of the port, it is an upstairs restaurant with picture windows allowing for harbor views. Inside, there's a formal Provençal atmosphere. A sun room under a canopy adjoins the restaurant. You make your dining selections—a Mediterranean classic repertoire—from the à la carte menu. If you're willing to pay for it, you can enjoy really superb viands. An excellent dish—just to get you started—is the moules (mussels) marinières. The two celebrated fish stews of the Côte d'Azur are offered here: a bourride provençale and a bouillabaisse. The fish dishes are especially good, particularly the loup (sea bass). If you're not in a fishy mood, try the grilled, tender entrecôte. The chef prepares two dessert specialties, a soufflé au Grand Marnier or with Cointreau. An average meal will range from 230F ($31.72) to 300F ($41.37). The restaurant is open from February to the first of November.

L'Auberge des Maures (The Inn of the Moors), 4 rue du Dr-Boutin (tel. 94-97-01-50), is an offbeat choice. You walk up a small street, really an alleyway, lying just off the rue des Allards. A short walk from the port, it is entered through gypsy-like curtains. You can have your meal either inside or al fresco under a flowering arbor. On any given night you're likely to run into a table of rock singers with their groupies, a filmmaker with his starlet of the moment, a conservatively dressed judge from the U.S. midlands, or a honeymooning couple from Paris. The menu is gilt-edged, and so are the tabs—but the cuisine is really good. The fish soup is made with rouille, a "combustible" sauce of garlic and red peppers. Other specialties are mullet cooked with fennel hearts and lobster with port. The dessert specialty is sabayon. Service is an extra 15%. Savory fish specialties will mean a bill in the 325F ($44.82) range. The restaurant serves dinner nightly from Easter to October 1.

Le Bistrot des Lices, 3 Place des Lices (tel. 94-97-29-00). On one of my favorite squares in St-Tropez, this informal bistro is filling a need in town for a reasonably priced yet glamorous dining room. The staff is dressed in shades of red and white, maintaining a casual chic. The suavely hyper-trendy clientele seems to enjoy the ambience and has made this place a popular favorite. The decor is pleasant, especially on a sunny day when the sunlight is filtered through the gauzy lace curtains that ring the innermost dining room. If you don't feel like eating, you'll have your choice of several "hangout" areas within the place. There's an outdoor café protected from the Mediterranean winds by a well-designed windbreak, and a piano bar and café in the outermost room which you'll pass through to reach the peach-colored interior. In summer, management sets up tables in the rear garden.

You may enjoy such dishes as chicken fricassée flavored with raspberry vinegar, stuffed artichokes, terrine of fish, filet of John Dory, sauté of rabbit with mustard sauce, and côte de boeuf for two persons, along with rich, creamy pastries made fresh daily. Music in summer begins at 7:30 p.m., and à la carte meals cost about 300F ($41.37) apiece. Set menus cost from 170F ($23.44) to 230F ($31.72). It's open daily all year.

The Medium-Priced Range

L'Escale (Port of Call), Quai Jean-Jaurès (tel. 94-97-00-63). One of the most compelling reasons for dining here—other than the good cuisine—is to be seen. The setting is hard not to like: outside tables under a canopy, with portside views. On the à la carte menu, specialties include sea bass (loup), a bourride provençale (a savory fish stew), and escalope à la crème, which is veal with fresh cream. There is also a piano bar. Expect to spend around 200F ($27.58) for a complete meal. The restaurant is open from March 1 to October 1.

Le Girelier, Quai Jean-Jaurès (tel. 94-97-03-87), is right in the mainstream of social activity. The food is excellent, and there are two price levels for dinners. Pierre Rouet, the patron and chef de cuisine, charges 95F ($13.10) for a meal, which might include soupe de poissons (fish soup), moules marinières (mussels), or gambas mayonnaise (big shrimp), followed by pipérade (omelet with pimiento, garlic, and tomatoes), croustade de fruits de mer, vol-au-vent of mussels, shrimp, and mushrooms, octopus américaine, or escalope pannée with rice or fried potatoes or a salad, plus a choice of cheese or dessert. The restaurant is closed from mid-November to mid-January.

ST-TROPEZ AFTER DARK: Café Sénéquier, sur le Port (tel. 94-97-00-90). Leslie Maitland once described the kind of clientele attracted to Sénéquier at cocktail hour. The reporter asked, "What else can one do but gawk at a tall, well-dressed young woman who appears *comme il faut* at Sénéquier's with a large white rat perched upon her shoulder, with which she occasionally exchanges little kisses, while casually chatting with her friends?" This and many other oddities have happened here, and if you want to meet someone in a relatively anything-goes kind of place, the café is for you. There are masses of red tables, red chairs, and red stools, all under a canopy facing the yachts moored in port. On the most crowded days of summer, yacht-watching is the favorite pastime. Whisky costs from 45F ($6.21); coffee, 15F ($2.07). The café is open all day and most of the night as well.

Café de Paris, sur le Port (tel. 94-97-00-56), under the Hôtel Sube, is one of the most consistently popular hangouts in town. An attempt has been made to glorify a fairly utilitarian room with turn-of-the-century globe lights and an occasional 19th-century bronze and masses of artificial flowers, but no one goes here for decor. They are attracted to the permissive ambience and the crowd, which is irreverent and animated, even in winter when the yachting crowd departs. The most consistently colorful personalities wind their way to the long zinc bar, where a café crème costs 15F ($2.07), a whisky going for 45F ($6.21).

Café des Arts, Place des Lices (tel. 94-97-02-25), might be the last establishment on the Place des Lices to avoid the interior changes that local restaurant managers usually feel their clients want. This is a local hangout, a stronghold of Provençal blue-collar sentiment and an occasionally rowdy nighttime carnival. Many of the local residents interrupt a game of *boules* on the square outside to come in for a glass or two of wine. The low-ceilinged room can cram in lots of locals mixing happily with tourists between its stone columns. Alcoholic drinks cost from 45F ($6.21).

Les Caves du Roy, Hôtel Byblos, Avenue Paul-Signac (tel. 94-97-00-04), is considered the chicest disco along the French Riviera. It certainly provides the most romantic background for dancing in the area. It also features the best live entertainment in St-Tropez (but don't count on this every night). The music is the latest in what's trendy. On the lower level of this unusual hotel, the disco combines Lebanese decorative features with those of Provence. This *caveau* attracts a very chicly dressed crowd (most within the post-25 set). Dress in your most casually elegant attire or else you won't get in. A circular dance floor is surrounded by decorative bas-relief columns. Drinks begin at 120F ($16.55).

Chapter XXIV

CORSICA

1. Bastia
2. L'Île-Rousse
3. Calvi
4. Porto
5. Corte
6. Ajaccio
7. Porticcio
8. Propriano
9. Sartène
10. Porto-Vecchio
11. Bonifacio

THE THIRD-LARGEST ISLAND in the Mediterranean, Corsica (*Corse* in French) is a rugged, mountainous land that seems more Italian than French. It has been fought over for centuries by rival seapowers, and has done plenty of internal fighting itself (the word "vendetta" comes from Corsica).

In spite of its size, it is one of the most thinly populated of Mediterranean islands, containing some 220,000 hearty souls. It measures about 115 miles from north to south, and at its widest point it is a distance of some 52 miles from east to west. Corsica is much closer to the Italian mainland, only 50 miles away, than it is to mother France, some 100 miles from the Côte d'Azur. However, at one point Corsica comes only 7 miles from the Italian island of Sardinia, to which it bears a certain similarity.

Most of the denizens of Corsica live either in Bastia in the northeast or around the capital of Ajaccio, to the south on the western coastline. There are vast stretches of uninhabited land, not only along the coastline (how unlike the Riviera), but mainly in the interior.

A large part of that interior is covered with a dense undergrowth called *maquis,* the hiding place for the legendary Corsican bandit of yesteryear. The maquis is thick with heather and other sweet-smelling shrubs. In fact it has so much vegetation that the English invaders nicknamed it "Scented Isle." Guy de Maupassant wrote of its "holm-oak, juniper, arbutus, lentisk, buckthorn, heath bay, myrtle, and box." But it was a Corsican himself in fact, the most famous of Corsicans, who issued the most famous statement about Corsica. Napoléon Bonaparte proclaimed, with a great degree of accuracy, that he could "recognize Corsica blindfolded." So strong is the sweet smell that many present-day Corsicans could probably make the same boast.

Of course Corsica is not all Mother Nature running wild. The strong-willed Corsicans who have chosen to take their stand there and struggle to make a living (many have emigrated to the mainland) have studded the island with olive groves, orchards, vineyards, and terraced gardens. It is amazing how far up certain hill sites cultivation has been extended. Corsica is a mountainous land, its highest point being Monte Cinto at 9,020 feet. It is also cut by deep valleys.

Its coastline stretches for some 600 miles. Ideally, many visitors who want to see most of the island take a motor route along the entire circuit, venturing inland for certain attractions such as the town of Corte. However, it should be pointed out that if you want to follow in that daring example you must literally take your life in your hands along certain rugged stretches. Roads are narrow and filled with hairpin curves.

On my most recent visit I tried blowing my horn constantly as I turned a curve. That certainly signaled an oncoming motorist that I was coming. For reasons known only to them, most Corsican motorists did not return my honk. Because of that, I faced a head-on collision several times, and did in fact see three accidents as I made my way along the coast from Calvi to Porto, which I found the most treacherous route. The scenery is spectacular along this run, but can you really enjoy it when you must face such terrible road conditions? If you want to play it much safer, you can skip the northwest corner altogether, heading from Bastia to Corte and from Corte taking a much better inland route via Vizzavona to the port of Ajaccio.

Corsica has a mild climate. If you are seeking beach action along the coasts in July and August, expect an average temperature of 73° Fahrenheit. The weather will be hot and dry. September and October are often ideal months to visit, experiencing temperatures of 68° and 61° Fahrenheit respectively. It's possible to enjoy sea bathing from early May to November, the longest beach season in France (if you exclude the départements of Guadeloupe and Martinique in the West Indies, of course).

Even winter can be comfortable if the wind doesn't blow too fiercely. The average temperature in December is 54°F. Many French people from the mainland—which Corsicans often contemptuously call *les continentaux*—visit Corsica to enjoy the "white spring," lasting from mid-April to mid-June when the white heather of the maquis bursts into full bloom.

THE QUESTION OF SAFETY: Some of those French visitors are not well received, especially those who'd like to have a "second home" in Corsica. During one of my visits, 26 bombs exploded on my first night on the island. The targets were not tourists staying in local hotels, certainly not North American visitors. The bombs were aimed at the banks and homes of mainland French people, who are bitterly resented on the island. The outlawed Corsican National Liberation Front (the FLNC) seeks Corsican independence from mainland France, from which it has long felt it's gotten a bum deal. Parisians are especially singled out for attack.

It should be noted that many Corsicans bitterly object to this separatist talk. One "far-right" politician told the press rather candidly that an independent Corsica was "doomed to becoming a Soviet air base or an Arab colony."

Oldtime travel writers spoke of the "tourist dawn" that has come to Corsica. I'm not so sure that the sun has come up yet. Corsica is only beginning to awaken to tourism, and many of its facilities remain underdeveloped. It certainly is not prepared for the mass kind of tourism that afflicts the Riviera. Sometimes it's the small things that can be frustrating, like getting a travelers check cashed on a Sunday. Or getting your gas tank filled. Also, don't count on finding many people who speak English, except in the most important hotels. Italian is widely understood, but French is, of course, the official language.

Since the hotels are likely to be fully booked in summer, you have an added inconvenience if you arrive in July and August without an ironclad reservation. Prices, for the most part, are much better on your wallet than they are in Provence.

CORSICA

N

LIGURIAN SEA

MEDITERRANEAN
SEA

80

Saint-Florent

Bastia

L'Île-Rousse

81

Calvi

197

Vescovato

Golo R.

Gorges de la
Restonica

Corte

Porto

Venaco

Tavignano R.

Mont Rotondo

Aleria

Cap de Feno

193

69

Mont d'Oro

Ajaccio

L'Incudine

Taravo R.

Zonza

Cucuruzzo

TYRRHENIAN
SEA

Propriano

Sartène

Porto-Vecchio

Bonifacio   Île Cavallo
Cap de Feno

Strait of Bonifacio

SARDINIA (ITALY)

A BIT OF BACKGROUND: The present invader, the tourist, joins a line of other invaders who have descended on Corsica during the course of its long and turbulent history.

The Greeks came this way, followed by the Etruscans and Carthaginians. The conquering Romans arrived, establishing their iron-fisted might, and by the 3rd century Christianity had come. The Middle Ages saw the arrival of the Vandals and the Ostrogoths, the parade continuing with the Byzantines, the Franks, and the Saracens.

In 1077 the Pisans took over the island, which in the decades ahead brought them into conflict with the Genoans. The Pisans were defeated in 1284. However, in 1296 the pope "assigned" Corsica to Aragon, a struggle that brought it into much conflict with Genoa. Once Genoa finally established its supremacy, it was to dominate Corsica on and off from 1453 to 1729.

In 1729 the Corsicans rebelled against the Genoans. In 1769 Genoa sold her rights in Corsica to France. That same year, on August 15 to be exact, Napoléon Bonaparte was born at Ajaccio.

Corsica has belonged to France ever since, except for a few interruptions. The English intervened at the time of the French Revolution, but France reconquered Corsica in 1796. And the Allies landed to liberate Corsica in September of 1943.

FOLKLORE AND FOOD: In addition to rugged mountain and coastal scenery, the island is rich in folklore. The music, especially the **lamenti,** is famous. Natural singers, the Corsicans have developed a sad and melancholy music which tells of their past struggles, the pain and suffering they have endured. This music can still be heard in the *caveaux* in the tiny port towns and in the dance cafés. Festivals also bring out the young singers of the island who appear in typical Corsican folkloric dress.

Many visitors like to come to Corsica just to eat. The wives of the fishermen, for example, have their own version of bouillabaisse. They call it **aziminu.** The pigs that live on the island and eat chestnuts produce a smoked ham or a smoked sausage unique in the world. The flavor comes from the aromatic shrubs used to feed the fires. Wild boar still is found on the island, as it is in Sardinia, and in season game is a feature in the local restaurants, the blackbird pâté singled out as a favorite delicacy (the birds feed on berries in the maquis).

The table is bountiful in fish caught in local waters around Corsica. There is also trout from mountain streams. Many Corsicans make their cheese from sheep's and goat's milk, and it has a distinctive flavor.

Corsican wines are becoming better known. The red wines are known for their color and flavor, and there are many rosés to amuse.

GETTING THERE: About the cheapest, and certainly the most convenient, way to get to Corsica is by air. Both **Air France** and **Air Inter** fly there. In summer there are more frequent flights to meet the increased demand. You can fly from Paris, Nice, or Marseille to either Bastia or Ajaccio. Check with travel agents to obtain certain discounts granted to stimulate travel to Corsica.

The **Compagnie Général Trans-Méditérranienne** will take you to Corsica on a car-ferry leaving from Nice (allow 6½ hours) or Marseille (11 hours, but you can rent a sleeping cabin). These ferries go to Bastia, Ajaccio, and Calvi. It's also quite reasonable to take your car, although space is almost impossibly tight in summer. If you have a rented car on the Riviera, you might prefer instead to make an arrangement with the same company to have a car waiting for you in one of the Corsican ports.

In my opinion you should rent a car on Corsica in spite of the driving problems on certain roads. Public transportation seems completely inadequate unless you have weeks to explore the island, which is unrealistic for today's hurried visitor.

1. Bastia

Chances are, your boat from the French mainland will deposit you at Bastia, the largest port on the island. Don't judge Corsica too hastily by this port, which is not an important sightseeing destination. If you're landing in Bastia by plane, you'll touch down at Poretta, 13 miles away. When the Genoese were the rulers of Corsica, Bastia was their capital. It still has the most population, more than Ajaccio, the present capital of Corsica.

If you're in Bastia waiting for the ferry to take you back to the mainland, you might do some exploring. At the old port, you can visit the **Genoese Governors' Palace,** at the Place de la Citadelle, which has been converted into a minor museum, the **Musée d'Ethnographie Corse,** open from 10 a.m. to noon and 3 to 6 p.m. in summer (from 9 to 11 a.m. and 2 to 5 p.m. in winter). It is closed on Sunday and charges 5F (69¢) for admission. A new wing houses archeological, botanical, and minerological exhibitions, as well as a collection of 17th- and 18th-century paintings. A collection of modern paintings is on view as well. Each summer different expositions are offered, and the palace is also a rendezvous for concerts. If you walk through the gardens of the museum you'll enjoy a magnificent view of the islands in the distance.

Vieux Bastia, or the old town, is also worth exploring. The hub of life in Bastia, with several cafés and restaurants, is the Place St-Nicolas.

Bastia also forms a good base for exploring **Cap Corse,** a small peninsula about 10 miles wide and 25 miles in length, the northernmost part of the island. It is filled with the houses of people who earn their living from the sea. Many are painted in bright colors. A corniche road provides a link to these many villages. Often the word "Riviera" is used to describe the landscape, but that seems far too sophisticated a term for the quiet life and local charm you will encounter.

FOOD AND LODGING: **Hôtel Pietracap,** Pietranera (tel. 95-31-64-63), is the best hotel in Bastia. It stands at the top of a winding road whose steep curves might present a challenge if you're a timid driver. Once you arrive, however, you're assured of total comfort. The Corsican architect designed many terraces with sea views if you're outside or big windows if you're inside. The decor is enhanced by a judicious use of marble and tiles. The Raffalli family, the owners, personally chose many of the watercolors in the attractive bedrooms. The family is active in business and politics in Bastia. They have a bar area, lying off the spacious pool lined with flagstones. The garden with olive trees is a few steps from the front door. Doubles range from 290F ($39.99) to 400F ($55.16), depending on the accommodation. All units contain private bath. Guests are received from March 1 to November 30.

Chez Assunta, 4 Place Fontaine-Neuve (tel. 95-31-67-06), is housed in a Mediterranean-style building with stucco walls and a view of the small public fountain ringed with carved dolphins. The porpoise motif is repeated in the iron lampposts of the garden area to one side of the building. Verdant shrubbery and latticework screens separate the restaurant from the street. The interior used to be a chapel whose brick-vaulted ceiling witnesses the consumption of the specialties thoughtfully prepared by Assunta Cianelli, the mistress of the house. These include carefully grilled fish, homemade pasta, herb tarts, cabri Corsican style, and fresh desserts. Assunta is the best restaurant in Bastia. When the bill arrives, you may be surprised at how reasonable it is, considering the quality of the food and wine. A dinner costs about 210F ($28.96). The interior is air-conditioned if the evening is too hot for the garden. Meals are served every day except Sunday and holidays. The place is also closed in January.

La Taverne, 9 rue du Général-Carbuccia (tel. 95-31-17-87). As you set out to find this restaurant in the depths of one of the most confusing sections of the old town, a series of signposts will guide you to its door. Chefs serve such specialties as stuffed squid, sea bass with fennel, bouillabaisse, various kinds of scallops, lamb cutlets, tripe maison, spaghetti fruits de mer, and a full array of omelets. You'll enter several warmly regional rooms, only a few of which have windows, and sit on French provincial chairs. Fixed-price menus are offered for 85F ($11.72), while à la carte meals usually average 180F ($24.82). Lunch and dinner are served every day until 10:30 p.m. except on Monday.

2. L'Île-Rousse

A small sea resort, L'Île-Rousse lies only 13 miles from Calvi. Created in the 18th century, the town takes its name from the trio of reddish granite rocks that lie outside the harbor. The center of town is a big plaza studded with plane trees. Its casino will hold little interest for the average North American visitor, although the sandy beach is a lure. On a summer day, several trains run between Calvi and L'Île-Rousse.

FOOD AND LODGING: **Hôtel de la Pietra,** Chemin du Phare (tel. 95-60-01-45), is a modern hotel set on a windswept rock near the end of the road which follows the edge of the harbor. The well-maintained but boxy façade is faced with gray stones from the nearby mountains. The view from many of the simply furnished bedrooms is of an old Genoese lighthouse, evoking the memory of another era. The sunny and airy lobby with its huge sea-view windows is inviting. Many of the accommodations of this three-star hotel have windows looking over the port from behind private loggias. The 40 rooms rent in high season for 400F ($55.16) in a double and for 280F ($49.64) in a single. Specialties in the panoramic dining room include snails doused in Corsican wine, John Dory in a confit of shallots, and a full and extensive array of fresh fish. If you've come just for a meal, fixed-price menus are offered for 120F ($16.55) to 180F ($24.82), while à la carte dinners cost 275F ($37.92). Both the hotel and restaurant are closed from November to April.

Hôtel Napoléon Bonaparte, 3 Place Paoli (Place des Plantanes) (tel. 95-60-06-09). This pink hotel rises grandly a short distance from the center of town. It has two crenellated towers set at either end, very much like a palace in Palermo or in Naples. Despite its fortress-like exterior, the public and private rooms are surprisingly modern and very comfortable. The 100 bedrooms cost between 280F ($38.61) in a single and 620F ($85.50) in a double. The in-house restaurant, La Piscine, is one of the choice dining spots of town. Partially located in the open air, the restaurant sits between two swimming pools in a well-kept garden. Closed December to mid-February.

On the Outskirts

À **Pastorella** (tel. 95-60-05-65), at Monticello, almost 3 miles southeast of L'Île-Rousse, is a restaurant and hotel in a Corsican mountain village high above the town. The winding route to it is well indicated. After exploring the narrow streets of the village, you can head for this restaurant on the main square. There Georges (Gogo) and Michelle Martini maintain a country-elegant restaurant with an outer bar and an inner dining room with a timbered ceiling. As an Alsatian bombé grandfather clock ticks against one wall, you'll enjoy well-prepared specialties that include six kinds of fish (including giant shrimps and terrines), a form of crêpe known as a brioccu (stuffed with boiled whey, parsley, garlic, and crème fraiche), and pork dishes along with baby lamb, which is usually raised on the Martinis' property. If you're not sure of the fish you'd like, someone will bring you a big platter so you can see the selections in their natural state.

A five-course fixed-price menu is served for 80F ($11.03), and it's usually accompanied by a large carafe of strong-bodied local wine. Mr. Martini is a charming, full-blooded Corsican who lived for a while in Montmartre in Paris, and Michelle spent part of her youth in the Loire Valley. They also rent out attractive rooms, some of which have a private terrace. Prices begin at 170F ($23.44) for two persons. Closed from November 1 to January 1.

3. Calvi

Instead of Bastia, you might also dock at Calvi, as this little resort is the closest port to the mainland of France. By ferry from Nice, the trip takes about 5½ hours. However, it is only a 45-minute flight from the Côte d'Azur. If arriving by air, you'll be about three miles from the center of town.

The major attraction is the **Citadel,** built by the Genoese conquerors and enclosed by ramparts. From its ramparts you can take in the best that Calvi has to offer: the high mountains in the background and the beautiful bay stretching before you. The four-mile-long bay, bordered by a long strip of sand, is studded with pine trees. Many water sports activities, such as waterskiing and skin-diving, take place here. In summer the yachting crowd arrives and the town takes on a somewhat festive air.

After the Citadel, you can walk the narrow, winding streets of the old town, viewing the **Église St-Jean-Baptiste** on the Place d'Armes in the center. Look for a Renaissance baptismal font inside, along with other ecclesiastical treasures.

Consider also a visit to the **Oratoire de la Confrérie St-Antoine,** open July 1 to mid-September from 10 a.m. to noon and 3 to 6 p.m. It is closed Sunday and charges 4F (55¢) for admission. Dating from the 15th century, it has been turned into a showcase of religious art of Calvi. Most of the sacred objects of art date from the 16th through the 19th centuries.

Of limited interest is the so-called maison natale, or **birthplace of Christopher Columbus.**

FOOD AND LODGING: **Le Grand Hôtel,** 3 Boulevard du Président-Wilson (tel. 95-65-09-74), is a central hotel whose façade curves gently around a street corner near the post office. Shutters cover the windows of the five floors of air-conditioned rooms. Inside, you'll find stone floors, vividly colored tapestries with nautical themes, and an airy bar area. Views from the dining room encompass the mountains and the sea through big windows partially protected with iron railings. The hotel is open only from April 1 until the end of September. Accommodation rates range from 450F ($62.06) in a single to 650F ($89.64) in a double.

Hôtel les Aloës, Quartier Donateo (tel. 95-65-01-46) is set at the top of a winding road about a mile before you reach Calvi on the road from L'Île-Rousse. The modern hotel stands in the midst of a tropical garden. Flagstone walkways surround the building, embellished with lots of potted vines trailing down from Mediterranean-style urns. The red-trimmed upper floors have rows of balconies which overlook the ancient fortress of Calvi, set on a neighboring mountaintop. Open from April to the end of September, the hotel charges 220F ($30.34) in a single, 325F ($44.82) in a double. An annex contains about 20 rooms with kitchenettes.

4. Porto

If you are still alive after having driven from Calvi to Porto along that treacherous road already mentioned, you will be rewarded with a pleasant stopover. That is, if you've reserved a room. Italian vacationers take up nearly all the accommodations in summer.

This little port, which is only halfway to Ajaccio, is one of the most beautiful in France, opening onto the Gulf of Porto. Set against a backdrop of red granite cliffs, it is deep as a Norwegian fjord. It is even more spectacular when viewed either at sunset or dawn. In the curve of the gulf, Porto comes at the end of a valley filled with scented eucalyptus trees. Overlooking the slopes is a watchtower built by the Genoese.

Porto only comes alive in summer. Many of its citizens have no work all winter, patiently waiting for the summer hordes. You can negotiate a boat trip around the gulf, which will be one of the scenic highlights of your visit to Corsica. You'll be back to listen to a singing group in one of the many cafés that ring the port.

FOOD AND LODGING: Hôtel Cyrnée, à La Marine (tel. 95-26-12-40). The name of this place means Corsica in local dialect. That might give a hint as to the regional character of this simple balconied hotel looking out over the port, within earshot of the crashing waves. Ten rooms are available for overnighters, and only half-board guests are accepted, paying from 220F ($30.34) per person daily. Meals inside the basic dining room are regional in character and often quite good, especially the fish soup. A dinner costs 90F ($12.41) to 150F ($20.69). Madame Poggioli directs an extended family who run this place. She usually beams a sincere affection for her guests, who are received from the first of April to the end of September.

Le Flots Bleus, Porto-Marine (tel. 95-26-11-26), enjoys one of the most scenic views in town. The establishment offers good, simple, modern rooms in the hub of activity. In summer the hotel will probably be fully booked, especially by Italians. In season, the hotel accepts only half-board guests, charging them from 280F ($38.61) per person daily. The place closes down between mid-October and April 1.

Le Maquis (tel. 95-26-12-19) serves some of the best food at Porto. It is in reality a *restaurant avec chambres,* presenting a severe stone façade pierced by an arched door and a big, multi-paned window. It faces a street that leads to the port. The restaurant is set below an extended open porch; however, in cold weather guests retreat into the rustically furnished country-style interior. Each of the simply furnished bedrooms looks onto a garden. All contain hot and cold running water, and a few possess private bath. If you're passing through, you can enjoy a meal here at prices ranging from 85F ($11.72) to 135F ($18.62). The seven bedrooms range in price from 140F ($19.31) to 200F ($27.58) for two persons. Le Maquis is closed from mid-March to mid-November and from mid-December to January 5.

5. Corte

Fifty miles inland from Ajaccio (or 43 miles southwest from Bastia), the little resort of Corte was the historic capital of Corsica. It is still the biggest town on the island not opening onto the coastline. Because it was inland, the Corsican Republic chose it as a capital since any port city was likely to be raided. Lying at the junction of the Restonica and Tavignano Rivers, Corte has traditionally been associated with the struggle for local independence.

The town is dominated by a **citadel,** which you may want to explore. Dating from the 15th century, it today affords a stunning panoramic view of the area. Otherwise, there isn't that much to see in Corte, except for connoisseurs. However, it does make an interesting base for excursions. A 12-mile road runs along the gorge made by the Restonica River, eventually taking you to **Lake Meloat** at 6,500 feet and **Lake Capitello** at 7,200 feet. Finally, you approach **Monte Rotondo,** the second-highest peak in Corsica at 8,600 feet.

FOOD AND LODGING: Hôtel de la Paix, Avenue de Gaulle (tel. 95-46-06-72), stands on one of the prettiest squares in Corte. The hotel is one of several Italianate buildings that line this almost Neapolitan-style block bordered with towering palms and dotted with heroic statues. Attractive bedrooms are available, fronting either the quietly residential square or an arid but still green landscape interrupted by a few buildings. In summer, half board is required, costing from 300F ($41.37) to 350F ($48.27) per person, depending on the accommodation. The rest of the year, doubles cost 280F ($38.61) per person, breakfast not included. The dining room has timbered ceilings and a bar opening just off the tile lobby.

Sampiero Corso, Avenue du Président-Pierucci (tel. 95-46-09-76), presents six floors of balconied white walls and white louvered shutters to the main road leading to Porto-Vecchio. The lobby area contains an early-'60s decor of red and white tiles, leather couches, and colorful wall murals of the medieval fortress of Corte. The rooms are simple and functional, renting for 220F ($30.34) to 250F ($34.48) in a double. The 31-room hotel is closed from October 1 to April 1.

6. Ajaccio

This town is forever linked with the legend of Napoléon Bonaparte, who was born there on August 15, 1769. The west-coast port of some 50,000 inhabitants is still rich in Napoleonic memorabilia.

Boats will take you to Ajaccio, the capital of Corsica, or you can fly there, arriving at the airport, Campo dell'Oro, which is four miles away.

Founded by the Genoese in the 15th century, Ajaccio is a town of large plazas and wide boulevards. It is commercial but also colorful, especially if you take the time to seek out its old town and fishing port.

One of the major attractions is the **Casa Bonaparte,** rue Saint-Charles (tel. 95-21-43-89), the birthplace of Napoleon. It is open in summer from 9 a.m. to noon and 2 to 6 p.m.; in winter from 10 a.m. to noon and 2 to 5 p.m. It is closed on Sunday afternoon and Monday morning. Admission is 8F ($1.10). Just off the rue Bonaparte, it is filled with many antiques.

If you're a true Bonaparte devotee, you may also seek out the **Musée Napoléonien de l'Hôtel de Ville** (tel. 95-21-90-15). It is open from 9 a.m. to noon and 2:30 to 6 p.m. (closes at 5 p.m. in winter, and also closed on Sunday). Admission is 4F (55¢). Among its many memorabilia is a death mask of Bonaparte in bronze.

The **Chapelle Impériale** is another monument to the Bonapartes, this one erected in 1855 as a tomb for members of the family. It stands on the rue Fesch, charging 7F (97¢) for admission.

Next door, the **Musée Fesch,** 50 rue Cardinal-Fesch (tel. 95-21-48-17), contains the major art collection of Ajaccio. Cardinal Fesch was the uncle of Napoleon, and he presented the nucleus of the collection to the city. Many Italian works are included, featuring the paintings of such illustrious artists as Veronese, Cosima Tura, Botticelli, and Giovanni Bellini. Some art critics claim that this painting collection is the "second most important" gallery of Italian paintings in French museums, after the mighty Louvre of course. The museum is open from 9 a.m. to noon and 2:30 to 6 p.m. in summer (from 9 a.m. to noon and 2 to 5 p.m. in winter). The museum is closed on Sunday.

At the **Syndicat d'Initiative,** Hôtel de Ville (tel. 95-21-40-87), ask about boat trips to the **Îles Sanguinaires,** which lie at the head of the gulf in a southwesterly direction from Ajaccio. These stunning grottoes are best visited at sunset when they glow a blood-red. You'll spend about 55F ($7.56) on boat fare to visit them. Vessels depart from the Quai Napoléon facing the Place du Maréchal-Foch from the end of April until the end of October.

WHERE TO STAY: Hôtel Albion, 15 Avenue du Général-Leclerc (tel. 95-21-66-70), is a modern hotel that looks surprisingly like an apartment building. It was built 12 years ago in a residential area near the Plage de la Ville, with many reproduction English details. The lobby bar, whose view opens onto the garden, has tried to re-create the aura of a London club. From the uppermost of the six floors, you can see the water. This is the best hotel in the very center of town, with each of the accommodations being air-conditioned and fitted with a phone and a private bath. Singles rent for 300F ($41.37), and doubles cost 350F ($48.27).

Hôtel Costa, 2 Boulevard Colomba (tel. 95-21-43-02). Set back about a block from the beach in a quietly residential part of town, this hotel is a gleaming (almost glaring) white mass of thick walls, unembellished rectangular windows, simple furniture, and marble flooring. It's surrounded with a small but verdant garden, and entered via a gently sloping double staircase, which adds some relief to the building's bulk. About half of the 53 comfortable rooms look out over the sea. According to the season (the hotel is open all year), singles cost 185F ($25.51) to 290F ($39.99), and doubles range from 250F ($34.48) to 330F ($45.51). Triples are available for 340F ($46.89) to 430F ($59.30).

Hôtel Eden-Roc, Route des Sanguinaires (tel. 95-52-01-47), is a dramatically modern hotel separated from the surf by a road leading to Ajaccio, several miles away. The façade is composed of blocks of local stone, white-painted concrete, and oversize glass windows angled toward the water. On the premises are a series of landscaped terraces dotted with semitropical plants and a heated swimming pool set into the rocks. Since the hotel is open only from May to September, the management prefers that clients take full board, which doesn't represent a hardship since the hotel is a Relais et Châteaux and the food is superb. All the rooms have a private terrace with views of the sea. Full board costs 600F ($82.74) to 650F ($89.64) per person, depending on the accommodation.

WHERE TO DINE: Chez Charlot (Pardi), 60 rue Fesch (tel. 95-21-43-08), is a cool enclave on a hot day. It's the kind of place where the local owners—in this case the Pardi family—are a visible presence among the steaming platters of fish soup, Corsican ham, tripe maison, and a choice of omelets. The establishment is so popular that a line usually forms promptly at noon on the stairs leading up to the second-floor room with the beamed ceiling where it's located. The fixed-price menus, served on bistro-style tablecloths, include wine and service (you should leave a small additional tip). There is no à la carte menu. You'll quickly get the feeling that this is practically everyone's favorite for a friendly and unpretentious restaurant, especially at lunchtime. Fixed-price menus cost from 60F ($8.27) to 85F ($11.72). The "social institution" is closed every Sunday and from just before Christmas until the end of February.

La Côte d'Azur, 12 Cours Napoléon (tel. 95-21-50-24), is ideal for a leisurely lunch. In an olive-drab room, which might have been a garrison for some of Napoleon's troops, you can enjoy Marc Lamic's tempting versions of saffron fish soup, a terrine of monkfish with a caper sauce, mussels flavored with thyme, the fresh fish of the day, and perhaps a lamb dish. Fixed-priced menus cost 115F ($15.86) and 185F ($25.51), with à la carte dinners averaging 165F ($22.75). Meals are served daily except on Sunday and from late June to late July.

7. Porticcio

This is a virtual suburb of Ajaccio, but it contains the finest accommodations. The location is 10½ miles south of Ajaccio. Chances are, from your hotel room you'll have a view of the Bay of Ajaccio, the Sanguinaires Islands, and a background of mountains. The trip from the Ajaccio airport to Porticcio takes about 15 minutes. It's a drive of about 20 minutes, but only 10 minutes if you go by boat from your hotel.

FOOD AND LODGING: Le Maquis (tel. 95-25-05-55). There's no question about this being my favorite hotel in all of Corsica. In an island punctuated with starkly angular properties that look like temporary housing in a war zone, this lushly decorated inn is a welcome relief. The land it sits on was used as a kitchen garden until 1952, when Catherine Salini built this Mediterranean-style villa on property that had been owned by her family for generations. In 1969, with the help of her by-now-grown children, she added a tastefully designed high-ceilinged addition which was decorated, like the original core, with antiques discovered at various shops in Alsace and Provence. The arched fireplace in the main salon is topped with copper pots and flanked with utilitarian art objects.

In the panoramic dining room, the huge ceiling truss came from the demolition of a 300-year-old seminary. The terracotta terrace seems to embrace the stretch of sandy beach whose colors and expansiveness give the impression of a private island in the Caribbean. While Madame Salini cannot speak English, she has surrounded herself with people who can.

The elegant establishment, which sits clustered like a collection of private villas on the slope of a flowering garden, requires that clients accept half board during middle and high season, lasting from April to October. Prices range from 565F ($77.91) to 750F ($103.43) in a single and from 480F ($66.19) to 900F ($124.11) per person in a double. Accommodations range from attractively furnished rooms with shower, toilet, and sink, to beautifully terraced units with full private bath. Apartments and duplexes are available for up to 2,300F ($317.17) per person per day in high season, with half board included.

Menu specialties include a wide range of grilled fish, including gambas provençales and lobster, veal with olives, a large selection of meat dishes, especially a succulent local lamb and an entrecôte with roquefort, a unique platter of hors d'oeuvres, unusual terrines, mussels marinières, and bouillabaisse. The hotel remains open all year, but the restaurant closes between mid-January and mid-February, during which period the staff cheerfully directs visitors to a nearby restaurant owned by Madame Salini's stepfather.

Hôtel Sofitel, Golfe d'Ajaccio (tel. 95-25-00-34). The airy, California-style format of this place is enhanced by its position on the bay, a 20-minute drive from the center of Ajaccio, and by the extensive gardens that surround it. Many of the clients come here for the spa facilities nearby. However, if you've come to swim, play tennis, boules, waterski, windsurf, or scuba-dive, you'll find what you need here. The public rooms are sometimes interconnected with a series of flower-bordered walkways leading (among others) to a pleasant bar and a spaciously sunny dining room. There, meals costing 210F ($28.96) might include civet of wild boar Corsican style, bouillon of swimming crabs flavored with tarragon, gratin of crayfish tails, and many other specialties. Your view will be of the dramatically landscaped pool, the sea, the mountains, pink napery, Spanish-style wrought-iron chairs, and, perhaps, of someone you love. In high season, half board is required of all guests. Tariffs range from 1,050F ($144.80) to 1,400F ($193.06) per person, depending on the accommodation. Each of the units contains color TV, air conditioning, and a modern bath.

8. Propriano

In the Sartène region, the small town and port of Propriano lies 65 miles south of Ajaccio and some 61 miles to the northwest of Bonifacio. Opening onto the Gulf of Valinco, it enjoys summer business as a resort. Water sports include skiing and underwater swimming. Most of the small restaurants specialize in seafood off the coast, especially Corsican lobster.

WHERE TO STAY: **Hôtel Miramar,** Route de la Corniche (tel. 95-76-06-13), is a large, white hotel set so high on a bluff above a curve in the road that it is visible as you drive toward the center of town from Ajaccio. The hotel, its terraces, its swimming pool, and its gardens have been set into the vine-covered rocks of the hillside. The interior is marked with thick stucco walls, terracotta tiles, and the kinds of Mediterranean pots that hold masses of ivy and flowers. If you want to go to the beach from your very large bedroom, the management has constructed a stairwell beneath part of the house and under the road that winds down to the sands. Views from many parts of the hotel encompass much of the town and bay. The 30 bedrooms rent for 420F ($57.92) in a single, 550F ($75.63) in a double. Open Easter to October.

9. Sartène

This is the name of the region that most citizens say is "the most typical" on the island, and it is also the name of a small town whose buildings, for the most part, were constructed from a darkish granite. Built on the side of a hill, Sartène rises above the Valley of the Rizzanèse. An archway through the town hall leads to **Vieux Sartène,** which is the most interesting part to explore, with its small Corsican houses and narrow streets. Here the Middle Ages live on. The heart of the town is the Place de la Libération, which has several cafés. It is also the site of a colorful market. Sartène is famed for its unusual procession, the *Catenaccio,* which takes place on the night of Good Friday and draws visitors from many parts of France. Sartène lies some 51 miles south from Ajaccio and some 32 miles northwest from Bonifacio.

WHERE TO DINE: La Chaumière, 39 rue du Capitaine-Benedetti (tel. 95-77-07-13), is in a stone, four-story house on a hillside street that winds past some of the most ruggedly twisted—and perhaps some of the oldest—houses in Corsica. If you prefer to park in the heartbeat Place de la Libération, it will require a brisk four-minute walk to get to the restaurant. The street changes its name from the rue San-Bastianu to the route du Lycée to the rue Capitaine-Benedetti. You might imagine that the owner of such a regionally conscious restaurant would be a pure-blooded Corsican, but Madame Bianchini is formerly of Paris.

However, virtually all of her menu items are locally inspired. They include such Corsican specialties as grilled suckling pig (for four persons; this must be ordered in advance), a ragoût of mutton, a terrine or a stew of wild boar, Corsican fish soup, boiled beef (daube) with olives, a terrine of blackbird, and a pâté of chestnuts. There's a fixed-price menu offered for 85F ($11.72), while à la carte meals range from 160F ($22.06) to 180F ($24.82). In low season the restaurant is closed on Sunday, and also shuts down in January.

10. Porto-Vecchio

By the time you reach the southeast of Corsica, you will be in a virtual subtropical climate. Sheltered by pine trees, the sandy beaches lure hordes of Italian visitors in summer. Many come from Genoa, the seat of the former conquerors of Corsica. The town is noted for its colorful fishing port, and beginning in late spring the yachting crowd arrives as well.

Once Porto-Vecchio was a fortified town because of its position at the head of a deep bay. In the 16th century the Genoese built walls around Porto-Vecchio, and behind these walls you can walk and explore along the medieval-like streets. The present residents have cut into these walls, opening up cafés, bistros, little shops, and often private residences.

You'll stand a better chance of getting a room at Porto-Vecchio in the crowded months of July and August than you will in the more colorful Bonifacio (see below). Bonifacio is 16½ miles to the south. If you're driving along the east coast of Bastia to Porto-Vecchio, the road is good and the distance more than 85 miles.

FOOD AND LODGING: Hôtel du Roi-Théodore, Route de Bastia (tel. 95-70-14-

94), lies about 1½ miles from the center of the port on the road to Bastia. It is a Mediterranean-style building—the best hotel in Porto-Vecchio—with wrought-iron window bars, vivid rose-colored stucco, a verdant semitropical garden, and a motel-like format of big-windowed rooms stretching out toward the back. In all, 39 attractively furnished rooms are rented, costing 350F ($48.27) in a single and 480F ($66.19) in a double. Guests are received from the first of April to the end of October.

Hôtel le Goëland, à La Marine (tel. 95-70-14-15), is an attractive house set directly on the water, with a garden and piers a few steps from the back door where fishing boats moor. A short walk from the port, the hotel contains a big breakfast room and bar area with a stone fireplace and modern chairs and tables. The bedrooms are simple, but clean and fairly comfortable. They are also a great bargain: doubles rent for 165F ($22.75) to 250F ($34.48).

Le Bistrot du Port, rue du Port (tel. 95-70-22-96), serves the best food in Porto-Vecchio and is especially known for its fresh fish. It's set directly on the water, with a view of the marina's boats bobbing a short distance away. In summer, most guests prefer to eat on the terrace below the globe-shaped lampposts. If you opt for the interior, you might want a drink in the oak-trimmed bar before heading to the rustic dining room scattered over two levels. I prefer the upper level, probably because of its fireplace and privacy. Chef Joel Robuchon makes a valiant effort to introduce a conservative form of La Nouvelle Cuisine to the island, including such dishes as veal scallop with lemon, his salade Bistrot, and red mullet with two kinds of pepper. For dessert, have a kiwi tart with an orange terrine. À la carte meals range from 210F ($28.96) to 285F ($39.30), and are served daily except Tuesday in low season and in November.

11. Bonifacio

One of the most dramatically situated coastal towns of Corsica, Bonifacio stands at the southern tip of the island, some 105 miles from Bastia. Lying at the foot of a promontory, it faces Sardinia, to which there are frequent ferry connections. The city is only 8 miles away. Once again, the conquering Genoese built Bonifacio behind massive walls in the 13th century. In many ways the town happily basks in the past. The **citadel** still crowns the port, looking out onto the Straits of Bonifacio. You can wander for hours in the old town, called **Vieille Ville.** The streets are cobbled, narrow, and winding, and it's easy to get lost. In 1792 Napoleon was an artillery officer here.

And if you have trouble understanding the local speech, don't despair. Even Corsicans have trouble understanding people of Bonifacio, because their speech is heavily influenced by Sardinia.

The hotels have severely limited accommodations, and reservations are imperative if you're contemplating a visit there. Several restaurants are found around the harbor, each one specializing in seafood. For a good beach, however, you'll have to head four miles to the east to Santa Manza.

If you want to go boating, you usually have to make your own arrangements at the harbor. One popular trip is to visit the uninhabited islands of Cavallo and Lavezzi. Cavallo, for instance, was once a Roman quarry, and many ancient remains are still there, including sculptures made by slaves.

FOOD AND LODGING: Hôtel Solemar (tel. 95-73-01-06) is a three-star modern stucco hotel whose ochre exterior is built like a row of harborside Mediterranean-style houses. The sunny interior has big windows looking out over the marina, within sight of some of the most glamorous boats in Corsica. The hotel is built between the bay and a wind-eroded cliff, whose weirdly sculpted rocks sometimes throw up a blinding dust storm when the wind gets strong. Utrillo featured this kind of angular architecture in some of his paintings. Guests are received only from April to October and housed in well-furnished bedrooms, 59 in all, at prices that go from 275F ($37.92) in a single to 410F ($56.54) in a double. There is no restaurant.

Hôtel Résidence du Centre-Nautique (tel. 95-73-02-12) is my personal choice in the south of Corsica, and if you're lucky enough to get a room here, it might be yours too. It was built in 1910 as the headquarters and dormitory for the French navy stationed in Bonifacio. That explains the high ceilings, and the efforts that Juliette Laurent Van de Put and her husband have expended during the past 20 years to transform the premises into a series of duplex apartments. Each of the ten rooms contains a sleeping platform and a starkly but comfortably furnished combined living room and salon below it, interconnected with a winding metal staircase. In high season the hotel is so popular that it's often booked entire seasons in advance.

You'll find one of the hotel's most unusual features at the top of a long and massive flight of stone steps. An upper-level sitting room contains the barnacle-encrusted anchor from an ancient Roman vessel which, although discovered by the hotel's owner, technically belongs to the French government. The hotel is closed from the end of October until the beginning of April. Depending on the season, rooms range from 260F ($35.85) to 310F ($42.75) for two persons. There are no meals other than the optional breakfast served here. However, in the same building is a popular paneled bar decorated with signal flags and lots of paneling. Under a different management, it is most popular with the yachting crowd.

Hôtel des Étrangers, Avenue Sylvère-Bohn (tel. 95-73-01-09), has been maintained by members of the Bohn family since 1907, when it was first built by the Alsatian grandfather of the present owner. The simple white-faced hotel sits close to the road from Porto-Vecchio, just before you reach the center of Bonifacio. There's a bar area on the ground floor for the use of guests. Accommodations are extremely simple, renting for 180F ($24.82) in a double. Don't expect the Ritz here, although the prices are just right for budget-conscious visitors. You'll be five minutes from the port, but about three miles from a good beach. The hotel stays open all year. The rooms away from the busy road might be quieter on a summer evening. There is no restaurant.

PRENTICE HALL PRESS Date_____
ONE GULF + WESTERN PLAZA, NEW YORK, NY 10023

Friends, please send me the books checked below:

FROMMER'S $-A-DAY GUIDES
(In-depth guides to low-cost tourist accommodations and facilities.)

☐ Europe on $25 a Day	$12.95	☐ Mexico on $20 a Day	$10.95
☐ Australia on $25 a Day	$10.95	☐ New Zealand on $35 a Day	$10.95
☐ Eastern Europe on $25 a Day (avail.		☐ New York on $45 a Day	$9.95
Oct. '86)	$10.95	☐ Scandinavia on $40 a Day	$10.95
☐ England on $35 a Day	$10.95	☐ Scotland and Wales on $35 a Day	$10.95
☐ Greece on $25 a Day	$10.95	☐ South America on $25 a Day	$9.95
☐ Hawaii on $45 a Day	$10.95	☐ Spain and Morocco (plus the Canary	
☐ India on $15 & $25 a Day	$9.95	Is.) on $40 a Day	$10.95
☐ Ireland on $35 a Day	$10.95	☐ Turkey on $25 a Day (avail. May '87)	$10.95
☐ Israel on $30 & $35 a Day	$10.95	☐ Washington, D.C. on $40 a Day	$10.95

FROMMER'S DOLLARWISE GUIDES
(Guides to accommodations and facilities from budget to deluxe with emphasis on the medium-priced.)

☐ Alaska (avail. Apr. '87)	$12.95	☐ Caribbean	$12.95
☐ Austria & Hungary	$11.95	☐ Cruises (incl. Alaska, Carib, Mex,	
☐ Benelux Countries (avail. June '87)	$11.95	Hawaii, Panama, Canada, & US)	$12.95
☐ Egypt	$11.95	☐ California & Las Vegas	$11.95
☐ England & Scotland	$11.95	☐ Florida	$10.95
☐ France	$11.95	☐ New England	$11.95
☐ Germany	$11.95	☐ New York State (avail. May '87)	$11.95
☐ Italy	$11.95	☐ Northwest	$11.95
☐ Japan & Hong Kong	$12.95	☐ Skiing in Europe (avail. Oct. '86)	$12.95
☐ Portugal (incl. Madeira & the Azores)	$11.95	☐ Skiing USA—East	$10.95
☐ South Pacific (avail. June '87)	$12.95	☐ Skiing USA—West	$10.95
☐ Switzerland & Liechtenstein	$11.95	☐ Southeast & New Orleans	$11.95
☐ Bermuda & The Bahamas	$10.95	☐ Southwest	$11.95
☐ Canada	$12.95	☐ Texas (avail. Oct. '86)	$11.95

THE ARTHUR FROMMER GUIDES
(Pocket-size guides to tourist accommodations and facilities in all price ranges.)

☐ Amsterdam/Holland	$5.95	☐ Mexico City/Acapulco	$5.95
☐ Athens	$5.95	☐ Montreal/Quebec City	$5.95
☐ Atlantic City/Cape May	$5.95	☐ New Orleans	$5.95
☐ Boston	$5.95	☐ New York	$5.95
☐ Cancun/Cozumel/Yucatán	$5.95	☐ Orlando/Disney World/EPCOT	$5.95
☐ Dublin/Ireland	$5.95	☐ Paris	$5.95
☐ Hawaii	$5.95	☐ Philadelphia	$5.95
☐ Las Vegas	$5.95	☐ Rome	$5.95
☐ Lisbon/Madrid/Costa del Sol	$5.95	☐ San Francisco	$5.95
☐ London	$5.95	☐ Washington, D.C.	$5.95
☐ Los Angeles	$5.95		

SPECIAL EDITIONS

☐ Bed & Breakfast—N. America	$7.95	☐ Shopper's Guide to the Caribbean	
☐ Fast 'n' Easy Phrase Book		(avail. Oct. '86)	$11.95
(Fr/Ger/Ital/Sp in *one* vol.)	$6.95	☐ Shopper's Guide to the Best Buys in	
☐ Guide for the Disabled Traveler	$10.95	England, Scotland & Wales	$10.95
☐ How to Beat the High Cost of Travel	$4.95	☐ Swap and Go (Home Exchanging)	$10.95
☐ Marilyn Wood's Wonderful Weekends		☐ Travel Diary and Record Book	$5.95
(NY, Conn, Mass, RI, Vt, NJ, Del, Pa)	$9.95	☐ Where to Stay USA (Lodging from $3	
☐ Motorist's Phrase Book (Fr/Ger/Sp)	$4.95	to $30 a night)	$9.95
☐ Museums in New York	$8.95		

In U.S. include $1 post. & hdlg. for 1st book; 25¢ ea. add'l. book. Outside U.S. $2 and 50¢ respectively.

Enclosed is my check or money order for $_____

NAME_____

ADDRESS_____

CITY_____ STATE_____ ZIP_____